Amphibious Assault:
Manoeuvre from the Sea

The Assault on Walcheren, 1 November 1944. (Courtesy of The Peter J. Sterkenburg Maritime Paintings Foundation)

Amphibious Assault: Manoeuvre from the Sea

from Gallipoli to the Gulf – a definitive analysis

Edited by Tristan Lovering MBE

SEAFARER BOOKS

First published 2005 by the Royal Navy

This revised and expanded edition published in the UK by Seafarer Books, 102 Redwald Road, Rendlesham, Woodbridge, Suffolk, IP12 2TE

www.seafarerbooks.com • www.amphibiousassault.co.uk

© Seafarer Books 2007

ISBN 978-0-9550243-5-1 paperback
ISBN 978-0-9550243-6-8 with slip case

Grateful acknowledgement is made to the following for permission to reproduce photographs, maps and illustrations:
The Peter J Sterkenburg Maritime Paintings Foundation; Naval Historical Branch, Portsmouth (NHB); The Royal Marines Museum, Southsea (RMM);
The Imperial War Museum (IWM); Fleet Photographic Unit, Royal Navy (RN); Britannia Royal Naval College (BRNC); The National Archives, Kew (NA);
Defence Graphics Centre (DGC); Ministry of Defence (MOD) (Crown Copyright); US Marine Corps (USMC); US Navy (USN); US Army;
US National Archives & Records (NARA), and The US Department of Defense (DoD).

Front cover main image: US landing craft at Omaha Beach, Normandy, 1944 (D-Day). The photograph by Robert Capa is a work taken or made
during the course of a United States Coast Guard serviceman's or employee's official duties. As a work of the US federal government, the image is in the public domain
(17 USC § 101 and § 105). Other front cover images (left to right): Australian infantry at Gallipoli, 1915 (IWM); Salerno, 1943 (NA); attack plan for Operation Husky,
Sicily, 1943 (NHB); Royal Marines landing in Sierra Leone, 2000 (RN). Back cover background image: US assignment of shipping for the assault on Okinawa, 1945 (USN).
Other back cover images (clockwise from upper left): US troops at Bougainville, Solomon Islands, 1943 (NARA); German troops near Ösel, 1917 (IWM);
HMS Ocean launches helicopters before Operation TELIC, 2003 (RN). Inside front cover montage: D-Day map (NHB), with superimposed images of a Royal Marines
amphibious exercise and HMS Ocean (RN). Inside back cover image: painting by Charles deLacey (1885 – 1930) of the raid on Zeebrugge, 1918 (RMM).

British Library Cataloguing in Publication Data
Lovering, T. T. A. (Tristan T. A.)
Amphibious assault : manoeuvre from the sea
1. Amphibious warfare - History - 20th century 2. Landing operations - History - 20th century
I. Title
355.4'6
ISBN-13: 9780955024351 (paperback)
ISBN-13: 9780955024368 (with slip case)

Editor: Tristan T A Lovering MBE
Typesetting, design and layout: Adrian J Williams and Michael Shaw
Cover design: Louis Mackay

Printed by 1010 Printing International Ltd, China,
via Nicky Clarke, MBC Print Consultancy
www.mbcprint.co.uk

Contents

Foreword

By Correlli Barnett CBE

All the wars fought by the English-speaking peoples in the twentieth century (and after) have been expeditionary wars nourished by seapower. This necessarily follows from the fact that the English-speaking peoples live on islands: famously Britain herself, but also Australia and New Zealand in the southern oceans, and, yes, even North America, a vast continental island except for the frontier of the United States with Mexico. And this frontier is hardly endowed with a strategic significance equivalent to that of the land frontiers of Europe in 1914-18 and 1939-45.

It is therefore right to recall that the army of 61 divisions in France commanded by Field-Marshal Sir Douglas Haig during his final victorious offensive in 1918 – by far the largest British army ever committed to a continental campaign – had begun the war as 'The British Expeditionary Force' of just four divisions, while the 90 American, British and Canadian divisions commanded by General Dwight Eisenhower in North-West Europe in 1944-45 remained to the day of Germany's unconditional surrender entitled 'The Allied Expeditionary Force'.

And in 1918 and 1945 alike, victory in a continental land campaign depended on a massive and continuous flow of seaborne supplies and reinforcements. This flow was in turn only made possible by the supremacy already won over the German surface fleet and U-boats by the allied navies, above all the Royal Navy, in two battles of attrition in the Atlantic, in 1917 and 1943. So for the English-speaking peoples, war on land was, and will always remain, an extension of maritime strategy and maritime power.

This extension is relatively simple to implement whenever there is a host nation to provide the port facilities and perhaps even an existing battle front where an expeditionary force can be deployed, as was the case in France during the Great War or in Vietnam in the 1960s. But otherwise the essential preliminary to successful extension must lie in an amphibious assault on a defended shore. From the fall of France in 1940 onwards, this was invariably true of the campaigns of the Second World War, no matter whether the enemy was Germany, Italy or Japan.

In the case of the Anglo-American invasions of French North Africa in 1942, Sicily and Italy in 1943, and Normandy in 1944, or the American 'island-hopping' in the Central Pacific and South-West Pacific in 1942-45, amphibious assault therefore served as the cutting edge of grand strategy. But it also acted – still acts today – as the key to planning and decision at the operational level. Which stretch of coastline offers the best possibilities for taking the enemy by surprise? Which offers the best opportunities for deep manoeuvre inland?

And below this operational level come the tactical decisions which determine whether the immediate assault will be successful or a bloody failure. Exactly which beaches offer the most favourable gradients and tidal flows for amphibious assault? Which are the least well-defended? Which has the best exits inland? These are questions only to be answered by painstaking reconnaissance – reconnaissance virtually absent before the landings on Gallipoli in 1915, but, along with elaborate aerial photography, fully carried out before the D-Day landings in Normandy in 1944.

In *Amphibious Assault: Manoeuvre from the Sea*, the editor and his contributors have produced a comprehensive but highly readable reference work covering every aspect of this hugely important subject, from grand strategy to tactics. This coverage takes the form of 37 richly varied and well-documented historical case-studies by distinguished historians and commanders. The case-studies range forward from Gallipoli, the supreme lesson in how not to do it, through the Second World War to the Korean conflict in 1950-51, the Suez operation in 1956, the Vietnam war of the 1960s, the recapture of the Falklands in 1982, and the first and second Gulf wars in 1991 and 2003. Moreover, the book also takes in seaborne assaults with a strictly limited purpose – raids really – such as the daring but abortive British attempt on St George's Day 1918 to block the exit from Zeebrugge harbour used by U-boats, or the successful attempt to put the dry-dock at St Nazaire out of action in 1942.

Today, when trans-oceanic armed intervention rather than mass continental warfare is likely to be the future norm, *Amphibious Assault* should be required reading for all officers, whether sailors, marines, soldiers, or airmen – and indeed all civil servants and politicians involved in the broad field of defence and foreign policy. In particular, the book serves as an antidote to the facile belief that advanced military technology ('net-centred warfare') provides a magic bullet, a sure recipe for success, so rendering all historical experience obsolete and redundant. The lessons afforded by the historical case-studies in this book stem from the failures and the successes in equal measure: reverse and obverse. The first such lesson is the need for a clear-cut tri-service organisational structure with a single overall commander at the top. Confused chains of command and uneasy relationships between land and sea commanders (sometimes very personal) have greatly contributed to the bungling of amphibious operations. The Anglo-French expedition to the Dardanelles in 1915 [Chapter II] provides the classic exemplar of such confusion, although similar command shortcomings also contributed to the muddles and fatal delays in the Anglo-French campaign in Norway in 1940 [Chapter VII], and, for that matter, the Japanese loss of Guadalcanal in 1942 [Chapter XII].

In sharpest contrast stands the elaborate tri-service organisational structure and crystal-clear chain of command created for Operation NEPTUNE, the D-day landings in Normandy on 6 June 1944, the largest and most complex amphibious operation ever [Chapter XXIII]. At the top was General Dwight Eisenhower as Supreme Commander Allied Expeditionary Force. Under him and responsible for planning and commanding the movements of 2,700 vessels (ranging from liners and battleships to towed barges) from British harbours to the invasion coast in the Bay of Normandy was Admiral Sir Bertram Ramsay. Under him in turn was Rear-Admiral Philip Vian RN (Eastern Task Force) and Rear Admiral Alan Kirk USN (Western Task Force).

Planning for the land battle once the amphibious assault had hit the beaches was the responsibility of Eisenhower's Land Force Commander, Field-Marshal Sir Bernard Montgomery. Ramsay and Montgomery not only worked together closely during the planning of D-Day, they even messed together, not entirely to Ramsay's pleasure.

The second lesson from history is that amphibious forces that are ill-trained and improvised at the last moment along with their headquarters and staffs are a sure recipe for calamity. This was certainly true of the hapless Dardanelles expedition of 1915; true of the bungled Anglo-French expedition to Norway in April 1940 [see Chapter VII]; and also true of the inept German preparations for Operation SEALION (the invasion of England in 1940). Comparable confusions nearly brought about disaster at Salerno in 1943 [Chapter XVI] and Anzio in 1944 [Chapter XX].

Instead, amphibious forces must be thoroughly well trained and rehearsed in what they have to do, and on a tri-service basis. This was, after all, another of the secrets of success in Operation NEPTUNE. Such a high degree of tri-service professional competence from commanders and staffs down to the rank-and-file enables an amphibious force to adapt swiftly to the unexpected setbacks that always occur at the sharp end in war. Training and rehearsal are in fact the secret of operational and tactical flexibility. Yet along with human preparedness must go adequate provision of specialised equipment such as landing ships, landing craft, and HQ ships. Lack of such equipment doomed the 1915 landings on Gallipoli, while abundance of it made possible the allied success on D-Day. Similar abundance facilitated the amazing advance of the US Navy, Marine Corps and Army from island to island across the Pacific.

The recurrent leitmotiv of *Amphibious Assault: Manoeuvre from the Sea* lies in using historical example to illustrate the now fashionable doctrine of 'manoeuvrism', whether by sea or land. As it happens, I was asked in 1993 to comment on an early draft of the British Army version of 'manoeuvrism'. I feared then,

and I fear now, that this might be a revival of Sir Basil Liddell Hart's concept of 'the indirect approach', which I along with other military historians have long believed to be dangerously seductive, even fallacious, because it offers an enticing vision of success easily won at small cost in casualties, and neglects a historical truth that conflicts between opponents roughly equal in combat effectiveness are decided by sheer attrition.

Among the successes for 'manoeuvrism' explored in *Amphibious Assault*, we may note the British landing at San Carlos Bay during the Falklands war of 1982 in preference to a direct attack on Port Stanley, as expected by the Argentinians. It was a classic outflanking manoeuvre, but it is fair to point out that the victim (denied all reinforcements by the Royal Navy) lacked the mobility and striking power to respond. Then again, MacArthur's seaborne leap-frogging of Japanese bases along the northern coast of New Guinea in 1943-44 [Chapter XXII], and his brilliant outflanking of the North Korean invaders of South Korea in 1950 by his landing at Inchon unquestionably constitute stunning achievements for 'manoeuvrism'. But in the New Guinea campaign MacArthur enjoyed a decisive superiority in naval and air forces over the Japanese. A more agile opponent would not have sat tight behind his defences waiting to be defeated in detail. In Korea the sensational success at Inchon was followed by a grim struggle of attrition ending in the stalemate of 1953.

Likewise, the allied victory in Normandy in August 1944 was the result of a two-month-long close-quarter battle of attrition won by sheer weight of men, material, and air-power. The German defenders simply ran out of reserves, whereupon their front broke up.

In Italy, 'manoeuvrist' allied attempts to bypass the strong German defence of the peninsula by landings at Salerno in 1943 and Anzio in 1944 failed in their strategic purpose, partly because of defects of allied operational planning and leadership, but largely because the German army was capable of swift redeployment to block off the beach-heads. Allied mobility by sea was matched by German mobility on land. So the actual fighting at Salerno and Anzio was decided by a process of attrition in which superior Allied strength eventually prevailed.

Even the strategic and operational manoeuvrism of the American forces in their advance island by island across the Pacific was only made possible by the weakness of the Imperial Japanese Navy owing to attrition by the United States Navy in fierce battles from Midway to Leyte Gulf.

Of course, it makes sense wherever possible to exploit the opportunity to outflank and take by surprise an enemy rather than pursue an obvious frontal approach, providing always that the enemy is inferior in combat effectiveness and above all in mobility. But it would be a dangerous mistake to become a mental prisoner of manoeuvrist doctrine, believing it to be the sure recipe for success. As all military and naval history goes to show, the primary intellectual requirement for success does not lie solely in doctrine, but in pragmatic good judgement founded on professional knowledge and experience, and on the classic principles of war.

Correlli Barnett

UK Principles of War

Selection and Maintenance of the Aim
Select and define the aim clearly, and ensure all strategy is directed toward achieving it.

Maintenance of Morale
Success in war depends as much on moral as on physical factors. Morale is an important element of war.

Offensive Action
Offensive action is the chief means to influence the outcome of a campaign or a battle.

Surprise
Seize the initiative. Surprise causes confusion and paralysis in the enemy's chain of command.

Concentration of Force
The concentration of superior force at the decisive time and place.

Economy of Effort
Make efficient use of forces, conserving energy and material to prevent unnecessary depletion.

Security
Physical protection and information denial is essential to all military operations.

Flexibility
Exercise judgement and flexibility in modifying plans to meet changed circumstances.

Cooperation
Coordinate the activities of all Arms, of the Services and of Allies, for optimum combined effort..

Administration
A clear appreciation of logistic constraints is essential.

US Principles of War

Objective
Direct every military operation toward a clearly defined, decisive and attainable objective

Offensive
Seize, retain, and exploit the initiative.

Mass
Mass the effects of overwhelming combat power at the decisive place and time.

Economy of Force
Employ all combat power available in the most effective way possible; allocate minimum essential combat power to secondary efforts.

Maneuver (UK: Manoeuvre)
Place the enemy in a position of disadvantage through the flexible application of combat power.

Unity of Command
For every objective, seek unity of command and unity of effort.

Security
Never permit the enemy to acquire unexpected advantage.

Surprise
Strike the enemy at a time or place or in a manner for which he is unprepared.

Simplicity
Prepare clear, uncomplicated plans and concise orders to ensure thorough understanding.

Preface

Crown Copyright

Amphibious landings are not simply about that moment when the Landing Craft comes to rest on the beach and the Coxswain shouts, '*Out Troops!*' The threat posed by a well-entrenched enemy positioned along a hostile shoreline, replete with man-made and natural obstacles, can never be underestimated. Although leadership, training and morale will always play a part in overcoming any threat, a professional knowledge of amphibious operations is paramount in littoral warfare; it underpins all else.

For centuries commanders have been identifying tactical, operational and strategic lessons from past campaigns and wars. Lessons from Gallipoli and Walcheren are as pertinent today as they were in 1915 or 1944. Although our capabilities, weapon platforms and doctrine may have developed, some key principles remain. Therefore, Royal Marines must be conversant with past amphibious operations.

Amphibious Assault: Manoeuvre from the Sea is an ideal starting point for junior commanders to build on their understanding of amphibious operations. It is also useful for a deeper appreciation of the role of the Royal Marines. For those attending bespoke Amphibious Warfare Courses, it will enhance the historical narratives in use. *Amphibious Assault: Manoeuvre from the Sea* illustrates cases containing those lessons that must be learned. Evidence from most recent operations suggests that we have learned from the past; but we should not become complacent for the future. It is our responsibility as experts in amphibious operations, to ensure that we remain familiar with the unique challenges that this type of warfare presents.

Major General J.B. Dutton CBE
Commandant General Royal Marines
(2004-2006)

Acknowledgements

This book would not have been possible without the wholehearted support and enthusiastic commitment of each chapter author. Thank you! The contributors have been extremely generous with their time, expertise and knowledge, unified in their desire to make their chapters as informative, interesting and relevant as possible. Their collective efforts are hugely beneficial to the Royal Marines and to other professionals who have an interest in the development of Amphibious Warfare.

I am particularly indebted to Mr Adrian Williams and Mr Mike Tanner from the Royal Navy Graphics Centre. They have worked tirelessly over the last four years making the myriad changes in order to make this book what it is.

Significant thanks are also due to Mrs Patricia Eve, Mrs Nicky Clarke, Mr Louis Mackay and Mr Hugh Brazier of Seafarer Books for their welcome support, their enthusiasm for this book and their wish to see it published.

I would also like to thank: Captain Christopher Page R.N., Mr Steve Prince and Kate Tildesley from the Naval Historical Branch; Mr Ian Hook, Curator of the Essex Regiment Museum; Mr Robert Wardle, Mrs Angela Twist and Mrs Rachel MacEachern from the Library at the Commando Training Centre Royal Marines; Mr Richard Kennell, Mrs Janet Kennell and Mrs Gill Smith from the Library at Britannia Royal Naval College Dartmouth; Mr Robert White, Mr Chris Plant, Ms Joan Carbard, Elizabeth Bowers and Mrs Yvonne Oliver from the Photograph Archive at the Imperial War Museum; Mr Paul Johnson from The National Archives at Kew; Mr Mathew Little and Mr John Ambler at the Royal Marines Museum Portsmouth; Captain John Hillier MBE RM; Lieutenant Colonel Andrew Noyes RM; Major Peter Willett HAC; Lieutenant Colonel Timothy Jackson, Lieutenant Colonel Michael West, Colonel Jon Hoffman and Major Brendan McBreen USMC; Chief Historian Charles D. Melson at the US Marine Corps History and Museums Division, Washington D.C.; Commodore Michael Clapp CB RN; Brigadier Ian McNeil; Lieutenant Commander Alex Manning RN; and Major General David Botting CB CBE. In particular I am deeply grateful to Major General Julian Thompson CB OBE for his guidance, advice and generous support; Professor John Forfar MC for his kind comments and continued encouragement and to Professor Kenneth J. Hagan for his professionalism, friendship and for acting as the 'bridge' across the Atlantic.

Thanks are also extended to serving and former Directors of the Advanced Amphibious Warfare Course delivered by the Defence Studies Department at the Defence Academy. Dr Robert Foley, Dr Stuart Griffin, Dr Harry Dickinson, Dr Ian Speller and Dr Tim Benbow have all contributed chapters, have been highly supportive of amphibious education and been enthusiastic in their desire to help with this publication. In addition many officers from the Royal Marines who have attended the Advanced Amphibious Warfare Course either as visiting lecturers or on the course, have been very generous with their suggestions, in particular those from Lieutenant Colonel David King RM, Lieutenant Colonel Mark Maddick RM, Lieutenant Colonel Jim Morris RM, Major Dai Davies RM, Major Richard Reardon RM, Major Neil Robertson RM, Major Richard Parvin RM, Major Matt Stovin-Bradford RM, Major Woody Page RM, Maj Ollie Lee RM, Maj Nigel Somerville MBE RM, Major John Collins RM, and Major Dave Nicholson RM. I would also like to pass on my thanks and gratitude to Reverend David Devenney for our partnership in encouraging the use of battlefield tours in making history come alive. Other officers who have provided very useful additional comment are: Lieutenant Colonel Rory Copinger-Symes RM, Lieutenant Colonel Rex Barnes RM, Lieutenant Colonel George Mathews RM, Lieutenant Colonel John Davies RM, Major Simon Chapman RM, Major Alex Case RM, Major Mark Searight RM, Major Ian Corner RM, Major Matt Hood RM, Major Bob Perry RM and Captain Jim Nicholas RM. I would also like to thank Mr John Lodge for his professional advice about medals.

I would also like to thank close work friends and colleagues, in particular Colonel Joss McCabe OBE, Commander Peter Adams RN, Major Clive Wilson RM, Major Chris Hazelwood RM and Lieutenant Commander Andrew Plackett RN who have also provided considerable support in ensuring the successful completion of this publication.

Finally a sincere and heart felt thank you to my wife and family for their patience, understanding and tolerance over the last four years: Lisa, Montgomery, Horatio, Tiggy, Alan, Bronwen, Pauline and Peter.

The editor takes full responsibility for any mistakes, errors or omissions in this book.

This book is dedicated to my friend and mentor Robin Neillands.
His love of military history was only surpassed by that for the Royal Marines.

Introduction
Amphibious Assault: Manoeuvre from the Sea

By Lieutenant Commander Tristan T A Lovering MBE RN

Between 1999 and 2004 the British Armed Forces were deployed in Bosnia, Congo, Rwanda, Sierra Leone, Kosovo, Afghanistan and Iraq. The Royal Marines were frequently at the vanguard of those deployments, working as an integrated part of the Royal Navy, delivering a significant battlefield effect in conjunction with the Army and Royal Air Force. Frequently those operations were not only *joint* between the different services of the British Military, but *combined*, in close cooperation with partners from the United States Marine Corps, the Royal Netherlands Marine Corps, the Australian Defence Force, and other important allies. That busy operational tempo did not allow the Royal Marines the opportunity to put their recent campaigns into context. Other than those who managed to smuggle a history book into their already heavy bergans, few had the opportunity to delve into the record of amphibious operations.

Aim

The principal aim of this book is to enhance Royal Marines' core knowledge of amphibious warfare. All are familiar with the names of assaults, raids, withdrawals and amphibious demonstrations, but not everyone is conversant with the detail. The intention of *Amphibious Assault: Manoeuvre from the Sea* is to act as one of the foundation stones in the understanding of amphibious warfare. Whatever the future holds for expeditionary warfare, history

demonstrates there will always be a need for the military to have a specialist capability of fighting in the littoral region.[1] The challenges posed by amphibious operations against a hostile (or potentially hostile) shore are uniquely difficult to overcome given that they demand a thorough awareness of both land and naval warfare. The adoption of the 'manoeuvrist approach', as we will see later, is key to overcoming the obstacles posed on an enemy shoreline and gaining theatre entry.

While today's Royal Marines are highly experienced, there are still lessons that can be identified from their forebears. Current amphibious doctrine owes much to the lessons from Suez, Korea, Dieppe or earlier. Therefore, a subsidiary aim of this book is to highlight the part that History plays. Such is the importance of its role that the Navy Board has instructed that all officers in the Royal Marines and Royal Navy should undergo formal study of the fundamental principles of British Maritime Doctrine. History has evolved and reinforced these principles. The value of History to the Royal Navy and Royal Marines is, perhaps, best summed up by the naval theorist Sir Julian Corbett. He reflected in 1913 that:

> 'No historian whose task has brought him in touch with this work can fail to appreciate its value, nor in the care and thoroughness of its methods can we fail to recognise a complete change in the attitude of the Services to history…It is, primarily at least, due to the sound and

philosophical method which the Historical Sections have adopted that has led them directly to an appreciation of the practical living value of history – that has revealed history not as a museum of antiquities, but as a treasure-house of rich experience…Officers no longer look upon history as a kind of dust heap from which a convenient brick may be extracted to hurl at their opponents. They no longer go to it to prove some empirical view of tactics or material, or to show that some battle or other was fought in the way they think it ought to have been fought. They go to it as a mine of experience where alone the gold is to be found, from which the right doctrine – the soul of warfare – can be built up'.[2]

History allows the professional, expert in current procedures and familiar with the latest technology and platform capabilities, to reflect on those operations of the past in order to place his experience in context. Corbett commented on this, he continued:

> 'A broad distinction will at once suggest itself between histories of bygone wars, waged with material that is now quite obsolete and under conditions that no longer exist, from which we can only derive the broader doctrines; and histories that deal with the wars of yesterday, in which, in spite of the rapid development of material, we seek for closer and more direct light on the wars of tomorrow'.[3]

---

[1] Generally accepted to mean the coastal sea areas and that portion of the land which is susceptible to influence or support from the sea.
[2] Julian Corbett, 'Staff Histories' in *Naval and Military Essays: Being Papers read in the Naval and Military Section at the International Congress of Historical Studies 1913* (Cambridge: University Press, 1914), p. 23.
[3] *Ibid.*, pp. 23 -38.

The Cost of Attrition: Allied dead in an abandoned landing craft following the Raid at Dieppe in August 1942. (NHB)

The Manoeuvrist Approach

'The manoeuvrist approach to operations is one in which shattering the enemy's overall cohesion and will to fight, rather then his materiel, is paramount. Manoeuvre warfare is the application of manoeuvrist thinking to warfighting. It aims to apply strength against identified vulnerabilities. Significant features are momentum and tempo, which in combination lead to shock action and surprise. Emphasis is on defeat and disruption of the enemy by taking the initiative and applying constant and unacceptable pressure at the times and places the enemy least suspects, rather than attempting to seize and hold ground for its own sake. It calls for an attitude of mind in which doing the unexpected and seeking originality is combined with a ruthless determination to succeed'.[4]

Elements of manoeuvre are encapsulated in the ideas of military thinkers as far back as Sun Tzu and Machiavelli, to the writings of military thinkers such as Clausewitz and Captain Sir Basil Liddell Hart.[5] The manoeuvrist concept gained credibility, at the expense of the attritional approach to warfare, in the late 1980's following its widespread acceptance in much of the US military. More recently there has been debate as to the merit of assuming that the period of the attritional style of warfare had passed.[6] Even one of the key proponents of manoeuvre has identified that in the new age, the threat encompassed in the '4th Generation war' has rendered some of the ideas of manoeuvre potentially obsolete.[7] Where a prospective adversary is unlikely to be a nation-state and not content to meet the most developed nations on a conventional battlefield, manoeuvre, it is argued, may perhaps be an outdated concept. However, in this era where the public have immediate access to the information from the battlefield via the global media, as well as a limited acceptance for casualties, the manoeuvrist approach still has merit. Not only does it encompass principles for warfighting that are still relevant today, significantly it is an approach that, unlike its attritional counterpart, will hopefully result in fewer casualties.

Manoeuvre relies on shock action, deception and suprise, fundamental to a successful military operation and key to achieving victory at the lowest cost to one's own side. It may not always be possible to meet all the criteria contained within the term 'manoeuvre' but the approach gives an indication of the manner in which victory should be sought. These ideas gained prominence in the late 1970's, and were advocated by Colonel John Boyd, U.S. Air Force. He introduced a concept which is key to the manoeuvrist approach, coining the term 'Observation, Orientation, Decision and Action' (OODA) loop. This gained support from commanders from all arms and services as they identified its value in enhancing their own ability to conduct war in the most efficient manner. He believed that the faster a commander could undertake those different actions on the battlefield (in any environment) the greater the likelihood that the enemy would lose the initiative. This in turn would allow greater freedom of action and enable a more effective battle winning strategy to be adopted. Getting

---

[4]*British Defence Doctrine* (JWP 0-01) (2nd Edition), Chapter 3.

[5]Important texts include: Paret, Peter, *Makers of Modern Strategy: from Machiavelli to the Nuclear Age*, (Oxford: Clarendon Press, 1990), Tzu, Sun, *The Art of War*, (Oxford: Oxford University Press, 1971), Machiavelli, Niccolo, *Art of War*, (Chicago: University of Chicago Press, 2003), Clausewitz, Carl von, *On War*, (London: Everyman's Library, 1993) and Liddell Hart, B. H., *Strategy*, (New York: Praeger, 1955).

[6]See: Bellamy, Professor Christopher, 'In Praise of Attrition', A Summary of his Inaugural Lecture at Cranfield University, in *The British Army Review, The Magazine of British Military Thought*, No. 134, Summer, 2004, p. 46 and earlier articles, 'Operational Maneuver From the Sea' by General Charles C. Krulak U.S. Marine Corps, *Proceedings* January, 1997, p. 26; 'Myths of Manoeuvre' by Brigadier Robert Fry RM, *RUSI Journal*, December, 1997, p.5; 'Liddell Hart and Manoeuvre' by Professor Alex Danchev, *RUSI Journal*, December, 1998, p. 33; and 'The Meaning of Manoeuvre' articles by Major General John Kiszely MC and Brigadier Robert Fry MBE, *RUSI Journal*, December, 1998, pp. 36-44.

[7]See: 'The Changing Face of War: Into the Fourth Generation' by William S. Lind *et. al.*, in *The Marine Corps Gazette*, Vol. 73, Number 10, (October, 1989), pp.22-26, and in the next Chapter by William S. Lind.

inside the enemy's OODA loop allowed quicker decision making and the opportunity to prosecute the battle in a manner which was more likely to result in defeat for the adversary. Commanders seek to achieve and maintain 'decision superiority' and optimum tempo at all levels in order to gain and retain initiative. This comparative advantage can be enhanced by the use of amphibious assets to assist in dominating all parts of the battlespace, particularly in joint operations.

Manoeuvre and Joint Operations

Manoeuvre is not simply confined to the land campaign. The Maritime Contribution to Joint Operations (MCJO) enhances the aspiration and prospect of manoeuvring into a position of advantage in a land campaign. The land component commander seeks to adopt an approach which gives him an advantage with respect to the enemy, from which force can either be threatened or applied. An important role, envisaged both in the MCJO and in the Future Maritime Operational Concept (FMOC), is the ability to position the land force in a manner which is likely to achieve surprise, confuse an adversary and be innovative in the way in which the force operates. Amongst the key attributes provided by the Naval force is the speed at which it can travel, the distances covered in any 24 hour period and its significant integrated logistical support. A maritime force can move as far as 400 miles in one day in order to establish a new position from which to strike. Land forces, without air or sea lift, are much more restricted. Operational Manoeuvre From The Sea (OMFTS) is a combat function, and considerably adds to the joint operational perspective. The attributes of an amphibious force are considerable, and as part of a multinational joint task force provide the strategic commander with an invaluable asset with which to shape the littoral battlespace. Concepts such as Ship to Objective Manoeuvre (STOM)

and Littoral Manoeuvre (LitM) seek to take advantage of the assets held by the amphibious force and turn the theory of manoeuvre into reality. The UK's maritime forces have always operated in the littoral regions of the world and "predictions of the future strategic environment indicate that little will change".[8] Britain's interests will inevitably continue to be influenced by those centres where population, resources, industry and trade are concentrated, and the ability to operate in that environment is of great importance. The amphibious force is an ideal tool to achieve this. Many outstanding examples of manoeuvre from the sea are included in this book, two of which are described in the chapters by Colonel Michael Hickey examining the Inchon landings in Korea and by Dr Tim Benbow's on Madagascar during 1942. The Maritime component of a joint force is particularly relevant when examining different campaigns of the past, but it does not offer the exclusive solution to any given phase of war. Indeed,

> 'All forces have the potential to offer ways and means of enhancing the manoeuvrist approach. To do this most effectively, all must be allowed to play to their particular strengths. Maritime, land and air forces have different but complimentary attributes. Access, mobility, versatility, sustained reach, resilience, lift capacity, forward presence, poise and leverage of the maritime forces are the Royal Navy's contribution to the joint solution'.[9]

Joint operations are not simply a matter of forces from different arms of the armed forces operating in the same theatre. The real essence of effective command, is demonstrated in the chapters on Normandy and Iraq where the relative strengths and weaknesses (both inherent and institutional) of each component of the force were recognised; the value of a joint force being more than merely the sum of its constituent parts. The strength of a joint approach to warfighting is nothing new, and strategists over the last century frequently identify the merits of a combined Naval, Land and Air solution in amphibious operations.

In the era of globalisation the importance of the sea is likely to grow.[10] The new strategic environment is now much less stable with the loss of the old east-west balance of power. The policy led Strategic Defence Review set the foundations for a more expeditionary UK defence strategy,[11] which is likely to result in future maritime operations being joint and often multinational/combined.

The well earned reputation of the Royal Marines and Royal Navy is based on many of the operations described in detail within *Amphibious Assault: Manoeuvre from the Sea*. These campaigns

[8]*British Maritime Doctrine BR1806*, Third Edition, (Norwich: Her Majesties Stationery Office, 2004), p. 27.
[9]*Ibid*, p. 48.
[10] See: The First Sea Lord's Address to RUSI (12 May 2004) 'Maritime Power in a Global Context', available at http://www.royal-navy.mod.uk/static/pages/content.php3?page=6817
[11]'Delivering Security in a Changing World: Future Capabilities', Presented to Parliament by The Secretary of State for Defence (TSO, July 2004).

help to explain the basis of their reputation. The high quality training, excellent motivation, versatility, close cooperation, teamwork and professionalism have ensured that the Royal Marines and Royal Navy remain a battle winning combination. The maritime component of national strategy is vital for the conduct of expeditionary operations that are likely to evolve following the 'end of the continental century'.[12] The relevance of the amphibious capability is clearly stated in the different operations examined in this book.

As in Corbett's time, modern forces have to be prepared for limited war. The need for mobile, pre-packaged expeditionary forces is likely to increase in the decade's ahead, and the result will inevitably require a force *from the sea*, along the lines of Corbett's predictions, as opposed to the power *at sea* maintained throughout the Cold War period. Professor Geoffrey Till has reflected, 'The ability to focus a higher proportion of naval effort on the projection of power ashore rather than on control of the sea would seem to imply that the leverage of seapower over the world's affairs will certainly not diminish in the future but on the contrary will probably grow.'[13,14] The Royal Marines are, therefore, likely to remain at the vanguard fulfilling their unique role, by sea and by land, encapsulated in their motto, *'Per Mare Per Terram'*.

At the end of each chapter is suggested 'Further Reading'. These lists have been compiled for those seeking more information about each operation. There are a number of other texts which give more detail about the development and history of amphibious operations. This list highlights a concise selection of some of those currently in use by the Royal Marines.

Royal Marines

Thompson, Major General Julian, *The Royal Marines: From Sea Soldiers to a Special Force, (Sidgwick & Jackson,* 2000)

Neillands, Robin, *By Sea and Land: The Royal Marines Commandos: A History, 1942-1982,* (Casemate, 1987)

Ladd, James D., *By Sea, By Land: The Royal Marines, 1919-1997: An Authorized History. Rev. Ed.,* (Harper Collins, 1998)

A Short History of the Royal Marines, 1664-2002, published by The Royal Marines Historical Society, Special Publication No. 25, (RMHS, 2002)

UK Doctrinal & Official Publications

British Defence Doctrine, 2nd Edition, (JWP 0-01*),* (JDCC, 2001)

British Maritime Doctrine, 3rd Edition, (BR-1806) (TSO, 2004)

United Kingdom Approach to Amphibious Operations, (MWC,1997)

NATO *ATP (8) B, Vol.1, Doctrine for Amphibious Operations.*

United States Marine Corps, MCDP 1, *Warfighting,* (1997)

The Application of Force: *An Introduction to Army Doctrine and the Conduct of Military Operations*, (Norwich: TSO, 2002)

Amphibious Operations

Bartlett, Lieutenant Colonel Merrill L., USMC (Rtd.) *Assault from the Sea: Essays on the History of Amphibious Warfare*, (Naval Institute Press, 1983)

Evans, Colonel M.H.H., *Amphibious Operations: The Projection of Sea Power Ashore,* (Brassey's, 1990)

Fergusson, Bernard, *The Watery Maze: The Story of Combined Operations,* (Collins, 1961)

Gatchel, Theodore, *At the Waters Edge: Defending Against the Modern Amphibious Assault,* (Naval Institute Press, 1996)

Hayden, Lieutenant Colonel H. Tom, *Warfighting: Maneuver Warfare in the U.S. Marine Corps,* (Greenhill Books, 1995)

Ladd, James J. D., *Assault from the Sea 1939-1945: The Craft, The Landings, The Men*, (David & Charles, 1976)

Ladd, James J. D., *Commandos and Rangers of World War II,* (Book Club Associates, 1978)

Speller, Ian & Tuck, Christopher, *Amphibious Warfare: The Theory and Practice of Amphibious Operations in the 20th Century,* (Spellmount, 2001)

Whitehouse, Arch, *Amphibious Operations,* (Frederick Muller, 1963)

---

[12] Fry, Brigadier Robert MBE, 'End of the Continental Century', from *RUSI Journal*, June, 1998, pp. 15-18.

[13] Professor Geoffrey Till is Dean of Academic Studies in the Department of Defence Studies at the Defence Academy. He is author of many key texts examining modern maritime history and contemporary maritime strategy, including: Series Editor of the Frank Cass Naval History and Policy series; *Amphibious Warfare*, (1997); *Seapower: Theory and Practice*, (1994); Geoffrey Till (ed.), *Seapower at the Millennium*, (2001); With G.D. Sheffield (eds.) *Challenges of High Command in the Twentieth Century*, (2003); *Seapower: A Guide for the 21st Century* (2003).

[14] Till, Geoffrey, 'Maritime Strategy and the Twenty-First Century' in *The Journal of Strategic Studies*, Vol. 17, No. 1, March 1994, p.186.

Commando Unit Histories

Beadle, Major J. G., *The Light Blue Lanyard: 50 Years with 40 Commando RM*, (Square One Publications, 1992)

Courtney, G.B., *SBS in World War Two: The Story of the original Special Boat Section of the Army Commandos*, (London: Robert Hale, 1983)

Churchill, Major General T., *Commando Crusade*, (London: William Kimber, 1987)

Durnford-Slater, Brigadier John, *Commando*, (Kimber, 1953)

Ford, Ken, *D-Day Commando: From Normandy to the Maas with 48 Royal Marine Commando*, (Sutton Publishing, 2003)

Forfar, John, *From Omaha to the Scheldt: The Story of 47 Royal Marine Commando*, (Tuckwell Press, 2001)

Hampshire, Cecil A., *The Beachhead Commandos*, (Kimber, 1978)

Lee, David, *Beachhead Assault: The Story of the Royal Navy Commandos in World War II*, (Greenhill Books, 2004)

Lockhart, Robert Bruce, *The Marines Were There: The Story of the Royal Marines in the Second World War* (Putnam, 1950)

Messenger, Charles, *The Commandos, 1940-1946*, (William Kimber, 1985)

Mitchell, Raymond, *They Did What Was Asked of Them: 41 (Royal Marines) Commando 1942-1946*, (Firebird, 1996)

Moulton, Major General J. L., *The Battle for Antwerp: The Liberation of the City and the Opening of the Scheldt, 1944* (Hippocrene,1978), & *Haste to Battle* (Cassell, 1963)

St George Saunders, Hilary, *The Green Beret; The Story of the Commandos 1940-1945*, (Michael Joseph, 1949)

Young, David, *Four-Five: The Story of 45 Commando Royal Marines, 1943-1971*, (Cooper, 1972)

Globe and Laurel Magazine

The Sheet Anchor Magazine (RM Historical Society)

Navy News

Historical

Amphibious Warfare Headquarters, *The History of the Combined Operations Organisation 1940-1945*, (London, 1956)

Aston, Sir George (Colonel of Royal Marine Artillery), *Sea, Land, and Air Strategy: A Comparison*, (London: John Murray, 1914) & *Letters on Amphibious Wars*, (1911)

Barnett, Correlli, *Engage the Enemy More Closely*, (London: Penguin, 2000)

Calwell, Colonel C. E., *Military Operations & Maritime Preponderance: Their Relations and Interdependence*, (Blackwood, 1905)

Combined Operations 1940-1942: Prepared for the Combined Operations Command by the Ministry of Information, (London: HMSO, 1943)

Corbett, Julian S., *Some Principles of Maritime Strategy*, (1911)

Corbett, Sir Julian S., *England in the Seven Years' War*, (Greenhill Books, London, 1992)

Creswell, Captain John, *Generals and Admirals: The Story of Amphibious Command*, (London: Longmans, 1952)

Grove, Dr Eric, *The Royal Navy Since 1815, A New Short History* (Palgrave Macmillan 2005)

Keyes, Admiral of the Fleet, The Lord, *Amphibious Warfare and Combined Operations*, (Cambridge, 1943)

Lorelli, J.A., *To Foreign Shores: U.S. Amphibious Operations in World War Two*, (Annapolis:NIP, 1996)

Maund, Rear Admiral L., *Assault from the Sea*, (Methuen, 1949)

Molyneux, Thomas More, *Conjunct Operations: or Expeditions that have been carried on Jointly by the Fleet and Army*, (London R. and J. Dodsley, 1759)

Roskill, Captain S.W., *The Strategy of Sea Power: Its Development and Application*, (Collins, 1962)

Vagts, A., *Landing Operations: Strategy, Psychology, Tactics, Politics, from Antiquity to 1945* (1946)

Additional Recommended Reading

Alexander, J. & Bartlett, M., *Sea Soldiers in the Cold War*, (1995)

Badsey, Stephen, *Normandy: Utah Beach* (Sutton, 2004) & *Normandy, 1944: Allied Landings and Breakout*, (Osprey, 1990)

Ballendorf, Dirk and Bartlett, Merrill, *Pete Ellis: An Amphibious Warfare Prophet, 1880-1923*, (Naval Institute Press, 1997)

Bruce, Colin, *Invaders: The British and American Experience of Seaborne Landings 1939-1945*, (Chatham, 1999)

Gardiner, Ian, *In the Service of the Sultan*, (Pen & Sword, 2006)

Hagan, Professor Kenneth, *The People's Navy: The Making of American Seapower*, (The Free Press, 1992)

Hickey, Colonel Michael, *The Korean War: The West Confronts Communism 1950-1953*, (John Murray, 1999) & *Gallipoli*, (John Murray, 1995)

Lind, William S., *Maneuver Warfare Handbook*, (Westview, 1985)

Page, Captain Christopher, R.N., *Command in the Royal Naval Division*, (Spellmount, 1999)

Southby-Tailyour, Ewen and Clapp, Michael *Amphibious Assault Falklands: The Battle for San Carlos Water*, (Orion, 1997)

Southby-Tailyour, E., (ed.), *Jane's Amphibious Warfare Capabilities*, (Coulsdons: Jane's Information Group, 2000)

Speller, Ian, *The Role of Amphibious Warfare in British Defence Policy, 1945-56*, (Palgrave, 2001)

Thompson, Major General Julian, *No Picnic: 3 Commando Brigade in the South Atlantic, 1982*, (Fontana, 1985)

Till, Professor Geoffrey, *Seapower: A Guide for the 21st Century*, (London: Frank Cass, 2003)

Crowl, P.A. and Isley, J.A., *The U.S. Marines and Amphibious War*, (Princeton:Princeton University Press, 1951)

United States Marine Corps Gazette

United States Naval Institute Proceedings

Whicker, Alan, *Whicker's War*, (London:Harper Collins, 2005)

Manoeuvre - Historical Significance
The Influence of History upon Sea Power

I

By Mr William S Lind

One of the many false ideas universally held true in present times is the notion that 'new' means 'good' and 'old' implies useless and irrelevant. I am certain it comes as a surprise to young Marine officers who ask me what to read on the subject of amphibious war when I suggest Sir Julian Corbett's two-volume work *England in the Seven Years' War* - a book published in 1907 that concerns a war fought between the years 1756 and 1763.

In fact, I know of no finer or more instructive study of manoeuvre in amphibious war on all three levels, strategic, operational and tactical. Wolfe's taking of Quebec is just one of many examples: it was an amphibious campaign, waged over a distance of 3000 miles, that was in turn part of Pitt's amphibious strategy - the 'Maritime War,' as it was called at the time - by which he endeavored to influence the outcome of the war in Germany. At the tactical level, the intimate cooperation of fleet and army, the use of amphibious mobility to bypass the main French defences, Wolfe's 'getting inside the mind' of his French enemies by presenting more threats than they could possibly counter, all speak directly to amphibious manoeuvre warfare of the present. Compare what Corbett writes about the British fleet commander at Quebec, Admiral Saunders, with the actions of the Royal Navy in the Falkland's War:

General James Wolfe used flat-bottomed boats to cross the St Lawrence River in order to take the Plains of Abraham during the Seven Years War with France. (Quebec, 13th September, 1759)

'To carry such a fleet as his up such a river, to maintain it there for three months in spite of gales and batteries and two attacks by fireships, to preserve it in perfect harmony with the sister service, to judge and take every risk soberly and yet to the extremity of daring; and finally, to bring it forth again at the last moment with the loss of but one ship, was a stroke of conduct without parallel. Such a method of proceeding requires, of course, the highest foresight, resource, and daring - indeed all the finest qualities a leader can possess. At the same time there is no force so well adapted for the work as one that is amphibious, not only in composition but also in unity of purpose and harmony of spirit between admiral and general. Such fortunately - perhaps in the highest degree on record - was the British force which sat astride the entrance of the basin of Quebec.'[1]

From the perspective of manoeuvre warfare doctrine, there is no question as to whether the study of history can and should influence the conduct of maritime war, the combination of naval warfare and operations ashore by amphibious forces, in the present time. There is a question, however, as to how history should be used. There are two different approaches, the analytical and the synthetic. One is supportive of manoeuvre doctrine and the other is not.

It may be helpful here to look first at manoeuvre warfare's opposite, what I call Second Generation war and is also known as firepower/attrition warfare or methodical battle (were I to be unkind to the Americans, I might also call it 'synchronized war').[2] Developed by the French Army during and after World War I, Second Generation war attempts to break war down into discrete actions which can then be combined into set methods or processes.[3] To give battle, one simply goes through the steps of the process in the stipulated order.

When history is studied in support of Second Generation war, it is studied analytically. The goal is to find rules or principles: in such a situation, one should do this. One thereby develops rules such as 'never hold artillery in reserve,' or 'amphibious operations cannot succeed without air and sea superiority' (a look at German amphibious operations in the eastern Mediterranean

[1] Sir Julian S. Corbett, *England in the Seven Years' War* (Greenhill Books, London, 1992), Vol. I, pp. 476 and 424

[2] The framework of the Four Generations of Modern War was first laid out in an article in the October, 1989 Marine Corps Gazette, *"The Changing Face of War: Into the Fourth Generation;"* the author of this chapter was one of five co-authors of the piece. The great American military theorist Colonel John Boyd argued strongly that synchronization was incompatible with maneuver warfare.

[3] Robert Allen Doughty, *The Seeds of Disaster: The Development of French Army Doctrine, 1919-1939* (The Shoe String Press, Hamden, Conn., 1985)

in 1943-44 soon puts paid to that one), or perhaps worst of all, the rule that amphibious manoeuvre requires specially prepared forces with unique equipment (to roast that chestnut, look at 'Panzer' Meyer's crossing of the Gulf of Corinth while chasing the British Army out of Greece in 1941).

War simply does not work this way. For every rule, there are many exceptions. For every infallible method or process, the enemy has a wide selection of spanners to toss in the works. It is no accident that the German Army, which pioneered Third Generation manoeuvre warfare, had no list of 'principles of war' derived from history. They knew that any such rules represented a misuse of history and a false image of war. Their first and perhaps only rule of war was that every situation is unique.

A young Marine officer might ask, 'If that is true, then what is the purpose of studying history at all?' The Third Generation, manoeuvrist answer is one word, a word central to manoeuvre doctrine: context.

In a Second Generation service, the young officer or new recruit is constantly having someone senior grab his head and push it down into the mud. 'Look down' is the message, down into the minutiae of minor tactics and techniques. Anything else, he is forcefully told, is 'above your pay grade.'

Some years ago, when the U.S. Marine Corps was moving toward adopting manoeuvre doctrine,[4] a group of Marine officers from Quantico met with some former *Wehrmacht* officers. The Marines said, 'Of course, you agree that in officer training, one has to start with the basics.' The Germans did not agree. They replied, 'The first thing we did with an officer candidate was to put him in the position of a battalion commander in war games and map exercises. If he could not understand how to fight a battalion he could never lead a platoon.'

The reason the Germans did this was to get the young officer candidate's head up, to begin to form the mental habit of always seeing his own military situation in a larger context. Because manoeuvre doctrine accepts the fog and friction of war, rather than trying to impose order on it, it relies on leaders at every level, down to the individual soldier or Marine, to make their own actions harmonise with and support what their superiors are trying to achieve. They can only do that if they think up and comprehend up, if they routinely can and do see their own situation in a broad context. In effect, manoeuvre warfare demands a **Gestalt** type of thinking, where the situation is seen as a whole and not analytically as a collection of independent parts. That, again, requires context and a constant search by all leaders for context.

It is here where the synthetic reading of history comes in. The manoeuvrist who is studying history is looking not for rules but for the largest possible picture, the broadest context, and an understanding of how all the pieces fit together (or, quite often, failed to fit together) in that context. He is less taking things apart than putting them together, not only putting them together as they actually did or did not fit but also as they might have fit differently. In doing so, he is developing a habit of mind that can and should carry forward into the actual situations he will face in war.

By studying history, he is experiencing far more situations and the mental problems they posed than he can ever hope to experience personally. To some advantage, he is doing so in ways where learning experiences need not be paid for in his own blood or the blood of his men. He can see results and outcomes more clearly than they are ever visible in ongoing operations. He can work from the large picture to the small and back again, developing an understanding of how his own actions may fit in the larger situations of which he will someday be a part. He will, in short, get his nose up out of the mud into which the sergeant major pushed it.

What sorts of history are best to study in order to develop an ability to see and think in context? Good case studies, such as

---

[4]It did so officially but not in practice.

those provided in this book, are invaluable. In school situations, they are ideally used in conjunction with map problems, where the student is first put in the historical situation as a commander and compelled to make and explain decisions. Then, he reads what actually happened and why. This is especially useful in developing the all-important ability to critique military exercises, because it develops an ability to see critical junctures - times and places in the action where events threw the result one way or the other.

But case studies are not where the new student of war should start. He should start reading history to develop the broadest of all contexts, the context of the evolution of war itself. The intellectual framework of the 'Four Generations of Modern War' is one such context, and there is a canon of seven books which, read in the right order, establishes that framework (as one U.S. Marine Captain teaching at The Basic School put it, 'Unless the guy is a rock, he can't read these books in the right order and not get it.').

The books (in the correct order) are:

1) *The Enlightened Soldier: Scharnhorst and the Militaerische Gesellschaft in Berlin, 1801-1805,* by Charles Edward White. This book explains why you are reading all the other books.

2) *The Seeds of Disaster: The Development of French Army Doctrine, 1919-1939,* by Robert Doughty. Here you will find the origins of the current 'American way of war,' which will

also necessarily be the way a combined Anglo-American force will fight. Every U.S. Marine officer to whom I have lent my copy has returned it saying, 'This is us.'

3) *Stormtroop Tactics: Innovation in the German Army, 1914-1918,* by Bruce Gudmundsson. The best book on the birth of modern manoeuvre warfare, it is also a wonderful study of how to change an army. The Germans applied their new manoeuvre tactics in amphibious operations in the Baltic, leading to a very different approach from that developed by the U.S. Marine Corps between the wars.

4) *Command or Control?:* by Martin Samuels. As Bruce Gudmundsson has said, in every generation one Briton is allowed accurately to understand the German way of war. In the present generation that man is Martin Samuels, and this contrast of the British and German approaches is of vast value to a British audience.

5) *The Breaking Point: Sedan and the Fall of France, 1940,* again by Robert Doughty (the chairman of the History Department at West Point). Here the reader sees Second and Third Generation war meet on the battlefield, in a book that reads like a good novel. Over and over, the Germans get the result the situation requires because subordinates (often NCOs) take initiative, while the French wait for orders.

6) *Fighting Power: German and U.S. Army Performance, 1939-1945,* by Martin van Creveld. This book compares and

contrasts Second and Third Generation militaries as institutions, showing how profoundly they differ in almost everything. Readers will quickly understand why it won't work to try to equip a Second Generation service with manoeuvre doctrine; the head and the body will reject each other.

7) *The Transformation of War:* by Martin van Creveld. The definitive book thus far on Fourth Generation war, this is also the most important book on war published in at least the last quarter century.

Especially for an audience interested in maritime war, I am tempted to expand the canon by one book: *The Rules of the Game,* by Andrew Gordon. In the second half of the 18th century, the Royal Navy developed what we now call manoeuvre warfare in almost all its central aspects. Gordon writes the account of how it lost it all again in the 19th century, and why. At the heart of the answer lies something that cuts close to home in the present time of computers and 'information dominance': signalling.

The canon offers a foundation, and a necessary one, because it provides the biggest of the ink-blots in the **Gestalt** of manoeuvre warfare. In building the structure of genuine understanding higher, the next level is probably memoirs that take the reader inside the mind of commanders who were successful in manoeuvre war. A few of my favorites are von Mafistein's *Lost Victories,* Rommel's *Infantry Attacks!* and the Civil War memoirs of American General U.S. Grant (his Vicksburg campaign in particular, which has amphibious elements; also, if you ever want to study model orders, look at Grant's). Surprisingly, good historical fiction can also offer first-rate studies in decision-making; some examples are C.S. Forester's Horatio Hornblower books and similar naval novels by C. Northcote Parkinson.

Then come historical case studies, such as those found in this book. Here, value is proportional to how the reader approaches them. If he reads them merely as good stories, he is likely to get little from them beyond some pleasant evenings in his favourite reading chair, hopefully with his pipe and a good bottle of Port. If the object is to develop military understanding, he needs to do more. He needs to stop frequently along the way, putting himself in the situation as it unfolds and asking, 'How might I have seen this? What, at this point, would I have perceived as the decisive elements? What orders would I have given?' Like Holmes, the reader needs not merely to see, but to observe.

Finally, there are some valuable tactics manuals that are written from an historical perspective and that are very much worth a read. Perhaps the best is H. John Poole's *The Last Hundred Yards,* one of the few books to effectively address the tasks facing small units leaders. Most official doctrine manuals are limited in value, but there are a few exceptions. The U.S. Marine Corps' MCI *Warfighting Skills Program*, like Poole's book, speaks directly to

the small unit leader from an historical, manoeuvrist perspective; so do the **original** versions of the U.S. Marine Corps' FMFM-1 *Warfighting* and FMFM 1-3 *Tactics*.

In all of this reading, even the tactics manuals, the goal is the same: to acquire context, to develop a habit of mind of looking up for the big picture. Without that habit, one cannot hope to practice manoeuvre warfare, because without the big picture one cannot determine what to do except by following processes and methods. That, of course, marks a reversion to the Second Generation of modern war.

I dare say no one reading this book would go to a doctor who had never read a medical book or take a case to a barrister who had never read a book of law. Sadly, both Britain and America still routinely send their sons off to war under officers who, in many cases, have never studied military history. Churchill wrote, 'Battles are won by slaughter and manoeuvre. The greater the general, the more he contributes in manoeuvre, the less he demands in slaughter.'[5] Leaders in amphibious manoeuvre warfare, be they generals or corporals, have little hope of greatness unless they have developed a contextual understanding that reaches far beyond their personal experiences. That is, or ought to be, the influence of history upon sea power.

---

[5]Sir Winston Churchill, The World Crisis, Vol. II, 1923

Biography

William Sturgiss Lind is the Director of the Center for Cultural Conservatism at the Free Congress Foundation graduated from Dartmouth College in 1969 and received a Master's Degree in History from Princeton University in 1971. He worked as a legislative aide for Senator Robert Taft, Jr., and later with Senator Gary Hart. He is the author of the *Maneuver Warfare Handbook* (Westview Press, 1985); co-author of *America Can Win: The Case for Military Reform* (Adler & Adler, 1986); and co-author of *Cultural Conservatism: Toward a New National Agenda* (Free Congress Foundation, 1987). He has written extensively for *The Washington Post, The New York Times*, *Harper's*, and professional military journals, including *The Marine Corps Gazette, U.S. Naval Institute Proceedings* and *Military Review*. Mr. Lind co-authored the prescient article, "The Changing Face of War: Into the Fourth Generation," which was published in *The Marine Corps Gazette* in October, 1989 and which first propounded the concept of "Fourth Generation War." Following the events of September 11, 2001, one of his articles was credited for its foresight by *The New York Times Magazine* and *The Atlantic Monthly*. He is the author of *George W. Bush's `War on Terrorism': Faulty Strategy and Bad Tactics?* (2002).

pre-world war II

Gallipoli
The Constantinople Expeditionary Force, April 1915

By Colonel Michael Hickey (Rtd)

Introduction

The campaign ashore on the Gallipoli peninsula, April 1915 - January 1916 was Britain's first attempt at opposed landings on enemy shores since 1801 at Alexandria. The naval actions in the Dardanelles and subsequent fighting ashore on the Gallipoli peninsula arose from the need for indirect action against the Central Powers and their Turkish allies. Britain was committed to a continental war for which she conspicuously lacked the necessary land forces. Her allies were equally under pressure. Russia had suffered crushing defeat in East Prussia, her homeland was threatened by the Austro-Hungarians, and Turkey's closure of the Dardanelles and Sea of Marmara, prevented the export of Russian strategic commodities (grain and oil) as well as supplies of armaments from the western allies. At the end of 1914 Grand Duke Nicholas, the Russian commander in chief, asked his allies to make a diversionary move against the Ottoman Empire.

Asquith's Liberal government had no experience of war on the scale now encountered. Lord Kitchener of Khartoum, appointed War Minister on the outbreak of war, predicted a long drawn-out war. Conscription being politically unacceptable, recruitment of an all-volunteer force, the 'New Armies', began at once, stimulated by the famous poster bearing Kitchener's formidable stare and the slogan 'Your country needs you'. Until this force had been trained for war the remains of the old regular army and the Territorial Force, would have to hold the line.

Britain relied upon the navy for its security. Its political head, as First Lord of the Admiralty, was Winston Churchill, in post since 1911. In October 1914, after his First Sea Lord, Prince Louis of Battenberg had been hounded from office because of his German origins, Churchill recalled the former First Sea Lord, 74-year-old Admiral Sir John (Jacky) Fisher. As far as Fisher was concerned the Army was no more than an imperial gendarmerie, a missile to be fired ashore by the navy as and when required. He believed that any war against Germany would be decided by the destruction of the main enemy battle fleet in the North Sea and a naval blockade of Germany followed if necessary by an amphibious descent on the north German Baltic coast, bringing an army ashore under the guns of the fleet only 90 miles from Berlin. He had initiated a naval building programme to implement this concept; it included a number of shallow-draught gunships or monitors, as well as ramped powered lighters, armoured against small arms fire and shell splinters and with bow doors which could be lowered to permit the rapid landing of men, field artillery and materiel.

On the outbreak of war the fully manned battle fleet, ordered to its war stations in the last week of July, was ready. Churchill favoured the strategy of indirect approach as a solution to the western front deadlock. His advocacy of an expedition to take Constantinople, thereby depriving the Central Powers of a key ally and freeing the southern sea passage to Russia, became insistent following the Russian plea for assistance.

By Christmas 1914 the Royal Navy had suffered a number of unfortunate reverses, and Churchill's political career could be endangered by further catastrophes. The chance to use the principles of Indirect Approach with an expedition against Turkey therefore offered a tempting solution. Although he had written, as recently as 1911, that to force the Dardanelles with a fleet unsupported by troops ashore would be impossible, he initially decided that the Anglo-French fleet blockading the straits should be used for this purpose, directing its commander, Vice Admiral Sackville Carden, to prepare his plans.

Fisher, anxious to avoid his battle fleet's dilution for what he regarded as a sideshow, would permit only the deployment of pre-dreadnoughts - which he considered expendable - to the eastern Mediterranean. 'Damn the Dardanelles', he wrote to Churchill, 'they will be our grave'. Once allied battleships appeared off Constantinople, it was hoped Turkey would surrender. However, entry to the Sea of Marmara depended on the destruction or neutralisation of the Dardanelles defences, in particular the forcing of the heavily fortified Chanak Narrows where the seaway is barely a mile wide. On the outbreak of war, minefields were sown in the Dardanelles by the Turks under German instruction, augmented by torpedo tubes and searchlights ashore.

Admiral Carden was no Drake or Nelson; he had never handled a fleet in action. He was also heading for a complete nervous

Some of the cap badges of the Royal Naval Division. (RN)

breakdown. In early March 1915 he reported that he was ready to launch the attack. All surprise had been lost by the sporadic bombardment of the outer forts. Landing parties of marines and bluejackets blew up the guns. This left numerous static and mobile batteries along the Dardanelles to be tackled, as well as the problematic minefields. Arrangements for sweeping these ahead of the battle fleet proved hopelessly inadequate; the impressed civilian trawlers and drifters used were easy targets for the Turkish guns and their crews understandably declined to continue. By the time saner counsels - of using destroyers - prevailed it was too late and all chances of forcing the narrows with the battle fleet had evaporated.

Recognising that land forces would indeed be required to occupy the battered defences once the fleet had passed through. Kitchener appointed General Sir Ian Hamilton as Commander-in-Chief of this part of the operation, reminding him that if he succeeded in entering Constantinople with his army he would probably win the war. As the official British observer with the Imperial Japanese Army in Manchuria during the Russo-Japanese war of 1904 Hamilton's perceptive eye had resulted in a highly critical appraisal of the Russian performance, citing poor intelligence, disregard of cover, secrecy or swiftness, lack of dash and initiative, and above all, lack of good generalship. As it turned out, these factors would all contribute to the allied defeat at Gallipoli.

The theatre of war

The Gallipoli peninsula stretches for some 50 miles into the Aegean Sea from its roots in European Thrace. Its greatest width is 12 miles and its narrowest, in the area of Bulair, less than 4. The landscape consists mainly of rugged hills intersected by steep gullies which flood in the seasonal rains. Its tip, Cape Helles, faces Asiatic Turkey (Anatolia) some four miles away across the mouth of the Dardanelles, protected by the so-called Outer Forts at Sedd el Bahr on the European and Kum Kale on the Asiatic shores. The few landing places are found around Cape Helles, near Gaba Tepe some 12 miles further north, in Suvla Bay, and along the shores of the Gulf of Saros.

By March 1915 the defence of the area lay with the Turkish army under command of the German general, Otto Liman von Sanders, granted the rank of Turkish Marshal. He had ample time to prepare. He correctly identified the most likely landing points on the Asiatic shore, around Cape Helles, around Bulair, and at Gaba Tepe further up the coast from Helles.

Hamilton arrived out from England in time to observe the attempt of the allied fleet to force the Chanak narrows on 18 March, under command of Vice Admiral de Robeck as Carden had finally collapsed on the eve of the operation. The attack was repulsed by the guns and mines of the Turks and their German advisers with the total loss of three battleships and serious damage to others.

The crucial ingredients

Success in amphibious operations depends on the fulfilment of a number of factors:

- Sound, unambiguous political and strategic direction
- Well practised joint staff procedures, and the careful selection of officers for key appointments.
- Well trained and equipped land forces
- Adequate weaponry and munitions
- Thorough attention to Logistics
- Reliable Intelligence based on the availability of good maps and charts and on thorough reconnaissance
- Accurate assessment of enemy capabilities based on the foregoing intelligence.
- Appreciation of geographical and hydrographical factors affecting the projection of power over what may be extended distances

In almost every way these factors were either ignored or insufficiently observed throughout the impending campaign.

Political and strategic factors

Hamilton was under constraints. Kitchener had forbidden extended operations on the Asiatic shore other than a diversionary landing. The Navy stood out against any landing

Cap badges of the ANZACs and the
Royal Marine Light Infantry. (RN)

Political direction from London lacked
resolution, willingness to listen to
professional advice, and suffered from
the baleful influence of divided counsels

at Bulair where, although the peninsula was at its narrowest, the Gulf of Saros was shallow and lacked modern survey. No air support was available from the Royal Flying Corps; it came instead from the Royal Naval Air Service (RNAS) whose overworked aircraft, airships (blimps) and tethered balloons performed outstandingly throughout. Political direction from London lacked resolution, willingness to listen to professional advice, and suffered from the baleful influence of divided counsels. Churchill and Fisher had become increasingly antagonistic to the other's point of view, leading to the admiral's resignation barely three weeks after the April landings, shortly followed by Churchill's departure from the Admiralty as the Liberal government was replaced by a coalition. From the outset the enterprise was holed below the waterline. None of the brilliant men in Asquith's cabinet possessed the strategic, naval or military knowledge to permit objective discussion in the face of Churchill's passionate advocacy. The Chief of the General Staff, Wolfe-Murray, the professional head of the army who should have been party to all major decisions, was overawed by Kitchener and reduced to the status of a cipher.

Staffing problems
Hamilton arrived in the eastern Mediterranean with only a cadre of his general staff, headed by Major General Braithwaite. The personnel ('A') and logistic ('Q') staff would have to be cobbled together from whatever could be found at home after meeting the ever-increasing priorities of the BEF in France. The 'G' staff grappled with the logistical problem of assembling the landing force. The 'A' staff, responsible for the medical evacuation and hospitalisation plans, were delayed in England (as was the Director of Medical Services for the expedition). The 'Q' staff straggled out from England as and when suitable appointments could be made.

Although Hamilton got on well with de Robeck, they answered to different masters. The Admiralty and War Office were separate entities, facing each other across Whitehall; there was no Joint command at the highest level and certainly no agreed joint staff procedures. Wireless telegraphy, telephone, signal lamp, heliograph and flag signals comprised the available means of communication at all levels. It was difficult to arrange planning conferences in Egypt or on the Aegean islands. Everything had to be worked out from first principles; fortunately Hamilton, a consummate diplomat, succeeded in maintaining harmonious relations between the two services and with his French allies.

Availability of well trained and equipped land forces
The troops available for landing on the peninsula were a mixed bag. Hamilton was reluctantly granted the loan of the last remaining regular division in England, the 29th. In addition was the Royal Naval Division (RND), consisting of Royal Marine Light Infantry battalions raised on much the same voluntary principle as the army's 'Kitchener' units, and battalions of naval reservists for whom no sea-going berths existed on mobilisation. The RND had already seen action at Antwerp in October 1914, when their lack of experience had been all too evident. The Australian and New Zealand Army Corps (ANZAC), en route to the western front, had been held back in Egypt, ostensibly for further training and defence of the Suez Canal. The French Corps was a mix of metropolitan, Foreign Legion and colonial troops. Also in Egypt, but not immediately available, was the 42nd (East Lancashire) Division of territorials. Unlike the RND or 29th Divisions the 42nd had been training hard in theatre for months, was fit, acclimatised and keen for the fight. There was a grave shortage of field and heavy artillery and in particular of high explosive shells needed to defeat defensive earthworks. Shrapnel, lethal against men in the open, was useless against wire or dug-in troops. Most significantly, Hamilton's ammunition railhead was at Marseilles at the far end of the Mediterranean, from where the sea routes became increasingly dangerous as the U-Boat threat developed.

Availability of suitable shipping
In March 1915 as the expedition prepared to embark in Britain it relied on civilian cargo ships, loaded without consideration for the sequence in which cargoes would be required on arrival at the seat of war. Negotiations with the Greek government had procured the use of several islands within easy distance of the Dardanelles as launching bases. Of these, Lemnos possessed in Mudros Bay one of the finest anchorages in the eastern

Mediterranean but it was devoid of wharfage, warehousing, and adequate cargo-handling, watering or refuelling facilities. The ships were diverted to Alexandria, where their cargoes were re-assigned and re-loaded, watched closely by intelligence agents of the Central Powers who noted crates clearly labelled as 'Constantinople Expeditionary Force'. Apart from the prior warning of the naval bombardments of the outer forts, security had been hopelessly compromised,

Training in amphibious warfare must cover every aspect from physical fitness to continuation training, as well as the boat drills ensuring rapid transfer from ship to shore. Some small scale trial exercises held under Admiralty auspices at Clacton-on-Sea in 1902 had identified the need for naval officers and beach parties to be placed ashore at the earliest possible moment in order to control the movement of inshore shipping and landing craft. This was the beginning of the Beachmaster organisation; its presence at Gallipoli would be instrumental in preventing calamitous losses and total chaos on numerous occasions.

The planners of Hamilton's arrival on a hostile shore therefore had to accept that the entire landing force lacked experience of landing from the sea. The 29th Division, regulars brought home from overseas garrisons, was billeted in the Midlands as far from the sea as possible. The Royal Naval Division, following its baptism at Antwerp, was made up to strength with raw recruits and trained on the downs above Blandford. The Australian and New Zealand troops in Egypt also lacked any amphibious experience. The fourth element, equally untrained for landing operations, was the French contribution of metropolitan and colonial troops. By degrees, the whole force assembled in the theatre of war. Many units, however, received little or no practice in boatwork.

Amphibious landings depend on naval gunfire support (and in the modern context, air support) and the main armament of the pre-dreadnought battleships assigned to the Dardanelles operation was the 12" gun. Firing on a shallow trajectory, its high explosive shell, suitable for the attack of fortifications, was only effective if a direct hit was secured. After 25 April naval gunfire support proved a mixed blessing; much of the fire passing over the defence. Once the battleships had been driven away from the peninsula by the U-boats, cruisers, monitors and destroyers had to provide support, but this was not entirely successful in a situation demanding plunging fire of the sort provided by land-based howitzers and field guns.

Logistics

The ammunition railhead for Hamilton's force was at Marseilles. Within weeks of the landings, U-boats were operating in the Mediterranean and Aegean Seas, picking off ships with impunity in the absence of a convoy system. Rations had to come from great distances; chilled meat from as far as New Zealand, Australia and Argentina. The troops had to accept a diet of hard tack and canned salt beef until the supply chain was improved. Water was a pressing problem; insufficient thought had been given to this and although the ANZACs quickly sank boreholes, the position at Helles was always critical, and at Suvla Bay in

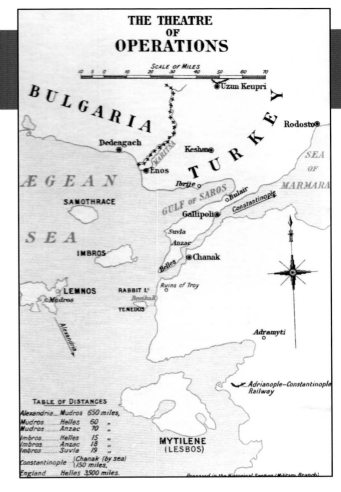

The Dardanelles: Theatre of Operations. (NHB)

August, where the water lighters first ran aground on uncharted shoals and where wells marked on maps often turned out to be non-existent, soldiers were frequently driven to drinking their own urine. Well trained troops with experienced leaders can generally cope with logistic problems as they occur, but at Gallipoli the junior leaders, though anxious to do their best, simply lacked the training or knowledge to cope.

No sooner had the campaign got under way when the folly of trying to plan it with only a partly formed staff became evident; in particular the medical plans drawn up by Hamilton's 'G' staff in Egypt proved totally inadequate to cope with the unexpectedly high casualty rate. In the first days following the April landings, hundreds of wounded lay on the beaches awaiting sea transport to Egypt and Malta as too few hospital ships had been provided. The so-called 'black ships' - transports which in many cases had been used to carry horses and mules to Gallipoli - had to be pressed into service and the casualties obliged to endure the horrors of the voyage to Alexandria lying in blood-soaked uniforms on soiled straw and with no other medical staff than veterinary assistants; the mortality rate was high. Their sufferings even then were not over as the base hospitals were unable to cope with the huge influx, leading to scenes reminiscent of those encountered by Florence Nightingale 60 years earlier.

Intelligence

Hamilton's briefing by Kitchener had consisted of no more than two short interviews. He was sent to the eastern Mediterranean with obsolete maps and no trained head of Intelligence. Yet there was a mass of up to date information available in Whitehall. In the summer of 1914 Lieutenant Colonel Cunliffe-Owen, the British Military Attaché in Constantinople, had made a covert reconnaissance of the Dardanelles and the Gallipoli peninsula, recording the locations and condition of the coastal defences. Until October 1914 the head of the Ottoman navy had been Rear Admiral Limpus, Royal Navy, whose intimate knowledge of the equipment and personnel of the Turkish army and navy were unsurpassed. Instead of using this, the Admiralty posted him as dockyard Superintendent at Malta. Hamilton was never given the opportunity to interview either of these men, nor was he shown Cunliffe-Owen's reports which had been circulated at the War Office, initialled, and then filed away. On his arrival off the Dardanelles the day before the allied fleet's abortive attempt to force the narrows, Hamilton viewed likely landing beaches from a light cruiser, the only opportunity granted to him before planning this perilous enterprise. There were no facilities for beach reconnaissance, the navy's charts, and such Ottoman maps as were issued to GHQ, were equally out of date. Hamilton was told by Kitchener that there would be no Royal Flying Corps support for aerial surveillance or photography. All aviation support at Gallipoli and the Dardanelles was provided by the Royal Naval Air Service, using dirigible airships (blimps), tethered balloons, land-based aircraft and seaplanes.

One cause of failure at Gallipoli was lack of accurate knowledge of Turkish dispositions, the exact positions of their beach defences, and of the fighting capabilities of their army. This led to a fatal under-estimation of the opposition, the effects of which became all too clear as the landings at 'V' and 'W' beaches ran into trouble.

Geography

This expedition was conceived and mounted far from the home base, over an extended sea line of communication vulnerable

to submarine attack, and with no specialist sea transport. The nearest island base to the Dardanelles with a decent anchorage was at Mudros, 50 miles further away. Alexandria, the main army base, where the military hospitals were to be found, was over 700 miles distant. These distances imposed not only serious constraints on movement within the theatre of operations but also on a communications system based on wireless telegraphy and the Morse code, and on land line telegraph. Communication within visual range relied on flag hoists, lamp and heliograph. Hamilton's expeditionary force was subject, in fact, to the limitations of late Victorian technology.

Planning for the April landings

Following personal survey of the peninsula on 17 March Hamilton formulated his outline plan for implementation by Major General Braithwaite and the staff. Their choice of possible landing beaches coincided almost exactly with that of Liman von Sanders. Assuming an earliest date for landings no earlier than the last week of April, the defence had nearly six weeks for preparation. Liman von Sanders had also identified the likely beaches. The choice in any case was limited, as Hamilton realised. He was obliged to use beaches close to Cape Helles at the tip of the peninsula, so that naval gunfire support could be provided without risking the fleet to the fire of numerous batteries further up the Straits. The two main beaches, 'V' and 'W', were close enough together to offer the chance of a rapid link-up before exploitation inland, where the objectives for the first day were the village of Krithia and the hump-back hill, Achi Baba, just over

a mile to the east. To reach them meant traversing some five miles of gently rising ground, hard for unopposed and unladen men but totally impossible under fire when burdened with up to 60 pounds of weaponry, ammunition and equipment. The plan was devised from a map far from the scene by men who had not reconnoitred the ground personally. Nor had a close examination of the beaches been possible; their defences actually consisted of fields of barbed wire laid underwater, electrically detonated mines, further dense wire fields ashore, and carefully sited infantry positions overlooking the beaches -both of which were likened to stages in a theatre, overlooked by an audience dug in on the balconies and galleries and well supplied with machine guns and ammunition. Recognising that the landings at 'V' and 'W' would be highly dangerous Hamilton initially called for them to be carried out at night but Admiral de Robeck vetoed this, citing navigational problems, suspect charts and lack of knowledge of enemy minefields. He did agree however to an approach under cover of darkness to the landing beaches selected for the Anzac corps north of the Gaba Tepe headland some 12 miles up the north east coast of the peninsula.

In the absence of landing craft the final approach to the beaches would have to be in ships' boats, towed in groups (or 'tows')

of six by steam pinnaces to a cast-off point a few hundred yards off shore. At Anzac there was at least the hope that the approach inshore might go unobserved until the last moment; but at Helles, where the landings were timed to take place in broad daylight it was assumed that the enemy's heads would be kept down by naval gunfire. In view of the risk level, an original idea was fielded by Lieutenant Commander Unwin, a destroyer captain who proposed that a collier, the *River Clyde*, be used as a sort of Trojan Horse. With sallyports cut in her side, from which gangways were hung, she would be run ashore under the walls of the ancient fortress at Sedd el Bahr; barges lashed alongside would then be pushed into position by a steam hopper to form a bridge to the shore across which the attacking troops would rush the defences. Unwin was appointed to command the *River Clyde* and set about converting her; machine guns were mounted in a sandbag emplacement on the foredeck to suppress defensive fire as the troops emerged from the sallyports and made their way down the ramps to the floating bridge. At the same time as

Australian infantry coming ashore at Anzac Cove on the morning of 25 April 1915. The preceding landings of the covering force at first light had achieved surprise but had come ashore nearly a mile north of the planned point and had almost immediately lost all cohesion as they stormed the heights of Sari Bair. (NHB)

the Clyde's arrival the Royal Dublin Fusiliers were to be landed from ship's boats further along the beach, which is little over 450 yards long. Simultaneously, landings were to be made at 'W', 'X', 'Y' and 'S' beaches, supported by the guns of the fleet, though instructions were given that fire was to be directed, not at the beach defences, but at the country beyond, presumably in hopes that this would deal with reinforcements hastening to the battle.

To draw attention from the Helles and Anzac landings, Hamilton planned two diversions: a landing by elements of the French Expeditionary Corps at Kum Kale at the entrance of the Dardanelles on the Asiatic side and a 'demonstration' by elements of the Royal Naval Division in the Gulf of Saros, on the northern flank of the isthmus linking the Gallipoli peninsula with European Turkey. It was in this area that the enemy main reserve was deployed; Liman von Sanders had ordered the Turks to hold the coastline lightly, holding their mass of manoeuvre back to launch decisive counter attacks once it was clear where the main thrust of the landings was taking place. The threat of a major landing in the Gulf of Saros remained in von Sanders' mind, as an allied success here would cut off all the Turkish formations deployed closer to Helles. Once Hamilton's staff had completed their work it was possible to prepare the naval plan.

Execution

Late on the afternoon of 24 April the invasion fleet got under way from anchorages around the Aegean islands of Lemnos,

Mitylene and Tenedos. During the hours of darkness final preparations were made for the transfer of the embarked troops, who were to encounter mixed fortunes on the morrow. The Anzac landing Lieutenant General Birdwood, commanding the Anzac force, had asked for the landing to take place in total darkness but on naval advice a compromise was adopted; moonset was at 0257, giving only an hour of darkness before dawn. It was agreed that the 3rd Australian Brigade, selected as the covering force, would land just before dawn. They would be followed, in broad daylight, by the rest of the 1st Australian Division, the New Zealand Brigade, and as much artillery as could be got ashore.

As the tows neared the land, it was clear that an unexpectedly strong current was carrying them further north than intended

and the first landing took place nearly a mile north, at Ari Burnu. The Turks were taken by surprise and initial opposition

by sunset the beach was piled high with unsorted stores, rations, and ammunition, and hundreds of wounded were awaiting evacuation

was sporadic. The troops soon realised they were in the wrong place; instead of a gently shelving beach they were faced with steep slopes. Undeterred they swarmed uphill against rapidly stiffening opposition. All cohesion was lost and units, sub-units and even formations became hopelessly mixed. Such was the fitness and aggression of the Anzac infantry that they managed

'V' beach today. The cemetery lies over the mass grave dug following the landings of 25 April 1915, in which lie hundreds of officers and men of the Royal Dublin and Munster Fusiliers and ratings and marines of the Royal Naval Division. (MH)

to get well onto the high ground of the Sari Bair feature by mid morning. Things now went seriously wrong, for the commander of the Turkish 29th Division, Lieutenant Colonel Mustafa Kemal, reacted quickly to the threat, launching a desperate counter attack. Birdwood's plans for exploitation inland were in ruins by midday and the only course open was to hold onto whatever ground his troops could secure. This actually became the Anzac front line for most of the rest of the campaign; at no point was it more than a thousand yards from the beach.

Although the pinnaces and tows carrying the covering force had been protected by darkness they suffered once the sun rose and accurate shrapnel fire was brought to bear on the beach. Had it not been for the work of the beachmasters and their parties of ratings and signallers there would have been a shambles. As it was, by sunset the beach was piled high with unsorted stores, rations, and ammunition, and hundreds of wounded were awaiting evacuation. Soon, the hospital ships were full and resort had to be made to the 'black ships'. With hundreds of stragglers filtering back to the beach in search of

their units and for water and rations, Birdwood was taking council of his fears and signalled his intention of re-embarking, citing widespread disorganisation and demoralisation ashore; wiser counsels prevailed and Hamilton ordered the ANZACs to hold fast and '…Dig, Dig, Dig….' unintentionally giving birth to part of the mythology that would forever characterise this campaign.

Helles. The landings of 29 Division consisted of simultaneous descents on five beaches -'Y', 'X', 'W', 'V' and 'S'. 86 Brigade was to go ashore after daybreak on 'V', 'W' and 'X' and secure the beach head. 88 Brigade would then land at 'V', advance up the peninsula and link up with the forces at 'Y' and 'S' on the extreme flanks. 87 Brigade would then come ashore and pass through 88 Brigade to seize the village of Kritthia by 1200 and the summit of the dominating high ground of Achi Baba by last light. All was to be conducted to a rigid timetable.

'Y' Beach. This was the extreme left flank landing, carried out by the Plymouth battalion RMLI (Lieutenant Colonel Matthews)

and the Kings Own Scottish Borderers (Lieutenant Colonel Koe) plus a company of South Wales Borderers. The landing took place at 0500 and gained complete surprise as there was no preliminary bombardment. There was no opposition; a significant force was ashore behind the Turkish flank, but then everything went wrong. The two COs bickered over their respective seniority, Matthews had no written orders and Koe had not even attended the divisional briefing. Both battalions dug in as best they could on top of the cliffs and awaited further instructions, which did not materialise. The Turks awoke to the danger and later in the day began to counter attack. After a night of fierce fighting the Turks pulled back but both the Borderers and the marines were running out of ammunition, Colonel Koe was dying, and men began to straggle back to the beach. There was only one solution and the navy took off the survivors. Hamilton was offshore during this performance but was unable to reverse the situation. There was no guidance at any time from HQ 29 Division whose commander, Major General Hunter-Weston, was obsessed with events at 'W' and 'V' beaches.

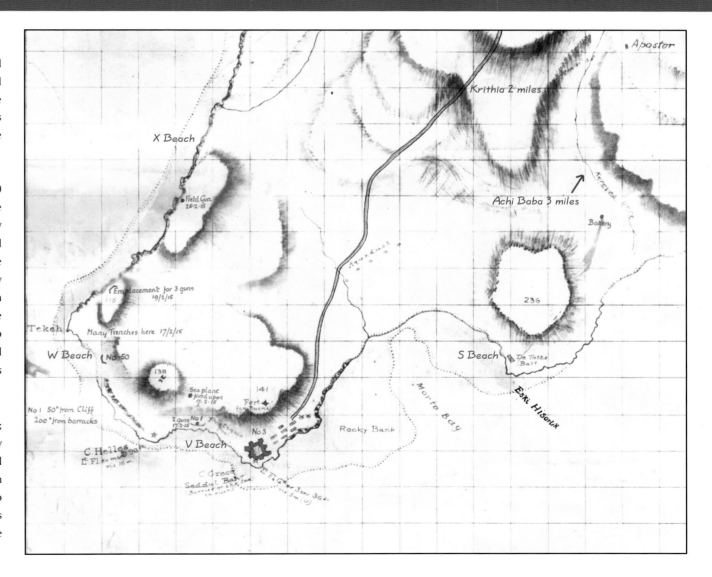

'X' Beach. This was the target for the 2nd Royal Fusiliers and defended by only 12 Turkish soldiers who were quickly dispersed by the main armament of HMS *Implacable*. The Fusiliers got ashore by 0630 and began to move inland, intending to link with troops ashore at 'W' and 'V' beaches, but this did not happen until the following day due to stubborn Turkish resistance.

'W' Beach. This resembled 'V' beach; both were about 400 yards wide, overlooked at both ends from cliffs where the Turks had emplaced machine guns. Wire had been laid thickly below the water a few yards offshore, electrically detonated mines placed along the beach and further wire laid above the strand. The defenders were one company of Turkish infantry with artillery support on call. First ashore were the 1st Battalion Lancashire Fusiliers with a beach party of a platoon from the Anson Battalion RND. The Fusiliers were under orders to link up as soon as possible with the troops landing at 'V' beach. Naval gunfire support would be from the cruiser *Euryalus*, standing less than a mile offshore.

All was calm until the tows cast off, 100 yards from the beach; a storm of fire then came down on the packed boats as they attempted to row ashore. Many soldiers leaped overboard in full marching order and quickly drowned; others were entangled in the submerged wire. Out of 24 boats in the first wave only two reached the beach and about half the battalion got ashore. Rifles became jammed with sand and the wire entanglements at the head of the beach proved too much for the wirecutters issued.

The second wave of boats included those carrying the brigade commander and his headquarters, a medical detachment, naval beach party and some sappers. With some Fusiliers they scaled the cliff to the left of the beach, outflanked part of the defence and rolled up the Turkish line. Gaps were now made in the wire and the Fusiliers surged forward. By 0830 a perimeter had been secured, the next wave of infantry were landing, and contact made with 'X' beach. But 11 officers and 350 men of the Fusiliers had fallen; six VCs were awarded for this extraordinary feat of arms.

'V'Beach. General Hunter-Weston made this the key to his division's assault. The first troops ashore were to take the ruins of the fort and village of Sedd el Bahr as the follow-up troops made contact with the landings at 'W' and 'X' beaches. 'V' beach formed a natural amphitheatre; on the left were the battered remains of a great gun battery already destroyed by landing parties from the fleet. At the other end, some 400 yards away, the ruins of the old castle. From either flank, machine guns could rake the foreshore. The beach was ringed with trenches and heavily wired above and below water. It was defended by no more than 70 Turkish infantry, admirably sited and led.

The first troops ashore were to be the 1st Battalion Royal Dublin Fusiliers, in ship's boats. Half a company of Dublins was to land on the far side of the castle at a point known as the Camber. As they approached the shore the '*River Clyde*', carrying the Royal Munster Fusiliers, most of the 2nd Hampshires, a beach party, signallers and sappers and a medical detachment, was to beach immediately below the castle and discharge its troops onto floating bridges. The tows carrying the Dublins were held up by a strong current and the Clyde had to slow in order to avoid a collision. Consequently she beached at a much slower speed than planned and stopped nearly 50 yards short. At once the Munsters

emerged, to be greeted by a tornado of fire. The Dublins were similarly engaged some 50 yards offshore and scenes reminiscent of 'W' beach were repeated. Within 30 minutes the pilot of an RNAS aircraft overhead was appalled to see that the sea was red with blood for 50 yards out from the shoreline. Despite the heroism of Lieutenant Commander Unwin of the *Clyde* and his devoted crew, the Munsters were cut to pieces. Those who made it ashore joined the 300 or so Dublins seeking cover in the lee of a low bank on the shore and below the castle walls. By 0930 it was clear that further attempts at landing would be suicidal and these were called off until after last light.

'S' Beach. This was the extreme right flank of the Helles landings, at the far extremity of Morto Bay. Here, the defence consisted of little more than part of an infantry company, occupying the remains of an 18th century defensive work known as De Tott's Battery. The assaulting force consisted of three rifle companies of the 2nd South Wales Borderers, a naval beach party and a detachment of sappers. They achieved almost total surprise due to a series of unforeseen events: the hour fixed for the landing was 0530 but adverse currents held the boats up. Admiral Wemyss, in charge of the naval side of the landings, postponed events at 'V' and 'W' beaches (thereby affecting the approach of the *River Clyde*, with results described above), and extended the largely ineffectual naval bombardment. The Borderers landed two hours late and found that the defenders' guard had dropped; the Turkish position was stormed with little loss. By 0830 'S' beach was secure and the surviving defenders

All that remains of the elaborate harbour facilities constructed by naval and army engineers following the landings of August 1915. In the far distance is the Sari Bair ridge and in the middle distance, on the far side of Suvla bay, the low hillock of Lala Baba. (MH)

had fled. General Hunter-Weston was signalled to this effect but gave no instructions for exploitation for the rest of the day and the Borderers sat tight on their objective, when they could have relieved pressure on the battalions pinned down on 'V' beach. As in the case of the 'Y' beach landing, Hunter-Weston's refusal to capitalise on these two successful landings resulted in the virtual destruction of 86 Brigade at Sedd el Bahr by little more than a weak Turkish rifle company.

By last light on 25 April it was clear that 29 Division's landings had stalled. The day's objectives of Krithia village and the high ground of Achi Baba remained in Turkish hands, as they would throughout the campaign. Far too much had been asked of troops called on to land on a fiercely contested shore and fight their way some five miles to objectives selected off the map without regard for the likely opposition, terrain and the sheer physical difficulties of cross-country movement with full fighting gear.

During the night of 25-26 April, Lieutenant Colonel Doughty-Wyllie, a GHQ staff officer who had been assigned to the *River Clyde*, went ashore at Sedd el Bahr, rallied as many of the traumatised survivors as possible, disembarked the rest of the troops from the ship, and led a desperate attack on the morning of the 26th which succeeded in taking the castle and the village, as troops from 'W' beach finally fought their way across the shoulder of Cape Helles to link up with the surviving Dublins, Munsters and Hampshires. Doughty-Wyllie was killed at the moment of his triumph and lies buried in solitary state where he fell.

Apart from sending troops ashore tightly packed in ships' boats the high casualty rate at Helles was due to the care with which the defences had been prepared, the resolution and good fire discipline of the defenders, and the ineffectiveness of the preparatory naval bombardment which despite enormous amounts of smoke, dust and noise, achieved almost nothing. The gunnery officers in their Gun Direction Platforms were looking into the eye of the rising sun. High velocity, flat-trajectory gunfire, using mainly armour piercing rounds, was almost useless and there was a severe shortage of the high explosive natures that could have been more effective.

After the landings. It was several days before the troops had recovered sufficiently from their ordeal to attempt any exploitation inland. When this came, the plan was over-ambitious and what became known as the 1st Battle of Krithia was a shambles, as were all subsequent attempts to take this objective. With stalemate at Helles and Anzac Hamilton had to consider what to do. He called for reinforcements, which were sent piecemeal into battle at Helles with dire results; eventually he was promised a new army corps from the UK.

Consisting of territorial and new Army divisions, none with combat experience, they arrived to take part in an early August offensive. The object of this was the seizure of the entire Sari Bair feature, the original target of the ANZACs, which was to be achieved by a bold left hook round the Turkish right flank whilst diversionary attacks were made at Anzac and at Helles to pin down Turkish reserves and the IXth Corps was put ashore at Suvla Bay. For this operation a quantity of dedicated armoured powered landing craft or 'X' craft was now available; known as 'beetles' they were the product of Fisher's eccentric notion of landing on the north German coast. They could carry up to 500 troops ashore, cruised at 5 knots and were ramped at the bows. Their design made them hard to handle in high winds and currents and they had an alarming tendency to broach to; for much of the time they had to be towed by picket boats when beaching in anything but calm conditions.

The Suvla landings

Although it was not expected that the landings of the night 6-7 August in Suvla bay would be hotly opposed, a number of factors reduced the operation to chaos. During the approach to the

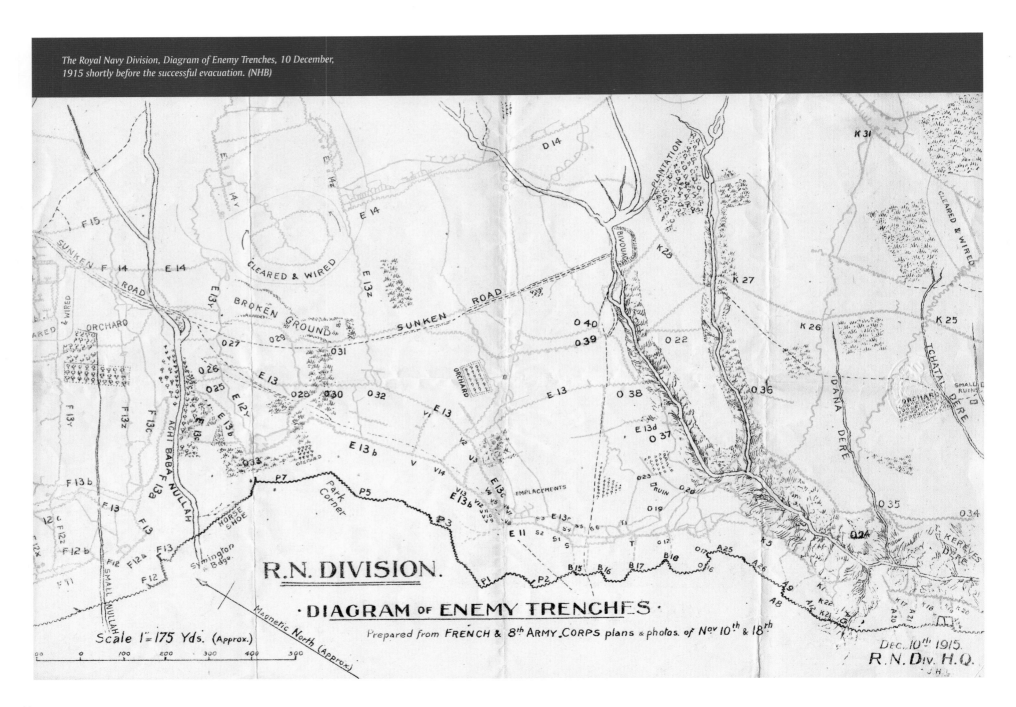

The Royal Navy Division, Diagram of Enemy Trenches, 10 December, 1915 shortly before the successful evacuation. (NHB)

designated beaches it was found that due to inaccurate charts, landing craft were running aground on shoals; the troops had to go ashore in many cases neck deep in water. Seven destroyers approached the bay after dark, towing 'beetles' and the picket boats for inshore work. Two cruisers provided desultory fire support, and trawlers followed, towing horse barges, guns and limbers.

The troops selected for the initial night landings were ill trained for this difficult task and heavy casualties resulted. Chaos reigned ashore. Whilst landings on 'C' and 'D' beaches went reasonably well, the troops destined for 'A' beach were landed well south of it and delays set in. Exploitation was halted as units ashore sorted themselves out. The water lighters ran aground in the bay and soldiers from all units fought for access to the canvas hoses when these eventually came onto the beach. Lieutenant General Sir Frederick Stopford, commanding IX Corps, displayed extraordinary torpor, remaining afloat and failing to report any progress to an anxious Hamilton at his HQ in the island of Imbros. Rear Admiral Christian, in charge of the naval part of the operation, was almost equally ineffectual and still aboard Stopford's boat in the bay, none of the divisional commanders displayed any sense of urgency or aggression and the whole corps remained motionless for almost 48 hours; by this time the high ground dominating the Suvla Plain, which was to have been in British hands by last light on 7 August, was occupied by the Turks in strength when the first British troops reached the summit early on 9 August, to be conclusively

routed. With the repulse of Hamilton's great attack at Sari Bair, deadlock set in once more. A last throw on 21 August by exhausted and demoralised troops resulted in another bloody reverse.

The evacuation

Although the navy had succeeded in setting the army ashore in April and in August, success on land was thwarted. Uncertain political direction from London; a change of government to coalition; growing disenchantment with the Gallipoli enterprise once Churchill had been ousted from the Cabinet; increasing influence of the 'westerners' in Whitehall; the continuing shortage of artillery ammunition and demands for priority to go to the BEF; the entry of Bulgaria into the war on the side of the Central Powers (thus opening direct rail communication from Germany to Turkey for passage of munitions); increasing hostile submarine activity in the Mediterranean and Aegean which drove the battleships away to safer anchorages. It was time for decisions.

Hamilton was removed from command in October and his successor, Monro, was carefully briefed by Kitchener in London. Whilst he was promised additional troops if he saw a chance of success, he was also given a remit to recommend withdrawal and this he did. Kitchener came out himself and was aghast at what he saw. Plans were made for what promised to be a very difficult operation. Cabinet authority to evacuate was given on 7 December; preparations were already well in hand. A great

storm had swept the peninsula in November, a portent of what might lie ahead. Two factors above all governed the planning of the withdrawal. First: total secrecy must be observed, for if the Turks gained a hint of what was in hand and attacked once the defences had begun to thin out, catastrophe would be certain. Secondly: all depended, as it had so often in the previous two centuries, on the navy's professionalism in the historically well-practised business of getting the army out of tight corners.

It was decided to evacuate the Anzac-Suvla sector first, in the third week of December. Helles would follow early in January 1916. An elaborate deception plan was devised aiming to convince the Turks that the force was ashore for the winter. Empty cases were brought ashore by day and vital stores carried off at night. Fires were lit in vacated tent lines. Then all units were ordered not to fire at the enemy for whole days, and resume without warning. Ingenious devices such as the water-activated rifle were installed throughout both sectors, complicated booby traps placed, and all stores which could not be moved without exciting suspicion were prepared for explosive demolition. At Anzac in particular, where the front lines lay within yards of each other, and the Turks, surging forward onto the high ground could dominate the evacuation beaches with small arms fire, the situation hung on a knife edge. Once it was decided that 19 December would be the final day at Anzac-Suvla, the final thinning out began. The wounded went aboard under cover of darkness, leaving the dressing stations a blaze of light as though business was normal. The artillery had been thinning out for some days, leaving dummy emplacements. In the forward infantry positions, all ranks bound sandbags around their boots to deaden sound and wired barriers were prepared for drawing across communication trenches as the last men passed. Check points were set up at section. Platoon. Company, battalion and brigade level as the silent columns made their way towards the beach. The Turks could still be heard working, only yards away, on their own wire and defences as the forward positions were finally abandoned. Well before the last files went aboard, demolition fuzes had been lit; after final checks of the beaches for stragglers revealed none, the boats cast off, and as they pulled out from the land a series of tremendous explosions racked the Anzac heights and Suvla Plain. The Turkish reaction was one of incredulity mixed (as it would be at Helles barely three weeks later) with admiration.

Despite the raised Turkish level of awareness at Helles, which could have had an adverse effect on the withdrawal there, the game of deceit was played out to the very end. On the night of 7-8 January the Turks' suspicions were aroused; they launched a fierce assault on the British extreme left flank, at Fusilier Bluff, held by a New Army Battalion, the 7th North Staffords, who threw the enemy back with heavy casualties albeit with the loss of their own CO. By midnight on the 8th the line had been abandoned and columns of troops were silently making their way to the evacuation beaches. Those at Helles were still under fire from Turkish heavy guns on the Asiatic shore. A bugler posted on the walls of the ruined Sedd el Bahr castle sounded a long 'G' whenever he saw a discharge flash, upon which the columns broke ranks soundlessly and took cover until the shell had landed. As at Anzac-Suvla, huge stocks remained ashore, prepared for demolition, and these were duly detonated as the ships put out to sea. The time was 0345 and some 17,000 men had been embarked on that final night, without sustaining a single casualty.

Lessons identified from Gallipoli

Selection and maintenance of aim

Diffuse from the start. No-one seems to have thought through what would have happened had the allies taken Constantinople; bitter contest between the Russians and Greeks over restitution of the orthodox Patriarchate in St Sofia would have been certain. The selection of objectives for 29 Division on 25 April would have been impossible to achieve even against the lightest of opposition.

Maintenance of Morale

Although spirits were high on the eve of the April landings, conditions ashore were so bad that huge demands were made on junior leaders. It is hard to keep morale high when under incessant fire, and in appallingly unsanitary conditions, when high sickness rates equalled those of the battlefield.

Security

Allied shipping movements in the Mediterranean and evident preparations in Egypt, where numerous enemy agents were active, compromised operations from the start.

Surprise

This was lost as early as the end of 1914 with the start of the desultory bombardment of the outer forts.

Offensive action

Once the energy of the initial landings at Helles and Anzac had been expended, Hamilton was obliged to adopt mainly defensive tactics, lacking the infantry and artillery to open a successful major offensive.

Concentration of force

By the dilution of landings at three points, Hamilton's staff produced a plan which enabled a small number of well deployed defenders to stop the attackers on the beaches, and to deny them the chance of successful exploitation.

Co-operation/Inter-service integration

In the absence of any Joint Service warfighting policies, this had to depend on good personal relations between army and naval commanders. De Robeck's caution and then his unilateral decision to withdraw the surviving battleships after three had been sunk offshore, did little for inter-service harmony.

Sustainability (Administration)

That the enormous logistic task of sustaining the forces at Gallipoli was even attempted, given the problems of time and space, is remarkable. There were many shortcomings, initially stemming from the piecemeal way in which the 'A' and 'Q' staffs were cobbled together. Lack of refrigeration, poor food handling ashore, and over-reliance on inferior canned food, contributed

Soldiers about to burn supply dumps immediately prior to the evacuation from the Peninsula. (IWM Q13663)

to disease. There was a well-perceived difference between living standards afloat and on the actual peninsula, where fresh bread and rations were regarded as a luxury.

Historical perspective

The army's last major amphibious operation had been at Alexandria in 1801; however, on that occasion success was ensured by preliminary training, carried out for weeks beforehand. At Gallipoli, where the defences included machine guns and wire, many units received little or no boat-work practice, and had little idea of plans for exploitation.

Unity of Effort

Because the Royal Navy and Army were run from separate ministries their commanders were answerable to different masters and were not in fact fighting for the same aims.

Winning of Sea Control

This was assured by the allied blockade of the Dardanelles and, within the Sea of Marmara, by the successful allied submarine campaign. With the arrival of U-boats in the eastern Mediterranean the balance shifted, and from mid May 1915 much naval gunfire support was withdrawn following the loss of three battleships.

Training

None of the regular, territorial or New Army troops sent out from England had undergone training relevant to conditions at Gallipoli, having been destined for the western front. Only the 42nd Territorial Division, stationed in Egypt since October 1914, was fit for open warfare.

Sound Intelligence

Almost non-existent, due to the War Office's failure to capitalise on Colonel Cunliffe-Owen's material and the experience of Admiral Limpus.

Deception

The withdrawal was a classic example of what can be achieved and immediately recognised as such by the Turkish and German high commands.

Air superiority

Almost irrelevant; The RNAS dominated the skies over the Dardanelles and Gallipoli, there was no air-to-air combat but much reconnaissance, gun fire spotting for the fleet, and some bombing.

Naval Gunfire Support

Due to the shortcomings of warships' main and subsidiary armament and lack of HE natures, this was marked more by spectacular noise than lethal effect once the troops were ashore.

Further Reading

Bush, Eric, *Gallipoli*, (London: Cox and Wyman, 1975)

Carlyon, L. A., *Gallipoli,* (London: Doubleday, 2002)

Chasseand, Peter and Doyle, Peter, *Grasping Gallipoli - Terrain, Maps and Failure at the Dardanelles, 1915*, (Staplehurst: Spellmount, 2005)

Haythornthwaite, Philip J., *Gallipoli 1915: Frontal Assault on Turkey* (London: Osprey, 1991)

Hickey, Michael, *Gallipoli,* (London: John Murray, 1995)

James, Robert Rhodes, *Gallipoli,* (London: B. T. Batsford, 1965)

Laffin, John, *Damn the Dardanelles! The Agony of Gallipoli,* (Stroud: Budding Books, 1997)

Moorehead, Alan, *Gallipoli,* (London: Hamish Hamilton, 1956)

Page, Captain Christopher, R.N., *Command in the Royal Naval Division*, (Spellmount, 1999).

Steel, Nigel and Hart, Peter, *Defeat at Gallipoli,* (London: Macmillan, 1994)

Travers, Tim, *Gallipoli 1915,* (Stroud, Gloucestershire: Tempus, 2001)

Biography

Colonel Michael Hickey is an expert on the Gallipoli campaign. He has led numerous visits to the Battlefield with the Gallipoli Association, advised television documentaries and has given lectures on aspects of the campaign to the Royal United Services Institute in Whitehall, the Staff College and other organisations. His interest was triggered by his father's service in the Cheshire Regiment in the First World War. His book *Gallipoli*, published in 1995, is one of the key texts recommended to Royal Marines who are interested in researching the campaign or discovering more about the units and men involved in the Constantinople Expeditionary Force.

Ösel & Moon Islands
Operation ALBION, September 1917
The German Invasion of the Baltic Islands

The First Operational Manoeuvre From the Sea?

By Dr Robert Foley

The First World War is not particularly remembered for its amphibious operations. First, the navies of this period were heavily influenced by the ideas of Alfred Mahan, in particular his concept of a great decisive fleet battle, and they put most of their energies into conducting such a battle.[1] As naval doctrine had not yet fully embraced the idea of landing an infantry force in the face of enemy opposition, the specialist techniques and procedures of combat loading or naval gunfire support that would characterise amphibious warfare during the Second World War had not been developed.[2] Following from this, amphibious technology was in its infancy. With no perceived need for specialist shipping or support, landing forces during the war were forced to rely upon ad hoc solutions for coming ashore and for sustainment once on the beach. Indeed, amphibious operations between 1914 and 1918 were decidedly ad hoc affairs. Without proper doctrine or specialist technology, the navy and army commanders charged with conducting warfare in the littoral were forced to make do with the primitive techniques and technologies readily to hand.

With its long history of expeditionary and amphibious operations and with its overwhelming naval supremacy in the First World War, one would have expected Great Britain to be able to develop its amphibious capabilities rapidly and effectively. However, British amphibious operations during the war did not demonstrate a flexibility of thinking or a willingness to develop new concepts and technologies. Instead, British operations, such as Gallipoli, were marked by command tensions, lack of cooperation between the services, and amateurish logistics.[3] Consequently, they made no meaningful impact upon the course of the war.

Ironically, it was the German armed forces, rather than the British, that conducted one of the most successful amphibious operations of the war. Despite never having conducted an amphibious operation before and despite the lack of a naval tradition, the German armed forces were able to put a large landing force ashore against enemy opposition and quickly and smoothly achieve their objectives. Moreover, the German armed forces were successfully able to integrate this amphibious operation into a wider campaign plan and thus achieve an effect

at the operational level, a concept that would not be fully incorporated into Anglo-American amphibious doctrine until the publication of 'Operational Manoeuvre from the Sea' (OMFTS) in the 1990s.[4] Indeed, the German landings and occupation in the autumn of 1917 of the islands in the Baltic Sea off the coast of modern-day Latvia could rank as the first true application of what we now term OMFTS.

The naval side of Operation ALBION, the German code name for this operation, has been well covered by A. Harding Ganz.[5] However, Anglophone historians have largely neglected the army side of the operation.[6] Thus, this chapter will examine the operation largely from the army perspective. To do this, it will make use of newly discovered material – the Kriegstagebucher (war diaries) of the units responsible for the landing and occupation of Ösel, Moon, and Dagoe Islands, the German XXIII Reserve Corps and the German 42nd Infantry Division.[7]

Strategic Context

In the autumn of 1917, German armies held fast against powerful Entente attacks on the Western Front, but faced a

---

[1] See Jan S. Breemer, 'The Burden of Trafalgar: Decisive Battle and Naval Strategic Expectations on the Eve of World War I,' Geoffrey Till, ed. *Seapower: Theory and Practice* (London: Frank Cass, 1994) pp. 33-62.

[2] On the development of modern amphibious techniques and technologies, see Kenneth J. Clifford, *Amphibious Warfare Development in Britain and America from 1920-1940* (Laurens, NY: Edgewood, 1983) and Jeter A. Isely and Philip A. Crowl, *The US Marines and Amphibious War: Its Theory and Its Practice in the Pacific* (Princeton: Princeton University Press, 1951).

[3] For the most-recent account of this debacle, see Michael Hickey, *Gallipoli* (London: John Murray, 1995).

[4] See Headquarters Marine Corps, 'Operational Maneuver From the Sea' (June 1996) and Marine Corps Combat Development Command, 'A Concept for Ship-To-Objective Maneuver' (November 1997).

[5] A. Harding Ganz, 'ALBION – The Baltic Islands Operation,' *Military Affairs* Vol. XLII (1978) pp. 91-97. Ganz made extensive use of German admiralty papers in his article.

[6] The standard source for the operation has been Erich von Tschischwitz, *Armee und Marine bei der Eroberung der baltischen*

Inseln im Oktober 1917 (Berlin: Eisenschmidt, 1931). This was translated by Col H.H. Hassfield, USA, of the US Army War College as 'The Army and Navy during the Conquest of the Baltic Islands in October 1917.' A typescript of the translation held in the Alfred Grey Research Center, Quantico, VA. (Hereafter, Tschischwitz, 'Conquest') Tschischwitz was the chief of staff of the XXVII Reserve Corps during the operation. In English, see Alfred Vagts, *Landing Operations: Strategy, Psychology, Tactics, and Politics from Antiquity to 1945* (Harrisburg, PA: Military Service Publishing Company, 1952) pp. 555-565.

[7] XXIII Reservekorps, 'Die Eroberung der baltischen Inseln,' *Anlagen zu Kriegstagebuch: Erfahrungen v. 17.10.16-1.7.18*, US National Archives and Records Administration, Record Group 165, Entry 320, Box 113; and 42. Infanterie-Division, *Kriegstagebuch v. 1.9-31.10.17* (Hereafter, 42 ID, Ktb); and *Anlagen zu Kriegstagebuch von 1.9-31.10.17*, NARA, RG165, Entry 320, Box 153 (Hereafter, 42 ID, Anl.z.Ktb). Also, 42. Infanterie-Division, 'Erfahrungen der 42. I.D. bei der Eroberung der Inseln Oesel, Moon und Dagö,' 29 October 1917, OberOst, *Anlagen zu Kriegstagebuch*, NARA, RG165, Entry 320, Box 153 (Hereafter, 42 ID, 'Erfahrungen').

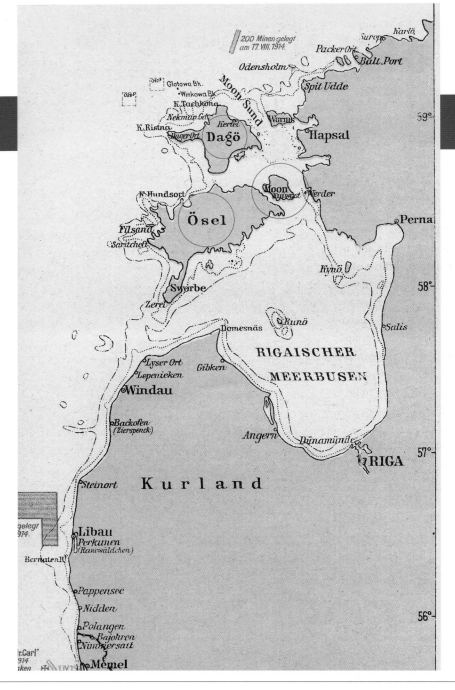

weakening enemy in the east. The revolution of 1917 demonstrated the parlous state of Russian morale and offered an opportunity for the German army to achieve meaningful results on the Eastern Front. If Russia could be knocked from the war, or her army at least substantially weakened, German forces could be transferred to the west for a potentially war-winning offensive there. The German Ostheer went on the offensive in an attempt to deal Russia a deathblow. In early September, Oskar von Hutier's 8th Army crossed the Dvina River, seized the important port city Riga, and threatened the Russian capital, St. Petersburg. However, the flank of the 8th Army's advance was exposed to the strong Russian naval forces operating in the Gulf of Riga and from the Gulf of Finland. These forces were protected from the German navy by the fortified islands blocking the entrance to both gulfs – Ösel, Dagoe, and Moon.[8]

Of the three islands, Ösel was the most significant. At 50 kilometres across, it was the largest of the three islands. It also had a relatively large population of 60,000. This population, largely farmers and fishers, was spread throughout the island in penny packets. Its sparse road network converged on the capital city, Arensburg. The island was separated from the mainland to the southwest, the Courland Peninsula, by the 28-kilometer-wide Irbe Strait. It was separated from Dagoe Island to the north by the Soela Sound, and was connected to Moon Island by a narrow causeway 3.5 kilometres long. The Russians had installed significant defences on the island. The Irbe Strait was covered by a battery of 25 cm guns and battery of 30.5 cm guns with ranges of 25 kilometres. Two additional batteries of 25 cm guns covered the Soela Sound and the western approaches to the island. A regiment of Russian infantry and numerous anti-aircraft guns covered each battery. As Vice Admiral Friedrich Schultz, Commander of the Reconnaissance Forces in the Baltic, noted, Ösel was 'the key, not only to the Gulf of Riga, but also to Riga itself.'[9]

Despite Ösel's importance, Dagoe to Ösel's north and Moon to the east were also important to the Russian defence of the Gulf of Riga. The sparsely populated Dagoe mounted 25 cm and 30.5 cm batteries on Cape Toffri in the south covering the Soela Sound, on Cape Dagerort covering the western approaches to the island, and on Cape Tachkona covering the northern approaches to the island and the western

---

[8]In August and September 1915, German naval forces attempted to force their way into the Gulf of Riga, but were halted by Russian defences on the Baltic Islands and Russian mines. Paul G. Halpern, *A Naval History of World War I* (Annapolis, MD: Naval Institute Press, 1994) pp. 196-199.
[9]Ganz, 'ALBION,' p.92.

approaches to the Gulf of Finland. The smallest of the three islands, Moon, contained a battery of 30.5 cm guns covering Moon Sound to the north. All told, 25,000 Russian soldiers occupied the three islands.[10]

The defence of the islands not only rested on the land, but also at sea. First, the Russian fleet in the Gulf of Riga consisted of four modern battleships, two pre-dreadnoughts, heavy and light cruisers, as well as torpedo boats and destroyers. Most worrying for the Germans, however, were the eight British submarines that were known to be operating with the Russians. In addition to the support that could be provided by the Russian navy, deep belts of mines protected the islands. Erich von Tschischwitz, the chief of staff of the landing force for the German operation, later commented upon the Russian mine fields:

> 'Mine defence seemed to be especially well organized. This is a field of activity in which the Russians have always shown great ingenuity and skill and in which their successful experiences during the Russo-Japanese War taught them valuable lessons. Mine-fields and mine-chains had gradually developed on a gigantic scale in the course of time. The sea areas under consideration were infested with many thousands of mines…' [11]

Any counter-mine operation was made all the more difficult by the Russian practice of placing small mines ('little fishes' as they were termed by the Russians) a metre or half-metre under water. These small mines would do no damage to a capital ship, but they would be deadly for small minesweepers.

The seizure of these islands would have a significant strategic and operational effect, and the German Admiralty had long advocated their capture.[12] If these islands could be occupied, the Russian navy would have nowhere to hide from the superior German navy. The Russian ships could either be defeated at sea or forced to remain in what ports they had left. Either way, the Baltic would become largely a German lake, and the vital lines of communication between Germany and Sweden would be fully secured. Further, the operation would provide useful employment and a morale boost to a German navy that had been bottled up in its ports for most of the war.[13] While the navy had long pushed for a seizure of the islands, it wasn't until advances on the land that the German army began to consider benefits of such an operation. If the islands could be taken and the Russian navy cleared from the Gulf of Riga, the threat to the flank of a German army advance on St Petersburg would be eased and further pressure could be placed on the already shaky Russian government.[14] Indeed, if the German navy was able to achieve

control of the Gulf of Riga, it could provide effective support for a land advance. Thus, by autumn 1917, both the navy and the army supported an operation to take the islands and preparations began for the German armed forces' first amphibious operation.

Planning and Preparation

With both the army and navy behind the idea of the invasion of the Baltic islands, events moved rapidly. In early September, the German Admiralty Staff wargamed an invasion of the islands. They concluded that considerable naval forces would be needed from the High Seas Fleet based in the North Sea to support the operation, as it had not only the numbers of ships, but also the modern ships necessary. Previous experience had shown that the operation needed to be supported by modern capital ships, as pre-dreadnoughts lacked the necessary armor to protect against mines and torpedoes. Based on this planning, 10 modern battleships and a battle cruiser were assigned to the naval protection force for the operation. On 15 September, a planning group was created from naval and army staffs under the direction of Captain zur See Magnus von Levetzow to complete the planning. The army was represented by Major Georg Wetzell from the Army High Command (Oberste Heeresleitung or OHL) and Major Brinkmann from the High Command of the German Armies in the East (Oberbefehlshaber

---

[10]Tschischwitz, 'Conquest,' pp. 11-20.
[11]Tschischwitz, 'Conquest,' pp. 16-17.
[12]Ganz, 'ALBION,' pp. 91-93.
[13]Reinhard Scheer, *Germany's High Seas Fleet in the World War* (London: Cassell, 1919) p.295.
[14]Paul von Hindenburg, *Aus meinem Leben* (Leipzig: Hirzel Verlag, 1934) pp. 203-204; and Erich Ludendorff, *Meine Kriegserinnerungen 1914-1918* (Berlin: ES Mittler, 1919) p.404.

Ost or OberOst). This group determined that the land forces for the invasion would comprise a reinforced infantry division operating under a corps-level staff, or a landing force of about 25,000 men. Crucially, command relationships between the naval and land forces were worked out clearly during this planning before the operation began.

On 20 September 1917, the order was given to begin Operation ALBION. It ran, **His Majesty has ordered:**

> 'To secure control of the Gulf of Riga and to guard the flank of the Ostheer, the islands of Ösel and Moon are to be taken through a coordinated attack by land and sea forces and the passage of enemy naval forces through the Moon Sound is to be blocked.'[15]

Hutier's 8th Army was given overall command of the operation, while General der Infanterie Hugo von Kathen's XXIII Reserve Corps was tasked with the land side and a specially created naval command, Flottenverband für Sondernunternehmungen, or Sonververband, under the command of Vice Admiral Ehrhard Schmidt, was charged with the naval side of the operation. The order enshrined the command relationship between the military and naval forces as agreed during the initial planning phase:

> 'The commander of the naval forces will direct the transportation of the troops by sea and the protection of the sea transportation. The embarked elements of the landing forces are under the orders [of the naval commander] for the duration of the voyage until the moment of disembarkation.'

After the successful landing, the naval commander will meet the requests of the 8th Army command or those of the commander of the landing corps with all means available. The islands of Ösel and Moon belong to the operations area of the 8th Army. The commander of the landing corps will direct operations on the islands. He will also later be responsible for their defence.[16] In other words, the navy would lead the operation until the landing and would thereafter take its orders from the army.

The main landing force would comprise Generalleutnant Ludwig von Estorff's 42nd Infantry Division. This unit would be reinforced by a large number of specialist units. All told the landing force would comprise six infantry regiments, a bicycle infantry brigade (32 companies), two independent stormtroop companies, two machinegun sharpshooter detachments, a cavalry regiment, a field artillery regiment, three battalions of heavy artillery, five independent heavy artillery batteries, a number of trench mortar companies, and an engineer battalion. The force totalled 24,600 troops, 8,500 horses, 2,500 vehicles, 40 guns, 85 trench mortars, and 225 machineguns.[17]

The naval Sonderverband comprised two elements: the transport fleet, under the command of Fregattenkapitän von Schlick, and the combat fleet, under Admiral Schmidt. The transport fleet consisted of 17 steamers, some of which were confiscated Italian and British ships, to be manned and commanded by German navy personnel, ranging from 1,750 to 11,500 tons. The assembly of a fleet capable of carrying the landing force as well as ammunition and supplies for 30 days was no easy task for Germany at this stage in the war. Many of the ships had been inactive for some time and had had much of their machinery stripped out as spares for navy vessels. Moreover, most vessels needed to be specially configured to transport men, horses, motor vehicles, artillery, and ammunition. Consequently, many needed to go into dry dock for emergency repairs and refits before they could be employed as transports.[18] Further, the navy had to work hard to assemble the large number of landing craft necessary to ferry the landing force ashore. How to move the horses from the transports ashore proved to be one of the most difficult problems to address. Ultimately, a consider number of 'horse-boats' were procured. These were 'pontoon-shaped boats, rather long and flat-bottomed, the broad reargate of which would fold down and serve as a landing bridge.' In the end, these served the landing force well to move horses and vehicles ashore.[19]

---

[15]OberOst to 8th Army, Ia Nr. 165 op.geh., 21 September 1917, Anlage 36 in 42 ID, Anl.z.Ktb.
[16]Ibid.
[17]'Belegung der Schiffe der Transportflotte durch die 42. Inf.-Division,' and 'Verteilung der 42. Infanterie-Division auf die Transportflotte,' in 42 ID, Anl.z.Ktb.
[18]XXIII Reservekorps, 'Eroberung,' p.5.
[19]Tschischwitz, 'Conquest,' p.31.

German troops loading into small boats alongside a troop ship near Ösel Island. (IWM Q48847)

Assembling the combat fleet offered problems of its own. Although Germany had the necessary warships, the modern ships needed for this operation were deployed in the High Seas Fleet as a defence against the Royal Navy in the North Sea. Withdrawing the 11 capital ships needed for the operation represented a significant weakening of the High Seas Fleet, and some German navy officers voiced their fears about the possible adverse consequences of detaching such a sizable force for the operation. However, planning had progressed too far and the necessary ships were seconded to the Baltic Fleet. In the end, the combat fleet would comprise 2 squadrons of battleships (10 ships), 2 divisions of cruisers (8 ships), 3 ½ flotillas of torpedo boats (100 boats), 6 submarines, 95 mine sweepers, and 60 submarine search boats, or close to 300 vessels in all.[20] The task of this considerable force was to provide cover for the transports as they approached the islands and to support the landing and the advance of the XVIII Reserve Corps.

While land and sea forces were clearly the most significant elements of the operation, airpower was not left out of the German forces arrayed for the invasion. About 90 aircraft, ranging from Zeppelins to seaplanes from both the army and the navy, were assigned to the operation. These air assets were intended not only to provide reconnaissance for the operation, but also support. Before the landing, aircraft would bomb the Russian positions, and once the landing had taken place, aircraft were designated to work with the artillery of the XVIII Reserve Corps.[21]

The joint force now faced the question of how to seize the islands. Clearly, Ösel was the most important island and would be the main target of the German operation. Given the significant Russian forces on the small island, it was apparent that the landing force would face an opposed landing. As the Germans possessed no specialist amphibious shipping or assault craft, they opted to attempt to surprise the Russian defenders as a means of diminishing the threat to the landing. This was to be accomplished in a number of ways. The removal of assets from the High Seas Fleet and the assembly of such a large

The Germans embarking horses in Libau Harbour for the landing at Ösel. (IWM Q48831)

---

[20]Tschischwitz, 'Conquest,' pp. 182-184.
[21]42. Infanterie-Division, 'Divisionsbefehl: Einsatz der 8 See-Flugzeuge der Seeflugstation Windau,' 4 October 1917,' Anlage 74, 42. ID, Anl.z.Ktb, pp. 113-116.

> **While the combat forces drove inland, logistical units would unload the 30 days of supplies the landing force required, which included 5 million rifle and machinegun rounds, 110,000 hand grenades, and 45,000 rounds of artillery munitions**

naval force in the Baltic could not go unobserved. To throw the Russians off the scent, the Germans operated a deception plan aimed at convincing the Entente that the target of the German operation was Kronstadt or St Petersburg rather than the Baltic Islands.[22] At the tactical level, surprise was to be achieved by keeping the Russians guessing as to where the actual main landing would occur. To confuse the defenders, diversions were to be staged. Battleships and cruisers were to bombard the heavy batteries on the Sworbe Peninsula and small-scale landings were to take place at various points on the islands.

Interestingly, these diversionary operations also had positive goals: The naval bombardment of Sworbe was designed to silence the Russian batteries there. The landing at Pamerort was designed to destroy the battery there and then to drive inland and cut off the Russian lines of retreat. A special, highly mobile force was created for this '*Nebenlandung.*' All of the XXIII Reserve

Corps' 1,650 bicycle-mounted infantry were assigned to this force, along with two field guns and a stormtroop company.[23] Part of this force was to drive on the capital, Arensburg. Its orders ran: 'The detachment … will initially support the advance of the division by means of a rapid advance on Arensburg. It is to attempt to take Arensburg by means of a coup de main. In case this does not succeed, the detachment should place itself in a wide front across the road leading to Orrisar. The sooner [the detachment] appears, the greater the enemy's confusion and uncertainty.'[24] Another detachment of this bicycle infantry force was to cut off Ösel from Moon by advancing rapidly to seize the Ösel side of the causeway that connected the island with Moon at Orrisar, which was heavily defended.[25]

The main landing was to take place in the sheltered Tagga Bay. An assault force of two infantry regiments without heavy weapons but with two detachments of strormtroops (about 3,700 troops) was to lead the landing. This advance force, loaded on torpedo boats and other fast vessels, was to reach the bay at first light and break the resistance of the Russians defenders. The two German regiments were then to drive inland, seize the high ground around the bay, and prevent the Russians from interfering with the main landing. Further, they

were to take the Russian seaplane station at Kielkond and the radio base at Papensholm. Once the remainder of the landing force was ashore, the force would be divided into four all-arms groups based around the four infantry regiments of the landing corps. In effect, they would form four regimental combat teams, each of which was capable of independent action.[26] Three of these groups would move inland and the fourth would serve as a reserve for the operation. While the combat forces drove inland, logistical units would unload the 30 days of supplies the landing force required, which included 5 million rifle and machinegun rounds, 110,000 hand grenades, and 45,000 rounds of artillery munitions.[27]

The Execution

Initially, German planners hoped to launch the operation on 27 September. However, the date that the operation would begin depended upon a number of factors. First, the necessary shipping had to be assembled and the army units had to reach the port of embarkation, Libau. This proved to take more time than anticipated. For example, the bicycle infantry did not reach Libau until 1 October. Further, lanes of approach to the islands had to be cleared of mines. As many of the German minesweepers proved incapable of weathering the Baltic

---

[22]See XXIII Reservekorps to 42. Infanterie-Division, Id Nr. 229/9, 30 September 1917 and 'Fernschreiben an N.A. Kiel für Admiralstab,' 1 October 1917, Anlagen 67 and 68, 42 ID, Anl.z.Ktb, pp. 102-103.
[23]XXIII Reservekorps, 'Eroberung,' p.4.
[24]42. Infanterie-Division, 'Divisionbefehl für Abteilung v.Winterfeld,' 28 September 1917, Anlage 64, 42 ID, Anl.z.Ktb, pp. 97-98; and 42. Infanterie-Division, 'Divisionsbefehl für Landungsabteilung Pammerort,' 4 October 1917, Anlage 75, 42 ID, Anl.z.Ktb, pp. 116-117.
[25]XXIII Reservekorps, 'Direktiven für Angriff auf den Brückenkopf Orrisar u. Übergang nach der Insel Moon,' 27 September 1917, Anlage 62, 42. ID, Anl.z.Ktb, pp. 94-95.
[26]42. Infanterie-Division, 'Divisionsbefehl für die Landung auf Ösel,' 27 September 1917, Anlage 60, 42 ID, Anl.z.Ktb, pp. 81-86.
[27]XXIII Reservekorps, 'Besondere Anordungen,' 26 September 1917,' Anlage 61, 42. ID, Anl.z.Ktb, pp. 90-94.

A German sailor on an improvised signal tower, flag signalling from Ösel to a German transport ship in the Gulf of Riga, October 1917. (IWM Q48855)

Sea in stormy September, this proved a time-consuming and dangerous process. Finally, the operation was dependent upon the meteorologists predicting a clear enough spell of weather to make the passage to the islands. By the end of the first week of October, the conditions were finally right, and on 8 October, the order to launch the operation was given. Embarkation took up the 9th and the 10th, but on 11 October, the fleet finally left Libau for the islands.[28]

The passage went largely according to plan. German submarines had marked the path through the minefields to Ösel with light buoys. However, to be safe, a flotilla of minesweepers led the long column of ships from Libau. The minesweepers were immediately followed by torpedo boats carrying the initial assault force. Then came the Third Battleship Squadron with the fleet's flagship, the SMS *Moltke*, followed by the Fourth Battleship Squadron. A considerable distance behind this force followed the 17 transport ships, escorted by the cruiser divisions. On either flank of the

column ranged torpedo boats providing protection from British and Russian submarines. Tschischwitz later described how the army saw the sailing:

> 'The transport fleet was especially well cared for, in so far as the rather limited number of torpedo boats rendered it possible. Groups of from three to five steamers, each, were headed by a light cruiser, mine-breakers preceding and hospital ships and salvage vessels following the group. Naval aviation and naval dirigibles provided security against hostile action from the air.'

Far ahead of the column submarines were stationed in the Gulf of Riga, in front of the southern and northern entrances to Moon Sound, and off the northwest point of Dagoe.[29]

Rough seas slowed the passage, however. The minesweepers leading the column were forced to slow to 3 knots. Faced with the prospect of arriving at the launch point well after dawn, the naval commander, Schmidt, decided to risk the mine threat and ordered the force to advance without a final sweep. In the end, the force reached its anchor point 7 nautical miles off the coast of Ösel at 0300 on 12 October, only one hour behind schedule. Shortly before reaching anchorage, the battleships *Friedrich der Grosse* and *König Albert* had been detached from the fleet so that they could bombard the Sworbe Peninsula at first light as a diversion. Similarly, a half flotilla of torpedo boats was detached to bombard the Russian seaplane base at Kielkond.[30]

Just before dawn, the fleet took up its positions for the landing. The ships of the assault force, joined by the fleet flagship, readied themselves to dash into the Tagga Bay. Three ships of the Fourth Battleship Squadron took up position to provide covering fire for the assault force against the Russian batteries on the western side of the bay. Four battleships of the Third Squadron were to bombard the batteries on the eastern side of the bay as the assault force landed. The battleship *Bayern* and the light cruiser *Emden* moved off with the ships carrying the bicycle force that was to land at Pamerort. These two ships were to cover this diversionary landing against fire from the Russian batteries at Pamerort and across the Soela Sound on Dagoe.

Shortly before dawn, the battleships *Bayern* and *Grosser Kürfurst* hit mines. Believing these to be torpedoes from a Russian submarine, their anti-submarine guns began firing, and this precipitated the general bombardment slightly earlier than planned. The covering force closed to within 8,000 metres of Ösel and quickly silenced the Russian guns. Although the battery at Hundsort fired three salvos at the *Moltke*, it had been put out of action before it could fire a fourth. The Russian battery at Ninnast did not even fire a round; the ships of the Third Battleship Squadron destroyed its command post on their first salvo.

Even before the dual between the ships and the batteries, the first elements of the assault force sailed into Tagga Bay. At 0600, the German infantry began wading ashore before the Russian

[28]Tschischwitz, 'Conquest,' p.38.
[29]Tschischwitz, 'Conquest,' p.39b.
[30]Ganz, 'ALBION,' p.94.

defenders even knew they were there. However, the fire of the German battleships alerted the defenders and the more tardy elements of the assault force were taken under artillery and machinegun fire as they landed. The two stormtroop detachments had to fight their way through Russian bunkers to take the batteries at Ninnast and Hundsort. Nonetheless, by 0800, the entire assault force had been disembarked and their initial objectives had been reached. The two infantry regiments fanned out to secure the breachhead, and disembarkation of the main landing force began.[31]

By mid-day, most of the transport fleet had reached the safety of the bay. One steamer, the *Corsika*, struck a mine coming into the bay, but torpedo boats were able to disembark her troops and supplies. The remainder of the disembarkation went smoothly. Tschischwitz described it thus:

> 'By 10:00 A.M. disembarkation from the transport fleet was already well under way. Motor-barges and motor-launches were towing to the shore long strings of boats, some containing troops, others, i.e. horse-scows, carrying horses and vehicles. The disembarkation-pioneer company and the 9th Pioneer Replacement Battalion had in the meanwhile provided improvised landing bridges for foot passengers and other purposes.'[32]

By evening, all of the infantry of the landing force had come ashore, but only one artillery battery.[33] Nonetheless, this force had advanced far enough inland to provide a secure lodgment for the remainder of the disembarkation.

While the main landing was taking place in Tagga Bay, the diversionary landing was also occurring at Pamerort. Here, the Russian defenders were somewhat more successful. The Russian battery on Cape Toffri on Dagoe hit a German torpedo boat. Immediately, the *Bayern* and the *Emden* took the battery under fire and quickly silenced it. By 0700, the bicycle detachment was landing. A force of sailors and a stormtroop company designated to take the battery at Pamerort found that intelligence had been wrong and there was in fact no such battery. The bicycle-mounted infantry force, assisted by commandeered horses and wagons, pushed rapidly inland after landing. By the second day, the two elements of this detachment had reached their objectives. One battalion combat team lay astride the road from Arensburg to Orrisar and the other, under the command of Hauptmann von Winterfeld, had reached the Russian fortifications at the Orrisar bridgehead 50 kilometres from Pamerort. Despite its relative weakness, this latter detachment managed to take the Russian field fortifications at Orrisar and, indeed, even advanced to within 30 metres of Moon before being forced back by Russian fire. However, this weak force, cut off from the rest of the landing force, soon found itself in an exposed position.[34]

Early on the 13 October, the main landing force began its advance. The 255th Reserve Infantry Regiment was to advance on Ladjall (7 kilometres northeast of Arensburg) and the 65th Infantry Brigade (the 17th and 138th Infantry Regiments) was to drive on Hasik (20 kilometres northeast of Arensburg). Once the advance of these two groups was successfully underway, Estorff ordered the 131st Regiment to cut off the Russian force on the Sworbe Peninsula. While the 131st succeed in bottling the Russian 425th Infantry Regiment up on the Peninsula, the other two combat groups were less successful in their missions. The Russian defenders facing these groups merely put up token resistance before retreating, and the poor roads, made worse by the rain that had started in the morning and continued all day, proved more of a hindrance to the German advance. Both groups fell short of their objectives by nightfall, and the Russian forces slipped through their fingers.

Instead of putting up a fight, the Russian units on Ösel were attempting to retreat to Moon Island. Standing between them and the comparative safety of Moon was Winterfeld's weak bicycle infantry force at the Orrisar bridgehead. This force, a battalion of infantry reinforced by a company of stormtroops, was attempting to cover a 7-km front. Through the course of the day, it came under increasing pressure from the retreating Russians desperate to reach Moon. Numerous small detachments of Russians had succeeded in penetrating

---

[31]Tschischwitz, 'Conquest,' pp. 42-45.
[32]Tschischwitz, 'Conquest,' p.48.
[33]Indeed, disembarking the artillery proved to be a more time-consuming process than initially envisioned and the operation was over before most of the heavy artillery was off the transports.
[34]Tschischwitz, 'Conquest,' pp. 49-51.

German landing craft embarking troops for the landings at Ösel. (IWM Q48850)

the German perimeter, and strong forces supported by artillery attacked from the north. The crisis came at night as the Russians attempted to wrestle the bridgehead from Winterfeld's control:

'An engagement came at this decisive point [i.e. the bridgehead] during the night, both sides fighting with extreme fury during a period lasting several hours. The Russian was determined to force open his line of retreat across the [causeway]. Winterfeld, on the other hand, refused to give in. His situation became more and more difficult when the enemy succeeded in closing up on him, and especially when the hostile contingent from Moon began to exert pressure across the [causeway] against his rear. The Germans were able to stand their enemy off with the aid of hand grenades, whenever he would come too close....'

When, at length, the ammunition supply began to run low, Captain von Winterfeld was obliged to give up the bridgehead. At 1030 he fell back, without being pressed by the enemy.[35]

Although it was not yet apparent to all within the landing force, the decisive battle for Ösel was being fought around the Orrisar bridgehead. On the morning of the 14th, the Russians attacked Winterfeld's detachment in an attempt to secure completely their line of retreat. The ever-weakening detachment was able

to hold off this attack, but was unable to retake the bridgehead. The best that Winterfeld could accomplish was to put his force in position to take the causeway under machinegun fire and to block the road from Arensburg. He was assisted in this by the arrival of the 5th Bicycle Battalion as reinforcement around midday. However, his situation was far from secure. More and more Russians continued to arrive at the bridgehead from around the island and Russian artillery firing from Moon Island put his force under great pressure.[36]

Due to a lack of radio communication, the bulk of the landing force around Arensburg was completely unaware of the Winterfeld detachment's desperate battle. It wasn't until late on the 13th that reconnaissance aircraft reported the situation back to Estroff's headquarters. Upon hearing the news, Estorff ordered that the 42nd Division advance immediately to assist Winterfeld.[37] The individual units were left to themselves to

make their way to Orrisar at night along the terrible roads as quickly as they could. They all recognized the gravity of the situation, and most units left behind all but the most necessary equipment to speed their march. The war diary of the 17th Infantry Regiment captured the spirit of the division: 'The knowledge that a great victory was impending electrified the men who were quite exhausted from the marches made under a continual down pour over soft roads and without subsistence. Every soldier was ready to use up the last ounce of strength left in him.'[38] Once the tired units of the 42nd Division reached Winterfeld's detachment, they were launched immediately into battle in an attempt to stabilize the situation. The XXIII Reserve Corps' official report noted:

'After an exhausting 40-kilometer long march, the 65th Infantry Brigade with only one battery of field artillery reached the area of [Orrisar] in the evening [of the 14th],

[35]Tschischwitz, 'Conquest,' p.61.
[36]Tschischwitz, 'Conquest,' pp. 67-69.
[37]XXIII Reservekorps, 'Eroberung,' p.13.
[38]Quoted in Tschischwitz, 'Conquest,' p.71.

just as the enemy began a new attack against the Winterfeld Detachment. The 17th Infantry Regiment entered the scrape immediately and by 7:00 P.M. the entrance to the causeway was again firmly in our hands.'

The Reserve Infantry Regiment 255 reached [the Orrisar area] around midnight after a 50-kilometer march and entered the battle....

'Thanks to the incredible marching ability of the infantry, the enemy, who had been retreating to the east, was prevented from retreating further to Moon and was forced to fight on two fronts. A great success appeared in sight.'[39]

The arrival of the main landing force effectively sealed the fate of the Russians on Ösel. However, even before their arrival at Orrisar, Winterfeld's detachment had been receiving enough support to block the Russian retreat across the causeway to Moon. After a sharp battle at sea, a flotilla of German torpedo boats under Captain von Rosenberg succeeded in forcing its way into the Moon Sound and make contact with Winterfeld's detachment. These ships were able to give ammunition and food to Winterfeld's tired troops and perhaps more importantly provide much-needed naval gunfire support against the Russian attacks. Further, the German ships were able to provide counter-battery fire against the Russian artillery on Moon Island and

were able to bombard the Russians as they attempted to make use of the causeway.[40]

This naval support put the final nail in the coffin of the Russian forces on Ösel. They were unable to use the causeway to retreat to Moon, were unable to be reinforced or rescued by sea, and were fighting against German infantry units to their front and rear. On the morning of 15 October, the 42nd Infantry Division renewed its attacked against the Russians. After several hours of hard fighting, the commander of the 107th Russian Infantry Division recognized the hopelessness of his position and at 1500 ordered his units to lay down their weapons. With him surrendered two brigade commanders and the remnants of two Russian regiments with their machineguns and guns.[41]

While this battle was taking place, the 131st Infantry Regiment was dealing with the 425th Russian Infantry Regiment and the heavy batteries on Sworbe Peninsula. With the support of fire from the German battleships off the coast and much of the landing force's heavy artillery, the 131st Infantry advanced south along the Peninsula on 13 October. By 1800 on the 14th, the Germans had inflicted enough damage on the Russian defenders for them to surrender.[42] With this, German minesweepers were

free to begin the dangerous process of clearing the Irbe Strait of mines and opening the Gulf of Riga to heavy German ships.[43]

While Ösel may have been taken, the landing force now faced the challenge of capturing Moon Island. Reconnaissance suggested that Moon had been heavily reinforced by the Russian 470th and 471st Infantry Regiments from the mainland. Moreover, to get to Moon, the German troops had to cross the long causeway that connected the two islands under fire from Moon's defenders. Estorff was preparing for a bloody assault across this causeway when an important piece of intelligence reached his headquarters. A German pilot had been shot down while reconnoitering Moon's defences. While in the water, he noticed a sandbar linking Moon with an undefended small island to the north – Kleinast. Estorff recognized that this offered an opportunity to avoid, or at least make easier, the assault across the causeway. If troops could be landed on Kleinast and make their way across the sandbar, they might catch the Russians unaware from the flank.[44]

During the course of 17 October, he made his plans for the capture of Moon. Under the covering fire of the still arriving artillery and the German ships around Moon, the 255th Reserve Infantry Regiment and the 18th Stormtroop Company would storm the across causeway on the morning of the 18th. On the

[39]XXIII Reservekorps, 'Eroberung,' p.14.
[40]Halpern, *Naval History*, pp. 215-217.
[41]XXIII Reservekorps, 'Eroberung,' pp. 14-15.
[42]Tschischwitz, 'Conquest,' p.105f. The Germans captured 120 officers, 4,000 men, and 49 artillery pieces on the peninsula.
[43]Halpern, *Naval History*, pp. 217-219.
[44]Tschischwitz, 'Conquest,' pp. 128-129.

German First World War medal.

night of the 17th/18th, the 138th Infantry Regiment would be landed on Kleinast by Rosenberg's torpedo boat flotilla and would cross the sandbar and attack the Russian defenders in their flank.

However, the 42nd Division did not even have to resort to this plan. Further reconnaissance showed that the there were not significant Russian forces on the Moon side of the causeway. Rather than land on Kleinast, the 138th Regiment was put ashore on Moon after dark and under the cover of fire and smoke from the torpedo boats. Meanwhile, as soon as darkness had fallen, the 18th Stormtroop Company began its crossing of the causeway, but was held up by Russian machinegun and rifle fire and could not make the final 500 metres to Moon. Finally, under pressure from the 138th Regiment on their flank and from the 18th Stormtroop Company to their front, the defenders fled their positions around 0200, leaving behind their artillery and an armored car. With surprising ease, the way to Moon was free.[45]

On the morning of 18 October, the engineers of the landing force repaired damage to the causeway and made it passable to vehicles. Once this had been done, the bulk of the landing force could cross to Moon with its artillery support and finish off the Russian defenders. However, this task proved easier

than anticipated. As the Russians fled from the Moon causeway bridgehead, they were pursued by elements of the Bicycle Brigade and the German cavalry. When the 5th Bicycle Battalion ran into strong Russian forces near the far side of the island, the latter laid down their weapons and surrendered. As the land battle was taking place, German ships had succeeded in driving the Russian fleet away from Moon, cutting off the Russian army from the mainland.[46] Consequently, most other Russian units also negotiated their surrender by nightfall. The exception was the so-called 'Death Battalion,' a crack Russian volunteer force. This had been landed on Moon on 14 October with orders to hold to the last man. However, after a brief fight with superior German forces, the 'Death Battalion' too laid down its arms. By the end of the day, Moon was securely in German hands and the landing force had captured a further 5,000 Russians, including a brigade commander.[47]

The XXIII Reserve Corps' report of the capture of Moon gave various reasons for its success. First, the corps acknowledged the importance of the navy:

'The unexpectedly rapid capture of Moon was, in the first instance, the service of the fleet. By their timely appearance in Moon Sound and the disruption of the

communications to the mainland, by their chasing off of the enemy sea power and their early destruction of the battery at Woi, they had here, in accordance with the frequently expressed will of the corps commander, prepared in a favourable way the conquest of the island by the 42nd Infantry Division.'[48]

While it acknowledged the key role played by the German fleet, the report did not forget the exertions of the infantry of the landing force: 'The rapid action of the landing corps, especially the brave conduct of the Winterfeld Detachment at the Orrisar bridgehead, could not but make an impact on the [Russian] units. They were destined to suffer the fate of the 107th Division.'[49]

After the seizure of Moon, the final large island of the group, Dagoe, needed to be secured. Already on 14 October, a 300-strong naval landing party had put ashore on the south of the island at cape Toffri. This force not only helped keep the Soela Sound and Kassar Wiek open for the German fleet, it also functioned as a beachhead for German army units.[50] On 18 October, despite the poor weather, the 17th Infantry Regiment with a field artillery battery was landed on the beachhead. Within a few days the 750-strong Russian garrison had surrendered and the island was firmly in German hands.[51]

[45]XXIII Reservekorps, 'Eroberung,' pp. 16-17.
[46]Ganz, 'ALBION,' pp. 95-96.
[47]Tschischwitz, 'Conquest,' pp. 128-131; XXIII Reservekorps, 'Eroberung,' pp. 17-18.
[48]XXIII Resevekorps, 'Eroberung,' pp. 16-17.
[49]XXIII Reservekorps, 'Eroberung,' p.17
[50]Ganz, 'ALBION,' p.95.
[51]Tschischwitz, 'Conquest,' pp. 141a-141c.

With the capture of Dagoe Island, the main objectives of Operation ALBION were accomplished. In the space of a week and for minimal casualties, the operation had inflicted a severe defeat upon the Russians. The islands guarding the approaches to the Gulfs of Riga and Finland were in German hands, and the navy was able to clear sea lanes of mines at will. A number of Russian ships had been destroyed during the course of the operation and the remainder fled to the comparative safety of the Gulf of Finland. The German navy had suffered minor losses for this result: Several battleships had been damaged by mines and a number of small craft were sunk with the cost of 130 officers and men killed or missing and 61 wounded.[52] Moreover, the Russian army had taken a heavy blow. For the cost of 9 officers and 186 men killed or wounded, the landing force had captured 20, 130 Russian soldiers and sailors, 141 guns, more than 130 machineguns, 10 aircraft, and 2 armored cars, as well as the garrison's treasury of 365,000 rubles.[53]

Praise for the landing force and for the fleet was not long in coming. Hutier thanked the military and naval units in a message dated 24 October: 'In a feeling of the utmost comradery [treuester Waffenbrüdershaft], the army and the navy can look back with pride at the great result, which belongs to both.'[54] Both Winterfeld and Rosenberg received praise and were decorated for their actions during the operation, with Rosenberg winning the pour le merite. Kaiser Wilhelm wrote to the Chief of the Navy Staff: '…during the seizure of the islands…cooperation between the Army and the Navy was achieved in a most perfect manner.' To OberOst he wrote: 'In cooperation with My Navy, your battle-tried troops prepared for, and achieved the wonderful results which culminated in the conquest of Ösel, Moon, and Dagoe.' To both, he expressed the gratitude of the German nation.[55]

Conclusion

The German capture of the Baltic Islands has been called by the British official historian of World War I 'a model enterprise of its kind' well deserving of our study.[56] Indeed, despite the German armed forces' complete lack of training or experience in amphibious operations, Operation ALBION was a remarkably sophisticated undertaking, one showing many traits that would not develop within Anglo-American amphibious thought until many years later and one that deserves to be known as one of the first operational manoeuvres from the sea. First, unlike the British practice during the war, the Germans quickly dealt with the thorny question of command. From the operation's start, it was clear who commanded when and where, and it was apparent which element was supported and which element was supporting at any point during the operation. Moreover, although one historian has called the naval forces deployed 'a classic case of overkill,'[57] the large numbers of ships allowed for many missions to be conducted simultaneously. The German fleet could provide naval gunfire support to multiple army

> *The German capture of the Baltic Islands has been called by the British official historian of World War I 'a model enterprise of its kind' well deserving of our study*

advances, while clearing mines and defeating the Russian fleet. Indeed, the entire German operation was marked by the use of simultaneity. By attacking a many different points at the same time from the very beginning of the landings, the German land operation was designed to break up the cohesion of the Russian defence. These attacks also had the effect of confusing the defenders as to where the main German landing was taking place. Further, contrary to the common practice of the day, the Germans did not wait for supplies to be built up ashore before beginning their advance. The initial orders made clear that all landing forces were to move rapidly to seize key features inland. The force landed as a diversion in the north at Pamerort had the task of advancing on the capital far to the south and of taking the vital bridgehead between Ösel and Moon. To accomplish these missions quickly, this landing force comprised bicycle-mounted infantry. In the process, this force cut the Russian lines of communication and made the islands roads impassable

---

[52]Halpern, *Naval History,* p.220.
[53]XXIII Reservekorps, 'Eroberung,' pp. 20-21.
[54]Hutier to the Chef des Sonderverbandes, the XXIII Reservekorps, and the 42. Infanterie-Division, 21 October 1917, Anlage 89, 42. ID, Anl.z.Ktb, p.135.
[55]Tschischwitz, 'Conquest,' p.178.
[56]J.E. Edmonds, 'A German Landing: The Capture of the Baltic Islands, Oesel, Moon and Dagö, October 1917,' *Army Quarterly,* Vol.10 (1925), p.270.
[57]Holger Herwig, *Luxury Fleet: The Imperial German Navy, 1888-1918* (London: Allen & Unwin, 1980) pp. 236-237.

to the defenders. Thus, from the beginning of the operation, the Russian defenders had been paralyzed by rapid German manoeuvre, unable to move reserves to face the multiple landings and unable to retreat off the island.

Indeed, the German commanders were clear that speed was crucial to success of the operation. Winterfeld drove his detachment hard to reach and capture the bridgehead at Orrisar before it could be reinforced. Once it became apparent that the Russians were retreating, Estorff ordered a relentless pursuit, which was designed to engage the Russian units before they could break through Winterfeld's anvil. Abandoning their artillery, the main landing force moved as quickly as it could over the poor Ösel roads to reach Winterfeld's position in time and entered into the attack after a night during which they had marched 40 to 50 kilometres.

Despite the exertions of the main landing force, Winterfeld's detachment would not have been able to hold if not for the support offered by Rosenberg's torpedo boat flotilla. Rosenberg had recognized the importance of blocking the Russian retreat to Moon and had taken considerable risks in the face of superior Russian naval forces to break into the Moon Sound. Rosenberg's action, combined with the navy's success in neutralizing the Russian batteries on Dagoe and Moon and the forcing of Soela Sound and the Irbe Strait, isolated the islands from the Russian mainland. With no prospect of reinforcement and no way of

retreating, the garrisons of Ösel, Moon, and Dagoe fell one by one to superior German land forces. The actions of the navy and the army complimented each other well.

However, despite the overwhelming success of Operation ALBION and despite how well the army and the navy had worked together, the staff of the 42nd Infantry Division still found room for improvement. In an appeal for more extensive joint training and education, they wrote:

> 'It appears necessary that a greater number of General Staff officers and Admiral Staff officers than before be trained for joint operations between the army and the fleet. The previous peacetime practice of training a few General Staff officers in the Sea Transport Section [of the Admiral Staff] is not enough. Training must be based on broader principles. It should not only take in the technical aspects of transportation by sea, but should arouse an understanding of sea tactics as well as land tactics. Simultaneously to this, a proper appreciation of the capabilities of land and sea forces should be gained. To accomplish this, secondment to the General Staff and the Admiral Staff seems to be as important as secondment to the army and the fleet.' [58]

Despite the progress that has been made towards joint training and education and towards joint doctrine, these words have resonance for armed forces even today.

[58] 42. Infanterie-Division, 'Erfahrungen der 42. I.D. bei der Eroberung der Inseln Oesel, Moon und Dagö,' 29 October 1917, OberOst, Anlagen zu Kriegstagebuch.

Further Reading

Edmonds, James E., *A Short History of World War I*, (London: Oxford University Press, 1951)

Ganz, A. Harding, *ALBION – The Baltic Islands Operation*, (*Military Affairs* Vol. XLII 1978)

Gilbert, Martin, *First World War*, (London: Weidenfeld and Nicolson, 1994)

Halpern, Paul G., *A Naval History of World War I*, (Annapolis, Maryland: Naval Institute Press, 1994)

Vagts, Alfred, *Landing Operations: Strategy, Psychology, Tactics, and Politics from Antiquity to 1945*, (Harrisburg, PA: Military Service Publishing Company, 1952)

Biography

Dr Robert T Foley is a senior lecturer in the School of History at Liverpool University. He received his BA in history and MA in modern European history from New York University and his PhD in war studies from King's College London. He also studied at George Washington University in Washington, DC, and the Charles University in Prague, and he has worked at the Joint Services Command and Staff College, where he was the academic director of the Advanced Amphibious Warfare Course. He is the author of *German Strategy and the Path to Verdun* (Cambridge University Press, 2004), for which he was awarded the 2005 Gladstone Prize for best book on a non-British subject by the Royal Historical Society. Dr Foley was the editor and translator of *Alfred von Schlieffen's Military Writings* (Frank Cass, 2002) and he has published extensively in journals such as *Marine Corps Gazette, RUSI Journal, War in History and War & Society*.

The Zeebrugge and Ostend Raids
Operation ZO, April 1918

By Dr Harry W Dickinson

The raid against Zeebrugge and Ostend, conducted in the early hours of St George's Day April 1918, constituted one of the most courageous exploits of the First World War - hailed as a great victory the bitter fighting, particularly at Zeebrugge, produced more than 600 casualties and eight Victoria Crosses in an action lasting little more than an hour. Of heroism and selfless devotion to duty there was no doubt. That it was anything like a victory was much more dubious, indeed in overall terms the operation must be counted on that peculiar British list of failures subsequently promulgated as success. If, however, stirring example and inspiration were required, and both qualities were in short supply at this point in the First World War, then Operation ZO, the so-called 'twisting of the dragon's tail' provided it in its most desperate and dramatic form.[1]

To understand the significance of the raids on the Belgian coast in April 1918 it is necessary to place them in the broader context of the First World War and particularly hostilities at sea.[2] While immediately prior to the outbreak of war it was possible to assert, as one French general did, that the British Navy was not worth a single bayonet, it soon became clear that with

stalemate on the Western front and opposing armies seemingly incapable of achieving decisive results, that sea power would play a crucial part in final victory. Exactly which particular part was more difficult to identify. From the beginning of the war the Royal Navy had demonstrated its prowess in distant waters with early setbacks more than compensated by a crushing victory at the Falkland Islands. Soon there would be little significant German blue water naval activity and British superiority, both in terms of number of ships and geographical position, could be applied more closely in home waters. It was however a slow acting business and for almost two years the war at sea was characterised by a series of minor skirmishes in which both sides attempted to lure the other into major fleet action, via raids and ambushes. These generally resulted in disappointment - for the Germans because they were unable to dent their opponents overwhelming advantage, but more particularly perhaps for the British, whose general public had been conditioned to expect news of a second Trafalgar. Even when the great set piece battle finally arrived, at Jutland in May 1916, the results were indecisive and although the Germans could claim a minor tactical victory, their fundamental strategic problem - how to wrest naval supremacy from their opponents - remained unresolved.

One of the effects of the battle fleet stalemate and the failure to achieve a decisive victory was a redoubling of German efforts towards the submarine war against commerce. By the end of 1916 the sterility of the surface conflict, the failure of the Allies to respond to German peace overtures, and what seemed the very real possibility that the U Boat might strangle the British lifeline to its Empire and the United States, encouraged a campaign of unrestricted undersea warfare. The offensive produced immediate results and by the Spring of 1917 monthly losses were averaging more than half a million tons. In April of that year more than 400 ships, totalling in excess of 800,000 tons, had been lost to just 75 U Boats and there had been virtually no attrition of the undersea threat. In the first three months of 1917 only nine U Boats had been sunk and two of these had been lost in their own minefields.[3]

The question of what to do about the U Boat was by far the most important issue within the Plans Division of the Admiralty in early 1917 and the answer was not found until the grudging introduction of the general convoy system at the end of April that year. The evolution of trade protection strategy lies outside of the scope of this chapter but it is relevant to note that while the introduction of the convoy system was stunningly

---

[1] Several published works deal with the Zeebrugge operation. For traditional accounts generally supportive of the Keyes plan and execution see Barrie Pitt, *Zeebrugge: St Georges Day 1918*, (1958) and Philip Warner, *The Zeebrugge Raid* (1978). For a more recent account, strongly critical of Keyes, see Deborah Lake, *The Zeebrugge and Ostend Raids 1918*, (2002). The operation is discussed in detail in Roger Keyes, *The Naval Memoirs of Admiral of the Fleet Sir Roger Keyes: Scapa Flow to the Dover Straits 1916-1918* (1935) and a further eye witness account appears in Alfred B. Carpenter, *The Blocking of Zeebrugge*, (1925).
[2] The official history of naval operations is the five volume, Julian S. Corbett and Henry Newbolt *History of the Great War: Naval Operations*. (1920-1931) The best and most accessible single volume account of the war at sea, 1914-1918, is Paul G. Halpern, *A Naval History of World War 1*, (1994).
[3] Halpern, *op cit* 341.

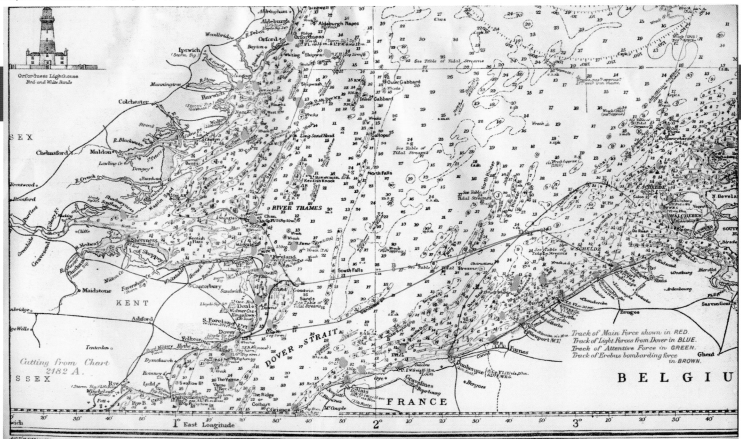

lock gates, invisible from the range of twelve or thirteen miles, proved daunting. Other plans, thankfully not brought to fruition, included an attack by Coastal Motor Boats, which would approach the ports at high speed and attempt to torpedo the canal entrances in what would have presumably been a one-way voyage. More bizarrely, an amphibious operation was envisaged that involved landing a 150 ton, 18" gun on captured enemy territory, where it would be shifted some miles, placed inside a disused hotel and then employed bombarding the target from close range. Incredibly, this plan reached the detailed planning stage but was thankfully abandoned.[4]

successful, it did take time to implement in full. Thus although there was an immediate and gratifying reduction in the number of merchant vessels sunk, the monthly returns for late 1917 were still substantial and worrying. In September some 353,000 tons had been lost, in October the figure rose to 466,000 tons and although it fell again in November, by the end of the following month it again exceeded 400,000 tons. The introduction of the convoys had also prompted a realignment of U boat attacks from deeper offshore waters into the Irish Sea and the English Channel - to the extent that the short sea routes to Ireland, and the inshore coastal passages along the south coast of England were still hazardous, whether convoyed or not.

The majority of submarines operating in littoral British waters started their journey to the killing grounds from the coast of Flanders and particularly from Bruges, which was about eight miles inland but connected to the coast at Zeebrugge and Ostend by a series of canals. The port of Bruges, which was also home to flotillas of destroyers, was virtually invulnerable to attack from the sea but throughout the war Allied planners, aware of the source of their submarine problems, had wrestled with how the canal basins and locks at the seaward end of the system might be destroyed. Long-range bombardment had been attempted from monitors standing offshore but the coastline was exceptionally heavily defended and the tasks of hitting a set of

Such was the state of play regarding operations against the coast when Rear Admiral Roger Keyes arrived as Director of Plans at the Admiralty at the end of September 1917. A former Inspecting Captain of Submarines and Commodore of the Submarine Service, he was an active and energetic leader, who notwithstanding his association with the disastrous 1915 Dardanelles expedition had moved rapidly up the promotion ladder. He had twice been mentioned in despatches and held both the DSO and CMG - evidence of both his gallantry and the quality of his political connections, particularly with Winston Churchill. After the Turkish campaign Keyes returned to England to take command

---

[4]The so called 'Great Landing' was the product of the fertile mind of Keyes predecessor at Dover, Admiral Sir Reginald Bacon. He apparently believed that if his plan had been implemented 'the destruction of the lock gates should have been a matter of comparatively few rounds'. R. H. Bacon, *Dover Patrol, 1915-1919,* (1919)

38

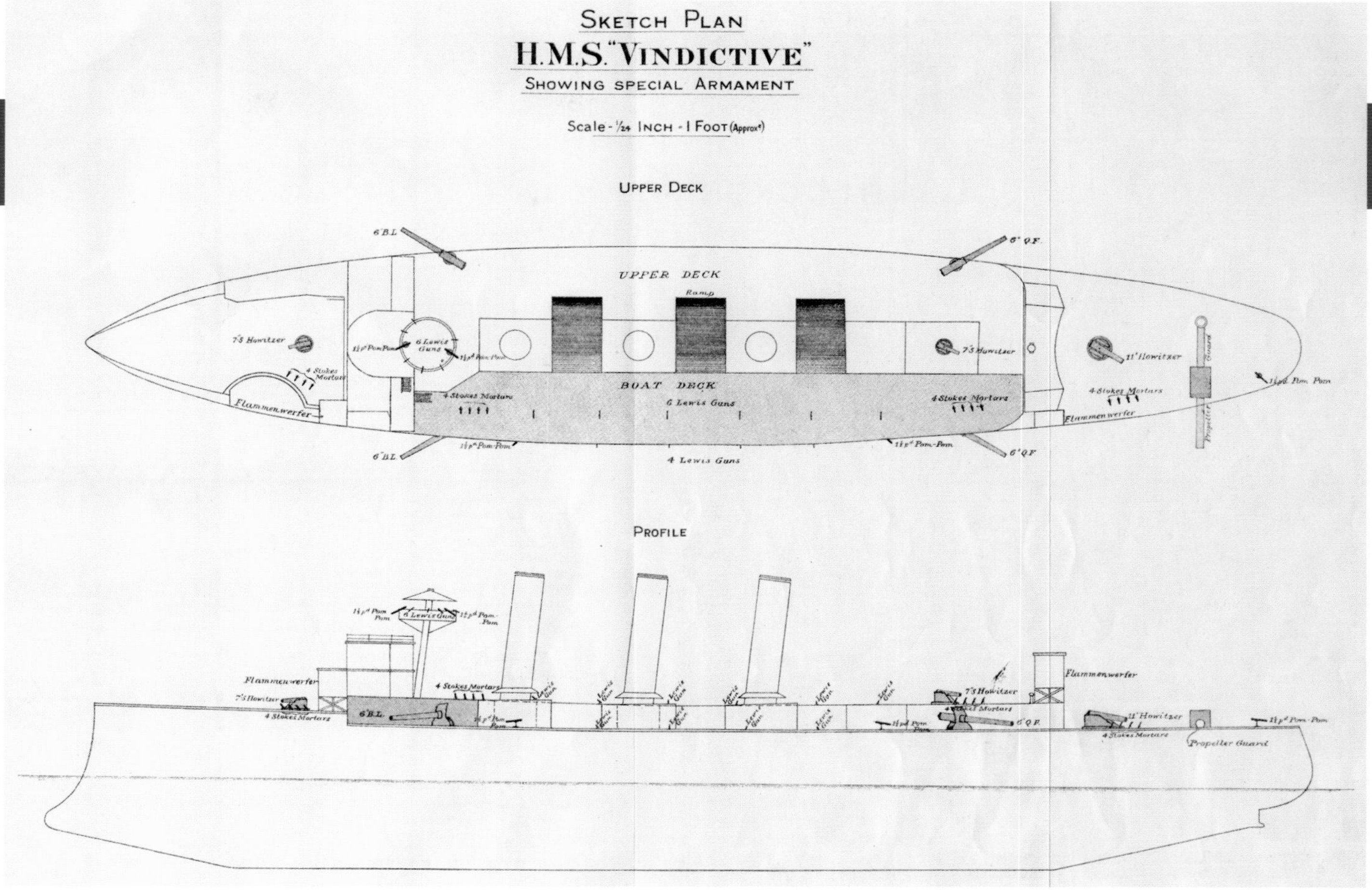

SKETCH PLAN
H.M.S. "VINDICTIVE"
SHOWING SPECIAL ARMAMENT

Scale - 1/24 INCH - 1 FOOT (Approx.)

UPPER DECK

PROFILE

of the battleship HMS *Centurion* and in April 1917 was promoted Rear Admiral, commanding the Fourth Battle Squadron. On arrival at the Admiralty his initial reaction to the dire situation in the Channel was to devise a series of improved measures to bar the Straits to submarines and then to formulate a longer-term plan to attack the problem at its source, via operations against the enemy coast. Unfortunately at this stage Keyes was the most junior Flag Officer in the Service and his aggressive and energetic ideas were not well received by more senior colleagues, particularly those who might have responsibility for implementing them. However, he was to become more intimately connected with the schemes he had first sketched on paper when, following the appointment of Sir Rosslyn Wemyss as First Sea Lord in December 1917, Keyes was given command of the Dover Patrol. He now had that rare naval opportunity – the chance to put his own plans into action.

The basic concept was relatively simple and attempted to achieve three objectives: to block the Bruges canal entrance to the extent that German submarines and torpedo boats would find it impossible to access Channel waters, to act similarly and simultaneously at Ostend, and to inflict as much generalised damage as possible on both ports and thus interfere with ancillary naval operations, particularly seaplane sorties. To achieve this an old 6,000-ton cruiser, HMS *Vindictive*, would

be fitted with an 11.5" howitzer, flamethrowers, mortars and machine guns and would be used as an assault vessel. She was to secure alongside the great harbour mole at Zeebrugge and specially designed brows would then be lowered to assist the landing of the Royal Marines and a 200 strong Bluejacket assault party. In this operation she would be assisted by the Mersey ferries *Iris II* and *Daffodil*, unarmed but protected by a combination of armour plate and mattresses. Meanwhile the blockships, obsolete 3,600 ton cruisers each filled with more than 1,000 tons of concrete, would steam into the harbours - *Iphigenia, Intrepid* and *Thetis* at Zeebrugge, and *Sirius* and *Brilliant*

at Ostend – and proceed to the locks where electrically fired charges would scuttle them. Additionally at Zeebrugge the old submarines C1 and C2, packed with explosives would be expended against the section of viaduct connecting the Mole to the land. The crews of both the blockships and the submarines would abandon ship immediately prior to impact and be picked up by supporting launches and motorboats.

If the plan was simple the execution represented a formidable challenge. Although the number of vessels undertaking the dual assault was relatively small, when the monitors required

BLOCKSHIPS AS USED AT ZEEBRUGGE AND OSTEND.

SHOWING ARRANGEMENT OF CONCRETE &c.

Scale, 1 inch = 40 Feet.

["SIRIUS".
"BRILLIANT."]

PROFILE.

Position of Charge

A.P.   D°   D°   D°   F.P.

PLAN OF PROTECTIVE DECK.

Concrete:—
Water Ballast:—

The water ballast shewn is that originally arranged for. It is understood however, that very little was actually carried.

["IPHIGENIA."
"INTREPID."
"THETIS."]

PROFILE.

Position of Charge

A.P.   D°   D°   D°   F.P.

PLAN OF PROTECTIVE DECK.

Plate 1.

10378. 38084. 36579

Malby & Sons. Lith.

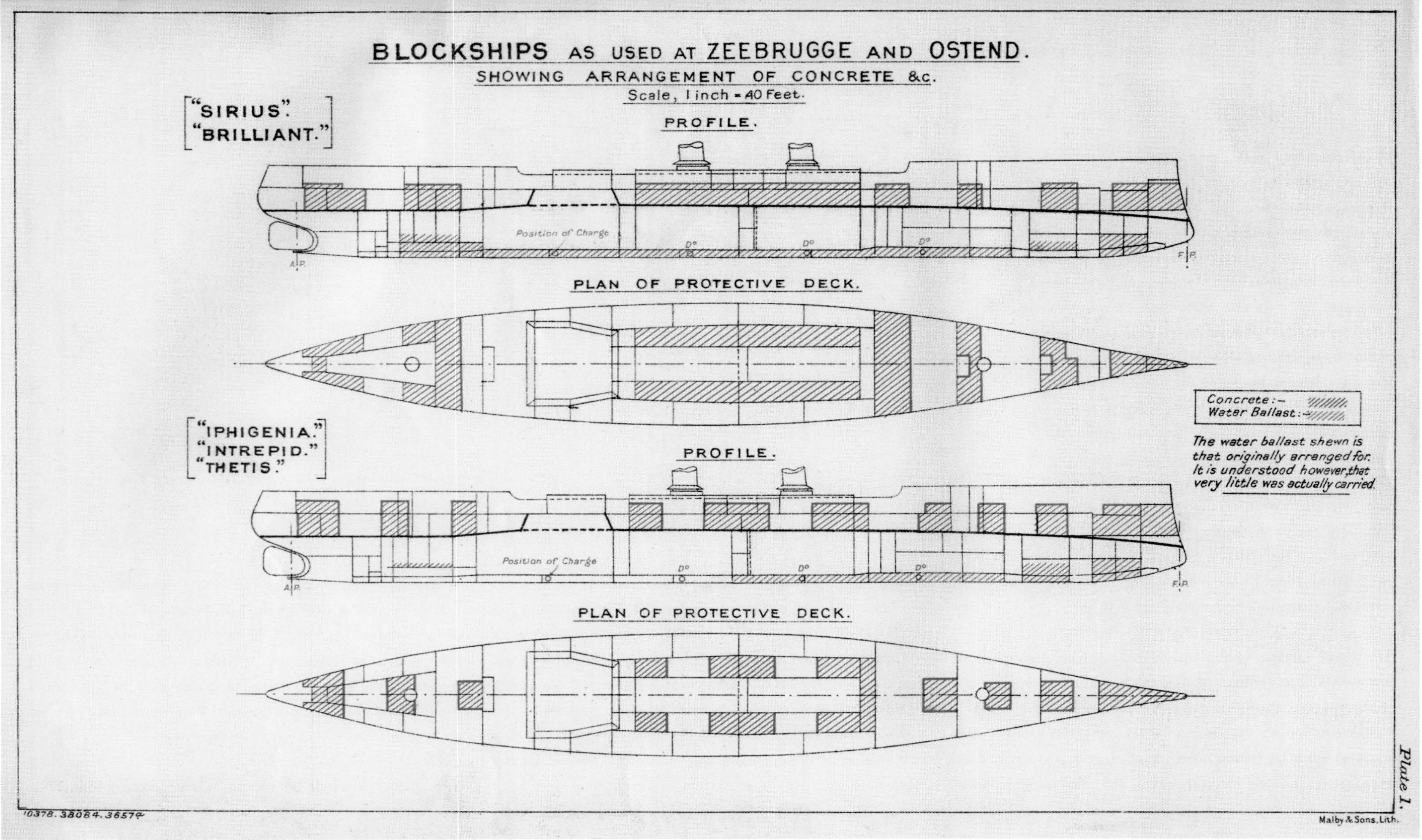

Intrepid, Iphigenia and Thetis blocking Zeebrugge Harbour. (NHB)

for the initial bombardment, together with screening light cruisers and destroyers, motor launches, coastal motor boats and the shallow draft Mersey ferries were considered, the striking force constituted an armada of more than 150 vessels. This sizeable force would approach a very heavily defended coastline that in the 12 miles that separated Zeebrugge from Ostend featured minefields and numerous gun batteries, many equipped with 15" guns. Dark, moonless conditions and extensive use of smoke on favourable winds were considered essential preconditions. Assuming that the initial approach was successful it was then necessary to assault the respective harbours. There was no Mole at Ostend but at Zeebrugge the harbour fortifications were a major piece of civil engineering. The Mole here was more than a mile long and 80 yards wide and carried a footpath, a road and a twin track railway. It was protected on the seaward side by a ten-foot high wall, which at High Water Springs was some thirty feet above the water, which meant that the assaulting troops would have to clamber up the ramps to land. Along the wall were various 5.9" guns, machine

gun posts and blockhouses, and at the seaward end was a Mole extension - a narrow pier about 300 yards long upon which several 3.5" and 4.1" co-axial guns and a huge flare cannon capable of illuminating the whole harbour were mounted. Coincidental with the assault on the Mole, the blockships and submarines would negotiate the sandbank-strewn harbour, locate their targets and taking tidal conditions into account, scuttle themselves. There then remained the question of withdrawal - about which little could be guaranteed beyond the fact that the enemy would no longer be surprised.

Dark, moonless conditions and extensive use of smoke on favourable winds were considered essential preconditions

Training and preparation for Operation ZO commenced in January 1918 and as befitted a sizeable naval force involving some 1800 officers and men, was intensive and demanding. Keyes dealt personally with the selection and appointment of the officers and recognising that many of the units would have to operate in a detached and independent mode, took care to interview singly the leaders who would serve under him. He seems to have relied heavily on personal contacts - particularly officers who had served with him at Gallipoli, or who had been recommended by close friends whose professional judgement

he respected. Once the key commanders had been selected, Keyes allowed each one to suggest two further officers who they could trust and to whom they could transfer command with confidence. Despite stringent security precautions news of the plan spread quickly in naval circles and its audacity and offensive character attracted some unorthodox and independent spirits. Yet each volunteer – and they were all volunteers – was carefully selected, with Keyes taking considerable pains to ensure that every officer was of proven and disciplined fighting pedigree.[6] Seamen and stokers came predominantly from Beatty's Grand Fleet, glad perhaps to end many months of frustration and the 200 or so who formed the naval assault parties were drawn largely from the trenches of the Royal Naval Brigade in France. The Royal Marine contingent consisted of officers and men of both the Royal Marine Artillery, who joined from the Grand Fleet on 1st March, and the bulk of the force, Royal Marine Light Infantry, who joined the 4th Battalion formed at Deal on 25 February 1918.

In his previous appointment as Director of Plans, Keyes had carefully defined the conditions for an attack. The stealthy approach required a moonless night and approach and withdrawal under cover of darkness. The assault on the lock gates needed to be conducted at, or close to, high water and the two ports needed to be hit simultaneously. This created a fairly restricted window of opportunity but at least it was

---

[6]Additionally one of the conditions for the selection of those taking a leading part in the assault, whose survival was considered doubtful, was that they should also be unmarried. See Pitt, *op cit* 33.

*Sketch plan of
Zeebrugge Mole. (NHB)*

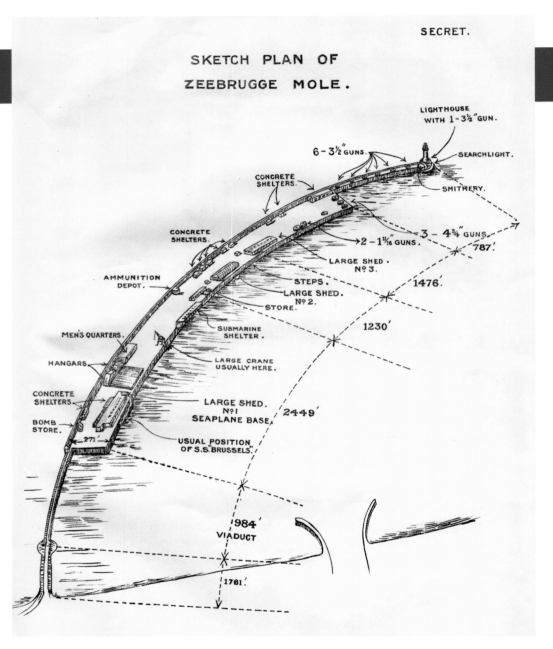

SECRET.

SKETCH PLAN OF
ZEEBRUGGE MOLE.

*Sketch plan of
Zeebrugge Mole. (NHB)*

calculable. More difficult to predict were the weather conditions that required a combination of the moderate seas required by the smaller craft and a reasonably favourable onshore breeze that would enable the small armada to approach behind an advancing smoke screen. Extensive preparatory operations were required including covert inshore mine clearance and the laying of vital marker buoys that would ensure an accurate initial approach – the last thirteen miles was to be conducted by dead reckoning across the tide. Some elementary deception operations were envisaged, in particular a plan to lay mines in the approaches to Ostend and Zeebrugge which would be time-detonated to sink and become ineffective. In this manner it was hoped to both persuade German patrol craft not to enter these waters and at the same time persuade them that the British had no intention of doing so either. Assuming that the timings for the mining operations were accurate this was judged to have a fair chance of success. Further confusion was sewn with the nightly bombardment of the area for several weeks prior to the main operation to accustom defenders into thinking that such activity was unremarkable. Similarly the target area was regularly over-flown by aircraft whose engine pitch was similar to that of the raiding Coastal Motor Boats (CMB). In the heat of the actual attack even momentary hesitation in defence would confer considerable benefits.

By the end of March 1918 Keyes was ready to go and the next available 'window' was identified between the 9th and the 14th of the following month. The ships of the assault force were assembled in the Thames estuary and the Royal Marines, who had embarked in transports supposedly bound for France some days earlier, were rerouted to join them. For some days the assault force and its screening flotilla waited pending satisfactory

The Zeebrugge Mole. (NHB)

defences and the difficulties that lay ahead.

The operation at Ostend had been similarly abandoned with the loss of one coastal motor boat but at this point Keyes and his subordinate Commodore Hubert Lynes felt, perhaps surprisingly, that the plan was intact and determined to try again. A second attempt was made on 13 April but within two hours of leaving the Thames, adverse wind conditions forced a further postponement. This date was also the end of the favourable phase of the moon for April and it would now be at least three weeks before the operation could be remounted. Fearing that the passage of time might influence continuing Admiralty approval Keyes now abandoned one of the essential pre conditions – a moonless night – and successfully petitioned the Board to carry out the operation at the earliest midnight high tide. It is hard not to conclude on the impetuosity of this decision. The original plan had stressed the paramount importance of an approach in total darkness and this was now summarily dismissed. In the failed first attempt Keyes had been given graphic evidence of the quality of the shore batteries and their ability to engage targets at great range, and the offshore bombardment of Ostend and the aerial attacks at Zeebrugge had clearly indicated British intent in

the area. Finally there was the question of the fate of the missing CMB and its crew – if they had been captured and interrogated, how far had the plan been compromised?

Keyes does not seem to have been unduly concerned about this possibility and although in his memoirs he admits to a degree of depression arising from the two postponed attempts; at no point did he consider the abandonment of the mission. On the night of 22 April, in brilliant moonlight, the force again commenced its cross channel transit. This time the weather conditions were favourable and within two hours of setting out the cloud had bubbled up, the wind lay astern and light rain began to fall. At 2230 the Ostend force - *Brilliant, Sirius,* two destroyers and two CMBs departed from the main group and about 15 minutes later the bombarding monitors *Erebus* and *Terror* opened up with their 15" guns pounding the enemy coast. At 2310 the first of the smoke screens was activated from supporting small craft and over the next half hour a blanket of dense grey-white smoke was thrown over the assault area.[7] The approach phase had gone very largely to plan and it was not until ten minutes to midnight that the enemy responded, with the firing of a white illuminating flare, probably from the harbour wall. Almost simultaneously the wind shifted, quickly dispersing the fog and revealing the assault ship *Vindictive*, visible against a blanket of retreating smoke, less than a thousand yards offshore and speeding towards the great harbour mole. There could now be no turning back.

weather conditions but at 1600 on 11 April they got under way. By 1930 the various elements off the assault force assembled at 'A' Buoy, the first of a series of way marks across the Channel, and led by Keyes, flying his flag in the destroyer *Warwick*, they began their carefully planned passage. At 2300 the force raised D Buoy some 35 miles from the target but within an hour the wind, which had been favourable throughout, dropped and shifted to the south thus denying any use of smoke in the final approach. With the defenders already fully alerted by a previously planned aerial bombardment there was no alternative but to abandon the mission. With a heavy heart Keyes gave the one word order and his staff officer began the hazardous operation of turning, in darkness and without lights some 74 vessels, many under tow and some packed with explosives, for home. This was achieved with no casualties but as the force disappeared into the gloom four 12" shells from the Knocke battery, some 32,000 yards away, straddled the flagship – a potent reminder of the quality of the

[7]The responsibility for the provision of smoke, flares and other pyrotechnics throughout the operation belonged to Wing Commander Frank Brock RNAS, son of the head of the firework company of that name. He was killed in fierce fighting on the Mole.

The Plan used in the report by the Royal Navy on the attack against Zeebrugge Harbour. (RMM)

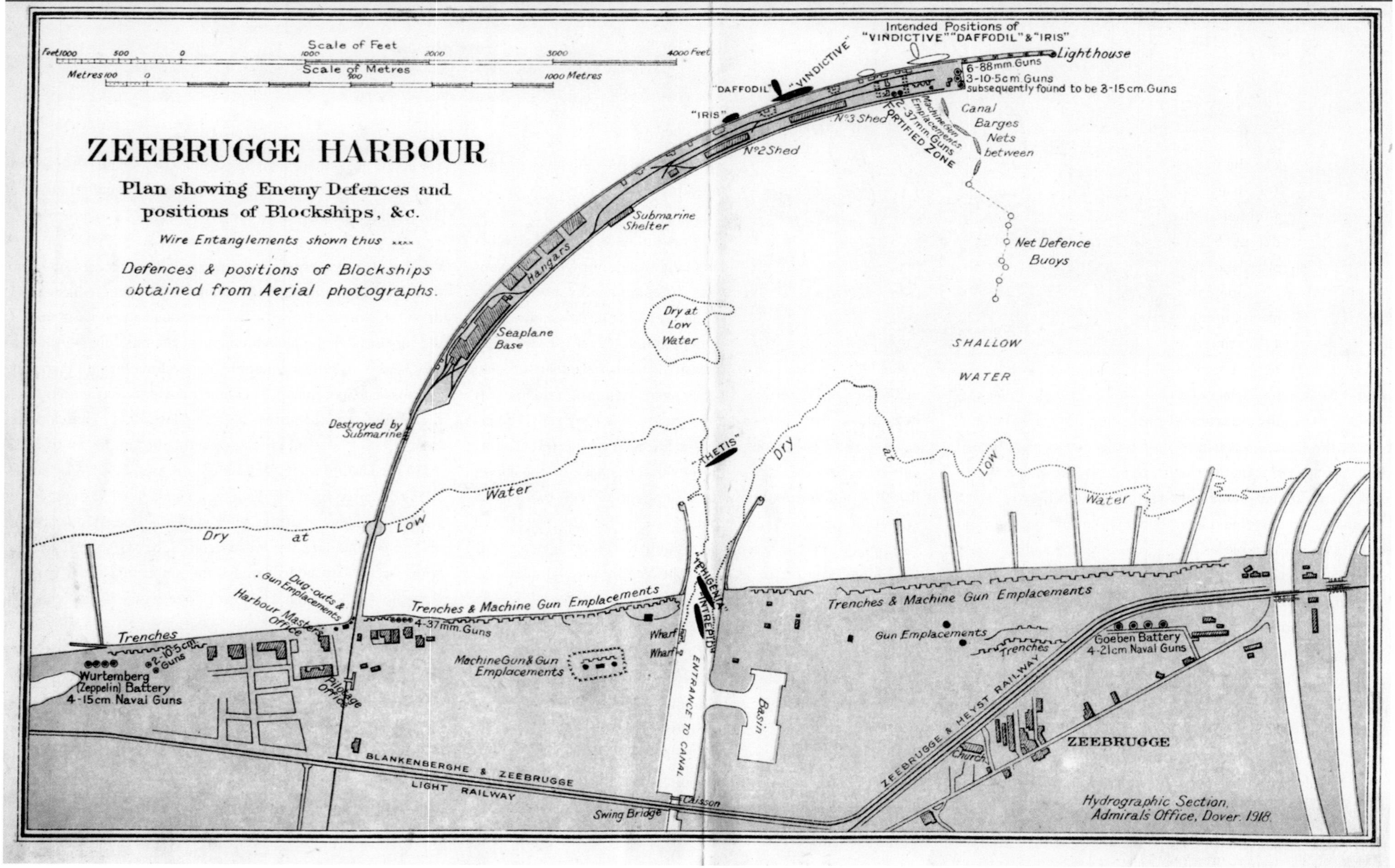

ZEEBRUGGE HARBOUR

Plan showing Enemy Defences and positions of Blockships, &c.

Wire Entanglements shown thus ....

Defences & positions of Blockships obtained from Aerial photographs.

Scale of Feet
Feet 1000   500   0   1000   2000   3000   4000 Feet
Scale of Metres
Metres 100   0   500   1000 Metres

Intended Positions of "VINDICTIVE" "DAFFODIL" & "IRIS"

Lighthouse

6-88mm Guns
3-10.5cm Guns
subsequently found to be 3-15cm Guns

"DAFFODIL"   "VINDICTIVE"

"IRIS"   Nº3 Shed   FORTIFIED ZONE

Canal
Barges
Nets
between

Nº2 Shed

Submarine Shelter

Net Defence Buoys

Hangars

SHALLOW WATER

Seaplane Base

Dry at Low Water

Destroyed by Submarine

"THETIS"   Dry   at   Low   Water

Water

Dry   at   Low

Dug-outs & Gun Emplacements

Harbour Masters Office

Trenches & Machine Gun Emplacements   Trenches & Machine Gun Emplacements

Trenches   4-37mm.Guns   Wharf   Gun Emplacements   Trenches

2-105cm Guns   MachineGun & Gun Emplacements   Wharf   Goeben Battery 4-21cm Naval Guns

Wurtemberg (Zeppelin) Battery 4-15cm Naval Guns   Pilotage Office   "INTREPID"   "IPHIGENIA"   ENTRANCE TO CANAL   Basin   ZEEBRUGGE

ZEEBRUGGE & HEYST RAILWAY

Church

BLANKENBERGHE & ZEEBRUGGE LIGHT RAILWAY

Swing Bridge   Caisson

Hydrographic Section. Admirals Office. Dover. 1918.

Medal commemorating the Raid on Zeebrugge and Ostend. (NHB)

The *Vindictive* closed the mole at full speed, an open target for the batteries of 105mm and 88mm guns on the mole extension, which opened up on her at about 200 yards. The guns had an immediate, murderous effect with the officer commanding Marines, his deputy, and the commander of the Bluejacket party, all killed in the opening salvos. The ship's propulsion and steering gear remained in tact however, and she was alongside the mole almost on time, but somewhat out of position. Securing alongside was more difficult and the 6,000-ton ship could only be kept in place by the continual efforts of the ferry *Daffodil* pushing the old cruiser against the mole continually for the next 50 minutes. It was only the efforts of the ferry that allowed the disembarkation ramps to be lowered; several were shattered by German gunfire and it was to be almost 15 minutes before the first landing parties were ashore. Bitter fighting took place on the mole as the reduced landing parties came under heavy machine gun and small arms fire. Some cover was provided from the *Vindictive*'s fighting top, where Royal Marine Sergeant Norman Finch already badly wounded was pouring fire down on to the jetty below. Men, and particularly leaders of men, were now being cut down from entrenched defensive positions. Lieutenant Hawkins made the perilous journey up a boarding ladder from the *Iris* but was killed as he reached the parapet. Lieutenant Commander Bradford was killed as he attempted to secure an anchor to the mole and Petty Officer Hallihan perished attempting to retrieve his body. All around them Royal Marine platoons were racing along the wall and the roadway beneath to secure their objectives but the advantage

was now firmly with the defenders and the Mole at Zeebrugge was fast becoming a vicious killing ground.

In contrast to the smoke and din atop the harbour wall some 3000 yards out to sea the submarine C3, her bows packed with five tons of high explosive, proceeded silently towards her objective. She commenced her final approach at 9 knots and went forward, in the glare of searchlights, but unchallenged by sustained fire, towards the viaduct connecting the mole to the land. The C3 grounded successfully and her crew began to abandon ship leaving the commanding officer, Lieutenant Sandford, to set the charges. The crew pulled away from the submarine and were immediately in trouble. They came under sustained small arms fire wounding three of the crew and almost simultaneously the engine of their small skiff failed, forcing them to pull against a tide that threatened to push them back on to the stricken vessel. They were scarcely 200 yards from the C3 when, briefly and spectacularly, night became day as the amatol charges exploded. The viaduct was no more and the mole was separated from the land - an island of misery, ruination and death.

In considering the destruction and the sacrifice bled out atop the harbour wall, it is sometimes difficult to remember that both these actions were diversionary, with the aim of disrupting enemy response and distracting attention to allow the main thrust - the blocking of the canal entrance - to proceed unhindered. The three old cruisers had deliberately maintained a slower

speed than the rest of the force with the intention of arriving in the midst of the *Vindictive* assault. Despite the attentions of the shore batteries they made the edge of the smoke screen unscathed and led by the *Thetis* rounded the Mole at 0020. From this point the lead blockship received the undivided attentions of the defending gunners, as shell and machine gun fire spewed from the harbour wall at a range of only 100 yards. Unable to properly defend herself she was hit incessantly - her forward progress hindered not so much by gunfire as by the harbour defensive nets which snagged her screws. Desperately she steered for the canal entrance but losing way all the time she was taken by the tide and grounded on the port side of the main channel about three hundred yards short of the lock gates. Her final helm order just managed to swing her bows into the dredged channel. The *Thetis* was short of her objective but her engines had now seized, communications from the bridge had ceased and she was slowly listing to starboard. There was little more to be done and her CO, Commander Ralph Sneyd, gave the order to fire the charges and blow the bottom out of his ship.

The second blockship HMS *Intrepid* reaped the benefit of the attentions devoted to the Thetis, for the boom defences had now been destroyed and she was given a relatively clear run through the harbour. Using the starboard navigation light of the stricken Thetis as a marker, the second cruiser proceeded unscathed to within about half a mile of the lock gates. There seems to have been no military or technical reason why Lieutenant Bonham Carter and his crew should not have now carried on and smashed

British Prisoners of War captured during the Raid. (NHB)

the blockship into the gates themselves - thus decisively cutting the umbilical between the Bruges base and the coast. And given that this was the overall objective of the operation anyway it could hardly be conceived as a serious divergence from the plan. Nevertheless, Bonham Carter stuck stolidly to his orders and proceeded to con his ship into a position athwart the main channel but at some distance from the lock. This proved to be more difficult than anticipated for although his engine and helm orders were answered with alacrity, the width of the channel proved to be somewhat less than the length of the ship. This meant that it was difficult to find the speed or the room to place her firmly in position. Ignoring the increasing attentions of the defenders and under dense cover provided by her smoke canisters, the *Intrepid* diligently attempted to bury her stem and stern into the Flanders mud.

Unfortunately much of this effort was wasted for, in the midst of the darkness and dense smoke, the third blockship, HMS *Iphigenia* announced her arrival by colliding with the port bow of the *Intrepid* - pushing her out of her carefully crafted position. The *Intrepid's* charges were immediately blown and she settled quickly but in the meantime *Iphigenia's* 22 year old commanding officer, Lieutenant Billyard - Leak, attempted to get his vessel to ground on the eastern shore. Engulfed in smoke both from the *Intrepid's* defensive screen and a fractured steam pipe in her own forecastle, the old cruiser sank her bows into the canal bank. There was nothing more to be done and the young captain gave the orders to scuttle. When the ship settled and her upper deck

was awash he joined the remainder of the crew in the one remaining cutter.

For many of the crew of the three blockships the most hazardous part of their mission now commenced as in a collection of cutters and skiffs they attempted to return to the rescue launches and larger ships that had stood off during the assault. One of *Intrepid's* cutters managed to exit the canal basin and proceed across the harbour and out into the open sea where the destroyer *Whirlwind* rescued her crew. ML 282, made slower progress with more than 100 men on board and a further party towed astern in a skiff, she came under continuous heavy fire from the shore but eventually ran into the Warwick searching the sea close to the harbour wall. Vessels large and small were now leaving the scene. A star shell illuminated the *Vindictive*, which together with *Iris* and *Daffodil* was now homeward bound. The remaining motor launches heavily overcrowded were also heading into the dark. But the defenders continued to hunt them out and the destroyer *North Star*, in the depths of the smoke screen, was caught first by a German destroyer and then, as the smoke cleared, by the Mole batteries. Desperately she fired torpedoes but was overwhelmed by 8-inch shells and despite supporting fire from the *Phoebe* was eventually sunk. This loss, timed at 0225, marked the effective end of the Zeebrugge action.

The complementary operation at Ostend had also concluded by this time although it was apparent to all participants that

it had ended in total failure and that the blockships had not managed to obstruct the canal entrance. The evolution foundered in the face of good enemy intelligence gained from the capture of CMB 33 in the abortive raid of 11-12 April. Fully aware of the nature and possibility of an assault, the Ostend defenders, unlike their Zeebrugge counterparts, took the precaution of adjusting the position of marker buoys offshore, thus sewing confusion in the approaching force. The result was that although the blockships were finally sunk they were hopelessly out of position and provided no obstruction to the passage of submarines from the canal to the sea. Two later attempts were planned to block the Ostend canal and although on the night of 11-12 May the old *Vindictive*, employed this time as a blockship was successfully sunk, her position was not accurate enough to close the canal. The third attempt planned for June was cancelled.

While the failure at Ostend was apparent to almost all who took part in the operation the desire to announce a success that would boost both the morale of the Service and the general public seems to have prevailed. Much emphasis was placed on the gallantry displayed and both national and local press recounted the thrilling deeds that would serve as a source of inspiration

German troops inspect the British dead. (NHB)

during the dark days of war. Even when it became apparent that Ostend had been less than a success, it seemed to strengthen the view that Zeebrugge had been more of a triumph. Eagerly the newspapers devoured the initial Admiralty account of events that recounted an operation achieving total surprise, running like clockwork and resulting in a decisive conclusion. The only incalculable was the height of British heroics and the depth of German cowardice. There were however calmer and more objective assessments that stressed that despite the gallantry and the appalling casualties, more than 600 killed and wounded, there was pitifully little to show for either operation. Obviously this was apparent to the Germans although their claims were instantly dismissed as propaganda but it was also clear to Naval Intelligence who analysing aerial photographs also concluded that the blockships at Ostend and Zeebrugge were probably not an effective obstacle.

In fact any interdiction of submarine operations due to the assault at Zeebrugge proved to be remarkably short lived. In the area around the blockships the channel between the obstructions and the canal bank was quickly dredged and widened and within two days submarines and torpedo boats were using the locks. Within two weeks vessels up to a thousand tons were entering the canal. It might also be pointed out that, regardless of the damage inflicted at Zeebrugge, with Ostend remaining open the ultimate intention to neutralise the Bruges base could not be realised. While it was true that the number of submarines and destroyers using the Flanders base did eventually decline it did not do so for some

time after the assaults and this change of posture was not a result of the physical obstructions placed by the British. Thus we are left with an operation which cost the lives of 170 men and whose contribution to the overall strategy of the war at sea was marginal. There can be little doubt as to its psychological value both on the home front and in a navy that had struggled for an opportunity to engage the enemy and achieve decisive results. It also had some limited military value as part of the broader activities of the Dover Patrol and, as Professor Paul Halpern has pointed out, from around the time of the Zeebrugge raid, the numbers of Flanders based destroyers and submarines attempting to pass through the Dover Straits went into steady decline. By this time however any initiative possessed by the Germans was beginning to slip away. In the face of increasingly successful convoy tactics and the advance of the allied armies into the fields of Flanders, the submarine menace that had originally prompted the Zeebrugge and Ostend operations was now receding. The U boats that had wrought such havoc were at last called home.

Lessons identified from Operation ZO

1.   There can be little doubt that the basic concept of attacking Zeebrugge and Ostend was a sound one. The notion of 'rooting out the U Boat at source' in the protected enclave of Bruges, and its canal links to the coast, rather than confronting the threat in

the North Sea was obvious. What was more difficult to understand was why the plan took so long to come to fruition. As early as the autumn of 1914, during the allied retreat from Antwerp, it was recognised that the canal entrances and basins should not be allowed to fall undamaged into enemy hands. When they did it was confidently assumed that repossession would soon be achieved. From this point onwards action against the Belgian coast was under continual discussion but never distilled into anything more than sporadic long-range bombardment.

2.   Bringing the eventual plan to fruition seemed to have as much to do with the personalities and changes of senior personnel, particularly the new First Sea Lord, as any broader shift in the broader strategic requirement. The particular appointment of Keyes was clearly fundamental to the conduct and style of the operation. His personal bravery was never in doubt but his tendency to alter plans at short notice and without consultation, have made him the subject of criticism. The decision to persist with the Ostend raids in the face of almost certain compromise following the capture of CMB 33 is a serious charge.

3. While there have been numerous criticisms of inadequate planning and a deadly lack of attention to detail in the execution of the operation, Keyes seems to have been successful in the selection and motivation of personnel – particularly those chosen for positions of leadership. The degree of gallantry and personal sacrifice evident in Operation ZO, particularly from very young officers, is testament to the quality of morale of the assault force. Set against this is the charge that few officers seemed to properly understand the operation beyond the strict requirement to gallantly obey orders – the failure of the *Intrepid* to ram the lock gates and thus put the outcome of the operation at Zeebrugge beyond doubt, is often cited as an example of this.

4. There can be little doubt that the operations at Zeebrugge and Ostend were a failure and that their principal value lay not in military achievement but in the effect they had on a war-weary British public who were allowed to believe that, in the midst of continuing bad news from the Western front, there were reasons to be confident of an eventual German defeat. This was of course a substantial and very real contribution to the overall war effort. Whether it could begin to justify the loss of so many lives is more dubious.

Further Reading

Carpenter, Alfred B., *The Blocking of Zeebrugge,* (London: Herbert Jenkins, 1925)

Corrigan, Gordon, *Mud, Blood and Popycock,* (London: Cassell, 2003)

Ferguson, Nial, *The Pity of War,* (London: Penguin, 1998)

Keyes, Roger, *The Naval Memoirs of Admiral of the Fleet Sir Roger Keyes: Scapa Flow to the Dover Straits 1916-1918,* (London: Thornton Butterworth, 1935)

Lake, Deborah, *The Zeebrugge and Ostend Raids,* (Barnsley: Leo Cooper, 2002)

Neillands, Robin, *The Old Contemtibles: The British Expeditionary Force, 1914,* (London: John Murray, 2004)

Pitt, Barrie, *Zeebrugge: St George's Day 1918,* (London: Cassell, 1958)

Sheffield, Gary, *The Somme,* (London: Cassell, 2003)

Terraine, John, *The First World War 1914-1918,* (London: Leo Cooper, 1965)

Thompson, Julian, *The Royal Marines: From Sea Soldiers to a Special Force,* (London: Sidgwick & Jackson, 2000) See Chapter 9.

Warner, Philip, *The Zeebrugge Raid,* (London: William Kimber, 1978)

Biography

Dr H W Dickinson teaches in the Defence Studies Department, Kings College, London at the Joint Services Command and Staff College. An MA and PhD graduate of the University of London he taught previously at the Royal Naval Colleges at Dartmouth and Greenwich, and at the United States Naval Academy. In 1997 he was awarded the Julian Corbett Prize for Modern Naval History, by the Institute of Historical Research.

Japanese Amphibious Warfare
Manoeuvre in the East, 1918 - 1942

By Mr Mark J Grove

If the tradition of successful and ambitious Japanese amphibious operations had its roots in the late 19th century, the equipment and doctrine which underpinned the capability unleashed across south-east Asia and the western Pacific in December 1941 had been in development since the 1920s and tested in operations in China during the 1930s.

> *It was a central belief of both the political and military elites that Japan's destiny lay in the acquisition of a greater Empire.*

The impetus for such a capability again came from Japanese ambitions, now further heightened.[1] The Imperial National Defence Policy was revised in 1918 in the light of the changed international situation. It was a central belief of both the political and military elites that Japan's destiny lay in the acquisition of a greater Empire. China appeared for the first time but the most likely opponent was still felt to be Russia. However, the Japanese Navy, with its eyes on a developing naval armaments race with the US increased its preparations against the latter. This accorded with the growing feeling in the Navy that the new Empire would not be found on the Asian mainland, as most in the Army believed. Instead, the Navy looked south,

towards resource-rich Malaya and especially the Dutch East Indies. This would necessitate taking French Indo-China and the US-held Philippines which flanked the approach. However, whilst the Army added to the 'Outline of the Employment of Forces' - the annual operational plans - a statement that if war did occur with the US it would immediately co-operate with the Navy in an attack on Luzon in the Philippines it appears to have made no realistic preparations for this.[2]

The ten years before the outbreak of the First World War had seen few changes in the Japanese approach to amphibious operations. However, following the operations against Tsingtao in 1914, the pace of development quickened. The Army General Staff's study of the British experience at Gallipoli led to a recognition of the difficulties posed by new defensive weapons and a requirement for more flexible, lighter forces conducting operations much more quickly with effective communications, naval gunfire and air support coming ashore ready to fight.

These changes in the role of the Army acted as a spur to the formulation of doctrine and the provision of training. A minor landing exercise involving the Hiroshima based 5th Division had taken place in 1918. But in 1920 a major exercise was

conducted under the supervision of the General Staff. The exercise, witnessed by General Uehara Masasaku, Chief of the General Staff, led him to order the development of an armoured, motorised landing craft.[3] The design of the simple, traditional Japanese fishing boat that had been used in the earlier campaigns was developed into a more specialised craft. This became the ubiquitous Daihatsu A landing craft which entered service in 1925 and would be used extensively and in large numbers by both the Army and Navy during the Second Sino-Japanese (1937-45) and Pacific Wars. Fitted initially with a petrol engine but later a diesel, it was equipped with a ramp, a double-keeled bow and a protected screw, and could carry a maximum payload of 15-tons or 40 to 50 troops (double that on short trips). This was a robust and versatile craft.[4] A smaller version, the kôhatsu, with about half the carrying capability, was completed in 1927.[5]

In 1921 the Army began formal training and instruction in amphibious operations,[6] and full-scale landing exercises at divisional level were held in Ise Bay during that summer with three divisions (out of a total Army strength of 17 divisions) taking part in the exercise of the following year. However, one senior officer later recalled that such exercises were still too

[1]Fujiwara Akira, "The Role of the Japanese Army", in Dorothy Borg & Shumpei Okamoto (Eds.), *Pearl Harbor as History: Japanese American Relations, 1931-1941*, (New York, 1973), [hereafter Fujiwara Akira, "The Role of the Japanese Army"], p.189. Mark J. Grove, 'The Development of Japanese Amphibious Warfare 1874 to 1942', in Geoffrey Till, Theo Farrell, and Mark J. Grove, *Amphibious Operations*, (Camberley: Strategic and Combat Studies Institute, 1997), pp. 30-32.
[2]Fujiwara Akira, "The Role of the Japanese Army", p.189.
[3]Edward J. Drea, 'The Development of Imperial Japanese Army Amphibious Warfare Doctrine', in *idem, In the Service of the Emperor: Essays on the Imperial Japanese Army*, (Lincoln: University of Nebraska Press, 1998), p. 17.
[4]U.S. War Department, *Handbook on Japanese Military Forces*, (London: Greenhill Books, reprinted 1991), pp. 327-330.
[5]Edward J. Drea, 'The Development of Imperial Japanese Army Amphibious Warfare Doctrine', p. 18.
[6]Allan R, Millett, 'Assault from the Sea: The Development of Amphibious Warfare between the Wars, the American, British and Japanese Experiences', in Williamson Murray and Allan R. Millett (eds), *Military Innovation in the Interwar Period*, (Cambridge: Cambridge University Press, 1996), p. 67.

*The ubiquitous Japanese 'Dihatsu A'
Landing Craft. (BRNC)*

rare, for despite the benefits, especially for inter-service co-operation, as the Army Transport Department was reliant on chartered transports, the cost was deemed to be prohibitive. So, alternative ways had to be found to train the men. Often, simple methods were employed: rope ladders were hung out of the upstairs windows of barracks, for example, to practice climbing down from transports into landing craft and mock-ups of landing craft, which could be rocked from side to side, were built, in which soldiers were taught how to position themselves in the boats, how to shoot from a moving craft and how to leap onto the beach.[7]

The practice whereby the initial landfall was made by landing parties supplied by the Navy from the fleet was largely ended, although the Navy continued to train its officers and men to conduct them. Instead, the Army undertook to execute beachhead operations on its own.[8] Japanese attention,

prior to the First World War, had been directed rather more to the business of transporting troops than landing them. For example, the section in the pre-War Field Duty Manual had been confined to problems of transportation, albeit at great length. Revised and renamed the Field Service Manual it provided instruction and guidance for the Army units now tasked with carrying out landings, whilst the Shipping Transport Duty Manual was also revised, detailed information relating to landing operations being added.[9] In 1924 a Landing and Landing Defence Operations Manual, the first dedicated manual covering landing operations was issued.[10] This was a major improvement on the Navy's guide to landing for units drawn from the fleet.[11]

By 1923, and a further revision of the National Defence Policy, the US had replaced Russia as the most likely enemy and a newly created Tactical Plan included a firmer statement of joint occupations of both Guam and the Philippines.[12] The following year saw the Army General Staff establish a 'Committee to Study Preparations for War Against the United States' and from 1925 the Army's annual operations plans included ever more elaborate strategic schemes in the event of war with the US.

That for 1925 specified that an emergency force of one and a half divisions would land at Lingayen and Lamon Bays on Luzon and capture Manila prior to occupying the whole of the Philippines before the arrival of the US main fleet from across the Pacific.[13] In 1926, three divisions had been earmarked for the Luzon operation.[14]

However, despite the strategic scheming, the Army's main area of interest remained continental Asia and amphibious preparations were conducted with this in mind. Such a state of affairs would continue until the late 1930s. This had much to do with the fact that by the early 1920s, with the demise of the authority of the genro,[15] the only co-ordinating body between the ministries and armed forces had disappeared. The resulting inter-service rivalry saw not only budget competition but, in the absence of centrally established priorities, the setting of increasingly mutually exclusive objectives. So, whilst it had 'reached the stage of formally adopting plans for war with the US...[the Army] continued to make no serious effort to implement them.' Indeed, whilst the 1937 plan earmarked the 5th and 11th Divisions for the assault on the Philippines, these divisions would prepare for operations against the USSR! Not

---

[7]Military History Section, Headquarters, Army Forces Far East, "Historical Review of Landing Operations of the Japanese Forces", Japanese Monograph No. 156, (Washington: Office of the Chief of Military History, Department of the Army, 1952), [hereafter Japanese Monograph No. 156], p.22.
[8]Japanese Monograph No. 156, pp.2-3.
[9]Japanese Monograph No. 156, p.21.
[10]Japanese Monograph No. 156, p.21. This was superseded in 1933.
[11]Millett, 'Assault from the Sea', p. 67.
[12]Fujiwara Akira, "The Role of the Japanese Army", pp. 189-190.
[13]Fujiwara Akira, "The Role of the Japanese Army", pp. 189-190.
[14]Japanese Monograph No. 156, pp. 8-9. Millett has the 5th, 11th and 12th assigned to the Luzon landing plan in 1926. Millett, 'Assault from the Sea', p. 67.
[15]W. G. Beasley, The Rise of Modern Japan, (London: Weidenfeld & Nicolson, 1990), p.159.

until after 1939 did the Army begin to plan in earnest for war against America.[16] It is certainly significant that the late 1920s saw the development of the Navy's own Special Landing Forces and that during the 1930s all naval officers passing through the Etajima Naval Academy received extensive training in the conduct of landing operations.[17] Nevertheless, both services continued to co-operate in the development of amphibious capabilities.

In the late 1920s a further series of reforms occurred. In 1928, amid concern over the quality of the Army Transport Department's civilian transport and landing craft crews, who tended to be of a lower physical calibre than those conscripted into the Army proper, the Transport Department lost responsibility for the operation of landing craft to the so-called Shipping Engineer Regiments. These consisted of 1,200 officers and men in an headquarters and three companies. It was from these that the Debarkation Commandos, which played such an important role in the Pacific War, developed.[18] These units were trained to operate landing craft on the basis of a Debarkation Manual issued the same year.[19] Those concerned with the debarkation of troops and supplies were now grouped together as the 'Debarkation Working Party', which was eventually commanded by a senior officer from one of the

Shipping Engineer Regiments. He was tasked with working out a landing plan in conjunction with the troop commander's staff. The landing plan was concerned with the landing of the troops and supplies efficiently, in good time and in the correct sequence and the creation of a beachhead: the unloading of landing craft from transports and their allotment to specific tasks; the placing of landing markers; the building of piers; if necessary, marking channels, mooring areas and dangerous waters; and the organization of communications facilities, assembly areas and ammunition dumps on or around the beach itself.[20] By 1930, some of the units involved were being specifically trained to remove beach obstacles as a preliminary to an assault landing.[21]

The Army and the Navy developed a clear understanding of the principal requirements for a successful opposed landing. The Navy would have to prevent an enemy air, submarine or surface attack interfering with the arrival of the amphibious convoy or the movement ashore and would be responsible for laying down gunfire sufficient to destroy beach defences and suppress the defenders. From 1926 the Navy conducted a series of gunfire experiments involving the Army. Whilst the results were disappointing they did serve to identify the necessary improvements in communications, range-finding and

shell design required - although there is no sign of significant investment in minesweeping capabilities. Between 1929 and 1931, a further series of amphibious exercises was carried out, in which major developments in ship-to-shore movement - notably the use of large numbers of Daihatsu A landing craft - were tested in both daylight and night-time landings, sometimes to destruction with landing craft wrecked and soldiers killed. These hard won techniques would soon be tested on the Asian mainland.

Japanese amphibious operations were an integral part of Japan's campaigns in China during the Shanghai Incident of 1932 and the Second Sino-Japanese War, 1937-1945. During the Second Sino-Japanese War Japan was able to capture at will all the Chinese ports - cities and towns which were the centres of political and financial support for the Kuomintang and through which the bulk of any foreign assistance would have to pass. In addition, and of particular interest, are the outflanking movements which were used to rescue Japanese land operations that had been successfully tied down by Chinese forces at Shanghai in both 1932 and 1937.

The Shanghai Incident was an attempt by Navy hard-liners to exploit a tense situation in Shanghai in a bid to emulate the

---

[16]Fujiwara Akira, "The Role of the Japanese Army", p.190.
[17]Cecil Bullock, Etajima: The Dartmouth of Japan, (London: Sampson Low, Marston & Co., 1942), pp.13-14.
[18]Hans G. Von Lehmann, "Japanese Landing Operations in World War Two", in Merrill L. Bartlett (Ed.), Assault from the Sea: Essays in the History of Amphibious Warfare, (Annapolis: USNIP, 1983), [hereafter Lehmann, "Japanese Landing Operations in World War Two"], pp. 197-198.
[19]Japanese Monograph No. 156, pp. 11, 21, 22.
[20]Japanese Monograph No. 156, p.42.
[21]Edward J. Drea, 'The Development of Imperial Japanese Army Amphibious Warfare Doctrine', p. 18.

Japanese Landing Ship Tank, troops disembarking armour. (BRNC)

Chinese 19th Route Army. Nevertheless, the Chinese, threatened with envelopment, retreated, allowing the Japanese to announce that they considered hostilities to be at an end.

Many operational deficiencies had been exposed during the Shanghai Incident of 1932 and improvements to both doctrine and equipment were made prior to 1937 as a result and with good effect. Particular emphasis was placed upon the need for Army and Navy co-operation and the responsibilities of commanders in this respect at all levels, although as will be seen at the highest levels this would remain an aspiration. The 1924 Landing and Landing Defence Operations Manual was re-written during 1932 by the General Staffs of both the Army and Navy as the Landing Operations Manual.[24] At the same time the existing Joint Exercise Manual was renamed the 'Army-Navy Joint Order No.1' - the only such joint order issued by the two services - at its heart the co-ordination of planning and direction of combined operations.[25] Efforts were also made to improve intelligence gathering of both topography and enemy dispositions,[26] and to increase the effectiveness of fire-support operations with Army officers being placed upon warships to act as liaison. Direction from the air was also explored.[27] Against a background of ever-increasing inter-service hostility, amphibious warfare was now

activities of their Army counterparts in Manchuria which they had seized in 1931. However, the Incident, in the first instance, was to show that the Navy was not equipped for autonomous amphibious operations on anything but a small-scale. With Admiral Shiozawa's powerful Yangtze squadron off Shanghai and the presence of two aircraft carriers, the *Hoshu* and the *Kaga*, the Navy believed that a Naval Landing Party would be sufficient.[22] But the Navy landed without heavy weapons and with insufficient ammunition. Despite the fact that China had

practically no navy or airforce the ensuing fight lasted for six weeks and necessitated an embarrassing call for help to the Army and the landing of more than 70,000 Japanese troops into the city from 15 February.[23] Not only strategic but also tactical shortcomings in Army-Navy co-operation were exposed. Nevertheless, the landing of the 11th Division up the Yangtze, 25 miles to the north of the city, behind the lines of the Chinese besieging force was to prove decisive. Whilst the landing went well, the Division suffered heavy casualties at the hands of the

[22]Stephen Howarth, Morning Glory: A History of the Japanese Navy, (London: Hamish Hamilton, 1983), [hereafter Howarth, Morning Glory], p.173.
[23]Alvin D. Coox, "The Rise and Fall of the Imperial Japanese Air Forces" in Air Power and Warfare: Proceedings of the 8th Military History Symposium, (USAF Academy, 1978), [hereafter Coox, "The Rise and Fall of the Imperial Japanese Air Forces"] p.91.
[24]Japanese Monograph No. 156, p.21.
[25]Japanese Monograph No. 156, p.22.
[26]Japanese Monograph No. 156, p.27.
[27]Japanese Monograph No. 156, pp.39-40.

the only subject that led to contact between the instructors and students of the respective staff colleges.[28] However, despite these positive developments, very few amphibious exercises were held - one source claiming only two prior to 1940, the Fifth Division's in October 1932 and the Eleventh's in 1934.[29] But rather than simply indicating a loss of interest in amphibious operations, it seems likely that given the demands placed on the relatively small Japanese Army by the occupation of Manchuria, units could simply not be spared.

Against a background of ever-increasing inter-service hostility, amphibious warfare was now the only subject that led to contact between the instructors and students of the respective staff colleges

Innovative improvements in equipment were certainly being made. As a direct result of difficulties experienced during the 1932 Shanghai landings a decision was made to build specialist amphibious warfare ships capable of carrying landing craft and troops. The first to be built, at the request of the shipping bureau of the Transport Department but designed by the Navy's design bureau[30], was the *Shinshu Maru* in 1933. Displacing 8,100 tons and 479 feet long it was constructed to an army specification along the lines of a whaler with a stern ramp, closed to the sea by doors. This led up to a large hangar able to hold twenty landing craft which could be lowered down the ramp giving the ability to launch 2,000 men in a single wave. Further, smaller landing craft could be carried on davits. There were also several side openings where landing craft alongside could be loaded. Hull openings also permitted vehicles to be directly off-loaded onto a pier from a deck-level parking hold. In addition, an upper deck hangar provided space for 12 catapult aircraft.[31] There are some indications that this was intended to be the first of a class of nine, however, effort was soon switched to a slightly larger class which also had a bigger flight deck. The first named, the *Akitsu Maru* - also seen as *Akitsushima Maru* - was completed in January 1942, to be joined by a second vessel the following year.[32] During the 1930s, the Army also converted two merchant vessels whilst under construction to LSDs, whilst several existing merchantmen were converted for use as conventional landing ships.[33] The quality and quantity of landing craft was also addressed in order to speed up landing operations.[34]

Despite these first attempts to build specialist amphibious warfare ships, operations would continue to be reliant on converted merchantmen. It is therefore not surprising that the stockpile of materials and equipment which would be used to convert merchant ships into military transports, which, under the Japanese Army's Army Stockpile Regulation, had always been a responsibility of the Army Transport Department, was enlarged. By the time of the outbreak of the Sino-Japanese War in 1937 the Department had amassed enough equipment to convert 300,000 tons of shipping,[35] which on the basis of United States intelligence estimates of shipping requirements during the Pacific War was sufficient to move about three divisions.[36] This is about the size of the largest operations conducted by the Japanese, at Shanghai in 1937, Canton in October 1938 and at Lingayen Gulf on Luzon in the Philippines in December 1941. In addition, Japanese navy warships were frequently pressed into

---

[28]Commander Masataka Chihaya, untitled, unpublished typescript, quoted in Arthur J. Marder, Old Friends and New Enemies: The Royal Navy and the Imperial Japanese Navy. Strategic Illusions, 1936-1941, (Oxford: Clarendon Press, 1981), [hereafter Marder, Old Friends and New Enemies], p. 291.

[29]Edward J. Drea, 'The Development of Imperial Japanese Army Amphibious Warfare Doctrine', pp. 18-19.

[30]Millett, 'Assault from the Sea', p. 81.

[31]Hansgearg Jentschura, Dieter Jung, Peter Mickel, (Translated by Antony Preston and J. D. Brown), Warships of the Imperial Japanese Navy, 1869-1945, (London: Arms & Armour Press, 1977; reprinted 1996), [hereafter Jentschura, Jung & Mickel, Warships of the Imperial Japanese Navy], p. 231. Norman Polmar & Peter B. Mersky, Amphibious Warfare: An Illustrated History, (London: 1988), [hereafter Polmar & Mersky, Amphibious Warfare], p.23. The Shinshu Maru was accidentally sunk in 1942 off Java. However, after a salvage operation she was rebuilt and operated until the early months of 1945.

[32]Jentschura, Jung & Mickel, Warships of the Imperial Japanese Navy, p. 61. Polmar & Mersky, Amphibious Warfare, p.23; Japanese Monograph No. 156, p.14.

[33]Polmar & Mersky, Amphibious Warfare, p.23.

[34]Japanese Monograph No. 156, p.37.

[35]Japanese Monograph No. 156, p. 14.

[36]U.S. War Department, Handbook on Japanese Military Forces, (London: Greenhill Books, reprinted 1991), p. 180.

service. In an emergency lift to reinforce Shanghai in February 1932, 10,000 men, mainly of the 24th Mixed Brigade arrived forty-eight hours after being requested, most crammed aboard Navy warships whilst transports were used to carry their heavy equipment which included tanks, motor vehicles and twelve crated aircraft.[37] Of note is that this force needed less than 60,000 tons of shipping. A British observer estimated that the Royal Navy would have needed over 200,000 tons![38]

Meanwhile, the poor performance of the Naval landing parties at Shanghai in 1932 hastened the formation of permanent Special Naval Landing Forces at the four main naval bases, Sasebo, Kure, Yokosuka, and Maizuru. These were reinforced battalions of 1,069 officers and men that included a heavy weapons unit equipped with light howitzers originally designed for mountain warfare.

Some sixteen amphibious operations were conducted by Japanese forces between August 1937 and March 1941.

The second Sino-Japanese War that broke out in 1937 was not expected by the Japanese. Some sixteen amphibious operations were conducted by Japanese forces between August 1937 and March 1941.[39] One of these, a second Shanghai outflanking movement would led to the defeat of Chiang Kai-shek's southern offensive in 1937 and deal his Kuomintang forces a blow from which they would not recover. Chiang had aimed to draw the Japanese away from their northern offensive into a war of attrition fought on the heavily prepared defensive lines with which the Chinese had surrounded Shanghai. The Japanese were caught by surprise, and initially six Japanese divisions were besieged by 71 Chinese (some 500,000 men), including the German-trained units of the elite Central Army containing nearly all Chiang's artillery and much of his air strength. Early attempts to repeat the 1932 Yangtze landings failed. Whilst the Japanese units succeeded in getting ashore in the face of considerable opposition they lacked local air superiority. It led to two months of slow progress, for once out of the range of the Navy's guns, the operation ground to a halt amongst poor terrain and effective Chinese defensive positions which made both re-supply and the provision of organic artillery support difficult. [40] The 11th Division, one of the three specialist amphibious divisions, suffered a casualty rate of 66%, including 2,293 killed out of a strength of 12,795, and was to never fight again.[41] But Chinese losses were greater and by 20 October their overall losses at Shanghai stood at some 130,000.[42]

But to the south of Shanghai lay Hangchow Bay. This had been dismissed by the Chinese planners as an 'unlikely' place for a landing on account of the offshore sandbanks which would force transports to remain at least two miles out, fierce tides, and the flat exposed beaches backed by salt-marshes. It was therefore only lightly defended by machine-gun emplacements. An old seawall protected the northern shore of the Bay. And it was here, at Chinshanwei, that on 5 November 1937 three under-strength divisions, some 30,000 troops, of the Japanese 10th Army under Lieutenant General Yanagawa Heisuke were landed from 40 transports. Undefended, the wall actually facilitated the Japanese disembarkation, and the attackers quickly overcame both the natural and the few man-made obstacles that remained.[43] This unexpected threat to the Chinese right flank and rear caused Chiang's forces to disintegrate.[44] Their discomfort was heightened when their northern escape routes were endangered by the Japanese 13th Division which had been quickly pulled out of Shanghai and landed further up the Yangtze with the help of the hitherto secret 'Military Landing Craft Carrier', the *Shinshu Maru*.[45] Within a few days, the army that Chiang had spent years building was destroyed. Chinese losses may have exceeded 300,000, and the way to his capital, Nanking, lay open.[46]

---

[37]Howarth, Morning Glory, p.174; Japanese Monograph No. 156, pp. 3-4, 13.
[38]Howarth, Morning Glory, p.174.
[39]Edward J. Drea, 'The Development of Imperial Japanese Army Amphibious Warfare Doctrine', p. 21.
[40]Meirion & Susie Harries, Soldiers of the Sun: The Rise and Fall of the Imperial Japanese Army 1868-1945, (London: Heinemann, 1991), [hereafter Harries, Soldiers of the Sun], p. 181.
[41]Edward J. Drea, 'The Development of Imperial Japanese Army Amphibious Warfare Doctrine', p. 20. After reconstitution, it was sent with the 12th as part of the garrison on the Soviet border in eastern Manchuria. Neither would fire a shot in anger during the Pacific War. Ibid.

[42]Edward L. Dreyer, China at War 1901-1949, (Harlow, Essex: Longman, 1995), p. 218.
[43]Dreyer, China at War 1901-1949, p. 218.
[44]Harries, Soldiers of the Sun, pp. 182-183.
[45]Harries, Soldiers of the Sun, p.183.
[46]Dreyer, China at War 1901-1949, pp. 218-219

The Shinshu Maru: A specialist amphibious warfare ship designed by the Japanese Navy in 1933, along the lines of Whaler with a stern ramp and sea doors. (BRNC)

To some extent the Japanese use of the blockade, outflanking movements, the seizure of ports during the second Sino-Japanese War is very reminiscent of past British operations against continental Europe. But whereas the British could usually rely on a continental ally the Japanese had none. Moreover, the Chinese, unlike in 1894-95 or the Russians in 1904-05, were not prepared to yield. Put simply, Chiang was not prepared to trade land for peace. This was despite the fact that the coastal cities, which were the political base for the KMT and the ports through which any foreign assistance would come, fell quickly to a series of Japanese amphibious operations. Instead, his forces retreated into the continental vastness of China, over-extending Japanese lines of communication and exploiting the traditional weakness of an amphibious power attempting to intervene on a large landmass. Despite maps showing great swathes of China under Japanese control, the Japanese only had sufficient men to hold the major cities and the rivers and railways that connected them.

Given the unexpected nature of the 1937 war it took time to mobilise Japanese reserves and the Japanese were forced to press its three amphibious divisions into general service. The Fifth Division found itself fighting in northern China where it was badly mauled by Lin Piao's Communist 115th Division in a narrow pass at Pinghsingkuan. It suffered about 3,000 killed to some 400 Chinese casualties.[47] Its fate, taken with that of the 11th Division near Shanghai, has led one writer to wonder if these 'especially designated' divisions had spent too much time in learning to land and too little in learning to fight.'[48] In any case, the Chinese War seemed to demonstrate that perhaps such specialist forces capable of undertaking opposed landings were not actually required, that the traditional approach to amphibious operations - landing at undefended sites - still worked. Certainly, the great swathe of coastline enabled the Japanese to select their landing places at will. When defenders were present the approach adopted by the Japanese, of night-time battalion-sized landings by a number of dispersed columns (rather than waves) of landing craft - bringing concentration of force at the point of contact - not surprisingly confused, overwhelmed and demoralised the Chinese. With no Chinese naval forces to interfere, landings could take place in a rather more measured, traditional way. The Japanese Army did however pay more attention to the air threat to its transports. Weaknesses in air cover had been demonstrated in 1932 and, again, in the early campaigns in 1937.[49] However, lessons were quickly learned, partly through the efforts of the Battle Lessons Committee set up during the Sino-Japanese War.[50] By 1941, for example, Japan possessed some of the best naval aircraft and pilots in the world and understood better than others that air superiority was a vital prerequisite to a successful operation.

That the Japanese avoided opposed landings has been criticised by some writers as a return to the doctrine of the Russo-Japanese War (in fact, it was a return to Japanese practise in the first year of that conflict).[51] Comparisons have been made with the approach later taken by US forces in the Pacific. In fact, the Japanese Army could and did undertake opposed landings. For example, the 5th Division with air and naval support forced their Daihatsus through the outer defences of the forts guarding the entrance to the Pearl River at Canton in October 1938. But such

[47]Dreyer, China at War 1901-1949, p. 215. One of its brigades would also be besieged along with the 10th Division at Taierhchuang in March and April 1938 by the KMT's 20th Group Army. Eventually only 2,000 survivors managed to fight their way out and flee leaving some 16,000 dead and most of the units' equipment behind. Dreyer, China at War 1901-1949, p. 227.
[48]Millett, 'Assault from the Sea', p. 68.
[49]Coox, "The Rise and Fall of the Imperial Japanese Air Forces", p. 89.
[50]R. J. Overy, The Air War, 1939-1945, p.87.
[51]Edward J. Drea, 'The Development of Imperial Japanese Army Amphibious Warfare Doctrine', pp. 21-22. Millett, 'Assault from the Sea', pp. 68-69. See Mark J. Grove, 'Japanese Amphibious Operations during the Russo-Japanese War, 1904-1905' in the present volume.

an opposed operation was rare. The Japanese instead used the sea to outmanoeuvre their Chinese opponents - an eminently sensible approach. Indeed, by 1938 the Japanese Army had begun to land at night to increase the prospects for surprise, for example the landings that year east of Hong Kong. Comparison cannot be made be made with US capabilities in the second half of the Pacific War - the prevailing conditions were completely different. The major problem with the Japanese approach was that its Chinese operations might have reinforced a mindset within some in the Army that opposed landings would never be required. One is tempted to draw parallels with the post-Pacific War United States Marine Corps mindset tending to over-emphasise the direct approach at the expense of a proper consideration of the possibilities of manoeuvre. Nevertheless, by 1941 Japan could draw on over fifty years of amphibious development and experience, and, at that time had a capability far more developed than either the United States or Great Britain which it was about to unleash.

Notwithstanding the spectacular success of the Japanese assault, it should be remembered that the mismatch between strategic planning and actual preparation had continued in the Army until 1940. During that year seven major exercises were conducted by the Army - not one involved amphibious operations.[52] And, despite, in 1936, at the Navy's instigation,[53] the inclusion in the National Defence Policy of the move south, throughout the 1930s the Navy itself continued to prepare intensively and well nigh exclusively for a decisive naval battle against a US fleet steaming west, a battle which by 1940 was envisaged as taking place in the Eastern Carolines and Marshall Islands.[54] As late as November 1939 the Navy's plan for operations against Malaya consisted of just two or three pages and despite the importance attached to Singapore it remained in this form until the end of 1940.[55] It makes the Japanese achievements all the more remarkable.

To most, the opening of the Pacific War means one thing: Pearl Harbor. But Admiral Yamamoto's *coup de main* had been a late addition to a plan that had always been intended to be a complex and ambitious projection of power from the sea. The operation was divided into two parts. The 'First Operational Stage' involved the seizure of Malaya, Singapore and the Philippines and Pacific islands such as Wake and Guam allowing forces to converge on the main objective, the oil and mineral rich East Indies. Perhaps the most important point to make is that the whole operation relied on only the 11 Army divisions which could be spared from China and Manchuria, where 27 were to remain. British and US naval power was known to weak in the region. But speed and surprise were vital to attain local superiority. This could only be achieved with good intelligence of enemy dispositions, very careful co-ordination and planning and the use of well-trained forces. In these respects the efforts of the Doro Nawa unit or the Taiwan Army Research Section, which was established at Taipeh at the end of 1940, were crucial,[56] as were the training and large-scale exercises that the forces involved undertook from October 1940.[57] Part of this training involved practising the difficult art of night landing that was a feature of the operations in 1941-42. This was in contrast to the traditional dawn landings used certainly up until the early operations of the Sino-Japanese War.[58] In this the Army was aided by the skill of the Imperial Japanese Navy (IJN).

There can be little doubt that Japanese amphibious operations during the (second) Sino-Japanese War and the early stages of the Pacific War benefited enormously from the drive for quality in both ships and crews to offset the quantitative restrictions placed by the Naval Armament Limitation Treaties and from the strategy aimed at defeating a quantitatively superior enemy fleet adopted by the Japanese Navy during the inter-war

[52]Edward J. Drea, 'The Development of Imperial Japanese Army Amphibious Warfare Doctrine', p. 51.
[53]Akira Iriye, The Origins of the Second World War in Asia and the Pacific, (London: Longman, 1987), p.35.
[54]Marder, Old Friends and New Enemies, p. 318, n.28.
[55]Marder, Old Friends and New Enemies, p.327.
[56]Stanley L. Falk, Seventy Days to Singapore: The Malayan Campaign 1941-1942, (London: Robert Hale, 1975), [hereafter Falk, Seventy Days to Singapore], pp.24-25. Masanobu Tsuji, Japan's Greatest Victory: Britain's Worst Defeat: The Capture of Singapore, (Staplehurst, Kent: Spellmount, 1997), pp. 3-27.
[57]Falk, Seventy Days to Singapore, pp.24-25; Marder, Old Friends and New Enemies, pp.327-328.
[58]Lehmann, "Japanese Landing Operations in World War Two", p.196.

A photograph of a Japanese Landing Boat Type A1, believed to have been taken by Victor H Krulak (later Lieutenant General) when serving as a young USMC officer with the 4th Marines in China. He was spying on the Japanese operating landing boats in Shanghai harbour in 1937, and this design powerfully influenced the development of the US Higgins boat. (USMC)

period. Whilst, under the 'baneful spell' of Tsushima, the tactical tradition of the Navy was very much an offensive one,[59] of particular importance was the intense effort that had gone into perfecting night-fighting techniques irrespective of conditions,[60] which complemented the Army's newly acquired preference for night landings. The clear superiority of the Japanese Naval Air Arm has already been mentioned and this was particularly true of their long-range land based fighters and bombers.

And airpower was now seen as crucial. Over 1,200 aircraft were available for support of the 1941 Pacific and South-East Asian operations. Indeed, the requirement for air support during and after landings drove strategy. For example, the move into French Indo-China in the summer of 1940 followed the first Army draft war plan which stated that it would need to set up air bases in Indo-China and Thailand before any move on the Dutch East Indies.[61] Most of the Army's fighters, designed for war against the Soviet Union when able to use airfields in Manchuria,

were of short range. But in the Type 0, the Mitsubishi A6M 'Zeke' or Zero, the Navy had a top-class fighter with a range of over 500 miles plus 15-minutes worth of combat capability. Intelligence had been available to the West about the combat capabilities of the remarkable Zero, but it had been ignored, for example, with many US aviators before Pearl Harbor refusing to take the information seriously.[62] The Zero increased Japanese options but there were never enough, especially as over 100 were to be ear-marked for the carrier-borne attack on Pearl Harbor. Initial air attacks always sought to knock out Allied airpower on the ground, usually using fighter-bombers which had been found to be more reliable than level bombing by conventional bombers during the Sino-Japanese War.[63] Before 8 December was out, British airpower in northern Malaya had been slashed from 110 to fewer than 50.[64] Ahead of the Japanese landings in the Philippines on 22 December 1941 the defending air group of nearly 300 aircraft, the largest outside the United States, had been reduced to just a handful.[65] Indeed, the initial attacks against American airfields there had been successful despite being made hours after the Pearl Harbor operation because of delays caused by bad weather over the Japanese airbases. And the majority of landings in Malaya, the Philippines and

the Dutch East Indies had as their initial target the seizure of advanced airfields from which supportive operations could be maintained and the air umbrella extended. Whilst Japanese landings were often indirect approaches to main objectives, allowing forces to be built up for the main assault, exceptions were made in the case of some of the attacks on airfields. In securing the airfields in northern Philippines the Japanese 14th Army took considerable risks with small forces, none larger than three battalions being expected to support themselves for up to three weeks.[66] Not only did Allied land operations suffer as a result of Japanese air supremacy, conventional naval operations became impossible, as the destruction of HMS *Prince of Wales* and *Repulse* so dramatically demonstrated. And this only increased the attackers' options.

Even more options were available to the Japanese by their possession of parachute forces, the only such units in the Pacific at the outbreak of the War. Japan had developed its airborne units in 1940 drawing heavily on German methods, equipment and by the autumn of 1941 the efforts of some 100 German instructors. Of particular interest are the naval units, which were specifically intended to assist seaborne landings by dropping inland from the beaches. By October 1941 there were two such units, the 1st and 3rd Yokosuka Special Naval

[59]Marder, Old Friends and New Enemies, p. 318.
[60]Marder, Old Friends and New Enemies, p. 319.
[61]Akira Iriye, The Origins of the Second World War in Asia and the Pacific, (London: Longman, 1987), p.102.
[62]Thomas C. Mahnken, Uncovering Ways of War: U.S. Intelligence and Foreign Military Innovation, 1918-1941, (Ithaca: Cornell University Press, 2002), pp. 79-81. One who did not was Lieutenant Commander John S. Thatch, commanding officer of Fighter Squadron Three based in San Diego, who had used the information he received in the spring of 1941 to develop the 'Thatch Weave' to counter the Zero's tighter turn radius, higher speed and faster time to height. Ibid. p. 80.

[63]Koichi Samada, 'The Opening Air Offensive Against the Philippines', in David C. Evans (ed.), The Japanese Navy in World War II, 2nd Edition, (Annapolis: USNIP, 1986), p. 84.
[64]H. P. Wilmott, Empires in the Balance: Japanese and Allied Pacific Strategies to April 1942, (Annapolis, MA.: Naval Institute Press, 1982), p. 166.
[65]H. P. Wilmott, Empires in the Balance, p. 148.
[66]H. P. Wilmott, Empires in the Balance, p. 149.

Landing Forces, each of 844 men. The 1st was responsible for the capture of Menado airfield in the Celebes in January 1941; the 3rd took part in the capture of Timor in February 1942 when it successfully disrupted the defenders' communications to the rear of conventional seaborne landings. The Timor operation was perhaps the most sophisticated amphibious operation of the Japanese onslaught.[67] Whilst having clearly mastered the techniques involved the forces were underused and hampered by the lack of suitable aircraft, those available tasked to the army logisticians who had first call.[68]

The Japanese plans were designed to extract as much advantage as possible from their geographic position. This allowed them to operate on internal lines and to swap forces from one target to another in quick succession - vital given the few divisions available. The inability of any of the dispersed Allied garrisons to tie the Japanese forces for any length of time meant that these quickly became available for the next target and so on. Allied garrisons were picked off one by one as the degree of sea and air control possessed by the Japanese gave them the initiative. General Wavell, in his unenviable role as Supreme Commander of the Allied ABDA (American, British, Dutch and Australian) forces described himself as faced with 'an option of difficulties'.[69] Unless a key installation such as an airfield or oil refinery had to be taken quickly, opposed landings were avoided. For the moment the Japanese could use the sea as a manoeuvring space able to select when and where overwhelming force was to be applied. In addition to airpower, landing convoys were protected by cruisers, destroyers and minesweepers. But the Japanese also used freshly laid minefields during their operations in both Malaya and the Philippines to protect their beachheads from Allied naval counterattacks. By mining the San Bernadino and Surigo straits, for example, Luzon was sealed off from American reinforcements coming by sea from the south.[70]

Operations were proceeded by a short, opening barrage from the sea or from land-based aircraft. The assaults were then launched in darkness by means of columns (rather than waves) of landing craft landing their troops onto multiple, narrow beachheads along long stretches of shoreline. The Japanese put a considerable premium on seizing the beachhead as quickly as possible. Consequently, transports carried as many landing craft as possible so that the first wave could be as strong as possible. Such a requirement is demonstrated by the design of the *Shinshuu Maru* landing craft carrier. Smoke was used if necessary. Forces were carried ashore in the correct tactical formations allowing them to fight immediately on landing.

Where possible, rivers and estuaries were used to infiltrate forces behind defenders

The first wave comprised infantry, advanced artillery units, engineers and signals teams. There is, however, some evidence to indicate that the Japanese underestimated the volume and reliability of communications required and that as a result the communications nets were insufficient. Units were landed with ten days of supplies.[71] Where possible, rivers and estuaries were used to infiltrate forces behind defenders. Airborne forces were raised and trained with a similar aim. Landing craft were to be used to shift the focus of the assault should it be required. By means of infiltration, speed and the concentration of force at

[67] John Weeks, Assault from the Sky; The History of Airborne Warfare, (Newton Abbot: David & Charles, 1988), [hereafter Weeks, Assault from the Sky], pp.90-94; R. A. Stewart, "The Japanese Assault on Timor, 1942" in Merrill L. Bartlett (Ed.), Assault From the Sea: Essays in the History of Amphibious Warfare, (Annapolis: USNIP, 1983), p.204.

[68] Weeks, Assault from the Sky, pp.72, 74, 89.

[69] Wilmott, Empires in the Balance, p. 311.

[70] Wilmott, Empires in the Balance, p. 152.

[71] Hans G. von Lehman, 'Japanese Landing operations in World War Two', in Merrill L. Bartlett (Ed.), Assault From the Sea: Essays in the History of Amphibious Warfare, (Annapolis: USNIP, 1983), pp. 199-201.

the point of contact, the objective was to confuse the enemy and exploit this, keeping him confused and off balance. And it was a similar story once ashore. Where necessary the sea could be used as a tactical manoeuvring space as much as a strategic one. The Japanese could thus negate the presence of larger forces, such as the British in Malaya. And by Christmas the Americans had been effectively defeated in the Philippines without heavy fighting in a major battle. As Wilmott has concluded: 'By their imaginative use of small bodies of troops the Japanese completely outmanoeuvred the Americans, the level of their generalship being markedly superior to that of a defending force whose problems were immense and probably insoluble.'[72] That what remained of the now isolated American garrison courageously lingered on for months was simply ignored by the Japanese, with their timetable for the moment remaining unperturbed. In fact, in Malaya, the Philippines, and the Dutch East Indies effective defence by land forces alone was probably impossible, and the Allies simply did not have the naval or air forces necessary: with the US refusing to adequately reinforce its naval presence and the British unable to.

The Japanese plan for the invasions of neutral Thailand and British Malaya were of necessity complex.[73] The approach had to be made concurrently with the Pearl Harbor operation in such a way as to not precipitate a British attack or movement into southern Thailand. Security was vital and deception operations, including the circulation of rumours of an imminent seaborne assault on Bangkok, were successfully employed. It was impossible, due to shipping constraints, to land all the forces at once and yet key objectives, notably a series of airfields in southern Thailand and northern Malaya, had to be seized quickly to support for operations. Two armies, the 15th (for operations in Thailand) and the 25th (Malaya) were to be mutually supportive.

The British defensive plan - Operation MATADOR - a pre-emptive move into southern Thailand, depended on firm intelligence of Japanese aggressive intent and a willingness to breach Thailand's neutrality. Given the intelligence available, one is hard pressed to conclude that the former could ever have overcome qualms about the latter. The Japanese went to expectable lengths to deceive the British and, in using the sea to outmanoeuvre the British, they had no concerns about violating a neutral state's sovereignty - it was an exploitable weakness.

The initial 26,000-strong landing force for the northern Malaya operation sailed in nineteen transports and, whilst having cruiser and destroyer escort, were largely dependent for protection from the 22nd Air Flotilla, reinforced to deal with the British Force Z. Japanese submarines formed advance reconnaissance lines. In order to maintain security the Japanese were willing to take risks: an RAF reconnaissance aircraft was shot down in the Gulf of Thailand hours before the Pearl Harbor attack.[74] In fact, reliable reports had already reached the British about the presence of Japanese transports but nothing was done as the British felt unsure about their intentions. This was despite the fact that with Japanese transports known to be south of latitude 10° North, the British Commander-in-Chief in the Far East, Air Chief Marshal Sir Robert Brooke-Popham had the freedom to launch MATADOR. He dithered. The Japanese were handed the initiative.

The Japanese objectives were Patani and Singora in the south of Thailand and Kota Baru in northern Malaya where airfields were to be seized and a beachhead established in order to receive the second echelon due to arrive on the 13th. The approach was made under cover of darkness. The Japanese started coming ashore in Thailand and Malaya about an hour before the attack on Pearl Harbor. A regiment of the 15th Army's 55th Division landed at four points along the Kra isthmus to seize the railway down which further units would come by train from Japanese-held Indo-China. With the British unwilling to sanction Operation MATADOR the landings at Singora and Patani were unopposed. However, at Kota Baru, it was a very different story. Protecting the nearby airfield was a triple line of pill-boxes and wire defended by the 3rd/17th Dogran, part of the 8th Indian Brigade, with the rest of the Brigade held in reserve. Tasked to land was the Takumi Detachment, based around the 18th Division's 56th Infantry Regiment with supporting arms making for a total of 5,300 men. The three transports anchored off the

---

[72]Wilmott, Empires in the Balance, pp. 153-54.
[73]Wilmott, Empires in the Balance, pp. 161-172; Major-General S. Woodburn Kirby, Singapore: The Chain of Disaster, (London: Cassell, 1971), Chs. 11-15; Masanobu Tsuji, Japan's Greatest Victory: Britain's Worst Defeat: The Capture of Singapore, (Staplehurst, Kent: Spellmount, 1997), Chs. 12-15.
[74]Wilmott, Empires in the Balance, p. 164.

beach at midnight and despite rough seas the men were loaded into their landing craft. As the three columns of craft neared the shore the escorting flotilla of a cruiser and four destroyers opened up on the beach. The defenders in the pillboxes were not suppressed and the assaulting force met heavy fire on landing. For some time they were pinned down on the beach and took heavy casualties. Shore-based artillery fire damaged a number of landing craft and the transports were soon attacked by Australian Hudson aircraft from the nearby airfield. At least one, possibly two Japanese transports were damaged but not before they could unload. However, despite the opposition the assaulting forces managed to infiltrate through the widely spaced defences. By dawn three battalions were ashore and they had a beachhead of reasonable size. The transports had already slipped away in the dark as a force of RAF bombers found when they arrived with first light. The Japanese resisted subsequent counter-attacks into their flanks by the 8th Indian Brigade's two reserve battalions which, ill-trained for mobile operations, had to contend with terrain riddled with creeks. By the 9th, the Kelantan airfields were in Japanese hands.[75]

As some writers have pointed out, not all of the Japanese landings were initially successful. But too much can be made of these failures.[76] Despite destroying most of Wake's fighter force on the ground on 8 December the first attempt by an

Imperial Japanese Naval force of 450 men to assault the atoll three days later was a disaster. Wake's five-inch batteries only opened up when the Japanese had closed to 5,000 yards. The destroyer *Hayate* blew up, and a cruiser, several other destroyers and transports were badly damaged in often furious exchanges before the Japanese withdrew. But the retiring force was to suffer further damage, including the loss of another destroyer, this time by the island's four remaining fighters that had been kept in reserve. This was the only occasion in the Pacific War when an amphibious assault was defeated.[77] By the time of the second Japanese assault on 23 December, the Americans having failed to reinforce Wake, the defenders had no more aircraft left. The Japanese had assembled a much more powerful force. The carriers *Soryu* and *Hiryu* returning from the Pearl Harbor strike provided air support. This larger naval force, which now included four cruisers, kept out of range of the shore batteries before the assaulting force of 2,000 men were sent ashore in darkness. On one island of the atoll, Wilkes Island, the Japanese naval infantry in concentrating their efforts against a single gun-emplacement were surprised by defenders raised from the other emplacements and wiped out. But on Wake itself by dawn the defenders were surrounded and, having been informed by US Pacific Headquarters that no assistance could be expected, they surrendered. The cost to the Japanese had been 1,000 casualties. Nevertheless, both operations were conducted by

all troops must be trained to an appropriate level if you want to make successful use of the sea as a manoeuvring space

the Imperial Japanese Navy and as such were atypical: 'the Japanese fielded their second team and it showed'.[78] They indicate that some of the problems experienced ten years earlier in Shanghai had not been rectified.

Attention has also been drawn to the Japanese failure to overcome the US defensive line on Bataan during January and February 1942 with a series of small amphibious assaults - the so-called 'Battle of the Points' - all of which failed. Contributory factors were most certainly want of numbers and artillery and armoured support.[79] But it might also be pertinent to mention that the assaults were being undertaken by the Sixty-Fifth Brigade, 'an occupation force of overage, overweight veterans 'absolutely unfit for combat duty', General Homma having lost his best division, the 48th, which was required for the next series of assaults against the Dutch East Indies.[80] Again, Bataan was not a typical operation. It does, however, reinforce the point that if you are going to embark upon operations in the littoral all troops (and their officers) must be trained to an appropriate level if you want to make successful use of the sea as a manoeuvring space.

Japanese success in earlier wars had led not only to a new national self-confidence and but within the Army an increasing emphasis

---

[75]Woodburn Kirby, Singapore: The Chain of Disaster, pp. 134-36; Masanobu Tsuji, Japan's Greatest Victory: Britain's Worst Defeat, pp. 75-78.
[76]Millett, 'Assault from the Sea', pp. 89-90.
[77]Wilmott, Empires in the Balance, p. 142.

[78]Wilmott, Empires in the Balance, p. 143-46.
[79]Millett, 'Assault from the Sea', p. 90.
[80]Ronald Spector, Eagle Against the Sun: The American War with Japan, (London: Viking, 1994), p. 112.

*the inherent complexity of their approach did leave
the Japanese dangerously prone to the effects of
inter-service disagreement*

being placed on seishin - human spirit - even in the face of superior technology or materiel.[81] Recent experience in China had reinforced this self-conceit and, set against the marshal traditions of the Samurai, the soldierly qualities of their new Western opponents were viewed with a contempt only approached by that of the Allies for those of the Japanese prior to December 1941. Japanese plans were undoubtedly made with a degree of risk but then it could be argued that many of the successful uses of manoeuvre warfare have been. It is a moot point as to whether the risks that the Japanese took in the First Operational Stage - that they attempted 'too much, with too little and too quickly' - were unacceptable. For, after all, the risks paid off. In fact, there was far less improvisation, far less left to chance than there might at first appear, which would in turn prove problematic. However, the Japanese fondness for using complex interrelated operations relying on the use of dispersed forces carried real dangers as the Midway operation in 1942 would prove. And the inherent complexity of their approach did leave the Japanese dangerously prone to the effects of inter-service disagreement - a problem never solved - the pernicious effects of which began to tell.

The Second Operational Stage which saw Japan being drawn into an attritional campaign in the Solomons and New Guinea during 1942-43 and included the disasters in the Coral Sea and at Midway, had been little considered. The phase highlights certain limits to the extent of Japanese 'manoeuvre-mindedness'. It was,

in sharp contrast to the First Stage, undertaken with no detailed planning - on which the Japanese were possibly over-reliant -and without it the Japanese began to come unstuck. Over confidence was rife - plans were raised to assault Hawaii, Australia, Ceylon and Madagascar. They were soon dispensed with. Those that were conducted were over-ambitious and most certainly under-resourced. And once the Allies had recovered their balance and were able to engage the Japanese on something like equal terms, even before the greater US superiority really began to tell and the Japanese lost the ability to use the sea freely, the limitations to Japanese capabilities and their approach became apparent.

In New Guinea, in the Buna-Gona area and in the Solomons at Guadalcanal, Japanese forces were beset by Allied forces. In both cases, the Japanese had naval and air power sufficient to support, and the land forces available to undertake, major amphibious counter-landings which the Allied commanders certainly feared. In neither case did such a threat materialise.[82] Given that the Japanese certainly had the ability to launch further amphibious assaults it is perhaps worth pondering the depth of their 'manoeuvre-mindedness'. But the relationship between the Japanese Army and Navy was breaking down. Each lacked information about the other's current capabilities to the extent of the Navy concealing the scale and implications of the Midway disaster. And both services lacked accurate information about the Allies. To begin with the Allies had conformed very

much to within Japanese expectations. But by the summer of 1942 the Japanese had lost the intelligence battle and therefore the strategic initiative had been passed across. The Japanese planners were being out-thought and out-manoeuvred.

Even so, new equipment continued to be acquired, such as large numbers of LST-type vessels. However, these would be pressed into service re-supplying the increasingly beleaguered Japanese defensive perimeters. In any case, after 1942 it didn't really matter whether or not Japan had sufficient amphibious capability in the narrowest sense. For the Japanese experience points to the true complexity of maritime power of which amphibious operations are but a part. In theory, Japan may have had the equipment to project power, but in practice it had certainly lost the ability to protect it. In the United States, their opponent was a maritime power with far greater resources and far greater reach. The US Navy with its superior carrier forces and very effective submarine arm could now seize control of the sea, indeed dominate the oceans. It was now Japan that was forced to defend everything and thus be weak everywhere. It was now the Allies who could pick off and defeat in detail the outlying Japanese garrisons and bases as they closed on Japan itself. The strategic advantages, for so long bestowed upon Japan by possession of a true maritime capability, were now held by its opponents.

---

[81]Leonard A. Humphreys, The Way of the Heavenly Sword: The Japanese Army in the 1920s, (Stanford, California: Stanford U.P., 1995, pp. 14-16.
[82]Millett, 'Assault from the Sea', p. 91.

Further Reading

Drea, Edward J., 'The Development of Imperial Japanese Army Amphibious Warfare Doctrine', in *idem*, *In the Service of the Emperor: Essays on the Imperial Japanese Army*, (Lincoln: University of Nebraska Press, 1998)

Grove, Mark J., 'The Development of Japanese Amphibious Warfare 1874 to 1942', in Geoffrey Till, Theo Farrell, and Mark J. Grove, *Amphibious Operations*, (Camberley: Strategic and Combat Studies Institute, 1997)

Harries, Meirion & Susie, *Soldiers of the Sun: The Rise and Fall of the Imperial Japanese Army 1868-1945*, (London: Heinemann, 1991)

Jentschura, Hansgearg Jung, Dieter Mickel, Peter (Translated by Antony Preston and J. D. Brown), *Warships of the Imperial Japanese Navy, 1869-1945*, (London: Arms & Armour Press, 1977; reprinted 1996)

Millett, Allan R, 'Assault from the Sea: The Development of Amphibious Warfare between the Wars, the American, British and Japanese Experiences', in Williamson Murray and Allan R. Millett (eds), *Military Innovation in the Interwar Period*, (Cambridge: Cambridge University Press, 1996)

Polmar, Norman & Mersky, Peter B., *Amphibious Warfare: An Illustrated History*, (London: Blandford Press, 1988)

Stewart, R. A. "The Japanese Assault on Timor, 1942" in Merrill L. Bartlett (Ed.), *Assault From the Sea: Essays in the History of Amphibious Warfare*, (Annapolis: USNIP, 1983)

Von Lehmann, Hans G., "Japanese Landing Operations in World War Two", in Merrill L. Bartlett (Ed.), *Assault from the Sea: Essays in the History of Amphibious Warfare*, (Annapolis: USNIP, 1983)

Wilmott, H. P., *Empires in the Balance: Japanese and Allied Pacific Strategies to April 1942*, (Annapolis, Maryland: Naval Institute Press, 1982)

Biography

Mr Mark J Grove was educated at Cardiff and Aberystwyth Universities and is a Senior Lecturer in the Strategic Studies Department at Britannia Royal Naval College, Dartmouth. He is responsible for a number of courses including the Royal Marines' Basic Amphibious Warfare Course. He is also the module leader for the Maritime Command, Logistics and Power Projection, and the Maritime Aviation Modules. Whilst known as a historian of naval and amphibious operations, he has lectured across the full spectrum of the Pillar's courses and has taught International Relations, including a foreign policy analysis course, at the University of Plymouth. He is also a regular contributor to the Advanced Amphibious Warfare Course at the Joint Services Command and Staff College, Watchfield. His publications include: 'The Development of Japanese Amphibious Warfare, 1874-1942' in Geoffrey Till, Theo Farrell and Mark J Grove, *Amphibious Operations*, (Camberley: SCSI, 1997), *The Second World War: The War at Sea*, (Botley, Oxford: Osprey, 2002) with his brother Philip D Grove and Alastair Finlan. He co-edited *The Falklands Conflict Twenty Years On: Lessons for the Future*, (London: Frank Cass, 2004).

The Genesis of the U.S. Marine Corps' Amphibious Assault Mission, 1890-1934

By Lieutenant Colonel Merrill L Bartlett USMC (Rtd)

From the founding of America's smaller naval service in 1798 to the turn of the 20th Century, duties performed by the U.S. Marine Corps remained wedded to the Age of Sail and changed little. Moulded in the same pattern as France's Regiment la Marine (1627) and the Royal Vaiseaux (1635), the Admiral's Regiment of Great Britain (1664), and Holland's Korps Mariners (1665), the American Marines served mostly as a naval constabulary. While occasionally forming the bulwark of naval landing parties deployed ashore, the marines' most important duties involved maintaining order and discipline among the riff raff that occupied the lower decks of warships. After failing to make a significant contribution to the Union side in the American Civil War, the U.S. Marine Corps continued to slide into mediocrity seemingly unable to embrace a naval mission beyond its traditional role in the Age of Sail.

Its role as policemen aboard the warships of the fleet diminished, coincident with the abolition of flogging and the serving of alcohol to the crews. Recruitment of sailors from a more stable segment of society decreased the requirement for marines to uphold order aboard ship. Critics and budget-conscience Congressmen began to question the requirement for a separate naval service that performed such an antiquated role. Although in the second half of the 19th Century, landing parties stormed ashore on 29 occasions, only 3 of them appeared of significance (Formosa,1867; Korea ,1881; and Panama, 1885).

During the last quarter of the century, luminaries within the Navy argued with increasing currency that the Marines had outlived their usefulness as security forces in the ships of the fleet, and should be formed into battalions and even regiments to deploy ashore at the behest of squadron and fleet commanders. Hidebound Marine Corps officers brushed off the entreaties, considering them veiled attempts to emasculate the smaller of the naval services by either transferring its functions to the Navy or even to the Army. In the pages of an influential and widely-read service journal, a prominent Navy officer of the era proclaimed that the word 'marine' had become 'a synonym for idleness, worthlessness, and a vacuity of intellect.'

> *...on shore and at sea must be considered as an expeditionary force for use in any part of the world and not merely as a collection of watchmen*

A single junior Marine Corps officer at the time demonstrated the temerity to respond to the Major General Commandant's (MGC) request for commentary on the inflammatory subject by exclaiming that the chief role of the Marines both 'on shore and at sea must be considered as an expeditionary force for use in any part of the world and not merely as a collection of watchmen.'

The prophetic young officer, George Barnett, had been among the handful of new officers migrating from the U.S. Naval Academy to the Marine Corps for the first time in 1883; the intellectual vigour and professional naval background that these young officers brought with them served to infuse the lesser and occasionally-maligned of the naval services with a keen appreciation for the responsibility of the U.S. Marine Corps in support of the fleet.

The short and nationally-invigorating Spanish-American War in 1898 ushered in new vistas for the U.S. Marine Corps. The successful establishment and defence of an advance base in support of the fleet at Guantánamo Bay, Cuba, during the opening month of the war unveiled an important and innovative role for marines. In 1900, the General Board of the Navy recommended the establishment of an Advance Base Force to provide security for forward bases in support of fleet operations. Initially, the board recommended the formation of a 400-man battalion to form the force. When the Brigadier General Commandant of the Marine Corps accepted the mission on 22 November of that year, he responded with a measured and cautious tone: '[This effort] will necessitate very careful consideration and considerable time will be necessary for accomplishing it,' and predisposed the new mission with practiced bureaucratic indifference.

The luminaries on the General Board of the Navy envisioned the battalion as a permanently-formed nucleus which might swell to 1,000 men capable of handling and emplacing heavy naval guns ashore, installing minefields, performing normal coastal defence activities, and preparing field fortifications. For the first

decade of the existence of the concept, the events that unfolded mirrored the meagre expectations of both the Department of the Navy and its Marine Corps. While a handful of senior officers in Navy blue bemoaned the lack of preparation, equipping, and outfitting the advance base force, the leadership of the Marine Corps treated the organization with benign neglect.

Although the size of the smaller of the naval services grew from 5,000 in 1900 to twice that number by the end of the next decade, practical imperatives rather than bold initiatives in the employment of manpower prevailed. Almost the entirety of its meagre personnel assets continued in support of traditional

missions: more than 2,500 men assigned to the Marine Guards in the ships of the fleet; security duties at the Navy's yards; and a 2,000-man brigade stationed at Subic Bay in the Philippines. Congressionally-approved fiscal allocations in support of the Department of the Navy flowed almost entirely to the Navy, leaving little remaining for the manning and equipping of the advance base force. Nonetheless, an advance base school was established at Newport in 1901 and relocated a year later for semi-permanent status at the Philadelphia Navy Yard.

After more than a decade of critical cajoling and wheedling commentary by advocates of the concept within the higher

councils of the Navy, the Secretary of the Navy ordered the concept of the advance base force tested during the fleet's winter manoeuvres of 1913-14. By then, the force had grown - albeit on paper - to two regiments totalling 1,300 Marines apiece. The fixed-defence regiment contained field artillery; large-calibre naval guns, to be hauled ashore and emplaced; engineers; signal units; searchlight batteries; and mining companies. The mobile defence regiment contained 5 infantry companies, a machine-gun company, and a battery of light field artillery. The site chosen for the winter manoeuvres, the sea lanes off the Puerto Rican island of Culebra, allowed close proximity to Mexico in case the flare of diplomatic tempers between the U.S. and its southernmost neighbour flared anew. In customary fashion, the manpower for the two regiments came from a culling of the barracks along the east coast of the United States. Upon the completion of the exercise, commanders expected all of the marines returned to their barracks to resume customary duties involving the security of their parent naval stations. No one among the ranks of senior Marine Corps officers implied any premise of permanence to the advance base force in their commentary.

The scenario for the manoeuvres envisioned a declaration of war by the BLACK nation (clearly, Germany), with its fleet converging on the Caribbean to seek an engagement with the U.S. fleet (or BLUE force). After a hasty assemblage from the Marine barracks on the Atlantic coast to man the two regiments and the headquarters of the advance base force, aged navy transports hauled the Leathernecks to the eastern Caribbean in December 1913. The BLACK fleet, a light-cruiser task force, simulated an attack on the shores of Culebra. For two weeks prior to the arrival of the BLACK forces, the advance base force had toiled under the fierce tropical sun to prepare the defences of the small island. On 23 January 1914, umpires declared a victory for the BLUE fleet and success for the initial test of the advance base force.

Events following the manoeuvre foreshadowed a gloomy future for the concept, however. Hard on the heels of the Culebra manoeuvre, the advance base force re-deployed to the waters off Mexico. After diplomatic tempers erupted anew between the U.S. and its southernmost neighbour over a minor incident of

protocol, the force deployed ashore at Veracruz in April along with composite battalions of Bluejackets and Leathernecks formed from the ships of the fleet. A month later, many of the American naval forces had returned to their ships. The remaining marines, mostly from the Advance Base Force, remained in Veracruz, along with an army regiment, until 23 November 1914. The landing at Veracruz foreshadowed similar commitments that would all but preclude further exercises involving the Advance Base Force and any refinements to it.

Even before the imbroglio with Mexico, the U.S had demonstrated a propensity to dispatch naval landing parties ashore in the Caribbean whenever domestic disturbances appeared to threaten American commercial interests or *Yanqui* perceptions of justice and democracy. Cabinet members and jurists advised sitting presidents that the deployment of soldiers onto foreign soil constituted an act of war, while a similar deployment of naval forces (usually Marines) did not. An American naval force had assisted rebels in wresting Panama from Colombia in 1902 in a blatant act of foreign intervention that allowed the U.S. to begin construction of a cross-isthmus canal. Marine forces returned there, and to other potentially-troubling areas of the Caribbean periodically during the first decade of the century. The Platte Amendment, inserted into the Cuban constitution at the behest of the American government after the Spanish-American War, allowed the U.S. to intervene militarily in the island almost at will. Naval forces deployed ashore in 1906, and again early in the second decade, to put down domestic disturbances. In 1915,

similar deployments to what had become known pejoratively as the 'Banana Republics,' resulted in semi-permanent brigades established ashore in Hispaniola, both in Haiti and then in the Dominican Republic. While these commitments drew heavily on the resources of the Marine Corps, and all but pre-ordained the withering away of the advance base force in Philadelphia to a skeleton of its authorized size, the exigencies of the World War doomed any future exercise of the concept.

When the U.S. entered the war in April 1917, the Major General Commandant (MGC) pressed both the Secretary of the Navy and the Secretary for War to include marines in the American Expeditionary Force (AEF) deploying to France. Although loathe to include marines, whom one senior Army officer described as 'adventurers, illiterates, and drunkards,' a brigade of marines served as one of the two infantry brigades in the 2nd Division, AEF throughout the war. Traditional naval requirements continued at home and overseas, however. Before the intrusive and unwanted Leathernecks had spent their first year in France, a more traditional naval mission appeared for them, albeit briefly and it never reached fruition.

In conferences in London with the Allied Naval Council during the late winter-early spring of 1918, Admiral William S. Sims, proposed the re-deployment of U.S. Marines from the Western Front and from other units forming up at Quantico, Virginia, to serve as an amphibious force in the Adriatic under the British Mediterranean Fleet. The council anticipated a requirement of at least 30,000 troops, a force of American marines and Italian troops, to prevent the use of ports in the region to support the employment of submarines by the Central Powers. Planners envisioned the seizure of an advance base between Curzola (Korčla), a Croatian island off the Dalmatian coast and the seizure of the Sabbioncello (Peljesăc) Peninsula on the southern coast of Croatia. In preliminary discussions on the scheme, no evidence exists to suggest that the planning section considered withdrawing the Royal Navy Division currently serving on the Western Front. By the late spring of 1918, the MGC had a brigade of infantry, two regiments of artillery, one regiment of engineers, and additional smaller units forming up and training at Quantico.

The notion of an amphibious thrust in the Adriatic never evolved beyond thoughtful rumination, either in London or Washington, and no evidence exists that the MGC favoured it. But rumours about the possible pre-deployment of the American Marines from the AEF did reach the ears of the Secretary of War. The Chief of Staff of the Army launched a secret cable to the Commander-in-Chief, AEF, to squelch the notion of sending off the Leatherneck interlopers to possibly adorn themselves with further glory and unearned publicity at the expense of the Doughboys:

'. . . If you are required to send troops to Italy, or anywhere else [outside of France], they will come from the ranks of the Army and not the Marines,' General Peyton C. March instructed.

Although the Marine Corps expanded to almost 80,000 men, deployed two brigades to France, and fulfilled its commitments in support of the fleet and in garrisons at home and abroad, post-war retrenchment resulted in muster rolls dropping to pre-war totals. With only 21,000 men in uniform by 1921, and pre-war requirements remaining essentially unchanged, it seemed unlikely that any serious training of the advance base force or amphibious play during fleet exercises might occur. The new MGC, John A. Lejeune, thought otherwise.

a frustrated Congressman asked the MGC: "Will we ever get out of Haiti?" to which Lejeune replied somewhat laconically: "That is for you to decide."

During his pre-war tenure as the assistant to the MGC, Lejeune (an alumnus of the U.S. Naval Academy and a graduate of the Army War College) had bemoaned the lack of interest in planning and strategic thinking that existed among the senior leadership of the Marine Corps. A disproportionate number of officers believed strongly that the future of the smaller of the naval services lay in fighting America's small wars, or in colonial infantry duties. But by the second decade of the 20th century, America's political leadership and even the body politic had grown disenchanted with the altruistic idealism that had stimulated the establishment of sizeable naval forces ashore in the Banana Republics. In 1922, a frustrated Congressman asked the MGC: 'Will we ever get out of Haiti?' to which Lejeune replied somewhat laconically: 'That is for you to decide.'

The MGC ordered the establishment of the Division of Operations and Training (DOT) at Headquarters Marine Corps as the fountainhead of leatherneck doctrine and planning. To it, he ordered an unusual friend and colleague but one with an unsavoury reputation as a morose alcoholic. Lieutenant Colonel Earl H. 'Pete' Ellis joined the DOT in 1921 as its intelligence officer after serving with notable success as the adjutant of the 4th Brigade (Marine), AEF, during the war and then on the planning staff at the Naval War College.

Even before his tour in the DOT had begun, Ellis had become intrigued with the possible role of the Marine Corps in the event of a naval war against the Empire of Japan. With an almost-monastic fervor, he undertook a study of the amphibious requirements to seize the islands in the Central Pacific that the League of Nations had given to Japan under a post-war mandate. In an unheard of premise, Ellis predicted the requirement for 4 brigades of marines to re-take the islands in the event of a war with the Empire of Japan. In his prophetic analysis, he envisioned the amphibious force assembling initially in Hawaii for outfitting and training. Then, it would deploy to the Marshall Islands to establish an advance base. Ellis's surprising conclusions suggested a final phase with amphibious forces assaulting and reducing first the Carolines and then the Marianas. Ellis predicted the establishment of additional advance bases as naval forces closed the ring on a bellicose Japan. When he submitted his study, 'Advanced Base Operations in Micronesia, 1921,' to the MGC, Ellis tendered a strange request.

Lieutenant Colonel Earl H. 'Pete' Ellis USMC, author of Advanced Based Operations in Micronesia, 1921. (DoD)

the leadership of the Marine Corps to press ahead with the development of amphibious expertise.

The events that followed, and established Pete Ellis's identity as a bona fide member of a small military organisation noted for fostering eccentrics and adventurers, remains enshrined in the rich lore of the U.S. Marine Corps. When Ellis submitted his request to the MGC, Lejeune passed it on to the Chief of Naval Operations and the Secretary of the Navy. In the Office of Naval Intelligence (ONI), it received an enthusiastic endorsement because of an increasing interest in War Plan Orange, the possibility of a naval war with Japan, and speculation that the Japanese had begun construction of fortifications in the mandated islands. ONI provided the funding for the ill-conceived and amateurish spy mission, and took steps to compartmentalize the scheme to effectively shield everyone involved within the Department of the Navy.

The Five-Power Treaty signed by Great Britain, Japan, and the United States (as well as France and Italy) contained a provision that prevented the signatories from constructing permanent fortifications or enlarging their naval bases in the western Pacific. An anathema to the U.S. Navy, this proviso prevented further development of facilities on Guam and in the Philippines. Navy planners wondered increasingly if Japan would honour its obligation not to fortify the islands in Micronesia. The same Navy planners concurred in the belief that in the event of war, Japan's fleet would likely challenge the U.S. fleet in the central Pacific.

Ominously in their view, the Micronesian islands appeared as the logical sites to support the Imperial Japanese fleet. American Naval theorists wondered increasingly if fortification of the Japanese-held Mandates had already begun.

Initially, Ellis attempted to enter the Japanese Mandates through a variety of steamship passages from New Zealand and Australia north through the British Mandates. When further transportation from there into the Central Pacific to the Japanese mandates proved impossible, he took passage to the Philippines and then on to Japan. Throughout his journey, he resorted to alcohol for comfort and each stop along the way was punctuated with hospitalisation for severe bouts of delirium tremens. After reaching Yokohama, his bizarre behavior came to the attention of the U.S. Naval Attaché in Tokyo, and resulted in Ellis' confinement to the naval hospital with orders to return home on the next available military transport. By then, he had reportedly disclosed the substance of his intelligence-gathering mission in a variety of bordellos and bars in the Japanese port city.

Ignoring the orders of his superiors at the American embassy, Ellis boarded a Japanese ship scheduled to steam south into the mandates. After passing through the Bonins and Marianas, he visited the Carolines and Marshalls. When his health worsened, Ellis returned to Jaluit in the Carolines. Although his native mistress and other islanders tended him, the dissolute Leatherneck died of chronic alcoholism on 12 May 1923. A variety of island natives bore witness to Ellis's demise, and all

He asked Lejeune for permission to visit the central Pacific, and observe first-hand what fortifications the wily and supposedly-duplicitous Japanese had completed in the mandated islands. Myth, legend, conjecture, and journalism sputtered and flowed around the events that followed after Ellis's death under mysterious circumstances on 12 May 1923. Generations of Marines, a loyal following of Ellis's friends and family, and admirers of bizarre adventurers supported a variety of fanciful contentions. Most ominously, the belief that Ellis reported the construction of Japanese defensive installations and that he was killed as a result, continued to persist. Ellis's study, and demise under mysterious circumstances, served to stimulate further refinement of War Plan Orange and convince luminaries within

An early Higgins Boat, with front loading design on an early trial with vehicles. (USMC)

Although his native mistress and other islanders tended him, the dissolute Leatherneck died of chronic alcoholism

of them discounted any complicity in his death by Japanese authorities in the Carolines. Because cremation followed before an examination of the remains by a U.S. Navy medical officer, and the subsequent demise of that officer before his debriefing, speculation persisted that agents of the Japanese secret police had poisoned the amateur spy. If the *kempeitai* did indeed kill Ellis, it was only by permitting the travel of a seriously-ill alcoholic into the Mandates and then allowing native venders to continue supplying him with the distilled spirits that brought about his demise.

None of Ellis' notes or reports made it home to the ONI. Materials that he left with friends and confidants in the Mandates, including a copy of ONI's code book, eventually turned up in Japanese hands. Briefly, his death threatened to become a *cause célèbre*. A forthright admission on the part of the Marine Corps by the MCG, albeit confusing, defused the potentially embarrassing disclosure of Ellis' mission and death. Ellis' prophetic study, and not his amateurish spying mission to the Central Pacific, represents his most significant achievement and earns him a place among the pantheon of luminaries in forest green. The bizarre and erratic Leatherneck provided a logical enemy at the time, along with reasonable geographical area, for a major naval confrontation. Operation PLAN 712, 'Advance Base Force Operations in Micronesia,' which Lejeune approved on 23 June 1921, marked the theoretical departure

from the employment of marines in their mission of defending advance bases to one of amphibious assault to seize enemy-held territory from platforms at sea.

Even before Ellis' ill-fated assignment, the General Board of the Navy had suggested the organization and maintenance of between 6,000 to 8,000 Marines on the West Coast of the United States. Planners on Navy staffs envisioned such a force as the amphibious spearhead of any naval thrust into the Marshalls and Carolines in the event of war with Japan. Subsequently, the Chief of Naval Operations recommended the positioning of a similarly-sized force of Marines on the East Coast for possible deployment to the Caribbean.

By 1923, both units appeared under the rubric of 'West Coast Expeditionary Brigade' and 'East Coast Expeditionary Brigade.' While, ostensibly, planners envisioned each brigade composed of two regiments of infantry, only rarely did either one contain more than just a single regiment. Naval commitments in support of the fleet, and overseas in the Philippines and Haiti continued. New overseas requirements emerged as well: In 1927, the West Coast Expeditionary Brigade deployed to China and, when it withdrew less than a year later, one of its two regiments remained behind until re-deploying to the Philippines just before the onset of the War in the Pacific. In 1927, the East Coast Expeditionary Brigade deployed to Nicaragua. By early 1929, more than 5,000 Leathernecks served in an attempt to bring peace to a countryside riddled with political strife. On New Year's Day,

1933, the last elements of the brigade re-deployed to Quantico. Both major deployments, a few minor ones earlier in the decade, the nagging commitment in Haiti that did not end until 1934, and traditional obligations in support of the ships of the fleet served to detract from amphibious manoeuvres held during annual fleet exercises beginning early in the decade before.

The fleet manoeuvres of 1922, conducted at Guantánamo Bay, Cuba; and Culebra, Puerto Rico, differed little in scope and imagination from that witnessed during the first test of the Advance Base Force in 1913-14. Even though the amphibious force bore its new title, expeditionary force, hardly anything had changed. Sailors ferried marines to the beach and the latter manhandled huge naval guns ashore and dug emplacements to defend the advance base. Two companies of marines practiced the displacement of a pair of 155mm field guns ashore, hauled by 5-ton and 10-ton tractors. The exercise proved that naval guns and heavy artillery could be deployed from ship to shore, but only in good weather and low surf, and without serious opposition from an opposing force. Senior Navy and Marine Corps officers agreed, for a change, that the concept of an amphibious assault had just begun.

During an exercise in the Caribbean, the USMC land a 75mm (2.95in) howitzer from a 'Beetle Boat' on Puerto Rico, 1923. (USMC)

In the manoeuvres of 1923-24, Navy and Marine planners increased the amphibious exercising considerably. The entire East Coast Expeditionary Brigade deployed to the Caribbean with the fleet. The 3,300 marines were divided between two regiments, one to defend an advance base at Culebra and the other to conduct a beach assault in the Panama Canal Zone. Still, the landings continued to remain plagued with faults and underscored significant problems that had remained since the abortive Dardanelles Campaign in 1915. Naval gunfire support appeared sporadic and inadequate, transports disgorged supplies on the wrong beaches or unloaded them in a disorganised fashion, and antiquated Navy landing craft landed marines at incorrect sites. An attempt at a night landing resulted in dismal failure. For the most party, the exercise provided only sufficient problems that required study and rumination for more than a decade. Senior marines returned to Quantico determined to overcome the shortcomings.

In the most ambitious escalation of amphibious manoeuvres in conjunction with any fleet manoeuvre to date, the Marine Corps managed to cobble together a force of over 2,500 men from almost every stateside barracks and marine detachment afloat. The body of marines that assembled in 1925 at Mare Island, California, formed into a constructive force of two divisions to form the Blue Force in the fleet's attack against the Black Force (mostly the Army garrison on Oahu) in the Hawaiian Islands. As a change from the usually-tepid naval support for amphibious exercises in peace-time scenarios, the Navy provided 11 battleships, 6 cruisers, and 56 destroyers for simulated naval gunfire bombardment of the

A Christie 'amphibious tank' during manoeuvres on Culebra, in 1924. (USMC)

amphibious objective area. In a novel and constructive addition, the staff and students from the Marine Corps Command and Staff College at Quantico participated as an ad hoc staff during the amphibious play of the fleet exercise. While the fleet exercise of 1925 demonstrated improvements in every area of the amphibious spectrum, increases in both overseas and domestic commitments precluded further participation by sizeable Leatherneck units in future fleet exercises for the remainder of the 1920s and into the early 1930s.

Doctrine evolved coincident with participation in fleet exercises. However, in 1927 the Joint Army-Navy Board gave the amphibious assault mission to the navy; by default, the Marine Corps became the tip of the amphibious spear. Nonetheless, many senior officers continued to look backward and espouse colonial infantry duties and small wars conducted by seaborne forces as the *raison d'etre* for the smaller of the naval services; in contrast, luminaries in forest green looked to the future and embraced the concept of large-scale amphibious assaults in support of the fleet. Significantly, the decision of the Joint Army-Navy Board failed to establish priorities to any of the missions of the Marine Corps and left intact assignments that had endured for more than a century. Thus, the initiatives and imperatives of inter-service politics, Congressional budgetary limitations, and strategic planning tended to focus on everything but the genesis of amphibious doctrine and the ability of the Marine Corps to practice that complicated aspect of naval warfare.

A variety of factors propelled the Marine Corps' pre-eminent role as the ultimate practitioner of amphibious warfare to fruition in the early 1930s. Planning staffs at the Naval War College, War Plans Division of the General Board of the Navy, and the Joint Army-Navy Board had all undertaken the study of possible major revisions to War Plan Orange. Of the major war plans in existence, some more than two decades old, only a potential conflict with Japan remained plausible. Ellis's prophetic study, and the necessary naval forces to implement the amphibious courses of action he foresaw, meshed nicely with the updated war plans.

Commitments for overseas deployments of marines in the last half of the 1920s, coupled with post-war antipathy on the part of the American body politic, precluded serious refinement of amphibious doctrine or exercising. Herbert Hoover came to the American Presidency in 1929 determined to keep his campaign promise of military and naval retrenchment. While commitments worldwide for naval forces remained extant, the administration of President Hoover continued to slash at budgetary and personnel figures. The world-wide depression only fueled the economic fervour of Hoover and his advisors to reduce the expenses of the armed forces. By 1931, the MGC noted ruefully that most of his Marines were either overseas or in the ships of the fleet, or coming from or going there. In Congressional testimony, he pointed out that '[the reductions] have made it impossible to carry out its primary mission of supporting the United States Fleet by maintaining a force in readiness to operate with the fleet.'

In 1933, the grim outlook for adequate amphibious forces in America's naval arsenal took an upturn. Critics within the Department of State and Congress had convinced the Oval Office to begin withdrawing Marines from Nicaragua, and otherwise to implement a 'Good Neighbour Policy' in Latin America. The election of Franklin D. Roosevelt, a consistent supporter of the Marine Corps, buoyed hopes for relief from almost a decade of intermittent retrenchment. During President Roosevelt's first term in office, a significant departure from the Marine Corps's traditional role as a shipboard landing party occurred; it marked the beginning of a firm commitment to maintain separate organizations of marines for deployment overseas.

In 1931, the MGC recommended the elimination of the two expeditionary brigades and their replacements by fleet marine forces under the direct control of fleet commanders. Accompanying his directive, the MGC criticised the lack of amphibious doctrine. The implausible gyrations of the General Board of the Navy over the previous two years underscored the concerns of the Marine Corps' senior leadership. Taking matters into his own hands, and separating the navy hierarchy from any input into the generation of suitable amphibious doctrine, the MGC ordered his general officer commanding at Quantico to 'proceed as expeditiously as practicable to prepare for publication a manual for landing operations.' He directed work to begin no later than 15 November 1933, and authorized the suspension of classes to use the staff and students at Quantico

Genesis of Modern Amphibious Warfare:
Marine Corps Generals from the last Century
Semper Fidelis

to work on the project. Actually, the effort had begun in 1931, but now it proceeded full-bore to fruition.

The publication of the draft manual in January 1934 signaled a sharp change in the sea dynamic of the U.S. Marine Corps. Since its founding in 1798, numerous and sometimes insipid secretaries of the Navy had mostly sided with a variety of parochial senior navy officers or budget-minded congressman in measures that pre-ordained America's marines emergence from traditional duties more characteristic of the Age of Sail or the Age of Mahan, and then into the Golden Age of Amphibious Warfare that punctuated the naval campaigns of World War II. The establishment of the Fleet Marine Force at the end of 1933 and the publication of the *Tentative Manual for Landing Operations* in 1934 serve as benchmarks in the genesis of modern amphibious warfare. Together, they signalled the inauguration of the U.S. Marine Corps as a progressive amphibious force preparing to fight in the two-ocean war that evolved in World War II.

Major General Joseph H. Pendleton retired in 1924 after 40 years service in the Marine Corps, during which time he had command of the Fourth Regiment in 1916. During his service he acted as Military Governor of Santo Domingo, commanded the Marine Barracks at Parris Island and was Commanding General Department of the Pacific. (USMC)

Lieutenant General John A. Lejeune was the 13th Commandant of the Marine Corps. He was the first Marine officer to hold an Army Divisional command (2nd Infantry Division) when deployed with the American Expeditionary Forces in France in 1918 where he was awarded the Croix de Guerre and Legion of Honour for his leadership. (USMC)

The highly decorated Lieutenant General Lewis 'Chesty' Puller was a 'Marine's Marine', veteran of the Korean War and of four campaigns in World War Two. He originally joined the Marine Corps in 1919 and retired in 1955. During the fighting at the Chosin Reservoir he was awarded the Distinguished Service Cross for heroism with the 1st Marines, 1st Marine Division. (USMC)

General Alfred M. Gray was enlisted into the Marine Corps in 1950, reached the rank of Sergeant and was then commissioned in 1952. During his service he was on active duty with the 3rd Marine Division in Vietnam serving as an Artillery Observer. After Commanding the 2nd Division he eventually went on to become the 29th Commandant General of the Marine Corps from 1987 until 1991. (USMC)

Further Reading

Ballendorf, Dirk A. and Bartlett, Merrill L., *Pete Ellis: An Amphibious Warfare Prophet, 1880-1923,* (Annapolis: Naval Institute Press, 1997)

Bartlett, Merrill L., *Lejeune: A Marine's Life, 1867-1942,* (Columbia: University of South Carolina Press, 1991; reprint ed., Annapolis: Naval Institute Press, 1991)

Cosmas, Graham A., and Shulimson, Jack, "The Culebra Maneuver and the Formation of the U. S. Marine Corps' Advance Base Force," pp. 293-308, in Robert W. Love, Jr. et al, ed., *Changing Interpretations and New Sources in Naval History,* (New York and London: Garland, 1980)

Millett, Allan R., *Semper Fidelis: The History of the United States Marine Corps* (New York and London: Macmillan, 1980)

Millett, Allan R., and Shulimson, Jack, ed., *Commandants of the Marine Corps,* (Annapolis: Naval Institute Press, 2004)

Simmons, Edwin Howard, *The United States Marines: a History,* (Annapolis, Maryland: Naval Institute Press, 1998)

Biography

Lieutenant Colonel Merrill L Bartlett, earned his undergraduate degree at Washington State University and was commissioned via the Platoon Leaders Class program in 1963. He has a Master of Arts degree from San Diego State University, and has completed his studies for a Doctorate in history at the University of Maryland, College Park. He taught history at the Naval Academy from 1977 to 1982, and retired from active service as a Marine Corps Officer. While serving in Annapolis, he won the prestigious William D. Clements Award as the outstanding military educator at the Naval Academy for 1980. He is the editor of the acclaimed *Assault from the Sea: Essays on the History of Amphibious Warfare* (Annapolis: Naval Institute Press, 1983; reprint ed., 1985), author of *Lejeune: A Marine's Life, 1867-1942* Naval Institute Press, 1996); co-author (with Colonel Joseph H. Alexander) of *Sea Soldiers in the Cold War: Amphibious Warfare in the Age of the Superpowers*, 1945-1991 (Annapolis: Naval Institute Press, 1994); and co-author (with Dirk Anthony Ballendorf) of *Pete Ellis: An Amphibious Warfare Prophet, 1880-1923* (Annapolis: Naval Institute Press, 1996). His essays and book reviews have regularly appeared in a variety of professional and scholarly journals.

world war II

The German Invasion of Norway
Operation WESERÜBUNG, April 1940

By Dr Stephen Badsey

The Norway campaign of 1940 was the first example of tri-service three dimensional manoeuvre warfare of the Blitzkrieg era. From April to June 1940 the British and French fought their first major campaign of the Second World War in a futile attempt to prevent the German conquest of Norway, then a country largely unfamiliar to them. The resulting defeat revealed serious shortcomings in the British approach to warfare that led politically to the fall of the British Conservative government of Prime Minister Neville Chamberlain, and militarily to the establishment of new fighting organisations including the first Commandos.

From the start of the war, it was logical for the British to take chief responsibility for strategic issues concerning Norway. Rather than lying off the west coast of Europe, the British Isles actually form the middle of a semicircle of land and sea with Norway to the northeast and southern France and Spain to the southwest, giving Britain the wartime advantage of interior lines for sea movement. Oslo, the Norwegian capital and largest city is a little north of the northern tip of Scotland, and closer to the Royal Navy's base at Scapa Flow in the Orkney Islands than London is. Almost all of Norway is mountainous, about a quarter covered with forests, over a third of its length lies north of the Arctic Circle, a frozen desert where in June the sun does not set even at midnight, and most of the population live in the south. In 1940 only three

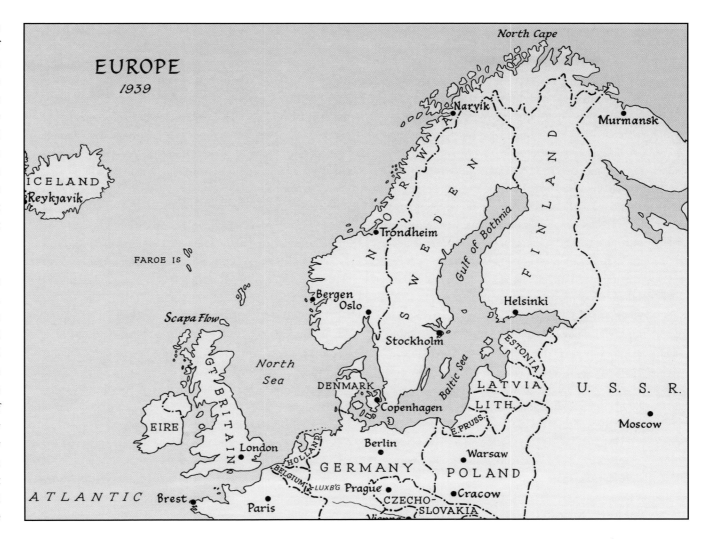

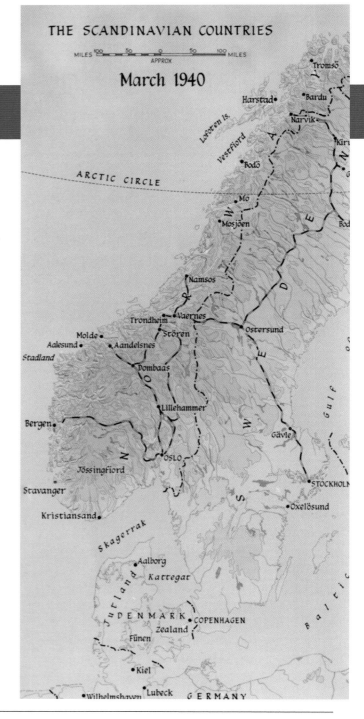

per cent of the land was used for agriculture, and Norway's major industries were all maritime, including fishing and a merchant marine that was the fourth largest in the world. Norway is 2,740 km long on the map, but has over 21,200 km of coastline due to the deep glaciated valleys known as fjords which radiate into the heart of the country like the roots of a tree, flanked by the mountains. The major Norwegian ports including Oslo lie considerably inland along these narrow twisting waterways, and the northern port of Narvik, which saw some of the heaviest fighting in 1940, lies only 70 km from the Swedish border, much closer than it does to the sea. Any ship entering the fjords was vulnerable to artillery, torpedoes or bombing from the air, with little room to manoeuvre. Communications in 1940 depended largely on a railway that reached only as far north as Namsos, and on roads running through and along the central mountain spine, continuous only as far north as Bodø, 180 km south of Narvik, and interrupted by ferry crossings over lakes and fjords, and by other choke-points. Winter 1939-1940 was unusually cold throughout western Europe, and deep snow persisted as far south as Åndalsnes well into May. Before the spring thaw, skis or snowshoes were essential for speedy cross-country movement, and moving artillery including anti-aircraft guns in particular was very difficult. The coastline of western Norway also includes numerous small islands mostly facing the Norwegian Sea, known to locals as the skerry guard. The narrow sea channels between these islands and the shore, called the Leads, never freeze in winter, meaning that even the far northern ports are ice-free.

In 1940 Norway was a constitutional monarchy under King Håkon VII, with a parliamentary government similar to that of Britain. It had been ruled as part of Sweden for almost a century until 1905, when it had achieved independence peacefully. Together with Sweden and Denmark it had stayed neutral in the First World War, and it had retained a policy of neutrality and non-alignment. Most Norwegian politicians were ignorant even of the basics of military organisation and operations. Norway's armed forces were small by the standards of the time, un-modernised and under-equipped, with an entirely defensive role. Based on conscription, the Norwegian Army consisted of cadres for six infantry divisions (each in reality of about strong brigade strength on full mobilisation), mostly with their depots located to defend the major population centres of the south: 1st and 2nd Divisions in the area of Oslo, 3rd Division near Kristiansand, 4th Division near Bergen, 5th Division near Trondheim and 6th Division near Narvik.[1] Oslo, with a population of 250,000, was defended by a single battalion of the Royal Guard Regiment. The Norwegians had no tanks and little training, but benefited from skiing and shooting being national sports, and from local knowledge of the terrain. The Norwegians had about 40 military and naval aircraft, fewer than half of them modern. Their largest airfield was at Sola near Stavanger, together with airfields at Fornebu near Oslo, and at Kristiansand and Trondheim, and in the winter frozen lakes could be used as improvised landing strips. The Royal Norwegian Navy had almost no modern warships, most of its operational fleet dating

---

[1] John Pimlott, *The Viking Atlas of World War II* (London: Viking, 1995) pages 52-3.

from the First World War or even earlier. Its largest vessels were two obsolete 'defence cruisers', plus seven destroyers and nine submarines, along with some heavy guns in the forts guarding the fjord entrances to its ports, which played an important part in their defence.

In September 1939 Nazi Germany invaded Poland, leading to declarations of war by Britain and France. Except for Austria and the Czech Republic, absorbed into Adolf Hitler's Third Reich in 1938-39, and the Soviet Union which occupied eastern Poland, all other European countries stayed neutral. After the defeat of Poland in October, some Polish forces escaped to fight on, including a few warships and submarines. The Germans drew up plans in October for an attack against France, which was delayed until the spring by the poor weather, and in December began planning for an invasion of Norway to precede it.

With Norway in its possession Germany could vastly increase its submarine threat to these convoys, and avoid another British blockade

The chief German motive for wanting to occupy Norway before attacking France was their experience in the First World War, when they had failed to win the war at sea and break the British naval blockade. From 1939 onwards, the Germans employed unrestricted submarine warfare, sinking without warning merchant ships of all nationalities (including neutrals, Norwegians among them) heading for British ports. In response

the British used convoys, protected by small, fast warships such as destroyers and frigates. With Norway in its possession Germany could vastly increase its submarine threat to these convoys, and avoid another British blockade. The Germans also tried to couple this submarine threat with surface raiders, battlecruisers or pocket battleships replenished by supply ships, against which the convoys and their escorts would be helpless. Possession of naval bases in Norway would greatly increase the chance of getting these big warships through the Greenland-Iceland-UK gap into the Atlantic. Norway was also an important, if indirect, source of strategic minerals for Germany, which was heavily dependent on iron ore mined in the northern part of neutral Sweden around Gällivare. Some of this iron ore was shipped to Germany from the port of Luleå at the northern end of the Gulf of Bothnia. But in winter these seas became impassable with ice, and most of the iron ore was transported by rail to Narvik and so by ship down the Leads and into the Baltic. The capture of Norway would secure this route, and also negate any possibility of Sweden siding against Germany. It would also pre-empt any British or French plans to bring Norway into the war on their own side and to establish naval and air bases there. Finally, since October 1939 Hitler had being secretly pressed to take over Norway for the Third Reich by Major Vidkun Quisling, leader of the Norwegian National Union Party and a fierce admirer of Nazism, who promised a military coup and an enthusiastic reception from his countrymen for German troops. Quisling had served as Norwegian defence minister 1931-33 and a few officers of the Norwegian Army were loyal to him and his

beliefs. Quisling's name was commonly used for years afterwards as a synonym for treachery in the face of enemy invasion.

The British understood the problems of amphibious warfare (their last experience had been the unsuccessful Gallipoli campaign of 1915-16), and even had a few assault landing craft which were used in the later stages of the Norway campaign. Their main problems if it came to a fight in Norway were the lack of dedicated amphibious forces and adequate air cover. The British were desperately re-arming over winter 1939-40, a process that would not near completion for another two years. They had despatched their few organised divisions to France in 1939, together with a force of RAF bombers and fighters. They were training other formations as rapidly as possible, but in addition to no amphibious troops they had no mountain troops or airborne troops either. This contrasted with the French, some of whose mountain troops, the *Chasseurs Alpins*, took part in the campaign, as did the Polish Carpathian Brigade (organised by the French as *Chasseurs de Montagne*, although some had no mountain fighting experience). It was recognised that any surface ships operating off the Norwegian coast were vulnerable to attack from the air. Southern Norway including Oslo and Stavanger were within range of RAF Bomber Command's medium bombers based in east and north-east England, and Trondheim was just about within range of bases in Scotland, but Norway was well out of range of RAF fighters. Air cover had to come instead from the three aircraft carriers with the Home Fleet, and from any air bases that the British could establish in Norway itself.

The British had neither planned nor expected to fight an amphibious campaign in Norway

In April 1940 the British had neither planned nor expected to fight an amphibious campaign in Norway. Their involvement and the haphazard manner in which it was conducted came about through divided political and military planning. Although the war at sea began at once, after the best British divisions had been sent to France there was very little else that the British government could do. Journalists called this period of military quiet the 'Phoney War' or the 'Bore War'. There were also some members of the Chamberlain government who hoped for a negotiated peace with Germany before the war escalated further, and the lack of resources was sometimes combined with a reluctance to act too aggressively. But this did not apply to Winston Churchill, appointed First Lord of the Admiralty on the war's outbreak, the political head of the Royal Navy. At this stage the British also had no tri-service planning organisation. The three professional service heads met as the Chiefs of Staff Committee, with oversight exercised by the Military Co-ordination Committee, usually chaired by Churchill. The opportunity existed for any one service to press its own case very strongly, Churchill was looking for ways to take the fight to the Germans, and Norway provided an opportunity.

In November 1939 the Soviet Union attacked Finland, and in response to the Soviet threat if Finland collapsed, Norway mobilised its 6th Division under Major General Carl Gustav Fleischer (about 8,000 strong) at Narvik. Although not declaring war on the Soviet Union, Britain together with France unsuccessfully sought Norwegian agreement for their sending troops through Narvik to fight alongside the Finns. A Finnish defeat and armistice on 12 March 1940 ended these plans. Winter 1939-40 also saw a series of 'incidents' in Norwegian coastal waters between the British and the Germans, typical of the pressures facing a neutral country in a war zone. The most publicised came in February 1940 when the destroyer HMS *Cossack* openly entered a fjord south of Stavanger where the German supply ship *Altmark* had taken refuge, boarded the ship and rescued British sailors. Looking for ways of pressuring Germany, the British also increasingly fixated on the supply of iron ore from neutral Sweden through Narvik and the Leads. By early 1940 they concluded that this inshore traffic was a legitimate target, and that cutting off the winter iron ore supply would be catastrophic for Germany. By April, Churchill had obtained Chamberlain's authorisation to place sea minefields blocking the passage through the Leads, a plan code-named Operation WILFRED by Churchill, who joked that he chose the name 'because by itself it was so small and harmless'.[2] The mining would be done without the permission of the Norwegian government, supported if necessary by the Home Fleet at Scapa Flow including its battleships, and by 2nd Cruiser Squadron. By this late date the sea routes to Luleå were already starting to unfreeze, and it was not clear that this mining would in fact have achieved anything.

An auxiliary to Operation WILFRED was Plan R4, the placing of troops from 24th Guards Brigade and 49th (West Riding) Division, a Territorial Army division lacking training and equipment, on board transports and the warships of 1st Cruiser Squadron. This was in the hope that, if the Germans responded to the mining by attacking or threatening Norway, its government would allow these British troops to land and help defend their country. There was a First World War precedent of sorts for this, when in 1915 the Allies had pressured neutral Greece into accepting their forces. The British were expecting a limited naval campaign, and possibly an unopposed landing in a friendly country from which they could establish a base, but any idea of their sending their troops to Norway depended on the German reaction to mining the Leads. Beyond this their thinking did not go.

While the British were planning to mine the Leads, plans were also being completed for the German invasion of Norway and Denmark, code-named Operation WESERÜBUNG ('The River Weser Exercise'). As chiefly a land power, Germany had no specialist amphibious assault troops or ships, and no doctrine or previous experience of amphibious landings other than the seizure of some small islands off Riga in the Baltic in 1917. The invasion took place mostly using troops landing directly at the harbour walls or ferried ashore from larger ships. Planning for the operation by-passed German Army headquarters, and XXI Corps commanded by *General* Nikolaus von Falkenhorst worked directly with Armed Forces High Command or *Oberkommando der Wehrmacht* (OKW). Although this decision was largely taken by Hitler to strengthen his own authority, it did provide

---

[2]Winston S. Churchill, *The Second World War Volume I: The Gathering Storm* (London: Cassell, 1948) page 522.

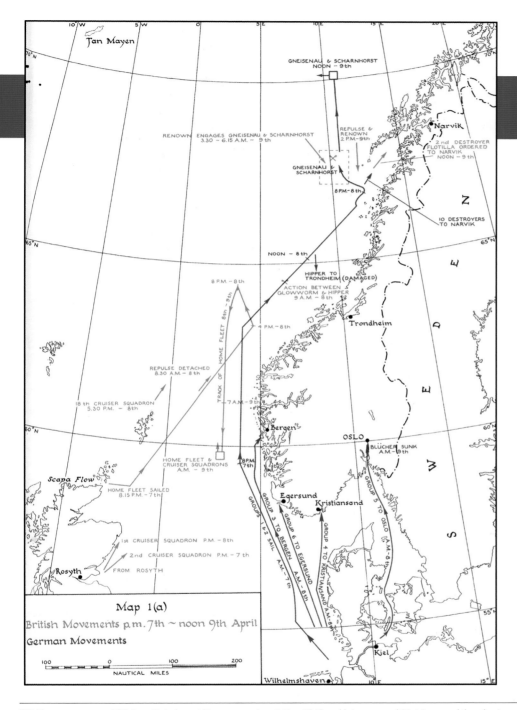

GNEISENAU & SCHARNHORST
NOON - 9th

RENOWN ENGAGES GNEISENAU & SCHARNHORST
3.30 - 6.15 A.M. - 9th

REPULSE &
RENOWN
2 P.M.-9th

Narvik

2nd DESTROYER
FLOTILLA ORDERED
TO NARVIK
NOON - 9 th

GNEISENAU &
SCHARNHORST

8 P.M.- 8 th

N

10 DESTROYERS
TO NARVIK

NOON - 8th

HIPPER TO
TRONDHEIM (DAMAGED)

8 P.M. - 8th

ACTION BETWEEN
GLOWWORM & HIPPER
9 A.M. - 8 th

4 P.M.-8 th

Trondheim

E

REPULSE DETACHED
8.30 A.M. - 8 th

7 A.M - 9 th

TRACK OF HOME FLEET 8th-9th

E

18 th CRUISER SQUADRON
5.30 P.M. - 8th

Bergen

OSLO

BLÜCHER SUNK
A.M.-9th

HOME FLEET &
CRUISER SQUADRONS
A.M. - 9 th

8 P.M
7th

W

Scapa Flow

HOME FLEET SAILED
8.15 P.M.- 7 th

Egersund

Kristiansand

GROUP 3 TO BERGEN A.M. 7 th

GROUP 1 & 2 SAIL A.M. 7 th

GROUP 6 TO EGERSUND A.M. 8 th

GROUP 4 TO KRISTIANSAND A.M. 8 th

GROUP 5 TO OSLO A.M. 8 th

S

1st CRUISER SQUADRON P.M. - 8th

2nd CRUISER SQUADRON P.M. - 7 th

Rosyth

FROM ROSYTH

Kiel

Map 1(a)

British Movements p.m. 7th ~ noon 9th April

German Movements

100   0   100   200

NAUTICAL MILES

Wilhelmshaven

*A Chart showing the German invasion of Norway
and the movements of the German Navy and the
Royal Navy between 7 - 9 April 1940. (NHB)*

a more co-ordinated planning structure.[3] A further advantage was that German military staffs, if not always the troops themselves, had considerable experience of prior military operations, stretching back to the Spanish Civil War 1936-39 and including the conquest of Poland. With the bulk of the German Army deployed along the French and Belgian border in preparation for an attack, from the start Norway would be a secondary theatre of operations, and the Germans could spare only six divisions. Hitler's directive for WESERÜBUNG, issued on 1 March, emphasised that 'Weakness in numbers will be made good by skilful action and surprise in execution'.[4] These were ordinary infantry divisions, except for the specially trained 3rd Mountain Division, although all were well equipped for operating in the mountains and snow. The Germans had a further big advantage in their formidable air force, the Luftwaffe, About 290 German bombers, 100 fighters and 50 dive-bombers took part in the campaign together with 571 Junkers JU 52 transport aircraft, commanded by X Air Fleet. The Luftwaffe forces also included some seaplanes, and a regiment of paratroopers.

As a neutral, Norway was vulnerable to the kind of military surprises and stratagems that could only work at the start of a campaign. For the Germans, the conquest of Norway was Blitzkrieg without tanks (one Panzer battalion mainly of light tanks did in fact take part), a single continuous military operation of great daring, showing their characteristic use of skill and violent shock to overthrow an enemy before he could recover, together with a great deal of bluff. The plan for WESERÜBUNG was based on capturing all the major coastal towns of Norway - Oslo, Kristiansand, Stavanger, Bergen, Trondheim and Narvik - simultaneously and by surprise, assisted by companies of paratroopers seizing the airfields at Sola and Fornebu. The Luftwaffe's fighter and dive bomber cover extended as far north as Oslo from its bases in Germany, and medium bomber range about as far as Trondheim. Against the might of the Royal Navy the Germans could not risk sending all their troops in slow-moving sea transports. Their plan was to position in Norwegian harbours merchant ships carrying fuel, supplies and equipment, some sailing under false neutral flags. Then five naval

[3]XXI Corps was renamed XXI Army Detachment (*Armeegruppe*) on 1 May 1940 and later renamed 21st Army, and then the Army of Norway. See Samuel W. Mitcham, *Hitler's Legions* (London: Leo Cooper, 1985), page 501; David Westwood, *The German Army: Organisation and Personnel 1933-1945* (London: MLRS, n.d.) pages 182, 193, 236-7; Len Deighton, *Blitzkrieg* (London: Jonathan Cape, 1979) page 80.
[4]H. R. Trevor-Roper (ed), *Hitler's War Directives* (London: Pan, 1966) page 62.

groups led by battlecruisers or cruisers would carry between 1,000 and 2,000 troops each in a swift dash to their objectives. Including the paratroopers, this first German lift totalled only about 9,000 troops. With the furthest to go, Group 1 led by the battlecruisers *Scharnhorst* and *Gneisenau* would take more than 36 hours to reach Narvik, and the landings would all start before dawn on the second day of the operation. The plan also meant most of the German warships sailing deep into the confined waters of the fjords, with every chance of the Royal Navy bottling up their escape, and once they had unloaded their troops and refuelled they were required to leave rapidly. At the same time, other German forces would invade and occupy Denmark.

If all went well, Norway would wake up to find itself helpless, and after Quisling's promises the Germans hoped that the people would accept the occupation peacefully, including their announcements that they had come to protect Norway against British invasion. If the Norwegians fought on after the first landings, then the capture of Sola and Fornebu would enable the Luftwaffe to extend its air cover up as far as Namsos.

Reinforced through the short sea route to southern Norway and by air transport, the German ground forces would then advance northwards up the two major valleys through the southern Norwegian mountains, the Gudbrandsdal past Lillehammer to Åndalsnes, and the Østerdal stretching up towards Trondheim. With their forces at Trondheim reinforced and relieved, they could then establish air bases bringing Narvik within range, and complete their conquest.

Co-incidences do happen even - especially - in wartime

Co-incidences do happen even - especially - in wartime. In the early hours of 8 April the Royal Navy started to lay its minefields in the Leads near Bodø and Narvik, only for this to be the same night that the German naval groups carrying their troops were sailing into position prior to their landings, having chosen the early hours of 9 April after several delays. Although indicators and warnings had reached London, the British were completely surprised by what was happening, and for a few days Chamberlain's government knew little more than what it could read in the newspapers. British intelligence was not properly co-ordinated, and the Royal Navy's prevailing view was that it would take 25-30 divisions to conquer Norway, and that any

German naval movements were instead related to the threat to the Atlantic. In fact both sides had surprised the other, and each found itself in perilous situations facing major warships with smaller vessels.

The Norwegians also were caught utterly by surprise at first, despite British warnings and the early sinking of a German transport, the *Rio de Janeiro*, by a Polish submarine on 8 April. As their troops landed, the Germans presented their demands to the Norwegians at 0515 local time on 9 April. The Norwegian government ordered mobilisation of its four southern divisions, but incredibly they did not grasp that the option they had chosen meant that the orders telling men to report to their depots would go out by letter, taking 48 hours. Denmark, invaded simultaneously by the Germans, surrendered that day. At 0730 the Norwegian foreign minister gave an impromptu radio interview mentioning the mobilisation, and many men took this as the order to report for duty, but the Norwegian mobilisation took place under chaotic circumstances of which the Germans took full advantage.

With the furthest to travel, over 2,200 kilometres from its home ports to Narvik, Group 1 with the *Scharnhorst* and *Gneisenau* and ten destroyers sailed on the morning of 7 April with 2,000 men of 139th Mountain Regiment, together with the commander of 3rd Mountain Division, Lieutenant General Eduard Dietl and his staff. Out in the Norwegian Sea gales were blowing at Force 8 and 9 with accompanying snowstorms. After escorting the

The Luftwaffe dropping supplies to the German Airborne Troops who had recently landed in Norway. (NHB)

destroyers close to the fjords, the two battlecruisers broke off northwards, where they ran into the British early on 9 April, and the *Gneisenau* was damaged in a running fight with the battlecruiser HMS *Renown*. The immediate British assumption was that this was an attempt by the German battlecruisers to break out into the Atlantic. In the event, they skirted round to the north and west of the British warships, and eventually regained safe harbour in Germany. The remainder of the group entered Narvik harbour where after a brief attempt at negotiation they sank both the obsolete defence cruisers *Eidsvold* and *Norge*, and landed their troops. The local Norwegian commander in Narvik, an admirer of Major Quisling, ordered his troops to surrender. This was the only major incident in which apparent 'Quisling' treachery affected the outcome of a battle, but at first it caused deep suspicion, both among the Norwegian forces, and from the Allies.

Group 2 heading for Trondheim was led by the heavy cruiser *Hipper* with four destroyers carrying 1,700 men also from 3rd Mountain Division, including two battalions of 138th Mountain Regiment. This group slipped past the British, except for a chance encounter on 8 April with the destroyer HMS *Glowworm*, which although vastly outmatched rammed and severely damaged the *Hipper* before sinking. Her captain, Lieutenant-Commander Gerard Broadmead Roope, was posthumously awarded the first Victoria Cross of the war. The *Hipper* continued on with her group to Trondheim, running the coastal fortress batteries and landing their troops to secure the port, which had a population

of 56,000, almost without loss, although the Norwegian 5th Division at Trondheim managed to mobilise some troops.

Group 3, led by the light cruisers *Koln* and *Königsberg*, carried 900 men of 69th Division including the divisional staff and part of 159th Infantry Regiment, heading for Bergen. The *Königsberg* was badly damaged by the Bergen coastal forts, but the Germans managed to land successfully and secured the port. On 10 April the *Königsberg* was sunk by British dive bombers flying at their maximum range from Scotland, the first major warship ever sunk by air attack in this way.

The critical airbase at Sola was captured from the air by the Germans by a company of 1st Paratroop Regiment, dropping at about 0800, followed by transport aircraft flying in the bulk of 69th Division, 5,000 troops over the next few days. The attack was heavily supported by the Luftwaffe which had no difficulty in destroying or driving off the few aircraft that the Norwegians could muster. An additional small naval landing was made at nearby Egersund to seize an important communications facility. Group 4, led by the light cruiser *Karlsruhe*, was destined for Kristiansand (and nearby Arendal), carrying 1,100 men of 163rd Division including a reinforced battalion of 310th Infantry Regiment. The Norwegian coastal batteries and destroyers in the harbour forced back the first two attempts at a landing, damaging the *Karlsruhe* in the battle, but a third attempt using false code signals succeeded. Later that day, the returning *Karlsruhe* was torpedoed by a British submarine and sank.

The German capture of Oslo was their largest single operation on 9 April, and came closest to failure. The plan involved paratroopers capturing Fornebu, followed as at Sola by transport aircraft flying in about 2,000 troops of 163rd Division. At the same time Group 5, led by the heavy cruiser *Blücher*, the pocket battleship *Lützow* and the light cruiser *Emden*, would enter the fjords and land at Oslo with another 2,000 men of 163rd Division, including two battalions of 307th Infantry Regiment and most of the divisional staff, together with the staff of XXI Corps. Oslo was guarded by five coastal fortresses and a few small warships. Group 5's first encounter came at 2315 on 8 April with a Norwegian patrol boat which managed to transmit a warning before being sunk. The Germans then tried to run the Norwegian coastal batteries in the dark, aided by a sea fog. The *Blücher* was hit and sunk, taking 1,000 troops

The WESERÜBUNG plan had succeeded, but the German forces at Trondheim and Narvik were still vulnerable. The Norwegian Army was mobilising and starting to fight back against the invaders, and the three British brigades of Plan R4, although they had no amphibious assault capability and only a limited fighting strength, had nevertheless been embarked on their ships and could have reached western Norway within 24 hours. A rapid response by the Allies could probably have regained the initiative. Instead the response was uncoordinated and confused. With the first news of the naval encounters, the Admiralty without consultation ordered the troops to disembark from 1st Cruiser Squadron so that it could put to sea to fight, (in the process many soldiers became separated from vital stores and equipment), only to have them re-embark later as orders changed. For almost a week British planning alternated between making Trondheim or Narvik their principal objective, finally settling on Narvik. No overall commander was appointed for Norway, or even three co-operating service commanders. Instead, operations were conducted from London, hampered by poor intelligence and communications.

This confusion in strategic and operational direction contrasted strongly with the Royal Navy's well deserved reputation for skill and aggression. On 10 April, five British destroyers entered the fjords leading to Narvik to engage the Germans. Two British destroyers were lost, but the German transports and two destroyers were sunk, and others damaged. On 13 April a Royal Navy squadron headed by the battleship HMS *Warspite* re-entered the fjords, sank the remaining German destroyers, and shelled the Narvik docks. All ten German destroyers from Group 1 were lost in these two battles.

Dietl's mountain troops were cut off at Narvik facing Fleischer's 6th Division, and in the days to come Hitler considered ordering them either to break out southwards or accept internment in Sweden. German transport aircraft flying onto a nearby frozen lake managed to land a mountain howitzer battery, and 2,500 sailors rescued from their sunken ships, officially known as *Marine-Battalion Erdmenger* and more familiarly as 'The Mountainsailors' (*Gebirgsmarine*), were used to crew dismounted naval guns and form fighting detachments. Plans to supply them by sea failed as the Allied navies controlled the approaches, but the neutral Swedes allowed some trains carrying supplies and medical stores through to Narvik.

While Dietl was organising his defences, there was still neither a plan nor any available troops for the British to seize the opportunity and land to retake Narvik. Admiral of the Fleet Lord Cork (the Earl of Cork and Orrey) was brought out of retirement to command the naval forces in northern Norway, and arrived in the theatre on 14 April, convinced that a sudden direct attack could succeed. But this was opposed by Major General

and most of 163rd Division staff with her. The *Lützow* and the *Emden* were both damaged, and the Germans had to divert their landing to a peninsula about 30 km south of Oslo. Advancing overland, the troops of 163rd Division did not reach the city until late at night on 9 April. The *Lützow* was also further damaged by a Royal Navy submarine while returning from the operation. At Fornebu airfield the parachute drop was called off due to the bad weather, and supported by fighters and light bombers the transport aircraft carrying two infantry battalions of 324th Infantry Regiment instead landed directly onto the runway against weak Norwegian opposition, followed later by the paratroopers. The Norwegians declared Oslo an open city to save it from bombing, and the Germans quickly organised a parade to impress the inhabitants with the apparent strength of their forces, which barely numbered 1,500 men at that stage. A brief diplomatic attempt to negotiate the surrender of Norway came to nothing as the Germans demanded that King Håkon accept a government under Major Quisling. After unsuccessful Germans attempts to capture and then to bomb the king and his government, both moved to safety in the north.

German Troops advance inland, carrying their skis as they march across Norway. (NHB)

P. J. Mackesy, appointed to command the ground troops, named as 'Avonforce,' (later 'Rupertforce') whose orders were only to contact the Norwegians and make an appreciation. On 15 April the first troops from 24th Guards Brigade began to arrive at Harstad in the Loften Islands, which cover the entrance to the fjords leading to Narvik, but time was needed particularly for their artillery and stores to join them. By the time that Major General Mackesy placed under Lord Cork on 20 April a week-long blizzard had blown up, and it was to take over a month from their first landings before the Allies were ready to attack. As the British official history put it, 'the effect of issuing incompatible instructions to two not wholly compatible commanders for Narvik' resulted in a lost opportunity.[5]

A very similar story occurred over Trondheim, which became the Allied secondary objective. An initial plan for 'Operation HAMMER' to force a landing through the fjords at Trondheim

itself was made, considered, and then dropped on 15 April, by which date most of the German 181st Division had already been transported to Trondheim by air. So, any chance to take Trondheim before the Germans could secure it passed. Instead, the new plan was to break up 49th (West Riding) Division, sending its 146th Infantry Brigade to Namsos, to the north of Trondheim, as part of 'Mauriceforce' under the enterprising Major General Adrian Carton de Wiart. This was to co-ordinate with a second brigade landing at Åndalsnes to the south of Trondheim, which at first was given the dual mission of co-operating with Mauriceforce to take Trondheim in a pincer movement from north and south, and also co-operating with the Norwegian troops then being driven back up the Gudbrandsdal valley from Lillehammer.

A contingent of Royal Marines secured Namsos on 14 April, 146th Infantry Brigade started to arrive two days later, and the 5th Demi-Brigade Chasseurs Alpins two days after that. Still lacking specialist equipment of any kind for fighting or even moving in the snow, the road-bound 146th Infantry Brigade advanced southward to Steinkjer, on one of the fjords about 80 km north of Trondheim. The Chasseurs Alpins also arrived lacking critical equipment, including even straps for their skies. The first arrivals could not land their artillery and specialist equipment because the ship that brought them was too long to get into Trondheim harbour, and the second ship was badly

damaged by German bombs.[6] By 21 April any idea of a further advance southwards was given up when the Germans exploited local command of the air and mobility through the fjords, using ships from Trondheim including a destroyer to land about three battalions with artillery in locations just behind the British positions at Steinkjer.

The Allied landing at Åndalsnes started on 18 April also with Royal Marines securing the port for a landing by 148th Infantry Brigade of two battalions, also from 49th (West Riding) Division, as the leading troops of 'Sickleforce'. Despite a similar lack of equipment and training, and losing the transport ship carrying their artillery and mortars, these troops advanced as far south as Lillehammer by 20 April, before falling back with the retreating Norwegians. They were reinforced on 23 April by two good infantry battalions of 15th Infantry Brigade, rushed from France but again sent into action without much of their artillery and equipment. Plans for further reinforcements and for co-operation with Mauriceforce to the north were shelved, since Åndalsnes and its nearby harbours, all little more than villages, did not have the capacity to support a third brigade.

Neither Namsos nor Åndalsnes could be held against German command of the air, and the Luftwaffe's bombs flattened both ports and the Allied supply bases there. On 16 April the cruiser HMS *Suffolk*, striking back by bombarding Sola airfield, was

---

[5] T. K. Derry, *The Campaign in Norway* (London: HMSO, 1952) page 236.
[6] Deighton, *Blitzkrieg*, page 83.

German Troops return fire with mortar and small arms while advancing through Norway. (NHB)

badly damaged by air attack. The RAF's 263 Squadron with obsolescent Gloster Gladiator biplane fighters was flown from the aircraft carrier HMS *Glorious* onto the frozen Lake Lesjaskog near Åndalsnes in order to provide some air cover. Arriving late on 24 April, over the next three days the squadron had almost all of its aircraft destroyed or rendered inoperable by the Luftwaffe and lack of fuel. Operating at the limits of its range, RAF Bomber Command flew 782 sorties during the campaign for the loss of 33 aircraft, but with little real effect on the German advance.[7]

Meanwhile the German 196th Division had also landed through Olso, and by 20 April together with 163rd Division it was pushing up the two main valleys through the mountains past Lillehammer towards Åndalsnes and Trondheim. Co-operation in this stage of the fighting between the Allies and the Norwegian forces under Major General Otto Ruge were hampered at first by mutual suspicion, but mainly by problems of off-road mobility and lack of artillery and air defences. The Germans did not have things entirely their own way: a company of paratroopers dropped at Dombås on 14 April to aid their advance was cut off and surrendered. But often with only smallarms to face tanks, artillery and bombing from the air, the Allies had no way to stop the Germans, and they had to fall back. By 29 April the first link-up had taken place between the 196th Division and the 181st Division from Trondheim. The Allied evacuation started next day from Åndalsnes, and from Namsos on 2 May. With Allied command of the sea there were few losses, other than one French and one British destroyer being sunk by the Luftwaffe on 3 May.

The best and strongest Allied forces had still not made a major attack on Narvik. It took until 24 April for operations to start, with a bombardment of the port by HMS *Warspite* and its escorts. Shortly afterwards, 24th Guards Brigade was reinforced by the 27th Demi-Brigade Chasseurs Alpins including some tanks, the 13th Demi-Brigade of the French Foreign Legion, and the Polish Carpathian Brigade, together with the Norwegian 6th Division a force of about 20,000 troops. On 28 April Lieutenant General Claude Auchinleck arrived to command Allied ground forces at Narvik under Lord Cork. But there was increasingly less justification for capturing the port. Naval bombardment had already wrecked much of Narvik and made it useless for loading iron ore. Giving up central Norway also meant that it was only a matter of time before more Luftwaffe bases were established there, and even if they captured Narvik the Allies felt that they could not hold it. Meanwhile, on 30 April, on Hitler's orders the infantry (*Gebirgsjäger*) battalions of 2nd Mountain Division were rushed to Norway and up to Trondheim area, to begin leading the advance northwards through the snow and mountains in an attempt to relieve Narvik.

On 7 May there were calls in the House of Commons for Chamberlain's resignation over the conduct of the Norway campaign, and on 10 May he stood down to let Churchill form a coalition government as Prime Minister. By another improbable co-incidence, it was also on 10 May that the Germans launched their main attack against France, Belgium and the Netherlands, with catastrophic results for the Allies as the French Army collapsed and the British were driven back to Dunkirk. Soon all forces were needed for the defence of Britain itself. On 24 May, Prime Minister Churchill and his advisers took the decision that the forces in northern Norway were to be withdrawn. But first it was decided to take Narvik, largely as a symbolic gesture to the Norwegians, and to confirm the infliction on Nazi Germany of its first major defeat of the war.

On 10 May, 24th Guards Brigade began a move south by ship to Bodø to help maintain a blocking position further south at Mo against the German advance, while the main assault on Narvik took

---

[7] John Terraine, *The Right of the Line* (London: Wordsworth, 1997) page 117.

place by French, Polish and Norwegian troops. One of the Guards' transport ships, the Polish *Chobry*, was sunk by the Luftwaffe, with considerable loss of life including the brigade staff. The British had also established a viable airfield in the snow about 80 km north of Narvik at Bardufoss, where they based 46 Squadron with modern Hawker Hurricane fighters and 263 Squadron once more re-equipped with Gloster Gladiator biplanes. Together with a few Norwegian seaplanes these pilots managed to maintain command of the air over Narvik for most of the battle.

As a further part of the attempt to slow the German advance northwards, from 17 May onwards the British landed five independent companies designated 'Scissorsforce' under Brigadier Collin Gubbins near Mo, equipped to carry out raiding and sabotage operations in small groups. Although they achieved little in Norway, these troops were the first parents of what would become the Commandos.

On 13 May the assaults on the German positions defending Narvik began under the command of the French *Général de Brigade* Antoine Béthouart, supported by a Royal Navy squadron led by the battleship HMS *Resolution*. This was the first time in the war that purpose-built landing craft were used in opposed amphibious landings. The German response was to reinforce the Narvik garrison with a series of parachute drops starting on 23 May, including troops of 1st Paratroop Regiment and two companies of 137th Mountain Regiment (from 2nd Mountain Division), hastily retrained with parachutes. These troops were badly scattered among the mountains and the fjords, but most got through to reinforce the garrison. On 28 May the Allies led by Norwegian troops captured Narvik, and the Germans were forced back into the mountains almost to the Swedish border. But rather than pursue, the Allies had already started their evacuation by sea, codenamed Operation JUNO, with the removal of forces from Bodø, and by 8 June Harstad and Narvik were also successfully evacuated. The only major loss came on 8 June when, in a highly controversial episode, the aircraft carrier HMS *Glorious* was intercepted at sea by the prowling *Scharnhorst* and the *Gneisenau*, and sunk together with two escorting destroyers. The *Scharnhorst* was damaged by a torpedo, but both German battlecruisers returned safely to port.

King Håkon and his government were transported by warship to Britain on 7 June. A few ships of the Royal Norwegian Navy also left to continue the war, most of the Norwegian merchant marine fleet escaped to be of value to the Allies, and other Norwegians served on as part of the RAF and with the British Army. Hostilities against the Germans on Norwegian soil were officially ended on 9 June with the surrender of the remaining Norwegian forces.

Naval losses on both sides in the campaign were considerable: the British lost one aircraft carrier, two cruisers and seven destroyers, the Germans three cruisers and ten destroyers, and both sides also lost several submarines. A further five large German warships were damaged, meaning that in July when Operation SEALION[8], the projected invasion of Britain, was being planned only the repaired heavy cruiser *Hipper* was seaworthy, together with two light cruisers and four destroyers. The figure for Norwegian military casualties for the campaign was 1,335; Norwegian civilian deaths were about 500, although all the major towns were bombed and several flattened by the Luftwaffe, in addition to the destruction of Narvik by the Allies. The figure for Allied casualties for the campaign was about 6,100 of which the British lost 1,869 and the French and Poles 533 in the land fighting, and the rest at sea. German casualties were 5,636 from all three services.

One of Churchill's first actions as Prime Minister was to announce the formation in June 1940 of the Commandos, recruited and trained from the Army with the co-operation of the Royal Marines; in 1942 the first Royal Marine Commando units were added.[9] Churchill also replaced the Military Co-ordination Committee with a strengthened War Cabinet overseeing all British strategy, giving himself the additional title of Minister of Defence.

[8]See next Chapter on Operation SEALION by Captain Christopher Page RN.
[9]The Army Commandos were disbanded after the war; see Hilary St. George Saunders, *The Green Beret* (London: Michael Joseph, 1949) pages 21-35 and 149-158.

The German possession of Norway together with France transformed the war at sea, as a Royal Navy that had expected to fight largely under air cover for the seas around Britain had to re-adjust to the Battle of the Atlantic. The Norwegian campaign secured for Germany the neutrality of Sweden, together with its iron ore supply, which began to flow through Narvik again in January 1941. Norway was also a source of heavy water which would have been vital had the Germans pursued their atomic bomb programme. Otherwise, there were few advantages to offset the German need to garrison Norway, especially in 1944 when Allied deception plans apparently threatening invasion kept significant German forces pinned there. Norway was liberated without fighting at the end of the war in Europe in 1945 when Germany surrendered.

Factors which led to success in Operation WESERÜBUNG

- Unified planning and command
- Command of the air
- Specialist troops and equipment
- Speed of decision and execution
- Intelligence and logistics as the basis for risk-taking

Further Reading

Ash, Bernard, *Norway 1940*, (London: Cassell, 1964)

Buckley, Christopher, *Norway: The Commandos: Dieppe*, (London: HMSO, 1951)

Derry, T. K., *The Campaign in Norway*, (London: HMSO, 1952)

Kersandy, François, *Norway 1940*, (London: Collins, 1990)

Macintyre, Donald, *Narvik*, (London: Evans Brothers, 1959)

Moulton, J. L., *The Norwegian Campaign of 1940*, (London: Eyre and Spottiswode, 1966)

Pimlott, John, *The Viking Atlas of World War II*, (London: Viking, 1995)

Biography

Dr Stephen Badsey is a senior lecturer at the Royal Military Academy Sandhurst and a Fellow of the Royal Historical Society. His most recent books include *Utah Beach* (Sutton, 2004) and *Omaha Beach* (Sutton, 2004), published as part of the *Battle Zone Normandy* series. He edited *The Gulf War Assessed* (with John Pimlott) (Sterling, 1993) and has written or contributed to over 50 more works of military history, including; *The Falklands Conflict Twenty Years On: Lessons for the Future* (Taylor and Francis, 2004); *Media and International Security* (Taylor and Francis, 2000); *Arnhem 1944: Operation Market Garden* (Osprey, 1993); *Hitler* (Harvey Books, 1994). He has also made numerous television appearances commenting on military history.

The Planned Invasion of Great Britain
Operation SEALION, July 1940

By Captain Christopher Page RN (Rtd)

Much has been written about this subject, and in the past, any attempt to highlight the Royal Navy's effect on Operation SEALION has been taken by some as somehow denigrating or devaluing the wonderful performance of the RAF in the Battle of Britain. This short account benefits from an unpublished incomplete account by the Naval Historical Branch written as a classified Battle Summary Report in 1942, which gives it immediacy not found in later works.[1]

What is sometimes forgotten is that another operation, the successful invasion of Norway in April 1940, had nevertheless resulted in serious and irreplaceable losses to the German Navy that would affect the outcome of war: In addition to 3 cruisers sunk, their 2 capital ships *Scharnhorst* and *Gneisenau* were damaged, and the latter suffered more serious hurt by a torpedo attack by the submarine *Clyde* on 20 June. Of the pocket battleships *Lutzow* was in repair after severe torpedo damage inflicted by Spearfish, *Scheer* was in refit, and Graf Spee had been scuttled at Montevideo. Other major losses included the 10 modern destroyers sunk during the 1st and 2nd Battles of Narvik. All that was left to Grand Admiral Raeder, Head of the OKM, High Command of the Navy, for operations in the early summer

of 1940 besides small craft and 2 antique pre-Dreadnoughts were the cruiser *Hipper*, the light cruisers *Nurnberg* and *Emden*, - the latter an old ship and normally used only for training – 8 destroyers, and 26 operational U-Boats, only 12 of which were fit for long range deployment. German comment on their naval casualties in the first few days of the Norwegian campaign was that 'These losses were severe, but they were approximately what Raeder had expected, and indicated what might be in store for Germany if they also tried to invade England.'[2] The Royal Navy had suffered too in Norwegian waters, but was much better able to stand the losses.

At the end of May 1940 the Germans were at the Channel coast and the British Expeditionary Force was being withdrawn from the Dunkirk perimeter by the Royal Navy. While more than 330,000 were rescued, they came home with almost no heavy equipment. Operation YELLOW, the conquest of France, initially set out in Directive No 6 on 9 October 1939, had succeeded beyond even Hitler's expectations.

Raeder was an able commander, and, shortly after the start of the war had established a small team within the Naval Staff to investigate the implications of a seaborne invasion of the UK in

the event of a successful outcome of an offensive in the west. The Naval Staff came up with two principal conditions for a major landing in Britain: first the complete destruction of the enemy's air power, and second, the annihilation or removal of any enemy forces which could threaten the area of approach of the landing forces. However, Raeder's first airing of these views to Hitler was not made until 25 May 1940, when the Fuhrer's comment was that he 'fully appreciated the exceptional difficulties of such an undertaking'.[3] No steps had been taken to construct suitable craft or pursue technical developments for the operation.

No more discussion took place in Hitler's headquarters as to whether the invasion should be prepared for another 6 weeks. Not until 2 July did the Supreme Command issue the first directive for the operation as theoretical preparations for the possible event. Again, the importance of the achievement of air superiority was emphasised.[4] On 9 July, the Naval Staff stated that, in their view, the invasion was for them only a matter of transportation, and that the invasion should take place in the area between North Foreland and the Isle of Wight. This played into the Army's hands who, on 12 July produced a general memorandum written by Jodl, the Chief of Operations at OKW,[5] who likened the invasion to a 'river crossing on a broad front'.[6]

[1]*Threat of Invasion 1940: A Rough Draft Battle Summary Report*, Paper TSD 105/43 of the Director of Tactical Torpedo and Staff Division of the Admiralty, the precursor of the Naval Historical Branch.
[2]*The Fuhrer Conferences on Naval Affairs 1940.* Copy held by the Naval Historical Branch p28. This collection of documents was among the captured German Archives. Minutes and record staff meetings between Hitler and his various commanders. The *Naval Conferences* were written up from rough notes taken by the Commander in Chief Navy or his deputy during the conferences.
[3]*Plans for the Invasion of England 1940. The German Navy's Part*, NID paper NID 24/ghs/1 of February 1947 pp1 and 2.
[4]*The Fuhrer Conferences on Naval Affairs 1940:* The record for 2 July begins: ' The Fuhrer and Supreme Command has decided: 1. That a landing in England is possible, providing that air superiority can be attained...'
[5]OKW was the OberKommando der Wehrmacht, the High Command of the German Armed Forces, but whose ethos and senior officers were all army officers.
[6]*The Breaking Wave: The German Defeat in the Summer of 1940,* by Telford Taylor, published byWeidenfeld and Nicholson , 1967

... not just a river crossing, but the crossing of a sea which is dominated by the enemy

Despite Raeder's enumeration to Hitler of the huge difficulties involved in a landing, on 15 July the Supreme Command informed the Naval Staff that the operation should be prepared to go ahead 'with surprise'[7] any time from the 15 August 1940. The resulting Directive No 16 of 16 July referred to the Navy's role as being that 'of engineers', which probably did not fill Raeder with a warm feeling.[8] His role would be to safeguard the invasion fleet, provide coastal batteries, and ensure adequate protection during the crossing. The use of this last word in the singular illustrates a certain airiness in the Fuhrer's mind about the need for continuous logistic support. The Directive also allocated the code name SEALION to the operation.

In the discussions between the Commanders in Chief of the Navy and Army in the following day the Navy gained the impression that the Army greatly underestimated the difficulties and dangers of the operation, for example in believing that the whole affair would last about one month, despite Raeder's stated view that there was a chance that the whole Operational Army could be lost in the enterprise.[9] He also flatly contradicted the Army's intention for the landings to take place in 3 separate areas, Ramsgate and Dover, Dover to the Isle of Wight, and a further group west of the Isle of Wight, as such a large sea area could not be swept of mines.

The Navy's consideration of Directive 16 is evidence of their dismay. On 19 July, their appreciation, sent to Supreme Command, was that: 'The task allotted to the Navy in Operation SEALION is out of all proportion to the Navy's strength...'. They highlighted the damage to inland waterways and harbour installations in the mainland invasion ports, unfavourable conditions in the Channel (weather, tides, currents, etc), the problem of mines, and the need for air supremacy. Raeder followed this up on 21 July pointing out that this was 'not just a river crossing, but the crossing of a sea which is dominated by the enemy...the most difficult part will be the continued reinforcement of material and stores'.[10]

During this time the Army were informing the Navy what sort of force they intended to put ashore, and on the 25 July the Naval Staff had received the news that more than 90,000 fully-equipped men, 4,500 horses, and 650 tanks would form the first wave. Further waves would have to follow in quick succession, with the second spread over 2 days consisting of another 170000 men, 57,500 horses[11] and 34,200 motor vehicles which would follow within 2 to 3 days These were regarded by the Army as the minimum numbers. The Navy's calculations to move this huge assembly resulted in estimates of 1722 barges, 471 tugs, 1161 motor boats, and 155 transport ships. Later trips would have to be carried out with vessels that had returned from the first and second waves. As a final stricture, the Army wanted the landing to be at dawn. Acrimonious disputes between the OKM and the OKW, the Headquarters of the Army ensued over the question of a broad or narrow front, with OKM wishing to restrict the assault beaches to two small strips near Dover and Beachy Head, while the Army clung to its desire for an area stretching from Ramsgate to Lyme Regis. On 31 July, Raeder obtained Hitler's agreement that the earliest date for the landing was 15 September, and that the narrow front should be used for the planning. Notwithstanding what Raeder thought had been agreed, the very next day the Supreme Command put out a new note stating that preparations should continue 'on the previously planned wide scope'.[12]

---

[7]*GC and CS Naval History, vol XIX, Western Europe and the Baltic,* written by Lieutenant Commander LA Griffiths RNVR p41, Copy No 23 is held in the NHB, and records that in the original German document, an exclamation mark appears in parenthesis after this word. It is interesting that this GC and CS history interprets Raeder's initiation of invasion plans in the autumn of 1939 as evidence that the OKM were proponents of such action. The opinion of the Naval Intelligence Department differs and states that the Grand Admiral was taking sensible precautions against being surprised by the Supreme Command in the future. The balance of evidence favours the latter view, however, it is possible that the OKM, before being confronted with the realities of their own relative maritime weakness, may have been a little optimistic in their own abilities in the early stages of the war.

[8]*The Fuhrer Naval Conferences: Directive No 16, Preparation for the Invasion of England dated 16 July 1940.* Copy held by the Naval Historical Branch, p67

[9]*Plans for the Invasion of England 1940.* op cit p8, also confirmed in *The War Diary of the German Naval Staff, Operations Division,* Part A Volume 2, entry for the 18 July 1940.

[10]*Fuhrer Naval Conferences* op cit p72,

[11]Throughout the war, the German Army relied on horse drawn transport to a much greater degree than the British and American Armies

[12]*Fuhrer Directives and other Top Level Directives of the German Armed Forces 1939-1941:* Document WFA/Abt. L I Nr.33189/40 g.K.Chefs dated 1 August 1940, signed by Keitel, Chief of Staff, Armed Forces High Command, P 112, Copy held in NHB. The NID post-war view, having interviewed the surviving main players in the drama, was that Keitel and Jodl had managed to persuade the Fuhrer that the broad front should still be planned.

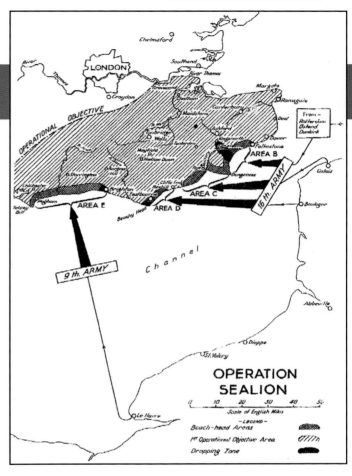

Raeder was not to be rail-roaded and, after nearly a fortnight of deadlock, Hitler had to be asked to decide: at the conference of 13 August Raeder asked for a final decision on the width of the invasion front, repeating his emphasis that operation SEALION should only be attempted 'as a last resort if Britain cannot be made to sue for peace in any other way'.[13]

In the end a compromise was reached, and by 3 September the final decisions were made: the Lyme Bay landing was abandoned. The earliest date for the assault was by now 21 September. The areas around Deal and South Foreland to Folkestone had been successfully rejected by the Navy, as the beaches were unsuitable, so the main landings would be on a narrow front in four areas: Folkestone to Dungeness, landing area B, 14 miles in length, using transports from Rotterdam, Ostend and Dunkirk; Dungeness to Cliffsend, landing area C, 11 miles supplied from Calais; Bexhill to Beachy Head, landing area D, 7 miles, transported from Boulogne; and Brighton to Selsey Bill, landing area E, from Le Havre consisting of a strong contingent of 4-5000 men would also be landed without heavy arms or heavy equipment by motorboats and motor sailing vessels. The resupply of this force would be from the group landed in area D and would be accomplished by road, more than 20 miles away. The first operational objective would be a line from Southampton to the mouth of the Thames. The available heavy ships, *Scheer* and *Hipper* would be sailed on to attempt to occupy RN units by a diversionary forays into northern waters, and the remaining light cruisers would escort a convoy feinting towards the north east coast between Aberdeen and Newcastle. The total numbers of German Navy vessels available for the escort of the 4 invasion forces were 2 Destroyer Flotillas (10 ships), 4 Torpedo Boat Flotillas, (20 ships), 40 –50 Motor Torpedo Boats, and up to 200 Motor Minesweepers. There was nothing else.

Loading of material would start on S minus 10, and troops S minus 3.[14] The invasion force would sail on S minus1.[15] The Germans hoped to land two consecutive echelons of 6 Divisions each within 6 days.

The Germans estimated that the British could muster about 20 divisions that were completely trained, but that their artillery was at about 50% strength. They assessed the coastal defences were strong in parts. Despite the predicted strength of the opposition, the Supreme Command went ahead with the assembly of the necessary transport for the invasion forces. Some 500 tugs of over 250 horsepower were requisitioned, 2000 barges from the Rhine and Holland, 140 merchant vessel transports and hundred of smaller motorboats. The effect of the withdrawal so much maritime and riverine transport proved a major blow to the German economy, but by 4 September the Naval Staff reported that they had achieved most of the requirement. On 6 September the Naval Staff had accepted the Admiral Commanding U Boats' proposals for submarine deployments, including 15 boats in the western English Channel, 6 small boats in the southern North Sea, 4 off the Pentland Firth, and 2 in English coastal waters. The minelaying operations to protect the flanks of the operating area would be complete by 19 September.[16]

The landings would rely on surprise, although how this was to be achieved was not stated, and would be supported by coastal force guns and army heavy artillery totalling about 100 pieces. The Naval Staff War Diary of 15 July had recorded: 'the Head of the Naval Ordnance Office again points out that it is impossible to carry out the artillery task on the Flanders coastline: long

[13]*Fuhrer Naval Conferences op cit p82*, Raeder's report to the Fuhrer, on 13 August 1940
[14]S Day was the code allocated to the day of the invasion
[15]*Fuhrer Naval Conferences p88*, entry for 3 September 1940
[16]*Plans for the Invasion of England 1940. The German Navy's Part*, NID paper NID 24/ghs/1 of February 1947 pp47 and 48

Invasion barges on the Rhine. (TNA)

Aerial photograph showing a concentration of 67 invasion barges berthed at the Quay Chazny and Basin Loubet in Boulogne Harbour. (TNA)

long range artillery cannot provide effective fire cover for a landing on the enemy coast

range artillery cannot provide effective fire cover for a landing on the enemy coast'.[17]

On 13 September, the day before a preliminary decision was due to be made by the Supreme Command on the invasion, Raeder's personal assessment was that 'The present air situation does not provide conditions for carrying out the operation...'[18] Hitler agreed that the air supremacy had not been achieved, but said that the air attacks had been very effective. Faced with growing evidence that Fighter Command remained far from defeated, and that the invasion transports were suffering constant attacks by the RAF,[19] and taking into account the decreasing chance of fine weather, SEALION was postponed until 27 September at the earliest, and on 17 September, the famous decision was recorded in the War Diary that 'The enemy air force is still by no means defeated. The Fuhrer therefore decides to postpone SEALION indefinitely.'[20] On the 9 January 1941 Hitler made the formal decision to abandon preparations for Operation SEALION.

German preparations were not, however, taking place in a vacuum. The United Kingdom, the target of their potential invasion was making plans to counter any such attempt.

From the time of the German onslaught in the west, the Admiralty's priority initially concentrated on the possession and retention of suitable ports. In May 1940 the coastline as a whole was largely unprotected. The initial fear in London was that of a sudden large-scale raid: The Chiefs of Staff admitted that such action might not be totally prevented by the RN and the RAF. This transient threat passed quickly and the considerations turned to a full invasion. On 16 July all Home Fleet cruisers and destroyers were ordered to be at half an hours' notice. One of the lessons learned from the Norwegian campaign was that of German attacks by small coasters or fishing vessels on small ports. The first steps were therefore taken to provide for port defences, and if these failed, by the use of blockships and demolition charges. Open beaches would be defended by guns, obstructions and mines. Also at the end of May 1940, the Coast Guard was taken over by the Admiralty. The scale of the problem confronting the Chiefs of Staff resulted in immobilisation precautions being put in place for ports in stages from Aberdeen to Swanage, certain ports in Northern Ireland, then round Land's End as far north as Holyhead on the west coast. By August, 77 ports had been fitted with additional defences including mines, fixed torpedo tubes, nets - as an anti-motor boat device, blockships and

---

[17]My emphasis: Quoted in *Operation Sealion*, by Ronald Wheatley, published by OUP in 1957

[18]*Fuhrer Naval Conferences* p98, entry for 14 September 1940

[19]It was estimated that, by 21 September, 21 of the 167 Steamships, 214 of the 1697 barges, and 5 of the 360 tugs had been lost or damaged, as had an unknown number of the 100 coastal motor vessels and 1200 motor boats. *GC and CS Naval History, vol XIX, Western Europe and the Baltic*, op cit p53. In September, a further 12% of the total assault shipping was lost.

[20]*Fuhrer Naval Conferences* p101, entry for 14 September 1940

DUNKIRK

BARGES — SUNK AND DAMAGED.

COMPLETELY DEMOLISHED BUILDINGS

A

Bombing results 19/9/40. 82 Squadron

Aerial reconnaissance photograph revealing German invasion barges at Dunkirk. (TNA)

demolition charges. The most likely period for the invasion was assessed by the Combined Services Intelligence Committee as falling between 13 September and 24 October, after a steady build-up of invasion ships and barges at the various assembly ports. Intelligence was received from the British Ambassador in Washington on 21st that the invasion was timed for the afternoon of 22 September.[21] The landing did not, of course, materialise, but British forces remained at a very high state of readiness until 24 October, when the Home Fleet reverted to normal notice for steam.

From early in June, the Admiralty had been concerned at the possibility of invasion. At the time they were still embroiled in Norway, and were uncertain about the operational status of major German warships, in particular *Scharnhorst* and *Gneisenau*. Nevertheless, the Admiralty's plans were built on the 'experience of centuries',[22] an excellent example of the applicability of naval history to current events. Despite the possibilities of attacks as far afield as Ireland, it was expected that any invasion would be concentrated at the shortest route – across the Channel. The Admiralty preferred to base their action on attacking the German forces before they deployed, and expected that there would be heavy losses in defeating the landings, but defeated they would be. The problem would be dealt with by the time-honoured

method set out by Sir Julian Corbett: 'we keep a hold on it [the invasion army], firstly by flotilla blockade and defence stiffened as circumstances may dictate by higher units, and secondly by battle fleet cover. It is on the flotilla hold that the whole system is built up.'[23] Anti-invasion measures would be based on obtaining as much warning as possible: RAF photo-reconnaissance was backed with the employment of 700 armed patrolling vessels of which 2-300 were always at sea in the area between the Wash and Newhaven. 25 fast minesweepers and 140 minesweeping trawlers kept a swept channel around the threatened coast. Attacks by naval vessels and the RAF on the invasion ports would be made. If and when the enemy was at sea aggressive action was the order of the day. Typical anti-invasion orders stressed the need for attacking vessels to concentrate on the transports rather than the warships, using depth charges among enemy troop carriers if possible. Admiral James', CinC Portsmouth, injunction to his officers was to repeat Nelson's dictum that 'no

captain can do very wrong if he places his ship alongside that of an enemy'.[24]

To deal with the enemy on passage, the Admiralty would rely on a striking force based on a core of about 36 destroyers, supported by cruisers, all based in the area from Portsmouth to the Humber. 17 corvettes, 17 sloops and about 15 MTBs were also in the area of greatest threat, and 35 submarines were in UK waters. This immediate reaction force was backed by significant numbers of ships, including battleships, cruisers, and aircraft carriers in Plymouth, Rosyth, and on the Clyde, most of which could be in the operational area within 24 hours. The question of whether capital ships should form part of the anti-

[21]*Threat of Invasion 1940 op cit p33*

[22]*The War at Sea* by Captain Stephen Roskill, Volume 1 p248 published by HMSO in 1954.

[23]*Some Principles of Maritime Strategy,* by JS Corbett, Published by Longmans, Green and Co in 1911, p245

[24]*Anti-Invasion Operation Order for Portsmouth Command, Operation JF October 1940.* quoted as Appendix 12 in *Defence Plans of the United Kingdom: 1939-1945,* compiled by Captain GC Wynne, of the Cabinet Office Historical Section in 1948. Copy No 8 of the draft is held in the Naval Historical Branch

German troops undertaking an amphibious exercise. (NHB)

even after a successful landing, the Army ashore would need to be resupplied

invasion units was firmly resisted by the CinC Home Fleet, Admiral Forbes. He was confident that no invasion would take place unless and until the Luftwaffe had achieved air superiority. His heavy ships would be held back to deal with their German equivalents. Forbes maintained that 'invasion is to all intents impossible without local control of the sea'.[25] He went on to dismiss any comparison of the German invasion of Norway with a similar attempt on the UK, and wryly reminded the Admiralty that it had taken us 24000 men just to capture Narvik in the face of only 2-3000 Germans ashore who had practically no tanks and guns. He pointed out that the Dunkirk evacuations illustrated that, despite lack of air superiority, the Royal Navy still maintained command of the sea. While not ruling out an irrational operation (as he saw it) to cross the Channel in the teeth of Royal Navy opposition, CinC HF added 'we should welcome the attempt as being an excellent opportunity to inflict a defeat on the enemy but we should not deflect our forces and energies into purely defensive measures to guard against it'.[26]

Forbes' sanguine view was not wholly shared by the Admiralty or some of the naval commanders nearer the possible invasion: The Admiralty, despite their confidence in the ability of the Royal Navy to defeat any invasion attempt, were always cautious enough to say that they could not guarantee that a surprise landing would not be made; Admiral Drax at the Nore on 22 September was apprehensive enough to insist on the need to keep the ships of the 18th Cruiser Squadron at Sheerness or Southend.[27]

Concern lingered on in Britain for some time after 1940 about the possibility of a German invasion: a document produced by the General Staff in April 1941 even considered and dismissed the utility of the existing Channel Tunnel workings as a means of getting across the Channel.[28] By then, the enemy had his hands more than full in other theatres.

Opinions are divided about whether the operation was ever a serious operation of war. In a war game held at The Staff College at Camberley in the 1970s, a distinguished group of players concluded that a successful landing could have occurred, but that the invasion would fail for reasons lack of follow up support because of lack of command of the sea.[29] Herein lies the key the German dilemma: even after a successful landing, the Army ashore would need to be resupplied, and it was this supply that was even more difficult than the landing itself.

A small German craft being landed during troop exercises. (NHB)

[25] Letter from CinC Home Fleet to Secretary of the Admiralty, dated 4 Jun 1940 on the subject of an invasion of the United Kingdom by the armed forces of Germany. Copy in NHB
[26] ibid
[27] Quoted in Roskill, op cit p 258
[28] National Archive WO208/2969 paragraph 19 *Notes on German Preparations for Invasion of the United Kingdom*. Prepared by the General Staff, January 1942.
[29] *Operation Sea Lion* edited by Richard Cox, published by Thornton Cox in 1974

A German author contends that the whole game was based on a false premise, 'since SEALION was never planned to be implemented'. Hitler only ever wanted it to be a threat.[30] A respected British commentator assessed that the invasion could have succeeded if it had taken place in the middle of July.[31] However, Macksey's account assumes an unbelievably feeble performance by all the various units of the Royal Navy in failing to intercept any of the transports or affecting the resupply of the landed German troops, together with an equally poor showing by the RAF.

The Dunkirk operation showed that ships could still be effective even in conditions where there was limited air cover, while the battle around Crete only a few months later in May 1941 demonstrated that, even in the complete absence of supporting air power, not one enemy soldier was put ashore on that island from the sea; naval losses were high, but not crippling. There would have been no such absence of air power in UK waters in 1940. Even had the RAF been defeated prior to the invasion. Enough aircraft would have remained operating from more westerly airfields to have played their part in any operation as desperate as this.

The prospect of virtually unarmed transports, motor boats, and hundreds of Rhine barges packed with troops coming under attack from just one destroyer, let alone several, hardly bears contemplation. In 1944, in the run up to D Day, a troop convoy was intercepted at night by German E boats off Slapton Sands in Devon. In the action that followed, 749 soldiers and sailors were killed. Five and a half miles off Cherbourg on Christmas Eve of the same year, the fast Belgian transport *Leopoldville*, escorted by destroyers, and carrying American soldiers was torpedoed: about 800 died. The German transports for SEALION were slow – the barges were to be towed at 4 knots – and the phrase 'sitting ducks' comes horrifically to mind.

In addition, these same transports and barges – or their survivors – would immediately have to begin the return journey to pick up the next wave of troops horses and material, and run the gauntlet again, and possibly repeatedly, only this time against an alert defence that by this time would have been greatly reinforced by units from Rosyth, Portsmouth and Plymouth. The assessment of Raeder in July therefore, that the enterprise risked the loss of the whole of the operational army, seems to be appropriate.

It is now a matter of historical fact that the operation that might be thought to be the inverse of Operation SEALION, the Allied invasion of Europe that took place four years later, revealed the scale of effort required to effect as successful seaborne assault on a well-organised, determined enemy. This huge undertaking took three years to plan. Even with complete command of the sea and air, years to plan, specialist assault craft, and enormous logistic support measures, the success of Operation NEPTUNE, the Normandy invasion, was far from inevitable.

In common with much of their prosecution of the Second World War, the Germans had failed to understand or learn the lessons of seapower. After the war, the German Admiral Weichold wrote a history of the German Navy in the Second World War, in which he concluded: 'In the greatest World War of all time, which depended for its outcome on issues determined at sea, the sea and its vast open spaces were regarded by the German Command as of secondary importance'. They never established a single operational command structure for Operation SEALION: the Navy was offended by the suggestion that the affair was merely like the crossing of a broad river, for which they would fulfil the function of a transport organisation, while they believed that there was no stomach for the fight in the Luftwaffe, who believed that the War could be won by air power alone without the need for an invasion of Britain. Raeder also believed that the Army had a greatly underestimated view of the difficulties and dangers of invading the United Kingdom.

As a summary, the inescapable conclusion is that Operation SEALION was never a practical proposition: it was something for which the enemy had not planned or organised early enough, nor did they put into place the necessary structures and resources to give the operation a fair chance of success. Or in the words of an American writer, 'the [German] generals of the air and the ground, if not the admirals of the sea, were also somnolent, lackadaisical, or blind to the strategic imperatives. By the time

---

[30] *Invasion of England 1940* by Peter Schenk, published by Conway in 1990, p.355
[31] *Invasion: The German Invasion of England July 1940,* by Kenneth Macksey, published by Arms and Armour Press in 1980

By the time everyone woke up, it was already too late to mount an invasion of Britain with any reasonable prospect of success.

everyone woke up, it was already too late to mount an invasion of Britain with any reasonable prospect of success.'[32]

Notwithstanding the lack of achievement of one of the necessary conditions for the invasion, the achievement of air superiority as a result of their defeat in the Battle of Britain, the other necessary and sufficient condition, that of gaining command of the sea would never have been satisfied.

In a post war conversation, Raeder explained that the reason for the failure of SEALION was the inability to obtain 'Command of the Sea, for lack of which Napoleon's invasion plans came to nothing in 1805'. Even had the Army been landed without excessive losses, the Grand Admiral concluded that: 'In the face of an all-powerful sea opponent – resolute and prepared for great sacrifices – it could not be assumed that the Luftwaffe alone - largely dependent on the weather – would succeed in permanently preventing the enemy's naval forces from disorganising supplies.'[33]

Further Reading

Barnett, Correlli, *Engage the Enemy More Closely: The Royal Navy in the Second World War*, (New York: Norton, 1991)

Collier, Basil, *The Defence of the United Kingdom,* (London: HMSO, 1957) Chapter XI

Cox, Richard, Ed., *Operation Sealion*, (London: Thornton Cox, 1974)

Fleming, Peter, *Invasion 1940: An Account of the German Preparations and the British Counter-measures,* (London: Rupert Hart-Davis, 1957)

Hattendorf, John B., *The Limitations of Military Power,* (Basingstoke: Macmillan, 1990)

Horne, Alistair, *To Lose a Battle: France, 1940,* (London: Macmillan, 1969)

Kieser. Egbert, *Hitler on the Doorstep. Operation "Sea Lion": the German Plan to Invade Britain, 1940,* (London: Arms and Armour, 1997)

Schenk, Peter, *Invasion of England 1940: The Planning of Operation Sealion,* (London: Conway, 1990)

Warner, Philip, *Invasion Road,* (London: Cassell, 1980)

Wheatley, Ronald, *Operation Sea Lion: German Plans for the Invasion of England 1939-1942,* (Oxford: Clarendon Press, 1958)

Biography

Captain Christopher Page RN took up the post of Head of the Naval Historical Branch of the Naval Staff of the Ministry of Defence in December 1999 after retiring from the Royal Navy following 37 years service. He specialised in Mechanical Engineering, and his sea service included aircraft carriers, frigates, a minesweeper, BRISTOL, and the Royal Yacht BRITANNIA. Ashore, his service included Portsmouth Dockyard; the Engineering Training School, HMS SULTAN; Director General Ships; The Head of Defence Studies in the MOD; Executive Officer of HMS HERON, the Royal Naval Air Station at Yeovilton; and on the staff of the UK Delegation to NATO as the Deputy Military Delegate to the Western European Union. He has been a Fellow of the Institution of Mechanical Engineers since 1991. In 1992 he gained his MA in War Studies from King's College, London. He is the author of *Command in the Royal Naval Division*, published in 1999, and has delivered many other talks, articles and chapters on various topics of naval and military history in books and journals. He is a member of the Western Front and Gallipoli Associations, the British Commission for Military History, and the Navy Records Society.

[32]*The Breaking Wave: The German Defeat in the Summer of 1940,* by Telford Taylor, published by Weidenfeld and Nicholson in 1967
[33]*Plans for the Invasion of England 1940. The German Navy's Part:* p52

Commando Raids at Lofoten and Vaagso
Operations CLAYMORE, GAUNTLET, ANKLET & ARCHERY, 1941

By Mr Philip D Grove

Background to the Raids

In the modern world the word 'Commando' has become synonymous with Britain's sea soldiers, the Royal Marines. Yet British 'Commandos' as a fighting force only officially originated in the dark days of 1940, and then most were army not naval personnel. However, they went on to carve a vital role for themselves and become invaluable in the war against Nazi Germany, fascist Italy and Imperial Japan.

In reality, however, British 'Commando' units had existed in all but name during the First World War. Although even then the true term and type of forces involved really began in the land operations during the Boer War in South Africa (1899-1902) where groups of Boers called 'Kommandos' would strike swiftly and suddenly at the British army. These Boer Kommandos would be the real inspiration behind the British Commando operations of the Second World War. Although the ability to strike swiftly and suddenly from the sea had been realised and employed by British Vice Admiral Roger Keyes in the First World War. Keyes had been the driving force behind Royal Marine forces used to raid German submarine bases, most notably against Zeebrugge on Saint George's Day, 1918[1]. Twenty years later, after two decades of amphibious neglect, the Commando idea was resurrected in June 1940 as a response to Prime Minister Winston Churchill's aim of unleashing 'a vigorous enterprising and ceaseless offensive against the whole German occupied coastline, leaving a trail of German corpses behind'. These potentially bloody hit and run raids would not just rekindle an offensive spirit within the British armed forces, they would also act to inspire confidence within the British public who in the summer of 1940 faced almost certain invasion by Nazi Germany. In July 1940, following a handful of commando reconnaissance raids against German occupied Europe, Admiral Keyes, of Zeebrugge fame, was confirmed as the head of the newly formed Combined Operations. This was the first attempt to create a tri-service body and its rationale was the combined raid against Europe. However, this novel organisation would have to wait until the Vaagso Raid in December 1941 for its first true tri-service combined operation. In the meantime the assault forces would go through a number of structural and title transformations, beginning life as Commandos before becoming Independent Companies, and then Special Service troops, before finally being renamed once more Commandos in March 1941.

For most of 1940 and the early part of 1941 the Commandos – increasingly army in composition – found themselves involved with training and familiarisation with new equipment. All the time the Commandos and their senior officers, men such as Lieutenant Colonel Charles Newman, CO of No.2 Commando and Lieutenant Colonel John Durnford-Slater, CO of No.3 Commando, were creating and instilling a new ethos of offensive thought and action, far more radical than anything then experienced within British armed forces. Yet this offensive spirit was denied any real outlet on the continent until the Norwegian raids of 1941 against Lofoten and Vaagso.

The First Lofoten Raid

The first Commando raid against the Lofoten Islands, off the coast of Norway, took place on the 3rd of March 1941. The raid, Operation CLAYMORE, was hugely important in giving a much needed boost to the flagging morale within the ranks of the Commandos following their months of 'inactivity'. Additionally, the country received the news as a well needed fillip as information concerning the raid became public. In fact the Commandos first major raid was seen by many as a great success, as it saw a large amount of destruction of German ships and herring and cod oil factories. Moreover, it gave free passage to the UK to large numbers of Norwegian volunteers, not to mention German and Quisling prisoners.

The Lofoten Islands (Svolvær and Stamsund) off the Norwegian coast are about 100 miles north of the Arctic Circle. In appearance and size they resemble the Outer Hebrides off the north-west coast of Scotland, which was useful as many of the men involved in the raid had trained in Scotland. The raid involved 'joint' naval and land forces. Two assault ships were employed, HMS *Queen Emma* (under Commander Kershaw) and the *Princess Beatrix* (under Commander Brunton). Both were converted cross channel ferries. Their lifeboats had been replaced with 6 LCAs a piece and additionally they carried two

[1]See Chapter IV By Dr Harry Dickinson

larger LCMs (each able to carry 70 troops). On board were No 3 & 4 Commandos. The assault force was escorted across the North Sea by the battleships HMS *King George V* and *Nelson*, a pair of cruisers and 5 destroyers. But for their final move towards the islands off Norway their escort was made up of only the 5 destroyers, HMS *Bedouin, Eskimo, Legion, Somali* and *Tartar*, under the command of Captain C Calson, and one submarine for final passage guidance.

The assault force flotilla originally left Scapa Flow in the Orkney's on 21 February, under the command of Brigadier Haydon. The initial destination was the Faroe Islands for final training. It was here that No. 3 and 4 Special Services Battalions reverted to No. 4 (Lieutenant Colonel Lister) and No. 3 Commando respectively. This was part of a much wider re-organisation of Special Forces which was completed by mid March 1941. On 1 March 500 commandos of No.3 and No.4 Commando, engineers for demolition purposes together with 50 Free Norwegian soldiers and sailors acting in the planning, guide and interpreter roles set off for the Norwegian coast.

The weather was foul on the three-day voyage and the cramped living conditions were made worse by the seasickness suffered by most on board. The two 'assault ships' had not been designed with the arctic sea conditions in mind, and were far from suitable for this enterprise. Nonetheless, the flotilla arrived off the Lofoten Islands in the early hours of 3 March as planned. As they boarded the landing craft, for four separate destinations

(No.3 Cdo to Stamsund and Hennigsvaer, with No.4 Cdo to Brettesnes and Svolvaer), the Commandos could see the lights of their targets in the distance. Obviously the Germans had not been expecting any raid. Surprise had been achieved. But they did experience one or two problems with the intense cold, as sea spray caused ice to form on the Commando's protective clothing, which all realised quickly was not thick enough. Additionally, the landings were more abrupt than usual as their

assault craft lowered their ramps onto solid ice. Additionally, it was impossible for the destroyers to escort the landing craft to the shore due to the terrain and ice. This forced the initial landing craft to act in the scout role in order to avoid all the craft being targeted simultaneously by any alert German defences.

However, the surprise was indeed complete. Locals going to work initially assumed that the sea borne activity was a German training exercise, but belated 'heil Hitlers' were soon replaced with cheering, hot coffee and gifts given to the Commandos. Very quickly German soldiers, officials and collaborators were rounded up and before long fish oil factories, military establishments and ships in the harbour were systematically blown up.

> ### belated 'heil Hitlers' were soon replaced with cheering, hot coffee and gifts given to the Commandos.

The high spirits of the Commandos was never in doubt, even in battle as Durnford Slater recounted in his autobiography, when relaying the case of Second Lieutenant R L Wills. The Second Lieutenant went as far as sending a telegram from the post office in Stamsund to Adolf Hitler in Berlin saying, 'You said in your last speech German troops would meet the British wherever they landed. Where are your troops?' Equally novel and humorous was the bus ride taken by Lord Lovat and some of his men to a nearby German seaplane base. The commander of the base later complained about the 'unwarlike' behaviour of the Commandos and undertook to report accordingly to Hitler. Lovat, besides taking the bus should not have been there at all as he had started the mission on board the *Princess Beatrix* as only an observer, but had then joined No.4 Commando en route to the islands becoming a troop commander before arrival off Lofoten.

British troops advance during the Lofoten Islands Raid. (TNA)

By midday on 3 March the demolition work had been completed. As Durnford-Slater wrote, 'great billowing funnels of smoke were rising into the sky. There was the smell of burning oil mingled with that of fish'. The charges had been set to cause maximum damage to the economic targets but with minimal impact on the surrounding civilian areas. Precision strike and avoidance of collateral damage were additional factors within this raid, and these were successfully achieved.

By 1400 the assault flotilla had left on the return journey to Scapa Flow, arriving back 48 hours later. There had been no significant resistance, bar one German armed trawler, the *Krebbs*, quickly dispatched by HMS *Somali*. The ease of the operation was for some Commandos a disappointment considering their training and their 'real' objective of hitting German forces. However, they had destroyed 11 factories, 800,000 gallons of oil and five ships (one of which was actually set ablaze by HMS *Tartar*). Additionally, they had acquired 315 volunteers for the Free Norwegian forces in Britain, but also captured 60 Quislings

Below: A map from a Combined Operations publication produced in 1943 giving the first outline of the raids. (NHB)

and 225 German prisoners (mostly merchant seamen). Moreover, the English manager of Allen and Hanbury, a chemist, who had been caught up in Germany's invasion of Norway in April 1940 was finally able to come home. All of this had been achieved at a price of one accidental self-inflicted wound to an officer's thigh! Any need for the 48 hours worth of rations each man carried in case the escorting destroyers were withdrawn suddenly were not required. None of the potential mishaps expected arose. One more Commando success not reported at the time was the recovery, from *Krebbs*, of a set of spare rotors for the Enigma coding machine. These were dispatched to Bletchley Park where they were of great use.

The months prior to this raid had been a frustrating time for the Commandos. They had volunteered in 1940 for hazardous duties at a dark time for the nation but were left with little to do, bar train and anti-invasion patrols. There were known disagreements at the highest levels concerning how these forces should be used and organised. Morale was thus understandably at a low ebb, but not during the mission. Although this raid was virtually unopposed it demonstrated what could be achieved by a relatively small force trained for the purpose of raiding and with the key element of surprise. The success of the raid was a fillip to morale in some quarters and was trumpeted by the press and public alike. Even the German press praised – if grudgingly – the raid for its secrecy and success. Yet there were some amongst

the Commandos themselves, who were disappointed and disillusioned that the hazardous duties they had volunteered and trained for, had been used for what seemed trivial purposes.

The aim, however, was an important one. The raid had been inspired by a number of factors. It was of course a demonstration to the doubters of the Commando capability by Admiral Keyes. There was also a real desire to hit back at Germany - Churchill's decree - and specifically it was a mission set by the Ministry of Economic Warfare which realised the importance of the Lofoten Islands to the German war effort. The primary targets were Norwegian fish oil factories. Their destruction would be a blow to German glycerine production as it employed herring oil in the process. As James Dunning wrote, 'following their conquest of Norway and having taken over the islands, the Nazis had established the laboratories, factories and storage tanks to process fish oil and export it back to Germany for a variety of uses, including the manufacture of nitro-glycerine for high explosives'. Dunning was one of the original volunteers of No.4 Commando and saw the objectives of CLAYMORE as 'simple and clear-cut, namely to deny the Nazis any further supplies of the fish oil by destroying the factories, storage tanks and the shipping used to export it to Germany. Further objectives were to capture Germans employed on the ships, enemy garrison troops and Norwegian Quislings, to bring back volunteers for the Free Norwegian Forces in Britain, and finally, to obtain useful military, naval and economic intelligence information'. All of theses were achieved.

*Director of Combined Operations
Vice Admiral Sir Roger Keyes. (NHB)*

*Keyes' successor, Vice Admiral
Lord Louis Mountbatten Chief of
Combined Operations. (NHB)*

**I want you to start a programme of raids...
so as to keep the enemy coastline on the alert
from the North Cape to the Bay of Biscay**

Thus the raid was indeed a great success, but it did little to sway the opponents of the Commando idea. The Commando forces would have to wait another nine months before their potential was finally recognised and accepted. That said during the first Lofoten raid all of the pre-requisites (bar the use of air power) for a successful 'Commando raid' were present. An aim, if not grand in stature, was selected, and it was carried through to conclusion, with a high level of morale throughout the operation. The morale of the forces involved was never in doubt, which is all the more impressive as they were being dispatched to the enemy coast, outside the range of air power, with limited firepower of their own, facing an enemy with an undetermined capability. This unknown quantity forced the two commanding officers of No.3 Cdo and No.4 Cdo to create very concise and clear, yet flexible, operational orders for their men whilst in transit to Lofoten. This style of concise but flexible planning would figure strongly in succeeding missions. Another crucial facet for the success of this operation was the level of secrecy behind the mission. The secrecy behind the Lofoten operation and the surprise achieved was total, forcing the Germans - after the event - to strengthen the garrison in Norway. Moreover the success could also be seen to lie in the co-operation between the land and naval forces involved. This was highly commendable, particularly with its very recent existence - less than 12 months. Quite obviously, the seeds for combined operations in the European theatre had been sown, but they would have to wait a few months before the real blossoming began.

The Spitzbergen Raid

Between the first (March) and second (December) raids against the Lofoten Islands there were no large scale Commando raids. However, there was another type of raid against Norway - Operation GAUNTLET. This raid took place between the 28 August and 2 September, 1941, with Spitzbergen (Svalbard) & Bear Island being the targets. This was not a Commando raid as the participating troops - some 1,500 - were mostly Canadian infantry led by Brigadier A E Potts; the naval force escorting the assault units was led by Rear Admiral P Vian. However, the assault force had been trained in 'amphibious warfare'. The aim of the operation was to destroy the coal mines on Svalbard to prevent them falling into German hands, to evacuate the 2,000 Soviet miners there to Archangel in Northern Russia and a further 800 Norwegians to Great Britain. More than 400,000 tons of coal and a further 250,000 gallons of oil were set alight. The radio and weather installations on Bear Island were also destroyed and the population evacuated.

Successful as the raid was, it created a problem for the Commandos, as it seemed to demonstrate to elements of the services that the Commando, and his special talents, were not required. In truth the Canadians had spent a considerable time at the Commando Training Centre in Scotland and could not be seen as 'normal' infantry. Partly, as a response to this and the months of active interference with and denigration of his forces by elements of the British military hierarchy, Admiral Keyes publicly resigned, and made a damning statement in Parliament

concerning the conduct of the war by senior officials in Whitehall. 'After 15 months experience as Director of Combined Operations, and having been frustrated in every worthwhile offensive action I have to undertake, I must fully endorse the Prime Minister's comments on the strength of the negative power which controls the war machine in Whitehall'.

His replacement on 27 October 1941 as Director of Combined Operations was Lord Louis Mountbatten. His unique position as a war hero and cousin to the King enabled Mountbatten to manoeuvre, cajole and understand inter-service relationships in a way that Keyes could only dream about. The result was a determination and the ability to take the war to Germany in the way Churchill had initially foreseen. According to Bernard Fergusson when Churchill briefed Mountbatten it was simple and to the point, 'I want you to succeed Roger Keyes in charge of Combined Operations. Up to now there have been hardly any Commando raids. I want you to start a programme of raids... so as to keep the enemy coastline on the alert from the North Cape to the Bay of Biscay'. Mountbatten's first operation was to be the raid against Vaagso, with a diversionary raid against Lofoten. Vaagso according to Peter Young has come to be seen as a 'minor classic of amphibious warfare, a raid which, despite the multitudinous accidents inseparable from warfare, actually went according to plan, in that all the groups into which the force was divided carried out their assigned tasks'. Interestingly, however, Mountbatten initially seemed a little dubious to the possible success of the Vaagso raid, until Durnford-Slater put his mind at rest following

LCA's returning to ship after the Raid on the Lofoten Islands. (TNA)

Anti-aircraft Bren gunners guarding landing craft in the Lofoten Islands. (TNA)

feints and major raids were now a legitimate tactic to divert attention and confuse the enemy

their preliminary briefing. From then on the Director of Combined Operations became a wholehearted supporter. However, before Vaagso came the second Lofoten raid.

The Second Lofoten Raid

Operation ANKLET, was the second Commando strike against the Lofoten Islands, and was conceived as a diversion in support of the much larger action against Vaagso, further south along the Norwegian coast. The Lofoten Islands had again been selected as a relatively safe target and one that would provide a measure of destruction against the Norwegian fish factories just getting back into production following the first Commando raid in March.

Since the first Lofoten raid earlier in the year the German forces in Norway had been strengthened, including their air and coastal units. The Germans (and British) had realised that feints and major raids were now a legitimate tactic to divert attention and confuse the enemy. Additionally, for the British the raids could promote the idea that Norway was a serious option for the launch of an invasion of mainland Europe from the UK. Some 300 men from No. 12 Commando and a number from

the Free Norwegian Army under the command of Lieutenant-Colonel S.S. Harrison landed at 0600 on 26 December. The planners had timed the raid in the expectation that the German garrison would be caught off guard following their Christmas celebrations of the previous day.

Still precautions would be needed. The assault ship had been camouflaged white for the venture and the Commandos were wearing white hooded overalls. The landings were unopposed as the Commandos entered the two harbours on the westerly island of Moskenesoy. The towns of Reine and Moskenes, the principal targets, were soon occupied and a small number of German prisoners and quislings were taken including those manning the wireless station at Glaapen. A large supply of French chocolates and cigarettes - part of the German garrison's Christmas present - were found and distributed to grateful locals. However, there was concern about reprisals and many locals wanted the British forces to stay.

Admiral Hamilton on his cruiser HMS *Arethusa*, with 8 destroyers in support, was tempted to consider a longer stay. There was

after all no sunrise in these latitudes between the 10 December to 3 January so the risk of attack from the air was much reduced. However, a German seaplane still managed to strike at the British ships. The bombs fell close to the *Aresthusa*, but without damage, so Harrison decided - after an almost two day stay - to withdraw having completed the mission successfully.

Two radio transmitters were demolished, several small German boats captured and a few Germans and Quislings taken prisoner. The raid had served its purpose and all men and equipment returned safely. Nonetheless, this was the last time that a Commando raid on this scale was mounted without any air support. The nature of this form of warfare was changing as both sides assimilated past experiences into future planning. That said, the force, which included men from the Norwegian Linge Company had again landed unopposed and captured the German garrison without a fight. When they left two days later they had destroyed installations and took with them 29 German prisoners as well as another 200 Norwegians. However, the ease of this operation was not going to be repeated further south at Vaagso.

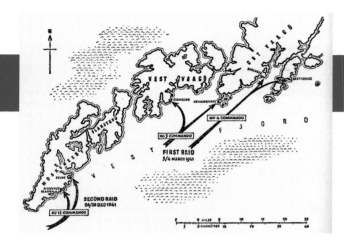

The Vaagso Raid

Operation ARCHERY, the raid on Vaagso and Maaloy took place on 27 December 1941. It broke new ground in terms of a 'combined operation' with the provision of air cover in the planning - a lesson learned from earlier raids around Europe when the lack of air cover had put missions in jeopardy - and execution. The force was to be supported by the RAF who provided air cover and strike against the local airfields, notably Herdla near Bergen. The ground assault would be made up of elements of four Commandos. The naval component of the force consisted of one 6in cruiser, HMS *Kenya*, four destroyers and two assault ships, HMS *Prince Charles* and *Prince Leopold*. ARCHERY is probably one of the most well known Commando raids, outside St Nazaire. It is certainly the best photographed as the raid was accompanied by official photographers and cameramen.

The Islands of Vaagso and Maaloy lie on the Norwegian coast between Bergen and Trondheim. Until the raids of December 1941 these small islands were little known outside the immediate area. Churchill had been keen to mount a major raid, ideally against Trondheim to take pressure off the Russians and to protect allied convoys to Murmansk. But this was not feasible

in late 1941. Mountbatten therefore decided that a raid of sufficient size to tie down German troops in Norway, thus denying their use on the Russian front, would best meet Churchill's aspirations. Following consultations with the COs of the Commando units, Vaagso was chosen. The raid was primarily designed to destroy German installations at Vaagso, but it would also demonstrate (again) the commando ability in an attempt to stifle criticisms from other areas within the military. Rear Admiral H M Burrough and Brigadier Charles Haydon were appointed on 6 December to be naval and military commanders of Operation ARCHERY (although Admiral Tovey, CinC Home Fleet was in overall command). At their disposal were No. 3 Commando, two troops of No. 2, a medical detachment from No. 4, a party of Royal Engineers from No 6 for demolition duties and a Free Norwegian Army detachment under the command of Major Linge (again for guide and interpreter duties). Additionally, there were Intelligence Officers and a Press Unit, the latter designed to capture the successful exploits of the commandos. In all around 51 officers and 525 other ranks. Colonel John Durnford-Slater, who had been closely involved in the detailed planning, was to be in charge of the landing party.

Many of the troops taking part had served under Brigadier Haydon on the first Lofoten raid earlier in the year. But Vaagso was an entirely different proposition, as this was known to be a

well defended and garrisoned target. There were German troops on both islands and significant coastal defences to neutralise at Vaagso and others within a few miles of the primary target. Intelligence sources indicated that 150 men from the 181st Division, a solitary tank (later destroyed in its garage by the Commando raiders) and 100 construction workers were billeted in the town. Four squadrons of fighters (Bf109s) and bombers (He111s and Ju88s), some three dozen aircraft in total, were operating in the area from bases at Herdia, Stavanger and Trondheim. However, no enemy warships were thought to be in the area, although German destroyers and fast attack craft were occasionally stationed there. On the small island of Maaloy, less than 500 metres by 200 metres, there was a concentration of coastal defences, ammunition stores, oil tanks and a German barracks. In addition the island was well placed to guard South Vaagso town where the main targets of an oil factory, several fish factories and power station lay. Convoys were also known to assemble in the vicinity of Vaagso offering the possibility of other targets.

Commandos on a hillside on Maaloy, overlooking the blazing town of Vaagso, December 1941. (RMM)

By the 15 December the raiding forces had been assembled and training exercises carried out. The training and briefings were extremely thorough, perhaps more so than any other British operation then carried out. Everyone was briefed. Everyone knew their role. The flotilla of the cruiser HMS *Kenya*, the four destroyers and two landing craft, HMS *Prince Leopold* and HMS *Prince Charles*, left Scapa Flow in the Orkney Islands for Sullom Voe in the Shetlands on Christmas Eve. However, they were struck by a severe westerly that caused serious damage. *Prince Charles* took onboard 120 tons of water that had to be pumped out at Sullom Voe. The raid was postponed for 24 hours while other damage was repaired and the men were given the chance to enjoy their Christmas dinner in relative comfort before they sailed again on the evening of the 26th.

The next morning they rendezvoused at 0700 with the submarine HMS *Tuna* on station at Vaagsfjord as their navigational check and guide. Landing craft (LSIs) were kept out of view of the main batteries on Maaloy. Fire was opened on the coastal defences by the warships at 0848, initially with a salvo of star shells from the *Kenya* to light up the island and then with 500 shells fired in 10 minutes from all five warships. A low flying attack by RAF Hampdens followed with aircraft successfully dropping smoke bombs to obscure the path of the advancing troops as they landed on the beaches. All the while air cover forward of the Luftwaffe was provided by Beaufighters and Blenheims making round trips from Wick (650 kilometres away) on the Scottish mainland and from the Shetlands (400 kilometres away). It was an excellent example of inter-service co-operation, bar one RAF

bomber, badly damaged, that dropped a phosphorous bomb into a landing craft.

The Commandos assault was broken into five groups. The first group landed at Hollevik - about two kilometres south of South Vaagso - to knock out the German defence there. The second group landed just south of the town itself. The third group landed on Maaloy Island to mop up any resistance following the bombardment. Whilst the fourth group was held as a floating reserve. The fifth group was carried past Maaloy into Ulvesund on the destroyer HMS *Oribi*, in company with the *Onslow*. They landed to the north of South Vaagso to ensure that no German reinforcements were able to get through to the town. A number of the forces landed directly underneath cliffs, much to the surprise of the escorting naval forces. However, scaling cliffs had been one of the elements of the Commando training in the run up to the operation. This ability enhanced their flexibility in the face of the German defences providing them with a much bigger choice of landing sites.

The German defenders were again, taken by surprise but soon resistance to the attack developed. The Germans were certainly in the town in greater numbers than the Commandos had expected and the group there called for reinforcements from the group to the West, from the floating reserve and from elements of the group on Maaloy. Three of the four coastal guns on Maaloy were soon knocked out, with the fighting there being over in 20 minutes due in part to the accuracy of the naval bombardment.

HMS *Kenya's* bombardment lifted when the 105 men of the third assault group were just 50 metres from the beach. The Germans barely had time to lift their heads before they were overrun. However, in the action Major Linge, the Norwegian commander was killed. The German survivors were rounded up, demolition work completed and the party crossed the short stretch of water to join the street fighting that had developed in South Vaagso. In the meantime the force at Hollevik experienced less resistance than expected since a number of the defenders were in South Vaagso having breakfast! These Commandos were soon able to reinforce the South Vaagso firefight. The floating reserve also had to be committed to deal with the unexpected level of German numbers. It soon became obvious that 50 extra German troops were in Vaagso on Christmas leave!

In the meantime the fifth group of Commandos were taken farther up the fjord past Maaloy by the two destroyers, *Oribi* and *Onslow*. The men were landed without opposition and blew craters in the road to block reinforcements from getting through from North Vaagso. They also destroyed the telephone exchange at Rodberg. A number of merchant ships came into view as well the armed trawler the *Fohn* and *Fritzen*. The German ships under power beached themselves when they saw the White Ensign on the destroyers. The *Fohn* and *Fritzen* were boarded under sniper fire from the shore in the hope of finding confidential papers or secret code books. With their mission a success the fifth group were also able to join the fighting in South Vaagso.

Resistance was not completely overcome in the street fighting but all the major demolition jobs were accomplished including the power station, coastal defences, the wireless station, factories and lighthouse. As a result of the fight 150 Germans were killed, 98 Germans and 4 Quislings made prisoner and 71 Norwegians took passage back to England. Farther up the fjord the destroyers sank ten ships totalling 18,000 tons and in the air four Heinkels were shot down. Both Herdia and Stavanger airports were bombed, the wooden runway of the former suffering sufficient damage to limit, not stop, German air activity.

Following his final troop commanders' meeting at 1345, Durnford-Slater ordered the withdrawal from South Vaagso to begin. It was led by No.2 troop, followed by No.6 with No.1 in rearguard. The force finally re-embarked at 1445 as the short arctic day came to a close. The assault force had suffered 81 casualties, including 20 killed. In addition six RAF Blenheims and two Hampdens were lost. The Blenheim fighters were no match for the single engined Luftwaffe Bf109s. This was the first time all three services combined their resources to mount an amphibious raid against a defended coast. As Mountbatten said at the outset '... nobody knows quite what is going to happen and you are the ones who are going to find out.' The RAF provided air cover for over 7 hours and undertook diversionary raids elsewhere. None of the attacking ships were hit by enemy bombs, nor by the shore batteries before they were silenced.

Much had been learned by both sides. Later the Germans over-stretched their Atlantic wall with the deployment of 30,000 extra troops to reinforce the Norwegian sector. Clearly Hitler had taken the bait that Norway might well be 'the zone of destiny in this war.' Photographs and eye witness reports were later used for morale boosting purposes at a time in the war when there was little good news to cheer about. The after effects of the raid had far reaching consequences, besides strengthening their garrison, the Germans took reprisals against the Norwegian population which prompted protests from the Norwegian King Haakon VII and the government-in-exile.

Conclusion

As with many previous operations there are lessons from Norway in 1941 for today and the future. From the planning and operational sides, but also the political. The Directors of Combined Operations, Keyes and Mountbatten and their immediate sub-ordinates were not operating in a politico-military vacuum, and they were fully aware of this. The importance and purpose behind their organisation and its true capabilities were not fully understood nor recognised until the

Vaagso Raid of 1941. From that raid onwards the Commando became an integral part of Britain's war machine against the Axis powers.

Numerous other large-scale operations against German forces in Norway were planned (and trained for) before being called off, although a number of smaller raids, often involving only a dozen men or so were carried out. It must also be remembered that the Special Operations Executive (SOE) which had responsibility for conducting espionage, sabotage and liaison with local resistance groups were heavily involved in planning and co-coordinating the raids carried out after Vaagso.

Without doubt for those involved and for the Director of Combined Operations, Vaagso had set the future pattern of sizeable raids and amphibious landings. Yet what exactly were the lessons for their subsequent deeds? Indeed what can be taken from the 1941 exploits of the British Commandos in Norway for those wishing to mount similar missions today?

From a crude point of view an observer quickly realises that all of the United Kingdom's Principles of War (as outlined in Maritime Doctrine, BR1806) were fulfilled. For instance, the selection and maintenance of the aim, a key principle was met by a combination of Churchill's directive of action against Nazi occupied Europe and the desire to do actual physical and financial harm to German interests in Norway. This was certainly achieved with all of the raids of 1941.

The maintenance of morale was always high. The Commandos were extremely well briefed, perhaps as British military units more thoroughly than any force before them. Additionally, their spirits were kept high knowing not only that they doing serious destruction to an element of the German war machine, but that they were also the vanguard in a new form of warfare. Durnford-Slater suggests that, 'everyone had enjoyed the (first) Lofoten Raid and felt that they had done useful work, yet they were disappointed at not seeing more action'. The Commando was indeed a new breed of British fighting soldier.

The principle of security was implemented with great success. All of the 1941 missions were carried out in the greatest of secrecy. The impressive points to take from this can be found in the nature of the raids themselves. They were not just combined and tri-service in formation which brings its own issues and problems, but they were joint, with allied (Norwegian) forces taking part not just in the execution of the raids but also in their planning. Yet information of the raids, the planning and even the arduous and lengthy training did not 'leak out' to the wider world until after the raids. In fact not until 1943 and the publication by HMSO of *Combined Operations*, 1940-1942, was the British public truly aware of the new type of forces involved, and the missions of the Commando units. All of this of course feeds perfectly into the principle of surprise. The first Lofoten raid and the mission against Spitzbergen by the Canadians came as total surprises to the Germans. By the time of the second Lofoten and Vaagso raids complete surprise could not be guaranteed

the Commando raids of 1941 demonstrated Britain's growing awareness of and increased ability in amphibious operations

as the Germans had strengthened their defences in Norway, yet the assaults still managed to catch the Germans (initially) unawares. Partly, the element of surprise could of course be accounted for in the nature of the offensive action employed by the Commandos, and by the fact that when the Commando forces struck they did so with a concentration of forces that out-numbered the defenders. This was true of all their raids in 1941. At the critical point of contact the assault forces in terms of sea, land and air units (the latter only employed at Vaagso) had the huge benefit of superiority in numbers on their side. This of course would not be guaranteed in future missions but in 1941 the British planners managed to achieve this principle. Yet they did so at a remarkably minimal price. Undoubtedly an economy of effort was part of the make up of Commando and Combined Operations. Several hundred troops, together with what was effectively a small naval force of fewer than ten ships were able to launch militarily and economically devastating assaults with minimal losses. Even by the time of Vaagso the air elements came at little cost. Seven hours of RAF air activity over the point of contact ensured a degree of air control then unknown for the Commandos, for the loss of only eight aircraft. This demonstrates the levels of co-operation that had been built up between the services within Combined Operations since 1940. Although in fairness it was not always representative as an example of normal inter-service co-operation, which were often far from effective and often hard to come by prior to Vaagso in December 1941. In fact they were not the norm in other theatres and missions until later in the war.

On the whole the Commando raids of 1941 demonstrated Britain's growing awareness of and increased ability in amphibious operations. Without doubt the forces that had taken part in all of the missions against the Nazi forces in Norway displayed crucial elements in the successful approach to amphibious operations. The training undertaken by the Commando forces during 1940 and 1941 had paid off. Their knowledge of weaponry, assault techniques, co-operation and command and control were far superior to standard British military forces of the time. Their *espirit de corps* was second to none. These factors along with air and sea control, when required, would provide Churchill and Britain with a versatile, effective strike force that would indeed see 'a vigorous and ceaseless offensive against the whole German occupied coastline'. As we now know as the war progressed the Commando units, first blooded in 1941, would become an integral and successful part of the allied war machine. Even in defeat the Commando units would emerge victorious, as No.4 Commando displayed at Dieppe, when they would be the only unit to come out of the disaster in August 1942 having achieved their mission successfully. And when part of and supported by an immense combined operation, as at D-Day in June 1944, the Commandos would prove themselves not to be simply another of 'Churchill's private armies' but one of the most effective and efficient military forces ever fired from the sea by Britain.

German prisoners captured during the Raid. (IWM N409)

Further Reading

Durnford-Slater, J., *Commando,* (London: William Kimber & Co Ltd, 1953)

Fergusson, B., *The Watery Maze: The Story of Combined Operations,* (London: Collins, 1961)

HMSO, Combined Operations, 1940-42, (London: HMSO, 1943)

Ladd, J., *Commandos and Rangers of World War II,* (Devon: David & Charles Publishers plc, 1989)

Messenger, C., *The Commandos, 1940-1946,* (London: William Kimber & Co. Limited, 1985)

Neillands, R., *The Raiders: The Army Commandos, 1940-1945,* (London: George Weidenfeld & Nicolson Ltd; 1989)

Seymour, W., *British Special Forces: The Story of Britain's Undercover Soldiers,* (London: Sidgwick and Jackson Ltd; 1985)

Young, P., *Commando,* (London: Ballantine Books Ltd, 1974)

Biography

Mr Philip D Grove, is a Senior Lecturer and the Head of Strategic Studies, Britannia Royal Naval College. He was educated at University College, Aberystwyth and has been a member of the Strategic Studies Pillar for twelve years. He has taught widely as a visiting lecturer in numerous naval establishments and universities, including the former Royal Naval Engineering College, Manadon. His main interest concerns the development and impact of naval aviation in the twentieth century and beyond, although he can be found teaching on all BRNC Strategic Studies modules. Philip Grove is a regular contributor to *The Naval Review*, and has published a *Concise History of the Sea War in World War Two* (Osprey, 2002) with his brother, Mark J Grove, and Alastair Finlan. His latest work, a new study of *Midway*, in the Brassey's Battles in Focus series was published in August 2004. He has also written a revisionist chapter on the air war in the Falklands Conflict, 1982 written for a new study of the conflict which was published in November 2004 by Frank Cass.

The British Invasion of Madagascar
Operation IRONCLAD, May 1942

By Dr Tim Benbow

At first glance, a relatively small-scale operation in a strategic backwater might seem a strange case to include in this volume, hardly deserving space alongside Gallipoli, D-Day and the Falklands. In fact, it is a fine case study. First, although it was small in comparison to some wartime operations, its size and the political restrictions imposed bear more resemblance to contemporary operations than does an operation on the scale of OVERLORD. Second, it was a significant point along the amphibious warfare learning curve for Britain, frequently cited as revealing important lessons that were taken up to good effect in North Africa, Sicily and Normandy. Third, it includes several interesting examples of a manoeuvrist approach to warfare and, in particular, it suggests that amphibious operations can be singularly conducive to that style of thought.

Madagascar lies off the east coast of southern Africa, some 9,000 miles from the UK. It is bigger than France and the third largest island in the world, about 1,000 miles long and (at its widest) about 300 miles across. Diego Suarez, on the island's narrow northern tip, boasts 'one of the finest natural harbours in the world' as well as the naval base of Antsirane with an airfield five miles south. To the south are smaller harbours at Tamatave and Majunga and the capital Tananarive.

Madagascar might seem a surprising objective for Britain at a time when the war was not going well. In late 1941, Britain's position was precarious and badly over-stretched exacerbated by a growing need to reinforce India and the Far East as a deterrent to any Japanese attack. It was feared that the situation could become even worse: in 1940 Japan had ruthlessly exploited the weakness of Vichy France to swallow up its colonial possessions in Indochina. Should it repeat the exercise to take Madagascar from Vichy control, it could station submarines, reconnaissance aircraft and even surface warships there, posing a grave threat to Britain's sea communications to the Red Sea, the Middle East and the Far East (along a route which was all the more critical due to the risks in the Mediterranean). There was therefore a case for pre-emptive action to seize Madagascar and forestall any Japanese occupation. The outbreak of war in the Far East and Japan's remorseless advances made the island's fate all the more important.

The Planning Process

Planning for an amphibious landing on Madagascar began in December 1941. The first decision made was that there was no need to take the whole island; rather, plans focussed on the harbour and airstrip at Diego Suarez. As Churchill put it, 'Portsmouth could be held with the enemy in Caithness, and so Diego Suarez with hostile forces still in Antananarivo and Tamatave.' The rest of the island could be occupied later, when circumstances permitted.

Confining the operation to Diego Suarez made the task more manageable but it was still a significant undertaking. The bay, the town and the Antsirane naval base and airfield lay behind formidable natural and man-made defences. The only channel through which the bay could be approached was the narrow (three-quarters of a mile wide) and heavily defended Oronjia Pass. A February 1941 intelligence appreciation stated that Diego Suarez 'is considered impregnable from seaward'; a surprise landing would be impossible, all the approaches were covered by commanding high ground, the narrow entrance was easily defendable and was dominated at point-blank range by well sited guns that were defiladed from outside view and supported by numerous well-sited observation points. The most obvious approach for any attacking forces was thus very hazardous. However, Diego Suarez is located on a narrow isthmus between two-and-a-half and six miles wide. If a force could be landed on the west coast, an advance over land would bring it to the defenders' rear. The western bays were considerably less well defended than the entrance to Diego Suarez bay, with just two gun batteries and a minefield. This was no mere oversight but was rather due to the extreme navigational difficulty of their approach, with unpredictable currents and many rocks, reefs and islets; indeed, the French considered that navigation at night was simply impossible. A Joint Planning Staff paper written in December 1941 identified several drawbacks in the west coast option. Landings there 'could only be attempted in daylight for navigational reasons and through mined waters and would entail land advances over difficult country which is easily defended'. Moreover, Courrier Bay was covered by modern coastal defence guns. The report concluded that the best

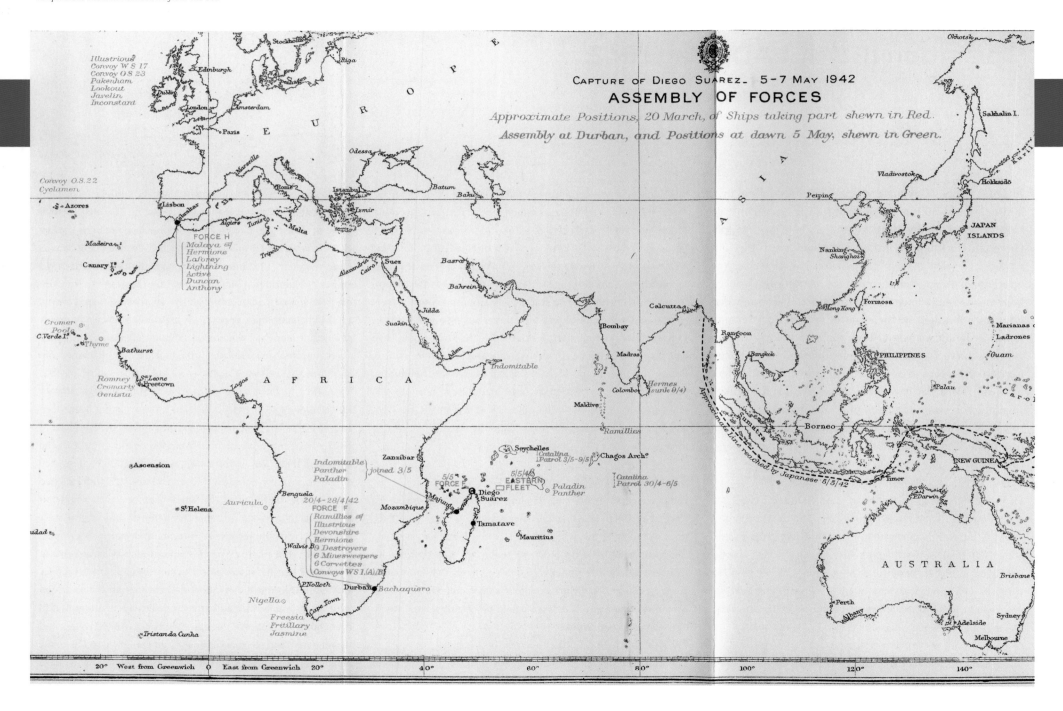

CAPTURE OF DIEGO SUAREZ. 5-7 MAY 1942

ASSEMBLY OF FORCES

Approximate Positions, 20 March, of Ships taking part shewn in Red.

Assembly at Durban, and Positions at dawn 5 May, shewn in Green.

*Left: A map showing the assembly of forces involved
in the capture of Diego Suarez. (NHB)*

option was to force entry into Diego Suarez harbour, though it conceded that this was risky. The decision of where to land was therefore a finely balanced one.

On 23 December 1941, Major General R.G. Sturges, Royal Marines, and Rear Admiral T.B. Drew were appointed joint commanders for Operation BONUS, the capture of Diego Suarez. By 31 December they had formulated a plan which reflected two key decisions. First, the landings would take place not directly at Diego Suarez but rather on the west coast, followed by an advance overland. They were aware of the problems involved, but: 'The force commanders decided that they could not afford the risk to shipping consequent upon a direct entry into the Harbour, and we therefore looked for alternative landing places which would take us in by the back door.' A second crucial decision taken by Sturges was to reject the Joint Planning Staff recommendation to begin the advance on D2 or D3, after a build-up period: 'I formed the opinion that this very orthodox plan gave the enemy far too much time to recover from the hoped for initial surprise'. He therefore decided that the first brigade to land should begin the advance on Antsirane immediately having secured the beaches: 'I considered that speed in the advance of this brigade, with limited armour, was more important than the completion of its supporting arms and equipment.'

Shortly after Sturges and Drew submitted their plan for BONUS, the operation was cancelled in favour of reinforcing India and planning for possible operations in North Africa. Nonetheless,

Exercise CHARCOAL, a full-scale rehearsal of the Madagascar operation, went ahead in February 1942. Much useful experience was gained, notably for landing craft crews, beach parties and signallers but also in allowing the naval and military staffs to practice working together.

On 14 March, the Chiefs of Staff told General Sturges that they had revived the operation to take Diego Suarez, which Japanese successes in Burma and the Indian Ocean had now made sufficiently important to justify the commitment of scarce resources. Rear Admiral E.N. Syfret, commander of Force H at Gibraltar, was appointed Combined Commander, while Sturges was to remain Military Commander under him. Further continuity was provided by the retention of much of the planning staff from BONUS, including Captain G.A. Garnons-Williams, Chief of Staff to Rear Admiral Drew, who was nominated Senior Naval Officer (Landings) and Naval Assault Commander. Brigadier Francis Festing, commander of 29 Independent Brigade, was made Military Assault Commander.

The military forces to conduct the operation were designated 'Force 121'. The lead unit was to be 29 Infantry Brigade Group, which was already embarked in assault ships in the Clyde ready for an amphibious exercise, and hence was immediately available. It was supplemented by No. 5 Commando and 17 Infantry Brigade, although the latter had no training or experience in combined operations (which the commanders sought to remedy by having experienced officers sail south with

them, 'to instruct them in the Do's and Don'ts of Combined Operations'). Later an additional reserve was added, in the form of 13 Infantry Brigade. No warships could be spared from the hard-pressed Eastern Fleet, so they were provided from Force H at Gibraltar. Re-designated 'Force F' for IRONCLAD, they included the battleship HMS *Ramillies*, the carriers HMS *Illustrious* and *Indomitable* with 42 fighters and 44 TSR aircraft, the cruisers *Devonshire* and *Hermione*, 11 destroyers, six corvettes and six minesweepers. The amphibious vessels comprised five Assault Ships, three Personnel Ships, six Motor Transport Ships, one Tank Landing Ship, two Royal Fleet Auxiliaries and a hospital ship. Although it was difficult to find forces for the operation in what was 'a dark period of the war', in total it involved 46 ships, 86 aircraft, 14,000 men and 340 vehicles and guns.

The politics of the situation complicated matters: Britain was not at war with Vichy France, so there was considerable reluctance to inflict casualties on the defenders. The prudent assumption was made that Vichy forces on the island would resist as best they could. However, for political reasons the force was ordered not to be the first to open fire, except against submarines and aircraft; unidentified surface vessels were to be ignored unless they took hostile action. In other circumstances, such constrained rules of engagement might have caused problems. Anticipated naval opposition comprised one or two French escort vessels, two armed merchant cruisers and five submarines. On land, the predicted enemy strength was 1,500 - 3,000 troops and nine coast defence batteries, backed by 17 fighters at Diego Suarez

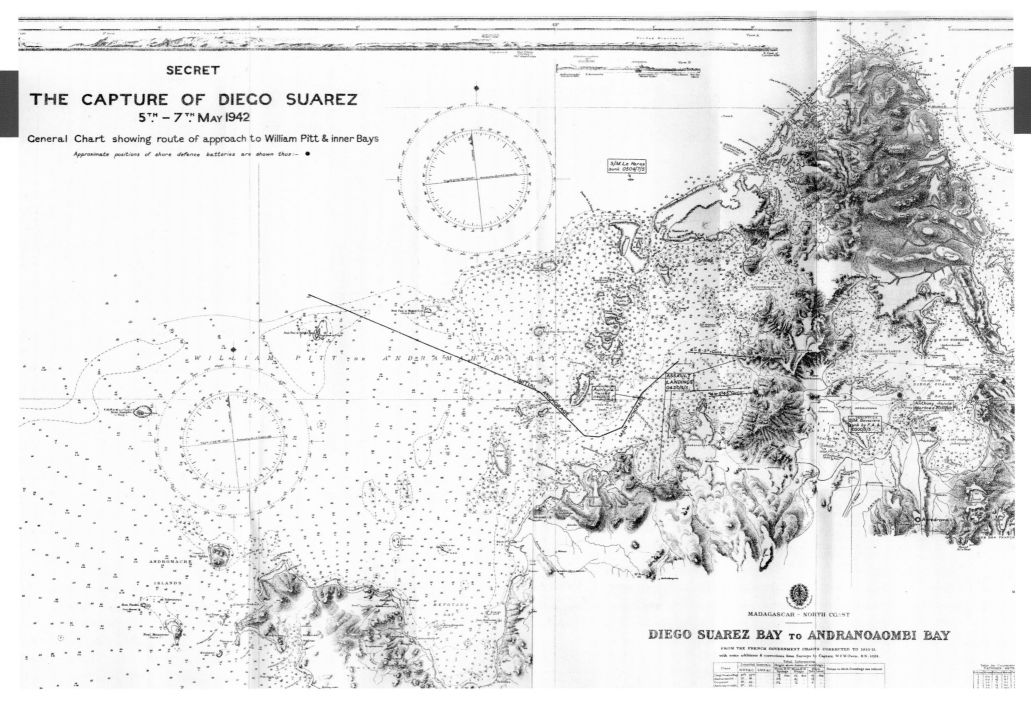

SECRET

THE CAPTURE OF DIEGO SUAREZ
5TH – 7TH MAY 1942

General Chart showing route of approach to William Pitt & inner Bays

Approximate positions of shore defence batteries are shown thus:- ●

MADAGASCAR — NORTH COAST

DIEGO SUAREZ BAY TO ANDRANOAOMBI BAY

FROM THE FRENCH GOVERNMENT CHARTS CORRECTED TO 1910-11.
with some additions & corrections from Surveys by Captain W.F.W.Owen. R.N. 1824.

*Madagascar Landing: The swift beach
assault of No. 5 Commando on the East
coast at Tamatave. (IWM K3517)*

and 18 bombers further south. It was also feared that Japanese forces might intervene, so part of the air striking forces was to be kept in reserve; orders for the operation stated that 'the destruction of Japanese forces is to be given priority over all other operations, except the attack on the aerodrome'. Cover was to be provided by the Eastern Fleet, which committed a force of two battleships, one carrier, cruisers and destroyers to cruise between 130 and 220 miles east of Diego Suarez, backed by Catalina patrols.

As Force 121 headed south, Sturges, Festing and Garnons-Williams (with reduced staffs) were all on MV *Winchester Castle*, so they were able to continue with detailed planning. On 6 April, Force F and Force 121 arrived in Freetown, Sierra Leone, allowing the naval and military commanders to meet for the first time. They left Freetown on 9 April, arriving in Durban from 22 April, where final preparations were made. As 17 Brigade had initially embarked to travel with a convoy, it was not tactically loaded for an assault and so had to be re-stowed. More broadly, fitness training for the troops was intensified, vehicles serviced and water-proofed, landing craft tested, communications set up, and maps, intelligence and final orders distributed. On the final day in Durban, General Sturges switched to the flagship, *Ramillies*, while the combined HQ of the Assault Force shifted into HMS *Keren*, 'as this ship disposed of the best communication facilities'. The slow convoy left port on 25 April and the faster convoy on 28 April. Various cover plans had been suggested but as the force sailed it was leaked

that the immediate destination was Mombassa, en route to the Middle East or India.

Even at this late stage, the possibility was raised once again of broadening the operation to take Tamatave and Majunga to the south. Asked on 26 April about the feasibility of doing so, Sturges replied that it would be possible if opposition at Diego Suarez ended by the evening of the day of the landings, and if he could retain 13 Brigade. He was told on 4 May that the extended objectives had been dropped, because of the need to move forces on to India. At 1500 on 4 May, Rear Admiral Syfret received the final go-ahead from London. As the force formed up into assault convoys on dusk, Sturges noted with more than a little understatement: 'I observed with some relief, that, when darkness fell, we did not appear to have been discovered by enemy air reconnaissance or surface vessels.'

The Landings

The final approach, at night and through notoriously difficult channels that were narrow, filled with scattered islets and reefs, subject to unpredictable currents and 'bristling with mines', was a stunning feat of navigation. Some assistance was provided by Special Operations Executive (SOE) agents who sailed out in a yacht and placed lights to assist the three leading destroyers tasked with buoying the channel. Once the destroyers had

marked the approach, minesweepers led the landing force in. By 0200 on 5 May, the assault ships were anchored outside the two main target bays, just beyond the range of the coastal batteries. While the landing craft were being manned and loaded, minesweepers swept the final channels to the beaches. Several mines were swept and two detonated, but without waking the garrison ashore. Around 0300 the landing craft began to depart for the beaches: further testament to the navigational skill involved is found in the fact that every landing craft found the correct beach at the correct time. To increase still further the chance of catching the enemy by surprise, the approach and initial landings were made at night, with H-Hour at 0430, some 80 minutes before sunrise.

The plan called for 5 Commando to land at Red Beach (sub-divided into Red North, Centre and South) in Courrier Bay, capture the two batteries there, and then advance to secure the Andrakaka Peninsula. Simultaneously, 29 Brigade would land further south at White and Green Beaches in Ambararata Bay and Blue Beach at Basse Point, between the two bays, and then

advance inland along the road to Antsirane. After the initial units were fully unloaded, 17 Brigade and, if necessary, 13 Brigade, would land and complete the capture of Antsirane and the Oronjia Peninsula.

The first landings went exactly according to plan. Complete surprise was achieved at Red Beach by 5 Commando, which landed unopposed and took all three beaches and the covering gun battery without loss. The extent to which the defenders were taken by surprise is indicated by the fact that all the battery's personnel were captured asleep in bed – with the single exception of the sentry, who was taken in the kitchen making a cup of coffee. As they pushed inland into the Andrakaka Peninsula, the Commandos encountered and overcame light opposition and by 1430 reached Diego Suarez village on the eastern edge of the isthmus.

South of Courrier Bay, 29 Brigade landed 'punctually and accurately' and met no opposition at Green and White Beaches. Blue Beach, described as 'a complete revelation', had been discovered very late by air reconnaissance. SOE agents had discovered that it was defended by 12 machine guns and about 60 troops, which were taken by troops landing at White Beach and then advancing to attack the defenders from the rear.

There were no preliminary or supporting bombardments during the landings. This furthered the aim of minimising French casualties and was made possible by the choice of lightly or undefended beaches, and by the advantage of surprise. The landings did receive support from another quarter: to coincide with the landings on the west coast, the cruiser HMS *Hermione* undertook a diversion off a likely landing beach on the east coast with star shell, rockets and smoke floats, while naval aircraft dropped dummy parachutists six miles inland. It was subsequently learnt that as a result the immediately available French reinforcements, which could have slowed the advance significantly, were initially sent here rather than to the west coast.

Complete surprise was achieved at Red Beach by 5 Commando

Half an hour after the initial landings, Fleet Air Arm aircraft attacked the airfield and shipping in the harbour. The results achieved were impressive: in the harbour an armed merchant cruiser and a submarine were sunk, while at the airfield, hangars full of aircraft were left burning. The effect of this strike was effectively to win air superiority for the British force at the very outset. Two or three ineffective strafing attacks against the beaches were made by French aircraft flying from bases to the south but Fleet Air Arm fighter patrols prevented any attacks on the transports. It also freed naval aircraft to support forces ashore, with reconnaissance, attacking enemy positions, spotting for naval gunfire and making further strikes against French warships and submarines.

By 0630 on 5 May, all of the beaches had been taken and some 2,300 troops had been landed. Unloading was hindered by the continuing mine threat and worsening weather, with the wind increasing to Force 8, yet the process continued and not a single landing craft was put out of action. Some difficulties were encountered in off-loading at Ambararata Bay; 'Green Beach was found to be unsuitable for vehicles and White difficult even for tracked vehicles', so only personnel were landed at these two beaches. Blue Beach was 'entirely satisfactory' and 'a model beach' for landing craft, though its utility was reduced by high winds and mines, which prevented the landing ships

The Betsiboka Bridge, blown up by the fast retreating Vichy French troops in Madagascar. Despite the demolition of the bridge, it was used by British and Commonwealth troops to get their vehicles across. (IWM K3522)

from approaching as close to the beaches as had been planned, leaving the landing craft with a two-mile trip. Particular problems were encountered with the Landing Ship Tank HMS *Bachaquero*. It proved difficult to find a suitable beach for her to off-load the 54 vital vehicles and artillery pieces that she was carrying, owing to her deep draught aft and an unexpected reef off Blue Beach. When a promising location was found at Red Centre, just before dark, she unloaded in an impressive 14 minutes, only to find that they were no roads inland so the guns could not join the main advance.

The Advance on Antsirane

The main advance towards the naval base and airfield at Antsirane initially encountered little opposition, due to the unexpected location and timing of the landings and the diversion on the east coast. During this early stage, the main problems for the troops of 29 Brigade were having to carry all their weapons and supplies through the dust and the tropical heat of the day, and over difficult terrain that included mangrove swamps and rocky ground. They were also irritated to discover that the distance from the beaches to their objective 'was considerably in excess of what was shown on the map.' The latter was on a 1/100,000 scale and highly inaccurate, showing the advance to be 17 miles whereas it was in fact 22 ½ miles, almost a third as far again as anticipated.

As the advance continued, the French began to recover from the initial surprise, manned their defences and offered more effective opposition. One factor in this stiffening of resistance was the

decision (described by Sturges as 'a great error' and by Garnons-Williams as 'a good example of the classic error of mixing politics and tactics') at about 0815 to send a captured French officer into the town with an ultimatum to surrender. He reported the main axis of the attack, allowing troops to be rushed into position and previously unmanned defences to be fully prepared. The advancing British troops were temporarily held up at Col de Bonne Nouvelle but tanks were brought up and knocked out the positions on the hill, as well as destroying several lorry loads of infantry moving forward. The tanks continued to push on, advancing to within about three miles of Antsirane, and then came upon strong French defensive positions which were located just beyond the point where aerial photograph coverage had ended. These positions were based on 'two old but solid and well concealed forts', connected by a line of trenches about a mile long, supported by anti-tank ditches, well-sited machine guns and two concrete pill boxes with 75mm artillery guns commanding the road running between the forts and towards the town. These defences were flanked by steep scrub leading down to mangrove swamps and then the sea, so they were difficult to by-pass. The British tanks, having advanced beyond infantry support, were hit by artillery fire and, unable to get off

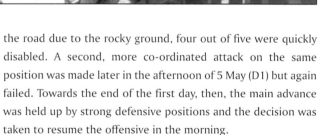

the road due to the rocky ground, four out of five were quickly disabled. A second, more co-ordinated attack on the same position was made later in the afternoon of 5 May (D1) but again failed. Towards the end of the first day, then, the main advance was held up by strong defensive positions and the decision was taken to resume the offensive in the morning.

At dawn on 6 May (D2), air strikes were carried out against the French positions, followed by attacks from land forces. One attacking battalion successfully moved through mangroves to penetrate the left flank of the defences but communications problems meant that the commanders were unaware of this success; indeed, they believed it had failed with casualties of up to 25%. This apparently grim picture was matched by the

A British Brigadier discusses the surrender of Tananarive with French Civil Authorities who met him some miles outside the city. (IWM K3525)

grinding to a halt of the attacks on the centre and right of the defences by two more battalions. The few British artillery pieces involved had to withdraw after coming under French fire and only five serviceable tanks remained. When Sturges arrived at battalion HQ, in his own words, 'It was quite clear that the attack had failed. It was an unhappy moment.' The British force seemed to be facing exactly what it had most wished to avoid, the prospect of prolonged operations, which would tie down forces badly needed in other theatres of the war.

General Sturges now instructed the brigade staff to plan a night-time assault, to begin between sunset at 1800 and the rise of the full moon at 2300. Throughout the remainder of the day, the British kept up harassing fire on French positions as Sturges returned to the flagship for discussions with Admiral Syfret. He reported his decision to bring forward his forces for a large-scale night assault and also proposed what would prove to be the masterstroke. Facing a strong defensive position that could not easily be out-flanked or by-passed, this was another opportunity to follow the traditional British practice against the French of exploiting the mobility provided to land forces by maritime power. Sturges suggested that a party of Royal Marines be landed in Antsirane from 'an expendable destroyer', as a diversion 'to take the Frenchmen's eye off the ball' and to dislocate the defences. A party of 50 Royal Marines from HMS *Ramillies*, under Captain Martin Price, therefore embarked on the destroyer HMS

Their mission was potentially of crucial importance but involved great risk

Anthony, which set off around the northern tip of Madagascar. Their mission was potentially of crucial importance but involved great risk. In Admiral Syfret's words, 'The *Anthony*'s chances of success I assessed as about 50 per cent., my advisers thought 15 per cent., and of the Royal Marines I did not expect a score to survive the night. The next few hours were not happy ones.'

Shortly after 2000, *Anthony* began to run the gauntlet of the French batteries protecting the entrance to the harbour, to which she responded with her own main armament with supporting fire from the cruisers *Devonshire* and *Hermione*. She was prevented by strong winds and the tidal current from going alongside the jetty at Antsirane, so her captain, Lieutenant Commander John Hodges, held the stern against it, allowing the Marines to scramble ashore while the ship's anti-aircraft weapons were used to suppress sniper and machine gun fire. Having disembarked the Marines, *Anthony* withdrew at high seed, under further and now more accurate French fire, and sailed to re-join the fleet on the west coast. As *Anthony* withdrew, the Marines set about

creating the requested diversion. They were hindered by the lack of a decent map, the only one available being 'on a page torn from an old tourist brochure that someone in the *Ramillies* had had, and it was fifteen years old.' Yet after scaling a cliff, climbing a wall and tearing a gap in a wire fence, they captured the artillery headquarters, seizing significant quantities of weapons, set several fires in the town to aid the diversion and then took the barracks at the French Naval Depot. Many French troops were captured asleep and several British prisoners were freed, including more than 50 captured troops, the crew of a downed Swordfish and one of the SOE agents on the island, who was due to be shot in the morning. The Marines also discovered a telephone exchange, where French officers had spread news of the attack in their rear, thus helping to do the party's work for it.

As the Marines were landing, 17 and 29 Brigades commenced their advance, pressing home the attack when the success signal from the town was seen. Many of the defenders, whose morale had already been shaken by the earlier penetration of their lines, retreated when they heard firing in the town behind them. By 0300 hours on 7 May the town and its defences were in British hands and Admiral Syfret was able to signal the Admiralty that the night attack by 17 and 29 Brigades had been '100% successful', with 'extremely slight casualties due to surprise and weight of the attack'. He noted that the impact of their assault had been 'combined with a surprise assault in the harbour area by 50 Royal Marines, who effected disturbance out of all proportion to their actual numbers.' The following day he stated that the *Anthony* operation was 'a fine achievement brilliantly carried out, and in my opinion was the principal and direct cause of the enemy's collapse'. What Churchill described as 'a daring stroke' succeeded in dislocating the French defences with minimal casualties among attackers, defenders and the civilian population, not least by avoiding the necessity of fighting in the town itself.

The one area ashore where resistance was continuing was on the Oronjia Peninsula. As 17 Brigade prepared to assault these positions the next morning, and negotiations were underway, *Ramillies, Devonshire* and *Hermione* undertook a short bombardment of the French batteries 'to encourage the enemy to surrender.' Ten minutes after they opened fire, French forces on the peninsula surrendered and the fighting ended. In the three days of the operation, British casualties were 105 killed and 283 wounded; one minesweeper was lost and seven aircraft destroyed (four shot down and three forced landings). French sources stated that their casualties were 150 killed and about 500 wounded, as well as seven aircraft shot down and ten destroyed on the ground, and the loss of 3 submarines and 2 minor warships.

The British force could now turn to the task of securing Diego Suarez. As planned, 31 aircraft from the South African Air Force were flown in to the airfield on 12-13 May. In late May, 13 Brigade sailed on to India, followed three weeks later by 17 Brigade, being replaced on Madagascar by an East African brigade. Force F dispersed once again, with most of its warships having left by 30 May when Ramillies was torpedoed and damaged, and a tanker sunk, by a Japanese mini-submarine. Between September and November, the rest of the island was taken by Operation STREAM-LINE-JANE, a campaign involving a series of amphibious landings, on both coasts, in combination with a land advance from Diego Suarez.

Critical Factors

As Churchill noted, the operation against Madagascar was 'our first large-scale amphibious assault since the Dardanelles twenty-seven years before'. Brigadier Festing took a still longer historical perspective, suggesting, 'it is not an exaggeration to say that an operation of this nature and at this range has not taken place since the period of the Napoleonic Wars'. The size

the operation against Madagascar was our first large-scale amphibious assault since the Dardanelles

of the operation, the fact that it was more than just a raid, the distance over which it was conducted and, of course, the success it enjoyed all mark IRONCLAD as worthy of attention.

Overall, ten main factors can be identified as the most important contributions to the success of Operation IRONCLAD. They can be further divided into three categories. The first group are those elements that worked well enough; they were considerably better than in previous (and some subsequent) cases, albeit demonstrating some weaknesses and needing to improve further. They are planning; intelligence; training and techniques for landings; and naval fire support.

The second cluster of factors worked very well and made a major contribution to the success of the operation, although this might have been in part due to favourable circumstances, notably the limited capabilities of the enemy. These factors are the command and control structure; sea control; and air superiority. The third and final group are the elements that were the most significant in the outcome of IRONCLAD, the strengths that more than compensated for minor weaknesses in other areas. These key factors are inter-service co-operation; surprise; and the overall operational approach.

Planning

Although IRONCLAD was launched on fairly short notice, it was able to draw extensively on the earlier planning for BONUS, not least because several of the key officers participated in both. The operation therefore benefited from careful, detailed and realistic planning, which was tested in a major exercise. One minor difficulty to arise was that Rear Admiral Syfret was not involved from the very beginning but was rather represented on the planning staff by an officer who was then unavailable for the operation itself. Syfret recommended that in future, the commander-in-chief should be present at the start of the planning stage. Further difficulty might have been caused had the operation been extended at the last minute to include the objectives further south in Madagascar, which was under consideration surprisingly late on. As it turned out, however, the focus on the principal objective was maintained.

> **the commander-in-chief should be present at the start of the planning stage**

Intelligence

The quality of the intelligence possessed by the forces undertaking Operation IRONCLAD is another area where the picture is mixed. Some was good, some was poor even taking into account the inevitability of it falling below perfection. In the context of so many factors going well, however, it was good enough.

Admiral Syfret reported that the information provided by SOE was 'most valuable'. General Sturges was realistic and satisfied: 'The topographical and enemy intelligence supplied, while not of course as complete as I would have desired, nor infallible, was, in view of the type of objective, good.' Festing, perhaps predictably as the commander with the more tactical focus, was more critical. He felt that much of the information provided was of dubious military relevance, discussing political undercurrents, the personality of the enemy commander and 'such information as is available from the encyclopedias Britannica and Baedeker. He rather required information about military facilities and defences, or number and quality of enemy troops. Festing also reported that the maps used were very poor, on too small a scale and also inaccurate, especially since far better maps were commercially available. Air reconnaissance photographs were highly valuable, but concentrated too much on the beach areas, with the result that their coverage stopped just short of the key French defensive line that surprised the British forces and this held up the advance on Antsirane.

Overall, however, the size and disposition of the French forces seem to have been accurately predicted, as was their fatal assumption that the west coast of the island could not be approached at night. There was doubt over whether the Vichy forces would resist but the prudent assumption was made that they would fight.

Training and techniques for landings

Although the operation drew attention to many important lessons for amphibious warfare, it also benefited from recent improvements in the techniques involved. There had been significant advances in concepts, planning, equipment and training since the beginning of the war, which had accelerated in the aftermath of Dakar, and at Madagascar these developments began to bear fruit. The use of trained and experienced troops as the bulk of the force involved in IRONCLAD was essential. The senior land commanders felt that the operation vindicated recent developments in training, especially the emphasis on increased speed of landing, the exploitation of surprise and night actions. Once again, some useful lessons were derived, based on shortcomings encountered. Sturges felt that the balance of the force embarked was not quite right as between fighting units and support, commenting that throughout the operation, 'we were suffering for the heavy cuts which had been made in HQ and signals to increase the number of fighting troops and vehicles.'

Specialised amphibious shipping was widely used and proved its utility. IRONCLAD was notable for the first use in action of the LST (tank landing ship) in the form of HMS *Bachaquero*. The Dakar operation had shown the need for what Churchill called 'ocean-going ships capable of landing tanks directly onto a beach'. Various purpose-designed ships were being built but three oil tankers were converted to provide an interim capability. *Bachaquero* was one of these, hence very much an improvisation,

he recommended that in future the commander-in-chief
should outrank all the officers serving under him

and although for Sturges she proved 'a disappointment', she vindicated the concept of purpose-designed LSTs and went on to participate in Operations TORCH and OVERLORD. According to Sturges, 'The rate of landing personnel and vehicles was an advance on anything yet achieved but a radical improvement in existing methods is still required.' In particular, he concluded that more landing craft had to be provided and better techniques devised to allow landing ships to be cleared quickly, especially where air attack was a possibility. The process of unloading after the initial landing also showed some weaknesses. It was widely recognised that the operation showed the need to develop a specialised beach organisation to manage unloading, and to store and distribute supplies in the aftermath of a landing. Garnons-Williams noted that the experience of unloading stores suggested 'that the supply problem for the 're-entry to the Continent' may find some extremely unpleasant surprises'.

Naval fire support

The French report on the operation stressed four critical factors in the British success: air support, tanks, numerical superiority and naval bombardment. The initial landings did not require preliminary or supporting bombardment due to the choice of lightly defended beaches and the considerable advantage of surprise. Nevertheless, subsequent stages of the campaign saw frequent use of warship firepower against defensive positions and to encourage the surrender of the batteries on the Oronjia Peninsula. Careful arrangements had been made to facilitate gunfire support, with each warship carrying a Royal Artillery

captain as a bombardment liaison officer, with two more acting as forward observation officers. Problems were encountered with aerial spotting for naval gunfire, which was often unavailable (due to the desire to maximise the number of carrier aircraft devoted to strike missions). In other circumstances, of course, naval gunfire support could have been still more prominent – if, for example, resistance had been more effective. In the event, however, it was possible for bombardment to be used in the relatively restrained fashion, intended to minimise casualties for political reasons and also to preserve shore batteries that would be needed for the defence of the harbour once it was in British possession.

Command and control structure

Operation IRONCLAD enjoyed a clear and effective command and control structure. This was an area that had undergone some change between the two world wars. The 1931 Manual of Combined Operations stated that, 'The command of a combined operation is vested equally in the commanders of the Services engaged', who must make decisions only 'after full consultation' with each other. In other than ideal circumstances, this system left the possibility of confusion and divided authority. The 1938 edition of the Manual set out three systems of command: Joint, where the commander of each service also has joint responsibility for the operation as a whole; Unified, with one commander-in-chief and the other commanders as his subordinates; and Command by One Service. For IRONCLAD, the 'General Outline of the Operation' specifically cited the 1938 Manual of Combined Operations with regard to the position

of Syfret as combined commander-in-chief, under the 'Unified Command' system, with Sturges taking command 'When the military are firmly established ashore and the supporting Naval Forces no longer required.' By chance, the rank of the Military Commander, Major General Sturges, was equivalent to that of the Commander-in-Chief. Syfret reported that owing to the excellent personal relationship between them this caused no problems but he recommended that in future the commander-in-chief should outrank all the officers serving under him.

Perhaps the greatest problems encountered during the operation related to communications, with those between the ships close inshore and those further out, for example, described as 'poor and undependable', and the overall complement of signallers proving 'totally inadequate for the task to be performed'. Even before this operation, the first Landing Ship Headquarters had been ordered but IRONCLAD confirmed the requirement for a dedicated amphibious flagship as well as the need to include more signallers, both for the commanders of the landings and to operate ashore.

One interesting comment, with a remarkably modern feel, was made in relation to command style. Brigadier Festing wrote that in amphibious operations it was quite impossible to devise a rigid plan that would cover every eventuality that could occur after a landing. Hence, he argued, it was 'of paramount importance that all ranks should be fully conversant with the Commander's intention so that they can be guided thereby in making up their

A map showing the Assault Landing locations
at Ambararata Bay and Courrier Bay. (NHB)

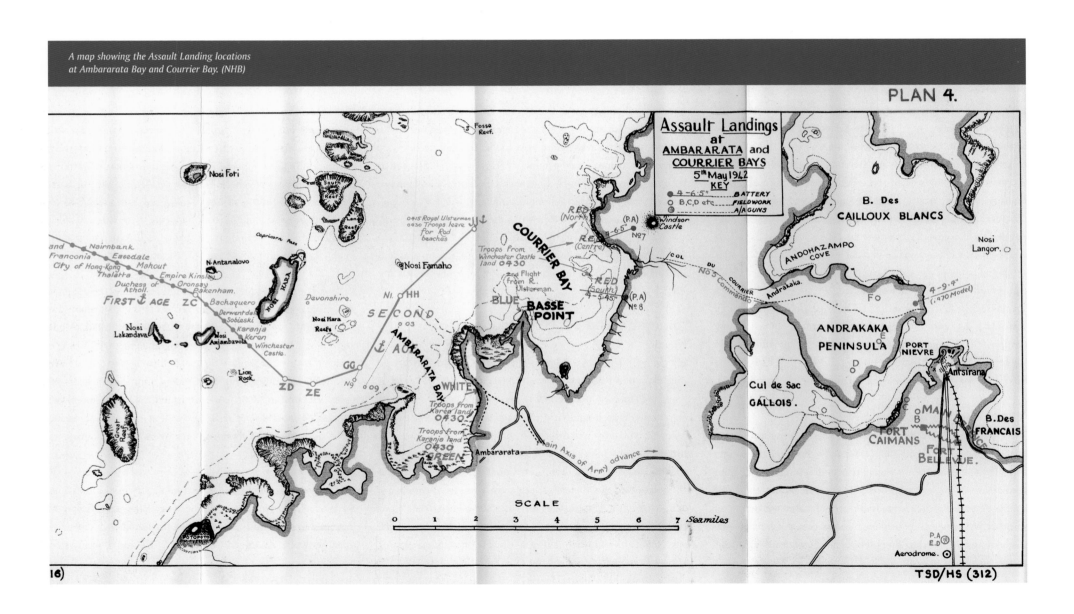

118

The ability of the Royal Navy to gain and exploit a high degree of sea control in the relevant area was an essential enabling factor

minds when confronted with the unexpected'. This view was echoed by Garnons-Williams, who wrote to Sturges that 'By working to 'Intention', the paucity of communications did not seem to matter.'

Sea control

The ability of the Royal Navy to gain and exploit a high degree of sea control in the relevant area was an essential enabling factor. Admittedly the naval forces of the French defenders were limited, but precautions needed to be taken against possible Japanese intervention. With the French surface warships and air forces swiftly neutralised, the main threats were submarines and mines, both grave dangers in amphibious operations, which by their very nature take place in conditions and locations highly conducive to these dangers. Constant anti-submarine patrols during the approach phase and the operation itself not only prevented any successful submarine attack but also led to the destruction of three French submarines. A total of 55 mines were swept at the cost of a single minesweeper (though without loss of life), allowing warships, amphibious vessels and landing craft to operate in heavily mined waters without a single strike by a mine. Gaining a high degree of sea control so quickly allowed Force F to concentrate on exploiting its dominance to influence events ashore, which it did by landing the troops, guns, vehicles and supplies that would capture the island, and by supporting them with naval gunfire, air strikes, tactical reconnaissance and, finally, transporting a force of Marines to land in the enemy's rear.

Air superiority

IRONCLAD demonstrated that carriers could provide the air power that was essential for combined operations, where shore-based aircraft were unable to do so. The surprise achieved by the operation allowed carrier aircraft to knock out the enemy air forces in the north of the island in a single early strike, which in turn enhanced surprise by denying the French any effective aerial reconnaissance. It also freed the Fleet Air Arm to support the land forces with air strikes against French positions, spotting for naval gunfire and tactical reconnaissance. The psychological effect on the defending forces should not be overlooked: interrogations of French prisoners of war revealed that fighter demonstrations over the town and naval base, as well as the continuous anti-submarine patrols provided 'a constant reminder of the British air superiority which did as much to reduce their morale as the earlier dropping of leaflets had raised it.'

The activities of the Fleet Air Arm in this campaign show attempts to learn from the experience of Norway, for example with the issuing of detailed operations orders and the production of relief models of the area to help the pilots to prepare. As in other areas that were broadly successful, a number of shortcomings can also be found. The issue of air support had been underestimated in the planning stage (close support of land forces, for example, 'had not been stated as a requirement in the original planning'), not least because no representatives from the carriers had served on the planning

team in the early stages. The Fleet Air Arm had not undertaken sufficient training in co-operation with the Army, a fact noted in their reports by General Sturges, Brigadier Festing and the captain of HMS *Illustrious*. While the contribution of carrier air power to the success of the operation was crucial, the lesson seems to have been that better integration of naval aviation in training and planning of amphibious operations would allow it to achieve even more.

Inter-service co-operation

One critical factor during IRONCLAD was the close and effective co-operation between the services. It is striking how frequently the harmony between the Army and Navy during the Madagascar operation is commented upon. The Report of 29 Brigade noted that the Naval and Military Assault Commanders (Garnons-Williams and Festing, respectively) embarked on the same ship and immediately established a common operations room: 'Throughout the entire operation the completest co-operation and friendship existed between the Royal Navy and the Army; it is considered that this was due in large measure to the immediate formation of what amounted to one staff.' This theme is echoed in the reports of the two commanders mentioned. Brigadier Festing mentioned 'the staffs of both the assault commanders constituted themselves one staff from the very first day of the planning period', while Captain Garnons-Williams wrote at a little more length, in comments that are worth citing in full:

'There is one lesson, however, which is so important and at the same time so common place to us all, that it nearly became overlooked. That is the prefect co-operation and friendship that exists between General Sturges and his Headquarters, Brigadier Festing and the 29th Independent Brigade Group Staff and my own Staff. This was not confined to the commands and Senior Officers, but went right down through to stewards and batmen, all of whom learnt to forget the word 'my' and referred to the Force as 'our'.'

The mutual confidence and understanding between the key commanders was heightened by their personal familiarity with each other: Syfret and Sturges had been acquaintances since 1910, while the latter (who had begun his career as a naval officer) and Garnons-Williams had been midshipmen on the same warship. Sturges also came to know Festing well, not least because he served as the chief umpire at the Exercise CHARCOAL rehearsal of the BONUS plan. Some minor improvements were suggested by various commentators: Army radio sets were found to be unable to cope with R/DF interference, the Army and Navy proved to have different understandings of indications of priority in signals and, in future, Garnons-Williams suggested that 'Naval personnel must be conversant with Army jargon.' Nevertheless, Operation IRONCLAD seems to stand out as a model of good inter-service collaboration. As the commander-in-chief wrote, 'Co-operation at all times between the Services was most cordial and to this must be attributed a great measure of the success of the enterprise.'

Surprise

One of the most significant factors in the success of the operation, so rapidly and at such a low cost, was the extent to which surprise was achieved. Many of the other factors considered here rested to a large extent on this impressive accomplishment, not least the gaining of complete air superiority and control of the sea, as well as the success of the initial landings. The commanders of the operation were keenly aware of the contribution of surprise to their success. Festing suggested that, 'It is no exaggeration to say that a successful surprise landing starts the attackers with at least 75% advantage.' He attributed the surprise gained in IRONCLAD to good security, good cover and the successful use of diversions. To this list should be added the contribution (noted by Syfret) of SOE in cutting telegraph wires to delay the warnings of the landings, and, at the wider level, the bold decision to attack from a direction and at a time that the French thought impossible, thus dislocating their whole defensive plan.

Operational approach

The final factor, which is partly the result of some of the other elements considered above, is the broad operational approach utilised in the planning and conduct of Operation IRONCLAD. Correlli Barnett described it as, 'an exemplary combined operation', that 'exemplified the principle of the 'indirect approach.'' This style of warfare, which might alternatively be labelled 'manoeuvrist', can be observed in the Madagascar campaign at various levels. First, at the grand-strategic and

a combined operation that exemplified the principle of the indirect approach

military-strategic levels, there was considerable boldness in taking decisive, pre-emptive action at a difficult stage of the war, when Britain was painfully over-stretched, to seize the initiative and exploit her maritime power to deny a critical position to an opponent and seize it for her own use. Second, the operational concept avoided the obvious approach of a direct assault on Diego Suarez Harbour – which was predicted and prepared for by the defending forces – in favour of attacking from a direction and also at a time that was completely unexpected. This bold move, reminiscent of the descents on Quebec and Havana during the Seven Years' War, achieved complete surprise and allowed the main French defences to be avoided, especially during the potentially most vulnerable stages of the landings.

Perhaps equally impressive, the surprise achieved was then effectively exploited, first, by knocking out the main enemy air forces to gain instant air superiority before most were able to conduct a single sortie, and second, by pushing inland rapidly from the beaches to deny the French the chance to recover from the initial blow. As explained above, General Sturges' original plan for BONUS rejected the orthodox approach of having the first units ashore secure the beaches and establish a covering position, with later formations continuing the advance: 'in the majority of cases such a plan forfeits most of the value gained by initial surprise.' Rather, he planned for the first units landing to begin

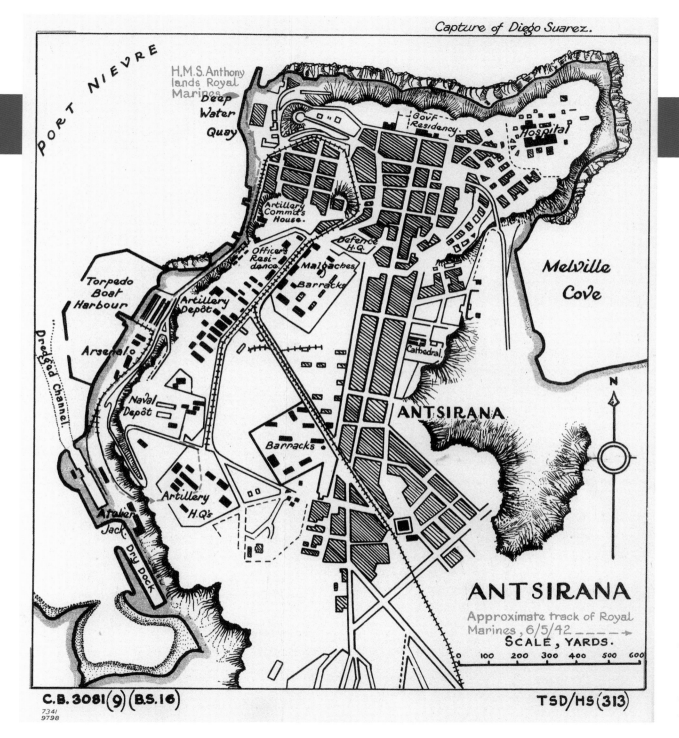

On the map:

PORT NIEVRE

H.M.S. Anthony lands Royal Marines

Deep Water Quay

Gov't Residency.

Hospital

Artillery Comm'd's House.

Defence H.Q.

Officers' Residence.

Malbaches

Barracks

Torpedo Boat Harbour

Artillery Depôt

Melville Cove

Arsenal

Cathedral.

Naval Depôt

ANTSIRANA

Barracks

Dredged Channel.

Atelier Jack.

Artillery H.Q's

Dry Dock

N

ANTSIRANA

Approximate track of Royal Marines, 6/5/42 -----→

SCALE, YARDS.

0   100   200   300   400   500   600

C.B. 3081 (9) (B.S.16)

7341 9798

TSD/HS (313)

The capture of Diego Suarez: A detailed map of Antsirane showing the landing of HMS Anthony and the route followed by the Royal Marines. (NHB)

their advance immediately, exploiting surprise and retaining the initiative. Festing fully agreed with Sturges about the importance of pushing inland fast: 'the time-honoured and traditional error of hanging about on the beaches was not committed on this occasion'. This view was echoed by the commanding officer of No 5 Commando, Lieutenant Colonel D.M. Shaw: 'After a successful surprise attack, rapidity of advance is essential'. Mopping up of isolated positions, he argued, should not be allowed to interfere with the speed of advance but should rather be left to following forces. Sturges and Festing also stressed other elements of what today would be called manoeuvre warfare, including the importance of imitating the mobility and speed of movement of the Japanese, emphasising night fighting and infiltration past rather than frontal assault on enemy positions, and recommending delegated command and ensuring that all ranks understand the intention of the commander.

Inevitably, the defenders eventually recovered from their initial confusion and reoriented themselves. Although this came too late to prevent the landings or to contest the initial British advance, it did enable them to man well prepared and strong defensive positions. These held up the attacking forces, which lacked the armour, fire support and time for an attritional battle and which due to the terrain lacked the option of manoeuvre on land. Nevertheless, there was still scope for tactical creativity, in the form of a successful – albeit not exploited – infiltration and then a large-scale night assault. These actions were complemented by the brilliant coup of landing a party of Royal

Marines behind the French defences. Before the operation, an attack into Diego Suarez bay would have been a painfully predictable, orthodox approach. After the successful initial landings and the reorientation of the French defences to meet the British advance, however, a landing in the bay now became an unexpected and truly manoeuvrist action. In combination with the frontal night assault on the main French position south of Antsirane, it collapsed the morale of the defenders thus avoiding costly attritional fighting against prepared positions and in the town itself.

It is striking that many mistakes were made and shortcomings revealed during the operation. Indeed, Bernard Fergusson wrote that IRONCLAD 'survived the breach of several basic rules which can rarely be broken with impunity'. Nevertheless, the overall impact of these problems was not sufficient to undo the positive effect of the manoeuvrist operational and tactical approach that was employed.

Conclusion

There is a tendency - as with Liddell Hart's 'indirect approach' mentioned above - to take a modern concept, the doctrinal *plat de jour*, and then anachronistically apply it to previous operations, each of which is found (surprise) to embody and justify the concept, demonstrating its status as the strategic

Holy Grail. This is not the case, however, in arguing that IRONCLAD epitomises a manoeuvrist approach. Manoeuvre warfare emphasises conceptual and physical agility, constantly looking to exploit surprise, mobility and tempo to throw the opponent off balance, disrupting and disorganising his ability to resist rather than physically destroying it.

Given the limited resources available to Britain in 1942 and the pressing priorities and commitments elsewhere, she could not afford to tie down large-scale forces for an extended period in Madagascar. Moreover, the political importance of minimising casualties among the French defenders, let alone the civilian population, also made an attritional approach undesirable. An approach with the attributes that would today be described as manoeuvre warfare was therefore deeply attractive.

It could also be argued that amphibious warfare lends itself particularly well to manoeuvre: as the internally produced History of Combined Operations Organisation 1940-45 (1956) puts it, in IRONCLAD, '... the power given to the attackers by amphibious expeditions is well illustrated. The principles of mobility and surprise were used to the full and produced successful results.'

Biography

Dr Tim Benbow is a Lecturer in the Defence Studies Department at the Joint Services Command and Staff College (JSCSC), Watchfield. He took undergraduate and graduate degrees at Oxford University, where he wrote his doctorate in strategic studies and naval history. He also studied at Harvard University and King's College, London. He taught at the University of Oxford, while conducting a research project for the UK Ministry of Defence, resulting in his book, *The Magic Bullet? Understanding the Revolution in Military Affairs* (Brasseys, 2004). He taught for two years in the Department of Strategic Studies at Britannia Royal Naval College, Dartmouth.

Further Reading

Battle Summaries No. 16 – Naval Operations at the Capture of Diego Suarez (Operation 'Ironclad') May, 1942 (1943)

Butler, J.R.M., *History of the Second World War: Grand Strategy Volume III June 1941 – August 1942, Part II,* (London, HMSO, 1964)

Fergusson, Bernard, *The Watery Maze: The Story of Combined Operations,* (London, Collins, 1961)

Roskill, S.W., *The War at Sea 1939 – 1945: Volume II The Period of Balance,* (London, HMSO, 1956)

Woodburn Kirby, S., *The War Against Japan, Volume II: India's Most Dangerous Hour,* (London, HMSO, 1958)

The author would like to record his gratitude for the very generous and immensely valuable assistance provided by Matthew Little of the Royal Marine Museum; Stephen Prince and Kate Tildesley of the Naval Historical Branch; and the librarians at Britannia Royal Naval College, Dartmouth.

The Raids on St Nazaire and Dieppe
Operation CHARIOT, March 1942 and
Operation JUBILEE, August 1942

By Mr Stephen Prince

The Strategic Context

'So we had won after all!…We should not be wiped out… Hitler's fate was sealed. Mussolini's fate was sealed. As for the Japanese, they would be ground to powder. All the rest was merely the proper application of overwhelming force'.[1]

Churchill's statement describes his reaction to the Japanese attack on Pearl Harbor and American entry into the Second World War. While his confidence would ultimately be fulfilled, achieving the 'proper application of overwhelming force' would prove to be a difficult and long-term task. In the short term, the period from December 1941 to October 1942 would be one of Allied, but particularly British, retreats and defeats. In the Far East, on 10 December 1941, the battleship HMS *Prince of Wales* and battlecruiser HMS *Repulse* were sunk by Japanese aircraft and, on Christmas Day, the garrison of Hong Kong surrendered. On 15 February 80,000 Commonwealth troops became Japanese prisoners at Singapore and this was followed by the British retreat through Burma. In North Africa the gains of the 'Crusader' offensive were rapidly eroded by Rommel's counter-attacks and on 21 June another 33,000 Imperial troops surrendered at Tobruk, with the 8th Army being pushed back to the El Alamein position. At sea, 1942 saw the peak of Allied shipping losses, with over eight million tons being lost. This included the

disastrous convoy PQ-17 of June-July 1942, in which 430 tanks and 2,500 aircraft were lost, and which led to the suspension of aid via north Russia. The mood of the time is well captured by the diary entry of General Sir Alan Brooke, Chief of the Imperial General Staff, for 31 March 1942:

> 'The last day of the first quarter of 1942, a fateful year in which we have already lost a large proportion of the British Empire, and are on the high road to lose a great deal more of it!'

> 'During the last fortnight I have had for the first time since the war started a growing conviction that we are going to lose this war unless we control it very differently and fight with more determination.'[2]

It was against this background of defeat and frustration that two of the most ambitious raiding manoeuvres of the Second World War were planned and executed.

Combined Operations

Britain's preparations for the Second World War had in no way allowed for the strategic earthquake that occurred in the summer of 1940. In a matter of weeks Britain's primary ally was defeated and Britain's host nation supported access to mainland Europe destroyed. While there had been greater consideration

and study of amphibious warfare in Britain than is commonly acknowledged, this had been implemented only on the basis of experimental investment to support long term development of capacity. While the prototype landing craft developed were of immediate value for evacuations, and would provide the basis for many of the fleets of landing vessels deployed later in the war, the tiny community of pre-war expertise was largely scattered on immediate tasks and its doctrinal publications frequently overlooked.[3]

In 1940 few resources were available for any offensive operations. However, there was a requirement for such action, largely to achieve a positive psychological effect, both domestically and with potential allies, during a period of defeats, conditions that would apply again as powerfully in 1942. Churchill's solution to this requirement was the establishment of a new organisation, Combined Operations, which would sponsor small scale 'commando' raids, as well as developing wider amphibious techniques. Though Lieutenant General Bourne RM briefly commanded Combined Operations, Churchill soon appointed the retired Admiral of the Fleet Sir Roger Keyes, the hero of Zeebrugge 1918, as Director of Combined Operations.[4] Keyes launched a series of small-scale raids, frequently against Norway and usually at company scale or less.[5] Keyes plans for much larger operations were always frustrated by resource

[1] Winston Churchill *The Second World War, Volume III, The Grand Alliance* (Cassell & Co.; London, 1950) p.539.
[2] Alex Danchev & Daniel Todman (ed) *War Diaries 1939-45 Field Marshal Lord Alanbrooke* (Weidenfeld & Nicolson; London, 2001) p.243.
[3] See Ian Speller *The Role of Amphibious Warfare in British Defence Policy, 1945-56* (Palgrave; Basingstoke, 2001) pp.16-27; The National Archives (TNA), Kew, DEFE 2/708 & 709, *Manual of Combined Operations*, 1931 & 1938 Editions.
[4] See Harry Dickinson's chapter in this volume.
[5] The exception was the raid against the isolated Norwegian Lofoten Islands by around 600 troops in March 1941. See Phil Grove's chapter in this volume.

constraints, magnified by the risks and diversions they would involve for units normally committed to enduring, defensive tasks. This situation led to frequent disputes with the Chiefs of Staff (COS), with whom Keyes had poor relations, and in October 1941 Churchill removed him.[6]

Keyes was replaced by Captain Lord Louis Mountbatten, who was appointed as a Commodore. A cousin of the King and a dashing destroyer captain, who had lost his ship off Crete, Mountbatten was a contrast to Keyes in age, seniority and charm. Churchill undoubtedly hoped to inject greater activity into Combined Operations through the appointment and reputedly told Mountbatten:

'Dickie, the trouble is that the British have lost the will to fight...The Chiefs of Staff are the greatest cowards I have ever met.'[7]

This statement evidently reflected Churchill's desire for offensive action. However, his ultimate support, after much argument, of the COS arguments for restraint concerning most of the planned raids also reflected his grudging acceptance of Britain's constrained strategic situation. This was further indicated both by Mountbatten's lower rank and his appointment as 'Adviser' on Combined Operations, rather than 'Director'.

The first significant raid during Mountbatten's command was an attack on the Norwegian port of Vaagso in December 1941, a raid initially planned under Keyes.[8] While Combined Operations produced the outline plans for raids and provided commandos, landing craft and specialist advice, the actual operation was commanded by co-equal land and naval commanders. Also the 'local' naval Commander-in-Chief (C-in-C), in this case Home Fleet, had the final decision as to whether the raid was launched. The co-equal system of commanders reflected British doctrine which prioritised environmental expertise over joint command, while the role of the naval C-in-C indicated the requirement for raids to conform to other operations in their local area.

The raiding force consisted of 600 assault troops, mainly commandos, supported by the six-inch gun cruiser *Kenya* and four fleet destroyers. The 125mm coastal defence guns near the harbour were effectively suppressed by an intensive nine-minute bombardment by the supporting warships, during which they fired 500 shells. This was followed by a rapid assault by the commandos, who, through bitter experience, put great emphasis on maintaining their momentum in assault, even as they took casualties. The 200 strong garrison was overcome, important fish oil facilities and 16,000 tons of coastal shipping destroyed and significant intelligence documents captured.[9]

The success undoubtedly owed much to the superiority of firepower deployed, the assault methods used, and the location of the target, where the distances involved limited exposure to counter-attacks.[10]

Mountbatten had been initially nervous about the prospects for this raid was encouraged by the results.[11] Together with his senior staff officer, Captain Hughes-Hallett RN, he produced an ambitious programme of raids for the 'raiding season' of 1942, with a new emphasis on the more difficult targets on the coast of north-west Europe. Two of the minor raids, at either end of this programme, were successfully executed with considerable effect. In February a company of paratroops captured valuable radar technology at Bruneval and were successful withdrawn by sea.[12] Then in December a small group of Royal Marine canoeists succeeded in damaging blockade-running shipping in Bordeaux (Operation FRANKTON), inflicting a three-month delay on the sailing programme.[13] While these raids were disproportionately effective they were still on a very minor scale compared to both the size of Combined Operations, and of existing campaigns, such as North Africa. Admiral Sir William James, C-in-C Portsmouth, who controlled the launching of the Bruneval raid, wrote to his wife, 'It seems rather silly to crow over this relatively unimportant little affair when so much is going on elsewhere, but

[6]See Jeremy Langdon 'Too old or too bold? The removal of Sir Roger Keyes as Churchill's first Director of Combined Operations', *Imperial War Museum Review*, No.8, 1993 pp.72-84.
[7]Quoted in Speller op. cit. p.33.
[8]See Phil Grove's chapter in this volume.
[9]F H Hinsley et al *British Intelligence in the Second World War, Volume Two* (HMSO; London, 1981) p.200.
[10] Brereton Greenhous *Dieppe, Dieppe* (Art Global; Montreal, 1992) pp.20-24.
[11] John Durnford-Slater *Commando* (William Kimber; London, 1953) p.69.
[12] Hinsley *Op. cit.* pp.248-9.
[13] See C E Lucas Phillips *Cockleshell Heroes* (Heinemann; London, 1956) & Hinsley *ibid* p.541.

even a tiny success lightens up the dark clouds.'[14] The first major raid on France by Combined Operations would derive much of its value from its relevance to the enduring campaign that was the 'centre of gravity' of the Anglo-American alliance, the Battle of the Atlantic.

The Assault on St Nazaire: Operation CHARIOT

When the damaged German battleship *Bismarck* was finally sunk by the Royal Navy in May 1941it was trying to reach the French port of St Nazaire. The Normandie dry-dock in that port offered the only facility on the Atlantic coast where battleships of that size could be repaired. From mid-1941, as *Bismarck's* sister ship, *Tirpitz*, approached operational status, there was increasing interest in how the threat of this battleship could be countered. While submarines inflicted the vast majority of losses on Atlantic trade the gradual nature of these casualties allowed them to be managed. If their attacks could be combined with the rapid, and potentially devastating, operations of a battleship the scope for fundamental disruption of communications was much greater.[15] While the only certain means to prevent this was by destroying the *Tirpitz*, German caution in deployment made this option difficult. That caution had also led to the withdrawal of other heavy units from the French coast in the 'Channel Dash' of

Anything that could significantly inhibit those intentions would have a valuable effect. Preventing Tirpitz from having access to the Normandie Dry Dock was identified as a way to achieve this

February 1942 – another embarrassment to Britain's military and political leadership– but the underlying threat still remained.[16] It distorted British maritime deployments and was primarily limited by the intentions of the German high command.[17] Anything that could significantly inhibit German options would have a valuable effect. Preventing *Tirpitz* from having access to the Normandie Dry Dock was identified as a way to achieve this.

The St Nazaire issue was first studied by the Naval Intelligence Division (NID) from July 1941. Utilising both open source publications and imagery, a considerable amount of intelligence on the dock and its environment was assembled, including the construction of an excellent scale model.[18] At the Admiralty's request the problem of assault was studied by both Admiral Keyes and the 'local' naval C-in-C, Admiral Sir Charles Forbes, C-in-C Plymouth. Principal problems were the 400-mile approach required and that the final six miles had to be through the narrowing Loire estuary, exposed to heavy concentrations of what might well be radar directed coastal artillery and then

rapid fire close-in weapons.[19] In addition the dock cassions had been hardened in order to protect them against accidental ship collisions.[20] Admiral Forbes thought any assault impractical; Admiral Keyes's concept of a large-scale conventional raid from landing ships and craft was seen as uneconomic, and finally the Special Operations Executive (SOE) reported crippling the dock was beyond their sabotage resources.[21] As a result of these opinions the concept of an attack became dormant.

It was revived in early 1942, when NID 'sold' the idea to Mountbatten and Hughes-Hallett during their 'keen search for targets.'[22] Hughes-Hallett suggested an innovative way of achieving the aim would be the use of a lightened warship, which could avoid the normal shipping channels and pass over shoal waters during the high spring tides. It would then be rammed into the dock gates, delivering commandos and then a concentrated explosive charge. The mass of existing information combined with more general ULTRA intelligence on German swept channels, recognition signals and routine patrols improved the viability of the concept and on 25 February the outline plan was approved by the Chiefs of Staff.[23]

The Force commanders appointed were Commander R. E. D. Ryder RN and Lieutenant Colonel Charles Newman of the Essex

[14]Sir William James *The Portsmouth Letters* (MacMillan; London, 1946) p.156.
[15]See Stephen Roskill *The War at Sea, Volume I* (HMSO; London, 1954) pp.371-77 & 550-1.
[16]James Op Cit. p.157-8; Roy Jenkins *Churchill* (MacMillan; London, 2001) p.681.
[17]German ship deployments to the Atlantic coast were also influenced by RAF bombing attacks and RAF/RN coastal minelaying.
[18]TNA, ADM 223/464 'Naval Intelligence 1939-1942' pp.53-55.
[19]In the harbour area there was a 20 or 40mm weapon for every 180m of waterside.

[20]Instead of gates the docks had cassions which did not open but were 'wound' into sub-docks by machinery into sub-docks at right angles to the main dock.
[21]C E Lucas Phillips *The Greatest Raid of All* (Pan Edition; London, 2000) p.22; M R D Foot *SOE in France* (HMSO; London, 1966) p.184.
[22]TNA, ADM 223/464 p.56.
[23]Hinsley Op Cit. p.192 & TNA CAB 79/18, COS 63rd Mtg, 25 February 1942.

Regiment and Number 2 Commando. When they studied the operation their plan was to forego the expendable ship in favour of sabotage parties delivered from a large number of small craft. This preference was based on the greater redundancy in a group of craft and due to practical doubts that a ship would be provided. Hughes-Hallett pressed for the ship plan, though he was unsuccessful over arguing for a second lightened ship to evacuate the raiders.

To a greater extent than possibly ever before did we rely on surprise

The final plan that emerged was therefore a hybrid, consisting of both the lightened ship and a group of small craft, a combination Ryder later thought improved on both originals.[24] Once this plan had been agreed, and a ship secured, the force commanders had no doubt that, 'To a greater extent than possibly ever before did we rely on surprise.' They also had no doubt as to their priorities in the assault. While it was feasible their warship could support the small craft in the assault, 'In our minds and in our plans…we envisaged sacrificing, if necessary, everything in order to get the 'Campbeltown' in'.[25]

we envisaged sacrificing, if necessary, everything in order to get the 'Campbeltown' in

HMS *Campbeltown* was the destroyer which had been selected as the expendable ship, one of the 50 'Destroyers for Bases' ships supplied to Britain by America in 1940. It arrived at the mounting base of Falmouth on 25 March, under the command of Lieutenant Commander S H Beattie RN. It had been adapted to reduce its draft from 14 to 11 feet,

---

[24]R E D Ryder *The Attack on St. Nazaire* (John Murray; London, 1947) p.11.
[25]TNA, ADM 199/1199, 'St Nazaire Raid. Report by the Naval Force Commander' (nd), Section A, Para.3.

One of the Force Commanders:
Lieutenant Colonel Charles E. Newman VC, Essex Regiment and
No. 2 Commando. (Essex Regimental Museum & IWM HB 16542)

enable the force to survive air attack on the return passage.[26] Including the RN crews the direct assault force totalled just over 600 men. Just before departure aerial photographs indicated the presence of five German torpedo boats at St. Nazaire. Ryder asked Newman how large his reserve was and was told twelve commandos. He replied, 'Then I suggest Charles, that you will probably need all of them.'[27]

Having secretly embarked the commandos the assault force, plus two escorting destroyers, left Falmouth on 26 March, following an indirect, intelligence determined route that would minimise its chance of detection. It maintained its 'cover' identity as the 10th Anti-Submarine Striking Force, on passage to Gibraltar, by steaming in an anti-submarine formation but also flew German ensigns against close visual contact. The cover measures were tested on the morning of 27 March when the force encountered and engaged a U-Boat, U 593, which was returning from its Atlantic patrol. Though the initial assessment was that the submarine had been destroyed, it had actually survived and surfaced that afternoon to report the action. The course and formation measures were successful in that German Naval Group Command West interpreted the encounter as having been with either a group heading towards Gibraltar or retiring following a mining sortie off the French coast. Actually, the result of this report was that the five German torpedo boats in St Nazaire

were ordered out to sea to sweep for the force, even as it approached their harbour. The possibility of a coastal raid was not considered.[28]

After sunset on 27 March Ryder & Newman transferred to the MGB as their command platform and the group formed its column formation for the attack. At 2215 they passed Position Z, a way-point 40 miles from St Nazaire indicated by the submarine HMS *Sturgeon* and where the escorting destroyers left the formation. At 2300 the fuse for *Campbeltown*'s explosives was set and, from midnight evidence of an air raid could be seen, an aspect of the plan arranged with Bomber Command. A raid by sixty aircraft was intended to divert the attention of the German defences and also hopefully drown out the extremely noisy engines of the Motor Launches, which were clearly audible at over three miles in still conditions. However, complete cloud cover over the target frustrated the efforts of all but four of the bombers, which were prevented from bombing France unobserved. Their strange 'loitering' did lead to suspicion amongst the German command of the possibility of some other form of attack, as well as leading to the complete manning of the artillery defences and at 0120 the warning 'Beware Landing' was made.[29] It is seldom noted, though, that the significant 'drowning out' effect of the assault force's engines was achieved.

to carry a three-ton explosive charge and to resemble a German torpedo boat. Together with 18 craft-16 Motor Launches (ML), a Motor Torpedo Boat (MTB) and a Motor Gun Boat (MGB), which had been assembling since 12 March- formed the assault group, which would carry just under 300 troops. The wooden MLs had the range to reach St Nazaire, though they needed vulnerable extra fuel tanks added to their decks to return. The MTB and MGB would have to be towed by destroyers for most of the journey. All vessels were, as far as possible fitted with 20mm cannons, in order to suppress defences once the force had been discovered. Ryder hoped these weapons would enable to force to move from 'surprise by stealth' to 'surprise by force' in the final stages of the attack. He also hoped their massed fire would

[26]Ryder *Attack* p.16.
[27]Lucas Phillips *Raid* p.99.
[28]Naval Historical Branch Collections (NHBC), BR1736(34)(48), *Battle Summary No.12, The Attack on St Nazaire* (Tactical & Staff Duties Division (Historical Section), Naval Staff, 1948) pp.4-5.
[29]Lucas Phillips *Raid*. P.130.

The assault force navigated across the shoal waters, guided by the radar of the MGB, which led the column. *Campbeltown* twice grounded lightly at 0045 and 0055 but was able to continue. The force was first detected at 0115 but not identified as hostile. It was then illuminated by searchlights at around 0125 when about a mile and three-quarters from the dock.[30] Ryder signalled the group was 'proceeding up harbour in accordance with instructions.' This satisfied most of the defences and when a light weapon on the shore opened fire the signal 'KK' for 'a vessel considering herself to be fired on by friendly forces' was sufficient to get the fire to cease. By around 0129 though German firing had become general and the RN vessels now revealed their identities and fired in return. However, by this point, *Campbeltown* was also less than a mile from the dock and beyond the firing arcs of the heavy German guns likely to do the ship fundamental damage.

Ryder later stated, 'It is difficult to describe the full fury of the attack that was let loose on both sides, the air becoming one mass of red and green tracer, most of it going over.'[31] British fire concentrated on searchlights and muzzle flashes, which they

were frequently able to suppress, though rarely destroy. Beattie later wrote:

'*Campbeltown* was repeatedly hit in all parts of the ship by shells and bullets from about 4' calibre downwards but no essential parts were damaged… apart from the layer and trainer the twelve pounder crew was composed entirely of stewards and cooks who deserve great credit for carrying out supply and loading of ammunition with great speed and efficiency until the gun was finally put out of action… The behaviour of the ship's company was magnificent.'[32]

It is difficult to describe the full fury of the attack that was let loose on both sides

On the final approach both the Coxswain and a rating were wounded at the wheel and Lieutenant Tibbets, who was also responsible for the explosive charge, took the wheel for the final approach at 18 knots. *Campbeltown* struck at around 0134, causing Beattie to comment, 'Well, there we are, four minutes late.'[33] The impact ran the ship 35 feet into the dock, placing the explosive charge immediately adjacent to the lock, though incredibly Beattie thought the ramming, 'a tame affair, and

---

[30]Reports by Ryder & Beattie have inconsistencies of up to five minutes but concur of the main sequence of events.
[31]TNA, ADM 199/1199, 'St Nazaire Raid. Report by the Naval Force Commander' Section B, Para.19.
[32]TNA, ADM 199/1199, Lt Cdr Beattie's 'Narrative of H M S Campbeltown at St Nazaire, 28 March 1942', 16 June 1945, pp.2-3.
[33]Lucas Phillips *Raid* p.141.

HMS Campbeltown struck the dock at St. Nazaire at 0134, 'Well, there we are', said Beattie, 'four minutes late.' (IWM HB 2242)

a great many men did not realise that the ship had actually rammed'.[34] Beattie's crew continued to man their guns until their commandos had been disembarked and the stern of the ship was scuttled to prevent any immediate attempt to remove it. They then left to meet Motor Launches for their evacuation.

Simultaneously the MLs were trying to disembark their commandos, both immediately south of the dock at the Old Entrance and further south at the Old Mole. While the commandos from *Campbeltown* came ashore as planned, both ML landing sites were subject to heavy enemy fire and only a single launch disembarked at each location, the vulnerability of the craft being illustrated. *Campbeltown*'s commandos were able to comprehensively sabotage the dock's winding and pumping machinery but only a minority of the commandos carried by the MLs made it ashore, so that damage was much less further south. By 0245 Newman's HQ party, which had been landed from the MGB, gathered together 80 to 90 surviving commandos near the Old Mole. Given the state of the MLs and continuing German fire on the river he knew there could be no withdrawal by sea and so led his men in breakout from St Nazaire Island into the wider town, from there hoping to escape in smaller groups. While the breakout was achieved, most of the commandos were now wounded and during the course of the following morning were taken prisoner, although one group of five made a remarkable escape via Spain.[35]

Ryder, commanding from the MGB, delivered Newman's headquarters and then went ashore to check *Campbeltown* had been properly scuttled. Having done this he ordered his MTB to torpedo the lock gates of the Old Entrance and then had all available craft take onboard *Campbeltown*'s crew. On leaving the Old Entrance, however, he could see the results of the shore guns, particularly those at the Old Mole, which were still operating:

The approaches were floodlit by searchlights from all directions and a deadly fire was being poured on the ML's still gallantly attempting to go alongside… With accurate fire from our Pom-pom we twice silenced the pill box [on the Old Mole] but it came to life again… All this time we were lying stopped about 100 yards off the Old Entrance and although fired on fairly continually by flak positions and hit many times we were by the Grace of God not set ablaze.

By 0250 Ryder found that, 'Looking around the harbour… I counted about seven or eight blazing MLs and was forced to realise that MGB 314 was the only craft left in sight.' With the MGB loaded with over 30 men, many of them wounded, Ryder finally resolved to withdraw, taking with him the two surviving MLs he could find. At 0745 the group made contact with the escorting destroyer force, which had already successfully engaged the German torpedo boats. At 0900 the combined force then met a further two destroyers which had been despatched from Plymouth. Ultimately, eight of the seventeen craft that had entered the Loire returned, although three were scuttled to prevent them delaying the return passage.[36] The group was able to return having frustrated air attacks, on lesser scale than the Ryder had feared, as the German command system was still recovering from the shock of the raid.

Campbeltown finally exploded just before noon on 28 March, about three hours later than the last time that the fusing should have allowed for. The caisson was completely destroyed and around 120 Germans experts and sightseers on the ship killed, despite the fact German naval command had been aware for several hours the ship contained explosives. The dock was not repaired during the war and the lack of its facilities was a powerful reinforcement to the caution that was already being

[34]TNA, ADM 199/1199, Lt Cdr Beattie's 'Narrative of H M S Campbeltown at St Nazaire, 28 March 1942', 16 June 1945, pp.2.
[35]*Battle Summary* pp.15-16.
[36]One of the MLs had turned back with engine trouble during the approach passage.

a deed of glory intimately involved in high strategy

applied to the use of *Tirpitz*, and other major units. This was on the basis both of the loss of facilities and because of the daring attitude the raid had demonstrated. Orders had already been given to withdraw major headquarters from the coastal region and immediately after St Nazaire Hitler extended this order with immediate affect to U-Boat Command. [37]

From the assault force of 630, 144 were killed, a proportion which can be compared with the 195 killed at Zeebrugge from a force of 1,780. In terms of total casualties the Royal Navy component suffered a loss rate of 55% and the commandos of over 80%. However, the success in the main objective, coupled with the daring nature and limited scale of the operation, meant this loss was not seen as controversial or disproportionate. Admiral Forbes stated in his despatch on the operation that, 'neither the losses in men or material can be considered excessive for the results achieved' and Churchill described the raid as, 'a deed of glory intimately involved in high strategy.[38] Eighty-three decorations were awarded to the attackers, including five Victoria Crosses, and the raid was celebrated not only to raise domestic morale but also to improve Britain's credibility in America.[39]

Dieppe: From Many Raids to Operation RUTTER

While the success at St Nazaire was a significant boost to both Mountbatten and Combined Operations, the situation of both was already improving. Earlier in the month, Churchill had insisted that Mountbatten be promoted to Vice-Admiral, with equivalent ranks in the other services, with a seat on the COS whenever issues concerning the major direction of the war were discussed. The origins of Mountbatten's elevation as Chief of Combined Operations have never been fully explained. It seems that Churchill wanted to raise Mountbatten's status as an ally against the other Chiefs caution, if required. The promotion also served to raise the profile of Combined Operations as an offensive organisation during a period of defeat.

The latter aspect was intimately linked to relations with America. While there was agreement between London and Washington over the grand strategy of beating 'Germany First' there were important differences in its application. American opinion was supportive of a cross Channel assault as early as possible; British opinion, while subscribing to the same ultimate goal, felt that the practical difficulties meant the operation would have to be delayed and that peripheral attacks should be mounted first to

wear Germany down. However, if this British view was pushed too strongly, there was a danger that American attention and resources would turn to the Pacific theatre, where they could be more readily applied. It was therefore important for Britain to remain as positive and demonstratively committed to cross Channel operations as possible, a role that Mountbatten and Combined Operations was well placed to fulfil.[40]

American pressure was reinforced by demands from the Soviet Union for operations directly against Germany. These were required to try and reduce the burden the Soviets were bearing as they confronted the vast bulk of the German Army, 163 divisions as opposed to 33 in western Europe.[41] This pressure increased during 1942 and with it Anglo-American fears about a Soviet collapse and the resulting freedom for German resources. From April 1942 senior British commanders, joined by General Eisenhower, worked on plans for a major landing in France in that year, designed as an emergency measure in the event of imminent Soviet collapse. The studies revealed that, given the scale of operation that could be sustained with the landing craft then available, Germany would be able to defeat such an invasion by simply concentrating its European occupation forces, without withdrawing any forces from the eastern front. As the troops that

---

[37]Horst Boog et al *Germany & the Second World War, Vol.VI, The Global War* (Clarendon Press; Oxford, 2001) p.436-37. The delayed action torpedoes fired into the Old Entrance exploded the next day. There is no evidence to support the story that there were also British officers' onboard Campbeltown who sacrificed themselves rather than indicate the presence of explosives.

[38]Admiral Forbes Despatch 'The Attack on St Nazaire', *London Gazette*, 30 September 1947, Para.4; Winston Churchill *The Second World War , Volume IV, The Hinge of Fate* (Cassell & Co; London, 1951) p.106.

[39]Brian Villa *Unauthorised Action Mountbatten and the Dieppe Raid* (OUP; Oxford, 1994) p.120.

[40]Villa *Op Cit*. pp.170 & 181.

[41]J R M Butler *Grand Strategy, Volume III, Part II* (HMSO: London, 1964) p.645.

An aerial photograph with annotations showing the double assault by No. 4 Commando led by Lieutenant Colonel Lord Lovat and Major Mills on the 6-Gun Hess Battery, West of Dieppe. (IWM D12874)

direct assaults on German held Europe and helped to develop forces and techniques for future operations, even when their current targets were not major priorities.[44] It was considered though that Fighter Command could have the greatest impact, in terms of supporting the Soviet front, by directly attriting the German Air Force (GAF) 's fighter force in the west. The result should be either diverting forces from the east, or at least constraining the rate of transfer to the east. The main problem with this method, which had been attempted with an exaggerated belief in its success since the spring of 1941, was compelling the GAF to fight, except when conditions were most favourable to it.[45] Almost the only way of guaranteeing a major air battle was through the mounting of a major raid and the significance of this role for raids is demonstrated by General Brooke's comment of:

> '...the importance of keeping in mind the object of these operations, namely to bring on a series of air battles in circumstances reasonably favourable to ourselves.'[46]

Combined Operations certainly had a major programme of such raids in support of this aim available from the spring of 1942. These included Operations IMPERATOR, for a 2-3 day divisional raid on Paris, and BLAZING for a Brigade level seizure of the

would probably be sacrificed in such an operation would still be largely be Anglo-Canadian in 1942, British refusal was decisive. This was confirmed to the American Joint Chiefs of Staff (JCS) on 22 July and by 30 July agreement had been reached, largely due to the support of President Roosevelt, for a less ambitious landing in Vichy French North Africa in October 1942.[42]

This programme, though, offered no aid to the Soviets. That could now only come from raids, either from the air or the sea. Bomber Command's increased tempo of activity, particularly its 1,000 Bomber raids from May, fitted well into this concept and to some extent paralleled the activities of Combined Operations.[43] Both pleased domestic and allied opinion by

---

[42]C P Stacey *Six Years of War* (Queens Printer; Ottawa, 1955) pp.314-18.
[43]See Sir Charles Webster & N Frankland *The Strategic Air Offensive Against Germany, Volume IV* (HMSO; London, 1961) Appendix 17.
[44]Max Hastings *Bomber Command* (Michael Joseph; London, 1979) Ch.6.
[45]Hinsley *Op Cit.* p.270.
[46]TNA, CAB 79/20, Chiefs of Staff, 163rd meeting of 1942, 28 May. Even after Dieppe planning for raids designed to provoke air fighting continued.

Channel Island of Alderney. Both were rejected by the COS, with General Brooke stating that Operation IMPERATOR's inland objective was unrealistic. Churchill personally confirmed the rejection of Operation BLAZING saying, 'we could not afford the risk of heavy casualties to our bomber force which this operation would probably entail. He considered this factor decisive...'[47] The cancellation of BLAZING illustrated the increasing problem Combined Operations faced when trying to plan large scale raids. Directly controlling only commandos and landing craft, it had to 'borrow' any further resources from the three services' operational commands, a requirement that inevitably impacted on that command's ongoing tasks. If the relevant Commander-in-Chief objected to this diversion, or the risks his forces would be exposed to, Combined Operations had only two choices. They could modify the raid's plan to avoid the requirement or Mountbatten could take the dispute to the COS for resolution - a resolution which, as in the case of BLAZING, usually came down in favour of the C-in-C. Simultaneously, however, the pressure on Combined Operations for major activity was maintained. At the same meeting where he confirmed the cancellation of

BLAZING Churchill also stated he was in favour of more minor raids, 'provided that these pinpricks were in addition, and not substitution, of larger scale operations.'[48] It was in this atmosphere that Operation RUTTER became the only major plan developed.

RUTTER was probably discussed within Combined Operations in March 1942, with the first formal consideration in April. It envisaged a one-day raid on the minor French port of Dieppe by two brigades, reinforced by an armoured regiment and paratroops. As this concept would require forces from C-in-C Home Forces, the COS required a representative of the C-in-C should be involved in the planning. General Paget nominated his C-in-C South Eastern Command, Lieutenant General B L Montgomery, and Home Forces staff officers joined the planning from 14 April. The Outline Plan, which emerged on 25 April, envisaged a dawn direct assault by a brigade with tanks on the beach adjacent to Dieppe harbour. This would be preceded by bombing of the town by around 150 aircraft and would be supported by two battalion level flank attacks. After holding the town for several hours and destroying minor local targets the units, including the tanks, would all then be withdrawn through the central beach. It has subsequently been claimed that Combined Operations preference was for an all flank attack and that Home Forces pressed for the plan that emerged. While there was certainly debate about the plan there is apparently

no contemporary evidence that refutes or confirms this claim. The Outline Plan was submitted to the COS on 9 May, with a target date of late June/early July. While Mountbatten stated in the submission one of the purposes of the raid was as assault training he also stated, 'It will not, however, throw light on the maintenance problem over beaches.'[49] The COS approved it as the basis of planning for the force commanders on 13 May. The force commanders the COS then approved were Air-Vice Marshal T Leigh-Mallory (AOC No.11 Group, Fighter Command); Rear-Admiral H T Baillie-Groham RN, who returned from Egypt for the raid, and Major-General J H Roberts (GOC of the 2nd Canadian Division).

The involvement of the Canadian Army, which would provide the vast majority of the landing force, arose from the keenness of the all ranks of the 1st Canadian Army to get into action. Canadian units had been based in Britain since December 1939 and by April 1942 had expanded to a complete Army of two Corps, the largest Dominion formation ever. However, the troops had been involved in no combat, elements of it having arrived in France in 1940 only in time to be evacuated and their expedition to the Arctic island of Spitzbergen in 1941 having been unopposed. With the exception of the two Canadian battalions lost at Hong Kong no Canadian troops had been engaged while troops from every other part of the Empire had seen extensive fighting in the Middle and Far East. Sending Canadian troops to the Middle East

[47]TNA, CAB 79/20, Chiefs of Staff, 146th meeting of 1942, 11 May.
[48]*Ibid*.
[49]Stacey *Op Cit*. p.326.

was an option but it would have meant dividing the Army with a loss of national cohesion and significance. This was avoided by retaining the Army in the UK, ready to ultimately participate in the key campaign of the war, but meant continuing its enforced inaction. Participation in raids would defuse this dilemma and Canadian commanders had been constantly pressing for it, increasing their autonomy from Ottawa in the process.[50] This pressure coincided with Montgomery's role as the commander of the region where Canadian forces were stationed and his high regard for the proficiency of the 2nd Division. On 30 April Montgomery had suggested 2nd Division's participation to General McNaughton, commander of 1st Canadian Army, who agreed subject to his staff approving the plan. This was achieved after a study by McNaughton's outstanding staff officer, Lieutenant Colonel Mann.[51]

As the force commanders subsequently developed the plan two major changes emerged. The first was that the gap between the flank and central landings was increased from 30 to 60 minutes, in order to increase the chance of those troops engaging the German defences on Dieppe's headlands by the time of the main landing.[52] The second was made at a command conference on 5 June which cancelled the preliminary bombing, despite the fact that a special dispensation had been gained from the Prime Minister for this bombing of a French town only a few days before. Montgomery made much of this change in his memoirs, stating it applied to the 'revived plan', Operation JUBILEE and that he would not have agreed to it but that he had, by then, left the command system.[53] In fact the change also applied to the original plan RUTTER, and he chaired the meeting that approved its cancellation. At the meeting Leigh-Mallory stated that 'a raid which was not over-powering might only result in putting everyone on the alert', a view which would seem to apply the experience of St Nazaire. General Roberts' views are not recorded, but he subsequently stated he agreed to the cancellation of bombing because he was convinced the rubble created would immobilise his tanks and that this effect outweighed the benefits of the bombing.[54]

It is difficult to reconstruct with certainty how far the reasons given were valid and how far they may have been rationalisations. The arguments had some merit and fitted with such doctrine as existed, which tended to stress surprise over firepower in landing operations. However, this would have been equally true earlier in the process and it is odd the objections should emerge just after so much effort had been applied to removing the restrictions on bombing. It may have been that there was an apprehension that Churchill's agreement could have easily been reversed, so that it was best not to rely on bombing. The likely underlying cause, though, is indicated by a post-operation report by Rear Admiral McGrigor. It stated that bombing was 'ruled out because of the dislocation which it would have involved in the country's bombing offensive against Germany owing to the need for prolonged training of the crews concerned.'[55] As the decision came only four days after Bomber Command's spectacular success in its first '1,000 Bomber' raid it seems likely the commanders simply decided to avoid asking for a resource they had previously been refused, a result that was now even more likely. Trying to insist on it would almost certainly lead RUTTER to go the way of BLAZING, a result none of them wanted.

The removal of heavy bombing, which was now to be utilised only for more limited strikes on German airfields in the region, left a definite lack of firepower in the planned firepower which had been intimately linked to the decision for a frontal assault. Lighter aircraft were to provide both cannon fire and smoke cover immediately before the assault, but the only heavy weapons left were the guns of the tanks and the four inch guns of the eight destroyers, two of which would restricted by their roles as headquarters ships. This was far less firepower than had been deployed at Vaagso, when the landing force had been only a tenth of the scale of Dieppe. Mountbatten apparently requested battleship or cruiser support from the First Sea Lord. Admiral Pound's objections apparently included the fact that heavy

[50]See Peter J Henshaw 'The Dieppe Raid: A Product of Misplaced Canadian Nationalism?', Canadian Historical Review, Volume 77, Number 2, 1996.
[51]Stacey Op Cit. pp.329-332.
[52]Peter J Henshaw 'The Dieppe Raid: The Quest for Action for All the Wrong Reasons' Queens Quarterly 101/1, Spring 1994, p.107.
[53]Field Marshal Montgomery of Alamein Memoirs (Collins; London, 1958) p.76
[54]Stacey Op Cit. pp.336-7.
[55]NA, DEFE 2/727 'McGrigor Committee Report', 5 December 1942, Para.5.

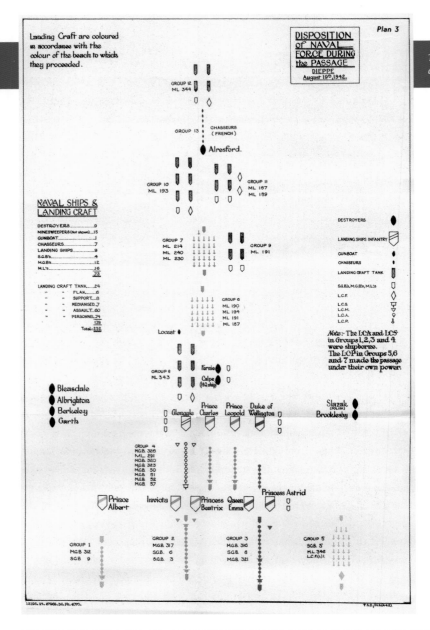

The Disposition of the Naval Force vessels during the passage to Dieppe. (NHB)

... if a battleship was used and should unhappily be sunk, we should never make a victory out of the operation

gunfire would create similar debris to bombing, and he is also supposed to have stated, 'Battleships by daylight off the French coast? You must be mad, Dickie!'[56] However the naval force commander, Rear Admiral Baillie-Groham continued to press Mountbatten for greater firepower and this led to an interesting account by him concerning the context of the raid in a 1957 letter to the Naval Historical Branch. Mountbatten reputedly told him:

> 'One of the main reasons for this raid was to give the British public something to cheer them up. For some months now there had been nothing but disaster. At sea alone, we had lost the *Prince of Wales* and *Repulse*, the *Barham*, the *Ark Royal*, two of our battleships had been put out of action in Alexandria; further, Singapore and its garrison had been lost, and so on. It was high time to help maintain morale at home. Experience had shown that in these times, the side which got its news and reports in first was believed; and that as we had the initiative in this (by knowing about the raid), we were going to make certain that it was we who got our propaganda in first. This was being most

carefully organised and arranged. Even if the raid was not an entire success, our propaganda would make it so. Now, the reason why the employment of a larger or capital ship had been turned down was that if a battleship was used and should unhappily be sunk, we should never make a victory out of the operation, no matter what propaganda was sent out, or how successful the raid was. There were, of course, other reasons for staging this operation, but this was the one which excluded the use of a large or capital ship.'[57]

Baillie-Groham accepted the restriction, which he believed derived from the Prime Minister, and preparations continued. This again followed the pattern of accepting severe resource compromises rather than confronting the COS with the issues and risking complete cancellation.

A major rehearsal YUKON, was held off the Dorset coast 11-12 June. Its poor execution led to YUKON II 22-23 June, where performance improved, and Montgomery reported to Paget that, 'I am now satisfied that the operation as planned is a possible one and has good prospects of success...'[58] On 30 June, Churchill, politically weakened by the fall of Tobruk and the imminent no-confidence vote in parliament, had a crisis

---

[56]Earl Mountbatten 'Operation Jubilee: The Place of the Dieppe Raid in History.' *Journal of the RUSI*, Vol.119, No.1, March 1974, p.27.
[57]NHBC, Battle Summary No.33 'Raid on Dieppe', Revision File, 'Statement by Vice-Admiral Baillie-Groham', 30 June 1957.
[58]Stacey *Op. Cit.* p.33.

of confidence. This seems to have been based less on any doubts about the viability of the operation than on his own vulnerable position. Brooke persuaded him the raid was still a reasonable operation and a necessary experiment for future landings.[59] At the start of July the task force assembled on the south coast, aiming at a window of 3-7 July for the raid. While it seems both Leigh-Mallory and Roberts had doubts, neither had was willing to defy their respective senior officers and jeopardise an operation that they were committed to and which was close to execution.[60] On 6 July Mountbatten briefed the COS on RUTTER and they formally approved the final plan, though apparently without more than an oral brief. As it was also at the same meeting that Mountbatten reported the raid was currently delayed by weather, this strongly indicated that the COS saw final approval as only a 'rubber stamp', with it being equally possible Mountbatten could have reported to them that the raid was already in progress.[61] It seems likely that the COS relied on the general information they received during a raid's preparation to inform them, but particularly on the consent of the force commanders to the plan and the lack of objections from the C-in-Cs whose forces were involved.

Early on 7 July two of the raid's landing ships were damaged by bombs, though the troops were successfully trans-shipped

Montgomery recommended the raid should be cancelled 'for all time'

and this damage did not, as is sometimes claimed, lead to the cancellation of RUTTER later that day. This was as a result of weather and, though it is usually assumed that it was the weather at sea that was too poor, Mountbatten stated that the critical factor was, 'owing to weather preventing adequate fighter cover.'[62] With cancellation of the raid the forces were dispersed and reverted to their normal tasks and commands.[63] Montgomery recommended the raid should be cancelled 'for all time', though this arose from his belief security would now have been compromised, rather than lack of faith in the plan.

Dieppe: From RUTTER to JUBILEE

Even before RUTTER's cancellation, Mountbatten had already secured from the COS agreement that he should 'consider remounting it at a later date.'[64] Though this was the formula that had already been used to mitigate other cancellations there is no doubt Mountbatten pursued the opportunity it offered vigorously. It was unlikely a new raid could be mounted, and, without a large-scale assault, Combined Operations record would seem slight compared to its resources. The situation and Mountbatten's reaction was best summarised by Hughes-Hallett in a post-war lecture:

'Suffice it is to say here that not the least remarkable feature of the operation was the fact of its having been carried out at all, and this was due to the united determination of the Chief of Combined Operations and his subordinates to drive on unless told otherwise by superior authority.'[65]

Mountbatten tried twice in July to have the COS enhance his powers to mount raids. Both attempts were without success, though it seems the COS were more concerned about Mountbatten trying to dominate the appointed force commanders, rather than avoid their scrutiny. On 27 July they agreed to a new directive to Mountbatten that removed the need for the COS to approve the final plan for a raid. Given the events surrounding RUTTER they may well have seen this as a fairly nominal alteration. They still effectively relied on the force commanders they appointed, and the C-in-C's whose forces were involved, as both more appropriate and more effective judges of the viability of plans they had already generally approved of.

Mountbatten sought to work within these constraints by again avoiding the involvement of those likely to question the raid. He made no requests for bombers or heavy ships for JUBILEE and

[59]Danchev & Todman Op Cit. p.275; Villa Op Cit. p.90.
[60]Henshaw Op Cit. pp.108-9.
[61]TNA, CAB 79/56, Chiefs of Staff(Operational), 64th meeting, 6 July 1942.
[62]TNA, ADM 202/87, 40 Commando War Diary, 3 July 1942.
[63]Villa Op Cit. p.13.
[64]TNA, CAB 79/56, COS(O), 64th mtg, 6 July 1942.
[65]Rear-Admiral J Hughes-Hallett 'The Mounting of Raids' Journal of the RUSI, Vol XCV, November 1950, p.585.

Cap badge of the Royal Hamilton Light Infantry, one of the Canadian Regiments which demonstrated exemplary bravery at Dieppe. (RHLI)

Right: Principal Landing Places at Dieppe. (NHB)

avoided requesting other forces that might extensively disturb their parent commands and so invite debate at the COS.[66] He substituted commandos for the airborne forces of RUTTER. This both removed British troops other than the commandos, whom he controlled, from the raid, and limited its ability to be affected by bad weather. With only Canadian troops participating from Home Forces, Mountbatten proposed Montgomery's place be taken by a senior Canadian officer, a proposal that General McNaughton enthusiastically endorsed.[67] Fighter Command was still eager for a major air battle and Baillie-Groham was replaced as the naval force commander by Hughes-Hallett, even though Baillie-Groham remained employed within both the UK and Combined Operations.[68]

The COS had approved the substitution of Hughes-Hallett for Baillie-Groham on 14 July and, when this was coupled with the new 27 July directive, Mountbatten had his basis for pushing on with preparations. In recent years there has been considerable debate over whether Mountbatten actually had sufficient authority to re-mount the raid, and it is significant that the various British and Canadian official historians who

have addressed the topic have offered contradictory dates as to the point of authorisation.[69] In internal accounts immediately after the raid, Mountbatten based his authority solely on the 27 July Directive.[70] Post-war he shifted his argument towards a claim of verbal authority from Churchill and the COS, which was not written down because of the extraordinary security required to re-mount a raid. This indicates he was not comfortable with the directive as the basis for his actions. To support this he cited Churchill's supportive account in his memoirs but without admitting that this was the account he had asked Churchill to include. His claims for verbal authority came back to a single source - himself.[71] It is, though, significant that Churchill was willing to accept and include Mountbatten's claim as his own. None of the COS ever refuted the verbal claim but none ever supported it.

Overall there is no doubt that the COS and Churchill were all aware of Mountbatten's preparations, preparations that required the active and widespread endorsement of their immediate subordinates and ministries. For example, the Assistant Chief of the Naval Staff (Home) (ACNS(H)) had to order

the allocation of destroyers from three different commands to participate in the raid. These ships were a significant resource, being 50% of the modern escorts available for important convoys on the south coast.[72] ACNS(H) provided daily briefings to the First Sea Lord and preparatory signals for JUBILEE have widespread distributions which include the First Sea Lord.[73] Any of the Chiefs could have easily challenged the preparations or required a formal decision on the operation if they had wished. However it seems all could see sufficient merit in the raid, even after TORCH had been agreed in late July, and none wished to be responsible for cancelling the only cross-channel offensive planned that year. Equally, Mountbatten could have asked for a formal endorsement from the COS and could have co-ordinated the preparations for the raid more widely, including organisations such as the Inter-Services Security Board, which co-ordinated actual operations with deceptions. Given the already widespread involvement JUBILEE required throughout the service staffs this would have represented no real risk but Mountbatten probably feared the awkward questions this might involve, which might have put JUBILEE in doubt. Ultimately, it seems both Mountbatten and the COS were unwilling to trigger

---

[66]One example the 'Rutter' plan included five 'Eagle' anti-aircraft ships, diverted from the Thames Estuary. As this diversion proved disruptive to anti-minelaying in the area Mountbatten had been ordered by the Admiralty to retain them for the one minimum possible period. Mountbatten did not request them for 'Jubilee'. See NHBC, Director of Operations Division (Home) Telegrams, Vol I, Signals 104 & 105.

[67]Stacey *Op Cit*. p.343.

[68]Ballie-Groham took command of the Combined Operations training establishments at Largs.

[69]The range of dates offered by Official Historian for the date of authorisation are 14 July, 20 July, 27 July, 12 August and that the date was never recorded. Interestingly Stacey only committed himself to a statement that approval was 'implied' by the appointment of Hughes-Hallett. See Stacey *Op Cit*. p.341.

[70]TNA, CAB 121/364, Mountbatten to Ismay, Enclosure, 24 December 1942.

[71]Villa *Op Cit*. Ch.2.

[72]NHBC, Director of Operations Division (Home) Telegrams, Vol I. Signal 1843B from Admiralty to C-in-Cs Portsmouth, Plymouth & Nore, 27 July 1942 & 'Pink List' of available warships, 4 August 1942.

[73]NHBC, Director of Operations Division (Home), Volume I.

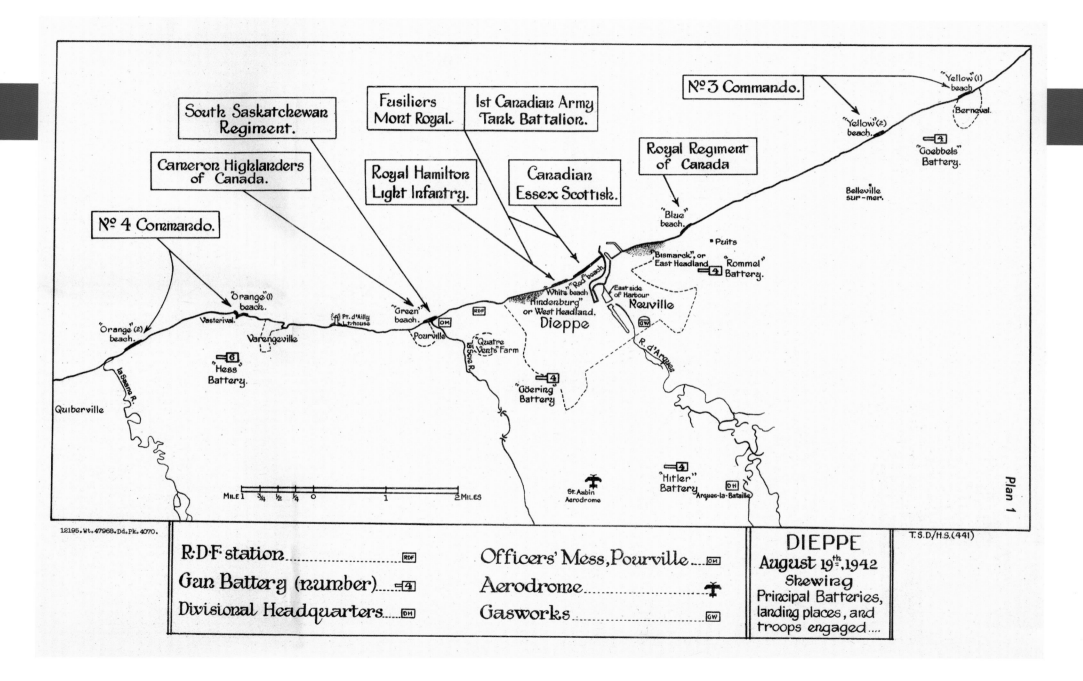

South Saskatchewan Regiment.

Cameron Highlanders of Canada.

Fusiliers Mont Royal.

1st Canadian Army Tank Battalion.

Royal Hamilton Light Infantry.

Canadian Essex Scottish.

Nº 3 Commando.

Royal Regiment of Canada

Nº 4 Commando.

"Yellow"(1) beach

Berneval.

"Yellow"(2) beach.

"Goebbels" Battery.

Belleville sur-mer.

"Blue" beach.

Puits

"Bismarck", or East Headland

"Rommel" Battery.

"White" beach "Red" beach

"Hindenburg" or West Headland.

Dieppe

East side of Harbour

Neuville

"Orange"(1) beach.

Vasterival.

Pt. d'Ailly Lt.-house

"Green" beach.

Pourville

OM

RDF

"Orange"(2) beach.

Varengeville

"Quatre Vents" Farm

la Scie R.

R. d'Arques

GW

"Hess" Battery.

"Göering" Battery

"Hitler" Battery

DH

St. Aubin Aerodrome

Arques-la-Bataille

Quiberville

la Saane R.

MILE 1   ¾   ½   ¼   0   1   2 MILES

Plan 1

12195. Wt. 47968. Dd. Pk. 4070.

T.S.D/H.S.(441)

R·D·F· station .... RDF

Gun Battery (number) 4

Divisional Headquarters ...... DH

Officers' Mess, Pourville ... OM

Aerodrome ....

Gasworks .... GW

DIEPPE
August 19th, 1942
Shewing
Principal Batteries,
landing places, and
troops engaged....

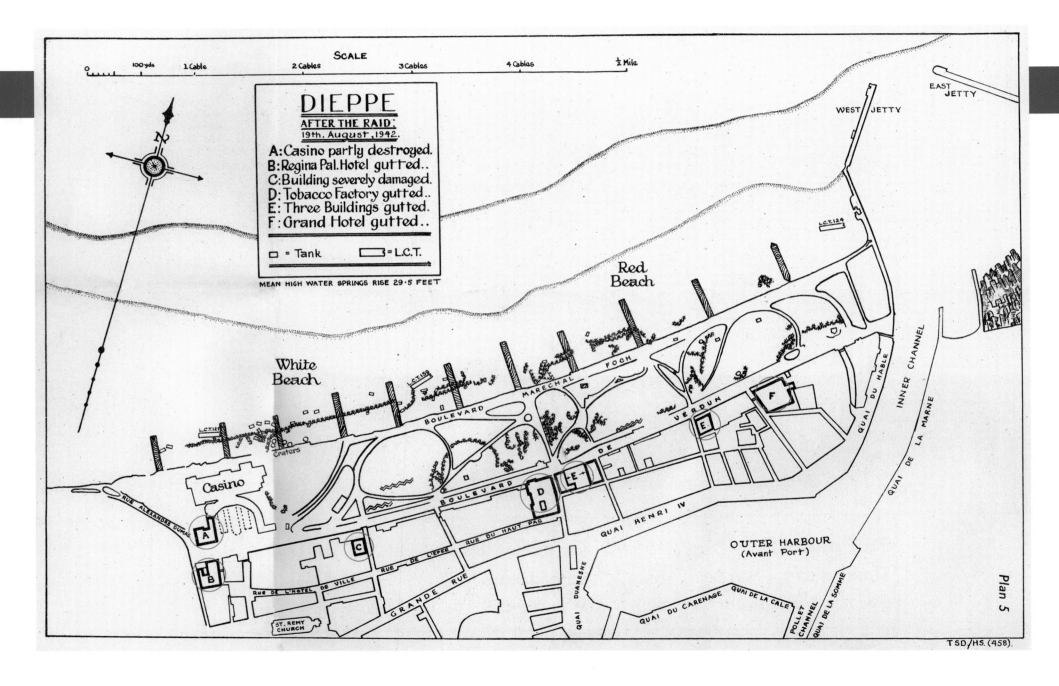

Left: Dieppe after the Raid. (NHB)

a formal consideration of the raid for fear of a result which would disadvantage them. Mountbatten's drive co-incided with the permissive environment provided by the COS and the support of the relevant C-in-C's and if any element had been absent then it is unlikely JUBILEE would have been launched. All parties hoped JUBILEE would be a success and none suspected it would be a disaster.

Many preparations for JUBILEE were determined by the enhanced requirements for security, against both German intelligence and, it seems, some internal audiences. Given the results of the raid there has been considerable speculation about German foreknowledge of the operation. Rumours of RUTTER do seem to have reached German intelligence after that raid was cancelled, possibly deliberately as part of the credibility building of 'turned' German agents using genuine but now apparently irrelevant information. However this information was only an insignificant fraction of the great mass of data available and was assigned no particular significance.[74] Security for JUBILEE preparations was maintained but German defence preparations were largely based on likely conditions. The result of this was that German forces were on a period on enhanced watchfulness on the French coast from 10-19 August but also that significant air assets had been diverted to Norway, as an anti-raid precaution, during the same period.[75]

While the JUBILEE task force was similar to that assembled for RUTTER it had some significant differences. Some of the 6,000 troops made their passage entirely in landing craft, rather than initially travelling in landing ships and then trans-shipping into craft for the assault. While this helped conceal the assembly of the force it added to navigation and timing difficulties in a group which now numbered 253 ships and craft. Sailing times had also been made later to reduce the risk of exposure to German air recconaisance that evening. The disadvantage of this however was that it resulted in the hour lead time for the flank attacks being reduced back to its original thirty minutes.

The Commander-in-Chief Portsmouth, Admiral Sir William James, gave the execute order for JUBILEE at 1002 on 18 August. The force sailed in thirteen groups and was broadly on schedule when at 0347 Group 5, carrying No.3 Commando for the assault on the Eastward German gun battery at Berneval, encountered a German coastal convoy. In a confused action the 23 landing craft carrying the commandos were scattered and the Berneval defences alerted. Only seven landing craft ever made a landing - six 20-25 minutes late at 'Yellow I', where the troops were pinned down on the beach. A single landing craft under Lieutenant H T Buckee RNVR landed Major Peter Young and 19 commandos at 'Yellow II' at 0445 - five minutes early. Young's party climbed a gully, circled behind the battery

and then sniped at it, suppressing it, until they ran out of ammunition, when they were evacuated by Buckee. Both Buckee and Young were awarded the DSO and Hughes-Hallett described the action as, 'the most outstanding incident in the operation.'[76] On the western flank at Varengeville No.4 Commando's assault was completely successful. Lord Lovat's commandos landed in two parties, on schedule and location. One party engaged the battery while the other rapidly encircled it. Immediately following an attack by cannon firing fighters at 0620 the battery was stormed, despite casualties during the assault across open ground. The six 150mm guns were destroyed and Lovat's force was evacuated, having suffered 45 casualties from its 252 strength.

The east flank convoy action did not, as is often stated in contemporary accounts, lead to a general alert in the Dieppe area. In fact, ironically, the action in some ways reduced the general German alert, as radar echoes off Dieppe were now interpreted as being ships from a normal night convoy action rather than a raiding force.[77] At Puys immediately to the west, however, the local commander did stand his small garrison to after hearing the firing, an initiative that would have devastating results. The troops landing here at the small 'Blue' Beach were mainly from the Royal Regiment of Canada. Given the very limited exit from the beach their assault relied on surprise and

[74]Greenhous *Op Cit.* pp.78-9.
[75]John Campbell *Dieppe Revisited* (Frank Cass; London, 1993) p.113.
[76]Captain Hughes-Hallett 'The Dieppe Raid' *The London Gazette*, 14 August 1947, Para.6.
[77]Campbell *Op Cit.* pp.139-42.

limited light. Surprise had already been lost and problems with forming up their landing craft meant the troops arrived about 17 minutes late, at 0507 rather than 0450. The combined effect of this was, despite the fact the German garrison did not exceed two platoons, the battalion was trapped on the beach. About 20 Canadians ultimately made it up the cliff but had little effect. Despite attempts by strafing fighters to assist the troops, they were unable to advance and were increasingly grouped under the cliffs to avoid enfilading fire. At 0835 the local German command reported the Canadian surrender at Puys and that about 500 Allied troops were dead or prisoners.

The other flank landing at Pourville to the west of Dieppe was the most successful of the Canadian operations. The South Saskatchewan Regiment landed at 'Green' Beach within two minutes of their target time at 0452 and were unopposed until they came ashore. They landed to the west of the River Scie, with the river between them and Dieppe, rather than on both sides of the river as had been intended. Despite this they pushed on, under Lieutenant Colonel Merritt, towards the town but met heavy resistance. By 0700 they were fighting on the western headland but never took the summit of it overlooking Dieppe. Though the landing was reinforced by the Cameron Highlanders of Canada the actions of the two battalions were never co-ordinated, with the Camerons following the original plan and trying to head inland. Withdrawal of units to the beach began

at 1100, as it was clear the troops at 'Blue' would now have to be evacuated from there rather than through Dieppe. Fourteen craft took off large numbers, although many were wounded and at least four of the craft were lost. Lieutenant Colonel Merritt surrendered his rearguard after 1300. He was subsequently awarded a Victoria Cross for his conduct throughout the day.

The failure of the flank landings meant that the main landing was now vulnerable to enfilading fire from both headlands. Though support was provided by the destroyers and five squadrons of Hurricanes with 20mm cannon exactly as planned the context of the raid meant there was no further firepower on call. The troops were landed within a minute of the 0520 H-Hour and also within about a minute of the lifting of covering fire. However, the three Landing Craft, Tank (LCT) were 10-15 minutes late and, as the Canadian Official Historian puts it:

> 'In any opposed landing, the first minute or two after the craft touch down are of crucial importance; and it may be said that during that minute or two the Dieppe battle, on the main beaches, was lost. The impetus of the attack ebbed quickly away, and by the time the tanks arrived the psychological moment was past.'[78]

Unsupported, and in a desperate situation, the Canadian troops largely went to ground on the beach and behind the sea wall.

While, as the commandos already emphasised, their best chance was to maintain their momentum, across the promenade and into the cover of the town, this was totally counter-intuitive. As such it could only be engendered by ruthless training, which stressed this requirement. While the Canadian troops were as well trained as any British division then in the UK it seems that normal infantry training of the time did not include this stress. Also, unlike for RUTTER, intensive mission training had withheld because of its security implications, a restriction, which did not apply to the commandos. The Canadians entered a situation, both at Puys and on the main beach, which was, almost certainly, worse than any the commandos had encountered until 'Yellow I' where they were also pinned down. An additional factor on the main beach, not normally recorded, was the opinion of the senior surviving medical officer of, 'the severe and almost paralysing effects of shingle thrown about by exploding bombs and shells.' This led to the, 'severely confused state caused by repeated blows from flying shingle.'[79]

At least two small parties were able to exploit the cover of the Casino at the west end of the promenade to get into the town but they numbered only about thirty. At the east end the Essex Scottish reformed for at least three local attempts to get to the town but were beaten back. Company Sergeant Major Stapleton

[78]Stacey *Op Cit.* p.375.
[79]J L S Coulter *The Royal Navy Medical Service, Volume II, Operations* (HMSO; London, 1956) p.417.

Landing Craft, Flak (Large) closed in to provide point blank range, and gave most effective support

managed to lead a group into the town but only about a dozen men made it. Twenty-nine tanks landed from 0535 onwards and at least 15 crossed the sea wall by mounting it at its ends where the gap between shingle and wall was only about two feet. Many accounts, including contemporary official documents, state the tanks did not cross the wall because after the raid they were recovered from the beach. This was in fact where they returned to later in the raid. While the tanks were impervious to the 37mm guns the Germans could bring to bear, they were unable to breach the concrete barriers the Germans had put over each road exit. With the surviving engineers unable to assist them, the tanks fell back to the beach to provide cover for the casualties.[80]

The air and naval components both did their best to assist with strafing and bombardment but lacked the firepower to have a major impact. Landing Craft, Flak (Large) 'closed in to provide point blank range, and gave most effective support. She was soon disabled and her captain killed, but her guns were fought until one by one they were put out of action, and the ship herself was finally sunk.'[81] At 0700 General Roberts committed his reserve battalion, the Fusiliers Mont-Royal, after exaggerated and fragmented signals suggested the Scottish Essex were in the town in large numbers. The battalion took heavy casualties on the run in and then joined the huddled force on the beach. The breakdown in communications though, meant that Roberts

was not aware of this and fragments of information still implied success in the town. He therefore ordered in his last reserve, the Royal Marine Commando, which had been intended as a cutting out party in the harbour, who were supposed to pass through the town and attack the eastern headland from the land. The Royal Marines suffered casualties on the run in and as they arrived at the beach their commanding officer, Lieutenant Colonel Phillipps RM, could see the real situation and tried to wave as many of the landing craft as possible off. He was killed while doing this but saved many of the commandos from adding to the carnage.[82] By 0900 Hughes-Hallett and Roberts were both agreed on the hopeless situation of the landing and a withdrawal was planned for 1100, the delay being required to organise the craft and air cover, including smoke laying. The withdrawal under fire had to be largely improvised and Stacey commented, 'These circumstances increase the credit due to the Navy for an evacuation carried out under conditions without parallel in the history of warfare.'[83] There was little control of troops on the beach and each landing craft had to make a dangerous independent passage, many of them being sunk or swamped by troops. While around 600 troops were saved from 'Green', only about 368 could be picked up from the main beach and only 6 from Puys. The destroyer HMS *Berkley* was lost to bombing during the evacuation but air cover prevented any further losses and the last units returned to England just before midnight.

Dieppe: Aftermath and Conclusion

Mountbatten asserted to the Chiefs of Staff that significant lessons would be learnt from Dieppe the day after the raid. What was beyond dispute was that the raiders had suffered heavily the previous day. The raid had involved over 15,000 Allied personnel who suffered 4,260 casualties, but the landing force had been just over 6,000. This group suffered a 59.5% casualty rate, of which 16% were fatal. This underestimates the loss of those who landed however as over 1,000 never made it off their landing craft. Stacey's figures show that 4,963 Canadian troops embarked and only 1,624 returned unwounded, of whom around 1,000 did not get ashore. This means a casualty rate for the Canadians who landed of 85%, killed, wounded and/or captured. Naval losses included a destroyer and 33 landing craft. The air battle, which had been a major driver of the raid, was fought with the Allied air forces flying well over 2,000 sorties. One hundred and six Allied aircraft were lost and 92 German aircraft claimed, with 39 probables.[84] The reality of the German air loss was 48 aircraft. Britain's official historians of intelligence have commented, 'In so far as one of its main objects was to impose wastage on the GAF and thus provide relief to Russia, the Dieppe raid was a resounding failure'.[85] Total German casualties were 591. Despite Mountbatten's plans, no amount of propaganda was able to disguise this situation.

---

[80]Stacey *Op Cit.* p.379-81.
[81]Hughes-Hallett, *Despatch*, Para.15.
[82]TNA, ADM 202/87, 40 Commando War Diary, Supplementary Statements, August 1942.
[83]Stacey *Op Cit.* p.384.
[84]See NHBC, BR1736(26) Naval Staff History *Raid on Dieppe (Naval Operations)(Battle Summary No.39)* Revised 1959, especially Appendix C.
[85]Hinsley *Op Cit.* p.270.

An abandoned tank near the Boulevard Marechal Foch on the seafront at Dieppe. (NHB)

In its longer-term aftermath there can be no doubt that the 'lessons learnt' argument has become the main justification for Dieppe, though this was only a partial justification before the raid. An extensive report on the raid was produced by Combined Operations and widely distributed later in the war. It included the claim, in Mountbatten's second foreword, that, 'It was considered essential, as a preliminary to a large-scale combined operation such as the occupation of North Africa, to gain battle experience of hitherto untried factors'.[86] The experience of the raid has been linked to many aspects of D-Day including the concept of the Mulberry Harbours, to substitute for assaulting a port; 'DD' floating tanks to provide immediate support for infantry; specialised command ships; intensive fire support, and Germany emphasis on defence of ports, permitting easier landings to be made over beaches. Mountbatten later went as far as to claim that, 'For every one man who died at Dieppe in 1942, at least ten or more must have been spared in Normandy in 1944.'[87]

The reality of the 'Lessons Learnt' was somewhat more equivocal, with simple comparison with later operations not demonstrating causal linkage.[88] Some significant lessons, such as the need to improve the professional skills and group cohesion of landing craft crews had been identified before Dieppe from the RUTTER training. Other innovations such as Mulberry

Harbours, special HQ ships and 'DD' tanks were already in development and, indeed, the Dieppe Report actually suggested that tanks should only be landed after infantry had secured the beach, the opposite of the method later developed.[89] As to German emphasis on defence of ports rather than beaches, this came from basic judgements about the most valuable terrain, which proved valid even though German resources as a whole were not adequate to resist invasion in 1944. As to firepower support there was never any doubt invasion would attract more support than a raid, as was soon demonstrated in TORCH and which Mountbatten had admitted even before the raid.[90] While the Dieppe experience would have been of more value had there been an attempt at D-Day in 1943 the invasions of North Africa, Sicily and Italy, which were much closer in scale and nature to D-Day, and their lessons rapidly eclipsed any value in JUBILEE. This limited relevance was reinforced by the fact that the Dieppe report, while dated in October, was not actually

printed until December, after the experience of TORCH. It was also subject to strong influence from Brooke, who thought it weak, and suggested to Mountbatten many of the lessons that 'should' be identified and others that he wanted suppressed. In his weakened situation after Dieppe Mountbatten eagerly had the report altered to fit Brooke's concepts, rather than an assessment of experience.[91] As John Campbell has put it in his thorough study of Dieppe's impact, 'An outdated or poorly conceived experiment often yields irrelevant data.'[92]

The Dieppe raid marked the end of the 'raiding period' at Combined Operations, as amphibious resources were increasingly committed to supporting enduring campaigns. Combined Operations continued to provide a vital role in infrastructure, training and concepts, but by 1943 its expanded fleet of landing craft was included in the normal Admiralty control of shipping. The St Nazaire raid had been Combined

[86]NHBC, CB 04244/ BR 1887, 'The Dieppe Raid (Combined Report)', October 1942, Second Foreword. As can be seen from this article there was actually no significant linkage between the Dieppe raid and 'Torch'.
[87]Lord Mountbatten 'The Dieppe Raid', *Naval Review*, 1965 p.40.
[88]See for example D & S Whitaker *Dieppe Tragedy to Triumph* (Leo Cooper; Barnsley, 1992) Ch.7
[89]Campbell *Op Cit*. p218-19.

[90]Mountbatten 'Operation Jubilee' p.27.
[91]See NA, WO106/44, Correspondence between Mountbatten and Brooke, 8-13 November.
[92]Campbell *Op Cit*. p.215.

Left: Burnt out landing craft at Dieppe.

Right: Allied troops taken as POWs. (NHB)

Operations greatest operational success. It had demonstrated sophisticated preparation and risk management, both in terms of the force relative to the objective and of the innovative methods used to compensate for the inevitable weakness of that force. There had always been a chance of complete failure but this had been minimised and redundancy had been actively included so that success was achieved despite failures in detail.

Dieppe provides a sharp contrast, where the high casualties were not compensated by success. There were areas of achievement, such as the force protection provided to surface units by the air forces, a necessary step before the evolution to greater direct support. Overall though the scale of the failure in planning was vast and any amount of gallantry on the ground could only have had a marginal effect on the outcome. While the encounter with a coastal convoy is often characterised as 'unlucky', the coastal traffic at that time meant it was always a

The requirement for more professional and thorough preparation in combined operations, supported by genuine unity of effort, was recognised

very possible scenario, which the planners had simply hoped to avoid. The really significant result from Dieppe, therefore, was that the commanders, principally Mountbatten but stretching from Churchill and the Chiefs of Staff, through the C-in-Cs to the force commanders, embarked on the operation on the basis of hope. Influenced by a wide variety of motives, they hoped they could 'get away with it' and chose not to analyse or challenge the judgements of either their seniors or their subordinates. After the result at Dieppe there was a much-enhanced appreciation of the dangers of hope. The requirement for more professional and thorough preparation in combined operations, supported by genuine unity of effort, was recognised.

Reflections on St Nazaire & Dieppe

- A weak strategic situation may permit or encourage high risk operations.

- St Nazaire demonstrates how an effect is achieved through innovation in both concept and method.

- Dieppe demonstrates how the desire of military organisations to participate in operations may affect their judgement.

- The danger of crediting 'lessons learnt' to a costly failure may help justify the reason behind the operation being launched in the first instance. This can distort where the innovation has really come from.

- There is an absolute requirement for unified professionalism in amphibious operations.

Further Reading

Atkin, Ronald, *Dieppe 1942: The Jubilee Disaster,* (London: Book Club Associates, 1980)

Campbell, John, *Dieppe Revisited* (London: Frank Cass, 1993)

Dorrian, James, *Storming St Nazaire: The Gripping Story of The Dock-busting Raid March, 1942,* (London: Leo Cooper, 1998)

Greenhous, Brereton, *Dieppe, Dieppe* (Montreal: Art Global, 1992)

Maguire, Eric, *Dieppe: August 1942,* (London: Jonathan Cape, 1963)

Mason, David, *Raid on St Nazaire,* (London: Macdonald, 1970)

Mordal, Jacques, *Dieppe: The Dawn of Decision,* (London: Souvenir Press, 1962)

Neillands, Robin, *Dieppe*, (London: Aurum Press, 2005)

Phillips, C. E. Lucas, *The Greatest Raid of All,* (London: Heinemann, 1958)

Robertson, Terence, *Dieppe: The Shame and The Glory,* (London: Hutchinson, 1963)

Ryder, R. E. D., *The Attack on St. Nazaire,* (London: John Murray; 1947)

Villa, Brian, *Unauthorised Action: Mountbatten and the Dieppe Raid,* (Oxford: Oxford University Press, 1989)

Biography

Mr Stephen Prince is a Historian in the Naval Historical Branch of the Naval Staff, where he has responsibility for operational records and the linkage between history and current policy. A graduate of Warwick University and King's College London he has previously been the Sir Robert Menzies Scholar at the Australian War Memorial, lecturer at Warwick and BRNC Dartmouth and Senior Lecturer at JSCSC. He has led many battlefield tours for all branches of the Services, including several to Dieppe. His publications include articles in the *RUSI Journal*, the *Journal of Strategic Studies* and *Defence and Security Analysis*.

Guadalcanal
Operation WATCHTOWER, August 1942

By Mr Colin Bruce

The landings on Guadalcanal and adjacent islands in August 1942 (Operation WATCHTOWER) marked the first offensive undertaken by American ground troops in the Second World War, and the first American amphibious operation since 1898.

The fighting graphically demonstrated the difficulty of seizing and holding a distant island objective without first achieving naval and air superiority. In contrast to the later Pacific island battles, where the Americans were able to isolate the defenders from external supply and reinforcement at the outset and then grind them down relentlessly, both sides found themselves executing amphibious operations concurrently, and both embraced a 'manoeuvrist approach' to a greater or lesser extent.

Guadalcanal was in many ways a textbook example of how not to conduct an amphibious assault, unless the situation seems desperate enough to call for it. Of course, when the operation was ordered in the Summer of 1942 the situation was regarded as desperate enough. The Japanese had successfully pushed to within striking distance of Australia. In May 1942 they occupied the island of Tulagi in the southern Solomons, in a move intended to cover the flank of further advances in New Guinea. To the Allies, the occupation of Tulagi also appeared to be the first stage of an attempt to sever the direct shipping routes between Australia and the USA, which ran up through

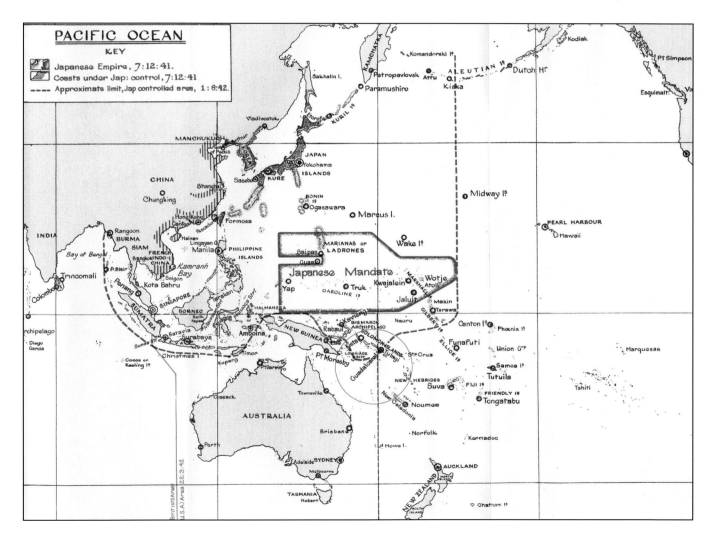

Left: Major General Alexander A Vandergrift. (USMC)
Centre: Rear Admiral Richmond Kelly Turner. (DoD)
Right: Vice Admiral Frank Jack Fletcher. (DoD)

*Right: South Pacific Area Naval
Operations 1 - 13 August, 1942. (NHB)*

New Caledonia and the lightly-garrisoned island groups of the New Hebrides (now Vanuatu), Fiji and Samoa. Overall American policy was to concentrate on the defeat of Germany and only to send to the Pacific such forces as were absolutely essential for containment, but it was acknowledged that to allow the Japanese to build airfields in these islands would be extremely costly in the long run.

In spite of plainly inadequate resources, on 2 July 1942 the US Joint Chiefs of Staff (JCS) approved a plan to recapture Tulagi 'and adjacent positions' and to occupy the nearby Santa Cruz islands as well. A target date of 1 August was set for the landings. As the orders passed down the chain of command, from the Joint Chiefs to the CinC Pacific Fleet, then to the Commander South Pacific, and finally to the officers who would exercise tactical responsibility, the importance of the Santa Cruz islands diminished but that of the 'adjacent positions' increased. Guadalcanal, unnamed in the original JCS instruction, came to be seen as the most important objective because it boasted a site on its north coast suitable for the construction of an airfield. An added impetus was given to the operation when firm intelligence arrived showing that the Japanese had already reached the same conclusion, and that construction work was under way.

The only available ground troops with the requisite amphibious training belonged to the US 1st and 2nd Marine Divisions, neither of which was organisationally complete or regarded

as fully combat-ready. The 1st was closer, being in the middle of a move to New Zealand, so was given the leading role. The 2nd was ordered to contribute a reinforced regiment (the 2nd Marines), most of which would act as landing force reserve. Assuming this was not needed in the initial landings, it would go on to occupy the Santa Cruz islands. Additional Marine Corps reinforcements in the form of the 1st Raider Battalion (raised as a copy of British commando units), the 1st Parachute Battalion and the 3rd Defense Battalion (composed principally of AA and coast defence gun batteries) began to be gathered from a variety of locations around the Pacific. Although the Marines were supposed to be relieved by Army units as soon as possible, so as to free them for further amphibious operations, no firm orders could be issued for this because no Army units were actually available. Similarly, no firm plan for the logistical support of the landing force could be made because no-one was sure where the supplies would come from, or indeed whether they could be found at all.

Major General Alexander Vandegrift, commanding the 1st Marine Division, had not expected his units to be committed to action before the start of 1943. One of his three marine infantry regiments, the 7th Marines, had previously been detached to garrison Samoa and could not be moved until a suitable substitute arrived from the USA. His second regiment, the 1st Marines, was at sea and could not reach him until 11 July

– only twenty-one days before he was expected to land in the Solomons. All its equipment and stores were transport loaded for an administrative move, not combat loaded for an assault. Only his third regiment, the 5th Marines, and the portion of Divisional assets which had recently arrived in New Zealand were able to make an immediate start on their preparations. The target date was eventually allowed to slip to 7 August, but the need to strike before the Japanese airfield received its first aircraft made any further postponements impossible.

In addition to the physical problems of re-stowing supplies and equipment in New Zealand, it quickly became apparent that Allied intelligence of the situation in the landing areas was woefully inadequate. Estimates of the opposition the Marines would face were pure guesswork, and no maps of the islands could be obtained.

However, the bulk of the invasion force was able to assemble off the Fiji islands on 25 July, in time for a few days of landing exercises. This was the first opportunity for Vice Admiral Frank Jack Fletcher, who had been named as the overall commander for the invasion force, to meet Vandegrift and the commander of the landing ships, Rear Admiral Richmond Kelly Turner, for a face-to-face discussion. By all accounts the meeting did not go well. Fletcher, who appeared to have little faith that the operation would succeed whatever support he gave it, dropped

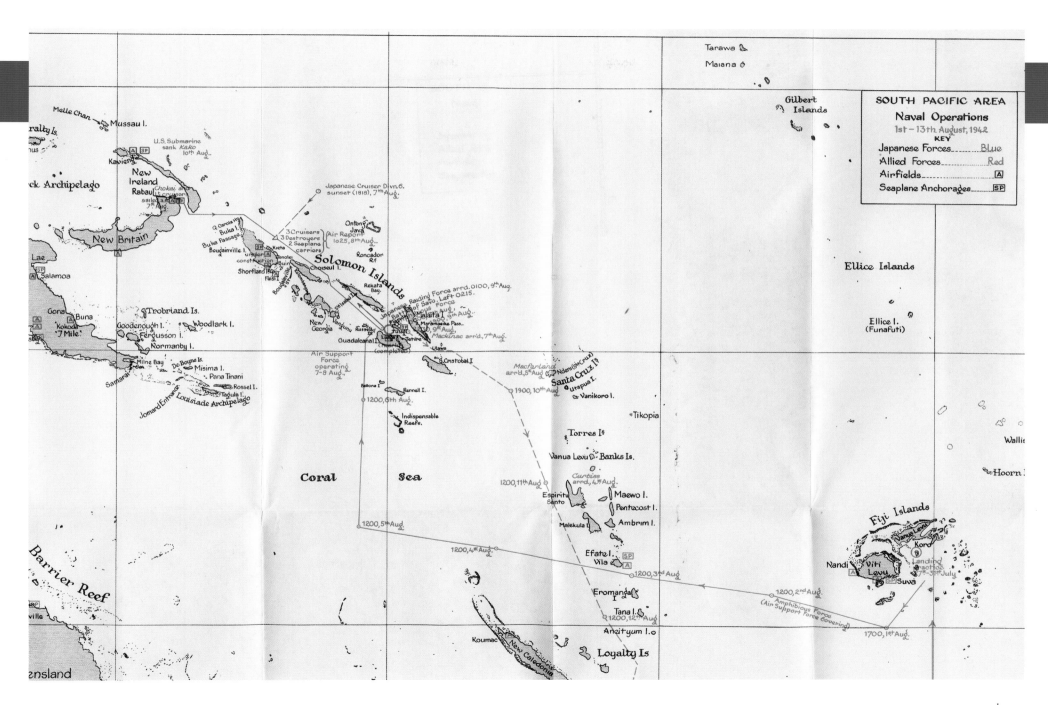

SOUTH PACIFIC AREA
Naval Operations
1st – 13th August, 1942
KEY
Japanese Forces............. Blue
Allied Forces................... Red
Airfields............................ [A]
Seaplane Anchorages........ [SP]

Melle Chan
Mussau I.
ralty Is
Kavieng
New
Ireland
Rabaul
sailed
7th Aug.
Chokai and
cruisers
U.S. Submarine
sank *Kako*
10th Aug.

ck Archipelago
New Britain

Lae
Salamoa

Gona
Buna
Kokoda
"7 Mile"

Q Carola Hbr
Buka I.
Buka Passage
Bougainville I.
Kieta
under
construction
Buin
Shortland I.
Faisi I.

Japanese Cruiser Divn.6
sunset (1818), 7th Aug.

Ontong
Java
(Air Report
1o25, 8th Aug.)

3 Cruisers
3 Destroyers
2 Seaplane
carriers

Ysabel
Choiseul I.

Roncador
Rf.

Santa Isabel I.

Solomon Islands

Trobriand Is.
Woodlark I.
Goodenough I.
Ferguson I.
Normanby I.

New
Georgia
Vangunu
Russell I.

Guadalcanal I.
(Air field
completed)

Rekata
Bay.

Japanese Raiding Force arr'd. 0100, 9th Aug.
Battle of Savo, Left 0215.
of US Force
9th Aug.
Malaita I.
Maramaike Pass
9th Aug.
Mackinac arr'd, 7th Aug.

Tulagi
Tetere
Ulawa

Milne Bay
De Boyne Is.
Misima I.
Pana Tinani
Samarai
Rossel I.
Tagula I.
Jomard Entrance
Louisiade Archipelago

Air Support
Force
operating
7-8 Aug.

S. Cristobal I.

Macfarland
arr'd, 5th Aug
Ndeni (Sta Cruz) Is

Santa Cruz
Utupua I.
Vanikoro I.

Bellona I.
Rennell I.

1200, 6th Aug.

Indispensable
Reefs.

1900, 10th Aug

Queensland
Barrier Reef

ville

Coral Sea

1200, 5th Aug.

1200, 4th Aug.

1200, 11th Aug.

1200, 12th Aug.

Tikopia

Torres Is

Vanua Levu
Banks Is.

Curtiss
arr'd, 4th Aug.
Espiritu
Santo

Maewo I.
Pentecost I.
Malekula I.
Ambrim I.

Efate I.
Vila

Eromanga
I.

Tana I.
Aneityum I.

Koumac
New Caledonia

Loyalty Is

Tarawa
Maiana

Gilbert
Islands

Ellice Islands

Ellice I.
(Funafuti)

Wallis

Hoorn I.

Fiji Islands
Vanua Levu
Koro
Nandi
Viti
Levu
Landing
Practice
17th-31st July
Suva

1200, 3rd Aug

1200, 2nd Aug.
Amphibious Force
(Air Support Force Covering)

1700, 1st Aug.

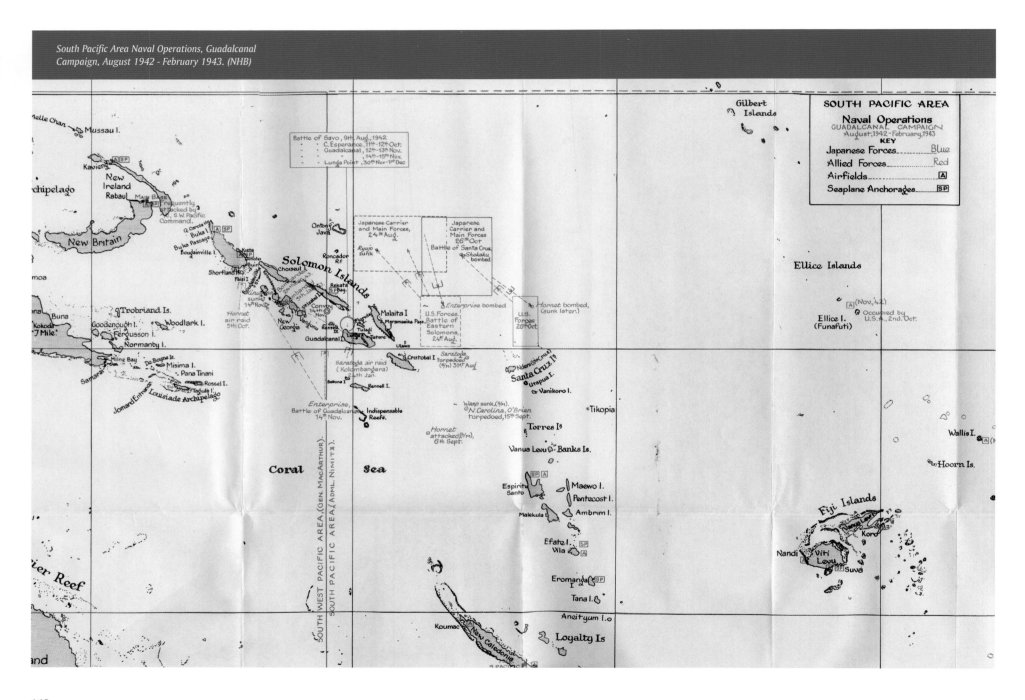

South Pacific Area Naval Operations, Guadalcanal
Campaign, August 1942 - February 1943. (NHB)

Annotated aerial photographs:
Left: Showing the Raider Battalion's advance along Tulagi. (USMC)
Right: Surprise was impossible at Gavutu. (USMC)

the bombshell that he intended to withdraw his carriers (and thus the Marines' only fighter cover) on D+1. Turner protested that this would not even give him enough time to fully unload, but Fletcher remained adamant. He commanded three of the five fleet carriers left in the entire US Navy (USS *Saratoga*, *Enterprise* and *Wasp* – *Ranger* was in the Atlantic, *Hornet* at Pearl Harbor having new guns and radar fitted), and he did not intend to expose these valuable ships to Japanese land-based air power for longer than two days.

On 31 July the invasion force left Fiji for the voyage to the landing areas. Joined on 3 August by the last of its ships (those bringing the 3rd Defense Battalion down from Hawaii), the force maintained radio silence and enjoyed the cover of bad weather, which restricted enemy air reconnaissance.

The Assault

The Japanese were taken completely by surprise when, on the morning of 7 August 1942, their positions in the southern Solomons came under air attack and naval bombardment. The first landings followed at 0740, when a company from the 1st

Bn, 2nd Marines occupied a promontory on Florida Island which overlooked the 1st Raider Battalion's planned landing beach on the western side of Tulagi. The Raider Battalion's landings, deliberately avoiding the south eastern end of

> **Only the belief that the Japanese did not hold Gavutu and Tanambogo in strength can excuse the decision to expose the landing force to such obvious dangers**

the narrow, 3 mile long island, where it was suspected the bulk of the Japanese garrison were located, went in at 0800. The Raiders quickly penetrated to the far coast and, in the absence of opposition, began to push south east. The 2nd Bn, 5th Marines, landing behind the Raiders, secured the north western end of the island and then joined the drive to clear the remainder.

At 0845 the 1st Bn, 2nd Marines (minus the company which had landed to secure the promontory overlooking Tulagi) occupied another promontory on Florida, this time to prevent the 1st Parachute Battalion's landing beach on Gavutu from being overlooked. Gavutu and Tanambogo, some 3,000 yards east of Tulagi, were two tiny islands linked together by a concrete causeway. Their small size afforded no possibility of using manoeuvre rather than a frontal assault, and neither was there any chance of surprise, given the fact that the 1st Parachute Battalion had to wait for the Tulagi force to finish disembarking

so that it could then re-use the same landing craft. Only the belief that the Japanese did not hold Gavutu and Tanambogo in strength can excuse the decision to expose the landing force (which although styled a battalion was only 350 strong) to such obvious dangers. Unfortunately when the Paras began landing on the eastern side of Gavutu at 1200 they quickly discovered that the garrison was much larger than they had been led to believe, and progress was slow.

Meanwhile at 0910 the remaining two battalions of the 5th Marines, followed closely by the three battalions of the 1st Marines, had begun an unopposed landing on the northern coast of Guadalcanal. As on Tulagi, the landing beach had been selected so as to avoid a frontal assault, and the Marines came ashore well to the east of the Japanese airfield. They were followed by their supporting artillery and tanks, together with the remainder of Vandegrift's division. The difficulty of movement through the dense jungle and the inaccuracy of the crude sketch maps which the Marines had been issued were more formidable obstacles than the Japanese, and the only American casualties were inflicted by bombers from Rabaul (the biggest Japanese base in the South Pacific, and the principal

Gavutu the Paras were requesting reinforcements, and in response to this the company from the 1st Bn, 2nd Marines which had made the first landings of the day was withdrawn from its promontory on Florida and ordered to assault Tanambogo. The attack was a total failure, and the company was driven back into the sea by the intensity of the Japanese fire. The other two battalions of the 2nd Marines, which Turner had hoped to keep back for use in the Santa Cruz islands, were then released from reserve. The 3rd Bn, 2nd Marines was ordered to land the following morning, and to assist the Paras on Gavutu.

On 8 August (D+1) the Guadalcanal beachhead was enlarged to absorb the almost-completed airfield, against negligible opposition. Having captured what he regarded as the vital ground, Vandegrift did not order a vigorous pursuit of the Japanese, who fled to the west, but instead concentrated on organizing his own defences, particularly against an amphibious counterstroke. The Japanese at Rabaul had, in fact, already dispatched a small relief force of around 400 men – all that could be gathered together immediately – aboard a single freighter, but this force was wiped out when the ship was picked off by an American submarine. Even had the force arrived, of course, it would have made no material difference to the situation on Guadalcanal.

air threat to the landings), which began to harass the invasion shipping during the afternoon despite the efforts of Fletcher's carrier-based fighters. Luckily for the Americans, the Japanese chose not to target the Guadalcanal landing beach, where large quantities of supplies had already begun to pile up due to a serious underestimation of the number of men needed to keep things moving. Despite the fact that the impending departure of the carriers made unloading a desperate race against the clock, the chaos on the beach became so bad that during the night the ships had to be instructed not to send anything else ashore.

By nightfall on 7 August it was also clear that the fighting on Tulagi and Gavutu would continue into a second day. On Tulagi the Japanese garrison had finally been located, well dug in at the south eastern tip of the island. After dark it counter-attacked the Marines repeatedly, expending a good deal of its strength in fruitless 'banzai' charges and attempts at infiltration. On

D+1 also saw organized resistance on Tulagi overcome after a renewed push by the Raiders and the 2nd Bn, 5th Marines. Individual Japanese continued to be a problem for several days, but the island was declared secure. On Gavutu and Tanambogo, however, the fighting continued all day and into the night, as the depleted 1st Parachute Battalion and the fresh 3rd Bn, 2nd Marines edged their way forward with the support of tanks, air strikes and continuing naval bombardment.

At 1807 on D+1 Fletcher formally requested permission from the Commander South Pacific, Vice Admiral Robert Ghormley, to withdraw his carriers. Ghormley raised no objections. A few hours later, in the early hours of the morning of 9 August (D+2), it was the Imperial Japanese Navy's turn to achieve complete surprise. A hastily-collected cruiser/destroyer force commanded by Vice Admiral Gunichi Mikawa arrived in the waters between Guadalcanal and Tulagi completely undetected, due to a combination of Japanese luck and inadequate Allied aerial reconnaissance. The resulting Battle of Savo Island was a crushing defeat for the Allied escort force supposedly providing close-in protection for the landings, with four of its eight cruisers being sunk and several other ships damaged. Only Mikawa's caution, which caused him to break off his highly successful action prematurely, saved Turner's helpless transports from certain annihilation. 'Had he done so', comments the US Army history, 'he could have effectively halted Allied operations in the South Pacific and completely cut off the 1st Marine Division from reinforcement and supply, for all the transports

Colonel Kiyono Ichiki, commander of the Japanese reinforcements. (USMC)

and cargo ships of the South Pacific Force were present in Sealark Channel.' The American carriers were too far away to launch any retaliatory air strikes at the Japanese ships as they retired towards Rabaul in daylight. The rest of D+2 saw Japanese resistance on Gavutu and Tanambogo finally mopped up, but during the course of the afternoon and early evening the Marines watched their transports and cargo ships sailing away, still with much of their equipment and supplies and even some of their personnel (including the regimental headquarters of the 2nd Marines) on board.

The period between 9 August (D+2) and 20 August (D+13), during which the Japanese enjoyed undisputed air superiority, was their best opportunity to defeat the American landings. The Marines were on short rations, and their stocks of ammunition were far below safe levels. They were also badly disposed, as the earlier decision to land all three battalions of the 2nd Marines on the Tulagi side had left Tulgai, Gavutu and Tanambogo (all of which were largely ignored by the Japanese for the rest of the campaign) over-generously protected while Guadalcanal was desperate for men. However, Vandegrift was given the time to progressively shift battalions from the Tulagi side to the main positions on Guadalcanal, owing to the tardiness of the Japanese counterblows.

Despite being able to bomb and shell the American positions at will, the commitment of ground troops by the Japanese was piecemeal. This was a direct result of the strategic surprise which

they had suffered (which meant that they had no large units of ground troops immediately available to retake the islands, nor ships to move them) and of their inflexibility. Although the forces available locally (principally those based at Rabaul) reacted promptly to news of the American landings, Imperial General Headquarters in Tokyo was very slow to appreciate that the decision by the Americans to fight for the Solomons had derailed all of its plans for the South Pacific. It was 29 August (D+22) before the Japanese 17th Army was ordered by Tokyo to make the recapture of Guadalcanal its first priority, and to relegate its ongoing operations in New Guinea to secondary importance. By this time the period of the Marines' greatest weakness (before they could get the airfield on Guadalcanal operational) had already passed.

The first Japanese reinforcements did not reach Guadalcanal until 18 August (D+11), when six destroyers landed a reinforced battalion of around 1,000 Army troops unmolested on the coast to the east of the Marine beachhead. The commander of the Japanese unit, Colonel Kiyono Ichiki, soon aware that his presence had been given away by a clash with an American patrol, and believing that there was only a token American presence on the island, decided not to await the further reinforcements he knew were on the way to him, but to attack westwards along the coast immediately. The use of speed and boldness (both good Manoeuvrist principles) had served the Japanese well in their earlier victories, such as the campaign which had won them Singapore. Unfortunately for Ichiki, on

this occasion he was not applying strength against weakness, but weakness against strength. On 21 August (D+14) his force launched a frontal attack on the Marine positions, and was virtually annihilated. That same day, D+14, American aircraft flew their first combat missions from the airfield on Guadalcanal, which had been completed (and was having bomb damage repaired daily) by the 1st Marine Division's organic engineer battalion. Nineteen F4F Wildcat fighters and twelve SBD-3 Dauntless dive bombers, all flown by Marines, had arrived the previous evening.

Their new base was christened Henderson Field, after a Marine Corps aviator killed at the Battle of Midway. Allied coastwatchers (recruited from local white residents of the Solomons and linked by radio with their headquarters at Townsville in Australia) were often able to provide advance warning of Japanese air raids heading for Guadalcanal, allowing the defending fighters time to position themselves for an interception. The arrival of aircraft at Henderson Field allowed American transports and supply ships to approach Guadalcanal with some degree of safety for the first time since the departure of Fletcher's carriers on D+1, and made daylight movement by Japanese ships much more dangerous.

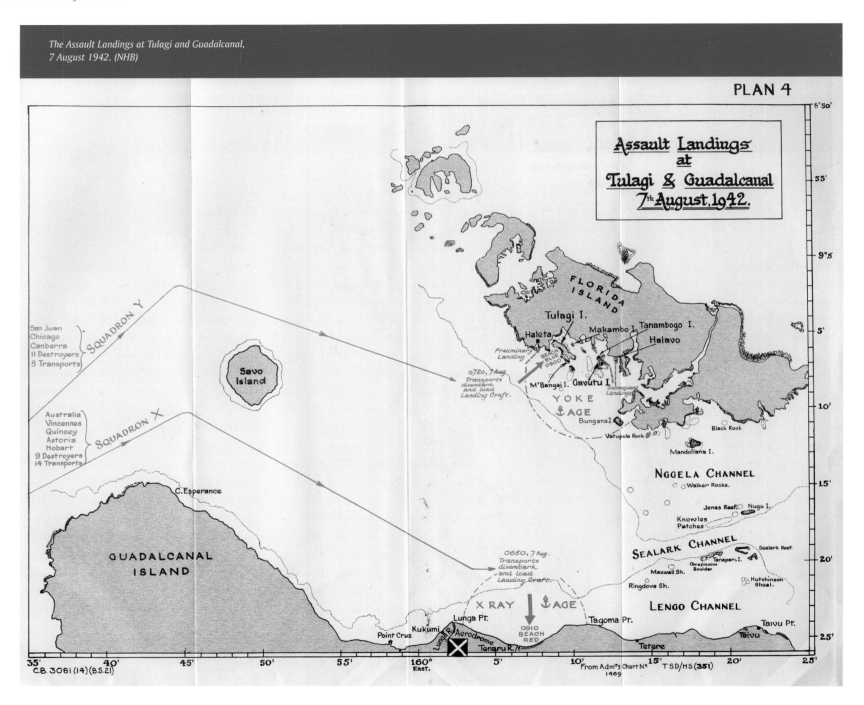

The Assault Landings at Tulagi and Guadalcanal,
7 August 1942. (NHB)

The Japanese now believed the Americans had around 7,500 men on Guadalcanal, when in fact the true figure was more than twice that

Loss rates for the aircraft and aircrews sent to Henderson Field were high, but the Americans realised the crucial importance of winning air superiority, and were prepared to fight a lengthy attritional battle to achieve it. Air reinforcements were fed in at irregular intervals, the Marines being joined by Army and Navy squadrons as they became available. Fletcher's carriers were meanwhile lurking to the east of the Solomons, protecting the sea route to the beachhead and awaiting any tempting targets, such as Japanese troop transports, for which it was worth hazarding their safety.

The first attempts by the Japanese to bring in troops and supplies in slow-moving transports rather than fast destroyers were thwarted by air strikes from Henderson Field and from Fletcher's carriers in a confused series of actions on 23-25 August (D+16, D+17 and D+18) now collectively known as the Battle of the Eastern Solomons. Both Navies showed a degree of timidity, but nevertheless the Japanese lost the carrier *Ryujo* sunk and the Americans the *Enterprise* damaged. The latter had to withdraw from the campaign for two months. When *Saratoga* was crippled by a Japanese submarine on 31 August (D+24) and *Wasp* was sunk by another on 15 September (D+39) the Americans were left with only one operational carrier – the newly-arrived *Hornet*.

The Tokyo Express

By the second week of September destroyers operating at night (a service referred to by the Marines as 'The Tokyo Express') had succeeded in building up Japanese Army strength on Guadalcanal in gradual increments until it stood at around 7,000. The largest concentration lay to the south and east of the Marines, where a brigade-sized force was deployed under the command of Major General Kiyotake Kawaguchi.

The Tokyo Express could carry personnel but not heavy cargo or weapons, leaving the Japanese short of artillery support, but Kawaguchi, like Ichiki before him, was completely unaware of the true ratio of forces. The Japanese now believed the Americans had around 7,500 men on Guadalcanal, when in fact the true figure was more than twice that. Consequently, the over-confident Kawaguchi refused to wait for more troops to arrive before launching the second Japanese attempt to retake Henderson Field. Between 12 September (D+36) and 14 September (D+38) he attacked the American beachhead from three sides, but without success.

The heaviest fighting was in the south, along some high ground dubbed Edson's Ridge by the Americans, after the CO of the defending 1st Raider Battalion. Japanese losses, compounded by the American superiority in artillery, were disproportionate, and they were forced to pull back into the jungle to regroup and await reinforcements.

However, the American position was further strengthened on 18 September (D+42) when six transports managed to evade the Japanese Navy and spend the daylight hours unloading Vandegrift's 'missing' regiment, the 7th Marines, together with the first shipment of ammunition received since D-Day. The depleted 1st Parachute Battalion departed on the same ships.

The Tokyo Express was by now ferrying in up to 900 men a night, and on 9 October (D+63) the commander of the Japanese 17th Army, General Haruyoshi Hyakutake, arrived to take charge of operations in person.

The Americans too were desperate to reinforce their troops on Guadalcanal, although in their case the only way to find additional units was to take them from the threatened island groups along the sea route between Australia and the USA. This they now felt they had to do, and Turner's transports were ordered to move the 164th Infantry Regiment – the first US Army ground troops sent to Guadalcanal - up from New Caledonia. A force of American cruisers and destroyers covering this movement clashed with the Tokyo Express on the night of 11/12 October (D+65/66), precipitating the Battle of Cape Esperance. Both sides inflicted losses and damage on the other, but both were able to land their troops and supplies, the American transports unloading the 164th during daylight on 13 October (D+67).

Aerial photograph of
Henderson's Airfield. (NARA)

Patch of the 25th Infantry Division
who relieved the 1st Marine Division
at Guadalcanal. (DoD)

Having failed to dislodge the Americans by using a battalion, and then a brigade, the Japanese were now assembling a division. In the early hours of 14 October (D+68) their battleships *Kongo* and *Haruna* arrived off Guadalcanal to clear the way for a convoy of transports carrying troops, supplies and artillery by subjecting Henderson Field to the heaviest shelling it would ever receive. The battleships spent eighty minutes methodically 'working over' the airfield with their 14 inch guns, setting fire to most of the Marines' precious aviation fuel and destroying or damaging half of the parked aircraft. Air strikes from Rabaul and intermittent artillery fire added to the destruction, but although Henderson Field itself was rendered unusable, a new grass airstrip (Fighter Strip No.1) which the engineers had laid out within the Marine perimeter was soon back in service. For a week 'Fighter 1' had to serve as the main runway.

The Japanese thus failed to prevent their convoy from being attacked by American aircraft, but at great cost they managed to complete the assembly of Lieutenant General Masao

Maruyama's 2nd Infantry Division (plus additional attachments), giving them roughly 20,000 men. American strength on Guadalcanal, boosted by the arrival of the 7th Marines and the 164th Infantry, was now around 23,000 (with 4,500 more on the Tulagi side), although many of them – like the survivors of the Ichiki and Kawaguchi Forces - were suffering badly from malnutrition, malaria, dysentery and other tropical diseases. Hyakutake ordered the bulk of the 2nd Division, which had assembled to the west of the Marine perimeter, to repeat Kawaguchi's tactical plan – a wide swing around the American beachhead followed by an attack from the south, accepting that the appallingly difficult terrain to be traversed would preclude taking any heavy artillery. The bulk of the guns remained grouped near the coast, to the west of the Marines. The few guns which did accompany the infantry on their jungle march had to be abandoned along the way.

Communications between the different Japanese units was very poor, with the result that between 20 October (D+74) and 26 October (D+80) they launched a series of uncoordinated attacks, starting with probes from the west and finishing with all-out assaults from the south, all of which failed. The Japanese again withdrew into the jungle to regroup and await reinforcement and resupply. At sea they had strong forces waiting to pounce on any American move to assist the Marines on Guadalcanal, and these were engaged by the carriers *Hornet* and

Enterprise (newly returned from having her previous damage repaired) on 26 October (D+80) in the bruising Battle of the Santa Cruz Islands. The Americans, who lost the *Hornet* sunk and the *Enterprise* damaged, hastily withdrew again to the south after the battle, leaving the Japanese with damage to the carriers *Shokaku* and *Zuiho*.

The first two weeks of November saw both sides continuing to feed in new ground units, with Vandegrift receiving more artillery plus the 8th Marines, the 182nd Infantry, the 147th Infantry and the 2nd Raider Battalion – the latter two to establish a new beachhead further east along the coast of Guadalcanal, where an additional airstrip was begun. Hyakutake began to receive a second infantry division – Lieutenant General Tadayoshi Sano's 38th.

In the early hours of 13 November (D+98) the American cruiser/destroyer force covering the delivery of the 182nd Infantry intercepted a Japanese force led by the battleships *Hiei* and *Kirishima* which had been tasked with repeating the 14 October bombardment (this time to clear the way for the largest convoy yet dispatched to Guadalcanal). The resulting naval action was a swirling melee fought at point blank range. Losses on both sides were heavy (including the *Hiei*), and the Japanese withdrew without accomplishing their bombardment. Only minor damage was inflicted on Henderson Field during a bombardment by Japanese cruisers a night later, with the result that the convoy,

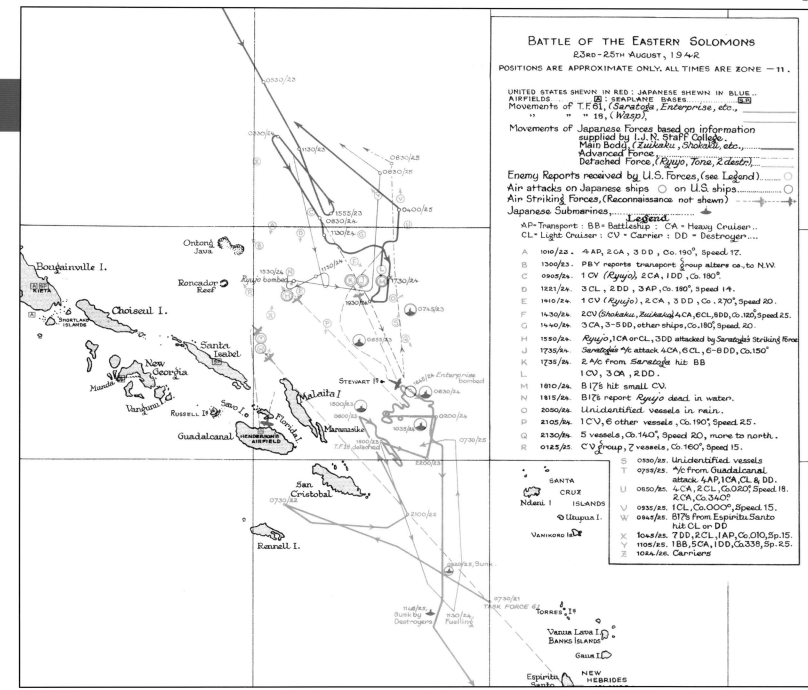

Battle of the Eastern Solomons. (NHB)

BATTLE OF THE EASTERN SOLOMONS
23RD - 25TH AUGUST, 1942
POSITIONS ARE APPROXIMATE ONLY. ALL TIMES ARE ZONE —11.

UNITED STATES SHEWN IN RED : JAPANESE SHEWN IN BLUE..
AIRFIELDS........ [A] : SEAPLANE BASES................[S.P]
Movements of T.F.61, (Saratoga, Enterprise, etc.,
   "   "   " 18, (Wasp),
Movements of Japanese Forces based on information
   supplied by I.J.N. Staff College.
   Main Body, (Zuikaku, Shokaku, etc.,
   Advanced Force,
   Detached Force, (Ryujo, Tone, 2 destr.)
Enemy Reports received by U.S. Forces, (see Legend)   ○
Air attacks on Japanese ships ○   on U.S. ships........   ○
Air Striking Forces, (Reconnaissance not shewn) ---→
Japanese Submarines,

Legend

AP = Transport : BB = Battleship : CA = Heavy Cruiser..
CL = Light Cruiser : CV = Carrier : DD = Destroyer....

A   1010/23 . 4 AP, 2 CA , 3 DD , Co. 190°, Speed 17.
B   1300/23 . PBY reports transport group alters co., to N.W.
C   0905/24 . 1 CV (Ryujo), 2 CA, 1 DD , Co. 180°.
D   1221/24 . 3 CL , 2 DD , 3 AP, Co. 180°, Speed 14.
E   1410/24 . 1 CV (Ryujo), 2 CA , 3 DD , Co. 270°, Speed 20 .
F   1430/24 . 2 CV (Shokaku, Zuikaku) 4 CA, 6 CL, 8 DD, Co.120°, Speed 25.
G   1440/24 . 3 CA , 3-5 DD , other ships, Co. 180°, Speed 20.
H   1550/24 . Ryujo, 1 CA or CL , 3 DD attacked by Saratoga's Striking Force
J   1735/24 . Saratoga's A/c attack 4 CA, 6 CL, 6-8 DD, Co.150°
K   1735/24 . 2 A/c from Saratoga hit BB
L   1 CV , 3 CA , 2 DD .
M   1810/24 . B 17's hit small CV.
N   1815/24 . B 17's report Ryujo dead in water.
O   2050/24 . Unidentified vessels in rain.
P   2105/24 . 1 CV , 6 other vessels , Co. 190°, Speed 25.
Q   2130/24 . 5 vessels , Co. 140°, Speed 20, more to north .
R   0125/25 . CV group , 7 vessels , Co. 160°, Speed 15.
S   0550/25 . Unidentified vessels
T   0755/25 . A/c from Guadalcanal
              attack 4 AP, 1 CA, CL & DD.
U   0650/25 . 4 CA , 2 CL , Co. 020°, Speed 18.
              2 CA , Co. 340°
V   0935/25 . 1 CL , Co. 000°, Speed 15.
W   0945/25 . B 17's from Espiritu Santo
              hit CL on DD
X   1045/25 . 7 DD, 2 CL , 1 AP, Co. 010°, Sp. 15.
Y   1105/25 . 1 BB, 5 CA , 1 DD, Co. 338°, Sp. 25.
Z   1024/26 . Carriers

Bougainville I.
Choiseul I.
SHORTLAND ISLANDS
Santa Isabel
New Georgia
Munda
Vangunu I.
RUSSELL I.
Savo I.
Guadalcanal
HENDERSON'S AIRFIELD
Florida I.
Malaita I.
Maramasike
Ontong Java
Roncador Reef
Ryujo bombed
Ryujo bombed
Stewart I.
Enterprise bombed
KIETA

San Cristobal
SANTA CRUZ ISLANDS
Ndeni I.
Utupua I.
Vanikoro Is.
Rennell I.

0730/22
0730/21 TASK FORCE 61
TORRES Is.
Vanua Lava I.
BANKS ISLANDS
Gaua I.
Espiritu Santo
NEW HEBRIDES

0530/23
0830/24
1130/23
0830/25
0830/25
0400/25
1555/23
0830/24
1130/24
1530/24
1730/24
1930/24
0745/23
0655/23
0630/24
1500/23
0800/23
0200/24
1035/24
0730/25
1800/23 T.F.18 detached
2200/23
2100/22
0920/25, Sunk
1145/25, Sunk by Destroyers
1130/24, Fuelling

US Marines landing at Guadalcanal, in the ubiquitous LVT, which was to prove its value throughout the Pacific Campaign. (NHB)

On 30 November (D+115) the Joint Chiefs of Staff approved the dispatch of a fresh Army division – Major General J. Lawton Collins' 25th Infantry Division – from Hawaii to Guadalcanal. By this time they felt secure enough to permit the long-overdue evacuation of Vandegrift's 1st Marine Division to begin even before the arrival of Collins' units,

same day, with departure of the 5th Marines for Australia. The rest of December and early January was a period of constant movement for the American transports and cargo ships, as burned-out units were evacuated and fresh ones brought in. By 15 January 1943 (D+161) the last of the original landing force had departed and American strength on Guadalcanal stood at three divisions, organized as XIV Corps. With these, Patch began to expand the American beachhead against stubborn resistance, unaware that the Japanese had already decided to evacuate as many troops as they could save. On the night of 7/8 February (D+184/185) the secret Japanese evacuation was completed, leaving the Americans - who had misinterpreted the upsurge in Japanese naval activity as another reinforcement effort – to finally declare organised resistance over on 9 February (D+186).

carrying a large proportion of Sano's 38th Infantry Division, was subjected to a severe mauling by Henderson Field aircraft (which included the Air Group from the damaged *Enterprise*) as it approached. The four surviving transports (out of eleven which had set out – six having been sunk outright and one having turned back, heavily damaged) arrived offshore on the night of 14/15 November (D+99/100), covered by a bombardment force, some of which had fought in the wild melee two nights previously. These found an even stronger American force waiting for them this time, including the new battleships USS *Washington* and *South Dakota*. In the only battleship-against-battleship action of the campaign, the *South Dakota* was damaged and the *Kirishima* crippled so badly that she had to be scuttled later in the day. The remaining Japanese transports were destroyed after daylight by bombing and shelling. These naval actions, later collectively known as the Battle of Guadalcanal, marked the end of any serious Japanese attempts to retake the island.

meaning that American troop numbers on Guadalcanal would actually fall in the short term.

Meanwhile, Japanese attempts to resupply their existing forces on Guadalcanal, so that these could at least resist the expansion of the American beachhead, continued to result in night-time clashes at sea between cruisers, destroyers and PT boats. On the night of 30 November, for example, another sharp defeat was inflicted on the US Navy just off Guadalcanal (an action later called the Battle of Tassafaronga). The growing American ascendancy at sea, however, was not adversely affected.

The 132nd Infantry Regiment of the Americal Division (parent formation of the 164th and 182nd Regiments) arrived on 8 December, and on 9 December Major General Alexander Patch of the Americal succeeded Vandegrift as commander of the troops on Guadalcanal. Relief of 1st Marine Division began the

At the campaign's end the Japanese, who had entered it on the strategic offensive, were unmistakably on the defensive. Their primary concerns were to fortify their positions higher up the Solomons, in expectation of further American advances. The Americans, who had entered the campaign on the strategic defensive, ended it with higher morale and in possession of the strategic and operational initiative.

Naval losses during the campaign reflected the intensity of the fighting. The Americans lost the carriers *Wasp* and *Hornet*, eight cruisers (one of them Australian) and fourteen destroyers. Many more ships were damaged, some of them – like *Enterprise* – more

The Waterstone's Card

for more rewarding reading

If you love reading as much as we do, you'll love the new Waterstone's Card

Earn three points for every £1 you spend and make reading even more rewarding

Just show your card every time you shop and we'll add your points to your account. The more points you earn, the more you can save and you can redeem your points whenever you wish.

Exclusive benefits for you:

- emails featuring book reviews, news on the latest titles and competitions to read and review books before they are published

- double points and bonus points on books by some of your favourite authors

- exclusive cardholder offers on selected books

- invitations to exclusive shopping events

- free copies of Waterstone's Books Quarterly magazine when you visit our shops

It's free and easy to join

You can start earning points as soon as you've signed up. Simply ask in store for an application form.

You can also register at **Waterstones.com** and can use your card to earn and redeem points when you shop online as well as in our shops

For full terms and conditions see the Waterstone's Card application form or visit **Waterstones.com/waterstonescard**.

BT Total Broadband

The UK's most complete broadband.
Now from only £8.95 a month
for the first 6 months[1].

Get £30 worth of e-vouchers to spend at **Waterstones.com**

Find out more at **www.waterstones.com/bt**
or call **0800 032 4630**

BT

No wonder its called BT Total Broadband

There's never been a better time to get BT Total Broadband as it now has more features than any other UK broadband provider.

Option 3

 Up to 8Mb[2]
 Norton Security[3]
 Unlimited Monthly Usage[4]
 Wi-Fi Minutes[5]
 5GB online storage[9]
 Inclusive UK Calls Package[6]
 BT Home Hub[7]
 BT Hub Phone[8]

only **£18.**⁹⁹ a month for the first 6 months[1] £24.99 a month thereafter. 18 month contract.

Option 2

 Up to 8Mb[2]
Norton Security[3]
8GB Monthly Usage[4]
 Wi-Fi Minutes[5]
 5GB online storage[9]
 Inclusive UK Calls Package[6]
BT Home Hub[7]

only **£13.**⁹⁹ a month for the first 6 months[1] £22.99 a month thereafter. 18 month contract.

Option 1

 Up to 8Mb[2]
 Basic Security[3]
 5GB Monthly Usage[4]

 250 MINS Wi-Fi Minutes[5]

 5GB online storage[9]

 Inclusive UK Calls Package[6]

only **£8.**⁹⁵ a month for the first 6 months[1] £17.99 a month thereafter. 18 month contract.

To claim your £30 Waterstones e-voucher

1. Sign up to BT Total Broadband at **www.waterstones.com/bt** (remember to write down your Order Reference Number as you will need this information to claim your £30 e-voucher)
2. Once your BT Total Broadband line is activated, go to **www.btyahoo.com/promotion** and complete the online redemption form
3. Your voucher will be sent to you within 28 days

BT

A wounded soldier from the 25th Infantry Division is assisted down a steep jungle hillside during the fighting at Guadalcanal. (NARA)

than once. The Japanese lost the carrier *Ryujo*, the old battleships *Hiei* and *Kirishima*, four cruisers and eleven destroyers, as well as around 300,000 tons of transports and cargo ships. Their naval air power was permanently damaged by the severe losses of aircraft and experienced crews. In terms of ground forces, the Americans lost 1,598 dead; the Japanese around 23,800 dead from all causes.

Factors identified at Guadalcanal

Surprise

The Americans achieved total strategic surprise, which put them in a position of advantage right from the start.

The US Forces exploited the enemy's critical vulnerabilities

The selection of Guadalcanal as a target was a classic application of the Manoeuvrist Approach at the strategic level. The Japanese were caught off balance and obliged to fight an unanticipated campaign for which they were ill-prepared logistically and which diverted them from their own objectives.

Principles ignored at Guadalcanal

Do not attack prematurely, with inadequate forces

Both sides were guilty of this - the Americans with their initial landings of 7 August, and the Japanese with all of their subsequent attempts at recapture. Had the Americans been able to land and maintain a force adequate to secure the whole of Guadalcanal they might have avoided having to fight a debilitating ground campaign there.

Base decisions on sound intelligence

Again, both sides were guilty of basing their plans on faulty or inadequate intelligence. The consistent underestimation of enemy strength by the Japanese was one of the primary causes of their defeat.

Sea control

Sea control remained contested throughout the campaign. Neither side was strong enough at any point to impose a complete blockade on the other, although the Japanese came close during the period between D+2 and D+13. Both sides should have made more aggressive use of their submarines for sea denial.

Air superiority

Daylight air superiority rested with the Japanese during the critical period between D+2, after the American carriers had withdrawn, and D+13, when fighters arrived at Henderson Field. During this period the American landing force was very nearly isolated, and was using up its limited stocks of supplies. It goes without saying that the Japanese should not have allowed the airfield to become operational.

Operational tempo

Both sides struggled to maintain operational tempo, but the Americans benefited from having seized the vital ground at the outset.

> **Army planning was often done in complete isolation from Navy planning, and vice versa. This had disastrous consequences when close cooperation was called for at the operational or tactical level**

Exploit opportunities

Mikawa squandered his opportunity to wipe out the American logistical support ships on D+2.

Sustainability

Both sides were guilty of pushing forces into the battle area without proper regard for whether they could be maintained there.

Unity of effort and operational coherence

Incredibly, Japanese Army planning was often done in complete isolation from Navy planning, and vice versa. This had disastrous consequences when close cooperation was called for at the operational or tactical level, as at Guadalcanal. The Americans were subject to the usual inter-service rivalries, but never to the degree that they endangered the national war effort.

Further Reading

Hough, Frank, *Pearl Harbor to Guadalcanal,* (Washington DC: US Marine Corps, 1958)

Loxton, Bruce, *The Shame of Savo: Anatomy of a Naval Disaster,* (St. Leonards, NSW, Australia: Allen & Unwin, 1994)

Miller, John, *Guadalcanal: The First Offensive,* (Washington DC: US Army, 1949)

Morison, Samuel Eliot, *The Struggle for Guadalcanal,* (Boston: Little, Brown & Co., 1950)

Mueller, Joseph N., *Guadalcanal 1942: The Marines Strike Back,* (London: Osprey, 1992)

Biography

Mr Colin Bruce was born in 1960 in Elgin, in North East Scotland. After obtaining an honours degree in History from the University of Aberdeen he moved to London to pursue a career as a military historian. Since 1985 he has worked for the Imperial War Museum, where he is now a Senior Curator specialising in public access to the collections as well as being the Museum's academic expert on amphibious warfare. He has written three books, the most recent of which was *Invaders: British and American Experience of Seaborne Landings, 1939-1945*, (Chatham Publishing, 1999) in the UK and by the US Naval Institute Press in the USA.

The Invasion of North Africa
Coalition, Compromise & Conquest: Operation TORCH, 1942

'Trying to follow the evolution of TORCH is like trying to find a pea in a three shell game.'

Captain Harry C. Butcher, U.S. Naval Reserve

Naval Aide to General Eisenhower[1]

By Professor Kenneth J Hagan

The Decision to Invade North Africa

TORCH was the code name for the Anglo-American amphibious invasion of French Morocco and Algeria that took place in November 1942. It was a compromise operation inspired by British Prime Minister Winston Churchill and opposed by the American Army Chief of Staff, General George C. Marshall. The general wanted a direct and immediate Clausewitzian strike at the Nazi German war machine on the continent of Europe by assault forces streaming across the English Channel from staging areas in the United Kingdom.[2] Churchill and his military advisors were dubious about the chances for success of a cross-Channel invasion if made in 1943, and they were categorically opposed to attempting one in 1942. Unlike the Americans, who remained neutral in the war until December 1941, the British could estimate their enemy on the basis of hard experience. They had been driven in gallant ignominy from the continent of Europe by the Wehrmacht at Dunkirk in May-June 1940, and their ongoing campaign in North Africa against the Afrika Korps of Field Marshal Erwin Rommel ('The Desert Fox') had deepened their respect for German armies. Chief of the Imperial General Staff Field Marshal Sir Alan Brooke much later expressed his bewilderment at what he saw as Marshall's naivety:

'I found Marshall's rigid form of strategy very difficult to cope with. He never fully appreciated what operations in France would mean – the different standard of training

of German divisions as opposed to the raw American divisions. . . . He could not appreciate the fact that the Germans could reinforce at the point of attack [in France] some three to four times faster than we could, nor would he understand that until the Mediterranean was open

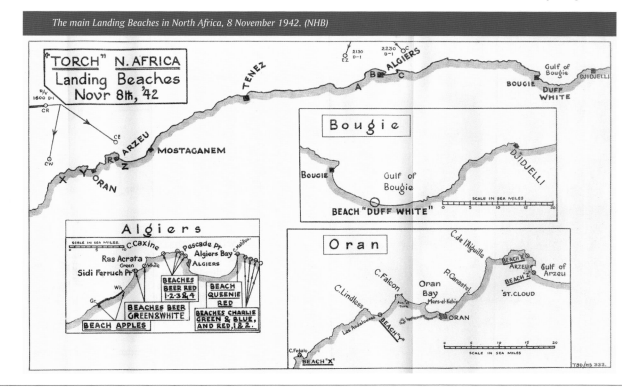

The main Landing Beaches in North Africa, 8 November 1942. (NHB)

again [to Allied shipping] we should always suffer from a crippling shortage of sea transport.'[3]

TORCH also displeased the most senior U.S. naval commander, the chief of naval operations, Admiral Ernest J. King. Described

---

[1]Butcher quoted in Barbara Brooks Tomblin, With Utmost Spirit: Allied Naval Operations in the Mediterranean, 1942-1945, (Lexington, KY: The University Press of Kentucky, 2004), p. 8.
[2]See Carl von Clausewitz, On War, Michael Howard and Peter Paret, trans. and eds. (Princeton, NJ: Princeton University Press, 1976) and Michael I. Handel, Masters of War: Classical Strategic Thought, 2nd ed., rev. (London: Frank Cass, 1996).
[3]Brooke quoted in Williamson Murray, 'WWII: Triumph of Operation Torch,' www.historynet.com/wwii/bloperation_torch/, accessed 18 Sep. 2004.

*Having won the political struggle for the offensive
of his preference, Churchill grandly surrendered its
implementation to the Americans*

by an admiring biographer as 'suspicious, cruel, vain, rude, and irascible,' King hated the British and loved his own navy.[4] He thirsted for a Mahanian naval war against the Japanese fleet in the Pacific.[5] For King, as for Marshall, TORCH was a strategic miscalculation destined to postpone favoured offensives. They were right about the postponement.

Faced in the summer of 1942 with Churchill's intransigent opposition to mounting an early invasion of continental France, Marshall and King entertained the idea of altogether abandoning transatlantic military enterprises and concentrating exclusively on America's war against Japan in the Pacific. This radical proposal flew in the face of Anglo-American prewar strategic planning, which always stipulated an offensive against 'Germany first.' The Pacific war was to be relegated to the strategic defensive until Hitler was defeated. The intransigence of Marshall and King so alarmed Field Marshall Sir John Dill, Churchill's representative in Washington, that he drafted a cable summarising the Americans' attitude: 'We are finished off with the West and will go out in the Pacific.'[6]

The senior American army officer in the Pacific would have been pleased with a Pacific-only war. General Douglas MacArthur,

the flamboyant and politically powerful army general who had fled the Philippines and taken up station in Brisbane, Australia. 'MacArthur was frustrated almost to the point of despair over the strategy of Germany first,' writes his biographer.[7] Unlike many senior American and British commanders, he believed that the vast Soviet Union would persist against the onslaught of the invading German army. Therefore, an Anglo-American attack on North Africa was pointless. Historian Geoffrey Perret has summarized MacArthur's position: 'There was nothing to be won in the Mediterranean that was worth the effort. The right strategy would be to build up the forces needed for a landing in France once air superiority had been secured over the Germans.'[8]

United in their strategic revisionism, the American top brass misjudged their president. Franklin Delano Roosevelt was an upper class Europeanist who throughout the darkest days of 1940 and 1941 had steadfastly seen England's survival in its war against Germany as indispensable to American security. Earlier, in World War I, he had served as assistant secretary of the navy, which was then the number two civilian position in the U.S. Navy Department. From that vantage point he had helped orchestrate the vital Anglo-American shipping and convoy campaign to

outflank the German submarines that were attempting to starve England into submission in 1917 and 1918. Even before the United States entered World War II, and certainly by 1942, Roosevelt and Churchill had forged a strong and remarkably personal cooperative relationship. Almost by instinct, therefore, Roosevelt favoured Churchill, the grand alliance, and TORCH over the self-serving provincialism of his own military and naval advisors. On 25 July 1942 the impatient president ordered Marshall and King immediately to begin final planning for an invasion of North Africa to take place not later than 30 October 1942. 'Roosevelt's decision for TORCH marked the defining moment of America's entry into World War II,' writes historian Douglas Porch.[9]

Having won the political struggle for the offensive of his preference, Churchill grandly surrendered its implementation to the Americans. He beguilingly informed Roosevelt, 'In the whole of TORCH, military and political, I certainly consider myself your lieutenant, asking only to put my viewpoint plainly before you.'[10] It was assumed that George Marshall would command the invasion, but the president felt Marshall's presence in Washington to be indispensable. On 31 July Roosevelt named recently promoted Lieutenant General Dwight D. ('Ike')

[4]Robert W Love, Jr., 'Fighting a Global War, 1941-1945,' in Kenneth J. Hagan, ed., In Peace and War: Interpretations of American Naval History, 1775-1984, 2nd ed. (Westport, CT: Greenwood Press, 1984), p. 264.
[5]See Alfred Thayer Mahan, The Influence of Sea Power upon History, 1660-1783 (New York: Dover Publications, Inc., 1987 [originally published in 1890 by Little, Brown, and Company]).
[6]Dill quoted by Leo J. Meyer, 'The Decision To Invade North Africa (Torch),' in Kent Roberts Greenfield, ed., Command Decisions (Washington, D.C.: Center of Military History, 2000 [first published in 1960]), p. 183.
[7]Geoffrey Perret, Old Soldiers Never Die: The Life of Douglas MacArthur (New York: Random House, 1996), p. 309.
[8]Perret, Old Soldiers, p. 303.
[9]Douglas Porch, The Path to Victory: The Mediterranean Theater in World War II (New York: Farrar, Straus and Giroux, 2004), p. 329.
[10]'Combined Operations: Operation Torch - North Africa – 8th to 12th Nov 1942', www.combinedoperations.com/TORCH.htm, accessed 18 Sep. 2004.

Eisenhower as the Commander in Chief, Allied Expeditionary Force in North Africa.

As far as the U.S. Army was concerned, the Pacific war had been put largely on hold, but Roosevelt did grant King, the navy and the U.S. Marine Corps one major offensive in the Southwest Pacific: an amphibious landing at Guadalcanal, in the Solomon Islands, in August - three months' prior to the TORCH descent upon North Africa.[11] This decision reflected Roosevelt's deep affection for the navy and his political need to take some offensive action against Japan, loathed by the American people for its sneak attack on Pearl Harbor, Hawaii, on 7 December 1941. The president's concession to King also meant that the United States was destined to fight two major wars simultaneously: one in the Pacific and the other in Europe. Prewar strategic planning was being jettisoned cavalierly in the summer of 1942, but the stupendous military-industrial potential of the United States immunised such behavior against long-term disaster.

From the presidential decisions of July 1942, until the end of the war in Europe in May 1945, the land, sea and air forces of Britain and the United States would fight in the Atlantic and Europe as integral parts of a joint command largely because their civilian heads of government shared a visceral sense of mutual strategic interdependence.

The Mediterranean in Anglo-American strategy

History presented the dominant personalities at the pinnacle of the Anglo-American partnership with certain realities, and as a result they could not entirely control the complex strategic situation in the Mediterranean. For the Americans of the World War II era, the Mediterranean Sea had always served as a highway for trading throughout its littoral. An avenue to riches for some merchants and ship owners, especially those in the New England states, the Mediterranean was strategically inconsequential to the North American continental colossus. Far more important were the waters of the western Atlantic, the Gulf of Mexico and Caribbean Sea, and the vast Pacific Ocean trapezoid bounded by the Panama Canal, Hawaii, Alaska and the continental West Coast.

By contrast, 'the Middle Sea' had long been central to the policy and strategy of the maritime and imperialistic British. 'Since the seventeenth century,' writes Douglas Porch, 'Britain had been active . . . fighting the French and Spaniard to insure that its shortest route to India was preserved.'[12] Completion of the Suez Canal in 1868 had begun 'what many saw as the dawn of Britain's Mediterranean hegemony over a segment of a geopolitical puzzle, a maritime link that London had to control to survive.'[13] The Mediterranean's strategic primacy to Britain was well understood by Vice Admiral Andrew Browne ('ABC') Cunningham, since June 1939 the Commander in Chief, Mediterranean Fleet. Cunningham 'argued that Britain had more political and economic interests in the Mediterranean than in the Far East.'[14]

In September 1939 England and France declared war against Germany. By the end of June 1940 Churchill was prime minister, Italy had declared war, France had surrendered, the Germans were occupying Paris, and the 'Battle of Britain' was about to begin. In the Mediterranean, Cunningham was increasingly frustrated by the Italian navy's refusal to engage with its capital ships at sea. He therefore staged an audacious night attack by carrier-borne bombers and torpedo planes against six Italian battleships moored at their base in Taranto, where the heel of Italy joins the arch. 'Taranto Night', 11 November 1940, cut in half the number of operational Italian battleships and graphically proved the vulnerability of battleships to carrier aviation.[15] Had the Americans paid heed they might have avoided the catastrophe at Pearl Harbor in December 1941.

[11]For the U.S. Marine Corps landing at Guadalcanal, see the Chapter by Colin Bruce, 'Guadalcanal,' in this volume.
[12]Porch, Path to Victory, p. 4.
[13]Ibid. p. 4.
[14]Ibid. p. 6.
[15]The phrase and evaluation are in Jack Greene and Alessandro Massignani, The Naval War in the Mediterranean, 1940-1943 (London: Chatham Publishing, 1998), p. 152.

Lieutenant General Mark Clark, Admiral Bertram Ramsay, Lieutenant General Brian Horrocks and Admiral Jean-Francois Darlan at a ceremony in Algiers soon after the Vichy French capitulated. (NHB)

Four months after his carrier raid on Taranto, Cunningham scored a major victory over heavy elements of the Italian surface navy. On 28-29 March 1941 off Cape Matapan - to the south and southwest of Crete - Cunningham's surface and air units sank three Italian cruisers and two destroyers at a cost of one damaged cruiser and one lost airplane and pilot. Making a favourable comparison to Horatio Nelson at Trafalgar, Churchill hailed Matapan as a 'timely and welcome victory' that 'disposed of all challenge to British naval mastery in the Eastern Mediterranean at this time.'[16] The prime minister's euphoria was premature.

The senior Axis power now asserted itself in the Aegean. On 6 April the German army invaded Greece, the Greek government surrendered on 24 April, and the Royal Navy faced an evacuation 'even more difficult than Dunkirk.'[17] Devoid of protective land-based air cover and forced to embark troops only in the darkness of night, Cunningham's ships nonetheless managed to evacuate 50,000 men from Athens and the Peloponnesus over a six-day period.

Then came the May 1941 German invasion of Crete. Cunningham's sailors fought valiantly to keep the Germans off the strategically placed island, but the Luftwaffe's land-based bombers would not be denied supremacy over the restricted waters surrounding the island. The Germans landed, and the Royal Navy evacuated about 17,000 British and ANZAC (Australia and New Zealand Army Corps) troops. The cost was high: three

cruisers and six destroyers sunk; one aircraft carrier, three battleships, six cruisers, and seven destroyers damaged; a total of about 13,000 army and navy casualties. The most disabling German loss was 5,000 men of their only airborne division, without which they could not overwhelm Malta.

Cunningham steamed east to Alexandria, Egypt, from which distant station he concentrated on getting convoys to and from Malta, the last vital Mediterranean choke point between Gibraltar and Suez still in British hands. The loss of Malta would have meant unhindered transit of Axis convoys from Italy to the North African port of Tripoli in Libya. It would have made absolutely impossible any trans-Mediterranean shipments or troop movements by the British. Suez, already seriously threatened by Rommel, would have been at fatal risk. Forfeiture of Suez would have cut the vital supply line from the United States, isolated the British from the India-Burma theatre of operations, and given the Germans access to Middle Eastern oil. The prospect was horrifying.

In March 1942, seven long months before General Bernard Montgomery ('Monty') would finally stop Rommel's eastward advance at the Battle of El Alamein, Cunningham was plucked from his precarious perch at Alexandria. He was ordered to head the British Admiralty delegation to the strategic planning meetings of the British-American Combined Chiefs of Staff

[16]Churchill quoted in http://home/freeuk.com/johndillon/matapan.htm, accessed 22 Oct. 2004.
[17]E.B. Potter, ed., *Sea Power: A Naval History* (Englewood Cliffs, NJ: Prentice-Hall, Inc., 1960), p. 530.

(CCS) in Washington, D.C. In the opinion of the Royal Navy, Cunningham was 'an ideal opposite number to the equally blunt American, Admiral Ernest King'.[18] His combat experience of the previous two years and his deep understanding of the forbidding strategic situation in the Mediterranean and North Africa, which he found 'depressing in the extreme',[19] made him an irresistible spokesman for TORCH in the summer of 1942. At the Washington meetings Cunningham's demonstrated ability to hold his own in a volatile quasi-diplomatic environment at the highest levels of the Anglo-American coalition resulted in his selection as Naval Commander, Allied Force, the senior naval position under Eisenhower.

Planning a transoceanic invasion

Eisenhower's London staff consisted of a balanced mix of American and British officers from all services. Vice Admiral Bertram H. Ramsay, RN, quickly took charge of overall planning for TORCH. This assumption permitted Admiral Cunningham to focus on establishing and maintaining operational command of the Mediterranean element of the Allied expedition. After sailing from Plymouth on the cruiser HMS *Scylla* Cunningham arrived at Gibraltar on 1 November. Ike joined him on 5 November, only three days' prior to the invasion, after a harrowing flight through bad weather in a B-17 'Flying Fortress' heavy bomber.

While still in London Cunningham had challenged the decision not to invade at Bizerte-Tunis, an operational restraint reflecting American fear of heavy counterattack by Axis airpower. On 31 August President Roosevelt wrote to Churchill, 'It is our belief that the German air and parachute troops cannot get to Algiers or Tunis for at least two weeks after the initial attack.'[20] This prediction proved woefully misguided; the Germans would beat the Allies in the race to Tunis. Cunningham later remembered, 'Once more I bitterly regretted that bolder measures had not been taken in Operation TORCH, and that we had not landed at Bizerte, as I had suggested.'[21]

The month of August witnessed many other disagreements within Ike's staff and with the American Joint Chiefs of Staff (JCS) in Washington. One cause was foot-dragging by Admiral King in Washington, but he had his reasons. In early 1942 German U-boats rampaged along the U.S. Atlantic and Gulf coasts, sinking hundreds of thousands of tons of cargo vessels and tankers bearing oil for the blast furnaces of the industrial northeast. Then, as King was coming to grips with the importance of convoys as the central weapon of antisubmarine warfare, Admiral Karl Dönitz shifted the mass of his U-boat 'wolf packs' to the North Atlantic, where they threatened to cut the shipping lines of communication between the United States and Britain, as well as

those leading over Norway to the Soviet Union. King also had his favorite operation, Guadalcanal, very much on his mind. It began on 7 August, but it would not officially end until February 1943. Its outcome was uncertain in the early autumn of 1942.

Once again the resolution of disputes within the military came from the political overlords. On 3 September President Roosevelt 'came up with a new plan in which he proposed three simultaneous landings - at Casablanca, Oran, and Algiers.'[22] The Americans would provide the transports, escorts and troops for the Casablanca prong of the three-pronged invasion; the British must supply the sealift and naval escort for the two landings of predominantly American soldiers within the Mediterranean. The U.S. Navy would steam from Norfolk, Virginia, across 3,900 miles of open ocean directly to Casablanca, on the Atlantic coast of French Morocco, an unheard of reach for an amphibious force. The two Mediterranean invasion forces would sail from the United Kingdom, past Gibraltar, to their destinations along the coast of North Africa. Churchill accepted Roosevelt's plan at once, in a message dated 5 September 1942.

For Eisenhower, Cunningham, and Ramsay this final directive from their political controllers meant delegation of authority and decentralisation, rather than concentration of command.

---

[18]'Royal Naval History: Admiral of the Fleet Viscount Cunningham of Hyndhope 1883-1963,' www.royal-navy.mod.uk/static/pages/3522.html, accessed 22 Oct. 2004.
[19]Cunningham quoted in Tomblin, With Utmost Spirit, p. 9.
[20]Roosevelt quoted in Tomblin, With Utmost Spirit, p. 9.
[21]Cunningham quoted in Tomblin, With Utmost Spirit, p. 9.
[22]Meyer, 'The Decision to Invade,' in Greenfield, Command Decisions, p. 194.

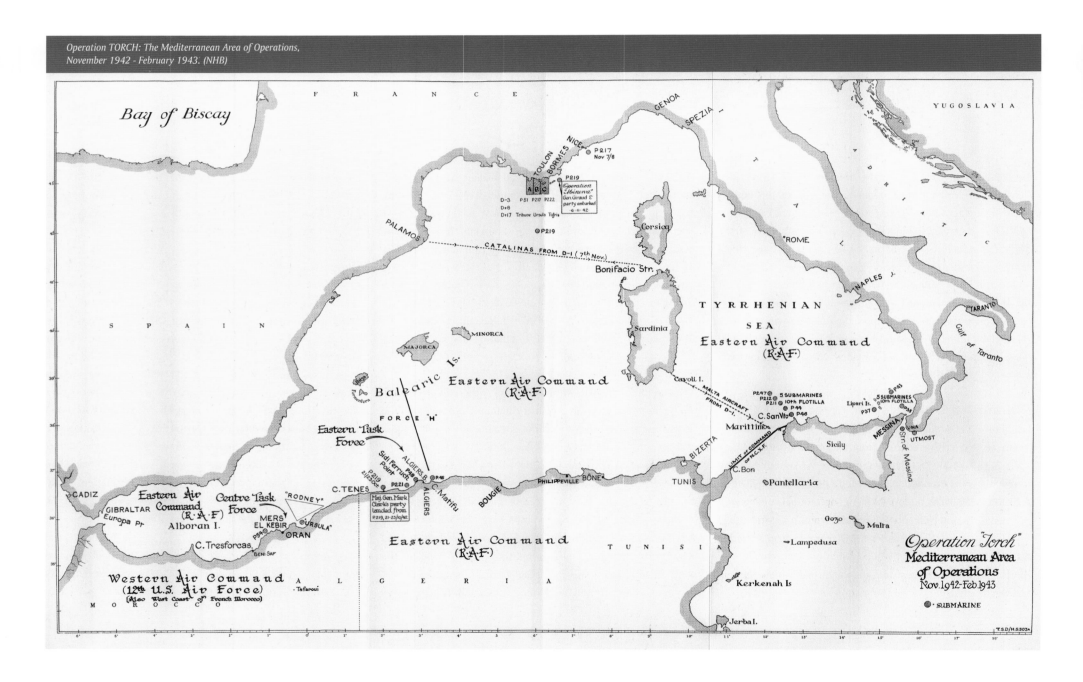

Operation TORCH: The Mediterranean Area of Operations, November 1942 - February 1943. (NHB)

They created three separate task forces, each autonomous of the other, and each ordered to attack a different objective. The Western Task Force would seize the Casablanca area on the Atlantic coast of French Morocco and speed toward Spanish Morocco 'to guard the vital communications through the Straits of Gibraltar.'[23]

Meanwhile, the Centre Task Force, the strongest of the three, would assault Oran in Algeria, on the Mediterranean coast of North Africa. Simultaneously with the other two landings, the Eastern Task Force would go ashore at Algiers, the capital of Algeria and the 'best port on the Barbary Coast,' and then rush into Tunisia, headed for the logistically pivotal coastal area of Tunis and Bizerte.[24] Despite what Cunningham thought, historian E. B. Potter has concluded, 'The venture was risky enough to satisfy the boldest'.[25]

TORCH was complex beyond imagination. Large ocean-going transports were few in number, and amphibious assault vessels could not be produced rapidly enough to provide abundant numbers for both Guadalcanal and TORCH. Escort vessels were in very short supply, and Dönetiz's U-boats could strike convoys almost at will. Their proven lethality was increasing by the month; they would not lose the 'battle of the Atlantic' until late 1943. Another hazard to TORCH was the weather, which ultimately determined the selection of 8 November 1942 as D-day. By meteorological calculation this was the very last date in 1942 when amphibious forces could safely land on beaches soon to be buffeted by the heavy Atlantic Ocean swells of the winter months.

Politics introduced another uncertainty. French Morocco and Algeria were governed and garrisoned by men loyal to the Vichy government, the French puppet of Nazi Germany. They commanded 120,000 troops, 350 aircraft of varying sizes, 200 tanks, considerable artillery and mortars, and a fleet comprised of a modern battleship and smaller warships. E. B. Potter has summarised the strategic dilemma: 'If all these forces fought with determination, and if the Germans moved into Spanish and French bases to assist them, cutting the Allied supply route at Gibraltar, it appeared to many Allied staff officers that the invasion might be defeated.'[26]

The planners had to hope that General Francisco Franco, the fascist dictator of Spain, would prohibit German overland movement through Spain to the rear of the British naval bastion at Gibraltar and that the French military and naval units in North Africa would offer minimal resistance, if any at all.

The American Landings: Morocco

With these apprehensions weighing on their minds, the Western Task Force architects of the Casablanca landings began to meet in the United States, principally at the Naval Operating Base in Norfolk, Virginia. Rear Admiral Henry Kent Hewitt, USN, had been chosen as the Commander, Western Naval Task Force (Task Force 34). He directed the planning and commanded the operation while at sea. Once the army landed and Major General George S. ('Blood and Guts') Patton, Jr., U.S.A., the Commanding General, Western Task Force, established his headquarters ashore, he would assume command of the operation, including the direction of naval vessels supporting the landing. Eisenhower, either directly or through Cunningham, exercised ultimate command over the Western Task Force, once it passed the meridian of 40° West Longitude. This command arrangement set a precedent for subsequent American army-navy operations in World War II. At Guadalcanal, which took place while Hewitt and Patton were planning TORCH, the admiral commanding the amphibious operation remained senior to the Marine Corps general commanding the troops throughout the operation. Bitter internecine conflict erupted, with the Marines claiming the navy had not provided sufficient air cover. The TORCH arrangement was therefore an inspired stroke intended to minimise interservice squabbling, some of which is inevitable in any joint operation.

[23]Potter, Sea Power, pp. 566-67.
[24]Ibid. p. 566.
[25]Ibid. p. 567.
[26]Ibid. p. 568.

Gaining valuable experience: The key Commanders from North Africa seen here at a later meeting in Sicily, Generals Patton, Eisenhower and Montgomery. (IWM NA6110)

The selection of Hewitt as the Western Naval Task force commander was prudent. Somewhat cerebral, he was in command of all Atlantic Fleet cruisers when the United States entered the war in December 1941. Since April 1942 he had been commander of the newly created Amphibious Force, Atlantic Fleet. In June, at Admiral King's direction, he had gone to England to learn about British combined operations. He recalled, 'We were there about two weeks and visited almost all the training bases of combined operations. We also attended landing exercises on the south coast that turned out to be the raid on Dieppe.'[27]

On 19 August 1942, 6,100 Anglo-Canadian amphibious troops assaulted the French Atlantic coastal port of Dieppe.[28] The daring venture lasted a few short hours and was an absolute disaster: fewer than fifty percent of the Canadians returned to England; twenty-seven tanks were lost, as were thirty-three landing craft and a Royal Navy destroyer. A staggering 106 RAF aircraft were shot down (the highest single-day total of the war.)[29] The calamity discouraged further serious consideration of continental landings. It also opened a rancorous debate about the value of heavy offshore bombardment prior to an amphibious operation versus the advantages gained by surprising the defenders. Hewitt, perhaps because he was a naval officer, favoured massive pre-landing naval bombardment.

Army officers preferred to maximise surprise. The issue was never fully resolved.

One tangible impact of Dieppe was the decision by Hewitt and Patton - prompted by Eisenhower - to avoid a frontal assault on Casablanca

One tangible impact of Dieppe was the decision by Hewitt and Patton - prompted by Eisenhower - to avoid a frontal assault on Casablanca, which 'had become France's main port on the Atlantic coast and 'France's most important naval base left after Toulon.'[30] It also had the definite liability of being heavily defended by the battery of the 'El Hank' fortress and by the battleship *Jean Bart*, which was immobilised but mounted a fully functioning turret of four 15-inch guns. They therefore subdivided the 35,000 men of the Western Task Force into three attack groups: the Northern (Task Group 34.8), Centre (TG 34.9), and Southern (TG 34.10). The Centre Attack Group was the strongest of the three. It was charged with landing on beaches near Fedala (modern Mohammedia), some fifteen miles northeast of Casablanca, and then heading overland to take Casablanca from the rear. The imponderable for the Centre and other two attack groups was how the French would react. In diplomatic and clandestine military contacts the Allies had urged the Vichy French leaders in North Africa not to resist, but the result could not be known

with certainty until D-day. Eisenhower's headquarters therefore had issued a precautionary directive that the French must be permitted to fire the first shot, and the task force troops must cease firing as soon as French resistance stopped.

Eisenhower promulgated the final operation plan for TORCH on 8 October, scarcely more than a month after Churchill cabled Roosevelt acquiescing to the overall concept, and only a month to the date before the landing. Now, in the last few weeks before deployment, Hewitt and Patton oversaw a vast preparation at widely separated military and industrial centres on the Atlantic

---

[27]Hewitt quoted in Tomblin, With Utmost Spirit, p. 11.
[28]See Chapter XI by Stephen Prince, on Raiding Europe: Assualts on St Nazaire and Dieppe.
[29]'The Raid on Dieppe: August 19, 1942,' http://users.pandora.be/dave.depickere, accessed 10 Nov 2004.
[30]Tomblin, With Utmost Spirit, p. 12.

'Never in history has the Navy landed an army at the planned time and place... but if you land us anywhere within fifty miles of Fedala and within one week of D-day, I'll go ahead and win'.

coast. The army's 2nd Armored Division manoeuvred in the marshes of the Carolinas. Naval gunfire support ships blasted at targets in the Chesapeake Bay; transports loaded troops and cargoes at Hampton Roads, Virginia; assault vessels practiced landings on the ocean coast of Virginia; the covering group of two heavy cruisers and a battleship outfitted at Casco, Maine; small-boat sailors who had been recruited in New York City boarded their landing vessels for the first time in Bayonne, New Jersey. None of these thousands of men in rehearsal knew where or when the curtain would go up. Lest Axis ears learn the truth from sailors on liberty, Hewitt's officers told their men that they were headed for more exercises in the Caribbean.

This frenzy was orchestrated by the staff at Norfolk, a collection of army and naval officers and one Marine Corps colonel. The rest of Hewitt's Marines had been called to Guadalcanal, so he lacked full representation by the one Allied service that in the interwar years had conceived and written the amphibious doctrine and designed the assault vessels that would prove absolutely fundamental to victory in both the Pacific and European theatres. Although missing the expertise more Marines would have provided, Hewitt was pleased with the uniquely interservice composition of his staff: 'I think it was probably one of the first joint staffs formed.'[31] His modest satisfaction was not shared by his partner, General Patton, who vented his opinion of the navy at the final staff briefing of 23 October. 'Never in history has the Navy landed an army at the planned time and place,' the U.S. Army's most belligerent general officer bellowed. He then explained how he might nonetheless achieve victory: 'But if you land us anywhere within fifty miles of Fedala and within one week of D-day, I'll go ahead and win.'[32] They did, and he did.

Task Force 34 set sail from Norfolk, Virginia, in different groups on two successive days, beginning 23 October. From the moment of weighing anchor until reaching its destination some 3,900 sea-miles to the east, the overriding tactical consideration of TG 34 was to avoid or to neutralise German submarines. Evasion and passive anti-submarine warfare (ASW) utilising 'Enigma' electronic intercepts of Dönetiz's commands to his wolf packs were the order of the day until the morning of 28 October, when the five-carrier air group (TG 34.2) rendezvoused with of all of the combatant and transport vessels. Four of the carriers were untested light escort carriers. A crewman aboard the USS Santee would reminisce about how 'her green hands' were thrown into combat: 'If there was one ship totally unprepared for war, it was the Santee. Anything that could have possibly gone wrong, did. Even some things that couldn't go wrong went wrong, too.'[33] USS Ranger was another matter. Commissioned in 1934, this veteran fleet carrier - the only one not in the Pacific - boasted a well-seasoned air wing of fighter and anti-submarine aviators whose squadrons bore bellicose names like 'Red Ripper' and 'Fighting Blue.'

Carrier aircraft immediately commenced patrols around the fleet, a morale-boosting form of active (ASW). Spirits were further buoyed by news of General Montgomery's victory over Rommel at El Alamein on 4 November. All eyes turned eastward, and in their few hours of rest between flights the airmen prepared for the war against the shore that awaited them in Morocco. They

[31] Hewitt quoted in Tomblin, With Utmost Spirit, p. 10.
[32] Patton quoted in and in Eric Larrabee, Commander In Chief: Franklin Delano Roosevelt, His Lieutenants, and Their War (New York: Harper & Row, 1987), p. 129.
[33] Sailor Frank Wotnik quoted in Tomblin, With Utmost Spirit, p. 18.

Left: Rear Admiral Henry Kent Hewitt of the US Navy (Commander Western Naval Task Force). (NHB)

Right: Vice Admiral Bertram Ramsay RN, who had much of the responsibility for planning Operation TORCH. (NHB)

would be backed by the capital-ship task group that had now joined up. TG 34.1 consisted of USS *Massachusetts*, a newly commissioned 35,000-ton battleship, and two heavy cruisers, *Wichita* and *Tuscaloosa*. Admiral Hewitt flew his flag aboard another heavy cruiser, the *Augusta*. Their combined large-bore gunfire should silence anything hostile in Casablanca.

For a few days, the heavies and the other gray hulls steaming toward Africa constituted an armada of 107 warships, transports, and auxiliaries blanketing more than 500 square miles of the Atlantic Ocean. On 7 November the sprawling fleet split into three invasion groups, each headed for a different destination on the Moroccan coast. Flagship *Augusta*, cruiser *Brooklyn*, fleet carrier *Ranger*, one escort carrier, and ten destroyers shepherded the fifteen transports of the Centre Attack Group to the designated anchorage six to eight miles off Fedala. The flagship signalled 'Stop' just minutes before midnight, and landing craft were immediately lowered into the choppy sea. The first elements of the 19,500 men scheduled to invade began debarking from the transports and clambering into the landing craft thrashing alongside.

H-hour, the time set for the landing craft to head for the beach outside Fedala, was set at 0400. It was missed by an hour because the darkness of night caused great chaos. The navy would have preferred to assault at dawn, after a pre-invasion bombardment with naval gunfire, but the army 'had insisted

on night landings - both to achieve surprise and because army officers were not yet convinced that naval gunfire could provide adequate support for a daylight landing.'[34] This disagreement would persist in Mediterranean operations, with the army usually getting its way, until the invasion of southern France (Operation DRAGOON) in August 1944, where Hewitt's desire for heavy naval bombardment and a daylight landing finally prevailed.

At Fedala the hope of not provoking the French into taking up arms had provided an additional reason for not blasting the coast prematurely, but all uncertainty about French intentions was resolved just after 0600. As 3,500 American soldiers were crossing the beach and rushing to occupy the town, French shore batteries opened fire on the troops and nearby destroyers. The 'Naval Battle of Casablanca' had begun.

It was a genuine mêlée. Aircraft from the two carrier wings engaged shore-based French fighters and attacked sortieing French warships. *Ranger's* airmen administered the *coup de grâce* to the light cruiser *Primauguet*, after gunfire from the

American cruisers had given her a drubbing. The *Augusta* and *Brooklyn* engaged French destroyers emerging from Casablanca under smokescreens to attack the vulnerable transports as they disgorged men, vehicles and equipment. Four French 'tin cans' went to the bottom before the day was over. The *Massachusetts'* covering battle group temporarily silenced the 15-inch guns of the French battleship *Jean Bart* and took on the coastal defense guns of El Hank battery. El Hank scored one hit, on heavy cruiser *Wichita*, wounding fourteen sailors.

The navy's major losses at Fedala on 8 November were in landing craft and crews. Exhausted by working all night, the crewmen had to continue shuttling soldiers from transports to shore throughout the day because there were not enough landing craft to bear the load without endless trips back and forth. Potter has described the disaster:

'Collisions and broachings continued. The numerous boats stranded and abandoned on the beach were banged together and shattered by the incoming tide and rising surf. By nightfall on D-day nearly half the 347 landing

[34]Potter, *Sea Power*, p. 572.

craft of the Centre Attack Group had been destroyed, and only 40 per cent of the 19,500 troops embarked in the transports had been brought ashore.'[35]

On their first day of ground fighting in the European theatre the Americans of the Centre Attack Group took only the town of Fedala, which surrendered easily before noon. The soldiers' movement toward their principal objective, the port of Casablanca, was hampered mostly by the restricted flow of men and matériel from the transports. Offloading and conveyance to the shore was so slow that the transports had to remain off Fedala for several days, four of them becoming targets for German U-boats. But by the time the U-boats converged on their sitting prey the Americans had surrounded Casablanca. General Patton, now reporting directly to Eisenhower at Gibraltar, was preparing an all-out attack from the air, sea, and land for the morning of 11 November.

Fortunately, in Algiers American diplomat Robert D. Murphy and U.S. Army General Mark Clark had persuaded French Admiral Jean François Darlan, second in command of the Vichy government, to order the overall French commander in chief in Morocco, General Noguès, and Contre-Amiral François C. Michelier to cease resistance at Casablanca. They sent a flag of truce to Patton fifteen minutes before the American attack was to start. Michelier, who had satisfied his sense of honour, told

Hewitt, 'I had my orders and did my duty; you had yours and did your duty; now that is over, we are ready to cooperate.'[36] By 16 November all of the Centre Task Group's remaining ships were safely inside the harbour at Casablanca.

Embarked on the *Brooklyn* to chronicle TORCH, the official naval historian Samuel Eliot Morison left a first-hand impression of the French transformation and its impact on Allied operations in North Africa:

> 'There was no surrender, no transfer of sovereignty; merely a cease-fire, which developed into full cooperation between, Allied and French authorities, military and civil. The French naval administration at Casablanca immediately placed port facilities, installations, tugs, pilots and divers at our disposal. Thus, after three days' sharp fighting, the traditional friendship was renewed under the happiest circumstance of making common cause against the Axis powers.'[37]

While Hewitt was making his attack, the Southern Attack Group made its contribution to the defeat of the French in Morocco. Some 150 miles southwest of Casablanca lay Safi, a small phosphate port. It had been chosen as an objective in order to preclude French reinforcement of Casablanca. Adding to Safi's importance was its modest quay, where Hewitt's planners hoped

to land 90 medium and light tanks. Getting tanks ashore was a difficult proposition because the soon-to-be famous landing ship tanks (LSTs), which could disgorge large armoured vehicles from their great bellies directly onto beaches, had not been built in time for TORCH.

Safi fell easily and according to plan. In the pre-dawn darkness of 8 November, two vintage World War I 'four-piper' destroyers steamed brazenly into the harbour with assault troops on board and landing craft astern. One of the destroyers, the *Cole*, simply came alongside the quay and tied up without losing a man. The soldiers jumped ashore, drove back a handful of French Foreign Legionnaires, stormed into the town and secured it. They swarmed in under the covering fire of the 14-inch guns of the old battleship *New York* and the 6-inchers of light cruiser *Philadelphia*, which were noisily silencing French coastal artillery batteries north of Safi. Escort carrier *Santee* launched its air wing to strafe and bomb French military aircraft resting at the Marrakech airfield.

Sailor-historian Morison completes the sketch: In the afternoon of the 8th the *Lakehurst*, a converted train ferry, 'made a dignified entry and began discharging tanks. They started rumbling along the road to Casablanca on 10 November; but before they had got very far word came through from Admiral Darlan that this little Franco-American war was over.'[38]

[35]*Ibid*. p. 576.
[36]Michelier quoted in Potter, Sea Power, pp. 577-78.
[37]Samuel Eliot Morison, The Two-Ocean War, (New York: Galahad Books, 1997), p. 232.
[38]*Ibid*. p. 232.

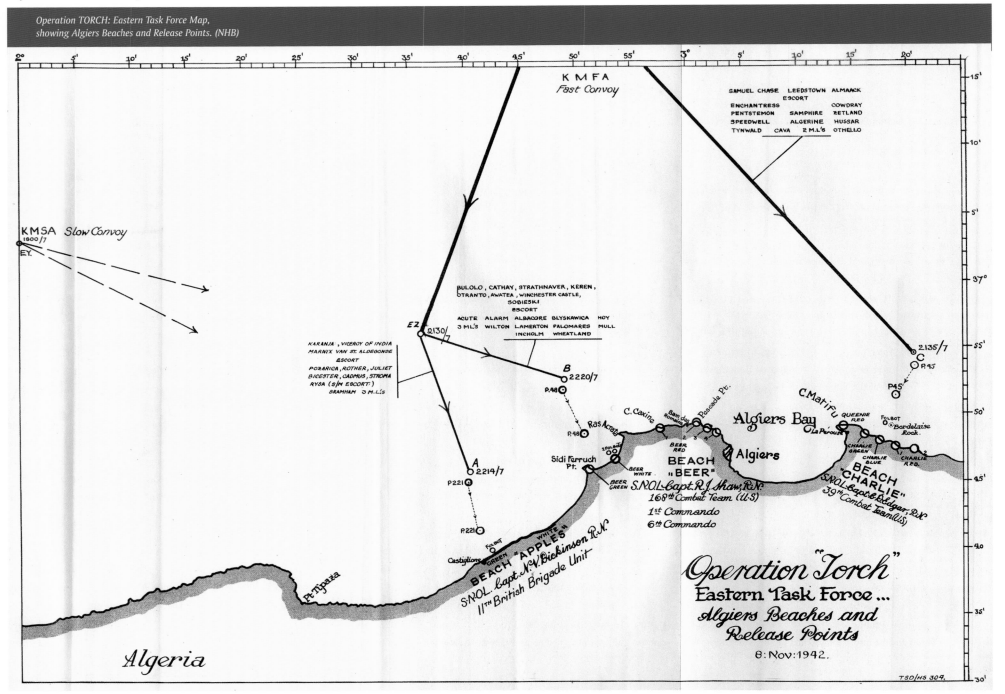

That combination of inexperienced landing crews, poor navigation, and desperate hurry from the lateness of the hour, finally turned the debarkation into a hit-or-miss affair that would have spelled disaster against a well-armed enemy intent upon resistance

The going had been much tougher for the Northern Attack Group, whose objective was the large airfield of Port Lyautey, the only one in Morocco with heavy-duty concrete runways. Its capture would enable the Allies to operate land-based fighters and bombers, freeing the carriers for other coastal operations and for ASW against the Atlantic wolf packs of Karl Dönitz. The airfield lay behind the seaside village of Mehedia, a short way up the Sebou, a barely navigable river blocked by an obstructing boom. Mehedia was protected by 3,500 troops, 14 tanks and the guns of an ancient citadel, the Kasba. Hewitt's plan called for pre-dawn landings at five beaches straddling Mehedia and a thrust upriver by another old four-piper, the *Dallas*. Razeed and loaded with a raider detachment of seventy-five men, she was to cut through an obstructing cross-river boom, head upriver and drop off her men. They were to join a battalion of the 2nd Armored Division in enveloping and capturing the airfield.

The plan may have been too complex, but in any case the French surprised the Americans with determined shelling of the landing beaches and transports, beginning as early as 0605. The transports had to pull back out of coastal artillery range, making the landings of additional troops all the more difficult and disorganised. The skipper of one transport noted ruefully, 'Subsequent waves on this day were subjected to both shell fire and strafing by enemy planes.'[39] By the end of the first day, only half the planned number of soldiers had been brought ashore. The American general commanding the army at Mehedia,

Lucian K. Truscott, Jr. described the landing as a very close-run thing: 'That combination of inexperienced landing crews, poor navigation, and desperate hurry from the lateness of the hour, finally turned the debarkation into a hit-or-miss affair that would have spelled disaster against a well-armed enemy intent upon resistance.'[40]

The French, in fact, exhibited considerable determination at Mehedia and Lyautey. Throughout the 8th and the 9th French soldiers and tanks counterattacked as the battery of the Kasba rained shells on the invaders, especially on the *Dallas*. Fighters from escort carrier *Sangamon* kept driving them back, and the covering fire of the 14-inch guns of battleship *Texas* and the 6-inch artillery of the light cruiser *Savannah* helped slow down the French. However, fear of hitting the besieging American soldiers prevented the commanders from ordering the *Texas* to train its guns on the Kasba and take it out quickly.

As a result of this hesitation, which was bred by inexperience with amphibious operations, it was not until early on 10 November that the *Dallas* crashed through the boom and scraped her way up the shallow Sebou to a point near the airfield. Her raiders rapidly joined up with the army regulars and seized the Lyautey airfield. Carrier bombers neutralised the Kasba, and infantrymen occupied it. In mid-morning the escort carrier *Chenango* launched its special wing of U.S. Army Air Forces (USAAF) fighters, and by 1030 P-40's were operating from Lyautey. Land-based air had

been added to the arsenal of the Western Task Force, which now possessed at Casablanca a major entrepôt for receiving masses of men and matériel directly from the industrial behemoth at the western edge of the Atlantic Ocean.

The Anglo-American Landings: Algeria
While Hewitt and Patton were securing Casablanca and Port Lyautey, two Mediterranean task forces under British naval command were wresting Algiers and Oran from the French. Vice Admiral Sir Harold M. Burrough, RN, commanded the 93 ship Eastern Task Force. Their destination was Algiers, the capital of Algeria, set on the North African coast at three degrees east longitude. Burrough and his sailors were to land a mixed force of 33,000 British and 10,000 American troops, all of whom would fall under the command of American Major General Charles W. Ryder after they landed. Commodore Thomas H. Troubridge, RN, controlled the 105 ship Central Task Force, headed for Oran, which lay on the Algerian coast at about 30 minutes of longitude west of the prime meridian. He was to land 39,000 soldiers, mostly Americans. After the landing they would be commanded by Major General Lloyd R. Fredendall, U.S.A. The two generals reported directly to Eisenhower, once they were free of naval oversight, and the two Royal Navy flag officers answered directly to Cunningham throughout the operation. This shifting of authority from the navy to the army replicated the arrangement that governed Hewitt and Patton.

[39]Captain A.T. Moen quoted in Tomblin, With Utmost Spirit, p. 26
[40]Truscott quoted in Tomblin, With Utmost Spirit, p. 29.

The relatively small number of landing craft, and the fact that
only two passenger ships are in this assembly at Gibraltar,
do not indicate any immediate landing in the Mediterranean

During the final approach and actual landings the two task forces of Burrough and Troubridge would receive protection from the heavily armed Force H of Vice Admiral Sir Neville Syfret. Operating out of Gibraltar, Syfret's specially reinforced fighting force consisted of three battleships and battle cruisers, three light cruisers, three fleet aircraft carriers and seventeen destroyers. Their responsibility was to defend the invading task forces from attack by the Italian navy, Vichy French warships based at Toulon, or German U-boats in the Atlantic waters near Gibraltar. As it turned out, Syfret had little to do during the landings at Oran and Algiers, other than 'patrolling to and fro further north', because the Italian fleet remained safely out of the area of combat.[41]

The perilous passage from the United Kingdom began on 20 October, with the departure from the Clyde of the aircraft carrier *Furious* and three destroyers. They were followed two days later by the first transports of the assault convoys, and on 30 October the main support and covering warships departed Scapa Flow and the Clyde. A combination of carrier aircraft and long-range RAF bombers stood ready to protect the convoys from attack by German airplanes, surface raiders, or U-boats. An apprehensive First Sea Lord Dudley Pound advised Prime Minister Churchill that the U-boats 'might well prove exceedingly menacing . . .

[to] the most valuable convoys ever to leave these shores.'[42] One U-boat was destroyed on 24 October; another was sunk by a B-24 Liberator bomber on 24 October. Other U-boats and German aircraft sighted some of the escorts and parts of the convoys.

The official Royal Navy historian, Captain Stephen W. Roskill, records the incomprehension of the Germans: 'But in spite of all these reports of exceptionally heavy southward movements between the 26 October and the 3 November the enemy did not guess what was in train.'[43] In a memorandum dated 4 November the German Naval Staff noted: 'The relatively small number of landing craft, and the fact that only two passenger ships are in this assembly at Gibraltar, do not indicate any immediate landing in the Mediterranean or on the north-west African coast.'[44] At that very moment, having largely if not entirely evaded detection, the ships of the Eastern and Central Task Forces were converging on the Straits of Gibraltar, through which they would begin to pass in orderly procession beginning at 1930 on 5 November.

The Germans had missed their moment in an area of the Atlantic historically vital to England's national security. 'No waters in all the wide oceans of the world, not even those which wash the shores of Britain herself,' writes the awe-struck Captain

Roskill, 'have played a greater part in her history, or seen more of her maritime renown than these, where the rolling waves of the Atlantic approach the constricting passage of the Pillars of Hercules.'[45]

The greatest danger to Burrough and Troubridge had passed once the armada cleared the Straits of Gibraltar and entered the Mediterranean. It did so by 0400 on the 7th, with the loss in the transit of only one torpedoed American transport, most of whose soldiers survived to fight. The fleet then assembled in the configurations to be used on D-day, 8 November.

Commodore Troubridge's Centre Naval Task Force of over seventy warships and thirty-two transports headed east, as if toward Malta. At the last moment, under cover of darkness, they broke into three landing groups and turned south toward three beaches outside of Oran. Battleship *Rodney*, the anti-aircraft cruiser *Delhi*, one heavy and two escort carriers, and thirteen destroyers met twenty-five miles off Oran at 0530 on the 8th. Thereafter they covered the expedition. Slightly before midnight on the 7th the 39,000 invading soldiers boarded their landing craft and headed for the coast. They began to hit the beaches between 0100 and 0130 on the 8th. They were almost all Americans from the 1st Infantry and 1st Armored Divisions.

[41]Captain Stephen W. Roskill, The War at Sea, 1939-1945: Volume II, The Period of Balance (London: Her Majesty's Stationery Office, 1956), p. 328.
[42]First Sea Lord quoted in Roskill, The War at Sea, p. 317.
[43]*Ibid.* p. 319.
[44]German staff quoted in Roskill, The War at Sea, p. 315.
[45]Roskill, The War at Sea, pp. 320-21.

Centre Task Force Map showing Oran Beaches and Release Points. (NHB)

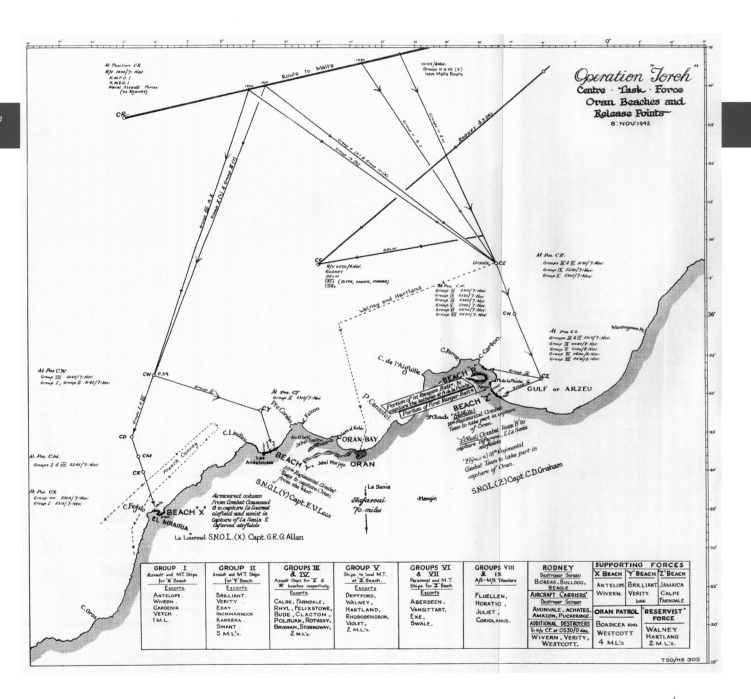

At the western landing sector a nasty current caused some of the landing craft to miss their exact point on the beach, but otherwise there were no mishaps of consequence. By 11 November more than 3,000 men, 458 tanks and vehicles, and over 1,100 tonnes of equipment had been brought ashore. The landings on the beach to the east of Oran were the largest. Facing no opposition and making few mistakes, thirty-four transports and eighty-five landing craft put ashore 29,000 men, 2,400 vehicles, and 14,000 tonnes of stores. The centre landing beach, which lay a short distance to the west of Oran, was another matter. Here an undiscovered sand bar trapped a portion of the forty-five landing craft, resulting in damage and loss. Not a few vehicles foundered while trying to make their way from the landing craft to the shore. Fortunately, once again there was no opposition from the French. Despite this minor catastrophe at the centre, by noon the soldiers had captured the main airfield fifteen miles south of Oran. In the afternoon of the first day of the assault Spitfires from Gibraltar arrived and became part of the force.

It was in the port city of Oran itself where the plans of the Centre Task Force came unglued. To prevent the French navy from scuttling ships and demolishing the port, two former U.S. Coast Guard cutters jammed with American troops were to dash into the harbour and put the men directly ashore, in so-called Operation RESERVIST. It was

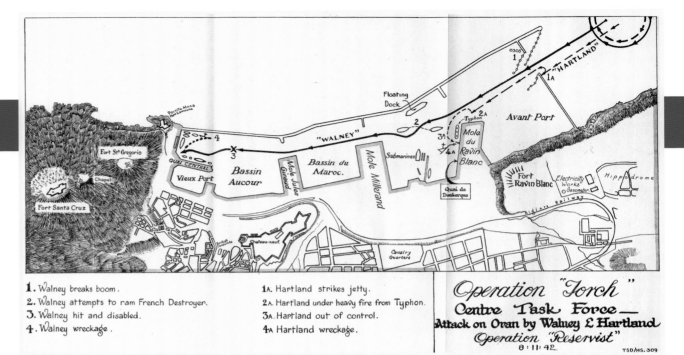

1. Walney breaks boom.
2. Walney attempts to ram French Destroyer.
3. Walney hit and disabled.
4. Walney wreckage.

1A. Hartland strikes jetty.
2A. Hartland under heavy fire from Typhon.
3A. Hartland out of control.
4A. Hartland wreckage.

*Operation "Torch"
Centre Task Force —
Attack on Oran by Walney & Hartland
Operation "Reservist"*
8·11·42.

not to be. The cutters were not dispatched until after the beach landings had alerted the French defenders, and the result was a disaster.

After ramming the harbour's defensive boom shortly around 0300 on the 8th, the lead cutter *Walney*, followed closely by her sister vessel the *Hartland*, 'broke into the harbour. She at once came under withering fire from ships and shore, was totally disabled, had most of her company killed and finally sank. The *Hartland* fared no better.' While trying to manoeuvre toward a quay the *Hartland* came under a French destroyer's fire at a range of 100 feet. Virtually all hands were killed, wounded or taken prisoner. The skipper of the *Walney*, Captain F. T. Peters, survived only to be killed accidentally a few days later. He received the Victoria Cross posthumously.

The navy's frontal assault had failed, leaving General Fredendall's men to take Oran and its sabotaged harbour from the rear. The American soldiers attacked at 0730 on the 10th, and the French capitulated at noon, a few hours before Admiral Darlan ordered all French forces to cease fighting. The Royal Navy's sense of relief was expressed by Captain Roskill: 'fifty-nine hours after the first assault, a base which had been a source of trouble and anxiety to us ever since June 1940 passed into Allied hands.'[46]

The Anglo-Americans of Vice Admiral Burrough's ninety-three ship Eastern Task Force won an even quicker victory in Algiers.

As at Oran, the invaders struck at three beaches flanking the major objective. The pre-dawn sea was calm, but there was a sharp westerly set to the current. This disturbance, added to lack of training in amphibious operations, resulted in confused ship-to-shore movement, great loss of landing craft, and intermingled military units. Absence of resistance at the beaches had a countervailing effect of enabling the troops to regroup quickly and move inland toward their objectives. At 0640 one of General Ryder's regimental combat teams captured the Maison Blanche airfield near Algiers. Pro-Allied sentiment on the part of French officers led to negligible resistance. By 0900 RAF fighters from Gibraltar were landing at Maison Blanche. They sucked up available fuel and began flying patrols over the landing beaches flanking Algiers.

The port was targeted by the navy for a pre-emptive frontal assault, as at Oran and at Safi in Morocco. Two destroyers

loaded with troops made their way toward the harbour, hoping to enter and debark the men hurriedly as a means of preventing sabotage. In the darkness the destroyers missed the harbour's entrance and came under heavy fire as they searched for the channel. On her fourth try, at 0520, destroyer *Broke* found the entrance, crashed through the defensive boom and berthed. She hurriedly disembarked her American passengers who were soon pinned down by small arms fire and captured. Forced by heavy fire to withdraw, the badly damaged *Broke* sank the next day. The outcome at Algiers might have been dire had not the French commander surrendered the city intact to the Americans in the early evening of the 8th. The dexterous hand of American diplomat Robert Murphy was again pulling the strings. He had persuaded Admiral Darlan to authorise the city's surrender.

In a somewhat farcical encore the next morning, Admiral Burrough's specially configured command ship, the *Bulolo*,

[46]Roskill, The War at Sea, p. 328.

HMS Bulolo in Algiers Harbour used during the landings on Operation TORCH. (NHB)

steamed into harbour and overshot her berth, coming to an undamaged rest on a nearby mud bank. No matter. By gaining possession of the capital of French Algeria, the best port on the western Mediterranean coast of Africa, the Allies had set the stage for the next act in the Mediterranean war: their race with the Axis armies for Tunisia, the real strategic goal of TORCH.

Strategic consequences of TORCH

Algiers was a major port, but it was too far west to be more than a base area in the struggle to expel the Germans from North Africa. Tunisia, with the important port and naval base of Bizerte, was separated from Sicily by a mere ninety miles of narrow Mediterranean Sea. In Allied hands, Tunisia would deny the Germans resupply and reinforcement as they now battled on two fronts: against Montgomery's Eighth Army in the east and Lieutenant General Kenneth Anderson's British First Army to their west. It also would serve as a launching point for an Allied invasion of Sicily or Italy.

The Germans could not tolerate the Anglo-American occupation of Tunisia, and they moved swiftly to preclude such a strategic disaster. As early as 9 November, they began flying reinforcements from Sicily to Tunisia. Several thousand German paratroopers descended on Tunisia on 13 November, blocking a swift Allied advance toward Bizerte and Tunis. General Anderson's soldiers, abetted by the Royal Navy's seizure of two small ports well east of Algiers, got to within eighty miles of Tunis. 'But supply lines were over-stretched and, as the First Army came under increasing pressure from newly arrived German forces, progress slowed.'[47] Ike ordered a pre-Christmas offensive that failed. The Allies were bogged down.

In mid-January Eisenhower was directed to plan for Allied landings in Sicily and Italy, so he turned the Tunisian campaign over to General Sir Harold Alexander. The British general commanded the newly created 18th Army Group, composed of the British First and Eighth Armies and the U.S. II Corps. These forces would battle with the Germans for control of Tunisia until May 1943. The Americans finally captured Bizerte on 7 May, just as Tunis fell to the British 11th Hussars. On 13 May, 175,000 Axis troops squeezed into Cape Bon at the northeastern tip of Tunisia surrendered to the British and to Major General Omar N. Bradley's American II Corps. Four days later a trans-Mediterranean convoy left Gibraltar for the first time since 1941; it arrived at Alexandria, Egypt, on the 26th. The Indian Ocean-Suez-Mediterranean-Gibraltar-Atlantic lifeline was at last open. Transports no longer had to round the Cape of Good Hope to reach India or Australia. Admirals Cunningham, Burrough and Troubridge had begun to restore the Royal Navy's historic domination of the Mediterranean Sea. The military struggle had been bitter, and the Americans had been forced painfully to learn a great deal about fighting a determined and able foe.

In the contest for Tunisia two of America's top commanders, Generals Bradley and Patton, mastered the skills that ultimately carried them to Normandy and into the heart of Germany, alongside Montgomery. Historian Rick Atkinson has described the American experience as creating 'an army at dawn.'[48] Valuable as this blood-drenched schooling may have been, there is still good reason to meditate on what American naval historian Samuel E. Morison has written: 'Bold as Operation TORCH was, and successful within its sphere, it could well have been a little bolder and secured Tunisia too, as Admiral Cunningham wanted.'[49]

With TORCH an irreversible amphibious success and with the Anglo-American armies slowly but inexorably extirpating the Germans from North Africa the time had come to determine what was next on the strategic agenda. President Roosevelt and Prime Minister Churchill decided to wrap up the affair the way they had begun it: with a personal meeting. Between 14 and 24 January 1943, the two leaders of the Anglo-American coalition met at the Casablanca Conference (codenamed SYMBOL), along with many of their most senior military and naval advisors. The original intention had been to include Premier Josef Stalin of the Soviet Union, upon whose people the Germans were inflicting enormous losses on the Eastern Front. But Stalin was thoroughly preoccupied by the Battle of Stalingrad, which was nearing its

[47] John, Pimlott, The Historical Atlas of World War II (New York: Henry Holt, 1995), p. 110.
[48] See Rick Atkinson, An Army at Dawn (New York: Henry Holt, 2002), passim.
[49] Morison, The Two-Ocean War, p. 236.

culminating destruction of a German army at the moment the Casablanca Conference convened. He did not attend, and he worried that in his absence Roosevelt and Churchill might once again defer opening of a 'second front' in France. Understandably distrustful of the democratic leaders, he cabled the president and prime minister: 'Allow me to express my confidence that the promises about the opening of a second front in Europe given... in regard to 1942, and in any case with regard to the spring of 1943, will be fulfilled.'[50] He was to be massively disappointed, and his sense of betrayal helped fuel the early Cold War.

The most famous outcome of the conference was the proclamation of the doctrine of 'unconditional surrender,' first proposed by Roosevelt. He derived the phrase from a demand made by U.S. Civil War General Ulysses S. Grant, whose initials are sometimes said to stand for 'Unconditional Surrender.' Churchill apparently accepted the idea, although not necessarily its public release. The president nonetheless announced it as an Anglo-American war aim the day after the conference closed. Roosevelt explained, 'I think... that peace can come to the world only by the total elimination of German and Japanese war power, [which means] the unconditional surrender by Germany, Italy and Japan.'[51]

Other monumental decisions of the conference were kept secret from the public for reasons of military security. Chief among these was the selection of Sicily as the next major amphibious objective. The decision was reached after a reprise of the 1942 debates that had led to TORCH. General George Marshall still wanted an early attack on the continent of Europe, preferably a massive one; the British chiefs of staff countered that the overwhelming number of available German divisions spelled certain defeat of any Allied assault on the coast of France. Far better to continue the peripheral strategy by which Germany would be forced to recall some divisions from the Eastern Front, where at that moment the hard-pressed Red Army was managing to encircle a large German army at Stalingrad. An Anglo-American attack from across the Mediterranean into southern Europe possibly would induce Italy to withdraw from the war, although the surprising doctrine of 'unconditional surrender' made that less likely. But the Germans would have to come further into southern Europe to counter any invasion, and this would give the Anglo-Americans a numerical advantage once the time came for a landing in France, now thought to be impossible before 1944. Faced with the meticulous staff work and persuasive logic of their counterparts, the American chiefs of staff capitulated. They accepted Sicily as the next objective, and Eisenhower was directed to plan Operation HUSKY.[52]

Before capitulating to the British, the Americans won a major concession demanded by Admiral Ernest King: the right to continue the Pacific offensive against Japan that had been started at Guadalcanal, an operation which was just winding down as the conferees met. This approval signaled a green light for General Douglas MacArthur to begin the protracted 'island hopping' campaign that would carry his army back to the Philippine Islands in 1944. In this manner the 'Germany first' strategy that had dominated Allied planning since about 1939 again fell to the wayside of American political, military, and naval imperatives. Whatever the wisdom of the individual decisions reached at Casablanca, the conference did shape the strategy for the remainder of the war in both the European-Atlantic and Pacific theaters. Casablanca in turn was a direct result of TORCH. Thus it can be said that an operation agreed upon with doubt and by compromise in the middle of 1942 had by January 1943 transformed the global strategy of all parties fighting World War II.

TORCH and The Study of Strategy

TORCH took place over sixty years before this essay was written, but it is alive with transcendent implications for modern students of military and naval strategy, especially for those studying amphibious warfare. With trepidation, the author lists below some of the 'lessons', that struck him as he was writing.

- **Complexity:** Douglas Porch writes, 'No other operation surpassed TORCH in complexity, in daring - and the prominence of hazard involved - or in the degree of strategic surprise achieved.'[53]

[50]Stalin quoted in Simon Appleby, 'SYMBOL: The Casablanca Conference, chapter 2, p. 1, http://casablancaconference.com, accessed 24 November 2004.
[51]Roosevelt quoted in Simon Appleby, 'SYMBOL: The Casablanca Conference,' chapter 3, p. 15, http://casablancaconference.com, accessed 24 November 2004.
[52]See Chapter XV on Sicily, by Lieutenant Commander Tristan Lovering.
[53]Porch, Path to Victory, p. 329.

No other operation surpassed TORCH in complexity, in daring - and the prominence of hazard involved

- **Coalition warfare:** TORCH showed that compromise at the highest political levels is the essence of a coalition, even one that was arguably history's most amicable.

- **Pre-war strategies:** TORCH led to the abandonment of four years' dedicated planning to fight 'Germany first.' This reversal suggests that war will irrevocably alter strategy, and it calls to mind Carl von Clausewitz's injunction always to keep strategy and policy in harmony by adjusting one when the other changes.

- **'Unconditional surrender':** Franklin Roosevelt's unexpected announcement of this goal stands as a warning against making public pronouncements not preceded by the most careful consideration of their impact. The concept of unconditional surrender runs counter to Sun Tzu's warning not to back an enemy into a corner because he will fight all the more desperately even though he knows he is defeated. [54]

- **'Jointness':** This 21st century American desideratum for judging military strategy and performance was more than met by TORCH, even though there was plenty of friction and disagreement.

- **Command of the Sea:** The historic Mahanian standard of judging navies and their accomplishments by the extent to which they exercised command of the seas in which they operated was proven null and void by TORCH. The Royal Navy did not command the Mediterranean until after TORCH, and neither the British nor American Navy, singly or jointly, commanded the Atlantic until the U-boats were brought under control nearly a year after TORCH.

- **Power projection:** The Western Naval Task Force (TF 34) traversed 3,900 miles of open ocean to reach its destination in Morocco without losing a single vessel to a U-boat. It lacked land-based air cover, and it had to replenish underway two times. This model is worth careful study by strategists and tacticians in the 21st century.

- **Direct versus indirect strategies:** The Americans wanted a direct Clausewitzian attack through France at the German heartland; the British favoured a peripheral strategy, and they won out. The debate classically pits Clausewitz against Sun Tzu, General Marshall against B. H. Liddell Hart.[55] The correct choice is indeterminable.

- **Boldness versus caution:** The Americans were bold in wanting to strIke immediately at the coast of France; they were cautiously unwilling to extend the reach of TORCH to Bizerte and Tunis. The British were cautious about striking France, but Cunningham wanted to include Bizerte and Tunis as objectives of TORCH. As with the direct and indirect approaches, it is impossible to issue a final judgement on which was correct, but the nature of the debate is timeless.

- **Tactical wisdom** of attacking beaches rather than ports. Oran and Algiers illustrate the hazards of a frontal attack on a city, even when the enemy's resistance is not resolute.

- **Deception and electronic warfare:** TORCH illustrates the importance of both, and their interconnectedness with one another. They are mainstays of the modern war against terrorism.

- **Surprise:** The debate over whether to attack before dawn without pre-invasion naval bombardment, or to lose the element of surprise by softening the target with naval gunfire before the landing, was never resolved. It in part reflects interservice rivalry between the U.S. Army and the U.S. Navy, a debilitating condition that still exists.

- **Innovation:** The interwar development, mostly by the U.S. Marine Corps, of radically new techniques for amphibious operations made TORCH and the simultaneous landings at Guadalcanal possible. It suggests the absolute necessity of creative thinking at every level of the military in periods of peace.

---

[54]For Sun Tzu, see Sun Tzu: The Art of War. Translated by Samuel Griffith. London: Oxford University Press, 1971.
[55]For the British writer who most explicitly considered himself a disciple of Sun Tzu, see B. H. Liddell Hart, History of the Second World War (New York: G. P. Putnam's Sons, 1970), passim.

Further Reading

Atkinson, Rick, *An Army at Dawn: The War in North Africa, 1942-1943*, (New York: Henry Holt, 2002)

Cunningham of Hyndhope, Admiral of the Fleet Viscount. *A Sailor's Odyssey*, (London: Hutchinson, 1951)

D'Este, Carlo, *Eisenhower: A Soldier's Life*, (New York: Henry Holt, 2002)

D'Este, Carlo, *Patton: A Genius for War,* (New York: Harper Collins, 1995)

Greene, Jack and Alessandro Massignani, *The Naval War in the Mediterranean 1940-1943*, (London: Chatham Publishing, 1998)

Hamilton, Nigel, *Master of the Battlefield: Monty's War Years, 1942-1944*, (New York: McGraw-Hill, 1983)

Hewitt, H. Kent, *The Memoirs of Admiral H. Kent Hewitt*, Edited by Evelyn M. Cherpak, (Newport, RI: Naval War College Press, 2002)

Howard, Michael, *The Mediterranean Strategy in the Second World War*, (New York: Praeger, 1968)

Morison, Samuel E., *History of United States Naval Operations in World War II, Volume II: Operations in North African Waters, October 1942-June 1943, Campaign, IL:*, (The University of Illinois Press, 2001) [new paperback edition of a classic]

Porch, Douglas., *The Path to Victory: The Mediterranean Theater in World War II.*, (New York: Farrar, Straus and Giroux, 2004)

Roskill, Captain S. W., *The War at Sea, 1939-1945: Volume II, The Period of Balance,* (London: Her Majesty's Stationery Office, 1956)

Tomblin, Barbara Brooks, *With Utmost Spirit: Allied Naval Operations in the Mediterranean, 1942-1945*, (Lexington, KY: The University Press of Kentucky, 2004)

Biography

Kenneth J Hagan is a Professor of Strategy at the US Naval War College, Monterey and Museum Director Emeritus of the US Naval Academy. He joined the US Naval Academy faculty in 1973, was a Professor of History between 1987 and 1993, and taught naval history at the Academy for over 20 years. He gained his PhD in History from the Claremont Graduate School, and his Bachelor's and Master's Degrees from the University of California at Berkeley. His academic specialty is the history of US naval strategy and policy. He has written extensively, lectured worldwide, delivered numerous articles and papers, and subsequently has one of the finest reputations as a naval historian today. He is the author of: *American Gunboat Diplomacy and the Old Navy, 1877-1889* (Greenwood Press, 1973), which is on the Commandant of the Marine Corps' Reading List, and *This People's Navy: The Making of American Sea Power* (The Free Press, 1991), is editing the third edition of *In Peace and War: Interpretations of American Naval History, 1775-1984* (Greenwood Press, 1984), and is the co-author with Ian J. Bickerton of *Unintended Consequences: The United States at War* (Reaktion Books, 2007) He also served as an intelligence officer in the US Naval Reserves for twenty-seven years retiring as a Captain in 1985.

The Capture of Attu Island
Operation LANDCRAB, May 1943

XIV

'Those men can take it. And you can't tell me an army travels on its stomach; because long after it gets through traveling on its stomach it continues to travel - on its guts.'[1]

By Professor William Allison

Lieutenant Charles K. Paulson,
Company F, 17th Infantry Regiment, 7th Division,
United States Army, Massacre Valley, Attu Island

Introduction

In May 1943, a joint United States Army and Navy task force made a bold amphibious assault against Japanese forces on the small American island of Attu, one of the more remote islands of the Aleutian chain southwest of Alaska. The operation, codenamed LANDCRAB, was only the third amphibious attack conducted by American forces in World War II and the first by the Army against an enemy-held island. The North Pacific campaign is one of the least known and most under-appreciated theatres of operations in World War II. In hindsight, the military operations of the North Pacific and its desolate wintry islands may indeed represent one of the more minor and relatively insignificant campaigns of the war. Yet from 1939 through 1944, the United States considered the North Pacific islands crucial to the defence of North America as well as a possible base of operations for a direct assault on the Japanese home islands. The amphibious assault on Attu succeeded in annihilating the Japanese force defending the island despite many serious flaws in planning, command, and logistics, and exceptionally rugged terrain and harsh climatic conditions. The American military learned valuable lessons from this often forgotten operation that helped improve the planning and conduct of amphibious operations in late 1943 and 1944.

Strategic Contours

From both the offensive and defensive points of view, the Aleutian Islands presented a complex strategic problem to both Japanese and American war planners. Weather, terrain, and distance dictated every strategic and tactical consideration. Stretching nearly one thousand miles from the tip of the Alaskan Peninsula west-southwest to within one hundred miles of Kamchatka, the Aleutians are comprised of over one hundred and twenty volcanic islands. Thin-crusted tundra, snow-capped mountains, near constant fog and freezing drizzle, and ferocious winds make the islands among the more inhospitable places on earth. Distances among the islands and to major military centers are impressive. The easternmost island of Unalaska is two thousand miles from San Francisco and Honolulu. Kiska, in west-central portion of the chain, is six hundred and ten miles west of Dutch Harbor, Unalaska. Attu is one thousand miles from the Alaskan mainland and seven hundred and fifty miles from the northernmost Japanese islands. Between these islands are rough seas filled with uncharted rocks and shoals that can rip apart the hull of any vessel. Air power could provide only a limited alternative to surface fleets, as few islands had potential for airfields and fog-filled skies made flying even the most simple of missions a risky adventure. It is no wonder that both Japanese and American high commands hesitated at pursuing major operations in the North Pacific.[2]

Before the outbreak of War World II in 1939, the United States gave Alaskan defence scant consideration. As Germany invaded Poland, the United States Army had an undersized garrison of two rifle companies at Chilkoot Barracks, Skagway, while the Navy maintained only a seaplane base at Sitka and a radio station, along with a Coast Guard base, at Dutch Harbor on Unalaska Island in the easternmost Aleutians. The United States had under construction seaplane and submarine bases at Kodiak and Dutch Harbor by late 1939. In 1940, a full naval air station was added to Dutch Harbor, along with a greater Army presence to defend the station.[3]

In 1936 Japan abrogated the 1922 Washington Naval Treaty, a move that forced the United States to reconsider hemispheric security in its War Plan ORANGE for possible war with the Empire of Japan. The American War Plans Division envisioned a security triangle stretching from Alaska to Hawaii then to the Panama Canal to defend North America. Although the Navy continued to insist that it alone could defeat Japan, as originally stipulated in War Plan ORANGE, the Army insisted upon the security triangle defensive concept in the 1938 revision of ORANGE. Alaska and the Aleutians would anchor the northern azimuth of the Pacific security triangle. To rectify the vast geographic and topographic ignorance of the Aleutians, the Army had already initiated its Alaskan Mapping Project in 1936. For the westernmost island of Attu, unfortunately, by 1943 only the coastline had been

---

[1]*The Capture of Attu: As Told by the Men Who Fought There* (Washington, D.C.: Department of War, 1944), p. 31.
[2]*The Aleutians Campaign, June 1942-August 1943* (Washington, D.C.: Naval Historical Center, 1993; reprint, Washington, D.C.: Office of Naval Intelligence, 1945), pp. 2-3.
[3]Stetson Conn, Rose C. Engleman, and Byron Fairchild, *The United States Army in World War II: Guarding the United States and Its Outposts* (Washington, D.C.: United States Army Center for Military History, 1962), pp. 223-24.

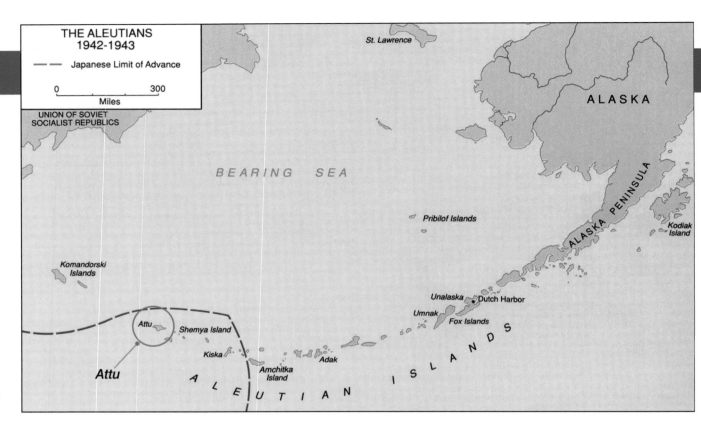

The Aleutian Islands: Highlighting the Japanese Limit of Advance, 1942 - 1943. (NHB)

mapped to any accuracy. The interior, with its abrupt peaks and steep ravines, remained uncharted.

The Navy also briefly brought the Aleutian Islands to the fore in 1936. A study by the Naval War College concluded that the Aleutians could only be held with the help of Soviet Russia and Canada, and that Japan would quickly take the long island chain to prevent American long-range bombers from using the islands as bases for operations against the Japanese home islands. The major drawback of the island chain was that none of the islands afforded a harbour adequate enough to accommodate a major fleet. Moreover, the climate, inhospitable at best, made what looked great on a map in Newport rather impractical. Still, such close proximity to the northern Japanese islands made the Aleutians quite inviting, but the harsh realities of year-round fog and mist, freezing temperatures, and extremely rugged terrain, the study concluded, would make major military operations in the region extremely difficult for both Japanese and American forces. Impressed by the study though ignoring the climatic warnings, the Navy began considering the base-buildup that came to fruition in 1940. Politics, however, stalled more aggressive plans. The United States did not want to unnecessarily provoke Japan by what could easily be misinterpreted as an offensive buildup in Alaska and the Aleutians.[4]

According to the 1940 RAINBOW war plans, which stipulated the defeat of Germany while fighting a defensive holding action in the Pacific against Japan, the Army and Navy had joint responsibility for defending Unalaska Island, the westernmost defended position in the Aleutian chain. Sitka, Kodiak, and Anchorage would also be garrisoned, with Anchorage providing the primary base of supply and operations. Major General Simon Bolivar Buckner, Jr., appointed commander of the new Alaska Defence Command in July 1940, quickly found the RAINBOW plan inadequate for Alaska and the Aleutians. The Army and Navy operated at crossed purposes in the region. The Navy, with its installations at Sitka, Dutch Harbor, Kodiak, and Anchorage,

assumed the Army would defend these bases, while the Army found the Navy either unwilling or unable to warn the central command at Anchorage of a Japanese attack and thus kept its main force on the Alaskan mainland. While the Navy claimed that Japan would not and probably could not stage an attack on the Alaskan peninsula and saw no need for the Army to keep its main garrison at Anchorage, the Army vehemently disagreed and would only assign minimal forces to defend Navy bases. Buckner worried that even though the Japanese might not want to stage a large offensive in the North Pacific, they certainly

[4]Galen Roger Perras, *Stepping Stones to Nowhere: The Aleutian Islands, Alaska, and American Military Strategy, 1867-1945* (Vancouver: University of British Columbia Press, 2003), pp. 28-42.

Left: Lieutenant General John L DeWitt.
Right: Admiral Chester Nimitz USM. (DoD)

would take advantage of the unoccupied and weakly defended Aleutians as a defensive move to protect the home islands of Japan. Buckner's prognosis was right - Japan did not intend to attack Alaska, but did campaign against the western Aleutians as part of a principally defensive strategy. To discourage Japanese designs, Buckner increased fighter and bomber support and began air patrols over the maritime approaches to the Alaskan peninsula. By July 1941, Buckner had increased the Alaska garrison to 24,000 men, and had promises of twenty-five fighters and twenty-six bombers by December. The Navy had only four surface vessels, two submarines, and six planes in the Alaskan theatre.[5]

December 1941, of course, changed everything. After the stunning Japanese attacks on Pearl Harbor, the Philippines, and other American and Allied possessions in the Pacific, the Alaska Defence Command, like everyone else, screamed for more men, more planes, more ships, more everything. With American air, naval, and ground forces stretched dangerously thin and with pressure from Great Britain to open operations in the European theatre, plans to expand defensive capabilities, and further establish offensive bases in Alaska ran into several practical roadblocks. Building airfields in the western Aleutians could be done but not for over a year, and besides there were not enough planes available to equip them. American planners even considered Siberia as a possible base of operations to

defend Alaska and attack Japan, but the Soviet Union understandably put a quick end to that idea. Radar sets, anti-aircraft guns, and other necessary equipment remained in short supply in the Alaskan theatre. At the beginning of the war the United States simply did not have enough of anything to fully equip the unprecedented scope of its theatres of operations. Meanwhile, the Japanese juggernaut continued to roll onward on all fronts, until May 1942, when the United States Navy, at heavy cost, stopped the Japanese Imperial Navy at the Battle of Coral Sea, the war's first great carrier battle.[6]

Despite the Coral Sea setback, the Japanese Imperial High Command sensed an opportunity to finally destroy the American carrier fleet. Japanese Admiral Isoroku Yamamoto proposed a bold plan to take the Western Aleutians and Midway Island. Holding both points would give Japan its own strategic security line while providing the bait to lure the weakened American fleet out of Pearl Harbor to meet its final destruction. An attack on the Aleutians, Yamamoto hoped, would force the American fleet north, leaving Midway unprotected. Once the Japanese attacked Midway, Yamamoto reasoned that American Admiral Chester Nimitz would then order the American fleet back to Midway, where the Japanese Navy would deliver the *coup d'grace*. The destruction of the American Pacific fleet would give Japan complete command of the central, western, and northern

Pacific. Of course, Yamamoto had to divide his fleet – two aircraft carriers and numerous support ships to attack the Aleutians and four carriers, nine battleships, and twelve transports and their support ships to attack Midway and set the trap for Nimitz and his Pacific fleet. In addition to breaking the Japanese naval code, which exposed Midway as the principle target, this division of force arguably gave Nimitz a decided advantage in the Battle of Midway in June 1942. Yet, Nimitz also had to divide his force, sending almost a third of his ships, but significantly no carriers, to defend the Aleutians, which American intelligence had also discovered was a primary target.[7]

Task Force 8, under command of Rear Admiral Robert A. Theobald, steamed to Dutch Harbor with orders to prevent Japan from landing on Alaskan soil at all costs. Once in the Alaskan Theatre, Theobald, under the chain of command of Nimitz at Pearl Harbor, took control over all naval and air forces (including the Army Air Corps 11th Air Force at Kodiak), while Buckner, who answered to Lieutenant General John L. DeWitt, commander of the new Western Defence Command at San Francisco, commanded all ground forces. Theobald set up Navy headquarters at Kodiak Island, while the Army maintained its prewar headquarters three hundred miles away

[5] Perras, *Stepping Stones to Nowhere*, pp. 42-52.
[6] Conn, et al., *Guarding the United States and Its Outposts*, pp. 253-57.
[7] George L. MacGarrigle, *The U.S. Army Campaigns of World War II: Aleutian Islands* (Washington, D.C.: United States Army Center for Military History, 1992), pp. 1-4; Samuel Eliot Morison, *History of United States Naval Operations in World War II, Volume VII: Aleutians, Gilberts, and Marshalls, June 1942-April 1944* (Boston: Little, Brown, and Company, 1961), pp. 3-5.

at Anchorage. According to the official Army history of the war, the joint operations centre at Anchorage was 'worthless.' A new joint command centre set up at Kodiak in August 1942 worked somewhat better. As was common in many theatres, the Army and Navy failed to effectively share intelligence and conflicts over the control and use of air assets caused friction. Moreover, in the Alaskan theatre personality conflicts muddied the normally clear waters of effective command. The Alaskan chain of command structure itself was awkward and, at times, unworkable. The Joints Chiefs of Staff in Washington, D.C., had to resolve disagreements between the two commands. Arguments to remove Alaska from Western Defence Command and give it independent command status fell upon deaf ears. These command problems would continue to hamper American efforts in Alaska and the Aleutians through 1943, the most critical year in the theatre during the war.[8]

Opening Salvos

Japanese aircraft from Admiral Boshiro Hosogaya's Northern Strike Force attacked Dutch Harbor on June 3 and 4, 1942, hitting oil storage tanks and killing 43 Americans. Stiff American resistance at Dutch Harbor convinced Hosogaya to abandon his original plan to occupy Adak and instead send 1,800 troops to occupy Kiska and Attu on 6 and 7 June. The Japanese landing parties met no resistance. On Attu, the Japanese captured

some forty Aleuts and one American missionary (another had apparently committed suicide), while on Kiska a ten-man American weather team on the island fell into Japanese hands. Without Midway, the Japanese strategic concept of a defensive line and ability to command the central and northern Pacific disappeared, but holding Kiska and Attu did provide a defensive point to block American attacks on northern Japan via air and sea. Japan had no intention of invading Alaska, and by this point, the United States had all but abandoned hopes of attacking Japan from the Aleutians. Yet, neither had realised the abandoned strategy of the other and both assumed the game was still on. From the American standpoint, at the very least Japanese forces had occupied American possessions and had to be removed.[9]

Throughout the late summer and winter of 1942-1943, the Americans and Japanese traded jabs, mainly through frequent bombing raids and naval bombardments that achieved only infrequent successes. In November 1942, through daring submarine and surface delivery, the Japanese increased their garrisons on Kiska and Attu to four thousand and one thousand troops respectively. The United States had increased its Alaska forces to 94,000 by January 1943. Without resistance, American forces occupied and built airfields on Umnak and Adak Islands. In January 1943, American forces landed on unoccupied Amchitka

Island and, despite incredibly harsh climatic conditions, built an airfield by mid-February.[10]

Finding their positions on Attu and Kiska increasingly difficult to re-supply because of the proximity of American air forces and intense patrolling by American destroyers and submarines, the Japanese made a daring run with four heavy cruisers and four destroyers escorting several transport and supply ships in March 1943. On 26 March, this Japanese fleet ran into an American fleet of two cruisers and four destroyers off the Komandorski Islands. The American and Japanese navies battled each other for over three hours at distances ranging from eight to twelve miles. In one of the largest and longest fleet actions of the war, both sides withdrew battered but suffered no serious damage. For the Japanese, however, it must be considered a defeat, as the transports and supply ships did not deliver their precious cargoes to Attu and Kiska and instead the entire force returned to Japan.[11]

Retaking Attu

General DeWitt made retaking Kiska the first priority in removing the Japanese from the Aleutians. Planning began as early as December 1942. With an airfield, built by the Japanese, and a decent harbour, Kiska would provide the better base for future operations than Attu. Intelligence suggested that Japan

---

[8]MacGarrigle, *Aleutian Islands*, pp. 5-6; Conn, et al., *Guarding the United States and Its Outposts*, pp. 266-67.

[9]Morison, *Aleutians, Gilberts, and Marshalls, June 1942-April 1944*, pp. 4-5; *The Aleutians Campaign*, pp. 17-19.

[10]MacGarrigle, *Aleutian Islands*, pp. 10-11.

[11]Morison, *Aleutians, Gilberts, and Marshalls, June 1942-April 1944*, pp. 22-36; *The Aleutians Campaign*, pp. 35-75.

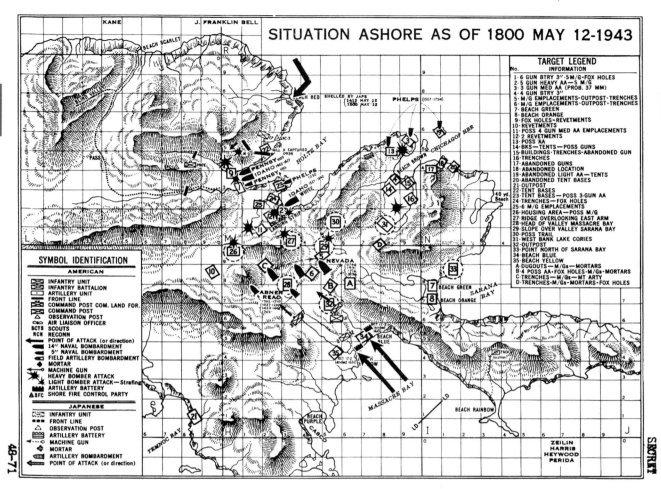

had over ten thousand troops on Kiska (actually much less), leading planners to propose a division-sized operation (twenty-five thousand men) to assault the island. The Joint Chiefs of Staff concurred, but replaced the desired 35th Division with the motorised 7th Division, which made little sense because Kiska had few roads and Attu had none. The 7th Division had been training for the unique desert warfare of North Africa; now, it suddenly had to learn the polar opposite – the rigours of sub-Arctic warfare, which few actually new much about. Moreover, several officers of the 35th Division, including its commander, had Alaska experience – the officers of the 7th Division had none. But the 7th Division had been training longer and seemed ready to ship out at short notice. It was still at Fort Ord, California, where amphibious training facilities existed, though practice landings on the Monterey Peninsula hardly equalled landing on Attu or Kiska. At San Diego, a joint Army-Navy planning staff under the command of Rear Admiral Francis W. Rockwell, who had also been appointed commander of Amphibious Force, North Pacific, coordinated planning for the Kiska assault. Commanding General of the 7th Division, Major General Albert E. Brown, would command the actual landing. At Fort Ord, United States Marine Corps Major General Holland 'Howlin Mad' Smith, former commander of the Marine 1st Division, organised and led the amphibious training course for the 7th Division. The Joint Chiefs of Staff had scheduled the assault for the spring of 1943, which was just an ambitious, if not unrealistic, few months away.[12] By this point in the war, the United States Army had staged one

major amphibious landing in North Africa and the United States Marine Corps had made its difficult assault on Guadalcanal. Planning for major operations against the Solomon Islands and Sicily were well underway. Transports and landing craft, and a myriad of other assorted equipment needed for amphibious operations, were few in number and in great demand. These transport and supply shortages convinced Rear Admiral Thomas C. Kinkaid, who had relived Theobald as commander of Task Force 8, that an assault on Kiska was not feasible. The more practical and perhaps even more strategic target was Attu Island. Thought

to be defended by a mere 500 Japanese, many of whom were labour troops busily building the airfield on the rugged little island, General Buckner and Admiral Kinkaid recommended that Attu could be taken with one infantry regiment and an artillery unit. Instead of the large number of transports needed for an entire division, for Attu the assault force would require only four attack transports and a few cargo ships to make the landing. Strategically, taking Attu instead of Kiska would separate Japan from Kiska, thus cutting off Kiska from its supply line with Japan. In only a short time, Kiska would fall to American hands. In

---

[12]Brian Garfield, *The Thousand-Mile War: World War II in Alaska and the Aleutians* (Garden City, New York: Doubleday and Company, 1969), pp. 193-95; Conn, et al., *Guarding the United States and Its Outposts*, pp. 277-78.

US Troops embarking onto a Landing Craft at Adak Island in the Aleutians. (NHB)

March 1943, the Joint Chiefs approved the change. The assault to retake Attu Island, designated Operation LANDCRAB, was on.[13]

Or so it seemed. On 1 April, DeWitt, Rockwell, Buckner, and others joined the joint planning cell at San Diego to work out the new assault plan. Deadlines loomed, June is traditionally the worst month for the normally thick fog that enshrouds the western Aleutians, so May 7, just five weeks hence, was set as 'D-Day.' The meeting disintegrated into a series of some serious but mostly petty arguments. DeWitt argued that the entire operation would take only three days, while Brown passionately retorted that the terrain alone would take at least a week to conquer before they even reached the Japanese garrison at Chichagof Harbor. DeWitt had never liked Brown and had even less confidence in him as a field commander, and even told Kinkaid and Buckner as much. He went so far as to request Brown be relieved and replaced by the 35th Division's Brigadier General Eugene M. Landrum, who had experience in the Aleutians. The War Department, however, stuck with Brown. Then DeWitt suggested that Brown appoint Landrum as his second in command. Brown flatly rejected the notion and instead took on Brigadier General Archibald V. Arnold, the 7th Division's artillery commander. Influenced by DeWitt, both Kinkaid and Buckner, who hardly knew Brown, began to treat Brown with poorly disguised disdain.

Other issues became contentious. Advisors from the Alaska Defence Command, many of whom had been in the Aleutians, found their advice either accepted with suspicion or completely ignored. Between the Army, Navy, and Air Corps, four different sets of map coordinates existed. Brown did nothing to rectify the discrepancies. Experience had clearly shown that Japanese air strikes rarely did

---

[13]Conn, et al., *Guarding the United States and Its Outposts*, pp. 278-80; Garfield, *The Thousand-Mile War*, pp. 195-96.

7th US Division, while preparing for desert warfare, had to quickly adapt to the rigours of sub-Arctic warfare. (DoD)

The remarkable aspect of the planning for LANDCRAB was that planners knew so little about Attu. Only the coastline had been mapped to any degree of accuracy.

any significant damage, so the cumbersome 90-mm anti-aircraft regiments would likely not be needed. Brown insisted that they stay as part of the assault force. Naval anti-air support could easily defend the landing force against any Japanese air strikes. Brown decided to take the heavy guns anyway. He refused to make a personal reconnaissance of Attu even though he had never been to the Aleutians. A colonel who had never been west of Kodiak put together the assault force's kit and equipment, both of which proved woefully inadequate.

Buckner added to the tense situation by requesting Brown take along some of the Alaska garrison's 4th Infantry Regiment. They had been in Alaska for months, indeed years, and felt they deserved a piece of the action. Brown refused. Rockwell could legitimately claim that transport was not available for extra troops, but DeWitt ordered room made for one Alaska combat battalion. DeWitt commissioned a commercial ship, the *Perida*, to transport the Alaska contingent and extra supplies. With limited landing craft and transports, Rockwell worried that he could not land the assault force quick enough if the Japanese fought to stop the assault on the beaches. DeWitt saw no problem and said the assault would go ashore as planned. Rockwell nearly derailed the entire operation by threatening to cancel it. Admiral Kinkaid overruled Rockwell and ordered him

to get the force on the beaches. Buckner finally got Brown to agree to allow the 4th Infantry Regiment to act as a ready reserve force at Adak that could be on the move in twenty-four hours if needed.

Then new intelligence estimates came in. Air reconnaissance indicated that the five hundred-man Japanese force on Attu had grown to sixteen hundred troops dug in on good defensible ground. In fact, the Japanese had reinforced Attu by submarine to bring the garrison's strength closer to twenty-four hundred. Some large guns had been spotted from the air, but in the fog no one could be certain what they were or indeed how many. And who knew what could be hidden in the many caves and tunnels that the Japanese surely must have used to stow away more guns, more troops, more supplies. Rockwell could not cancel the operation now only three weeks before D-Day. Doctrine dictated that only overwhelming force could defeat an entrenched, well-fortified defensive position. Twenty-five hundred American soldiers could not defeat sixteen hundred dug-in Japanese troops. The Pacific island battles were already showing that outnumbered Japanese troops would put up a massive fight. Rockwell made a momentous decision to commit the entire 7th Division (ten thousand troops) to the assault.[14]

The remarkable aspect of the planning for LANDCRAB was that planners knew so little about Attu. Only the coastline had been mapped to any degree of accuracy. A Coast and Geodetic Survey

chart warned ships to give the island at least a two to three mile-wide berth. The interior remained mysterious, shrouded in dense fog and violent snow squalls. Attu's forty-mile length (east to west) and twenty-mile maximum width of mountains, ravines, and valleys was foreboding to say the least. From the sea the island appeared to have no beaches. The mountains seemed to abruptly jut out of the surf. The few beaches that did exist were rocky, often surrounded by high cliffs with narrow gullies carved by streams coming down the mountainsides. The snow-covered mountains went as high as three thousand feet, and had no cover and no trees, only barren jagged rocks. The valley floors consisted of a shallow layer of volcanic ash that had over time became muskeg-like mossy tundra, underneath which lay several feet of muck. A man walking along could easily feel the earth beneath him give and bounce back, then suddenly break, sinking the person up to his knees in thick black mud. Vehicles had no chance crossing this boggy ground. Because of the Japan Current, temperatures remained moderate, normally ranging from -5° C to +5° C, so the ground never froze and the island remained habitually socked in by fog, mist, and the frequent 'williwaws,' violent winds that pounded the island for days. The sun could be seen only eight to ten days a year, and on average five days a week a thick foggy drizzle fell upon the island. By far, more American and Japanese aircraft had been lost in the Aleutians to weather than to enemy action. The terrain model the American planners developed included only the eastern half of the island, where the Japanese had established

[14]Garfield, *The Thousand-Mile War*, pp. 196-98.

garrisons at Chichagof Harbor and Holtz Bay. The only passes the model indicated running through the steep mountains and deep ravines were found along a saddle west of Massacre Valley and near Henderson Ridge. The assault force would not even see this mock-up until just days prior to landing on Attu.[15]

Defending the island were twenty-four hundred Japanese troops under the command of Colonel Yasuyo Yamazaki. The garrison included what amounted to little more than one infantry battalion, three anti-aircraft batteries, two platoons of mountain artillery, and a large engineer unit charged with building the airfield. Yamazaki placed the anti-aircraft batteries, whose 75-mm. guns could also be used as artillery, on the west and east arms of Holtz Bay and on high ground at Chichagof Harbor. The mountain artillery's 75-mm. pack howitzers guarded the pass between Holtz Bay and Massacre Valley. Machine gun and mortar positions ringed these defensive ridges, often enfilading the valleys below. What little aerial reconnaissance there was indicated the Japanese had not put in place fixed defences on the beaches at Massacre Bay or around Holtz Bay. Yamazaki had instead chosen to leave the beaches open and dig in on high ground where he could best use his guns and mortars. His men dug foxholes and two-man machine-gun and mortar holes along as many strategic points as time allowed. He had to spread is small force thin to guard possible approaches from what he considered the ideal landing sites. Through the strategic placement and concealment of these small positions, Yamazaki's men could pin down a much larger force, and thus allow the Japanese time to stage a fighting withdrawal to Chichagof Harbor when necessary. Yamazaki hoped to retain the initiative until reinforcements could arrive from either Kiska or Japan.[16]

As the assault force sailed from San Francisco on 24 April, five optional plans had been chosen for the Attu assault, all of which were based upon faulty and incomplete intelligence and flawed perceptions of terrain, weather, and Japanese defences. Plan A called for a major landing at Massacre Bay with secondary landings at Beach Red west of Holtz Bay. Plan B placed the major assault at Sarana Bay, while Plan C landed the entire force at Massacre Bay. Plan D had two landings: one at Holtz Bay and the other at Beach Red. Plan E had options for three separate simultaneous landings: one at Beach Red or Holtz Bay, one at Massacre Bay, and the last at Sarana Bay. Rockwell, commanding the sea borne force, did not like Plans B and C, while Brown, commanding the actual landing force, did not favour the all or nothing landing of Plan C. At the rendezvous point off Cold Bay on the tip of the Alaskan Peninsula, the commanders agreed on Plan E less the assault on Sarana Bay. Massacre Bay would receive the major landing – Southern Force – while a secondary landing – Northern Force – would seize Beach Red, while the Provisional Scout Battalion would land further west at Beach Scarlet as a decoy to lure Japanese forces away from Massacre Bay. Alaskan and Nisei Scouts would accompany all units. The two forces, approaching each other from the northwest and the southeast, would converge and join for an assault on Japanese positions defending Holtz Bay, then turn northeast to destroy the primary Japanese garrison at Chichagof Harbor. Rockwell worried that poorly charted shoals and reefs at Holtz Bay would delay the landings there and possibly result in the loss of landing craft. Instead, he argued for landing the entire force at Massacre Bay. Brown could only accept multiple landing points and still maintained that the operation might take weeks. Three days, however, remained the target for completing the operation.[17]

The Operation

Not surprisingly, weather delayed the invasion fleet from leaving Cold Bay on 3 May. Leaving the next day, the delay pushed D-Day to 8 May. When the fleet rendezvoused one hundred and fifteen miles north of Attu, the weather worsened. Admiral Kinkaid delayed the landing to 9 May. Circling hidden in the foggy rough seas, the transports and their destroyer screen waited for a break in the weather. Rockwell ordered the cruisers west to head off a rumored Japanese reinforcement fleet. At great danger to their planes and lives, air reconnaissance crews reported heavy surf on the landing beaches. Kinkaid moved D-Day back another day. With no break in the weather foreseen, Kinkaid ordered Brown and Rockwell to make the assault on 11 May.[18]

[15]Conn, et al., *Guarding the United States and Its Outposts*, pp. 280-81; *The Aleutians Campaign*, pp. 2-4.
[16]Brendan Coyle, *War on Our Doorstep: The Unknown Campaign on North America's West Coast* (Surrey, British Columbia: Heritage House, 2002), pp. 167-68; Conn, et al., *Guarding the United States and Its Outposts*, pp. 281-82.

[17]Conn, et al., *Guarding the United States and Its Outposts*, pp. 283-84; Garfield, *The Thousand-Mile War*, pp. 202-05. The Nisei role on Attu and later Kiska is described in Otis Hays, Jr., *Alaska's Hidden War: Secret Campaigns on the North Pacific Rim* (Fairbanks: University of Alaska Press, 2004).
[18]Conn, et al., *Guarding the United States and Its Outposts*, pp. 283-84; Garfield, *The Thousand-Mile War*, p. 284.

He could not see twenty yards to his front because of the fog and howling winds threatened to blow his men over an unseen cliff or down a hidden ravine

The air bombardment of Attu had been scuttled because of the foul weather. The Japanese knew an attack was imminent and remained on high alert. In the dawn hours of 11 May, lead elements of the Provisional Scout Battalion left their submarines to paddle ashore at Beach Scarlet. Heavy fog delayed landing the rest of the battalion to about noon, some eight hours after the scout company had landed. The Provisional Scout Battalion experienced some of the bitterest fighting of the operation. Equipped only with what they could carry, Captain William H. Willoughby's handpicked force of two hundred and fifty men suffered terribly on the exposed mountainsides west of Beach Red as they fought against the elements and small units of Japanese defenders to link with the main force that had landed at Beach Red. By midnight of D-Day, Willoughby had reached a long ridge overlooking a still distant Holtz Bay, and had reached the blank space on his map, which left the ravines and cliffs beyond a complete mystery. The temperature had dropped to -22° C. Willoughby decided to stop. He could not see twenty yards to his front because of the fog and howling winds threatened to blow his men over an unseen cliff or down a hidden ravine.[19]

On Beach Red, an advance scouting party landed to make sure landing on the beach was even feasible. Finding it good enough for two or three landing craft to disembark troops at one time, the order was passed along to land the rest of the Northern Force.

Troops of the 17th Infantry and 32nd Infantry had been in landing craft and transports since 0800 that morning – it was now well past 1300. Fog continually delayed giving the order to head for shore. Finally, at 1530, Brown gave the order for Battalion Combat Team 17-1 (1st Battalion, 17th Infantry) to head inland. By 1700, over fifteen hundred men had been landed on Beach Red with no sign of the Japanese. Meanwhile, the Navy had begun its radar-controlled bombardment of Chichagof Harbor, alerting the Japanese that the invasion had begun. At Massacre Bay, the original H-Hour of 0740 had been pushed back to 1040, then 1530. The landing approach required the landing craft to follow the minelayer *Pruitt*'s whistle to navigate the thick fog and avoid jagged rocks lying just beneath the surface. One landing craft bottomed on a rock while another capsized. The first wave met no resistance, nor did the second – BCT 17-2 (2nd Battalion, 17th Infantry) and BCT 17-3 (3rd Battalion, 17th Infantry) held the beach at Massacre Bay. Casualties thus far resulted from accidents. One landing craft dropped its ramp too soon, swamping the boat and drowning several men.[20]

By the end of the day, over 3500 American troops had landed on Attu. At 1800, advance parties from Beach Red and Massacre Bay came under Japanese fire for the first time. The main force of BCT 17-1 was to get to an 800ft camel back two miles inland from Beach Red. By 2230, it had reached a hill that it hoped was

the camel back, but it could not be sure. Again, the maps proved inadequate. BCT 17-2 advanced along the east slope of Massacre Valley before meeting sporadic gunfire. After halting for over half an hour, BCT 17-2 moved out under increasingly intense gun and mortar fire. At 2100, BCT 17-2 stopped for the night, having advanced three thousand yards from Massacre Bay. BCT 17-3, moving along the west arm of Massacre Valley, also ran into intense Japanese gunfire and dug in, separated from BCT 17-2 by a long hogback that ran up the centre of Massacre Valley.[21]

At the end of the first day, BCT 17-2 and BCT 17-3 had come close to reaching their D-Day objectives. BCT 17-2 thought it was less than one thousand yards shy of the pass to Sarana Bay, while BCT 17-3 concluded it had come within six hundred yards of the pass to Holtz Bay. The next morning, D+1 (May 12), both units found themselves much further from their objectives than originally thought and exposed to enemy fire from the flanks as well as front. BCT 17-2's commander, Colonel Edward P. Earle, was killed by Japanese machine gun fire while scouting a forward position. Brown's chief of staff, Colonel Wayne L. Zimmerman, took Earle's place. For two more days, both BCT 17-2 and BCT 17-3 staged frontal attacks to get past strongly entrenched Japanese positions on the ridges, but to no avail. BCT 32-2 (2nd Battalion, 32 Infantry) reinforced BCT 17-3, but only created a logjam of supplies on the beach. As at Beach Red, vehicles could

[19]Conn, et al., *Guarding the United States and Its Outposts*, pp. 283-84; Garfield, *The Thousand-Mile War*, pp. 285-86; Garfield, *The Thousand-Mile War*, pp. 208-09, 213-215.
[20]Garfield, *The Thousand-Mile War*, pp. 210-213; Conn, et al., *Guarding the United States and Its Outposts*, pp. 283-84, 287.
[21]Conn, et al., *Guarding the United States and Its Outposts*, pp. 288-89.

not drive on the thin-crusted tundra without sinking over their axels, so supplies and ammunition had to be carried forward on the backs of the troops, which took men off the front line where they were needed. By D+3, the Massacre Bay front had become stationary. On the Beach Red front, BCT 17-1 had only advanced three hundred yards and the Provisional Scout Battalion had been trapped in a canyon for three days, fighting for its life. Willoughby's men had run out of food and began vomiting on the white snow. They suffered from frostbite and trench foot. Their jackets and boots had been soaked since the first day. They built small fires in snow caves as Japanese soldiers taunted them in English via megaphones. While Willoughby's men froze, naval gun and Army air support found few targets on Attu in the thick fog. It was going to take longer than three days to take Attu.[22]

It was difficult to tell if the island itself or the dogged Japanese defence was having the greatest impact in stalling the Attu assault. General Brown called for reinforcements. So many soldiers had to be used to transport supplies to the front line and return with wounded that the effective fighting force of each battalion combat team had been cut by almost two-thirds. BCT 32-3 (3rd Battalion, 32nd Infantry) and BCT 32-1 (1st Battalion, 32nd Infantry) had come ashore to support BCT 17-1 and BCT 17-2 respectively, but Brown now wanted the 4th Infantry Regiment ready reserve sent from Adak along with a large order for engineering equipment and supplies. Rockwell at first did not believe the situation merited such massive reinforcements, but forwarded Brown's request to Kinkaid and Buckner nonetheless. Rockwell wanted to withdraw his naval force because of Japanese submarine activity in the area of Attu Island. Several torpedoes had been dodged since the landings 11 May, leading Kinkaid to approve Rockwell's request to withdraw the fleet by 17 May. In the meantime, Kinkaid and Buckner, who never had much confidence in Brown in the first place, grew concerned over

Naval gun and Army air support found few targets on Attu in the thick fog. It was going to take longer than three days to take Attu

what they interpreted as panic in Brown's desperate requests for reinforcements. On 16 May, Buckner and Kinkaid, motivated by personal prejudice and a stalemated operation, relieved Brown of command, replacing him with Brigadier General Landrum. From Brown's perspective, his relief was unwarranted. He had warned that the operation would take longer than three days, that the terrain would be just as tough as the Japanese, and that the Japanese would be tougher still.

BCT 17-3 had been hit hard trying to take Jarmin Pass to link up with BCT 17-1 from Beach Red on Friday, 14 May. It had to be withdrawn from the line. The hastily set up field hospital at Massacre Bay overflowed with combat and frostbite casualties, where many wounded men lay uncovered in the steady drizzle for over forty-eight hours. Companies had to be rotated in and out of the line to warm themselves in improvised heating tents. Landing craft loaded with supplies and wounded swamped and sank in the rough seas. Air support remained grounded because of the miserable weather. The cruisers and destroyers had run out of shells and thus could no longer provide any fire support, not that it had made much difference anyway. Supplies were not getting to the beaches, and what was on the beaches was not getting to the front lines. Bickering broke out among Army and Navy commanders on shore and aboard ship. But with the arrival of reinforcements from the 32nd Infantry, Brown had confidence that the link up could be made in a matter of days, then the final push on the Japanese garrisons at Holtz Bay and Chichagof Harbor could begin. His protests had worn thin. Considering the casualties and the myriad of other problems threatening the campaign, Kinkaid and Buckner believed they had little choice but to relieve Brown.[23]

The Japanese then stepped in to help things along. On 14 May (D+3) Colonel Yamazaki decided to abandoned the Holtz Bay base and withdraw the garrison east to Chichagof Harbor for a final stand. Reinforcements from Japan were out of the question. Japanese air support, like that of the Americans, could do nothing because of the weather. A relief fleet formed at Paramushiro and sailed for Attu, but not knowing that the

---

[22]Conn, et al., *Guarding the United States and Its Outposts*, pp. 289-92; Garfield, *The Thousand-Mile War*, pp. 214-21.
[23]Garfield, *The Thousand-Mile War*, pp. 223-33; Conn, et al., *Guarding the United States and Its Outposts*, p. 293.

The first wave of Assault Boats make their way through the Aleutian fog towards Attu, two miles ahead. (NARA)

American fleet had withdrawn the Japanese ships hovered three hundred miles west of Attu waiting for some opportunity to get to their beleaguered comrades. Even Japanese transport submarines dared not approach the island. Now that the Japanese had abandoned their defensive positions around Holtz Bay, Willoughby's Provisional Scout Battalion and BCT 17-1 could link and move to join with the Southern Force. The breakthrough occurred just as Brown left and Landrum arrived to take command.[24]

As in all campaigns, the fighting is ultimately done by small units of men trying to simultaneously achieve minor objectives and stay alive. The Attu campaign is filled with valiant stories of small unit action under extreme conditions. Lieutenant Charles K. Paulson's infantry platoon, part of Company F, BCT 17-2, on the right side of Massacre Valley, became separated from the main advance on 12 May while making its way across the ridge to Sarana Bay. In a small valley Paulson's platoon got pinned down by heavy Japanese fire and dug in, trying unsuccessfully to make contact with the main battalion. The next morning Paulson awoke to find his platoon nearly surrounded by Japanese positions on the hillsides around the valley. Low on food and ammunition, several men began vomiting green bile and many others suffered frostbite in their soaking wet boots and clothes. Some men shut down completely. By 15 May, after four days of fighting for their very lives, the platoon received not only the familiar machine gun fire from the Japanese but also found themselves the unwitting target of a naval gun barrage – friendly fire. Realizing that they had to move or be blown to bits, Paulson ordered a squad to assault a Japanese machine gun position on their front. The men did not respond. Paulson advanced himself, then finally got a group of men together to move out and take the Japanese machine gun nest. Using grenades, the squad took the position, which allowed the rest of the platoon to move under the cover of yet another heavy fog. Following the sounds of tractors and trucks in Massacre Valley, they stumbled and felt their way across a ridge and down a steep slippery slope out of the fog and into the welcoming arms of friendly troops. One can only guess at how good their first warm meal in nearly five days made them feel.[25]

The link up between Northern Force and Southern force occurred when advance patrols from both forces met each other on Jarmin Pass at 0230 on 18 May. On 19 May through 21 May, BCT 32-2 and BCT 17-2 attacked Japanese positions in and around Clevesy Pass, which guarded the approach to Chichagof Harbor. Reinforcements from the 4th Infantry ready reserve force also saw action along Prendergast Ridge, gaining hard-fought ground halfway up its steep southern slope. Having made abandoned Holtz Bay defensible with BCT 17-1, Northern Force also made its assault toward Chichagof Harbor on May 19. Attacking up the equally steep northern slope of Prendergast Ridge, BCT 17-1 advanced yard by yard up the slope into intense Japanese fire. Not until 25 May did BCT 17-1 gain the top of the ridge and begin making its way along another ridge of snow-covered mountains called the Fish Hook. In the meantime, Southern Force assaulted the Sarana Nose, where many Japanese defenders fought to the death, and secured the southern slope of Prendergast Ridge. All that stood in the way of the Americans and the main Japanese garrison at Chichagof Harbor was the Fish Hook.[26]

[24]Garfield, *The Thousand-Mile War*, p. 236; Morison, *Aleutians, Gilberts, and Marshalls, June 1942-April 1944*, pp. 43-44.
[25]*The Capture of Attu*, pp. 27-31; Garfield, *The Thousand-Mile War*, pp. 227-28.
[26]*The Capture of Attu*, pp. 9-18; Garfield, *The Thousand-Mile War*, pp. 236-46.

7th Infantry Division landing at Massacre Bay, Attu, May 1943. (NARA)

Landrum planned the attack on the Fish Hook just as he had all assaults since taking command of American forces on Attu. Taking the high ground was critical to defeating stiff Japanese resistance. Once the Japanese had been driven from the high ground, American forces could maintain the initiative. Such was the case in the battle for the Fish Hook. The attack began late on the afternoon of 23 May. BCT 17-2 advanced about two hundred yards before Japanese fire stopped them in their tracks. The next day, BCT 17-1 of Northern Force had advanced far enough on the west side of the Fish Hook to support Southern Force's assault. In a coordinated attack, both BCTs struggled all day against stiff Japanese fire and by dark had to withdraw back to their jumping-off points. Some progress was made against a Japanese stronghold, a two hundred-yard trench virtually invisible in the deep and swirling snow, on 25 May. Landrum attempted numerous assaults over the next two days and finally gained control of the Fish Hook on 28 May. The closer the Americans came to Chichagof Harbor, the more fiercely Japanese soldiers defended their shrinking and increasingly defenceless positions.[27]

Yamazaki had only 800 men left and over 600 wounded to tend. He now faced an American force of over 14000 most of whom continued to play a supportive role. Surrounded at Chichagof Harbor, Yamazaki knew he had no hope of reinforcement and that surrender was not an option. Food and ammunition had run out. Yamazaki made a bold decision. Waiting for a final American assault at Chichagof Harbor had no purpose, but he could attack and gain honor for himself and his men. Historian Brian Garfield called Yamazaki's plan 'ingenious as it was simple.'[28] By hitting the thinnest part of the American line, that part on the valley floor, in the dark so as to avoid enfilading fire from the surrounding ridges, Yamazaki hoped to reach the American supply dump that he assumed must be toward the rear of the American position. With supplies he might be able to hold out a bit longer, but the odds of surviving such an assault were slim indeed.

At 0300 on 29 May, Yamazaki issued the order for his eight hundred troops to advance. Most of the six hundred wounded had been injected with lethal doses of morphine while the rest committed ritual suicide. Company B of BCT 32-3 received orders to leave their frontline position and return to the rear for a hot meal. At about 0330, as the weary American soldiers tramped through the snow rearward, the horrific Banzai cry filled the air. With bayonets fixed and grenades at the ready,

the Japanese swiftly cut through the shocked Americans, most of whom simply ran in whatever direction afforded safety. The Japanese next encountered Captain William H. Willoughby and fifteen men at an observation post on the side of Engineer Hill. The Japanese quickly overran Willoughby's position, killing 11 of the 15 and severely wounding Willoughby. One Japanese unit ran into an American aid station, completely surprising medics, wounded and other personnel. The Japanese bayoneted the wounded and killed several others. Miraculously, 12 men inside the medical tent played dead and eluded Japanese steel.

On Engineer Hill, several support units awoke from their frigid encampment to the sounds of battle. The 50th Engineers, 7th Medical Battalion, 13th Engineers, and the 20th Field Headquarters reacted quickly to the brisk orders of Brigadier General Archibald V. Arnold, who had taken this position to command the assault on Chichagof later that morning. Using grenades and intense rifle fire, Arnold and his assortment of engineers, cooks, and medics momentarily halted the Japanese onslaught. Yamazaki fell back, regrouped his men, and charged forward again. Arnold and Yamazaki's men fought hand to hand, then the Japanese fell back again. They made one more desperate charge – Yamazaki fell and the last Japanese resistance crumbled. Attu was secure. Later that day, an American patrol discovered the bodies of over five hundred Japanese soldiers who had committed suicide by pulling grenades on themselves.[29]

---

[27]*The Capture of Attu*, pp.18-20; Garfield, *The Thousand-Mile War*, pp. 247-51.
[28]Garfield, *The Thousand-Mile War*, p. 251.
[29]*The Capture of Attu*, pp. 20-22; Garfield, *The Thousand-Mile War*, pp. 252-56.

... stepping stones to nowhere

Soldiers firing their mortars over a ridge into a Japanese position, 4 June 1943. (NARA)

Aftermath and Conclusion

With its mountains, ravines, caves, and desolate slopes, Attu provided several Japanese soldiers excellent places to hide out, some for as long as three months after Yamazaki fell on 29 May. None surrendered, choosing instead to kill themselves. After mopping up for several days, the Americans settled into building an airfield on Attu. Operation LANDCRAB had involved over 14,000 American soldiers. For the Americans, the cost of taking Attu was much higher than anyone had imagined possible: 549 killed; 1,148 wounded; 1,200 cold weather casualties (mostly trench foot); 614 out of action from sickness due to exposure; and 318 from self-inflicted wounds, mental breakdowns, and other incidents. Considering numbers engaged Attu was one of the bloodiest campaigns of the Pacific War. For every 100 enemy found on the island, over 70 Americans had been killed or wounded. Of the approximately 2,400 Japanese defending the island, 2,351 died. Only 29 Japanese soldiers had been captured alive.[30]

With Attu in firm hands, the Americans next turned to Kiska. In August, a combined force of mostly American and some Canadian troops attacked Kiska after a long naval and air pre-invasion bombardment. Over 10,000 Japanese troops were thought to hold the island. Unbeknownst to the Americans, the Japanese had withdrawn their entire force by submarine and surface transport throughout the month of July. The island was deserted. The invasion of Kiska cost almost 100 American lives, including over 20 soldiers killed in friendly fire incidents and 70 sailors died when the destroyer *Abner Read* hit a mine. With the Aleutians under Allied control and over 144,000 Allied troops in the Alaska theatre, the possibility of an assault on the northern Japanese home islands seemed possible. By the time such plans could be realised, however, American forces had begun attacks on Iwo Jima and the amphibious attack on Okinawa was well into the planning stages. The western and southern path to Japan had eclipsed the northern approach. The threat to Alaska had long since past, and the possibility of offensive operations against Japan from the Aleutians had become strategically obsolete. The Aleutians had become, in the words of historian Galen Roger Perras, 'stepping stones to nowhere.'[31]

Operation LANDCRAB had been somewhat of an amateurish campaign. Too many commanders presumed too many things. They wrongly presumed accurate intelligence on Japanese strength, a clear understanding of Attu's topography, and a trouble-free landing. They under-appreciated distance, climate, and the fanaticism of the Emperor's loyal soldiers. The Joint Chiefs of Staff failed to create a unified Pacific command under one commander, which contributed to a convoluted chain of command, petty personal bickering, and operational confusion. Relieving the land component combatant commander at D+5 only highlighted these and other problems. Brown had been pessimistic but right, and was in the process of adapting the battle plan to meet the unexpected conditions, namely topography, climate, and Japanese resistance, when Kinkaid and Buckner relieved him. Fortunately, Brown's replacement, Landrum, understood the tactical problems that confronted both landing forces and was able to carry on much as Brown had originally planned.

The Army quickly implemented some lessons learned from Attu before the major campaigns of late 1943 and 1944. Buckner and his naval counterpart made certain the Kiska invasion force would have winter parkas and waterproof boots. The men would come from veteran Attu units and other components that had been stationed in Alaska for some time. Medical aid stations on Attu had been nothing short of disastrous. The Surgeon General's office reorganised combat medical teams and their medical kits to be more efficient and better prepared for a wider range of causalities. The Army made improvements in boots, jackets, gloves, tents, and bedrolls that probably saved many a life in Europe during the winter of 1944-1945. Combat air support and forward air control, both of which failed at

---

[30]Conn, et al., *Guarding the United States and Its Outposts*, p. 296; MacGarrigle, *Aleutian Islands*, p. 22; *The Aleutians*, p. 26.
[31]Conn, et al., *Guarding the United States and Its Outposts*, pp. 296-300; Perras, *Stepping Stones to Nowhere*, p. 278.

Operation LANDCRAB succeeded because:

- A ready reserve force was available
- Effective small unit combat capability
- Abilty to overcome weather and terrain
- Enemy inability to re-supply and reinforce

Attu because of weather, poor communications, and command problems, received a great deal of attention before the next amphibious operation at Rendova in June 1943. Greater effort was given to up-to-date and accurate charts and maps, weather prediction, and security. Training in a like environment also became a priority. Most of all, planning, which took time and tremendous effort, had to be detailed, complete, but flexible. Other lessons went unheeded. Joint operations continued to be contentious and riddled with turf conflicts for the remainder of the war. Allied theatre commands around the globe contested for preciously limited supplies and equipment, and continued to be disrupted by personality conflicts. Naval fire support continued to be used as a destructive tool rather than a means to neutralize the enemy, as it had when weather permitted on Attu. Still, Attu had been a success, though a costly one. The Army gained invaluable experience in amphibious warfare. Training improved, as did communications between officers in the field, command posts, and commander headquarters.[32]

Attu had been a close run thing. Among the senior commanders, except for perhaps Brown, confidence going in had been high. Then the unexpected happened at nearly every slope, every ravine, and every ridge. It is hard to say which commander had or had not read their Clausewitz. The fog of battle on Attu had been both literal and Clausewitzian. Perhaps the Americans did not know their enemy quite yet. Accurate intelligence, thorough planning, clear chain of command, aggressive training, proper outfitting, and necessary support give an amphibious operation the greatest chance for success. Attu had none of those, thus three days became three weeks, and many American and Japanese soldiers suffered because of it.

Further Reading

Army Center for Military History, *Aleutian Islands,* (Washington, D.C.: United States Army Center for Military History, 1992)

Conn, Stetson Engleman, Rose C. and Fairchild, Byron, *The United States Army in World War II: Guarding the United States and Its Outposts,* (Washington, D.C.: United States Army, 1962)

Coyle, Brendan, *War on Our Doorstep: The Unknown Campaign on North America's West Coast,* (British Columbia: 2002)

Garfield, Brian, *The Thousand-Mile War: World War II in Alaska and the Aleutians,* (New York: Doubleday and Company, 1969)

Hays, Jr., Otis, *Alaska's Hidden War: Secret Campaigns on the North Pacific Rim,* (Fairbanks: University of Alaska Press, 2004)

Morison, Samuel Eliot, *History of United States Naval Operations in World War II Vol 7 Aleutians, Gilberts, and Marshalls, June 1942-April 1944,* (Boston: Little, Brown, and Company, 1951)

Perras, Galen Roger, *Stepping Stones to Nowhere: The Aleutian Islands, Alaska, and American Military Strategy, 1867-1945,* (Vancouver: University of British Columbia Press, 2003)

Biography

William Thomas Allison, PhD, is the Associate Professor of History at the Weber State University. He was Visiting Professor in the Department of Strategy and International Security at the United States Air Force Air War College at Maxwell Air Force Base, Alabama for the 2002-2003 academic year. As part of the Air War College visiting professor programme his responsibilities included teaching Strategy, Doctrine & Air Power core course and the academic portion of the Central Europe Regional Studies sylabus. A native of Texas, he earned his bachelor's and master's degrees from Texas University at Commerce in 1989 and 1991, and then earned his doctorate in history from Bowling Green State University in Ohio in 1995. His books include *American Diplomats in Russia, 1916-1919: Case Studies in Orphan Diplomacy* (Praeger 1997), *Witness to Revolution: The Russian Revolution Diary and Letters of J. Butler Wright* (Praeger 2002), and *To Protect and To Serve: A History of Police in America* (Prentice Hall, 2004), *Military Justice in Vietnam: The Rule of Law in American War* (2006). He is writing a survey of American military history for undergraduate courses, which will be published by Prentice Hall.

[32] MacGarrigle, *Aleutian Islands*, p. 23; Garfield, *The Thousand-Mile War*, p. 256-58; *The Aleutians Campaign*, pp. 111-117.

Sicily
Operation HUSKY, July - August 1943

XV

By Lieutenant Commander Tristan T A Lovering MBE RN

Brigadier Maxwell Taylor was woken by one of his staff at 0200 on 11 July, 1943. He was at an airfield in Tunisia, and on the previous night had overseen the departure of U.S. parachute troops for Sicily. They had been sent to support General Omar Bradley's II Corps who had landed on that Mediterranean island the day before. The news was not good; the 2,304 men in the 504th Parachute Regimental Combat Team had been the victims of 'friendly fire' the likes of which make modern incidents of fratricide seem tame. Of the 144 Dakota transport planes carrying Colonel Reuben Tucker's airborne force, only a few were as lucky as their commander and managed to land at the Farello airstrip near Gela. The troop laden aircraft, only flying at 700 feet (at 100 mph) were engaged by scores of allied vessels off the Sicilian coast, as well as the land-based anti-aircraft guns which had been landed 24 hours previously. The lethal barrage resulted in 23 aircraft[1] being shot down, approximately 410 casualties and the death of 81 paratroopers and aircrew.[2]

Despite warnings from General Matthew Ridgeway to all units that parachutists from the 82nd Airborne would be dropping at Farello, nervous soldiers and sailors had filled the sky with flak as the Dakotas approached the beachhead.[3] Following a recent bombing by the Luftwaffe, allied troops were unwilling to risk another attack from the unseen enemy without at least returning fire. The allied flight formation quickly divided as planes received hits, exploding in flight or falling to the ground in flames. Some of the aircraft which survived the barrage were valiantly crash landed in the choppy sea, the planes remaining afloat just long enough for the parachutists to exit safely and ditch their weighty equipment. They then found themselves at the mercy of sailors who lowered their sights and fired their 20mm canon believing them to be German troops. General Patton, (Commander U.S. Seventh Army), and General Ridgeway, (Commanding the 82nd Airborne Division) witnessed the debacle, unaware that the assistant Divisional Commander, Brigadier Charles Keerans had been killed in the fire directed at the aircraft.[4] On the night of 9/10 July a similar fate had befallen the British airborne forces. Owing to poor weather and bad navigation a Brigade had been sent to the west of Syracuse to seize the Ponte Grande bridge but 12 gliders of the 134[5] were crash landed in the sea and only seven reached their objective. Soldiers from the 1st Air Landing Brigade were spread across the 120 mile by 90 mile island. If this operation had intended to be manoeuvrist, for the likes of Keerans and other allied airborne troops, the unfolding disaster probably appeared to have all the attributes of an attritional war.

The landings made by the U.S. and British in Sicily and the subsequent Campaign (July and August 1943) are examined on three levels, followed by analysis of the German evacuation:

Defending the beachhead from the Luftwaffe: An Anti-Aircraft gun deployed on the beach in Sicily, July 1943. (NHB)

At the strategic level, the attack was launched in an attempt to shatter the enemy's overall cohesion. The allies were responding to pressure from Stalin to open the Second Front in order to lift the pressure on the hard pressed Red Army. The allies were also hoping to break the axis unity by putting further pressure on the Germans and reducing the Italian will to fight. The ultimate aim was to force the Italians to capitulate and to remove Mussolini. Some argued that Sicily was a 'side show' and critics claimed that the operation, (codenamed Operation HUSKY) was a 'backwater war' while Churchill argued that it was targeting the 'soft underbelly' of Europe.

---

[1] Battle Summary No. 35, *The Invasion of Sicily: Operation 'HUSKY'*, CB. 3081, 1946, (London: Tactical & Staff Duties Division, Naval Staff, Admiralty, S.W.1., February 1946), p. 172.
[2] Garland, Albert N. Lt. Col., & Mc Gaw Smyth, Howard, *U.S. Army in World War II, The Mediterranean Theater of Operations: Sicily and the Surrender of Italy*, (Washington, D.C.: Office of the Chief of Military History, Dept. of the Army, 1965), p. 182.
[3] See: Breur, William B., *Drop Zone Sicily: Allied Airborne Strike, July 1943*, (Novato CA: Presido Press, 1983), p. 137.
[4] Whiting, Charles, *Slaughter over Sicily*, (London: Leo Cooper, 1992), p. 129.
[5] *Op Cit*, Battle Summary, p. 172.

The operational dilemma of where the allies would attack highlights a number of elements of the manoeuvrist approach. This reflects an attitude of mind, and both Patton and General Montgomery (GOC) demonstrated some of these tenets during the campaign in Sicily but manoeuvre as understood in terms of today's doctrine was not in the common lexicon of their day. The key to their success was their adherence to the principles of war, aggressive attitude and focus on the enemy centre of gravity. Both prosecuted battle plans along those lines, although their attitude and planning reveal different elements of the 'manoeuvrist approach'.

The campaign will be assessed at the tactical level, where Battalion sized units were employed in amphibious operations by both Army commanders. Attacks were launched across the island and the use of the maritime flank lent itself to manoeuvre from the sea using amphibious forces. The U.S. and the British Armies recognised the possibility, but initiated landings at different times with varied degrees of success. The concentration of force, economy of effort and surprise offered by amphibious forces were understood but were not utilised effectively. Although some elements were put into effect, the manoeuvrist approach was not consistently followed at all levels of war by all services.

Patton and Montgomery shared many qualities, including; great flexibility; skill at identifying and seizing opportunities; an ability to inflict on the enemy a series of violent and unexpected actions; innate aggressiveness; a desire to create a turbulent and deteriorating situation for the enemy – all consistent themes and elements of manoeuvre as understood today. Had they utilised all these advantages, particularly in terms of maritime power projection, sea control and air superiority (all used highly effectively for the initial landings) success may have come more swiftly and at greater cost to the axis. This failure enabled the axis troops to withdraw in good order and in large numbers across the Straits of Messina. Parallels have been drawn with Operation DYNAMO (the allied evacuation from Dunkirk) but the Germans escaped *both* well equipped *and* ready to fight another day.

Strategic Level

Significant features of manoeuvre are momentum and tempo which in combination lead to shock action and surprise. Churchill recognised these features and wanted to capitalise on the allied victory in Tunisia, keeping up pressure on the retreating German and Italian forces. Action had to be taken swiftly in order to both impress on Stalin the allied commitment to the cause and to add further pressure on the German military machine. To support the strategic plan, a key part was to deceive the Germans as to the exact location of the next allied attack in the Mediterranean. Not only would the surprise benefit the allies in terms of catching the enemy off guard, but it would ensure that the axis troops were located at points other than the intended site for the amphibious landing.

The ingenious deception, codenamed Operation MINCEMEAT and designed by Lieutenant Commander Ewen Montagu RN, used a body which was then given the false identity of Major Martin Royal Marines. In April 1943 the body was floated ashore in Spain, and top secret files were put in a case handcuffed to his wrist. The Spanish authorities copied and forwarded these to the Germans, before handing the body and files back to British diplomats. The objective was to lead the Germans into believing that the allies were planning an invasion of Sardinia with the Western Army (General Alexander) and also the Balkans with the Eastern Army (General Maitland Wilson). Hitler was anxious about Greece and he redeployed more troops (and briefly General Rommel), 'with defensive measures concerning Sardinia and the Peloponnese taking precedence'[6] over Sicily. The twist in the plan was that the allied deception would target Sicily. Deceit and sleight of hand are very much part of the manoeuvrist approach to war and MINCEMEAT achieved that aspiration. War may not necessarily require any physical movement at all, using deception in order to mentally out manoeuvre as an alternative to attrition, much in the spirit of Sun Tzu. 'The results were gratifying and did much to reinforce the view that one of the great purposes of deception measures was to comfort the enemy by confirming his preconceived ideas'[7], and the allies achieved that goal.

If the concept of manoeuvre warfare is 'the employment of forces through movement in combination with fire, to achieve a position of advantage with respect to the enemy in order to accomplish the mission... with a warfighting philosophy that seeks to defeat an enemy by shattering his moral and physical cohesion – his ability to fight as an effective, co-ordinated whole'[8] then HUSKY achieved that objective at the strategic level. The impact of the Allied invasion of Sicily (as well as reports of impending Soviet attacks) contributed to Hitler's lack of willingness to commit a further three experienced Panzer Divisions to the stalled German offensive (Operation CITADEL) in the armoured engagement at Prokhorovka in the Battle of Kursk on the Eastern Front. The German Army also had to reposition its own Divisions to defend Italy (2nd Parachute Division deployed to Rome), and had to reposition Army Group B in September 1943 into northern Italy to counter the Italians' 'devilish ideas'[9] in seeking negotiation and capitulation with the allies. Field Marshal Kesselring (German C-in-C Southern Italy) said that the landings in Sicily resulted in 'constant bickering about disposition of the German and Italian formations'[10]. He feared a guerrilla war in Italy in addition to the regular war at the front with the allies, and poisoning of the relations at the highest level between the axis powers. In terms of the allied ambitions in opening the second front to ease the military pressure on the Russian forces in Eastern Europe, the Sicily operation resulted in German troops being diverted from deployment on the eastern front, to secure Germany's southern border to counter the threat of further landings along the Italian peninsula and in the Aegean aimed towards the Balkans. The anxiety amongst the German High Command was so heightened that they considered launching Operation FELIX, an invasion of Spain in order impose on the allies an even more demanding strategic predicament.

Mussolini was convinced that if the allies wanted to create a second front, the most convenient door to Germany was not Sicily, but Greece. HUSKY triggered a series of events which resulted in Mussolini's removal from power on 25 July. Despite his replacement by fellow fascist, Marshal Badoglio, it acted as a catalyst to greater Italian opposition to the war. According

[6]Strawson, John, *The Italian Campaign*, (London: Secker and Warburg, 1987), p. 104.
[7]*Ibid.*, p. 106.
[8]BR 1806 *British Maritime Doctrine*, (3RD Edition), (London: HMSO, 2004), p. 47.
[9]Kesselring, Albert, *The Memoirs of Field Marshal Kesselring*, (London: William Kimber, 1954), p. 172.
[10]*Ibid.*, p. 168.

> **They could not see that the two allies were like climbers on a precipice; if one should fall, he would so strain the rope that the other could make no further progress**

to Kesselring it resulted in pronounced antagonisms, with the Italians demonstrating no further eagerness to fight. If manoeuvre seeks to defeat an enemy by shattering his morale and physical cohesion and by reducing his ability to fight as an effective, co-ordinated whole, HUSKY succeeded at the strategic level. Admiral Sir Andrew Cunningham (Allied Naval Commander) believed the landings were the 'greatest amphibious assault ever'[11], and in terms of scale it was the largest up until that point. With 160,000 allied troops, 14,000 vehicles, 600 tanks and 1,800 guns to be landed it required a fleet of more than 3,200 vessels and over 1,600 aircraft to transport and protect what became known as Force 141. While planning continued as the Eighth Army's campaign in North Africa was coming to a successful conclusion, there was still disagreement about whether Sicily should be the next objective or if there was any efficacy in pursuing further operations in the Mediterranean theatre, such as Operation BRIMSTONE, the planned capture of Sardinia. General Marshall[12] came out against 'interminable operations'[13] in the Mediterranean, arguing that 'every diversion or side issue from the main plot acts as a suction pump'[14], to that which he considered the grand strategic objective of Germany. Marshall believed the British were simply exhibiting opportunism for a local operational advantage, as opposed to addressing the

requirement for a cross channel assault aimed at the Wehrmacht and Nazi heartland. However, the powerful case mounted by Sir Alan Brooke[15], won the day. Brooke argued that since the Germans had 44 Divisions in France, Hitler could deal with any cross channel threat without withdrawing forces from Russia. If the allies attacked Italy, however, and forced Mussolini and the fascists out of the war, it would compel Germany not only to occupy the Italian peninsula, but to replace the Italian forces in the Balkans as well.

The significance of the capture of the island should not be underestimated. One German General reflected, 'It is amazing how little even the more important German leaders foresaw the consequence of the Italian collapse. They could not see that the two allies were like climbers on a precipice; if one should fall, he would so strain the rope that the other could make no further progress…I realised the war was lost.'[16] The situation posed serious problems for Hitler, chiefly amongst those how to prevent the Italians from surrendering and if they did how to minimise the effect of that surrender. It also created the problem of whether to abandon Sicily or to hold on as long as possible. Minutes from Hitler's Headquarters indicate that relations were becoming strained, 'there are further indications that the Italian

government is double crossing us'[17] and plans to evacuate Sicily were ordered by the Fuehrer on the 27 July, but 'we must gain time to strengthen our position in the Balkans and Italy with reinforcements. Even if we can hold Sicily for only a short period, the time won will be of great strategical value to us'[18].

Operational Level

Liddell Hart differentiated between the direct approach, highly attritional in nature, and its antithesis, the indirect approach which would, he argued, deliver victory at minimum cost. Montgomery did not want to land in the teeth of the enemy, choosing the indirect route for the launch of HUSKY. The original plan was for Patton to land at the western end of the island to seize Palermo and its valuable harbour, while Montgomery landed on two fronts in the south east. Montgomery was very unhappy about this division of forces and argued that it made his inland flank vulnerable to German counter attack from the Herman Goering Division. The enemy knew that an invasion was pending, and with the allied bombers switching to attack Trapani, in the west of Sicily, the Italian High Command concluded that the invasion would be launched against the western tip of the island. They argued that since this was the shortest sea passage (190 miles) from Tunis the allies would seek to launch

[11]Cunningham of Hyndehope, Viscount, Admiral of the Fleet, K.T., G.C.B., O.M., D.S.O., *A Sailors Odyssey*, (London: Hutchinson & Co. Ltd., 1951), p. 534.
[12]President Roosevelt's key military adviser & U.S. Chief of Staff.
[13]Higgins, Trumbull, *Soft Underbelly: The Anglo-American Controversy over the Italian Campaign 1939 – 1945*, (London: Collier-Macmillan Ltd., 1968), p. 46.
[14]*Ibid.*, p. 47.
[15]British Chief of the Imperial General Staff.
[16]Von Senger und Etterlin, General Frido, *Neither Fear Nor Hope: The Wartime Career of, Defender of Cassino*, (London: Macdonald, 1964), p. 153.
[17]TNA: NHB, AL 721/6, *Fuehrer Conferences on Naval Affairs 1943*, (May 1947), p. 71.
[18]*Ibid.*, p. 68.

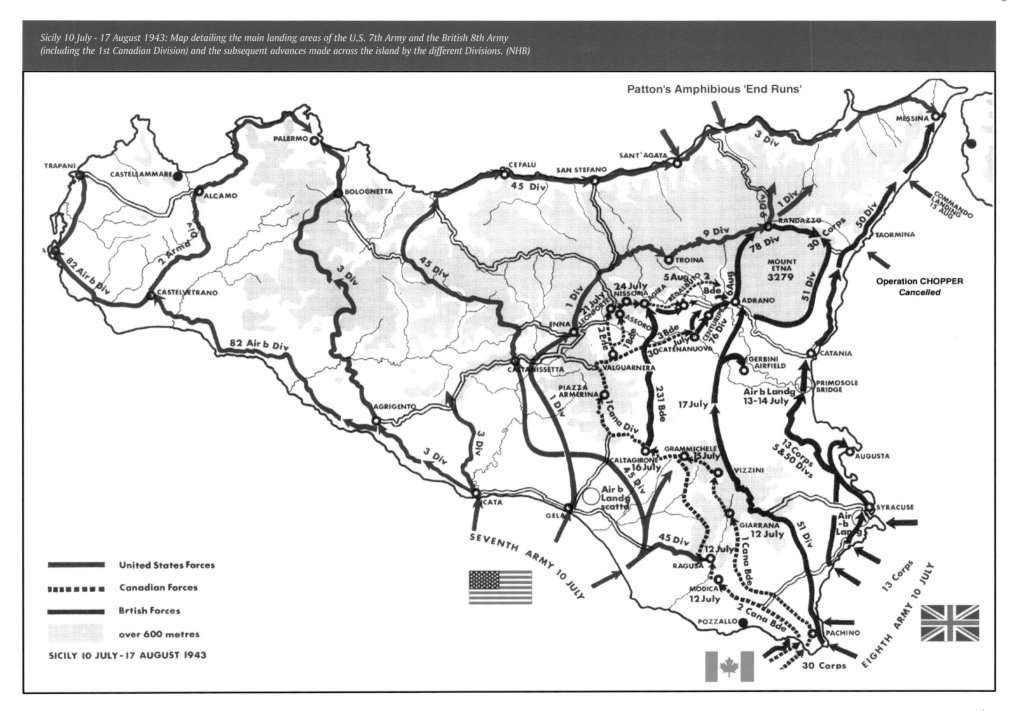

Sicily 10 July - 17 August 1943: Map detailing the main landing areas of the U.S. 7th Army and the British 8th Army (including the 1st Canadian Division) and the subsequent advances made across the island by the different Divisions. (NHB)

Patton's Amphibious 'End Runs'

TRAPANI
CASTELLAMMARE
PALERMO
ALCAMO
BOLOGNETTA
CEFALU
SAN STEFANO
SANT'AGATA
MESSINA
COMMANDO LANDING 15 AUG
2 Armd
45 Div
3 Div
1 Div
RANDAZZO
30 Corps
50 Div
TAORMINA
82 Air b Div
CASTELVETRANO
3 Div
45 Div
9 Div
78 Div
MOUNT ETNA 3279
51 Div
Operation CHOPPER Cancelled
82 Air b Div
ENNA
LEONFORTE
1 Div
21 July
24 July
NISSORIA
AGIRA
REGALBUTO
TROINA
5 Aug
2 Bde
6 Aug
ADRANO
CALTANISSETTA
ASSORO
1 Bde
38 bde
CENTURIPES
76 Div
CATENANUOVA
2 Bde
VALGUARNERA
30
July
GERBINI AIRFIELD
CATANIA
AGRIGENTO
PIAZZA ARMERINA
1 Cana Div
1 Div
231 Bde
17 July
Air b Landg 13-14 July
PRIMOSOLE BRIDGE
3 Div
3 Div
CALTAGIRONE
16 July
45 Div
GRAMMICHELE
15 July
VIZZINI
13 Corps
5 & 50 Divs
AUGUSTA
Air b Landg scatto
GELA
ICATA
45 Div
GIARRANA
12 July
1 Cana Bde
51 Div
Air -b Landg
SYRACUSE
12 July
RAGUSA
MODICA
12 July
2 Cana Bde
SEVENTH ARMY 10 JULY
13 Corps
POZZALLO
PACHINO
30 Corps
EIGHTH ARMY 10 JULY

━━━━━ United States Forces

▪▪▪▪▪▪▪ Canadian Forces

━━━━━ Brtish Forces

░░░░░ over 600 metres

SICILY 10 JULY - 17 AUGUST 1943

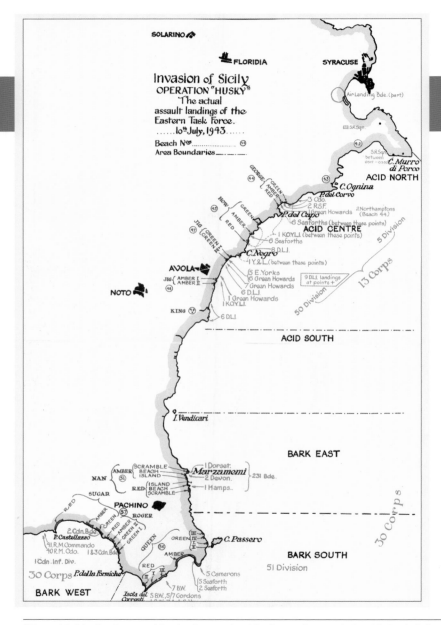

Operation HUSKY: The actual assault landings of the Eastern Task Force, 10 July 1943. (NHB)

the invasion from there. The surviving German and Italian fighters were then transferred to the west of the island, over 100 miles from the allied landing beaches. Although the allied aerial bombardment of enemy airfields and decisive points had not intended to be a feint at this stage, the result was an impression that at the operational level, the allies would come from the west. The Allied air attacks had resulted in significant reductions in the German and Italian capability to dominate the skies, evidenced by General von Senger und Etterlin's[19] comment that 'the enemy at that time [June 1943] entirely dominated the air. The majority of German air units which had been stationed on the island had already been destroyed on the ground, and the aerodromes were more or less out of use'.[20] He was also worried because the allies had 'the three branches of modern warfare, navy, army and air force, in combined action, whereas the Axis side had only ground force'.[21] Little did he realise in June 1943, just how limited the 'combined' nature of the allied attack would be.

The use of shock action and surprise at the operational level could have been lost on two occasions; during the secret reconnaissance of Sicilian beaches by the Royal Navy's Combined Operations Pilotage Parties (COPPS) and following the allied attack of Pantellaria.

The COPPS reconnaissance of the 300 miles of coastline was undertaken by volunteers from the Navy and Army in March 1943. The tasks they undertook included; beach surveys; measuring shore gradient; recording sandbars; taking samples of sand, and assessing enemy obstacles. One team missed the rendezvous with their submarine HMS *United* and subsequently had to decide their next course of action while sheltering from the wind, spray and rolling storm waves in a Sicilian bay. Losses from other COPPS teams had been mounting quickly, and the paddlers did not want to become prisoners of war (or worse), or to give away Allied future plans, and decided to make for Malta. They eventually crossed the 70 miles, despite high winds and rolling seas, having fought off exhaustion, dehydration and sunburn, eventually reaching Malta 48 hours later.[22] A motor torpedo boat went to intercept them, but the commander insisted on canoeing the final mile to landfall. *United* never came back from the mission, neither did a number of other COPP teams, 'their casualties in this operation being unfortunately heavy'[23], but the Allied plans remained intact and secret despite this.

---

[19]General Fridolin Von Senger und Etterlin, Commander of the German Forces in Sicily in 1943, who before the First World War had been a Rhodes scholar at Oxford.

[20]Von Senger und Etterlin, General Fridolin, 'The Sicilian Campaign – 1943 Part I', *An Cosantoir* Journal, June Issue, 1949, p. 256.

[21]*Ibid.*, p. 259.

[22]*Op cit*, Whiting, pp., 9 – 17.

[23]*Op cit*, Battle Summary, p. 143.

British Troops wading ashore from an LCI(L) in Sicily. (NHB)

The second indication of allied intent was the attack on the island of Pantellaria (which dominates the Mediterranean between Tunisia, Malta and Sicily) and had remained a 'thorn in our side'[24] according to Churchill. When a landing was launched on 11 June 1943 (following heavy air and naval bombardment), 11,000 prisoners were taken with no casualties to the allies other than 'one soldier bitten by a mule'.[25] The predominantly Italian garrison signalled their intended surrender by declaring that they had run out of drinking water. Although an obvious stepping stone to Sicily, the allied intent was still not entirely transparent as the use of surprise was further compounded by the deception plan Operation MINCEMEAT. Although Field Marshal Kesselring suspected Sicily to be the next allied objective, Hitler continued to believe that the Balkans were the target.

In practice, the operations undertaken by the allies were a balance of manoeuvre and attrition, the emphasis on one or other depending on when and where they perceived success to lie. Although Montgomery used airborne troops in the manner of manoeuvre at Primasole Bridge, and No. 3 Commando to attack Malati Bridge on the same night, the subsequent amphibious assault (Operation CHOPPER), using 40 and 41 Commando was cancelled a short notice. When an amphibious flanking attack was finally undertaken on the eastern coast, the result was of limited value. Operationally he was frustrated at his inability to break through the Catanian plain and to outflank the enemy to the left by pushing up the Vizzini-Enna road. It wasn't so much a war of attrition, but a battle dictated by the Germans who were fighting a defensive withdrawal in order to ensure a successful evacuation.

Manoeuvre characteristically combines the resources of all arms and services, with air power being of crucial importance. This was not lost on either Air Chief Marshal Tedder (Allied Air Commander) or Admiral Cunningham who both stressed the importance of securing enemy airfields as early as possible. The RAF and USAF did endeavour to destroy all axis aircraft on Sicilian airfields. Tedder believed that 'it would be hard to imagine a better demonstration of the flexibility of air power than that provided by the attacks on airfields in the first nine days of July 1943'.[26] They concentrated on engaging the enemy airfields and installations, using bombers primarily to destroy as many axis aircraft as possible and between 6 July and 19 October 1943 'lost on the ground alone 322 bombers and 268 fighters, and 207 bombers and 700 fighters destroyed in the air'.[27]

The allied Air Forces were pre-occupied with broader strategic targets as opposed to integrated aviation support above the beachhead or on other battlefield air interdiction tasks. The lack of close air support was not at all good, with Rear Admiral S.E Morison referring to the North African Tactical Air Force 'giving no advance assurance to Army or Navy as to the kind and quality of support they could expect on D-day or thereafter. This refusal stemmed from the reluctance of top air commanders to sacrifice flexibility: 'Tactical' might be wanted to support 'Strategic' in action'.[28] Vice Admiral Hewitt commented that as far as assurances for air support were concerned, requests 'had to be submitted with not less than twelve hours' notice to a target

---

[24]Churchill, Winston S., *The Second World War: Vol. V Closing the Ring*, (London: Cassell & Co. Ltd., 1952), p. 30.

[25]*Ibid.*, p. 30.

[26]Tedder, Marshal of the Royal Air Force, Lord Tedder, G.C.B., *With Prejudice: The War Memoirs*, (London: Cassell, 1966), p. 447.

[27]*Ibid.*, p. 446.

[28]Morison, Samuel Eliot, *History of United States Naval Operations in World War II, Vol. IX, Sicily, Salerno, Anzio, January 1943 – June 1944*, (Boston: Little, Brown and Company, 1960), p. 22.

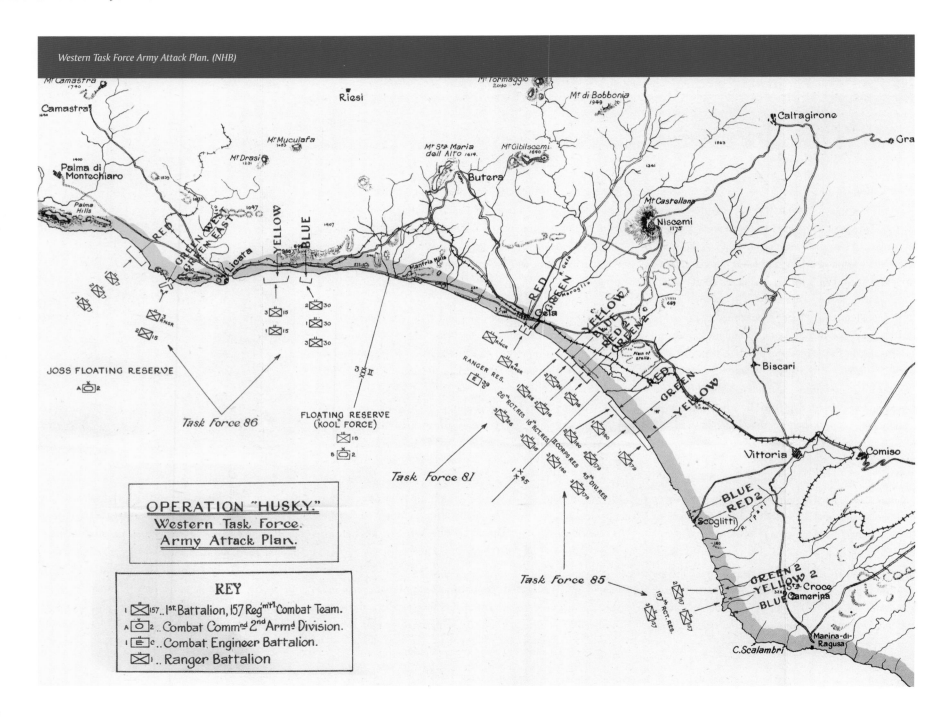

Western Task Force Army Attack Plan. (NHB)

OPERATION "HUSKY."
Western Task Force.
Army Attack Plan.

KEY

1 ⊠ 157 .. 1st Battalion, 157 Reg'm't'l Combat Team.
A ⌼ 2 .. Combat Comm'nd 2nd Arm'd Division.
1 E c .. Combat Engineer Battalion.
⊠ 1 .. Ranger Battalion

JOSS FLOATING RESERVE

Task Force 86

FLOATING RESERVE
("KOOL" FORCE)

Task Force 81

Task Force 85

committee located in North Africa' complaining that 'You can get your Navy planes to do anything you want, but we can't get the Air Force to do a goddam thing!'[29]

Although the RAF considered its role and cooperation most effective, the relationship between the services was seriously tested. This tension is apparent in Tedder's criticism of the Royal Navy when announcing that it was physically impossible to share a combined command post for communications at Bizerta in Tunisia. Tedder believed that his place was with his squadrons in order to provide close control and support for his subordinate commanders, rather than being with General Alexander in Malta.

Naval gunfire support (NGS) had mixed results. According to Morison the naval gunfire used to support the seaward flank of the Eighth Army, was 'not impressive'[30], but other accounts differ. Other than the light cruiser HMS *Mauritius* and two destroyers bombarding Giarre on 8 August, and *Uganda* and *Flores* on the 10th, NGS does not appear to have been used frequently on the eastern coast. However, the British Eastern Naval Task Force (under the command of Admiral Sir Bertram Ramsay), clearly understood the utility of NGS in support of the land campaign. The element of surprise at the operational level

was aided by the diversion, Operation FRACTURE when the Battleships HMS *Howe* and *King George V* engaged three enemy coastal batteries at Levanzo and Trapani in the north east. This led the Axis to consider an allied landing most likely in western Sicily. Alexander recounted that, 'We had quite clearly, contrary to all reasonable expectations, achieved strategic surprise and evidence appeared to show that the Germans were, as we had hoped, thinning out in the assault area to reinforce western Sicily'.[31]

The U.S. component commanders had a close relationship and the intimate support from the NGS from Rear Admiral L.A. Davidson's Naval Task Force 88 (NTF 88) was extremely effective. When the bulk of the Italian Livorno Division joined the Herman Goering Division to counterattack on 11 July, the U.S. 180th Infantry were tasked with holding the Biscari road. The *Beatty* gave heroic support, and later the Rangers also called for NGS. Captain Lyle who commanded the Rangers near Highway 117 was personally briefed by Patton to 'Kill every one of the god dam bastards'[32] as the Italians counter attacked. The *Savannah* responded, and fired over 500 6-inch shells, the results of which were 50% of the Italian unit killed or wounded, with reports of bodies 'hanging from the trees'[33], such was the accuracy and ferocity of the naval guns.

Cunningham was frustrated, not only in the fact that his relationship with Montgomery did not mirror that between Patton and Hewitt, but because the British failed to launch any further effective amphibious landings following D Day. He reflected that;

'No use was made by the 8th Army of amphibious opportunities. The small LSI's were kept standing for the purpose at the call of Rear Admiral McGrigor and landing craft were available on call: but the only occasion on which they were used was on the 16th August, after the capture of Catania. There were doubtless sound military reasons for making no use of this, what to me appeared, priceless asset of sea power and flexibility of manoeuvre: but it is worth consideration for future occasions whether much time and costly fighting could not be saved by even minor flank attacks which must necessarily be unsettling to the enemy. It must be for the General to decide. The Navy can only provide the means and advice on the practicability from the naval angle of the projected operation….It may be that had I pressed my views more strongly more could have been done'.[34]

[29]*Ibid.*, p 22.
[30]*Op cit*, Morison, p. 208.
[31]TNA: NHB, Alexander of Tunis, His Excellency Field Marshal The Viscount Alexander, G.C.B., G.C.M.G., C.S.I., D.S.O., M.C., Despatch by, *The Conquest of Sicily*, Copy No. 5. File M48L, (1943), p. 20.
[32]Garland, Albert N. Lt. Col., & Mc Gaw Smyth, Howard, p. 170.
[33]*Ibid.*, p. 170.
[34]'The Invasion of Sicily', Supplement to the *London Gazette*, of Tuesday, 25th April, 1950, p. 6.

the best thing of all was the way the destroyer came right in close to the headland and gave us fire support

Other than the landings of No. 3 Commando under Lieutenant Colonel Durnford-Slater, no other use was made of amphibious forces by the Eighth Army despite the Royal Navy having suitable shipping available. According to a letter[35] from Lieutenant Colonel J.C. Manner's (Commanding Officer of 40 Commando RM) written on 16 August 1943, a subsequent operation was cancelled because two German Regiments had arrived in the area of their proposed objectives. The Colonel was told by a Divisional Commander that the Commando was not going to be employed unless there was 95% certainty of achieving its mission. The lack of amphibious landings surprised the Germans particularly since the allies maintained total sea control from the outset. The failure to utilise this maritime flank resulted in the axis feeling 'mighty lucky... the absence of any large-scale encirclement of the island or of a thrust up the coastline of Calabria gave us long weeks to organise the defence with really weak resources'.[36] An amphibious landing by 40 Commando Royal Marines was launched on the night 15/16 August (in front of General Leese's 30 Corps near Scaletta) but the enemy had already withdrawn, evading the trap.

In an amphibious operation, every component commander should ideally be given control of the artillery, air and naval gunfire assets if required, but in Sicily (particularly in the British area) it relied upon the ships to move in close to the shore to identify their own targets. On occasion they managed this very successfully. When 3 Commando landed at Agnone the intimate fire support was described as being most effective, 'When we were about 100 yards out, the coast defence battery and several light machine-guns opened up on us. The destroyer *Tetcott* immediately opened up on the battery, while the pillboxes were taken on by machine-guns...the streams of bullets converging on pillboxes was most encouraging, but the best thing of all was the way the destroyer came right in close to the headland and gave us fire support'.[37] Coordinated fires were not as effective as they could have been, and simply relied on the courage of the Navy and initiative of the ships Commander.

Tactical Level

As Patton's U.S. Seventh Army advanced eastwards along the northern coast of Sicily, he and Bradley quickly appreciated the potential for amphibious hooking operations to out manoeuvre the German defensive line and to avoid any unnecessary attrition. These flanking moves unlocked the enemy's centre of gravity, and enabled them to reach Messina prior to Monty's Eighth Army. Unfortunately Patton's military success was overshadowed by the 'slapping incidents' in which he reprimanded casualties, who were victim of battlefield trauma.

It was an embarrassment to General Eisenhower, and only with persuasion did he let Patton remain in command.

The campaign by the Seventh Army reflected Patton's aggression and personal desire to see American troops prove their worth in combat. He continually pushed General Bradley's II Corps to such an extent that the U.S. Military account from the operation states that the advance on Palermo 'had been so swift that it had been necessary to call in many close support air missions, with the result that most tactical sorties had been flown well ahead of the advancing units attacking targets of opportunity'. But the cooperation was not always seamless. In one incident during the advance on Messina, the 180th Infantry could not seize the opportunity to pursue withdrawing 29th Panzer Grenadier Division, because 14 naval vessels (including 4 cruisers) were sighted off the northern coast. Fearing these were axis ships, General Bradley halted the 45th Division and instructed them to prepare to defend from a possible amphibious attack. The 180th and other units redeployed in order to defend the beaches to their rear, and it was not until 24 hours later that an aircraft identified the vessels as American. Coincidentally the German General Hube (Commander 14th Panzer Corps) believed that they were U.S vessels, and alerted his units as far as Calabria to be ready to defend against amphibious landings. Despite Admiral Hewitt[38] creating a bespoke Naval Task Force,

[35]TNA : PRO, ADM. 202/87 (40 Commando War Diary), Letter Manners to General 16th August, 1943.
[36]*Op cit.*, Kesselring, p. 165.
[37]Young, Peter, *Storm from the Sea*, (London: Greenhill Books, 1989), p. 89.
[38]Vice Admiral Henry K. Hewitt, Western Naval Task Force Commander.

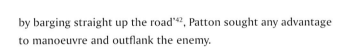

Sherman Tanks disembarking from an LST in the Eastern Task Force Area. (Crown Copyright)

specifically to support Patton's request for a series of amphibious operations along the north coast, it was not used to undertake an amphibious 'end run' until all land based operations seeking to outflank enemy defensive positions had been exhausted.

Admiral Davidson's NTF 88 was created to 'support the eastward advance of the Seventh Army by gunfire support and by effecting advance landings of military units'[39] ready to launch when the right opportunity presented itself. It was in effect 'General Patton's Navy'.[40] At the village of San Fratello the Germans had laid out defences on a 2,200 ft peak overlooking the coastal road. Unable to force that position with a frontal attack over the mountains, Patton had explored the likelihood of outflanking the coastal road block by amphibious envelopment.

General Lucian Truscott's[41] assessment was that the Germans were utilising the high ground and key points along the narrow coastal road, denying any freedom of movement or flanking manoeuvre. Therefore a battalion of Infantry, one tank platoon and two batteries of self-propelled field artillery were landed near Terranova. Landings were undertaken by Colonel Bernard's 30th Infantry on the night of 7 August. They were bold, daring and designed to disrupt the defensive cohesion of the enemy. They landed in complete surprise, and their attack was designed to apply force against an identified point of weakness.

That this operation has not been called manoeuvrist is a matter of nomenclature. It was swift, decisive and bold, inflicting shock action against the Panzer Grenadiers and resulted in the capture of over 1,200 German troops.

Patton was pleased with the results of II Corps amphibious assault, and decided to keep Bernard's task force intact. If a landing could be made deeper behind the 29th Panzer Grenadier Division, Patton could cut off large numbers of German soldiers and prevent their evacuation from the island. Despite some misgivings Truscott launched another operation using Bernard's Regiment at Brolo beach against the Panzer Grenadiers. Initially they met no resistance but soon found tougher opposition due to the greater concentration of enemy troops in north eastern Sicily. This amphibious landing was not as effective, resulting in a slower link-up with the U.S. 3rd Division. Trying to aid Bernard's men, the *Philadelphia* opened at prearranged targets, and moved close enough to engage enemy vehicles and infantry attempting to counter attack. Despite advice from Truscott that that there was 'No need for another landing, we can outrun an amphibious force by barging straight up the road'[42], Patton sought any advantage to manoeuvre and outflank the enemy.

Montgomery's advance was slow and he failed in his attempt to cut the axis route for withdrawal. The defensive posture adopted by General Hube appeared to be well balanced between having coastal and mobile defences, although the former proved almost totally ineffective. Following the landings the axis had the advantage of moving forces to a number of pre-prepared positions in-land, fighting a delaying action against Montgomery, and maintaining a mobile force in the form of General Conrath's armour. Subsequently the race to Messina was won 'neither by the British or the Americans, but by the German commander General Hube'[43], who succeeded in the

[39]*Op cit*, Battle Summary, p. 132.

[40]*Op cit*, Morison, p. 191.

[41]Commander 3rd Infantry Division, part of General Bradley's II Corps.

[42]Bradley, Omar, *A Soldier's Story of the Allied Campaigns from Tunis to the Elbe*, (London: Eyre & Spottiswoode Ltd., 1951), p. 162.

[43]Stawson, John, *The Italian Campaign*, (London: Secker & Warburg, 1987), p. 121.

Neither by land nor by sea does the strategist wish any mobile force to be permanently tied to local defence, any more than a chess player would appreciate some of his pieces being glued to their squares

evacuation of the numbers of troops, weapons and vehicles to reinforce the German Army in southern Italy. The Germans proved themselves skilful and creative in defence and masters of delay and withdrawal.

Montgomery's concerns about German defence are a possible explanation of why he did not authorise more effective and larger scale amphibious landings than the single operation initiated. This was launched towards the end of the campaign, just prior to the final assault on Messina. The issue of how best to overcome shore defences had been recognised as early as 1914 by General Sir George Aston (Colonel of the Royal Marine Artillery) who reflected that, 'Neither by land nor by sea does the strategist wish any mobile force to be permanently tied to local defence, any more than a chess player would appreciate some of his pieces being glued to their squares'.[44] Ultimately, this attitude and ability to understand the value of mobility, and more importantly manoeuvre against the enemy is as relevant to those in defence as it is to those launching an attack from the sea. Montgomery had the facility and capability to use the maritime flank, as opposed to the more cautious inland approach adopted when sending 30th Corps around the western side of Mount Etna. Meanwhile his 13th Corps mainly fought a battle of attrition along the coast road heading northwards. Montgomery would have benefited from seeing his 'chessboard' extending

out to sea and using the potential it offered to launch attacks in order to disrupt and destroy the enemy where the axis were most vulnerable. That it was not launched was more a reflection of Montgomery's limited experience in the littoral environment than any lack of manoeuvrist aspiration on his part. Some historians reflect that 'a sea borne hook well behind the German defenders at Catania, perhaps in the area of Taormina, would have paid off. There are beaches there. Such a lodgement could have been reinforced thus trapping the Germans and preventing large numbers of them escaping, as well as restoring manoeuvre to the Eighth Army'.[45]

Montgomery's anxiety prior to the operation was revealed in notes taken at the planning meeting on 2 May 1943, 'I know well that I am regarded by many people as being a tiresome person…I try hard not to be…but I have seen so many mistakes in this war, and so many disasters happen, that I am desperately anxious to try to see that we have no more…disaster in Italy would be dreadful'.[46] Success was his aim, not the style of victory, 'It is not merely a matter of capturing some beaches, or some airfield or some ports…we require the whole island'.[47] For a man who fought in the First World War it is not surprising that on occasion his advance was conventional and cautious. He wasn't prepared to gamble success in a large scale *coup de main* operation in a maritime environment in which he was less familiar.

The German Evacuation

The Germans used the codename Operation LEHRGANG for their withdrawal. The UK Approach to Amphibious Operations states that a withdrawal is when an 'Amphibious Force re-embarks onto parent shipping in preparation for redeployment after the seizure of amphibious objectives or as part of a pre-planned evacuation operation from a hostile shore'.[48] Although the German evacuation does not meet the strict criteria of the definition in terms of tactical reload and reconfiguration of the landing force, LEHRGANG was highly effective. The principles employed by 14th Panzer Corps included maintaining strict discipline throughout, men took priority over material and no German soldier was allowed to board a ferry without his personal weapons.

Allied intelligence had reported Germans crossing the Straits on 3 August. Alexander warned Cunningham and Tedder that preparations for an evacuation were underway and that they must be in a position to take advantage of such a situation using the full weight of naval and air power. Much to Kesselring's surprise, 'The enemy failure to exploit the last chance of hindering the German forces crossing the Straits of Messina, by continuous and strongly coordinated attacks from the air, was almost a greater boon to the German Command than their failure immediately to push their pursuit across the straits on

[44]Aston, Sir George, *Sea, Land and Air Strategy: A Comparison*, (London: John Murray, 1914), p. 227.
[45]Correspondence with Major General Julian Thompson, Ref: Op HUSKY, dated, 01/10/2004.
[46]Montgomery, Field-Marshall, The Viscount, K.G., *The Memoirs of Field-Marshal Montgomery*, (London: Collins, 1958), p. 178.
[47]*Ibid*, p. 179.
[48]The United Kingdom Approach to Amphibious Operations, Stationary Office, Dd8454297.5/97 J7894, April, 1997 p. 33.

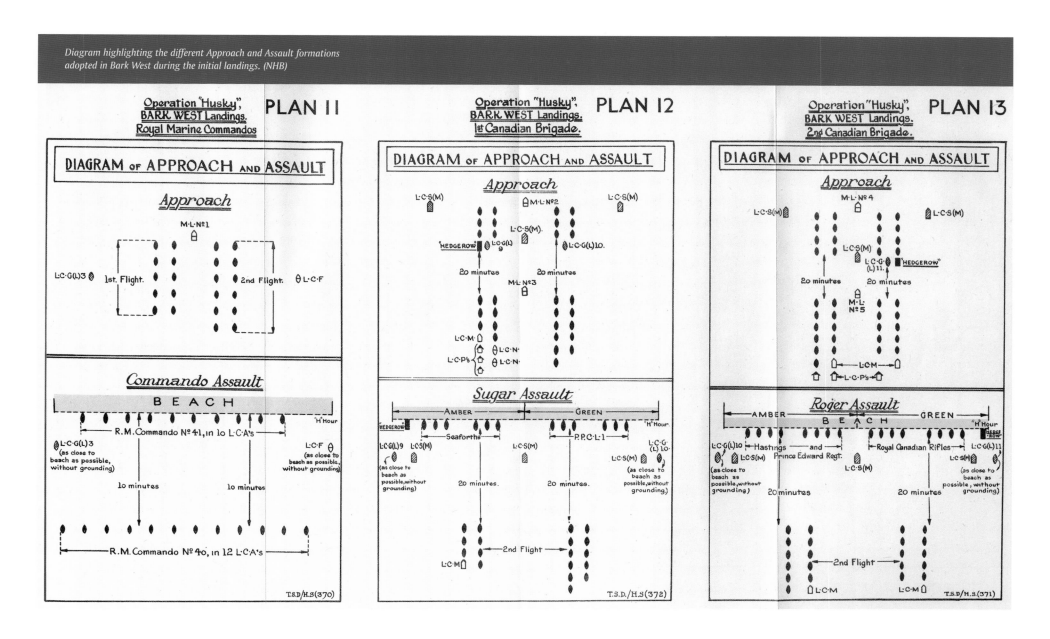

Diagram highlighting the different Approach and Assault formations adopted in Bark West during the initial landings. (NHB)

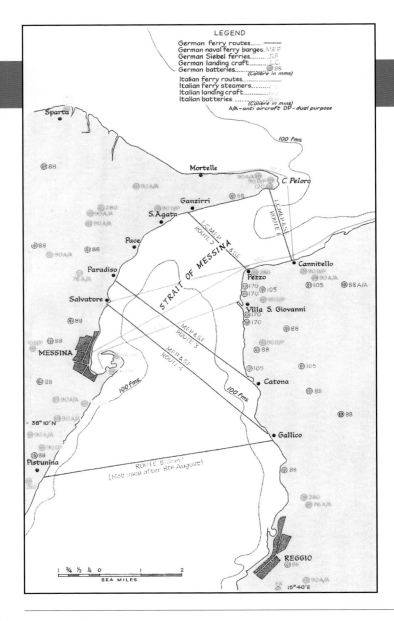

17 August'.[49] The vulnerable German troops could not believe their good fortune at the inaction of the allies to hit them as they loaded or disembarked. General von Senger und Etterlin, Commander of 14th Panzer Corps even termed the evacuation as a 'glorious defeat'[50], due to allied air supremacy and abundant sea power failing to stop the axis retreat.

Montgomery was also irritated by the fact that most of the Germans escaped from Messina. 'We took some five weeks to complete the capture of Sicily and the Eighth Army suffered 12,000 casualties. With close co-ordination of the land, air and sea effort we would, in my view, have gained control of the island more quickly, and with fewer casualties'.[51] He lamented about the heavy axis traffic crossing on 6 August, noting 'I have tried to find out what the combined Navy-Air plan is in order to stop the enemy getting away; I have been unable to find out. I fear the truth of the matter is that there is NO plan'.[52] In his view the failure was not with individuals, or services, but rather their locations and lack of appreciation of the overall picture, 'Cunningham is in Malta; Tedder is at Tunis; Alexander is at Syracuse. It beats me how anyone thinks you can run a campaign in that way, with the three Commanders of the three

Services about 600 miles from each other'.[53] Montgomery persuaded his commander General Alexander to write a signal to Tedder and Cunningham highlighting the possibility of a German withdrawal, and a requirement for both the allied Navy and Air Force to prevent the axis from getting any troops or materiel across the Straits of Messina. He was determined that the benefits of attritional war and exploiting the allied success should not be lost.

Despite this frustration, overall he was highly satisfied with the manner in which the Eighth Army had adapted after North Africa. It had undertaken a very successful landing on a hostile shore, tackled demanding terrain and had overcome stiff German resistance despite the demands of insufferable temperature and a large number of casualties caused by malaria.

Cunningham was adamant that the responsibility to interdict was not the senior services alone. He gave clear guidance in a signal to the Fleet in July that, 'great risks must be and are accepted. The safety of our ships and all distracting considerations are to be relegated to second place'[54] although losses were relatively light.[55] While the Royal Navy still reflected with pride Nelson's desire to close with the enemy, that war fighting philosophy did not appear to have been followed when faced with a shore based enemy in Sicily. The

[49]Op cit., Kesselring, p.165.
[50]Op cit., Morison, p. 216.
[51]Op cit., Montgomery, p. 188.
[52]Hamilton, Nigel, Monty: Master of the Battlefield, (London: Hamish Hamilton, 1983), p. 348.

[53]Ibid., p. 348.
[54]Op cit., Cunningham, p. 551.
[55]Ibid., p 558. Two submarines, three motor torpedo boats, one motor gunboat and a few landing craft.

allies were anxious about the enemy submarine threat, shallow water, mines, shore based artillery, as well as the danger of counterattack by the Italian Navy.

'My thinking on the Messina Straits has always been influenced by what we underwent in the approaches to the narrows at Gallipoli'

Cunningham had been given command of the destroyer HMS *Scorpion* in 1914, and had 'always been in the forefront of the action'[56] while serving in the Dardanelles in 1915. Morison poses the question that perhaps the 'powerful deterrent [to action in the Messina Straits] was British memory, and American knowledge, of the Gallipoli campaign in World War 1. The topography of the Dardanelles is roughly similar…amphibious assaults were a costly failure, and battleships were unable to cope with mobile artillery and coastal batteries'.[57] Knowledge of the toll at Gallipoli, as well as the naval costs spread a dark shadow, across both time and the Mediterranean. In private correspondence, Morison's suspicions about the Navy's reluctance to interdict the withdrawing enemy are confirmed, when Cunningham wrote that 'My thinking on the Messina

Straits has always been influenced by what we underwent in the approaches to the narrows at Gallipoli and our night raids there where the defences were nothing like as efficient as Messina'[58], although he was never to admit that publicly.

The RAF also had problems preventing a German 'Dunkirk'. It was difficult because crews 'had to contend with powerful concentration of flak…and found much difficulty in attacking enemy shipping in this confined space under the shadow of the steep cliffs'.[59] Over the period of HUSKY, '533 enemy aircraft were destroyed in the air…20,000 tons of bombs had been dropped on ports and bases, nearly 7,500 tons on airfields, and no less than 15,500 tons on lines of communication. So intense an effort certainly helped to undermine Italian morale on the island and to prepare the way for imminent Italian collapse'.[60] The strategic value of the approach adopted by the RAF was clear, but at the tactical level, the German's believed that the effectiveness of allied airpower had not been as good as it had the potential to be. However it was not until the captured Italian airfields were repaired and in good order that allied aircraft could use bases in Sicily. Critically, Messina was 150 miles from Malta, and until 13 July, beyond the range of allied single-seater aircraft. While Tedder claimed that the Allied Air Forces had operated without distinction

of nationality with their contribution to victory in Sicily being 'capital'[61], the Germans were not as complimentary. Although the RAF did sink two Siebel[62] ferries and one ship, the smaller craft were too agile and well defended to be endangered by high level bombing or the brave attempts of fighter bombers to penetrate the flak screen. The Italians observed that 'they could count on peace in the Strait for an hour each side of first light'[63] and Admiral von Ruge critically remarked that 'knowing Anglo-Saxon habits, he found the lunch hour also a quiet time for crossing'.[64]

Personal letters about the evacuation reveal that 'dive bombing of the Siebel ferries was tried but proved to be suicidal so that all subsequent bombing during the evacuation was from a high level and hit nothing'.[65] Allied aircraft had a difficult task, but were probably not aware of the shortage of anti-aircraft (A.A.) ammunition experienced by the axis. The German Naval Officer-in-Charge reflected that, 'If there had been sufficient supplies of ammunition, the A.A. defences in the Messina Straits would certainly have been able to achieve much greater success'.[66] It appears that the fear of attrition and the high costs anticipated by the allied air force acted as a considerable deterrent, which gave the escaping axis Army the window they needed to escape relatively unscathed.

[56]Royal Navy Museum, Research Collections Team, 'Andrew Browne Cunningham', from http://www.royalnavalmuseum.org/library/factsheets/andrew_cunnigham.htm (Accessed 12/08/2004).
[57]Op cit., Morison, p. 219.
[58]Churchill Archives, Cambridge, *The Roskill Papers*, ROSK 05/100, Letter dated 9th November (Year unknown), to 'My Dear Roskill'.
[59]Op cit, Tedder, p. 453.
[60]Ibid., p. 453.
[61]Ibid., p. 454.

[62]TNA: NHB *Weekly Intelligence Reports*, No. 92-104, WIR 100, 6th February, 1942, p. 27, describes the Siebel as a twin hulled vessel, with a speed of 6-7 knots, which could be transported in sections, armed with 3 x 8.8 mm A.A. Guns.
[63]Op cit, Morison, p. 214.
[64]Ibid., p. 214.
[65]Churchill Archives Centre, Cambridge, *The Roskill Papers*, ROSK, 05/100, Letter from Rear Admiral S.E. Morison USNR (Rtd.) to Admiral of the Fleet Viscount Cunningham of Hyndhope, dated 16 November, 1953.
[66]Churchill Archives Centre, Cambridge, *The Roskill Papers*, ROSK 05/100, War Diary of Naval-Officer-in-Charge, Sea Transport, Messina Strait (Captain von Liebenstein), 1 August 1943 – 17 August 1943, Admiralty Ref: PG 45898, p. 29.

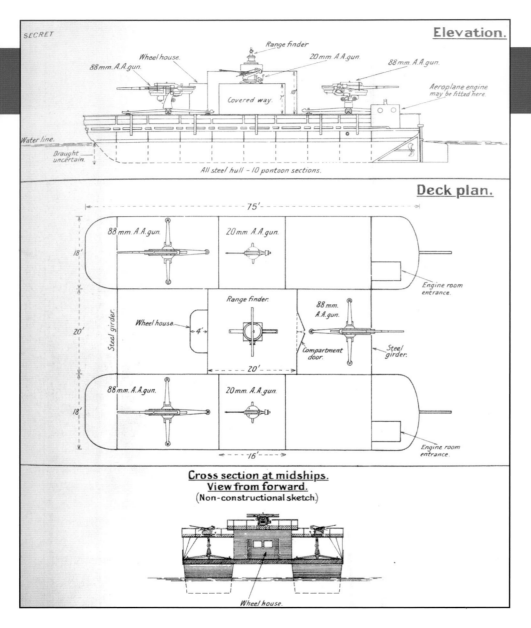

Left: Secret drawings taken from the Allied Weekly Intelligence Report, showing the Siebel Ferry elevation and deck plan.

Below: The Siebel Ferry could transport over 200 personnel at a time. (NHB)

The operation on Sicily concluded with Patton entering Messina on 17 August. 'The U.S. Seventh Army, thanks to their amphibious tactics and prodigious road engineering feats beat the British Eighth Army by a short head'.[67] A key lesson identified was that subsequent to the initial assault, there was a 'need to form, in advance, an amphibious force for the exploitation of outflanking opportunities and its existence and value to be firmly indicated in the plan'.[68] The value of manoeuvre and the effective exploitation of the maritime flank were seen as particularly relevant.

On 21 August 1943, General Eisenhower, Allied-Commander-in-Chief issued a report on the invasion of Sicily;

> 'It cannot be too clearly recognised that a combined operation is but the opening... of a purely army battle. It is a function of the navy and of the air to help the army to establish a base or bases on the hostile coast from which the military tactical battle... must be developed. It is upon the army tactical plan... that the combined plan must depend. The navy and air commanders must join with the army commander to ensure that base or bases selected for seizure are capable of achievement without prohibitive loss'.[69]

[67]*Op cit*, Battle Summary, p. 149.
[68]*Ibid*. p.149.
[69]*Op cit*, Battle Summary, p. 141.

This was designed to encourage all commanders to recognise the requirement to mount a joint and combined campaign, and where possible avoid unnecessary casualties through attritional style warfare. In the space of 38 days Sicily had been recaptured, relatively successfully, with allied casualties totalling 20,000 men; the axis suffering 31,000 dead and wounded, with over 140,000 POW's.[70] A greater awareness of the potential of manoeuvre via the sea and a more effective use of the maritime flank could have resulted in a less pyrrhic victory for the allies and a more convincing defeat against the axis.

In a letter written by General Alexander to the Prime Minister dated 17 August, 1943, he reflected that during the whole operation the 'Air Forces have maintained domination throughout…and the Royal Navy have kept our sea-lanes open and supplied us with everything we need',[71] which raises the question that if they had been so successful how did the axis troops depart with so much materiel? Alexander's letter tells as much about the campaign in terms of what he left out as that information which he included in this correspondence with Churchill.

A critical weakness was the failure for the commanders to communicate and work effectively with each other. Three separate plans were run in parallel throughout the campaign, resulting in significant failures in terms of the combined and joint

battle. Their personal relationships appear to be strained, and although little of this tension appears in official biographies and accounts, private correspondence reveals the anxieties between them. Montgomery stated in a letter to Ramsay that 'the 'Old Man of the Sea' [Cunningham] got very troublesome. In the end he really became beyond a joke, and refused to produce what was necessary for our next business'.[72] Cunningham believed the failure of the allies to stop the axis evacuation lay with Montgomery, 'As it was there is no doubt the honours went to the Yanks who used their sea power in landing behind the enemy. Nothing would induce Monty to do the same till the last when he wasn't bold enough and landed in front of the enemy…I fear Monty has not profited by the lectures on sea power which I'm sure you gave him'.[73]

The Germans had achieved the unthinkable recovering three Divisions to the mainland, ready, equipped and prepared for further battle. This withdrawal bestowed an operational level of capability which the allies could have prevented had they adopted a joint approach throughout the campaign and clearly articulated this to each component commander.

Conclusion

Some historians, such as Professor Richard Harding, argue that the Allied victory in Sicily is tainted by questions as to the nature of the success. Carlo D'Este's *Bitter Victory* and Martin

[70]Italian Personnel: POW's 123,000; killed 2,000; wounded 5,000; evacuated 35,000. German Personnel: POW's 7,000; killed 5,000; wounded 20,000; evacuated 60,000. (From Battle Summary No. 35, p. 140).
[71]*Op cit*, Churchill, p. 38.
[72]Churchill Archives Centre, Cambridge, *Ramsay Papers*, 9/4, Letter dated 26-8-43.
[73]Churchill Archives Centre, Cambridge, *Ramsay Papers*, 9/4, Letter dated 20th September, Bizerta, 1943.

Blumenson's *Sicily: Whose Victory?* reflect suspicions that HUSKY was not as successful as it could have been. There were some notable achievements, such as advances in over the beach supply using the new landing ships and DUKW[74], and the time it took to deliver logistical support. Naval Gunfire was accurate, the airforce neutralised the axis aircraft and the 'combined' nature of allied co-operation was clearly evident, but criticisms were raised contemporaneously[75], as well by historians today. Despite this the operations on D-Day were a tremendous feat of planning, co-ordination, inter-service co-operation and allied unity. The largest amphibious invasion of enemy territory had succeeded in the face of fierce axis counter attacks, a result of which was a significant psychological boost to the allies.

The doctrine of manoeuvre addresses the public reluctance to take casualties, which was as relevant in Sicily in 1943 as it is in the world of mass media today. Attritional warfare was unacceptable to a generation who had been scarred by the number of deaths in the previous war. The political, cultural and societal reluctance to accept undue casualties relied on good military leadership. General Ridgeway argued that any commander, who in the confusion of battle forgot that he was dealing in men's lives, and needlessly sacrificed them, was 'more butcher than battle leader. He is a fool and not a guiltless

one'.[76] While Ridgeway admired courage and valued gallantry, having witnessed the fratricide over the sea en route to Gela he favoured the battle which would secure victory at the lowest cost to one's own troops.

This was also identified by Bradley, recognising that 'Men must be subordinated to the effort that comes with fighting a war, and as a consequence men must die that objectives might be taken. For a commander the agony of war is not in its dangers, deprivations or the fear of defeat but in the knowledge that with each new day men's lives must be spent to pay the costs of that day's objectives.'[77] There are benefits to be gained from the process of attrition[78] (reducing the enemy's manpower and materiel) but manoeuvre has the advantage of ensuring that the 'cost' is as small as possible. Although manoeuvre could have been the key to unlocking the campaign and achieving an earlier victory, attrition was equally important in order to prevent the German Army from evacuating with so many soldiers, and with much of their armour and artillery intact.

Manoeuvre succeeded in Sicily in terms of shattering the enemy's will and cohesion. Montgomery and Patton achieved their aim of taking the island and HUSKY met the grand strategic ambitions outlined eight months previously at the Combined Chiefs of

Staff meeting in Casablanca. The allies made the Mediterranean Sea lines of communication more secure, diverted German pressure from the Russian front and intensified pressure on Italy. However, this was an occasion when the application of overwhelming strength could have paid significant dividends. The axis troops departed from Sicily relatively unscathed with 110,000 troops, 9,600 vehicles, 47 tanks and approximately 200 artillery guns. An attritional approach could have potentially yielded a more substantial success. In reality if the Seventh and Eighth Armies had enveloped the Germans and Italians, and the allied air and naval forces had cut off the 2 km stretch of water between Messina and the mainland, the victory could have been more significant and less bitter than some historians reflect. The allies had 'two superior elements, sea and air power which should have more than compensated for the terrain. These they failed to use intelligently.'[79]

Not all those attributes of manoeuvre were put into practice consistently at all levels of war during this campaign. A balance was required between Patton's high tempo approach, advocating 'a good plan now being better than a perfect plan later' and Montgomery's methodical, cautious and highly meticulous attention to detail. Neither commander appears to have the perfect solution. Manoeuvre utilises Patton's aggression and

---

[74]DUKW (an acronym based on D-model year 1942, U-amphibian, K-all wheel drive, W-dual rear axles), called 'duck'.
[75]See for example; Butler, Captain Harry C., *Three Years with Eisenhower*, (London: William Heinman Ltd., 1946), p. 330. Eisenhower admitted 'mistakes' and reflected that the Allies should have made simultaneous landings both sides of the Messina Straits.
[76]Soffer, Johnathan M., *General Mathew B. Ridgeway, From Progressivism to Reaganism 1895 – 1993*, (London: Praeger, 1998), p. 28.
[77]*Op cit*, Bradley, p. 154.

[78]Bellamy, Professor Christopher, 'In Praise of Attrition', A Summary of his Inaugural Lecture at Cranfield University, in The *British Army Review*, *The Magazine of British Military Thought*, No. 134, Summer, 2004, p. 46.
[79]*Op cit.*, Morison, Samuel Eliot, p. 202.

The 'Soldier's Guide To Sicily': A British infantry soldier, armed, equipped and informed about the next step in the Mediterranean campaign. (IWM NA4500)

desire for maintaining momentum and Montgomery's well considered options to achieve overwhelming battlespace domination. Although both commanders sought to out-think their opponent they did not fully utilise their maritime flank. They demonstrated an appreciation of the potential of amphibious landings, but neither launched a large enough attack to prevent the axis evacuation.

The lessons from the past still have powerful resonance today. Sicily represented a failure in terms of prosecuting the battle on a joint basis following the initial landings. Although the first few days were a great success, OP HUSKY could have been even more victorious if the services had combined their staffs and planning, incorporating land, naval and air assets at each stage of the campaign. Prescient warnings had been given by General Aston as early as 1911, 'For fleets and armies to work together for a common object the most loyal co-operation is required between all ranks of both services. In the old days the want of such co-operation between our own naval and military commanders was notorious'[80] and by 1943 that message had still not been fully understood.

Lessons identified from Op HUSKY

- **Surprise:** The OP MINCEMEAT deception plan was highly effective and deceived the enemy as to allied intentions in the Mediterranean.

- **Security:** The security of the plan was well guarded. It was not until after the troop ships and escorting vessels departed from port that their destination was revealed.

- **Fires:** Fires for an amphibious landing should combine decentralisation and mission command with the ability of the landing force commander to exploit success rapidly.

- **Joint Mission:** Each service focussed on what they considered to be the most important objective in the battle, rather than adopting an integrated approach and maintaining liaison. The tensions in Sicily highlight the importance of close professional relationships between commanders from different services.

- **Amphibious Knowledge and Experience:** Generals Patton and Bradley's amphibious 'end runs' encapsulate the manoeuvrist spirit, catching the enemy off guard with speed and surprise to gain tactical advantage. They understood what operational manoeuvre from the sea could contribute to their campaign plan.

- **Specialist Amphibious Shipping:** The development of specialist vessels (LST, DUKW) was highly significant in aiding theatre entry. Once the landings had occurred, the rapid build up of logistical support from across the beach was enhanced by these vessels, thereby avoiding the immediate requirement to capture a heavily defended port.

- **Aircraft Recognition:** Improved identification of aircraft (friend or foe markings) and longer warning of the passage of airborne forces.

---

[80]Aston, G.G., C.B., Brigadier-General, *Letters on Amphibious Wars*, (London: John Murray, 1911), p. 360.

Further Reading

C.B. 3081 (27) Battle Summary No. 35. The Invasion of Sicily: Operation HUSKY, (T.S.D. 21/46, Naval Staff, Admiralty, Feb 1946)

Blumenson, Martin, *Sicily: Whose Victory?* (Macdonald, 1969)

D'Este, Carlo, *Bitter Victory: The Battle for Sicily 1943*, (Collins, 1988)

Garland, Albert N. Lt. Col., & Mc Gaw Smyth, Howard, *U.S. Army in World War II, The Mediterranean Theater of Operations: Sicily and the Surrender of Italy*, (Washington, D.C.: Office of the Chief of Military History, Dept. of the Army, 1965)

Grigg, John, *1943 The Victory that Never Was*, (London: Methuen, 1980)

Montagu, Ewen, *The Man Who Never Was*, (Evans, 1953)

Morris, Eric, *Circles of Hell, The War in Italy, 1943 - 1945*, (London: Hutchinson, 1943)

Pack, S.W.C., *Operation HUSKY The Allied Invasion of Sicily,* (London: David & Charles, 1977)

Strawson, John, *The Italian Campaign*, (London: Secker and Warburg, 1987)

Whiting, Charles, *Slaughter Over Sicily*, (Cooper, 1992)

Whicker, Alan, *Whicker's War,* (London: Harper Collins, 2005)

Winton, John, *Cunningham: The Greatest Admiral Since Nelson* (London: John Murray, 1998) Chapter 20.

Biography

Lieutenant Commander Tristan Lovering was the Royal Marines Corps Tutor (2001-2005) and was responsible for the delivery of the Advanced Amphibious Warfare Course at the Defence Academy. He was also responsible for other Royal Marine educational courses delivered at the Commando Training Centre Lympstone and Britannia Royal Naval College, Dartmouth. He has a First Class Honours Degree in International Relations from Southampton University and a Masters degree in International Relations from Cambridge University. Before joining the Royal Navy he was in the Royal Artillery, serving in Germany, Northern Ireland, Cyprus, Bosnia and Serbia. He was awarded an MBE in the Queen's Birthday Honours 2006 for his services to Royal Marines officer education and for advancing the study of amphibious warfare.

Salerno
Operation AVALANCHE, 9 September 1943

By Dr Christopher Tuck

Operation AVALANCHE, the landing at Salerno in September 1943, provides an excellent case study of amphibious operations and manoeuvre warfare.[1] Operation AVALANCHE had great potential as a manoeuvre warfare success: the strategic and operational conception for the landing was manoeuvrist in outlook; the theatre geography was conducive to amphibious operations; and the handling of the landings at a tactical level was generally good. Yet the Salerno landings proved to be a profound disappointment for the Allies. Why was this, and what lessons can be drawn about the relationship between amphibious operations and manoeuvre warfare? An examination of the conception and execution of the landings throws important light on some of the wider challenges in using amphibious operations as part of manoeuvre warfare. This chapter will explore these challenges first by outlining the main tenets of manoeuvre warfare. It will then consider, in general terms, the opportunities and problems associated with the use of amphibious operations in manoeuvre warfare. It will then use Salerno as a case study to amplify one of the important challenges in making amphibious operations

manoeuvrist: maintaining the momentum of the landing through exploitation. The analysis makes two general observations that explain the outcome at Salerno. First, manoeuvre warfare is relational - realising the tenets of a manoeuvrist approach to war depends to a great extent on the co-operation of the enemy. Second, the material conditions of war still matter; geography and the balance of forces may constrain the ability of a commander to operate in a manoeuvrist manner.

Manoeuvre Warfare, Manoeuvrism and Amphibious Operations

Contemporary British doctrine defines manoeuvre warfare as 'the application of manoeuvrist thinking to war fighting.'[2] Manoeuvrism is therefore a way of thinking; manoeuvre warfare is a way of fighting that expresses manoeuvrist thinking. Manoeuvrist thinking places an emphasis on the intangibles of war. It focuses on attacking the enemy's system rather than his physical strength through targeting morale, will and decision-making capacity. Manoeuvrist thinking emphasises pre-emption, dislocation, maintaining the initiative and directing one's own strengths against the enemy's weaknesses.[3] The

purpose is the shattering of enemy cohesion, both physical and moral, and his ability to fight as a cohesive whole, rather than destruction.[4] Manoeuvrist thinking is often wrongly portrayed as the antithesis of 'attrition' and attritionist approaches to war. Whereas manoeuvre warfare is often associated with attacks on enemy intangibles, attrition is characterised by a focus on the physical destruction of the enemy. However, manoeuvrist thinking does not preclude the use of attrition; it does, however, place an emphasis on encouraging the commander to create attrition on one's own terms. For example, Soviet operational art embraced favourable attrition as a desirable outcome of operations. There are several concepts central to a manoeuvrist way of thinking about war; these include the principles of simultaneity, surprise, and maintaining the initiative. A foundation principle for manoeuvrist thinking is the concept of tempo. Tempo is an important relational concept; it is associated with 'time competitive observation-orientation-decision-making cycles'[5] ; the proposition that if one side can move through the process of relevant decision-making faster than the enemy then that side can accrue a decisive battle advantage.[6] Manoeuvre warfare therefore stresses the temporal dimension of war: war is competition in time.[7] Because manoeuvrism is a way of thinking,

[1] The analysis, opinions and conclusions expressed or implied in this chapter are those of the author, and do not necessarily represent the views of the JSCSC, the UK MOD or any other government agency. The author would like to thank Dr Stuart Griffin and Dr Deborah Sanders for their comments and observations on earlier drafts of this chapter.
[2] Joint Warfare Publication 0-01, *British Defence Doctrine* (2nd Edition) (HMSO: 2001) p.3-5.
[3] *The Application of Force: An Introduction to Army Doctrine and the Conduct of Military Operations* (HMSO, 2002) p.39.
[4] Ibid., p.40.
[5] Often referred to as a 'Boyd' or 'OODA' loop after the observations of Colonel John Boyd on the importance of Observation-Orientation-Decision-Action cycles. See William S.Lind, *Maneuver Warfare Handbook* (Boulder: Westview, 1985), pp.4-6.
[6] Lind, *The Maneuver Warfare Handbook*, pp.5-6.
[7] William S. Lind, 'The Theory and Practice of Maneuver Warfare' in Richard D. Hooker, Jr (Ed), *Maneuver Warfare: An Anthology* (Novato: Presidio, 1993) p.9.

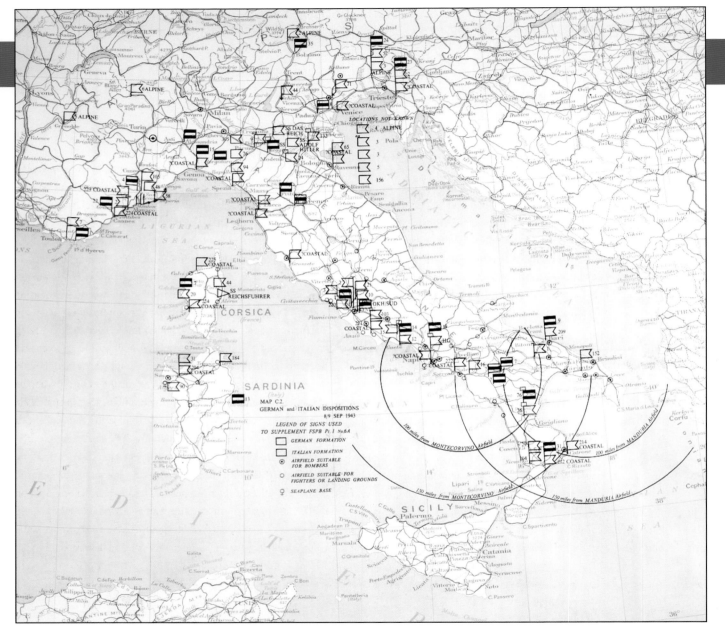

German and Italian dispositions on the 8/9 September prior to the Allied landings at Salerno. (NA)

proponents of the idea of manoeuvre warfare argue that it can apply to all levels of warfare: strategic, operational and tactical. At Salerno, therefore, the manoeuvrist approach encompassed the operational concept behind the landing, not just the tactical implementation.

Manoeuvre warfare can be realised through a number of enablers. The first is de-centralised command and control to allow more rapid decision-making. Known as 'mission command' this approach to command and control focuses on a subordinates understanding of the commander's intent, which he then sets about realising in a manner of his choosing. Mission command requires a strong understanding at all levels of the aims of an operation if unity of effort is to be sustained.[8] The second is the need for a 'reconnaissance pull' approach to operations. This means acceptance of confusion and disorder, a rejection of rigid timetables of advance that may constrain a sub-ordinate's initiative. The commander needs to reinforce success as it emerges on the ground and avoid too rigid a plan. Third, manoeuvre warfare puts a focus on avoiding a mechanistic approach to fighting; encouraging spontaneity and lateral thinking, avoiding fixed ways of doing things. These precepts

---

[8]For some of the problems associated with Mission Command See B Tan, *Auftragstaktik: a critical analysis and its viability in the future* (Camberley: The Staff College, 1994)

AVALANCHE was designed to try to avoid a campaign of attrition on the Italian mainland

rely to an extent on having the appropriate military structures to realise them. Fundamentally, though, the manoeuvrist approach is a state if mind.

The basis of manoeuvre warfare is the desire 'to circumvent a problem and attack it from a position of advantage rather than straight on'.[9] Theoretically, manoeuvre warfare 'offers the prospect of rapid results or of results disproportionately greater than the resources applied.'[10] It is no wonder, then, that manoeuvre warfare is of such interest to the military. The concept remains controversial not least because some have argued that the focus on manoeuvrism reflects a Western fascination with German military practice in the Second World War; indeed, one commentator has criticised the current focus on manoeuvre warfare as a bad case of 'Wehrmacht envy'.[11] Nevertheless, the British and American militaries continue to attach great importance to the concept of manoeuvrism.

Amphibious operations might seem to sit naturally within the manoeuvrist tradition. Amphibious capabilities confer a number of generic advantages: strategic reach, through the ability to extend the reach of land and air forces; mobility, capitalising on the instrumental advantages of moving in the medium of the sea;

flexibility, through the range of forces that can be embarked.[12] Amphibious capabilities extend the range of options available to a commander and may, therefore, help to provide the means to realise a more manoeuvrist approach to operations.[13] In the past, amphibious operations have often been viewed as the means to avoid or to escape from attrition. The origins of the Gallipoli campaign, for example, lay in part in its potential to escape from the grim attritional struggle on the Western Front and to deliver disproportionate political success. [14]

Nevertheless, since the manoeuvrist approach is fundamentally a state of mind, there is nothing inherently manoeuvrist about amphibious capabilities; it is the manner in which they are employed that will determine how manoeuvrist they are. Gallipoli again provides us with an example of this point. Despite the high hopes regarding its potential success, the landings at Gallipoli ultimately only created a new front for attrition because of the poor execution of the operation. One of the main reasons for the failure of the landings were the problems associated with translating the successful amphibious landing, into operations further in land that would exploit the initiative obtained by the landings and maintain the momentum of the operation.

In fact, maintaining the momentum of a landing is an inherently difficult thing to do. Amphibious landings are complex and problematic operations. The complexities associated with the joint nature of amphibious operations, such as command and control, compound more generic problems of planning, force protection and landing. Even a successful landing is unlikely, in itself, to deliver more than temporary initiative over the enemy. In order to have a broader effect on the enemy, the momentum of the assault needs to be maintained by exploiting the landing through follow-on operations in-land.[15] The success in bridging the gap between consolidation of a landing and exploitation operations can be a determining factor in the overall impact of an amphibious landing. Operation AVALANCHE provides an object lesson in the problems that can constrain the successful exploitation of a landing and which can rob an amphibious operation of its manoeuvrist dimension.

Salerno: The Operational Concept

From the beginning, the strategic and operational conception behind the landings at Salerno was manoeuvrist. AVALANCHE was designed to try to avoid a campaign of attrition on the Italian mainland. In July 1943, the Allies had landed in Sicily, and despite, its problems, this operation gradually succeeded

---

[9] John F. Antal, 'Thoughts About Maneuver Warfare' in Hooker, Op. Cit. p.63.

[10] JWP 0-01, p.3-5.

[11] Daniel P. Bolger, 'Maneuver Warfare Reconsidered' in Hooker, Op. Cit. p.27.

[12] See *BR1806: The Fundamentals of British Maritime Doctrine* (London: HMSO, 1995) pp.81-104.

[13] For details of the complex dimensions of amphibious landings see Col MHH Evans, *Amphibious Operations: The Projection of Sea Power Ashore* (London: Brassey's, 1990) Especially Part II.

[14] N Steel and P Hart, *Defeat at Gallipoli* (London: Macmillan, 1994) pp. 1-10.

[15] The relevance of such exploitation will depend on the type of operation: raids, feints, demonstrations and withdrawals naturally involve less in the way of exploitation than theatre entry scenarios.

Some hoped that, with Italian surrender, the Salerno landings might involve no fighting at all

in driving back the Axis forces. Winston Churchill pushed for follow-on operations against mainland Italy itself.[16] For Churchill, a campaign in Italy was replete with strategic potential. Not only would it take Italy out of the war, but it might also have important implications for the situation in the Balkans, by bringing Turkey into the war, and would also expose Austria to attack from the south.[17] By August 1943 operational orders for the next phase of the war against Italy had been formulated.[18] This consisted of a two-pronged advance. In Operation BAYTOWN, the Eighth Army was successfully transported across the Straits of Messina onto the toe of Italy. From there, they would commence an offensive through Calabria and push northwards into central Italy. The second prong was more ambitious. In operation AVALANCHE the US 5th Army (which included as many British troops as American) commanded by Lieutenant General Mark Clark would be landed 30 miles southeast of Naples in the Gulf of Salerno; AVALANCHE would threaten the communications of Axis forces in the whole of southern Italy and, it was hoped, lead to a rapid collapse of their positions: Mussolini had been deposed and the new Italian government was making peace overtures. Some hoped that, with Italian surrender, the Salerno landings might involve no fighting

at all. Others hoped that the landing would result in a German withdrawal all the way back to northern Italy.[19] Whatever the general impact, the intent behind AVALANCHE was firmly manoeuvrist. Rather than commit Clark's troops with the 8th Army to a long and potentially difficult thrust up the length of Italy, AVALANCHE was designed to collapse the German defence by placing Allied troops on their lines of communication. As Churchill put it, why 'crawl up the leg like a harvest-bug from the ankle upwards? Let us rather strike at the knees ....' .[20] The landings promised to deliver the initiative to the allies, to knock the Germans off-balance and to deliver results out of proportion to the forces involved. Clark commented that 'From the first this operation... looked good to me.'[21]

The Plan

On 26 August, Clark issued his plan to the 5th Army, directing his forces 'to seize the port of Naples and to secure the airfields in the Naples area with a view to preparing a firm base for further offensive operations.'[22] The ground forces allocated to AVALANCHE included major elements of the US VI Corps and British X Corps. The former consisted of 36th and 45th Divisions under the command of Major General E J Dawley. The

latter included the 46th and 56th Divisions with two brigades of commandos and rangers under the command of Lieutenant General Richard McCreery. The landing beach was 36 miles from end to end and ran from the village of Maiori in the northwest down to the villages of Paestum and Agropoli. The two army corps would initially be landed 10 miles apart, with subsequent movements to expand the bridgehead. Expanding the bridgehead was necessary in order to seize airfields, especially the one at Montecorvino, to take the high ground beyond the beach, and cut to German communications with Naples. The 7th Armoured Division would provide the main element of the initial reinforcements. The 82nd Airborne Division would be available to conduct landings from the air. Naval support for AVALANCHE was organised into the Western Naval Task Force under Admiral Hewitt. This was further sub-divided into a Northern Attack Force under Commodore G N Oliver, which would support X Corps, and a Southern Attack Force under Rear-Admiral J L Hall, USN, to support VI corps. The Salerno operation was built around a massive maritime operation; including merchant shipping the landing involved around 900 ships, numbers that would generate their own planning and force protection challenges.[23]

---

[16]Corelli Barnett, *Engage the Enemy More Closely: The Royal Navy in the Second World War,* (Penguin: London, 2001), p.685.

[17]In this, the operation was again reminiscent of Gallipoli. See T Higgins, *Winston Churchill and the Dardanelles* (London: Hindman, 1963).

[18]Though not without major disagreements between the Allies: see Carlo d'Este, *Fatal Decision: Anzio and the Battle for Rome,* (London: Fontana, 1992), p.32-33.

[19]General Mark Clark, *Calculated Risk: His Personal Story of the War in North Africa and Italy* (London: Harrap, 1951) p.183

[20]Barnett, p.655.

[21]Clark, p. 171. The choice of the landing site was subject to much debate. Clark was against Salerno, but representations from the airforce and navy ruled out operations further north. See Carlo D'Este, *Eisenhower: Allied Supreme Commander* (London: Weidenfeld & Nicolson, 2002) p.447.

[22]From Brigadier CJC Molony, *History of the Second World War, Vol. 5: The Mediterranean and Middle East* (London: HMSO, 1973) p.257.

[23]Barnett, p.662.

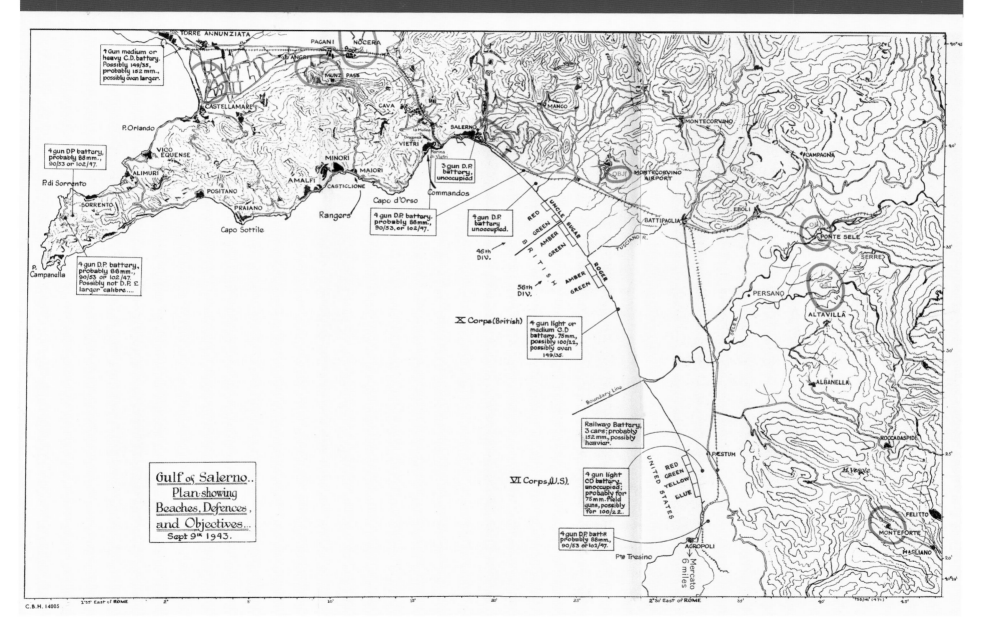

4 Gun medium or heavy C.D. battery. Possibly 149/35, probably 152 mm., possibly even larger.

4 gun DP battery, probably 88 mm., 90/53 or 102/47.

4 gun D.P. battery, probably 88 mm., 90/53 or 102/47. Possibly not D.P. £ larger calibre....

3 gun D.P. battery, unoccupied

Commandos

4 gun D.P. battery, probably 88 mm., 90/53, or 102/47.

Rangers

4 gun D.P. battery unoccupied.

46th DIV.

56th DIV.

X Corps (British)

4 gun light or medium C.D battery. 75 mm., possibly 100/22, possibly even 149/35.

Railway Battery, 3 cars; probably 152 mm., possibly heavier.

VI Corps (U.S.)

4 gun light CD battery, unoccupied; probably for 75 mm. Field guns, possibly for 100/22.

4 gun D.P. batt.ᵞ probably 88mm., 90/53 or 102/47.

Gulf of Salerno.. Plan showing Beaches, Defences, and Objectives... Sept 9ᵗʰ 1943.

C.B.H. 14005

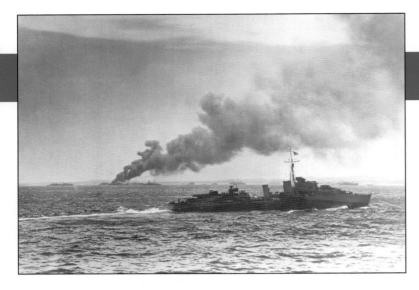

Royal Navy Ships providing NGS at Salerno. (NA)

Protection from the air, en-route and in the assault area, would be provided by Northwest African Coastal Air Force and Malta Air Command. In the assault area the air force would provide 660 fighters.[24] Air power was also used extensively to prepare the ground prior to AVALANCHE. The North African Air Force launched 4,500 sorties against command and transport and infrastructure targets, including airfields, dropping 6,500 tons of bombs.[25] Landing at Salerno would put the force towards the edge of the ranges of available land-based air cover. For this reason the assault force was allocated 'Force V': a carrier group including HMS *Illustrious* and four ex-US escort carriers (HMS *Attacker*, HMS *Battler*, HMS *Hunter* & HMS *Stalker*). Force V would be protected by 'Force H'; HMS *Nelson*, HMS *Rodney*, *Illustrious*, HMS *Warspite*, HMS *Valiant*, HMS *Formidable*, supported by the 4th, 8th and 24th destroyer flotillas.

Unless the momentum of the landing was maintained, the German defence might well have time to bring considerable forces to bear. The German commander responsible for central and southern Italy was Field Marshal Albert Kesselring. Less his unreliable Italian allies, Kesselring's forces consisted of the Tenth Army plus supporting forces. The Tenth army consisted of the 14th Panzer Corps and 76th Panzer Corps, totalling three Panzer, one Panzer-Grenadier and one parachute division. In addition. Kesselring had under his command the 11th Flak Corps (one Panzer Grenadier and one parachute division). The threat to the Allied operation was multi-dimensional; Kesselring also had under his command Air Fleet 2, and Naval Command Italy, which had light forces deployed in the Tyrrhenian Sea.[26] Although the Allied superiority in air and naval assets was considerable, it was certainly not complete. Additional German forces were deployed on Corsica and Sardinia. Kesselring was outnumbered, but not overwhelmingly so. Moreover he might also be able to call on reserves held in northern Italy.

A rapid exploitation of the landing at Salerno was vital for the success of the operation as a whole. First, although the beach itself was a good landing point, the surrounding terrain provided potential problems if it was not cleared quickly. The plains behind the beach were surrounded by the southern Apennines.

Not only did this high ground dominate the landing area, it was through these mountains, in particular two key passes, that 5th Army would have to pass in order to reach Naples. Unless the landing moved inland quickly, the terrain would provide a good base for a German defence. Second, unless the beachhead was developed with celerity, then either in defence or counter-attack the Germans would be able to exploit potential weaknesses in Clark's plan. These potential weaknesses included: the gap between the two landings; the need to capture airfields to allow land-based air power to be brought in; the obstacle provided by the river Sele and its tributary streams, which split the beachhead in two and could only be crossed by bridges; and the terrain beyond the beach, which was heavily obstructed by farms, gullies, groves and broken ground.[27]

Execution

In many respects the initial stages of the Salerno landing were a model of effective amphibious landings. As one army eyewitness commented 'It was all splendidly carried out …'.[28] Salerno was an expression of the experience that the Allies had accumulated from the landings in North Africa and Sicily as well as past failures such as Dieppe 1942. Co-ordinating the movement and assembly of the invasion forces was challenging because the forces were dispatched from different ports and organised

[24]Molony, p.271.

[25]WF Craven & JL Cate (Eds), *The Army Air Forces in World War Two, Vol 2: Torch to Pointblank, August 1942 to December 1943* (Washington: Office of Air Force History, 1983) p.504.

[26]Albert Kesselring (translated by Lynton Hudson), *The Memoirs of Field-Marshal Kesselring* (London: William Kimber, 1953) p.182.

[27]Eric Linklater, *The Campaign in Italy* (London: HMSO, 1977) p.62.

[28]Molony, p.275.

**by 10 September, the operation had begun to fail
even though the landing had succeeded**

by different headquarters. Nevertheless, informed by the experiences of TORCH and HUSKY, the assembly and dispatch of forces was handled well and the assault convoys sailed on 3 September 1943 without any major mishaps. D-day had been set at 9 September, with the landing at 0330.

Force protection was provided by air and naval assets. The naval covering force of four battleships, with two carriers and an escort of destroyers under Vice-Admiral Willis entered the Tyrrhenian sea on the 8 September. Here it was subjected to heavy attack by 30 torpedo bombers but suffered no damage and was able to place itself to provide air and naval gunfire support for the landing forces as they marshalled in their assembly positions and then advanced towards the beach. Vian's escort carrier force arrived from Malta to provide fighter cover. The threat situation was much reduced when, on the 8 September, the Italian's surrendered, removing the threat posed by their fleet.[29]

The landing itself was conducted in the same general manner as Sicily: the assault troops were embarked from transports to landing craft at sea, or were already deployed on larger infantry and tank landing craft, and moved in to shore in waves, the assault beaches being marked by vessels with beacons. The assault waves were supported by a variety of fire support landing craft, including three fitted with rockets.[30] The assault was directed from a headquarters ship, the *Ancon*. A belated attempt was made to achieve tactical surprise by using only a very abbreviated preparatory bombardment. This attempt failed: the German defences were already on alert and the assault was fired upon as it moved towards the shore by units of 16th Panzer Division. The last seriously opposed landing in Europe had been at Dieppe, in which the landing force had suffered 60 percent losses. At Salerno, however, the landing force fared much better. Although lit by flares and coming under fire from German artillery and machine guns, the assault forces were able to take the beach and move inland, though the fighting was often heavy, especially in the U.S. sector.

Despite the inevitable initial confusion, in which maintaining radio communications proved especially problematic, the Allies past experience allowed the establishment of a functioning beach organisation. Lessons from previous operations had shown the importance of deploying shore engineers and beach masters early on in order to organise the marshalling of troops and stores on the beach. Functioning logistic lines were established very quickly. Salerno was taken on D+1 and infantry landing craft and landing ships were used to establish a rolling supply link between Salerno and the supply ports in Sicily.[31]

Effective experience and training also facilitated the clearing of German minefields.[32] The difficult job of shifting troops ashore was facilitated by a 'shore to shore' logistic plan; landing craft were loaded with supply lorries in North Africa sailing to the beach via a refuelling stop in Sicily. They then disbursed their lorries onto the beach, taking on empty lorries for the return journey.

There were many elements of the landing which might have been improved upon in retrospect. The plan itself has been the subject of criticism. Clark landed three divisions over a front of thirty six miles. Indeed, the more successful the early stages of the landing, the weaker the landing forces position would get since the troops would be spread out over a progressively wider front.[33] The problems that this caused at Salerno were one reason for Eisenhower's insistence on a greater concentration of force at Normandy. In addition, the time available for planning the operation was certainly less than desirable. The objective, Naples, not finally agreed upon until seven weeks before D-Day, and D-Day was not confirmed at 9 September until the 17 August.[34] Command and control arrangements were hardly ideal by the standards of current doctrine; there was no joint force commander for the amphibious operation. Another area of controversy was the lack of preparatory bombardment

[29]S.W. Roskill, The War at Sea, Vol.III, Part 1, (London: HMSO, 1960) p.170.
[30]C. J. Bruce, *Invaders: British and American Experience of Seaborne Landings 1939-1945*, (Annapolis: Naval Institute Press, 1999) pp.5-6.
[31]Roskill, p.297.
[32]L.E.H. Maund,, *Assault From the Sea*, (London: Methuen, 1949) p.225.
[33]d'Este, *Eisenhower*, p448.
[34]Barnett, p.662.

British troops and vehicles from 128 Brigade, 46th Division are unloaded from LST 383 onto the beaches at Salerno, September 1943. (IWM NA6630)

of the beaches, which in retrospect was probably a failure. Nevertheless, these problems did not, of themselves cause the landing to fail. By nightfall of 10 September the assault had not taken all of its objectives, but the landing was firmly established ashore, and ready to develop the bridgehead that was now around five miles deep. In relative terms the initial stages of the operation had gone very well.

Challenges

In war, failure often is not self-evident. The early success of the landing obscured a number of quite basic difficulties. In fact, by the 10 September, the operation had begun to fail even though the landing had succeeded. This was because Clark was unable to maintain the momentum of the operation and so could not translate the landing at Salerno into a meaningful push towards Naples. To understand why this was the case, we need to examine two factors: the problems associated with tactical build-up; and the actions of the enemy.

Tactical build-up refers to the rate at which the landing force can be reinforced. For some enthusiasts, manoeuvre warfare derives part of its attraction from the way in which it may put less emphasis on numbers and more on technique.[35] In the case of the Allies at Salerno, however, numbers mattered; the rate at which the Allies built up their forces and logistics at the beachhead

needed to exceed the rate at which the Germans built up theirs if the Allies were to have the wherewithal to engage in exploitation. However, the Allied plans had an inbuilt logistic bottleneck. Early on in the planning, the Royal Navy raised the issue of the difficulty in confirming the availability of landing craft.[36] There were a limited number of landing craft and competing claims from the Pacific and European theatres. Indeed, it was for this reason that BAYTOWN and AVALANCHE were launched sequentially, rather than in parallel – there was not enough landing craft to support both.[37] The Royal Navy worried that the available amphibious transport would limit their ability to reinforce the beachhead sufficiently quickly. By the time this became a recognised issue in early September, however, it was too late to do anything about it.[38] The Deputy Chief of Staff at Allied Forces Headquarters told the War Office that 'The follow-up problem is perhaps more complicated than anything we have met hitherto'.[39]

The lack of amphibious transport meant two things. First, from the outset the overall balance of numerical advantage would

not be overwhelmingly in the Allies favour. Even if everything went as planned, the margin of error was slim. The Allies estimated that on D-Day German forces would amount to one Panzer division and up to five parachute battalions. It was estimated by Allied intelligence that this would increase to five divisions by D+5 and to six and a half divisions by D+22. By D+22, however, the Allies planned to have available one armoured division, three tank battalions, one airborne division and four infantry divisions.[40] This was hardly an overwhelming advantage, if the Germans decided to make a fight of it. Indeed, Clark had originally wanted to combine the Salerno operation with an airdrop along the Volturno River by the 82nd Airborne Division. It was intended that this drop would help to interdict the movement of German reinforcements to the beachhead and

---

[35]Especially so from a contemporary British perspective, although this makes a virtue out of necessity. However, as the earlier comments on attrition and the manoeuvrist approach indicate, the approach can equally well be associated with mass.
[36]Roskill, pp.155-159.
[37]D'Este, *Eisenhower*, p.447.

[38]Roskill, p.297.
[39]Molony, p.260.
[40]Bartlett, p.666.

sow confusion and uncertainty in the German commanders. In the event, late in the planning, Clark had the division removed from his command and it was instead allocated to a drop on Rome (later cancelled).[41]

Second, the shortage of transport meant also that the Allies had to make detailed assumptions about how the battle would unfold in order to best tailor the flow of reinforcements. The reinforcement schedule had to be carefully choreographed and reflected an assessment of what kind of forces would be required, and when they would be needed. The reinforcement schedule assumed that the main need would be armour (hence the use of 7th Armoured Division as the main reinforcing element) and

that this force would need to be brought in between D+12 and D+17.[42] The lack of flexibility in the reinforcement plan, which was a function of a shortage of transport, was a potential problem. Clearly, if the battle developed in a manner that differed from Allied assumptions then serious difficulties might emerge. The problem of reinforcements was worsened by two other factors. First, if there were a crisis, where would additional reinforcements come from? Four additional divisions were available, two in North Africa and two in Sicily – but not all of them were at full strength and they would, of course, still need to be transported to Salerno.[43] Second, because the landing had failed to achieve all of its initial objectives, the beachhead was still relatively shallow and therefore cramped and heavily obstructed. Even if more troops could be funnelled in, would the existing logistics framework cope?[44] The problem of tactical build-up would have important potential consequences for the Salerno operation. Realising manoeuvre warfare requires not just flexibility in mind set, but also flexibility in capabilities; one needs the means to be manoeuvrist as well as the intent. If the Salerno landing did not go exactly according to plan, Clark was likely to be critically short of the military means to respond to

the changed military situation. The problem of tactical build-up would have been of less salience if the Germans had acted as Allied optimists anticipated; however, they did not. The landing did not precipitate a wholesale German retreat. Kesselring was an able and energetic commander. In pondering potential developments after the end of the Sicily campaign he based his defensive dispositions on a number of assumptions. First, he believed that an attack on mainland Italy was likely. Kesselring recognised, as Churchill did, the potential opportunities that this might deliver for applying additional pressure on Germany. Second, he was cognisant that the combination of the geography of Italy and the demonstrated Allied amphibious capabilities made a landing against the mainland likely. His analysis of the strengths and weaknesses of the potential landing sites led him to believe that attacks via the Adriatic and north of Rome were unlikely. Attacks further south he viewed as sufficiently likely that they would have to be planned for. The Bay of Salerno was, in Kesselring's view, 'uniquely suitable' for an amphibious landing and would need to be defended.[45] Eisenhower himself was clear that the greatest disadvantage of the Salerno landing was that 'its logic was obvious to the enemy as well as to us.'[46] Eisenhower went into the landings 'with no illusions of surprising the enemy'[47] but he believed that air and naval gunfire support would allow the Allies to land successfully.[48] Kesselring, too, believed that Allied air and naval gun support were sufficiently

[41]Clark, p.177.
[42]Molony, p.304.
[43]Ibid., p.305
[44]Ibid., p.286
[45]Kesselring, p.183

[46]Dwight D. Eisenhower, *Crusade in Europe* (New York: Doubleday, 1952) p.185. To draw another parallel with Gallipoli, the same point was made about the Bulair landing beach. For this reason the Allies used an amphibious feint at Bulair and landed elsewhere.
[47]Eisenhower, p.186.
[48]He applied this same view to the Normandy landings.

overwhelming that the Allies would crush a defence focused on the water's edge; he therefore favoured a mobile defence concept based on defence in depth with reserves held back for the counter-attack.[49]

Kesselring's analysis would have an important bearing on the outcome of the Salerno landings. War is, amongst other things, an adversarial activity: it is fought against another human entity. In Clausewitz's words, 'war is always the shock of two hostile bodies in collision, not the action of a living power upon an inanimate mass'.[50] Clearly, the success of the Salerno landings would relate in part to the competence of the Allies in planning and execution. However, the important facets of manoeuvre warfare such as initiative, surprise, and tempo are essentially relational concepts; one holds them only in relation to the actions and mind-sets of the enemy. Many of the theoretical

benefits that the Salerno landings might deliver in terms of shock and dislocation were unlikely to be delivered in reality, simply because Kesselring had already second-guessed Allied intentions. One of the perennial dilemmas of amphibious defence is whether to focus on the forward defence of the beach, or whether to adopt a mobile defence based on counter-attack. This dilemma was at the heart of the differences between Rommel and Von Runstedt over how to respond to an Allied invasion of France. Kesselring established a defensive deployment that focused on allowing the Allies to land and then attacking them with reserve forces deployed further in land. The 14th Panzer Corps was deployed in the Naples area, and the 76th Panzer Corps further to the south with orders to conduct a slow withdrawal if southern Italy were invaded. The 16th Panzer Division was split into four battle groups, each group separated by around six miles, the bulk of which were deployed at Eboli-Battipaglia, near Salerno and about 3 to 6 miles from the beach. At Salerno, therefore, the beach was defended by limited numbers of troops. Most of the division was deployed several miles to the rear in position to counter attack.[51] In addition, the defences around the Salerno beach were augmented with the deployment of new mines, artillery and mortars. With the Hermann Goering

Divison near Naples and the 15th Panzer Grenadier Division at Gaeta, Kesselring had around 20,000 men in the vicinity of Salerno with another 100,000 available to reinforce them once a landing had been confirmed.[52]

Kesselring's reading of the situation made surprise more difficult to achieve at the operational and tactical levels. Since manoeuvre warfare is associated with the concept of doing the unexpected, surprise is an important enabler. Kesselring's deployment in depth made tactical surprise less relevant. The Allies first tried to confuse the Germans as to the general target of the landing. The assault shipping sailed via the west of Sicily, partly to avoid as much German air attack as possible, but also partly to convince the Germans that the landing might be directed against Sardinia or Corsica. German aircraft spotted the allied fleet on 7 September; at that point it was clear that the target was mainland Italy, but its exact destination remained a mystery. The mobility of the amphibious force meant that Kesselring could not be clear whether the objective might be Naples, Rome or Campagna. The Royal Navy conducted preparatory operations in order to achieve tactical surprise, using smaller craft to conduct shelling and raids at Naples and to the north. However, the continued presence of the invasion fleet in the Tyrrenhian sea convinced Kesselring that the landings would come at Salerno.[53] Ultra intelligence revealed that the

[49]Theodore L. Gatchel, *At the Water's Edge: Defending Against the Modern Amphibious Assault,* (Annapolis: Naval Institute Press, 1996) p.50.
[50]Carl Von Clausewitz, *On War* (Ware: Wordsworth, 1997) p.8.
[51]Gatchel, p.52.
[52]Clark, p.180.
[53]Kesselring, p.184.

less like an avalanche and more like a snowball

LCT-222 landing U.S. Army vehicles on an Italian beach. (NARA)

Germans expected an attack and that troops had been alerted on the 8th to expect an attack the next day. Lieutenant General Hermann Balck, commander of 14th Panzer Corps, was alerted by scattered aerial reports of the presence of the Allied armada. He put his troops on maximum alert.[54] Even with air superiority, it was impossible to keep such a large amphibious armada hidden from view on an extended sailing. Uncertainty remained about the scale of the landing there and whether it might be a diversionary operation as a prelude to an invasion further north. This meant that a concentration against the Salerno beachhead was not ordered until later on 9 September when the German commander became convinced that this was the main assault. However, since the German defensive concept was founded on destroying the landing through counter attack, not at the water's edge, this did not constitute a major difficulty.

Failure

The combination of the problems of tactical build-up and the German defensive concept robbed the Allied landing of its momentum and its ability to sustain initiative and tempo relative to the Germans. From 10 - 12 September, the Allied assault attempted to expand the bridgehead, gaining some ground. By the end of this period, however, the Allied attack culminated,

as the greater rate of German reinforcement forced the Allies onto the defensive. Alexander sent a signal on the 12th to the Chief of the Imperial General Staff that 'I am not satisfied with the situation at AVALANCHE. The build-up is slow and they are pinned down to a bridgehead which has not enough depth.'[55]

To compound matters, the 8th Army's advance from the south was slower than anticipated. Montgomery had always been sceptical about the possibility of a rapid advance up the Italian mainland. Montgomery's orders were opaque and failed to convey the importance of the 8th Army's role with the necessary clarity.[56] Even when Montgomery's orders were made more explicit the excellent defensive terrain and German tactical skill dramatically slowed the 8th Army's advance. It became clear that the link with the AVALANCHE landings would occur much later than anticipated.[57] The 76th Panzer Corps conducted a staged withdrawal northwards and Kesselring was able to effect a concentration of German forces against the Salerno bridgehead. German reserves moved up and the local German commander believed that there was a genuine opportunity to crush the landing forces. The Germans occupied the high ground around the beachhead, giving them the opportunity to observe allied movements, to shift reserves to meet allied thrusts and to bring

artillery fire along the depth of the Allied lodgement. By the 12th, Clark's assault has stalled. As Geoffrey Perret comments dryly, the landing had become "...less like an avalanche and more like a snowball'.[58]

From the 13th to the 15th the Germans began a series of counter-attacks. The German defence had been less co-ordinated than it might have because of fears that additional landings might take place closer to Naples, and because fuel shortages slowed the arrival of reinforcements from the south. Once the scale of the amphibious operation had been clarified, the German 10th Army was committed to larger scale counter attacks. Kesselring was not unhappy with the results: 'The fighting on the beaches ... went better than I had dared hope.'[59] The Allied position was worsened by the fact that the Germans proved to be competent enough exponents of manoeuvre warfare at the tactical level. Using infiltration tactics, probing for weak spots and using good all-arms co-ordination, German forces were progressively able

[54] Molony, p.267

[55] Ibid., p.299

[56] Field Marshal B. Montgomery, *The Memoirs of Field-Marshal Montgomery* (London: Collins, 1958) p.192

[57] Field Marshal Lord Carver, *The Imperial War Museum Book of the War in Italy 1943-1945*, (London: Pan, 2001), p.62.

[58] Quoted in d'Este, *Eisenhower*, p.448.

[59] Kesselring, p.186.

to push the Allies back, taking Persano and drive the allies back from Ponte Sele and Altavilla. The German offensive threatened to drive apart VI and X corps.

The reinforcement plan, so carefully crafted, proved wholly inadequate. The crisis had emerged much earlier in the campaign than expected, D+5 to D+7 rather than D+12 to D+17. Moreover, Clark's overwhelming need was for more infantry not tanks.[60] The shallowness of the beachhead meant that German artillery could play the full depth of the lodgement. German shelling forced the closure of Salerno harbour. Combined with fire onto the beach, this resulted in logistic chaos with shipping packed into the bay unable to unload. With the exits from the Salerno beachhead blocked by the Germans it proved difficult to maintain an ordered logistic system for the materiel that could be unloaded. One eyewitness described the beaches as '...like the car park at Ascot on Gold Cup Day.'[61] Lacking troops, Clark was simply unable to create an effective reserve force with which to influence the battlefield. Clark was forced to use a scratch force, including mechanics and even a regimental band, to halt the spearhead of the German assault.[62]

Clark's options were limited. Reinforcements were brought in, but because of the obstacles to an effective tactical build-up these were not numerous enough to allow the Allies to do more than maintain a defence. The 82nd Airborne's mission to Rome had been cancelled and was once again available for Clark to use. On 13 September

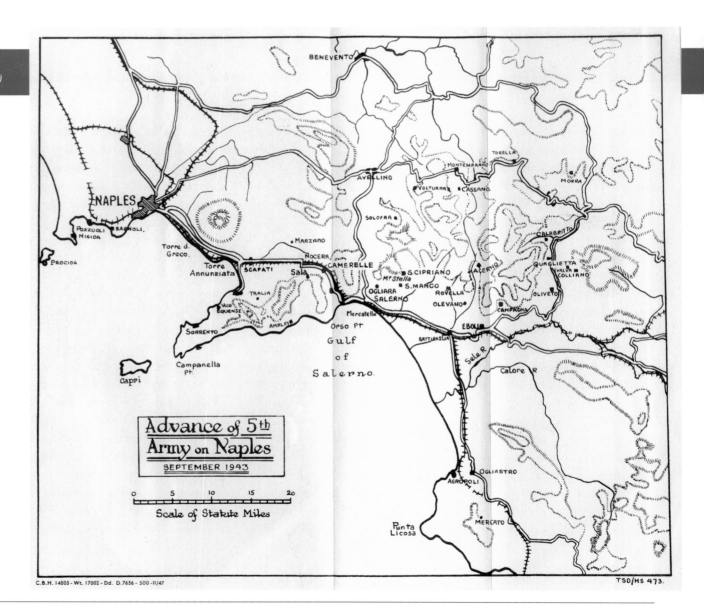

[60]Molony, p.304.
[61]Maund, p.225.
[62]Clark, p.196.

The continued threat posed by German airpower placed high value assets such as Vian's carriers at great risk

elements of the division were airdropped into the beachhead, with the remainder following by sea. Cruisers were used to transfer more troops from Tripoli and to provide additional logistic support. However, the total number of additional troops made available to Clark during the critical period of the crisis amounted to only two parachute battalions and around 1,500 infantry.[63]

Since the 5th Army could not restore the situation at Salerno through reinforcement, Clark was forced to search for alternatives. One source of succour was naval gunfire support. After D-Day, Bombardment Liaison Officers (BLOs) were pushed ashore with the troops to help co-ordinate naval gunfire.[64] US and Royal Navy ships added considerably to the weight of firepower available to the Allied troops: for example, HMS *Mauritius* fired off over 1,000 6-inch shells from 10 - 13 September. *Warspite* and *Valiant* were used to bring fire and air attack to bear on German lines of communication. Some destroyers were deployed so close to the shore that they were fired upon by German tanks.[65] On the 12th additional warships were brought in to augment the 5th Army's firepower including the cruisers *Aurora* and *Penelope*. A reliance on naval gunfire support was not without its penalties. The need for this kind of support kept naval assets tied to the vulnerable assault area leaving them exposed to air attack. The Allies paid the price for failing to have a more complete air superiority. Dornier 17 bombers posed a particular threat:

these aircraft were armed with radio controlled FX-1400 radio guided bombs. Air attacks from wireless controlled bombs hit three cruisers and on 16 September the battleship *Warspite* was hit and immobilised.[66] This damage was particularly dangerous because the Allied navy was operating beyond its established sea bases. The continued threat posed by German airpower placed major ships such as Vian's carriers at great risk. This risk was multiplied because of the high attrition suffered by the Royal Navy's Seafires, mostly through damage caused by deck landings rather than enemy action. On 12 September Vian was forced to withdraw the vulnerable carriers and send the remaining Seafires to a makeshift airfield ashore.

Clark also turned to airpower for help. Airpower had already made an important contribution to 5th Army's assault on Salerno. Preparatory air attacks had inflicted heavy damage on German airfields. Amongst other targets, on D-day itself air attacks were launched on German headquarters, railways, and critical transport nodes. The weight of air attack was dramatically increased from 12 September, with strategic bombing assets pressed into a tactical airpower role. From 12 - 15 September Strategic Air Force dropped 3,000 tons of bombs.[67] On the night of 14/15 September the air force launched 2,000 sorties, redoubling strikes on German troop and gun positions, and on German communications and logistic targets.[68] This sortie level needs to be compared with that of the German

airforce which made only 162 sorties, most of these delivered on Allied shipping, rather than against 5th Army's troops.[69] The 29th Panzer Grenadier Division recorded that '...the strafing we underwent at this time, and particularly on 14 September, put all our previous experiences in the shade.'[70]

Clark also looked to another alternative means of supporting his beachhead; an airdrop. Clark ordered the 509th Parachute battalion to be dropped into the area of Avellino on the night of 14 September. In theory, this would put the battalion into the German rear. The results of this move were disappointing. Unable to use gliders because of the difficult Italian terrain, the Allies suffered many of the problems that had plagued the Germans in Crete and which would afflict the Allied drops on Normandy as part of D-Day. The paratroopers were landed in a scattered manner, and Clark did not have the strength to launch an assault to link up with them. Although the landing did cause much confusion, it failed to relieve much of the pressure on the beachhead. Few of the paratroops reached Allied lines; indeed it took around two months for the survivors of the drop to be gathered together again.[71]

German pressure on the beachhead nevertheless continued. Clark therefore considered another option: withdrawal. With German forces within two miles of the beach, Clark asked the Navy to prepare plans for an amphibious withdrawal. In the first instance

[63]Molony, p.307.
[64]JD Ladd, *Assault From the Sea*, (Vancouver: David & Charles, 1976) p.115.
[65]Bartlett, p.675.
[66]Gatchel, p.55.
[67]Craven & Cate, p.535.
[68]Molony, p.306.
[69]Ibid., p.282
[70]Ibid., p.315
[71]Craven & Cate, p.533.

Axis aerial reconnaissance photograph revealing Allied shipping in Naples harbour following the city's liberation on 1 October 1943. (NHB)

Clark considered a partial withdrawal, preparing to evacuate one beach in order to reinforce the other.[72] The navy were not at all keen given the potential pitfalls associated with withdrawal operations; Admiral Sir Andrew Cunningham arguing that it 'would have resulted in a reverse of the first magnitude'.[73] Oliver argued '…in my view it would be suicide.'[74] Transferring forces from one portion of the beach would allow the smaller beachhead to be enfiladed, making the lodgement even less secure. Full withdrawal would have proved even more problematic. It would have been conducted without the benefit of a port, without air superiority, and in close proximity to the enemy.[75] From 12 September, the Salerno landing had failed as a manoeuvrist enterprise. It had instead become an exercise in attrition on German, not Allied, terms in which Clark's priority was not exploitation but survival.

In the end, however, withdrawal proved unnecessary. The allied troops hung on; air and naval firepower pounded the German forces; and pressure from the 8th Army mounted. The Allies benefited from the decision by the German High Command not to sanction the release to Kesselring of German reserve divisions in northern Italy. By the 15 September Kesselring had abandoned the idea of driving the landing back into the sea. Recognising that the moment to crush the landing had passed, Kesselring executed a staged withdrawal from the Salerno area. On 16 September advance elements of 8th and 5th Armies finally made contact.

---

[72]Bruce, p.102.
[73]d'Este, *Fatal Decision*, p.41.
[74]Quoted in Bartlett, p.675
[75]For some of the problems see I Speller and C Tuck, *Amphibious Warfare: The Theory and Practice of Amphibious Operations in the 20th Century* (Staplehurst: Spellmount, 2001) pp.119-133.

But there was to be no vigorous pursuit. Even as German counterattacks were underway on 12 September, Kesselring has already been considering how he could develop a more prolonged defence of central Italy and hold Rome for as long as possible. He ordered the preparation of a thick defensive belt, which would become known as the Gothic Line. This defensive line was 135 miles wide running from Gaeta to the Adriatic, Italy's narrowest point. Rather than a single linear defence, the line consisted of an array of fortified strong points deployed in depth and making the best use of the good defensive terrain. When the Tenth Army began a measured withdrawal from Salerno to a line on the Volturno river, Kesselring began the process of falling back on this strong new prepared position. The Allies took Naples on 1 October, but it was hardly the hoped for victory. The Germans had held the Salerno landing for eight days, threatening to drive it back into the sea. When this proved impossible they were able to withdraw in stages to a pre-prepared defensive position of great strength. Clark commented that 'We had come along a rough road to get there [Naples] from Salerno, and we had paid a heavy price for the short progress...'[76]

Conclusion

Tactical action failed to realise the manoeuvrist operational concept that underpinned the Salerno operation. Some critics simply regarded the operation as a mistaken venture: Alexander regarded the operation as 'a dangerous gamble'.[77] Lieutenant General Fridolin von Senger und Etterlin, commander of the defences of Corsica and Sicily and then later of XIV corps on mainland Italy, was critical of the Allied choice of a landing at Salerno. Von Senger argued that, since Corsica and Sardinia were the German soft spots, they should have been invaded first. The islands could then have been used to provide air cover for amphibious operations between Pisa and Elba. Amphibious operations so far north might have forced a major re-alignment of German lines.[78] Others saw Salerno as a valid concept undermined by poor execution. Montgomery argued before the landings took place that 'In my view, AVALANCHE was a good operation to carry out', but that not enough effort had been put into making it work.[79] Instead, he argued that the 8th Army should have been made available to reinforce the Salerno landings, or to poise in opposition to threaten additional landings.[80]

More modern critics might attack the deliberate conduct of the landing operations. Less deliberate, more manoeuvrist approaches to amphibious operations at the tactical level might include replacing landing waves and beachhead consolidation with landing at multiple points accompanied with rapid advances into the enemy depth. In theory this would allow the commander to 'test' the enemy defences, exploring weakness and allowing reconnaissance pull.[81] This approach would be facilitated by de-centralisation of command, better joint integration, a 'floating supply' logistic structure and deep attacks using air power.[82] Aside from the problems of implementing such as a concept with the technology and logistics that existed in 1943, such an approach would only have worked if sufficient reserves had been available to reinforce the key axes sufficiently, which they were not. In the final analysis, the Salerno operation failed to realise its potential because the 5th Army could not maintain the momentum generated by the initial landing. The failure to effect a breakout from the beachhead was less about too little dispersal and de-centralisation in the conduct of the operation and much more about the failure to attain the desirable conditions for a favourable tactical build-up. In-built logistic constraints were contained within the plan that made it difficult to reinforce the beachhead quickly. Allied commanders at the strategic and operational levels failed to anticipate the adoption by the Germans of an elastic mobile defence. Lacking any great advantage of surprise or numbers the Allies could not maintain the momentum of Operation AVALANCHE. Without momentum the operation could not hope to maintain the initiative over the Germans or to generate a favourable tempo of operations. On 9 September, 1943, the failure of Clark's initial plan and the lack of the means to the generate alternatives meant that the degeneration of the Salerno landings from offensive manoeuvre warfare into an unfavourable defensive battle of attrition was not just a possibility; it was almost inevitable.

[76]Clark, p.208.
[77]d'Este, *Eisenhower*, p448
[78]F. Von Senger und Etterlin, *Neither Fear Nor Hope* (London: MacDonald, 1970) p.178.
[79]Montgomery, p.190.
[80]d'Este, *Eisenhower*, p.449.
[81]Lind, *Maneuver Warfare Handbook*, p.36-37.
[82]Ibid., p.38-39.

Developing themes post-Salerno

- **Approach in darkness.** Under the cover of darkness, the landing force should approach as quickly as possible using fast ships carrying special landing craft.

- **Speed and Surprise.** With the landing ships still out of sight of land, landing craft flotillas should assemble and then approach from ship to shore en masse, at speed, under cover of both smoke and naval gunfire support to achieve tactical surprise.

- **Reserves.** Once surprise has been achieved sufficient floating reserves should be in place and landed in waves in order to exploit any early gains.

- **Air superiority.** Air cover is essential in an amphibious operation, and therefore aircraft carriers should be available or local airfields should be secured as early as possible. In the case of Salerno, this might have been easier to achieve had the islands of Corsica or Sardinia already been in allied hands.

- **Maintaining momentum.** Commanders at every level should be reminded that the momentum generated by the initial landing should be maintained. Without that momentum, the initiative and tempo of operations is likely to be lost.

- **Securing the beachhead.** Following the landing of the floating reserve, where success has been won, the requirement is to capture a covering position sufficiently far inland to make the beach and anchorage secure from enemy gunfire and air attack.

- **Logistic support.** Logistics are the 'lifeblood of war' and it is essential that the build up of materiel is rapid and efficient. This enables the commander the opportunity to maintain the offensive spirit. (This does not necessarily require a land based logistic structure).

- **Safe anchorage.** Once logistic supplies were being off-loaded, the discharge of personnel, vehicles, ammunition and stores should be undertaken using other special landing craft as quickly and efficiently as possible.

Further Reading

History of the Commandos in the Mediterranean Sept. 1943 to May 1945

Bruce, Colin John, *Invaders: British and American Experience of Seaborne Landings 1939-1945,* (London: Chatham, 1999)

Churchill, Thomas B. L., *Commando Crusade,* (London: William Kimber, 1987)

Gatchel, Theodore L., *At the Water's Edge: Defending Against the Modern Amphibious Assault,* (Annapolis, Maryland: Naval Institute Press, 1996)

Mitchell, Raymond, *Marine Commando: Sicily and Salerno, 1943 with 41 Royal Marines Commando,* (London: Robert Hale, 1988)

Morison, Samuel Eliot., *Sicily-Salerno-Anzio January 1943 – June 1944.* Vol. 9 of *History of United States Naval Operations in World War II,* (London: Oxford University Press, 1954)

Pond, Hugh, *Salerno,* (London: William Kimber, 1961)

Biography

Dr Christopher Tuck is a Lecturer at the Defence Studies Department, King's College London, based at the Joint Services Command and Staff College. He joined JSCSC in 1997. Prior to this, he was a lecturer at the Royal Military Academy, Sandhurst (1994-1997) where he worked in the Department of Defence and International Affairs. He has also worked as a researcher for a foreign policy lobbying, investigating aspects of Global Governance. His publications include: *Amphibious Warfare: The Theory and Practice of Amphibious Operations in the 20th Century* (Spellmount: 2001), co-authored with Dr Ian Speller.

Termoli
Operation DEVON, October 1943

By Major Mark Bentinck RM (Rtd)

The allies landed in Sicily on 10 July 1943 – the 8th Army under Montgomery, and the U.S. 7th Army under Patton, and by early September they were ready to cross the Straits of Messina. On 3 September Montgomery landed on the toe of Italy, with the U.S. 5th Army landing at Salerno on 9 September, and Italian capitulation followed immediately. Also on this date the British 1st Airborne Division took Taranto, and moved on Bari, where they were joined by the British 78th Division. Foggia fell a week later. The outline plan was for the 5th Army to fight up the west coast, and the 8th Army the east.

The Germans retreated in good order, making good use of the mountainous terrain, demolitions, and mines to delay the Allied advance. However by the beginning of October allied troops were in contact with the enemy 8 miles south of the River Biferno. This river runs at a right angle towards the coast, entering the sea near the small town of Termoli. The natural obstacle that the river presented offered the Germans another opportunity to hold the Allies up, and was covered by the 1st Parachute Division, part of Kesselring's 10th Army. It could be quickly reinforced and strengthened if threatened.

The 2nd Special Service Brigade (later, with the others, they were more aptly renamed 'Commando' Brigades) was led by the Deputy Commander, Lieutenant Colonel John Durnford-Slater, and arrived in Bari by landing craft on the same day as the Germans evacuated it, 30 September 1944. Instead of the expected 'run-

3 Commando, Operation DEVON, October 1943. (RMM)

ashore' they were told to prepare for an operation, and busied themselves in replenishing ammunition and regrouping in the landing craft. They then sailed to Manfredonia for final orders.

The plan (Operation DEVON) was to make an amphibious right hook round the coast to Termoli, which would turn the river

Biferno defence line and the Germans' right flank, and attack their rear. It would also gain us a useful harbour, and give us the key road west to Campobasso and Naples. For this operation the Brigade consisted of the following elements: 40 RM Commando (Lieutenant Colonel JC Manners); 3 Commando (Captain AG Komrower); Special Raiding Squadron (1st SAS - Major Mayne). It

was a remarkably small force for the task: owing to casualties 40 Commando was 100 men under strength (a Commando Unit was nominally 450 men, but they were rarely up to complement), and Captain Komrower, in the absence of Lieutenant Colonel P Young who was ill, commanded 4 troops of 3 Commando (normally 60 men per troop, but here mustering only 180 men in all).

Termoli itself is a small coastal town and fishing port 120 miles from Bari, and offered the allies a small, but much needed harbour. The older buildings and church stand on a small promontory with the houses on the northern side overlooking the harbour. The east side of the town is bordered by a cultivated valley which extends inland beyond the built up area, and to the west the ground falls away gradually to sea level. A minor road follows the line of a narrow plateau southward and inclines gently to a moderate crestline (Point 169) before descending again to Guglionesi, a large village about 10 miles inland. Information regarding the enemy in the vicinity of Termoli was

limited, with no aerial photographs available, and only a small-scale and inaccurate map. The primary routes of communication in 1943 were the railway, which followed the line of the coast and marked the inland boundary of the town at that time, and Highway 16, the coastal road from which the winding Highway 87 connects with Naples to the west.

It was decided to land the force on the night of 1/2 October, about a mile west of the town. 3 Commando would land in six LCAs and establish a small beachhead. Lieutenant Colonel Durnford-Slater's HQ would follow them ashore in a seventh LCA and 40 RM Commando and 1st SAS would land from four LCI(L)s. There was to be no fire support. The task of 40 Commando was to pass through the beachhead and capture the town and harbour. The SAS would also pass through 3 Commando, capture the road junction of the Highways 87 and 16, and reconnoitre eastwards along Route 16. If the road and rail bridges over the River Biferno were still intact they were to guard these until

contact was made with 11th Brigade coming from the East. The understanding between Durnford-Slater's force and the landing craft flotilla was so close that only half a sheet of notepaper was necessary for the operation order. Major Brian Franks the principal (and often only) brigade staff officer had a great dislike for paperwork, 'The Brigade filing system is here' he would say, tapping the pockets of his uniform!'[1]

After a postponement of 24 hours for an improvement in the sea conditions the detachment sailed from Manfredonia at noon on 2 October in LCIs and LCAs of the 22nd Landing-craft Flotilla, under the command of Lieutenant Commander R Lammert RNVR. The weather was settled, the sea conditions were good and the LCIs, with LCAs in tow, made steady headway, until LCI 136 grounded on a sandbank about a mile off-shore, and four miles short of the objective. The problem was resolved, and 3 Commando were transferred to the LCAs, and made a dry landing, quickly forming a bridgehead, at about 0230. 150 yards inland on the railway line 3 Commando captured a train, complete with driver and fireman, and 12 sleeping German soldiers in a coach: a large metal hook on a flat-bed carriage was ready to tear up the track as the train moved forward. The other units followed, with many men not so lucky, and having to swim ashore: every radio set of 40 Commando was 'drowned', and remained non-operational throughout the subsequent action, while the medium machine guns, sorely missed later, had to be left behind.

[1]*The Green Beret - The Story of the Commandos* by Hilary St George Saunders

40 Commando paraded for inspection, and being congratulated by General Montgomery following the Termoli Operation. (RMM)

Some 20 enemy in this area were killed and 50 captured, and by 0800 3 October the force had taken all its objectives

Surprise was maintained until 40 Commando, now well into the town, encountered an Italian civilian who, frightened out of his wits, screamed loudly: surprise was lost, and a fierce battle with German soldiers took place in the area of the railway station. Demolitions were found in place ready to destroy both the station and its water tower. Some 20 enemy in this area were killed and 50 captured, and by 0800 3 October the force had taken all its objectives. The Royal Marines then secured Pt 169, 4 km south-west of Termoli, while the SAS made contact with a battalion of Lancashire Fusiliers at the demolished road bridge over the Biferno. So complete was the surprise that up to 1100 hours various German vehicles continued to drive into the area, only to be ambushed, thus confirming that the presence of the British was quite unsuspected - the German NAAFI supplies were much appreciated! Meanwhile, using a temporary bridge over the Biferno, reinforcements from 78 Division boosted the Allied numbers in town during the day and following night. The next morning, the Commandos were withdrawn into the town, their task seemingly finished.

The Germans did not intend to let this key town slip from their grasp. On 4 October at about mid-day, it became apparent that a counter-attack was inevitable. 3 Commando and a SAS Troop were sent back to positions they had occupied previously, where they joined 8th Battalion The Argyll and Sutherland Highlanders and elements of the Reconnaissance Regiment, together with 4 x 6-pounder anti tank guns, a 19-pounder anti-tank gun and 3 Vickers machine guns operated by the Kensingtons. This sector was commanded by Lieutenant Colonel Chavasse DSO. Dug in, now lashed by driving rain, they awaited the inevitable attack. The remainder of the SAS and the Royal Marines were allowed to rest in the town, having had little sleep in the last seven days - the move up the coast had been marked by rough weather before the start, allowing no rest while at sea. Apart from making the conditions miserable, the rain had caused the Sappers' temporary bridge over the Biferno to be washed away, and the force was now isolated. To add to their worries a patrol brought in an ominous prisoner - a member of 26th Panzer Division.

At dawn on 5 October a major German attack commenced, with air support, and 40 Commando were sent to reinforce the western perimeter of the town, while Lieutenant Colonel Durnford-Slater assumed overall command of the defence of Termoli. In the sector manned by 3 Commando most of the Argylls and the Reconnaissance Regiment were driven back, with the anti-tank gunners opening fire too early, and giving their position away. A tenuous radio link brought support from field artillery and, later, Kittyhawk fighters. Pressure was kept up on the position throughout the day and following night, with tanks, mortar fire and infantry all thrown against them. During the night 3 Commando was forced to withdraw into Termoli itself. The town remained under continuous heavy and accurate shellfire for several days to come: this was found to be directed by a German in the clock tower of the church, who was eliminated. 40 Commando, covering the railway line, was subject to intermittent fire, but with the arrival of further allied troops and tanks its position was less hard pressed. The last efforts of the enemy were against 40 Commando in the morning of 6 October on the outskirts of the town, but by midday the enemy was retreating, and the battle of Termoli was over.

British 8th Army
shoulder patch. (NHB)

Conclusions

This operation was a classic use of the sea to outflank strong enemy positions, and to restore the ability of the Allies to manoeuvre by forcing the enemy to withdraw. Security was excellent, and the speed with which the operation was mounted clearly caught the enemy by surprise. The ability to mount the operation quickly, and to overcome unexpected problems, was due to flexibility, and the high degree of well practised co-operation with other arms, especially the landing craft crews. The ability to move fast and surprise the enemy was critical, but equally important was the ability of lightly armed troops to fight with tenacity, skill and bravery to hold what they have taken.

Further Reading

40 Cdo War Diary ADM 202/87

Beadle, J.C., *The Light Blue Lanyard – 50 Years with 40 Commando Royal Marines*, (Worcester: Square One, 1992)

Farran, Roy, *Winged Dagger: Adventures on Special Service*, (London: Cassell, 1998. Reprint) Book II Chapter 5.

Ladd, James, *Commandos and Rangers of World War 2*, (London: Macdonald and Jane's, 1978)

Liddell Hart, Basil H., *History of the Second World War*, (London: Cassell, 1970)

Saunders, Hilary St George, *The Green Beret – The Story of the Commandos*, (London: Michael Joseph, 1949)

N.B. The author of this Chapter is most grateful to Major Beadle for his help and advice in preparing this text.

Developing themes in Amphibious Warfare

- The need for overwhelming bombardment from the sea right up to the moment of landing, and naval gunfire support on call thereafter

- The need for intimate fire support alongside the landing craft

- The need to get the armour ashore early in working order

- The requirement for better security

- Aviod landing at a defended port or the obvious place if possible

- A Headquarters ship is vital for Command and Control

- Thorough preparation supported by genuine unity of effort

Biography

Major Mark Bentinck joined the Royal Marines as a 2nd Lieutenant in 1963, and saw active service in 45 Commando in Aden in 1965-66. Four further Commando Unit postings followed, based in UK, Singapore and Malta, with an operational tour in Northern Ireland, and a 6 month attachment to the Imperial Ethiopian Marines. He qualified as a military parachutist, Forward Air Controller, and Arctic Warfare Instructor. As a Jungle Warfare specialist he instructed in the Army Jungle Warfare School in Brunei in 1976-1979, returning to a spell in RM Officer Training at Lympstone, followed by the RN Staff course at Greenwich, and a posting in MOD. He retired in 1985, with the rank of Major, and 1992 became the Historical Records Officer for the Royal Marines as a Civil Servant. He now works in the Royal Naval Historical Branch in Portsmouth.

Soviet Amphibious Landings in the Black Sea, 1941 - 1944

By Professor Donald Stoker

When one thinks of amphibious operations, especially large-scale landings, one does not immediately think of the Soviet Union. Most writing on Soviet military operations in the Second World War focuses upon vitally important battles such as Leningrad, Stalingrad, Kursk, or the destruction of Army Group Centre. But restricting our search for the war's military lessons to these titanic events ignores the broader scope of Red Army, Navy and Air Force operations during what the Soviets referred to as the Great Patriotic War.

One element of the Soviet war effort against Nazi Germany was amphibious operations. During World War II the Soviets made extensive amphibious landings, putting ashore 330,000 troops on all fronts. Soviet Naval Infantry conducted 120 major amphibious attacks. The Soviet Black Sea Fleet and Azov and Danube Flotillas conducted 41 operations, landing a total of 210,000 troops. In the war's early stages the Soviets launched small, tactical amphibious operations to hinder or hold up German advances along the coast, or to force the Germans to protect their coastal flanks. Later, the Soviets used amphibious assaults to breech German coastal fortifications, 'to seize beachheads for offensive operations, and to capture ports, enemy bases, and strongpoints' and 'cut off the retreat of enemy forces.'[1]

Pre-War Soviet Amphibious Doctrine

Drawing upon experience gained during World War I and the Russian Civil War, Admiral Ivan Isakov laid out the framework of Soviet amphibious doctrine in 1931. Later, during World War II, Admiral Isakov served as the Chief of the Soviet Navy Main Staff, which meant he was responsible for coordinating all Soviet naval operations, including amphibious assaults.[2]

In his writings, Isakov classified landing operations as three types: strategic, tactical, and raiding. As an example of a strategic operation he cited the British landings at Gallipoli in 1915. Strategic landings were meant to open another front, to be long term, and to be made by large forces, including corps level units. A division would be considered the minimum force necessary. Isakov defined a tactical landing as an assault on a flank as part of an effort to envelope an enemy force in order to try and influence the course of a particular battle. Forces from a battalion to a division would be used here. Raiding landings involved the insertion of small units to stir up trouble in the enemy's rear areas, or conduct minor operations such as blowing up gun emplacements. Unlike Isakov's other landing types, raiding forces also required extraction. Isakov's sequence of events for an amphibious operation can be described by the acronym PERMA: Planning, Embarkation, Rehearsal, Movement, and

Assault. But, the 'Planning' stage might more accurately be described as 'Preparation', and 'Rehearsal' was not really viewed as a separate stage. Isakov also insisted that 'Planning' should include preparation for evacuation, in case that became necessary.[3]

Isakov viewed amphibious landings as the most difficult of all military operations, insisting that they all shared the following characteristics: 1) The need for a joint plan covering all of the forces involved; 2) That they were all subject to the influence of the same air, sea, and shore conditions, including the weather and astronomical factors, i.e. the phases of the moon; 3) That success depended upon choosing a proper landing site, timing, properly preparing the forces, and insuring operational secrecy. Isakov though, made no allowance for the necessity of having air superiority over the landing site.[4] This oversight is likely a result of the then minimal capabilities of ground attack aircraft.

Soviet planners expanded upon Isakov's ideas in 1937, adding operational landings. This was an intermediate sized attack between the tactical and strategic landings and was meant to hit the enemy harder than a tactical assault, or add a new direction

---

[1]Dominik George Nargele, 'The Soviet Naval Infantry: An Evolving Instrument of State Power,' Georgetown University, PhD dissertation, 1983, 82-4; V. I. Achkasov and N. B. Pavlovich, *Soviet Naval Operations in the Great Patriotic War, 1941-1945* (Annapolis, MD: Naval Institute Press, 1973), 96-7.

[2]Charles B. Atwater, 'Soviet Amphibious Operations in the Black Sea, 1941-1943,' (CSC, 1995), http://www.globalsecurity.org/military/library/report/1995/ACB.htm, 5.

[3]Atwater, 'Soviet Amphibious Operations in the Black Sea,' 5-7.

[4]Ibid., 6.

Odessa, 1941

On 22 June 1941 the Germans launched Operation BARBAROSSA, their invasion of the Soviet Union. During the initial period of the war when the Germans were on the offensive, the Soviets used tactical and operational landings in an effort to shift the war's initiative out of Nazi hands. More than one third of Soviet World War II amphibious operations were conducted during this period, with the Soviets landing 57,000 troops during 1941-1942. This was accomplished with insufficient air cover, troops with no specialised training, and no landing craft designed for the task. The lack of specialised equipment is surprising, particularly since the Russians developed the first modern landing craft in the Black Sea in 1916.[6] The absence of these vessels would be sorely felt throughout the course of the war. On 22 September 1941, in an effort to take pressure off the defenders of Odessa, the Soviets launched a combined amphibious and airborne assault behind the Rumanian lines near Grigoryevka. Soviet writers consider this one of the two most important tactical landings of the war. Tied to this assault was an attack from troops defending the port. The counter-offensive threw back the surprised Rumanians and the Soviets recovered the positions from which their enemies had shelled Odessa's port facilities. The Soviet naval force in this operation was commanded by Captain 1st Rank Sergei G. Gorshkov, who later became the distinguished head of the Soviet Navy.[7]

The operation at Grigoryevka was far from flawless. The commander of the amphibious assault force was Rear Admiral L. A. Vladimirskii. He, and the landing vessels, did not make the rendezvous with Admiral Gorshkov's supporting cruiser brigade, which was carrying the 3rd Naval Infantry Regiment, the unit scheduled to make the landing. Vladimirskii's ship was sunk on the way and command devolved to Gorshkov. He elected to begin the landings using the ships' launches and boats, which was possible only because the Soviets had studied this option beforehand and put additional such craft aboard the cruisers and destroyers transporting the landing forces. These boats could not land troops as quickly as desired, but the pre-

of attack. The Naval Provisionary Regulations of 1937, which made the addition, argued for the seizure of a beachhead 300-600 metres in depth, which would keep the follow on forces out of the range of enemy machinegun fire. Expansion of the beachhead's borders to push them out of artillery range would then follow. Pre-war Soviet doctrine also called for making amphibious landings at dawn.[5]

[5]Ibid., 8; Achkasov and Pavlovich, *Soviet Naval Operations*, 99.

[6]Jacob W. Kipp, 'The Second Arm and the Problem of Combined Operations: The Russian-Soviet Experience, 1853-1945,' in *The Sources of Soviet Naval Conduct*, Philip S. Gillette and Willard C. Frank, Jr., eds. (Lexington, MA: Lexington Books, D.C. Heath and Co., 1990), 151; Donald W. Mitchell, *A History of Russian and Soviet Sea Power* (New York: MacMillan, 1974), 413.

[7]Friedrich Ruge, *The Soviets as Naval Opponents, 1941-1945* (Annapolis, MD: Naval Institute Press, 1979), 66-7; Kh. Kh. Khamalov, *Naval Infantry in Combat for the Motherland* (Moscow: Military Publishing House, 1966), 103.

designated landing vessels arrived soon enough to get the rest of the troops ashore.[8]

The assault began at 0130, with the attackers speeding to the beaches on launches. All of the troops were ashore by 0500, and began advancing toward Grigoryevka. The enemy withdrew to the north, and the Soviets eventually advanced five kilometres.[9] When the Soviet High Command eventually decided to abandon Odessa in the face of Axis pressure and the initial success of BARBAROSSA, the Soviet Navy, from 1-16 October 1941, evacuated 150,000 civilians and 121,000 troops, all under the nose of the Axis forces.[10]

The Kerch-Feodossiya Operation

The largest Soviet amphibious operation in the early period of World War II (the phase in which the Germans held the initiative) was the Kerch-Feodossiya landing. The Soviets mounted this operation from 25 December 1941 to 2 January 1942. It had two objectives: 1) Liberating the Kerch Peninsula; and 2) Establishing a bridgehead to weaken the Axis blockade of Sevastopol which could serve as a base for launching future operations supporting the liberation of the Crimea.[11] Operationally, the Soviets planned a broad front of landings, with the most important being those near Ak-Monai on the Kerch Peninsula's northern

shore, and those on the south coast at Feodossiya. Smaller landings at other sites, including in the Kerch Straits, provided support. They planned to land 44,000 men of the 44th Army at Feodossiya, about 13,000 of the 51st Army in the Kerch Straits vicinity, and another 3,000 of the 44th Army at Cape Opuk. A blocking force of airborne troops was dropped near Arabat. None of these operations had air support. Moreover, the Kerch landings were conducted under heavy shelling by German artillery. In general the units came ashore under intense enemy fire. Some troops landed in frozen water and waded to the beach, cutting paths through the ice with their chests.[12]

> **The naval gunfire supporting the landing alerted the Germans, forcing the attackers to endure withering enemy fire**

In order to shorten the duration of the operation the Soviets planned to land the Feodossiya force directly into the harbour, a type of operation that became known as 'Coast-Coast'. The naval gunfire supporting the landing alerted the Germans, forcing the attackers to endure withering enemy fire. The Soviets struck Feodossiya hard, blasting their way into the port and dropping 23,000 men in the first wave, overwhelming the thin German defences. Special units on small boats took the piers, holding them for the warships bringing in reinforcements. The first vessel into the harbour was a coast guard cutter, *SKA-0131*. In the face of German fire the ship's captain, Commander A. D. Kokarev, landed an assault group on the protective breakwater. The troops captured the lighthouse and turned on its light. The first wave of 300 seamen, the main assault detachment, followed up this success, being brought directly into the port by escort ships and disembarked. They captured part of the port and seized the moorings for the follow-on forces.[13]

[8]Kipp, 'The Second Arm,' 150-1.
[9]Khamalov, *Naval Infantry*, 104-5.
[10]Ruge, *The Soviets as Naval Opponents*, 66-7.
[11]Achkasov and Pavlovich, *Soviet Naval Operations*, 106.
[12]W. I. Atschkassow, 'Landing Operations of the Soviet Naval Fleet during World War Two,' Michael C. Halbig, trans., in Merrill L. Bartlett, ed., *Assault from the Sea: Essays on the History of Amphibious Warfare* (Annapolis, MD: Naval Institute Press, 1983), 301; Jürg Meister, *Der Seekrieg in den osteuropäischen Gewässern 1941-45* (München: J.F. Lehmanns Verlag, 1958), 245; Khamalov, *Naval Infantry*, 105.
[13]Atschkassow, 'Landing Operations of the Soviet Naval Fleet,' 301; Ruge, *The Soviets as Naval Opponents*, 73; Khamalov, *Naval Infantry*, 106.

Soviet Naval Gunfire Support circa 1943.
A 130mm gun on the cruiser Krasnyy Krym firing.
In the foreground is a 100mm AA gun. (NHB)

The Kerch-Feodossiya Operation was hindered by 'the complete absence of special amphibious transport and landing craft.' The Soviets had discussed developing such vessels before the war, but done nothing more. The result was that they mounted landings in a ragtag collection of craft ranging from barges and dredges, to fishing boats and small warships. Use of such varied vessels, and the fact that they operated at different speeds, made coordination, organisation, and execution of landing operations very difficult. None of the units hit their assigned landing sites on time. Additionally, in support of such landings, or to harass the Germans, the Soviets would send Motor Torpedo Boats (MTBs) into harbours and fire torpedoes at facilities. For example, in a late 1942 Soviet attack on Anapa, torpedoes destroyed the enlisted mens' quarters on a wharf.[14]

But the operation did succeed. The port of Feodossiya was cleared by 30 December and the Soviet success blocked any immediate German advance across the Kerch Strait to the Taman Peninsula, leading to the creation of the new Soviet Crimea Front. Moreover, the Germans assaulting Sevastopol were forced onto the defensive.[15] The local German commander, Field Marshal Erich von Manstein, had to break off the attack he had begun against Sevastopol, giving the Soviets time to bring in reinforcements. The siege went on for six months longer than the Germans planned, tying down forces that could have been better used in other areas.[16] The successful amphibious assault was not the only factor causing the lengthening of the siege, but it contributed. In January 1942 the Germans counterattacked to retake the positions they had lost on the Kerch Peninsula. Initially, they failed to push the Soviets out of the peninsula's neck, but they would succeed in May, breaking through the Soviet lines and pressing the Soviet defenders against the sea. Here, unlike Odessa, Soviet evacuation efforts failed, and the Germans took 150,000 prisoners.[17]

The Novorossiysk Area and Malia Zemlia

On 28 June 1942 the Germans launched their summer offensive in the southern Soviet Union. Much of it was directed at the Caucasus region and one of the German operational objectives was the capture of the Soviet Black Sea ports. The Germans took the city of Novorossiysk in August 1942, but failed to penetrate south of it.[18] Elsewhere, the Germans continued to advance, but they did not inflict any decisive damage to the Soviet Union's ability to wage war. In late 1942 and early 1943, the Germans endured disaster in and around Stalingrad and the war's initiative shifted to the Soviets, who went on the offensive against the invader.

In early February 1943, the Soviet Black Sea Fleet launched amphibious operations against Novorossiysk. The Soviet 47th Army was advancing towards Verkhne-Bakanskii in the hopes of driving the Germans from the port city of Novorossiysk. To assist them the Soviets planned a two-pronged amphibious assault. The primary landing aimed at Yvzhnaya Ozeryeka, a town southwest of Novorossiysk. The secondary and diversionary attack targeted Stanichka, south of Novorossiysk, but closer to the city. When the attack began paratroopers were also dropped at Yvzhnaya Ozeryeka a quarter of an hour before the beginning of the preparatory naval bombardment of the landing areas.[19]

The Soviets began planning for the landings around Novorossiysk, at what became known as the Myskhako beachhead, in November 1942. They found it difficult to keep their preparations secret

---

[14]Achkasov and Pavlovich, *Soviet Naval Operations*, 109-10; Ruge, *The Soviets as Naval Opponents*, 86.

[15]Atschkassow, 'Landing Operations of the Soviet Naval Fleet,' 301; Khamalov, *Naval Infantry*, 105.

[16]Ruge, *The Soviets as Naval Opponents*, 76-7.

[17]Ibid., 77-8.

[18]Albert Seaton, *The Russo-German War 1941-45* (New York and Washington: Praeger, 1971), 266, 272; E. Eustigneev, 'On Course to Novorossiisk,' Jane E. Good and James A. Malloy, Jr., trans., in Merrill L. Bartlett, ed., *Assault from the Sea: Essays on the History of Amphibious Warfare* (Annapolis, MD: Naval Institute Press, 1983), 286.

[19]Nargele, 'The Soviet Naval Infantry,' 115; Khamalov, *Naval Infantry*, 109.

The former Soviet Premier, Leonid I. Brezhnev, decorated for his actions as a Colonel when undertaking amphibious operations in the Black Sea. (NHB)

because they had to make them so close to the German lines and under the eyes of German reconnaissance flights. To counter prying German observers, the Soviets devoted much effort to increasing their anti-aircraft defences and camouflage. Figuring out the timing was also a problem because the landings were dependent upon the progress of the ground forces.[20]

Another difficulty was ensuring proper preparation of the men and equipment, particularly the moving of the all-important *bolinders* to the beach. The *bolinders*, half landing craft, half miniature Mulberry, were towed landing barges of 530 tons, 45.8 metres in length, and 7.2 metres in width. They could carry 10 tanks, or a battalion of troops. Their cargo was offloaded via bow ramps, and then they were positioned offshore for use as docks for unloading other equipment. Gunboats and minesweepers then made profitable use of the *bolinders*, drawing close inshore and disembarking their troops down their own ramps, while simultaneously mooring to the *bolinder* and unloading equipment.[21]

Since the naval forces that were going to be involved in the operation were constantly employed moving men and equipment in support of operations around the Black Sea war zone, they did not get as much specific training for the Novorossiysk operation as the Soviets wanted. They did manage to conduct five daytime

Without such thorough training a daring landing and especially the initial night assault was quite out of the question, for everything had to be done in the dark by touch

and four night-time exercises with the tugs and barges. The transports and gunboats held four day and nine night drills, and the minesweepers and patrol boats also conducted some training missions. Landing troops were also trained using mock-ups of vessels built on beaches.[22] Leonid I. Brezhnev, the future Soviet dictator, and a participant in some of the Black Sea operations, described the training for the landings at Stanichka:

'We chose the men carefully and they had special training. Assault groups were trained at Cape Toniky in Gelendzhik; they were taught jumping into the water with machine guns, scaling rocks and throwing grenades from awkward positions. They learned to handle every kind of enemy weapon, to throw knives, to strike blows with rifle butts, to bandage wounds and arrest bleeding. They memorised agreed signals, learned to load submachine-gun magazines blindfolded and to tell by ear where the fire was coming from. Without such thorough training a daring landing and especially the initial night assault was quite out of the question, for everything had to be done in the dark by touch.'[23]

The plan for the initial Novorossiysk area landings called for a 30-minute preparatory bombardment, followed by gunfire support for the forces on shore. The Soviets held two joint exercises as training. The fire-correction teams formed for these missions, which consisted of a gunnery officer, a chief petty officer, and three radiomen, conducted 40 practice drills. The Soviets also made a thorough reconnaissance of the German gun emplacements to provide accurate information to their supporting coastal artillery. This included occasional firing at the Germans to get their guns to reply, then locating the positions of the enemy batteries for future counter-battery attacks. Much attention was paid to reconnaissance in general, which included the landing of 22 reconnaissance teams. Preparations also included 'party political work aimed at successful performance of the combat mission'. Meanwhile, Soviet weather-guessers tried to figure out when they would have two or three consecutive days of calm, a difficult task because of the many days of stormy weather in the Novorossiysk area in the fall and winter.[24]

The Soviet forces sailed from Batum, Tuapse, and Gelendzhik. They had bad weather during the crossing, which delayed the landing at Yuzhnaya Ozeryeka. It had been scheduled for 0130

[20]N. Belous, 'Soviet Amphibious Preassault and Landing Operations in World War II,' Kendall E. Lappin, trans., in Merrill L., Bartlett, ed., *Assault from the Sea: Essays on the History of Amphibious Warfare* (Annapolis, MD: Naval Institute Press, 1983), 292-3; Khamalov, *Naval Infantry*, 109.
[21]Belous, 'Soviet Amphibious Preassault and Landing Operations,' 293, 298 fn4.
[22]Ibid., 293.
[23]L. I. Brezhnev, *Trilogia*, (Trilogy), (Moskva: Politizidat, 1978), 24, quoted in Nargele, 'The Soviet Naval Infantry,' 118-19.
[24]Belous, 'Soviet Amphibious Preassault and Landing Operations,' 294-5.

Russian Marines of the Black Sea fleet in action after being landed in the rear of enemy positions, on German occupied territory on the Black Sea coast. (IWM Rus Navy file 4873)

on 4 February 1943, but began later. At 0045, according to plan, Soviet aircraft bombed Yuzhnaya Ozeryeka and the airborne troops were dropped in the Vasil'yevka-Glebovka area. The air raid started fires that illuminated the landing beaches. The Soviets hit Yuzhnaya Ozeryeka before dawn on 4 February, landing 1,427 men and 16 tanks between 0345 and daybreak. Fearing air attack, they stopped their landing operations at sun-up. Because of this they never landed the main elements intended for Yuzhnaya Ozeryeka.[25] The late start and bad weather injured the Soviet plan, leaving the landing force much weaker than it needed to be.

The experience of the 563rd Independent Tank Battalion gives us a picture of what it was like for one of the units participating in the Yuzhnaya Ozeryeka landing. At 0200 on 4 February the first two of their three towed *bolinders* reached the shore, each carried 10 American Lend-Lease M3 Stuart Light Tanks, two GAZ trucks, in addition to infantry. Under German artillery fire the Soviets began unloading the tanks directly into the water. The first *bolinder* received a direct hit that damaged the gangway,

preventing unloading. It also set the tanks on fire and the vessel began to burn. Its crew and the troops on board abandoned ship. The second *bolinder* unloaded seven tanks, and with these, and supporting infantry, the Soviets mounted their attack, pushing to the outskirts of the village of Glebovka. The Germans cut them off by the end of the day. Trapped, the Soviet troops received an order via an airdrop to try and reach Stanichka. Their tanks out of fuel, they stripped out the machineguns, then disabled the vehicles.[26]

The third *bolinder* involved in the assault, 'during its approach to shore, was dropped from the tow and moving by inertia stopped some 30-40 meters from the shore.' The Soviets began unloading these tanks directly into the water as well, safely disembarking seven, and losing the other three in the surf. With these, and the accompanying infantry of the 140th Battalion, the Soviets fought off German counterattacks until 6 February, receiving no reinforcements. But by the 6th, the Soviet commander saw that the situation was hopeless. His men also removed the machineguns from their surviving and now fuel-less tanks, disabled them, and tried to break out, eventually being forced by their German and Rumanian attackers to disperse into small groups. This failed landing cost the Soviets 30 tanks and 151 men killed or missing.[27] At 0130 on 4 February 1943,

Soviet artillery at the Novorossiysk Naval Base across the bay (the Soviets held positions bordering the city) opened fire on the Stanichka beaches. Ten minutes later Soviet Naval Infantry under the command or Major Ts. L. Kunikov began landing. The Soviets deposited a 900-man force of volunteers at dawn, all combat veterans, who completed the initial assault in two minutes. Colonel Leonid I. Brezhnev, a political officer with the 18th Army, wrote of the Stanichka landing:[28]

'It was a very dark night of February 3, 1943, the motorboats with the task force on board left Gelendzhik quietly for Tsemesskaya Bay. Deploying there, they headed for the shore as signal flares rose in the air. Simultaneously our artillery bombarded the shoreline that was already in our sights. Into the rolling thunder of explosions burst blazing volleys from a 'Katyusha' – it was the first time in military practice that a multiple rocket launcher had ever been mounted on a trawler, the *Skumbriia*. Two torpedo boats going full out across the bows of the assault craft laying a smoke screen in their wake to shield the craft from shore-based enemy fire. A patrol boat opened fire on the area of the fish cannery, neutralizing any gun posts that had survived the bombardment. The moment Kunikov's men rushed ashore our batteries lifted their barrage.'[29]

[25]Ibid., 296; Nargele, 'The Soviet Naval Infantry,' 115-16.
[26]'Report About the Combat Actions of 563rd IndepTBn,' 8 March 1943, James F. Geberhardt, trans., http://www.battlefield.ru/library/battles/battles17.html, 2.
[27]Ibid., 2-3.
[28]Belous, 'Soviet Amphibious Preassault and Landing Operations,' 296; Nargele, 'The Soviet Naval Infantry,' 116; Khamalov, *Naval Infantry*, 110-11.
[29]Brezhnev, *Trilogia*, 28, quoted in Nargele, 'The Soviet Naval Infantry,' 116-7.

Soviet Navy observer with the Russian fleet in the Black Sea spotting for German aircraft. (IWM Rus Navy file 240)

The Soviets attributed their eventual success at Stanichka to Kunikov's heroic leadership and the bravery of his men. He was mortally wounded during the operation and for his conduct was named a Hero of the Soviet Union.[30]

The main landing force included two naval infantry brigades, a rifle brigade, an anti-tank artillery regiment, a tank battalion, and a machinegun battalion. Air support comprised 167 planes from the Red Navy and Air Force. Over 70 vessels of all types were used. In addition to the two main landings and the airborne drop, the Soviets made 'demonstration landings' at Zheleznyy Rog Cape, Anapa, Varvarovka, and other spots.[31]

The Soviet assault force suffered heavy casualties carving out a tiny, fire-swept beachhead of 300 to 400 metres near the fish processing plant on the southern side of the town of Stanichka. This secured a landing zone for the main assault force. The fighting here drove the Soviet soldiers to desperate measures. Junior Sergeant M. M. Kornitskiy enabled his infantry company to retreat in the face of a German counterattack by strapping anti-tank grenades in his belt, holding another in his hand, throwing

himself at an attacking German detachment, and detonating the held grenade. Vitya Chalenko, a 15-year old infantryman in the 144th Battalion crawled through a curtain of German machinegun fire and single-handedly knocked out the crew of the weapon that was ravaging his comrades and stopping their advance. He then killed three more Germans who appeared, whereupon 'Inspired by the heroism of' young Vitya, 'the battalion rose to the attack with new force. Vitya rose as well, but at this moment an enemy bullet brought the hero down.'[32]

On 5 February, in the face of stiff German resistance at Yvzhnaya Ozeryeka, the Soviet commander decided to make Stanichka the primary landing and redirected the main assault forces to the where the Soviets had met lighter resistance. One Soviet author argues that this should have been done sooner. Reinforcing success, they built up the Stanichka beachhead, then withdrew the forces landed at Yvzhnaya Ozeryeka. On the night of 6 February they put ashore 4,500 men. The forces at Stanichka suffered grievous losses, both ashore and while attempting to land. The casualties proved so heavy that the operation almost collapsed. Enemy fire prevented any landings the next night, but despite their casualties, two 18th Army engineer battalions had already begun building moorings on Sudzhuk Spit. On the night of 7 February patrol boats began running men to the beaches and between 4 and 9 February the Soviets landed over 17,000

men. The position they established made it impossible for the Germans to use the port. The Soviets steadily expanded their Stanichka holdings and by the end of March, and despite their losses, the 45,000 Soviet troops held a 45 square kilometre beachhead that became known as *Malia Zemlia* -- Little Land.[33]

On 17 April 1943 the Germans launched Operation NEPTUNE, their last offensive aimed at destroying the Stanichka beachhead. The German-Rumanian push ended on 25 April. The Soviets held, consolidated their positions, and after 225 days, began operations that led to a breakout from the beachhead.[34]

On to Novorossiysk

As the general German position in the Soviet Union began to deteriorate in the summer of 1943, the Soviets prepared a combined amphibious assault and army operation aimed at driving the Germans from the Taman Peninsula, as well as finally retaking Novorossiysk. In August 1943, the Soviet forces in the North Caucasus were ordered to break the German defences known as the Golubin (or Blue) Line. The Soviets aimed at cutting the Germans up and destroying them piecemeal. The Front commander, Lieutenant General I. E. Petrov, 'decided to strike the main blow on the left wing in hopes of breaking the Golubin Line in the area of Novorossiysk.' The Soviets hoped to retake the city and port by attacking it simultaneously from three sides with units

---

[30]Belous, 'Soviet Amphibious Preassault and Landing Operations,' 296; Nargele, 'The Soviet Naval Infantry,' 119.
[31]Belous, 'Soviet Amphibious Preassault and Landing Operations,' 295.
[32]Khamalov, *Naval Infantry*, 111, 113.
[33]Nargele, 'The Soviet Naval Infantry,' 115-6, 118; Achkasov and Pavlovich, *Soviet Naval Operations*, 114; Belous, 'Soviet Amphibious Preassault and Landing Operations,' 114.
[34]Nargele, 'The Soviet Naval Infantry,' 120-1.

of the 18th Army. Two of the attacking prongs would be by land, one from the west of Novorossiysk, and one from the east from Little Land. The third prong was 'a daring amphibious landing directly in the port.' Meanwhile, the Soviets began converting the tactical beachhead at Stanichka into a strategic one. [35]

The Soviets planned to land two assault groups in the port, the eastern, under the command of Colonel V. A. Vrutsky, and the western, led by Commander N. A. Shvarev. The amphibious force was supported and transported by 150 ships under the command of Rear Admiral G. N. Kholostyakov. The Soviets had the benefit of experienced personnel as 'More than half of the soldiers and sailors in the assault were participants in previous landing operations.'[36]

The Soviet's launched their offensive against the Golubin Line on the night of 10 September 1943. At around 0230 a force of 25 torpedo cutters, 'under the command of Captain V. T. Protsenko burst at full speed into the port to attack weapon emplacements on the docks, mooring lines, and shore. Assault groups blew up the boom net obstacles. Then the landing began.' Some of the Soviet forces, probably because of poor visibility and the intensity of German fire, failed to land where they were supposed to. This

spread the attacking forces over a six-kilometre front, instead of the originally planned 1,200 metres. Rear Admiral Cholostyakov conducted the landing of the 255th Marine Brigade utilizing a flotilla of about 130 small craft. After a 90-minute barrage the Soviet Marines, reinforced to about 9,000 men, landed in two waves beginning at 0315. The first 2,000 men hit the piers in small detachments. The Soviets also lacked proper landing craft for this operation, contributing to the heavy losses among the Naval Infantry. The 240 man German naval detachment was prepared for the attack and mounted a strong defence, holding out long enough to be reinforced by an under strength German battalion. The remaining Marines landed at other points. A small detachment, 80 men, went ashore on the harbour's west side. The Germans pounded them with 210-mm mortars and they were 'scattered into [the] hinterland.'[37]

The Soviets decided to reinforce the eastern group on 10 September. Five days of fighting followed until the Germans were forced from Novorossiysk on 15 September. On 16 September the Soviets broke through the Golubin Line. They drove the last Germans from the Taman Peninsula on 9 October 1943. A Soviet historian attributed their eventual success at Novorossiysk to solid preparation, which included three

weeks devoted to training for the landing, achieving surprise, substantial air and artillery bombardment, air superiority, the torpedoing of enemy positions and obstacles, as well as 'the unprecedented bravery of the personnel of the assault landing force and well organised and effective party-political work in the troops.'[38] Some doubt could be cast upon the applicability of the last reason given for Soviet success at Novorossiysk, but there is no disputing the penultimate one. The bravery of the Soviet servicemen involved made Soviet operations work, in spite of their leaders, the lack of specialised amphibious equipment, and the barbaric and often primitive conditions under which they were forced to live and fight.

The Germans began evacuating what soon became known as the Kuban bridgehead. During this one month operation the Soviets harassed the Germans with repeated landing attempts behind German lines, most from the Sea of Azov, though at least one was mounted on the Black Sea side. Most of these never reached the coastline, but the Soviets did succeed in putting ashore a 400-man battalion at one point, which the Germans annihilated. Despite Soviet pressure, the Germans evacuated across the Kerch Strait 256,000 troops, including 16,000 wounded and vast quantities of equipment.[39]

---

[35]Ibid., 123; Khamalov, *Naval Infantry*, 117; Eustigneev, 'On Course to Novorossiisk,' 287-8.

[36]Eustigneev, 'On Course to Novorossiisk,' 288-9.

[37]Ibid.,' 289; Ruge, *The Soviets as Naval Opponents*, 110-11; Nargele, 'The Soviet Naval Infantry,' 123-5; Khamalov, *Naval Infantry*, 117, 119. One source gives the number of troops being landed as 6,000, Khamalov, *Naval Infantry*, 117. It is possible that the western landing force was completely destroyed. Some units certainly were, Ruge, 111, insists upon this, and the Soviet sources tend to not mention the destruction of attacking forces. The fact that the Soviets followed their traditional practice of reinforcing success by giving additional support to the eastern force also encourages the belief in the destruction of the western force.

[38]Eustigneev, 'On Course to Novorossiisk,' 289; Nargele, 'The Soviet Naval Infantry,' 125; Khamalov, *Naval Infantry*, 120.

[39]Ruge, *The Soviets as Naval Opponents*, 111-112; Nargele, 'The Soviet Naval Infantry,' 125.

The Allied view: A Russian newspaper cartoon celebrates a 'rat' leaving a sinking ship following the fall of Mussolini in 1943. (IWM Rus file)

While the Germans were being driven from the Black Sea coast, the Soviets also began pushing them out of areas bordering the northern littoral of the Sea of Azov. During August and September 1943, the Soviets made a number of tactical landings, primarily to hinder the retreat of German forces. At the end of August they made two landings around Bezymyanovska and Veselyy to keep the Germans retreating from Taganrog (southwest of Rostov) from using the coastal road. Similar landings in this area followed and on 10 September a Soviet force came ashore near Melenkino and seized the port of Mariupol. This helped break open the German defensive lines on the Kalmius River. A number of similar landings occurred during September, providing solid support to Red Army advances.[40] The Soviets launched renewed offensive operations in southern Russia in the last week of October 1943, soon reaching the Perekop isthmus and isolating the German forces in the Crimea. Hitler ordered the Crimea held as a fortress.[41] The Soviets prepared to breach it.

The Kerch-Eltigen Landings

From 31 October to 11 December 1943 the Soviets conducted the Kerch-Eltigen landings in support of Red Army efforts to clear the Crimea and the North Caucasus in preparation for the eventual liberation of the Crimea. Their plan called for three, simultaneous landings: 'The 56th Army was to be put ashore on the spit of land north and east of Kerch and then occupy this area as well as the city of Kerch. The amphibious forces of the 18th Army were to land near Eltigen and build a beachhead near Kamysch-Burgun-Cape Takil. The subsequent mission of both amphibious units was to liberate the eastern part of the Kerch peninsula.' The operation, conducted by the 56th Army on 1 and 2 November 1943, was perhaps the largest Soviet amphibious landing. Because of the area's geography and mine laying operations, the Soviets only used light craft and only made the landings after careful minesweeping. Land-based artillery and about 600 aircraft provided support, as did the Black Sea Fleet.[42]

Stormy weather upset much of Soviet pre-invasion planning and kept the landings from being made simultaneously. It also damaged and disabled many of the landing craft of the Azov Flotilla, delaying their attack until 2 November. A planned simultaneous attack became successive landings and this gave the Germans a chance to concentrate their counterattacks against the Soviet 18th Army, which withstood 37 German assaults during two and one-half days.[43]

On 1 November 1943, a battalion of Soviet Marines crossed from the east bank of the Kerch Strait and made a surprise landing at Cape Yenikale, seizing the battery and establishing a beachhead that the Soviets proceeded to enlarge. Troops also landed south of Kerch at Eltigen. The Eltigen landings proved a disaster for the Soviets. The Germans established a close blockade of the Eltigen beachhead that they continued for five weeks. Nearly every night saw bitter fighting between the German blockaders and the Soviet naval forces struggling to bring supplies and reinforcements into Eltigen. The Soviets tried to keep the beachhead supplied by air as well, but all their efforts proved unsuccessful. In December, the Germans began liquidating the pocket, clearing it by the 11th, capturing 3,000 prisoners, and finding 10,000 dead. Around 800 Naval Infantry managed to breakout and reach the other beachhead.[44]

The Germans succeeded in stopping some other Soviet landings, but on 10 January 1944 the Soviets struck a severe blow at the German position. In an effort to enlarge their Yenikale beachhead, the Soviets landed about 2,000 Naval Infantry from 40 motorboats at Cape Tarkhan, ten miles west of the Sea of Azov entrance to the Kerch Straits. It was an area the Germans had neglected and the landing succeeded. German counterattacks forced the Soviets to withdraw from Cape Tarkhan, but they continued to hold their Yenikale positions at the time.[45]

[40]Achkasov and Pavlovich, *Soviet Naval Operations*, 123.
[41]Ruge, *The Soviets as Naval Opponents*, 114.
[42]Atschkassow, 'Landing Operations of the Soviet Naval Fleet,' 301; Achkasov and Pavlovich, *Soviet Naval Operations*, 119; Nargele, 'The Soviet Naval Infantry,' 127-8.
[43]Atschkassow, 'Landing Operations of the Soviet Naval Fleet,' 301; Achkasov and Pavlovich, *Soviet Naval Operations*, 121.
[44]Ruge, *The Soviets as Naval Opponents*, 115, 116-18; Nargele, 'The Soviet Naval Infantry,' 129.
[45]Mitchell, *A History of Russian and Soviet Sea Power*, 416; Ruge, *The Soviets as Naval Opponents*, 124; Nargele, 'The Soviet Naval Infantry,' 130.

Russian sailors on patrol along the sea frontiers. (IWM Rus 276)

Right: The extent of the Soviet advances around the Sea of Azov and Black Sea, in March 1944. (NHB)

of a Naval Infantry battalion 'on the north mole of Kerch in an attempt to enlarge the Yenikale position in this direction.' This assault succeeded, but a subsidiary landing to the south was repulsed. One writer states that 'It is interesting to note that the Soviets repeated their amphibious attacks on the Kerch Peninsula at the same places where similar operations had met with limited success in the winter 1941-1942.'[46]

The situation in the area stabilized until Soviet successes elsewhere forced the Germans to begin withdrawing during 1944. In April 1944, the Soviets attacked into the Crimea. On the 7th they recaptured Feodossiya. By 8 May Soviet troops were fighting in Sevastopol.[47] In August 1944, Soviet armies under the command of Generals R. Ya. Malinovsky and Feodor Tolbukhin began offensive operations in the region between the Black Sea and the Carpathian Mountains. In support of this, on 22 August, a force of 600 small, Soviet naval craft landed an amphibious force behind the German lines. The Soviets made another landing at the mouth of the Danube River two days later. Things began

falling apart for the Germans along the Black Sea. Jassy fell to the Soviets. A coup in Rumania toppled the pro-German government and the nation's new leaders declared war on Germany. Bulgaria soon did the same.[48]

Conclusions

Obviously, Soviet Black Sea amphibious operations did not have a decisive impact on the outcome of the war on the Eastern Front, but they did provide valuable support for the Red Army's land offensives. Having the capability of making landings, and the willingness to make daring and sometimes even suicidal ones, forced the Germans to be constantly vigilant against strikes on their vulnerable southern flank, one that their own lack of naval power in the Black Sea left consistently exposed.

In general, Soviet landings, and not just those in the Black Sea, took place over short distances, and almost always had air support (though there were exceptions to this early in the war, i.e. those around Odessa in 1941, and at Kerch-Feodossiya). Additionally, most Soviet landings were prepared quickly. Of the 113 landings made, 62 'were prepared in less than twenty-four hours.' Later in the war, landings generally took place at night in order to maximize the chance of surprise, but doing this limited the effectiveness of artillery and air support. Moreover, airborne drops were found useful in support of landing operations, confirming pre-war thinking.[49]

The Cape Tarkhan operation was merely the first of several Soviet efforts to enlarge their Yenikale beachhead. On 23 January 1944, using 15 motorboats the Soviets landed 450 men

[46]Ruge, *The Soviets as Naval Opponents*, 124; Nargele, 'The Soviet Naval Infantry,' 130.
[47]Nargele, 'The Soviet Naval Infantry,' 130; Mitchell, *A History of Russian and Soviet Sea Power*, 416.
[48]Mitchell, *A History of Russian and Soviet Sea Power*, 418.
[49]Atschkassow, 'Landing Operations of the Soviet Naval Fleet,' 305.

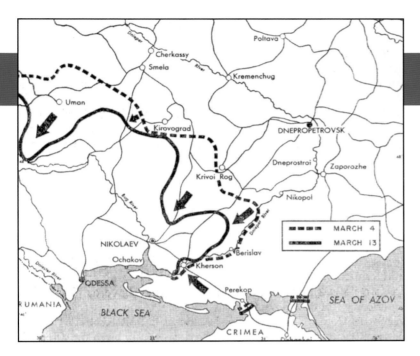

The Russian front line in March 1944. (NHB)

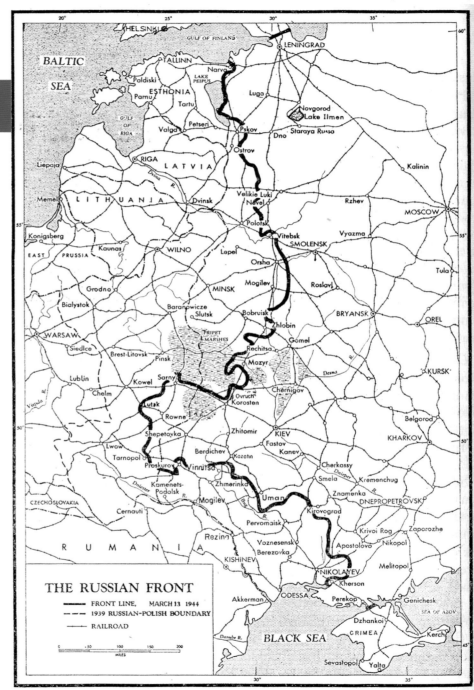

Though the Soviets did derive operational and strategic benefits from the use of their amphibious forces, and often used them with a skill generally ignored in the West, there is much about the conduct of their operations to criticise. The first and foremost is that they were far, far too generous with the lives of their men, a standard criticism of Soviet military operations. Casualties are a bitter reality of war, but the Soviets made little effort to keep these to a minimum. One way of doing so would have been to provide their men with proper amphibious equipment, especially some type of landing craft. This was not beyond the capability of Soviet industry (which generally out-produced the Germans), and having proper equipment would have enabled the Red Navy to put men, their weapons, and their supplies ashore more quickly, and in larger numbers, thus speeding the conduct of any operation and increasing the chances of its success. This would have meant fewer failed landings, fewer evacuated beachheads, and a smaller loss of life.

Amphibious operations were not the key to eventual Soviet success in the Black Sea during World War II, but they were an important component of the Soviet military effort that kept the Germans off-balance, threatened their unguarded flank while drawing away resources needed elsewhere, and gave the regular land forces of the Red Army valuable support against the Nazi invasion of the Soviet Union.

Russian Naval sailors of the Black Sea fleet standing by their anti-aircraft guns ready for action. (IWM Rus file 4443)

Further Reading

Achkasov, V. I. and Pavlovich, N. B., *Soviet Naval Operations in the Great Patriotic War, 1941-1945*, (Annapolis, Maryland: Naval Institute Press, 1973)

Atschkassow, W. I. "Landing Operations of the Soviet Naval Fleet during World War Two." Michael C. Halbig, trans. In Merrill L. Bartlett, ed., *Assault from the Sea: Essays on the History of Amphibious Warfare*, (Annapolis, Maryland: Naval Institute Press, 1983, 299-307)

Belous, N., "Soviet Amphibious Preassault and Landing Operations in World War II." Kendall E. Lappin, trans. In Merrill L Bartlett, ed., *Assault from the Sea: Essays on the History of Amphibious Warfare,* (Annapolis, Marlland: Naval Institute Press, 1983, 292-298)

Eustigneev, E., "On Course to Novorossiisk." Jane E. Good and James A. Malloy, Jr., trans. In Merrill L. Bartlett, ed., *Assault from the Sea: Essays on the History of Amphibious Warfare*, (Annapolis, Maryland: Naval Institute Press, 1983, 286-291)

Khamalov, Kh., *Naval Infantry in Combat for the Motherland*, (Moscow: Military Publishing House, 1966)

Kipp, Jacob W., "The Second Arm and the Problem of Combined Operations: The Russian-Soviet Experience, 1853-1945." In Philip S. Gillette and Willard C. Frank, Jr., eds., *The Sources of Soviet Naval Conduct*, (Lexington, MA: Lexington Books, D.C. Heath and Co., 1990, 121-163)

Meister, Jürg, *Der Seekrieg in den osteuropäischen Gewässern 1941-45*, (München: J.F. Lehmanns Verlag, 1958)

Mitchell, Donald W., *A History of Russian and Soviet Sea Power*, (New York: MacMillan, 1974)

Nargele, Dominik George, "The Soviet Naval Infantry: An Evolving Instrument of State Power", (Georgetown University, PhD dissertation, 1983)

Ruge, Friedrich, *The Soviets as Naval Opponents, 1941-1945*, (Annapolis, Maryland: Naval Institute Press, 1979)

Biography

Donald Stoker is Professor of Strategy and Policy for the US Naval War College's Monterey Program. He is the author of *Britain, France, and the Naval Arms Trade in the Baltic, 1919-1939: Grand Strategy and Failure* (Frank Cass, 2004), and the co-editor of *Girding for Battle: The Arms Trade in a Global Perspective, 1815-1940* (Praeger, 2004). Currently, he is co-editing two works: *Conscription in the Napoleonic Era* and *Strategy in the American War of Independence: A Global Approach*, and developing another, tentatively titled, *The Origins of Middle Eastern Naval Power*. He is also at work on his second book, *The Strategy of the U.S. Civil War, 1861-1865,* and awaiting the 2005 publication of his first novel.

The Liberation of the Gilberts
Operation GALVANIC, November 1943

By Mr Branden Little

Strategic Background and Planning

In the fall of 1943 Allied forces clearly held the initiative across the many fronts of the Pacific theatre. They were poised to conquer Bougainville, the northernmost and last redoubt of the Solomons; coiled at the doorstep of the fortress Rabaul on New Britain Island; collected after evicting the Japanese from the northern Pacific Aleutians; and intent on driving into the central Pacific. But the Allies lacked the strength to penetrate deeply into Japan's defensive perimeter in order to secure the right flank of General Douglas MacArthur's southwest Pacific thrust and to carry the war directly to the Japanese home islands.

The contours of Allied strategy in the Pacific theatre had already been determined in planning conferences that year at Casablanca, Washington, D.C., and Quebec. The Combined Chiefs of Staff (CCS) agreed that in 1943-44 American forces would commence a central Pacific campaign to conquer enemy-occupied island chains from the Marshalls to the Marianas. Although Allied in name, operations in the central Pacific would remain exclusively an American enterprise until 1945. Preliminary plans conceived of staging an attack into the Marshall Islands from the growing network of U.S. air and naval bases in the Ellice, Samoan, and Canton Islands. Admiral William F. Halsey had launched a carrier raid on the Marshalls in early 1942, but little was learned about enemy fortifications. Afterward, regular aerial reconnaissance or preparatory bombings proved impossible due to the extreme distances from U.S. bases. By mid-1943, the CCS expected the Japanese to have heavily reinforced defences in the Marshalls with ground troops and aircraft operating from numerous airfields.

> *The Solomons campaign demonstrated the validity of landing operations doctrine and procedures, but U.S. amphibious forces still lacked vital equipment and experience for conducting assaults against strongly defended islands*

Allied naval forces were rapidly growing in strength, but matériel weaknesses and inexperience made commanders cautious. The failure of the Allied task force to remain on station during the invasion of Guadalcanal, compelled by Japanese warships to withdraw, constantly reminded the U.S. Navy of the hazards of supporting amphibious landings, and made the U.S. Marines eternally wary of their comrades-in-arms who abandoned them during the initial phase of the battle. Thereafter, the navy's leadership insisted that future amphibious operations be swiftly concluded to free the surface fleet for anticipated engagements with the powerful Japanese Combined Fleet. The Solomons campaign demonstrated the validity of landing operations doctrine and procedures, but U.S. amphibious forces still lacked vital equipment and experience for conducting assaults against strongly defended islands. The brief but intense opposition confronted during the Bougainville landing hinted at what lay ahead for Allied ground forces in the central Pacific islands, where far greater difficulties were expected because coral reefs promised to restrict the passage of landing craft, and as the proximity to the Japanese home islands multiplied dangers.

In light of these considerations, the U.S. Joint Chiefs of Staff (JCS) reconsidered an invasion of the Marshalls as the commencement of the central Pacific campaign. Wake, Nauru, and the Gilbert Islands ranked prominently on the list of alternates. Pacific Fleet commanders quickly discounted Wake and Nauru because of their remoteness from U.S. bases; Nauru's garrison, estimated at 3,700 troops-strong, also discouraged its selection. The JCS chose the Gilberts instead - a chain of atolls and islands southeast of the Marshalls - and appreciably closer to U.S. bases located in the Ellices at the atolls of Funafuti, Nukufetau, and Nanumea. These locations were over three times closer than Pearl Harbor to the Gilberts.

The Gilberts, a British colony since 1916 (and now part of the Republic of Kiribati), comprise sixteen, low-lying coral atolls and islands and are located 480 km to the southeast of the Marshalls, 3,800 km southwest of Hawaii, and 4,500 km northeast of Australia. All the islands are less than 4 metres in elevation. A total of 26,000 natives and about 100 foreigners inhabited the islands before the war. Japan invaded the Gilberts in December 1941, seized the Makin Atoll, and expanded its control over the Tarawa and Abemama (also called Apamama) Atolls in angry response to a raid by U.S. Marines in August

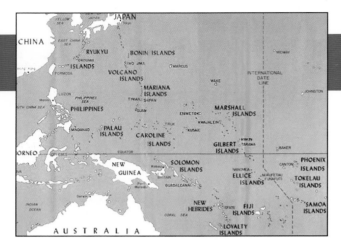

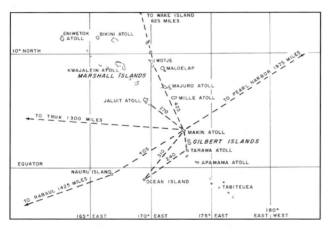

1942. Operating clandestinely from two submarines, Lieutenant Colonel Evans F. Carlson and two companies of the 2nd Marine Raider Battalion conducted an amphibious raid on Butaritari, an island in the Makin Atoll. Although a modest boon for American morale, this action prompted the Japanese to augment defences in the Gilberts and aggressively destroy the clandestine network of New Zealand Coastwatchers who relayed intelligence to Allied forces from these islands.

Despite these developments, the full scope of which was not known, selecting the Gilberts eased many strategic concerns and logistical burdens. The capture of an enemy seaplane base at Butaritari and an airfield at Betio (pronounced Bay-sho) in the Tarawa Atoll promised to eliminate the most immediate threat to interallied lines of communication between the United States, Australia, and New Zealand. It would diminish enemy threats to Allied bases in the Ellices, Samoas, and elsewhere. Future reconnaissance and attacks on the Marshalls could also be staged from the Gilberts. Given the familiarity of U.S. commanders with implementing a reduced-risk, incremental approach such as that employed in the move toward Rabaul, the Gilberts were strategically situated for initiating operations against the Japanese-controlled central Pacific.

Operational Planning and Deployment
In July 1943, the JCS directed Admiral Chester W. Nimitz, Commander in Chief, Pacific Fleet and Pacific Ocean Areas, to prepare for the Gilberts' liberation, presciently dubbed Operation GALVANIC. It informed Nimitz that the timetable for the Gilberts was late November 1943; for the Marshalls it was January 1944. The Gilberts were to be immediately turned into a launching pad for reconnaissance and bombing missions in preparation for the assault upon the Marshalls. The rapid schedule was designed to accelerate the operational tempo of the central Pacific campaign and generate strategic momentum in support of the combined Allied efforts against Japan.

Tarawa is of more strategic importance to us than it is to the enemy

The navy's leadership echoed the JCS's directive by insisting that the assault troops swiftly seize the objectives to restore the mobility of the carrier and invasion task forces and thereby elude retaliation by Japan's still-formidable navy and air forces. It was widely believed that a brief naval bombardment would destroy fortifications on the Gilberts and expedite their capture by ground troops.

Chief of staff of the 2nd Marine Division, Colonel Merritt A. Edson, was involved in the planning. He produced a contrary 'estimate of the situation' that predicted Japan would not counterattack with its Combined Fleet. 'It is doubtful' he argued, 'if they will risk a major fleet engagement to retain it or to reinforce it... Tarawa is of more strategic importance to us than it is to the enemy'. Edson desired for the navy to remain on-station, deliver a lengthier bombardment, and prevent a reoccurrence of the epic struggle for Guadalcanal where Japanese warships bombarded American ground forces after Allied vessels withdrew from the vicinity. He fully expected the U.S. Navy to retreat and leave the marines vulnerable to enemy reprisals. Moreover, he believed that the enemy at Tarawa would 'endeavour to hold it and to make its capture as costly as possible'. Edson spoke as a veteran of Guadalcanal, where he earned the United States' highest award for valour, the Congressional Medal of Honour.

A briefing prior to the assault on Betio. (USMC)

His analysis fell on deaf ears - the admirals wished to avoid another naval clash like that which occurred off Guadalcanal - and confidently predicted the destruction of enemy defences with a minimal preparatory bombardment. Although reconnaissance indicated defences at Betio were growing more formidable, marine requests to land artillery on nearby islets and for a lengthy bombardment were denied in deference to the overriding requirement for speed. Speed, in the admirals' calculus, was the foremost consideration for achieving success, to complete the operation before encountering a powerful counterattack and the completion of fortifications. These unbending constraints placed a heavy burden on the forces assigned to the mission.

Nimitz tasked Vice Admiral Raymond A. Spruance, commander of the Fifth Fleet, with liberating the Gilberts. The Fifth Fleet comprised nearly two-dozen new fleet carriers and smaller escort carriers. *Essex*-class fleet carriers displaced 27,100 tonnes and carried over 100 aircraft. *Casablanca*-class escort carriers displaced a mere 7,800 tonnes and carried 28 aircraft. The navy ordered numerous carriers in late 1941 and early 1942, and they were rapidly built and commissioned. In addition to the carriers, twelve battleships, fourteen cruisers, and an even larger complement of destroyers, transports, cargo vessels, landing craft, and vehicles formed an armada of over 200 ships manned by nearly 74,000 sailors.

To conduct the operation Spruance nominated Rear Admiral Richmond Kelly Turner, commander of the Fifth Amphibious Force, a flotilla of warships, transports, and landing craft, and Major General Holland M. Smith, commander of the V Amphibious Corps (VAC), whose purview included the marine and army assault troops assigned to the Fifth Fleet. Planning for GALVANIC began in earnest in August and coalesced in October at a staff conference in Hawaii.

Spruance, Turner, and Smith decided to conduct simultaneous amphibious assaults on two locations: the island of Betio in the Tarawa Atoll, and 170 km to the north, Butaritari, in the Makin Atoll. Both islands functioned as Japanese administrative centres of the Gilberts' central and northern districts, and possessed an airfield and seaplane base, respectively. Securing the remaining islands within the two atolls, along with the rest of the Gilberts, notably Abemama Atoll, became the secondary objective.

Accurately charting the hydrography was highly important because coral reefs surrounded each atoll within the Gilberts' archipelago; water depth over the reefs varied greatly and under certain conditions could prohibit landing craft from crossing. Reefs varied in size: some were hundreds of metres wide and enclosed lagoons that also stretched hundreds of metres from reef to shoreline. Should a Landing Craft Vehicle Personnel (LCVP) or Landing Craft Mechanised (LCM) fail to cross the entire reef, troops and vehicles would be stranded, forced to debark on the reef, and wade ashore. The depths of water in the lagoons also varied and craft capable of negotiating reefs might still beach well before their destination. Dry landings were a remote possibility. The challenges of assaulting an atoll were thus pronounced, and the timing of GALVANIC reflected tidal considerations.

Intelligence collection prioritised hydrographic conditions at Betio and Butaritari. Spruance's staff gathered a cadre of Australian and New Zealander reservists and civilians familiar with the Gilberts to determine tidal ranges. Dubbed the 'Foreign Legion', its calculations provided Turner and Smith with fairly accurate charts. The Legion anticipated a depth of 1.5 metres over the reef at Betio in late November, for example, but cautioned that regularly occurring (but unpredictable) 'dodging tides' caused the water to plummet to depths insufficient for landing craft to pass. Major F. L. G. Holland, an advisor from the New Zealand army who had lived in the Gilberts, took exception to their advice. He strongly protested that the invasion would founder because he predicted the water depth would only be 1 meter, thus preventing the passage of landing craft, which required at least 1.06 metres. The margin of error was very small.

The commanders understood that they might encounter a dodging tide but believed the risk to be low based upon the

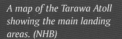

A map of the Tarawa Atoll showing the main landing areas. (NHB)

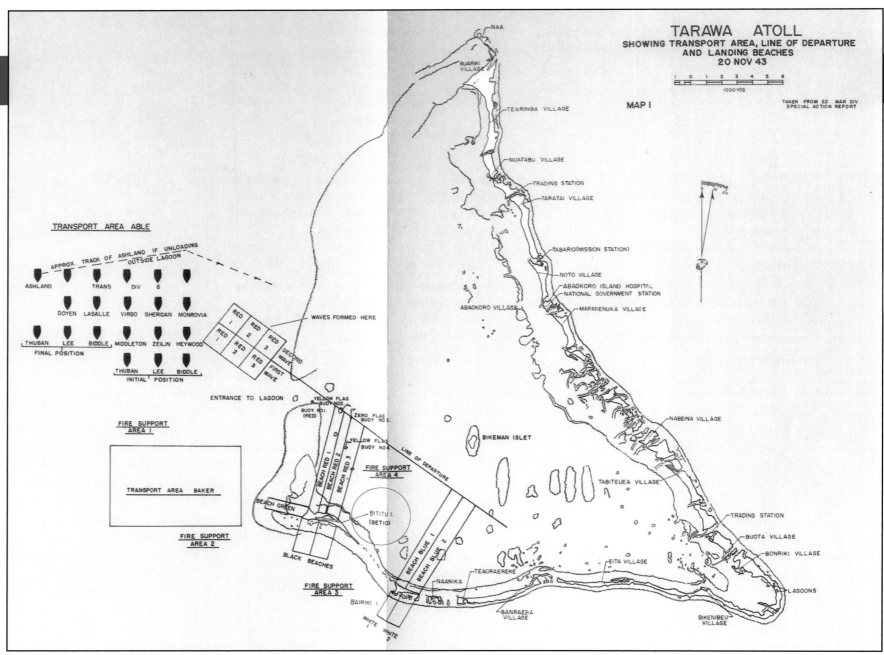

experts' majority opinion. They recognised the dangers involved and trusted that the high tides on the morning of 20 November would be sufficient for the landing craft to cross. During optimal conditions, however, high tide would only last for about four hours; no boats could cross during low tide. All the waves of landing forces needed to debark their troops and equipment within this narrow span of time.

As a precautionary measure, Marine Corps planners recommended the use of amphibian tractors - the unarmoured Landing Vehicle Tracked (LVT) - for transporting the initial waves of landing forces. The 'amtrac' featured tracks that functioned like paddlewheels and could operate on land and sea. Previous tests suggested it could negotiate coral reefs at low tide unlike conventional landing craft, but exhaustive trials were warranted. Tests conducted at Noumea, Fiji, and in the United States between May and October 1943 verified the LVT's capability to operate in high surf, over reefs, and barbed wire. In the event the tide 'failed', a shuttle system was devised to convey the troops and cargoes in successive waves from the reef to the shore. Unfortunately, operational LVTs were not yet available in quantity; only enough existed to carry the initial waves. While planners arranged for LVTs to be employed in a combatant role, attempts were made to determine the strength of enemy forces at Tarawa and Makin.

Early estimates of enemy strengths, revised later as a result of reconnaissance in mid-September 1943 from army and navy aircraft and submarines, provided detailed composites of the transformation of Betio and Butaritari into island fortresses. After Carlson's raid in August 1942 the Japanese had fervently prepared for an invasion of the Gilberts. For over a year highly skilled engineers and enslaved Korean labourers built fortifications. The Japanese continually improved upon the defences, which included erecting an impenetrable steel fence around Betio, and employing along the reef concertina wire, mines, and concrete tetrahedrons to channel landing craft into zones defended by numerous heavy weapons. They built a 1 to 1.5 metre-high seawall of coconut logs around nearly the entire island. At Butaritari elaborate, water-filled tank ditches segmented the island to hinder the movement of Allied forces. Rear Admiral Keiji Shibasaki arrived in July 1943 to coordinate these efforts. He fully understood that his men needed to resist an Allied attack for 3 to 7 days before the Combined Fleet could arrive to contest the invasion. Cognisant that his men were creating a potential nightmare for an invasion force, Shibasaki boasted that a million men in a hundred years could not conquer Tarawa. Marine planners conceded 'that the topography and hydrography of the area definitely favour the enemy'.

U.S. intelligence accurately estimated the number of defenders in the Gilberts. An ingenious method of counting latrines helped determine how many Japanese resided on the islands by correlating their army regulations for sanitation with aerial photos. At Betio the Americans anticipated about 4,600 enemy forces and at Makin 800; the number of combatants was somewhat lower in reality because Korean labourers were factored into the totals. The invasion forces were the beneficiaries of the sinking of the *Bangkok Maru*, an auxiliary transport carrying 1,200 Japanese soldiers to Betio, by a U.S. submarine in May 1943. Intercepted Japanese communications alerted American forces to the transport's route.

VAC commander Holland Smith designated two divisions to conduct the seizure of Tarawa and Makin: the 2nd Marine Division (of which Colonel Edson was the chief of staff) commanded by Major General Julian C. Smith, and the army's 27th Infantry Division, commanded by Major General Ralph C. Smith. Julian Smith's marines were stationed in Wellington, New Zealand and Ralph Smith's soldiers in Pearl Harbor, Hawaii, and their staffs actively participated in the October conference. Substantive differences existed between the divisions' combat effectiveness - the majority of marines were battle-hardened veterans of the Solomons campaign and versed in amphibious doctrine and training, but the soldiers comprised a National Guard unit called to federal service with little or no combat experience. They lacked traditions of interoperability with the fleet, but endeavoured to compensate for inexperience in amphibious operations through an intense, pre-deployment regimen. These disparities, however, repeatedly appeared during operational planning and execution.

Accordingly, Holland Smith directed the more experienced organisation, the 2nd Marine Division, to accomplish the more difficult task of seizing Tarawa. He believed that a regimental

*Admiral Turner's flagship the
USS Pennsylvania (BB-38). (DoD)*

combat team (RCT) from the 27th Infantry Division would overwhelm the small number of defenders at Makin. But Admiral Turner insisted that Smith remain on-scene with him during the Makin operation, aboard the flagship *Pennsylvania* (BB-38). Turner's main concern was retaliation by Japanese air and naval forces from the Marshalls and Truk which were closer to Makin than Tarawa; Smith felt he should be present at Tarawa where heavier fighting was expected.

The scheduled date for the invasions of Makin and Tarawa was 20 November. The 27,600-strong army and marine force would conduct a simultaneous, two-pronged assault on islands 170 km apart, in combination with a series of attacks on lesser defended atolls. To orchestrate this initial phase of the central Pacific campaign, Spruance divided the powerful Fifth Fleet into four task forces (TF). Coordinating this trans-Pacific manoeuvre was extraordinarily complex. Its successful execution required detailed planning and precise timing. Deception featured prominently in plans for GALVANIC, which commenced with carrier raids on numerous enemy bases throughout the central and southwest Pacific.

The Fast Carrier Task Force, commanded by Rear Admiral Charles A. Pownall, spearheaded the assault by launching preparatory raids and intercepting threats in the target area throughout September and November 1943. Employing four separate carrier groups that sortied from Hawaii and the New Hebrides, Pownall endeavoured to deceive the Japanese as to

what the Allies' intentions were and where an invasion might take place by bombing the Marshalls, Rabaul, Wake, Marcus, and Nauru, in addition to the Gilberts. These actions permitted aerial reconnaissance of invasion sites, and, it was later learned, effectively degraded the capabilities of enemy air forces to counterattack the invasion. Moreover, Japanese defenders expended large quantities of irreplaceable ammunition to repel the raids. Japan's failure to re-supply its garrisons diminished their capacity to resist.

Task Force 52, the Northern Attack Force, was formed to conduct the assault on Makin. It remained under Turner's direct control and sortied from Pearl Harbor in mid-November. Four battleships, four cruisers, three escort carriers, six troop transports carrying elements of the 27th Infantry Division, and one tank transport plus miscellaneous vessels steamed together toward the Gilberts after conducting rehearsals off Maui in the Hawaiian Islands. They were preceded by three Landing Ship Tanks (LSTs), derisively called 'Large Slow Targets', which carried amtracs and had departed several days earlier to ensure that they arrived on time with the faster elements which followed them.

To effect the seizure of Tarawa and Abemama, Task Force 53, the Southern Attack Force under Rear Admiral Harry W. Hill, was established. In early November, it transported the 2nd Marine Division from New Zealand to Efate in the New Hebrides for rehearsals. The Mobile Service Squadron, an innovative support organization, refuelled TF 53 underway before it reached the

Gilberts. Three battleships, five cruisers, five escort carriers, sixteen troop transports, one tank transport, and nearly two dozen destroyers steamed separately from amtrac-laden LSTs. The LSTs departed San Diego, California for the Samoas to collect vehicle crews that feverishly worked to add armour to the vehicles, before rendezvousing with TF 53 off Tarawa on the morning of the invasion.

TF 52 and 53 initially deployed on geographic tracks converging on the Ellices, southeast of the Gilberts. In the event Japanese surveillance detected the convoys the feint would not be readily obvious. The LSTs' early departure from Hawaii and the Samoas created a higher but acceptable level of risk to the commanders who debated the issue but were persuaded by Holland Smith's arguments that Betio could not be taken without amtracs. The deception worked; the convoys remained undetected until 18 November when they were nearly on station.

The fourth task force departed last and was scheduled to arrive on 24 November. Divided into two elements, the Garrison Group of 7,600 troops steamed from Hawaii and the Samoas. Its vital mission was to relieve the assault troops and transform the war-torn islands into functioning bases.

Liberating Butaritari

Butaritari Island is the largest land mass in Makin, the northernmost atoll in the Gilberts. It stretches like an elongated letter 'T', and is 16 km long and 410 metres wide. A fringing

2nd Battalion, 165th Infantry assault Yellow Beach, Butaritari Island, in the Makin Atoll. (NARA)

reef surrounds the atoll and ranges from 90 metres wide on the southern side to 1,100 metres wide on the northern side.

The Japanese had established a seaplane base and radio station on the island. A conglomerate force of 600 Japanese soldiers and sailors defended it from Allied invasion; about half of those troops were deemed 'combat effectives'; the rest included aviation and construction personnel. 200 Koreans worked on Butaritari. Defences were concentrated in an area the Allies called the 'Citadel', an 1,800 metre-long segment in the island's centre. Strengthening their position, the defenders constructed deep tank ditches that intersected the island on the western and eastern sides of the Citadel.

General Ralph Smith conceived the invasion plan for Butaritari. He intended to land two battalions of infantry on the west coast of Butaritari, and to land a third battalion on the northern coast, two hours later. The third battalion would then divide into two elements, one moving westward to unite with the initial force and the second to drive eastward to secure the remainder of the island. Smith believed he could crush the enemy stronghold with a pincer movement. Holland Smith favoured a single assault, but he did approve the more complicated plan with its sequential landings. The army received no guarantee of LVT availability and planned accordingly, expecting and hoping for a high tide.

Ralph Smith formed the 165th RCT (Reinforced) from the 27th Infantry Division to effect Butaritari's seizure. Elements of various units also joined the 165th, including part of the 105th Regiment, and a marine reconnaissance platoon. The force totalled 6,500 men. Fortunately for the soldiers, 50 LVT(2)s arrived in Hawaii two weeks prior to the invasion.

Bombardments by naval gunfire and carrier planes preceded landings on the morning of 20 November. The troops landing on the western beaches encountered no resistance until moving further inland. A diminishing tide pressed the LVTs into ferry service, conducting trips to and from the reef to collect troops and equipment loaded in LCVPs. Inexperienced beach masters, fluctuating tides, and rocky beaches brought congestion to the shoreline with the deleterious effect that of 250 LCVP loads only 31 made it ashore on D-Day, but the larger LCM obtained a better record by landing 18 out of 28 loads. Supplies were not a critical issue because the regiment was not engaged in fierce combat.

Poor coordination between the infantry and tanks that made it ashore, exacerbated by an inability to aggressively attack the enemy, meant that the western landings bogged down before reaching the tank ditch. Sporadic sniper fire and a 15-man redoubt delayed two battalions during the first day. The landings on the northern coast encountered minimal enemy fire.

LVTs deposited their passengers on the beaches, although the majority of infantry in later waves waded across 275 metres of shallow water without difficulty.

What Holland Smith expected Ralph Smith to accomplish in one day took four instead. The assault was haphazard, hampered by poor fire discipline and communications. The failure to effect the enemy's destruction as rapidly as planned was attributable to the inadequate training of green army units in amphibious tactics. After overwhelming the western barrier defences the soldiers methodically drove eastward, captured the Citadel, and reached the island's furthest tip by the morning of the 23rd.

The army suffered 66 killed and 187 wounded. The entire Japanese garrison was destroyed, and most of the Koreans surrendered. An enemy submarine, one of nine despatched by the Japanese navy to contest the invasion, sank the escort

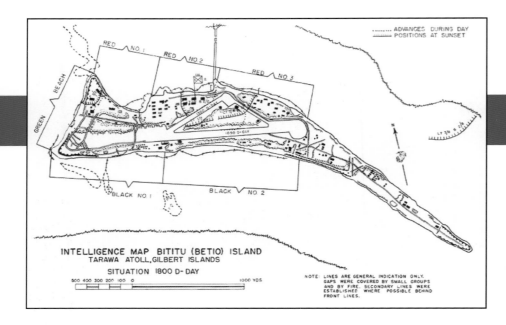

INTELLIGENCE MAP BITITU (BETIO) ISLAND
TARAWA ATOLL, GILBERT ISLANDS
SITUATION 1800 D-DAY

An intelligence map of Betio Island. (USMC)

carrier *Liscome Bay* (CVE-56) on 21 November with the terrific loss of 644 officers and men, including the commander of the air support group for TF 52, Rear Admiral Henry M. Mullinnix.

Naval historians have long argued that had the army conquered the island with the desired speed, the screening force to which *Liscome Bay* was attached would have departed before I-175 arrived to sink it. This loss undeniably reinforced the imperative naval officers felt concerning amphibious operations, namely that they be quickly concluded to release the fleet from its supporting role in a restricted area of operations, within range of enemy forces.

Interservice strain between the army on one side and the navy and marines on the other intensified as a result of the *Liscome Bay* episode. One positive result of the catastrophic sinking, however, was that it inspired the navy to strengthen the armour protecting other escort carriers' magazines. These structural changes undoubtedly mitigated future losses.

Liberating Betio

The Tarawa Atoll consists of over forty small islands and islets in a triangular shape, virtually enclosed by a coral reef. The southern (bottom) chain of islands is about 19 km long and the right side, angled in a northwestern direction, is about 29 km long. The left, or western side of Tarawa, is a reef with one major break that provides an entrance to the lagoon.

Betio Island is located at the southwestern tip of the atoll. It is 3,500 metres long, 730 metres across at the widest point, and is 117 hectares in area. A reef with a width of between 450 and 1,100 metres surrounds Betio; the lagoon measures between 180 to 730 metres from the reef's edge. In 1943 its bird-like shape with beak and abdomen inside of the lagoon, was emphasised by a pier extending into the lagoon, giving the impression of skinny legs. Betio possessed a 1,300-meter runway that the Japanese started building in October 1942 and the Allies discovered in late January 1943. A force of 4,700 Japanese, including Special Naval Landing Forces (*rikusentai*), manned virtually every part of Betio and had constructed elaborate fortifications across the island, along the reef, and in parts of the lagoon. They built some 500 reinforced bunkers and pillboxes with concrete, steel, sand, and coconut logs that contained dozens of heavy weapons.

The geography of Betio presented the marines with the daunting task of frontal assault. Given the island's small size they had little opportunity to achieve tactical surprise or avoid contact with the enemy. Faced with these impediments, General Julian Smith's 2nd Marine Division developed a plan that would prove Admiral Shibasaki's 'million men' proclamation wrong. Colonel Edson and Colonel David M. Shoup were the chief architects of that plan. Defences were weakest along the northern lagoon side and they decided to strike there with three battalions of infantry, understanding that invading from this approach was more complicated and required the landing craft to travel 16 km before reaching the reef. The Japanese did not anticipate the Americans would approach from this direction and consequently had not fortified the lagoon beaches as substantially as the approaches from the sea.

As a former president of the Marine Corps Equipment Board, Smith knew about the LVT's promise, but he generously credited Shoup with the proposal to use the LVT as an assault conveyance for the Gilberts' invasion. To augment their 75 LVT(1)s, they arranged for 50 LVT(2)s to be shipped from the United States to arrive in time to conduct the assault. The first three waves of assault troops would therefore be carried in amtracs; the remaining forces would follow in LCVPs and LCMs, hoping the tide would remain high enough to cross the reef.

On the morning of 20 November, TF 53 arrived off Tarawa and commenced an intense bombardment of Betio lasting four

hours. No deviations from the plan to extend the bombardment or position artillery on adjacent islets were permitted. Naval gunfire disrupted enemy communications, providentially obliterated Shibasaki and his staff, and destroyed many heavy weapons. Glitches in U.S. communications, however, severely disrupted the coordination of naval gunfire and close air support with the landing waves.

The marines soon discovered the tide was too low for conventional landing craft to cross. Due to an uncommon 'apogean neap tide' it remained low well into the second day. The LVTs functioned according to plan and proved indispensable, first, by depositing the initial three waves ashore; second, by ferrying men and equipment from the reef to the beach; and third, by evacuating wounded to the reef where they could be withdrawn by raft or LCVPs to ships for treatment. Although the low tide shattered the invasion's momentum, it preserved a dry beach upon which to land. If the tide was higher and the beach submerged, it would have denied the marines a shelter beneath the fire-swept seawall, drowned many of their severely wounded who received care on the beach, and made the collection of supplies exceedingly difficult if not impossible. The LVTs and the dry beach became key ingredients to the operation's success.

Enemy fire or related action disabled 90 of the 125 LVTs and compelled many marines to wade ashore from burning amtracs or from LCVPs hung-up on the reef. Betio's defenders mercilessly cut down men who waded hundreds of metres through the lagoon. Those who made it ashore fanned out from the narrowest of beachheads, through withering fire, and systematically reduced enemy positions with satchel charges, grenades, flamethrowers, and small arms. A leader among them was Major William D. Hawkins, whose scout-sniper platoon seized the long pier and pushed inland. Major John F. Schoettel's impassioned radio communications to Shoup revealed the precariousness of the assault: 'Receiving heavy enemy fire all along beach. Unable to land all [forces]. Issue in doubt'. 'We have nothing left to land' he

soon reported. Smith committed the regimental and divisional reserves within hours, signs of the marines' desperation. The corps reserve landed the following day.

Shoup's steadfast leadership of the ground forces ensured that the battle, although in grave doubt on several occasions, was ultimately resolved in the marines' favour. Organised resistance ceased in 76 hours at the cost of 1,027 Americans killed, 2,292 wounded, and 88 missing; 4,690 Japanese died, and 19 were captured alongside 127 Koreans. Shoup received

Securing the Gilberts

In addition to the conquest of Butaritari and Betio, U.S. forces seized adjacent islands in the two atolls to eliminate counterattacks by nearby bastions and to establish additional airfields. At Makin an infantry detachment surged forward to Kuma Island, the nearest to Butaritari, on the afternoon of the 22nd. The other few tiny islets contained no Japanese. The four vessels of the Makin Garrison Group arrived on the 24th to commence construction of an airfield for fighter planes. It was operational in early January 1944.

Just as the fighting had been heavier at Betio, the mopping up process in the Tarawa Atoll required more effort too. A reinforced battalion incurred 90 casualties while eradicating the last of the Japanese between 21-28 November. The four vessels of the Tarawa Garrison Group arrived on the 25th and quickly rehabilitated and expanded facilities on the atoll. Limited docking capacity and a shortage of transports made their task far less efficient than planned. Nevertheless, by late December medium bombers and fighters were attacking the Marshalls from airfields on Betio and Buota, an island at the southeastern tip of

The contribution of logistics to operational manoeuvre was clearly demonstrated by the synchronisation of the assault landings with the arrival of garrison units

Tarawa. The runways were built over the bulldozed graves of many marines - one veteran sardonically reflected that the dead literally 'paved the way to Tokyo'. Heavy bombers commenced operations from Tarawa in early January.

Abemama Atoll is situated 120 km southeast of Tarawa and features a deep lagoon suitable as an anchorage for ships. The largest of the atoll's islands, Abemama, is a 'J'-shaped island over 11 km in length, and is between 900 to 1800 metres wide. The Japanese had intended to establish an airfield on the island, but the Americans did so first. On 21 November, a company of marines conducted a raid from a submarine using rubber rafts. They overran two dozen Japanese with the assistance of native islanders, their submarine's deck gun, and a nearby destroyer. By mid-January medium bombers and fighters were operating from an airfield constructed by the Abemama Garrison Group.

These relatively minor endeavours were essential to ensure the safety of the garrison personnel from residual enemy outposts. Allocating the resources to accomplish these tasks was not an inconsequential consideration for commanders eager to redeploy assault forces and the ships supporting them. The contribution of logistics to operational manoeuvre was clearly demonstrated by the synchronisation of the assault landings with the arrival of garrison units.

the Congressional Medal of Honour, the British Distinguished Service Order (DSO), and Purple Heart; Major Henry G. Lawrence, executive officer of the 2nd Amphibian Tractor Battalion, earned the Navy Cross, the DSO, and Purple Heart. 'Bloody Tarawa' became an epithet for critics who argued the navy should have bypassed the atoll, and believed the exorbitant casualty list testified to poor judgement. Unfavourable comparisons were made to Guadalcanal where similar casualties were incurred but over a duration of six months. The senior commanders, among them Spruance, Turner, Hill, and Julian Smith, rejected this view. They agreed that this high price purchased them much needed experience to make future amphibious operations less costly and provided an invaluable position from which to invade the Marshalls.

Lessons Learned and Applied

In hindsight, the liberation of the Gilberts demonstrated the strategic value of opening a central Pacific campaign in tandem with the southwest Pacific drive. But if the marines had failed at Tarawa the JCS might have cancelled this campaign, and regrettably concentrated on MacArthur's singular thrust. Instead, because of the marines' victory, MacArthur's and Nimitz's forces 'cartwheeled' from objective to objective, established advanced bases, and bypassed numerous enemy strongholds. Japanese commanders were exasperated because they could not predict where the next attack would occur and could not repel the dual forces that operated over such a vast geographical expanse. At the time, however, U.S. commanders did not fully understand that Japan was incapable of responding effectively to the grand pincer movement. They were relieved and felt fortunate to have avoided tangling with the Combined Fleet before mustering sufficient strength to defeat it. They now appreciated that the unflinching emphasis on speed proved counterproductive, insofar as the landing forces were concerned. The refusal to extend preparatory bombardments and establish artillery on nearby islands risked defeat.

Exhaustive planning and preparation made GALVANIC possible, but the narrow victory at Tarawa demonstrated the need for even greater exertion, to include extended commitments by the fleet to support amphibious assaults. Raiding airfields, sinking transports, and wreaking havoc on Japanese bases were necessary but not sufficient factors in achieving victory. Likewise, the operational flexibility provided to the fleet and its amphibious forces by the Mobile Service Squadrons and Garrison Groups, which could replenish ships at sea and establish airfields and fleet anchorages, was of little importance without the capacity to actually seize the advanced bases where these facilities would be built.

The electrifying lessons of GALVANIC were earnestly sought, categorised, and disseminated throughout the armed services. Credit is due to the commanders who insisted that future operations must benefit from the Gilberts experience. The need for improved intelligence, unit-level firepower, enhanced naval gunfire and close air support, and greater numbers of amphibian tractors constituted the central 'lessons learned'. Better procedures and equipment for command, control, and communications between surface and landing forces were also imperative.

Periodic aerial and submarine reconnaissance, signals intercepts, and intelligence provided by Australian, New Zealander, and indigenous personnel were indispensable to formulating plans for GALVANIC. Routine surveillance of enemy movements and fortifications, and better hydrographic intelligence, would have greatly benefited planning and execution. To enhance their awareness of conditions in the Marshalls, U.S. forces immediately used aircraft based in the Gilberts to collect intelligence for the impending operation.

Flamethrowers and satchel charges proved invaluable on Betio, and bazookas and rockets were used effectively on Butaritari. An unfortunate administrative oversight prevented the marines from obtaining bazookas and rockets. More weapons of all types were needed to destroy ingeniously prepared defences. The need for specialised swimming teams to clear obstacles under water and on reefs was also recognised. Thereafter, underwater demolitions teams (UDTs) were formed and weapons' allocations were increased - for example, a division's allotment of flamethrowers skyrocketed from 24 at Betio to 243 at Saipan - a mere seven months later.

The GALVANIC commanders agreed upon recommendations to establish improved communications procedures, to modify munitions for increased effectiveness against ground fortifications, and to expand the duration and intensity of bombardments. Speed had been the primary justification for keeping the bombardment to a minimum, but it would have been of little value had the marines failed. They endorsed

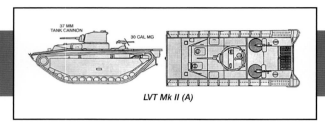

Left: High loss rates suffered by inadequately armoured amphibians indicated that changes were necessary.

Right: The armoured LVT mounting a 37mm cannon promised to enhance firepower. (USMC)

LVT Mk II (A)

arrangements for improved ship-to-shore communication to permit gunfire support after troops landed. Japanese defences encountered in the Gilberts were studied in detail and replicated on gunnery ranges in Hawaii to permit realistic training. Ships could fight forts contrary to the adage they could not. Their officers needed to learn how to do it better, and the imperviousness of defences on Betio made this readily apparent.

Perhaps the greatest operational lesson learned at Tarawa was the requirement for more LVTs. Senior commanders, including Spruance and Holland Smith, insisted that every division receive 300 LVTs with which to conduct amphibious operations. They did not want tidal fluctuations to impede future operations. The reef not only destroyed the marines' tactical momentum, but in combination with enemy fire and the low tide, threatened the Betio invasion with defeat. Admiral Hill affirmed, 'the assault [on Betio] would undoubtedly have failed if sole reliance had been placed on boats'. The LVT, therefore, was the critical technology that made success possible. Reassigning the army's LVTs to the marines would have facilitated the landing at Betio, but further retarded the conquest of Butaritari aptly characterised by Holland Smith as 'infuriatingly slow'; larger problems than this existed.

The risky contingency of receiving 50 LVT(2)s the morning of the invasion, and the high loss rates suffered by inadequately armoured amphibians at Betio indicated what changes were necessary. Programmes for LVT maintenance, combat repairs, crew training and interoperability with transport shipping and ground forces were soon implemented. New versions, including an armoured LVT mounting a 37mm tank cannon promised to enhance landing forces' firepower. Armoured troop-carrying models would dramatically increase the protection afforded to the vehicle crews and assault personnel. Amtrac production soon soared from a mere handful of LVT(1)s and (2)s to the manufacturing of thousands of vehicles at plants across the United States. As a result of its performance at Tarawa, the LVT earned a place as the lead assault conveyance for amphibious operations in the Pacific.

The enormous strategic benefits to amphibious operations of carrier raids and U.S. submarine attrition of Japanese maritime elements were not yet apparent. By exploiting the speed, range, and firepower of its carriers, and the stealth of its submarines, the U.S. Navy would relentlessly degrade Japan's island defences. Airbases, ground installations, and transports bearing troops and materials to enhance fortifications succumbed to these highly mobile components of U.S. naval power. Enemy garrisons, such as those at Butaritari and Betio, became increasingly isolated strong points rather than part of an interconnected defensive system. They were denied replenishment and stripped of protection from Japanese fighters and warships unable to

pierce the screens erected by American forces. The steady attrition of Japanese defences, and the ability to achieve sea and air control during an invasion, would immeasurably contribute to the success of U.S. amphibious assaults. U.S. commanders were justifiably cautious about GALVANIC, but commencing the central Pacific campaign was an undeniably bold endeavour. By seizing the initiative and opening this second Pacific front, the Allies directly challenged the Japanese to halt both campaigns. On the eve of 1944, U.S. forces had conclusively demonstrated their ability to conduct amphibious assaults against a determined foe.

The narrow victory at Tarawa revealed that they could offset matériel shortcomings and inexperience with sound strategy, doctrine, organisation, and personal intrepidity. U.S. forces proved adaptable to the ever-changing face of battle, whether on large jungle islands in the southwest Pacific or on tiny central Pacific atolls. They systematically integrated the myriad tactical and operational lessons of combat, and the new weapons of war rolling off American assembly lines, into an increasingly powerful military.

GALVANIC greatly facilitated the Marshalls' rapid conquest in January-February 1944, but thereafter the Gilberts' geostrategic importance diminished. Makin and Tarawa quickly became backwaters because, by their capture, they emboldened U.S. forces to brazenly exercise their expanding mobility and strength.

A Japanese Command Post with enemy tank in the foreground. Shells and bombs had little effect on this reinforced concrete structure. (USMC)

The experience gained there continuously benefited each new step toward the Japanese home islands. Slightly over two months later during the Marshalls invasion, nearly 500 LVTs were utilised, naval gunfire proved far more destructive, and the U.S. incurred fewer than 3,000 casualties. Within 18 months U.S. forces landed at Okinawa, the greatest of all amphibious operations in the Pacific, where 1,300 ships, 1,100 LVTs and over 191,000 marines and soldiers defeated an island fortress of 100,000 Japanese in three brutal months.

Betio took just over three days and incurred ten times fewer casualties than this culminating battle. But after Betio, and as a result of it, the outcomes of subsequent amphibious assaults in the Pacific war were never in doubt. The name of the atoll, Tarawa, remains indelibly etched in the American memory as a symbol of sacrifice and valour.

Lessons identified from the Gilberts

U.S. forces accelerated the strategic momentum in the Pacific theatre by initiating a central Pacific campaign in November 1943 to complement the southwest Pacific campaign. Commanders adopted a limited-risk campaign plan that balanced the desirability of offensive action with the comparative strengths and weaknesses of Allied and enemy forces. Operational manoeuvre depended greatly upon integrated logistical capabilities, to replenish multiple task forces at sea, and to swiftly convert Japanese-controlled islands into advanced bases from which to stage future operations. The establishment of sea control by

> **Operational manoeuvre depended greatly upon integrated logistical capabilities, to replenish multiple task forces at sea, and to swiftly convert Japanese-controlled islands into advanced bases from which to stage future operations**

the U.S. Navy was a function of preparatory raids and maintaining a preponderance of naval power in the Gilberts during Operation GALVANIC.

Carrier aviation and surface task forces protected the assault troops from counterattack by enemy air or sea power. Inadequate naval gunfire and close air support jeopardised the landing operation at Betio Island in the Tarawa Atoll. The duration, intensity, and timing of the preparatory bombardments proved woefully insufficient to destroy Japanese fortifications.

The amphibian tractor (LVT) negotiated coral reefs at low tide and delivered intact the initial waves of assault troops ashore. At Betio the failure of conventional landing craft to cross reefs destroyed the tempo generated by the LVTs and threatened the entire operation with failure. Numerical shortages of LVTs revealed that the much-vaunted industrial capacity of the United States was insufficiently mobilized in late-1943 to satisfactorily provision the Allies with critical military hardware.

Further Reading

Alexander, Joseph H., *Across the Reef: The Marine Assault of Tarawa. Marines in World War II Commemorative Series*, (Washington, D.C.: MCHC, 1993)

Alexander, Joseph H., *Storm Landings: Epic Amphibious Battles in the Central Pacific*, (Annapolis, MD: Naval Institute Press, 1997)

Alexander, Joseph H., *Utmost Savagery: The Three Days of Tarawa,* (New York: Ivy Books, 1995)

Morison, Samuel Eliot, *Aleutians, Gilberts and Marshalls, June 1942-April 1944*. Vol. 7 of *History of United States Naval Operations in World War II*, (Boston: Little, Brown and Co., 1951)

Shaw, Henry I., Bernard C. Nalty, and Edwin T. Turnbladh, *Central Pacific Drive*. Vol. 3 of *History of United States Marine Corps Operations in World War II*, (Washington, D.C.: MCHC, 1966)

Sherrod, Robert, *Tarawa: The Story of A Battle*, (New York: Duell, Sloan, and Pearce, 1944)

Stockman, James R., *The Battle for Tarawa*, (Washington, D.C.: MCHC, 1947).

Biography

Mr Branden Little is a PhD candidate in history at the University of California, Berkeley, and earned an MA in national security affairs from the US Naval Postgraduate School in 2002. He formerly served as Chief Operations Officer for the US Department of Defense's Center for Civil-Military Relations, where he coordinated international security assistance programmes. His publications examine aspects of modern naval history and civil-military relations. He is writing a doctoral dissertation on American-led humanitarian relief operations in First World War-era Europe, and is also completing a book manuscript, tentatively titled *A Means to an End: the Amphibian Tractor, Industrial Mobilization, and the Defeat of Japan.*

Anzio
Operation SHINGLE, January 1944

'Don't Stick Your Neck Out, Johnny': Exploitation, Risk, and Allied Failure at Anzio.[1]

By Dr Christopher Tuck

One of the foundations of manoeuvre warfare is a willingness to exploit circumstances as they emerge; manoeuvre warfare feeds upon 'the calculated risk, and the exploitation of chance circumstances.'[2] The purpose of this chapter is to examine the issues of exploitation and risk in relation to Operation SHINGLE, the Allied landing at Anzio on 22 January 1944. At Anzio, the Allies achieved complete tactical surprise, opening up a period of perhaps two days in which the landing force might have plunged inland in pursuit of its wider objectives. Instead, the landing force placed its focus on consolidating the landing rather than exploiting it; the Allies dug in, ceding the initiative to the Germans who sealed off the beachhead area, counter-attacked and threatened to overrun the Allied lodgement. Operation SHINGLE is a source of great controversy. One view sees a failure in tactical command; this image of failure regards Anzio as an excellent opportunity wasted by the vacillation of an incompetent land force commander unwilling to take the risks necessary to achieve success. Another view sees Anzio as an operation that could never have worked, in which the 'calculated risk' associated with exploitation would actually have amounted to a reckless and probably futile gamble.[3]

The debates regarding the sources of failure at Anzio are of enduring relevance. The contemporary focus on manoeuvrist approaches to war encourages risk-taking as a route to success. Yet the consequences of failure can be particularly high for amphibious operations; if things go wrong, the sea complicates seriously the ability to reinforce a landing or to evacuate it. For the landing force commander this creates a difficult tension between consolidation and exploitation. Consolidation is necessary so that an amphibious lodgement can resist enemy counter attacks. The consolidated beachhead also acts as the strong base into which reinforcements and logistic support can be brought and from which further operations are supported. Yet without exploitation an amphibious landing is meaningless; worse, it risks ceding the initiative to the enemy and being sealed in or pinched out.

This chapter argues that Operation SHINGLE did not fail to achieve its objectives because of the incompetence of one man. Instead, the commanders judgement regarding the risks that he should take in choosing the balance between consolidation and exploitation were shaped by factors largely outside of his control, not least: the unrealistic assumptions that underpinned the operation; the failure to maintain unity of effort from the strategic down to the tactical levels; and the failure to provide

forces adequate for the task. The chapter begins by examining the overall objectives of the Anzio landing. It then moves on to examine the plan and the assumptions that underpinned that plan. The analysis then focuses on the execution of the plan, showing how the early success of the operation was lost as too long was spent on consolidation. Finally, the analysis focuses on key areas that shaped the commanders' willingness to risk early exploitation of the Anzio landings.

Anzio: The Operational Concept

An examination of the wider objectives of Operation SHINGLE is necessary for two reasons: first, it is important to understand what strategic and operational level decision-makers believed the objectives of the operation to be; second, it highlights the number of optimistic assumptions that had to be made in order for the plan to work.

With the link up of 5th and 8th Armies after the Salerno operation in September 1943, the Allies gained firm control of the south of Italy. The Allies managed to take the Foggia airfields and this allowed Allied bombers to attack the Rumanian airfields. However, follow-on operations designed to push further north became bogged down. In the face of a skilfully handled defensive withdrawal by the Germans, facilitated by difficult terrain and

---

[1] The analysis, opinions and conclusions expressed or implied in this chapter are those of the author and do not necessarily represent the views of the JSCSC, the UK MOD or any other government agency. The author would like to thank Dr Deborah Sanders for her comments and observations on earlier drafts of this chapter.

[2] John F. Antal, 'Thoughts About Maneuver Warfare' in Richard D. Hooker, Jr (Ed), *Maneuver Warfare: An Anthology* (Novato: Presidio, 1993) p.64.

[3] In relation to this chapter, the distinction between 'risk' and 'gamble' is taken to lie in the issues of probability and consequences; risks are taken when there is still a reasonable probability of success and where the consequences of failure can be mitigated by precautions; gambles involve 'all or nothing' scenarios in which the chance of success is unknown and the consequences of failure are high.

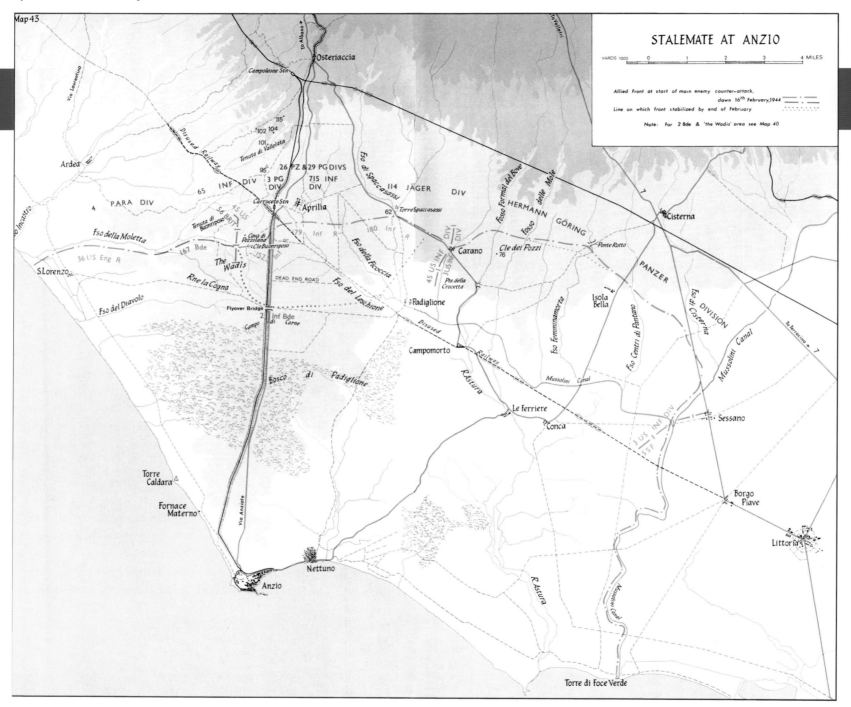

Map 43

STALEMATE AT ANZIO

YARDS 1000   0   1   2   3   4 MILES

Allied Front at start of main enemy counter-attack,
                              dawn 16ᵗʰ February,1944
Line on which front stabilized by end of February

Note: For 2 Bde & 'the Wadis' area see Map 40

atrocious weather, the Allied advance ground to a halt in front of the Gustav Line. Montgomery was critical of the whole approach of the Allies in Italy. He criticised the ad-hoc approach taken by the Allies to the Italian campaign with insufficient thought given to how operations in Italy would be developed, and a failure to establish an adequate logistics framework to cope with the widening scope of the campaign.[4] For example, by October 1943 the Allies logistic framework could only support 16-17 divisions, but the Germans already had 23 in Italy at that time, 9 of them in the South.[5]

By November 1943, the 5th and 8th Armies had suffered heavily in their attempts to crack the Gustav Line and Eisenhower had become convinced that a decisive breakthrough could not be achieved. The use of amphibious operations to turn the German flanks had an obvious logic; indeed, were it not for the shortage of transport caused by the needs of Operation OVERLORD Eisenhower recognised the logic of simultaneous amphibious attacks on both German flanks.[6] With only enough transport for one major landing, Churchill argued that the 'stagnation' in Italy could be ended by landing an allied division on the west coast of Italy at Anzio; a point fifty miles in front of the allied positions and 26 miles south of Rome. This force would then push 20 miles inland in order 'to cut the enemy lines of communication and threaten the rear of the German 14th Corps'.[7] Codenamed Operation SHINGLE, its successful execution and exploitation promised to unlock the whole Gustav Line and re-energise the Allied push northwards to Rome. Revised to include an expanded landing force of two divisions drawn from Lieutenant General Mark Clark's 5th Army, the landing would be co-ordinated with a major push from the south by II Corps, X Corps and the French Expeditionary Force. It was hoped that the landing at Anzio would force the German commander in southern Italy, Field-Marshal Albert Kesselring, to divide his forces to meet the multiple threats and that this would allow a breakthrough to be made either at Anzio or on 5th Army's front up Highways 6 and 7 forcing the Germans to withdraw and uncover Rome.

Even at the time, the Anzio landings were acknowledged as a risky venture. General Dwight D. Eisenhower, at that time Allied overall commander in the Mediterranean, pointed out to Churchill the potential pitfalls of landing a relatively small force well beyond the main Allied lines. Churchill, though, was absolutely committed to the operation, and overrode Eisenhower's concerns on the basis of the potential results that might be achieved.[8] In exasperation, Eisenhower commented: 'Prime Minister, when you want to do something you dismiss logistics with a wave of your hand.'[9] Eisenhower, though, was soon to be moved to the position of Supreme Commander Allied Expeditionary Force, and his place was taken by General Sir Henry Maitland Wilson, a British officer and thus more malleable in the face of Churchill's pressure.

The viability of Operation SHINGLE was based on an assumption made by higher-level decision-makers of the successful conjunction of a number of favourable factors.[10] First, Allied intelligence sources believed that the Germans would simply attempt to seal off an Allied landing, rather than focus on crushing it. Second, it was hoped that ex-theatre reinforcements would not be made available to Kesselring. Third, it was hoped that assaults by 8th Army on the Allied right would prevent Kesselring from shifting forces from that part of his front. Fourth, the Allies hoped that the overwhelming allied airpower could successfully isolate the landing area making it very difficult for the Germans to shift troops to meet the SHINGLE landing force. As Clark commented in his memoirs, however: 'That would have been according to the school-books; but in warfare things very seldom happen according to the book.'[11]

[4]Field Marshal B. Montgomery, *The Memoirs of Field-Marshal Montgomery* (London: Collins, 1958) pp.190-200.
[5]Eric Linklater, *The Campaign in Italy* (London: HMSO, 1977) p.152.
[6]Dwight D. Eisenhower, *Crusade in Europe* (New York: Doubleday, 1952) p.212
[7]Alexander's orders quoted in Field Marshal Lord Carver, *The Imperial War Museum Book of the War in Italy 1943-1945*, (London: Pan, 2001) p.108.
[8]Eisenhower, pp.212-213
[9]Carlo D'Este, *Eisenhower: Allied Supreme Commander* (London: Weidenfeld & Nicolson, 2002) p.470
[10]General Mark Clark, *Calculated Risk: His Personal Story of the War in North Africa and Italy* (London: Harrap, 195) pp.272-273.
[11]Ibid., p.272

HMS Mauritius, providing Naval Gunfire Support. (NHB)

Set against the risks of the operation, the Allies could rely on a number of favourable factors. One advantage was the theatre geography. Anzio was the best beach south of Rome, although it did have some problems, not least offshore sandbars and the fact the beach was soft and sandy which would make the going difficult for vehicles. Nevertheless, there were other places that the Allies could land which created a degree of uncertainty for Kesselring; even if the logic of Allied amphibious landings were clear, the exact place in which they might occur was not. Another advantage lay in Allied capabilities. Allied amphibious capabilities had been progressively improved through the introduction new techniques and equipment; the former included shore-to-shore logistic practices, the latter included Landing Ship Tanks, capable of offloading directly onto the beach, and DUKW amphibian vehicles. Amongst other things, these capabilities and techniques made the logistics of amphibious assaults less difficult.

The Allies could also rely on other advantages. By this stage of the campaign the Allies had sea control and air superiority. The Allies would have 2,700 aircraft to support the operation as opposed to around 400 German aircraft.[12] Moreover, Anzio was well within range of Allied air bases around Naples making it easier to bring this advantage to bear. The assault shipping would be well protected on the journey to the amphibious objective area. The Allies also had the benefit of effective intelligence resources; these included information from ULTRA sources, but also more detailed tactical information on the beaches and on the inland area thanks to beach reconnaissance and the activities of the Photograph Reconnaissance Wing.

Underpinning all that the Allies would do, however, was the advantage of experience. Commenting after the successful landings at Sicily, Montgomery's Chief of Staff Major-General Francis de Guingand argued that: 'We thought it was a great achievement, and we also thought we knew all about amphibious warfare.'[13] The experience at Sicily and Salerno may have illustrated that the Allies did not know all that there was to know about amphibious warfare, but it had shown that the Allies knew enough to effect successful landings at relatively short notice.

Planning

The Allies needed their experience. The final go-ahead for Anzio was only given late in the day. Planning was completed in two weeks and orders for the operation were distributed on 16 January. When D-Day was finally set at 22 January, it left only 15 days to carry out training and preparation for the landings.[14] The navy, in particular, were sceptical about the operation. There were continuous problems obtaining the necessary sea-lift, because of the growing demands elsewhere. Not only that, the Navy would almost certainly be locked in a protracted period of difficult logistic support for the Anzio beachhead until a link up could be effected with armies from the south; a particular problem given that the weather was expected to be bad.[15] Sir John Cunningham, the new naval commander in the Mediterranean,[16] nevertheless agreed to the plan given the prize at stake and because he felt that there was a good chance

---

[12]Brigadier CJC Molony, *History of the Second World War, Vol. 5: The Mediterranean and Middle East* (London: HMSO, 1973) p.563.
[13]These didn't go at all well. See Major-General Sir Francis de Guingand, *Operation Victory* (London: Hodder and Stoughton, 1947) p.310.
[14]Carlo D'Este, *Fatal Decision: Anzio and the Battle for Rome,* (London: Fontana, 1992) p.108.
[15]Ibid., pp.97-98.
[16]Sir John Cunningham, who replaced Sir Andrew Cunningham (no relation) in October 1943.

An LST approaching the assault area, while destroyers lay a smoke screen. (NHB)

Assault area, showing LSTs unloading. (NHB)

that the Germans would retreat once the landings had been made. Some of the problems of this short planning time were mitigated by the continuity in staff at the higher level.[17] The Allied command structure was conventional, but tested. The theatre commander was General Wilson in his capacity as Allied Commander-in-Chief, Mediterranean Theatre. Allied land forces were commanded by the Honourable Sir Harold Alexander, who commanded the 15th Army Group comprising the US 5th and British 8th Armies.

The Anzio landing force would consist of the US VI Corps of Clark's 5th Army, commanded by Major-General John P. Lucas. Allied airforces were commanded by Lieutenant-General Ira C. Eaker, USAAF. Naval command was vested in Admiral Sir John Cunningham, the Allies' naval Commander in Chief, Mediterranean, whose command included the American Vice Admiral Hewitt.[18] The command structure involved a high degree of integration between the British and American personnel. The US VI Corps, for example, contained almost as many British as American troops. In addition, the senior commanders were based in the theatre allowing them to visit the key areas of fighting.[19]

The final plan divided the Anzio assault area into two zones - the north and the south. In the north would be deployed the

Northern Assault Force (codenamed Peter) carrying the reinforced 1st British Infantry division (Major-General W.R.C. Penney), the 46th Royal Tank Regiment, and the 2nd Special Service Brigade consisting of 9 and 43 Royal Marine Commandos. In the south, the Southern Attack Force (codenamed X-Ray) would carry the 3rd US Infantry Division (Major-General Lucian K. Truscott), the 751st Tank Battalion, three battalions of Rangers, and the 504th Parachute Infantry Battalion. Following on from these initial landings would be a second wave consisting of half of the US 1st Armoured Division, the 157th Regimental Combat Team of the US 45th Infantry Division and elements of the Corps artillery. All told the SHINGLE force would amount to a total of 50,000 men and 5,000 vehicles.

This assault force would be carried or supported by 379 vessels of varying sizes. Peter force would be carried on three infantry landing ships, 33 tank landing ships and 56 other smaller craft; protection would be provided by the cruisers HMS *Orion*, HMS *Spartan*, HMS *Palomares* (an anti-aircraft and fighter direction ship) eleven destroyers, sixteen minesweepers, four anti-submarine/minesweeping trawlers, three tugs and another twenty assorted craft. This force would be commanded by Rear Admiral T.H. Troubridge in the Headquarters ship *Bulolo*. X-Ray force would be transported in five infantry landing ships, 50 tank landing ships and over 100 other types of landing craft; protection would come

[17]Theodore L. Gatchel, *At the Water's Edge: Defending Against the Modern Amphibious Assault*, (Annapolis: Naval Institute Press, 1996) p.57.

[18]Major-General Julian Thompson, 'Command at Anzio and in the Falklands: A Personal View' in G.D. Sheffield (Ed), *Leadership and Command: The Anglo-American experience Since 1861* (London: Brassey's, 1997) pp.159-160

[19]Thompson p.160. No command arrangement is perfect, and to set against the experience of the Allied commanders were the significant personal tensions between the US and the British. Alexander, for example, was sceptical of the abilities of the US Generals. Clark loathed Alexander whom he called 'a feather duster'. Clark, in turn, was disliked by his X Corps subordinate Lieutenant General Richard McCreery. See D'Este, *Eisenhower*, p.454-456

from HMS *Penelope* and USS *Brooklyn*, as well as 13 destroyers and assorted smaller vessels. The submarines HMS *Uproar* and HMS *Ultor* would act as beacon vessels. In total the Royal Navy would provide about half of the vessels for the operation with most of Peter Force carried by British vessels.[20] In addition to British and US ships there would also be Greek, Polish Dutch and French vessels involved in the operation.

Naval assets would also support the operation in other ways. With much of the transport due to be sent to Europe soon after the landing, the Anzio beachhead had to be able to support itself logistically after a month. The navy would therefore be involved in bringing in 30 days supply for the troops.[21] Naval assets were also earmarked for preparatory and diversionary activities. The former included reconnaissance of the landing area and beaches. The latter included attacks on coastal targets. On 20 January ships of the 15th Cruiser Squadron bombard coastal defences at Terracina to the south of Anzio. Diversionary bombardments and amphibious feints were carried out at Civitavecchia, north of Rome.

As with previous operations, airpower would also have an important part to play in the operation. Air power was tasked with several roles: the destruction of as much of the Luftwaffe as possible on the ground; interdicting the movement of enemy troops on the ground; protecting the landing force; and the provision of Close Air Support on the battlefield. Many of these attacks were conducted as preparatory operations; by 21 January Allied air forces had dropped 4,000 tons of bombs on German rail targets and 1,900 tons on German airfields.[23]

All of these efforts were designed first to land the assault force on Anzio beach and then to allow VI Corps to push northeastwards. The landing area was bounded to the south by the Pontine Marshes and to the north by wooded land and cultivated fields, interspersed by deep cuttings, that extended to the Tiber river. The landing area was cut through by a main road that ran from Anzio to Highway 7, one of the main routes to Rome. The plains beyond the Anzio beach spread inland for around 20 miles before reaching the Alban Hills, a massif rising to around 3,000 feet. Allied control of these hills would threaten the communications of the German right flank of the Gustav Line forcing the Germans to react.

Operation SHINGLE

The early part of the execution of the Allied plan went exceptionally well. Attacks on the Gustav Line began on January 15th. These succeeded in drawing south the main elements of 90th and 29th Panzer Grenadier Divisions, leaving the Anzio area virtually denuded of German troops. On 21 January the invasion force set out from the Naples area, reaching the amphibious objective area unseen; one fruit of Allied air superiority was that it severely curtailed German air reconnaissance capabilities. After an abbreviated bombardment immediately prior to the landing consisting of 758 5-inch rockets launched from a landing craft, the assault force went forward under cover of darkness with H Hour at 0200. The general structure of the landings in terms of command and control, logistics, movement ashore and so forth resembled that of Sicily and Salerno. In this the Anzio landings simply reflected accumulated amphibious 'best practice'.

The landings managed to achieve complete tactical surprise due to a combination of Allied deception and German intelligence failures. The only German formation in the area was a single depleted battalion of the 29th Panzer Grenadiers. Some challenges were posed by mines, shallow beach gradients and offshore sand bars, but otherwise resistance was minimal; Anzio was quickly seized by Ranger units and the first tank landing ships and landing craft were able to offload on D-Day. VI corps casualties on the first day amounted to only 13 dead and 87 wounded.[24] Offloading into the port commenced and 36,000 troops and 3,000 vehicles were landed without a casualty. By 23 January the Allies had established a firm perimeter. By 24

---

[20]S.W. Roskill, *The War at Sea*, Vol.III, Part 1, (London: HMSO, 1960) pp.302-303.
[21]Clark p.274.
[22]Molony, p.652.
[23]Ibid., p.660.
[24]Thompson, p.164.

A mine or bomb explodes among DUKWs carrying stores on to the Anzio beaches. (NHB)

January the beachhead was 15 miles wide and 7 miles deep. The development of the beachhead was not wholly without its problems. German air attacks on the 23rd inflicted some losses on shipping. Bad weather on 24 and 26 January also posed some logistic challenges. Nevertheless, within a week Lucas had available a force of 70,000 men, over 500 guns, nearly 240 tanks and more than 27,000 tons of stores.

Despite its very promising beginnings, in a larger sense the operation had already begun to unravel. Proponents of manoeuvre warfare argue that when on the offensive an emphasis needs to be placed on aggressive reconnaissance operations. It is only by doing this that a commander can 'feel' out the enemy, test him, finds weaknesses, and focus on levering these apart whilst flowing around enemy strength. Reflecting Basil Liddell-Hart's idea of the 'expanding torrent', aggressive reconnaissance is the foundation for maintaining the momentum of an attack.[25] However, having landed, Lucas failed to engage in active reconnaissance. In his diary, Clark noted that: 'I have been disappointed by the lack of aggressiveness on the part of VI corps [at Anzio] although it would have been wrong in my opinion to attack to capture our final objective [the Alban Hills] on this front.'[26] Instead, Lucas' focus was simply on digging in and trying to consolidate his position as rapidly as possible. Lucas himself did not go ashore until D+2.[27] Without

active reconnaissance in the direction of the Alban Hills, Lucas' force had little concrete information on what their enemy was doing. A member of the Scots Guards commented that: '...We found ourselves able to move about, form up and generally conduct ourselves as if we were on an exercise. Looking back, it all seemed ridiculously easy but it did not appear so at the time; we thought that we were liable to be attacked at any moment.'[28] Indeed, this was part of the problem. The example of Salerno indicated to Lucas that a German riposte to his landing was likely to develop early and in strength. Therefore Lucas focused on building up his forces to meet this expected threat, rather

than pushing forwards to gauge the true extent of the forces facing him.

More Allied troops moved into the bridgehead; the initial landing force was joined by 1st US Armoured Division, the 45th US Infantry Division and a brigade of the British 56th Division. Lucas made limited moves in the direction of the Alban Hills, towards the intermediate objectives of the towns of Campoleone and Cisterna; these were beaten off on 24 and 25 January. It was not until 27 January that Lucas decided to engage in a full assault towards the Alban Hills and not until the 30th that the

[25]William S.Lind, *Maneuver Warfare Handbook* (Boulder: Westview, 1985) p.9.
[26]Clark, p282.
[27]Thompson, p.167.
[28]Quoted in Molony, p.666.

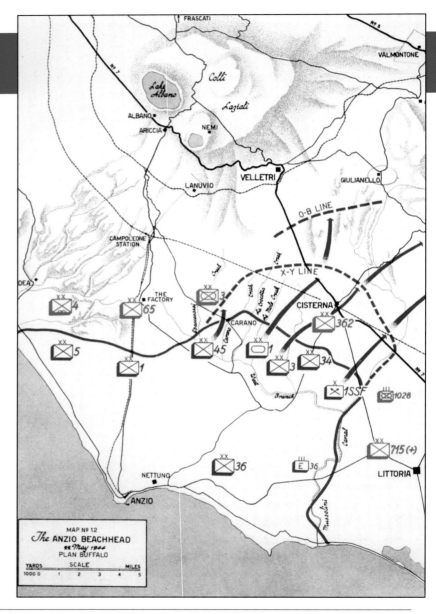

Towards the breakout from the Anzio Beachhead in May 1944. (NHB)

The balance between the consolidation of a landing and exploitation is not an easy one to strike

attack was ready to be mounted.[29] By 27 January Alexander was communicating to Clark his fears that the operation was not proceeding fast enough. On the 28th Churchill sent a message to Alexander indicating that: 'It would be unpleasant if your troops were sealed off there [at Anzio] and the main army could not advance up from the South.'[30] By this stage, Lucas' problems were also mounting in other areas; enemy air raids, shelling, and torpedo boat attacks, along with bad weather were making his logistic situation difficult.

The balance between the consolidation of a landing and exploitation is not an easy one to strike. There are certainly important benefits to be gained by pausing to bring in additional troops, to build up logistic support and to prepare the way for an advance through air and naval support. However, Lucas' overlong pause at Anzio had serious implications for his ability to develop the landing. As with Salerno, the rate of German reinforcement of the forces opposing the landing was much greater than anticipated by the Allies. By D+2, the German rate of reinforcement was double that predicted by the Allies and by D+10 the Germans has 34,000 men ready to oppose the landing. By 24 January Kesselring believed he had in place enough troops to hold his position. By the 26th he had elements of six divisions available. Because of Lucas' failure to exploit, the Germans were also able to base their main defence

forward of the Alban Hills so that the towns of Campoleone and Cisterna were not advanced positions but instead constituted the main line of defence. By 30 January the Germans could muster 33 battalions, divided into four battlegroups, supported by 238 field guns and 32 Nebelwerfer rocket launchers.[31]

How had Kesselring managed to muster these reserves? In the first instance Kesselring had managed to convince Hitler that southern Italy should not be abandoned lightly and that the best place for a defence was along the Gustav Line, especially around Cassino.[32] Because of this, and contrary to Allied expectations, Kesselring was heavily reinforced by forces outside of his command; these included one and half divisions from Yugoslavia, a division from France, virtually all of the German reserves in northern Italy as well as troops from Germany.[33] To make matters worse, the Allied attacks against the Gustav Line were beaten off. General Frido Von Senger und Etterlin, commander of the German XIV corps against whom the attacks were made,

[29]Linklater, pp.190-191.
[30]Quoted in Molony, p.671.
[31]Molony, p.672.
[32]D'Este, *Eisenhower*, p.460.
[33]Clark, p.281.

General Mark Clark and Air Marshal Coningham walking along a beach road at Salerno. General Clark was particularly critical of VI Corps under Major General Lucas. (IWM NA6825)

was later critical of the rigidity of the Allied plan.[34] But it is also true that the terrain was perfectly suited for the defence. The assaults by the 5th Army from the south yielded only months of heavy fighting in the iconic battles around Monte Cassino. Neither could the 8th Army make good their objective to prevent Kesselring from shifting forces from his left to support his right. Kesselring was also able to comb out the Tenth Army for more troops, yielding another three divisions.[35] In addition to ground troops, Kesselring also received air reinforcements including bombers armed with radio-controlled glider bombs.

Kesselring also benefited from the failure of Allied air interdiction operations to seal off the bridgehead. Whilst Allied air interdiction caused the Germans many problems with their build-up, these problems proved not to be insurmountable. The weather worsened, reducing the effect of Allied air superiority. In addition, by expedients such as moving at night, and de-training troops outside of the beachhead area, marching them in Kesselring was able to ensure an adequate flow of reinforcements to the bridgehead. By late January, when Lucas began to muster his forces for his major push, the German defences were already strong. There position was made even stronger by the use of defence in depth. The Germans were sceptical that a single defensive line could be held. They opted

instead for a deep defensive belt, utilising fortified defensive strong points and armoured reserves. The defence in depth included advanced and intermediate lines so that even initial Allied breakthroughs could be beaten off in the German rear areas.[36] Visiting his troops positions, Kesselring commented that: 'As I traversed the front I had the confident feeling that the Allies had missed a uniquely favourable chance of capturing Rome and of opening the door on the Garigliano front. I was certain that time was our ally.'[37]

When the Allied offensive was finally launched, it was beaten off with heavy casualties; in a particularly damaging encounter the 1st and 3rd Ranger battalions were ambushed losing all but 6 of their 800 men.[38] By 2 February, Lucas realised that VI Corp's attack had culminated and he ordered his troops to prepare defensive positions in preparation to meet a German counter-attack. In addition to fortifying existing positions, an inner defensive line was created between five and seven miles from Anzio. The failure of Lucas' attack left VI Corps holding a bridgehead around 18 miles deep towards Campoleone on the Allied left and 15 miles deep towards Cisterna on the right. The initiative now passed to the Germans signalling the end of any hope that the landings could achieve a rapid breakthrough towards the Alban Hills.

Having been ordered by Hitler to crush the Anzio 'abscess', the German forces put into action a planned counter-attack. Kesselring was optimistic about the potential outcome, believing: '…even taking their powerful naval guns and overwhelming air superiority into consideration, that with the means available we must succeed in throwing the Allies back into the sea.'[39] During

[34]F. Von Senger und Etterlin, *Neither Fear Nor Hope* (London: MacDonald, 1970) p.196.
[35]Linklater, p.191.
[36]Albert Kesselring (translated by Lynton Hudson), *The Memoirs of Field-Marshal Kesselring* (London: William Kimber, 1953) p.198
[37]Ibid., p.194.
[38]Linklater, p.194.

February, heavy fighting continued as the Germans attempted to dislodge the allies. German artillery was able to pound Allied airstrips and ports. Nettuno airfield had to be abandoned. German air attacks were made against Allied batteries, supply dumps, ports and troops though at heavy cost. Shipping off Anzio became subject to attack from a fearsome array of German weaponry – air attack, utilising torpedoes and bombs, small attack craft, U-boats, land-based artillery, mines and 'special weaponry': radio controlled glider bombs and human torpedoes. On 8 February Lucas asked for further reinforcement, but there were none available. Moreover, even if sizeable reinforcements had been available the bridgehead would have been unable to sustain them logistically.[40] Despite Allied counter attacks, and lulls in the fighting, by 17 February, German attacks had driven elements of the Allied force back to the inner line of defence. By 18 February, Lucas was fighting to hold the original landing area and a critical two-day struggle ensued in which the integrity of the whole Allied lodgement was seriously threatened. US counter-attacks were launched on the 19th and the last major German attack was beaten off.

Like Operation AVALANCHE, Operation SHINGLE managed to weather the storm. The Allies were helped in part by the terrain; if it had made the Allied advance difficult it also hampered the German counter-attack. With broken or marshy terrain to the north and south the German forces were forced to advance from the front and their losses were heavy. In fighting off the German counter-attack the allies were also helped by powerful artillery and air support. Allied artillery fired off an average of 25,000 rounds per day during the fighting, as opposed to the German daily total of 1,500.[41] Allied artillery was bolstered by naval gun support: four RN and one US cruiser, and all available destroyers were used in this role. VI Corps first asked for direct air support on the 27th receiving support from 87 Kittyhawks that dropped 25 tons of bombs.[42] Air attack maintained as much pressure as the weather would allow with an average rate in January of 1,300 sorties per day. The German air effort was much weaker, mustering 125 sorties on 27 January, but then tailing off.[43]

Since his effort to pinch out the Anzio bridgehead had finally culminated, Kesselring instead settled for containing it. For nearly four months the beachhead was hemmed in and a massive logistic effort was required to keep it supplied. The allied 'main effort' therefore ground to a halt and instead had to be rescued by the 'subsidiary' assault from the south. Eventually, an offensive

from the south broke through the Gustav Line at Monte Cassino and on 25 May 1944 spearheads from the Anzio lodgement and the southern forces linked up. Even then, opportunities were squandered; Clarke diverted the troops northwest to capture Rome rather than northeast to cut off the Germans[44] - Rome fell on 4 June but the German 10th Army escaped, falling back on its next defensive position, the Gothic Line.

Challenges

After the failure at Salerno, much of the blame fell on Major-General E.J. Dawley, the then commander of VI Corps. Dawley had been replaced by Lucas, and now it was Lucas' turn to face criticism. Many argued that it was Lucas' unwillingness to take risks after he had landed successfully that robbed the operation of its chance to achieve its wider objectives. Was there any truth in this? Lucas had certainly performed less well than many expected. Lucas was not an inexperienced commander. He had commanded a division and a corps in the US; he had been part of a team sent to collect the tactical lessons of the Sicily and North Africa campaigns; he had been Eisenhower's Liaison officer with 5th and 7th Armies and he had commanded US II Corps in Sicily and on mainland Italy. Before Operation AVALANCHE, Lucas had had powerful backers; General Marshall favoured Lucas as a man with 'military stature, prestige, and experience.' Alexander, not

[39]Kesselering, p.195.
[40]Clark, p.289.
[41]Linklater, p.200
[42]Molony, p.685.
[43]Molony, p.678.
[44]Carver, p.205.

Bren carriers move inland at Anzio after landing from LCTs. (TNA)

generally a fan of US generals, argued that Lucas was 'the best American Corps Commander.'[45]

... his weaknesses included a lack of willingness to go forward and see the ground

The Anzio landings had shown areas in which Lucas may have fallen short as a commander. His subordinate, Truscott, argued that: 'I was not blind to the fact that General Lucas lacked some of the qualities of positive leadership that engender confidence.'[46] His weaknesses included a lack of willingness to go forward and see the ground and the development of the battle, and a lack of direction and co-ordination for his command; he failed

to visit 1st Infantry Division until 18 days after D-Day.[47] Clark claimed in his autobiography that he believed Lucas to be physically and mentally unsuited to the rigours of commanding the force.[48] For this reason, Truscott was earmarked to replace Lucas, first being made his deputy and then taking over VI corps. Lucas' approach to command illustrates that mission command requires more than a 'hands off' approach to the detailed execution of a plan. The commander must instil a sense of purpose and energy into his command; mission command still requires leadership. However, to blame Lucas for the failings of Anzio is to posit too simplistic an explanation. Blaming Lucas for failing to take the necessary risks to reap the rewards of the landing places too much emphasis on hindsight. A more balanced assessment of Lucas' performance, and of the problems of Operation SHINGLE more generally, can be found in the answers to two questions: first, how much of a risk did an early exploitation of the landings entail; was there any reasonable chance that the Alban Hills could be taken and held? Second, how far did Lucas understand that he needed to take the risks associated with early exploitation? In answering the first question, we must look at the resources

available to Lucas. Lucas' unwillingness to take risks was related in part to his concerns over the weakness of his landing force. Before the operation was mounted, Lucas had already criticised: 'the diminutive size of the proposed expedition'[49] Like Salerno, the Anzio landing force was severely constrained in size by the available transport. This lack of troops engendered a clear sense of pessimism in Lucas about the viability of the operation as a whole. Writing in his diary, Lucas commented that: '...some of the higher levels think that I have not advanced with maximum speed. I think more has been accomplished than anyone has a right to expect. This venture was always a desperate one and I could never see much chance for it to succeed, if success means driving the Germans north of Rome.'[50] In Lucas' opinion pushing on to the Alban Hills would simply have resulted in disaster: 'being completely beyond supporting distance, [the advancing forces] would have been immediately destroyed.'[51] Lucas' views coincided with those of Ira C. Eaker, the Commander in Chief of Mediterranean Allied Air Forces. Writing to the U.S. Chief of the Air Staff in March 1944, Eaker argued that he had been initially very critical of Lucas' failure to push forward. However, 'having seen the ground, Eaker argued that he had come to believe that, with only two divisions available, an attempt by Lucas to push forward to the Alban Hills would simply have resulted in Lucas' force being cut off and smashed.[52] Writing in 1950,

---

[45]Molony, p.649.
[46]Quoted in Thompson, p.172.
[47]Thompson, p.168.
[48]Clark, p.291.
[49]D'Este, *Fatal Decision*, p.105.
[50]Quoted in Molony, p.670.
[51]Ibid.

German prisoners watching vehicles being discharged on the Anzio beaches, 22 June 1944. (TNA)

Alexander, too, had come to view Lucas' mission as impossible to achieve with the forces available, arguing that: '…6th Corps, with the resources available to it, would have found it very difficult both to be secure on the Alban hills and at the same time retain the absolutely necessary communications with the sea at Anzio.'[53]

Asked why the Confederates had lost the battle of Gettysburg the rebel General George Pickett replied: 'I always thought the Yankees had something to do with it.'[54] Likewise, the problems caused by the relatively small size of the landing force were multiplied by the actions taken by the Germans defenders in Italy. The important role that German actions would play in deciding the dynamics of the landing were recognised by Alexander: 'We had the initiative in operations but the Germans had the initiative in deciding whether we should achieve our object since they were… free to refuse to allow themselves to be contained in Italy.'[55] In parallel, many of Lucas' problems were created by the swift and effective response that Kesselring made to the landings, despite the fact that the landings attained surprise. In his memoirs, Kesselring was critical of the 'systematic' approach of the Allies.[56] The circumstances that faced the Allies on mainland Italy made amphibious landings highly likely. Kesselring therefore set in train preparations to meet new landings. These preparations included combing out his forces to create mobile reserves and in keeping his reserves at between four and 24 hour readiness. The Germans also established pre-prepared plans for ex-theatre reinforcement of Kesselrings positions. Contingency plans were put in place, governed by pre-arranged code words, for the concentration of reserves at various points. Kesselring could not be clear where the next landing would come from; his intelligence resources were poor, not least because air reconnaissance had virtually stopped in the face of Allied air superiority. He was nevertheless able to establish an effective enough system of mobile defence to ensure that any Allied landing would be met by a German in a reasonably short time. Eisenhower had recognised the bones of the problem before the landing took place; he had commented; '…there is no place where a full enemy division cannot be concentrated against us in 12 hours.'[57] Kesselring had little intention of conforming to Allied desire to retire.

Instead he favoured maintaining the Gustav Line because it was narrower than a fall back position to the North of Anzio; it is also clear that he believed that offensive operations against an Allied landing stood every chance of driving it into the sea.[58] The improvisational skills and the aggression of the Germans in defence had already been demonstrated at Salerno, where German counter-attacks materialised very quickly. The lessons of Salerno had a powerful effect on the mind-sets of Lucas and his subordinates. Lucas fully expected a determined German counter thrust to the landing to be mounted very quickly. Lucas and his subordinates had not expected to achieve tactical surprise. Once landed, the general focus was therefore on establishing a strong defensive position.[59] With this in mind pushing a portion of his relatively weak command forward simply risked having them surrounded and overwhelmed. The loss of these troops would render his whole position, including the beachhead, untenable. Manoeuvre warfare may be about the 'calculated risk', but from Lucas' perspective, he might have been forgiven for viewing a premature advance on the Alban Hills as less a calculated risk than a reckless gamble in which failure would threaten seriously the viability of his whole force.

In answer to the first question, then, the risks and costs associated with early exploitation appeared (and indeed probably were) very high. To turn to the second question, did

---

[52]Molony, p.686.
[53]Ibid.
[54]Gabor S. Boritt, *Jefferson Davis' Generals* (Oxford: Oxford Univeristy Press, 1999) p.175.
[55]Quoted in D'Este, *Eisenhower*, p.460.

[56]Kesselring, p.192.
[57]Molony, p.643.
[58]Senger und Etterlin, p.194.
[59]Molony, p.658.

Churchill's vision of Op SHINGLE was of 'hurling a wildcat onto the shore'

Lucas' understanding of the purpose of SHINGLE compel him to take those risks? In reality, Lucas' orders were vague, reflecting competing perspectives in the levels of command above him on what the priority should be between consolidation and exploitation. In its original conception it is clear that higher level commanders envisaged a landing force with a strong mobile exploitation element. Churchill's vision of SHINGLE was of 'hurling a wildcat onto the shore.' Cunningham referred to the operation as a 'lightening thrust'[60] Alexander's Operating Instructions of 12 January gave orders to 'land a Corps of two divisions and necessary corps troops, followed by a strong and fully mobile striking forces based on elements of a third division….,' in order to '…cut the enemy's main communications in the Colli Laziali area South-east of Rome, and to threaten the rear of the German 14th Corps.'[61] The focus on exploitation was reflected in the initial 'planning' missions that were handed to Lucas. These missions were threefold: first, to establish a secure beachhead at Anzio; second, to take the Alban Hills; third, to ready his force for an advance on Rome.[62]

However, the focus on exploitation was not reflected in Clark's orders to Lucas. Clark had serious reservations about the operation – his own experiences at Salerno had instilled in him a wariness of exploitation. Whereas Lucas' planning instructions were explicit in the order to take the Alban Hills, Clark's final orders to Lucas were not. Clark's orders to Lucas identified two main objectives: first to seize and secure a beachhead in the area of Anzio; second, to advance on the Colli Laziali. In considering how to exploit the landings, the second part of his orders neither required Lucas explicitly to take the Alban Hills, only to advance on them; nor did it lay out a time-scale for achieving this. To ensure that Lucas understood his orders, Clark sent his Chief of Staff to explain the orders; the priority was the seizure and consolidation the landing area; Lucas should push on if he thought that the situation was favourable.[63]

Nor did this dichotomy between the strategic and operational goals resolve itself once the landings took place. Both Alexander and Clark arrived at the beachhead on D-Day declaring themselves pleased with the progress of the operation. Alexander visited the beachhead several times, sometimes for 2 or 3 days. Clark established a forward command post in the beachhead area. By 25 January, Clark still viewed the progress of the operation as 'satisfactory'.[64] Neither of Lucas' immediate superiors was ignorant of the development of the battle. Both were generally supportive of the very deliberate way in which Lucas conducted his fight. According to Alexander's Chief of Staff, Lieutenant-General Lemnitzer: 'General Alexander realised that we did not have the strength to hold the [Alban] Hills even if we did take them. He thoroughly approved of the

caution with which the Corps commander was acting.'[65] Clark commented that 'in my opinion we most certainly would have suffered far more heavily, if not fatally, had our lines been further extended against the reinforcements the enemy was able to move in rapidly.'[66]

Clark was critical of Lucas' failure to take the intermediate objective of Cisterna and Campoleone early on, but he did not believe that an early assault on the Alban Hills was viable.[67] When, on 28 January, Clark urged Lucas to take Cisterna and Campoleone it was as a means to strengthen his defensive line not as a jumping off point for the Alban Hills. Lucas' orders did not compel him to take the risks associated with early exploitation; indeed implicitly he was encouraged by Clark not to do so. According to the official American historian of the campaign 'Clark did not want to force Lucas into a risky advance that might lose his corps.'[68] Clark, mindful of his problems at Salerno, counselled Lucas: 'Don't stick you neck out, Johnny. I did at Salerno and got into trouble'.[69]

Conclusions

Operation SHINGLE was a huge disappointment for those, like Churchill, that had envisaged it as a dynamic, decisive blow against the enemy in Italy. Cunningham drew parallels with the Suvla landings. As at Suvla, the Anzio landings had successfully

---

[60]Molony, p.645.
[61]Quoted in Molony, p.645.
[62]Thompson, p.161.
[63]Thompson, p.162.
[64]Clark, p.275.

[65]Thompson, p.173.
[66]Clark, p.276.
[67]Ibid., p.282.
[68]Quoted in Molony, p.646.
[69]William Breuer, *Agony at Anzio*, (London: Robert Hale, 1989) p.44.

made it ashore, only to fail to take the high ground further inland that would have given the landing an operational meaning. With the benefit of hindsight, Lucas probably had at least 48 hours after the landing in which he could have made advances against negligible opposition. Lucas can be criticised for not taking and holding Cisterna and Campoleone which would have given him useful defensive terrain.[70] However, to blame Lucas for more than this would be grotesquely unfair. Clark argued that commanders on both sides recognised that: 'the real outcome of the struggle would depend on which side could increase his forces most quickly, and they could not afford to get out on a limb until they were strong enough to prevent it from being chopped off.'[71] Lucas lacked the initial strength, or the relative rate of tactical build-up, to develop the resources for simultaneous consolidation of the landing area and early exploitation.

Manoeuvre warfare may well require a measure of audacity and risk-taking, but as the operation at Anzio shows, sometimes the only 'audacious' options are the reckless gambles. For Lucas an early advance on the Alban Hills would not have been a calculated risk. The landing force was too small, the opposition too well organised to admit any real prospect of taking and holding the Alban Hills without seriously compromising VI Corp's beachhead. Nor did Lucas' orders require him explicitly to take such a gamble. Under such circumstances Lucas' focus

on consolidation was entirely understandable and, indeed, sanctioned by his immediate superior. If the Anzio operation did not succeed, it was not because of Lucas' failure to take the necessary risks but because the grandiose objectives envisioned by individuals such as Churchill were beyond the capabilities of the landing force to achieve. The net result of this mismatch between ends and means was a hard fought 'soldier's battle' in which the Allies hung on but made only limited gains; as Clark commented laconically 'We had won a foothold at Anzio, and we had edged into the mountains above Cassino, and that was about all we got on the field of battle'.[72] With his gift for the bon mot Churchill put it best: ' [instead of]…hurling a wild cat on the shore … all we got was a stranded whale'.[73]

Further Reading

History of the Commandos in the Mediterranean Sept. 1943 to May 1945

Bruce, Colin John, *Invaders: British and American Experience of Seaborne Landings 1939-1945,* (London: Chatham, 1999)

D'Este, Carlo, *Fatal Decision: Anzio and the Battle for Rome,* (London: Fontana, 1992)

Hunter, Robin, *True Stories of the Commandos,* (Virgin, 2000)

Morison, Samuel Eliot, *Sicily-Salerno-Anzio January 1943 – June 1944,* Vol. 9 of *History of United States Naval Operations in World War II,* (London: Oxford University Press, 1954)

Saunders, Hilary St George, *The Green Beret – The Story of the Commandos,* (London: Michael Joseph, 1949)

Sheffield, G.D. (Ed), *Leadership and Command: The Anglo-American Experience Since 1861,* (London: Brassey's, 1997)

Trevelyan, Raleigh, *The Fortress: A Diary of Anzio and After,* (London: Collins, 1956)

Trevelyan, Raleigh, *Rome '44: The Battle for the Eternal City,* (London: Secker & Warburg).

Biography

Dr Christopher Tuck is a Lecturer at the Defence Studies Department, King's College London, based at the Joint Services Command and Staff College. He joined JSCSC in 1997. Prior to this, he was a lecturer at the Royal Military Academy, Sandhurst (1994-1997) where he worked in the Department of Defence and International Affairs. He is co-author of *Amphibious Warfare: The Theory and Practice of Amphibious Operations in the 20th Century* (Spellmount: 2001).

---

[70]Molony, p.686.
[71]Clark, p.281.
[72]Ibid., p.316.
[73]Carver, p.118.

The Conquest of the Marshalls
Operation FLINTLOCK, January - February 1944

By Mr Branden Little

Strategic Background and Planning

In the 1920s and 1930s, U.S. Marine and Navy strategists predicted a war in the Pacific with Japan. They viewed the Marshall Islands, the easternmost island chain in the Japanese Mandates, a central Pacific territory that Japan had controlled since the First World War, as an initial target for attack by U.S. amphibious forces in support of a naval strategy to defeat Japan. The long-anticipated war finally erupted with the devastating raid on Pearl Harbor in December 1941. Between August 1942 and December 1943, Allied forces fought in the southwest, northeast, and central Pacific to reverse the rapid territorial conquests of the Japanese in the Pacific theatre. Thus, over two years would pass before the Allies were positioned to penetrate Japan's pre-war defensive sphere and strike the Marshalls in January 1944.

At conferences in Casablanca, Washington, D.C., Quebec, Cairo, and Teheran in 1943, the Allied Combined Chiefs of Staff (CCS) were determined to project U.S. forces into the Mandates. The CCS hoped that the commencement of operations in the central Pacific would accelerate the Allied strategy to 'procure the unconditional surrender of Japan'. Two operations were eventually proposed: GALVANIC for the Japanese-held British Gilbert Islands and FLINTLOCK for the Marshall Islands.

In 1943, the Marshalls were admittedly too far from U.S. bases in the Hawaiian, Ellice, Samoan, and Canton Islands to invade. What little information the CCS knew about the disposition of enemy forces in the Marshalls was obtained from several sources including a carrier raid in early 1942, photographs taken by submarines, and signals intercepts. The intelligence collected suggested that the defences were formidable and included multiple airfields and naval bases. Proximity to additional bases in the Caroline and Mariana Islands provided the Japanese with numerous options to contest an invasion. The inability of the U.S. Navy to conduct routine surveillance also hampered the development of hydrographic intelligence on tidal fluctuations and water depths. As a result, beach conditions and the characteristics of coral reefs were virtually unknown. Moreover, the U.S. Joint Chiefs of Staff (JCS) believed American forces lacked sufficient experience and matériel to conduct amphibious assaults without this vital intelligence.

In July 1943, in deference to these considerable challenges, the JCS directed Admiral Chester W. Nimitz, Commander in Chief, Pacific Fleet and Pacific Ocean Areas, to conduct two sequential operations that would mitigate the risks of invading the Marshalls. First, in November 1943, Operation GALVANIC would recapture the Gilberts. U.S. forces would rapidly convert the airfield in the Tarawa Atoll into the first of several bases to launch aerial reconnaissance and bombing missions in the Marshalls. Second, the experience to be gained from an amphibious assault against the heavily defended Gilberts, together with the new intelligence obtained from reconnaissance flights, would greatly enhance the odds of successfully conquering the Marshalls during Operation FLINTLOCK, in January 1944.

Collectively, these two operations were designed to penetrate the outer ring of Japanese defences, and dramatically reduce the threat posed to interallied lines of communication between the United States, Australia, and New Zealand. After the completion of GALVANIC and FLINTLOCK, U.S. forces would be strategically positioned for future operations in the central Pacific and have built momentum for Allied offensives throughout the Pacific theatre.

In late November 1943, at great cost, American amphibious forces had liberated the Gilberts from Japanese control. This guarded first step into the central Pacific provided a strategic

Planners reviewing the Roi-Namur Atoll prior to the assault. (USMC)

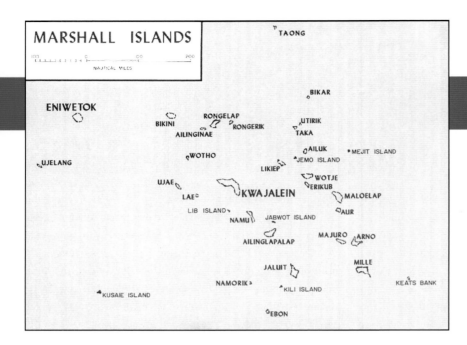

launching pad for operations against Japan. It demonstrated that Allied forces possessed the initiative and capability to seize strongly defended advanced bases. But it also revealed the dangers of the navy's overriding emphasis on speed in the execution of amphibious operations. The desperate naval battles for the Solomon Islands in August 1942, where some two dozen U.S. warships were sunk off Guadalcanal Island, haunted senior admirals who feared a reoccurrence. These admirals denied marine requests for extended bombardments prior to assaulting Tarawa because the time it took might enhance the likelihood of a devastating counterattack on the fleet. The startlingly high number of American casualties and the tenuousness of victory at Tarawa, however, compelled the admirals to reconsider their conservatism; never again would they make similar demands on an invasion force

For FLINTLOCK they would sacrifice speed to concentrate on the destruction of the enemy garrisons at invasion sites. With

a growing fleet and the Gilberts secured, the U.S. Pacific Fleet became far less fearful of powerful Japanese reprisals. In December 1943 and January 1944, the navy proceeded confidently in its final preparations for the long-anticipated conquest of the Marshalls.

The Marshalls comprise 34 atolls and islands in two parallel chains spread across 640,000 square km of ocean. Averaging 2 metres in elevation, these low-lying islands and adjacent waters are interspersed by over 860 coral reefs. A total of 131,200 natives and Japanese inhabited the islands in 1940. The western 'Ralik' chain includes the Eniwetok, Bikini, Kwajalein, and Jaluit Atolls. At an equidistant location from Pearl Harbor and Tokyo (3,500 km), the Kwajalein Atoll forms the largest atoll in the world with 93 islands. Kwajalein is situated 870 km northwest of Tarawa, 1,500 km east of Truk, and 2,200 km southeast of the Mariana Islands. Approximately 160 km to the east, the 'Ratak' chain consists of the Wotje, Maloelap, Majuro, and Mille Atolls. This vast territory would become the focus of intense scrutiny by U.S. war planners.

Operational Planning

In July 1943, Nimitz ordered the planning for the Gilberts and Marshalls operations to be conducted concurrently. The responsibility for GALVANIC and FLINTLOCK fell to the U.S. Fifth Fleet commander, Vice Admiral Raymond A. Spruance. His

increasingly powerful armada would soon swell to nearly 300 ships, consisting of some two-dozen aircraft carriers, fifteen battleships, eighteen cruisers, and numerous smaller warships and transports. His amphibious component commander, Rear Admiral Richmond Kelly Turner, controlled the naval task force that supported the marine and army ground troops assigned to Major General Holland M. Smith's V Amphibious Corps (VAC). In August 1943, Major General Julian C. Smith's 2nd Marine Division and Major General Ralph C. Smith's 27th Infantry Division were designated as the assault forces for the Gilberts. One month later in September, Major General Harry Schmidt's newly formed 4th Marine Division and Major General Charles H. Corlett's veteran 7th Infantry Division were assigned to conquer the Marshalls. Together these highly capable commanders orchestrated the planning and preparations for the two operations.

The planning staffs at the various headquarters selected the invasion objectives within the island chains. The Gilberts comprised 16 atolls and islands, and the Marshalls, 34. Several islands in each group became candidates for invasion. Ultimately, islands with pre-existing airfields or the capacity to be developed into airfields or fleet anchorages were selected. Wake, Nauru, Kusaie, and Eniwetok Islands were considered, but not chosen as objectives for either of the operations because of their distances from the centre of attack, or the strength of their garrisons. Planners determined the main objectives in the Gilberts to be the Makin and Tarawa Atolls because the first possessed a seaplane base and the second an operational

Some of the designated assault forces: US Marines 2nd Marine Division and the US Army 27th Infantry Division. (DoD)

The LVT was the only ship-to-shore conveyance unaffected by tidal variations, able to cross the reef, and ferry men and supplies to the shore

airfield. In the Marshalls, the Maloelap, Wotje, and Kwajalein Atolls were initially selected because they contained the majority of the enemy airbases in the archipelago. These three targets were later revised after the Gilberts' operation.

In November 1943, U.S. amphibious forces liberated the Gilberts. Four naval task forces - one carrier group, two assault armadas, and one garrison group - conducted an extraordinarily complex manoeuvre across vast stretches of the Pacific, from multiple directions and points of origin, to descend upon the Gilberts en masse. Nearly 110,000 personnel directly participated in GALVANIC, but countless more supported this endeavour from rear echelons. The Americans launched a simultaneous, two-pronged invasion of Butaritari Island in the Makin Atoll and Betio Island in the Tarawa Atoll, 170 km apart. An army Regimental Combat Team (RCT) attacked Butaritari, whereas a marine division assaulted Betio. Within four days Butaritari and Betio had fallen, and in five more days the Gilberts' archipelago was secure for garrison troops to begin their transformation of the atolls into forward bases to support the Marshalls invasion. What made the Gilberts' liberation such a remarkable accomplishment, however, was not so much the detailed operational planning and movement of forces. It was the tactical victory at Betio, where 4,700 Japanese had prepared the most sophisticated defences confronted in the entire war, on a tiny, 117-hectare island. During the battle, the marines came precariously close to being repulsed on several critical occasions, but stubbornly resisted. They vanquished the enemy

in 76 hours, at a cost of 3,407 casualties; only 19 Japanese survived. Had the marines lost at Tarawa the JCS could have concluded that it was impracticable to conduct assaults against coral atolls, thereby terminating future campaigns in the central Pacific. In this scenario, the Allies and the Japanese would have confronted each other along a single route, the southwest Pacific axis. A loss at Tarawa, therefore, would have compelled a major re-examination and likely readjustment of Allied strategy in the Pacific. Victory erased all doubts about the soundness of amphibious doctrine and techniques. The marines' intrepidity and sacrifices earned reverent praise. To ensure that future attacks were less costly U.S. commanders diligently studied the electrifying lessons of GALVANIC.

Lessons from Tarawa

An invaluable lesson learned from the assault on Tarawa was that amphibious forces required far more intensive naval gunfire and close-air support, properly sequenced with the landings, and that bombardments needed to be of an extended duration and utmost precision. The marines at Tarawa landed after less than four hours of preparatory bombardments, which were lifted so early that the Japanese regained their composure to fire on the landing forces before they touched shore. The bombardment had been so brief that it destroyed relatively few fortifications and undermined the prospects for victory.

Another lesson, perhaps the greatest of consequence to the marines, was the need for more amphibian tractors (LVTs).

These unarmoured vehicles had tracks that functioned like paddlewheels, enabling them to operate on land and sea, and to negotiate heavy surf and coral reefs. The first three waves of marines at Tarawa were delivered ashore via 125 'amtracs'. Their tactical value was fully recognised when subsequent waves of conventional landing craft were unable to cross the reef during a low tide of extended duration. The LVT was the only ship-to-shore conveyance unaffected by tidal variations, able to cross the reef, and ferry men and supplies to the shore. U.S. commanders recognized that without the LVT they would have failed at Tarawa. As evidence of the amtracs' vulnerabilities and valiant service, seventy-two percent of the LVTs - 90 in all - were lost in action. Post-battle analyses determined that at least 300 LVTs with factory-installed armour were needed to transport a division's assault troops. Other critical shortages of specialised equipment were identified, such as flamethrowers and bazookas, which were necessary tools to destroy Japanese pillboxes. The requirement for detailed intelligence about beaches, reefs, and to remove obstacles, indicated that underwater demolition teams were essential to improve the conduct of landing operations.

Japan's Response to the Fall of the Gilberts

After GALVANIC the Japanese conducted a last-ditch effort to bolster the Marshalls' defences. When Admiral Keiji Shibasaki sent his final broadcasts from Tarawa to Fourth Fleet headquarters at Kwajalein on the morning of 20 November it

*Admiral Chester W. Nimitz, Commander in Chief,
Pacific Fleet and Pacific Ocean Areas. (DoD)*

was apparent that he had underestimated the Americans who were using 'little boats on wheels' - LVTs - to cross the coral reef from inside the atoll's lagoon. Despite Shibasaki's warnings about the LVTs, Vice Admiral Masashi Kobayashi's Fourth Fleet and Sixth Base Defence forces were unable to reorient defensive positions in the Marshalls to ensure that all avenues of attack - from the ocean and lagoon - were sufficiently guarded. Their preparations were interrupted by constant U.S. air attacks that began in late December. These attacks damaged construction supplies, killed defenders, and soon destroyed every Japanese aircraft stationed in the Marshalls.

Kobayashi diverted shipments of construction matériel to the eastern atolls in anticipation of an American invasion. Kwajalein, located in the central Marshalls, did not receive the same priority even though it functioned as the nerve centre for the archipelago. He did not believe an invasion of Kwajalein was within the realm of American capabilities or intentions. Nevertheless, the late November arrival of 1,500 Japanese soldiers from Truk, rerouted from Makin to Kwajalein because of GALVANIC, was undoubtedly a welcome site to the island's defenders even though it revealed that the Gilberts' invasion caught them by surprise.

The ineffective response by Japanese naval and air forces to GALVANIC hinted at broader fissures in Japan's defensive strategy: it was failing to defeat the combined campaigns of the Allied forces in the southwest and central Pacific, to repel aggressive carrier raids, and to compensate for the unrelenting submarine attacks on its merchant shipping. In November alone, U.S. submarines sank a record total of 45 Japanese cargo ships. In a futile attempt to protect its fortress Rabaul on New Britain Island from Allied attacks, Japan expended virtually all of its carrier aircraft. In response to these foreboding developments, Japanese naval commanders decided in early December to withdraw the Combined Fleet from Truk to the Palau Islands where it would be less vulnerable to U.S. air attacks. In so doing, the Japanese had effectively forfeited the Marshalls to the Allies eight weeks prior to FLINTLOCK, and condemned the archipelago's defenders to meet the Americans at the water's edge.

FLINTLOCK Postponed

U.S. commanders argued for a postponement of FLINTLOCK, tentatively scheduled for 1 January 1944. Foremost on their minds was that in less than two years the Japanese constructed highly sophisticated defences resulting in a nightmare for the marines at Tarawa. The Americans shivered at the thought of the defences Japan could have constructed during thirty years in the Marshalls. But they did not yet fully appreciate Japan's rapidly deteriorating position. In early December 1943, as a powerful carrier raid pummelled targets and photographed the Kwajalein and Wotje Atolls in the Marshalls, Nimitz lobbied the JCS to authorise a delay.

Nimitz's forces required sufficient time to remedy vital deficiencies. They needed a postponement of at least 2 weeks but wanted 5 weeks. Airfields in the Gilberts would not support systematic reconnaissance and bombing missions before late December, which impeded the finalization of plans for the attrition of enemy strength in the Marshalls. At first the U.S. Fifth Fleet was hard-pressed to locate enough transports to carry two divisions of troops. Delays would permit landing force equipment depots along the west coast of the United States to distribute shipments of supplies and vehicles to the task force preparing to depart from San Diego, California. LVTs ranked most prominently among the lists of demands because their unique capabilities mitigated the effects of unpredictable tides. The 4th Marine Division, with its training nearly completed, required two weeks to transit between California and Hawaii where it would rendezvous with the other forces gathering for FLINTLOCK. Nimitz convinced the JCS to permit two delays for D-Day: from 1 to 17 January and then to 31 January. The invasion was set for the 31st.

Meanwhile, Nimitz's commanders repeatedly debated and revised the list of island candidates for invasion before their final selection. Earlier, in October 1943, Nimitz had issued the first operation plan for the Marshalls that scheduled simultaneous attacks on the Maloelap and Wotje Atolls in the eastern Marshalls because of their proximity to Pearl Harbor. Kwajalein Atoll, the nexus of Japanese activity in the Marshalls was also selected because it contained a major enemy headquarters on Kwajalein

The Kwajalein Atoll. (USMC)

Island, an airfield on Roi-Namur Island, and a seaplane base on Ebeye Island. In combination, their capture would rob Japan of this strategically vital position and consolidate Allied territorial gains in the central Pacific.

In the wake of the Gilberts, Holland Smith conceded 'that the Marshalls' plan was too ambitious' because his ground forces were insufficiently strong to seize three Tarawa-like atolls. He advocated a strike on Maloelap and Wotje followed by a later attack on Kwajalein. Nimitz's counterproposal to bypass the two atolls and strike directly at the heart of Japanese defences at Kwajalein shocked Spruance, Turner, and Smith. They feared powerful reprisals from Japanese aircraft at Maloelap, Wotje, Jaluit, and Mille. Nimitz overruled them. During a mid-December conference he told them 'the next objective will be Kwajalein'. He authorised a secondary objective in deference to a request by Spruance to acquire a suitable anchorage from which the U.S. fleet could operate during FLINTLOCK. Majuro Atoll, which they believed was lightly defended, was chosen. They also agreed to accelerate the invasion of Eniwetok, an atoll located at the extreme northwest tip of the Marshalls, and ideally situated to stage additional attacks into the central Pacific. The initial schedule for Eniwetok was 1 May, but Nimitz's decision to strike Kwajalein first made it feasible to adjust the date to 1 March.

FLINTLOCK Begins

Allowing for adequate preparatory bombardments and the collection of intelligence on enemy dispositions were vivid

lessons of GALVANIC fully implemented in the preliminary phases of FLINTLOCK. In late December 1943, aircraft started flying missions over the Marshalls from two airfields at Betio and Buota Islands in the Tarawa Atoll. Airfields at the Makin and Abemama Atolls in the Gilberts launched their first flights in early and mid-January, respectively. It was soon learned that the Japanese had developed six airfields and four seaplane bases in addition to three naval bases in the Marshalls. Construction on these facilities had begun in November 1939 when the Japanese Fourth Fleet was activated to defend the islands. Kobayashi's forces consisted primarily of an amalgam of soldiers and miscellaneous support troops. Intelligence indicated that within the Kwajalein Atoll enemy strengths totalled about 9,200 men: 5,000 on Kwajalein Island, 3,000 on Roi and Namur, 500 on Ebeye, and a smattering of personnel on other islands within the atoll. About 6,400 Japanese were located on Maloelap and Wotje. In total about 26,500 Japanese were scattered across the Marshalls, but most were concentrated at a few strategic locations.

VAC commander Smith designated two divisions to conduct the seizure of Majuro and Kwajalein: the 7th Infantry Division commanded by General Corlett, and the 4th Marine Division commanded by General Schmidt. In Operation FLINTLOCK the army would seize the southernmost objective, Kwajalein Island,

and the marines the northernmost, Roi-Namur. Joint forces would storm Majuro and Eniwetok. Corlett's division was stationed in Hawaii after conducting operations in the Aleutians. Only two of his Regimental Combat Teams (RCTs) had actually fought the Japanese on Attu Island. Schmidt's division, in contrast, was a green unit with no battle lineage. Activated 14 August 1943, the 4th immediately underwent an intensive period of training in southern California.

Specialised units were formed at this time. The marines' 4th Amphibian Tractor Battalion, freshly created, spun-off half of its personnel to form the 10th Battalion and one company of the 11th Battalion. Less than a month later, the 4th and the reinforced 10th embarked for combat in the Marshalls. The 1st Armoured Amphibian Battalion enjoyed a lengthier genesis. It used the LVT(A)1, a new, armoured LVT variant equipped with a gyroscopically mounted 37mm tank cannon and turret.

Three waves of 22nd Marines assault troops approach Engebi as smoke from the preliminary bombardment drifts across the landing lanes. (USMC)

Although ordered to lead the assault, the 1st Armoured had neither crossed a coral reef, nor conducted a full-scale rehearsal. Majors Victor J. Croizat and Louis Metzger provided sound leadership to these newly formed units. In addition to the amtrac battalions, underwater demolition teams (UDTs) were created in response to the requirement identified at Tarawa to clear obstacles and mines from the landing routes. Their personnel were affectionately dubbed 'frogmen'.

Scheduled for 31 January, FLINTLOCK consisted of five major phases to be accomplished by several naval task forces. First, a powerful carrier task force would bombard the objectives and interdict threats. Second, a 53,400-strong joint force would conduct a simultaneous, three-pronged assault on islands in two atolls; Roi-Namur and Kwajalein Islands in Kwajalein Atoll, and the adjacent islands of Dalap and Uliga in Majuro Atoll. Roi-Namur and Kwajalein were 69 km apart, whereas the Kwajalein and Majuro Atolls were separated by 354 km. Planners anticipated a victory in two days. Third, 10,300 assault troops would seize the Eniwetok Atoll in early March. Fourth, a marine regiment would conduct numerous smaller landings to secure key islands in other atolls. To avoid amphibious assaults of the more strongly defended Wotje, Maloelap, Mille, and Jaluit Atolls, U.S. commanders preferred to neutralize them

with aerial and naval bombardments. Fifth, 31,000 garrison forces would rehabilitate war-damaged facilities, construct new airfields, and prepare the Marshalls to function as advanced bases for the next series of operations in the central Pacific campaign.

An independent Fast Carrier Task Force, TF 58, commanded by Rear Admiral Marc A. Mitscher initiated events. Mitscher divided his twelve carriers and 750 aircraft into four groups of three. Three groups approached the Marshalls from the southwest and one from the east while refuelling underway. Eight battleships, six cruisers, and dozens of destroyers accompanied the carriers, and together they bombarded enemy positions in the Marshalls beginning 29 January. The establishment of complete air and naval superiority in the region was not difficult because previous attacks and TF 58's new strikes destroyed every Japanese aircraft in the Marshalls, and additionally so because the Japanese commanders refused to counterattack in strength from other locations.

To orchestrate FLINTLOCK, Spruance authorised the formation of a Joint Expeditionary Force (JEF) under Turner's direct control in Hawaii. The JEF, also designated Task Force 51, drew upon bases throughout the Allied sphere of control to provision the assault troops and warships gathering under his command. Turner divided the JEF into three assault and garrison groups; each contained aircraft carrier, naval gunfire, and transport vessels.

Task Force 51.2 was assigned the capture of Majuro. Rear Admiral Harry W. Hill commanded the small force to defeat an anticipated contingent of 300 to 400 Japanese. Hill expected a swift victory after which engineers would construct an airfield and fleet anchorage. Two escort carriers, one cruiser, and several smaller warships accompanied 1,600 soldiers and marines embarked in transports. TF 51.2 would depart from Hawaii as part of the JEF, but would detach just prior to its arrival at Kwajalein, to invade Majuro.

To effect the seizure of Roi-Namur, Task Force 53, the Northern Attack Force under Rear Admiral Richard L. Conolly, was established. Conolly directed operations from the newly commissioned *Appalachian* (AGC-1), a ship built specifically for the purposes of enhancing the command and control of amphibious forces. The AGC-class housed the commanders, their staffs, and modern communications gear. Prior experience at Tarawa revealed the inadequacy of conventional warships to serve this function. TF 53 included three battleships, three escort carriers, five cruisers, fifteen LSTs, and 65 other vessels. On 5-6 January, TF 53's slow-moving LSTs carrying the 4th Marine Division's amtracs departed California for Hawaii, a distance of 3,530 km; they were followed on 13 January by the division's ground troops and the bulk of the task force's ships. TF 53 rendezvoused with Task Force 52, already located in Hawaii, on 21 January. TF 52, the Southern Attack Force, was formed to conduct the assault on Kwajalein Island. Turner and Holland Smith directed operations from another specialised ship, the *Rocky Mount* (AGC-3). The

Japanese defences on the Roi and Namur Islands. (NHB)

task force included four battleships, three escort carriers, three cruisers, sixteen LSTs, and 58 assorted ships, and transported the 7th Infantry Division. Ships containing garrison and defence forces accompanied each of the assault forces. Garrison groups were skilled at the transformation of islands into advanced bases and had performed efficiently in the Gilberts, converting battle-damaged Japanese bases into fully functional Allied bases. Defence forces primarily consisted of anti-aircraft units to protect the gathering accumulation of matériel at these sites. 31,000 personnel, including 6,200 soldiers, 9,500 marines, and 15,300 sailors would serve in these capacities. They were organised into four groups: Kwajalein (Southern), Kwajalein (Northern), Majuro, and Eniwetok. Each possessed its own small flotilla of LSTs, destroyer escorts, and auxiliary ships. On 22-23 January, Turner's JEF steamed from Pearl Harbor in a southwest direction toward the Marshalls. It crossed 3,500 km of ocean and penetrated the eastern Marshalls before reaching Kwajalein on the 29th. At this point TF 51.2 and its garrison forces departed for Majuro, and TF 52 and TF 53 positioned themselves at opposite ends of the Kwajalein Atoll. They entered the lagoon to directly support to the invasion.

Capturing Majuro

The Majuro Atoll is 450 km southeast of the Kwajalein Atoll and its 57 islands and islets stretch 42 km (east to west) by nearly 10 km (north to south). Majuro Island is the largest mass within the atoll and is a mere 270 metres wide but 34 km long. An abandoned seaplane base was located on Darrit Island in the northeastern corner of the atoll, defended by a shipwrecked Japanese sailor. The Japanese had secretly withdrawn their troop contingent in November 1942. The thirteen ships of the Majuro Attack Group (Task Group 51.2) arrived on 30 January. Late that evening a marine reconnaissance company landed on several islands using rubber boats and quickly captured the hapless sailor. The next day the remaining ground forces, soldiers from the 2nd Battalion, 106th Infantry Regiment occupied Dalap, Uliga, and Darrit Islands. Within two more days 30 U.S. ships were anchored in the lagoon. The timely arrival of garrison forces and a marine defence battalion relieved the assault troops and revitalised the seaplane base. They built an 1,800 metre airfield within two weeks, and a second airfield shortly thereafter. A large naval base was also constructed to diminish the fleet's dependency on rear bases. Majuro soon housed 4,000 native Marshallese people that had been evacuated by U.S. submarines to ensure their safety and to rob the Japanese the use of their labour.

Conquering Roi-Namur

The loosely triangular-shaped Kwajalein Atoll stretches 106 km in length and is 32 km wide. Although it stretches across a large territory the cumulative acreage of all islands and islets in the atoll is just over 16 square km. At its northernmost point are located the twin islands Roi and Namur, which are connected by a manmade causeway and a narrow stretch of sand that is submerged during high tides. Both form roughly box-like shapes, but Namur is slightly smaller (730 x 810 metres) than Roi (1,070 x 1,140 metres). Runways formed the most prominent features on Roi, whereas dense vegetation covered Namur. The reef varies between 115 to 410 metres wide. A series of eight islands were located closely, between 0.40 and 6.4 km from Roi-Namur.

Whereas stealth characterized the Majuro invasion, the assault forces at Kwajalein announced their presence with a thunderous bombardment. Two days prior to D-Day, on 29 January, warships and aircraft from TF 53 saturated targets with 6,000 tons of ordnance. Compared to Tarawa, the preparatory fires lasted three times longer and with double the tonnage of shells. Moreover, naval gunfire systematically reduced fortifications with pinpoint accuracy that proved far more destructive than earlier techniques. Rocket-firing LCI(G) ships and 75 LVT(A)1s

Left: 24th Marines assault troops on the beach
at Namur await the word to move inland.

Right: Kwajalein Island. (USMC)

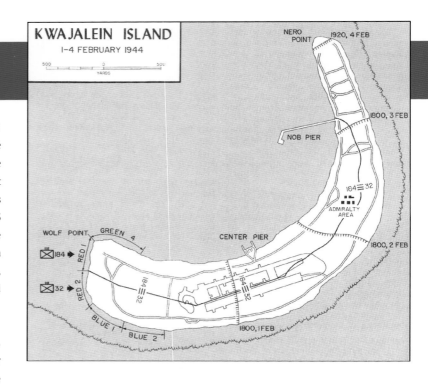

provided close-in fires. Rough seas made it exceedingly difficult for the 244 armoured LVT(2)s to rendezvous with troop-carrying LCVP landing craft, to maintain their formations, and to conduct the scheduled landings on D-Day (31 January). Waterlogged radios forced crews to rely on semaphore and other signals. Although the landing forces employed nearly double the number of LVT(2)s compared to Tarawa, they were still short of the 300 necessary to land the entire division.

The marines' initial destinations were six of the adjacent islands to Roi-Namur to preposition the 14th Marine Regiment's 75mm howitzers and 105mm artillery for the main attack on the following morning. RCT 25 seized each of the islands. Once the troops were ashore it took them less than two hours to eradicate the light opposition on each island. Hampered by darkness and dispersion across many islands the LVT battalions struggled to regroup for the main attack. LST crews disregarded scheduled rendezvous points and many amtracs ran out of fuel trying to locate their 'mother' ship. 23 LVTs sank before dawn because their electric bilge pumps drew power from the engine, an engineering flaw not remedied since encountered in the Gilberts.

Early in the morning of D+1 (1 February) UDT-1 frogmen cleared mines and obstacles along the lines of ingress to the Roi-Namur beaches. The familiar pattern of pre-invasion bombardment devastated the islands and destroyed numerous enemy strong points. An estimated 50 to 75 percent of the Japanese defenders died in these preliminary attacks. RCT 23, equipped with a lethal combination of LVT(A)1s, medium tanks, and assault troops, quickly overran Roi and declared the island secure that evening.

Conquering Namur required far greater effort. Confusion plagued the final preparations for Namur because of the disorganisation of the LVTs. These problems did not significantly impede the overall assault, but clearly revealed the need for better coordination between the crews of amtracs and transport vessels. Anti-tank ditches along the beach slowed the progress of the LVT(A)1s and tanks.

The island's dense vegetation further hindered the infantry of RCT 24. Tragically for Company F, its sappers unwittingly flung satchel charges into a bunker filled with torpedo warheads instead of enemy troops. This caused a massive explosion, created a huge water-filled crater, and generated a plume of smoke towering into the Pacific sky. In an instant, 120 marines were killed or wounded. RCT 24 pressed on and secured Namur

the following day, D+2. The 25th Marine Regiment proceeded thereafter to secure 50 of the remaining northern islands. Schmidt's 4th Marine Division incurred 1,004 casualties, 387 of whom died. They killed 3,570 Japanese and captured 90.

Conquering Kwajalein

Kwajalein Island occupies the southernmost position in the atoll and is curved like a crescent. It is 4 km long, an average of 730 metres wide, and tapers to 275 km at its northern tip. A reef with a width between 460 and 730 metres surrounds Kwajalein. 4,300 troops occupied the island. An uncompleted 1,500 metre runway intersected the island's interior, but a fully functional radio direction-finding station searched for signs of the Allies.

Men of the 7th Division use flamethrowers against the Japanese, 4 February 1944. (NARA)

Defences were concentrated along the ocean approaches. Nearby Ebeye measures 1,600 km long and 230 meters wide and featured two seaplane ramps, a radio direction-finding station, and the third strongest defences within the atoll.

On D-Day (31 January) TF 52 entered the Kwajalein lagoon. A powerful bombardment by U.S. ships commenced shortly thereafter. Using rafts, LCVPs, and amtracs, RCT 17 secured several islands close to Kwajalein to site four battalions of 105mm artillery and one battalion of 155mm howitzers. After UDT-2 verified the landing beaches were free of obstacles the main assault commenced on D+1. RCT 184 and RCT 32 landed from LVTs and DUKWs without difficulty on the island's western end and moved inland behind an unrelenting artillery barrage from the pre-positioned U.S. guns. The advance was slowed when fierce fighting erupted between soldiers and the surviving Japanese. Corlett concurrently released a reserve regiment to clear the remaining islands within the atoll on D+3. He declared Kwajalein secure on the afternoon of D+4 (4 February). It cost the 7th Infantry Division 989 casualties to capture Kwajalein and the remaining southern islands. 5,335 Japanese were killed. Kwajalein fell, but not as quickly as VAC commander Smith preferred. 'I fretted considerably at the slowness of the Army advance', he recalled. 'I could see no reason why this division . . . could not take the island quicker'. In a gesture toward interservice harmony Smith contained his impatience with the army's tactics; he had been far less generous during the invasion of Makin.

I fretted at the slowness of the Army advance... I could see no reason why this division could not take the island quicker

Conquering Eniwetok

Nevertheless, by 2 February, Spruance, Turner, and Smith recognized that Kwajalein was falling fast enough that they could revise the date set for the invasion of the Eniwetok Atoll from 1 March to 17 February. Detailed charts of the Eniwetok lagoon captured at Kwajalein considerably helped U.S. forces prepare for invasion. Eniwetok is a large atoll (34 x 27 km) located 540 km northwest of Kwajalein. It is circular in shape and consists of four moderately sized and 36 smaller islands. With two main entrances to its lagoon, Eniwetok provided a massive anchorage for ships. In December 1942, the Japanese commenced building an airfield on Engebi Island in the northernmost part of the atoll, but it was not completed until mid-1943, and was first used as a refuelling station for aircraft in November 1943. Thereafter Engebi became a major transit point for Japanese aircraft in the central Pacific. About 1,300 troops occupied the island, which was triangular-shaped and less than 2,000 km on all three sides. Eniwetok Island, located in the southernmost part of the atoll, had a steep, natural seawall that could present a formidable obstacle to landing forces. Over 800 Japanese resided on Eniwetok. Another 1,300 Japanese defended

a seaplane base and radio direction-finding station on Parry Island, northeast of Eniwetok.

Because of its distance from Kwajalein - a two day-long transit - Spruance dubbed the Eniwetok invasion Operation CATCHPOLE. The JEF Reserve was not employed during FLINTLOCK, so it was assigned the Eniwetok mission. Intense planning between 3 and 15 February ensured that the 63 ships of the newly formed Eniwetok Expeditionary Group (TG 51.11) would meet the revised schedule. It departed from Kwajalein on 15 February with a total of 10,300 soldiers and marines, protected by three battleships, three cruisers, and seven carriers. Two days later TG 51.11 arrived at the atoll. On the same day, 600 km to the west, Mitscher's Fast Carrier Task Force (TF 58) launched a devastating raid on Truk that destroyed 39 ships and 200 aircraft. Operation HAILSTONE, as it was designated, shattered the myth of the

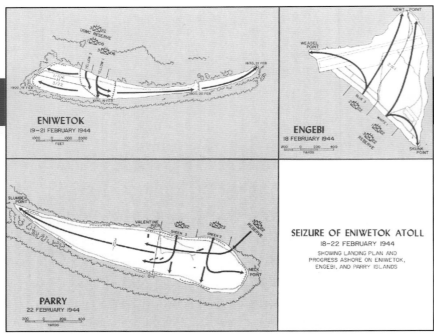

impregnability of Japan's 'Gibraltar of the Pacific', as Truk was often called. Once neutralised, Truk could not oppose the Eniwetok assault. Elements of TF 58 then raided Japanese bases in the distant Marianas before returning to the Marshalls.

On 17 February, D-Day, naval and aerial bombardments pounded enemy emplacements before assault forces secured two diminutive and weakly held islands to establish artillery. Frogmen cleared the landing routes. RCT 22 led a major attack against Engebi on D+1 and secured it the following day. Owing to inadequate intelligence that underestimated the Japanese presence on Eniwetok, the pre-landing bombardment proved woefully insufficient. Therefore, when RCT 106 landed on the 19th, it encountered stiff resistance and took three days to capture the island. Numerous 'spider holes' - camouflaged tunnels from which many Japanese sniped at U.S. troops - were encountered. These defences prefigured the growing sophistication of underground Japanese fortifications on other islands. A series of concurrent landings on Japtan Island and its nearby islets paved the way for a larger scale invasion

of Parry Island by RCT 22. The attack on Parry commenced on D+4 (22 February) and ended the next morning to conclude CATCHPOLE. Defence battalion and garrison personnel arrived on 25 February. In conquering Eniwetok Atoll, U.S. forces killed nearly 3,400 Japanese and took 105 prisoners, at a cost of 1,300 U.S. casualties.

Securing the Marshalls

To illustrate the dangers of advanced base duty, six Japanese aircraft from Saipan (in the Marianas) bombed Roi-Namur on 12 February, ten days after U.S. forces secured the island. The planes inflicted terrific damage by scoring hits on the massive U.S. supply dump that contained the accumulated fuel, ammunition, and other matériel on the island. Nearly 85 percent of the supplies were destroyed. Fortunately for U.S. forces they could recuperate from such devastating losses because of the accelerating rate of U.S. industrial production and an efficient logistics system. This attack encouraged the defence forces to remain vigilant while construction battalions built new airfields and naval facilities in support of the continuing operations in the Marshalls, and in preparation for the Marianas invasion. Between 7 March and 23 April, the 22nd Marine Regiment conducted Operation FLINTLOCK, JR. to secure several of the Marshall atolls remaining in enemy hands. Staged from Kwajalein, the regiment conducted 29 landings in six weeks, eliminated the

residual Japanese forces, and established a provisional military government to administer Marshallese affairs.

Marine and army aircraft neutralised the remaining garrisons on the islands of Kusaie, Wake, and Nauru, in addition to the atolls of Mille, Maloelap, Wotje, and Jaluit. Air power performed an invaluable role because it provided the means to isolate 13,000 enemy forces distributed on these islands. Aircraft and warships pounded these sites throughout the war to perfect close-air and naval gunfire techniques. Nearly 7,500 Japanese died in these attacks.

Lessons Learned and Applied

Nimitz's decision to strike Kwajalein directly and bypass the heavily defended eastern Marshalls surprised American and Japanese commanders alike. He was increasingly confident in the fleet's capacity to remain on station and repel any counterattack, even that of the Combined Fleet, because at every turn U.S. forces were defeating the Japanese in detail. This newfound boldness was built into FLINTLOCK's concept of operations. The U.S. Fifth Fleet would forfeit operational speed and tactical surprise in the Marshalls, in order to provide its amphibious troops the maximum opportunity for success. The earlier emphasis on speed gave way to a concept of comprehensive support for invasions. Preparations to deliver several days' worth of naval gunfire and aerial bombardments revealed how committed the navy was to advanced base operations.

Respite: After two days of heavy fighting on Eniwetok, this Marine heads back to the assault transport ship. (NARA)

Nimitz's gamble paid handsomely. The rapid conquest of the Marshalls shattered the outer ring of Japan's defences. Japan consistently misinterpreted U.S. intentions, but it better appreciated America's capabilities once the Gilberts and Marshalls fell. U.S. intentions were understandably hard to discern from a Japanese perspective because the combined southwest Pacific and central Pacific campaigns were using amphibious and air forces to assault some objectives while neutralising others. This grand pincer movement made it exceedingly difficult for Japan not only to predict the timing and location of the next American strike, but to respond effectively. Japanese forces expressed their respect for U.S. capabilities by the removal of the Combined Fleet to Truk, and their unwillingness to contest the Marshalls invasion. Even had the fleet sortied it is highly unlikely that Spruance and Turner would have responded in a manner that would have jeopardized U.S. landing operations because they appreciated their defensive strengths and the imperative to succeed. After February 1944, Japan's defensive sphere suddenly shrank.

FLINTLOCK was masterfully executed, but not without flaws. Concurrent planning of the Gilberts and Marshalls operations severely burdened the staffs by dividing their attention between two extraordinarily complex operations. Compressed timetables, however, placed a premium on efficiency and coordination, valuable skills put to good use in planning for future operations of even greater magnitude. But accelerated plans made it truly difficult to incorporate the lessons learned

from previous operations. Engineering flaws discovered in LVTs - bilge pumps and non-waterproof radios - for example, were less easily rectified than many procedural changes because it either took longer to alter designs at manufacturing facilities, or to distribute repair kits to the widely dispersed troops in the field. Nevertheless, a steady stream of ships, vehicles, and supplies from American factories meant that what could not be repaired could be replaced.

Just as they had studied GALVANIC, U.S. commanders scrutinised the 'lessons' of FLINTLOCK. Naval gunfire, close-air support, and pre-positioned artillery performed superbly; the landing forces demanded more of the same for the next operation. Similarly, rocket-firing LCI(G)s and cannon-firing LVT(A)1s closed the gap in firepower between the lifting of naval gunfire and the landing of the troops. They set a precedent by leading the waves of LVTs and landing craft, and U.S. commanders ensured that future plans emulated this pattern. The troops, however, demanded improved LVT designs such as a more powerful gun on the LVT(A)1. Industry responded with a new LVT(A)4 mounting a 75 mm howitzer. Enough were built to equip an amtrac battalion in less than four months. By December 1944 nearly 12,000 LVTs of all varieties were constructed to satisfy the insatiable appetite for the vehicle's unique capabilities. The difficulties of amtrac-LST coordination stimulated initiatives to enhance interoperability. UDT teams functioned according to plan and thereafter many more were created to provide beach reconnaissance and obstacle-clearing capabilities. The agility of

the industrial base and the government to meet tactically and operationally important requests for LVT(A)s and UDTs imbued U.S. forces with confidence. The chief 'lesson learned' in the Marshalls was the confirmation that the rigorous application of previous 'lessons learned' from GALVANIC endowed U.S. amphibious forces with unprecedented capabilities.

Possession of the Marshalls and the neutralisation of Truk strategically positioned U.S. forces for continued operations in the central Pacific at a pace hitherto inconceivable to both sides. In March 1944 plans to invade Truk were discarded in favour of accelerating the Marianas invasion by six months, from December to June, a mere four months in the future. B-29 heavy bombers based at Kwajalein pounded the Marianas without delay. Likewise, reconnaissance flights launched from the Marshalls began immediately to accumulate intelligence on the Marianas.

LVT(A)ls and LVT(2)s maintained the tactical momentum generated in the pre-invasion bombardments. Their enhanced firepower and armour lessened U.S. casualties and contributed greatly to the defeat of the enemy.

Building upon this operational momentum the JCS directed Nimitz to attack the Palaus in September and provide support to General Douglas MacArthur's subsequent invasion of the Philippines. The strategic benefits of MacArthur's and Nimitz's pincer movement became fully evident by year's end as the dual-pronged advances of the southwest and central Pacific campaigns began to converge: Japan's Mandates had fallen and the Philippines' liberation was underway. At the battles of the Philippine Sea in June 1944 and Leyte Gulf in October 1944 the U.S. Navy conclusively defeated the naval and air forces of Japan. These decisive battles revealed that the pattern set by FLINTLOCK, where naval task forces remained on station to support the invasion forces, had become the new standard for U.S. amphibious operations. Nimitz praised Spruance's decision to support the Marianas invasion forces to the utmost despite a desperate counterattack by the Combined Fleet, whereas he thought Admiral William F. Halsey's whimsical quest to destroy Japanese carriers at Leyte Gulf (thereby abandoning the invasion forces) was foolish.

FLINTLOCK provided the American people and their forces with the expectation of victory in the Pacific. The United States could now project joint air, land, and naval forces with such power that Japanese island fortresses crumbled under the onslaught. Once firmly planted in the Marshalls, U.S. forces viewed the prospects of defeating Japan with a measure of hope, certainty, and grim determination.

Further Reading

Chapin, John C., *Breaking the Outer Ring: Marine Landings in the Marshall Islands. Marines in World War II Commemorative Series*, (Washington, D.C.: MCHC, 1994)

Croizat, Victor, J., *Across the Reef: The Amphibious Tracked Vehicle at War*, (Quantico, VA: Marine Corps Association, 1992)

Crowl, Philip A. and Edmund G. Love, *The War in the Pacific: Seizure of the Gilberts and Marshalls. U.S. Army in World War II*, (Washington, D.C.: Department of the Army, 1955)

Heinl, Robert D., Jr., and John A. Crown, *The Marshalls: Increasing the Tempo*, (Washington, D.C.: MCHC, 1954)

Isely, Jeter A. and Philip A. Crowl, *The U.S. Marines and Amphibious War: Its Theory, and Its Practice in the Pacific*, (Princeton, NJ: Princeton University Press, 1951)

Rottman, Gordon L., *The Marshall Islands, 1944: Operation Flintlock, the Capture of Kwajalein and Eniwetok*, (Oxford: Osprey, 2004)

Sherrod, Robert, *On To Westward: War in the Central Pacific*, (New York: Duell, Sloan, and Pearce, 1945)

Biography

Mr Branden Little is a PhD candidate in history at the University of California, Berkeley, and earned an MA in national security affairs from the US Naval Postgraduate School in 2002. He formerly served as Chief Operations Officer for the US Department of Defense's Center for Civil-Military Relations, where he coordinated international security assistance programmes. His publications examine aspects of modern naval history and civil-military relations. He is writing a doctoral dissertation on American-led humanitarian relief operations in First World War-era Europe, and is also completing a book manuscript, tentatively titled *A Means to an End: the Amphibian Tractor, Industrial Mobilization, and the Defeat of Japan*.

My chapters in this volume are dedicated to the memory of my grandfather, Master Sergeant Robert J Little, USMC (Retd), Second Marine Division, Eighth Regiment, veteran of Guadalcanal and the central Pacific campaigns; and in memory of his brother, Thomas D Little, who as a Marine corporal was grievously wounded but survived the savage contest at Tarawa.

New Guinea
Operation RECKLESS, 1943 - 1944
The Forgotten Lesson from The South West Pacific Theatre

By Lieutenant Colonel Mark Maddick RM

The West's experience of amphibious operations, derived mainly from World War II, has falsely left behind a belief that they only have utility as early entry invasion forces. Had the lessons of the U.S. Army's experience from the South West Pacific Theatre[1] (SWPT) not been forgotten this might not be the case today. However, a resurgence of interest in expeditionary warfare and amphibious manoeuvre has given more relevance to the lessons from the SWPT.

This chapter covers the campaign in the SWPT, examining the period following General Douglas MacArthur's decision to move onto the offensive in New Guinea. As case studies it uses the landings at Lae and Hollandia in New Guinea on 4 September 1943 and 22 April 1944 respectively. The success of the amphibious capability is best typified by the landing at Hollandia during Operation RECKLESS, where over 60,000 Japanese troops and 400 miles of jungle were bypassed by a considerably smaller US force but still secured their objective. World War II has been widely described as the greatest amphibious war in history. However, it is generally forgotten that the types of amphibious operation varied dramatically between the different theatres of operation. It is usually assumed that there were two distinct styles of amphibious warfare in World War II: The European invasions[2] and the Central Pacific Theatre (CPT) island hopping conducted by the US Navy/Marine Corps team. There was, however, a third style. The third distinctive style was that conducted in the SWPT under the command of Army General Douglas MacArthur. In the SWPT amphibious operations largely avoided frontal assaults on positions well defended by the Japanese. They were generally intended as a method of achieving manoeuvre. Even here there were amphibious assaults which approached the ferocity of those in the CPT, if not on the same scale[3].

The Strategy

Owing to its size and to accommodate the personalities of MacArthur and Nimitz, the Pacific had been divided in to the SWPT and CPT. The SWPT ranged from Australasia through New Guinea to the Philippines. In 1942 the Australian plans for the defence of Australia centred on a wholly defensive strategy. MacArthur, who was appoint commander of the SWPT, decided to move the defence of Australia forward to New Guinea and began offensive operations in order to wrest the initiative from the Japanese, prevent them from consolidating their gains and keep them fighting in an area where their numerical superiority was less advantageous. His strategy called for an arrow straight advance along the northern New Guinea coast to gain a position from where it would be possible to liberate the Philippines and cut Japan's supply of raw materials for its military industrial base.

The terrain, scale of the theatre and to a certain extent the nature of the Japanese dispositions, opened the way for deep manoeuvre to bypass and isolate Japanese defences, this was in stark contrast to the CPT's requirement to direct assault. At the time, the best and perhaps only method to conduct this deep manoeuvre was through amphibious landings. Landings generally took place in areas lightly defended by the Japanese the so-called 'hit'em where they ain't'[4] strategy. Even if landings were conducted in direct support of the close battle[5], efforts were made to ensure that the landings took place on beaches weakly held by the Japanese even if this meant additional distance from the objective. The reach of air cover, about 150-200 miles, primarily dictated the depth of manoeuvre as the SWPT rarely enjoyed the support of the CPT's aircraft carriers. Although amphibious operations in this theatre were primarily those of amphibious envelopments, invasions were also used to gain the Philippines and many islands in the theatre.

The plan generally focussed on attacking weakly defended logistic supply areas and bypassing Japanese defensive positions, isolating them and making them largely irrelevant. The Japanese defensive positions were fixed by the close battle, geography or other means[6]. These positions were then starved out or the weakened remnants mopped up. An area away from any local Japanese strong points would normally be selected for

---

[1]SWPT is also referred to as the SWP Area (A).
[2]The one significant attempt at amphibious manoeuvre was the landing at Anzio[2]. See Dr Christopher Tuck's Chapter on Operation Shingle for further detail.
[3]See Willoughby and Chamberlain. MacArthur 1941-51. William Heinemann Ltd 1956 pp 177-179.

[4]Attribution is difficult. It is uncertain whether this was originally used by MacArthur or one of his staff.
[5]ADP Ops breaks down operations into close, deep and rear. Army Doctrine Publication Volume 1 Operations AC 71565 Pt1 pp 513
[6]Deception, air or naval bombardment.

US troops go over the side of a Coast Guard manned combat transport ship to enter the landing barges at Empress Augusta Bay, Bougainville, November 1943. (NARA)

landing and it would usually be near an airfield or a site suitable for the development of one. The reason for this was to allow the next manoeuvre to be achieved under the parallel advance of air and maritime cover. In tandem with the preparations for the amphibious operation, the airforce's long-range bombers would conduct a bombing campaign of Japanese air and naval bases that might be able to interfere with the landings, so easing the task of achieving air superiority over the landings. Once accomplished the 7th Amphibious Force, the SWPT's private navy, would deliver the landing force with the Airforce providing what cover it could. Even if the area did contain concentrations of Japanese troops, careful selection of the beaches, fixing operations or deception was used to prevent the immediate

interference of ground forces. Once the objective had been taken the airfield would be built, repaired or expanded and the process would then be repeated another bound along the coast, continually bypassing the Japanese in the process[7]. It was only with the support of the CPT's aircraft carriers that these bounds were beyond the range of land based aircraft.

Tactical Manoeuvre – The First Attempt

The operation to seize the Lae-Salamaua on the North Coast of New Guinea was the first major amphibious landing operation of the Campaign and is an excellent example of amphibious manoeuvre at the tactical level. Operationally Lae had to be taken to allow the establishment of an air and sea base on the north coast, however, it was well defended and the overland advance was proving slow and costly. At the time, the theatre had minimal access to CAS or NGS, therefore a direct landing was to be avoided. A small landing was made 20 miles short of Salamaua, bringing up artillery and supplies to join an overland advance. The Allies then advanced slowly on Salamaua. The sole intention of which was to draw troops from Lae and not to take Salamaua at that point. Lae was the more important objective because of its airfield and sheltered anchorage[8]. The landing to take Lae was scheduled for 4 September just over 2 months later and by then all but 2,000 troops had moved from Lae to Salamaua and become effectively fixed there. The landing took place 15 miles beyond Lae, 7,800 men were put ashore in 3

hours with opposition only from the air. The next day, parachute and air landed forces were landed on a disused airstrip to the west of Lae, so completing the encirclement of some 20,000 Japanese troops and precipitating the ultimate collapse of Lae. As a result, the Japanese abandoned the position and attempted to escape through the jungle to rejoin their other forces but the majority perished in the long over land trek through the jungle.

Operational Reach

The situation in Hollandia was fundamentally different. The operation involved simultaneous landings at Hollandia, Tanamera Bay and at Aitape. The beaches were over 500 miles to the west of allied forces and well beyond the range of land based air support. They were the first amphibious landings beyond the range of land based air cover in the SWPT. The aim was to strike so deep that the Japanese would not have prepared their defences. The target was a major enemy supply area. Hollandia was the logistic hub for Japanese forces. It was from here that they forwarded major supplies to their front line. As a result the majority of the troops in this area were logistic service troops. The purpose of the subsidiary landing at Aitape was to protect the flank of the main landings in Hollandia from the bypassed Japanese positions. The major challenge was that Hollandia was beyond the range of land based aircraft. MacArthur requested and received the support of the carriers from the CPT. The landing was a complete success with virtually

[7]Willoughby and chamberlain Op Cit pp 96 – 99.
[8]Further detail is best found in D E Barbey. MacArthur's Amphibious Navy. United States Naval Institute 1969 Chapter 9.

Allied Operations in New Guinea. (NHB)

no opposition to the landings. General Marshall the Army Chief of Staff described the operation as 'a model of strategic[9] and tactical manoeuvre'[10]. The result was that over 60,000 Japanese troops were bypassed isolated and defeated by a landing force of 26,000. Consequently this caused a complete rethink of Japanese strategy in the SWPT[11].

Mechanised Forces

By the autumn of 1944 a foothold had been established in the Philippines on the island of Leyte. Whilst New Guinea was ideally suited to this style of manoeuvre, the terrain and Japanese strategy as much as allied operations fixed the Japanese and made them vulnerable to deep manoeuvre. However, the terrain in the Philippines was fundamentally different. There were wide plains, which allowed the use of mechanised and armoured forces. Here it was up to the Allies alone to fix the Japanese main body to prevent interference by ground forces in the initial phases of the landings. This was the case with the landing of the 77th Infantry Division at Ormoc Bay on the West Coast of Leyte. The objective of the operation was to seize the port of Ormoc, through which the Japanese were re-supplying and reinforcing their troops, more importantly its aim was to bypass the Yamashita line, the Japanese main defensive position in the Ormoc corridor[12]. The landing was so successful that the Yamashita line was all but abandoned thus saving the Allies

considerable effort and lives. The same effect aimed for, but never achieved at Anzio.

Lessons of The Campaign

The strategy of amphibious manoeuvre proved to be remarkably effective. The overall effect is summed up by a captured Japanese officer 'this was the strategy we hated the most. The Americans attacked and seized, with minimum losses, a relatively weak area, constructed airfields and then proceeded to cut the supply lines to our troops in that area. Our strong points were gradually starved out.'[13] Between Lae in September 1943 and

July 1944 15 major amphibious manoeuvre operations were conducted. In total over 144,000 out of 250,000 troops were operationally bypassed and rendered strategically impotent. This figure does not include the tens of thousands that died trying to regain position by marching through the jungle and throwing themselves in suicidal attacks on the allied positions. The total cost to the allies of the New Guinea campaign was the loss of 18,757 casualties of which 2,472 were killed. This was only slightly larger than the total for the capture of Saipan[14] in the CPT. In addition to the specific requirements for conducting successful amphibious landings the campaign in the SWPT

[9]The term operational level of war is relatively new to the West. Here the terms are interchangeable.
[10]Willoughby and Chamberlain Op Cit pp 176.
[11]Willmott H P. The Great Crusade. Pimlico 1992. Pp 337.
[12]See The Reports of General MacArthur, Op pp 120-124.
[13]The Reports of General MacArthur, Op Cit pp 95.
[14]Direct comparisons at the tactical level should be avoided, as once the decision to assault one of the 'Island Fortresses' was taken there was little scope for innovative manoeuvre.

Left: Marines wading through the surf as they leave their LSTs at Cape Gloucester, New Britain, December 1943.

Right: 163rd Infantry Regiment exit Higgins Boats on Wadke Island, Dutch New Guinea, May 1944. (NARA)

Consequently air, maritime and close combat operations effectively shaped the Japanese, increasing their vulnerability to manoeuvre warfare in the form of amphibious manoeuvre. This unity of effort was achieved through an effective joint and combined command.

The SWPT enjoyed a truly unified command along the combined and joint lines that we have now come to expect. All efforts were designed to achieve the common mission. General MacArthur was in overall command in his Combined and Joint HQ. MacArthur had command not only of the US forces in the theatre but also of the Australian, British and Dutch forces. His HQ was based on a US Army HQ but included representatives of all 3 services. MacArthur did not exercise direct command over the Army, he did in fact have subordinate Land, Air and Maritime HQ's, all of which had command of the appropriate single service allied forces assigned to the theatre. Though the 7th Amphibious Force had a separate status for planning and tasking purposes on larger operations, of the scale of the invasion of the Philippines, it was subordinated to the appropriate maritime HQ. Initially the Maritime and Air HQs were collocated with MacArthur's and the Land HQ was nearby. The system steadily evolved. By the Hollandia operation, even the subordinated HQs had become joint[17] with integrated planning and liaison cells. This allowed the unity of effort that was achieved at the

operational level to be duplicated down the chain of command. Without it the parallel operations conducted by the 3 services would have been disparate and uncoordinated.

The unified command structure was also applied to managing the meagre resources and Combat Service Support was always stretched. Much of the management of these scarce resources was done centrally through the theatre combined operations service command with quieter and less important areas often going without, in order to keep the critical combat areas, in whichever service, supplied.

The only times that SWPT unified command structure was not employed was when forces from the CPT were assigned to support operations. This happened in the Hollandia landings and again for the invasion of the Philippines at Leyte. In both of these operations MacArthur had to rely on the air cover and support of the aircraft carriers of the CPT in order to achieve his objectives, as they were beyond the range of his own land

highlighted main requirements for amphibious manoeuvre to be successful as; Unity of effort; Tempo; Intelligence, Deception and surprise; Objective focused landings and the avoidance of establishing a beachhead.

Unity of Effort

Unity of effort was critical to the success of all operations in the SWPT as resources were comparatively scarce and the Allies were initially fighting a numerically superior enemy. Unity of effort allowed the resources of all 3 services[15] to be focused on one aim whether directly or indirectly. It allowed the theatre to manage and co-ordinate operational pauses between all 3 services whilst maintaining the tempo with the other 2, which prevented the Allies from reaching their culminating point[16].

---

[15] The US Air Force was still the US Army Air Force but did effectively operate as a separate service.

[16] An operation reaches its culminating point when the current operation can just be maintained but not be developed to any great advantage. The UK Doctrine for Joint and Multinational Operations. JWP 0-10.

[17] The Reports of MacArthur Op Cit pp 31-34.

In unison: A Sherman advances through the jungle with Infantry in close support, Bougainville, March 1944. (NARA)

based air cover. However, Nimitz was not prepared to place CPT forces under MacArthur's command. This presented no problem in Hollandia, as the command relationship was not tested. However, in the Philippines circumstances changed dramatically where had it not been for some quick and determined action by the amphibs' escorts the landings may have been a disaster. This was because Nimitz had given Halsey, the maritime commander, two missions. The first was to provide support to MacArthur and the invasion, whilst the second mission was to miss no opportunity to decisively defeat the Japanese Imperial Fleet. Consequently Halsey was busy chasing Japanese carriers when the amphibs were attacked by a powerful surface group. This contrasted dramatically with the earlier landings at Saipan, where landing, amphibious forces and escorts were under the unified command of the CPT. Here again Nimitz directed the escorting naval commander to exercise every opportunity to destroy the enemy fleet but not at the risk of uncovering the amphibious forces.

Tempo

In order for the campaign to succeed it was essential that the Allies maintained a higher tempo of operations than the Japanese. If this had not been achieved the Japanese would have had time to react and to bring their initially superior forces to bear in an effective manner, at which point the conflict would have degenerated to one of attrition. The maintenance of a

high tempo was relevant both at the operational and tactical level. At the operational level a low allied tempo would have allowed the Japanese to reconfigure their forces to meet the new threat. At the tactical level, it would have allowed the landing force and amphibious operation to be attacked during transition between maritime and land force and prior to the establishment of sufficient combat power to meet any local threats. The ability to achieve this higher tempo of operations was directly enhanced by the unity of effort provided by the combined and joint command structure. In contrast the Japanese ability to respond was hampered by their separate naval and land commands[18]. Its effect was to improve the efficiency with which operations were planned and conducted and the effectiveness with which the enemy were targeted.

Central to achieving and maintaining the high tempo of operations was the ability to rapidly plan, prepare and conduct amphibious landings of a divisional size. There were several instances in the campaign in New Guinea where landings were planned at very short notice, the schedule advanced, or an objective changed at the last minute. The intention was to

achieve a higher frequency of operations than the Japanese. By doing so greater tempo was gained in relation to their decision making cycle. This resulted in consistently taking objectives that were not prepared for defence and making existing Japanese troop deployments largely irrelevant. Often the allied operations had been predicted, but the Japanese had believed that the operation could not take place in the time scale that it did or they were helpless to do anything about it as in Hollandia[19].

The major key to achieving the short time scale required to plan and conduct the amphibious operation was the amphibious forces themselves, both the landing force and the 7th Amphibious Force. It was the initial absence of any amphibious trained troops that delayed the start of amphibious manoeuvre and it

[18]The Imperial Land and Naval command disagreements are clear in. Spector Ibid.
[19]The Reports of MacArthur Op Cit pp 146.

US Marines holding back a Japanese counter attack at Cape Gloucester, January 1944. (NARA)

was to take 18 months to build sufficient expertise in both naval and landing forces. Ultimately the 7th Amphibious Force and its Army landing forces were to become thoroughly proficient in conducting short notice operations which perhaps reached their zenith in the landing of a division (with 48 hours of supplies) in just under 3 hours at Ormoc Bay with just 10 days notice. This speed of planning and execution would not have been possible without experienced amphibious forces. It was only experience that allowed short cuts to be taken and standard procedures to be developed and used effectively. If that had not been achieved it was doubtful whether amphibious manoeuvre would have had any utility at the tactical level, as they would have been too slow to respond, and sufficient tempo could not have been maintained.

Intelligence, Deception and Surprise

Extensive use of intelligence, deception and surprise was made throughout the campaign. This helped in offsetting the initial

inferiority of allied forces and the inability to achieve enduring air superiority maintaining the tempo and was critical to the indirect approach adopted in the SWPT.

The Allied Intelligence Branch (AIB) formed early in the campaign had 2 main sources. Firstly it consisted of a network of coast watchers[20] inserted in to enemy territory who reported back on air and surface movements, giving advance warning of air and surface attacks but also allowing accurate assessments of the size of troop concentrations. Secondly, an early break of the Japanese code system, along the lines of the ULTRA[21] intelligence in Europe was equally valuable in assessing the operational and strategic intentions of the Japanese leaving them particularly vulnerable to deception. The AIB also made extensive use of interrogation and air reconnaissance. At the tactical level, the value of intelligence was counter-balanced by the risk of compromise in gathering it. Landing area and beach reconnaissance involved a significant risk of compromise for little more information than that which could be provided by air reconnaissance.

Intelligence was not only used to identify suitable landing areas, objectives and determining the size of the forces required but it also proved invaluable in planning successful deception measures and allowing surprise to be achieved.

The allied invasion of Hollandia and Aitape was a complete surprise

Surprise at Lae was achieved with a simple deception plan. Intelligence confirmed that the Japanese were expecting an overland attack from the direction of Salamaua. The allies reinforced this belief by mounting an overland diversionary attack at Salamaua which drew the majority of forces away from Lae. Deception perhaps played its greatest role in the Hollandia operation, as it was the first time that a move of such depth had been attempted and this relied heavily on good intelligence[22]. Crypto-analysis identified that the Japanese expected the next attack to be in the area of Madang and Hansa Bay, 150 miles along the coast[23]. It also identified an elaborate mobile trap for any landing. This spawned the idea of a deception plan to reinforce this false perception. This area was consequently prepared for a landing far more intensely than the Hollandia area. Japanese surprise was complete both at the operational and tactical level, the latter assisted by a circuitous sea route to the objective. Post war intelligence debriefing revealed the extent to which the deception and advanced timing of this operation caught the Japanese unawares. 'The allied invasion of Hollandia and Aitape was a complete surprise'[24] said the Commander of the 2nd Army. One Japanese Staff Officer of the 2nd Army reflected that the first he knew that the Americans were going to Hollandia was when he saw them in the harbour[25]. The same officer also informed

[20]See Lord Walter. Lonely Vigil Coast Watchers. Viking New York. 1977.
[21]See Drea E. MacArthur's Ultra. University Press of Kansas. 1992
[22]See Spector R. Op Cit 287.
[23]This was the normal bound as it would have been within range of land based air.
[24]The Reports of General MacArthur Op Cit., pp 146.
[25]Idem.

them that they had expected to be attacked eventually, but not so promptly and for the landings to occur in Hansa Bay. The number of hastily evacuated positions discovered by the landing force demonstrated the level of tactical surprise achieved, in some, the fires and meals were still warm.

Objective Focused Landings and the Avoidance of Beachheads

For this style of amphibious manoeuvre it was vital that the beach was seen only as a method of regaining the shore, an obstacle that had to be crossed and not a foothold or a beachhead in enemy territory that had to be defended at all cost. Had this not been the case the tendency might have been to adopt a defensive posture until combat power and supplies had been built up, rather as happened at Anzio. Had it occurred it would have allowed the Japanese to react to the landing, and the advantage gained by the Allies would have easily been lost. However, the Allies rarely stopped on the beach, allowing it only to become their rear supply area for their move

to the objective. The beaches protection came from the sea and by the fact that the Japanese were either fixed by other forces or the immediate threat the landing force was posing to its objective. Only on rare occasions were the landing force interposed between the Japanese and the beach. Often the beach area's best security was the exploitation of the landing force and the threat that this posed.

Considerable advantage was achieved both by the choice of weakly defended objectives deep in the rear of the Japanese defensive positions and the high tempo of operations. Though, this alone was insufficient to account for the success of the individual operations particularly at the tactical level. At the beginning of the campaign the Allies faced a foe superior in the air, on the ground and at sea. In the early days the Allies were only able to sustain air parity for 3 hours over the objective area. They constantly faced the threat of the imperial fleet and they were up against a numerically superior ground force often prepared, to fight to the last man.

To achieve this, a rapid offload capability was developed. Combat troops were taken from their normal duties to assist with offloading. The maximum amounts of stores were placed on wheeled vehicles and only 48 hours of supplies would be

landed. This element of risk taking and emphasis on speed allowed forces up to a division in size to be offloaded in less than 3 hours. This reduced exposure time, maximised the use of allied air and effectively minimised the losses of ships allowing them to clear the objective before Japanese aircraft appeared in strength. On the following nights the landing force would be re-supplied in a similar manner, from shore basis in the more secure rear area. It was only when the air situation was stabilised, usually once the forward airfield was established that significant stocks were moved forward. This technique was to prove very successful at Lae where, despite the unexpected close proximity of a flight of Japanese, bombers only 2 landing craft were lost to enemy action. This method of minimising the stock placed ashore is similar to that envisaged by sea-basing in the Littoral Manoeuvre concept.

Conclusion

The operations of the SWPT clearly demonstrate that when amphibious forces exploit the maritime manoeuvre space they can have an effect out of all proportion to their size. The landings in Papua New Guinea and later in the Philippines campaign were unique, and demonstrate the utility of amphibious manoeuvre. Importantly, Operation RECKLESS and those other landings undertaken in the SWPT provide a number of enduring lessons on how to conduct amphibious manoeuvre in a hostile environment, which continue to be of relevance today.

Summary of Lessons Identified pre-Normandy

- Heavy pre-bombardment from air and sea
- Get armour ashore early, preferably ahead of infantry, hence the need for
- Specialised armour
- Close support from gun/rocket craft on run-in
- Naval gunfire support on call
- Amphibians to cross water gap, and get inland away from the waterline

Further Reading

Barbey, D. E., *MacArthur's Amphibious Navy,* (Annapolis, Maryland: Naval Institute Press, 1969)

Drea, E., *MacArthur's Ultra,* (Kansas: University Press of Kansas, 1992)

Leonhard, Robert R., *The Art of Maneuver: Maneuver-Warfare Theory and AirLand Battle,* (Novato, California: Presidio, 1991)

Leonhard, Robert R., *Fighting by Minutes,* (Westport, Connecticut: Praeger, 1994)

Lorelli, John A., *To Foreign Shores: U.S. Amphibious Operations in World War II,* (Annapolis, Maryland: Naval Institute Press, 1995)

Lord, Walter, *Lonely Vigil Coast Watchers,* (New York: Viking, 1977)

Prefer, N., *MacArthur's New Guinea Campaign,* (Pennsylvania: Combined Books, 1995)

Spector, Ronald H., *Eagle Against the Sun,* (New York: Macmillan, 1985)

Van Der Vat, Dan, *The Pacific Campaign,* (Edinburgh: Birlinn, 2001)

Willoughby, Charles A. and Chamberlain, John, *MacArthur 1941-51: Victory in the Pacific,* (London: William Heinemann, 1956)

Biography

Lieutenant Colonel Mark Maddick was commissioned in to the Royal Marines in April 1985, and later appointed to 45 Commando Royal Marines. He then trained as a Landing Craft Officer and subsequently served in 539 Assault Squadron Royal Marines. After an exchange tour with the Royal Netherlands Marine Corps, he completed a tour in Bosnia as the Factions Liaison Officer, in NATO. He attended the United Kingdoms Advance Command and Staff Course in 1998. After which he served as the 3 Commando Brigade Operations Officer, which included deployments to Sierra Leone and Kosovo. He commanded a Company in 42 Commando Royal Marines, where he returned for a second tour to Sierra Leone. On promotion to Lieutenant Colonel he was appointed to the staff of Commander United Kingdom Amphibious Forces as the SO1 Future Plans and Policy. During his tour he was involved in the planning for Operation IRAQI FREEDOM. He is currently the Amphibious Concept Development Officer within the Maritime Warfare Centre.

The Normandy Landings
Operation OVERLORD, 6 June 1944
The Myth of Manoeuvrism

By Dr Stuart Griffin

D-Day is justifiably regarded as one of the greatest military undertakings ever. The scope of its ambitions and the scale of its achievements are remarkable. As an amphibious assault, Normandy remains unparalleled. However, with success often comes the temptation to ascribe characteristics and draw conclusions that simply do not apply as if successful operations provide panaceas for all other military endeavours. This is the inherent danger of the selective use of history to support current doctrine, as if everything is manoeuvrist. In the case of Normandy, such false history does all a great disservice. Instead, the best lessons from Normandy with regard to manoeuvre warfare and the manoeuvrist approach, are revealed when one explores the limitations of these concepts to OVERLORD not from attributing dubious levels of manoeuvrism to its design. Essentially, *Normandy was not especially manoeuvrist nor was it an exemplar of manoeuvre warfare*. The crucial point is *not* that this lack of manoeuvrism reveals a failure in the operation but that it emphasises that such concepts are a means to an end not an end in themselves.

Naturally, the Allies employed manoeuvrism, as we now understand it, to disguise their plans as best as possible and maximise their potential advantages. They also intended to conduct manoeuvre warfare to defeat German forces in the field once the Allied bridgehead was established. However, the realities of the situation in 1944 severely circumscribed the opportunity to fully exploit either of these related concepts. First, the truth of the matter was that suitable sites for an amphibious assault on the scale required, *a theatre - level entry with direct strategic intent*, were limited. As the Allies were not employing Liddell Hart's 'indirect approach', a drive on Germany through northern France was always the most likely course of action. Second, neither the Allied armed forces nor the Normandy countryside were particularly well suited to manoeuvre warfare and the nature of the German defence also mitigated against this, hence the attritional battle that eventually ensued. This chapter will explore the rationale behind the Allies' choice of Normandy as their beachhead. It will also examine the nature of the German defence and ask why it was so hard to break down though a detailed analysis of the entire Normandy campaign is beyond its scope. The chapter's primary focus is the planning and execution of the amphibious landing itself and what it says about manoeuvrism.

Planning the Normandy Landings:
The origins of Operation OVERLORD

Speculation about the nature and timing of a future Allied invasion of continental Europe began as early as 1942.[1] Within a few months of the United States' entry into the war after Japan's surprise attack on Pearl Harbor on 7 December 1941, Britain, the Soviet Union and the USA began serious discussions about the future direction of military strategy and the prospects for a cross-Channel invasion of Nazi-occupied France. Deciding upon the location of the assault became a vexed question but more immediately acrimonious was debate about timing. Since Germany's 1941 invasion of the USSR, Operation BARBAROSSA, the Soviet Union had borne the brunt of the fighting with Hitler's Axis. Owing to the scale of the conflict in the east, the Wehrmacht (German army) had been forced to deploy the vast majority of its best formations in Russia. However, spectacular battlefield triumph after spectacular battlefield triumph failed to bring decisive strategic victory and the Wehrmacht's 1942 drive into the Caucasus presaged shifting fortunes as Germany's elite 6th Army became bogged down at Stalingrad. Though the 6th Army would not be fully defeated until February 1943 and the tide would not turn irretrievably until after the Battle of Kursk in July of the same year, German military over-stretch was becoming increasingly apparent by the autumn of 1942. In October, Montgomery's 8th Army finally defeated Rommel's Africa Korps at the Third Battle of Alamein, Britain's first major victory against German land forces. Operation TORCH, the Anglo-American landings in North Africa, followed hot on the heels of this victory in November providing invaluable experience of large-scale amphibious assaults in advance of the Italian campaign of the following year and the Normandy landings of 1944.

These early indications of a shifting strategic balance re-invigorated discussion of the opening of a Second Front,

---

[1] Kirkpatrick, C, 'The Second Front Debate', in no-named author, *D-Day: Operation Overlord from its Planning to the Liberation of Paris*, (London: Salamander Books), 1999, pp.7-23.

The crucial point is not that this lack of manoeuvrism reveals a
failure in the operation but that it emphasises that such concepts
are a means to an end not an end in themselves

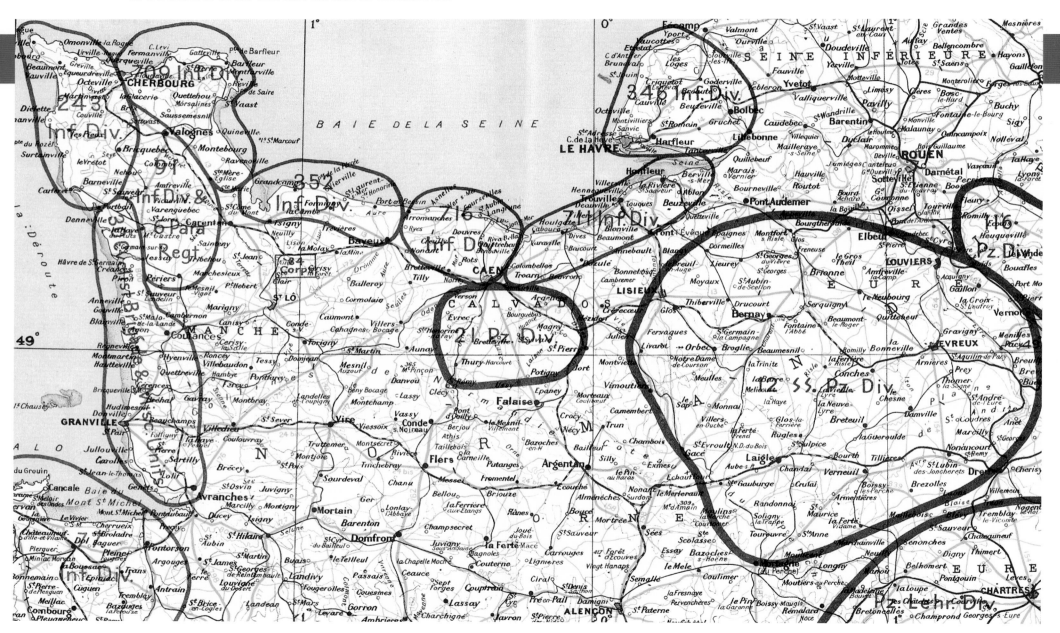

something that Stalin had been desperately pursuing since the Soviet Union's catastrophic start to the war in the east. By spring of 1942, Red Army losses were in excess of 5 million men and threatened to force the capitulation of the Soviet Union.[2] In the event, the Soviet Union had little choice but to fight on and its tenacity gave the western Allies invaluable time to prepare. This was of little consolation to Stalin who needed breathing space and implored Churchill and Roosevelt to counter-attack in the west. Roosevelt and his Chief of Staff, General Marshall, were keen to do so and pressured their British counterparts, Churchill and General Brooke (later Lord Alanbrooke), to open the second front.[3] Britain's refusal to do so caused friction between the two western allies and a serious rift with the Soviets. Churchill and Brooke resisted the opening of a second front in 1942 on the grounds that a precipitate counter-stroke was likely to go wrong. Both felt that their US allies seriously under-estimated the scale of such an endeavour and failed to grasp the fundamental fact that they were currently incapable of prosecuting a major invasion successfully. Until Operation BOLERO, the strategic build-up of US forces in Britain, could decisively shift the balance of forces in the west and the Royal Navy and RAF could win the Battle of the Atlantic and the struggle for air superiority over France, a full-scale cross-Channel invasion was simply untenable. The truly disastrous

Dieppe Raid (Operation JUBILEE) of August 1942 confirmed the potentially dire consequences of a false stroke.

British obstinacy resulted first in the postponement of the proposed Operation SLEDGEHAMMER of 1942, then its revision into Operation ROUNDUP planned for 1943, and finally the abandonment of an invasion of France until 1944. Instead, the western Allies opened the second front in the Mediterranean theatre with the invasion first of Sicily (Operation HUSKY) and then mainland Italy. This was regarded as a temporary expedient by both Russia and America, thus representing an unsatisfactory compromise with Britain.[4] These grand-strategic differences are highly relevant to the analysis of Normandy because they go to the very heart of debate about manoeuvrism. Churchill and Brooke wanted to open the second front in the Mediterranean for a host of reasons, most notably resource constraints.[5] Churchill certainly entertained vague hopes that an indirect assault upon Germany through its weaker Axis partner, Italy, and via the Balkans may lead to victory at a more acceptable price particularly with regard to restricting the future extent of Soviet influence in eastern Europe.[6] However, his perceived 'soft underbelly of Europe' was anything but and the Allies protracted crawl up Italy confirmed the necessity for a decisive strike into northern Europe: almost inevitably an amphibious assault on France.

The Italian campaign vividly highlights the limits of manoeuvrism. It was also a useful reminder to the Allies of the challenges to amphibious assault, demonstrating how well conceived plans and favourable odds do not guarantee success. Though each Allied landing was successfully executed, exploitation proved problematic every time. Further, attacking Germany indirectly through the Balkans was manoeuvrist but offered a slim chance of grand-strategic victory in itself. Its primary value lay in the diversion of German resources away from northern Europe and the Eastern Front though the extent of even this more limited assistance has been challenged.[7] To decisively defeat Germany, the Allies required military-strategic victories in either the west or the east and preferably both. In the west, this meant that a

[2]Overy, Richard, *Russia's War*, (London: Penguin), 1998.
[3]D'Este, Carlo, *Decision in Normandy: The Unwritten Story of Montgomery and the Allied Campaign*, (London: Penguin), 2001 (reprint), pp.23-28.
[4]ibid.
[5]Fraser, David, 'Alanbrooke', in Keegan, John (ed.), *Churchill's Generals*, (London: Abacus) 1999 (reprint), pp.96-7.
[6]Churchill, Sir Winston, *The Second World War*, (Boston), 1953.
[7]Molony, Brig CJC, *The History of the Second World War, Vol.V: The Mediterranean and Middle East*, (London: HMSO), 1973.

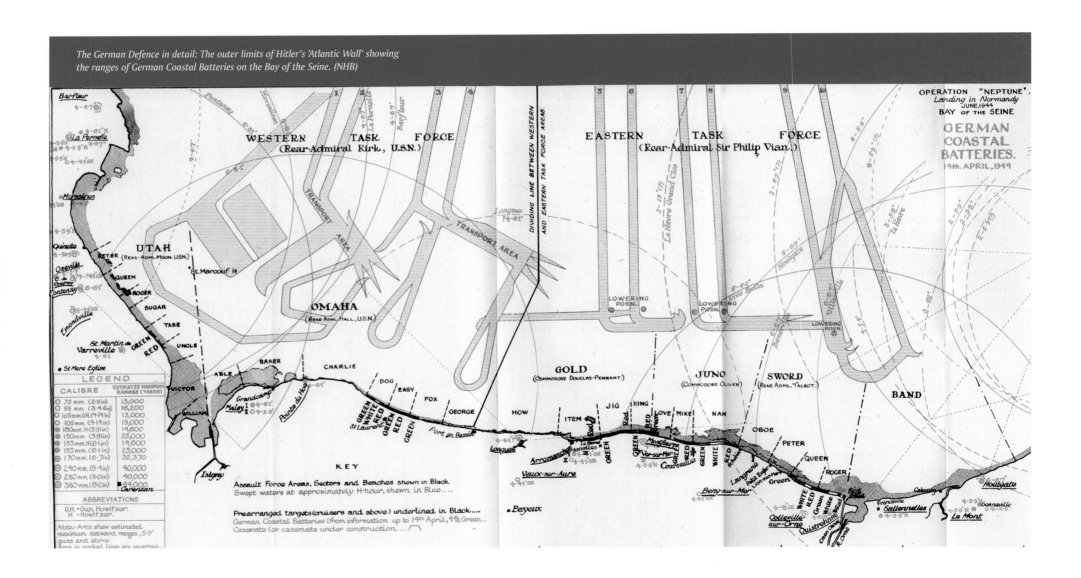

The German Defence in detail: The outer limits of Hitler's 'Atlantic Wall' showing the ranges of German Coastal Batteries on the Bay of the Seine. (NHB)

cross-Channel invasion was ultimately unavoidable, a fact that Britain conceded at the Casablanca Conference of January 1943 even before the Italian campaign got under way. Operations in Italy, however, did have the desired effect from the British perspective of stalling US and Soviet attempts to force a precipitate invasion of France. Only after the Tehran-Cairo Conference of November-December 1943 did Britain accept that the time was right to launch the primary counter-attack upon Germany, a decision that history tells us was correct but caused serious coalition frictions at the time.

US-Soviet perceptions of British recalcitrance were understandable given the former's desire to bring its material superiority fully to bear and the latter's need for support to relieve the pressure on its own beleaguered armed forces. However, British reticence had good cause. It was not until 1944 that the relative balance of military power swung decisively in favour of the Allies. Soviet victories the previous year had effectively broken German offensive power in the east[8] while the defeat of Germany's Atlantic U-Boat campaign finally re-secured Britain's SLOCs.[9] The Anglo-American bombing campaign over Germany was also beginning to have a major impact on Germany's ability to wage war.[10] Though Operation POINTBLANK, the strategic targeting of Germany's industrial base and air force, had begun in January 1943, it was the subsequent introduction of long-

Forced to engage Allied aircraft in an attempt to protect German industry, the Luftwaffe began to suffer critical losses

range fighter escorts that did the most damage to the Luftwaffe. Forced to engage Allied aircraft in an attempt to protect German industry, the Luftwaffe began to suffer critical losses. Air combat accounted for most of the 2262 German fighter pilots killed in the six months preceding D-Day[11] and allowed the RAF and USAAF bombers to inflict significant damage on the German aircraft industry. By June 1944, the Luftwaffe was largely incapable of replacing its losses both in terms of men and materiel. 'Put quite simply, the Allies did not merely possess air *superiority*, but air *supremacy* as well.'[12] General Eisenhower, appointed Supreme Allied Commander in December 1943, acknowledged that without air superiority the invasion would not have been possible, thus implicitly recognising the validity of British caution.

British conservatism had another very obvious source: Normandy was not a particularly surprising objective. Prior to the initiation of serious planning for the invasion of France, the Directorate of Combined Operations (DCO) had already undertaken extensive beach, defensive and topographical surveys of potential landing sites in northern France and concluded that Pas de Calais and Normandy were the only genuinely viable options for a major

amphibious assault.[13] On the one hand, Dieppe had proven that an assault on a well-defended port was extremely risky. Both Britain and Germany concluded that a direct amphibious desant to seize major port facilities was unviable if those ports were properly defended, leading Germany to concentrate its coastal defences around the major ports and Britain to look for more unconventional alternatives. Though hindsight demonstrates that the Normandy landings could have been sustained without the advent of the famous floating harbours, the so-called Mulberries, the psychological impact of creating alternatives to port facilities in the absence of evidence that adequate re-supply could be conducted over the beaches was an important factor in the decision to go.[14] On the other, Italy had emphasised the point that a successful lodgement was of limited value if it could not be properly sustained or exploited. These were not major revelations in themselves but served to focus attention on essential prerequisites for full-scale amphibious assault and, more importantly, its application to the desired strategic end-state. First, any potential landing site had to be vulnerable enough to amphibious assault to provide the Allies with the best opportunity to land the majority of their forces safely. Second, was the necessity for a large and defensible beachhead to allow appropriate sustainment. Finally, both had to be combined with the requirement to choose a geographic location allowing breakout and subsequent attainment of strategic goals.

[8]Glantz, David, *When Titans Clashed: How the Red Army Stopped Hitler*, (Kansas), 1995.
[9]Roskill, Stephen, *The Navy at War: 1939-1945*, (London: Wordsworth), 1998 (reprint), pp.262-268 and 351-364.
[10]Richards, Denis, *RAF Bomber Command in the Second World War*, (London: Penguin), 2001 (reprint), pp.221-231.
[11]Hallion, *Strike from the Sky*, (Shrewsbury: Airlife), 1989, p.190.

[12]ibid.
[13]D'Este, op.cit., pp.32-33.
[14]Van Creveld, Martin, *Supplying War*, (Cambridge: Cambridge University Press), 1977.

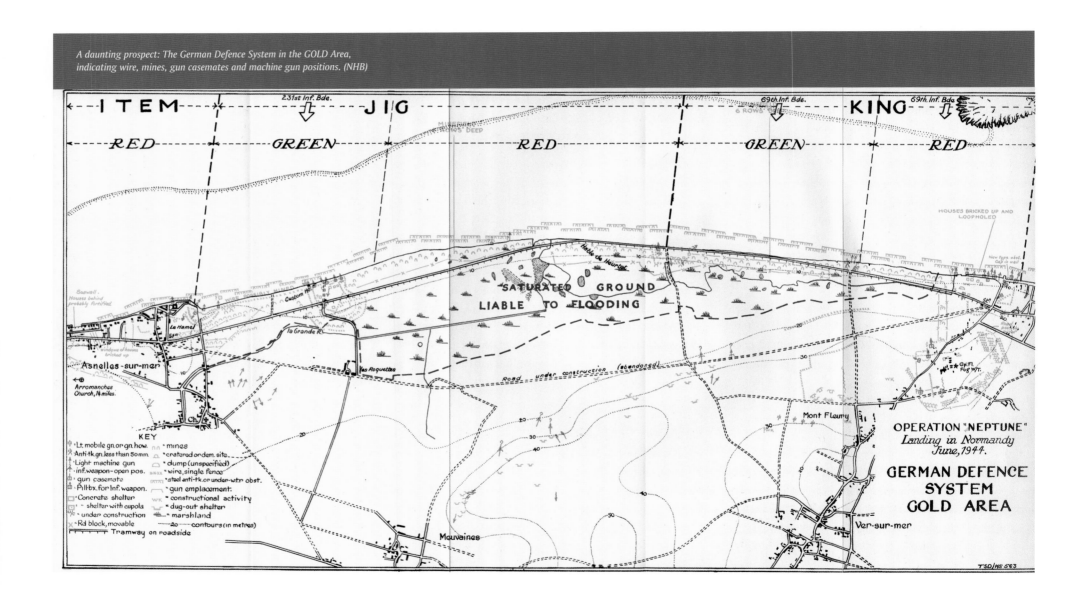

*A daunting prospect: The German Defence System in the GOLD Area,
indicating wire, mines, gun casemates and machine gun positions. (NHB)*

Lieutenant General Sir Frederick E. Morgan, named COSSAC after his post. (NHB)

Supreme Headquarters Allied Expeditionary Force badge. (NHB)

When Lieutenant General Sir Frederick Morgan was appointed Chief of Staff to the Supreme Allied Commander (Designate) early in 1943, his joint and combined planning team (named COSSAC after his post) drew the same conclusion as Mountbatten's DCO. In the summer of 1943 it presented its report and outline plan to the Joint Chiefs of Staff, concluding that the most direct route via the Pas de Calais should be over-looked in favour of the less well-defended Calvados-Cotentin peninsula.[15] The Normandy landings should be conducted, at minimum, as a three division assault over three beaches with rapid reinforcement to five divisions and a steady troop build-up as the bridgehead expanded, keeping the Allies ahead of the Germans in the race to reinforce. D-Day for Operation OVERLORD was initially set as May 1944.

General Eisenhower was appointed to command in December 1943 but did not formally take up his position until February. Though he and his subordinate commanders revised the plan once enhanced resources were confirmed, Overlord's basic concept remained the same.

'Our main strategy in the conduct of the ground campaign was to land amphibious and airborne forces on the Normandy coast between Le Havre and the Cotentin peninsula and, with the successful establishment of a beachhead with adequate ports, to drive along the lines of the Loire and the Seine Rivers into the heart of France, destroying the German strength and freeing France.'[16]

The ultimate aim was to decisively defeat German forces in the west, hence the requirement to land close to somewhere that the German army would be forced to defend vigorously. The Allied plan required the Wehrmacht to be brought to battle but on their terms after a foothold had been firmly established. Pas de Calais was discounted because it was the obvious choice due to the short transit across the Channel and the directness of approach to Germany. It was therefore the most heavily defended part of northern France. Normandy was the next best option, with a longer transit but weaker defences and better topography for lodgement and exploitation. To enhance the chances of a successful lodgement and breakout, Eisenhower and his land component commander, General Sir Bernard Montgomery, pressed for an expansion of the beachhead from three to five beaches roughly doubling the length of the beachhead to 61 miles, allowing a five division assault wave and bringing the westernmost edge of the landing onto the Cotentin peninsula within striking distance of a major port, Cherbourg. Airborne landings became integral to the plan with the British 6th and American 82nd and 101st Airborne Divisions employed to protect the exposed flanks and seize key bridgeheads for breakout operations.

If Normandy was a prime target, Allied chances of effecting a successful assault were enhanced by German defensive overstretch. Past Wehrmacht victories resulted in a weakened German army now having to defend over 3,000 miles of coastline in the northern European theatre from Norway to the Pyrenees. With the Eastern Front fixing the vast majority of Germany's armed forces, occupations in Greece, Yugoslavia and (effectively) Italy tied down more critical resources in the Mediterranean and Adriatic. Though there was no sensible alternative to shortening German lines Hitler forbade it. General Blumentritt, von Rundstedt's Chief of Staff in France, said simply: 'we were bound to arrive too late every time.'[17] Field Marshal von Rundstedt was German Commander in Chief West (OB West) with an area of operations whose right flank was delineated by the German-Dutch border in the north and left flank by the Franco-Italian border in the south.[18] OKW (Armed Forces High Command) correctly judged northern France the most likely target for the Allies' killing blow so von Rundstedt was able to prepare as best as possible though he, like most of his peers, judged Pas de Calais the probable location.

Ambiguous command responsibilities and limited resources combined with the geographic size of OB West's responsibility to undermine his ability to defend Normandy. In practice, von Rundstedt did not exercise direct control over many of his

[15]COSSAC (43) 32 (Final), *Digest of Operation Overlord*, 30 July 1943.
[16]Eisenhower, General Dwight D, *D Day to VE Day; Official Report*, (London: HMSO), 2000 (reprint), p.8.
[17]Blumentritt, G, 'Report of the Chief of Staff (B-283)', in Isby, DC (ed.), *Fighting the Invasion: The German Army at D-Day*, (London: Greenhill), 2000, pp.19-30.
[18]Blumentritt, op.cit., p.23.

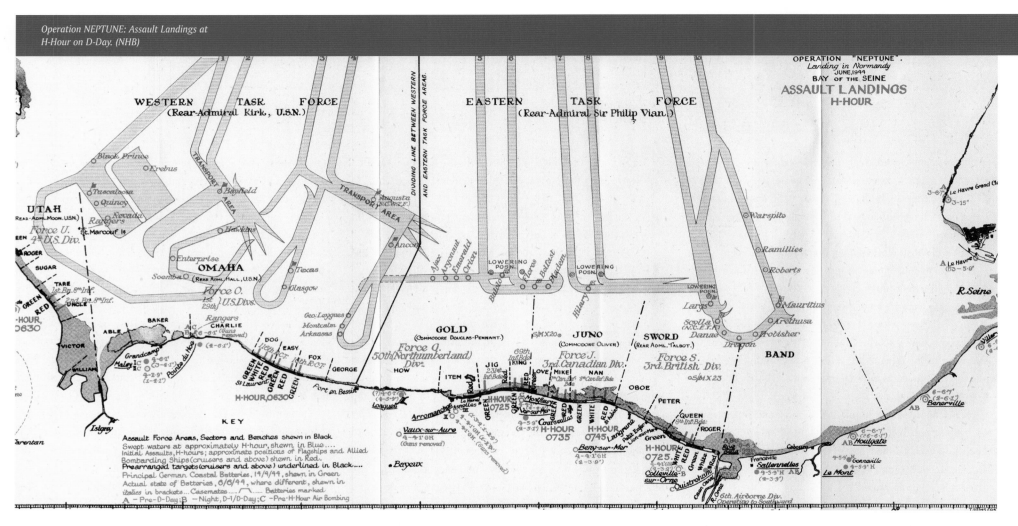

Operation NEPTUNE: Assault Landings at
H-Hour on D-Day. (NHB)

forces. Field Marshal Erwin Rommel was Commander of Army Group B, which included 7th Army in the Normandy sector, and had overall responsibility for coastal defences along the much-vaunted Atlantic Wall. They disagreed profoundly over the best defensive strategy, with von Rundstedt favouring a mobile reserve held well back near Paris and Rommel preferring a forward defence on the waterfront.[19] Both viewpoints had merit, illustrating the paradox that the German armed forces were presented with. It was true that strategic reserves based outside Paris would be unlikely to arrive in time to undertake decisive counter-attacks especially given the extent of allied air superiority but it was equally correct that, without definitive intelligence of the location of the invasion, forward deployment of the Wehrmacht's limited reserves could prove disastrous. One approach lacked mobility, the other flexibility, and neither offered a battle-winning approach in itself. The compromise of some forward deployed panzer divisions with more held back as a strategic reserve was even more unsatisfactory because the

[19]Gersdorff, F, 'Preparations Against the Invasion', in Isby, op.cit., pp.31-36.

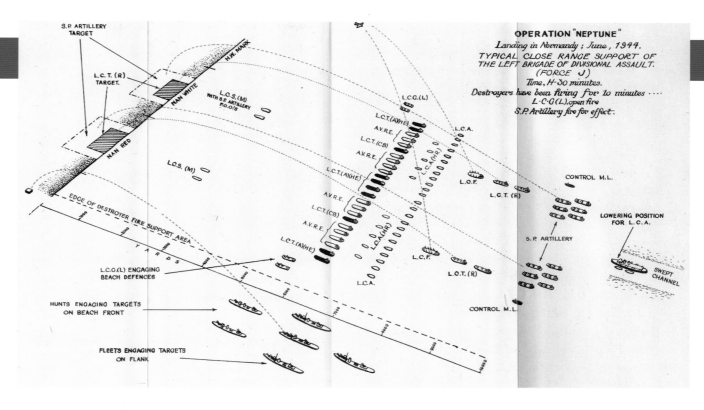

Typical Close Range Support of Landing Craft
as they approached the beach. (NHB)

reserves were not placed under either man's control, requiring Hitler's personal permission before they could be released. This had consequences on D-Day itself when the delay releasing Panzer Lehr surrendered all strategic initiative to the Allies.

A complicated division of responsibilities within OB West's area further encouraged command paralysis. Rommel had theoretical control over Army Group B's panzer forces but OKW held the reins of those in reserve, with General Geyr von Schweppenburg commanding Panzer Group West itself and Hitler wielding final authority. The Waffen SS was a law unto itself so SS panzer and infantry divisions could not be relied upon to follow orders from nominal superiors outside their own chain of command. Intelligence gathering was never centralised, with different agencies competing rather than collaborating and failing to properly assess its implications as a result. Finally, neither the Luftwaffe nor the German Navy operating in OB West came under von Rundstedt's command, which, frankly, was the least of his problems as neither was in any fit state to provide substantial assistance anyway. Fundamentally, OB West lacked the resources to match his responsibilities. Hitler's so-called Fortress Europe was anything but.[20] Though the Atlantic Wall boasted over 12,000 fortifications by June 1944 most were far weaker than intended in terms of men and equipment. German defences were stretched so thinly that OB West stood little chance of defeating an invasion at the waterfront unless the Allies landed in the most obvious places against major fortifications.

Von Rundstedt's best forces, 15th Army, protected Pas de Calais whilst Dollman's 7th Army had responsibility for the Normandy sector. The defences consisted of LXXXIV Corps in the Caen-Carentan sector, XXV and LXXIV Corps defending Brittany and the westernmost elements of 15th Army to the east across the River Dives. However, these forces were of mixed abilities with some decent regular infantry divisions supporting mainly poor static infantry divisions on the coastline. Some powerful panzer divisions were in reserve but the problematic command structure described above would inhibit their effectiveness too. Immediately available were 3 poor static infantry divisions consisting of second rate immobile troops in coastal defence roles, 2 good semi-mobile infantry divisions and 21 Panzer Division, the poorest of the armoured formations to be engaged

in the battle. The formidable formations of Panzer Lehr, 12 SS Panzer Division and 2 Parachute Corps could rapidly be brought into the line with other elite units also capable of reinforcing though not at such short notice.

From the Allied perspective, German defensive overstretch provided them with a very good chance of landing successfully but the lack of numerous suitable beaches meant that surprise would be absolutely crucial. Without it, the concentration of the Wehrmacht's best forces in northern France would allow the Germans to put up fierce resistance, perhaps beating the Allies in the race for reinforcement. It is in this more limited sense of strategic and operational deception that manoeuvrism played its most prominent role. The Allied deception plan,

[20]Ruge, Friedrich, 'The Invasion of Normandy', in HA Jacobsen and J Rohwer, *Decisive Battles of World War II: The German View*, (London: Andre Deutsch), pp.317-330.

Operation BODYGUARD, was an outstanding operation, previously unparalleled in the western theatre.[21] Though the Soviets regularly employed strategic level deception (the concept of *Maskirovka*), the Allies had never attempted anything so ambitious. BODYGUARD's subsidiary operations included the deliberate misdirection of the Allied bombing effort, which dropped twice as many bombs outside the Normandy sector as inside it. This also had the direct practical effect of causing severe damage to France's physical infrastructure and inhibiting German movement into Normandy. Most prominently, Bodyguard included the spectacularly successful deception Operation FORTITUDE.[22] FORTITUDE NORTH and FORTITUDE SOUTH were strategic level deceptions that aimed to convince German High Command (OKW) that the Allies main thrust would be in the Pas de Calais. FORTITUDE NORTH and SOUTH consisted of the invention of two entire army groups in Scotland and southern England. General Patton's imaginary First US Army Group (FUSAG), based in the south-east, was the masterstroke as the Allies knew that the Germans regarded Patton as their best general and therefore most likely to lead the main assault. BODYGUARD was ultimately so successful that the majority of 15th Army remained fixed in Pas de Calais over two months into the Normandy campaign with OKW still convinced that OVERLORD was a feint.[23]

D-Day and the Normandy Campaign

The achievement of strategic, operational and even tactical surprise on D-Day itself was an astonishing accomplishment. Equally remarkable was the secret assemblage, training and transit of the assault forces themselves. By the time the revised OVERLORD

The naval phase of OVERLORD, including the amphibious assault itself, was code-named Operation NEPTUNE

plan got under way on the morning of 5 June 1944 after a 24-hour weather delay, the Allies had assembled an invasion fleet second to none. Nearly 4600 vessels undertook the voyage to Normandy carrying 130 000 troops, 12 000 vehicles, 2000 tanks and 10 000 tons of supplies.[24] The naval phase of OVERLORD, including the amphibious assault itself, was code-named Operation NEPTUNE. It was planned and executed by Admiral Sir Bertram Ramsay with operational command on the day going to Rear-Admiral Kirk for the US (Western) Task Force and Rear-Admiral Vian for the British (Eastern) Task Force. Admiral Ramsay's meticulous naval orders[25] proved their worth as the entire invasion fleet left their berths in numerous ports around

Britain on (revised) schedule, came together off the Isle of Wight at position Z (nicknamed Piccadilly Circus) and arrived in good order off the Normandy coast, having cleared routes through the minefields for minimal loss. The crossing passed unmolested by U-boats with the destroyer screens only having to fend off one subsequent attack, from E-boats, which resulted in the single Allied loss to naval action, the Norwegian destroyer HNorMS *Svenner*. The first assault wave of the 1897 smaller landing craft carried across the Channel on board the 2700 larger vessels was launched in the Bay of the Seine before dawn on 6 June and appeared off the Normandy coast at first light.[26] Meanwhile, the Allied airborne forces dropped just after midnight, were already engaged in heavy fighting to secure the flanks.

The US beaches, UTAH and OMAHA, were protected by 3 battleships, 1 monitor, 9 cruisers and 25 destroyers while the British and Canadian beaches, GOLD, JUNO and SWORD, were covered by 2 battleships, 1 monitor, 11 cruisers and 40

[21]Cruikshank, C, *Deception in World War II* (Oxford: OUP), 1979.

[22]Hesketh, Roger, *Fortitude: The D-Day Deception Campaign*, (New York: Overlook), 2002.

[23]Haswell, J, *The Intelligence and Deception of the D-Day Landings*, (London), 1979.

[24]Ellis, LF, *Victory in the West*, vol.1, (London: HMSO), 1962, pp.222-223.

[25]Admiralty, *Operation Neptune – Naval Orders*. For an excellent summary of their content, see Barnett, op.cit., pp.781-809.

[26]Barnett, Correlli, *Engage the Enemy More Closely*, (London: Penguin), 2000 (reprint), pp.810-814.

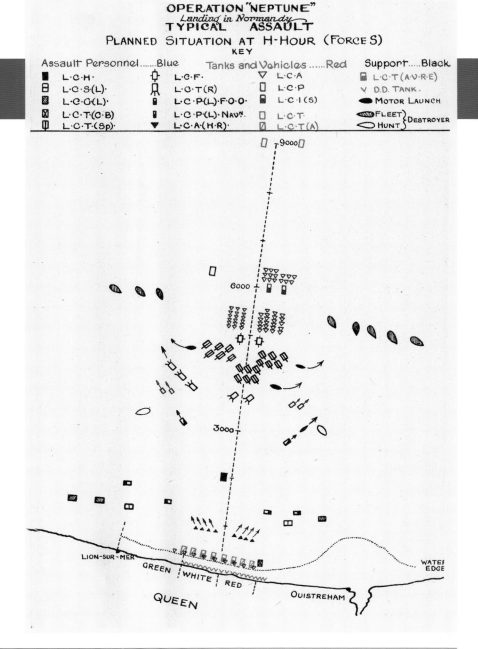

Operation NEPTUNE: Plan of a Typical Assault Formation on SWORD Beach. (NHB)

destroyers (with another battleship and cruiser in reserve).[27] Their mission was threefold: first, to secure the lodgement, second, to rapidly sustain 26 to 30 divisions in that lodgement and finally, to augment it as it expanded at a rate of between 3 and 5 divisions per month.[28] The extent of Allied pre-bombardment subsequently became a controversial issue. In outline, it consisted of heavy aerial bombardment by 1,136 RAF heavy and medium bombers between 0000 and 0500, a second wave of 1083 US 8th Air Force bombers in the hour before landing and naval bombardment from 0550 (when the light would be good enough for spotting).[29] Interestingly, each Task Force took a different approach to NGS with the British and Canadians, who were landing one hour later than the Americans, opening up before their US partners. Kirk's rationale for conducting a mere 40 minute pre-bombardment (H-Hour was 0630 for the Western Task Force) was to maintain tactical surprise to the very last but this went against the advice of USMC officers seconded from the Pacific theatre where heavy naval and air bombardment were proven prerequisites for opposed landings.[30] Kirk subsequently acknowledged that he got it wrong.[31] With the early H-Hour and fear of blue-on-blue casualties in poor weather conditions contributing to the ineffectiveness of the aerial bombardment as well, the Allies were unable to use their firepower to suppress beach defences to the degree intended. This was most damaging in the US-sector where seizing OMAHA beach proved extremely difficult.

OMAHA was the scene of the bloodiest fighting on D-day itself. The Allies knew that its 12 inter-locking gun emplacements with 60 major artillery pieces supported by numerous mortar and machine gun nests situated in strong defensive positions on the bluffs behind the beach made it the most problematic major landing site of the invasion but were unaware that the defence had been bolstered by the addition of regiments from the good 352nd Infantry Division to those of the mediocre 716th Static Infantry Division. As a result, with the defences left intact by the failure of the combined aerial-naval bombardment, the assault waves of the 29th National Guard Division and 1st Infantry Division met fierce resistance from the shore and suffered heavy casualties. A Company of the 116th Regiment suffered 96% casualties and engineers, crucial for the clearing of beach obstacles, sustained 41% casualties overall during the first wave. By the time the second wave landed amongst the wrecks and casualties piling up in the surf, General Omar Bradley,

[27]Barnett, op.cit.
[28]Operation Neptune – Naval Orders (ON1).
[29]Eisenhower, op.cit.
[30]Murray, Williamson, 'The Evolution of Joint Warfare', *Joint Force Quarterly*, Summer 2002, p.34.
[31]Ellis, op.cit., p.187.

commanding 1st US Army, was already considering re-routing follow-on forces to UTAH or GOLD. This eventuality was only avoided by the infiltration of small groups led by Brigadier Cota up the bluffs supported by more accurate NGS from destroyers that had closed to assist the landing forces. Once holes appeared in the defensive line it was no longer able to provide mutually supporting fire and the US forces were able to roll it up. By early afternoon all the beach defences had been overcome and the lodgement was secure though still shallow. *Omaha* casualties amounted to nearly 2,200, the majority during the initial assault waves, contrasting sharply with Utah where US 4th Division had got ashore for the loss of only 197 men.[32] US Airborne losses were higher again, with the 82nd Airborne alone taking over 1,000 casualties on D-Day and bringing total US losses to around 6,000 for the day. Casualties in the British and Canadian sector were

comparatively light, though the nearly 1,000 Canadian casualties on Juno were the next worst on the actual beaches. In all, 3,300 British casualties were sustained by the airborne and amphibious forces pushing inland on 6 June.[33] Placed in context, overall D-Day Allied casualty figures of approximately 10,300, though high by modern standards, were acceptable given the scale of the enterprise. For those losses, 132,715 men were put ashore by nightfall[34] and some 326,547 men, 54,186 vehicles and 104,428 tons of supplies were landed by D+6.[35] Further, the fractured nature of the German response was testament to the effectiveness of the Allies deception plan and the totality of surprise.

To the maximum possible extent, the landings had been aided by strategic and operational manoeuvrism, in the shape of deception, but they were still not especially manoeuvrist. Tactically, this is reflected in the difference of approach between the British and Americans when dealing with two particularly dangerous coastal batteries. In the US sector the decision was made to physically seize the imposing gun battery at Pointe du Hoc whilst in the

British sector the attackers relied upon the Royal Navy simply to suppress the German naval battery at Longues. The batteries' 155 mm guns enabled them to shell the approaches (out to about 12 miles) to three of the beaches: UTAH and OMAHA from Pointe du Hoc and GOLD from Longues. Both batteries were in strong defensive positions at the top of cliffs set back from directly observable naval fire. Pointe du Hoc was particularly awkward, situated on a defensible spit of land with another strongpoint, Point de la Percee protecting its eastern flank yet the Americans decided to assault it directly from the sea with elite forces from the US Rangers. The attack went in at 0630 alongside the OMAHA assault and took heavy casualties from the start. Nevertheless, the Rangers managed to take and hold both strong points only then discovering that the guns had been moved in land. By contrast, the 4 gun emplacements at Longues were working and opened fire on the Eastern Task Force at 0620, straddling the flagship of GOLD's naval commander, Rear Admiral Douglas Pennant. The battery was then immediately engaged by the cruiser HMS *Ajax* which fired 114 shells in 20 minutes with extraordinary accuracy, destroying two of the four guns and disabling the others. It was subsequently taken without loss the following morning by the Devonshire Regiment advancing from GOLD.

The contrast between Pointe du Hoc and Longues is a small but apposite example of the limits of manoeuvrism in the context of

[32]Ambrose, Stephen, *D-Day*, (London: Touchstone), 1995.
[33]Barnett, op.cit., p.825.
[34]Roskill, op.cit., p.378.
[35]Eisenhower, op.cit., p.91.

Discovered by the Allies, a German 'Beetle Tank', packed with HE ready to be deployed against the Allied invaders in the SWORD Beach area. (IWM B5115)

OVERLORD. Much criticism has been levelled at the US approach because of the perceived inaccuracy of NGS and the high casualty rate (173 of the 289 Rangers who assaulted both Points were killed or wounded by D+1) but there were key differences between the two batteries that account for the Americans' more high-risk tactics. First, intelligence on the relative gun positions was markedly better for Longues where the Resistance had provided exact distances and 34 Tactical Air Reconnaissance Wing was able to range over the battery providing aerial observation (weather conditions were worse off OMAHA). At Pointe du Hoc, there was no way of knowing the gun emplacements were empty or of accurately observing naval fires. Further, NGS from the battleship USS *Texas* and destroyers HMS *Talybont* and USS *Satterlee* did help protect the Rangers while they scaled the cliff. Second, Pointe du Hoc's geographic position was more dangerous in itself than Longues. Pointe du Hoc occupied a spit of land that jutted out between the Calvados and Cotentin peninsulas. It therefore had the potential to unhinge the US beachhead, splitting OMAHA and UTAH. As the shallowness of the initial lodgement testified, this could have been extremely dangerous.

What this illustrates once again is the limits of manoeuvrism. With hindsight, one can question the costly direct approach taken to seize Pointe du Hoc but under the circumstances of D-Day it was a perfectly reasonable decision not to risk leaving the battery in German hands. Faced with a similar possibility at Port-en-Bessin, which divided the British and US sectors, Lieutenant General Dempsey (Commanding 2nd British Army)

also made the decision to physically take the port, albeit from the rear, risking significant casualties to 47 Commando who captured it overnight on D+1. There are even stronger parallels with British 6th Airborne's assault on Merville Battery at the eastern edge of the landing in the early morning of D-Day. When elements of the scattered 9th Parachute Battalion, under Lieutenant Colonel Otway, charged the battery they took almost 50% casualties only to find the gun emplacements filled with old French guns incapable of threatening SWORD. The discovery of a lack of real threat, however, is not the point: available intelligence suggested that both Pointe du Hoc and Merville needed silencing. In both cases the more 'manoeuvrist' approach of suppression, whilst appealing, risked leaving potentially dangerous gun batteries operational. The benefits of physically securing them were therefore deemed to outweigh the costs in terms of casualties and the Allies accepted the necessity for a more direct approach.

The major disappointment of D-Day was that a successful lodgement did not precipitate a German collapse and rapid breakout. Though the British seaborne troops did link successfully with their airborne colleagues, plans for the lead elements of British 3rd Division to capture Caen on D-Day were ambitious and

contact with 21 Panzer Division outside the city brought them up short. The bridgehead was secured in a continuous line on D+1 but determined, if confused, German counters coupled with some cautious decision-making from the Allies stalled the advance. Several of the operational level commanders, most prominently General Montgomery (commanding all of 21st Army Group) and Lieutenant General Bucknall (commanding British XXX Corps), have been heavily criticised for this loss of initiative.[36] The static nature of the German defence, which was highly professional and supported by armour, also played a critical role in slowing Allied progress through the difficult terrain behind much of the beachhead which was characterised by dense 'bocage' country (boxed hedgerows enclosing small fields often with stone walls

---

[36]Hastings, Max, *Overlord*, (London: Pan) 1999 reprint.

Below: The floating breakwater in heavy weather surrounding the Mulberry Harbour. These were vital for the build up of logistical support until a port was captured. Each of the Phoenix caissons were hollow concrete units with flooding valves and were key to the success of the 'portable port' concept. (NHB)

and farmhouses making excellent defensive strong points) in the east, flooded marshland in the west and commanding wooded ridgelines further inland. As German resistance stiffened with the arrival of the Panzer Divisions, so the Allied advance halted barely inland from the original bridgehead and 'troops trained in England for open, mobile warfare had to re-think their tactics rapidly'.[37] Critically, the nature of the close-quarters defence and the enclosed countryside prevented the Allies from properly exploiting their massive firepower advantages, evening out the contest.

Detailed analysis of the land campaign is not the remit of this chapter but 21st Army Group's slow progress does emphasise another important point about the role of manoeuvrism in the Normandy campaign. Once safely ashore, it was always the intention to engage in manoeuvre warfare across the Normandy

countryside to decisively defeat German forces in the field. However, it had also been assumed that the best German armoured formations would need to be written down before rapid progress could be made, and that this was most likely to occur in the British and Canadian sector. The loss of tempo after D-Day led to an unexpected extended period of attrition but Montgomery, for all his faults, did draw the majority of the Panzer Divisions onto the British and Canadian lines as planned, eventually allowing the breakout to occur from the American sector. Operation COBRA, 25-28 July, effected the Allied breakout and, after the disastrous German Mortain counter-attack (Operation LUTTICH) the tempo of the campaign quickened dramatically with Patton's 3rd US Army making a rapid advance on Paris, which was liberated before schedule by 2nd French Armoured Division on 25 August 1944. The key to the Normandy campaign was not Patton's spectacular advance, which was practically unopposed, but the

methodical writing down of German strength before he even arrived in theatre. It was Bradley's 1st US Army and Dempsey's 2nd British (with 1st Canadian under Lieutenant General Crerar from 23 July) that wore German defences so thin that they eventually broke. Thus, manoeuvre warfare, which current British doctrine describes as 'the application of manoeuvrist thinking to warfighting',[38] was not a decisive factor in Normandy.

Conclusion

One of the most interesting aspects of the manoeuvrist approach is often over-looked. This is the fact that the concept developed partly in order to offset potential numerical inferiority. JWP 0-01 recognises this when it states:

'Such thinking offers the prospect of rapid results or of results disproportionately greater than the resources applied. Hence it is attractive to a numerically inferior side or to a stronger side

---

[37]Badsey, Stephen, Normandy 1944, (Oxford: Osprey), 2004 (reprint), p.42.
[38]Joint Warfare Publication 0-01, 2nd Edition, p.3-5.

Arromanches: One of the 1km long 'Whale' floating roadway piers. These enabled stores vehicles to exit directly from the ship to shore, regardless of tidal movement. (NHB)

that wishes to minimise the resources committed. *However, it does entail the risk that disruption of the enemy will not occur as predicted and hence can be less certain than an operation which relies on the use of overwhelming force as a means of destruction'.*[39]

Operation OVERLORD was too important to leave anything to chance and this is reflected in the limited scope for manoeuvrism in the campaign

The sentence in italics (added by the author) is the crucial point to keep in mind when analysing Normandy. Operation OVERLORD was too important to leave anything to chance and this is reflected in the limited scope for manoeuvrism in the campaign. In the end, it was the 'proper application of overwhelming force' that won the day not manoeuvrist brilliance. Though the Allies planned to conduct manoeuvre warfare once beyond the coastal defences, this course of action was denied by the obstinacy of the German defence and caution displayed by the Allied armies. However, there is a strong case to justify that caution even if it was not entirely intentional. Once the lodgement had been secured, the Allied navies began a masterful reinforcement effort that brought their material advantages fully to bear. The statistics are staggering: 39 divisions (2,052,299 men), 438,471 vehicles and 3,098,259 tons of supplies ashore by the end of

the campaign.[40] Though well over a million Germans were also poured into Normandy by the end of the campaign, the Allies won the race for reinforcement and re-supply, enabling them to fully bring their material superiority to bear. The casualty figures were high for both sides, over 200,000 Allied and around 450,000 German (including 200,000 POWs),[41] but it was the Allies who could suffer these losses and recover.

In the skies, the Allied air forces dominated to such an extent that German re-supply and reinforcement became a tortuous affair. The Allied interdiction campaign that preceded OVERLORD

and continued throughout it dropped bridges, blocked roads, destroyed railways and rolling stock and generally wreaked havoc upon German communications.[42] Allied tactical air took a heavy toll on German armoured columns attempting to reach the front[43] and became absolutely devastating once the Germans were forced back onto the roads in daylight after their defensive line broke.[44] On average, British 2nd Tactical Air Force and US 9th Air Force flew 3,000 sorties per day throughout the campaign, ten times more than Luftflotte 3's best effort.[45] In the face of the Allies material superiority, Hitler continued to

[39] JWP 0-01.
[40] Badsey, op.cit., p.85.
[41] Hastings, op.cit., p.367.
[42] Meilinger, Phillip, *Airwar: Theory and Practice*, p.141.
[43] Hastings, op.cit. It should be noted that most of the Panzer Divisions managed to get their armour into theatre relatively unscathed but suffered heavy losses to support vehicles.
[44] Buckley, J, *Air Power in the Age of Total War*, p.151.

pour reinforcements into the theatre long after OB West had recommended a retreat and it is this that accounts for the extended stalemate. It's feasible that a faster, greater or more imaginative push from 21st Army Group in June could have accelerated the breakout but it's also possible that German tactical superiority would have inflicted a bloody reverse that the Allies had no real incentive to risk once they were properly established.

In a sense, Normandy was more about the proverbial safe pair of hands than the military genius, which is why, at the operational level, Montgomery and Bradley were arguably better choices to lead the assault than the unpredictable Patton who came into his own once Bradley had created enough room for him to manoeuvre. Division between the two paramount US commanders over closing the Falaise Gap provides a revealing glimpse into their different psyches. Patton was keen to take a gamble in order to cut the Germans off at Falaise, later stating that if he had spent the war worrying about his flanks, he never would have won. Bradley, however, overruled Patton, famously saying he preferred the 'solid shoulder of Argentan to the possibility of a broken neck at Falaise'.[46] Though delays completing the encirclement did allow many Germans to escape Falaise, the scale of the carnage within the pocket was still massive, with perhaps 60,000 Germans killed or captured and

10,000 vehicles, including nearly 600 tanks and self-propelled guns, destroyed.[47] In the final analysis, Montgomery and Bradley presided over an overwhelmingly successful campaign that decisively defeated Wehrmacht forces in France and controversy surrounding their decision-making should always be placed in this context.

Finally, accepting the appeal of the manoeuvrist approach does not mean rejecting the value of more direct action; they are not anathema to one another. Again, current British doctrine recognises this: 'in practice, direct and indirect forms of attack are not exclusive styles of warfare and any strategy is likely to contain elements of each. Similarly, the manoeuvrist approach does not preclude the use of attrition.'[48] Put bluntly, as a senior British

[45]Badsey, op.cit., p.40.
[46]Bradley, Omar N, A Soldier's Story, (New York), 1951, p.377.
[47]Badsey, op.cit., p.84.

The rapid build up of combat power begins with US self-propelled 155mm Guns on Sherman chassis being unloaded from LSTs on 7 June 1944. (IWM B5131)

officer recently said 'it's about knowing when to be clever and when to just give them a bloody hard thwack up the middle'.

The Allies used manoeuvrist thinking to help win the Normandy campaign but operational necessities, physical constraints and strategic end states limited its value. The requirement to attack Germany as directly as possible led the Allies to conclude that 'only on the historic battlefields of France and the Low Countries could Germany's armies in the west be decisively engaged and defeated.'[49] Remaining focused on this main effort naturally constrained wider freedom of action. Suitable invasion sites were limited as were resources for complimentary manoeuvrist efforts. Plans for Operation ANVIL, simultaneous Allied landings in the south of France, had to be shelved in order to concentrate enough assets in Britain to maximise the chances of both a successful landing and a decisive campaign which was, after all, the military-strategic end state. ANVIL eventually re-emerged as DRAGOON in August, by which time the Normandy campaign was effectively won. Disagreement between Eisenhower and the strategic bomber chiefs, Harris and Spaatz, about how to prosecute strategic bombing in the run up to OVERLORD was decided in Eisenhower's favour. Ramsay eventually got his amphibious assets, naval protection and more. Air Chief Marshal Tedder, Commander Allied Expeditionary Air Force, was allocated over 250 squadrons of various types as well as strategic air assets under Eisenhower's control. Air, land

accepting the appeal of the manoeuvrist approach does not mean rejecting the value of more direct action; they are not anathema to one another

and naval assets were therefore all directed towards winning in Normandy and where competing demands required tough decisions, OVERLORD had primacy.

Normandy remains unparalleled as an amphibious assault. Its achievements are astonishing and it led directly to victory in the west. However, it is no disrespect to the planning and conduct of Operation OVERLORD to acknowledge that it was not really predicated on manoeuvrism. Instead, it reminds us that direct and indirect approaches to warfare are often complimentary,

not mutually exclusive, and that successful commanders choose the most appropriate, not always the most spectacular, course of action. Manoeuvre warfare and manoeuvrism only remain helpful concepts if they are viewed in this light. In the case of Normandy, manoeuvrist thinking was constrained by the requirements of the task at hand, playing an important, but not primary, role in victory.

---

[48] JWP 0-01.
[49] Eisenhower, op.cit., p.7.

Further Reading

Ambrose, Stephen, *D-Day, June 6th 1944: The Climactic Battle of World War II,* (New York: Touchstone, 1995)

Badsey, Stephen, *Normandy 1944: Allied Landings and Breakout,* (London:Osprey, 1990)

Barnett, Correlli, *Engage the Enemy More Closely,* (London: Penguin, 2000) (Reprint)

D'Este, Carlo, *Decision in Normandy: The Unwritten Story of Montgomery and the Allied Campaign*, (New York: Harper Perennial, 1991)

Eisenhower, General Dwight D., *D Day to VE Day; Official Report*, (London: HMSO, 2000) (Reprint)

Hastings, Max, *Overlord: D-Day and The Battle for Normandy,* (London: Guild Publishing, 1984)

Isby, DC (ed.), *Fighting the Invasion: The German Army at D-Day,* (London: Greenhill, 2000)

Keegan, John, *Six Armies in Normandy: From D-Day to the Liberation of Paris,* (London: Penguin, 1983)

Neillands, Robin, *The Battle for Normandy 1944,* ((London: Cassell, 2002)

Biography

Dr Stuart Griffin is the Deputy Dean of Academic Studies at the UK Joint Services Command and Staff College. He joined Defence Studies Department in 1999 having taught for several years at the University of Birmingham where he also undertook both his MA and PhD in the Department of Politics and International Studies. His undergraduate degree was in Renaissance and Modern History at the University of Warwick. Stuart's primary research areas in recent years have been international peacekeeping and the evolution of joint warfare. He has been a core member of JSCSC and joint MoD-FCO-DfiD peacekeeping training in support of the UN all over the world, including Argentina, Bangladesh, Ghana, Kenya, Kuwait, Nigeria, Romania, Senegal and South Africa. Stuart has written widely on UN and Commonwealth peacekeeping, the conflict management role of the OSCE, sources of conflict in the CIS and joint and combined warfare. He is currently working on the theory and practice of stabilisation operations. His most recent publications include *Understanding Peacekeeping*, with AJ Bellamy and Paul Williams (Polity) 2004 and *Joint Operations: A Short History*, (MoD) 2005. He is also a senior lecturer and has been responsible for the delivery of the Advanced Amphibious Warfare Course.

D-DAY, 47 Commando Royal Marines
Port-en-Bessin, Battle For The Oil Port

XXIV

By Professor John Forfar MC

The Planning Prelude

As the Second World War entered its fourth year in the autumn of 1943 British and Dominion troops had already been engaged in battles all over the world but until German hegemony over Europe had been destroyed and Germany defeated the war would go on. Europe would have to be invaded and Allied Armies, primarily British and Canadian, and now also American, would have to be pitched against the massive concrete and gunnery defences of the 'Atlantic Wall' in the biggest sea-borne landing ever contemplated. The planning was entrusted to an Allied task force under Chief of Staff to the Supreme Allied Commander (COSSAC), British General F. Morgan.

The shortest approach to the French coast was across the 22 miles wide Straits of Dover to the Pas de Calais but there the defences were strongest and concentration of German troops greatest. Weighing up the advantage of avoiding the Pas de Calais by landing on the Normandy coast COSSAC recognised that the 100 miles of ocean crossing involved, together with the time that the ships would be exposed at sea, carried the risk that the invasion fleet would be more vulnerable to aerial and naval attack. Offsetting that was the Allies naval and aerial superiority and Normandy was within the range of protective Spitfire fighter planes. COSSAC discounted the longer crossing and recognised that it would have the advantage of surprise if strict security could be maintained and the enemy deceived into thinking that a landing on the Pas de Calais, or Norway, was intended.

Normandy provided a 50 mile stretch of coast westward from Ouistreham within which over 130,00 men would be landed on D-Day on five beaches each about 2½ miles wide and designated, east to west, as SWORD, JUNO, and GOLD in the British sector and OMAHA and UTAH in the American. Thus the British Second Army (General Sir Miles Dempsey) and the Canadian First Army (General H. D. G. Crerar) would land on the Eastern (left) section of the front and the American First Army (General Omar Bradley) on the Western (right) section. The US First Army would come under command of 21st Army Group (General Sir Bernard Montgomery) in the early phase of the invasion.

Port-en-Bessin

Between the western edge of GOLD and eastern of OMAHA was a 12 mile stretch of steep cliffs 200 feet high. In a break in these cliffs - the ends of the break forming the so called Eastern and Western Features - lay Port-en-Bessin 8 miles west of GOLD and 3 miles east of OMAHA. 47 Royal Marine Commando would land at the extreme right of the British front and be responsible for capturing Port-en-Bessin and establishing a link with the Americans at OMAHA.

Port-en-Bessin was to be the terminal through which petrol would be piped to dumps serving the armies, and later also the air forces, on the British front. During the first few days petrol in 'jerrycans' would be landed over the beaches but thereafter 6 inch buoyed pipes would lead to the port from tankers off-shore, and shortly thereafter a pipe-line under

the ocean (PLUTO) would run directly from the Isle of Wight. For the invasion armies with their vast array of tanks, armoured vehicles and motorised transport

petrol was the lifeblood; without it the invasion would die. Paradoxically, the vital task of satisfying the thirst for petrol of this mechanised behemoth was going to depend on one small unit of 420 foot soldiers who would undertake an opposed landing and then engage in a long solitary march behind enemy lines and an assault on, and capture of, the of heavily defended port.

Port-en-Bessin, population 1,600, had an outer circular harbour 700 yards across and two in-line inner harbours extending to 500 yards. The streets were narrow, houses crowded together. The main landward entrance was the Rue de Bayeux running north through Escures 1½ miles from the port.

The Eastern Feature had a flat top 700 yds, east to west and 400 yds deep with 3 concrete pill boxes, 4 deep dug-outs, 2 Oerlikon type guns, 2 open emplacements with heavy machine guns, 4 light machine guns, 2 three inch mortars and smaller mortars. A trench and minefield ran along the seaward side: facing the harbour was a broken line of slit trenches at 30-40 yard intervals fronting a wire fence and a minefield. Near the mid point of the ridge somewhat below its summit was a concrete bunker at the site of an old reservoir.

The Western Feature was 400 yards wide, east to west, and 200 yards deep with 8 concrete bunkers/ pill-boxes, light machine guns, mortar emplacements and trenches. To the south and west it was protected by a thick belt of barbed wire and a minefield. There were several sunken flame-throwers on the harbour slope. Beside the Rue de Bayeux, 600 yards south of the port, were a series of Weapon Pits with machine gun emplacements, concrete shelters and trenches protected by barbed wire.

Port-en-Bessin was defended by the 352 Infantry Field Division (which decimated American troops at OMAHA on D-Day) extending westward from le Hamel. The British landing beaches were defended by the static 716 Infantry Division. There were also German troops at a sniper school at Fosse Soucy. 47 RM Commando had been given a formidable task. With the Dieppe raid (67% casualties) in mind its commanding officer Colonel C F Phillips decided to assault Port-en-Bessin from the rear rather than from the sea.

47 Royal Marine Commando

The Chief of Combined Operations described commandos as, 'small formations of troops, drawn from the Army and Royal Marines, trained for employment on expeditions calling for a high degree of disciplined daring and initiative such as the raiding of an enemy coast or the quick seizure of an enemy strong point'. Such was 47 Royal Marine Commando.

Embarkation and Cross Channel Voyage

The Commando embarked on Friday 2nd June on the *Princess Josephine Charlotte* and SS *Victoria*, two merchant ships adapted as mother ships for Assault Landing Craft (LCAs) - flat bottomed shallow-draft craft with a hinged ramp at front, carrying 36 men. D-Day was to be 5th June but by the 4th a depression approaching southern England enforced delay. Thousands of soldiers and sailors steeled up with expectation had to wait, crowded together, some already sea-sick. As Monday dawned the wind had abated and the sea had calmed. Soon, the fateful words was echoing round the invasion fleet – 'It's on'.

That morning a strange craft with an enormous drum of piping amidships, was setting sail. As the commandos waved to it they could only hope that the confidence of the ship's crew that Port-en-Bessin would be in friendly hands when they got there would prove justified. The ships sailed on the evening of the 5th. Below, final briefings and checking of weapons and equipment was taking place. As the night wore on the 6' guns of the cruiser *Orion* nearby, bombarding the French coast, boomed out defiance. After a fitful hour or two of sleep watching eyes were straining ahead and soon the edge of the enslaved continent came in sight – a low grey line of coast eight miles away. It was 0500.

The Landing

By 0730 the loud-speakers of the mother ships' were cracking out the order, 'To the landing craft' and fourteen LCAs were lowered, filled, and soon on their way bobbing up and down on an undulant sea. Early progress was uneventful but as the off-shore distance shortened the grey line ahead transformed into green fields and individual houses. A mile from the shore the scene was changing: enemy batteries were now ranging on the approaching LCAs. First to be hit, listing and sinking, was a Q troop LCA. Men were jumping into the water: others were not - the troop commander and eleven others including the troop medical orderly had been killed or drowned and fourteen including the adjutant wounded, 26 of the 36 aboard. Wounded men from sinking LCAs were in a parlous situation. Rescue by incoming craft was forbidden as stopping would disrupt landing schedules, make incoming craft easier targets and obstruct following craft. Only returning craft would rescue. Disabled wounded, supported by inflatable life belts usually had to float in cold water for one and a half hours, if they could, before aid came.

The commando was now approaching the westmost subsection of GOLD beach. That should already have been captured but was deserted bar two stranded motionless tanks. The plan that an RM Support Group should land 10 old Centaur tanks there as a form of advanced mobile artillery had been a failure. Five of the tanks had been lost when their landing craft capsized and 4 were knocked out by shell fire as they beached. The

A crowded scene on the beaches following the initial landing in the GOLD beach area. (IWM B5093)

commando's orders were to land on a captured beach, so, following the 1st Hampshire regiment ahead, it began an easterly traverse of 1½ miles. This would lengthen the commando's march to Port-en-Bessin and, more immediately, expose it to gunfire from enemy coastal guns and the band of mine-tipped obstacles running parallel to the shore which a rising tide was beginning to hide. Now the LCA containing half of Y troop struck a mine and sank in a cloud of spray killing 8 and wounding others including the troop commander and troop medical orderly.

When the remaining LCAs were opposite the Hampshire's landing beach they turned shore-wards. As they did an LCA of A troop blew up killing two and wounding others. Then two more LCAs struck mine-tipped obstacles and blew up. More were killed and injured and there was now a new hazard for those in the water as incoming tank landing craft (LCTs) could not see them and might run them down. The LCTs passed by, but the swimmers, amid their struggles, could still hear the rattle of bullets striking their sides.

By 0920 most of the commando was ashore opposite Les Roquettes but scattered widely along the beach. Many of the swimmers had lost their weapons and acquired others from dead men. Three of the four long range wireless sets had been lost and the remaining set was dead. The only 3 inch mortar rescued had lost its sight. All but one of the Bangalore torpedoes for blowing gaps in barbed wire had been lost. The beach,

narrowing with the incoming tide, was a mass of ammunition boxes, all kinds of equipment, creaking vehicles, Bren carriers, clanking tanks, damaged landing craft, shouting men and churned up sand. Tanks were manoeuvring towards the beach exits. A few prisoners were being hustled along. A Brigadier lay on the sand giving orders into his wireless. There was a background of the crack of rifles, stacatto of machine guns and crunch of exploding mortar bombs.

Gradually the commando gathered below the sea wall beyond which the road was being subject to enfilade fire. Seventy six officers and men, including Colonel Phillips, were missing: 28 had been killed or drowned and 21 wounded.

The Approach March

It was now past noon and with a 12 mile march ahead the Second-in-Command decided that he should wait no longer. At this stage concealment, not confrontation with the enemy, was the commando's role and with the planned route through le Hamel blocked he led through Les Roquettes. In a field ahead, a sign displayed a skull and cross bones with 'Achtung Minen'. Many of these were said to be bogus, designed to delay advancing troops, but the presence of two bloated cow carcasses nearby raised doubt, confirmed when a flail tank rumbling across the field exploded an anti-tank mine. Proceeding unobtrusively the commando reached the Meauvines-Buhot road. Shortly thereafter, Colonel Phillips rejoined: reconnoitring

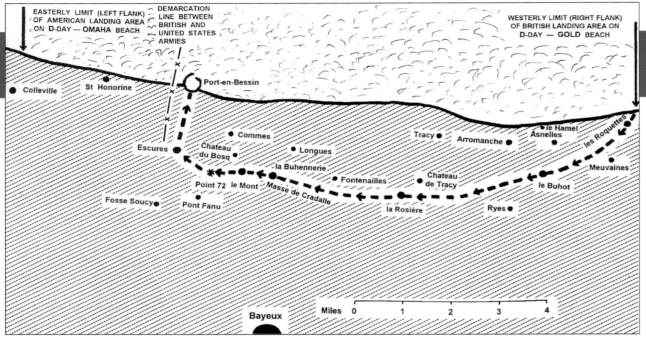

Attacking Port-en-Bessin from the landward side required a considerable walk behind enemy lines after 47 Commando had landed at the Western end of GOLD beach. (JF)

Further ahead a German officer was seen riding a horse but suddenly turned away. The risk that he had seen the column could not be ignored. A single shot rang out and he fell from the saddle. The horse looked, apparently somewhat querulously, towards the still form of its erstwhile master and it too turned away. Then a German jeep-like vehicle was seen approaching round a bend ahead. It suddenly slewed round at right angles and the driver jumped out into a ditch manning a MG-34 machine gun. He was promptly hit by commando fire. Lying dying he was asking for his mother. Confronted with British troops he had decided to face them alone rather than surrender.

Later, some Germans were heard shouting '*Lauft runter, das sind Indische Truppen*' (Run down there, these are Indian troops). Some of the commandos had blackened their faces! The most serious encounter was near la Rosière. Under fire, A troop shot up a machine gun post and took prisoners but X troop met the main opposition. Captain Walton led the troop straight into attack and quickly overran the position. A little later, a machine gun firing from the flank wounded two corporals and six marines as they crossed a gap in a hedge in single file. Seven of the wounded moved away quickly but one had been hit in the spine paralysing his legs. There was no nearby accommodation and he had to be left to the care of his wounded companions until further help arrived. In these encounters a number of German weapons were seized and put to good use in view of the commando's own depleted weaponry. Used by commandos their characteristic sounds confused the enemy.

towards le Hamel he had lost touch with the commando and had had to find his way back again. Moving stealthily through enemy occupied territory engenders intense concentration and vigilance. Every tree or animal that moves, every fold in the ground or bend in the road, every copse or culvert, every shadow, every sound tends to assume an ominous significance. Early on in the journey a shot rang out and one of the marines fell, killed by a sniper.

The first direct encounter with the enemy was with three soldiers. They were approaching down a field to a sunken road unaware of the marines' presence there until one of them, suddenly sensing danger, raised his sub-machine gun. Several shots rang out and he fell. His companions promptly threw down their weapons and put their hands up. The injured soldier,

hit in the abdomen, staggered down, collapsing at the roadside muttering 'Kaput, Kaput'. Possibly fearful of what his captors might do he fumblingly produced from his tunic his field pocket book showing a photograph of his wife and two children. There was little that could be done for him. Soon, the commando was on the march again: looking back a slumped figure lay alone by the roadside clutching the photograph of the wife and children he would probably never see again.

The two prisoners had to travel with the commando and one was detailed for non-combatant duties. Relieved at his escape, it was surprising how many stretchers (light airborne) this frightened but surprisingly jolly man was anxious to carry and how ready the erstwhile bearers were anxious to accommodate his enthusiasm!

In a column moving surreptitiously across country one sees little of one's companions except the few in front and behind. If troops sustain casualties the 'doc' has to catch up with the wounded, alerted by word passing, but he must not lose touch with the column and has to try to make some arrangement for the care and evacuation of wounded who cannot proceed. For such, field dressings and the nearest house, reached by stretcher if necessary, were usually the best that could be done. The farmhouses or cottages approached all readily admitted wounded marines despite the risk of German retribution.

Close to la Rosière the commando halted. It was 1530. One marine had been killed on the march by an unseen sniper and eleven wounded. The commando now numbered 360 - a few stragglers had caught up. The march resumed at 1945. Shortly hereafter an unarmed German Sergeant-Major appeared on a bicycle declaring that he had had enough of war and was going to see his girl friend before giving himself up. The route was now over fields and by the time le Mont was reached it was almost dark. Limited vision in the dark creates difficulties for a column moving in single file. Concentration on the silhouette and sound of the man in front becomes intense. If you lose him you will find yourself the inadvertent and probably very inappropriate leader of the remainder of the column!

Mont Cavalier (Point 72) was unoccupied although there were signs of defence work in progress The troops had to dig in and were allowed only two hours sleep. At the base of Mont Cavalier was a large concrete bunker. As one of the commando sergeants approached it two German medical officers were standing outside smoking. Turning round they suddenly found themselves facing British sub-machine guns. Entering the bunker the sergeant saw a soldier in bed make a movement under the bedclothes and in a split second had to decide whether the man was trying to shoot and whether to shoot him first. Instead he grabbed the bedclothes and pulled them off the bed. The man had not been trying to shoot. At personal risk the sergeant had been unwilling to shoot a German who might be defenceless.

The commando's regimental aid post (RAP) was established in the bunker. The senior German doctor declared that there were strong German forces nearby and that shortly the position would be reversed and the commandos captured. During the night a German soldier with a bullet wound of the abdomen was brought in but died shortly thereafter. As 7th June arrived the medical bunker had a morning call. A German NCO was marching a group of soldiers towards the bunker thinking that they were going to attend a German morning sick parade! They were given incarcerated medical attention! Lack of adequate wireless communication was creating a problem. The attack on Port-en-Bessin was to be supported by American artillery but no contact was possible. The cruiser Emerald, lying 5000 yards off port, could be contacted however. It was

Disaster On The Western Feature

While X troop was preparing to attack the Weapon Pits A and B troops led by a local gendarme were passing these by along a roadside ditch. A proceeded towards the Western Feature along Rue Nationale and B towards the harbour along Rue de Bayeux. They were followed by the RAP.

Reaching the barbed wire barrier in the Rue du Phare A troop found it was visible to the enemy. A three man party went forward and blew it with the only remaining Bangalore torpedo. Now advancing up the Western Feature A troop deployed in two halves, one going right the other left. The right hand group was in view of the outer harbour but latest intelligence reports indicated that the harbour was empty. Two French civilians had agreed this, but they were dramatically wrong. Two flak ships had entered the harbour just before D-Day. Unlike an aerial photograph taken a few days earlier showing the harbour empty, a U.S. Air Force photograph dated 6th June showed two flak ships. The right hand group of about 25 men was in full view of these. As the marines advanced to the defences above the flak ships opened fire on them. Exposed to fire from front and rear, the men were in a hopeless position. Within minutes more than half had been killed or wounded.

Simultaneously the left hand group had advanced. Less exposed to the flak ships they came under intense fire from the defences above. Crawling forward firing and lobbing grenades, they squeezed through two bands of barbed wire and had almost

arranged that in mid-afternoon it would bombard the Western and Eastern Features, followed by an attack by RAF rocket-firing 'Typhoons'.

The Attack On The Port
The Weapon Pits Overrun

On Mont Cavalier the plan of attack was formulated. Q and Y troops would occupy Escures, Q in its half strength state acting as reserve and Y, also seriously depleted, defending against possible counter-attack. Rear HQ would remain on Mont Cavalier with responsibility for its own defence. Troops A, B, and X would lead the attack. In the early afternoon Emerald bombarded the Eastern and Western Features for an hour, followed by the RAF attack.

As A, B and X troops moved away from Mont Cavalier about 1500, followed by the RAP, they came under and returned fire from the Fosse Soucy direction. The Germans were reacting and Y troop also came under fire.

X troop now proceeded towards the port, halting behind a group of trees bordering a 200 yard wide open field leading to the Weapon Pits. From there it charged at the double, bayonets fixed, firing, and shouting menacingly as it attacked. The defenders occupied slit trenches and a concrete bunker but despite this advantage the menace of the advancing marines was too much for them. Soon they were putting their hands up and climbing out of their trenches.

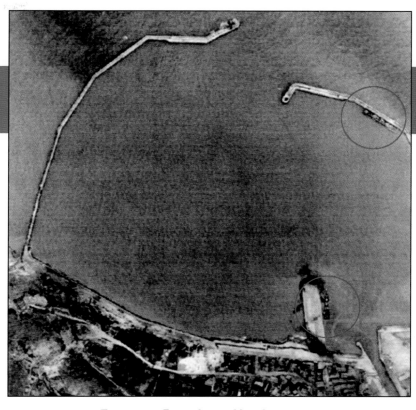

Left: Captain T. F. Cousins, A Troop Commander, who led the attack on the Western Feature and was later killed leading the assault on the Eastern Feature. (JF)

Right: The two Flak ships which had arrived after reconnaissance photographs had been taken for 47 Commando's briefing prior to D-Day. (NHB)

reached the defences when a machine gun opened fire from a pill-box. The officer leading threw a grenade, revealing his presence. This brought down a shower of hand grenades and as the group flattened themselves to the ground to avoid flying shrapnel he saw a grenade from a communication trench ahead coming at him. He lost consciousness and knew no more until he found that 'bullets were cracking above him'. He was covered with blood and his right arm was useless. He managed to crawl back through the barbed wire obstructions.

Faced with these disastrous events the troop commander Captain Cousins withdrew his men. During this carnage the troop medical orderly had gone out repeatedly to rescue wounded. Out of about 50 marines 12 had been killed and 17 seriously wounded. As the troop withdrew Corporal Amos delayed to apply a field dressing to his troop sergeant, lying gravely wounded. As he did a grenade exploded beside him without seriously injuring him but left him lying dazed. As he recovered he felt himself being pushed by a foot and turned to find a German standing over him. In charge of a guard who kept a rifle against his temple Amos was taken into a bunker where he was interrogated in front of a notice bearing Hitler's 1942 edict that all captured commandos were to be shot. A corporal was urging this course of action. Covered with the blood of his sergeant Amos was thought to be a medical orderly and told to deal with a German with a

compound fracture of his arm. He deemed it expedient to comply, then, left alone and exhausted, he fell asleep.

The Harbour Cleared but Threatened by the Flak Ships

Meanwhile, B troop had reached the inner harbour area where fortified buildings and a pill box near the top of the Eastern Feature commanded much of the ground. Confronting 10 Germans at the harbour and 2 coming down from the Eastern Feature the commando's German speaking sergeant from 10 (Inter-Allied) Commando shouted to them to surrender. All came forward with their hands up but while they were being searched a machine gun opened up from a harbour buildings and another from the Eastern Feature. One marine fell dead and 11 were wounded. The marines had to withdraw into harbour-side houses taking the wounded with them. Some were also wounded by mortar fire from the Eastern Feature. Gradually, however, the fortified harbour houses were cleared but the flak ships in the outer harbour remained a continuing threat to movement there. Meantime the Germans withdrew the bridge at the seaward end of the inner harbour denying the commando any direct access to the Eastern Feature but at the same time making any enemy counter-attack from the Feature much more difficult.

German Counter-attacks

The rump of Q Troop had now been called forward from Escures leaving the depleted Y troop there, and the small Rear HQ at Mont Cavalier. Back-up Bren carriers had arrived at Escures about 1700 and unloaded their ammunition. The Medical Officer having followed A and B troops into the port and attended some of their wounded there now returned to the RAP about 1900 with a view to bringing it into the port. He found a developing crisis. Two counter-attacks had been made against Rear HQ which numbered less than 20 and possessed in total only 8 rifles. These attacks had been repelled. The Germans had cut the Bayeux Road just south of the RAP: they could be seen moving a field's length away. Now the RAP was fired on. Just before that, the Bren carriers had been reloaded with ammunition for delivery to the port. As one of them left Escures it was fired on and the NCO in charge seriously wounded and left at the RAP.

A Copy of the original SECRET D-Day Map issued to Allied troops prior to the invasion. This mud stained map was carried by Captain John Forfar MC during the Battle for Port-en-Bessin and highlights the known German Defensive positions along this stretch of coastline. For the purpose of this Chapter additional annotations highlight the Eastern and Western features as well as the Flak Ships which were discovered during the battle, positioned in the harbour. (RN)

Y troop in Escures now came under increasing attack. It had been called forward to assist at the port but could not explain its position due to outgoing wireless failure, and could not immediately respond. About 2200 in fading light Rear HQ was attacked again and the position overrun, an officer being killed and a corporal and sergeant wounded. An hour later one of Y troops defensive outposts was overrun, three in it being wounded. With the road to the port blocked the Y troop commander now sought to reach the port by a circuitous march across country in the dark to 231 Brigade with which 47 RM Commando had an administrative link. There he obtained an armoured truck with which he reached the port by the coastal road, too late however, to participate in the battle. Twelve wounded in the RAP by the Escures road could not immediately be moved as any attempt to do so attracted enemy fire but as darkness fell the RAP moved into the port. Due to loss of stretchers at the landing seriously wounded men had to be carried pick-a-back.

The Battle at its Nadir

Thus, as that evening advanced the tide of battle was running heavily against the commando. The Western Feature assault had been repulsed with heavy losses. Y troop was cut off. Rear HQ was under attack and later overrun. Ammunition was running low prior to the arrival of the Bren carriers. The commando was isolated. Inadequate wireless communication made control very difficult. The position at the harbour was still precarious due to the proximity of the two flak ships. Access to the Eastern Feature across the mouth of the inner harbour was not possible.

The toll of killed and wounded was rising and the commando's strength down to about 280. The troops were scattered and also tired having had little more than two hours sleep since leaving England. The RAP was under serious threat.

Nemesis for the Flak Ships

Despite these predicaments two further moves were initiated. The destroyer *Ursa* and a Polish ship *Krakowiak* were about 800 yards from the harbour's eastern breakwater. At 2100 at high tide, they came under fire from one of the flak ships: both fired back. It was not known what damage, if any, they had done and they were asked if they could neutralise the flak ships. As darkness fell each sent out an armed motor boat. *Ursa's* boat attacked one and *Krakowiak's* the other, both firing rifles, Lewis guns and Lanchester guns. They came under fire from the shore and found that one flak ship had been partially sunk by the naval fire: in it 3 Germans lay dead and the survivors had fled. The other flak ship had been abandoned.

From Nadir to Zenith

The second move was to try and maintain the momentum of attack by sending out fighting patrols from A and B troops to make armed reconnaissances of the Eastern Feature. With the harbour bridge withdrawn the patrols had to proceed from the southern end of the inner harbour. The B troop patrol, out first, ran into heavy mortar fire as it moved through the buildings at the base of the Eastern Feature: nine marines were wounded. The A troop patrol – survivors from the Western Feature debacle – met the remnant of the B troop patrol and both, 3 officers and 10 other ranks, combined under Cousins' command. Near the southern end of the inner harbour they found a zig-zag path leading up the Feature. It was not apparently mined and except at the bends and near the top was not easily visible from above. The party moved up the path but 30 yards from the summit plateau met machine gun fire and thrown grenades. Further progress was not possible. Cousins, was convinced, however, of

Part of the zig-zag path. Captain Cousins advanced up this route protected from fire by the high bank on the right. He was killed as he rushed the blockhouse ahead. (JF)

Left: Royal Marines on Exercise PLUTO Return, follow in the footsteps of 47 Cdo. (DD)

the vulnerability of the Feature to an attack in darkness and on returning said to Colonel Phillips, 'If you give me 24 or 25 men I'm quite certain I can get to the top'. As the Bren carriers had arrived Heavy Weapons troop, from a position 400 yards south of the end of the inner harbour, could give some covering fire and lay smoke across the zig-zag path. Enemy could be seen on the Feature's skyline and replied with machine gun fire.

In gathering darkness Cousins now led off and moved up the zig-zag path. The marines were not visible to the enemy above but the latter were aware of their presence. Cousins had arranged that when he reached the exposed upper reaches he would fire a red Very light and that half the attackers would then assault to the left (west) and half to the right (east). At 2230 both groups were well up the path and the Very light was fired. Cousins led the left hand group through several wire fences, encountering fire from nearby trenches, and near the crest of the hill came under fire from the reservoir bunker at close range. He halted his men in some unoccupied trenches and taking his Bren gunner and three other marines with him went through a gap in a wire fence under fire and rushed the bunker. All were shooting as they went and grenades were being thrown at them. One of these exploded in front of Cousins and he fell forward, killed outright. One of the marines received a severe head wound and one was concussed. The waiting group heard bursts of fire, exploding grenades and a lot of shouting. They then ran forward. Forty yards ahead Cousins lay dead with the severely wounded marine beside him. The concussed marine had recovered quickly and

he and his two colleagues were continuing their fire. A captured German was then ordered to shout to the men in the bunker to surrender. A white flag appeared and the occupants came out. Cousins' sacrifice had not been in vain. A critical defensive position had been captured and the determined manner in which that had been done had weakened the enemy morale. The right hand group under Captain Vincent now advanced to the summit, firing as they went, and then traversed a further 100 yards to the right (eastward). Possible mines and trip wires had to be ignored. Determined attackers scarcely visible in the dark, explosions, gunfire, the menace of feared opponents and the possibility of fixed bayonets had doubtless further weakened the will of the defenders. As Vincent's men turned to close with them an officer and 7 Germans surrendered. Sending 2 prisoners ahead to avoid mines the commandos now moved westward along the ridge. An Oberleutenant now surrendered and other shadowy figures began to emerge from the darkness. Having traversed the ridge westward Lieutenant Stickings found the residue of Cousin's party immobilised in the open by fire from a concrete defence position which they could not easily see. He led a charge against the position and overcame this last resistance: another 4 officers and 34 other ranks surrendered. Outnumbered 4 to 1 Cousins' party of 4 officers and 24 other ranks had faced an enemy with the advantages of knowing the terrain, much greater fire power and the benefit of concreted, entrenched, barbed-wire and mine-protected positions which looked down on their assailants: but the commando had succeeded against all these odds. The critical point in the battle for Port-en-Bessin had been reached and the

determined action and superior will power of a few dedicated courageous men had turned the tide of battle.

The Final RAP

The RAP had now completed its move into the port. It was nearly midnight. A single Tilley lamp provided the only light. Gathered together were 40 British and 3 German soldiers and 3 French civilians, all strangely united in their common battle for survival. Men previously so active and committed lay prostrate, uncomplaining, without self-pity or recrimination, turned in on themselves and now fearful not of the enemy but of their own physical fallibility.

Dénoument at the Western Feature

In the Western Feature bunker Amos awoke at 0400 to a developing drama. News of the capture of the Weapon Pits, Harbour area, and Eastern Feature; the destruction of the flak ships and the aggressive determination of the marines had reached the Western Feature. A collapse of morale had occurred as its defenders contemplated a further attack. The corporal who had wanted Amos shot disappeared and an officer offered Amos a cigar with 'Kamerad prisoner'. Amos was shown a large red cross flag and some Germans, indicating their intention of leaving the bunker, shook him by the hand and saluted. Gratified by this subservience Amos led 23 Germans down the Feature and handed over his 'prisoners' to a somewhat astonished commando preparing for a further assault. The commando adjutant, Captain Spencer, fluent in

'one of the great feats of arms by any unit, Royal Marines, Army, Navy or Air Force of any nation in the Second World War'
Major General Julian Thompson

On 9th June an Army Port Company entered Port-en-Bessin. Already one of the pipe-laying ships was in sight. Soon large petrol pipes were snaking round the streets of Port-en-Bessin. The petrol supplies for the 21st Army Group were secure.

Port-en-Bessin: Conceptual Considerations

The manoeuvrist approach to warfare can be defined as nullification of the enemy's will to fight rather than the destruction of his materiel or the attrition of his forces. The invasion of Europe and the long campaign which followed was attritional in nature. In contrast the battle for Port-en-Bessin exemplified the manoeuvrist concept:

- The enemy surrendered because his will to fight was broken by the will of the commando.

- A particular significance of the battle was that its military importance was proportionately greater than its size and the number of men and the amount of military hardware involved.

- Success was not attended by great loss of enemy personnel.

- Excepting the flak ship, the enemy materiel (as recovered by the commando) was essentially intact at the end of the battle including the physical structure of his defences (concrete bunkers etc) and his weaponry. It was the enemy personnel who gave way.

- The battle was short, lasting only three days.

- Learning from the enemy, it is likely that manoeuvre warfare is best conducted and more likely to succeed when high quality intelligence guides its conduct and

German, led a party up the Feature to take the surrender of the other occupants: all had fled.

On the Western Feature 12 marines who had been killed lay where they had fallen, cold, pale and stiff, their wounds congealed with blood, a sad testimony to what they had endured. Lying close to the nozzle of a flame thrower the butt of a rifle was charred. The same day the commando's transport sergeant drove a Bren carrier through Escures, still occupied by the Germans. Under fire he rescued the 3 wounded Y troop marines from a ditch where they had lain all night. Later in the day Escures was reoccupied against little resistance.

That evening a 2 man officer patrol was sent out along the road leading to OMAHA to establish a link with the Americans. Nearing OMAHA they met an American patrol. 47 RM Commando had fulfilled its second task, linking the British and American Armies.

The Aftermath

On 9 June General Montgomery visited the commando to congratulate it and next day Generals Dempsey and Bradley joined him there. Of the 420 commandos who had left the mother ships 276 could be mustered on 9 June. 46 had been killed or drowned, 70 wounded, 6 captured and 22 missing. General Sir Miles Dempsey said:

'When all did so well it is rather invidious to pick out anyone for special mention but the two outstanding examples of initiative and the value of tough individual training were on my right and left flanks carried out by 47 Royal Marine Commando and the 6th Airborne Division respectively'

Sir Robert Bruce Lockhart, described the action as:

'the most spectacular of all commando exploits during in the actual invasion'

General Montgomery arrived at Port-en-Bessin on 9 June 1944. (IWM)

Re-visiting the site of street fighting in Port-en-Bessin, commemorating the actions of 47 Cdo. (DD)

determines the point where an enemy should be struck. If the Germans had understood and applied the concept of manoeuvre warfare they might have seen the advantage of devoting far more resources to a counter-attack against the petrol supply point which was being established at Port-en-Bessin to sustain the British front; but that orientation of thinking could only have evolved from better intelligence than the enemy possessed concerning the planned usage of the port.

- 'Manoeuvre warfare' is an attitude of mind to be applied in a flexible way as required. Many commando operations have been free-standing manoeuvrist affairs but the manoeuvrist Port-en-Bessin operation was part of a wider whole. Under different circumstances the manoeuvrist principle can be either the sole basis on which a military campaign is conducted or can be applied within an attritional campaign as a contribution towards the latter's success. Current international political developments suggest that the former is now an increasingly likely scenario, particularly outside formal war situations.

Key Lessons

- **Motivation, training, physical fitness, fellowship, cohesiveness and morale:** 47 RM Commando was not a 'battle hardened' (often battle weary) unit. It had never been in action and consisted of young volunteers, highly motivated to undertake battle actions, who had trained intensely in respect of military skills and physical fitness for the duties likely to be theirs. They had for long lived, worked and fed together, and developed an understanding with each other and their officers. 'Mates' would do almost anything for each other. The outcome was a high degree of cohesiveness underpinning morale. Accepting that the exigencies of war may at times mandate scratch formations, such cohesiveness will increase any fighting unit's effectiveness.

- **Courage:** The determination of the commando's leaders to maintain an unremitting initiative and fight on in the face of daunting repulses and serious losses of men and equipment, and the matching response of the men they led, were paramount.

- **Planning judgement:** The judgement that a small, lightly armed mobile unit would have a higher chance of success in capturing the port from the rear following a long cross country march on foot through enemy territory rather than a frontal sea-borne assault was vindicated.

- **Darkness:** The Port-en-Battle battle exemplifies the advantage which darkness can confer in that type of battle. Twice the Rear HQ resisted daylight assaults but was overrun in a third attack in the dark. Likewise, darkness contributed significantly to the successful assault on the Eastern Feature. Contrariwise, daylight, to the defenders of the Western Feature in their secure defences was to their advantage. In different circumstances, where numbers are more evenly matched and enemy defences less secure, as at La Rosiere and the Weapon Pits determination and tactical skill are able to decide a daylight battle.

- **Marine casualties:** Regretfully, the marines paid for their success in casualties. They were willing to take greater risks than the enemy and displayed skill, courage and determination to a degree which enabled them to reverse the balance of advantage held by the enemy in respect of defensive positions, weaponry and numbers. There may be circumstances where higher casualties are accepted in one specific manoeuvrist operation in the interest of lower casualties in a wider whole.

- **Manoeuvrism within a manoeuvrist operation:** Cousins attack on the Eastern Feature was this. It initiated a

'It is doubtful whether in their long distinguished history the Marines have ever achieved anything finer'
General Sir Brian Horrocks

domino effect which spread and brought a successful end to the battle.

- **Integration:** Port-en-Bessin showed that a small commando unit, part of the Royal Navy could work successfully in an integrated way within the Army in fulfilling and providing the expertise required for an amphibious task.

Key Principles Unmet

- **Intelligence:** Any military unit facing a battle should have available to it all relevant intelligence. If the commando had known beforehand about the flak ships in Port-en-Bessin harbour its losses would probably have been fewer. Admittedly, the commando attacked only 24 hours after the American Air Force knew of the flak ships but some of the local inhabitants knew several days before.

- **Landing tactics:** In amphibious operations where risk at the time of landing against established defences is so high something more trustworthy than makeshift landing craft and outdated tanks is necessary.

- **Communication:** At Port-en-Bessin communication was seriously hampered by the inadequacy and vulnerability of the wireless sets to shock and water.

Further Reading

Ellis, L. F., *Victory in the West, Volume I, the Battle of Normandy*, 1960, (Her Majesty's Stationery Office, London)

Forfar, John, *From OMAHA to the Scheldt, the Story of 47 Royal Marine Commando*, (Tuckwell Press, East Lothian, Scotland, 2001)

Hamilton, Nigel, *Monty, Master of the Battlefield, Vols I, II & III*; (London: Hamish Hamilton, 1987)

Ladd, James, *The Royal Marines, 1919-1980, An Authorised History*, (London: Jane's Publishing Company, 1980)

Montgomery of Alamein, Viscount, *The Memoirs of Field Marshall Montgomery*, (London: Collins, 1958)

Thompson, Julian, *The Royal Marines: from Sea Soldiers to a Special Force*, (London: Sidgwick & Jackson, 2000)

The Application of Force. An Introduction to Army Doctrine and the Conduct of Military Operations, 2002; Her Majesty's Stationery Office, London.

Biography

Professor John Forfar was Mentioned in Despatches after the capture of Port-en-Bessin and later won the Military Cross during the assault on Walcheren Island as part of 47 Commando Royal Marines, (one of the few units to assault Hitler's Atlantic Wall twice). Having studied medicine at St Andrews University he joined the Royal Army Medical Corps in 1942 and then undertook Commando Training before joining 47 Commando Royal Marines as their Medical Officer. In addition to landing on D-Day he also operated from his Regimental Aid Post at the Orne bridgehead in support of 6 Airborne Division. He is the author of *From Omaha to the Scheldt: The Story of 47 Royal Marine Commando* (Tuckwell Press, 2000). He later went on to eminence as one of Scotland's leading paediatricians, being one of the founders of the Royal College of Paediatrics and Child Health. He is the author/editor of five professional Textbooks and over 150 research papers, was the Vice President of the Great Ormond Street Hospital for Sick Children appeal, a Trustee of the Malcolm Sargent Cancer Fund for Children and a Fellow of the Royal Society of Edinburgh. In addition to his role as Professor Emeritus for Child Life and Health at the University of Edinburgh, he still finds time to lecture at the Joint Services Command and Staff College.

The Marianas Campaign
Operation FORAGER, June 1944

XXV

The Marianas were strategically important since they were considered part of the Japanese homeland

By Lieutenant Colonel Michael West USMC

A Case Study Through the Lens of 'Operational Fires'

This analysis of the Marianas campaign will focus on the operational level of war and how the warfighting function of fires was employed in concert with the other functions in combat to produce significant momentum and tempo that led to a critical victory in the Pacific in the summer of 1944. First, we will examine the strategic setting of the campaign and then the campaign concepts as they were reflected in the Marianas effort. Next, we will review a brief summary of the campaign execution and how the allied forces were better able to deal with the uncertainty and confusion inherent in any campaign and adapt quickly to confront and manage the risks associated with the operational uncertainties. We will then analyze the campaign from a fires perspective in the context of manoeuvre warfare. After illustrating the interaction of operational fires with the other warfighting functions, we will conclude with a look at the significance of the campaign and lessons learned.

Strategic Setting

At the Cairo Conference in late 1943, the Anglo-American Chiefs of Staffs reaffirmed the coordinated advances of Nimitz and MacArthur as the principal offensive effort of the Pacific War.[1]

Though often overshadowed by the main event at Normandy in June 1944, Operation FORAGER provides an excellent historical example of operational manoeuvre from the sea.[2] The U.S. 'storm landings'[3] in the Marianas Islands in the summer of 1944 followed closely after the strategic success of the Marshalls campaign in February that had significantly quickened the tempo in the Pacific.[4] In accordance with the two-pronged counteroffensive strategy in the Pacific, General MacArthur started his New Guinea drive in early 1944, while Admiral Nimitz secured the heavily fortified Marshalls in the Central Pacific by 21 July. When the Joint Chiefs approved Nimitz's recommendation to bypass Truk in the Carolines the stage was set for Operation FORAGER.[5] All the naval, air, and ground forces necessary for a bold concentration of overwhelming forces in the Marianas were now available. As a case study, Operation FORAGER provides a superb example of multiple services and

An LVT (Water Buffalo) loaded with Marines, bound for the beaches of Tinian Island, near Guam, July 1944. (NARA)

fires platforms integrated to isolate an operational area and fully complement an aggressive operational manoeuvre plan. Military Factors that affected this campaign are found at the operational and tactical level, where lessons learned from the Gilberts and

---

[1] The U.S. Marines and Amphibious War, p 304.
[2] MCDP 3: Expeditionary Operations, p 94.
[3] Storm Landings, Introduction. "The sudden American proclivity for bold amphibious assaults into the teeth of prepared defenses astonished Japanese commanders, who called them "storm landings" because they differed sharply from earlier campaigns."

[4] The U.S. Marines and Amphibious War, p303.
[5] MCDP 3: Expeditionary Operations, p 95.

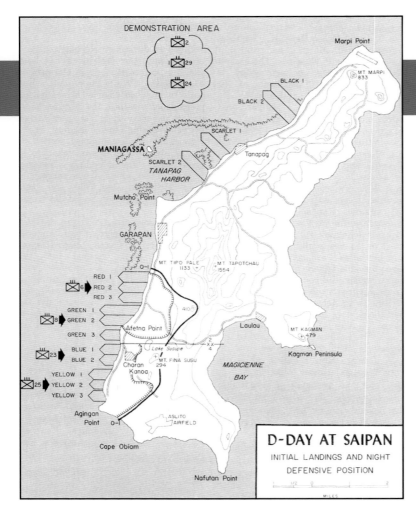

D-DAY AT SAIPAN

INITIAL LANDINGS AND NIGHT
DEFENSIVE POSITION

Left: Saipan on D-Day.

Right: The Marianas Island Group. (USMC)

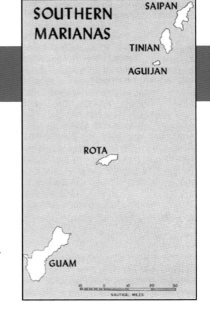

experiences of War Plan ORANGE development. The officers who had participated in war games at the Navy War College were well prepared to plan and execute the Marianas offensive. Though they were developed and in use since the '30s, fast carrier task force operations did not become an effective aspect of the war in the Pacific until the end of 1943. At this point, the industrial complex of the U.S. had produced enough new ships and aircraft to support the war in both Europe and the Pacific. At that time, the Essex and Independence classes of carriers started to appear in numbers in the Pacific. This powerful combined arms force was the operational linchpin in the isolation of the Marianas objective area.[7] Besides reducing the number of carriers, destroyers, and submarines available in the Pacific, the War in Europe and the preparations for Operation OVERLORD affected the number of amphibious transports, cargo ships, and landing craft available to Admiral Nimitz in the Pacific.

The Marianas were strategically important since they were considered part of the Japanese homeland. Their capture by the Allies would have an important political and psychological

effect on both sides. Allied possession of the Marianas isolated the Carolines to the south and provided a step closer to protecting the right flank of MacArthur's upcoming invasion of the Philippines. Controlling the Marianas would expose most of the remaining Japanese possessions in the Pacific and would provide more operational options to the Allies than the Japanese could defend against. Finally, the Marianas could provide critical air bases for long-range bomber strikes against the Japanese mainland.[8,9]

Campaigning Concepts

In order to attain the bold strategic objectives outlined in D.C. and Pearl Harbor, Admiral Nimitz assigned Operation FORAGER to Admiral Raymond Spruance, Commander of the U.S. 5th Fleet. Admiral Spruance built his joint service team around three main forces to execute a hard-hitting campaign plan: (1) the Joint Expeditionary Force, with Lieutenant General Holland M. Smith's V Amphibious Corps of 127,000 troops and Major General Roy S. Geiger's new III Amphibious Corps (2) Task Force 58, the Fast-

the Marshalls were applied in the Marianas. LCI gunboats, deception landings, advance force operations with UDT teams and minesweepers, and new landing vehicle tracks (LVTs) were characterised as significant improvements by Tarawa veterans.[6] At another level, the Marianas campaign benefited from the

the Pacific.

[6]Storm Landings, p 68.
[7]Spearhead - The Fast Carrier Task Force, p 19.
[8]MCDP 3: Expeditionary Operations, p 96.
[9]MCDP 3: Expeditionary Operations, p 97.

Cross decking Sherman tanks onto an LCT in preparation for Operation FORAGER. (NHB)

Carrier Attack Force, under Admiral Marc Mitscher (3) and all U.S. Army, Navy, and Marine land-based aircraft assigned to support the operation, including the Army's 7th Air Force.[10] Given the limited ground forces he had been assigned, Admiral Spruance was ably assisted by Admiral Kelly Turner and Lieutenant General Smith in creating subordinate task forces to accomplish the three phased campaign plan. Altogether, Spruance led 535 ships and over 165,000 troops into the Marianas.[11]

The campaign objectives were three of the southernmost Marianas islands, Saipan, Tinian, and Guam with their accompanying airfields and harbours. An example of effective operational sequencing, the FORAGER campaign phasing began with a detailed plan to secure the northernmost island first. Saipan would be attacked first to deny airfields to any Japanese support flying from Iwo Jima or from mainland Japan and to prevent these fields form supporting Japanese attacks on the southern two islands. Additionally, Aslito airfield was 100 miles closer to Japan than Guam and therefore a better base for bombers. Saipan was more than a thousand miles from Eniwetook in the Marshalls which was the nearest U.S. advanced naval base. This was by far the longest amphibious assault attempted yet in the war and demonstrated considerable 'operational reach.' Prior amphibious advances had been limited to about 300 miles; the range of land-based fighters providing close air support. In Operation FORAGER, all close air support was sea-based; flying

off Task Force 58's carriers.[12] If Saipan could be taken, Tinian and Guam would be cut off. In the initial plan, the second phase of a well-orchestrated sequence of operations was to begin soon after Saipan commenced, but due to a tougher than expected fight, the assault on Guam was delayed until Saipan was secured. The third phase of the initial plan, which essentially remained unmodified, was the capture of Tinian. The less formidable Tinian was southwest of Saipan across a channel only 3 miles wide. It had a small airfield, but no large harbour, so its military value would have been low if it was not so close to Saipan and offer such potential for air base development.[13] Throughout the campaign plan development, Admiral Spruance and his subordinate commanders demonstrated great forethought, flexibility, and teamwork. They modified their original plans as needed to best take advantage of the developing situation.

Though Admiral Spruance did not use the current concepts of centre of gravity and critical vulnerability, lessons from the Marshalls had proven that all of the Japanese capabilities had to be destroyed piece by piece as their national pride and fanatical devotion prevented any form of surrender. Given an enemy, isolated on islands, who would not surrender, there was no point so vulnerable that its destruction would produce the collapse of their fierce and loyal resistance. Spruance's desired endstate was to secure the decisive points of Aslito airfield on Saipan and Apra harbor on Guam in order to safely support

further operations to the west. To that end, he would need to effectively employ all available fire assets against a strong-willed enemy.

Campaign Execution Summary

Planning for Operation FORAGER started early and was continuous across all of Spruance's commands. The combined staffs leveraged any (but not all) of the costly lessons learned in previous operations. Once task force units and missions were assigned, the respective staffs worked diligently to ensure all operational and logistics requirements would be met in spite of a schedule that was considered by many to be too fast for proper planning, training, and combat loading. The embarkation phase of FORAGER was complex as it involved the Joint Expeditionary Force assembling in California, Hawaii and Guadalcanal before rendezvousing in the Marshalls. Following early tenants of amphibious doctrine, Admiral Conolly and Major General Geiger's staffs planned and executed full-scale rehearsals at the end of May 1944 at Cape Esperance on Guadalcanal. Though not

[10]Ibid., pg 96.
[11]Storm Landings, p 67.
[12]Ibid., pg 98.
[13]The U.S. Marines and Amphibious War, p 311.

Marines assault Saipan, taking cover behind a small sand bar. (USMC)

feasible for all the amphibious landing forces to conduct one, this rehearsal resulted in many critical deficiencies being exposed. After very honest and productive critiques that probably ended up saving many lives, the task force sailed to their staging point (movement) at Kwajelin. Mitscher's Task Force 58 arrived east of Guam on 11 June and soon commenced to bombard Saipan with aviation and naval gunfire.

In the temporary absence of General Obata, who was the commander of the Marianas defence and was off island on a defensive tour, Lieutenant General Saito had taken command of the Saipan and Marianas defence and had adhered to the defend-at-the-waters edge philosophy. Though not fully prepared for the coming storm, the Japanese ensured all key points on each island coastline were covered by howitzers, heavy mortars, and dismounted naval guns. Admiral Spruance's forces did not lack a target rich environment.

According to Holland Smith's plan for the first objective, the 2nd and 4th Marine Divisions (MarDiv) assaulted abreast at Saipan on 15 June against heavy resistance on an 8,000 yard front. The 27th Infantry Division under Major General R.C. Smith, USA was available as a floating reserve. The assault forces made slow progress, requiring the Guam landing to be delayed by a month. This chance delay was actually providential as it allowed a much-needed deliberate preparation of the objective. For organic fires, the 10th Marine Artillery Regt supported the 2nd MarDiv, and 14th Marines Artillery Regt supported the 4th MarDiv. In addition, Lieutenant General Smith had the US Army XXIV Corps Artillery with 155-millimeter guns and howitzers. Air support was provided by Vice Admiral Marc A. Mitshcer's fast carriers (TF 58) and by the escort carriers of Turner's Northern Attack Force and Conolly's Southern Attack Force. The day after the invasion of Saipan, navy submarines sighted Vice Admiral Ozawa's Imperial Fleet heading toward Saipan and caused Admiral Spruance to delay the assault on Guam. Admiral Spruance and his four carrier battle groups then engaged in the last great aircraft carrier battle of the War on 19 June and successfully isolated the Marianas,[14] thus providing the air and sea control needed for a secure environment within

which to sequence the FORAGER assaults. In this great carrier battle west of the Marianas, Admiral Mitscher's 15 U.S. carriers and 950 planes struck a Japanese force of 9 carriers and 550 aircraft. Before the day was over, the Battle for the Philippine Sea (The Great Marianas Turkey Shoot) saw the Japanese lose 240 planes and two carriers. U.S losses were only 29 planes and damage to one battleship. An overwhelming concentration of offensive capability demonstrated well the importance of this principle of war. Saipan was finally secure on 13 July after a final 'banzai charge' saw the last 3,000 survivors throw themselves at the Marines only 3 weeks after the Marines first waded ashore. The Guam landing then began on 21 July and the Tinian landing closely thereafter on 24 July. The Japanese had no means to react by sea or by air and were on the defensive throughout the campaign. The Tinian operation generated great pride as a planning, logistics, and operational deception masterpiece. It was executed with such ferocity by the veteran landing force that the island fell in nine days at a casualty rate of less than five percent.[15] Before Guam was officially secured on 10 August 1944, more than 8,000 tons of naval projectiles had been fired in support of the operation over a 13-day period.

Regardless of the diversion, disruption, delay, and destruction produced by preparatory fires, all three storm landings resulted in hard-fought assaults against fortified defences. The

---

[14]Saipan in Flames, p 14.
[15]The U.S. Marines and Amphibious War, p 357.

The real significance of the FORAGER landings lay in their direct operational and strategic effects

real significance of the FORAGER landings lay in their direct operational and strategic effects. The Marianas operation not only broke the inner perimeter of Japan's national defence sphere,[16] but caused a significant effect at the strategic level. As a result of the losses, the Japanese cabinet, led by General Tojo, was forced to resign in disgrace. By November of 1944, B-29 bombers operating from Saipan were attacking Japan on a daily basis, eventually reaching a rate of over a thousand sorties a week. Although the war in the Pacific continued for another year after FORAGER, this sequence of storm landings against the Marianas helped determine Japan's ultimate fate.[17]

Campaign Analysis

As demonstrated by Admiral Spruance and his team, a successful joint force commander must synchronise a variety of fires in time, space, and purpose to increase the total effectiveness of the joint force. According to AFSC Pub 2, 'operational fires focus largely on one or more of three general tasks: facilitating manoeuvre, isolating the battlefield, and destroying critical functions and facilities.' Operational fires are also one means to conduct interdiction operations.[18] These fires are designed to achieve a decisive impact in the conduct of a campaign or major operation. The current joint conceptual framework of fires consists of fires, joint fires, fire support, and joint fire support.

By today's definitions, all forms of fires were present in the Marianas campaign. From a service perspective, the Navy brought the most capability to the fight. When combined with the other service assets in a cohesive manner, Admiral Spruance led a powerful, joint fires team. His submarines, carrier air, battleships, cruisers, and destroyers provided ample close fire support to facilitate manoeuvre and destroy critical Japanese facilities. The Navy alone had the capability to produce fires that had effects on operationally significant objectives, as illustrated by their far ranging subs and carriers which helped to isolate the Japanese in the Marianas from their distant supplies, reinforcements, and air attacks. The Army contributed close air support, most often in the form of P-47's and a full corps of artillery to directly support the land operations. Likewise, the Marine Corps' contribution to fire support was solely from organic artillery and limited land-based air.

The best example of extremely effective non-lethal fires in the Marianas is illustrated by the success of the Navy's 'star shells'. During the night of W-Day on Guam, several fire support ships supplied harassing and illuminating fires through out that night while the Marines were becoming established ashore. This critical and often repeated procedure was very successful in preventing the Japanese from using their favorite tactic of infiltrating ground perimeters after darkness.[19] By leveraging

this non-lethal fire capability and integrating lethal fires, the U.S. was able to keep the Japanese off balance and minimise what had previously been one of the Japanese key strengths.

Effective firepower against an enemy requires that many functions are closely coordinated and executed efficiently. In reviewing the targeting and prioritisation processes used in this campaign, the navy, air, and ground fires appear to have been integrated in a progressively successful manner. After a slow start on Saipan, where naval gunfire support was not totally effective and air support was always too late,[20] fires accuracy and efficiency were improved when a panel of officers, called the target information board, was formed to evaluate target information. This initiative demonstrated the flexibility and adaptability so critical to success in the fluid environment of any campaign. This targeting board included representatives from the naval, air, gunnery, and intelligence staff sections as well as from the landing force. This group studied all reports of fires damage, as well as photo interpretation of new targets and maintained a current file on every target until destroyed.[21] Their work ensured the best weapons systems were matched against appropriate targets to maximise the effectiveness of the fires and brought a methodical discipline to the process that enabled important issues to be identified for further work.

[16]Storm Landings, p 62.
[17]MCDP 3: Expeditionary Operations, p 95.
[18]Joint Pub 3-03, p V.
[19]Naval Gunfire at Guam, p 55.
[20]The U.S. Marines and Amphibious War, p 362.
[21]Naval Gunfire at Guam, p 55.

The first flag on Guam, raised on a boat hook mast, by two US Officers 8 minutes after the US Marines and Army landed on the Island, 20 July 1944. (NARA)

the Battle of the Philippine Sea and isolate the ongoing assault of the Marianas from any Japanese air or naval interdiction.[23] The second operational objective was to gain and maintain air superiority with counter-air missions provided by both carrier air and mutually supporting army land-based P-47s. Once the assaults were in process at Saipan, Guam, and Tinian, carrier planes increased their close air support strike frequency, concentrating particularly on the landing beaches just before the first waves hit. Interdiction missions were continued to fix, disrupt, and destroy enemy island concentrations and defenses as the troops drove inland. Fortunately, close air support failures[24] to the front line forces were covered by the more familiar artillery support that was quickly landed to support the ground manoeuvre.

Naval gunfire support in the Marianas campaign demonstrated great versatility in adapting to new situations and accomplishing all three of the operational fire tasks. Because of inadequate time allotted for preparation fires and inefficient execution[25] at Saipan, Admiral Spruance's ships were much more productive on Guam and Tinian. On Saipan, strikes against beach defences, heavy fortifications, land planes and facilities of Aslito Field were ordered for only the two days before D-Day to fulfil the destruction taks. Additionally, all transportation and communications facilities on both Saipan and Tinian were planned for and attacked to isolate the beachhead and protect the landing force from enemy reinforcements. Once assault forces were ashore in all three islands, naval gunfire played a key role in facilitating manoeuvre to operational depths by creating exploitable gaps in Japanese and tactical defences.[26] The truth is that at Saipan, though, neither air nor naval gunfire support was adequate. This problem was rectified at Guam and Tinian.[27] Guam was the culmination of all that had been preciously learned about gunfire support. Extensive, thorough, pre-assault bombardments were required to minimise assault force loss of life. This lesson would be applied in most future amphibious assaults across the Pacific.

U.S. destroyer divisions played a key anti-submarine role in providing operational destruction fires that eliminated a majority of the Japanese undersea capabilities in the Central Pacific. During the Marianas campaign, Mitscher's sub hunters successfully destroyed many Japanese submarines that might

Air operational fires were both deep and close in the Marianas campaign. The deep operational fires were those bombing runs on surrounding islands in the months prior to the ground offensive. These fires from carrier air targeted Japanese airfields and ships that might be able to intervene and interfere with the U.S. offensive if not neutralised. A typical fast carrier force like Admiral Mitscher's TF 58 contained an incredibly large and capable mix of fires platforms to accomplish this objective.[22] Using a newly developed operational procedure called a 'deck-load' strike, a carrier task force like Admiral Mitscher's was able to begin a fleet engagement with a strike potential of over 3300 sorties each day. This innovative change helped TF 58 dominate

[22]Spearhead - The Fast Carrier Task Force, p 22.
[23]Ibid., pg 23.
[24]The U.S. Marines and Amphibious War, p 362.
[25]Naval Gunfire at Guam, p 56.
[26]The U.S. Marines and Amphibious War, p 318.
[27]Ibid., pg 381.

Army reinforcements disembarking from LSTs crossing a coral reef heading towards one of the beaches on Saipan, July 1944. (NARA)

have affected TF 58's success in the Battle of the Philippines and their ability to protect and isolate the amphibious forces in the Marianas. When the destroyers and escorts received the new ahead-thrown weapons ('hedgehog') in mid 1944, the South Pacific became a happy hunting ground.[28] Post war analysis indicates that 17 of the approximately 25 Japanese submarines that were deployed as part of Japanese operation A-Go or used for supply runs to by-passed garrisons were lost as a result of U.S. destroyer escorts.[29] The Japanese year long delay in completing the defences of the Marianas after the fall of Tarawa was in large part due to U.S. submarine fires. Ship after ship left Japan for the Marianas loaded with troops, weapons, and material, but the Western Pacific was no longer a safe transit zone.

> 'American submarines, their faulty torpedo fuses finally fixed, now prowled the underseas with a vengeance. Aided by ULTRA intercepts of routine reports of ship schedules between Japanese port captains, the subs began to eat the heart out of Japanese maritime power. Time and again, these subs positioned themselves to torpedo Japanese cargo ships laden with tanks, heavy guns, cement, and steel bound for Saipan. The 'silent service' likewise helped even the odds for the Marines ashore by sinking five of seven transports carrying the veteran 43rd Division from Korea to Saipan.'[30]

This example of timely intelligence coupled with the capability to project lethal fires illustrates well the operational benefits of synergism between the warfighting functions. By have the capacity to act on critical intelligence, our submarines were able to prevent crucial resources and manpower from reaching the campaign objective area. This saved U.S. lives.

Artillery's three basic characteristics of mobility, stability, and flexibility were all highlighted in the Marianas. The 'king of the battle' came ashore early on Saipan and Guam to take the hand off from the task force big guns afloat. On all three islands, the artillery provided accurate, massed, interdiction fires to facilitate manoeuvre and help isolate the battlefield. The 'Saipan first' campaign sequencing allowed massive amounts of artillery to support the landing on Tinian from the southern coast of Saipan. Just as at Guadalcanal, the Army artillery served very effectively with the Marines as a harmonious team. Organizing Marine Corps artillery for the Guam invasion was a big job, but it paid off well in more effective control and massing of fires to interdict enemy strong points and formations. With any air threat eliminated, most 90-mm anti-aircraft batteries were effectively employed as fiend artillery.[31]

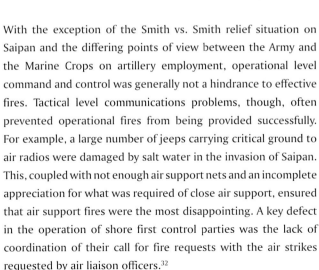

With the exception of the Smith vs. Smith relief situation on Saipan and the differing points of view between the Army and the Marine Crops on artillery employment, operational level command and control was generally not a hindrance to effective fires. Tactical level communications problems, though, often prevented operational fires from being provided successfully. For example, a large number of jeeps carrying critical ground to air radios were damaged by salt water in the invasion of Saipan. This, coupled with not enough air support nets and an incomplete appreciation for what was required of close air support, ensured that air support fires were the most disappointing. A key defect in the operation of shore first control parties was the lack of coordination of their call for fire requests with the air strikes requested by air liaison officers.[32]

---

[28]New Guinea and the Marianas, p 223.
[29]Ibid., pg 230.
[30]Storm Landings, p 70.
[31]The U.S. Marines and Amphibious War, p 362.
[32]Ibid., pg 383.

On the constructive side, when Rear Admiral R.L. Conolly leaned that he was designated Commander Task Force 53 for the attack on Guam, he departed for Guadalcanal, via air, as soon as possible in order to establish his headquarters close to that of Major General Geiger. This was the beginning of an ideal command and control team that significantly affected the quality of the operational fires provided at Guam.[33] The shore fires control parties (SFCP) controlled every type of fire that had ever been thought possible and actually even discovered many new schemes for employing naval gunfire support. On one occasion, SFCP spotters embarked in LCI gunboats and directed the machine guns and rockets of these craft to Japanese targets on the beach. The LCIs were particularly effective against the Japanese coastal caves.[34]

Admiral Spruance's task forces leveraged their intelligence advantages well in supporting operational fires. ULTRA's contribution to U.S. naval successes in the Pacific were many and greatly helped to shape the direction of operational fire assets. Two principle examples of indirect effects on the Marianas campaign were the ability to interdict known re-supply shipments to the islands and the assistance that intercepts provided in the Battle of the Philippine Sea. In the ground campaign, ULTRA was not as pivotal. In spite of the heavy casualties from the first two days of fighting on Saipan, the choice of the western beaches was wise, and a large measure of tactical surprise was achieved by the assault at that location.[35] After Saipan was secure, intelligence sections of all echelons involved in the assault on Tinian proceeded to step up their reconnaissance missions. They accumulated the most detailed and accurate intelligence data yet available to Marines in the war. Daily reconnaissance flights were flown to obtain targeting data and provide situational awareness for officers all the way down to the company commander level.[36] As a result of this increased terrain and target awareness, common target reference points were established and used to quickly bring destruction fires to bear on critical targets.

Throughout the Marianas campaign there was only limited latitude for tactical manoeuvre ashore, although both Saipan and Tinian involved the use of amphibious feints. With the help of deception fires, the Tinian operation achieved tactical surprise. The fast carrier task force with its speed and mobility allowed the U.S. to push the offensive perimeter in the Pacific over 3000 miles in less than one year. The aggressive jump from the Marshalls to the Marianas demonstrated an impressive operational reach that was unexpected. Prior to and after the Marianas campaign, fast carrier forces struck repeatedly at targets that were first precisely located and then just as precisely destroyed or neutralised. 'These operations proved that carrier air power, properly employed, embodies within itself an even greater range and mobility than that of what land air calls 'strategic' air power, plus all the precise destructive potency of so-called 'tactical' air power…in unified form.'[37]

One significant shortcoming that resulted from the Normandy competition for resources was Admiral Nimitz's lack of sufficient cargo ships. As a result, Lieutenant General Smith's ground units were unable to fully embark all their needed organic vehicles. Extended fighting ashore on the larger Marianas islands required a major operational logistics effort to keep the front line units stocked with sufficient ammunition.

As an example of the interaction between the fires and logistics functions, consider that the operational fires and accompanying manoeuvre were so effective at isolating the assault beach at Tinian that not so much as one pound of supplies had to be handled on the beach in the usual shore party manner. In effect, a reinforced corps was landed over less than 200 yards of beach and over a difficult reef, and was supplied through nine days of heavy combat without the normal beachhead buildup.[38] Less than fifty percent of required artillery trucks, for example, could

---

[33]Naval Gunfire at Guam, p 52.
[34]Naval Gunfire at Guam, p 56.
[35]The U.S. Marines and Amphibious War, p 338.
[36]Ibid., pg 355.
[37]Spearhead - The Fast Carrier Task Force, p 21.
[38]The U.S. Marines and Amphibious War, p 368.

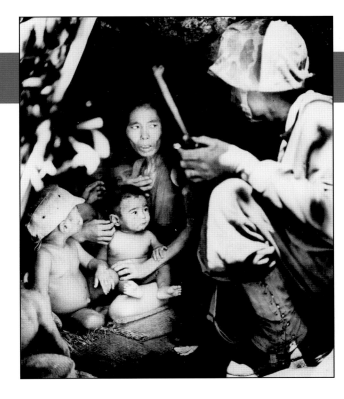

A member of a Marine patrol on Saipan found this family sheltering in a hillside cave, June 1944. (NARA)

the tremendous curtain of fire delivered during the landings on W-Day at Guam, determined that only light opposition would be offered to the assault waves

be embarked for operations at Guam. This greatly affected the artillery's ability to displace and provide operational fires to support the rapidly advancing infantry's manoeuvre plan. On a higher level and a more positive note, the navy's ability to keep its ships and aircraft supplied with sufficient fuel was a key difference in the U.S. ability to project operational fires well beyond the security of logistics bases. The Japanese did not enjoy such a rich and efficient logistics system, and it significantly hampered their capabilities.[39]

Obviously the best example of the 'fires' function interacting with the force protection function is when operational fires completely reduces the threat to operating forces. In the case of the Marianas, one sees a significantly more deliberate, thorough, and hence, successful plan for pre-assault fires result in significantly less assault casualties than had been experienced in the Marshall island campaign.

> 'The cumulative effect of the softening up bombardment, together with the tremendous curtain of fire delivered during the landings on W-Day at Guam, determined that only light opposition would be offered to the assault waves.'[40]

Summary and Significance

As indicated previously, Operation FORAGER campaign planning began early, was aggressive, and brought together the maximum amount of joint forces available to ensure a well-rounded team started the fight. Based on sound operational concepts like tempo and balance, indirect vs. direct, and gaining air and maritime superiority, the FORAGER plan helped set the stage for success. With respect to execution, the Operation FORAGER campaign definitely succeeded in obtaining strategically meaningful results (B-29 airfields) from an intelligently sequenced series of operational and tactical efforts. Though several problems were encountered, mass, momentum, and fortune favoured the brave and the prepared. Admiral Spruance and his subordinate commanders were able to synchronise the wide variety of fires available to them in time, space, and purpose to increase the total effectiveness of their joint force.

'The U.S. invasion forces had crippled the Imperial Mobile Fleet and practically annihilated an entire field Army after isolating them. From all reports, the Americans had outfoxed, outfought, and literally steamrollered each of the Marianas garrisons into oblivion.'[41]

Concerning FORAGER's impact on future operations, the rapid success in the Marianas prompted the Joint Chiefs of Staff to decide to move the assault of Leyte in the Philippines up by two months. The Fast Carrier Force and aggressive amphibious assaults had created an operational tempo that put the Japanese on their heels[42] and kept them there for the rest of the war. Many of the lessons learned in FORAGER are still being incorporated in the force structure and training of today's expeditionary forces around the world. Most recently, for example, the U.S. development of the Expeditionary Strike Group (ESG) concept captured the need for and benefits of a cohesive, well-rounded strike group to conduct amphibious operations. The additions of an attack submarine, a destroyer, a frigate, and a cruiser to the standard U.S. Amphibious Ready Group (ARG)/Marine Expeditionary Unit (MEU) team will enable an ESG commander to better apply the lessons learned in Op FORAGER.

[39]New Guinea and the Marianas, p 214.
[40]Naval Gunfire at Guam, p 56.
[41]Storm Landings, p 86.
[42]Spearhead - The Fast Carrier Task Force, p 20.

Further Reading

Alexander, Joseph H., *Storm Landings: Epic Amphibious Battles in the Central Pacific,* (Annapolis, Maryland: Naval Institute Press, 1997)

Bradley, James, *Flyboys: A True Story of Courage,* (London: Aurum Press, 2004)

Isely, Jeter A. Crowl, Philip A., *The U.S. Marines and Amphibious War Its Theory and Its Practice in the Pacific,* (Princeton, New Jersey: Princeton University, 1951)

Reynolds, Clark G., *The Fast Carriers: The Forging of an Air Navy,* (Annapolis, Maryland: Naval Institute Press, 1992)

Biography

Lieutenant Colonel Michael West was commissioned into the Marine Corps through The Pennsylvania State University in 1985. His operational tours include 1st Battalion, 3rd Marines in Hawaii, company command with 3rd Battalion, 6th Marines in Camp Lejeune, NC and command of MARFOR Unitas as a Major. Training and exercise deployments and contingency operations have taken him to Okinawa, Korea, the Philippines, Haiti, Cuba, South America, South Africa, the Mediterranean, and most recently the Gulf region. His education highlights include a masters degree in Operations Research from the Naval Postgraduate School, a masters in Military Studies from Command & Staff College, and the School of Advanced Warfighting. Staff tours include duty with Headquarters Marine Corps as a manpower analyst, and Operations and Planning Appointments with 2nd Marine Division, II Marine Expeditionary and with the 2nd Marine Expeditionary Brigade as the Lead Planner for Combat Operations in Iraq. He currently serves as the Future Operations officer at COMUKAMPHIBFOR battlestaff headquarters in Portsmouth, England.

The Invasion of Southern France
Operation ANVIL-DRAGOON, August 1944

By Dr Steve Weiss, Officier, French Legion of Honor

'Over this defended beach the men of the 36th Infantry Division stormed ashore 15 August 1944 together with their French Allies. They began here the drive that took them across France, through Germany and into Austria to the final destruction of the German Armies and the Nazi regime.' Monument at St Raphael, France[1]

The last sentence of the above quote defines the objective of millions of people caught up in the Second World War, but to translate this purpose into action would take years, as the planning and execution of an almost forgotten amphibious operation will demonstrate. The controversy over ANVIL-DRAGOON, the last major amphibious operation of World War II in Europe was the manifestation of two divergent strategies, one British, one American. It symbolised the emerging domination of one partner at the expense of the other that would change the polarity of the power structure within the Anglo-American coalition, a rising star for one, and a fading comet for the other. The British, in the ensuing debate, sought to maintain primacy of its Mediterranean strategy, insisting that a major catastrophic enemy collapse in Northern Italy and Central Europe would result, if followed; the Americans opted for a new front in Southern France and the seizure of the port of Marseilles; as part of the OVERLORD strategy, it would trap the German Army in a vast pincer movement. To Churchill, ANVIL-DRAGOON was considered a non-event, a poor return on investment, a

dispersion of military force better employed as indicated above. Implementation in mid-August, ANVIL-DRAGOON was too late to assist the allied armies which had broken out of Normandy and were racing across France; although the German Seventh Army was nearly destroyed at Falaise and the road to Berlin lay open, an allied victory by Christmas was denied. As subsequent events were to show in the fall and winter of 1944, the validity of the southern strategy, according to General Dwight D. Eisenhower, Supreme Allied Commander, was proven beyond question. ANVIL-DRAGOON was an awesome display of power, precision, and process, the proper application of military technology and manpower.

Since the end of hostilities in 1945, few historians have chosen the amphibious landing code-named ANVIL-DRAGOON as their subject of investigation. Might one obvious explanation be that it lacked the drama, impact, and portent of OVERLORD, one of the decisive battles of the war? In his speech on 6 June, 2004, commemorating the 60th anniversary of the D-Day landings, President George W. Bush at the Normandy American Military Cemetery at Colleville-sur-Mer, paid tribute to those soldiers who fell on that day and in the battles that followed. Although he mentioned the hell on the beach named OMAHA at least three times, not once did he mention the D-Day landings unfolding at the same time on UTAH, eight miles further west.[2] Much like ANVIL-DRAGOON, the landings at UTAH Beach succeeded

beyond expectation with a minimum loss of life, but it too failed to ignite the public's imagination.

To land in Southern France was highly controversial and remained a divisive strategic argument between the Anglo-American military staffs almost to its enactment; one of the protagonists, Prime Minister Winston S. Churchill attempted to use his power and influence, and the prestige of his office to eliminate it completely from contention. Only President Franklin D. Roosevelt and his military chiefs believed in its strategic value and remained steadfast. Military historians Liddell Hart, Chester Wilmot, and J. F. C. Fuller, agreeing with Churchill, in their post-war analyses of the war, considered its objective ill advised, its contribution to the German defeat negligible.[3] The American Admiral, H. Kent Hewitt, commander of both the Eighth Fleet and the Western Naval Task Force, in his autobiography said little of his participation in ANVIL-DRAGOON and left it for others to describe those events. What might have been a font of information by one of the major participants was lost. British Admiral Sir Bertram Ramsay, Commander of Operation NEPTUNE, felt that Marseilles and Toulon, now in allied hands, were too far away to sustain the victorious armies on the Channel Coast. Historian, Alan F. Wilt tried in 1981, to give a full account of the operation in his book, 'The French Riviera Campaign of 1944', and an American official history, 'From the Riviera to the Rhine,' was published in 1993, forty-nine years

[1] V. M. Lockhart, *T - Patch to Victory*, (Canyon, 1981), p. 16.
[2] US President, G. W. Bush, D-Day Speech, Normandy, 6 June 2004.
[3] B. H. Liddell Hart, *A History of the Second World War*, (London, 1970), pp. 537-538 [no index citation]; J. F. C. Fuller, *The Second World War*, (London, 1948), pp. 321-326 [no index citation]; C. Wilmot, *The Struggle for Europe*, (London, 1952), pp. 449-457.

if Britain wins decisively against Germany, we could win anywhere, but if she loses, the problem confronting us would be very great

after the event. What follows may offer some answers to the controversy of ANVIL-DRAGOON that exists to this day.

East of the ancient seaport of Marseilles and the naval fortress of Toulon, the beaches of the French Mediterranean, became the focus of intense allied military deliberations and negotiations at conferences designed for those at the highest levels of government during the later stages of World War II. The major actors at these meetings were such notables as the British Prime Minister and American President, leaders of the Free World, and their Chiefs of Staff, Generals George C. Marshal and Alan F. Brooke. During this lengthy and sometimes rancorous inter-allied debate, which ran from mid 1943 to August 1944 over the search for a war-winning strategy, one possibility for consideration included this strip of coastline. Known to the world as the French Riviera or the Cote d'Azur [4], and for our purposes, encompassing Cape Cavalaire on the west to Antheor Cove on the east, a distance of forty-five miles, this geographic entity almost faded into obscurity more than once during the course of the ANVIL-DRAGOON deliberations. British and Americans troops, having landed on the coasts of North Africa in late 1942, Sicily in the summer of 1943, and Southern Italy in the autumn of 1943, had succeeded in driving the German and Italian armies out of North Africa and Sicily. Only Italy required resolution. Each campaign had fulfilled part of a British strategic

grand design, although reluctantly agreed to by the Americans that brought the war closer to Italy and Germany. Success was achieved by island-hopping across the Mediterranean, challenging the enemy's ability to fight, and invading the European mainland, even if that region was alluded to by Churchill as the 'Soft Underbelly,'[5] defying the harsh reality of the Italian mountain landscape. Now, in late 1943, certain issues related to the 'higher strategy of the war'[6] demanded action.

The Crossroads: Anglo-American Summit Conferences, the beginning of discord.

Three years earlier, in 1940, based on an exchange with the president, the prime minister concluded that the United States would enter the war on the side of Great Britain.[7] Churchill received additional support from American Admiral Harold R. Stark, Chief of Naval Operations, who warned his political superiors and military colleagues against a 'Japanese first' policy in his Rainbow-5[8], Plan Dog Memorandum which read, '…if Britain wins decisively against Germany, we could win anywhere, but if she loses, the problem confronting us would be very great and, while we might not lose everywhere, we might possibly not win anywhere.'[9] Immediately after the Pearl Harbor attack in December, 1941, with the American public outraged at Imperial Japan's betrayal and demanding vengeance, the 'Germany First' policy remained the strategy of choice, even

if it were sorely tested by disastrous events in the Pacific. Travelling to the Arcadia Summit Conference of 22 December, 1941, in Washington, the first since America's declaration of war, Churchill said to his son, Randolph, 'Now that she (America) is in this harem, we talk to her quite differently.'[10]

ARCADIA was a most difficult conference because a new alliance was being forged, an amalgam of partners meeting soon after Pearl Harbor as so-called equals. The resulting discussions were long and wearisome.[11] To defeat the Axis in Europe, a portion of the total list of requirements follows: 1). The Ring around Germany is to be closed and tightened. 2). German resistance is to be worn down by air bombardment, blockade, subversive activities, and psychological warfare. 3). The inexorable goal of offensive action, as exemplified by a return to the Continent is, a). Via the Mediterranean, b). from Turkey into the Balkans, c). By landings in Western Europe.[12] Preoccupied with the latest events in the Pacific, the Americans were ill prepared to question the British proposals. Although they had signed the document, having made only slight changes, it remained largely a British design. The Americans were uneasy, and in the ensuing months their uneasiness was to increase.[13]

In this regard, it may be of considerable value to assess the results of those summit conferences that followed, labyrinthine

---

[4]S. E. Morison, *The Invasion of France and Germany, XI*, (Oxford, 1957), p. 234.
[5]Gen. W. G. F. Jackson, *'Overlord': Normandy 1944*, (London, 1978), p. 88.
[6]*The Higher Strategic Decisions of the War, 1941-1945*, prepared by the Historical Section of the Cabinet, (London), pp. 199-203.
[7]J. Leutze, *The Secret of the Churchill-Roosevelt Correspondence, September 1939-May 1940*, JCH, 10, 3, (1975)

[8]C. Chant, *The Encyclopedia of Code Names of World War II*, (London, 1986), p. 2.
[9]T. Higgins, *Winston Churchill and the Second Front*, (New York, 1957), pp. 43-46
[10]Sir A. Bryant, *Turn of the Tide*, (London, 1957), p. 234
[11]J. Leasor & Gen. S. Hollis, *War at the Top*, (London, 1959), p. 29
[12]COS to JCS, 'American-British Strategy', Washington, 22-24 Dec. 1941, *Arcadia Papers*, RG. 165, Exec. 4.
[13]Sir M. Howard, *The Mediterranean Strategy in the Second World War*, (London, 1968), pp. 19-20

and convoluted they may be, leading up to the allied invasions of Western Europe. The purpose of this evaluation is throw additional light on the central issue of our study in order to discover why arguments regarding a Southern France landing were so contentious and how it was forever inextricably linked to Operation OVERLORD and the Italian Campaign.

Soon after ARCADIA, ARGONAUT, the codename for an inter-allied Washington meeting, convened on 19 June, 1942 and lasted until the 25th. Reacting to the results of the meeting, historian, Martin Blumenson, criticised the coalition, in a journal article, for concocting a strategy whose primary purpose was to liberate territory rather than to destroy the German Army in France during 1942. It were as if they doubted the quality and effectiveness of their own land forces, fearful of a direct confrontation with German forces in Northern France, choosing instead a Mediterranean strategy, which prolonged the war beyond 1944. Blumenson, however, failed to define the Anglo-American strategic controversy, which resulted in an additional move to the periphery.[14] Moreover, by failing to draw a distinction between the British and American strategic positions, as did Michael Howard, Blumenson disregarded Churchill's awareness of the prevalent American attitude: its military leaders, suspicious of British intentions, favoured a massive Cross-Channel attack and suspected that TORCH, a

landing in North Africa, would serve to protect British interests rather than to defeat Germany. Seeking consensus, Churchill pressed Roosevelt for a full and irrevocable commitment to British strategy.[15]

Soviet leader, Joseph Stalin demanded a Second Front in Northwest Europe to ease the plight of the Russian Army fighting for its life against the German invasion of its territory. Reacting to Stalin's insistent demands but incapable of coming to the required aid of his ally, Roosevelt defined a Second Front in the broadest practical terms. Having determined that German combat strength and fighting-power in the Mediterranean was only a fraction of what it wielded in Europe, he concluded that the benefit of employing green American troops and inexperienced leaders against the enemy positions in North Africa afforded them the opportunity of gaining combat experience on more favourable terms. American forces could be in action sooner and in greater strength in the Mediterranean, however remotely situated from Northwest Europe. America had been at war eleven months, having begun the conflict with scant, archaic equipment and a small peacetime cadre. With such meagre beginnings, transforming its military into a large, modern and aggressive fighting force capable of amphibious operations under combat conditions was daunting.[16] Somehow, by the president's indirect efforts, Russia might survive.

SYMBOL, the Summit Conference of 14-23 January at Casablanca, by definition attended by Roosevelt and Churchill, was the 'watershed' conference of the war. With the North African littoral cleared of Germans, it was here that decisions were made to politicise the war in an utterly irretrievable manner[17] and to develop a military strategy based on attrition rather than on manoeuvre, on the acquisition of space rather than the destruction of the German Army.[18] The outcome was stalemate. Incompatible differences increased the tensions between the British delegates who advocated this type of warfare, ending with a landing in France as the *coup de grace* and the Americans who advocated a war of concentration beginning with a collision of forces. After days of intense negotiating between the two sides, some of which was acrimonious, Chief of Staff, General Alan Brooke wrote the following words in his diary,

> 'It is a slow and tiring business, which requires a lot of patience. The Americans can't be pushed and hurried…It is a slow and tedious business, as all matters have to be carefully explained before they can be absorbed. I was in despair and in the depths of gloom…It is no use, we shall never get agreement with them.'[19]

If the SYMBOL ended in enfeebled compromise, resulting in the British feeling satisfied and the Americans disappointed, with

[14]M. Blumenson, 'A Deaf Ear to Clausewitz: Allied Operational Objectives in World War II', *Parameters, US Army War College Quarterly*, XXIII 2, Summer (1993), pp. 16-27.
[15]H. Loewenheim, M. Jonas, H. Langley (eds.), *Roosevelt and Churchill, Their Secret Wartime Correspondence*, (New York, 1990), pp. 254-256; Marshall to Dill 'CCS-94,' Washington, 14 Aug. 1942, RG. 165 Exec 10 Box 59; Sir M. Howard, *Op. cit.* pp. 122-140.
[16]M. Stoler, *The Politics of the Second Front*, (Westport, 1977), pp. 53, 65.
[17]A. Wedemeyer, *Wedemeyer Reports!* (New York, 1958), p. 169.
[18]Sir Michael Howard, *Op. cit.*, p. 35.
[19]FM Lord Alanbrooke, 3/A/VIII, 16-18 Jan. 1943, pp. 600-608.

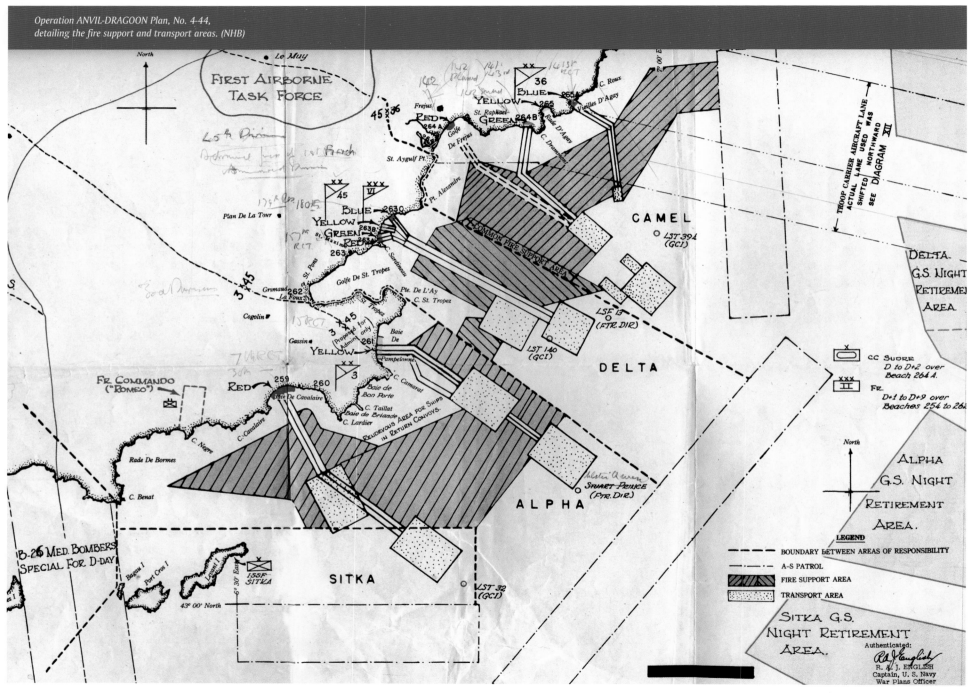

Operation ANVIL-DRAGOON Plan, No. 4-44,
detailing the fire support and transport areas. (NHB)

Roosevelt and Churchill sharing the view that the agreement fell short of great power capabilities and strategic intentions, included was the creation of a special inter-service Anglo-American planning staff. To be based in London, this new organisation was to plan for the execution of a Cross-Channel attack, and assigned to lead the enterprise was British General Sir Frederick Morgan, COSSAC (Chief of Staff to the Supreme Allied Commander) designate. He and his staff were to assemble the strongest possible force, to plan minor amphibious operations, to prepare for a possible landing on the Continent and the seizure of a continental bridgehead in 1943, leading to a rapid exploitation by a large-scale invasion in 1944.[20] However, General Marshall's reaction to the outcome was immoderate; he was concerned that future British operations in the Mediterranean would demand more and more American involvement, the outcome of which would preclude the assembly of sufficient forces in Britain required to execute a successful Cross-Channel operation.[21] The end of the conference left many matters unresolved.

Five months passed before TRIDENT, another Summit Conference, convened in Washington from 12-25 May 1943. It was to confirm the earlier Casablanca decisions, to clarify Anglo-American planning, and to specify long-term military goals. As the conferees gathered, they were informed of allied dominance in all theatres of war and the success at Stalingrad. General Alan Brooke was apprehensive of the American drift toward the Pacific since the Casablanca Conference, and in Washington, would seek reassurance that the 'Germany-First' formula remained intact. Nor did he envisage an easy time of it, because, in his view, American Admiral, Ernest J. King, Chief of Naval Operations, an Anglophobe, continued to divert large forces to the Pacific, with General Marshall's implicit support. Brooke dreaded the up-coming meetings, knowing that they would entail hours of argument with an ally trying to depart from the agreed basic strategy. Strained and depressed at the thought, he reasoned that if the Americans were allowed to succeed, if the Pacific were to absorb the bulk of the allied effort, the war could go on forever.[22] Even though the Americans disagreed with Brooke's Mediterranean strategy, Marshall counted on him to blunt some of Churchill's impractical schemes, and Roosevelt was determined to see 'Germany-First' through to the end.[23] Regarding the negotiations themselves, the principal American objective was to solicit British support for an early Cross-Channel operation, for which the JCS (American Joint Chiefs of Staff) had Roosevelt's backing for the first time. Even so, the difficulty of convincing the British of the operation's immediacy required a major change in their Mediterranean strategy. The Americans predicted that the British would only respond half-heartedly to an incidental landing tied to a German collapse. King expressed irritation, saying, 'The British limp along with an attitude of expediency. Nothing will make us sure what operations can be anticipated in 1944, unless there is a firm commitment to do ROUNDUP (later changed to OVERLORD).[24] Moreover, the Americans accepted that portion of 'closing the ring' in which continued Mediterranean operations, however, vague, would lead to an eventual Cross-Channel attack. At least in the Pacific wastes, controlled as they were by the Americans, there was to be no 'limping along', because King's view prevailed. Brooke privately recorded at the end of the conference,

'…in the light of the results that ensued the 'compromise' that emerged was almost exactly what I wanted!…King, however, was the unconvertible one, and I knew well that shipping and landing craft would continue to be sucked up in the Pacific irrespective of the requirements for the war in Europe.'[25]

At QUADRANT, a summit conference, also known as 1st Quebec, which ran for one week in mid-August, 1943, matters of immediate and long-term importance were considered. One of the speakers, General Morgan, COSSAC, reported that it was possible to undertake an amphibious operation to secure a lodgement area on the Continent from where further offensive operations can be carried out with forces from the United

[20]*Casablanca Conference Papers, Papers and Minutes of Meetings*, CCS-155/1, Office of the CCS, Jan. 1943, pp. 99-101.
[21]CCS 83 Meeting, Washington, 12 May 1943, Reel III.
[22]FM Lord Alanbrooke, 3/A/IX. 10 May 1943, p.86
[23]F. Pogue, interview with Gen. G. Marshall, 13 Nov., 1956.
[24]JCS 81 Meeting, Washington, 14 May, 1943, p. 3, Reel I.
[25]FM Lord Alanbrooke, *Op. cit.*, 3/A/VIII, 25 May 1943, p. 705.

American troops embark on shipping in Italy in preparation for the landings in Southern France. (NHB)

American position with qualifiers, Brooke evoked a strong JCS (Joint Chiefs of Staff, American) response. His qualifiers were seen as a British excuse to press for further Mediterranean operations or as a defence against being accused of breaking faith with their agreements. Although the president supported OVERLORD, the JCS, prior to his arrival, realised that after three days of intensive debate, a compromise was developing in which 'overriding priority' for the operation would be lessened, which would include future operations in Northern Italy. Because of the continuing build-up of American soldiers and materiel, an American officer would become supreme commander in Northern Europe. [27]

As the conference ended, the CCS (Combined Chiefs of Staff) directed General Eisenhower, serving as SACMED (Supreme Allied Commander Mediterranean) to submit an outline plan for a possible operation in Southern France. Operation ANVIL, as part of Operation OVERLORD was originally conceived during the conference and included in the Chiefs of Staff's Final Report, of 23 August 1943. It stipulated that,

'Offensive operations against Southern France (to include the use of trained and equipped French forces) should be undertaken to establish a lodgement in the Toulon-Marseilles area and to exploit northward in order to create a diversion in connection with OVERLORD. Air nourished guerrilla operations in the Southern Alps will, if

Kingdom, and for their build-up with additional divisions and supporting units that might be shipped from the United States or elsewhere. He cautioned, 'OVERLORD will be launched as an assault from an island against an extended continental mainland coastline. Consider that in the Mediterranean the tidal range is negligible and the weather reasonably reliable, in the English

Channel, the tidal range is considerable and the weather capricious. Target date, 1 May 1944.[26]

Brooke and his COS (Chiefs of Staff, British) accepted the viability of OVERLORD in 1944, but found the American insistence of giving it overall priority too restrictive. Seeking to soften the

---

[26]Gen. Sir Frederick Morgan, 'Operation OVERLORD', QUADRANT Conference, Appendix B, Washington, 15 Aug., 1943, Reel IV.
[27]E, Cray, *General of the Army, George C. Marshall*, (New York, 1990), pp. 408-413.

possible, be initiated…the necessary resources would be drawn from the Mediterranean Theatre. The examination of ANVIL on the basis of not less than a two division assault need be pressed forward as fast as possible; if the examination reveals that it requires strengthening, consideration will have to be given to the provision of additional resources.'[28] Henceforth, ANVIL would be inextricably entwined with OVERLORD.

Eisenhower's October report lacked enthusiasm, because there were not enough resources to launch a full-scale attack. He reasoned that only one division, used as a feint, could be in the initial assault, because of a shortage of landing craft. Even concerted operations might prove more valuable to OVERLORD than ANVIL itself, the report continued, the landing at best being a small-scale operation. Morgan disagreed, asserting that OVERLORD and ANVIL must take place simultaneously if two of the German mobile reserve divisions, stationed in Southern France, were to be tied down by formations under AFHQ (Allied Force Headquarters) control. He opposed Eisenhower's recommendation that the operation should be considered only as one of seven possibilities[29] British experts at the conference had disagreed with Morgan and at the first plenary session on 19 August, the CCS presented the results of five days of continuous discussion to the president and the prime minister:

'OVERLORD-target date, 1 May 1944, to land in France and strike at the heart of Germany and destroy her forces. Between OVERLORD and Mediterranean operations, the sharing of scarce resources is to be distributed and employed to ensure OVERLORDS's success. Consideration of a Northern Norway landing (Operation JUPITER), only if OVERLORD is rendered impossible. Unremitting pressure on the German forces in Italy, Southern France - a diversion and lodgement between Toulon and Marseilles, in conjunction with OVERLORD, with exploitation northwards. Air-nourished guerrilla warfare in Southern France. Balkan operations limited to supply, special operations and bombing of strategic objectives.'[30]

QUADRANT was a crucial conference in the evolution of Anglo-American strategy in the war against Germany. If planning at Casablanca represented the beginning of coalition warfare's offensive phase, and TRIDENT the halfway mark, QUADRANT was the beginning of the end for Germany, even though negotiations at Quebec fell short of the final showdown desired by Marshall.[31] Moreover, French forces needed to be integrated into overall allied planning, but the resolution of that issue would have to wait for another conference.

Churchill and Roosevelt accepted the paper with reservations related to OVERLORD.[32] During the second plenary session on the twenty-third, the prime minister, favoring the OVERLORD concept for 1944, but fearful of excessive casualties, requested that a rule be applied, as prepared by Morgan, that if there were more than twelve mobile German divisions in France at the intended moment of the allied landing, the landing would be cancelled. He also insisted that the assault force, including landing craft, to be increased by 25 per cent and allied fighter superiority achieved before the landing. The perennial landing craft problem persisted, the shortages of which limited all prospective operations, including the passage to Italy. The two sides also disagreed over landing craft procurement. The British desired a definite allocation per month or a percentage of monthly construction, while the Americans wanted to allocate them as needed for specific operations. The Americans, whose Navy controlled landing craft production and distribution, refused to give the British Navy a 'blank cheque,' particularly when it was using the craft for net protection at its naval base at Scapa Flow.[33] Even though two hundred and four Landing Craft Tank (LCT) and Landing Craft Infantry (LCI) were to be deployed against Germany by December 1943,[34] lacking was an oversight bilateral committee to reduce the incentive for deception and manipulation and to insure proper apportionment. Marshall was heard to say:

---

[28]CCS 116 Meeting, 'CCS 319/5: Final Report to the President and Prime Minister', Washington, 24 Aug. 1943, Reel IV.

[29]J. Ehrman, Grand Strategy, V, (London, 1956), p. 6.

[30]Minutes, 1st Meeting, CCS, 'President and Prime Minister,' QUADRANT Conference, Washington, 19 August 1943, Office of the CCS.

[31]M. Matloff, Strategic Planning for Coalition Warfare, (Washington, 1953), pp. 242-243.

[32]CCS 319/5, 'Final Report to the President and Prime Minister,' QUADRANT Conference, Washington, 24 Aug., 1943, Reel IV.

[33]JCS 108 Meeting, QUADRANT Conference, Washington, 23 Aug., Reel IV.

[34]M. Matloff, Op. cit., p. 398.

The armada arrives off the coast of Southern France. (NHB)

'My military education and experience in the First World War had all been based on roads, rivers, and railroads. During the last two years, however, I have been acquiring an education based on oceans and I've had to learn all over again. Prior to the present war, I never heard of any landing craft except a rubber boat. Now I think about little else.'[35]

Concurrently, the inevitable Italian collapse, accelerated by the Sicilian surrender on 17 August, lured allied forces toward Italy. Churchill suggested it take them beyond Rome to the Ancona-Pisa line and the northern Italian airfields.[36]

SEXTANT and EUREKA

OVERLORD and ANVIL, projected amphibious operations for 1944, were considered as inter-dependent parts of the same operation, the hammer and the anvil that would crush the German armies in Western Europe. Their acceptance and activation, however, were dependent upon the attitudes and changeable moods of the major participants, particularly those of Roosevelt and Churchill. Stalin, by contrast, was completely and steadfastly set on the Anglo-Americans invading Northern France. Churchill, on the other hand, convinced that the OVERLORD strategy was simply satisfying a political

expedient, pressed for further Mediterranean operations as a means of countering Russian advances into Central Europe.[37] Roosevelt, however, remained unwilling to accept any delay or postponement beyond May 1944 in order to fulfill his Second Front promise to Stalin. Mounting a threat against Southern France was first mentioned, then shelved at the TRIDENT Conference, revived by Anthony Eden, British Foreign Minister on a visit to Moscow, and accepted as a landing at QUADRANT.

Between 1939 and 1941, as the United States moved from ambivalent neutrality toward active belligerency, American and British policies toward Vichy France diverged. This disunity aggravated already delicate negotiations - particularly affecting ANVIL and French Resistance activities. The integration of the Resistance into allied planning was dependent upon the decisions reached by Churchill, Roosevelt, and Stalin at the EUREKA Conference in Tehran, November 1943.

Before the EUREKA was to convene, Churchill requested a summit meeting in Cairo, code-named SEXTANT, in order to resolve and co-ordinate Anglo-American strategic policy before meeting Stalin at Tehran. Because of disastrous British military excursions in the Eastern Mediterranean, which were proving highly prejudicial to a deteriorating allied Italian campaign, Churchill sought a modification of the QUADRANT agreement, in which seven Mediterranean-based allied divisions and sixty LST's

---

[35] J. A. Isely, & P. A. Crowl, *The U. S. Marines and Amphibious War*, (Princeton, 1951), p. 1.

[36] Minutes, 2nd. Meeting, President, Prime Minister, QUADRANT Conference, Washington, 23 Aug. 1943, Reel IV.

[37] J. Harvey, (ed.), *The Diplomatic Diaries of Oliver Hardy, 1937-1949*, (Eden's Secretary), (London, 1970), pp. 313-314; FO 371/370, 31 Oct. 1943.

US troops hitting the beaches at
St Raphael, Southern France. (NHB)

were scheduled for transfer to Britain, beginning in November, 1943.[38] The attritional battles south of Rome, in which eleven ill-prepared and under-manned allied divisions encountered nineteen experienced and well-positioned German divisions, foreshadowed a long and arduous winter campaign (1943-44). To relieve a growing anxiety over the front's tactical imbalance, Churchill and his COS sought to cast the seven idle divisions and the sixty landing craft, designated for the Cross-Channel attack, into battle.[39] Churchill petitioned Roosevelt, questioning the practicality of the relevant QUANDRANT decisions, as measured against the reality of the deteriorating conditions in Italy. He felt that by accepting QUADRANT, despite Roosevelt's insistence, would be both negligent and irresponsible. Roosevelt entertained Churchill's entreaties related to the following issues. In addition to the Italian debacle, the request for increased American support of British efforts, Operations ACCOLADE and HARDIHOOD[40] in the Eastern Mediterranean, and the merger of the two Mediterranean commands into one, subsumed less than one commander. Both Roosevelt and his JCS were alarmed and irritated with Churchill who sought to re-negotiate these salient features of QUANDRANT. It appeared to them that the prime minister was again abandoning OVERLORD in preference to an intensified Mediterranean policy.[41]

Cairo: SEXTANT I

The participants at this conference between 22 - 26 November tried to do too much work in too little time, exhausting the conferees before they travelled to Tehran. The conference registered two plenary sessions, and five meetings each of the CCS[42], COS, and JCS. There were numerous informal military and political meetings, and four out of the nine items on the agenda related to operation OVERLORD and the Mediterranean. On the 26th, Eisenhower presented his views. As AFHQ (Allied Force Headquarters) Commander, in the Central Mediterranean, he supported an all-out winter offensive in Italy and a build-up of of allied forces capable of moving east or west beyond the Po River. Owing to the shortage of landing craft, he would consider a cancellation of an invasion of Southern France. If additional means were available, he recommended limited operations in the Eastern Mediterranean and the Balkans, and garnered support from his British colleagues.[43] Marshall

was not deterred, recognising that Eisenhower like all theatre commanders, fought their own corner and said, 'that the JCS tentatively accepted the British proposals implied in the capture of the Rimini-Pisa line and the capture of Rhodes, but further discussions were required when the CCS returned to Cairo from Tehran.[44]

Tehran: EUREKA

Five days later the Americans returned from Tehran with a binding agreement based on Soviet strategic preferences comparable to their own, regarding operations in the West. Binding because it

[38]F. Loewenheim, et al, (eds.), Op. cit., pp. 386-388.
[39]CAB 79 (COS), 14, 19 Oct., 1943
[40]F. Loewenheim, et al, (eds.), Op. cit., pp. 370-374, pp. 312-313.
[41]JCS 117 Meeting, Washington, 5 Oct. 1943, Reel II.
[42]CCS (Combined Chiefs of Staff, composed of the American JCS and the British COS created in 1941). It served both allied leaders as a decision-making body.
[43]JCS 131 Meeting, Washington, 26 Nov. 1943, Reel II
[44]Ibid.

US aircraft and parachutists of the First Airborne Task Force over the drop zone in the Le Muy area. (NHB)

was as if the Americans had written the agreement themselves. Operations in the Eastern Mediterranean were made obsolete in three days during the full length of the EUREKA conference of 28th-30th November. Replacing these activities in the Mediterranean were OVERLORD and ANVIL, considered by Stalin as a single, indivisible military undertaking.[45] Both were planned to coincide with a Soviet summer offensive and increased allied operations in Italy. Moreover, Stalin insisted that a Supreme OVERLORD Commander be named quickly. Roosevelt and Stalin had achieved primacy over an angry Churchill, who felt marginalised by Roosevelt's attempts to carry favour, however naïve, with the Russian leader. He had no other course but to

comply, after arguing with the Americans against their overall 1944 plan in front of the Russians at Tehran.[46]

Cairo: SEXTANT II

By 2 December, the major participants had returned to Cairo exhausted, only to be locked in debate for another five days. The Americans had left Cairo for Tehran in a despondent mood, believing that Stalin wanted an allied operation close to his own front, near the Eastern Mediterranean, which would conform to the British position. When Stalin supported the American view, the British were astounded. They said that the Southern France operation could not be done due to a lack of resources, but when American plans, organised on the spot, demonstrated it could, the British lost the argument.[47] The president abandoned Operation BUCANEER, an amphibious operation planned for the recapture of the Andaman Islands in the Indian Ocean, in order to preserve OVERLORD on the required scale. Both conferences recorded some of the bitterest arguments of the war, but the British military hierarchy increased

its dominance in the Mediterranean. General Sir Henry Maitland Wilson assumed supreme command of a unified Mediterranean Theatre on 24 December 1943, General Sir Harold Alexander was appointed C-in-C Italy and Admiral Sir John Cunningham, became Naval C-in-C Mediterranean. Eisenhower relinquished his Mediterranean command and transferred to OVERLORD as SCAF (Supreme Commander Allied Expeditionary Force). Under the agreement 68 landing craft would remain in the Mediterranean until January 1944 as part of projected amphibious operations in Italy and the intended allied advance beyond Rome. The Cairo and Tehran conferences were tripartite summits whose results represented a form of coalition warfare based on an alliance of distinct parties combining to fight a common foe, but not united enough in their efforts to form a coordinated strategy. Moreover, Churchill's influence with Roosevelt waned after 1943, and many important military questions were hardly addressed.[48]

ANVIL versus the Italian/Balkan Debate

The decision on the timing, preparation, and size for both French operations was unavoidable, because of the May guarantee. On 6 January, Generals Montgomery, Smith (Walter B. Smith, Eisenhower's Chief of Staff), and Morgan deemed ANVIL unfeasible if mounted simultaneously with OVERLORD due to

[45]CCS 132 Meeting, EUREKA Conference, 30 Nov. 1943, Washington, Reel IV; G. A. Harrison, *Cross Channel Attack*, (Washington, 1951), p. 125.
[46]CAB 65/40 WM (43) 169, 13 Dec. 1943.
[47]Gen. T. Handy Interview, Washington, 28 Sept. 1956, RG 165 'Plan for Invasion for Southern France.' JPS 249, Washington, 5 Aug. 1943, 'Study, Operation Against Southern France.'
[48]D. Kaiser, 'Churchill, Roosevelt and the Limits of Power,' *International Security*, 10:1, (Summer, 1985), pp. 204-221.

US troops disembarked at St. Maxime in the Gulf of St. Tropez. (NHB)

ANVIL will be vigorously pressed and that it is the firm intention to mount this operation in support of OVERLORD

the shortage of landing craft. If ANVIL could not be eliminated entirely, they suggested, it should be used as a diversion and reduced to a one divisional threat.[49] Then Generals Montgomery, Smith, and Admiral Ramsay suggested a diversionary role for ANVIL, adding to the confusion.[50] On 4 February, Churchill concluded that OVERLORD and ANVIL were not strategically entwined, as perceived by Stalin. On 21 February, the president and his JCS met and concluded that since Eisenhower maintained he had enough landing craft for both operations, they strongly opposed the COS desire to cancel ANVIL. The president noted that ANVIL's cancellation would displease the Russians. Because of the stalemate in Italy, on 19 February, Eisenhower and the COS agreed that Italy required immediate assistance; ANVIL would revert to the scale originally intended, although planning would continue.[51] The JIC (Joint Intelligence Committee) assisted the Joint Planners in recommending that ANVIL be reduced to a threat, stating that there was no evidence that any reduction in ANVIL would lead to substantial changes in enemy dispositions. The JIC evaluations indicated that the Germans appeared 'nervous' about a threat to Southern France, but suggested an assault in the Adriatic on the Istrian Peninsula, immediately after OVERLORD would offer greater assistance than ANVIL.[52] The onerous conditions in Italy prompted Montgomery to reverse his position, and on 21 February wrote the following petition to Eisenhower, 'I recommend very strongly that we now throw the whole weight of our opinion onto the scales against ANVIL. Let us

have two really good major campaigns, one in Italy and one in OVERLORD[53] Conferring on 18 February in Italy, Generals Wilson and Alexander agreed that either a one divisional assault in the spring or a two divisional assault later against Southern France was dead.[54] It took one more month of discussions for Eisenhower to accede to Montgomery's recommendations which echoed those of the COS and Churchill's. By 24 February all the principals involved agreed to the above arrangement, amidst the search for landing craft. Since ANVIL was being crushed between the demands of OVERLORD and the Italian campaign, Eisenhower, with CCS approval, cancelled ANVIL on 21 March.[55] At one stroke, by agreeing to postpone ANVIL until Rome was captured, the Americans threw away their most important card, the operation conceived to siphon German reserves from OVERLORD, the hammer without its anvil.

Marshall agreed to ANVIL's postponement but refused to cancel it. He proposed that if the COS would accept a two divisional ANVIL, mounted on 10 July in support of OVERLORD, the JCS

would transfer 26 LSTs and 40 LCIs (L) from the Pacific to the Mediterranean[56] King concurred and the COS accepted the American proposal, assuming that when the strategic situation was reviewed in June, the additional landing craft would be used in a Mediterranean operation offering the most support to OVERLORD, not necessarily ANVIL. This assumption was in direct opposition to the JCS meaning. Field Marshal Sir John Dill, the senior British representative on the CCS, warned,

'...That the delayed ANVIL will be vigorously pressed and that it is the firm intention to mount this operation in support of OVERLORD with the target date indicated. The JCS are firm in their conviction that a decision must be taken to launch ANVIL on a specific date. They consider it

[49]COSSAC (44) 5m Op, ANVIL, Wa. 6 Jan. 1944, RG 331, SHAEF SGS FILE 370.
[50]FM Lord Wilson, Report- SACMED to the CCS on Ops in So. France Aug. 1944 p. 8.
[51]A. Horne & Lord D. Montgomery, Montgomery, The Lonely Leader, (London, 1994), pp. 78-79.
[52]F. Hinsley, British Intelligence in the Second World War, III, I, (London, 1984), pp. 24-26.
[53]Montgomery to Eisenhower, Washington, 21 Feb. 1944 RG. 165, Exec. 9, Book 15., Box 45.

[54]FM H. Wilson, Op. cit., pp 7, 11-12.
[55]Eisenhower to Marshall, Washington, 21 March 1944, RG 165 OPD CM-IN 15429.
[56]CCS 158 Meeting, Washington, 28 March 1944, Reel IV.

History will never forgive them for bargaining equipment against strategy and for trying to blackmail us... by holding the pistol of withdrawing craft at our heads

Part of a static defensive position near Toulon. French naval guns being inspected by allied troops.(NHB)

is clearly evident that the operation will not be launched unless such a date is taken...'[57]

An Istrian Alternative

In early 1944, General Alexander, supported by many of the military principals in the Mediterranean, including Wilson and Mark Clark (Commander, 5th Army), considered a plan, Operation ARMPIT, to break through the Apennines and carry the Ljubljana Gap, nor more than 30 miles wide, through which ran the main road and railway from Italy into Northern Yugoslavia. Vienna lay at the end of this 250-mile narrow transportation network, an objective of great political, military, and psychological importance.[58] Admiral Hewitt disagreed with Clark, suggesting that naval operations in the Northern Adriatic would put too much strain on the US Navy. US General Jacob L. Devers, Wilson's theatre deputy agreed. One survey of the region revealed that, 'The western shore of the Istrian peninsula is made up of numerous cliffs, scattered coves, occasional anchorages, a few small beaches and nowhere is it suitable for the classical, broad scale, textbook style of landing.[59] Alexander closely questioned Lieutenant Colonel Peter Wilkinson of SOE (Special Operations Executive) in March 1944 concerning the feasibility of an Istrian landing. Wilkinson replied, 'that it contained formidable technical difficulties and great risks.[60] It was doubtful that a force of more than six divisions could be sustained through the Ljubljana Gap, because its many railroad

tunnels were vulnerable to destruction by German demolition experts.[61] Roosevelt, in a letter to Churchill, expounded further: he was convinced that not only was it an area of poor beaches, limited natural cover, undeveloped mountain roads, impassable in winter's heavy snows and easily defended exits leading to the Danubian plain, through the Ljubljana Gap, but that an operation here did not support OVERLORD and therefore was unacceptable.[62] Two weeks after the Normandy landings, Eisenhower cabled the following message to Marshall, 'It is my belief that the prime minister and his Chiefs of Staff are honestly convinced that greater results in support of OVERLORD would be achieved by a drive toward Trieste rather than to mount ANVIL.[63]

Marshall was obdurate toward the British point of view and refused to withdraw landing craft from the Pacific to assist a course of action in Italy or the Adriatic. Brooke wrote in his diary,

'History will never forgive them for bargaining equipment against strategy and for trying to blackmail us... by holding the pistol of withdrawing craft at our heads.'[64] Without the extra landing craft, ANVIL, in support of OVERLORD was dead, regardless of Anglo-American strategic differences. The COS tried compromise by stating, '...a threat against Southern France and the seizure of any opportunity with available amphibious forces, either arising in France or elsewhere, would be most beneficial..'[65] The JCS added two amendments: 1). All offensive action in Italy would be discontinued when the mission was accomplished and

[57]CCS 159 Meeting, Washington, 29 March, 1944, Reel IV
[58]Sir M. Howard, *Op cit.*, pp. 61-62
[59]T. Barker, 'The Ljubljana Gap Strategy: Alternate to Anvil/Dragoon or Fantasy?' JMH, 56, (I Jan. 1992), pp. 73-74.
[60]T. Barker, *Op, cit.*, p. 61.

[61]R. Weigley, *Eisenhower's Lieutenants*, (Bloomington, 1981), p. 332.
[62]'JCS Operations to Assist OVERLORD,' Washington. 29 June 1944, Reel VII
[63]Eisenhower to Marshall, 29 June 1944, RG 218, JCS, Box 4, Chair. File.
[64]FM Lord Allanbrooke, *Op. cit.*, 3/B/XII, 19 April 1944, p. 937.
[65]CCS 465/22, Washington, 17 April 1944, Reel IV.

Part of a French Artillery Battalion in close action in the city of Toulon. (NHB)

2). ANVIL would be given top priority. Dill wrote, 'No formula can be a substitute for honest agreement.'[66]

The ANVIL controversy flared once again between the two staffs when Eisenhower's forces suffered logistically from a severe Channel storm, (wind velocity 22 knots, 7 foot waves) that lasted from 19-24 June and jeopardised the time-table of Montgomery's 21st Army Group. A British offensive toward Caen was postponed for a week. The delayed attack held hostage by the storm, demonstrated the need for the additional port that ANVIL could provide.[67] Eisenhower's anxious concerns were expressed in a cable to Marshall, 'AFHQ apparently fails to appreciate that the achievement of a successful bridgehead in France does not of itself imply success in operation OVERLORD as a whole….that it will be in urgent need of any assistance possible from elsewhere for sometime to come.[68] The two ports under consideration were Marseilles and Bordeaux. Marseilles, if cleared quickly, was much better suited to handle large-scale replacements than Bordeaux, which closer to the battle area, had constricted beaches. Tired of the wrangling and sure of its position, the JCS ordered Wilson to launch a three divisional ANVIL against Southern France by 15 August. It stated,

'We are convinced that the best use to which we can put our resources in the Mediterranean is to launch an ANVIL

at the earliest possible date. This is the only operation which will provide early and maximum support for OVERLORD, provide for additional major port required by SCAF and will put the French forces into battle for their homeland… The resources to be employed in ANVIL will be predominately US and French. We do not believe that extensive and long preparation to achieve perfection of arrangements is necessary or justifiable.[69] In response, the British turned the order down cold; the Americans countered in no uncertain terms, insisting the order be carried out. They were adamant that ANVIL must not be reduced to a threat in favour of a major campaign in Italy beyond the Pisa-Rimini line.'

A new ULTRA intercept revealed that the Germans were prepared to fight for Northern Italy, south of the Apennines, to prevent a breakthrough into the Po Valley. A loss here would have severe military and political consequences. This new information supported Churchill and Brooke's view of ANVIL, i.e., there would be nothing gained by a landing in the South of France, which was not already ensured by the Italian campaign. Cryptographic difficulties delayed the delivery of the intercepts. 'This may have been one of the turning points where history failed to turn: this single piece of intelligence had it been available might have led to a different decision. If presented earlier, the Americans might

have opted for a quick and overwhelming victory in Italy, an end to the war in 1944 and a different partition of Europe.' [70]

In view of the hardened American attitude, after a flurry of cables and an exchange of letters between Roosevelt and Churchill, Brooke agreed to American demands stating,

'All right, if you insist on being damned fools, we shall be damned fools with you, and we shall see that we perform the role of damned fools damned well.' [71]

On 27 July 1944, Churchill requested that ANVIL be renamed DRAGOON; chosen to deceive the Germans, it also stood for the contempt he felt for the operation. 'Done,' he later wrote, 'in case the enemy has learned the meaning of the original code word.[72]

[66]CCS 154 Meeting, Washington, 8 April 1944, Reel IV.
[67]Lt. Col. R. Lee, *48 Million Tons to Eisenhower*, (Washington, 1945), pp. 17-21.
[68]FM Wilson, *Report by SACMED to the CCS on the Italian Campaign*, (London, 1948), pp. 33-36.
[69]CCS 166 Meeting, 15 June 1944, Reel IV.

[70]R. Bennett, *Ultra and Mediterranean Strategy*, 1941-45, (London 1989), p. 362.
[71]FM Lord Alanbrooke, *Op. cit*, 3/B/XII, 29 June 1944, p. 971.
[72]W. Churchill, *The Second World War*, VI, (London, 1953), p. 58.

DRAGOON, at the tactical level, was a magnificent and well-timed operation

ANVIL's Metamorphosis

Planning for ANVIL had gone through many stages since its beginning on 19 December 1943, when AFHQ asked General George Patton's Seventh Army Headquarters planning staff to consider drawing up plans for an amphibious operation. During the last week of December, they were instructed to plan an operation codenamed ANVIL, which would involve American and French forces. The scale of the assault increased from three to ten divisions and required the acquisition of the port of Marseilles and the naval base at Toulon. On 12 January 1944, Force 163, the cover designation of General Garrison H. Davidson's US Seventh Army planners, which included representatives from the three services, took over from AFHQ. By 28 February, General Clark, relinquished his ANVIL responsibilities as Seventh Army Commander 'designate' to General Alexander Patch, a veteran of the Pacific 1942 Guadalcanal campaign. As the ANVIL debate raged at the higher levels, Force 163 planners, groping for something definite on which to plan, believed that the operation had been relegated to a 'command post exercise.' Was ANVIL to be abandoned, postponed, diminished or expanded? If an operation is scuttled, what is the purpose of planning for it? General Devers at AFHQ insisted that planning continue, and Patch asked him for a firm target date. In early spring, Force 163 planners, now based in Naples, were joined by French staff officers who shared their knowledge of the French Provencal coast and surrounding areas; French Resistance fighters, in support of the landings, added to the planner's supply of tactical information.[73]

On 29 April, ground, naval, and air plans were presented, modified, and accepted by Generals Wilson and Eisenhower, although the target remained indefinite. Under Patch, General Lucian Truscott would serve as 6th Corps Commander, consisting of the veteran 3rd, 45th, and 36th Infantry Divisions, the assaulting forces. Truscott had this to say: 'General Patch and Adm. Hewitt moved their headquarters to Naples. Afterwards our relations were very close, misunderstandings rare, and planning proceeded without any major difficulty. Any differences of opinion were always adjusted without rancor or reserve. Few operations of such magnitude have been planned more cooperatively or mounted more efficiently than ANVIL.'[74] On 15 March, French General De Gaulle visited Wilson in Naples, and after withdrawing his demands that a senior French general serve as ground commander, declared his full support for the operation. One month later, de Gaulle chose General Jean de Lattre de Tassigny, a difficult and opinionated officer, to command the French II Corps during the landings and eventually all of the First French Army. Air Corps General Gordon Saville of the XII Tactical Air Command was designated Air Task Force Commander and charged with all detailed air planning for the operation.[75]

Topography, Beaches, Enemy Defences, and Weather

The Cavalaire-Agay area was chosen as being the most favourable. It is in fighter range from Corsica with its fourteen airfields and supply depots; the sea approach was good and not heavily mined. The coastline is cut by some small streams and the River Argens; its valley is of great importance, because it is a natural exit from which to break out of the beachhead. This sector is less heavily defended than most landing places on the coast, the beaches were good, and three small ports offered shelter and good anchorages for shipping, which would provide a suitable base for the advance on Toulon and Marseilles. No roads of any importance run directly inland from any of the beaches, while the main railroad line runs from the Italian frontier, skirts the coast as far as St Raphael and follows the road through Frejus, Les Arcs, to Toulon, Marseilles, and up the Rhone Valley to Paris. Smaller gauge local lines run through the region.[76]

The Gunfire Plan

Admiral Hewitt's criticisms after the Salerno landing of the military insistence on the doctrine of tactical surprise with the corollary that there must be no bombardment of the enemy's position immediately before a landing, was changed. Hence plans were made for a heavy naval bombardment by about sixty warships to be carried out from dawn to H-Hour. The weight

[73]A. Wilt, *Op. cit.*, pp. 50-53.
[74]L. Truscott, *Command Missions*, (New York, 1954), p. 408.
[75]J. F. Turner & R. Jackson, *Destination Berchtesgaden*, (London, 1975), p. 33.
[76]'Invasion of the South of France,' Tactical and Staff Duties Division, Historical Section Naval Staff, (London, 1950), pp. 2-4.

of the bombardment was limited by the restricted quantity of heavy calibre ammunition. The principal targets were four heavy coastal defence batteries in the Toulon Marseilles, but light and field batteries were also included.[77]

Strategic Deception

From the concentrations that were apparent in the allied ports of the Western Mediterranean, the Germans knew that we would invade Southern France, but it was further believed that they did not know when or exactly where. Certain strategic deceptions were employed, such as troops were combat loaded from North Africa and sent to Italy, pre D-Day bombing was so coordinated with the entire theatre bombing campaign that no direct indication could be drawn. Many units in AFHQ, OSS (the Office of Strategic Services), and the US 8th Fleet, participated in the strategic deception. One such unit, the Beach Jumpers (BJ), was active in seaborne raids, special assault landings, and special operations.

The Hollywood actor, Douglas Fairbanks Jr., now a Lieutenant Commander USN was in tactical command of a BJ group of PT boats, Motor Torpedo Boats (MTBs), and a small flotilla of amphibious raiding craft. Before the DRAGOON landing took place, his unit made a feint towards Genoa to deceive the Germans. On a night mission, on D-1, he and his unit landed French Commandos west of Cannes. At dawn on the 15th, he

engaged two small enemy warships, which, with the help of an American destroyer, were sunk. The attacking convoys loaded with men and material were only an hour from debarkation.[78]

Enemy Forces

Opposing our assault forces was the German 19th Army under General Johannes von Blaskowitz, a holdover from the Old Prussian imperial army. The 19th had at one time a strength of thirteen divisions, but reinforcements had been sent to Normandy, and in late July only six undermanned infantry divisions and one armoured division remained. Early in August another infantry division and another armoured division were moving south as reinforcements, while other units in the assault area were considered to be of poor quality. The 242nd Infantry Division was stationed nearby, but three days after the assault, the enemy had the potential of concentrating another three to four infantry divisions and one armoured division in the field.[79]

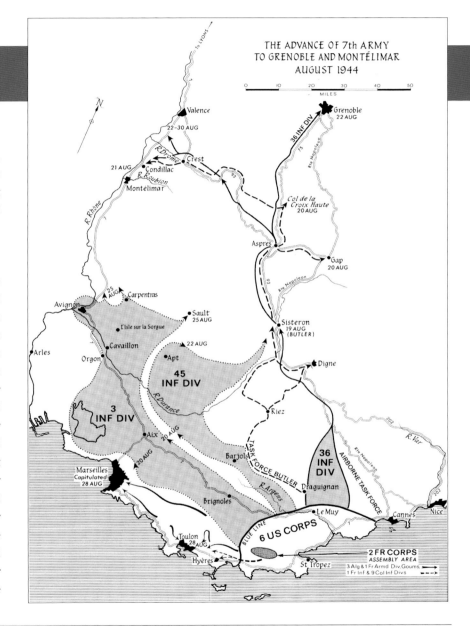

The advance of US 7th Army to Grenoble and Montelimar, August 1944. (NHB)

---

[77]*Ibid*, p. 4.
[78]D. Fairbanks, Jr. *One Hell of a War*, (New York, 1993), pp. 232-240.
[79]'Invasion of the South of France, *Op. cit.*, pp. 15-16.

The 'T Patch' of the 36th Infantry 'Texas' Division. (DoD)

Across the Alpha, Delta, and Camel beaches, naval attack forces were simultaneously to land the 3rd, 45th, and 36th US Infantry Divisions. The most difficult area for assault, the Frejus/St Raphael area, which shall be dealt with in detail later, was to be given the added support of 5,700 paratroopers of the 1st Airborne Task Force dropping inland on D-1 in the Le Muy area. The assault at 0800 on 15 August was to be preceded by the neutralising effort of 1,300 aircraft under XII Tactical Air Command and 53 gunfire support ships. Before H-Hour, commandos were to execute landings on either flank, and the 1st Special Service Force was to neutralise heavy enemy artillery batteries, a potential threat, on two offshore islands. A French armoured combat command was to follow the assault troops on D-Day over the Camel Beaches and push up the Argens Valley. French Army B, following the assault troops of the 3rd and 45th Divisions across their beaches, would spearhead the drive to Toulon and Marseilles.[80]

Training, Approach, Assault

Training on the Salerno beaches began with the suspension of twenty-four hour furlough passes and the completion of British Battle Drill exercises. Having been pulled off the line eight miles below Siena, the 36th Infantry Division, in which I served as a rifleman, began a series of amphibious training operations that included attacking from landing craft onto 'enemy-held' beaches. Two combat engineers demonstrated the use of plastic explosives against barbed wire entanglements and reinforced concrete pillboxes. After a day of practical exercises with Bangalore torpedoes, one soldier who witnessed the display, held a dynamite cap filled with fulminate of mercury in his hand while taking a shower. Sensitive to body heat, the cap exploded and blew his hand off. The next day, conducting another class, the two engineers, lacking basic teaching skills and arrogant in manner, were killed while demonstrating explosives to another group of soldiers.

Coupled with specialised amphibious training, our schedule included 25-mile hikes, the usual close order drill and calisthenics, bayonet drill and rifle practice, and map reading. For the next three weeks, during night and day exercises, some lasting up to 48 hours, we trained in every type of landing craft. Sizes varied, speed was essential. Sea smells mixed with diesel fumes; below decks on the larger craft, the air was humid and still, and the drone of generators merged with the sounds of pounding turbines; blue engine exhaust dissipated on the sea breeze. LSTs (Landing Ship Tank) loomed as large as Channel ferries and LCVPs (Landing Craft Vehicle & Personnel) looked as small as harbour powerboats. Streams of armed men went over the sides of the LSTs, and facing inward, feeling their way down hemp cargo nets, searched tentatively for footing onto the LCVPs below. Even in a smooth sea, the boats rocked and bumped against each other, widening and lessening the gap between. Men that easily misjudged the height and distance, particularly at night, were locked in a wet, dangerous, and shifting world. The possibility of breaking a leg or being crushed was a major concern, but once we were aboard, the navy coxswain and his full complement of human cargo joined a circle of identical craft milling about. Signals were exchanged, and on command, the boats peeled off and increased speed, formed a line abreast, and headed for shore from eight miles out. Fifteen or more landing craft were timed to hit the beach together. They never did.

Our training destinations and times aboard ship varied; sometimes we practiced in the Gulf of Salerno, or sailed north of Naples into the Gulf of Gaeta, each time attacking an 'Enemy-held' beach strewn with a variety of beach obstacles interlaced with concrete gun emplacements. Only enemy mine fields were missing. All units of the division, much like the 3rd and 45th, participated in these realistic 'dry run' exercises that included naval and air support, simulating the conditions to be met later. Live ammunition, phosphorous shells, and naval gunfire, the laying of smokes screens, and multiple rockets firing from landing craft contributed to wartime reality.

As a consequence of our non-synchronous landings, those rifle companies arriving late on the beach were fully exposed to adjacent companies arriving on schedule. Bangalores, long slender metal pipes filled with dynamite and bursting 'Bee Hives', satchel charges containing 30 pounds of explosive, blew up with resounding force. Jagged bits of barbed wire and shards

[80]*Riviera to the Rhine*, J. J. Clarke & R. R. Smith, (Washington, 1993), pp. 76-81.

'C' Company of the 143rd Infantry RCT (part of the 36th Infantry Division) boarding an LCI(L) on 13 August, 1944 at Puzzoli, Italy to make for the South of France for Operation ANVIL-DRAGOON. The author of this Chapter is walking up the right hand gangway. (SW)

of concrete zinged through the air, adding to the danger and confusion at the water's edge. As we lay bunched up on the wet sand, our legs half in and half out of the surf, a colonel observer, kept shouting, 'You will never get off the beach alive! This is an absolute disaster!' We knew we needed more training, but time was running out, and the deadline loomed. It was the unforgiving moment all over again. As General Vasily Chuikov, Commander of the 62nd Russian Army, remarked at Stalingrad in 1942, 'Time is blood.' Exiting from the beach behind schedule, we worked our way inland, climbing, it seemed forever over the coastal range to find a railroad line in the inland valley below. Like beasts of burden, we found the work exhausting and unrewarding, but we were tough and in excellent physical shape.

Unlike the G. I. who vomited from simply inhaling a boat's diesel fumes, I was never sick throughout my time at sea, regardless of the conditions, hour, or type of craft. Eventually, my Company was assigned to an American built LCI (Landing Craft Infantry); it was 158 feet long, fitted with external ramps, one on each side of the hull that could be lowered into the surf for unloading. A veteran British naval crew who had participated in every assault landing in the Mediterranean manned it. Theirs had been a long war. Every time the skipper tried to run his boat onto the beach, we were dropped into water above our waists. 'Don't worry mate,' one of the crew said, 'when we do this for real, you won't even get your feet wet.' The rest of the crew nodded in agreement.

In early August, our commanding officer told us we were going to invade Southern France, as part of an operation called DRAGOON. The beaches we'd practiced on were similar to the beaches we were headed for. One afternoon, we were introduced to the paratroopers of the British 2nd Independent Parachute Brigade, wearing their distinctive red berets and battle smocks, assigned to drop inland on D-1, along with American paratroopers of the 509th, 517th, and 551st. We familiarised ourselves with each other's uniforms, weapons, and equipment in order to prevent 'friendly fire' casualties during the planned link-up once the beachhead extended to a geographical objective, the imaginary Blue line.

Separate from the chaos during the previous training, I felt distracted by the lack of teamwork. The required minimum of small group cohesion within my squad seemed difficult to attain for a variety of reasons, one being the infusion of replacements; another was the commanding officer's lack of leadership, and our squad leader's desire to transfer to the paras.

Pozzuoli, a small fishing village west of Naples was our port of embarkation. The village, until now overlooked by the enemy, was transformed by our arrival. Thousands of soldiers, weighted down by the accoutrements of war, filed into its harbour where a score of landing craft rode at anchor. Fourteen years later, while working for CBS network television in Los Angeles, I met Sophia Loren, the international movie star, who told me that she had been born there, and as a little girl, remembered our arrival and departure.

I watched in awe as its black 2,000-pound projectiles sailed through the air effortlessly

On 12 August, our British LCI weighed anchor with the Company on board and slowly motored out of the harbour to take up station with hundreds of other ships steaming away from the Italian coast. Everywhere LSTs and LCIs, like armoured metal strands, plowed through the gentle swells. Navigating through the Strait of Bonifacio, between the mountainous headlands of Sardinia and Corsica, our flotilla anchored off Ajaccio on Corsica's west coast. From two miles off shore, on a bright summer's morning that accentuated the red-tiled roofs of the town against the azure blue sky, our LCI rolled gently on the swell. Founded by the Genoese in 1492, remembered as Napoleon's birthplace, Ajaccio nestled against the broom covered hills and the steep mountains beyond. Some of us leapt from the deck into the clear blue water twenty feet below. Swimming and cavorting in the bay, as playful as dolphins, it was difficult to believe that over the horizon, a war was raging. We emerged from the sea, climbing hand over hand to the deck above, our wet bodies glistening in the sun, the interlude over. It was great to be alive!

Relaxation gave way to a persistent ache in my stomach, evoking thoughts of the invasion, as we steamed towards the invasion coast. I turned to a few of my friends and asked, 'Will we survive?' 'Who knows.' What will the opposition be like?' Could be severe, if the fighting in Italy is any guide!' 'Will we get off the beach on time?' 'Not likely, if our rehearsals mean anything.' The answers to these questions were only hours away, but the waiting seemed interminable, and while pacing the deck, the

tightness in my stomach increased. It never dawned on me to write a 'last letter' home, nor did I carry a lucky charm to ward off personal destruction; survival could not be personally guaranteed.

The supply sergeant passed out American flag arm bands, a booklet entitled, 'A Pocket Guide to France,' small boxed rations for five days, and two packs of Lucky Strikes. Weighing anchor off Corsica on the 14th, we took up station with other ships of the invasion fleet. It was one of the few times I stood in awe of America's military power. Looking in any direction, I saw warships of every description, from battleships to attack transports. These ships and the convoys they protected, a total of eight hundred, had come from a number of Mediterranean ports such as Oran, Taranto, and Naples. 1,200 landing craft were deck-loaded on the transports, sharing space with the men of the American VI Corps (three divisions) and the French II Corps (four divisions).

Early the next morning, everything was grey, the ships, the sea, the sky. Visibility was four miles, hazy and improving, with a gentle shifting wind and negligible sea. We slithered through a swarm of cargo ships standing perpendicular to the French coast, noting our passage, waiting for us to secure the beaches before they move closer in shore. We weaved between cruisers and destroyers firing their 8 and 5 inch guns in support at the unseen enemy on shore. The American battleship, *Arkansas*, hammered targets beyond the beaches, with its complement

of 14-inch guns. Each time the guns fired a massive yellow-red muzzle flash and shattering explosion followed. The *Arkansas*, displacing a massive 27,000 tons, reacted as if it were stung, wallowing and rocking from the combined recoil, and slapping the sea before righting itself. I watched in awe as its black 2,000-pound projectiles sailed through the air effortlessly. The *Texas* and other warships were giving the other beaches an hour's pounding, the crack of their guns adding to the existing dissonance. The armada of eight hundred ships waited.

Large formations of allied fighter aircraft patrolled the skies above against the Luftwaffe, while twin engine medium and four engine heavy bombers flew missions further inland. Air superiority was achieved. Just before we hit the beach, specially equipped landing craft streaked in front of our flotilla and blasted enemy emplacements with masses of rockets, their trajectory at speed created a high-pitched swooshing sound on take-off. The sounds were deafening, a cacophony of banging frying pans and ripping paper; the neutral grey sky was a backdrop for yellow-red explosions and black spiraling smoke trails. Cordite stung my nostrils. Exploding enemy shells sent geysers of seawater skyward. Hidden German machine gunners fired in spurts from the bluffs above the beach, their Mg. 34s generating immense firepower.

Our landing craft picked up speed, and we jolted across Gulf of Frejus toward the beach. The LCI's hull grated on the stony shore at Dramont; between St Raphael and Agay at 0945, the crew moved quickly and lowered the ramps. We trotted along their length, and in clusters hit the stony shore. The crew had kept its promise, and none of us got our feet wet! Enemy machine gun fire slowed. Our beach was in a small cove surrounded by rust coloured hills and covered with pine. A coast road and railroad line ran parallel to each other on the high ground about two hundred yards beyond us. German opposition, after the opening stages of the battle became sporadic and isolated.

Although a First Scout in a rifle squad, I had landed carrying a flame-thrower, a weapon which sprayed a long stream of burning oil at a temperature of 2,000 degrees F., having volunteered to haul it for another G. I. whose newly discovered back pain had become progressively worse, as we approached the French coast. Both he and I knew the potential danger inherent in flame-throwers: if a bullet or shell fragment penetrated the tank and ignited the highly flammable petroleum jelly (Napalm) made from naphthalene and coconut oil within, I would be converted into an unrecognisable part of the beach, rather than an active participant of Camel Force. Although I didn't qualify, the most hated man in an outfit was usually assigned this dangerous instrument. 'Bad Back', his knowing smile and informative shrug, soon after, confirmed my suspicions, but before I could square the account, the company commander sent him home for being underage.

German JU-88 twin-engine light bombers hit LST 282 with radio-controlled bombs in a daylight raid on the first day of the landing. I watched as the ship's super structure disappear in a tremendous explosive flash that killed and wounded forty sailors. LST 282 burned for hours, a pall of black smoke hovered above it, and from its interior, ammunition popped and crackled all day. Soon after, above the beach, standing beside the open turret of a Sherman medium tank, we listened to fragments of a Bing Crosby-Bob Hope radio show on its receiver. The tankers were arrogant, having little time for the infantry. Revving its engines, the driver sped away leaving us choking in a cloud of dust beside the road, and suddenly crashed seconds later seventy-five yards further along. We raced to help. The driver had lost control, causing the tank to tip over at an extreme angle with one track rotating slowly in the air; some of the crew were injured, we administered first aid, but we felt the tankers had it coming.

On the coast road, an overzealous artillery truck driver had overturned his 105mm howitzer, causing a traffic jam that stretched all the way back to the beach, and delayed the movement of heavily laden motorised transport and tanks coming off the LSTs in increasing numbers. Our regiment travelled west and captured the beach resort of St Raphael against little enemy resistance. During a momentary lull, my squad relaxed next to an empty pillbox beside a bridge, only minutes away from the town's famous seaside villas, visible in the middle distance. I was taking a sip of water from my canteen, when an enemy shell came in and exploded against the pillbox. The explosion tore the reinforced concrete apart, and almost sheared off a soldier's leg. The dust hadn't settled when he disappeared on a stretcher underneath a pile of olive-drab blankets, hustled away by two company medics. A third performed a balancing act by holding a bottle of plasma above the pile, its hollow line attached to the wounded G.I.s exposed arm. At eighteen, the squad member's war ended abruptly, and shaken by the loss, with one man short, we gathered our gear and moved out. His leg was amputated soon after at the aid station.

Skirting the beach, we captured the local airfield overlooking the sea in a firefight and cut the east-west railroad line that ran across a viaduct. Planes caught on the ground were destroyed, and rifle fire set others alight. We ran into sporadic resistance and took some prisoners who knew, 'For you the war is over.' They were dispirited and confused, as they shuffled to the rear, some without tunics, their suspenders showing, some with their arms in the air, others with their hands clasped behind their heads, submissive, compliant. One young German soldier smiled at me in relief. How different were they from the Afrika Corps prisoners I had guarded as a raw recruit in 1943 at Camp Blanding, Florida, an arrogant lot believing that Nazi domination was only months away.

Beyond the airfield, we attacked through Frejus, causing little damage to this former Roman town, and moved into the dry Provencal hills beyond. There were some small firefights in which we surprised the enemy, but in one melee, we received word that our squad's rocket launcher 'bazooka' team was

1st Airborne Task Force which landed at Le Muy during Operation DRAGOON. (DoD)

trapped in a gully. I volunteered to help, but others were chosen. The rescue attempt failed, and we never saw the bazooka team again. Rumour had it that they were either captured or killed. Beyond the beachhead, moving north in an armoured convoy, Grenoble, the alpine town at the end of the Napoleon Highway, beckoned. Wilson cabled his superiors in London,

> 'Secret Operation DRAGOON - slight opposition only encountered by 36th Division landing on beaches either side of Agay road. Isle port Cros captured. Pre-assault naval gunfire bombardment reported very effective and very little naval gunfire was required later. After the airborne landings, the assaulting infantry cracked the beach defences and no allied aircraft was reported lost. No air enemy attacks up to noon. Two small enemy ships sunk during initial assault.'[81]

Conclusion

The British knew from the successful allied May offensive in Italy and from current ULTRA intercepts, in mid 1944, that the German army could be destroyed north of Rome. Therefore, they insisted on a continuation of their Mediterranean strategy, as long as the seven divisions and seventy percent of the air force there was not lost to the Southern France operation. The Americans, now the dominant partner, refused on logistical and political grounds, certainly not strategic, leaving the British no choice but to reluctantly agree.

DRAGOON, at the tactical level, was a magnificent and well-timed operation. The assault infantry divisions landed against light opposition and were followed ashore by reserve elements of the Seventh and First French Army. In little more than a month 380,000 troops crossed the beaches. Movement was swift. French forces took Toulon in 11 days instead of the predicted 20; Marseilles fell in 13 days rather than 45, even though Hitler designated both seaports as fortresses, to be defended at all costs. Seventh Army's Task Force Butler and elements of the 36th 'Texas' Division drove 190 miles in two days to liberate Grenoble on the 22nd.[82] Eisenhower wrote to Marshall in late summer, 'Every day I thank my stars that I held out for ANVIL in the face of almost overwhelming pressure.'[83] The retreating German 19th Army was battered and almost trapped by the three American divisions at Montelimar. The landing, the liberation of Southern France, the advance northward astride the Rhone Valley ended in the capture of 79,000 enemy troops and the destruction of large amounts of equipment. On 12 September, Seventh Army patrols made contact with General George C. Patton's Third Army near Dijon, thereby sealing the fate of thousands more of the enemy, and on the 15th, Eisenhower assumed operational control under Dever's newly constituted 6th Army Group which comprised the 7th American Army and the 1st French.

In less than one month, and not the three that Churchill had gloomily predicted, these two armies had surged northward 400 miles from their Mediterranean landing sites. Their lines of communication at the end of the first 45 days were twice as long as the operational planners had estimated for DRAGOON. Considered by Liddell Hart as the operation that went according to plan but not according to timetable, ANVIL-DRAGOON came ten weeks too late to help OVERLORD. Eisenhower claimed in his book, 'Crusade in Europe,' that, 'There was no development of that period which added decisively to our advantages or aided us more in accomplishing the final and complete defeat of the German forces than did this secondary attack coming up the Rhone Valley.' This post war view does not support American military doctrine of the time, that of inflicting a massive defeat upon the German Army. Those left behind to face the DRAGOON forces were incapable of defending against them.

Thus the operation's professed objective, to keep the 19th German Army occupied in the South of France and away from OVERLORD failed. Moreover, DRAGOON's two armies were given the role of protecting Eisenhower's southern flank in late August, when allied air power, having functioned in this role since the Normandy breakout, could have continued to do so. On 17 August, ULTRA intercepts revealed that Hitler's response to DRAGOON was not reinforcement but evacuation; ULTRA had unmistakably indicated that a Southern France invasion would

[81]S. Weiss, *Allies in Conflict,* (London, 1996), p. 158.
[82]J. Clarke & R. Smith, *Op. cit.* pp. 80, 142.
[83]J. P. Hobbs, ed. *Dear General: Eisenhower's Wartime Letters to General Marshall,* (Baltimore, 1971), p. 203.

The Assault areas of Operation DRAGOON on 15 August 1944. (NHB)

accomplish no more than threatening to do so.[84] A threat no longer, DRAGOON sounded the alarm for the 19th to begin a hasty but well coordinated retreat northward. Dragoon's timing served and benefited the 19th, whose retreat coincided with German forces retreating headlong from Normandy. In September both enemy remnants successfully organised a strong line of defence along the Franco-German border. If DRAGOON simply posed as a threat, the enemy would have stood fast in Provence-and would have been cut off by the advancing OVERLORD forces advancing eastward.[85] Instead, DRAGOON was part of Eisenhower's 'broad - front policy', a reflection of the US Army's preference for moving directly forward behind overwhelming fire-power supported by massive productive resources, rather than by feint, exploitation, and manoeuvre.[86] Politically, the newly created French Army under De Tassigny, whose participation in the operation inspired the French people to participate in their liberation, overshadowed DRAGOON'S strategic shortcomings.[87]

Any soldier who is prepared to leap onto a hostile and defended shore from a tossing landing craft under fire, not knowing the extent and depth of the enemy defences or the level of its fighting power is a hero. Whether it was attacking in Normandy, the Pacific islands, or the beaches rimming the Mediterranean, martyrdom is not a measurement for bravery, but the willingness to do so, regardless of the consequences, is.

[84]R. Bennett, *Op. cit.*, pp.297-299.
[85]W, Deakin et al, *Op. cit.*, p. 9.
[86]Maj. G. Higgins, 'German and US Operation Art: A Contrast in Maneuver,' *Military Review*, (Oct. 1985), pp. 22-29.
[87]Interview with French General F. Binoche, Nice, Aug. 1995.

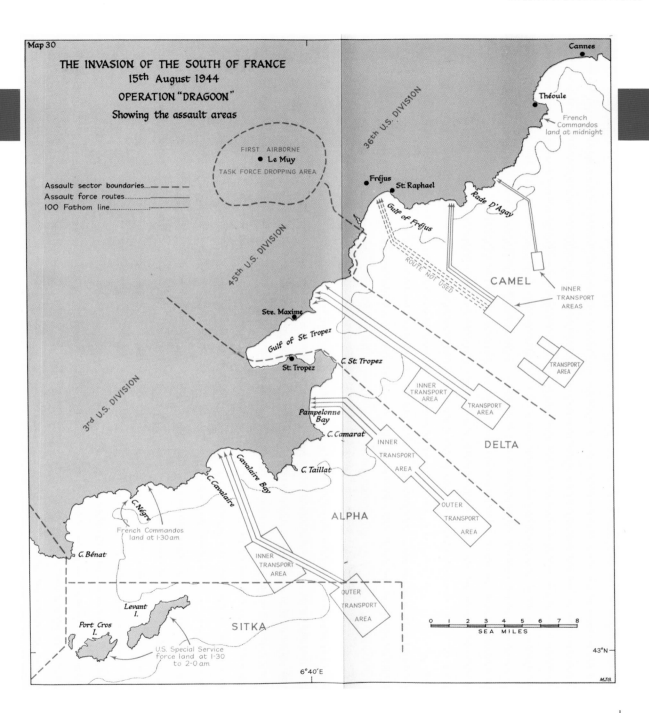

Further Reading

A Pictorial History of the 36th 'Texas' Infantry Division, (Austin: 1946)

Adelman, R. H. & Walton, G., *The Champagne Campaign*, (Boston: 1969)

Bourderon, R., *Libération du Languedoc Mediterranean*, (Paris: 1974)

Cherpak, E. M., (ed.), *The Memoirs of Admiral H. Kent Hewitt*, (R. I., 2004)

Clarke, J. & Smith, R., *Riviera to the Rhine*, (Washington: 1993)

Ducros, *Montagnes Ardéchoises dans la Guerre III*, (Valence: 1981)

Funk, A. L., *Hidden Ally*, (New York: 1992)

Howard, M., *The Mediterranean Strategy in the Second World War*, (New York: 1968)

Leslie, P., *The Liberation of the Riviera*, (New York: 1980)

Lockhart, V. M., *T-Patch to Victory*, (Texas: 1981)

Morison, S. M. E., *The Invasion of France and Germany 1944-1945*, (Oxford: 1957)

Robichon, J., *The Second D-Day*, (New York:1969)

Truscott, L., *Command Missions*, (New York: 1954)

Weiss, S. J., *Allies in Conflict*, (London, 1996)

Wilt, A. J., *The French Riviera Campaign of August, 1944*, (IL: 1981)

Biography

Steve Weiss is a Senior Visiting Research Fellow in the Department of War Studies at Kings College London, after being awarded his Masters and PhD in the same subject. Earlier, he was granted a Masters in Clinical Psychology from Goddard College in Vermont. In 1998, in combination with the University of Maryland and the US Army, he taught soldier-students based in Hungary. He is the author of *Allies in Conflict, Anglo-American Strategic Negotiations, 1938-1944,* (Macmillan Press, 1996), and a contributor to *'La Résistance et Les Français*, (Rennes, 1994) and *Time to Kill*, (Pimlico, 1997). He has contributed to the Imperial War Museum Oral History Programme, and provided a written story of some of his combat encounters to the D-day Museum, New Orleans, LA. He is the recipient of the French Legion of Honor, two Croix de Guerre, the French Resistance Medal, the American Bronze Star, the Combat Infantry Badge and three battle stars, and one arrow head for the ANVIL-DRAGOON assault landing. The towns of St Raphael, Valence and Grenoble have bestowed upon him the title of Citoyen d'Honneur. He has three grown children and eight grand children; he resides in London when not conducting battlefield tours.

The Invasion of Peleliu
Operation STALEMATE, September 1944
What Was Nimitz Thinking?

By Colonel Joseph H. Alexander USMC (Rtd)

Few World War II veterans on the 1st Marine Division and the Army's 81st Division ever made sense of the awful sacrifices it cost to wrest Peleliu from a stubborn foe entrenched in the badlands of the Umurbrogol, a moonscape known as 'Bloody Nose Ridge.' Many survivors consider Peleliu's worst legacy to be that their fleet commander, Admiral William F. Halsey, Jr., had recommended cancelling the landing at the last moment – only to have the suggestion rejected by Admiral Chester W. Nimitz, commanding the Pacific Fleet and the Pacific Ocean Areas (CinCPac/CinCPOA). Nimitz has since been excoriated for this decision. 'CinCPac here made one of his rare mistakes,' observed Samuel Eliot Morison in 1963. Three decades later, a naval historian Nathan Miller described the event as 'Nimitz's major mistake of the war.'[1]

Yet Nimitz made few rash decisions in 44 months as CinCPac/CinCPOA. He picked discerning staff officers, sought the advice of tactical commanders, and hearkened to his outspoken boss, Admiral Ernest J. King, Commander-in-Chief, U.S. Fleet (CominCh), and Chief of Naval Operations. How did Nimitz reach his decision about Peleliu, and upon what information did he base his judgement? The 72-hour period during 12 to 15 September 1944, essentially the three days leading to D-Day at Peleliu, was a time of significant westward movement by U.S.

forces. As one attack force converged on Peleliu and Angaur in the southern Palaus, another embarked in Hawaii for Yap and Ulithi in the Western Carolines, the second phase of Operation STALEMATE, and yet a third amphibious unit advanced on Morotai in the Moluccas. Complex as they were, each operation had the principal objective of paving the way for even larger campaigns soon to follow – MacArthur's return to the Philippines (see Chapter XXX), Nimitz's conquest of Formosa or (as some planners were beginning to suggest) Iwo Jima and Okinawa (see Chapter XXXI).

The key players were scattered widely. King and the other Joint Chiefs of Staff (JCS) were engaged in the Octagon Conference in Quebec with their British counterparts and Sir Winston Churchill. Nimitz held forth in his headquarters in Pearl Harbor. General Douglas MacArthur, counterpart to Nimitz as commander-in-chief of the Southwest Pacific Area (CinCSowesPac), sailed with the Morotai invasion force. And Halsey, less than three weeks in command of his newly designated Third Fleet, strode the flag bridge of the USS New Jersey (BB-62) in the throes of indecision.

Halsey had just arrived in the Philippine Sea, linking up with Vice Admiral Marc A. Mitscher, commanding the fleet's principal striking element, Task Force 38. Mitscher reported the results of air raids conducted by his fast carriers throughout Mindanao,

scheduled to be MacArthur's first major objective in the islands in late fall, following Peleliu and Morotai. Mitscher told Halsey the lack of Japanese opposition had rendered the mission useless.[2]

Mitscher's report surprised Halsey. He had assembled the Third Fleet in the Philippine Sea to cover Nimitz's two STALEMATE task forces and begin setting the stage for MacArthur's Mindanao landing. Halsey expected a hard fight for air supremacy throughout the Philippines. Perhaps Mindanao had been a fluke. But Mitscher then launched 2,400 sorties against the central Philippines during 12 to 13 September with similar results – scant opposition and little evidence of front-line enemy air units.

At that point, Halsey's forces extracted a downed U.S. aviator from Leyte. In an interview with Halsey, the pilot said that the natives who had rescued him told him that the Japanese were not in Leyte in force. The island was ripe for invasion.

Halsey knew the 11th hour had come for Operation STALEMATE. He also knew the complex campaign had already gathered its own momentum under Vice Admiral Theodore S. Wilkinson, Commanding Task Force 31, with its joint-service III Amphibious Corps destined to hit Peleliu on 15 September and its U.S. Army XXIV Corps slated to seize Yap and Ulithi on 3 October.

[1] Samuel Eliot Morison, The Two-Ocean War (Boston: Little, Brow, 1963), 425; Nathan Miller, War at Sea: A Naval History of World War II (New York: Scribners, 1995), 456.
[2] E.B. Potter, Bull Halsey (Annapolis: Naval Institute Press, 1985), 276.

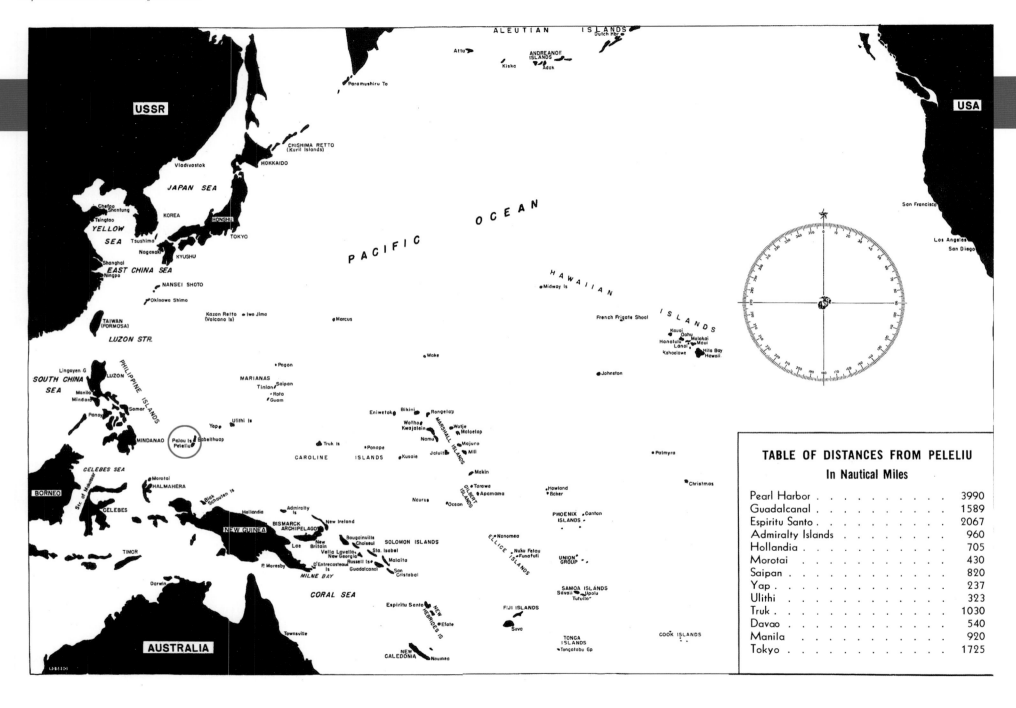

TABLE OF DISTANCES FROM PELELIU
In Nautical Miles

Pearl Harbor	3990
Guadalcanal	1589
Espiritu Santo	2067
Admiralty Islands	960
Hollandia	705
Morotai	430
Saipan	820
Yap	237
Ulithi	323
Truk	1030
Davao	540
Manila	920
Tokyo	1725

Halsey sought the advice of his chief of staff, Rear Admiral Robert B. ('Mick') Carney, and his newly appointed chief of staff for fleet administration, Commander Harold E. Stassen, the former three-term governor of Minnesota. As Stassen recalled the debate: 'Halsey was sobered by the significance of what he was recommending. We had our marching orders, now we were asking the Joint Chiefs to change their script.'[3]

In June, Halsey had gone out on a limb by expressing his personal belief to the JCS that any amphibious campaign against Peleliu, Angaur, Babelthaup, or Yap (the STALEMATE objectives) would be prohibitively costly, contribute little to MacArthur's return to the Philippines, and constitute an unnecessary detour on the road to Tokyo. Neither Nimitz nor King supported Halsey's view, and STALEMATE kept its destiny. Halsey knew Nimitz and King would suspect him of trying to reopen that issue at this late date.[4]

'The clincher was the report of the rescued aviator,' said Stassen. Halsey concluded that if Leyte was indeed ripe for invasion, then the Mindanao campaign was superfluous and therefore the pending seizure of the heavily defended Palaus no longer essential. Halsey then authorized Stassen to release two Top Secret messages.[5]

Halsey's first message (COM3RDFLT 130230Sep44) went to Nimitz, MacArthur, and King. 'Downed carrier pilot rescued from Leyte informed by natives no Nips on Leyte.' Halsey reported, adding 'Planes report no military installations except bare strips on Leyte.'[6]

Halsey used the first message to set the stage for the real bombshell (COM3RDFLT 130300) to Nimitz, King, and MacArthur. 'Am firmly convinced Palau not now needed to support occupation of Philippines,' wrote Halsey. 'Western Carolines not essential to our operations (except Ulithi) …. Believe that Leyte fleet base can be seized immediately and cheaply without any intermediate operations. … Suggest that Task Force 31 could be made available by CinCSowesPac if STALEMATE II cancelled.'[7]

This was heady stuff. Cancel STALEMATE entirely, except the seizure of lightly defended Ulithi Atoll, scratch Mindanao, move the Leyte campaign to front burner – in effect, accelerating the entire Pacific campaign plan by months – and offer Wilkinson's III Amphibious Force (a Nimitz asset) to MacArthur for the Leyte job. Interestingly, Halsey never used his oft-quoted prophesy about Peleliu – 'I fear another Tarawa' – in any of these pre-D-Day messages. Those were post war words.

The date was still 12 September in Pearl Harbor when Nimitz received Halsey's messages. His reaction remains lost to history. His flag lieutenant, H. Arthur ('Hal') Lamar, recalled no flashes of stormy impatience, as Nimitz rousted his key advisors for a council of war. He knew time was short.[8]

---

[3]Author interview with Mr. Harold E. Stassen, 31 March 1998.
[4]Potter, Bull Halsey, 272-73.
[5]Stassen interview, 1998.
[6]COM3RDFLT 130230Sep44 to CINCPOA, CINCSOWESPAC, and COMINCH, copy contained in CINCPAC Graybook Summary, Bookfive, 1Jan-31 Dec 44, p. 2353, Operational Archives, Naval Historical Center, Washington [hereafter 'Graybook Summary'].
[7]COM3RDFLT 130300Sep44 to CINCPOA, Graybook Summary, 2353.
[8]Author interview with Cdr H. Arthur Lamar, USNR, 26 February 1996.

As commander of a million-man force, Nimitz proved to be an exceptional judge of the character and potential of his principal lieutenants. By picking such resourceful tactical commanders as Raymond Spruance, Halsey, Mitscher, Kelly Turner, Holland Smith, and Roy Geiger, Nimitz could afford to keep his eye on the big picture. In time he became an accomplished strategist. A partial-insomniac, he converted his sleepless hours after 0300 into careful study of his charts of the Western Pacific.[9]

Halsey's message required Nimitz to face two chief issues. Operation STALEMATE took top priority because of its immediacy, but the bigger strategic issue was the accelerated invasion schedule for the Philippines. Nimitz had the authority to decide the fate of STALEMATE – re-shuffling the Philippines sequence would require MacArthur's considered input and a JCS resolution.

STALEMATE, especially the first-phase assault on Peleliu, needed an immediate resolution. It was not simply a matter of turning around the troop transports. Rear Admiral George H. Fort, commanding the Western Attack Force, already had committed shore-bombardment ships, dive-bombers, minesweepers, and underwater demolition teams to the battle. Frogmen were in the shallows, shoreward of the reef, attaching explosives to moored mines and antiboat obstacles.

Nimitz rendered his decision to Halsey in three terse sentences (CINCPAC 130747Sep44 to COM3RDFLT, info King and MacArthur): 'Carry out first phase of Stalemate as planned. Am considering eliminating occupation of Yap… In any event will occupy Ulithi as planned…' Minutes later Nimitz sent a message to MacArthur (CINCPOA 130813 to CINCSWPA, info King and Halsey) advising that 'if occupation of Yap is eliminated, 24th Corps, including 7th, 77th and 96th Divisions… would be potentially available to exploit favourable developments in the Philippines. Your view on this and COM3RDFLT's 130300 requested.'[10]

With MacArthur en route to Morotai under radio silence, his chief of staff, General Richard K. Sutherland, quickly mustered

his advisors in Hollandia, New Guinea, eager to project the views of the Southwest Pacific Area into the debate. Meanwhile, watch officers in the Pentagon forwarded each of the messages from Halsey and Nimitz to Quebec for delivery to King.

Halsey had foreseen the flurry of top-level activity. His recommendations, he admitted later, 'in addition to being none of my business, would upset a great many apple carts, possibly all the way up to Mr. Roosevelt and Mr. Churchill.'[11]

The Joint Chiefs made no specific mention of Peleliu, but picked up quickly on Halsey's other proposal to cancel Yap and use those sizable forces to augment an accelerated invasion of Leyte. 'Highly to be desired,' they signalled to MacArthur on 13 September. Sutherland soon responded in MacArthur's name, first dispensing with Halsey's intelligence coup – 'report by rescued carrier pilot incorrect according to mass of current evidence' – but concurring with the cancellation of Yap and Mindanao. Sutherland's rambling discourse in his name was likely too much for MacArthur, who broke radio silence one day later with a cryptic message in his emphatic style: 'I am prepared to move immediately to execution of K2 [Leyte] with target date October 20th.'[12]

---

[9] E.B. Potter, Nimitz (Annapolis: Naval Institute Press, 1976), 315.

[10] CINCPAC 130747Sep44 to COM3RDFLT, and CINCPOA 130813Sep44 to CINCSWPA, both messages Graybook Summary, 2353.

[11] Potter, Bull Halsey, 277.

[12] JCS to MacArthur, info Nimitz, Halsey, 'Octagon 24,' 13Sep44, resubmitted as COMINCH to CINCPOA 141325Sep44, Graybook Summary, 2356. See also Grace P. Hayes, The History of the Joint Chiefs of Staff in World War II: The War Against Japan (Annapolis: Naval Institute Press, 1982), 620-21 [hereafter Hays, JCS: The War Against Japan]. GHQ, SWPA, MacArthur [actually Sutherland] to JCS, CINCPOA, info COM3RDFLT, CX 17697, 13Sep44, listed under DTG 140316 in Graybook Summary 2354-55. MacArthur to JCS, C17744, 15Sep44 [local], listed under DTG 142359 in Graybook Summary, 2356.

Assault waves approaching Peleliu's smoke-covered beaches. (USMC)

Peleliu landings and subsequent operations. (USMC)

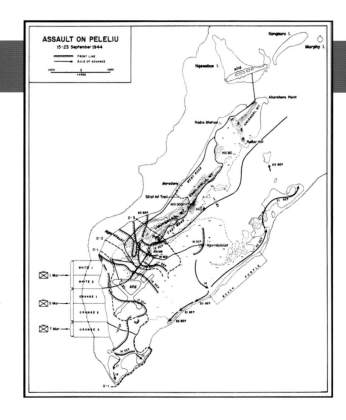

MacArthur's message was dramatic enough for aides to break the Joint Chiefs away from a formal dinner in Quebec the night of the 14th. In 90 minutes the two admirals and two generals agreed. Their enabling message to Nimitz and MacArthur, 'Octagon 31-A,' compressed the Pacific War strategy by two full months – a nice evening's work.[13]

But Peleliu remained on the boards. The JCS may have purged Operation STALEMATE of its mission to Yap, but the requirement for forcible seizure of the southern Palaus did not change. Indeed, at the same time the Joint Chiefs disrupted their dinner in Quebec, the assault elements of the 1st Marine Division were just crossing the line of departure at Peleliu, discovering to their horror that an abbreviated naval gunfire bombardment hardly had dented Japan's vicious matrix of anti-invasion weaponry.

So, what did Nimitz know about Peleliu? Why cancel a two-division assault on Yap and retain a similar-sized assault on Peleliu and Angaur? One set of clues may exist in a pair of messages released by Nimitz on 13 September during the lull between his early-morning signals to Halsey and MacArthur and his receipt of the first JCS response. Nimitz took the time to share with Halsey a bit more of the theatre commander's perspective on the Palaus. The purpose for seizing Peleliu, Angaur, and Ulithi, he wrote, 'include[s] not only support of occupation of Philippines, but also completion of neutralisation of highway and support of advances into Formosa-Luzon-China coast area and operations against objectives to northward.' Nimitz then sent a personal message to King, stating 'The occupation of Palau and Ulithi are of course essential and it would not be feasible to re-orientate the plans for the employment of the Palau attack and occupation forces as rapidly as Halsey's 130230 appears to visualize.'

Nimitz added a zinger. If MacArthur hesitated to employ the proffered 24th Corps, 'it may be possible to take Iwo Jima in mid-October using the Yap force.' The Eastern Task Force then loading in Hawaii was huge- more than 100 amphibious ships, escorted by 21 destroyers, a 50,000-man landing force. Coupled with the fast carriers of Mitscher's Task Force 38, 'the Yap Force' may well have succeeded in taking Iwo Jima four months ahead of schedule. But King did not bite, MacArthur quickly claimed the Yap force, and Iwo Jima would have to wait its bloody turn.[14]

Historians have often assumed that Nimitz retained Peleliu because of his personal assurance to MacArthur, in the presence of President Franklin D. Roosevelt at the Pearl Harbor 'Summit' of 26 July 1944, that he would seize the island on 15 September to coincide with MacArthur's capture of Morotai, thus facilitating the westward passage of the Philippines invasion force. Yet Operation STALEMATE had taken its final wrinkle, including reaffirmation of D-Day, weeks earlier. That Nimitz intended to land on Peleliu on 15 September should have been nothing new either to MacArthur or Roosevelt at Pearl.[15]

---

[13]JCS 150258Sep44 to Nimitz, MacArthur, info Halsey, 'Octagon 31-A,', Graybook Summary, 2357. See also Potter, Nimitz, 323.
[14]CINCPOA 132100Sep44 to COM3RDFLT. Graybook Summary, 2356. CINCPOA 140101Sep44 to COMINCH, 'Nimitz to King,' Graybook Summary, 2356. Joseph H. Alexander, 'The Americans Will Surely Come,' Naval History 9 (Jan-Feb 1995), 12-18.
[15]See CINCPAC/CINCPOA Staff Study 'STALEMATE II' of 14 July 1944, Record Group 38. Box 33, National Archives.

Marines going into battle. (USMC)

Assault Waves on the Orange beaches. (USMC)

Nimitz's personal reasons for deciding to retain the Peleliu landing can be deduced only by hindsight. We can safely rule out, it seems, factors of self-doubt, resentment toward Halsey's initiative, or callousness toward the likely costs. Nimitz's style of hands-off leadership would encourage exactly the kind of initiative that Halsey had just demonstrated. Nor did any evidence surface of callousness in Nimitz's character, according to those who knew him intimately. As Hal Lamar, his personal aide throughout the war, stated afterward: 'This used to hurt him very much, but I've heard him say to me, 'This is going to cost me ten thousand people.' ... He hated to know that he was issuing an order that would mean the loss of so many lives.' Similarly, in one of his few surviving letters to his wife, Nimitz

wrote from Iwo Jima of the 'spite mail' he received from grieving parents, admitting 'I am just as distressed as can be over the casualties but don't see how I could have reduced them.'[16] He was waging a grim war. Indeed, Nimitz's amphibious drive across the central Pacific ultimately incurred 100,000 American casualties.

Analysis of Nimitz's Peleliu decision within the context of his total performance in the protracted war suggests four likely contributing factors: a political sensitivity to fragile 'Home Front' morale, loyalty to King, his own sense of strategic priorities, and overconfidence.

Nimitz probably sensed that Halsey's message had come too late for Peleliu. Japanese gunners on Peleliu that day had shot U.S. Navy carrier aircraft out of the sky. Their swimmers this night were boldly laying new mines in the boat lanes cleared earlier by underwater demolition teams. Nimitz knew if he broke contact at this point, he would he handing the Emperor of Japan a priceless propaganda gem and creating a political disaster for President Roosevelt.

Among these four factors, Nimitz's close relationship with King is likely to have proved most crucial. They had not always seen

eye-to-eye on the necessity of invading the Palaus, but a sharp memo from King on 8 February 1944 (after the initial success of the Marshalls campaign) spelled out for Nimitz his objectives for the remainder of the year. 'Central Pacific general objective is Luzon,' said King, '[which] requires clearing Japs out of Carolines, Marianas, Pelews [sic] – and holding them.' This strategy, King argued, would cut the Japanese lines of communication to the Dutch East Indies and protect the flank of MacArthur's forces advancing to Mindanao.[17]

A month later, Nimitz went to Washington to provide this same rationale to the Joint Chiefs, the Joint Staff Planners, and President Roosevelt. Nimitz's memorandum, 'Sequence and Timing of Operations, Central Pacific Campaign,' contained King's earlier words, then added Nimitz's own views on the importance of Ulithi as a fleet anchorage in the westward drive, which would require the neutralisation of nearby Yap and

---

[16]Oral history interviews with Cdr H. Arthur Lamar, USNR by John T. Mason, Jr., 3 May 1970, New Orleans, contained in 'Recollections of Fleet Admiral Chester W. Nimitz,' 102-03, Center for Pacific War Studies, admiral Nimitz Museum, Fredericksburg, Texas. Nimitz to wife, 17 March 145, copy retained in same repository. Lamar also said the 'spite mail' to Nimitz began after Tarawa.
[17]COMINCH Memorandum for Admiral Nimitz, 8 Feb 44, contained in 'Personal Correspondence of Fleet Admiral Nimitz with COMINCH, 1942-45,' Operational Archives, Naval Historical Center, Washington. Note that the JCS throughout much of 1944 considered the principal objective in the Pacific to be Formosa, or the adjoining China coast, usually in conjunction with an intermediate seizure of Luzon. In this context, capture of Peleliu made much more sense. Developments late in the year – MacArthur's accelerated advance through the Philippines, the abandonment of Formosa as an objective, and the emergency of Iwo Jima and Okinawa as the new objectives of Nimitz's forces, combined to reduce Peleliu's strategic value.

Long range flame-throwers were first used at Peleliu. LVT mount was thereafter replaced by the tank. (USMC)

thus the seizure of the Palaus (Peleliu or Babelthaup). Nimitz suggested a November landing. The Joint Staff planners upped the ante, recommending a September date and declaring the capture of Palau to be 'essential to an invasion of the Philippines and an assault on Formosa' as a main naval base, citing the Palaus' airfields, sheltered anchorages, staging areas, and water depth sufficient for a floating dry-dock to be brought forward from Espiritu Santo.[18]

The Joint Chiefs then issued strategic guidance to MacArthur and Nimitz concerning the forthcoming Pacific campaigns. They set a target date of 15 September for the Palaus and specified the objective: 'to extend the control of the eastern approaches to the Philippines and Formosa, and to establish a fleet and air base and forward staging area for the support of operations against Mindanao, Formosa and China.'[19]

Peleliu could have been had for the asking in March. A light force of Imperial Navy antiaircraft gunners comprised the island's principal defence. But Nimitz's bold success in the Marshalls – leapfrogging first to Kwajalein, then all the way west to Eniwetok – caused consternation among Imperial General Headquarters. For the first time, the Japanese began pulling units from their elite Kwantung Army defending Manchuria against the Soviet

Far Eastern Army to face the U.S. threat in the Central Pacific. On 10 February 1944, the 14th Division received orders to leave its positions along the Nonni River above Tsitsihar. By June the build up of Imperial Army forces in the Palaus caused Nimitz enough concern to abandon Babelthaup and concentrate instead on the smaller islands of Peleliu, Angaur, Yap and Ulithi. King would not take kindly, Nimitz sensed, to further tinkering with STALEMATE's objectives.[20] In short, Nimitz and King had hammered out their plans for the Palaus campaign over an intense seven months.

On a personal level, Nimitz is likely to have determined that he had a clearer concept of the strategic situation in the Pacific than did Halsey. Halsey's galvanic messages provided good rationale for accelerating the Philippines and bypassing thorny Yap, but Nimitz found nothing in the fleet commander's report that tempted him to cancel Peleliu.

During his sleepless hours, as he studied the maps and charts of Palaus, Nimitz surely saw compelling reasons to wrest their control from the enemy. The Japanese maintained at Koror the headquarters for all their Pacific islands mandated by the old League of Nations. Kossol Passage, to the north, was a decent protected anchorage. If Babelthaup was too large and defended too heavily, Peleliu was certainly a suitable alternate objective because it was smaller, could be invested by the task force, and had a first-class airfield. Nimitz could readily see that seizing Peleliu would remove all these Japanese capabilities from the

---

[18]JCS Memorandum for Information No 200, 'Sequence and Timing of Operations, Central Pacific Campaign,' (which enclosed Nimitz's memo of same subject), 7 March 1944; Nimitz to King 8 March 1944, same subject, circulated by JCS as an addendum to the foregoing; Joint Staff Planners, 'Future Operations in the Pacific,' circulated as JCS 713/1 of 10 March 1944, page 17; all three documents contained in Record Group 218, Box 163, National Archives.
[19]JCS message 122319 March 1944 to MacArthur and Nimitz, Graybook Summary, 2312. An excellent account of these proceedings during 7-10 March can be found in Hays, JCS: The War Against Japan, 555-61.
[20]Saburo Hayashi with Alvin D. Coox, Kogun: The Japanese Army in the Pacific War (Quantico: Marine Corps Association, 1959), 76, 78. Hays, JCS: The War Against Japan, 607. Interview with former Lt. Ei Yamaguchi, Imperial Japanese Army, 2d Infrantry Regiment, Peleliu, translated by Mr. Isao Ashiba, May 1998.

Bloody Peleliu lasted longer than the other two most desperate assaults in Marine Corps history – Tarawa and Iwo Jima – but it produced the fewest visible strategic benefits

board and bottle up tens of thousands of troops on Babelthaup and throughout the western Carolines, including Yap. As Nimitz had been testifying for months, U.S. forces might be able to take Ulithi without Yap, but it could not be done without first taking Peleliu. Possession of Peleliu's airfield – and construction of a heavy bomber strip on the flat terrain of nearby Angaur – would permit Nimitz to support MacArthur, suppress Yap, protect Ulithi, and project reconnaissance and bombing missions far to the northwest as well.

Here, the factor of overconfidence likely weighed on Nimitz's decision. Arguably, he could have assigned one of Mitscher's carrier task groups to spend the rest of the war rendering the Palaus toothless from the air, but Nimitz believed it to be a more efficient use of his assets to seize, occupy, and defend Peleliu with his veteran landing force. Where Nimitz's earlier assault landings at Tulagi, Gavutu, and Tarawa had been executed at painful cost against fiercely resisting rikusentai (Japanese special naval landing forces), his principal opponents in the Marshalls and Marianas had been units of the Imperial Japanese Army, good fighters but poorly led in those battles. Ill-advised, grandiose Japanese counterattacks at Saipan and Guam had served only to accelerate the U.S. victories against an otherwise hidden and deadly enemy. At Tinian, the most recently executed landing before STALEMATE, the marines had seized the island in

nine days, inflicting a casualty ratio of four-to-one against the defenders.

Throughout the war, Nimitz kept posted over his desk a small sign whose lead question asked 'Is the proposed operation likely to succeed?'[21] Based on what he knew and assumed on 13 September 1944, the imminent invasion of Peleliu had every likelihood of success at an affordable cost. The resulting carnage at Peleliu doubtlessly shocked Nimitz as it did the amphibious force. And while tactical errors were committed by senior Navy and Marine officers who should have known better, the greatest shortfall of the campaign proved to be unsatisfactory combat intelligence.

Theatre intelligence teams published the precise enemy order of battle at Peleliu weeks in advance, but Nimitz, Halsey, and the Western Attack Force were served poorly by the omission of two critical enemy factors. No one knew that they would be facing one of the best-trained best-led infantry regiments in the Imperial Army; or that in Colonel Kunio Nakagawa the Marines would fight against a commander surpassed only by Iwo Jima's Tadamichi Kuribayashi as their most redoubtable opponent of all time, a Colonel with such an eye for terrain and such a gift for close combat that the Japanese government promoted him posthumously to Lieutenant General. Nor did anyone

appreciate the fact that the Japanese had just modified their counterlanding tactics. The Japanese at Peleliu would introduce the U.S. invaders to cave warfare, deep positions arrayed in honeycombed echelons, a new war of attrition. The tortured terrain of the Umurbrogol provided a perfect setting.[22]

Into this lethal landscape came an overconfident landing force, whose assault numbers barely equalled the defenders (much less the three-to-one ratio found necessary for success in earlier operations), whose operational reserves were too few and committed too readily to lower-priority missions against Angaur and Ulithi, with preliminary naval gunfire support reduced nearly to Tarawa levels, and with insufficient tank and mechanized flame-thrower assets. That the Marines and Soldiers eventually prevailed under these conditions is a tribute to their small-unit leaders and individual riflemen. That the bulk of the fighting was conducted at such close ranges that the Marines, to cite one example, expended 116,000 hand grenades, is not surprising. Nor is the fact that the operation cost 9,600 casualties and took ten weeks to complete.

Halsey's reaction to Nimitz's decision was muted. On D-day at Peleliu he wrote to his commander ('My dear Chester …') expressing delight at 'the prospective speed-up of the war,' but avoiding mention of the Palaus. As the battle progressed, Stassen

[21]Lamar Interview, 1996.
[22]Senshi Sosho [Japanese War History series], No.13, Chuba Taiheyo homen rikugen sakusen (2) (Army Operations in the Central Pacific, vol. 2), Tokyo: Asagumo shimbunsha, 1968, 151-52. See also Theodore L. Gatchel, At the Water's Edge: Defending Against the Modern Amphibious Assault (Annapolis: Naval Institute Press, 1996), 143-145, and Joseph H. Alexander, Storm Landings: Epic Amphibious Battles in the Central Pacific (Annapolis: Naval Institute Press, 1997), 108-111.

Bunker, or pillbox, of the type that infested Peleliu's low ground. After assault troops had overrun such positions, Japanese often sought to reoccupy these by infiltration. (USMC)

recalled Halsey discussing the high casualties and wondering if he should have made one final effort to persuade Nimitz to cancel Peleliu, 'but then he concluded it was too bad, that they had 'pushed it to the edge' and gotten as much concession from Nimitz and the Joint Chiefs as they had a right to expect.'[23]

Halsey visited Peleliu on 30 September, 15 days after D-Day, appalled at what he saw and shaken by a near miss from a Japanese mortar shell. A week later he downplayed the experience in a brief mention at the end of a routine letter to Nimitz, saying: 'Peleliu and Angaur were the usual thing on recent visit. The interconnecting caves in the hills, with many entrances and exits, and various connecting tiers were a new phase. It is a slow progress in digging the rats out. Poison gas is indicated as an economical weapon.'[24]

Nimitz did not visit Peleliu, the only major beachhead he skipped. Nor did he engage in public discourse when Halsey declared the campaign an unnecessary mistake in his outspoken postwar memoirs. Nimitz's sole retrospective consists of a 1949 note to historian Philip A. Crowl in which he cited two purposes for seizing Peleliu: 'first, to remove from MacArthur's right flank, in his progress towards the Southern Philippines, a definite threat of attack; second, to secure for our forces a base from which to support MacArthur's operations into the Southern Philippines.'[25]

Bloody Peleliu lasted longer than the other two most desperate assaults in Marine Corps history – Tarawa and Iwo Jima – but it produced the fewest visible strategic benefits. Many veterans became more outspoken as the years passed. Said former Marine mortarman Eugene B. Sledge in 1994: 'I shall always harbour a deep sense of bitterness and grief over the suffering and loss of so many fine Marines on Peleliu for no good reason.'[26]

Yet Peleliu was not devoid of redeeming values. Ulithi became a superb advance naval anchorage for the Iwo Jima and Okinawa invasion fleets. A Peleliu-based search plane found the forlorn survivors of the sunken cruiser Indianapolis (CA-35) in August

1945. Capture of Peleliu effectively bottled up some 43,000 other Japanese troops in the neighbourhood without a fight. And the tactical lessons in cave warfare learned at such cost by the III Amphibious Force proved invaluable in the struggle for Okinawa half a year later. In fact, the 1st Marine Division's masterful use of tanks, flame-throwers, siege guns, and close air support during its fierce battles for Awacha Pocket, Wana Draw, and Kunishi Ridge made a world of difference in the Okinawa campaign.

Lacking all this hindsight, Nimitz made the best decision he could with the information available at the time. The subsequent unpleasant surprises and terrible costs were painful to bear, but the result was a clear victory. Nimitz succeeded in driving another stake into Imperial Japan's heart, a chilling warning that U.S. forces could prevail despite the most ingenious of defences and skilful of island commanders – even on a bad day.

[23]Halsey to Nimitz, 15 September 1944, contained in 'Personal Correspondence of Fleet Admiral Nimitz with Commander Third Fleet,' Operational Archives, Naval Historical Center, Washington. Stassen interview, 1998.
[24]Halsey to Nimitz, 6 October 1944, contained in 'Personal Correspondence of Fleet Admiral Nimitz with Commander Third Fleet,' Operational Archives, Naval Historical Center, Washington. Nimitz marked the original letter with his customary red pencil but left no annotation around Halsey's comment on poison gas. That fact, plus the fact that Halsey sent his comments by mail a week after his visit instead of an immediate message, indicates the realisation by both admirals of President Roosevelt's long standing opposition to American offensive use of poison gas in the war.
[25]Nimitz to Dr. Philip A, Crowl, 5 October 1949, contained in 'The Princeton Papers,' Section IX, Personal Papers Collection, Marine Corps Historical Center, Washington.
[26]Eugene B. Sledge, 'Peleliu 1944: Why did We go There?' Naval Institute Proceedings 120 (September 1994), 74. Dr. Sledge is also the author of With the Old Breed at Peleliu and Okinawa, widely considered the definitive enlisted account of the Pacific War.

Lessons Identified from Peleliu

- Know Your Men - Nimitz proved to be an exceptional judge of character and hand picked the best commanders.

- Research the objective - Nimitz was a consummate professional who spent hours examining all available charts and maps of the enemy objective to gain as much information as possible.

- Assess the necessity of taking each objective - Political directives and strategic benefits do not necessarily require the taking of the same military objective.

- Naval Gunfire Support - The value of an intensive and prolonged naval bombardment cannot be underestimated.

- Intelligence - The absolute requirement for timely and accurate intelligence is essential.

- Defence - Enemy held defensive positions are likely to be in depth and positioned to take full advantage of the natural terrain.

- Reserves - Operational reserves should always be available, regardless of even the most optimistic of planning assumptions.

- Leadership - The courage and leadership displayed by sub-unit commanders and riflemen can overcome even the most unfavourable odds in close combat.

Further Reading

Davis, Burke, *Marine! The Life of Chesty Puller*, (Mass Market, 1964)

Gailey, Harry A., *Peleliu 1944*, (Amer, 1983)

Gayle, Brigadier General Gordon D., USMC (Rtd), *Bloody Beaches: The Marines at Peleliu*, (USMC: World War Two Commemorative Series, 1996)

Hallas, James H., The Devil's Anvil: *The Assault on Peleliu*, (Praeger, 1994)

Moran, Jim & Rottman, Gordon, *Peleliu 1944: The Forgotten Corner of Hell*, (Osprey, 2002)

Sloan, Bill, *Brotherhood of Heroes: The Marines at Peleliu, 1944 - The Bloodiest Battle of the Pacific War*, (Simon & Schuster, 2005)

Acknowledgements: The author is grateful for the assistance of Scott C Anderson, Isao Ashiba, Lt Col Jon T Hoffman, USMCR, Mary C Hoffman, Cdr H Arthur Lamar, USNR (rtd), Zunichi Ohtsuka, the Honorable Harold E Stassen, Paul Stillwell, Paula Ussery and Peleliu survivor Ei Yamaguchi.

Biography

Colonel Joseph H Alexander, USMC (Rtd) served for 29 years on active duty in the USMC as an assault amphibian officer, including two tours in the Republic of Vietnam and five years at sea on board amphibious ships. He was NATO operations officer at Fleet Marine Force Atlantic headquarters and Chief of Staff of the 3d Marine Division. He is a distinguished graduate of the Naval War College and holds degrees in history from North Carolina, Jacksonville, and Georgetown. He has written five books and six monographs on military history and has appeared as an on-screen authority for 25 military documentaries on cable television networks. His book *Utmost Savagery: Three Days of Tarawa* (1995) won the General Wallace M Greene Award of the Marine Corps Historical Foundation. During 2001-2006 he was chief historian and writer for the exhibit design team of the highly acclaimed National Museum of the Marine Corps in Washington DC.

Walcheren
Operation INFATUATE II, November 1944

By Professor John Forfar MC

Assault from the Sea: RN - RM Synergy

Three months after D-Day the Allied Armies were approaching the Dutch border but their supply ports, primarily Cherbourg, Arromanches, Boulogne and Calais, were 200-300 miles away. Dieppe and Ostend, just captured, had insufficient capacity. The key to the increasingly critical supply problems of armies now approaching two million men was Antwerp, the second largest port in Europe, which on 4 September 1944 had been captured undamaged by the British 11th Armoured Division: but Antwerp was 50 miles from the sea at the head of the tortuous, heavily mined, Scheldt estuary, 5 miles across at its widest.

The 80,000-strong German 15th Army made no attempt to retake Antwerp but denied its use by closing the Scheldt with the powerful defences they had established in the 'Breskens Pocket' to the south, and South Beveland and Walcheren to the north. The Allies would require to overcome these before Antwerp could be used. At this time General Montgomery was intent on a direct narrow front strike into Holland with the objective of reaching Arnhem and capturing the bridges over the Maas, Waal and Rhine in one incisive action, Operation MARKET GARDEN. This would require men, materials and transport: concurrent pursuit of the retreating German Army or attempt to open the Scheldt would have to wait. The Germans now reorganised their forces on both sides of the Scheldt and 3,000 German troops moved to strengthen the Walcheren garrison.

The key to the increasingly critical supply problems of armies now approaching two million men was Antwerp

For his part, the Supreme Commander General Eisenhower favoured a 'broad front' policy which would require the opening of Antwerp first. Both Admiral Ramsay, Eisenhower's (British) Naval Chief of Staff and Air Chief Marshall Tedder, Deputy Supreme Commander (British) shared that view. Eisenhower, however, was not prepared to veto Montgomery's plan and saw some attractions in it. MARKET GARDEN began on 7 September but by 25th it was clear that it had failed. Substantial resources of men (7,000 killed, wounded and captured) and much materiel had been lost, prejudicing the ability to mount an operation to free Antwerp. At the same time the importance of that operation had increased because a broad front prolongation of the war would increase supply needs and the recent liberation of semi-starving Paris and Brussels meant that the Allies now had an additional requirement of 4,000 tons of food, fuel, medicines, etc. per day.

Increasingly concerned about the need for Antwerp and fearful that preoccupation with Arnhem would blunt appreciation of that Eisenhower, in the middle of MARKET GARDEN (22 September), urged Montgomery that Antwerp must be opened as a matter of urgency but even after the 25th Montgomery was still reluctant to abandon the idea of a direct advance to the Rhine: the British Chief of the Imperial General Staff, Sir Alan Brooke, expressed his concern about this. On 9 October Montgomery received a more prescriptive message that unless Antwerp was functioning

by the mid-November all operations would come to a standstill and on 16 October he issued an order to his Army Commanders emphasising the importance of freeing Antwerp. He expected heavy casualties. In later years Montgomery admitted that he had been wrong in not first freeing Antwerp.

Montgomery sought to include American airborne troops for an attack on Walcheren but these were refused on the questionable ground that its terrain was unsuitable for airborne landings. Also the programme of preliminary bombing of the Walcheren coastal defences which Montgomery wished was only approved by Tedder in a very limited form. Directly, the operation would be under control of the Canadian Army.

The German high command considered that denial of the Scheldt to the Allies was vital. Hitler ordered that the Breskens pocket, South Beveland and Walcheren must be held to the last. The Commander of the German 15th Army, issued an order (7 October) emphasising how decisive the defences of the approach to Antwerp were and that their loss could be a death blow to Germany. His Breskens subordinate announced that any man who surrendered would be considered a traitor, his name made known to the German people and his next of kin vilified.

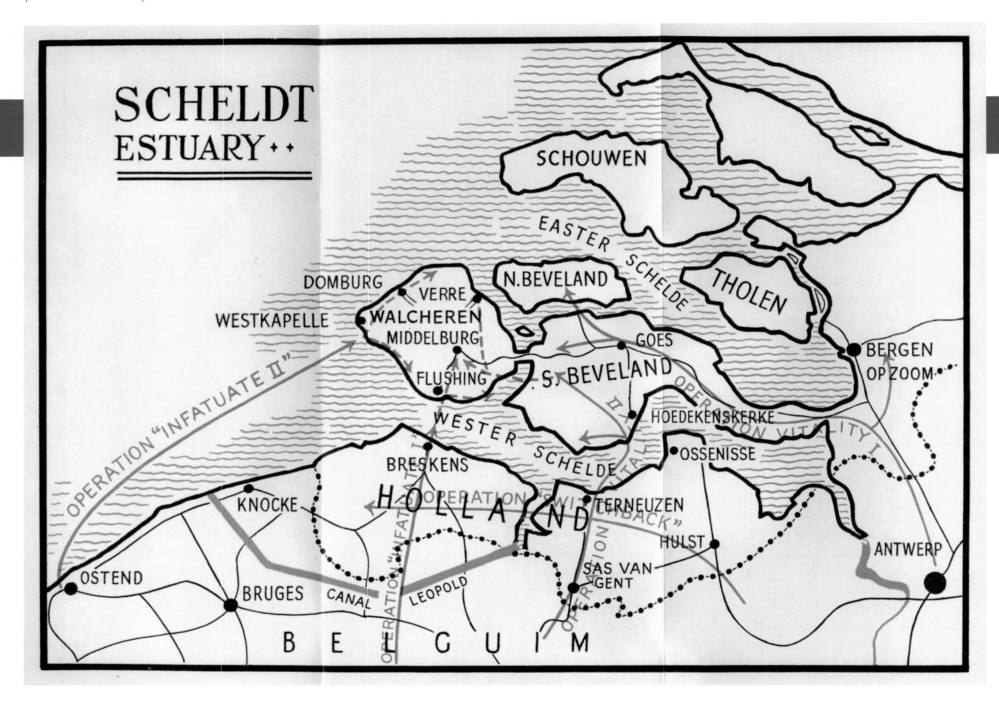

SCHELDT
ESTUARY ✦ ✦

SCHOUWEN

EASTER SCHELDE

N. BEVELAND

THOLEN

DOMBURG

VERRE

WESTKAPELLE

WALCHEREN

MIDDELBURG

GOES

FLUSHING

S. BEVELAND

BERGEN OP ZOOM

OPERATION "INFATUATE II"

HOEDEKENSKERKE

OPERATION VITALITY II

WESTER SCHELDE

OSSENISSE

OPERATION VITALITY I

BRESKENS

KNOCKE

OPERATION "INFATUATE I"

OPERATION "SWITCHBACK"

TERNEUZEN

HOLLAND

HULST

ANTWERP

OSTEND

SAS VAN GENT

BRUGES

CANAL

LEOPOLD

BELGUIM

Left: The Scheldt Islands and Operations to liberate them. (NHB)

Breaching the Dykes: A gap blown through the sand dunes at Westkapelle by RAF Bomber Command. (NHB)

The Breskens Pocket, South Beveland and Flushing (Vlissingen)

The first step in liberating Antwerp was an attack on the 'Breskens Pocket' (Operation SWITCHBACK) allocated to the Canadian 3rd Infantry Division and part of the British 52nd Division. After three weeks of bloody fighting over flat, cold, water-logged polders against a determined well armed enemy Breskens was cleared by 31 October. By the same date the Canadian 2nd Infantry Division along with British 52nd Division had cleared South Beveland (VITALITY I & II). Now, preventing land access to Walcheren was the Sloe. By blocking its northern end the Germans created an uncrossable swamp on the east side of the island. Any further attack would require to be mounted from the south and west. An army assault on Flushing across the Scheldt would be mounted from Breskens by 4 (Army) Commando and the (British) 52nd Division with elements of supporting arms (INFATUATE I). The west coast would be approached from the sea (INFATUATE II) by 4 Commando Brigade consisting of 41, 47 and 48 Royal Marine Commandos in conjunction with the Royal Navy.

Plans and Preparations

The time available for planning was very short. The naval commander, Captain Pugsley, was appointed on 16 September, the military commander, Brigadier Leicester, on 1 October. The western coastal defences of Walcheren were assessed by Combined Operations as 'some of the strongest in the world'. They consisted of about 30 batteries mounting approximately 60 major 3.0 to 8.6 inch coastal guns – some in concrete

casemates up to 14 ft. thick, anti-aircraft guns, concrete pill-boxes and bunkers, sand-bagged machine gun emplacements, mortar positions and trenches, mines, barbed wire, a concrete 'dragons teeth' tank barrier, vertical steel girders concreted into the dykes; off-shore mined underwater obstacles. The dunes were an almost continuous line of fortifications. A strong coastwise tidal current and off-shore sandbanks, would make the deployment of landing craft difficult.

General Crerar, commanding First Canadian Army, considered a sea-borne attack impracticable but took ill and was replaced by General Simonds, aged 42, on 26 September. Against considerable resistance Simonds conceived the idea of flooding the largely sub-sea-level island by blowing the dykes at Westkapelle, Veere and Flushing and isolating the western coastal defences on the dunes which were above sea level. RAF Bomber Command originally doubted the possibility of breaching the dykes - 120 yards wide at the base, 30 feet above sea level at low tide and 16 at high tide, constructed from large blocks of basalt and enormous wooden piles - but agreed to try 'earthquake' bombs which would penetrate to the base of the dyke before exploding.

On 3 October, the citizens of Walcheren, accustomed to RAF bombers flying high overhead en route to Germany, saw that the bombers (259 in all) were flying lower; and the throb of their engines was not fading. From the western tip of the island came the sound of crashing bombs. For a while the dyke held but as bomb after bomb embedded in it and exploded the dyke's height fell and water began to flow over it, gradually creating a tidal inrush 300 yards wide. Ninety per cent of Westkapelle was destroyed and nearly 200 of its inhabitants killed among them 47 women and children who had sheltered in a mill and were

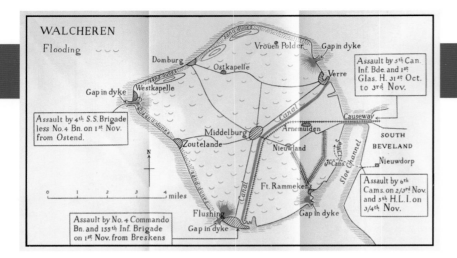

trapped inside - yet there was no recrimination by the islanders. A few days later the dykes north of Flushing (Nolle) (7 October) and at Veere (11 October) were similarly breached. Walcheren now became a lagoon ringed with dunes and dykes, streets became canals and people took to upper floors.

For this operation a naval Support Squadron (Captain Sellar), was assembled, manned by RN seamen and RM gunners. It consisted mainly of converted LCTs (Landing Craft Tank) with ramps welded shut, decked over to form a gun platform, shallow enough to get close to the Walcheren shore, yet capable of a 40 mile sea journey. These craft included 6 LCG(L) (landing craft gun: 4.7 inch and other smaller calibre guns), 2 LCGs(M) (landing craft medium: 17 pounder guns), 6 LCFs (landing craft flak:20 mm Oerlikon and 2 pounder 'pom pom' guns), 5 LCT(R)s (landing craft rocket) and 6 LCS(L) (converted, partially armoured, wooden infantry landing ships (6 and 2 pounder guns). The role of the Support Squadron, as learnt at the Dieppe raid, was to provide covering fire during the 'one hour gap' from the time that an aerial/naval bombardment ceased and the assaulting troops went ashore. The squadron was told that its mission would be dangerous.

In addition, the battleship *Warspite* and the monitors *Erebus* and *Roberts*, with 15 inch guns, would support the operation. The commandos would be transported in 35 standard LCTs and 3 LCI(S) (small timber, infantry landing craft holding 90 men). Two new amphibious transport vehicles were provided, Landing Vehicles Tracked (LVTs or 'Buffaloes', holding 24 marines, lightly armoured, with maximum water speed of 5 knots and land speed of 25mph under charge of the Royal Engineers 80th Assault Squadron; and smaller 'Weasels' also tracked and driven by commando drivers. Four stretchers could be fitted into a weasel. 41 Cdo would have armour in the form of Sherman tanks, AVRES (Armoured Vehicles, Royal Engineers) and armoured bulldozers (in the event only 2 tanks and 2 AVRES could be used) but there was no possibility of using these on the steep shifting sands of the dunes in the Westkapelle-Flushing section where small arms and mortars would have to be the main weapons.

Embarkation and Outward Voyage

The preliminaries were not encouraging. There was no possibility of maintaining security as preparations in Ostend harbour were obvious to all. There was a fear that, with prior warning, German E boats known to be harboured in Brouwershaven, 15 miles away, might attack the invading force at sea.

Time did not allow sweeping of the outer reaches of the Scheldt for mines – as a result the only hospital ship and a number of supply ships would be lost on their outward journeys – or rehearsal for the operation by all the units involved.

Over a few nights beforehand a special unit reconnoitred the gap and found a negotiable 8 knot tidal flow through it, but the immediate hostile reaction of the coastal defences showed that there could be no surprise. By 0115 on 1 November the assault force was assembling at the rendezvous off Ostend, 150 ships led by the Headquarters frigate *Kingsmill* with the commanders aboard.

The sea was fairly calm and there was little wind. A moon shone intermittently through cloud cover. To those aboard it appeared that the operation was 'on' but this was not so. The two commanders had been informed on leaving Ostend that due to fog in England the heavy Lancaster bombers and fighter bombers, essential for the aerial 'one hour gap' cover, were grounded. Some support from rocket-firing Typhoon aircraft might be available but not spotter aircraft to monitor the accuracy of the battleship fire. The two commanders had been instructed to set sail using their discretion as to whether the operation should proceed – tidal conditions would allow only a few more days on which the operation could be mounted. The commanders decided and the armada sailed on. By 0745 they received yet another disturbing message: there would be no Typhoon aerial support. The support squadron would now have to subsume the preliminary 'softening up' expected of the RAF.

The Assault on Walcheren, Operation INFATUATE II,
1 November 1944. (NHB)

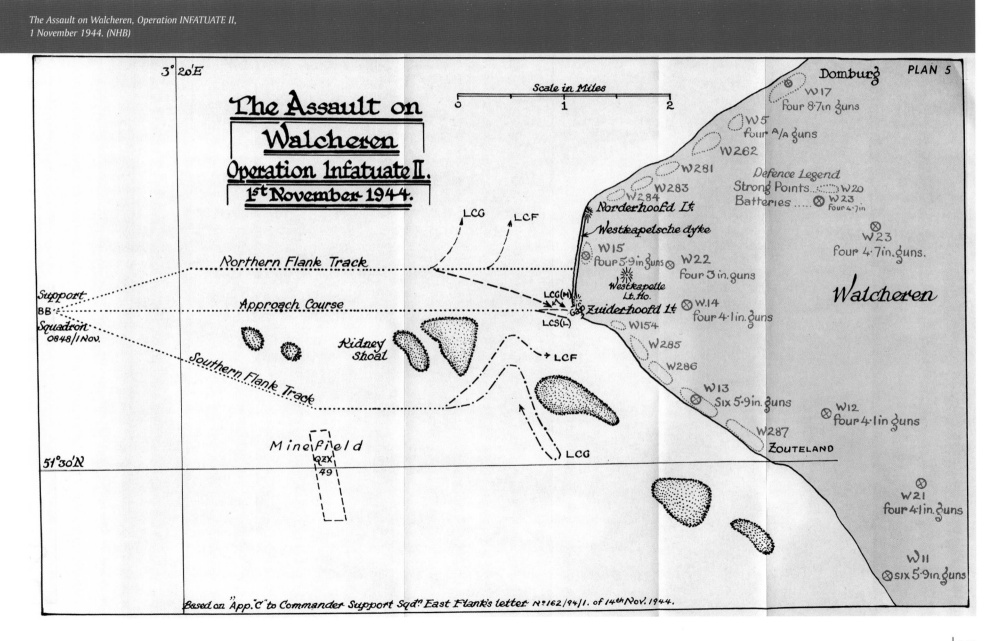

PLAN 5

The Assault on
Walcheren
Operation Infatuate II.
1st November 1944.

Scale in Miles

Domburg

W17
Four 8.7in guns

W5
four A/a guns

W262

W281

W283
W284

Defence Legend
Strong Points W20
Batteries W23
four 4.7in

Norderhoofd Lt.

Westkapelsche dyke

LCG   LCF

Northern Flank Track

W15
four 5.9in guns

W22
four 3in. guns

W23
four 4.7in. guns.

Walcheren

Support
BB

Approach Course

LCG(M)

LCS(L)

Westkapelle
Lt. Ho.

Zuiderhoofd Lt.

W14
four 4.1in. guns

Squadron
0848/1 Nov.

W154

Kidney
Shoal

W285

LCF

W286

Southern Flank Track

W13
Six 5.9in. guns

W12
four 4.1in guns

W287
Zouteland

Mine Field
QZX
49

LCG

W21
four 4.1in. guns

W11
six 5.9in. guns

Based on "App.'C' to Commander Support Sqdⁿ East Flank's letter N°162/94/1. of 14th Nov. 1944.

3° 20'E

51° 30'N

LCG(M) 101 closed with the German shore Battery to provide intimate gunfire support and also drew enemy fire away from the LCAs. It was hit by German rounds and the crew had to abandon ship. (IWM)

Little Ships and Big Guns

The morning of 1 November was cold and grey. As the armada turned toward the Walcheren coast the outline of the dunes, eleven miles distant, began to break the line of sea and sky. The lighthouse tower at Westkapelle revealed itself, standing high like a signpost to the coming battle. By 0830, in the LCTs, the marines were climbing into their buffaloes and by 0845 the *Warspite* and *Erebus,* 13 miles off-shore, were joining battle, the boom of their guns sounding across the water and the crash of their shells echoing back. Soon the lower half of the Westkapelle tower was obscured by a creeping pall of enemy smoke, the upper half standing proudly above it: but the wind was dispersing the smoke.

The 25 craft of the Support Squadron led in. The coastal defences had all the advantage including now no harassment from the air. Thirteen of the 25 craft attacked the defences north of the gap (W15) and 12 the defences south of it (W285, W286 and W13). The coastal guns held fire until the squadron was 3,000 yards

away. Three LCG(L)s positioned north of the gap and 3 south of it replied with their guns - the biggest in the Support Squadron. The LCG(L)s then moved to within 800 yards of the shore, sailing back and forward parallel to it, engaging the defences and zig-zagging to avoid the shells being blasted at them from muzzles projecting from concrete embrasures menacingly close. One of the LCG(L)s was soon severely damaged and sinking: an LCT went to its assistance, taking it in tow, but both struck mines and sank. Another LCG(L) struck by shells was sinking and an LCS(L) went to its assistance, unavailingly - the damaged LCG(L) slowly sank. Three others were hit, one set on fire, one severely damaged aft and one flooded. All kept firing until ordered to withdraw. Two LCG(M), adapted with special ballast tanks for stability, were given the dangerous assignment of beaching, one on each side of the gap, and engaging two pill-boxes on the landing areas which could seriously interfere with the commandos as they landed. LCG(M)102 beached south but within minutes was hit and engulfed in flames: all perished.

LCG(M)101 on the north side opened fire from 2000 yards and, firing as she went in, beached 40 yards away. The pillbox had an anti-tank gun. The forward half of LCG(M)(101) was below the

lowest point of depression of the larger guns firing at her but the stern half was not and was repeatedly hit, the whole craft being subject to small arms fire. The pillbox was blasted with the LCG(M)'s gun for 15 minutes but the shells were bouncing off. The craft then pulled away to make a fresh attack but as it did so began to sink, keeled over and foundered 800 yards from the shore. Four of the 5 rocket firing LCT(R)s made successful shoots and also laid smoke screens. The ranging of the rockets depended on positioning the LCT(R)s correctly, a difficult thing to do. One of the them fired short hitting two of the LCFs including the magazine of one which went on fire: the LCF had to be abandoned with many casualties. Another LCF took on her survivors, was herself hit but continued to engage the enemy at close range.

These (LCFs) had much lower fire power and had to go close to draw enemy fire. Another was hit on the water-line and the crew blocked the hole with hammocks: she was hit again and, putting out a smoke screen, went full steam ahead towards the enemy. More hits blew off her bows and forward magazine and a final hit then struck her main magazine – 100,000 rounds of Oerlikon and 2 pounder gun ammunition exploded blowing most of the personnel into the sea, 43 perishing. Other LCFs were hit and continued to fire.

The lightly armed 6 LCS(L)s also had to sail close to be effective. Three on the southern flank were hit, blew up and sank with heavy casualties. One on the northern flank was hit and set on fire, its engines destroyed; another towed the stricken vessel

The Opposition: Steep dunes, shifting sands and no roads. Here German Marines train near Battery W11 at Westkapelle. (IWM)

Great credit for the success of these amphibious operations is due to the support craft of the British Navy

to safety and returned to the fight. As the survivors of sinking craft paddled away on rafts and floats the enemy gunners fired at them.

These actions lasted for 3 hours from 0900 and gradually as the 'little ships' sank, went on fire, were severely damaged or exhausted their ammunition the few which could still float were withdrawn – 9 had been sunk or abandoned on fire, 7 others had suffered severe damage and 4 minor damage. They had more than fulfilled the dangerous task allotted to them. Their casualties were high, 19 officers and 151 other ranks were killed or missing and 15 officers and 110 other ranks wounded. The final casualty count for the total complement of LCT crews was 172 killed and 210 wounded.

General Eisenhower said:

'Great credit for the success of these amphibious operations is due to the support craft of the British Navy, which unhesitatingly and in the highest tradition of the service attracted to themselves the point-blank fire of the land batteries, thus permitting the Commandos and assault troops to gain the shore with much lighter casualties than would have otherwise been the case'.

As this uneven contest drew to a close, a few rocket firing Typhoons managed to take to the air and gave the little ships some belated assistance. The commandos owed the men of the Support Squadron an immense debt of gratitude.

Ashore - Dykes, Dunes and Dug-in Defences Day I

As the support craft engaged the shore batteries the landing craft carrying 41 and 48 Commando were moving in.

41 Commando

Delayed by hostile fire, 41 (Lieutenant Colonel Palmer) landed half its complement in LCI(S)s at 1012 on the north shoulder of the gap with a view to giving cover to half landing from buffaloes and weasels in the gap. The gap party landed 5 minutes later, overcame a pillbox after a sharp fight, and quickly captured Westkapelle village. Fire from the Westkapelle Tower was met by fire from 41 and its accompanying tanks and the defenders surrendered. Batteries W14 and W22 were found to be flooded and unoccupied. By noon the commando had advanced to Battery W15 and after half an hour of sharp fighting captured it by approaching it from the flooded side of the dyke, 120

prisoners were taken. One troop then proceeded beyond the battery. Battery 17 near Domburg was active and in the early afternoon a squadron of rocket-firing typhoons attacked it and *Warspite* shelled it. Two hours later the commando moved forward reaching W17 four miles away in gathering dusk. The battery apparently showed little fight, prisoners were taken and the commando entered Domburg; but it transpired that the main body of the enemy had pulled back into the wooded country beyond. Later that night one of the commando's troops encountered a group of enemy in a wire-protected position high on a dune. This group put up a stern fight and the 41 troop had to withdraw. In the dark the absence of the troop commander and a marine was not noted. They had been wounded in the advance towards the position. Overnight two unsuccessful attempts were made to rescue them.

An LCT discharges its LVTs and Weasels directly onto the beach at Walcheren. (IWM A26268)

48 Commando

The first elements of 48 (Lieutenant Colonel Moulton) touched down at 1010 – unscathed, as the 'little ships' were attracting the enemy fire – and quickly advanced to a Radar Station just ahead, unoccupied but under enemy small arms fire. They then advanced to Battery 285 capturing it without serious resistance. With the Support Squadron largely eliminated the LCTs offshore were now attracting the fire of the coastal guns and the later elements of 48 suffered. An LCT received a direct hit killing the driver and wireless operator and seriously wounding two marines. The landing area was now under heavy and sustained shell fire, casualties were occurring and when some of the amphibians went round on the inshore side of the radar station they were blown up on mines.

These setbacks to the later elements of 48 did not hinder the progress of its forward elements which occupied Battery 286 without difficulty. Wishing to maintain momentum, a small assault party then launched an attack against Battery 13. It was repulsed, the troop commander killed and most of the assault party wounded.

A more organised attack on W13 by the whole commando was then planned. HMS *Roberts* and artillery from Breskens would bombard W13 and 15 minutes later Typhoons firing cannon would attack it. While this support was being arranged 48's forward position was heavily mortared: one troop commander was killed and all the other officers and NCOs in the troop killed or wounded. Two other officers including the Medical Officer,

his MOA and a telegraphist were also killed. 47's medical officer went forward to assist. The artillery and aerial attack lasted 20 minutes and at 1610, 48 moved in. The command post was captured and progressively over several hours the other elements of W13 were attacked and occupied. As darkness descended the last of the W13 positions was overcome. One casemate had been smashed by bombs and all the crew killed. Many prisoners were taken but others withdrew and retreated through Zoutelande.

47 Commando

For over 2 hours 47 (Lieutenant Colonel Phillips) waited offshore for the order to land, spectators of the 'little ships' epic battle. At 1230 , two hours beyond the planned landing time, a naval launch shouted by loud hailer, '47, go in and land and good luck to you'. As 47 moved in it was subject to intense shelling. Amid a turmoil of gunfire, explosions and spray the Westkapelle tower and the smoking ruins from which it seemed to emerge came ever closer.

47 now encountered other difficulties. The delay meant that mine-tipped obstacles visible at a lower tide were now just covered and the Westkapelle gap was becoming increasingly obstructed by sunken or damaged craft and manoeuvring LCTs and LVTs. The coastal current added navigational difficulties. Once in the water LVT's sink deeply and with the eye of a navigator only a little above sea level the main channel through the gap was now difficult to identify. Also, with a 5 knot speed

the LVTs had difficulty in coping with the 8 knot current in the gap. The beach was now a mass of mud, tangled barbed wire, 'hedgehogs', large boulders and rubble; and was under fire.

47's leading LCT carrying the CO received a direct hit as a shell passed through the driving compartment of one of the LVTs killing the driver and wireless operator, setting flame-thrower fuel ablaze and inflicting burns on a number of marines, including one who already had a compound fracture of his leg. An RE corporal drove the burning LVT into the water and those in it had to swim. Another LVT had sustained a broken track and could not move: its occupants, avoiding the spreading flames in the LCT, had to jump into the water and swim ashore. The other LVTs advanced ashore.

Two other LCTs were hit by shell fire before beaching and the Regimental Sergeant Major and a Troop Sergeant Major wounded. Thus three of the four LCTs carrying 47 were hit before landing resulting in 30 known casualties and a number missing. Three LVTs landed on the wrong side of the gap and the re-cross proved difficult. Further casualties also occurred on the shell and mortar swept beaching area; a 47 officer and a marine died from wounds inflicted there.

Wounded

On the evening of 1 November one of the LCTs which had brought in troops but was in no way equipped as a hospital ship took off over 100 casualties.

DAY 2
41 Commando

The morning of 2 November was cold and grey. At first light 41 sent a troop forward to the position where the wounded troop commander went missing the previous night. The enemy had withdrawn. The troop commander was dead but the marine was alive. Later in the day, feeling that 47 might need help in its sector, the Brigadier ordered part of 41 to return to Westkapelle leaving the other part behind but due to shortage of LVTs 41 was not in a position to cross the gap until next day.

48 Commando

48 Commando now advanced to and overcame Battery W287 after a short encounter and the capture of 20 prisoners. By 1100 Zoutelande was reached just after HMS *Erebus* had subjected it to a bombardment. Two battles were fought in the dunes above the village and a few shots fired in the village itself. The German commander surrendered and 150 prisoners were taken.

47 Commando

Zoutelande was the point at which 47 Commando was to take over and clear the longer, more distant, 5 miles sector extending to the outskirts of Flushing. For 47 there were no 'little ships' to distract the enemy gunners and when the CO asked for air support he was told that none was available. Leaving Zoutelande

about 1300, 47 continued along the undulating 200 feet high dune ridge. Due to the terrain the LVTs found it difficult to keep up and it was heavy going manhandling mortars and machine guns up and down loose sandy slopes. Just beyond Zoutelande 47 Cdo's advance elements overcame lightly defended Battery W288 but when they had advanced further to the tank barrier they had to overcome an entrenched position: a sergeant was killed by a sniper and an officer shot in the neck.

The Tank Barrier prevented LVTs from going any further. The ridge now widened out to 600-800 yards. Battery 238 was 600 yards ahead and as the leading troop approached it a salvo of mortar fire killed 11 including the Sergeant Major and seriously wounded another 12 including the troop commander. The enemy mortar position was charged: its occupants fled.

Battery W11, a mile beyond the Tank Barrier, represented 47's major task. It included three large calibre field guns in concrete casemates, three anti-aircraft guns, sandbagged machine gun and mortar posts, trenches, 9 pillboxes. The machine gun, mortar and trench positions were spread out up to 300-400

yards on each side of the battery. There were also large calibre mortar positions along the inland side of the dunes which could harass the advancing commando but were too far away to allow a diversion towards them. Their fire killed a corporal and wounded an officer.

For 15 minutes before 47 attacked, W11 received an artillery barrage from Breskens. The attack was a confused close contact engagement, an 'up at the double, down' affair whose success depended on the field-craft, training, skill with small arms and grenades, and the dash and determination of the marines involved. One section often kept a position under fire while another crept round to take it by surprise. As they advanced the marines had to make good use of dead ground, stalk skilfully,

avoid raising their heads in the same place twice, be willing to dash across open ground under fire.

As the troop leading moved down the forward slope of a dune an enemy shell caused seven casualties. An unused searchlight base 400 yards short of the main part of W11 was passed and the troop advanced 100 yards beyond: in doing so its commander was seriously wounded and its Troop Sergeant Major and another marine killed. Leading elements were now reaching the central 'umbrella' feature of W11 and conducting probing attacks but casualties were rising.

It was now 2100 and dark. The various troops were somewhat disorganised and relative positions not very clear. The commando was seriously depleted with all 5 fighting troop commanders, 2 other officers, 3 troop sergeant majors, 12 other NCOs and many of the marines killed or wounded. Wireless communication had failed. Wounded were lying on the ground in dispersed positions and would have to be collected soon or some would die in the cold of that November night.

They received, on the spot, such first aid as was possible. Those who could not walk had to be carried for nearly a mile to the Tank Barrier and, lacking enough stretchers, doors removed from captured bunkers had to be used. Prisoners had to be employed as stretcher-bearers. At the Tank Barrier casualties were then loaded into LVTs. Other prisoners required guarding and removal from the fighting area.

Colonel Phillips decided that the attack could not continue and withdrew the commando, 350 yards back, under command of the Adjutant. As the latter was organising this position, a counter-attack took place. Fifty soldiers, more than the adjutant had at that stage, came over a ridge and opened fire: they were driven off, attacked again, and again were repulsed.

During these events other important matters were under discussion at 47's command post. The Brigade commander had come forward with 48's CO. Both urged 47's CO to mount a further attack that night but the latter considered that his commando was too disorganised to do that, that a new battle plan should be worked out and further ammunition and supplies brought forward first. He waited.

Supply ships

The first of the supply ships landed that day. In a mounting storm one which tried to beach became lodged on a broken part of the dyke and another dragged from its moorings. Others had to withdraw.

British Troops advancing along the waterfront near Flushing. (NA)

DAY 3
47 Commando

The battle for W11 resumed next morning. 47's CO again asked for rocket firing typhoons. None materialised but a 15 minute bombardment from the guns at Breskens took place. 47's Second in Command then led an attack on one of the flank positions which had caused much trouble the previous day and overcame it. At the same time a troop from 48 Commando gave covering fire to the 47 marines as they again attacked the main W11 position with a series of leap-frogging moves. W11 reacted with small arms, machine gun and mortar fire and grenades. The marines closed-in inexorably, however, and finally the adjutant led the troops, including the Dutch section, in a bayonet charge up a soft sandy slope and along an access trench. The fighting was now close contact and the enemy morale began to crack. They began to surrender and soon the whole battery was in the hands of 47. It was 1130 and the CO's judgement had been vindicated. One marine had been killed and 16 wounded, including some of the Dutch Troop. The main body of the commando, reduced to a third of its strength, now moved south. Ahead, 1½ miles away and ½ a mile north of the Flushing gap were the last remaining major batteries in the sector, W4 and W3. A captured officer prisoner was instructed to call upon the defenders to surrender. As W4 was approached a shot rang out and killed one marine. A period of expectant strained tension followed and then the area commander emerged. 47's CO gave him a stern ultimatum (somewhat hyperbolic regarding the forces ranged against him!) and after due delay he returned in full uniform and handed over

his hand gun in surrender. As far as 47 Commando was concerned the Walcheren battle was over.

41 Commando

During that day 41's LVTs had crossed to the southern side of the gap and advanced to Zoutelande to find that 47 had already reached the Flushing gap having captured W11, W4 and W3 and then made contact with 47 Commando across the gap.

DAY 4
41 Commando

The elements of 41 who had reached Zoutelande retraced their steps northwards across the Westkapelle gap and the reconstituted commando supported by tanks mounted an attack against W18. Prisoners were taken but heavy enfilade fire from woods on the right forced the commando to withdraw 500 yards to a consolidated position with a view to attacking next day.

DAY 5
41 Commando

41 resumed its attack on W18 at 1500 following an air strike. Supported by one Sherman tank and an AVRE the commando overran the battery. Four men including a troop commander were killed: 130 prisoners were captured.

Supply ships

The storm of Day 2 had now raged for 3 days causing supply problems. The supply LCT blown on to the dyke could only be very slowly and partly unloaded. Food shortages were now partly relieved by utilising captured German food supplies but an air drop of food and other commodities was also necessary.

Prisoners

These created a problem in respect of their numbers and the difficulty of disposing of them, particularly when they had to be marched for a long distance over the dunes.

DAY 6
41 Commando

41 consolidated its position in an area strewn with mines and brought forward supplies.

Casualties had to be evacuated by sea to the Base Hospital on an improvised LCT which would then take them to Ostend. (IWM)

Wounded

Due to the storm no casualties could be evacuated between days 2 and 5. They were crowded together in tents at the beach area in cold miserable conditions. Three of 47's wounded died there. With the storm abating and no hospital ship an empty LCT was loaded with 70 wounded, many on stretchers plus, 250 German prisoners. The stretcher cases were further traumatised as they had to be manhandled over other beached craft to reach the LCT. During the 10 hour journey to Ostend the wounded lay in the open, soaked by spray from the 8 feet waves breaking over the ship's bows: one marine died.

DAY 7
41 Commando

41 moved forward towards W19 but encountered minefields in which its supporting armour, a Sherman tank and an AVRE became immobilised. Coming under heavy mortar fire 12 marines were wounded, one fatally. The commando withdrew and in conjunction with the Brigadier decided on an early morning attack in the dark early next morning.

DAY 8
41 Commando

41 resumed its attack at 0615. Having to work its way through a minefield it was daylight before the attack went in but the enemy was taken by surprise and surrendered in droves. The battle for Walcheren was effectively over.

48 Commando

A 48 LVT passing through Serooskerke in transit struck a submerged mine: 16 marines and 5 Royal Engineers were killed and 8 wounded.

Casualties

41 lost 16 all ranks killed and an unknown number wounded. Including the losses at Serooskerke 48 lost 29 all ranks killed and 86 wounded. 47 Cdo lost 34 all ranks killed and 84 wounded. Among the 22 officers of 47 Cdo 36% were casualties and among 378 other ranks 28% Among the assault troops in closest contact with the enemy (i.e. excluding HQ and Heavy Weapons troop) numbering 288 (including medical personnel attached) as opposed to HW and HQ Troops (numbering 112) the casualty rates were 39% and 9% respectively. Among the officers in the assaulting troops the casualty rate was 57% (8 out of 14) and among the other ranks in these troops it was 37% (100 out of 274).

Antwerp Opens

With the Walcheren guns silent 100 minesweepers were soon in operation and by 1 December 10,000 tons of cargo had been unloaded at Antwerp. General Eisenhower described the capture of Walcheren as 'one of the most gallant and aggressive actions of the war'.

KEY ISSUES AND LESSONS
Priority

An assessment of a battle's importance requires the ultimate analysis of history but even at that undue historical dramatisation can distort military significance. Twenty-five years after Walcheren, General Simonds observed wistfully, 'If the assault on Walcheren had failed it would have been as famous today as the gallant airborne landing at Arnhem'. In September 1944, the Allies had the prize of Antwerp in their hands but failed, timeously, to exploit it. In manoeuvre warfare terms the attack on Walcheren, should have come before any other European operation at that time. Gallant as Arnhem was, Walcheren was the successful counterpoise which offset an expensive failure and enabled the war to continue to its successful conclusion.

*If the assault on Walcheren had failed it would have been
as famous today as the gallant airborne landing at Arnhem*

*The Commanders responsible for Walcheren: General Bernard Law Montgomery,
Lieutenant General Harry Crerar and Lieutenant General Guy Simonds. (NHB)*

Boldness and Surprise

In the face of much opposition both military and political General Simonds decided to flood the island. He took a calculated risk, a move which the enemy had not contemplated. It paid off by disrupting the enemy's ability to move troops and reinforce positions under threat (there were many unused German troops in Middelburg) and left the defenders on the dunes isolated with no possibility of reinforcement or retreat. Two of the batteries overlooking the gap (W14 and W22) were disabled by flooding.

German misjudgements

Considering the adverse circumstances confronting the assault on Walcheren, and yet its success, it is relevant to examine the lessons which might be learnt from the enemy's failures:

- The failure of the German Commander to destroy Antwerp's harbour facilities before abandoning them was a serious mistake.

- In the context of manoeuvre the assaulting force at Walcheren was possibly most vulnerable during its 40 mile journey from Ostend. The naval and air supremacy which the Allies possessed had their limitations and even at best would probably not have been very effective against the fast E-boats and the midget submarines which the Germans had at Brouwershaven close by, especially on the morning of 1 November with no Typhoons flying. E-boats could have played havoc with an armada consisting mostly of slow,

vulnerable LCTs. The Germans must have known that the assaulting force had set sail but their military thinking was not apparently properly attuned to their opportunity.

- The 'little ships', left alone to close 'the one hour gap' due to RAF grounding suffered severely but because the enemy gunners concentrated on them the first waves of commandos got ashore with comparative ease. If the German gunners from the start had concentrated on the LCTs carrying the commandos ashore the outcome of the battle might have been very different.

- There were two groups of defenders on Walcheren, the marines who were dominant, and the soldiers. The former were fanatical and highly motivated to defend 'the fatherland' to the last. The soldiers were less committed. Many had been there for a long time and some had established close emotional attachments to local girls which may have impaired their response to the 'do or die' exhortations of their leaders.

Other issues

Accepting that all battles, even the most successful, have their retrospectively implausible elements it is not too difficult to find such in Walcheren. That they did not affect the ultimate outcome is a tribute to those who did the fighting.

- **Planning and preparation time**. Preoccupation with Arnhem resulted in a handicapping shortage of planning

time for Walcheren and affected the adequateness of preparation.

- **Local resistance.** Unlike the situation on D-Day when the enemy forces opposing the assault from the sea were weakened by the subversive activities of widespread civilian resistance the attacking forces at Walcheren could not receive such assistance. The defending forces were beneficially sequestered on the dunes from which civilians had long been banned and the flooding of the island, while it conferred some advantage on the attackers, rendered any civilian movement which might assist the latter virtually impossible.

- **Use of airborne troops unreasonably refused**. After Arnhem, losses of British airborne troops meant that such were unavailable for Walcheren and Montgomery sought to include American airborne troops (had this been granted there would not have been any flooding of the island by breaking the dykes). His request was turned down on the basis that Walcheren was unsuitable for airborne landings, a surprising conclusion in view the island's flat interior and defences which were largely dispersed to its periphery, pointing outwards, leaving the centre relatively clear. It is

An LVT exiting the water. (IWM)

a moot point whether the number of military and civilian casualties would have been lower had there been an airborne component to the attack. The massive destruction of the island's physical and administrative structure would probably have been avoided.

- **Too limited use of air cover**. Although the operation was triphibious and the contribution of the RAF in breaking the dykes was seminal to its success, the degree of priority given to preliminary softening up of the defences by bombing and to air support during the ground attacks did not appear to be as high as the operation merited.

- **Failure of inadequately tested equipment**. The newly introduced LVTs were successful although they had difficulty in currents and in keeping up with troops moving on foot over loose shifting sand on steep dunes. They were brought to a complete standstill by the tank barrier. Weasels proved to be unreliable in the face of open sea, strong currents, soft sand, steep sand dunes and the actions of a hostile enemy. The misplaced reliance which had been put on them meant that much essential equipment (e.g stretchers which were lost and could have been carried by other means) was lost.

Further Reading

Ellis, L. F., *Victory in the West, Volume 2, the Defeat of Germany,* (London: HMSO, 1968)

Forfar, John, *From Omaha to the Scheldt, the Story of 47 Royal Marine Commando,* (East Lothian, Scotland: Tuckwell Press, 2003)

Forfar, John, *Towards Victory in Europe, the Battle for Walcheren,* (Proceedings of the Royal College of Physicians of Edinburgh; 25: 451-475, 623-628. 1995)

Ladd, James, *The Royal Marines, 1919-1980, An Authorised History,* (London: Jane's Publishing Company, 1980)

Linnell, T. G., *48 Royal Marine Commando, The Story,* (Published privately, 1946)

Mitchell, Raymond, *They Did What Was Asked of Them: 41 (Royal Marines) Commando,* (Firebird books, Poole, Dorset, 1996)

Moulton, J. L., *The Battle for Antwerp,* (Ian Allan Ltd: London, 1978)

Rawling, Gerald, *Cinderella Operation,* (Cassell: London, 1980)

Thomson, R. W., *The Eighty Five Days,* (Hutchinson: London, 1957)

Whitaker, W. D. & S., *The Battle of the Scheldt,* (Souvenir Press: London,1984)

Biography

Professor John Forfar was Mentioned in Despatches after the capture of Port-en-Bessin and later won the Military Cross during the assault on Walcheren Island with 47 Commando Royal Marines, (one of the few units to assault Hitler's Atlantic Wall twice). Having studied medicine at St Andrews University he joined the Royal Army Medical Corps in 1942 and then undertook Commando Training before joining 47 Commando Royal Marines as their Medical Officer. In addition to landing on D-Day he also operated from his Regimental Aid Post at the Orne bridgehead in support of 6 Airborne Division. He is the author of *From Omaha to the Scheldt: The Story of 47 Royal Marine Commando* (Tuckwell Press, 2000). He later went on to eminence as one of Scotland's leading paediatricians, being one of the founders of the Royal College of Paediatrics and Child Health. He is the author/editor of five professional Textbooks and over 150 research papers, was the Vice President of the Great Ormond Street Hospital for Sick Children appeal, a Trustee of the Malcolm Sargent Cancer Fund for Children and a Fellow of the Royal Society of Edinburgh. In addition to his role as Professor Emeritus for Child Life and Health at the University of Edinburgh, he still finds time to lecture at the Joint Services Command and Staff College, and at CTCRM Lympstone.

Commando Operations
The Bardia Raid (North Africa 1941) and Myebon (Burma 1945)

By Mr Robin Neillands

Some years ago, the late and much-lamented historian Dr David Chandler wrote an essay entitled 'What is Military History?' and began with the point that this was not the question. The question was - 'What is military history for?'

That is a good question and the answer largely depends on who one is talking to. To the layman, military history is entertainment. To the military historian, often the chance to score off rivals and grind a personal axe. To the professional soldier, sailor or Royal Marine, history offers an opportunity to learn the lessons of the past and – or so one hopes – profit from them. At that point, however, a problem often arises. Professional soldiers are notoriously reluctant to learn from the past, usually on the grounds that matters have changed since then and the lessons of the past are no longer applicable – if not positively dangerous.

There is some merit in this view. Clinging grimly to the lessons and methods of the past has contributed to the disasters on many stricken fields and, as a rule the professional soldier would be well advised to concentrate on the problem confronting him in the here and now and hope to get over it with a combination of professional expertise and low animal cunning. Ruminating on what Wellington would have done in similar circumstances may not be of much help. However, let us not throw out the baby with the bath water. There are few absolutes in life and no soldier is any the worse for having a sound grasp of military history. The kit and the tactics may change but there are eternal

verities even in the military world and history provides some lessons from which modern soldiers – and even modern Royal Marines, might profit. This point was well made shortly before the Second World War by General Sir Archibald Wavell in a series of history lectures to officer cadets;

> 'To learn that Napoleon in 1796 beat a superior force by something called 'economy of force' or 'operating on interior lines' is a mere waste of time. But if you can understand how a young, unknown man inspired a half-starve, ragged, rather Bolshie crowd; how he filled their bellies; how he out-marched, out-witted, out-bluffed and defeated men who had studied war all their lives and waged it according to the textbooks of the time, then you will have learnt something.'

Think on it. The lessons are there for those that have the wit to find them but you will find it by studying history, not merely reading it. Be critical; get a history book, an account of some battle or campaign and go through it carefully, annotating the words lines or paragraphs that interest, annoy or intrigue you. Above all, study the matter of WHY. Why did this engagement or campaign go wrong – and why did no one do anything about it? Was this a wise decision and if not, why not? Use the word 'why' - and keep on using it until you get to the answer and there are no more whys to ask. Do that and add a little common sense, and you will surely learn something to your advantage. Good history is full of lessons; it is not simply a narrative studded with dates.

At this point, let me declare an interest. I love history. I have loved it all my life and I admit to being biased in its favour. History has provided me with a constant source of pleasure and interest and is a basis for many other pleasures, like travel and reading - yes, and soldiering too. Over the years I have also discovered that many great soldiers - and hard-fighting men - were also lovers of history and that my own merry men, when compelled to listen and drag their minds away from the pleasures of

North Africa Star, Jun 1940 - May 1943.

the flesh and hard liquor, also found history compelling. This being so, I would now like to pass on a few stories concerning Commando operations in two very different theatres of war – the coastal desert of North Africa and the hills and jungles. Different too are the actions described, the one a none-too-successful raid, the other a highly successful all-out battle. Both, I think, provide lessons that one might absorb with profit. Much of what follows is oral history, the memories of the survivors, which are never less than entertaining and if carefully examined, can provide some useful lessons. They may provide some examples of good military practice – the need for training, discipline, aggression and the need to maintain the aim but they will also, I hope, illustrate the great truth about history; it is never, ever, dull.

HMT ship 'Glengyle' used to carry No. 7 Commando to the Bardia Raid on the night of 19/20 April, 1941. (NHB)

The Bardia Raid, 1941

' The object of Commando operations is to harass the enemy'

Commando Training Notes,
CTCRM, Bickleigh, 1950

From 1940 to 1943, the land battles against the Axis Powers of Germany and Italy took place mainly in the deserts of North Africa. The main problem which faced Army Commanders on either side during the Desert War was one of supply. The Desert War was a highly - mobile affair, fought out by tanks and lorried infantry, and the armies advanced or withdrew in relation to their ability to bring forward supplies of petrol, food, ammunition and reinforcements. The North African campaign also produced a surprising number of irregular forces on the British side, notably the Long Range Desert Group, the SAS, and three Army Commandos - Layforce - which carried out reconnaissance or raids behind the enemy lines by driving round their southern flank through the Great Sand Sea.

In fact, with the desert on one flank and the Mediterranean on the other, there were two flanks open for British raiding operations and so in February 1941 Colonel Robert Laycock embarked Nos. 7, 8 and 11 (Scottish) Commandos in the infantry assault ships HMTs *Glenearn*, *Glenroy* and *Glengyle* and sailed for the Middle East. Lieutenant Milton sailed with No. 7 Commando:

'I found myself on *Glenroy* with a group of officers which included Evelyn Waugh and Winston's son, Randolph Churchill. They seemed to spend most of their time gambling. This small brigade arrived in Egypt on 7 March and was then joined by two locally - raised Commando units, Nos. 50 and 52 Commandos, the composite formation then being known as Layforce. Layforce promptly fell victim to the Staff and was designated a Brigade in the 6th Division of General Wavell's Desert Army, the units being re-named as battalions. No 7 became the A Battalion, No 8, the B, No.11, the C, and the now - amalgamated Middle East Commando, the D Battalion. These battalions, like the brigade itself, lacked the usual accoutrements of heavy infantry units - engineers, transport, artillery, signals.'

Worst of all, though, the Middle East theatre was on the defensive and the British were constantly teetering on the brink of defeat. After a long string of successes against the Italians, the Eighth Army met a much more redoubtable opponent at the end of

March 1941, when the German General, Erwin Rommel landed in Cyrenaica at the head of the Afrika Korps. After that matters went seriously awry and staff officers, harassed to find reinforcements for frontline units, were soon casting greedy eyes at Laycock's brigade of well-trained infantrymen in the Canal Zone. This was bad enough but the Middle East was an active theatre where other units were already fighting and the Commandos could not fill that public and popular aggressive role they had come to occupy in the UK. Out here there was enough war for everybody and a brigade of trained soldiers could not be kept in idleness at such a time. Laycock knew this; the only way to keep Layforce intact was to give it something to do.

Laycock was therefore extremely glad when he was ordered to mount a raid on the Axis-occupied port of Bardia, 300 miles west of Alexandria. This operation was mounted on the night of 19/20 April 1941 by No. 7 Commando carried in HMT *Glengyle* and covered by a powerful escort, including the anti-aircraft cruiser HMS *Coventry*, three destroyers from the Royal Australian Navy and the submarine HMS/M *Triumph*.

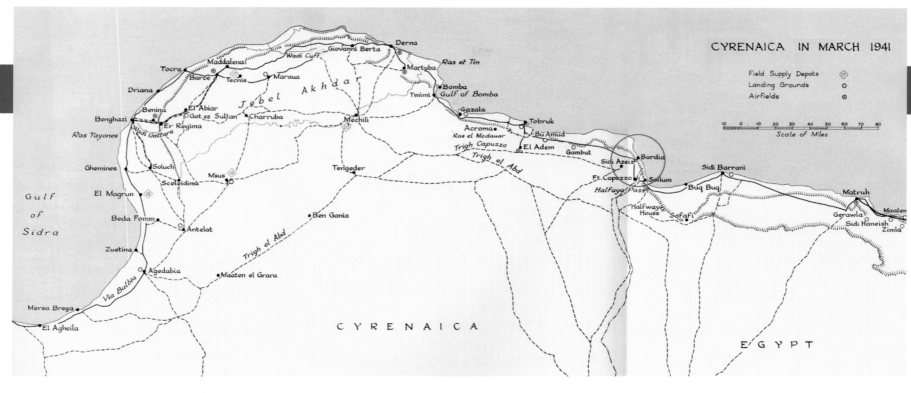

The Bardia raid met with an all-too-familiar series of amphibious problems. HMS/M *Triumph* was detected and attacked en route by Allied aircraft and was late at the off-loading point. The leading LCA was damaged and landed late. LCA compasses were faulty and put the men ashore at the wrong place, and a Commando officer, moving about the beach after the landing, was shot and killed by one of his own men.

The Commando stayed ashore for a short while and managed to destroy four guns before withdrawing, leaving about seventy men behind to be captured so it was not a successful debut. On the other hand, the Bardia raid did include one element not always found on military operations – comedy.

One bright spot at Bardia was the presence in the No. 7 Commando ranks of Admiral Sir Walter Cowan Bt., KCE, DSO,

MVO, a lively old gentleman, seventy-one years of age, bored with life on the retired list who, as an old friend of Admiral Sir Roger Keyes, Head of Combined Operations, had wangled his way into the Commandos. Admiral Cowan had first appeared in the Middle East as a young sub-lieutenant in charge of a Nile gunboat during Kitchener's campaign against the Dervishes that culminated in the Battle of Omdurman in 1898. In 1941, during the Second World War, the Admiral, now aged 73, had been captured by an Italian armoured division while engaging their advancing tanks with his service revolver. After some thought, the Italians politely returned the Admiral to the British lines, as 'an elderly officer, no longer fit for active duty'. They could not have been more wrong for Admiral Cowan attached himself to various Commando units and raided about the Mediterranean and Adriatic for the rest of the war. As the saying goes 'They don't make them like that any more'!

Lieutenant Milton takes up the story;

'As I remember, we were divided into two groups - a smaller group to enter the harbour, land and attack the town's water supply, while the major part landed west of the town to attack a defence battery and do other odd jobs, blow up road bridges and so on. My job was to take my section into the harbour in the leading LCA, ascend a cliff path, then march inland to find and demolish a valve that pumped the town's water supply. This, I was assured, would cut off the water for some time. We were accompanied on this raid by Admiral Sir Walter Cowan, a real fire-eater about five feet three inches tall. He was a friend of Sir Roger Keyes and, with Evelyn Waugh, was embarked for the landing in my LCA'.

operations will go awry and despite that the object of the
operation can still be achieved; that resolute men never give
up – and that it always helps to have a sense of humour

'We arrived off the port at about 22.00 hrs, it was quite
rough and choppy and in those days the first wave
climbed into the assault craft at deck level and were
then lowered into the water. For some reason our bow
davit lowered quicker than the stern one and we hit the
water bows first, smashed into the side of Glengyle and
damaged our starboard engine. I could see the shore and
worked out where we were, but when we were about a
hundred yards from the beach we touched bottom on
a sandbar and Admiral Cowan ordered our coxswain,
Sub-Lieutenant England, to "lower the door." England
complied and Admiral Cowan and Evelyn Waugh dashed
out and disappeared under the water. I held my men back
until, relieved of their weight, we scraped over the bar and
arrived at the real beach, dry-shod.'

'We went up the cliff path and towards our objective in
complete silence, until I saw figures ahead. These turned
out to be a Troop commanded by the unit's Second-in-
Command, Kenneth Wylie, who were going to blow up a
bridge. He told me it was too late to go on to the water-
pipes and to recce some buildings nearby. One of these
was found to be full of gelignite in a very critical state,
sweating and most unhealthy. I had no means of setting
it off, having only short fuses for our pipeline charges;
besides, if that lot had gone off it would have removed
7 Commando and most of Bardia to the middle of the
Mediterranean.

'I was detailed by Wylie to act as rearguard and so we
embarked late in our damaged craft and went slowly out
to sea, having an awful struggle to get our LCA off the
beach. When we got to the RV, the *Glengyle* had gone and
we were all alone on the ocean.

'Sub-Lieutenant England and I then had a conference and
we decided that the best thing we could do was to sail
to Tobruk, sixty miles or so to the west, which was then
surrounded by the enemy but held by the 9th Australian
Division. So off we went. I can't remember much about the
night except that it got very rough, and sleeping with my
head on my haversack, which contained some plastic 808
explosive and this gave me a peach of a headache.

'At dawn we were not far off the shore and it was still
rough. Then a vessel appeared on the horizon, flying no
flag, guns turned upon us. As she came closer I asked
England what we should do if she turned out to be Italian,
expecting him to say we would have to surrender, but
not a bit of it. He was signalling with his lamp and said
he would carry on signalling until we got alongside. Then
we would board her, capture her and sail her back to
Alexandria: the Nelson spirit was alive and well!

'Fortunately, she turned out to be a British boom-defence
vessel. We eventually sailed into Tobruk harbour, the men
went off to be fed and I was told to report to General
Morshead, commanding the 9th Australian Division. On

the dockside I found a truck driven by a very scruffy
Australian soldier, who looked me up and down and said,
"I suppose you went to Sandhurst ?" I looked him up and
down and said, "As a matter of fact, I did. Do you want to
make anything of it?"

'That was obviously the right reply, which was a good
thing as he was much bigger than I was and we drove
to Div. HQ, getting thoroughly shelled on the way. The
HQ was hidden away deep in some tombs, and there I
met the General, who also looked me up and down and
said, "What you need is a drink." One of his Staff Officers
went off and returned with a half- tumbler of whisky and
stood there while I drained it. As I swallowed the last
mouthful he sighed and I said, "What's the matter ?" and
he said, 'You have just drunk the last mouthful of whisky in
Tobruk'!

There are some lessons here; operations will go awry and
despite that the object of the operation can still be achieved;
that resolute men never give up – and that it always helps to
have a sense of humour.

Burma

For our next example of Commando operations we move from
the sandy beaches and arid wastes of North Africa to the muddy
chaungs and jungle-clad hills of the Arakan in Burma. Here in
1944, No. 3 Commando Brigade, commanded by a formidable

An Allied estuarian patrol prior to the build-up against Japanese positions in the Chaung area in Burma. (HNB)

Burma Star,
Dec 1941 - Sep 1945.

Royal Marines officer, Brigadier Campbell Hardy and consisting of Nos. 1 and 5 Army Commandos and Nos. 42 and 44 Royal Marine Commandos had been deployed for raiding operations against the Japanese. 'Campbell Hardy was a very good officer and I rate him highly', says Lieutenant Colonel Peter Young, who arrived in Burma as Deputy Brigade Commander in August, 1944.

'He had a somewhat Prussian air and was not someone to take lightly but since no one dared to cross him, we all got along very well. As for the units, it was a dammed good brigade with some fine people in it. I would rate 42 Commando highly for steadiness and No. 5 for dash but the outstanding unit was No. 1 Commando, one of the best of all the Commando units.'

The units of 3 Commando Brigade duly commenced a raiding programme along the coast of the Arakan but their big day came in early 1945 when the Brigade landed at Myebon and advanced inland to a feature called Hill 170. On Hill 170 the brigade fought one of the hardest Commando battles of the war and demonstrated that these wartime Commando units, though small, were capable of fighting full-scale battles against considerable odds.

This operation began badly. Put ashore some 200 metres from the shore at Myebon, the men had to wade in through mud that in places was waist or chest deep. Getting ashore was exhausting and took hours - and then they had to do battle with the Japanese who had arrived just too late to oppose the landing but were present in strength in Myebon village. The battle for Myebon lasted a day and a night and ended up with the Japanese retreating, having lost 150 men; Brigade losses came to 3 men killed and another 28 wounded. The Japanese had not gone very far. The Brigade re-embarked in their landing craft, sailed up the coast and came ashore again at Kangaw to find the Japanese dug in on a low hill just to the south east called Hill 170.

Peter Young takes up the tale;

'The Brigade task was to cut the communication lines of the Japanese Army which was now attempting to escape to the south. We disembarked and attacked Hill 170 with No. 1 Commando and took it, then gradually unrolled, taking further hills. Eventually the Japs got fed up with this and counter-attacked. They attacked one end of the Hill, which was held by one Troop of No. 1 Commando; this Troop was cut off from the rest of the Brigade by a re-entrant and this Troop behaved quite brilliantly; they massacred the Japanese but were massacred themselves. We took 100 casualties in a long day, wounded men being carried past

constantly and the following morning we changed No. 1 Commando for No. 5 Commando, to get fresh troops into the line.'

The main Japanese assault on the first day came in against No. 1 Commando, which seems to have borne the brunt of the fighting. The pattern of every Japanese attack was the same, a heavy artillery bombardment followed by a massed infantry

3 Commando landing at Myebon in the Burma Campaign. (NHB)

attack, pressed home to close quarters with the bayonet. The big attack came in against 4 Troop of No. 1 Commando, holding the northern edge of Hill 170, reinforced when possible by men from Nos 5, 42 and 44 Commandos. The Japanese man-handled their artillery close to the front line and were soon engaging the Commando positions over open sights, the Commandos replying with rifle and Bren gun fire. This change of unit came not a moment too soon as one of the Brigade signallers, Charles Hustwick relates:

'The battle on Hill 170 lasted a full 24 hours and most of it took place in an area no more than 100 yards square. The loss to the enemy was at least 300 killed and goodness knows how many wounded. When the hill was cleared the following day the back slopes were covered with enemy dead, small, dwarf like, armed with long rifles and long bayonets'... 'It was here that Lt. George Knowland of 4

Troop, newly commissioned and just out from the UK won a posthumous VC. He left his trench and moved about the position, throwing grenades, cheering the lads on. He engaged the enemy with a Bren when the crew was shot down, and then took up a rifle. He was last seen firing a 2-inch mortar from the hip when the Japs were just 30 yards away. Casualties were heavy among all the Bren gunners – we had one gun that twelve men manned in the course of the battle and eleven of them were hit before it ended. I have no idea what our casualties were, but the price of victory was not small.'

Peter Young again:

'On the morning of the second day I visited Robin Stewart of No. 5 Commando and he told me that in his opinion, if we gave the Japanese one more shove, they would go. I told him that the Brigadier had forbidden any more counter-attacks but if he wanted to put one in I would support him... Robin was one of those chaps who do not give a bugger, so without thinking of his commission, he gave them another shove, and that was that. There they were, all over the ground – dead. You could not step on the ground in front of the Brigade positions without

stepping on dead or dying Japanese. I have never seen anything like it, never... They had great gashes in them, a lot of head wounds. We had killed over 300 and only found two or three with enough breath left to croak. I took one prisoner although the Sikhs wanted to cut his throat, one prisoner in a battle that went on for two days. Afterwards we got a nice letter from 'up-top', saying we had won the decisive battle of the Arakan campaign but it is all forgotten now. No one knows what happened in Burma.'

The Brigade lost 44 killed and 90 wounded in the battle of Hill 170 and that letter from up top, an 'Order of the Day' from the Corps Commander, should not be forgotten:

'3 Commando Brigade, for indifference to personal danger, for ruthless pursuit in success and for resourceful determination in adversity, has been an inspiration to all their comrades in arms. The battle of Kangaw has been the decisive battle of the Arakan campaign and was won due to the magnificent courage shown by 3 Commando Brigade on Hill 170.'

This eulogy states no more than the truth, but what are the lessons of Hill 170? First, that sound leadership pays off; these men trusted their commanders; in all the accounts that came from Hill 170, there is not one word of panic. Secondly, that when British soldiers are well dug-in on a position they have

LCMs landing with Sherman tanks in the Kangaw, Burma. (NHB)

been charged to defend they will not be easily dislodged – so dig in well and get organised. That a good little 'un can beat a big one, if he uses his brains – you have to out-think them in order to out-fight them. That even all-out attacks can be defeated if the troops will hold their positions, know their weapons and fight back hard; discipline and training always pay off, so keep a grip and train hard. All basic stuff, perhaps, but it wins battles. And finally, as Lieutenant George Knowland demonstrated so well, nothing can be done without courage, the ultimate virtue.

Reflection

The Commando units of the Second World War bear little resemblance to their modern counter-parts. Just to begin with they were much smaller. When No. 4 Commando stormed the great guns at Varengeville during the Dieppe Raid he took just 242 men ashore – but they did the job and came home victorious. Size is not everything; what matters is training, discipline, good leadership and the will to win – those qualities were endemic in the wartime Commando units; put simply, they did not think they could be beaten. In October 1945, the Army Commando units were disbanded. The hard task of telling these men that they were no longer wanted was given to Brigadier Robert Laycock and his words are worth recalling;

> 'It has fallen to my lot to tell you, the Commandos, who have fought with such distinction in Norway and the islands of the North, in France and in Belgium, in Holland and in Italy, in North Africa and Egypt, in Crete and Syria, on the shores and islands of the Adriatic and in the jungles of the Arakan and Burma, it is with great regret that I must tell you today that you are to be disbanded...'

Fortunately, the Commandos have survived. The retention of 3 Commando Brigade, which served in every theatre in the 'End of Empire' period and latterly by the creation of various Army Commando units which for the last several decades have served in and with the Commando Brigade. There are plenty of brave tales from that post - War period as well and they too provide part of the on-going Commando history. They will also provide some of those eternal verities, those elements that transcend the present that General Wavell was talking about. At Achnacarry the instructors told the volunteers that it was, ' All in the heart and the mind' - that however hard it is, you can do it if you believe you can. They knew that at Dieppe and Varangeville and they knew that on the Bardia raid and on Hill 170. They did it, and we can do it too... if we believe we can and profit by the example this history provides. Long may we do so - and long may the Commando tradition stay alive.

Further Reading

Barnett, Correlli, *The Desert Generals,* (London: George Allen and Unwin, 1960, reprinted 1983)

Durnford-Slater, Brigadier, DSO* MC, *Commando*, (London, 1953)

Fergusson, *The Watery Maze*, (London, 1956)

Lepotier, Rear Admiral, *Raiders from the Sea*, (London, 1954)

Lovat, Brigadier The Lord, *March Past*, (London, 1978)

Neillands, Robin, *By Sea and Land; The Royal Marines Commandos, 1942-1982*, (London, 1987)

Roberts, Brigadier Derek Mills, DSO MC, *Clash by Night*, (London, 1956)

Saunders, Hilary St George, *The Green Beret*, (London, 1949)

Thompson, Julian, *The Imperial War Museum Book of the War in Burma, 1942-1945,* (London: Sidgwick & Jackson, 2002)

Young, Brigadier Peter, DSO MC**, *Storm from the Sea*, (London, 1958)

Biography

Robin Neillands was described as 'one of Britain's most readable military historians,' and was noted for his analytical approach to some of history's more pervasive myths. He was the author of more than 30 books, including: *D-Day, 1944: Voices from Normandy* (2004); *Grant: The Man Who Won the Civil War* (2004); *End Of The British Empire* (2004); *The Eighth Army: The Triumphant Desert Army That Held the Axis at Bay From North Africa to the Alps, 1939-45* (2004); *Winston Churchill: Statesman of the Century* (2003); *Attrition: The Great War on the Western Front, 1916* (2003); *By Sea, By Land: The Story of the Royal Marine Commandos (1996)* and other titles on subjects as diverse as the Hundred Years War and a history of Special Forces since 1945. Rob Neillands served in the Royal Marines Commandos and read Modern History at Oxford and Reading Universities. He lectured on military matters at Oxford University and the National Army Museum in London and led battlefield tours to Europe and the USA. He was both a Fellow of the Royal Historical Society and the Royal Geographical Society, Rob was also a member of the British Commission for Military History and a former Chairman of the Confraternity of St James, the pan-European pilgrim association. Rob sadly passed away in January 2006.

The Philippines
Striking into Emptiness: General MacArthur and the retaking of the Philippines (1944 - 1945)

By Professor Michael W Jones

When most historians associate General Douglas MacArthur with amphibious operations they invariably refer to Operation CHROMITE,[1] his brilliant plan to strategically outflank the North Korean army during America's 'Forgotten War.' They make only superficial references to well over 100 amphibious landings he commanded during the Second World War. Of these many offensives, the Allied army's return to the Philippines stands as one of the best examples of successful amphibious operations in history. Intricate staff work in the years leading to World War II had left MacArthur and many of his senior officers with a mastery of Philippine terrain and geography. From the outset of the Japanese invasion, Philippine guerrillas and the Allied Intelligence Bureau (AIB) inundated Allied planners with the Japanese order of battle.[2] The Allied operation tempo and the nature of amphibious warfare underscored the importance of speed and to attack an enemy in a vulnerable position.[3] Through naval superiority, MacArthur kept his forces concentrated and was strong at the decisive point.[4] By returning to the Philippines, MacArthur forced the Japanese to defend a valuable region far from their homeland, allowing him to eliminate the Japanese centre of gravity, its navy.[5]

Perhaps MacArthur's most significant attribute was the realisation that rapid, coordinated action would keep Japanese forces off balance. Within four months of MacArthur's retreat from Corregidor, he established headquarters in Port Moresby, New Guinea and began planning a counter-offensive. In the next two years he translated these plans into eighty-seven amphibious landings driving the Japanese out of the Southwest Pacific so that by July 1944, Allied combined forces were poised on the Vogelkop Peninsula in northwestern Dutch New Guinea to attack the Philippines.[6] The original plan called for a series of invasions starting with Mindanao in the south; however, Admiral William F. 'the Bull' Halsey's fleet carriers had discovered in the course of their raids that the island of Leyte in the central Philippines was lightly guarded. MacArthur rapidly shifted his plans to strike the island thirty days before his original schedule for Mindanao. Leyte offered him the most direct route to Luzon and ultimately, Manila and its harbours which could accommodate many of Vice Admiral Thomas C. Kinkaid's 738 ships. MacArthur's fertile mind demonstrated Clausewitz's concept of genius embodied in the combination of '*coup d'oeil*', the inward eye, and the 'determination' to follow its dictates.[7] He immediately grasped the essence of Leyte in his strategy. It allowed him to, 'take advantage of the enemy's unpreparedness; attack him when he does not expect it; avoid his strength and strike his emptiness.'[8]

Leyte Island was not without its dangers. October monsoons would relegate almost all the island's airfields to inoperable status and Lieutenant General George Kenney, in charge of Allied airpower, warned that Leyte was 500 miles from land based air cover.[9] These two problems would leave amphibious operations

US 6th Army

vulnerable to Japanese airpower. However, combined operations would ameliorate these dangers. Halsey's carriers decimated Japanese land based air power in the whole theatre starting with Formosa. In a three day battle beginning 10 October 1944, two-thirds of the Imperial air force was destroyed with only 100 U.S. planes lost. Halsey then shifted south to rain blow after blow on airfields around Manila.[10] After these engagements, Halsey refuelled his carriers at Ulithi and returned to the Philippines to attack Japanese logistical lines and troop transports attempting to reinforce Leyte from the islands of Cebu, Mindanao, Panay and Luzon.[11] Spearheading the assault on Leyte would be General Walter Kreuger's crack 6th Army. These 200,000 hard bitten veterans had strode across the Southwest Pacific retaking New Guinea, New Britain, the Admiralties, Biak, Noemfoor and Morotai. MacArthur could ask for no better instrument to demonstrate the capabilities and advantages of amphibious operations.[12]

---

[1]See: Michael Hickey's Chapter on the landings at Inchon in Operation Chromite.
[2]William B. Breuer, *Retaking the Philippines*, (New York, 1986), 12-13.
[3]Sun Tzu, *The Art of War*, translated by. Samuel Griffith, (Oxford, 1963), 134.
[4]Carl von Clausewitz, *On War*, translated by Michael Howard and Peter Paret, (Princeton, 1976), 204.
[5]Sun Tzu, 97.
[6]Breuer, xvii.

[7]Clausewitz, 102-03.
[8]Sun Tzu, 89.
[9]Spector, 512 and Breuer, 28-29.
[10]Gavin Long, *Macarthur as Military Commander*, (London, 1969), *151*.
[11]Spector, 511-12.
[12]Breuer, 39, 45.

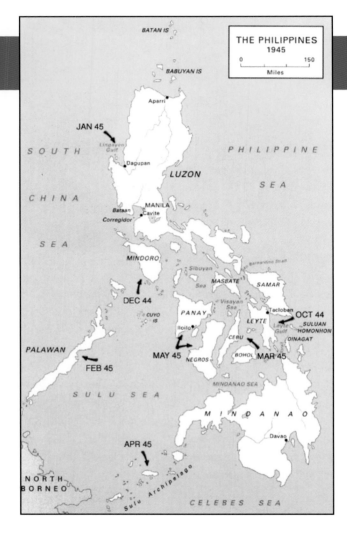

THE PHILIPPINES
1945

0   150

Miles

Map of the Philippines, 1945. (US Army)

The mobility offered by amphibious operations would break the deadlock

corps rapidly moved inland keeping the Japanese off-balance. Leyte Island's centre of gravity was the port of Ormoc on the west coast because it served as the entry point for Japanese reinforcements. Field Marshal Hisaichi Terauchi, against the advice of his commander in the Philippines, General Tomoyuki Yamashita 'the Tiger of Malaya', would make Leyte the decisive battle.[13] By doing so, he fell into the American trap. As Sun Tzu stated, 'those skilled at making the enemy move do so by creating a situation to which he must conform.'[14] The flower of the Japanese army in the Philippines would be isolated and destroyed at Leyte Island.

The struggle for Leyte Island pitted Allied advantages in manpower, air cover and naval assets against an entrenched and resolute foe. The mobility offered by amphibious operations would break the deadlock. Within days of the initial landings, X Corps captured the important crossroads town of Carigara on the northern coast, before the Japanese could reinforce it, and was poised to move on Ormoc. However, General Walter Krueger, fearing a seaborne attack on his beachhead, slowed the advance, giving Lieutenant General Suzuki Sesaki, commanding the 35th Japanese Army, time to establish a defensive perimeter west of Carigara in high mountainous terrain. The elite Japanese 1st Division imbued the terrain they defended with the nickname

Breakneck Ridge for their defence in the bloodiest battle of the Leyte campaign.[15] Despite the Allied edge in artillery the Japanese were able to slow Krueger's advance to a crawl. To break the impasse MacArthur would use his 'hit'em where they ain't' strategy, once again drawing on the 6th Army's experience using amphibious operations in New Guinea to outflank strong Japanese positions. The only flaw in the assault was a two week delay owing to insufficient shipping because of plans to invade Mindoro.[16]

The battle for Leyte was building toward its crescendo and the Japanese were determined to throw back the American advance. During the short operational pause, General Terauchi instructed Yamashita to 'muster all strength to totally destroy the enemy on Leyte.' His order doomed the Japanese army to defeat farther from its supply base and air support. At the beginning of the American invasion, 15-20,000 Japanese were on Leyte, but Yamashita reinforced this number to 60-70,000. During the transition, American fliers sank transports carrying 10,000 troops. Nevertheless, Yamashita's ability to reinforce the island, despite the enormous setback of Leyte Gulf, demonstrated that control of the sea was not an absolute term.[17] These numbers did fortify the Japanese position and led MacArthur to utilise another amphibious end run on the Japanese defences

The Allied invasion consisted of two amphibious landings on the eastern shore of Leyte, with X corps attacking south of Tacloban and XXIV corps striking Dulag. Once ashore both

[13]William Manchester, *American Caesar*, (Boston, 1978), 403.
[14]Sun Tzu, 93.
[15]M. Hamlin Cannon, *Leyte: The Return to the Philippines*, (Washington D.C., 1954), 211.
[16]Breuer, 83.
[17]Julian Corbett, *Some Principles of Maritime Strategy*, (Annapolis, 1988), 103.

The gun crews of a Navy cruiser covering the American landing on the island of Mindoro, 15 December, 1944, scan the skies in a effort to indentify a plane overhead. (NARA)

Our defeat at Leyte was tantamount to the loss of the Philippines

surrounding Ormoc. Although General Suzuki had erected no beach defences, the operation was daring because American leaders feared kamikaze attacks in the narrow waters around Ormoc.[18] On 7 December, the 77th Division of XXIV Corps, which had been held in reserve, went ashore unopposed three miles south of Ormoc. By 10 December two regiments of the division had fought its way into the town, thereby isolating Suzuki's men in the central highlands of Leyte by a three-pronged assault.[19] With the capture of Ormoc, MacArthur declared the Leyte operation merely required mopping up despite Suzuki still commanding 26,000 fanatical fighters. It would be left to Lieutenant General Robert Eichelberger's newly created 8th Army to dig them out.[20] Strategically, the battle for Leyte cost the Japanese 70,000 crack troops, decimated the Imperial Navy and destroyed the air force, leaving only kamikazes. Mitsumasa Yonai, the Japanese Naval Minister stated, 'Our defeat at Leyte was tantamount to the loss of the Philippines.'[21]

The second stage of MacArthur's strategy to liberate the Philippines was the capture of Mindoro, an island 260 miles northwest of Leyte and ninety miles south of Manila. Mindoro would provide land based air for the Luzon offensive.[22] The problem with this operation was that it outran air cover from Leyte leaving the amphibious invasion fleet vulnerable. Despite

these dangers, MacArthur knew the island was lightly defended, holding only 1200 Japanese, and it would quickly fall. He was correct. Soldiers came ashore on two beaches divided into White I and Blue I immediately capturing four abandoned air strips outside the village of San Jose. Whereas Japanese resistance on Leyte had delayed MacArthur's timetable for the Philippines, Mindoro fell so fast that the first airfield was operational two days after the landings. The second was ready in thirteen days. The amphibious assault on Mindoro struck into the emptiness of Japanese defences, however, kamikazes again exacted a toll, striking the *Nashville*, MacArthur's flagship, and left two LSTs disabled.[23] Also significant was that the Mindoro operation forced the Japanese in Luzon to protect against a southern advance further stretching Yamashita's resources. George Marshall stated, 'The Japanese were in an impossible situation.'[24]

Luzon was the prize of the Philippines. For MacArthur to fulfill his oath to return, Manila had to be recaptured. His force structure was larger than that in North Africa, Italy and southern France. It consisted of the 6th and 8th Armies, ten divisions strong. General Krueger would command the invasion force. In 1908 he had created a topographical map of much of Luzon and was an expert in Philippine geography. Together Krueger and MacArthur would adhere to Sun Tzu, 'Know the enemy,

know yourself: your victory will never be endangered. Know the ground, know the weather; your victory will be total.'[25] S-Day was set for 9 January 1945. Krueger's two Corps assault would be seventeen miles apart. XIV Corps, the 37th and 40th infantry divisions would hit the western beaches near the town of Lingayen and I corps, 6th and 43rd Infantry Divisions, would attack the eastern beaches near San Fabian.[26]

Meanwhile, General Yamashita, who had lost his best troops and air support on Leyte Island, crafted a strategy to draw out the defense of Luzon to attrite US forces.[27] The Japanese numbered 275,000 men, making Luzon the largest battle in the Pacific.[28] Yamashita correctly surmised the amphibious landing would take place at Lingayen Gulf, 120 miles north of Manila, because it had perfect beaches, a wide anchorage and was north of the central plain.[29] In contrast to MacArthur's defence of Bataan and Corregidor, Yamashita placed his headquarters in the mountains

[18]Manchester, 403.
[19]MacArthur, *Reminiscences*, (New York, 1964), 232-33.
[20]Long, *MacArthur as Military Commander*, 156.
[21]Manchester, 405.
[22]Breuer, 83.
[23]Spector, 518.

[24]Manchester, 411.
[25]Sun Tzu, 129.
[26]Breuer, 109.
[27]Spector, 518.
[28]Manchester, 406.
[29]Breuer, 107-08.

Rockets being fired at Japanese positions from an LCU off Mindoro. (NHB)

north of Manila and divided his defence into three groups. The first position, named Shobu, was the strongest and it defended the fertile region of the Cagayan Valley where Yamashita sought to draw his supplies. Kembu, the second group, was placed in the Zambales Mountains west of the central plains and was ordered to defend Clark Field. Yamashita placed his last group, Shimbu, in the mountains east of Manila to control the capital's water supply.[30]

The invasion fleet was so large that it was divided into four components with Rear Admiral Jesse B. Oldendorf's escorts

sailing first to clear the invasion route of Japanese air and remaining naval assets.[31] Once again, kamikazes exacted a heavy toll on Oldendorf's fleet, sinking twenty-four ships, including the escort carrier *Ommaney*, and damaging sixty-seven, in Lingayan Gulf. Yet the operation was a success because the Japanese impaled their remaining 200 aircraft on the escorts, allowing the transports and amphibious craft to arrive two days later relatively unscathed. With the landing uncontested from air and land, General Krueger put 175,000 men ashore in a few days, quickly capturing the 5000 foot Lingayen airstrip, which was in good condition.[32]

MacArthur's plan for the land campaign was for XIV corps to drive south for Clark Field and Manila while I corps attacked north and east to capture the junctions of route three and eleven. The latter road was a two-lane asphalt highway running northeast to the town of Baguio, Yamashita's headquarters. Control of the road would protect the XIV Corps' rear and the beachhead. However, seizing it would be difficult because troops had to pass through Japanese held mountain areas to arrive at the junction.[33] Allied forces landed unopposed and General MacArthur came ashore five hours later to order General Krueger to make all haste for Manila. At age sixty-five, MacArthur was a *tour de force* racing across the front to coordinate, assess and energise the offensive.[34] Despite his desire for speed, General Krueger

wanted to slow XIV Corps' advance until I corps could achieve its objectives and secure its flank and rear. MacArthur disagreed. He correctly analysed the inability of Japanese forces to launch a counter-attack and forced Krueger to push immediately for Manila on January 18. Five days later, advance elements began engaging Kembu group protecting Clark Field, which possessed a dozen airfields.[35] Control of this base would provide Allied forces with airlift and air cover. Yamashita had dug his troops into thirty fortified caves in the hills overlooking the airbase. His men fought a rugged defence that took the Americans a week to clear out, making MacArthur increasingly frustrated with the slow progress.[36]

General Yamashita initially planned to evacuate Manila, making it an open city; however, Rear Admiral Sanji Iwabuchi refused to abandon it and placed 16,000 sailors in the city. Yamashita grudgingly reinforced him with three battalions. This decision doomed Manila to severe destruction and high civilian casualties.[37] The city housed 800,000 people and was primarily constructed of reinforced concrete buildings, making it a strong defensive position. Admiral Sanji placed the Japanese troops in a line of camouflaged steel and concrete pillboxes four miles outside the city.[38] To break these defences, MacArthur would once again rely on amphibious operations combined with airborne landings. As Sun Tzu stated, 'War is based on deception. Move

---

[30]Spector, 518-19.
[31]Breuer, 111.
[32]Spector, 519-20 and Breuer, 119.
[33]Spector, 520.

[34]Breuer, 121, 24.
[35]Spector, 520-21.
[36]Breuer, 124.
[37]Manchester, 414.
[38]Carol Morris Petillo, *Douglas MacArthur, the Philippine Years*, (Indiana, 1981), 223.

when it is advantageous and create changes in the situation by dispersal and concentration of forces.'[39] With Japanese forces deeply engaged against the northern advance, the 11th airborne division, commanded by General Joe Swing, would come ashore at Nasugbu Bay, fifty-five miles south of Manila.

As in most of the 6th army's landings, the Nasugbu Bay amphibious attack relied on surprise, deception and speed. The 187th and 188th Glider Regiments would storm ashore January 31. They needed to immediately capture the Palico Bridge, five miles inland, spanning a 250 foot wide and eighty-five foot deep gorge, because this would give them control of Route 17 running to Manila. If the Japanese blew the bridge, the landing would be for virtually naught. Thereafter, they planned to drive north on Route 17 and strike the Tagatay Ridge, guarding the southern access to Manila, simultaneous with the rest of Swing's paratrooper division landing directly on the Ridge. The operation met with success, owing to the skill of the 11th Division. Palico Bridge fell before the Japanese engineers could react. The airborne troops never halted, pushing through the night for Tagatay Ridge and linking up with the rest of the 11th Division. This successful amphibious operation opened a second front on Manila, effectively hitting the city from the back door.[40]

With the XIV Corps pressing from the north and 11th Division hitting them from the south the Japanese troops were squeezed by an enormous pincer. Despite these incredibly mobile operations, the Japanese defence of Manila raged for a month. MacArthur had forbid the use of airpower for fear of collateral casualties but artillery and Japanese reprisals, including setting fire to the extremely flammable residential areas, drove up the casualty count to 100,000 Filipino deaths. The fighting finally died down on 3 March with the Allies in sole possession of the devastated city.[41]

For MacArthur, America's honour could only be restored with the retaking of Bataan and Corregidor. The two positions also secured Manila harbour and shifted the Allied supply line to a more defencible position in case of air attacks from Formosa. For Bataan MacArthur planned an amphibious landing on the Zambales coast of west Luzon with the XI Corps of the recently created 8th Army under Lieutenant General Robert L. Eichelberger.

As with most army amphibious operations in the Pacific, it struck at the weak exposed limb of the Japanese defences. The 38th Division of the corps landed unopposed and quickly captured the port of Olongapo on Subic Bay.[42] Once ashore, the division moved eastward to cut across the base of the peninsula. American forces began to encounter stiff Japanese resistance at 'Zig Zag Pass' where the jungle canopy obscured pillboxes and trenches. While the 38th Division continued with heavy fighting, another regiment of the XI Corps landed at Mariveles on the southern tip against light opposition. These forces enveloped the 1,400 Japanese defenders and in cooperation with air power destroyed them in seven days, thus freeing Bataan.[43]

The 38th Division had fought hard at Bataan and MacArthur called for another prodigious effort to recapture Corregidor. This tadpole shaped island lay astride the channel into Manila

[39]Sun Tzu, 106.
[40]Breuer, 137-41.
[41]Spector, 524.
[42]Manchester, 411.
[43]Spector, 525.

was their battle that only twenty Japanese were alive when the fighting ended. By 2 March 1944, after two weeks of fighting, 223 killed and 1,107 wounded the Stars and Stripes once again flew over the destroyed landscape of Corregidor.[45] The Japanese had lost thousands against US Marines in 1942.[46]

Bay. Over 6,000 Japanese guarded the island and they were expected to exhibit the usual fanaticism using their network of caves and mines. MacArthur again relied on surprise, airpower, naval support and the indomitable will of the American fighting soldier to overcome strong Japanese defences. The operation for Corregidor was an extremely dangerous affair with a nearly simultaneous parachute drop and amphibious landing. The two drop zones measured less than 1,000 feet long and 430 feet wide, with steady winds of twenty-five miles per hour capable of blowing soldiers over the island and into the water. Splintered trees became stakes, impaling helpless men. Meanwhile, a battalion of the 24th Infantry Division would come ashore in the centre of the island to split it in two.[44] So tough

While the fighting for Luzon continued MacArthur launched invasions against seven southern Philippine Islands. He decided upon this course of action against the wishes of the JCS who had briefed the British at Yalta that there were no plans to continue the Philippine campaign beyond Luzon. MacArthur's strategic objective was to control a belt of air bases flanking the South China Sea, thereby cutting off the Japanese line of communications.[47] Among other reasons, MacArthur sought airbases to cover future Borneo operations.[49] Prominent historians, among them MacArthur's leading biographer, have criticised the General's decision by claiming these islands were strategically unimportant. The Japanese navy was already shattered and the home islands were cut off from oil in the

In forty-four days, the 8th Army carried out fourteen major and twenty-four minor amphibious landings

Dutch East Indies.[48] The operations absorbed five divisions of General Krueger's 6th Army into General Eichelberger's 8th Army weakening Allied offensive capabilities on Luzon. Nevertheless, these forces again displayed the dash and élan for which their advance had grown famous. In forty-four days, the 8th Army carried out fourteen major and twenty-four minor amphibious landings. Supporting the army was Admiral Thomas Kinkaid's 7th Fleet, Daniel Barbey's 7th Amphibious Force and General Paul Wurtsmith commanding the 13th Air Force.[50] Due to the Battle of Leyte Gulf, in which Japan lost three battleships, four carriers, six cruisers and over twelve destroyers, forty percent of the Japanese fleet, the amphibious operations proceeded unmolested by Japanese naval and air assets.[51]

The recapture of the southern islands once again illustrated many aspects of manoeuvre warfare. MacArthur compared Eichelberger's campaign to J.E.B. Stuart's operations during the American Civil War. Manoeuvre was again critical in striking the Japanese at undefended beaches. Once ashore, Allied forces used terrain to cut the Japanese from supplies and drive them

[44]Daniel E. Barbey, *MacArthur's Amphibious Navy*, (Annapolis, 1969), 305-07.
[45]Breuer, 184, 256-57.
[46]Manchester, 411.
[47]MacArthur, 254.

[48]Manchester, 429.
[49]D. Clayton James, 'MacArthur's Lapses from an Envelopment Strategy in 1945,' in *MacArthur and the American Century*, Ed. by William Leary, 175.
[50]Barbey, 310.
[51]Spector, 440-41.

into pockets that could be harried by Filipino guerrillas. The 8th Army captured the islands of Negros, Cebu, Panay, Zamboanga, Palawan, Tawitawi and Guimaras. Few statistics can capture the success of American forces more than the disparity of casualties in the fight for these islands, 21,000 Japanese were killed as compared to 820 Americans.[52] George Marshall stated, 'General MacArthur instituted a series of amphibious thrusts with such lightning speed that the bewildered enemy, completely surprised, was successively overwhelmed.'[53]

Regardless of these victories, General Yamashita still possessed a formidable Japanese army on Luzon and his strategic objective to delay American victory had not changed. After the fall of Manila, Yamashita pulled back to the harsh mountain terrain in the northern portion of the island. He centered the Japanese defence on a triangle around the towns of Baguio, Bontoc and Bambang. MacArthur concentrated 6th Army's efforts on recapturing

Manila's water supply at the Wawa and Ipo Dam. The first dam was irrelevant to Manila's needs but it cost Americans two months of bitter fighting, while the more valuable Ipo Dam fell to Filipino guerrillas supported by 5th Air Force fighter-bombers. The fighting then shifted to Yamashita's position. Heavy infantry combat once again supported by tactical air isolated Baguio, slowly starving the Japanese defenders and driving them out of the town. However, this was as far as American forces would progress until the end of the war, when Yamashita surrendered with 50,500 well armed troops. Historian Ronald Spector blames the slow fighting and lack of further amphibious landings on MacArthur's operations in the southern Philippines but it is difficult to ascertain how amphibious landings could have achieved any more against Japanese forces dug into mountainous inland positions.[54]

General Yamashita met with General Jonathan Wainwright to sign the articles of surrender on 2 September 1945.[55] The Japanese referred to the campaign for the Philippines as the *sekigahara* or decisive battle. They were correct. On the eve of the Allied invasion, Japan had 400,000 soldiers in the Philippines because the archipelago was critical to the maintenance of its empire.[56] Recovering the Philippines, denied the Japanese access to oil, rubber, tin and other valuable resources. Over 100,000 Japanese soldiers were killed, captured and wounded with another

Because of this mobility MacArthur was able to mass superior forces at the decisive point, despite the Japanese advantage of numbers

280,000 scattered and isolated. The Imperial Navy and Air Force, with the exception of kamikazes, was shattered, isolating the Japanese home islands from their most important resource base in the South Pacific.[57]

The Campaign for the Philippines was a triumph for Allied arms and a model for the application of three prominent theorists. Sir Julian Corbett wrote, 'The object of naval warfare is the control of communications,' however, 'the destruction of your enemy's forces will not avail for certain unless you have in reserve sufficient force to complete the occupation of his inland communications and principal points of distribution.'[58] The naval battle of Leyte Gulf gave the Allies control of communications while the 6th and 8th Armies captured the inland communications. Strategically, General MacArthur followed Clausewitz's theory that a battle plan should be simple. Allied forces assaulted poorly defended beaches and once they encountered opposition ashore, MacArthur used further amphibious operations to outflank the Japanese. Because of this mobility MacArthur was able to mass superior forces at the decisive point, despite the Japanese advantage of numbers. In October 1944, the Japanese

[52]Manchester, 429-30 and William F. McCartney, *The Jungleers, A History of the 41st Infantry Division*. (Washington, 1948), 157.
[53]MacArthur, *Reminiscences*, 254.
[54]Spector, 526-30.
[55]Stanley Franckel, *The 37th Infantry Division in World WarII*, (Washington, 1948), 361.
[56]Manchester, 374.
[57]Breuer, 259.
[58]Corbett, 94.

Western Pacific Theatre US Army patch. (US Army)

had nine divisions available against six Allied divisions. Through adroit manoeuvres, MacArthur secured a force ratio of 6:1 at the Leyte beachhead. Thereafter, his rapid operation tempo, at the expense of thorough preparation, followed Clausewitz's theory to land blow after blow at the centre of gravity, keeping the Japanese off-balance.[59] During interrogations after the war, General Yamashita acknowledged the incredible accuracy of Allied intelligence and the speed with which the Allied armies moved; thereby validating two of Sun Tzu's core theories.[60] Although the Japanese were soundly defeated in the Philippines the Allies sustained 47,000 battle casualties making it proportionally one of the bloodiest campaigns in the Pacific.[61]

Further Reading

Barbey, Daniel E., *MacArthur's Amphibious Navy*, (Annapolis: Naval Institute Press, 1969)

Breuer, William B., *Retaking the Philippines*, (New York: St. Martin's Press, 1986)

Cannon, M. Hamlin, *Leyte: The Return to the Philippines*, (Washington D.C.: United States Army, 1993)

Gatchel, Theodore L., *At the Water's Edge*, (Annapolis: Naval Institute Press, 1996)

Krueger, Walter, *From Down Under to Nippon*, (Washington D.C.: Combat Forces Press, 1953)

MacArthur, Douglas, *Reminiscences*, (New York: McGraw Hill Book Company, 1964)

Manchester, William, *American Caesar*, (Boston: Little, Brown and Company, 1978)

Spector, Ronald H., *Eagle Against the Sun*, (New York: Vintage Books, 1985)

Biography

Dr Michael W Jones is a Professor of Strategy and Policy at the US Naval War College, Monterey, where he has taught for four years. Dr Jones received his Bachelor and Master's degrees in history from the University of New Orleans and his doctorate in history from Florida State University. He taught at Florida State for four years. A scholar with broad interests, his research has focused on modern military, diplomatic and political strategy, with specific emphasis on the Anglo-French wars of 1793-1815. Dr Jones is a Lieutenant in the US Navy.

[59]Theordore L. Gatchel, *At the Water's Edge*, (Annapolis, 1996), 115-16.
[60]General Walter Krueger, *From Down Under to Nippon*, (Washington, D.C., 1953), 328.
[61]Michael Schaller, *Douglas MacArthur, the Far Eastern General*, (Oxford, 1989), 98.

Iwo Jima and Okinawa
Operations DETACHMENT & ICEBERG
February - April 1945

By Mr Tim Bean

In the opening half of 1945 US forces mounted successive amphibious assaults against the islands of Iwo Jima and Okinawa, to secure bases for Operation DOWNFALL, a two-phase invasion (OLYMPIC-CORONET) of the Japanese Home Islands. Scheduled for 1 November 1945, Operation OLYMPIC would secure advance bases in southern Kyushu to support Operation CORONET on 1 March 1946 – which was to deliver a decisive blow against the Tokyo-Kanto plain. Occupation of Japan's political and industrial heartland was intended to leave her leaders no option but to accept Allied demands for 'Unconditional Surrender', promulgated at Cairo in December 1943 and re-affirmed at Potsdam in July 1945.

With the dropping of the atomic bombs on Hiroshima and With the dropping of the atomic bombs on Hiroshima and Nagasaki, and the Soviet Union's declaration of war in August 1945, DOWNFALL proved stillborn as Japan capitulated. The decision by US political and military leaders to use atomic weapons to end the war was underpinned by serious concerns that an invasion of the Home Islands would repeat the fighting experienced on Iwo Jima and Okinawa, but at a cost far in excess of their combined 98,583 casualties.[1] This scale of loss was a result of prolonged attritional fighting against heavily fortified Japanese defences characterised by depth and unparalleled density. Underpinning

formidable physical strength was the fanatical determination of Japanese troops to fight to the death. The combination of these elements created a situation in which American forces were forced to fight on terms set entirely by the Japanese. Modern concepts of a manoeuvrist approach 'in which shattering the enemy's cohesion and will to fight, rather than his material, is paramount'[2] were in fact reversed. On Iwo Jima and Okinawa, against an enemy whose will was virtually unbreakable, material and physical destruction became paramount.

Strategic Dilemmas

On 3 October 1944 Admiral Chester W Nimitz, Commander-in-Chief Pacific Fleet and Commander Pacific Ocean Areas, was instructed by the US Joint Chiefs of Staff (JCS) to draw up plans for seizure of one or more positions in the Bonin and Ryukyu islands. This decision emerged under the shadow of a lengthy argument over future strategy as US forces began the final operations to breach the Japanese 'Inner Defence Zone' along the Marianas-Palau-Mindanao axis. The essence of the arguments centred on the underlying strategy of the Pacific war that envisaged the Formosa-China coast-Luzon area as the main objective. This was seen as fulfilling two essential criteria: first, providing aid to China; second, cutting Japanese communications to South East Asia. In a 12 March 1944 JCS directive, Formosa had been marginally prioritised over Luzon.

Summer 1944 witnessed four events reverse these priorities, and then undermine the rationale for Formosa-China coast operations. First, from April, the impotence of Chinese Nationalist Kuomintang forces to prevent the Japanese overrunning US airbases in southwest China dealt a dual blow to American interests. Loss of its bases saw the Army Air Force's interest in Formosa-China coast operations diminish. Second, occupation of the Marianas revealed that Saipan and Guam could not provide the Navy with the logistic facilities to mount against Formosa: Luzon could. Third, in September a series of fast carrier raids revealed the weakness of Japanese positions in the Philippines. Cancellation of preliminary operations on Mindanao to strike at Leyte, in the centre of the archipelago, on 20 October opened up the possibility of landings on Luzon by 20 December, two months ahead of Formosa. Despite the inexorable logic of the combination of these three factors, it was the fourth that proved critical in finally convincing the principal advocate of Formosa, Admiral Ernest J King, Commander US Navy and Chief of Naval Operations, to agree to Luzon. At a 29 September – 1 October conference with his senior Pacific commanders King was persuaded by their doubts over the availability of troops and logistic support for Formosa. On the other hand they pointed out that Nimitz possessed sufficient marine and army forces at hand for an attack against Iwo Jima, in the Bonins, and Okinawa, in the Ryukyus, in early 1945.[3]

---

[1]Figures cover United States Army, Navy and Marine Corps killed, wounded and missing in action. Drawn from Ian Gow & H. P. Willmott, *Okinawa 1945: Gateway to Japan* (London, 1986), p.195; S. E. Morison, History of United States Naval Operations in World War Two, *Victory in the Pacific 1945*, vol. xiv (Castle Books, 2001), p. 69; Ministry of Defence (NAVY), *War With Japan; The Advance to Japan*, vol. vi (HMSO, 1995), p.209.
[2]*British Defence Doctrine* (JWP 0-01) (2nd edition), Chapter 3.
[3]Based on G. P. Hayes, *The History of the Joint Chiefs of Staff in World War II: The War Against Japan* (Naval Institute Press, Maryland, 1982), Chapters xix and xxiv.

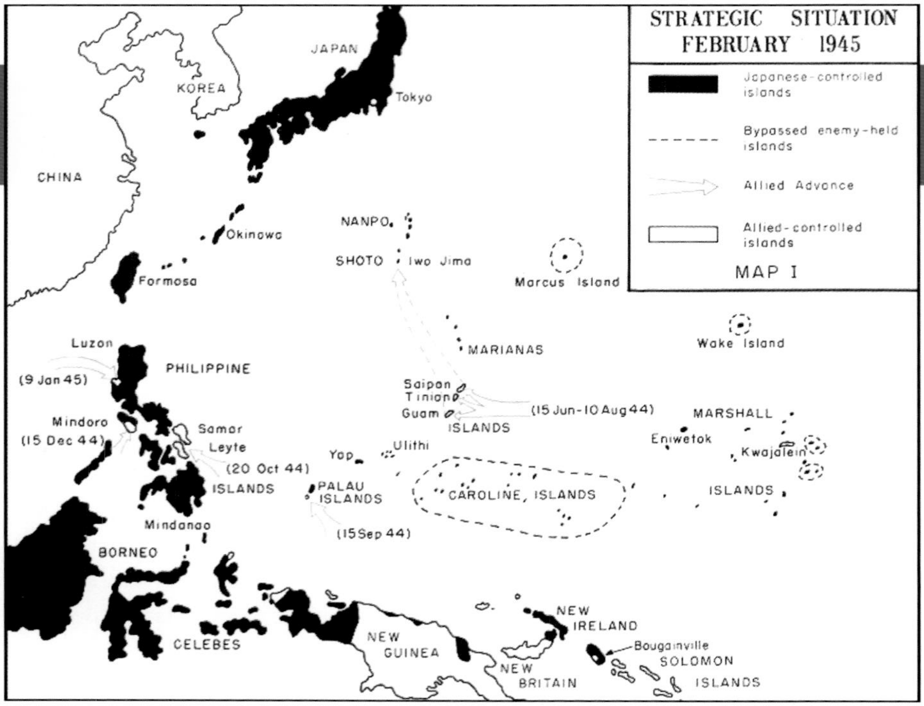
STRATEGIC SITUATION
FEBRUARY 1945
Japanese-controlled islands
Bypassed enemy-held islands
Allied Advance
Allied-controlled islands
MAP I
JAPAN
KOREA
Tokyo
CHINA
Okinawa
Formosa
NANPO
SHOTO
Iwo Jima
Marcus Island
Wake Island
MARIANAS
Luzon
(9 Jan 45)
PHILIPPINE
Saipan
Tinian
Guam
ISLANDS
(15 Jun-10 Aug 44)
MARSHALL
Eniwetok
Kwajalein
ISLANDS
Mindoro
(15 Dec 44)
Samar
Leyte
(20 Oct 44)
ISLANDS
Yap
Ulithi
PALAU
ISLANDS
CAROLINE ISLANDS
(15 Sep 44)
Mindanao
BORNEO
CELEBES
NEW GUINEA
NEW IRELAND
NEW BRITAIN
Bougainville
SOLOMON
ISLANDS

Map showing the strategic situation in the Pacific, February 1945. (USMC)

The occupation of these island chains, 750 and 350 miles from the Home Islands, would facilitate American tightening of the blockade of Japanese access to vital and increasingly scarce resources from South East Asia, China, Korea and to a degree Manchuria. Additionally, aerial bombardment of Japan, already scheduled to commence in November by B-29 bombers based in the Marianas, would be intensified. Whether these newly acquired positions would be required to support an invasion of Japan remained undecided, though in June 1944 the JCS had accepted the possibility of such an eventuality. Indirectly, Nimitz's orders effectively killed the Formosa-China coast options.[4]

Japanese Defence

The gradual evolution of US strategy, and the selection of the Bonins and Ryukyus as objectives for 1945, was reflected in growing Japanese measures for the defence of the islands. American seizure of the Marshalls in February provoked Imperial General Headquarters (IGHQ) to activate 32nd Army in the Ryukyus and place the Bonins under 31st Army on Saipan. A trickle of reinforcements and equipment was dispatched in April and May. The first breaches in IGHQ's 'Inner Defence Zone' signalled by American landings on Saipan (15 June), and the US Fifth Fleet's overwhelming victory at the battle of the Philippine Sea (19-21 June), forced a re-casting of Japanese plans. IGHQ drew up the four Sho-Go defence plans calling for all-out combined efforts by army and navy units in each of the areas including the Ryukyus and Bonins.[5] The 109th Division was assigned to the Bonins, the 9th, 24th and 62nd Divisions to Okinawa. Defeat of the Combined Fleet at Leyte Gulf (24-25 October) and US landings in the Philippines placed even greater stress on preparing the approaches to the Home Islands.[6]

By the time of the American landing on Iwo Jima in February 1945 over 21,000 army and naval personnel, backed by an impressive concentration of artillery including 361 field pieces of 75mm calibre, 65 150mm mortars and over 200 20-25mm anti-aircraft guns, defended the eight-square-mile island.[7] Deploying his forces, Kuribayashi downgraded beach defence, positioning his two operational groups either side of the landing beaches. The bulk of his forces were concentrated in the north along two defence lines running east-west along the plateau to the south and north of Motayama number 2 airfield. In the south a semi-independent group occupied Mount Suribachi, whose 550-foot summit dominated the landing zones. On Okinawa Lieutenant General Mitsuru Ushijima supplemented 32nd Army's 65,000 regular troops by drafting in service troops, 8,800 naval personnel and 20,000 Okinawans, bringing the island's defenders to a total of 110,000. The artillery concentration on Okinawa proved the greatest concentration deployed by the Japanese during the Pacific war, with over 270 guns of 70mm calibre or larger and with an ample supply of mortars. 32nd Army's main strength was concentrated in the south around the ancient capital of Shuri. The 62nd Infantry division defended three lines in this area while the 24th Infantry division covered potential landing sites around Minatoga on the southeast coast. The centre and north were covered by 44th Independent Mixed brigade and a few service troops intended to harass and delay the enemy.[8]

---

[4]Later claims that Iwo Jima was seized as an emergency landing area for stricken B-29s and to counter Japanese attacks on their bases in the Marianas are revealed as special pleading in hindsight in: *War With Japan*, vol. vi, p. 5, 151; 'Breaking the cycle of Iwo Jima mythology: a strategic study of operation detachment', by R. S. Burrell, *Journal of Military History* 68 (October 2004).

[5]H. P. Willmott, *The Battle of Leyte Gulf* (Indiana University Press, 2005), p. 47; Sho-1 Philippines; Sho-2, Formosa-Ryukyus; Sho-3 Kyushu, Shikoku and Honshu; Sho-4 Hokkaido and the Kuriles. Sho-3 acknowledged the possibility of a decisive battle off the Bonins in special circumstances; *War With Japan*, vol. vi, p. 8

[6]W. S. Bartley, *Iwo Jima: Amphibious Epic* (Washington, 1954), p. 6-9; Gow & Willmott, p. 30-42

[7]G. W. Garand & T. R. Strobridge, *History of United States Marine Corps Operations in World War II: Western Pacific Operations* (Washington DC, 1968), vol iv, p. 453-4.

[8]B. M. Frank & H. I. Shaw, *History of U.S. Marine Corps Operations on World War II: Victory and Occupation* (Washington DC, 1968), 46-51.

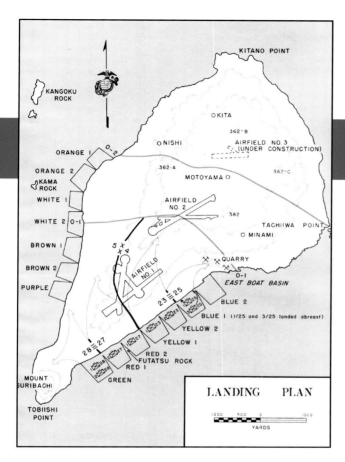

Left: Landing Plan map for the assault on Iwo Jima. (USMC)
Right: The first five waves moving into the beach, D-Day (H-Hour minus 6). (USMC)

Impressive as the forces on Iwo Jima and Okinawa were, it was their operational and tactical employment that proved the catalyst to the prolonged and costly struggles that occurred from February to June 1945. By January 1945 Kuribayashi and Ushijima had abandoned the standard Japanese practice of forward defence of the beaches supported by major counterattacks. Kuribayashi was motivated by the realisation that such tactics were futile in the face of overwhelming US firepower. Ushijima remained committed to a standard defence until January 1945, when withdrawal of the 9th Division and cancellation of the replacement 84th Division undermined 32nd Army's capability for offensive operations. Equally significant for both commanders was the IGHQ's strategy of using the islands

for delaying operations, to gain time to prepare the Home Island defences. As prolonged resistance was now the operational aim, conservation of strength became paramount. Costly large-scale counterattack was forbidden. Troops were to hold fire until US forces were ashore in order to lessen the effectiveness of US preliminary bombardment. Massive dense complexes of mutually supporting and interlocking fortified positions in depth were constructed to draw the Americans into a battle of attrition and inflict maximum casualties. IGHQ had recommended such measures in August: the 'Defence guide to Islands' disparaged 'rash counterattack' in favour of a policy of 'endurance engagement'.[9] At Biak in May and Peleliu in September Japanese garrisons had fought in a similar manner. What was to be unique on Iwo Jima and Okinawa was the scale of defences.

Planning

Planning for DETACHMENT and ICEBERG began in October 1944. The final drafts were submitted in December 1944 and February 1945 respectively. Interdependence in timing and resources meant that the two operations were essentially different phases of the same campaign. Together they constituted the most audacious and complex amphibious operations to be undertaken by US forces. As the scale of operations was beyond existing US shipping and naval resources, DETACHMENT would have to be completed before ICEBERG could be mounted. Both, in turn, were dependent on MacArthur releasing resources after landing

on Luzon on 20 December. Postponement of these operations to 1 January 1945 forced Nimitz to re-schedule his operations. The final dates set were 19 February for DETACHMENT, 1 April for ICEBERG.

Naval organisation saw a close correlation between the two operations. Overall responsibility for planning and conducting both operations was vested in Admiral Raymond Spruance as Commander Fifth Fleet, and during ICEBERG Commander Pacific Task Forces. Redesignation of Spruance's command reflected the greater size and complexity of the Okinawa operation. As Commander Joint Expeditionary Forces, Task Force 51, Vice-Admiral Richmond Kelly Turner was in overall charge of the amphibious operations, and his role was to coordinate a series of task groups whose individual commanders varied in the two operations, but which retained their specific roles. Notable amongst these was the newly formed Task Force 52, 'Amphibious Support Force', designed to coordinate all pre-invasion operations more effectively until the attack groups arrived.[10]

---

[9] Joseph H. Alexander, *Storm Landings: Epic Amphibious Landings in the Central Pacific* (Naval Institute Press, Maryland, 1997), p. 110.
[10] *War With Japan*, vol vi, p. 182-83.

Left: Marines of the 5th Division on Red Beach, Iwo Jima, 19 February, 1945. (USMC)

Right: LSTs and LSMs unloading on green and red beaches. (USMC)

For DETACHMENT the plan consisted of three broad phases. First, air and naval forces would bombard the island over a period of several months. In phase two Task Forces 52 and 54 would conduct a three-day preliminary bombardment. In phase three the island would be assaulted across the eastern shore and secured in ten days by Major-General Harold Schmidt's 5th Amphibious Corps. The 4th and 5th Marine Divisions would land abreast on the eastern beaches between Suribachi and the East Boat Basin. The latter would wheel one regiment against Suribachi, securing the position in the opening days. The remainder of 5th Division with the 4th would wheel north and drive to the north coast. The 3rd Marine Division was in reserve. Originally it was to wait ashore on Guam, but Commander Fleet Marine Force Pacific, Lieutenant General Holland M Smith, as photo-reconnaissance gradually revealed the scale of Japanese defences, redeployed it as a floating reserve off Iwo Jima. Smith and Schmidt also wanted the navy to extend its bombardment from three to ten days in order to carry out a methodical reduction of an estimated 450

Japanese positions. The navy's refusal, based on arguments concerning ammunition supply (re-supply at sea was, tentatively, due for the first time on 19 February), and unwillingness to expose its forces whilst the Fast Carriers dealt with enemy air power were, and remain, controversial. Both services held sound positions in terms of their own operational requirements, but these did not, or could not be made to, complement each other to the Marines' satisfaction.[11]

In ICEBERG, Spruance's plan of attack was conceived in four phases. Phase one was to be conducted by Vice-Admiral Marc Mitscher's Fast Carriers of Task Force 58 and B-29 'Superfortress' heavy bombers of General Curtis Le May's 21st Bomber Command. Attacks by these forces were intended to isolate Okinawa by neutralising Japanese air power in the Ryukyus, Japanese Home Islands and Formosa. Once this was completed Mitscher's Fast Carriers were to take station east of Okinawa to provide support to the other phases of ICEBERG. Additionally, Mitscher was responsible for eliminating any enemy surface threat. Joining American naval forces for the first time would be the British Pacific Fleet. Commanded by Vice-Admiral Sir Bernard Rawlings, the British carriers of Task Force 57 were to protect the left flank of the invasion by mounting strikes against Japanese air assets in the Sakishima Islands and Formosa. In phase two Vice-

Admiral Richmond Kelly Turner's Joint Expeditionary Force was to support landings by the 24th Army and 3rd Amphibious Corps of Lieutenant General Simon Buckner's 10th Army. These forces were initially to secure the Keise Shima and Kerama group islands west of Okinawa. Once secured, the Keramas would become a forward fleet base. Keise Shima was designated as a fire-base for 155 m 'Long Tom' field guns against southern Okinawa. The main landings would then take place on the Hagushi beaches along the centre of Okinawa's west coast. The second phase would end with the securing of the southern part of the island. In phase three the remainder of the island would be occupied along with Ie Shima island off the northwest coast. In the fourth, additional positions would be occupied in the Ryukyus.[12]

[11] Bartley p.40-1.
[12] Frank and Shaw, p.67-8.

Smashed by Japanese mortar and shellfire, trapped by Iwo's treacherous black-ash sands, Amtracs and other vehicles of war lie knocked out on the black sands of the volcanic fortress, March 1945. (USMC)

Operation DETACHMENT

Attacks against the Bonin islands had begun in June as the Fast Carriers undertook suppression of Japanese air power across the Central Pacific in preparation for the invasion of the Marianas. Similar raids in support of the Palau and Philippines operations were conducted from July to October. With Nimitz's 7 October directive outlining the invasion of Iwo Jima, Seventh Army Air Force and B-29's of 21st Bomber Command began a series of attacks that month. On 8 December a concerted and sustained aerial preparation of the island began. Over the next 72 days Seventh Air Force hit Iwo Jima daily, staggering attacks throughout the day and night to cause maximum physical and psychological disruption of defences. Four naval bombardments were undertaken by advance cruiser and destroyer formations. Overall in the ten weeks before the start of the pre-invasion bombardment Iwo Jima was the target of 6,800 tons of bombs and nearly 22,000 5-16 inch naval shells.[13] Final pre-invasion operations commenced on 16 February as Task Force 54, 'Gunfire and Covering Force', began fire missions to destroy Japanese positions and protect the minesweepers, underwater demolition teams and beach reconnaissance forces under the direction of Blandy's Task Force 52. Between 16 and 18 February 14,250 tons of shells were fired, but the effects of this bombardment proved as limited as the preceding attacks. Rear Admiral Blandy admitted that the first day was largely spent learning how to identify the superbly concealed enemy positions, while bad weather on the second limited operations. Consequently effective destruction of Japanese positions only began on the third day, to the disquiet of Holland Smith and Schmidt.[14] Even so 'As General Kuribayashi would ruefully admit in an assessment report to the Imperial General Headquarters, "we need to consider the power of bombardment from ships: the violence of the enemy's bombardments are beyond description." '[15] Simultaneously, Task Force 58's carriers made the first attacks against Japan since the punitive Doolittle raid of April 1942. Over a two-day period, Vice-Admiral Mitscher's sixteen fleet and light carriers delivered shattering blows against the enemy, claiming over 631 enemy aircraft from a total of 2,761 sorties. On 18 February Mitscher's force split. Two groups deployed west of Iwo Jima to provide close air support, three moved southwest to replenish from oilers and store ships of the new floating mobile fleet Logistic Support Group, and two fast battleships joined the bombardment force off Iwo Jima.[16]

In the early hours of 19 February Task Force 53, carrying the Marines of 5th Amphibious Corps (VAC), joined Blandy's groups off Iwo Jima. Joint Expeditionary Force commander Vice-Admiral Richmond Kelly Turner now assumed overall supervision from Blandy. In all, 450 ships lay off the island. As nearly 50,000 Marines ate a hearty breakfast at 0640 seven battleships, four heavy cruisers, three light cruisers and ten destroyers opened fire, bringing to a crescendo the bombardment started 80 days previously. In the heaviest pre-H-Hour bombardment in history they fired 38,500 5-16 inch shells.[17] At 0830 Turner signalled 'Land the Landing Force' and 482 Amtracs began the two-mile approach to the beach. The final closely choreographed stages

---

[13]*War With Japan*, vol vi, p.153-4.

[14]Morison, p. 13.

[15]Joseph H. Alexander, *Closing In: Marines in the Seizure of Iwo Jima*, Marines in World War Two Commemorative Series (US Marine Corps Historical Centre, Washington DC, 1994), p 11.

[16]Morison, p. 25.

[17]Morison, p. 34-5.

What impels a young guy landing on a beach in the face of fire?

As Kuribayashi instructed, the Japanese remained inactive until the Marines' lead units were around 200 yards inland, and then opened fire, throwing the advance into chaos. With movement halted, or at a crawl, congestion built up on the beaches. As the day went on smashed and burning vehicles, landing craft, stores and equipment littered the beaches. 'Japanese artillery and mortar fire continued to rake the beachhead. The enormous spigot mortar shells (called 'flying ashcans' by the troops) and rocket-boosted aerial bombs were particularly frightening – loud, whistling projectiles, tumbling end over end. Many sailed completely over the island; those that hit along the beaches or on the south runway invariably caused dozens of casualties. Few Marines could dig a proper foxhole in the granular sand ('like trying to dig a hole in a barrel of wheat').[18] Increasingly rough surf conditions were to make unloading difficult throughout the operation, damaging craft intended for Okinawa. Seizure of the western beaches and their opening with the fall of Suribachi on 23 February relieved the pressure.

Throughout 19 February the 4th and 5th Divisions pushed forwards. The individual courage and determination of the Marines, with their emphasis on improvisation and initiative, saw ad-hoc groups composed of several units push on to their objective. This situation impressed itself upon Lieutenant Colonel Donn J Robertson, commander 3rd Battalion, 27th Marines, as he landed that afternoon. 'He watched with pride and wonderment as his Marines landed under fire, took casualties, stumbled forward to clear the beach. "What impels a young guy landing on a beach in the face of fire?" he asked himself.'[19] The concept of an all-arms battle diminished as tanks threw tracks whilst endeavouring to scale the steep volcanic terraces, and organic divisional artillery could not be landed until late in the day. Casualties at the close of the day totalled 2,450. The Marines had fallen far short of their objectives, airfield number 1 was still to be overrun, and 4th Division had reached only 500 yards inland. Even so 30,000 troops and increasing amounts of heavy equipment and stores were ashore, and beachhead development was slowly commencing.

Over the next six weeks, until the island was officially declared secure on 19 March, VAC ground its way forwards. The fighting can essentially be viewed in three broad phases. In the first, from 20 to 23 February, a dual advance was mounted. Advancing methodically, 4th and 5th Divisions cleared airfield number 1 to reach their D-Day objective, and Kuribayashi's main line

of support for the troops commenced as naval guns lifted the trajectory of their fire to permit aircraft to deliver a series of close attacks. Continuity of naval gunfire, closely coordinated with air strikes delivering rockets, bombs and napalm, was achieved for the first time. The first wave of LVT(A) armed with a short-barrelled gun for suppressing enemy defences landed at H-Hour, 0900. One minute previous the navy began a pre-timed rolling barrage inland, predicated on the troops' expected rate of advance. At 0902 the second wave landed, followed by eight others at five-minute intervals. This carefully organised assault plan put 9,000 troops ashore across a 3,000 yard front in 45 minutes.

[18]Alexander, *Closing In*, p. 19.
[19]Alexander *Closing In*, p. 19.

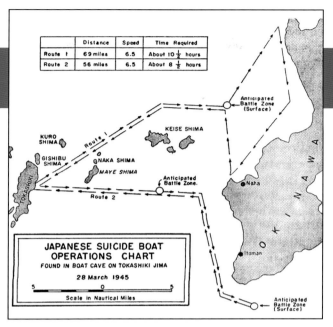

Japanese suicide operations chart discovered on Tokashiki Jima. 'Suicide boats' (far right) looked like small speedboats but were poorly constructed and slow. These two craft were captured in their cave shelters by American troops on Okinawa. Note booby trap warnings and crude depth charge racks at stern. (US Army)

JAPANESE SUICIDE BOAT OPERATIONS CHART
FOUND IN BOAT CAVE ON TOKASHIKI JIMA
28 March 1945
Scale in Nautical Miles

	Distance	Speed	Time Required
Route 1	69 miles	6.5	About 10½ hours
Route 2	56 miles	6.5	About 8½ hours

on the southern edge of airfield number 2. To the south 28th Marine Regiment doggedly pushed against positions along the base of Suribachi. The first breach was made by a platoon of E Company, and following eight hours of fighting a Congressional Medal of Honor, three Navy Crosses, a Silver Star and 17 Purple Hearts were won.[20] Once the top of Suribachi was reached on 23 February (several days of clearing Japanese out from caves on its slopes), observed fire onto the landing beaches slackened, easing logistic operations. The second phase lasted from 24 February to 10 March and involved breaking Kuribayashi's two lines along the Motoyama plateau either side of the second airfield. The intensity of fighting forced Schmidt eventually to commit two regiments of 3rd Division into the centre. This justified Holland Smith's earlier decision to base it close by as a floating reserve, though the piecemeal commitment of the formation could be argued as dissipating its potential effectiveness. The advance was supported by armour, naval and air support. In the case of the latter new command and coordination procedures enhanced its effects, and the deployment of Marine air groups, operating from carriers and skilled in point-blank attacks, was justified.

Even so the fighting remained dominated by small-unit actions in which closing with small arms, grenades and flamethrowers were the principal means of destruction. In the third phase a series of isolated pockets along the northern fringes of the island were painstakingly reduced. Conquest of the island cost the Marines 5,931 dead and missing, 18,770 wounded. All but

just over 1,000 Japanese (who were too wounded to commit suicide) were killed. Holland Smith's summary of the battle serves to emphasise the irrelevance of manoeuvre concepts to Iwo Jima: 'It was an operation of one phase and one tactic. From the time the engagement was joined until the mission was completed it was a matter of frontal assault maintained with relentless pressure'.[21]

Operation ICEBERG

Operation ICEBERG commenced on 14 March when Vice-Admiral Marc Mitscher's Fast Carrier Force, Task Force 58, totalling 10 fleet and 6 light carriers supported by 8 fast battleships and 80 other combat vessels, sortied from Ulithi for preparatory operations. Commencing strikes on 18 March, over the next two days a running battle developed with the Japanese Fifth Air Fleet. Three carriers were damaged and another permanently forced to retire. Task Force 58's claims of 528 aircraft destroyed

were countered by Japanese admissions of 163. What is beyond question is that Mitscher's attacks, complemented a week later by B-29 raids, succeeded in dislocating Fifth Air Fleet's ability to mount major air raids until 6 April. On 22 March Mitscher's carriers replenished at sea and then conducted two days of strikes and photo-reconnaissance of Okinawa. On 24 March Task Forces 52 and 54 initiated the standard preliminary landing procedures of minesweeping and beach reconnaissance. Six fast battleships were detached by Mitscher to bombard the beaches around Minatoga as part of the diversion plan. The following day Admiral Durgin's 18 escort carriers and Rear Admiral Blandy's Gunfire and Covering Forces commenced softening up the Kerama Rettos and Hagushi beaches. From 26 March to L-Day, 1 April, Task Force 54's ships expended 5,162 tons of ammunition. At 0801 on 26 March four battalions of the 77th Division began landing to secure the Kerama Rettos. This move caught the Japanese by surprise. Defences proved weak, and critically the capture of over 350 Shinyo suicide boats was a blow to Japanese plans. The islands were secured by 29 March, and development of an advance fleet anchorage began. Keise Shima was secured two days later, ending the preliminary stage of ICEBERG.

---

[20]R. Wheeler, *A Special Valor; The U.S. Marines & The Pacific War* (Castle Books, 1996), p. 377.
[21]Alexander *Storm*, p.126.

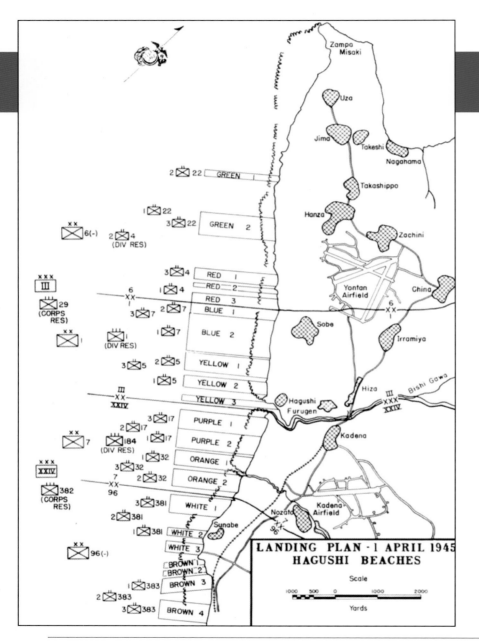

Landing Plan map for the assault on Okinawa. (USMC)

Dawn on Easter Sunday, 1 April, disclosed over 1,300 American ships riding in the waters adjacent to Okinawa. 'A Japanese soldier observing the huge armada bearing down on Okinawa wrote in his diary, "it's like a frog meeting a snake and waiting for the snake to eat him." '[22] Just after 0400 Vice-Admiral Richmond Kelly Turner signalled 'Land the Landing Force'. Soon thousands of marines and soldiers began climbing down scrambling nets into landing craft alongside their transports. Specialised tank landing ships spread their yawning bow doors and launched the first wave, composed of amphibious M4A4 Sherman tanks. Behind them five to seven waves of Amtracs formed up 4,000 yards from the beaches. As hundreds of assault craft moved into position, warships and other fire support craft continued to saturate the beaches. Over 44,000 shells, from 5 to 16 inches in calibre, were fired. At 0800, along an eight-mile front, the 1st and 6th Marine and 7th and 96th Army Divisions began their final approach to Okinawa. At 0842 the first wave hit the Hagushi beaches. To the

southwest off Minatoga 2nd Marine Division's feint was under way, launching 'amphibian tractors and Higgins boats, loaded conspicuously with combat-equipped Marines, then dispatched them towards Minatoga Beach in seven waves. Paying careful attention to the clock, the fourth wave commander crossed the line of departure exactly at 0830, the time of the real H-Hour on the west coast. The LVTs and boats then turned sharply away and returned to the transports'.[23] On the actual landing beaches throughout the day the whole complex and minutely choreographed landing procedure continued. In the first hour alone 16,000 troops were landed. By nightfall 60,000 troops with stores, vehicles and artillery were secure in a large bridgehead. The opening day of Operation ICEBERG had surpassed all expectations. Airfields at Yontan and Kadena were secured with negligible casualties. During the night the anticipated Japanese counterattacks failed to materialise.

Advance to the Shuri line

The absence of all but sporadic enemy resistance both confused US commanders and gradually led to optimism that enemy strength had been overestimated. Unable to obtain accurate intelligence about the location of the main Japanese positions, the seasoned troops of the Third Amphibious and 24th Army Corps continued to push quickly inland against sporadic enemy resistance. Exploiting this situation on 3 April, Buckner advanced Third Amphibious Corps' strike north. A

---

[22]Joseph H. Alexander, *The Final Campaign: Marines in the Victory on Okinawa*, Marines in World War Two Commemorative Series (US Marine Corps Historical Centre, Washington DC, 1994), p 11.
[23]Alexander, *The Final Campaign*, p. 12.

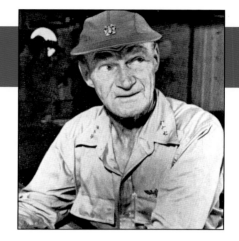

Left: A marine of the 1st Marine Division shoots at a Japanese sniper, Wana Ridge. (USMC)

Right: Vice Admiral Marc A Mitscher USN in USS Randolph. (USN)

machine guns, supported by seven 50mm mortars. From these positions the Japanese could shelter during US artillery barrages then rapidly emerge, placing concentrated fire on US infantry struggling over the wire and mines or canalised by them into prepared killing zones, all covered by pre-registered artillery. These positions were gradually overcome through a combination of frontal assaults, infiltration and sheer courage.

Operations at sea

During the Iwo Jima landings the Japanese had made no concerted effort from the air, preferring to conserve strength for their Ten-Go plan, which envisaged use of massed suicide groups (Kikusui) in the decisive battle for Formosa, the Ryukyus and Home Islands. When ICEBERG commenced Imperial General Headquarters had authorised its Operation Ten-Go defence plan for Okinawa on 25 March but Mitscher's strikes ensured that it was 6 April before Japanese forces recovered their balance. In all the Japanese mounted ten mass suicide attacks during the Okinawa campaign involving over 1,900 aircraft. These achieved a hit rate of only one in ten, far lower than IGHQ had hoped. Over 4,800 conventional aircraft had also been involved. In total the Japanese sank 36 ships and damaged 368 others.

Considering the concentration of shipping in the Kerama road anchorage it is surprising that losses were not higher. Japanese air losses totalled over 7,800, to just 773 American aircraft.[24]

The failure of Ten-Go, and in particular the Special Attack Groups (Kamikaze), was the product of many factors, not least US quantitative, qualitative and organisational superiority. In specific relation to Kikusui tactics it is critical to note that any attempt to overwhelm US defences to register significant shipping losses could not be based on overall numbers but could be achieved only by concentration of force. On any single day the various formations moving against US forces needed close coordination in timing to deliver sufficient strength. Concomitant was the need to mount attacks for sustained periods of daily attack to knock US forces off balance and prevent recovery. There are two obvious provisos to this argument. First, American quantitative and qualitative superiority in 1945 made it a big 'if'. Second, this method of attack was beyond Japanese forces, lacking forward airfields, and thereby suffering from inadequate command facilities, logistic weaknesses, enormous losses in air groups and delays in replenishment caused by the necessity to disperse replacement aircraft for protection.

rapid advance saw the only Japanese resistance on the Motobu Peninsula reduced by 17 April. Simultaneously, 77th Division secured Ie Shima by 22 April.

In contrast, on 5 April the southward advance by Major-General John Hodges' 24th Army Corps stalled against the Shuri line's outer positions. The three days of fighting to overcome Japanese positions revealed many of the problems US troops would face during fighting for the rest of the island. Typical of Japanese positions was the 450-foot ridge near Arakuchi, nicknamed the 'Pinnacle'. Elements of the 14th Independent Battalion occupied a honeycomb of trenches, fire pits and underground passages. All the main approaches were mined and covered with barbed wire. The base of the hill was defended by ten light and heavy

[24]*War With Japan*, vol vi, p. 194-6.

Corsair fighter fires rockets against a Japanese stronghold, June 1945. (NARA)

Securing the outer Shuri line

As Vice-Admiral Spruance's Fifth Fleet rode out the massed kamikaze attacks, 10th Army spent 14-19 April reconnoitring enemy positions and securing jumping-off points for a major offensive. To ensure maximum chance of success Lieutenant General Buckner landed the 27th Division. The attack opened on 19 April preceded by the greatest concentration of fire in the Pacific war, involving field guns, warships and hundreds of aircraft. Japanese defences were not significantly disrupted, and the three-division attack quickly collapsed into a series of individual battles. Conducting a skilful river crossing outflanking the Kazaku ridge to the west, 27th Division was halted at the western end of the Urasoe-Mura ridge. In the centre 96th Division struggled to gain a series of toeholds on the Nishibaru ridge. To the east, 7th Division made no progress. Some of the bitterest fighting over the next few days occurred around a salient centred on the Kazaku ridge. As Japanese positions here threatened the flanks of the 27th and 96th Divisions, they had to be reduced. Moving methodically west to east, elements of the 27th Division had nearly cleared the ridge by the afternoon of 20 April. However, the desperate fighting on the Urasoe-Mura ridge required the diversion of forces away from Kazaku. The aggressive Japanese defenders immediately rushed more troops and mortars back onto the ridge. With enemy troops in its rear, and no reserves, 27th Division was in a serious position. The central position of the Nishibaru ridge made 96th Division's advance difficult. Fire from flanking positions and massed artillery took a heavy toll. Six days of fighting finally brought the Americans to the verge of penetrating 32nd Army's outer defensive ring on 24 April, only for Ushijima to withdraw to the inner Shuri line. Skilfully timed and executed, his decision denied the Americans the chance to seize the initiative and fight a fluid battle in the open, where their firepower might devastate Japanese forces.

Buckner now relieved the exhausted 27th and 96th Divisions, bringing part of Third Amphibious Corps into the line. Slow progress and heavy losses in shipping raised inter-service tensions. Army and Marine officers were disquieted by Buckner's fixation on frontal attacks. On two occasions in late April proposals were made to land either 77th Division or 2nd Marine Divisions in 32nd Army's rear at Minatoga. Buckner refused, citing the danger of placing a single division so deep behind enemy lines and the additional burden on logistics and warships to protect another anchorage. The Navy was divided over the idea. Interestingly Nimitz agreed with Buckner and Spruance, but Turner did not. Unknown to the Americans, Ushijima had already moved 24th Division from Minatoga to reinforce the battered 62nd Division.[25] This was not the first, or the last, time that poor intelligence dogged the American conduct of the Okinawa campaign.

[25] R. E. Appleman, J. M. Burns, R. A. Gugeler & J. Stevens, p 195-6.

Japanese prisoners on Okinawa, carrying the wounded. (USMC)

Breaking the Shuri line

By the start of May Buckner's forces had completed their reorganisation, with the 1st Marine and 77th Divisions moving into the line for another multi-division assault. On 4 May these repulsed a major Japanese offensive. Ushijima had agreed to this disastrous attack after intense pressure from Imperial General Headquarters and elements of 32nd Army's staff for a more aggressive strategy. The immediate cost to 32nd Army was 6,237 good troops, but a longer-term consequence for sustaining its resistance was the revealing of many artillery positions and depletion of its limited ammunition supplies.

On 11 May 10th Army attacked in strength, and again fighting splintered into localised actions. In the west the two marine divisions pushed slowly south towards the Asato river behind the Shuri heights, from where the Japanese poured in constant harassing fire. The hinge of the enemy positions in this sector was a complex of three hills. One of these, 'Sugar Loaf', proved the 6th Marines' toughest fight of the campaign. Despite tank, artillery and air support, and naval gunfire, the 6th Marines repeatedly failed to move over the crest against Japanese rear slope positions. It took four days of bitter fighting before 'Sugar Loaf' fell. It cost the marines 2,662 casualties, and significantly a further 1,662 from combat fatigue.[26] The 1st Marine and 77th Division experienced equally hard opposition, but progress was made as new weapons and tactics were utilised. It still took ten days to break the Shuri line.

Again Japanese skill, assisted by torrential rain, enabled 32nd Army to withdraw its remaining 14,000 troops from under a swift American blow to the formidable Yuza-Dake and Yaeju-Dake escarpments. Yet, Japanese resistance was finally beginning to show signs of crumbling under the American onslaught. Although fighting for outposts in front of the Yuza-Yaeju escarpment was heavy, Japanese soldiers increasingly ran from their positions, and a steady stream of prisoners was taken. On 6 June 1st Marine Division began a gruelling six-day battle on the Oroku peninsula to eliminate the Naval Defence force. In the centre US 96th Division initially struggled to take a low ridge below the main Yuza-Yaeju escarpment until a coordinated attack with neighbouring 7th Division. By 11 June several tenuous toeholds had been secured on the heights, once again with the aid of powerful air strikes and naval gunfire. Fighting for the Yuza-Yaeju position, and the supporting position of Kunishi ridge to the west, lasted until 17 June, when an exhausted Japanese defence finally collapsed under unremitting American pressure. The island was officially secured on 25 June

.

The Americans paid a high price for this island fortress. Over 7,213 soldiers and marines were killed and 31,000 wounded, and non-battle casualties reached 26,211. The navy had 4,907 killed and 4,824 wounded, making it the only service where deaths exceeded wounded. Japanese losses were over 100,000, though 7,400 prisoners was the largest single haul of the war to date. Over 7,800 Japanese planes were lost to just 773 American. *Yamato*, the largest battleship ever built, had been ruthlessly dispatched by the US Navy, though the campaign cost it 36 ships sunk and 368 damaged. [27]

CONCLUSIONS

Air Support

Forces benefited to a considerable extent from new techniques of close air support. The Marines preferred their own dedicated air groups, and by Iwo Jima these were available. Army and Navy support were improved by the introduction of Land Force Air Support Control Units and Air Liaison parties, and greater integration of land and air operations was achieved.[28]

[26]Gow and Willmott, p. 152.
[27]Gow and Willmott, p. 195.
[28]Allan R. Millett, *SemperFidelis: The History of the United States Marine Corps* (New York, 1991), p. 408-9.

Japanese kamikaze attacks were a constant menace to the US fleet. Top: A Kamikaze plane plunges into the sea after being hit by anti-aircraft fire. Below: The aircraft carrier USS Franklin was not as fortunate. Hit off Kyushu by two armour-piercing bombs, the ship's fuel, aircraft and ammunition went up in flame; more than a thousand of her crew were lost. (USN)

Naval Gunfire

The scale of gunfire provided was, and remains, unparalleled. Its effectiveness was reduced because Japanese defences required destruction, which was beyond all but the heaviest guns, and this was the reason that doctrine advocated the principal role as suppression or neutralization.

Carrier Air Support

Though US forces emphasised the importance of quick base construction to establish land-based air power for ground support and defence of the beachhead, carrier support was vital to both operations. The Fast Carrier Force comprised five task groups operating in close proximity for better coordination and mutual support. Utilising strategic and operational mobility the Fast Carrier Force could concentrate over 1,000 aircraft for coordinated and sustained attacks to overwhelm enemy land-based airpower. Experience of Japanese suicide attacks off the Philippines in late 1944 led to a strengthening of the carriers' defences. VT proximity fuses were increasingly used, and the heavier 40mm anti-aircraft gradually replaced ineffective lighter weapons. Carrier air complements were reorganised for greater defence by increasing fighters from 40 to 70 per cent.[29] The resulting loss in a carrier's individual striking power was compensated by the collective strength of the task groups. Off Okinawa, despite heavy damage, US carriers defeated the Japanese air threat to the invasion forces.

Logistics

Supporting the Fast Carrier Force was an impressive logistic train. A Fleet Oiler and Transport Carrier Group of 24 oilers and seven escort carriers

[29]C. G. Reynolds, *The Fast Carriers: The Forging of an Air Navy* (New York, 1968), p.289-90

Fifth Fleet consumed nearly 9 million barrels of oil: more than Japan as a nation imported in 1944.

provided fuel and replacement aircraft. Additional support came from the Fleet Train, which for the Okinawa campaign consisted of 206 support ships. These included repair ships, floating dry docks, hospital ships, salvage vessels, ammunition ships, victualling and store ships. Two impressive features of operations in 1945 were, first, the ability to re-ammunition heavy ships at sea and, second, the rotation of aircrews between sea operations and rest ashore. During the Okinawa campaign these factors enabled the Fast Carrier Force to maintain a high level of combat effectiveness over 92 days of action without ever having to return to port. In the first six weeks of the operations Fifth Fleet consumed nearly 9 million barrels of oil, more than Japan as a nation imported in 1944. [30]

Logistics for both operations were conducted on an enormous scale, involving pre-ordering and dispatch of supplies to theatre. ICEBERG was larger than any other operation of the Pacific War. For the assault 183,000 troops and 747,000 tons of supplies were loaded into over 430 assault vessels and landing ships at 11 different ports from Seattle on the west coast of the United States to Leyte in the Philippines. A further 115,000 service troops would land once Okinawa was secured, to begin developing port and base facilities and airfields. Including naval forces, by the end of the campaign 548,000 personnel participated in the campaign. Though smaller in extent, Iwo Jima reflected most of the organisational factors and was a huge undertaking. Perhaps the best illustration of the immense capability of the USA at this stage of the war was the fact that the 5th Marines could be afforded the luxury of a packet of twenty cigarettes a day for every man for eight months. [31]

Tactical Flexibility

Within the manoeuvrist approach, all-arms coordination and the devolving of responsibility to the lowest levels through application of mission command are stressed for generating tactical and operational momentum. General artillery barrages were slowly rejected in favour of pinpoint fire against specific targets. Armoured flame-throwing medium tanks, and VT proximity shells (rushed to Okinawa), which burst directly over enemy trenches, showering them with lethal splinters, were employed. Extensive use was made of infantry-tank teams in both battles. Most effective was the combination of neutralising fire from small arms followed by flame-throwers and demolition charges to destroy positions – termed 'blowtorch and corkscrew' by Buckner. [32]

Combined Operations

During ICEBERG, US forces were supported by the British Pacific Fleet. Designated Task Force 57, four British carriers covered the US left flank, conducting strikes against airfields in the Sakashima Gunto islands. The deployment of this force was vociferously opposed by Admiral King. His principal argument was that British forces lacked the logistic capability to cope with Pacific operations and would have to rely on stretched US resources. King and some of his senior commanders also wanted to exclude the British from any part in what they saw as an American theatre. Despite this stance Nimitz and Spruance proved grateful for the British contribution.

Inter-Service Co-operation

At times both operations saw fierce inter-service disputes. Mounting losses and lack of progress ashore at Okinawa saw Nimitz inform Buckner, 'I'm losing a ship and a half a day. So if this line isn't moving within five days, we'll get someone here to move it.' [33] The Marines felt the Navy had let its own priorities deny the Marines an adequate bombardment off Iwo Jima, whilst the Army wasted lives with its refusal to countenance an amphibious landing to outflank the Shuri line. Spruance clashed with air force commanders when he found that development of bomber facilities had been unofficially pushed ahead of those for fighters. Yet overall, US commanders managed to square the demands of each of their services to plan and implement these most demanding of operations – highly effectively, in this unparalleled theatre of war.

---

[30] W R. Carter, *Beans, Bullets and Black Oil*, Washington, 1953), Chapters xxii for Iwo Jima, and xxv-xxviii for Okinawa.
[31] Garand and Strobridge, p.
[32] Gow & Willmott, p.203-4.
[33] E. B. Potter, *Nimitz* (Naval Institute Press, Maryland, 1976), p. 375.

Lessons Identified from Okinawa

- **Amphibious mastery** - By coincidence, the virtually flawless amphibious assault on Okinawa occurred 30 years to the month after the debacle at Gallipoli.

- **Attrition** - Disregarding the great opportunities for surprise and manoeuvre available in the amphibious task force, much of the campaign for Okinawa was conducted in an unimaginative attrition mode which played into the strength of the Japanese defenders. Several opportunities for tactical innovations were lost.

- **Joint Service** - The battle for Okinawa represented joint service cooperation at its finest.

- **First rate training** - The Marines who deployed on Okinawa received the benefit of the most thorough and practical advanced training of the war.

- **Outstanding leadership** - Many of those Marines who survived Okinawa went on to positions of top leadership within the USMC, including two Commandants and two Four-star Generals, and at least 17 others achieved the rank of Lieutenant General.

Further Reading

Alexander, J. H. *The Final Campaign: Marines in the Victory on Okinawa*. Marines in World War Two Commemorative Series, (Washington DC: US Marine Corps Historical Center, 1996).

Bartley, W. S. *Iwo Jima: Amphibious Epic*, (Washington, 1954).

Bradley, J. & Powers, R. *Flags of Our Fathers: Heroes of Iwo Jima*, (Bantam, 2000).

Garand, G. W. & Strobridge, T. R. *Western Pacific Operations*, Vol. IV, *History of U.S. Marine Corps Operations in World War Two*, (Washington DC: Historical Division, HQMC, 1971).

Millett, A. R. *Semper Fidelis: the History of the United States Marine Corps*, (New York, 1991).

Morehouse, C. P. *The Iwo Jima Operation*, (Washington DC, 1946).

Nalty, B. C. *The U.S. Marines on Iwo Jima: the Battle and the Flag Raising*, (Washington DC: Historical Branch, 1960).

Newcombe, R. F. *Iwo Jima*, (New York: Bantam, 1982).

Ross, B. D. *Iwo Jima: Legacy of Valor*, (New York: Vanguard Press, 1985).

Wheeler, R. *Iwo*, (New York, 1980).

Yahara, H. *The Battle for Okinawa*, (New York, 1995).

Biography

Mr Tim Bean is a Senior Lecturer in the Department of War Studies, Royal Military Academy Sandhurst. He holds a Bachelor's degree in history from the University of York, and a Masters in war studies from King's College London. He specialises in naval and amphibious operations, with particular emphasis on the late seventeenth century and the Second World War. His publications include *Omaha Beach* (Sutton: 2004), co-authored with Dr Stephen Badsey, and an introductory essay to *Forests and Seapower: the Timber Problem of the Royal Navy, 1652-1862*, by R G Albion (reprinted in the Naval Institute Press Classics of Naval Literature series, ed. Jack Sweetman, 2000).

post-world war II

The Inchon Landings, Korea
Operation CHROMITE, 15 September 1950

XXXII

By Colonel Michael Hickey (Rtd)

A student attending the 1961 Camberley Staff Course was tasked by his Directing Staff with chairing a syndicate presentation on Operation CHROMITE, the bold stroke by which General Douglas MacArthur used the principle of Indirect Approach in order to restore the fortunes of the United Nations' forces in Korea. Thinking to steal a march on fellow syndicate chairmen he wrote in suitably flattering terms to the old general, then living in retirement in New York, asking him if he would record a short message outlining the operation and his decision to carry it through in the teeth of robust opposition from his own staff and the dismay of the Pentagon.

MacArthur's response was courteous and prompt. Whilst not exactly meeting the applicant's fondest hopes its unselfconscious vanity throws an interesting light on the man's character:

2 June 1961

Dear Capt Hickey,

I have just received your letter of May 29th with reference to the Inchon Campaign. A full account of this operation is contained in General Courtney Whitney's book, 'MacArthur - His rendezvous with History'. I have spoken to him of the matter and he is sending you under separate cover a copy of the history for the Staff College.

With best wishes to you all,

Most Sincerely

Douglas MacArthur

The book, written by one of MacArthur's time-serving courtiers, had been written months after his master's precipitous fall from power in 1951 and remains a classic example of adulatory obfuscation, the work of a toady. Whitney was no warrior; as a trained attorney he was MacArthur's personal legal advisor throughout the Pacific campaigns of World War II, and had remained on the staff as head of the Government Section in HQ Supreme Commander Allied Powers (SCAP) in Tokyo. With unfettered personal access to his master at all times he was also his fawning biographer, confidential and legal secretary, and a man feared and mistrusted by the majority of the SCAP staff.

Despite Whitney's abject apologia, however, MacArthur's political, strategic and tactical handling of the Inchon operation merits inclusion in any list of boldly planned and executed strokes of war. It was a classic example not only of indirect approach but of the use of available resources in order to achieve maximum effect. MacArthur knew that despite the mediocre performance of the United States Army in Korea in the opening weeks of the war, he could draw on a wealth of experience gained by the US navy and marines in the Pacific, providing this could be re-assembled in the limited time available for mounting the operation. He also knew he had the ability to carry through his project, if necessary, against all opposition, whether from his own staff or from the Pentagon.

Following the defeat of Imperial Japan in 1945 the Korean peninsula, occupied by the Japanese and administered from Tokyo

since 1910, had to be returned to its people. An arbitrary line was therefore drawn approximately half way down, on the 38th Parallel of Latitude. To the north the Soviet forces and their political apparat set about the creation of a Stalinist vassal state. The south, under American occupation, became the Republic of Korea under Washington's client president Syngman Rhee. In Pyongyang, the northern capital, the Russians installed their own carefully trained dictator, Kim Il Sung and the business of setting up an industrialised communist police state went ahead. The Russians also ensured that Kim Il Sung's authority was backed by a large, well equipped army capable of waging aggressive war when called on to do so against the south. Syngman Rhee's armed forces, created under cautious American supervision, were little more than a lightly armed constabulary. The Republic of Korea Army (ROKA) possessed no tanks and very little field artillery. Whereas the North Koreans disposed of numerous light bombers the ROK Air Force had no more than light observation and training aircraft. This policy emanated from Washington, where Rhee's frequent bellicose pronouncements of imminent invasion of the north were taken for much more than the bluster they were. Between 1945 and 1950 there were numerous bouts of fighting along the 38th parallel but even these failed to convince the Americans - and in particular General MacArthur in Tokyo - that there was a serious risk of aggression against the south.

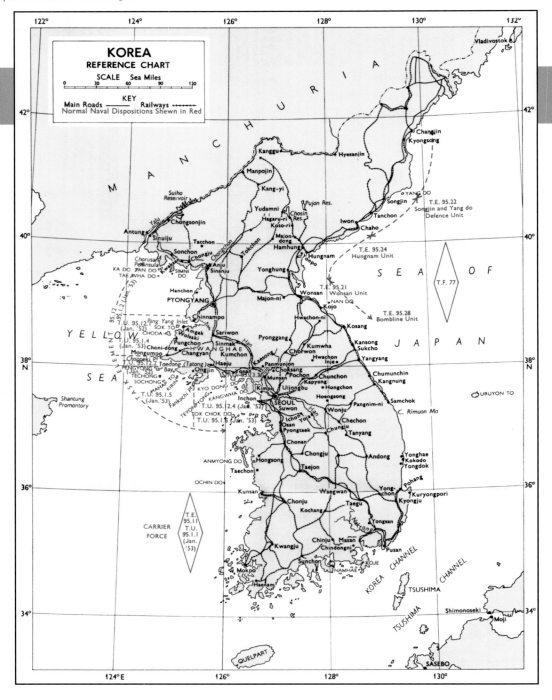

Map showing Naval dispositions. (NHB)

On 25 June 1950, when many of the ROKA formations guarding the frontier were enjoying a weekend's leave, the North Korean Peoples' Army (NKPA) erupted across the 38th parallel. Its armoured columns, equipped with Russian T-34 tanks and self-propelled guns, overwhelmed the defence. Late that night the American Secretary of State, Dean Acheson called President Harry S. Truman urgently back to Washington and succeeded in persuading the UN Security Council to brand North Korea as an aggressor. As the invasion continued and the ROKA dissolved into rout, the Security Council called on UN member nations to contribute forces to withstand the attack; but in the immediate short term the burden of assistance had to fall on the United States. MacArthur was appointed Commander-in-Chief of the UN forces, renamed the 8th US Army, Korea (EUSAK). Immediately available was the US 7th Fleet already in far Eastern waters. The US Army of occupation and US Far East Air Force were close at hand. The USAF had little difficulty in driving the North Korean air force out of the sky but the provision of American army units capable of taking on the formidable NKPA would prove another matter.

Immediately the extent of the Korean crisis was observed in Washington a huge logistic apparatus swung into action; a fleet of mothballed naval and merchant shipping was ordered back into service and before long reservists were being called back to man them. Following the end of the war against Japan hundreds of landing craft of all sizes, from LSTs (landing ships, tank) to fast assault craft, had been consigned to heavy preservation and moored in dozens of anchorages on both sides of the United States. A number of LSTs had been passed over to the newly forming Japanese Self Defence Force and these were hurriedly made available for the Inchon operation, manned by highly competent ex-Imperial navy officers and ratings. The heterogeneous support fleet which began to assemble in Japanese waters within two weeks of the outbreak of war had few claims to elegance but it was soon fully operational and ready to carry out its tasks. Fire

At the same time MacArthur privately decided to assemble a task force which would be capable of bringing off an amphibious landing well in the enemy rear

support for any landings on the hostile Korean coast would be more than adequately backed by the massive firepower of the 7th US Fleet, notably that of the USS *Missouri* and its main battery of 16-inch guns, reinforced by elements of Britain's Far East Fleet – several elements of which were exercising in Japanese waters at the start of hostilities, including the 6-inch cruiser *Jamaica*. The policy was adopted whereby the Far East Fleet operated off the Korean west coast and the US 7th off the east; there were normally two British (or Commonwealth) light fleet carriers, with their escorts, on station.

By the end of June the South Korean capital, Seoul, had been lost and the ROKA continued to flee south. MacArthur flew from Japan to assess the situation for himself; his advisers told him that in the past four days the ROKA's bayonet strength had evaporated from around 100,000 to 8,000, most of whom were heading away from the fighting. MacArthur, standing on the banks of the Han river near Seoul , decided to send troops of the 8th Army from Japan to Korea at once; he also knew that these troops had fallen prey to all the vices of an occupation force; lax discipline, poor skill at arms, inattention to field training, and low all-round fitness for war. Within two weeks the dismal performance of units of the 24th Infantry Division would confirm his worst predictions. At the same time MacArthur privately decided to assemble a task force which would be capable of bringing off an amphibious landing well in the enemy rear. Fully aware of the deficiencies of the US Army at this time he pinned his hopes on the US Marine Corps, whose matchless experience of amphibious operations in the Pacific fitted them ideally for the task in hand.

Between the two world wars the USMC had devoted much time to the study of historical precedents and the Gallipoli campaign had long featured in their studies. Directed by their Commandant, General Lejeune, these centred on the works of a visionary USMC officer, Earl Ellis, who had lectured before 1914 at the US Naval War College on the thesis that war against Japan in the Pacific was inevitable. In 1921, he had unveiled War Plan Orange, describing what he termed as 'Advance Base Operations in Micronesia', and which proved to be an uncanny forecast of the shape of operations in the western Pacific, 1942-45. (Ellis disappeared under mysterious circumstances in the 1930s, probably when conducting a covert reconnaissance of the Japanese Pacific islands). A parallel study of Gallipoli by Colonel Robert Dunlop USMC concluded that there had been nothing wrong with its strategic concept but that it had foundered due to inept execution, lack of proper shipping and equipment, the absence of sound command and control infrastructure, poor intelligence and the loss of surprise. After Lejeune's retirement in 1929 the USMC studies and exercises continued whilst in Britain the dead hand of the Treasury made such activities impossible. In the 1930s a series of major USMC publications had set the stage for operations in World War II. Following 'Joint Action, Army and Navy' came 'Marine Corps Landing Operations' of 1932, then the 'Tentative Manual for Landing Operations' of 1934, destined to become the Gospel for modern amphibious warfare.

It covered Joint Command and Control, ship-to-shore movement, communications, air and naval gunfire support, techniques and drills for disembarking, and the organisation of beach parties. A number of exercises refined the techniques and enabled the marines to arrive at organisations and war establishments that would be used from the outset once MacArthur, as allied supreme commander in the Pacific, went over to the offensive in 1943 with his triumphant 'island-hopping' campaign. Lessons still had to be learned but by VJ day, when MacArthur was poised to attack the Japanese home islands, the drills had been perfected. He and his forces knew that the final phase would certainly be bloody but were spared this once the two atomic bombs had been dropped on Hiroshima and Nagasaki.

A US government policy of 'Get the boys' home' led to precipitate demobilisation of all branches of the American armed forces. The USMC was speedily cut from a war peak of 485,000 personnel to 156,000 in the middle of 1946 and further to 92,000 by June 1947. A fight for very survival now began in the light of the US Army's campaign to take over all operations ashore in the face of the nuclear threat. The newly created US Air Force demanded the monopoly of all types of air operations including those previously carried out with extreme efficiency by the USMC Air Arm. As had been the case with the newborn RAF in the 1920s the USAF, obsessed with the doctrines of strategic nuclear bombing, 'flew away' from the army, navy and marines who were left to work out their own salvation for battlefield aerial support. In the marines' case this soon embraced a doctrine of 'vertical

envelopment', using the nascent capabilities of the helicopter. In the shorter term, however, the marines still held a reservoir of highly experienced officers and men with Pacific experience, and had managed to hold onto enough specialist assault craft and amphibious vehicles to equip one division. Although USMC strength had fallen even further in mid 1950 to 75,000 the fight for survival was won and the National Defense Act of 1947 permitted the USN to retain its carrier-borne aircraft and the USMC its organic aviation, armour, artillery and specialist shipping.

Following his assessment of the situation in Korea and aware of this rundown of USMC capability but convinced that only the marines could bring off the bold coup he had in mind, MacArthur summoned the Commandant of the USMC, General Lemuel Shepherd, to Tokyo. Shepherd, once appraised of the plan, immediately undertook to assemble a marine division from detachments scattered worldwide. Meanwhile General Walton Walker, EUSAK's field commander, was ordered to hold out in the Pusan bridgehead until reinforcements arrived. This he managed to do, in a remarkable display of personal courage and determination. Other UN elements were now joining him,

including the British 27th Brigade from Hong Kong and a battalion of Australian infantry from Japan.

There now began a race for time. It was essential to relieve Pusan and therefore the Inchon landing had to take place no later than mid-September, when a favourable series of spring tides would enable the landing force to approach the objective, using the tremendous 36 foot high water to get ashore; these diurnal tides occurred at Inchon at 0700 and 1800 on 15 September and to miss them would involve a fatal postponement. At low water the sea retreated (as it advanced) at the speed of a trotting horse to lay bare vast mud flats The date also coincided ominously with the height of the typhoon season in those waters. No updated charts were available, the approach channels were thought to be mined, and navigational marks had been removed or tampered with. A high element of risk thus coloured all aspects of the planning phase. In great secrecy MacArthur's staff therefore enlisted the professional skills of former Japanese coastguards and inshore pilots with knowledge of the Inchon approaches. These were allocated to key ships in the task force. There was even some uncertainty as to the strength, dispositions and state of morale in the NKPA troops defending the port. As Wolmi island (Wolmi-Do), dominating the final approaches to the landing beaches, was known to be garrisoned and with artillery pieces well dug in, it clearly had to be neutralised beforehand by naval gunfire and aerial attack. Cautious reconnaissance revealed that few if any of the small islets lining the Flying Fish channel, the principal shipping approach, were garrisoned. MacArthur now

created the Xth Corps and placed it under his direct command. It comprised the 1st Marine Division and the US 7th Infantry Division, which had no experience of amphibious operations and had already been stripped of many of its personnel to flesh out earlier reinforcements for the Pusan bridgehead. To make up its strength to something approaching war establishment its ranks had been augmented with raw Korean recruits.

The appointment of Major General Edward Almond as X Corps commander was greeted incredulously by Walker at EUSAK who knew Almond as little more than a court favourite, MacArthur's chief of staff in Japan, an effective staff officer who craved martial glory as a field commander. Unlike many of the staff in Tokyo, the so-called 'Bataan Club' who had served MacArthur throughout the Pacific campaign, he had spent a somewhat unhappy and undistinguished war in Europe, commanding a black infantry

In great secrecy MacArthur's staff therefore enlisted the professional skills of former Japanese coastguards and inshore pilots with knowledge of the Inchon approaches

Planning went ahead in Tokyo under stringent security restrictions; a former aircraft hangar in the suburbs was wired off and became a huge planning cell. By 23 August sufficient work had been completed for MacArthur to invite a distinguished group of service chiefs over from Washington for a preliminary briefing. These included Admiral Sherman, General Lawton Collins and Lieutenant General Edwards of the USAF. Throughout the formal presentations the audience sat motionless, hardly daring to believe what they were being asked to sanction. Even Admiral Doyle, the designated commander of the Amphibious Task Force entrusted with getting X Corps ashore, felt obliged to end his contribution with the words: 'The best I can say about Inchon is that it is not impossible'. The VIPs in the front row were too stunned to comment and in any case MacArthur himself now took centre stage. Brandishing his famous corncob pipe, discarding his script, and standing with his back to an enormous map of Inchon and its approaches, he delivered a memorable summary of the operation. The enemy, he said, had concentrated 90% of their strength around the Pusan perimeter; they were still trying to drive Walker and his troops into the sea. If the forces now earmarked for Inchon were to be fed into the bridgehead they would be wasted and even if they succeeded in a break-out

division in Italy which consistently underperformed and was only kept in the line at times by threat of dire punishment; this was at a time when black combat units were firmly segregated and with which white officers were most reluctant to serve. Described by one distinguished American historian as being '… endowed with intelligence and skill, yet cursed with a wretched personality' and by a fellow US Army general as 'The Big A - and I don't mean Almond', he had at least done his best to improve the operational efficiency of the occupation army in Japan. Major General Oliver Smith of the 1st Marine Division was of an

altogether different mould. Revered throughout the Corps, he had fought in some of the most ferocious Pacific battles and knew his trade backwards. His combat experience had made him frugal of mens' lives and he was now inclined to caution as the outline plans for CHROMITE were revealed. Almond brushed his comments aside, accusing Smith of 'lack of response'. Walker, the tough unsentimental fighting soldier who had saved the UN from ignominious defeat at Pusan, fumed as he saw Almond creaming off the glory for CHROMITE whilst EUSAK slogged up the peninsula to link up with X Corps.

Struble, MacArthur and Smith at Inchon, 1950. (NARA)

this could involve up to 100,000 casualties. A landing at Inchon, MacArthur concluded, would create an anvil on which Walton, advancing from the south, would smash the NKPA.

Although MacArthur appeared to have carried the day against even the doubts of his own staff, two of the Washington visitors, General Collins and Admiral Sherman, returned to him for reassurance the next day. His reply was pithy and typical of the man: 'Gentlemen, I have the opportunity, for a five-buck ante, to win $50,000 and that is what I am going to do'. The die was cast; the visitors returned to Washington and Pentagon approval was granted on 28 August. By now, further reconnaissance had revealed more details of the Inchon defences; it seemed that Wolmi Island was held by no more than 500 troops, with a battery of field artillery, and that some 1500 troops in and around Inchon City were little more than line-of-communication and administrative soldiers. Lieutenant Eugene Clark USN was secretly put ashore on the offshore islands with a remit to transmit details of tides, navigational beacons and possible mining activity. He also updated the local charts, reported on the state of the defences and was still hard at it when the landings took place on 15 September; he even succeeded in turning on a key lighthouse at the entrance to the Flying Fish Channel. Elsewhere along the west coast a number of deception operations were carried out, in which British and Commonwealth frigates and destroyers played a leading part. Low level oblique aerial photography of the area identified all the NKPA positions on Wolmi and a bombardment plan was prepared. Wolmi had

first to be eliminated and captured, followed on the next high tide by landings on and around the inner harbour.

Although an intermittent bombardment of Inchon had been in progress for several weeks, and a remarkably lax sense of security prevailed in Japan, where the landings had been openly discussed in clubs and beer halls for some time, the north Koreans made little attempt to stiffen the Inchon defences, possibly because they had pinned all their hopes on overwhelming the Pusan perimeter by mid-September. The scales were in fact tilting in the UN forces' favour. By 15 September the NKPA in the south were outnumbered two to one by Walker's hard-pressed troops, now receiving a stream of reinforcement daily. It was time to co-ordinate the great *schwerpunkt*. Walker was ordered to go over to the offensive on 16 September (D+1 of CHROMITE) and advance north on two axes to link up with X Corps. On the way it was expected that the remnants of the NKPA would be destroyed or rounded up. The UN now enjoyed total command of the air and sea and the advance would be heralded by an intense aerial interdiction programme.

The Inchon invasion fleet put to sea from Yokohama on 5 September. It comprised a total of over 250 ships under Vice Admiral Dewey Struble, Commander US 7th Fleet, and included a number of RN and Commonwealth ships. The troops carried were hardly a well-trained and practised force for the gamble in hand. In June 1950 Smith's 1st Marine division disposed of only one regiment, the 5th Marines. This was hastily organised into

the 1st (Provisional) Marine Brigade and thrown into the Pusan perimeter to stiffen the defence, which was showing signs of demoralisation after the long and ignominious retreat. The 1st Marine brigade was held in the perimeter until the last minute before embarking at Pusan to join the Inchon task force on 13 September. Its 1st Marine Regiment had been assembled in the USA on the outbreak of the war and the 7th Marines, also formed after the outbreak of the war from miscellaneous drafts, embassy guards worldwide, and others abstracted from the 6th US Fleet in the Mediterranean, were still en route to Japanese waters and did not arrive in theatre until after the Inchon landings. There was thus no time for collective training; but General Smith knew he could rely on the hard-won experience of a large proportion of his division. To make up his strength he was allocated the 1st Korean Marine regiment and a number of US Army units – field artillery, Medium Tank, combat, port construction and specialist engineers, and some logistic units. None had any experience of amphibious operations or of serving alongside the US Marines. The 7th US Infantry Division, under Major General Barr, was also a last-minute collation of units lacking amphibious experience.

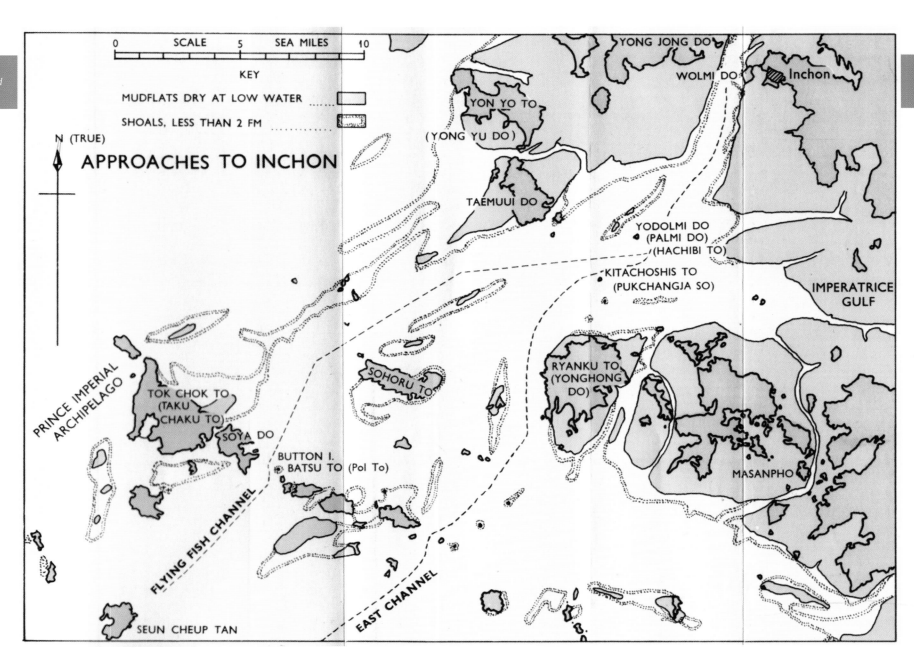

SCALE 0 5 SEA MILES 10

KEY

MUDFLATS DRY AT LOW WATER ....

SHOALS, LESS THAN 2 FM ....

N (TRUE)

APPROACHES TO INCHON

YONG JONG DO

WOLMI DO — Inchon

YON YO TO

(YONG YU DO)

TAEMUUI DO

YODOLMI DO
(PALMI DO)
(HACHIBI TO)

KITACHOSHIS TO
(PUKCHANGJA SO)

IMPERATRICE GULF

PRINCE IMPERIAL ARCHIPELAGO

SOHORU TO

RYANKU TO
(YONGHONG DO)

TOK CHOK TO
(TAKU CHAKU TO)

SOYA DO

BUTTON I.
BATSU TO (Pol To)

MASANPHO

FLYING FISH CHANNEL

EAST CHANNEL

SEUN CHEUP TAN

be in a state of shock and the island was secured by 0800. Only 17 marines had been wounded. Over 100 NKPA soldiers lay dead and a further136 were taken prisoner. At this point the great ebb tide set in and the task force withdrew into the main channel to await the next flood, due after 1700 hrs. The bombardment rose again to its climax as the 1st and 2nd battalions of the 5th Marines stormed the sea wall on Red beach at 1733, and the 1st Marines started to land on Blue beach. By 0130 on 16 September all the primary objectives were in the marines' hands and resistance had petered out.

Almond moved his tactical HQ ashore on the evening of 15 September as the marines exploited beyond the built-up area and into the country along the road to Seoul. The main body of the 7th Infantry Division came ashore on 20 September and joined in the push for Seoul as well as thrusting south-east towards Suwon where it was intended to link up with 8th Army's leading elements. On 21 September overall command of the operation passed from Admiral Struble to General Almond, whose main concern now was to oblige MacArthur's well-publicised promise to liberate Seoul by the 25th.

The break-out from Pusan, however, had not been as instant as had been hoped; the NKPA was still full of fight and seemed disinclined to flee north. Almond began to castigate Smith for his cautious approach to Seoul; this further exacerbated the poor relationship between the two men, which deteriorated even further when Almond re-assigned the capture of the capital to 7th Division and ordered Smith to transfer his Amtraks for 7th Division's crossing of the River Han and into the city. MacArthur's moment of triumph had to be postponed until the 29th, when Syngman Rhee was formally taken back to his capital. On the same day, elements of 8th Army, advancing north, made contact with X Corps troops near Osan.

CHROMITE is often cited as MacArthur's crowning glory, the victory which set the seal on his long career. It has certainly acquired mythological status as a classic example of the indirect approach and of manoeuvrist warfare. It will stand as a memorial to the extraordinary self-confidence of its begetter, even though the result was in little doubt once the bombardment got under way and the landing craft went ashore. The professionalism and experience of the US Marines ensured that casualties on D-day, 15 September had been remarkably light; 1st Marine Division lost 20 killed in action and less than 200 wounded. CHROMITE continued as the marines drove north from Seoul towards the 38th parallel until relieved early in October; by this time the division had lost 366 killed in action, 49 died of wounds, 6 missing and 2029 wounded in battle. The 7th Division's casualties amounted to 366 killed in action, 49 died of wounds, and over

If General Smith and other subordinate commanders felt more than a little apprehensive about the outcome their fears were not shown by their supreme commander. MacArthur established his tactical headquarters aboard the USS *Mount McKinley* where he kept to his cabin until early on the morning of the assault when he took post on the bridge, surrounded by his senior staff and a troop of newsmen and cameras. As he had done since 1942 he wore his personally-designed forage cap of a Filipino Marshal and presided imperturbably over the operation as it unfolded, smoking the inevitable corncob pipe, and ensuring that the cameramen got the most favourable angles.

The seizure of Wolmi Island was entrusted to the 3rd Battalion, 5th Marines; as they headed for the land in their Amtraks, the naval and aerial bombardment rose to a climax. At 0633 the first marines went ashore against little resistance. The garrison appeared to

Naval Gunfire Support: The USS Missouri bombarding Chongjin, Korea, October 1950. (NARA)

2000 wounded. X Corps captured some 7000 NKPA soldiers and killed a further 14,000.

The NKPA was reduced for the time being to a shattered rabble fleeing north, leading MacArthur to commit his fatal error by pursuing it north of the 38th parallel. Promising President Truman that the war would be over by Christmas he permitted EUSAK to advance as far as the banks of the Yalu River, bordering the newly-emerged Chinese Peoples' Republic, with results that were to prove almost fatal to the UN cause.

Key Lessons

- **Selection and maintenance of aim:** MacArthur's will prevailed over all doubters.

- **Maintenance of Morale:** That of the USMC was high. In 7th Infantry Division, an amalgam of inexperienced troops and hastily embodied raw Korean recruits, it was far lower, but signified little in view of the division's subordinate follow-up role.

- **Surprise:** It was clear to the enemy that an amphibious landing was imminent on the west coast, but the choice of Inchon, with its strong tides, took the defence by surprise.

- **Offensive action:** The USMC, confident in their training, and well led at all levels, maintained their momentum throughout.

- **Concentration of Force:** MacArthur threw all his assets into Inchon, apart from minor feints elsewhere, and this guaranteed success.

- **Economy of Effort:** Had the troops who took Inchon been used as part of EUSAK, fighting their way out of Pusan, it is unlikely that so decisive a tactical result would have been achieved and the NKPA decisively defeated.

- **Co-operation/Inter Service integration:** By having their own integral supporting arms and logistics services the USMC were able to work easily with the USN on well practised drills.

- **Historical perspective:** The USMC had devoted much study between the wars to the Gallipoli campaign and made use of their knowledge to develop, in World War II, an amphibious capability equalled by no other nation.

- **Unity of Effort:** Excellent throughout, with joint command and control exercised smoothly from the HQ ship where the commanders (including MacArthur) had their fingers on the pulse.

- **Air Superiority:** This was virtually total as the North Korean air force had been destroyed within days of their invasion; only two attempts were made to bomb the invasion fleet.

- **Security:** Good, thanks to sophisticated communications systems.

- **Training:** Although many of the Marines were reservists, their World War II experience enabled them to perform well up to standard.

- **Sound Intelligence:** Preliminary surveillance by small parties landed on the approaches to Inchon, enabled charts to be updated and enemy dispositions fixed.

- **Readiness:** Although the CHROMITE force was hastily assembled, it contained such a strong reservoir of experience that the operation was feasible without extended rehearsal.

- **Deception:** The enemy appear to have thought that landings on the offshore islands or further south down the west coast were more probable than the head-on attack.

- **Winning of Sea Control:** There was no North Korean navy and the arrangements for minehunting and countermeasures worked well.

- **Naval Gunfire Support:** In the absence of opposition, the fleet closed in to give overwhelming support, from the main armament of the USS *Missouri* to light automatics.

- **Top-Down planning:** A classic example, in which the begetter and planner, MacArthur, was present on the day to see the conclusion of his plan.

Further Reading

Alexander, Joseph H. and Bartlett, Merrill L., *Sea Soldiers in the Cold War: Amphibious Warfare, 1945-1991,* (Annapolis, Maryland: Naval Institute Press, 1995)

Ballard, John R., *Operation Chromite: Counterattack at Inchon,* (Joint Forces Quarterly Spring/Summer 2001 p.31-36)

Bartlett, Merrill L. ed., *Assault from the Sea: Essays on the History of Amphibious Warfare,* (Annapolis, Maryland: Naval Institute Press, 1983)

Farrar-Hockley, Anthony, *Official History. The British part in the Korean War: Volume 1 A Distant Obligation,* (London: HMSO, 1990)

Hickey, Michael, *The Korean War: The West Confronts Communism 1950-1953,* (London: John Murray, 1999)

Speller, Ian and Tuck, Christopher, *Strategy and Tactics: Amphibious Warfare,* (Staplehurst, Kent: Spellmount, 2001)

Biography

Colonel Michael Hickey FRUSI MRAes took part in the Korean War as a Young Officer. He is a graduate of the Staff College Camberley, the Joint Services Staff College and the Royal Military College of Science at Shrivenham. He was a Defence Fellow at King's College London, Commandant of the Joint Air Transport Establishment and later Director of the Museum of Army Flying. His most recent books include the critically acclaimed *The Unforgettable Army* (Kent: Spellmount Ltd, 2002) on Slim and his 14th Army in Burma, *Gallipoli*, *Out of the Sky: A History of Airborne Warfare*, and *The Korean War: The West Confronts Communism 1950-1953*, (London: John Murray, 1999).

The Suez Crisis
Operation MUSKETEER, November 1956

XXXIII

By Dr Ian Speller

On 26 July 1956 the Egyptian President, Gamal Abdul Nasser, announced to a jubilant crowd that the Suez Canal Company was to be nationalised. Simultaneously, Egyptian forces seized the offices and facilities of that organisation, an international company in which the British and French governments were major shareholders. Both governments reacted angrily to this unilateral act and both began preparation for a military response almost immediately. In the absence of a political settlement satisfactory to all parties Britain and France initiated military action against Egypt on 31 October, culminating in an amphibious landing at Port Said on 6 November. Despite the apparent success of Anglo-French military operations, a combination of political and economic pressure caused the allied forces to halt operations at midnight that day.[1]

The result was a political disaster that did much to undermine the British position in the Middle East. It is not uncommon to hear the debacle over Suez described as a military success but a political failure. This argument is superficially attractive. Military operations were conducted in a competent professional manner. By the time of the cease fire Anglo-French forces had achieved sea control and air superiority and had firmly established

themselves ashore. Opposition in Port Said was limited to uncoordinated small arms fire and British tanks were driving south down the causeway alongside the canal towards Qantara and Ismailia. The land force commander, Lieutenant General Sir Hugh Stockwell, expected to have secured the former by midday on 7 November and to be attacking the latter by last light. His French deputy, General de Division Andre Beaufre, believed that Suez could have been taken as early as 8 November if a vigorous advance had been pursued. That this did not occur was the result of *political* decisions taken in London rather than any purely *military* consideration.

This line of argument is flawed. One does not need to be a student of Carl von Clausewitz to understand that it is impossible to separate military success from political failure. Clausewitz is famous for reminding us that war is a political act and that the means (war) can never be considered in isolation to their purpose (political objectives). No battle or campaign that fails to achieve its purpose can be considered a success. A military operation that can only offer success at a price that political leaders are unable or unwilling to pay is fatally flawed no matter how sound it might appear in the sterile world of the military textbook. It must, therefore, be accepted that Suez was a military failure. Nevertheless, one could still argue that, while the operation was

a failure, the military performed as well as could be expected and were undermined by non-military circumstances beyond their control rather than by any events on the battlefield. This chapter will try to assess the degree to which this is true. In the process it will aim to highlight issues of significance to those studying amphibious warfare today and will relate the conclusions that will be drawn to the contemporary concept of Manoeuvre Warfare.[2]

Naval General Service Medal, Near East 31st Oct – 22nd Dec 1956

MILITARY PLANNING

From the outset of the crisis the British Prime Minister, Anthony Eden, contemplated the use of military force to restore the canal to 'international control'. The Chiefs of Staff were asked to prepare contingency plans on the same day that Nasser made his momentous announcement and their initial plan was submitted to a special Egypt Committee[3] on 2 August. Ideally the British would have been in a position to launch an immediate operation, seizing control of the canal before Egyptian ownership could be established as a fact and while there was still a sense of outrage at Nasser's unilateral action. Unfortunately the forces that would have been required to conduct such an operation were not

---

[1] British forces used Greenwich Mean Time throughout Operation *Musketeer*. This was two hours behind local time in Egypt. Unless otherwise stated all times given in this chapter are GMT.

[2] The ensuing account is based upon the following sources: General Sir Charles Keightley, *Operations in Egypt – November to December 1956*, National Archives: DEFE 7/1081. General H.C. Stockwell, *Report by Commander 2 (Br) Corps on Operation Musketeer*, National Archives: WO 288/77. Brigadier R.W. Madoc, *3 Commando Brigade Royal Marines – Operation Musketeer Report*, National Archives: ADM 202/455. Vice Admiral M Richmond, *Naval Report on Operation Musketeer*, National Archives: ADM 116/6209. Air Marshal D Barnett, *Report by Air Task Force Commander on Operation Musketeer*, National Archives: AIR 20/10746. Meetings and Memoranda of the Egypt Committee, National Archives: CAB 134/1216 and 1217. For further details see Ian Speller, *The Role of Amphibious Warfare in British Defence Policy, 1945-1956* (Basingstoke: Palgrave, 2001) chapter 7.

[3] The Egypt Committee was established to formulate policy during the crisis and consisted of the Prime Minister, Lord President, Chancellor of the Exchequer, Foreign Secretary, Commonwealth Secretary and the Minister of Defence.

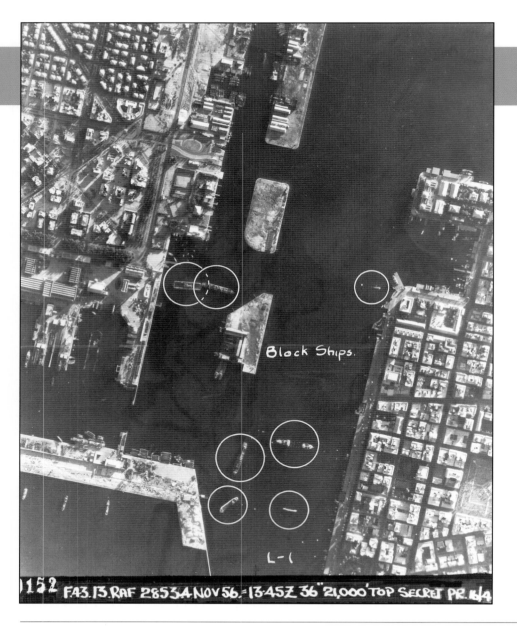

Block Ships.

L-1

)152 F.43.13.RAF 2853 4 NOV 56. - 13.45Z 36" 21,000' TOP SECRET PR. 1/4

TOP SECRET RAF aerial photograph of the Block Ships in the Suez Canal, November 1956. (NA)

available at short notice. The 16th (Independent) Parachute Brigade, based in Cyprus, was employed in counter-insurgency operations and had not conducted parachute exercises in over nine months. The Royal Marines of 40 Commando and 45 Commando were similarly employed in Cyprus and had not conducted any amphibious training for almost a year. The Commando Brigade's third unit, 42 Commando, was based back in the UK at cadre strength. In any case there were not enough transport aircraft to embark the Parachute Brigade in one lift nor were their sufficient amphibious ships or craft to embark and land the Commando Brigade. The Strategic Reserve in the UK consisted of the 3rd Infantry Division but this was under strength and unprepared for immediate operations. The Royal Navy had only one aircraft carrier in the Mediterranean while the Royal Air Force (RAF) assets in theatre were not in a position to guarantee air superiority over an opponent that had recently taken delivery of 120 modern Soviet Mig-15 fighters and 50 Ilyushin Il-28 bombers.

The First Sea Lord at the time, Lord Mountbatten, was later to claim that he informed Eden on 26 July that the Mediterranean Fleet could have embarked the Marines at Cyprus before landing them at Port Said in a matter of days. They could then advance down the causeway connecting that town to the mainland *'without a shot being fired'*.[4] There is no evidence that he actually made this suggestion. Indeed, the evidence shows that Mountbatten and his fellow Chiefs of Staff were opposed to putting ashore a lightly armed force, even had the capability to do so been available. In their initial discussions with the Cabinet on 27 July the Chiefs argued that the equivalent of three divisions would be required to overcome Egyptian opposition and that it would take several weeks to prepare for such an operation. The capabilities required to launch a rapid *coup de main* simply did not exist.

The Chiefs of Staff appointed Lieutenant General Sir Hugh Stockwell, Vice Admiral Sir Maxwell Richmond and Air Marshal Sir Denis Barnett as the army, navy and air force task force commanders for any operation and their staff gathered in Whitehall between 1 and 4 August. The first Joint

[4]Philip Ziegler, *Mountbatten. The Official Biography*, (London: Collins, 1985) p. 537.

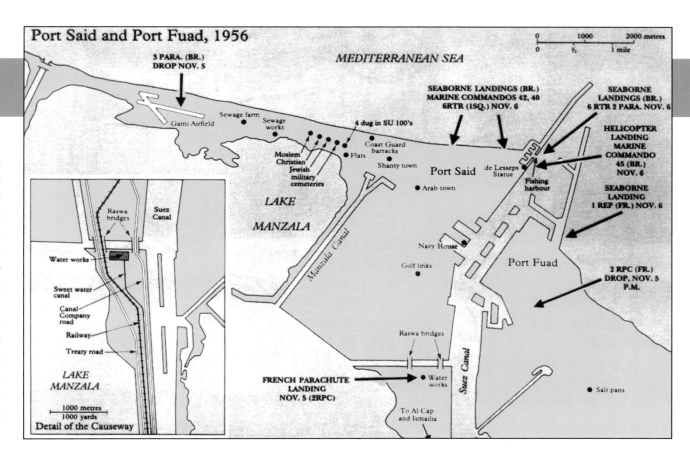

The Port Said, the Port Faud area and the main British and French landing zones. (NHB)

Task Force Commanders meeting took place on 6 August. Three days later General Sir Charles Keightley took up his position as Allied Commander-in-Chief. The French provided officers to act as deputies to their British counterparts and to command French forces in any actual operation. Integrated planning with the French began on 16 August. The initial plan developed by the Chiefs of Staff catered for a maritime blockade and air action against Egypt followed, if necessary, by a landing at the northern end of the Suez Canal and a feint towards Alexandria. Port Said would be secured by a combined amphibious/airborne operation, after which follow-on forces would be built up before breaking out to secure the canal and occupy Suez. It was recognised that it would take at least six weeks to mobilise sufficient amphibious shipping to support such an operation, involving two Commando units, only one of which would be landed in the assault wave.

Neither Stockwell nor Beaufre were particularly enamoured with this plan. The beaches at Port Said were shallow and thus less than ideal for any amphibious assault. The port had limited unloading and cargo handling facilities which would slow down the build-up of follow-on forces. Worse still, it was connected to the mainland by a narrow causeway running along the course of the canal for 25 miles, with impassable salt marshes on either side. This could cause obvious problems for any force breaking out. Port Said also lacked an airfield capable of taking modern high performance aircraft and the nearest such facility, at Abu Sueir, was 50 miles away. Alexandria, on the other hand, had

first rate harbour facilities and a modern airfield that could be captured at an early stage. Coastal defences were stronger than at Port Said, but these, it was believed, could be suppressed by naval gunfire and air attack. Stockwell and Beaufre therefore developed a plan to land at Alexandria. The plan, codenamed Operation MUSKETEER, consisted of three stages and was to be preceded by two or three days and nights of air action designed to destroy the Egyptian air force. The Commando Brigade would land on beaches close to Alexandria or directly into the harbour itself, while airborne forces secured the airfield and causeways from that city. Air strikes and naval gunfire would neutralise

coastal defences. The leading units of 3rd Infantry Division would go ashore once the harbour was secured. British and French forces would then be built up to a strength of around 80,000 troops including two infantry and two armoured divisions. This force would advance towards Cairo before moving off to occupy the Canal zone. It was assumed that the main force of the Egyptian army would be engaged and defeated within fourteen days of the initial landing. It was hoped that this would prompt the fall of Nasser. The Egypt Committee accepted this as the basis for planning on 10 August, with a landing provisionally scheduled for 15 September.

was completed by 12 October and was due to come into effect on 21 October. However, three days before this date Keightley signalled that MUSKETEER *Revise* was to remain in force. The *Winter Plan* had been overtaken by political developments.

Military Preparations

A considerable time was required in order to prepare for operations against Egypt. The French had to recall the Landing Ship, Dock (LSD) *Foudre* from Saigon, sailing the long way around the Cape rather than through the Suez Canal. Parachute troops required refresher training and forces previously allocated to counter-insurgency operations in Algeria had to prepare for more conventional operations in Egypt. All of this training and preparation took time. As late as the end of August the 7th Division Mécanique Rapide, one of the units allocated to MUSKETEER, had still not received gun sights for its AMX tanks.[5]

The British faced similar problems. A small Amphibious Warfare (AW) Squadron capable of embarking a battalion group was kept in commission at Malta. This was clearly inadequate for an operation the size of MUSKETEER. Britain still had the remnants of the large amphibious fleet that had existed at the end of the Second World War but a lack of priority meant that most of the ships and craft were kept in reserve, mothballed and unmanned. Ships and craft therefore had to be brought forward from reserve in the UK and Malta and their crews had to become familiar

The date for the landing was pushed back from 15 September to 19 and then 26 September. The need to co-ordinate the movement of a large number of ships from the UK, North Africa and Malta made the plan rather inflexible. In order to meet the latter date a decision to proceed was required on 9 September with the first ships sailing from the United Kingdom six days later. These dates passed without the necessary action being taken. It became clear that an alternative concept of operations was required, one that could be held at readiness for an extended period of time. As a result General Keightley developed an alternative plan, eventually known as MUSKETEER *Revise*. This plan was centred upon an air offensive designed to

target Egyptian military forces and strategic targets, notably oil supplies, until Nasser was forced to capitulate. The bombing campaign was to be supported by a major psychological warfare effort. A military force, consisting of three divisions, would be landed at Port Said and would proceed to occupy the Canal Zone once the Egyptians were incapable of organised resistance. The new concept was first presented to Anthony Eden on 7 September and was formally adopted by the Egypt Committee on 19 September. As time passed and there was still no call to activate the plan Keightley prepared yet another concept, designed to offer military options during the poor weather that could be expected in autumn and winter. This *Winter Plan*

---

[5]Andre Beaufre, *The Suez Expedition 1956*, (Faber and Faber, 1966) p.45.

Above: Aerial photograph of the beach at Port Said where the Commandos went ashore. (RMM)

Below: A view of the same beach looking westwards. (IWM C(AM)2345)

with operating them. Inevitably vessels that had been held in reserve for years were not in any state to conduct immediate operations. The ships and crews were eventually brought to a satisfactory state of training and material, but they could not have been considered ready for active operations before the end of September.

The situation regarding landing craft was particularly problematic. The limited availability of Landing Craft Assault (LCA) forced the Chiefs of Staff to limit the assault wave in their initial plan to a single Commando unit. Thus, the assault wave was to be determined by the shortage of landing craft rather than the nature of the objective or the likely opposition. Sufficient LCA were brought out of reserve to alleviate this problem, although many of these were old LCA Mk1 rather than the more modern Mk 2. This caused some difficulties as the old Mk 1s were in a poor state of repair and this had an impact on training. It was recognised that the beaches at Port Said were very shallow and that LCA would beach some distance from the shore, forcing troops to wade ashore before crossing a further 200 yards of open beach. For this reason it was decided to employ old tracked amphibious vehicles (LVTs) known as *Buffaloes*. These old war veterans had initially been intended only for use in the build-up phase, and thus had no fitted machine guns, radios or pin-on armour. This was to cause the assaulting marines some discomfort on 6 November. Only 16 such vehicles were available. As there was no unit trained to operate them No. 1 Troop LVT, Royal Armoured Corps was

quickly formed and their crews eventually became proficient in their use. Not, however, before they had rammed the Appledore lifeboat when training off the coast of Devon. The British were forced to go to extraordinary lengths to ensure the availability of some amphibious vehicles that were no longer maintained by the armed forces. One reservist officer recalled his friend's surprise as they saw a number of DUKWs (amphibious trucks) arrive at the Amphibious Warfare Centre at Fremington.

Edward's interest was occasioned by the fact that this particular DUKW was decorated in a manner reminiscent of a barber's pole, in red, white and blue stripes. It passed by us, near enough for us to see painted on the gunwale the name *Saucy Sue*, and on a notice board still attached to the side, the legend '*Long Trips on the Briny. Adults 2s 6d. Children Half Price.*'[6] It is remarkable to note that only twelve years earlier the Royal Navy had provided the majority of amphibious ships and craft employed in the largest amphibious operation in history.

The men of the Parachute Brigade conducted refresher training in the UK with the aircrew who would drop them in any operation. 42 Commando was brought up to strength and joined the remainder of 3 Commando Brigade in Malta where they undertook a series of amphibious exercises through September and October. The Commando Brigade was reinforced with Air Control Teams, reservists from 116 Amphibious Observation Battery and anti-tank platoons from 3rd Infantry Division. The

Despite the difficulties the armed forces of both Britain and France were eventually ready for operations. By mid-September most of the key elements of the force had been gathered

3rd Infantry Division mobilised in the UK. Two battalions of the Royal Tank Regiment (RTR) were earmarked for operations in Egypt, the 1st and the 6th. The latter was chosen to participate in the initial assault and sailed for Malta between 23 August and 2 September. C Squadron practised loading into Landing Craft Tank (LCT) but, due to a lack of waterproofing supplies and a shortage of suitable beaches, only one vehicle actually practised landing across the beach. Similarly, the Royal Navy and the RAF concentrated forces in the Mediterranean, basing at Malta and Cyprus respectively.

The issue of bases posed a particular problem of the planners. Malta, the headquarters of the Mediterranean Fleet, possessed all of the facilities necessary to mount a major amphibious operation. Unfortunately it was over 900 miles from the Suez Canal, far too far for land-based fighter aircraft to be of any use. British administered Cyprus was closer but lacked the harbour facilities necessary to support the invasion force. Therefore it could not be used to mount the amphibious operation. It did have sufficient airfields to be used for air and airborne operations. However, at the outset of the crisis only Nicosia's civilian airfield was in operation, and that was under reconstruction and not operating at full capacity. The RAF airfield at Akrotiri was still under construction and the third airfield, at Tymbou, was only an emergency landing strip. The airfields did

not become fully operational until late October. Even then they were all packed to capacity. Given that Cyprus lacked a modern radar early warning system the planners were understandably concerned about the vulnerability of the airfields to a strike by Egypt's Ilyushin bombers.

Despite the difficulties the armed forces of both Britain and France were eventually ready for operations. By mid-September most of the key elements of the force had been gathered. By the end of that month they were more or less ready for operations. The requirement to get the military forces ready to act thus imposed a delay of around two months on operations. Subsequent delay was to reflect political rather than strictly military imperatives.

In the immediate aftermath of the nationalisation of the Suez Canal Company there had been an outcry against Nasser's action. At this point, in the heat of the moment, military action may have been credible. Unfortunately for Britain and France they were not ready to act. By the time they were ready, there no longer seemed to be any need. To the frustration of both governments the Egyptians proved perfectly capable of administering the canal at least as well as had the old company and they refused to allow themselves to be provoked into taking any action that might seem to justify a military response. Britain and France thus lacked a suitable *casus belli*. This was particularly problematic as in the United States President Eisenhower was opposed to the

---

[6]D.M.J. Clark, *Suez Touchdown. A Soldiers Tale* (London: Peter Davis, 1964) pp 8-9.

use of force to settle the dispute. A rather disreputable solution was found. In secret negotiations between Britain, France and Israel it was agreed that the latter would attack the Egyptians in the Sinai. Britain and France would then issue an ultimatum to both sides, requiring that they both accept a cease-fire and withdraw to ten miles on either side of the canal. If Nasser refused, as he was certain to do, they would have an excuse to intervene in the guise of peacekeepers. A protocol was signed to this effect at Sevres on 24 October. The Israeli offensive was to begin five days later.

Operation MUSKETEER

In accordance with the agreement at Sevres Israel attacked Egyptian forces in the Sinai on 29 October. The following day Britain and France issued their ultimatum, demanding that both sides accept a ceasefire, withdraw their forces to ten miles either side of the Canal and that Egypt accept the temporary occupation of the Canal zone. As expected, Israel accepted and Egypt rejected what were always intended to be unacceptable terms. As a result the British and French initiated high level bombing raids against Egyptian airfields during the night of 31 October and these were followed, rather more effectively, by low-level daylight raids by fighter and ground attack aircraft. Lacking

proficiency with their new Soviet aircraft the Egyptians did not put up any serious resistance in the air and by 2 November their air force was neutralised.

As a result of collusion with Israel there was no time for the extended period of bombing and psychological warfare originally envisaged for MUSKETEER *Revise*. On the contrary, with world opinion opposed to military action it was imperative for the allies to conclude the fighting as soon as possible. Unfortunately, in order to preserve the veneer of impartiality and to hide the fact of collusion it was decided not to sail the main amphibious force until after the expiry of the ultimatum to Egypt. As such, and given the slow speed of Britain's

ageing amphibious fleet, no landing would be possible before 6 November. In the meantime the allied air forces attacked Egyptian military targets and, after some delay, put out of action Nasser's key propaganda tool, Cairo Radio.

The plan for MUSKETEER envisaged a combined amphibious and airborne landing on 6 November. Two Royal Marine Commando units (No.40 and No.42) would assault the main beach astride the Casino pier 35 minutes after sunrise. The assault wave would be carried in LVTs with the remaining troops wading ashore from LCAs. These troops would be reinforced by tanks landed from LCTs. Simultaneously British paratroops would secure Gamil airfield to the west of Port Said while French paratroops

sealed off Port Fuad on the east bank of the canal in support of a French amphibious landing. French paratroops would also secure two bridges at Raswa to the south of the town vital for the subsequent break-out down the causeway.

It had previously been planned to seize these bridges using the marines of 45 Commando landed from helicopters from two aircraft carriers offshore. The British were aware of American developments in the use of helicopters in the amphibious assault but had never practised such operations themselves. In late September two redundant light fleet carriers, HMS *Ocean* and HMS *Theseus* were earmarked to act as LPHs embarking a very makeshift airgroup comprising helicopters from the navy's No.845 Squadron and a joint army and RAF formation, the Joint Experimental Helicopter Unit (JEHU). Prior to their adoption of this role in October neither unit had ever practised assault operations. HMS *Theseus* and *Ocean* arrived at Malta with their new air groups on 19 and 31 October respectively. Limited training was possible with the marines of 45 Commando on 1 November but a full dress rehearsal of their planned role was not permitted due to concerns over security. The two ships sailed for Port Said on 3 November catching up to the slow amphibious force by sailing at a respectable 17 knots. However, on 31 October the force commanders cancelled the helicopter assault at Raswa. There were not enough aircraft to land in one lift a force sufficient to meet the likely threat at the target and the commanders were understandably nervous about employing helicopters in such a novel role. Instead 45 Commando was to

remain offshore, acting as a floating reserve.

A combination of factors led the force commanders to consider revising their invasion timetable. Severe criticism of British and French action both at home and abroad increased the need for the quick resolution of military operations. The crisis in Egypt was debated in the United Nations (UN) Security Council on 30 October. Britain and France were twice forced to veto Security Council resolutions calling for a cease fire and the withdrawal of Israeli forces. The first such resolution, proposed by the United States, represented the first time that Britain had ever used its veto. To make matters worse, on 2 November the United Nations General Assembly, using the 'Uniting for Peace' mechanism for the first time, passed a resolution calling for an immediate cease fire and a withdrawal of all military forces to their pre-crisis positions. The Egyptians agreed to this demand. Worse still, the Israeli offensive was so successful that there appeared every chance that they would achieve all of their objectives before British or French troops could intervene. Indeed, Israel secured its last objective, Sharm-el-Sheikh, on the morning of 5 November. The war that Britain and France were purporting to stop was already as good as over before any Anglo-French troops were on the ground.

The French were rather more aware of the need for speed and rather more willing to take risks than were their British counterparts. Prior to the initiation of hostilities General Beaufre devised a scheme to deploy French infantry rapidly from Algeria in the fast battleship *Jean Bart*. These troops, combined with vehicles and equipment based in slow amphibious shipping off Cyprus, could provide a limited but rapid intervention capability. This 'Plan A' was approved, but was only to be implemented if Egyptian opposition was expected to be negligible. This was not to be the case. As early as 31 October the French proposed to implement Operation OMELETTE, involving the landing of airborne forces before the arrival of seaborne reinforcements. The British were reluctant to do this, noting the redeployment of Egyptian forces from the Sinai towards the Canal Zone. The British did, however, agree to Operation TELESCOPE, the plan to land the airborne element on 5 November instead of simultaneously with the amphibious landing the next day. TELESCOPE catered for parachute landings at Gamil (British) and at Port Fuad and Raswa (French) on 5 November, the day before the seaborne landings. This had the advantage of placing troops

on the ground twenty-four hours earlier than had been planned, and offered the possibility of facilitating a more rapid break-out from Port Said once seaborne reinforcements had arrived.

At 0515 668 soldiers of 3 Parachute Battalion (3 Para) were dropped at Gamil airfield, four miles west of Port Said. Shortly afterwards 500 men of the 2nd Regiment Parachutistes Coloniaux jumped at low level on a narrow strip of ground to the south of Port Said, at Raswa. These were followed in the afternoon by a second French airdrop to secure Port Fuad. Both the British and French airborne operations were successful. French troops, battle hardened in Algeria and Indo-China and benefitting from better equipment and more appropriate transport aircraft than their British counterparts, seized all of their objectives and cleared Port Fuad, removing the possibility of any opposition to the French amphibious landing the next morning. British paratroops secured Gamil airfield and pushed into the outskirts of Port Said, where they were held up by a shortage of ammunition and a lack of heavy weapons. They then spent a rather uncomfortable night in the town sewage works, waiting for the main seaborne force to arrive the next day.

The amphibious landing went well, although it was not without some hiccups. There was a temporary ceasefire during the fighting on 5 November when it appeared that the local Egyptian commander was willing to surrender to the allied forces. Although this proved not to be the case it did mean that for a time the marines offshore were under the impression that they might not have to conduct an opposed landing the following day. More significantly, politicians back in London were becoming increasingly concerned by both domestic and international criticism of their actions. They were extremely concerned about the possibility of heavy civilian casualties caused by any naval bombardment. As a result Keightley was instructed that only naval guns of 4.5-inch calibre or less could be employed. This ruled out the 6-inch guns of the two British cruisers offshore and the 15-inch guns of the French battleship, *Jean Bart*. At the last minute the force commanders were told that no bombardment was permitted. This order, while sensible in political terms, opened up the possibility that assaulting troops might face heavy fire from unsuppressed defenders. As a result the instruction was ignored. The semantic difference between 'bombardment' and 'naval gunfire support' was exploited and four British destroyers provided fire support to the two assaulting Commando Units, drenching the beach with 920 rounds over 45 minutes.

It was the first time in history that helicopters had been used in this manner during an amphibious operation.

In the absence of specialist assault craft, designed to suppress defenders once the destroyers lifted their fire during the assault wave's final approach, carrier borne aircraft strafed the beach for ten minutes. Naval gunfire was controlled and accurate, although one shell did start a major fire that destroyed many homes in the shanty town area of Port Said. After the initial landings NGS did not play an important part in operations ashore. The force commanders were not allowed to call upon the fleet's heaviest guns to destroy Egyptian strongpoints such as the Navy House and the Custom House. The only fire that was required was provided by the destroyers HMS *Chaplet* and HMS *Decoy* which were given permission to silence an SU-100 armoured vehicle that had opened fire. The provision of fire support during the landings proved adequate. This does not mean that it would have been sufficient against a more capable opponent. After the landings it was discovered that twin six-pounder gun emplacements on the breakwater at Port Said were still intact. These had been targetted by air strikes and

abandoned. Had their crews possessed greater resolve these guns could have inflicted significant casualties on the assaulting Commandos.

The leading waves of 40 and 42 Commando came ashore in their LVTs at 0450, facing light opposition. The second wave, landing in LCAs, had to endure a 35 yard wade. The marines were followed at 0500 by four LCTs that landed 14 waterproofed Centurion tanks of C Squadron, 6 RTR in four and a half feet of water. Seven of the tanks towed one-ton trailers filled with ammunition and supplies for the marines, they dumped these at the back of the beach after wading ashore. Due to the limited availability of suitable craft and the shallow beach gradient the only other vehicles that were landed over the beach were five Austin Champs landed from LCA Mk2s. The first LCTs, carrying anti-tank platoons, discharged their cargo at the quayside in the fishing harbour at 0520 and these were followed by others containing the remainder of C Squadron 6 RTR. The first LST began unloading at 0830 and by nightfall a total of 14 LSTs had discharged men, vehicles and stores at the Casino Palace Hotel wharf and the Fishing Harbour. Unfortunately it was not possible to utilise the main harbour facilities at Port Said due to blockships and other obstacles. The French assault force consisted of 1st Regiment Etranger Parachutists and naval commandos. These were supported by a squadron of AMX light-tanks that were landed in Landing Craft Mechanised (LCM) from the LSD *Foudre*. The success of the parachute landing the previous day meant that their landing was unopposed.

At 0520 45 Commando was ordered to land within the beach area already secured by the marines. In 89 minutes 22 helicopters flew in a total of 425 men and 23 tons of stores from the carriers situated nine miles offshore. The marines landed on the beach near the de Lesseps statue, but not before the commanding officer had a close escape during a recce in which his helicopter landed him in a sports stadium still held by the Egyptians. The ability of the helicopter to sustain hits was demonstrated as the Whirlwind Mk22 being used was hit at least 20 times before the pilot was able to re-embark his passengers and fly to safety. In many respects this was a remarkable operation. It was the first time in history that helicopters had been used in this manner during an amphibious operation. The US Marine Corps had pioneered developments in this field, but had not yet had the opportunity to put them into practice on the battlefield. Even given the improvised nature of the British force, and the rather conservative way in which it was used, the potential for helicopters to add speed and flexibility to amphibious operations was readily apparent. This success was slightly marred by a friendly-fire incident in which a Royal Navy fighter-bomber attacked the marines on the beach, wounding the commanding officer and causing seventeen other casualties. These were swifly evacuated back to their ship by helicopter.

A detailed examination of the tactical conduct of operations is beyond the scope of this chapter. Fighting in Port Said continued throughout the day. Resistance consisted largely of sniping, although stiff opposition was encountered at Egyptian strongholds such as the Customs House and the Navy House, both of which were eventually subdued with the assistance of tanks and air strikes. By mid-afternoon the French paratroops at Raswa had been joined by marines from 42 Commando and tanks from 6 RTR. The French paratroops and British tanks then began a somewhat leisurely advance south towards Qantara. By nightfall they had reached the small Canal station at al-Tinah, where they halted. Later that evening they received an order to resume the advance to Qantara immediately. Stockwell informed them that a ceasefire was to begin as 1200 GMT (0200 local time). An ad hoc force of British tanks and paratroops then advanced as far as al-Cap, 25 miles south of Port Said and four miles short of Qantara, before they were forced to halt because of the cease fire.[7] This was as far as they were to get. International pressure forced the British, and because of them, the French, to accept a ceasefire before they had obtained their objectives. The ceasefire was followed by the withdrawal of Anglo-French forces from Egypt, to be replaced by a UN peacekeeping force. The last British and French troops left on 22 December. The British Prime Minister, Anthony Eden, resigned 13 days later. British casualties during MUSKETEER were 16 killed and 96 wounded. The French lost 10 dead and 33 wounded. Egyptian casualties are harder to estimate but certainly included hundreds of soldiers and civilians.

Doing The Unexpected, Seeking Originality and A Ruthless Determination To Succeed?

Joint Warfare Publication 0-01, *British Defence Doctrine*, describes '*the manoeuvrist approach*' as an approach to operations '*in which shattering the enemy's overall cohesion and will to fight, rather than his material is paramount*.' It pits strength against weakness and seeks to exploit momentum and tempo to create shock action and surprise. Emphasis is placed on disrupting and ultimately defeating the enemy by seizing the initiative and applying constant and unacceptable pressure where and when they least expect it. The focus is on the enemy's decision making cycle rather than necessarily being on his armed forces. This approach is supposed to be applicable at all levels of war and is inherently joint, requiring the co-operation of land, sea and air forces. It calls for '*…an attitude of mind in which doing the unexpected and seeking originality is combined with a ruthless determination to succeed*'.[8]

Manoeuvre in the traditional sense of the word does not automatically result in '*manoeuvre warfare*'. This requires more than mere mobility. Manoeuvring slowly and in a predictable fashion is unlikely to shatter the enemy's will and cohesion. Equally, manoeuvring rapidly and in an unexpected fashion is unlikely to lead to success in warfare unless such actions are directed against an appropriate and realistic target. Manoeuvre warfare may involve an element of risk not associated with more traditional approaches based on numerical superiority and slow, methodical techniques. However, in some circumstances risks must be run in order to provide satisfactory outcomes within an appropriate timeframe at an acceptable cost. This is particularly the case when political considerations are taken into account. This point is rather more apparent to British military planners today that it was in the 1950s.

Operation MUSKETEER cannot be taken as an example of *manoeuvre warfare*. British and French forces certainly manoeuvred and their sea and air borne mobility conferred specific advantages that could be, and sometime were, exploited. However, at no stage could they truly be said to have shattered Egyptian will and cohesion. It could be claimed that had operations continued such an effect would have become evident. It is certainly the case that, despite some isolated cases where British troops encountered stubborn resistance from Egyptian defenders, the Egyptian armed forces appeared completely incapable of generating an effective and co-ordinated response to the allied invasion. However this appears to have been more a result of *force majeure* than tempo and momentum. Unlike their Israeli co-conspirators British and French operations were not particularly characterised by speed or surprise. British commanders were averse to taking any risks, even when the need for speed was becoming very obvious to their French allies. As a result the pedestrian pace of Anglo-French military operations completely undermined any chance

---

[7]In reality they reached al-Cap 20 minutes after the cease-fire, but decided to push on until they reached this point.
[8]*British Defence Doctrine. Joint Warfare Publication (JWP) 0-01*, pp. 4.8-4.9

of political success. Indeed, the inability to conclude operations within a satisfactory timeframe meant that it was the British will to fight that was shattered as a result of constant and unacceptable pressure applied beyond the battlefield.

This does not mean that the British and French were defeated by the Egyptian armed forces. They were not. Nor should it be suggested that the soldiers, sailors and airmen participating in Operation MUSKETEER lacked the will or capability to overcome what remained of Egyptian resistance. They did not. However, while the Egyptian armed forces could not hope to protect the country against the combined attention of Britain, France and Israel, Nasser was able to exploit world opinion to the point that the British and French at least were ultimately thwarted. In the conditions that now prevailed military superiority was no longer enough. Issues of legitimacy and proportionality were at least as important. A permissive diplomatic environment was as important as either sea control or air superiority. In this sense Operation MUSKETEER was a very '*modern*' operation.

A number of features apparent in twenty-first century operations were evident during the crisis. Political factors influenced every aspect of the crisis. The need for an acceptable excuse to intervene delayed the operation and led the British to accept collusion with Israel. The absence of significant support on the international stage added to political pressure being applied to Eden's government at the domestic level. The resulting run on

Sterling, and American obstructionism at the World Bank forced Eden to accept that the costs of continuing to fight outweighed the benefits. The use of the US Sixth Fleet to harrass and obstruct the Anglo-French invasion convoy as it approached Egypt provides a classic example of the use of maritime forces to send a political message. It also demonstrates that such signals are not always heeded.

Political considerations also had an impact at the tactical level. The fleet offshore was constrained in its ability to provide naval gunfire support due to a fear of collateral damage. Indeed, the switch from landing at Alexandria to Port Said was as least partially influenced by the fear of the impact on civilian lives and property of the heavy bombardment that would be required to support the planned assault directly into Alexandria harbour. The desire to avoid civilian casualties caused numerous problems. British troops in Port Said encountered difficulties distingishing between civilians and combatants as many Egyptian soldiers discarded their uniforms in favour of civilian clothes. Prior to the landings the Egyptians had distributed arms to the civilian population, making the distinction between combatant and non-combatant even more difficult. The French, hardened by counter-insurgency operations in Indo-China and North Africa, appear to have been rather less concerned about such issues.

The most obvious way in which political considerations influenced the conduct of military operations was in the constraints that

they imposed on the application of air power. Attacks on targets in built-up areas or other places where civilian casualties might result were problematic. For example, it was not possible to neutralise Illuyshin bombers stationed at Cairo West Airport due to the fear of hitting Amercian civilians who were being advised to evacuated along a route adjaent to the airport. These aircraft were able to escape to airfields in the south where they were eventually destroyed by French ground-attack aircraft. The truncated aero-psychological phase of MUSKETTEER was a complete failure. It is hard to coerce people to the point of surrender with a target list that is necessarily constrained by political and humanitarian considerations. It is harder still to convince people that the real enemy is their own government when they are being bombed by foreign aircraft. As Beaufre was later to claim, 'A guarded air threat is illusory, politcally dangerous and psychologically disastrous'.[9] He could also have noted that in the real world all '*air threats*' would be guarded to a greater or lesser degree.

Even with these constraints failure was not inevitable. Quick and decisive action in the immediate aftermath of nationalisation might have secured control of the canal before opinion had time to harden against the military option. Current British thinking, as expressed in *The United Kingdom Approach to Amphibious Operations*, emphasises that properly executing amphibious manoeuvre from the sea '..requires specialist amphibious shipping and equipment, bespoke command and control arrangements, an appropriate philosophy of command and an

[9]Andre Beaufre, *The Suez Expedition*, p 138.

in being and ready national amphibious force.'[10] In July 1956 this did not exist. By the time that an appropriate amphibious (and airborne) force had been mustered, the opportunity to employ military forces successfully may already have passed.

Even with the extended delay prior to MUSKETEER there may still have been a chance for success in November. Ideally the allies would have been in a position to launch a combined airborne and amphibious operation to seize Port Said and exploit down the canal as soon as air superiority had been assured by 2 November. They could not do so because, for political reasons, the British fleet based at Malta could not sail before the expiry of the ultimatum to Egypt and Israel. In retrospect the shipping could have sailed under the thin disguise of an amphibious exercise. Indeed, the headquarters' ship HMS *Tyne* did just this in order to ensure that the force commanders could be offshore at the appropriate time. That no-one would have been fooled by such a manoeuvre would hardly have mattered as few people were fooled in any case. There was also an added complication. Old Second World War type landing ships and craft, loaded beyond their intended personnel capacity, did not have the endurance or habitability to allow troops to be kept poised offshore for an extended period of time. Had the fleet sailed early from Malta any subsequent delay in the landing, caused by hiccups in the air campaign or other unexpected events, could have caused some difficulty.[11] What was really required was a

fast modern amphibious capability, able to sail to the objective area at high speed and to poise offshore for an extended period of time without a serious reduction in the fighting efficiency of its embarked force. In 1956 the United States possessed such a capability, the British did not. Despite all of the various difficulties

there were opportunities to conclude operations more rapidly. Beaufre suggested that the battleship *Jean Bart* should transfer its cargo of infantry into the waiting landing craft at sea off the coast of Egypt instead of sailing to Cyprus to do so. By doing this they would, at least in theory, have been available to go ashore a

---

[10]Headquarters Royal Marines and the Maritime Warfare Centre, *The United Kingdom Approach to Amphibious Operations*, (1997) p.21.
[11]Stockwell claimed that the amphibious fleet could not stay at sea for more than seven or eight days. The passage to Port Said was expected to take six days.

day early, on 5 November. Neither Admiral Durnford-Slater[12] nor his French deputy would agree to this. The British amphibious convoy had been expected to sail at a modest six knots. In the event the old amphibious craft managed to maintain eight knots. On 4 November they received the information that TELESCOPE was to be implemented. At this stage they could have been off Port Said at 0930 (1130 local time) on 5 November. As such it would have been possible to land the marines in support of the airborne forces that were already ashore. This would have entailed changing existing assault and fire support plans, and landing in broad daylight against an alert opponent or else finding a new landing site close to the airborne landing ground at Gamil. It is perhaps understandable that Durnford-Slater preferred to stick to the original plan and land his force at dawn the next day. Apparently, Vice-Admiral Manley Power, commanding the British aircraft carriers, suggested landing 45 Commando by helicopter at Gamil. This too was rejected. Similarly, no attempt was made to airlift additional forces into Gamil airfield despite the fact that it proved possible to operate Dakota transport aircraft from the short runway. An opportunity was thus missed to reinforce the paratroops at Gamil and to then push on and secure Port Said before the seaborne assault. Given the urgent need to secure physical control of the canal before pressure at the UN brought a halt to operations, this is a little hard to understand.

The command arrangements for MUSKETEER were less than ideal. Keightley acted as the commander-in-chief at a theatre level but had no direct role in the conduct of the actual landing. This remained in the hands of the three task force commanders and their three deputies, under the chairmanship of Stockwell. In effect, therefore, there was no joint commander at the operational level. Beaufre believes that this caused a degree of confusion and contributed to the situation where the task force commanders became isolated from the political atmosphere that would ultimately determine the fate of the operation. British commanders were particularly disadvantaged in this respect. Stockwell did not learn that MUSKETEER was to be implemented until 26 October after a chance encounter with Beaufre in Paris. Prior to this British planners had been more concerned with preparations for CORDAGE, a plan to intervene against Israel in the event of their attacking Jordan. On a more mundane level, the British depot ship HMS *Tyne* acted as headquarters' ship for MUSKETEER. Unfortunately this vessel had a limited command and control suite and as a result the Joint Fire Support Committee was accommodated in the small headquarters' ship HMS *Meon*, along with the staff of the AW Squadron. Beaufre was so dissatisfied with arrangements in *Tyne* that he moved his command to a separate vessel, the *Gustave-Zede*. After the seaborne landings on 6 November both Stockwell and Beaufre went ashore, initially at least to investigate reports of an Egyptian surrender. After surviving an attempt to land them at a point still held by Egyptian forces both commanders went ashore where they remained separated and incommunicado for most of the afternoon. Thus, through his own actions, Stockwell was not in a position to discover and respond to the political pressure that was building towards a cease-fire. Keightley, based in Cyprus, was aware of the requirement to halt operations by mid-afternoon, but he was not in a position to influence the conduct of operations ashore.

Had military operations in October/November been concluded more quickly it is possible that the British and French might have secured control of the canal before pressure to halt operations became acute. It is easy to criticise the Force Commanders for the slow pace of operations during MUSKETEER. It should be noted, however, that they had no reason to believe that they would be ordered to halt offensive operations less than twenty-four hours after the main seaborne landings. The French in general, and General Beaufre in particular, were quick to criticise their allies for their cautious approach. However, British officers did not have to think back as far as Arnhem (1944) to recognise the vulnerability of airborne forces dropped inland in the face of an undefeated enemy and without the prospect of immediate support by conventional forces. The catastrophic defeat of French airborne forces at Dien Bien Phu (1954) offers a cautionary tale, albeit in very different circumstances. Had the Force Commanders known in advance that they had but a few short hours to secure their objectives they may have accepted the need to run greater risks. This requirement was not communicated to them. In the circumstances perhaps they were justified in taking things slowly.

---

[12]Admiral Durnford-Slater replaced Admiral Richmond as task force commander prior to *Musketeer*.

The British learned a number of harsh lessons during the Suez crisis. It became clear that they were no longer a great world power and that they could not afford to ignore world opinion without the support of the United States

What would have happened after an Anglo-French victory is an interesting question, but one that is beyond the scope of this paper. Possession of the canal would have given the two governments some leverage in the discussions leading to eventual withdrawal. It would also have provided them with the opportunity to clear the waterway of the numerous obstructions that had resulted from Operation MUSKETEER. In many ways the restoration of the Suez Canal to international control was only a cover for wider British and French objectives. These revolved around the removal from power of Nasser and the consequent boost to their own prestige and power in the Middle East and North Africa that this would bring. It is possible that Nasser's government would have fallen to be replaced by one more amenable to the British. It is equally possible that it would not have done and that the British and French would have become engaged in a low-level guerrilla campaign at least as violent as the one that had earlier forced the British to decide to abandon their military presence in Egypt in 1954.[13] Had the allies extended operations beyond the Canal Zone and occupied Cairo they might have faced considerable difficulty in containing such resistance activity. This was certainly an outcome anticipated by General Beaufre.

The British learned a number of harsh lessons during the Suez crisis. It became clear that they were no longer a great world power and that they could not afford to ignore world opinion without the support of the United States. The inability of the military to provide suitable options within an appropriate timeframe reinforced existing plans to reshape the British armed forces, relying more on nuclear weapons to keep the peace in Europe and reinvesting in conventional forces designed to provide the capability for rapid intervention in limited conflicts overseas. In the years after 1956 British amphibious capabilities underwent a renaissance with the construction of two new Landing Ships Dock, six new Landing Ships, Logistic and the conversion of two aircraft carriers into LPHs. The Royal Marines received a new priority and 3 Commando Brigade expanded with the addition of two new Commando units and new administrative and support elements. The value of the aircraft carrier was confirmed, albeit temporarily. The Royal Navy had deployed three aircraft carriers in support of MUSKETEER and their air groups had flown 1614 sorties, damaging or destroying 289 enemy aircraft, 150 armoured vehicles and sinking six E-boats.[14] The ability of the aircraft carrier to provide a flexible power projection capability was something that the navy would continue to stress in their bitter dispute with the RAF over the future provision of air support beyond the NATO region.

An examination of the crisis reveals numerous factors that remain important today. The way in which **political considerations** have a necessary and profound impact on military activity at all levels is manifest. If commanders fail to take account of this and if they become isolated from the political results of actions on the battlefield success in the military sphere is likely to count for little. The consequences of maintaining armed forces unable to react rapidly to unforseen events in areas of vital national interest are also apparent. By the time that the military were able to provide their political masters with useable options it was probably already too late. In operations of this nature **tempo** is likely to be critically important, both at the tactical and operational levels and also at the strategic level. Maintaining small but capable military forces at an appropriate state of **readiness** may therefore be at least as important as the ability to generate a larger force at a later date. In order for such forces to achieve the desired effect appropriate **command and control** structure need to be in place and supported by the necessary equipment, infrastructure and outlook. One can find numerous examples of tension between the British and French commanders during MUSKETEER. These were overcome due to the French reliance on the British, their acceptance of a subordinate position within the command structure, and the physical separation of French and British ground forces during most of the short-lived campaign. Nevertheless, it is clear that the ability for allies to cooperate and coordinate effectively during **multi-national operations** was not something that could be taken for granted and was an area where difficulties could emerge. This problem was illustrated rather starkly from the French perspective as they were subject to the idiosyncrasies

---

[13]The last British troops had left the Suez Canal base in June 1956.
[14]Department of Operational Research – Report No.34, *Carrier Operations in Support of Operation Musketeer*, National Archives: ADM 219/610.

of the British with only a limited ability to influence decisions that were of enormous national importance. Perhaps this is the inevitable fate of the junior partner during coalition operations. An approach to the planning and conduct of operations more in tune with the principles that underlie the concept of manoeuvre warfare might have increased the chances of success during the crisis. However, one must question whether Britain's real aims - as opposed to the declared ones - could ever have been achieved by force of arms. Thus, perhaps, the overriding lesson of MUSKETEER is the requirement for **realism** during the decision making process that leads politicians to decide on the use of military force. There are simply some things that cannot easily be solved through the use of military force no matter how expertly it may be applied.

Further Reading

Beaufre, Andre, *The Suez Expedition 1956*, (London: Faber and Faber, 1969)

Cull, Brian, *Wings over Suez: The First Authoritative Account of Air Operations During the Sinai and Suez Wars of 1956*, (London: Grub Street, 1996)

Fullick, Roy and Powell, Geoffery, *Suez: The Double War*, (Hamish Hamilton, 1979)

Jackson, Robert, *Suez 1956: Operation Musketeer*, (London: Ian Allan, 1980)

Kyle, Keith, *Suez*, (New York : St. Martin's Press, 1991)

Speller, Ian, *The Role of Amphibious Warfare in British Defence Policy, 1945-1956*, (Basingstoke: Palgrave, 2001)

Varble, Derek, *The Suez Crisis*, (Oxford: Osprey, 2003)

Biography

Dr Ian Speller is a Lecturer in the Department of Modern History at the National University of Ireland, Maynooth. He also lectures in defence studies at the Irish Defence Forces Command and Staff School and provides occasional lectures at the UK Joint Services Command and Staff College (JSCSC). Prior to this he was a Senior Lecturer in Defence Studies at King's College London and the JSCSC where, in addition to a range of other duties, he had particular responsibility for the Maritime Phase of the Advanced Command and Staff Course and for the Advanced Amphibious Warfare Course. Dr Speller is the author *of The Role of Amphibious Warfare in British Defence Policy, 1945-56* (Palgrave, 2001) and the editor of *The Royal Navy and Maritime Power in the Twentieth Century* (Routledge, forthcoming). He is currently completing a volume for the Navy Records Society on *British Amphibious Forces, 1945-1975*.

Kuwait
Operation VANTAGE, July 1961

By Dr Ian Speller

The '*manoeuvrist approach*' represents a way of thinking about war fighting. It places an emphasis on matching strength against weakness and on pre-emption, dislocation and maintaining the initiative. The aim is to shatter the enemy's will to fight, rather than necessarily targeting their material. Tempo represents a core principle as does the associated ability to '*get inside*' the enemy's decision making cycle by forcing them to make decisions at a rate faster than they can cope with. The approach rests on an acceptance that, in certain circumstances, a degree of risk must be accepted in order to achieve positive results.[1]

The principles of the manoeuvrist approach were enshrined in British military doctrine in the 1990s. This does not mean that the principles associated with this approach did not apply before then, just that they were articulated in a different way. In 1961 the British undertook Operation VANTAGE, an operation to reinforce Kuwait rapidly in the face of a perceived threat of Iraqi invasion. The operation revolved around the use of both amphibious and air transported forces, building up a brigade-sized force in Kuwait in a matter of days. The British action was timely and effective and no Iraqi attack materialised. It could be argued that in many respects the success of Operation VANTAGE rested on the application of military force in a way that was

inherently '*manoeuvrist*'. VANTAGE provides a useful case study to examine the advantages of amphibious forces when employed in support of government policy in crisis situations short of war. It also provides an opportunity to compare and contrast the different strengths and limitations of sea based and air transported forces operating in a situation where political limitations compounded military challenges. This chapter will examine these issues.

The failure of British arms to secure a satisfactory outcome to the Suez crisis demonstrated the inability of Britain's armed forces to react quickly and effectively to limited but unforeseen challenges overseas. This reinforced the need for a change in priority. The 1957 defence review conducted by the Secretary of State for Defence Duncan Sandys placed an emphasis on the nuclear deterrent as a means of keeping the peace in Europe while smaller, more mobile conventional forces would deal with trouble further afield. In line with this approach the review also announced an end to National Service (conscription). In future Britain would rely on smaller, better trained and better equipped professional armed forces. The Defence White Paper described the navy's role in major war as '*somewhat uncertain*' but went on to stress the utility of both the Royal Navy and the Royal Marines as an '*effective means of bringing power rapidly to bear in peacetime emergencies or limited hostilities*'.[2] This was in line with existing Admiralty plans

to reduce the emphasis placed on sea control operations in any future war against the Soviet Union and to develop a new capability to support British interests overseas. The use of aircraft carriers in power projection operations against shore targets and the introduction of helicopter equipped 'commando carriers' was approved by the Board of Admiralty even before the value of both was illustrated during Operation MUSKETEER.[3]

The flexibility and mobility provided by maritime forces was seen as particularly valuable given the uncertain tenure of many of Britain's existing overseas facilities. The danger of relying on overseas bases as a means of projecting power was illustrated in 1956 when political restrictions meant that existing facilities in Jordan, Libya and Ceylon could not be used to support operations in Egypt. Bases in the British administered territories of Malta and Cyprus were available, but their distance from the area of operations had a deleterious impact on the conduct of operations. In the aftermath of the Suez crisis access to overseas facilities became even more problematic as the British were forced to withdraw from their bases in Jordan and Ceylon in 1957 and from the air bases at Habbaniyah and Shaibah in Iraq after a coup in that country ousted the pro-British government in 1958. By the end of the decade there was a growing appreciation that such problems could only get worse as the process of decolonisation accelerated.

---

[1] JWP 0-01, *British Defence Doctrine*, 1996, pp. 4.8 – 4.9.
[2] *Defence: Outline of Future Policy*; Cmnd.124, (London: HMSO, 1957)
[3] National Archives: DEFE 5/70, COS (56) 280, *The Future Role of the Navy*, 20 July 1956.

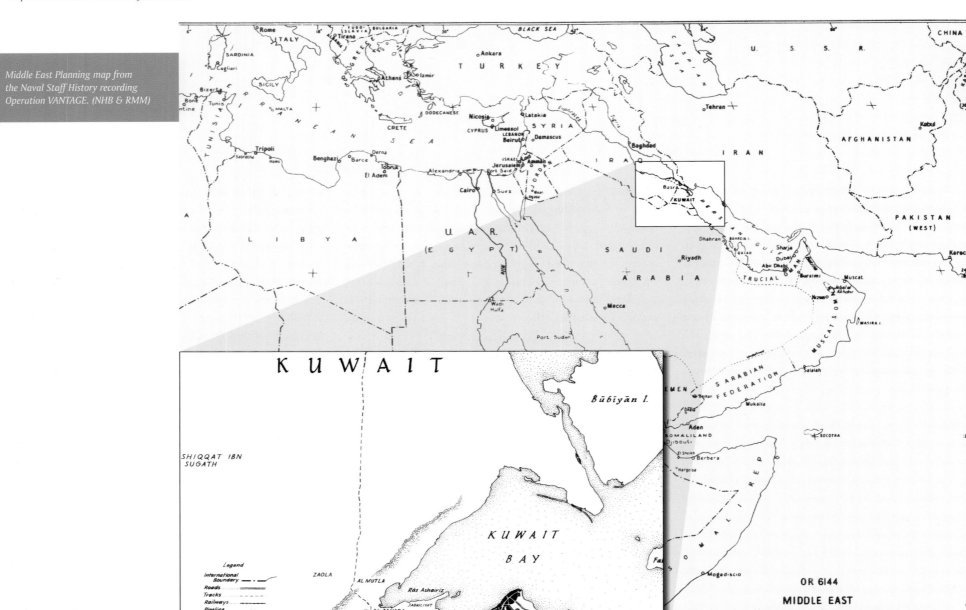

*Middle East Planning map from
the Naval Staff History recording
Operation VANTAGE. (NHB & RMM)*

In June 1959 the Prime Minister, Harold Macmillan, initiated a study of future policy by a high level working party chaired by the Cabinet Secretary, Sir Norman Brook. The report of the working party noted that, as war in Europe was unlikely, the armed forces should concentrate on winning small wars in the Middle East and the Far East. Due to the uncertain tenure of some overseas bases it was recognised that a mobile force structure was required. In the light of this report in 1960 the Chiefs of Staff undertook a study of *Military Strategy for Circumstances Short of Global War*. Their conclusions formed the basis of a later paper entitled *British Strategy in the Sixties*, prepared in the light of a directive issued by Macmillan in October 1961. During this review process the Admiralty articulated the case for a navy whose primary role was the provision of presence and limited military force east of Suez. To support this role a full range of maritime capabilities were required, from submarines and minesweepers to frigates, destroyers and cruisers. Aircraft carriers would provide a mobile and independent platform for both air defence and strike missions and a rejuvenated amphibious capability would offer the ability to land and support in combat a balanced military force including, if necessary, tanks and artillery. If all existing bases were retained then existing plans to maintain four aircraft carriers[4], two commando carriers and two new assault ships (LPDs) would suffice. This would provide Britain with *a 'Joint Services Seaborne Force'* able to land and support in action a balanced brigade group independent of local base facilities. If Britain was forced to relinquish all of its bases east of Suez, except for facilities in Australia, then the Admiralty proposed to deploy two such forces. By rotating these as required a powerful military presence could be maintained off a trouble spot almost indefinitely. Unfortunately this would require a total of four commando carriers, four LPDs and six aircraft carriers with four air groups.[5] Both the Chiefs of Staff Committee and the Cabinet Defence Committee accepted that this so called *'double stance'* was desirable as a means of maintaining British power and influence east of Suez but that it would be too expensive. The proposal for a single Amphibious Task Force east of Suez was approved and this was announced in the 1962 Defence White Paper.[6]

The navy's case was based upon the supposed ability of maritime forces to provide a unique range of capabilities. Aircraft carriers could provide air defence and close air support at sea and on land without reliance on local basing facilities. Amphibious forces were similarly independent of local facilities and could steam to a crisis area unobtrusively without having to agree the over-flight arrangements that were already beginning to prove a problem for air-transported forces. An amphibious task group had a heavy lift capability that could not be rivalled by air transport and, once ashore, could be supported by a range of other maritime assets, including the heavy guns of any accompanying cruisers or destroyers. The Admiralty did not claim that maritime forces alone could provide for all of Britain's defence needs overseas. They were scrupulous in their recognition of the need for a range of joint capabilities, both land and sea based. However, they were clear that the mobility, flexibility and versatility provided by a balanced maritime capability made a vital contribution to the maintenance of British interests overseas. These assumptions would be tested during Operation VANTAGE.

The navy's case for maritime expeditionary capabilities received support from some high profile commentators. In the conclusion to the official history of the Royal Navy in the Second World War, published in 1961, Stephen Roskill stressed that *'of all the lessons of history, none was more strikingly reaffirmed than the value of amphibious power, and its far-spread influence as a factor in both major and minor strategy'.*[7] In a series of lectures given at Cambridge in 1960, and subsequently published as *The Strategy of Sea Power*, Roskill expanded on this theme. He argued that after the provision of the strategic nuclear deterrent the second most important requirement in British defence policy was the provision of two joint service task forces capable of landing and supporting a brigade group or its equivalent at short notice wherever the situation should demand. Given the problem of basing and over-flight of third parties, he imagined

---

[4]With three air groups.

[5]National Archives: ADM 205/192, *Presentation of Alternative Long Term Naval programme*, 17 May 1961.

[6]*Statement on Defence 1962: The Next Five Years*; Cmnd 1639, (London: HMSO, 1962).

[7]S.W. Roskill, *The War at Sea 1939-1945. Volume Three, Part Two, The Offensive*, (London: HMSO, 1961) pp.-403-4.

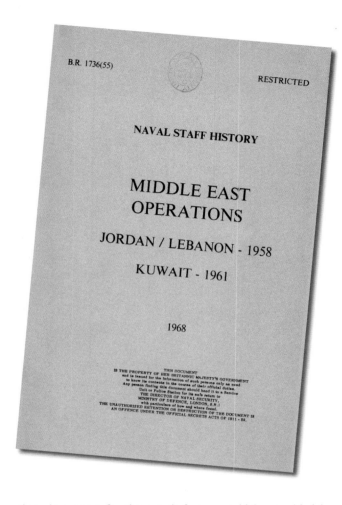

NAVAL STAFF HISTORY

MIDDLE EAST OPERATIONS

JORDAN / LEBANON - 1958

KUWAIT - 1961

1968

amphibious companion' as a means of bringing limited military power to bear in circumstances short of all-out war. Modern amphibious forces had strategic reach without reliance on facilities in other countries. At a tactical level they could land and sustain in combat a balanced military force without reliance on ports, airfields or beaches. If necessary they could also re-embark that force much more quickly and easily than would be possible with a conventional military deployment. Liddell-Hart also noted the utility of airborne forces in such circumstances, but stressed their limitations, including the problems of cost, range, over-flight restrictions, reliance on bases, reliance on facilities on arrival and the tactical limitations inherent in that mode of transport. He concluded that it was desirable to have an airborne force as it provided the quickest means of intervention where its use was possible, but that it was essential to have an amphibious capability, and that it should be '*the bigger of the two*'. He stressed that, '[a] *self-contained and sea-based amphibious force…is the best kind of fire-extinguisher because of its flexibility, reliability, logistic simplicity, and relative economy*.'[9]

had demonstrated the limitations of using old equipment and outdated techniques in limited military interventions. A new concept of operations designed specifically for limited war contingencies was required. As a result the seaborne/airborne concept was developed.[10] Reflecting the new emphasis on limited war operations, the concept stressed the need for seaborne and airborne forces to operate in concert in order to provide a mobile and flexible intervention capability. The need to respond quickly to crises meant that most of the initial forces employed would be provided from within the particular theatre. Follow-on forces would come from adjacent theatres and from the UK. Some land forces would remain afloat although the bulk of troops would be air transported from the UK. Heavy equipment such as tanks would continue to be transported by sea. Air transported follow-up forces would rely heavily on stockpiles which would be established in likely areas of operations. It was appreciated that opposition could vary in intensity but assaults against heavily defended coastlines were not contemplated.[11]

The Seaborne/Airborne Concept

In common with Liddell-Hart, British military planners appreciated the value of both airborne and amphibious forces in circumstances short of war although they did not all share his prioritisation between the two. Operation MUSKETEER

The details of the new concept were set out in 1962 by the Joint Warfare Staff:

'In the present concept of limited war our forces must be ready to counter sudden enemy intervention in a country

that air support for these task forces would be provided by aircraft carriers. In essence he was speaking in support of the '*double-stance*'.[8]

Similarly, in 1960 Basil Liddell-Hart also wrote about the value of '*amphibious flexibility*', extolling the virtues of '*seapower and its*

---

[8]S.W. Roskill, *The Strategy of Seapower*, (London: Collins, 1962) pp.254-255.
[9]B.H. Liddell Hart, 'The Value of Amphibious Flexibility and Forces', in *Journal of the Royal United Services Institution*, Vol. CV, Feb-Nov, 1960 pp 483-492. Also published in B.H. Liddell-Hart, *Deterrent or Defence. A Fresh Look at the West's Military Position*, (London: Stevens and Son Ltd, 1960).

[10]Sometimes known as the seaborne/airborne/land concept.
[11]National Archives: COS (61) 180, *Seaborne/Airborne/Land Concept*, 8 June 1961; DEFE 5/114. Also see J.L. Moulton, 'Amphibious Warfare in the Late 1960s: Seaborne/Airborne Operations', in *Journal of the Royal United Services Institution*, Vol. CVII Feb-Nov 1962, pp. 19-28.

In this concept of joint seaborne/airborne operations, the amphibious and air transported forces are part of a single team

that is neutral or friendly to us. The enemy will have the initiative and will be able to strike at the time and place he chooses, even if his moves can be foreseen, our forces may not be able to land before his active intervention, for political reasons. The requirement is for a force that can act quickly and is ready to fight immediately in an area that may be far from its base; and that has the hitting power and mobility to take offensive action and get quick results, to prevent the war from extending or from escalating to global war.'

It was anticipated that a properly balanced force was unlikely to be achieved unless airborne and seaborne forces operated in unison:

'In this concept of joint seaborne/airborne operations, the amphibious and air transported forces are part of a single team, sea and air providing those elements of the force best suited to their characteristics and to the kind of operations expected.'[12]

The requirement to land troops as quickly as possible would sometimes conflict with the requirement to land balanced forces. It was recognised that as the air transported force and the seaborne force might arrive at different times or land far apart they needed to retain the ability to operate independently, at least in the initial stages of an operation. In 1961 this concept was still in its infancy. The basic principles that lay behind it were to be tested during Operation VANTAGE.

Protecting Kuwait from Iraq

The security and stability of Kuwait was an issue of vital importance to the British. Kuwaiti oil accounted for around forty percent of Britain's total oil supplies and provided over fifty percent of the state-owned British Petroleum's crude oil production. Kuwaiti oil was paid for in Sterling, representing a significant saving in foreign currency for the hard pressed British exchequer. As a result, the Kuwaiti government had amassed a large Sterling reserve and Kuwaiti investments in Britain were estimated to be worth $100 million per annum. Formerly part of the Ottoman Empire, Kuwait had in effect been a British protectorate since 1899 under the terms of an Anglo-Kuwaiti Treaty. On 19 June 1961 this Treaty was replaced by an Exchange of Notes that recognised the full independence of Kuwait under the ruling authority of the Amir, Sheikh Abdullah as-Salim as Sabah. The British recognised the right of the Amir to conduct his own foreign and defence policies, but they agreed to provide military assistance to support the independence of Kuwait if requested to do so.

Historically Kuwait had had a difficult relationship with its neighbour to the south, Saudi Arabia. However, by 1961 Saudi-Kuwaiti relations were cordial. The main threat to Kuwaiti independence appeared to come from its northern neighbour, Iraq. In 1958 a bloody coup had seen the pro-British monarchy replaced by the nationalist government of General Qasim.[13] Qasim was hostile to imperialist influence in the Arab world, and was particularly hostile towards the British. He saw himself as a revolutionary Arab nationalist leader in a similar vein to Nasser, prompting a rivalry between the two leaders that helps to explain Nasser's tolerant attitude towards the British intervention. In common with his predecessors, Qasim considered Kuwait to be an integral part of Iraq.

In a key speech on 25 June 1961, just six days after the Exchange of Notes, he declared that both this and the 1899 Treaty were illegal and illegitimate and that Kuwait was an *integral and indivisible* part of Iraq. The language that he used was inflammatory, but he stopped short of threatening to annex or occupy Kuwait. Despite this, the speech caused much concern in both Kuwait and the UK. Kuwait had not yet been accepted into the United Nations or the Arab League. Qasim, therefore, had a window of opportunity to pursue Iraq's historic claim to this oil rich state before the fact of Kuwaiti independence became established.[14]

[12]National Archives: DEFE 2/2074.
[13]Often misspelled *Kassim* in British sources.
[14]For further details see Monice Snell-Mendoza, 'In Defence of Oil: Britain's Response to the Iraqi Threat towards Kuwait, 1961', in *Contemporary British History*, Vol.10, No.3 Autumn 1996, pp 39-62; Nigel Ashton, 'Britain and the Kuwait Crisis, 1961' in *Diplomacy and Statecraft*, Vo.9, No.1, March 1998, pp. 163-181; and, Mustafa Alani, *Operation Vantage. British Military Intervention in Kuwait, 1961,* (Surbiton: LAAM, 1990).

Headquarters Company, 42 Commando leaving Kuwait New Airport, about to prepare for the immediate defence of Kuwait. (NHB)

The British had been aware of the possibility of an Iraqi move against Kuwait since the Iraqi coup of 1958. As early as 1959 two alternative plans were drawn up. The first catered for intervention at the request of the Amir with the aim of averting internal insurrection or deterring an Iraqi attack. The second plan was based upon intervention without a request by the Amir, in a state of affairs where he had lost control of the situation in Kuwait. There was no plan to evict Iraqi forces after a successful invasion. The British did begin to consider such a plan. However, it was recognised that any counter-invasion would require large-scale operations and would take at least 24 days to prepare. It was considered unlikely that international political support would be forthcoming for such action.[15] The permissive international political environment that enabled the liberation of Kuwait in 1991 did not exist thirty years earlier. With the memory of Suez in the forefront of their minds the British planners were forced to accept that, for political reasons, such an operation was unrealistic. This had important consequences. It meant that it was imperative that the Iraqis should not be allowed to establish themselves in Kuwait as a *fait accompli*. British forces might be able to forestall or halt an invasion, they would not be given the opportunity to eject the Iraqis should they succeed in seizing Kuwait.

Unfortunately for the British the Amir of Kuwait was unwilling to allow them to station troops on his territory. His own army included a Frontier Force of 1200 and a Security force of 1500 men. They were equipped with jeeps, armoured cars, armoured personnel carriers and a total of 18 Centurion tanks. They could not be expected to hold off an Iraqi invasion force that could, it was believed, consist of two brigade groups and an armoured regiment with up to 70 tanks. British plans, therefore, were based upon the need to reinforce Kuwait rapidly in the event of a major crisis. The majority of troops would arrive by air, with heavy equipment and stores arriving by sea from stockpiles at the British bases in Bahrain and Aden. A series of plans were developed. The existing plan in June 1961 was Reinforced Theatre Plan VANTAGE. This was in the process of being replaced by a new plan, codenamed BELLRINGER, and while it was VANTAGE that was actually implemented, the operation reflected many aspects of the new plan.[16]

Plan VANTAGE was founded upon the ability to airlift sufficient troops into Kuwait to forestall any Iraqi attack. The reluctance of the Amir to accept British forces based in Kuwait and the inability of transport aircraft to lift heavy military equipment brought a requirement for seaborne support. In October 1959 ministers approved a plan by the Chiefs of Staff to deploy the Amphibious Warfare (AW) Squadron from Malta to Aden in conjunction with the move of a squadron of tanks and a Royal Marine Commando unit. At a cost of £407,000 the ageing vessels of the AW Squadron were fitted with air conditioning and moved to their new station in June 1960. The primary task of the squadron was to provide follow-up lift for troops transported by air. As it would take nine days for a slow Landing Ship Tank (LST) to sail from Aden to Kuwait it was decided to keep one LST with half a squadron of tanks embarked permanently on station in the Persian Gulf.

[15]National Archives: DEFE 13/89, 'Intervention in Kuwait'.

[16]Unless otherwise stated the following account of Operation Vantage is based on the following sources; National Archives: DEFE 5/118, COS (61) 378, *Report by the Commander in Chief Middle East on Operations in Support of the State of Kuwait in July 1961*, 18 Oct 1961; W.B.R. Neave-Hill, *British Support of the Amir of Kuwait 1961*, (The Historical Section, Ministry of Defence Library, 1968); National Archives: ADM 234/1068, BR1736(55), *Naval Staff History, Middle East Operations: Jordan/Lebanon 1958, Kuwait 1961.*; and Sir David Lee, *Flight from the Middle East. A History of the Royal Air Force in the Arabian Peninsula and adjacent territories, 1945-1962,* (London: HMSO, 1989) chapter nine.

any pre-emptive deployment of troops to Kuwait was undesirable as without an obvious and immediate Iraqi threat such a move would be represented as aggressive

This *Seaborne Tank Force* would be provided by two Royal Navy ships, rotating as required. When two such ships were not available a civilian manned LST would fill the role. As only the Royal Navy LSTs had air conditioning the crews for tanks carried in other LSTs would stay ashore during the summer months, flying forward to join their tanks if required. In addition, the Amir agreed to stockpile in Kuwait half a squadron of Centurion tanks and their ammunition. These tanks were Kuwaiti owned, and thus could not be portrayed as part of a permanent British presence, but would be made available to British crews in the event of any intervention. In order to provide the necessary lift of vehicles and stores from the military stockpile at Bahrain to Kuwait, the Landing Craft Tanks (LCTs) *Bastion, Redoubt* and *Parapet* were permanently based at Bahrain.

Given the absolute requirement for British forces to arrive in Kuwait *before* the Iraqis there was clearly a need for good intelligence to provide sufficient warning. VANTAGE was based upon an assumption that prior to any invasion the Iraqis would need to reinforce their forces as Basra with an armoured brigade from Baghdad. It was believed that this move would take seven days to complete. There was also an expectation that any Iraqi invasion would be preceded by internal subversion in Kuwait. It was believed that the two factors combined would provide the British with four days warning of any attack. Given this, two battalions with supporting arms could be flown in direct to Kuwait within twelve hours. Subsequent reinforcement would lead to the deployment of a reinforced brigade group, supported by RAF fighter and ground attack aircraft. This was deemed to be sufficient to deal with any likely Iraqi invasion force. Unfortunately, in the aftermath of Qasim's speech, intelligence reports began to suggest that an Iraqi invasion might occur without any real warning.

Initial intelligence assessments emanating from the British embassy in Baghdad stressed that they felt that military action was unlikely. However, by 28 June the Military Attaché had concluded that the possibility of an Iraqi attack could not be excluded, and that if it did occur it was likely to involve a '*quick dash*' using forces already stationed at Basra and without any prior reinforcement from Baghdad.[17] This was something of a nightmare scenario for the British. Without any troops in Kuwait they were poorly placed to deal with an invasion without warning, and they had already accepted that they could not eject the Iraqis once they had seized Kuwait. Unfortunately, advice from the embassy in Baghdad continued to stress that any pre-emptive deployment of troops to Kuwait was undesirable as without an obvious and immediate Iraqi threat such a move would be represented as aggressive and another case of anti-Arab imperialism by the British.

In the UK the government was aware of the need to tread carefully. They appreciated that, at the very least, any intervention would have to be seen to be at the request of the Kuwaitis. On 29 June the Cabinet Defence Committee sanctioned a number of precautionary moves to improve military readiness, but these did not include the deployment of any troops to Kuwait. The same day the ambassador in Baghdad was instructed to inform the Iraqi government that they had given the Amir of Kuwait an assurance of military support if it were required. Meanwhile the British Political Agent in Kuwait informed the Amir of the serious nature of the Iraqi threat. He was asked to request British help.[18]

In response to the growing tension the commando carrier HMS *Bulwark*, equipped with 16 Whirlwind helicopters and with the Royal Marines of No.42 Commando embarked, was ordered to proceed from Karachi to Kuwait. The following day the headquarters' ship HMS *Meon* and the LST HMS *Striker* were also ordered to Kuwait where, like *Bulwark*, they were to remain out of sight of land. *Bulwark's* presence in the region could be described as somewhat fortuitous. It was at Karachi, en route to the Gulf where it was scheduled to conduct hot weather trials. Unlike *Striker* and *Meon* it was not part of the force permanently assigned to VANTAGE. It may not have been entirely coincidental that the British chose to deploy their newest and most capable

---

[17]National Archives: PREM 11/3427, Telegram no. 639, Baghdad to the Foreign Office, 26 Jun. 1961 and Telegram no. 658, Baghdad to the Foreign Office, 28 Jun. 1961.
[18]National Archives: CAB 128/35 part 1, CC (61) 36th conclusions, 29 June 1961; DEFE 131/26, D (61) 41, 30 June 1961; CAB 131/25, D (61) 11th meeting, 29 June 1961; PREM 11/3427, Telegram no. 644, Baghdad to the Foreign Office, 27 June 1961 and Telegram no. 413, Foreign Office to Kuwait, 29 June 1961.

amphibious vessel to the Gulf with a visit scheduled for Kuwait only weeks after that country had gained independence. In any case, HMS *Bulwark* had been deployed east of Suez to meet precisely this type of contingency and therefore its availability should not be considered to be purely the result of good luck. The British were, however, lucky in that the LST *Striker* was due to be relieved by the civilian manned LST *Empire Gull*. As a result there were two LSTs in the Gulf each carrying half a squadron of tanks instead of just one. On 29 June the crews for the tanks in the *Empire Gull* were ordered to proceed to Bahrain. The air-conditioned *Striker* already had its tank crews onboard. The aircraft carrier HMS *Victorious*, en route to Hong Kong, was ordered to proceed to Bahrain, where it was expected to arrive on 8 July. A second carrier, HMS *Centaur*, was ordered from Gibraltar to the eastern Mediterranean and a third, HMS *Hermes*, sailed from the UK to Gibraltar.

In addition to the maritime redeployments, land and air assets prepared for the possibility of intervention. Troops in Kenya and the UK moved to their concentration areas in preparation for a possible air-lift. Hunter FGA9 fighter/ground attack aircraft from No. 208 Squadron deployed from Nairobi to Bahrain where they were joined by Hunters from No.8 Squadron from Aden. The presence of these aircraft at Bahrain offered the possibility of limited air cover for any operation in Kuwait. Two Shackletons from No. 37 Squadron were also deployed to Bahrain to provide a night reconnaissance capability. In addition to this the Ministry

of Defence ordered a squadron of Canberra light bombers to re-deploy from Germany to Sharjah. The Bahrain stockpile and the emergency camps at Bahrain and Aden were activated.

In the light of events in Iraq and the rather worrying advice that he was receiving from the British, Sheikh Abdullah issued a formal request for British intervention on 30 June. That evening the British joint Commander-in-Chief Middle East, Air Marshal Sir Charles Elworthy, received instructions to implement VANTAGE. In retrospect it is by no means clear that the Iraqis did intend to invade Kuwait. There is certainly no real evidence that they did. British assessments of Iraqi intentions were made difficult by a pre-planned military parade in Basra, to celebrate Iraq's national day on 14 July. A heightened degree of military activity in the area could therefore be expected. Alternatively the parade could have been a cover for a build-up prior to invasion. Political restrictions on Canberra photo-reconnaissance flights over Iraq made it hard for the British to be sure. Intervention came at the request of the Amir, but in issuing this request he was acting on British advice. Some authors have portrayed this as a cynical British ploy to discredit the Iraqis and to demonstrate to the Kuwaitis their enduring dependence on British military support.[19] This may have been the case. This is not the place to examine this issue in detail. Suffice to say that given the need for the British to deploy to Kuwait before that country was seized by the Iraqis it was inevitable that VANTAGE would operate on something of a hair trigger. This was particularly true given the

inflammatory messages emanating from Baghdad. Even if he had no intention of invading Kuwait, Qasim would have done well to realise that rattling the sabre can sometimes cause an opponent to draw his sword.

Operation VANTAGE

Given the possibility of an imminent Iraqi attack Elworthy decided to prioritise the movement of fighting forces into Kuwait, if necessary at the expense of logistic and transport personnel. Inevitably this had a deleterious effect on the subsequent smooth running of the transport operation. With the first troops arriving on the morning of 1 July Elworthy aimed to have two infantry battalions, a squadron of tanks, an armoured car squadron and two squadrons of Hunter aircraft in Kuwait by the following day. He was fortunate in that the lack of an Iraqi presence in Kuwait or of any internal insurrection meant that an airborne or amphibious assault was not required to secure entry points. He was less fortunate in other respects. The ability to transport troops by air to Kuwait was central to VANTAGE. The existing barrier to such movements created by the refusal of the United Arab Republic (Egypt and Syria), Saudi Arabia and Iraq to allow over-flight of their territory meant that military aircraft en-route to the Gulf had to fly south, via Libya, Sudan and Aden or north via Turkey and Iran. Unfortunately permission to fly over the territory of another state could be withdrawn. On the night of 30 June/1 July both Sudan and Turkey withdrew this permission. It appears likely that Sudan was waiting to see how

---

[19]See Alani, *Operation Vantage*.

42 Commando set up defensive positions on the Al Mutla Ridge. (NHB)

British intervention would be received by world opinion before restoring such permission. As a neighbour of Iraq Turkey had an obvious interest in wishing to appear impartial, despite being allied to the UK through NATO[20] and CENTO.[21]

Both Turkey and Sudan lifted their over-flight bans on 1 July. However, Turkey was only willing to allow flights at night and away from centres of population. They clearly wished to avoid any political fall-out from being seen to support the British. Permission to use this route was withdrawn again, on 4 July, when news that the British were using this route leaked out. The immediate consequence of these developments was to delay the arrival of the Parachute Regiment from Cyprus and to seriously complicate the whole movement plan. The worse consequences of the ban were circumvented by the decision to allow RAF Canberra bombers, re-deploying from Germany, to covertly over-fly Sudan, presumably on the assumption that there was not much that the Sudanese could do to stop this, even should they be aware of it. Similarly, the rapid air transport of forces from Aden was aided by the decision to allow some covert flights over Saudi territory.[22] This says much for British pragmatism and little for their respect for the finer details of international law.

The maritime forces devoted to VANTAGE did not share the problems of their air transported counter-parts. Able to steam to the northern Gulf through international waters and to poise unobtrusively out of sight of land, HMS *Bulwark* and *Striker*

provided the key initial contribution to the defence of Kuwait. *Bulwark's* helicopters landed the first marines of No.42 Commando at Kuwait New Airport soon after 0900 on 1 July. Later that day *Striker* landed its half squadron of tanks using a Rhino ferry after it was discovered that the designated landing 'hard' had been removed the previous week. Once ashore the marines deployed forward to the Mutla Ridge, a defensive feature to the north of Kuwait town. They were supported by an additional platoon of marines from the frigate HMS *Loch Alvie* which was in support offshore in company with HMS *Meon*. In addition, two companies of Coldstream Guards were flown forward from Bahrain where they had been on internal security duties. Ten Hunter fighter/ground attack aircraft from No.8 Squadron deployed forward to Kuwait, where they were joined by the appropriate ground control personnel. Unfortunately, poor visibility caused by blowing sand made air reconnaissance difficult and would have ruled out any ground attack missions.

According to Elworthy, in these initial stages his plan was to:

'deploy two battalions along the Mutla Ridge, supported by British and Kuwaiti tanks and artillery, to hold a further battalion with a squadron of British tanks as a counter-attack force, to keep a fourth battalion in Kuwait Town as a

mobile reserve, with a fifth in Bahrain. The screen between the Ridge and the frontier was to be provided by British and Kuwaiti armoured cars.'

This land force was to be supported by two squadrons of Hunters and Kuwaiti Twin Pioneers at Kuwait New Airfield, the Canberra squadron at Sharjah and the Shackletons at Bahrain.

No.45 Commando began to arrive by air on 2 July, completing the move from Aden the next day. On 2 July the Parachute Light Battery arrived, less mortars and vehicles, as did an armoured car squadron from the 11th Hussars. HMS *Bastion* and *Redoubt* landed equipment, stores, ammunition and armoured cars from Bahrain. The half squadron of tanks was landed from *Empire Gull*. The following day the first battalion from the Parachute Regiment began to arrive by air and the crews for the stockpiled tanks arrived. The build up was not complete until 9 July, by which time there were 4,112 Army personnel, 596 RAF personnel and 960 Royal Marines ashore. This military force was under the tactical command of Brigadier D G T Horsford,

[20] North Atlantic Treaty Organisation
[21] Central Treaty Organisation.
[22] National Archives: WO 32/20719 and CAB 131/26, D (61) 43, notes from a meeting held on 30 June.

42 Commando RM board Whirlwind helicopters of 848 Squadron for the flight to Kuwait airport. HMS Bulwark, 1 July 1961. (RMM)

officer commanding 24th Brigade. With the arrival of the 24th Brigade by air, the two Commandos were able to fall back from the Ridge and form a reserve. The Coldstream Guards returned to their internal security duties at Bahrain on 6 July. In contrast to operations against Egypt in 1956, British intervention in Kuwait in 1961 received much international support, with the obvious exception of Iraq and the Communist bloc. The United States, in particular, backed their British allies strongly. There was even some suggestion that a small US Navy task force currently off the coast of east Africa, could be deployed in support of VANTAGE. This task force, known as *Solent Amity*, consisted of two destroyers and some other vessels, including an LST, and around 500 US Marines. In addition, the US also had two destroyers in the Gulf. *Solent Amity* quietly sailed north in case it was needed. It was expected to be able to reach the US destroyers at Bahrain by 5 July, although in the event both governments decided that it was not required and the idea was dropped without the general public ever being aware that it had been an option.[23] Criticism of British action by Arab countries was muted. The Saudi government backed Kuwait against the Iraqi threat, even deploying to Kuwait a tiny force of 31 troops that provided symbolic assistance to their neighbour. On 20 July the Arab league voted to accept Kuwait as a full member. The League was keen to see the British leave Kuwait and agreed to provide 4,000 Arab troops to take the place of the British,

who were equally keen to go. The government in London was aware that a permanent British presence in Kuwait was likely to have damaging political repercussions. The Arab League presence removed the need for this. The last British troops left Kuwait on 19 October. Nevertheless, the possibility remained that VANTAGE might need to be repeated. The British were not overly optimistic about the ability of the Arab forces to hold Kuwait if the Iraqis launched a major offensive. Fortunately, this did not happen. Iraq finally recognised the independence of its southern neighbour in October 1963 after Qasim had been deposed and shot in a coup the previous February.[24]

The best kind of fire extinguisher?

As an exercise in foreign policy Operation VANTAGE was a great success. Five years after the debacle over Suez, Britain had demonstrated an ability to intervene rapidly in support of a friend and ally. The Iraqis were seen to be deterred, whether or not they had ever really intended to invade. Britain had demonstrated a firm resolve and real capability to defend its interests in the region. The operations demonstrated the value of amphibious capabilities as a potent deterrent to hostile military action and provided a chance to test the seaborne/airborne concept. The Secretary of State for Defence, now Harold Watkinson, saw the operation as a vindication of his support for amphibious capabilities. As early as 3 July he explained to his Cabinet colleagues that:

'The Operation had demonstrated both the value of amphibious forces in providing military assistance at relatively short notice and the political difficulties which might be expected in obtaining overflying rights, even from allies, when their was a risk of actual hostilities.'[25]

As Watkinson noted, VANTAGE demonstrated some of the problems in relying on long-range air transport. By 4 July RAF Transport Command had committed 53 transport aircraft to VANTAGE, in addition to the 18 aircraft held within theatre. These were supported by 17 chartered civil airliners and three aircraft provided by the Royal Rhodesian Air Force. This proved sufficient to meet requirements. Unfortunately, and despite the conclusion of the Chiefs of Staff that air transport had performed well, VANTAGE showed that in the real world where political considerations would always be a complicating factor, air transport could not always be relied upon. The delays caused by the over-flight restrictions suddenly imposed by Turkey and Sudan confirmed the existence of a Middle East *'air barrier'*. It showed up the flaws in the idea that a strategic reserve could be held in the UK and airlifted to trouble spots by the long-range aircraft of Transport Command. In his report on VANTAGE Elworthy concluded that, for long-range air reinforcement to be viable, either sufficient aircraft would have to be maintained on *both* sides of the air barrier, or the RAF would have to accept the need to over-fly countries without

[23]See National Archives: PREM 11/3428.

[24]Hussein Hassouna, 'The Kuwait-Iraq Border Problem', in Joseph A. Kechicgian, *Iran, Iraq, and the Arab Gulf States,* (Basingstoke: Palgrave, 2002) p.239.

[25]National Archives: CAB 128/35 part 1, CC (61) 38th conclusions, 3 July 1961.Also see, Harold Watkinson, *Turning Points. A Record of Our Times,* (Salisbury: Michael Russell,) pp. 134-135.

Marines of 5 Company, 42 Commando, land near the Al Mutla Ridge from a Whirlwind of 848 Squadron, 2 July 1961. (RMM)

The problems at Kuwait New Airport illustrate the dangers of relying on host nation support

their permission.[26] The former approach would be expensive financially, the latter would bring a political cost. The need to overcome the problem of over-flight permission was one of the factors that led the RAF to develop their scheme for a series of '*Island Bases*' from which to deploy long-range air power east of Suez.

An examination of VANTAGE reveals a number of other problems. Most obviously, and unlike their amphibious counterparts, transport aircraft relied on the existence of airfield facilities within Kuwait to be able to unload their cargo. As hostilities did not commence, civilian flights into the old airport at Kuwait continued throughout the operation. Ironically, these flights relied on Iraqi air traffic control. As a result, military flights used Kuwait New Airport. Unfortunately this airport was so new that it lacked proper cargo handling facilities. This, and the decision to prioritise '*teeth*' arms, led to a somewhat chaotic situation developing where it was often difficult for units to find the appropriate equipment and where it was not always possible to unload particular items. To make matters worse the RAF appear to have been a little idiosyncratic in their prioritisation of cargo. Units frequently arrived in Kuwait to find that equipment that had accompanied them at the start of their journey was no longer available. When No. 45 Commando arrived from Aden they found that the base plates for their mortars were missing and they had no ammunition for their MOBAT anti-tank

weapons.[27] It was believed that these had been unloaded in order to make space in the aircraft for camp beds for RAF personnel.[28] Poor visibility in Kuwait meant that some aircraft were unable to land, being diverted instead to Bahrain. Elworthy noted that this made it difficult to concentrate whole units or sometimes even to locate reinforcing personnel. Had hostilities commenced both airports would have represented obvious targets for a pre-emptive Iraqi air strike or for attacks by Iraqi sponsored insurgents. Unlike the amphibious ships offshore, they could not be moved out of danger.

The problems at Kuwait New Airport illustrate the dangers of relying on host nation support. VANTAGE was based on the provision of substantial support from the Kuwaiti government, particularly in terms of accommodation and transport. Neither was made available in either the quality or quantity expected. This was particularly problematic in respect of military transport. The difficulty of transporting vehicles by air led to an agreement that the Kuwaitis would provide 688 vehicles to British forces should intervention occur. Unfortunately only 355 were actually provided and of these only 78 had four-wheel drive. The remaining vehicles were of little use in the desert. This had a serious impact on the mobility of the British force. An Army Operational Research Group sent out to study events in Kuwait was forced to conclude that British forces lacked mobility and would have been incapable of anything other than

a static defensive battle had the Iraqis attacked. The one unit that had all of its vehicles with it was No.42 Commando, landed from HMS *Bulwark*.[29] Fortunately a considerable degree of support was provided to the British by the Kuwait Oil Company (KOC), including access to KOC facilities and even the homes and dinner tables of some company personnel.

One issue that received considerable attention in 1961 was the problem of heat exhaustion. Newspaper reports suggested that troops airlifted to Kuwait from beyond the Persian Gulf had suffered a high number of casualties due to the heat. In Kuwait City temperatures in the shade varied between 40 and 45 degrees centigrade. These figures were exceeded in the desert. Conditions were bound to be difficult, particularly for the crews of the armoured vehicles. In these conditions some of the personal equipment issued to troops proved inadequate. It was fortunate that there was a plentiful supply of water, and even ice, provided from local sources. In his report Elworthy claimed that incidents of heat exhaustion had been exaggerated. This view was repeated by the internal Ministry of Defence history of the operation prepared in 1968. These views were based on the conclusions of the HQ Middle East Medical Report. As such they may not be reliable. This report based its conclusions on the number of hospital admissions. It did not include troops dealt with at unit level, by field ambulances or in HMS *Bulwark*. The latter proved

[26]COS (61) 378.
[27]National Archives: WO 32/20721, *Army Operational Research Group No. 6/61, 'Operation Vantage'.*
[28]Julian Thompson, *The Royal Marines. From Sea Soldiers to a Special Force,* (London: Sidgwick and Jackson, 2000) p.495. Also see, David Young, *Four Five: Story of 45 Commando Royal Marines, 1943-1971,* (London: Leo Cooper, 1972).
[29]WO 32/20721.

Marines of 42 Commando on the Al Mutla Ridge, Kuwait, with a Centurion Tank of 3rd Dragoon Guards, July 1961. (RMM)

particularly popular with troops as it was air conditioned and provided a valuable opportunity for rest and recuperation. On the basis of their own research, the Army Operational Research Group concluded that the number of personnel unavailable for action due to heat illness during the first five days of VANTAGE was 2.9 per cent, 4.5 per cent and 9.7 per cent in individual units air lifted from Cyprus, Kenya and the UK respectively. This could be compared with an absence of any incidence of heat illness amongst the personnel from a squadron of armoured cars that had been based in Sharjah and was therefore acclimatised to local conditions.[30] It seems reasonable to conclude that had hostilities broken out and active operations ensued the incidence of such illness would have increased. Clearly there were some problems with the idea that troops could be airlifted straight from the UK to operations in the desert without some opportunity to become accustomed to local conditions. Had hostilities actually broken out the ability to control the skies over Kuwait would have been critical to British success. British and Kuwaiti forces and facilities would have needed protection from Iraqi air attack, as would the transport aircraft flying to and from Kuwait and the ships and craft offshore. Equally, given the limited size and nature of the British force in Kuwait, close air support would play an important part in any attempt to halt and turn back an Iraqi invasion. The

Iraqi air force had a squadron of Soviet supplied IL-28 bombers, two squadrons of MiG-17 fighters and two squadrons of British built Hunters and Venoms. It was in the process of upgrading these with more modern MiG-19 fighters. The British Joint Intelligence Committee assessed that this force had a '*moderate*' capacity in the role of army support. Air defence capabilities were believed to be '*indifferent*'.[31]

Unfortunately, the RAF was poorly placed to achieve air superiority prior to the arrival of the aircraft carrier, HMS *Victorious*, on 9 July. Before this a limited daytime air defence capability was provided by the RAF Hunters based at Kuwait, directed by *Bulwark's* radar. Kuwait lacked a radar early warning system. The RAF deployed a Type Sc-787 transportable radar to Kuwait but this was a lightweight system with limited performance and no height-finding capacity. It did not become operational before 18 July. Radar cover was later provided by a frigate off Kuwait. Unfortunately, the need for the frigate to remain close inshore in order to be able to provide naval gunfire support caused problems of blanking due to the proximity to the Mutla Ridge. This could have caused problems in detecting low-flying aircraft. HMS *Victorious'* Type 984 three-dimensional radar was unable to provide effective cover ashore due to dust conditions, hence the need to deploy the frigate in an early warning and fighter control role for which it, and its replacements, had had little recent practice.[32]

According to Air Chief Marshal Sir David Lee, before the arrival of HMS *Victorious* air defence '*could have posed almost insuperable problems for the two Hunter Squadrons*'.[33] The arrival of *Victorious* with its complement of Sea Vixen fighter/ground attack aircraft eased the situation considerably and for the first time provided a sophisticated day and night air defence capability. Nevertheless some problems remained. In his report on VANTAGE, Rear Admiral Smeeton concluded that while the Navy was able to improvise a workable air defence organisation he doubted whether they would have been able to repulse an Iraqi attack on the carriers, Kuwait harbour, the airfield or the army forward defended localities.[34] This was worrying for a pre-planned operation, within range of existing RAF bases in the Gulf and with airfield facilities provided in theatre. It is significant that the RAF's preferred option, destroying enemy aircraft on the ground in a pre-emptive strike, was ruled out for political reasons. The British could not be seen to initiate military action. Thus RAF or RN aircraft could intercept Iraqi aircraft intruding into Kuwaiti airspace but they only had permission to enter Iraqi airspace in '*hot pursuit*' of an intruder. Even then restrictions applied. An intruder could be followed back to its base where rockets and guns could be used to destroy it on the ground but bombs could not be used.[35] Obviously such restrictions were likely to be relaxed after the outbreak of any hostilities but this would only occur after the Iraqis had had the opportunity to launch the first blow.

[30]Ibid.

[31]Richard A. Mobley, 'Gauging the Iraqi Threat to Kuwait in the 1960s', in *Studies in Intelligence* (unclassified edition), Fall-Winter 2001, No.11.

[32]See Ministry of Defence Naval Historical Branch, Whitehall; Box T2644-T2673, *Summary of lessons learnt by Flag Officer Aircraft Carriers from the Kuwait Operation*, 26 Oct. 1961.

[33]Lee, *Flight from the Middle East*, p. 180.

[34]Ministry of Defence Naval Historical Branch, Whitehall; Box T2644-T2673, *Summary of lessons learnt by Flag Officer Aircraft Carriers from the Kuwait Operation*, 26 Oct. 1961.

[35]National Archives: WO 32/20719.

*A Marine of 42 Commando mans a Bren
gun on the Al Mutla Ridge, Kuwait, with
3rd Dragoon Guards, July 1961. (RMM)*

Their actions were most definitely audacious, dynamic and ruthless

Maritime force played a critical role in the success of VANTAGE. Without the presence of *Bulwark* and *Striker* off Kuwait on 1 July there would have been no significant British ground presence in Kuwait on the first day of the operation. The LSTs and LCTs of the AW Squadron played an important role in bringing stores and equipment forward from Bahrain to Kuwait. HMS *Meon* provided vital communications facilities during an operation in which all parties accepted that communications between Kuwait, Bahrain and Aden were stretched to breaking point. *Bulwark* not only landed and supported its own embarked force, it also provided rest and recuperation facilities for large numbers of very grateful troops from other units. The guns of the frigates offshore offered some measure of fire support for a land force that was very short of artillery. Air defence capabilities, always somewhat inadequate, were totally unsatisfactory before the arrival of an aircraft carrier. Nevertheless, some limitations in the maritime capability were apparent. HMS *Bulwark* and *Striker* were able to sail to Kuwait before the operation began and thus were ready to land their embarked force at very short notice. Other maritime assets took longer to arrive. It was nine days before HMS *Victorious* arrived with its escorts. Prior to the arrival of the frigates *Loch Fyne* and *Loch Ruthven* on 5 and 7 July respectively there was only one frigate escorting *Bulwark* off Kuwait. This was inadequate to deal with the threat of an attack by Iraqi light forces and as a result *Bulwark* withdrew south each night to keep out of harms way. This, of course, illustrates a capability as well as a weakness. One notable shortcoming was in the provision of mine counter measures vessels. None had been deployed in theatre prior to VANTAGE. The 108th Minesweeping Squadron was deployed from Malta, but did not arrive until 21 July. Prior to this it is unclear how the British would have dealt with any mine threat.

Conclusion

With reference to Operation MUSKETEER Liddell-Hart wrote in 1960 that the British habit and motto *'slow but sure'* was *'all to sure to prove unsure – by being too slow'*. He went on to claim that national character proved a handicap in 1956 as *'…swift success in offensive action requires qualities – audacity, dynamism and ruthlessness – that are no longer natural to the British as they were in the times of Drake and Nelson'*.[36] This was not to prove the case during VANTAGE. The British acted swiftly, pre-empting a possible Iraqi move into Kuwait and reinforcing their own influence in the region. Their actions were most definitely audacious, dynamic and ruthless. The military force ashore in the early stages of the operation was small and lightly equipped. As such, it may have faced serious difficulties if the Iraqis had indeed decided to invade in strength. Nevertheless, the ability to put ashore at short notice a light but credible force that could simultaneously act as a concrete sign of British commitment, provide a visible deterrent to any Iraqi attack and cover the rapid build up of a bigger more balanced force proved more valuable than the larger but slower intervention capability generated for MUSKETEER. The British had to accept a degree of risk in order to stop the Iraqis from being able to seize Kuwait as a fait accompli. The risk was acceptable because, unlike 1956, the necessary intervention capabilities were in place and these were supported by an appropriate mind-set.

The British had reorganised their armed forces to enable them to meet limited challenges overseas. In the case of Kuwait, a specific threat was identified and measures were taken to ensure that an appropriate and timely response would be possible should the need arise. VANTAGE was enabled by some new equipment, notably transport aircraft and the commando carrier, but it also relied on old amphibious vessels, the same ships and craft that had been employed at Suez. The most important difference between 1956 and 1961 was the change in mind-set. Most obviously, the seaborne/airborne concept reflected an appreciation of the political limitations that were likely to influence the conduct of operations, and placed an emphasis on tempo and an acceptance of risk that was absent in 1956. In this sense it can be said to have encompassed what would now be called *'manoeuvrist'* principles, although, of course, they were not defined in those terms in the 1960s. The concept received its first test during VANTAGE and was deemed to have passed with flying colours. Shortcomings were identified and remedial action sought but overall VANTAGE was taken as an indication that British defence policy was heading in the right direction. It should be noted that VANTAGE was a

---

[36]Liddell-Hart, *Deterrence or Defence*, p.28.

pre-planned operation within range of established bases and as such did not represent the greatest challenge to the seaborne/ airborne concept. Nevertheless, both Ministers and the Chiefs of Staff were pleased with the results. Amphibious forces, in particular, were recognised to have played a major part in the success of the operation. The navy were to use the experience of VANTAGE to support their case for maritime expeditionary capabilities in the years that followed. The modern Royal Navy is at least as aware of the utility of amphibious forces as it was in the 1960s. British Maritime Doctrine explains the value of joint maritime/amphibious forces, emphasising the utility of *'maritime manoeuvre'* as *'the ability to use the unique access provided by the sea to apply force or influence at a time or place of political choice, taking into account the conditions of the modern world and the advances offered by technology'.*[37] Maritime forces are described as being inherently *'manoeuvrist'*, in particular because of their combination of mobility, firepower, flexibility and responsive command and control systems. This can make them particularly well suited to operations where political considerations, and restraints, are paramount. The current definition of a maritime expeditionary force is *'a self-sustaining forward deployed joint maritime force which demonstrates UK interest with its physical presence and latent power. Operating from international waters, the joint maritime force is free of political and economic encumbrances, and independent of overseas bases or host nation support, which may*

not be accessible due to domestic or international concerns'.[38] This provides a useful description of the role played by maritime forces off Kuwait in 1961 and of the key advantages that they had over their land based, air transported alternatives. British defence priorities have changed considerably since the early 1960s. Nevertheless, the ability to exploit a capacity to project military force overseas in order to secure political objectives remains important to defence planners. This is reflected in the recent investment in amphibious capabilities and in plans to build two new aircraft carriers. In many ways the basic rationale for such capabilities has changed little since the 1960s. The ability to project a small but potent force at extended range and without undue reliance on overseas bases remains key.

Further Reading

Alani, Mustafa, *Operation Vantage. British Military Intervention in Kuwait, 1961*, (Surbiton: LAAM, 1990)

Darby, Phillip, *British Defence Policy East of Suez 1947-1968*, (London: Oxford University Press, 1973)

Lee, David, *A History of the Royal Air Force in the Arabian Peninsula and Adjacent Territories 1945-1962*, (London: HMSO, 1980)

Neave-Hill, W.B.R., *British Support of the Amir of Kuwait 1961*, (The Historical Section, Ministry of Defence Library, 1968)

Biography

Dr Ian Speller is a Lecturer in the Department of Modern History at the National University of Ireland, Maynooth. He also lectures in defence studies at the Irish Defence Forces Command and Staff School and provides occasional lectures at the UK Joint Services Command and Staff College (JSCSC). Prior to this he was a Senior Lecturer in Defence Studies at King's College London and the JSCSC where, in addition to a range of other duties, he had particular responsibility for the Maritime Phase of the Advanced Command and Staff Course and for the Advanced Amphibious Warfare Course. Dr Speller is the author *of The Role of Amphibious Warfare in British Defence Policy, 1945-56* (Palgrave, 2001) and the editor of *The Royal Navy and Maritime Power in the Twentieth Century* (Routledge, forthcoming). He is currently completing a volume for the Navy Records Society on *British Amphibious Forces, 1945-1975*. He regularly returns to the Defence Academy in order to lecture to the Advanced Amphibious Warfare Course.

[37]BR1806, *British Maritime Doctrine*, 2nd Edition, (London: The Stationary Office, 1999) pp.43-44.
[38]Ibid., p.218

The Second Indo-China War
Vietnam, 1965 - 1973

XXXV

By Lieutenant Colonel H Thomas Hayden USMC (Rtd)

DEFINITION: Amphibious Operation

'An amphibious operation is an attack launched from the sea by naval and landing forces embarked in ships or craft involving a landing on a hostile shore.' (JCS Pub 1-02)

U.S. Marine Corps and U.S. Joint Chief's of Staff doctrinal publications describe the types of amphibious operations as follows:

1. **Amphibious Assaults.** The principle type of an amphibious operation that involves establishing a force on a hostile shore.

2. **Other Amphibious Operations.** Other types of amphibious operations which are governed by U.S. doctrine, but do not involve establishing a landing force on a hostile shore, are as follows:

   - Amphibious Withdrawal
   - Amphibious Demonstration
   - Amphibious Raid

Vietnam

The US Marine Corps began its formal involvement in the Republic of Vietnam following the January 1962, decision by President John F. Kennedy to establish the US advisory effort under the Commander U.S. Military Assistance Command (COMUSMACV). In April 1962, the first Marine Corps tactical unit, Marine Medium Helicopter Squadron-362 (HMM-362) deployed to Soc Trang, about 85 miles south of Saigon, in

the Mekong Delta. Operation SHUFLY saw Marine CH-34D helicopters involved in supporting Vietnamese army units fighting the Viet Cong (Vietnamese Communist). Marine Corps advisors were in the Republic of Vietnam as early as 1955. The first arrival of amphibious forces of the U.S. Marine Corps, in the Republic of Vietnam, 8 March 1965, was more an administrative landing than an amphibious operation. The 9th Marine Expeditionary Brigade (MEB), led by Battalion Landing Team 3/9 (3rd Battalion, 9th Marine Regiment or BLT 3/9) came ashore to a welcoming committee and not enemy forces. The 9th MEB, with support aviation and logistics/combat service support quickly established itself around the Da Nang airfield already in use by Marine helicopter units since 1964.

BLT 3/9 had been the Special Landing Force (SLF) of Seventh Fleet. The SLF was the forerunner of today's Marine Expeditionary Units (Special Operations Capable). On 7 May 1965, the 3d MEB landed at Chu Lai, around 55 miles south of Da Nang. Both brigades were under the operational control of III Marine Expeditionary Force (III MEF). III MEF changed its name to III Marine Amphibious Force (III MAF), presumably because the Marines did not want to be equated to the former French Expeditionary Corps. The 9th MEB became the 9th MAB.

The landing of the 9th MAB, followed by the 3rd MAB, seriously depleted the Fleet Marine Force (FMF) in the Seventh Fleet. Lieutenant General Victor H. Krulak, USMC, CG FMFPac, and Vice Admiral Paul P. Blackburn, USN, CinCPacFleet, decided

that the Special Landing Force (SLF) needed to be reconstituted for contingencies, requiring amphibious operations, in support of Vietnam and the region. General William C. Westmorland, USA, COMUSMACV, and CinCPacFlt, decided upon a costal surveillance and interdiction campaign. Operation MARKET TIME was designed to interdict North Vietnamese re-supply to the Viet Cong in the South. Doctrinal and command relationships soon complicated the role of the US Marines but it was finally decided that amphibious forces would operate as part of Commander Seventh Fleet (COMSEVENFLT) in support of COMUSMACV, usually under III MAF. On 7 May 1965, the Marines made an unopposed amphibious landing at Chu Lai with Regimental Landing Team-7 (RLT-7) - all units were taken under the operational control of III MAF and 3d Marine Division.

Amphibious Operations

The first major example for Marine Corps manoeuvre warfare in Vietnam occurred with Operation STARLITE, which took place between 18-24 August 1965. A deserter from the 1st Viet Cong (VC) Regiment indicated that the 1st VC Regiment was just 12 miles south of Chu Lai, with an estimated strength of 1,500 men, and was preparing to attach the Marine base at Chu Lai. The 7th Marines were given the job to dispatch the 1st VC Regt.

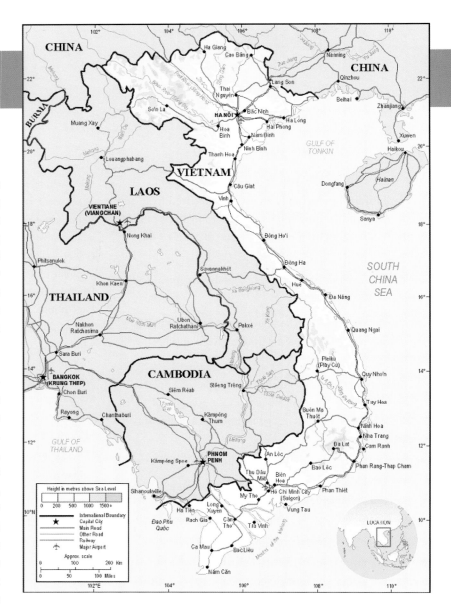

Map showing the main towns and cities of Vietnam. (DGC)

amphibious operations forced the Viet Cong away from the coastal peninsulas where they had found sanctuary

The Marine plan of manoeuvre included a river crossing in amphibious assault vehicles (LVTPs) from the north, a helicopter-borne assault on the west (inland side) and an amphibious assault from the sea. BLT 3/7 was fortunate that the ships of Amphibious Squadron 7 (Phibron 7) were still at Chu Lai disembarking 3/9, and at Da Nang disembarking 3/7. Accordingly, Phibron 7, Seventh Fleet, was available for the amphibious operation.

BLT 3/7 was designated to make an amphibious assault across 'Green Beach,' at 0630, 18 August 1965. BLT 2/4 made a heliborne assault into three LZs. Fire support was provided by 3rd Bn, 12th Marines (Artillery Bn) helo-lifted into positions, Marine F-4 Phantom and A-4 Skyhawk attack aircraft, and Navy Surface Fire Support. It was a converging movement with Marines in blocking positions and amphibious and helo-lifted Marines sweeping the area. By 24 August, the battle was over and initial estimates reported 623 VC dead and 54 Marines killed in action (KIA). However, subsequent Intelligence reports put the VC dead at nearer 1,000. The 1st VC Regiment was no longer combat effective.

The next opportunity to use the SLF and embarked Marines came during Operation PIRANAH, 7 September 1965, on the Batangan Peninsula, just eight miles south the Operation STARLITE area. Two Marine battalions embarked in Seventh Fleet amphibious shipping, while another battalion would conduct a heliborne assault into the objective area to set up a blocking position.

Small boats from the Republic of Vietnam's Navy blocked fishing boats from the landing area. Two Vietnamese infantry battalions later were helo lifted into the area. During Operation PIRANHA, allied forces killed 178 VC and captured or detained 360 enemy soldiers or suspected enemy personnel. Two Marines and five Vietnamese soldiers were KIA with 14 Marines and 33 Vietnamese wounded.

Manoeuvre warfare in the Second Indo-China War was exemplified by U.S. Marine Corps amphibious operations with the Seventh Fleet's Special Landing Force (SLF). Brigadier General Edwin H. Simmons, USMC, in an article for *Naval Review,* 1968, 'Marine Corps Operations in Vietnam, 1965-1966', wrote: 'A more lasting result was that the Viet Cong were disabused of any illusion that they could defeat Marines in a stand-up battle. Moreover, this and later amphibious operations by the Marines forced the Viet Cong away from the coastal peninsulas where they had previously found sanctuary from their enemies.' There were four more amphibious operations from the SLF in 1965, and the second most successful amphibious operation of the year was Operation HARVEST MOON, where BLT 2/1, the SLF, came ashore. In 1966, the SLF was the only CinCPacFlt amphibious force in-theatre because all of III MAF operated in conjunction with the land campaign 'in-country'.

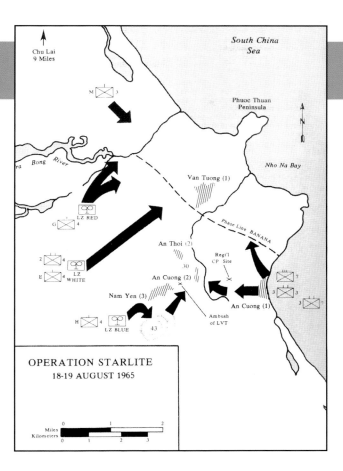

OPERATION STARLITE
18-19 AUGUST 1965

Operation DOUBLE EAGLE was the largest amphibious operation up to that time, 28 January - 7 March 1966, which landed Marines in Quang Ngai Province but failed to engage any significant enemy forces. However, in Operation JACKSTAY, 26 March - 6 April 1966, the SLF moved out of the III MAF Area of Operation (AOA) and landed in the Rung Sat Special Zone, south of Saigon.

By 1967, the SLF was under extensive scrutiny by COMUSMACV, CinCPacFlt and the Pentagon. The SLF was not part of the manpower restriction imposed by the Pentagon and the White House. Nevertheless the various command headquarters agreed that the SLF was a critical asset and increased the Navy Amphibious Ready Group (ARG) to a total of five amphibious assault ships. Vietnamese Marines and the SLF moved further south of Saigon and landed in Kien Hoa Province, for Operation DECKHOUSE V, 6 January 1967. This was the first use on US ground combat forces in the Mekong Delta. Following the first SLF landing of 1967, there would be 22 more amphibious landings in the I Corps area.

The Seventh US Air Force controlled all air space in South Vietnam while Seventh Fleet controlled most of the air space over North Vietnam. The air arm of the SLF and supporting Navy air units, operating so far from the III MAF AOA, gave the Air Force an opportunity to again challenge the independence of the Navy/Marine Corps aviation assets. The result of the confrontation was that the SLF would operate in the future only in the III MAF AOA, the northern provinces of I Corps Tactical

Zone – commonly called 'Eye Corps'. In the 1967, due to the heavy requirements for amphibious forces, Seventh Fleet created SLF Alpha and SLF Bravo, called ARG Alpha or ARG Bravo, which saw the two ARGs participate in 23 amphibious operations in I Corps. The two landing forces, Alpha and Bravo, continued at sea to be under Seventh Fleet but once they moved ashore they were under the operational control of III MAF. According to Joseph H. Alexander and Merrill L. Bartlett in their *SEA SOLDIERS in the Cold War*, US amphibious operations were very successful in continuing to improve amphibious doctrine, shipping, and Navy and Marine equipment; however, there was little excitement for

amphibious operations in COMUSMACV who always viewed the SLFs as only battalions and aircraft squadrons and not Marine Air-Ground Task Forces (MAGTFs) of combined-arms.

Riverine Operation

Many faulted the US Marine Corps for not embracing riverine warfare in the Mekong Delta of the Republic of Vietnam. However, there is a large difference between blue water and brown water military operations. Again, by definition, an amphibious operation is an assault launched from the sea by amphibious forces embarked in ships and craft. With the US Marine Corps forcible entry capability, Navy landing craft, UDT, beachmasters, deepwater navy surface fire support ships, etc., to be used in river patrolling, would be a waste of a valuable operational asset.

Riverine warfare in Vietnam was conducted by the US Army's 9th Infantry Division headquartered at My Tho, on the Mekong River, south of Saigon. The Mekong River has three large tributaries - Bassac, Co Chin, and Rach Ba – along with thousands of inlets, canals and waterways. The 2nd Brigade of the 9th Infantry

Division arrived in Vietnam in 1967, and formed part of the Mobile Riverine Force (MRF). The initial plan called for the MRF to be stationed aboard US Navy 'barracks ships'. The ground combat forces were to be carried into battle on river assault boats called Armoured Troop Carriers (ATCs) and were backed by monitors (named after the Yankee USS *Monitor* of the American War between the States fame). The monitors carried 20mm or 40mm guns and 81mm mortars. The Navy element was known as Task Force 117.

In one operation a VC Battalion was located near the confluence of the Rach Ba and Mekong near Dong Tam. The plan was to send one Army battalion in ATCs to sail past the suspected enemy position and land north of their positions, while another battalion went ashore south of the enemy positions and another moved overland on Army M-113s. Unfortunately, the enemy had been alerted to the movement of the MRF and laid a carefully planned ambush. Only one ATC made it to the northern landing site. The Army forces quickly regrouped and launched an attack from the southern landing sites. With the help of Navy and Army helicopter gunships, and USAF attack aircraft, stubborn VC resistance was overcome and the enemy melted into the jungle

leaving behind over 80 VC dead and a large number of weapons. The pattern of mobility, manoeuvre, speed, and surprise, became the trademark of the MRF. They conducted a series of operations under the code name CORONADO. In one operation, the MRF moved its floating base 60 miles in just over 48 hours and were almost immediately available for combat operations upon arrival.

TET Offensive 1968

The battalion landing teams of the SLF Alpha and Bravo, had been busy in I Corps during January 1968, and there would be 13 SLF amphibious operations in 1968. However, the world would remember the events of January - March 1968, far more than any other event in the Republic of Vietnam. In December 1967, massive movements by the North Vietnamese Army (NVA) and VC units provided indications and warnings that something big was in the making. The enemy were moving their forces closer to Saigon, and the major cities in the Republic of Vietnam. In January 1968, three NVA divisions were moving toward Marine targets near the DMZ.

The TET Offensive of 1968 by the NVA and Viet Cong forces was an operational disaster but a strategic victory. The Viet Cong were almost totally destroyed and VC personnel had to be replaced by NVA troops to fill local and regional guerrilla units. However, exaggerated news media reports and disgruntled politicians concerned over the American losses in Vietnam, would change the direction of the war. Khe Sanh, a relatively

unknown Marine combat operating base, had not seen major combat operations for almost a year. On 20 January, a Marine company made contact with what was later determined to be a battalion size NVA force around Hills 881 South and 881 North, just two miles from Khe Sanh. On 21 January, the NVA over ran the village of Khe Sanh and refugees began to flood the roads. There were five infantry battalions at Khe Sanh including US Marines and Vietnamese Rangers, reinforced by three batteries of 105mm howitzers, a battery of 4.2" mortars, and a battery of 155mm howitzers. Additionally, the Army had 175mm guns in range and, of course, close air support was available, weather permitting. The North Vietnamese mistakenly thought that Khe Sanh was a very inviting target. While the communist announced a seven-day 'truce', in honour of the TET New Year (27 January - 3 February), there was no confusing that three NVA divisions were trying to surrounding Khe Sanh.

On 29 January, the enemy started their attack in I Corps, which was actually premature for what was supposed to be a coordinated attack all over the Republic of Vietnam. Attacks against Da Nang and Hue City on 30 January, signalled major assaults. Many in the U.S.A. and the COMUSMACV headquarters saw visions of Dien Bien Phu, and the major French Army defeat during the First Indo-China War, and many counseled to withdraw from Khe Sanh. Khe Sanh could not have been abandoned before the offensive. It was the major combat base setting just south of the DMZ and the line of march into the coastal cites. It had to be defended and it was. Khe Sanh proved to be a death trap for many NVA, thanks

A USMC Lieutenant inspects a combined squad of Vietnamese Popular Force troops and U.S. Marines at Phu Bai. (USMC)

to the tenacious Marines and superb U.S. air power with close air support backed up by B-52 bombers. The NVA, and much weakened VC forces, tried two more 'offensives' in 1968. Each was weaker than the first and met the same results. It is believed that after the third failed 'offensive' there was a major change of command in North Vietnam and the NVA began to adopt new tactics. Unfortunately, more for the Vietnamese but for the Americans also, the President of the United States announced his decision not to seek re-election and began a US withdrawal plan to be called 'Vietnamisation.' 0n 10 April, President Johnson announced that General William C. Westmoreland was to be replaced by General Creighton W. Abrams. Many thought that Abrams was a far more proficient commander for the Vietnam war, but regardless of Abrams' warfighting skills and his full understanding of the tactics, techniques and procedures needed to win, the political situation at home made the decision for a pull out of American forces irreversible.

Marine strength peaked in September 1968, with over 85,500 Marines in-country. The year 1969 saw 14 SLF amphibious operations, as compared to 13 in 1968, and 25 in 1967. Operation BOLD MARINER, 13-24 January, was the largest amphibious operation since the Korean War. A MAB size landing force which included both SLFs, joined with US Army units of the Americal Division, south of Chu Lai.

Pacification and rural development was thought to be highly successful in Vietnam. The primary mission was to keep a village under the control of the Republic of Vietnam. Of all the Marine programmes to provide security in the rural area, the most successful was the Combined Action Programme (CAP). This programme combined a specially selected and trained Marine rifle squad combined with a Vietnamese Popular Force Platoon (like the Home Guard). From the beginning of the CAP platoons in 1965 to 1971, no Vietnamese village under the protection of a CAP platoon was ever lost to the VC or NVA forces.

Vietnamisation was the term given to the cover for the withdrawal of US forces from the Republic of Vietnam. The term was to convey that the US military forces had completed its mission in preparing the Republic of Vietnam to take on the burden of defence of its country. With the announcement of the Vietnamisation programme the NVA and VC reverted almost completely to guerrilla and terrorist activities while they awaited the major US troop withdrawals.

As part of Vietnamisation, toward the end of 1969, the 3rd Marine Division was redeployed to Okinawa and reverting back to U.S. national strategic reserves, provided manning of the SLFs. Accordingly, SLFs could no longer deploy to South Vietnam without specific authorisation of the Joints Chiefs of Staff. The 31st Marine Amphibious Unit (31st MAU) participated in the last U.S. Marine Corps action in the Republic of Vietnam, February-March 1971, in Operation LAM SON 719, providing the Vietnamese helicopter support. The operation ended with the 31st MAU conducting an amphibious demonstration in the southern part of North Vietnam.

Easter Offensive 1972

In 1972 there were around 500 hundred Marines in the Republic of Vietnam, which included Embassy guards, staff officers, and advisors to the Vietnamese Marine Corps. The NVA began their offensive on 30 March, with a three-division attack across the DMZ. This was over 45,000 enemy troops reinforced with Russian tanks, heavy artillery and extensive anti-aircraft weapons. The test for Vietnamisation had come to the Republic of Vietnam. The 3rd ARVN Division was overrun and the brigades

Left: Marines from the 3rd Battalion, 9th Marines near Da Nang. (USMC)

Right: Marines on board the LPH Iwo Jima, having just returned from a raid on the Vung Mu Peninsula, September 1965. (USMC)

of the Vietnamese Marine Division were the only troops to stand and fight.

The 9th Marine Amphibious Brigade (9th MAB) sailed from Okinawa into a position off the coast near the DMZ. The 9th MAB had four Marine Battalion Landing Teams and two helicopter squadrons aboard. MAG-15, with F-4 Phantoms, flew from bases in Japan to Da Nand Air Base. MAG-12 moved two squadrons of A4 Skyhawks to a former USAF base at Bien Hoa. A-6 Intruders also flew combat missions from the USS *Coral Sea*. The new AH-1J, Sea Cobras, arrived in-theatre and operated off Navy shipping and ashore. MAG-15 was later moved to Nam Phong, Thailand, and continued to provide close air support to the beleaguered Republic of Vietnam.

No ground combat Marines went ashore. However, the Vietnamese Marines and ARVN forces were additionally provided with extensive naval fire support from every cruiser and destroyer in the Seventh Fleet that could get to the coastal waters off the DMZ and the northern provinces. On 15 April, NVA forces crossed the Cambodian border threatening the Tay

Ninh Provincial Capital west of Saigon with a second offensive. USAF B-52 flew mission in Tay Ninh that caused serious damage to the NVA forces. A third offensive was launched by the NVA in the central part of the country at Kontum. Ironically, the NVA capture of Quang Tri City and their concentration on the northern provinces, caused the NVA attacks to stall at An Loc, Tay Ninh Province, and Kontum in the central highlands. The Vietnamese Marines and Airborne Divisions fought a delaying action in the north until the enemy was stopped at Hue. US Marine Corps helicopters lifted the Vietnamese with their US Marine advisors into many battles. US Marine amphibious vehicles and navy landing craft were used for an amphibious operation to land the Vietnamese Marines behind the NVA.

In September, Quang Tri was retaken and the NVA offensive ground to a halt. The inability or unwillingness of the NVA to concentrate its forces and not piecemeal attacks all over the country, gave the Republic of Vietnam the opportunity to blunt the three NVA attacks and counterattack each NVA thrust in turn. The weight of US air and naval fire support was a decisive factor. It was estimated that from 30 March, to 15 August, US

aircraft destroyed over 258 NVA tanks. The Easter Offensive of 1972, proved that the Republic of Vietnam could defeat NVA main force units with Soviet armour and extensive support of their communist allies, if given proper support at or near the same support the communist were giving to North Vietnam.

The Final Offensive

The Great Spring Offensive, 11 March - 30 April 1975, should not have been a surprise to seasoned observers in Vietnam. By 1973, American promised financial support began to wane. The US Congress began to cut aid to the Republic of Vietnam and the North Vietnamese began to see the difference. In 1974, a military aid package of $1.6 billion was cut to $700 million. Further aid requests from the US Congress were also refused. Between 1973 and 1975 the NVA, in violation of the Paris Peace Accords, moved to triple their forces in the south. The Republic of Vietnam was not ready to stand-alone and the North Vietnamese smelled blood. In early March 1975, three NVA divisions were concentrated against Ban Me Thout, in the central highlands. With no U.S. air support the central highlands fell on 11 March.

Marines from the 2nd Battalion, 3rd Marines move into the hamlet of Le My. (USMC)

It is hard to imagine a more disastrous plan than the decision to abandon the central highlands and concentrate forces around Saigon. With the northern provinces cut off and many ARVN forces surrounded in the provincial capitals, the north I Corps area quickly fell to the enemy. Hue fell on 25 March and Da Nang four days later. The NVA had learned from their mistakes in 1972, and carefully concentrated their forces in a slow deliberate move on Saigon. A gallant stand was made by ARVN units at Xuan Loc, north of Saigon, but they were overwhelmed by superior numbers and superior equipment. At 0500, 30 April 1975, the NVA armoured columns entered Saigon. It was not a barefoot peasant guerrilla, fighting a 'civil war', who marched into the Presidential Palace, as many political pundits described the war in Vietnam, but a Russian T-54 tank driven by regular North Vietnamese communist soldiers.

With the collapse of the Republic of Vietnam, partially due to President Richard M. Nixon being embroiled with an investigation for the Watergate scandal, and most certainly the US Congress failure to honour commitments to the Republic of Vietnam with logistics and financial support, there was little chance the Republic of Vietnam could survive the Russian and Chinese supported NVA. Amphibious elements of the Seventh Fleet and 9th MAB participated in the enormous effort to evacuate the remnants of the U.S. personnel from Cambodia and South Vietnam. In Operation EAGLE PULL U.S. personnel in Cambodia were evacuated without serious incident and in Operation FREQUENT WIND, 29-30 April 1975, U.S. personnel

and many Vietnamese officials, but not nearly enough, were evacuated form Saigon. This unusual amphibious withdrawal operation, exceedingly difficult to execute, was carried out exceptionally well by forward deployed amphibious forces of the US Seventh Fleet and the Fleet Marine Force, Pacific.

Aftermath

Brigadier General Ed Simmons, USMC, again writing an article for *Naval Review*, 'Marine Corps Operations in Vietnam, 1969-1972,' summarised the final chapter of Marine Corps involvement in the Republic of Vietnam:

> 'Most of the Marines, as they went up the ship's gangplank
> or aircraft's ramp on their way home, probably left
> Vietnam with a feeling that they and the Marine Corps had
> done the job assigned to them'.

According to Norman Friedman in his *Seapower as a Strategy: Navies and National Interest,* one irony of Vietnam was when President John F. Kennedy was asked why he was willing to fight there instead of Laos, said that Vietnam was much closer to the sea, and much more subject to U.S. naval action. Most knew that in fact a key line of communication of the VC in South Vietnam ran, not along the coast, but through Laos. Sea-based forces could certainly strike any where in North or South Vietnam,

but one key element to the war was surrendered when the U.S. failed to resist communist control of strategic parts of Laos. Another handicap to US strategic foreign policy, according to Friedman, was that as early as 1965, the U.S. secretly assured the Peoples Republic of China that the U.S. would not invade North Vietnam, to preclude something like the Chinese intervention in Korea. Also, it is reported that the North Vietnamese demanded and received reassurance from the Chinese that they would intervene if the U.S. invaded North Vietnam.

Many political leaders on both sides of the Atlantic Ocean thought that the ultimate task of the U.S. in the 1960s was to preserve the NATO alliance. After the disaster in Vietnam some in Europe felt that the tide had turned in favour of the Soviets. Europeans did not see Vietnam as a 'proper' Cold War confrontation. To them, the Cold War was about Europe. Some even thought that many Europeans lacked sympathy because the U.S. had failed to appreciate the European perspective during their period of decolonisation and withdrawal from Empire.

Factors Identified from the Amphibious Operations undertaken in Vietnam

- Tactical and operational manoeuvre capabilities were achieved by the Special Landing Force, which the enemy had no ability to oppose and therefore ceded the entire coast of Vietnam to the US naval forces.

- Surprise was achieved every time an independent US naval amphibious force was able to conduct an amphibious operation without possible Vietnamese counter-intelligence failures.

- Exploiting vulnerabilities and opportunities.

- In order to generate the tempo of operations we desire and best cope with the uncertainty, disorder, and fluidity of combat, command must be decentralized.

- Manoeuvre warfare requires that we must shape the battle to our advantage in terms of both time and space.

- *Coup d'oeil* is the ability to look at a military situation and immediately see its essence, especially the key enemy weakness, which if exploited, can lead to a decision.

Further Reading

NWP-22 (B)/LFM-01, *Doctrine for Amphibious Operations*.

The Marines in Vietnam 1954-1973: An Anthology and Annotated Bibliography, (Washington, D.C.: History and Museums Division, Headquarters Marine Corps,1974)

Alexander, Joseph H. and Bartlett, Merrill L., *Sea Soldiers in the Cold War: Amphibious Warfare 1945-1991*, (Annapolis, Maryland: Naval Institute Press, 1995)

U.S. Marines in Vietnam, 1954-1975, 9 Volumes, (Washington, D. C.: History and Museums Division, Headquarters Marine Corps, 1977-1997)

The Vietnam War: The History of America's Conflict in South-East Asia, (London: Salamander Books, 1996)

Melson, Charles D., *The Marine Corps in Vietnam*, (Oxford: Osprey, 1998)

Biography

Lieutenant Colonel H Thomas Hayden recently concluded over 35 years of service, which included working in the Agency for International Development, the US Marine Corps, and the Pentagon. His specialties are Intelligence, Counter-insurgency Operations, Counter-terrorism, and Joint Concepts Development and Experimentation. His Marine Corps assignments have included command of two separate battalions; working as a Staff Officer in the 4th Marine Division; Branch Head at the Headquarters US Marine Corps and later Special Assistant to the Assistant Secretary of Defense for Special Operations and Low Intensity Conflict; and Senior Program Analysts with the Joint Staff at the Pentagon. He spent two years in Southeast Asia (1967-1969), and other assignments including, Japan & Okinawa, Europe, Central America, Saudi Arabia and Kuwait, Somalia, Singapore, Philippines, and Colombia. He has an MBA (Pepperdine) and an MA in International Relations (University of Southern California). He has written two books, *Shadow War: Special Operations and Low Intensive Conflict* (Pacific Aero Press, 1991) and the popular *Warfighting: Maneuver Warfare in the U.S. Marine Corps* (Greenhill Books, 1995).

---

[1] It is important to note that the US Marine Corps has U. S. Congressional statutory requirement for primary responsibility to develop, in coordination with other Services (US Army, Navy and Air Force), the doctrine, tactics, and techniques for landing forces in amphibious warfare.

[2] The author wishes to acknowledge the contributions made to this chapter by the History and Museum Division, Headquarters, US Marine Corps, through their 9 volume series on the "US Marines in Vietnam, 1954-1957" and "The Marines in Vietnam: 1954-1973, An Anthology and Annotated Bibliography."

Falkland Islands
Operation CORPORATE, May-June 1982

By Major General Julian Thompson CB OBE (Rtd)

Introduction

Operation CORPORATE, the amphibious operation to repossess the Falkland Islands in 1982, should be viewed against a background of diminishing interest in the UK in the future of amphibious operations. The planned disposal of the two LPDs was cancelled in late 1981, an eleventh hour decision. No replacements were planned. The carriers (CVS) were to be sold or scrapped. The British maritime headquarters in Northwood was organised for peacetime training, foreign visits and escalation to the lower levels of a NATO war. Because amphibious operations were the responsibility of the United States Navy, Striking Fleet Atlantic, there was no obvious need for the Northwood headquarters to include a staff with amphibious expertise; the sole Royal Marine officer being retained for security duties.

The operation to retake South Georgia is not included in this case study.

Outline of Operations

The operation was mounted in response to the Argentine invasion and seizure of the islands on 2 April 1982. Alerted by intelligence, a British Task Force began assembling before the Argentine invasion, and the first elements sailed south on 2 April. Over the following days the Amphibious Task Group sailed with the Landing Force, a greatly expanded 3 Commando Brigade, embarked in a host of Ships Taken up From Trade (STUFT), Royal Fleet Auxiliaries (RFA) including LSLs, and yet more warships. The final major element to sail south was the 5 Infantry Brigade.

It was necessary for the amphibious ships and 3 Commando Brigade to pause at Ascension Island to restow STUFT and RFA. In the interests of speed to convey a political signal, the ships had departed UK not combat loaded. At the outset neither a campaign plan nor an initiating directive had been promulgated to the Landing Force and Amphibious Task Group Commanders. Re-stowing and planning was not made any easier for lack of a Campaign Plan and Initiating Directive. Indeed the Amphibious Group and Landing Force Commanders were never made aware that either ever existed. On 10 April the mission given was: Plan to land on the Falklands with a view to repossessing them. This was subsequently changed late in the campaign to the more positive mission: repossess the Falklands as quickly as possible. From Ascension the Carrier Battle Group went ahead to establish air and sea control. By which time the command organisation was as shown below.

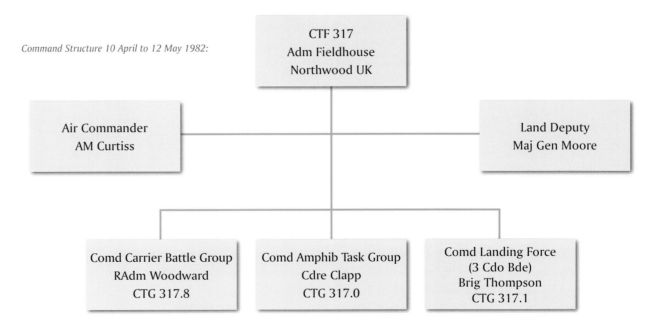

Command Structure 10 April to 12 May 1982:

The Sub-Surface and South Georgia Task Groups are not shown. Both reported direct to CTF 317.

Command Structure 12 May to end of Operations:

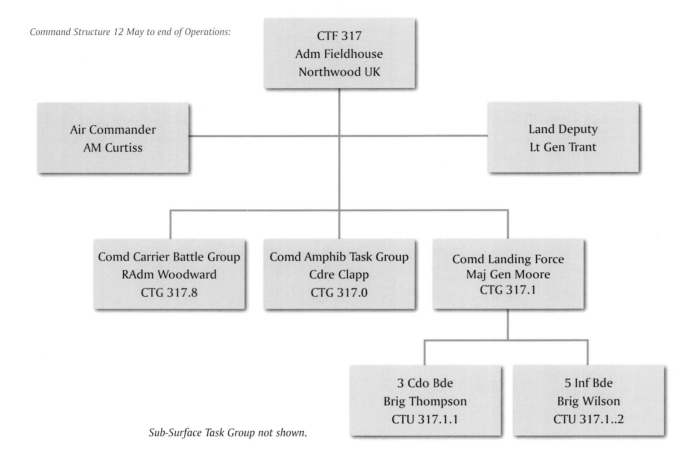

Sub-Surface Task Group not shown.

who had no knowledge of amphibious operations. He brought with him a staff all without amphibious training or experience. Despite the Commodore Amphibious Warfare (Commodore Clapp), sending his Staff Officer Operations, who had welfare problems, to Northwood to assist their staff, he was sent away as unnecessary. One Royal Marine officer, Lieutenant Colonel Donkin was posted to the Northwood Headquarters, but his advice was largely ignored and he was not kept fully in the operational picture.

The normal command structure for an amphibious operation with the amphibious task group commander being appointed CATF was never instituted. Clapp and Thompson worked as if it was in place, although neither the superior headquarters nor the Carrier Battle Group commander appeared to understood the relationship between a CATF and a CLF, and conducted business including issuing orders, as though such a command arrangement did not exist.

Planning

Planning for the amphibious operation was done by Commodore Clapp and Brigadier Thompson and their respective staffs travelling together in the LPD HMS *Fearless*. No other headquarters were involved. The plans were handed to Major General Moore when he visited the two Task Group Commanders at Ascension, and taken by him to Northwood for approval. It is understood that the plans were also presented to the Chiefs of Staff.

Major General Moore did not leave UK until 20 May, and travelled south in the STUFT *Queen Elizabeth II*. He did not appear in-Theatre until D plus 9, and because the communications in the ship in which he was travelling broke down, he was out of touch during the landings and initial battles and key moves, and unable to influence the operation until 30 May. Thus the command structure change on 12 May

above was academic, and Brigadier Thompson was the landing force commander for the planning right up to D-Day, for the initial amphibious assault, and subsequent moves out of the beachhead.

Major General Moore's place at Northwood as Land Deputy was taken by Lieutenant General Trant, then GOC South-East District,

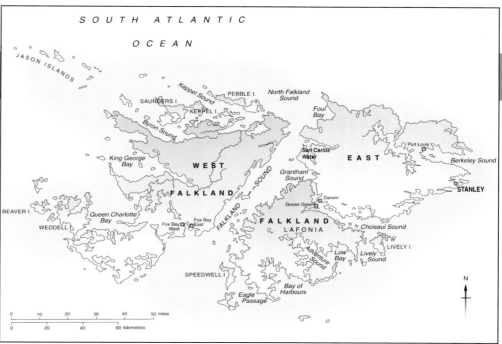

The place chosen for the initial landing was San Carlos Water, which fulfilled both the Landing Force and Amphibious Group requirements. The main drivers in deciding the location were (not in any order of priority), the beachhead:

- Was impossible to attack using Exocet.

- Was difficult, although not impossible to attack from the air.

- Was difficult to attack by submarine.

- Was easy to defend from seaward and landward.

- It provided a sheltered anchorage allowing an uninterrupted offload by day and night whatever the weather.

- Was lightly defended. This was very important in view of total lack of armoured amphibians and gun-equipped landing craft to give intimate support on landing, thus precluding any direct assault on a well defended shore.

- Was too far from main enemy land forces for them to move and mount an attack quickly.

- Had plenty of good beaches.

- Had ample 'elbow room' in which to deploy troops inland from the beaches.

- Had good exits for tracked vehicles: CVRT, BV 202.

- Had space for a Brigade Maintenance Area.

- Although it could be easily mined, both at sea and ashore, Special Forces reconnaissance saw no evidence of either.

- Was assessed, correctly as it later transpired, as a surprise choice, in the light of the enemy expecting an assault in the area of Stanley.

The shortage of medium helicopter lift, combined with there being no LPH being available, necessitated a surface assault for the first two waves, including the use of LCUs to take in troops, a purpose for which the craft is not designed.

Narrative of Operations

The landings in the early hours of 21 May were entirely successful, and achieved with very few casualties to the Landing Force. Two light helicopters of 3 Commando Brigade Air Squadron were shot down by ground fire from retreating Argentine troops, three aircrew were killed and one wounded. Casualties in ships in the AOA were greater due to the enemy air attacks which started soon after first light. Enemy air interdiction caused most of the casualties in the beachhead area throughout the operation.

On the night of D-day, the Commando Brigade Reconnaissance Troop (Mountain & Arctic Warfare Cadre) pushed patrols well forward some 20 to 30 miles to give warning of enemy activity and surveillance over the routes that Brigadier Thompson intended to use to advance on the high ground leading to Stanley.

Shortage of helicopter lift, exacerbated by the loss of the Atlantic Conveyor with all but one Chinook, led to two of the Brigade's manoeuvre units (45 Commando (45 Cdo) and 3rd Battalion the Parachute Regiment (3 PARA)), marching to secure the key high ground leading to Stanley, and ultimately all the way to that town. While this was in progress, the Battle of Goose Green was being fought and won by 2nd Battalion The Parachute Regiment (2 PARA). This was a diversion in the tactical sense, and carried out at the insistence of the CTF who was concerned that the

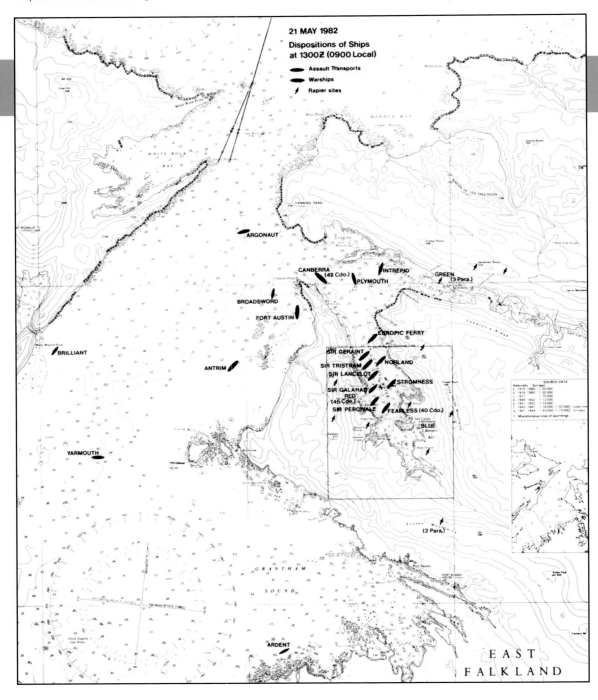

21 MAY 1982

Dispositions of Ships
at 1300Z (0900 Local)

➤ Assault Transports
➤ Warships
⚑ Rapier sites

ARGONAUT

CANBERRA
(42 Cdo.)   INTREPID   GREEN
PLYMOUTH   (3 Para.)

BROADSWORD

FORT AUSTIN

EUROPIC FERRY

SIR GERAINT
                    NORLAND
SIR TRISTRAM
SIR LANCELOT
                    STROMNESS
SIR GALAHAD
RED
(45 Cdo.)
SIR PERCIVALE   FEARLESS (40 Cdo.)
                        BLUE

BRILLIANT

ANTRIM

YARMOUTH

(2 Para.)

GRANTHAM

SOUND

ARDENT

EAST
FALKLAND

SOURCE DATA

A Naval chart detailing the disposition
of ships on 21 May 1982 (NHB)

loss of ships sustained to that date needed to be balanced by a victory. Apart from providing a much needed filip to sagging morale at the politico-strategic level of command back in the UK, a number of useful lessons were learned, or more accurately, re-learned at the tactical level, and the operation was, therefore, thoroughly worthwhile from most points of view, except that of causing an unwelcome diversion of effort.

A helicopter lift over two successive nights was carried out by 42 Commando (42 Cdo) to secure Mount Kent, while 45 Cdo and 3 PARA were marching forward. The route for the main axis of advance by 3 Commando Brigade was deliberately chosen to take advantage of the sea flank for logistic supply. Teal Inlet on Salvador Water was accessible to LSLs, thus reducing the distance for helicopter lift to supply the Brigade forward on the Mount Kent line, by two thirds.

While 3 Commando Brigade was moving forward, 5 Infantry Brigade arrived in the beachhead. Despite the employment of anti-submarine helicopters in support of ground forces, the overall shortage of helicopters necessitated the move forward of this brigade by sea by a combination of LPD/LCU and LSL. During one of these moves, two LSLs were bombed in Port Pleasant, near Fitzroy. One, the *Sir Galahad*, was damaged beyond repair, and subsequently scuttled out at sea. Poor procedures and communications in this brigade, combined with lack of training in, and awareness of the imperatives of, amphibious operations led to unnecessarily heavy casualties among troops of 5 Infantry Brigade in the two LSLs.

With the bulk of the enemy force (a brigade plus, and numerically stronger than both British brigades) now situated in the triangular peninsula leading to Stanley and the airport, with nowhere else to go, attacks were mounted by both

J Company, 42 Commando digging in above San Carlos Water. (RMM)

A Seaman beside a 7.62mm GPMG for use against low-level air attack on the ships in San Carlos Water. (IWM CICD82)

British Brigades, with all but one key battle being fought by 3 Commando Brigade. The aim being to pin the enemy back on the narrow isthmus leading to the airport, here he would either see sense and surrender, or be subjected to air and artillery bombardment until starved into submission. The attacks on the nights 11/12 and 13/14 June were successful, and the enemy signed the surrender document in the presence of Major General Moore at 2100 hours on 14 June 1982.

Analyis of the Operation

The analysis of the operation will be considered under the following headings:

1. The Manoeuvrist Approach
2. Unity of Effort
3. Winning Sea Control
4. Achieving Surprise
5. Generating Tempo
6. Sound Intelligence
7. Readiness
8. Training
9. Deception
10. Air Superiority
11. NGS
12. Navy and Landing Force Integration
13. Top-Down Planning
14. Command and Staffs Same Locality
15. Logistics

The Manoeuvrist Approach

From the outset of the operation, the intention was to attack where the enemy least expected it, and to capitalise on support from the sea to enable the advance to take the least obvious route. It is clear from subsequent interrogation and conversations with Argentine officers, that the enemy expected the main effort to be from the South-West or South via Fitzroy or even closer to Stanley, and his deployment as shown in his after-action report bears this out. In fact the main effort was by 3 Commando Brigade from the North-West.

The actions of 3 Commando Brigade Reconnaissance Troop in destroying or neutralising the enemy special force reconnaissance on key high ground overlooking the Brigade's axis of advance and helicopter Main Supply Route (MSR), denied the enemy acquiring information on the moves of 3 Commando Brigade.

The battles for Stanley were fought on the principle of converging axes, which allowed maximum fire support to be employed, while successive attacks from different axes kept the enemy guessing where the next one would come.

Unity of Effort

Unity of effort was achieved by the Amphibious and Landing Force Commanders and their staffs working together on mutually agreed lines. The success of this effort risked being jeopordised by:

Brigadier Julian Thompson and Major General Jeremy Moore on the slopes of Mount Kent before the final battle for Stanley. (IWM)

- There being no overall in-theatre commander to co-ordinate the efforts of the three co-equal task group commanders.

- Lack of understanding of the amphibious imperatives on the part of staffs in Northwood once Major General Moore and his staff had departed, and a similar failing on the part of the Carrier Battle Group Commander.

Winning Sea Control

Sea control was established well before the amphibious operation when the heavy cruiser *General Belgrano* was sunk by the submarine *Conqueror*. Thereafter the Argentine surface fleet took no further part in the war. Upon the arrival of the Carrier Battle Group in the theatre of operations, no supply or reinforcement of the Argentine garrison by sea was possible.

Achieving Surprise

Surprise was achieved for the initial amphibious operation by selecting a beachhead well away from the main enemy concentration around Stanley. As alluded to earlier, the amphibious and landing force group commanders assessed that the Argentines expected an assault in the vicinity of Stanley, and the deployment of their troops reflected this.

Once the beachhead had been identified by the enemy, surprise was maintained by selecting an axis of advance from an unexpected direction, the North-West. This also allowed use of the sea flank for logistic support via Teal Inlet in Port Salvador in the north of East Falkland.

Despite the LSLs being overflown while in Teal Inlet, surprise was largely maintained by denying the enemy observation over the axis of advance, thanks to the activities of the Brigade Reconnaissance Troop (see above). The insertion of part of 5 Infantry Brigade through Port Pleasant inadvertently helped maintain surprise, because the enemy believed that this heralded a major attack from the direction they expected.

Generating Tempo

The shortage of medium helicopter lift, and total absence of roads for wheeled transport, made generating tempo very difficult. Moves of troops were ponderous and slow, as was the build-up of supplies to support land operations.

Sound Intelligence

In the early part of the lead-up to the operation intelligence was thin. This was rectified as time went by, mainly, it is assumed, by GCHQ intercept. There was no air-photographic cover, and if there was any satellite imagary, none was made available to the operational commanders in-theatre. Nor was there any satellite meterological forecast available to the Amphibious and Landing Force Commanders. Excellent intelligence for the Amphibious and Landing Force commanders in the pre-landing phase was provided by the SAS, and especially the SBS. In general the SAS were tasked by Landing Force Commander and the SBS by the Amphibious Force Commander. The CO 22 SAS and OC SBS were located in HMS *Fearless*. The SBS carried out the usual advance force functions. After landing, the best intelligence as far as the landing force was concerned, was obtained by patrolling and contact intelligence, including captured maps. In this respect the Brigade Reconnaissance Troop were especially valuable.

Readiness

The amphibious and landing forces had no warning of the impending operation. This state of affairs was brought about by MOD (Navy) failing to warn either that some units of the fleet were being brought to short notice two days before the Argentine invasion of the Falkland Islands. In the event, both the amphibious and landing forces demonstrated a high degree of readiness, by loading and sailing in five days from a standing start, having been at seven days notice to move.

Training

Despite a lack of amphibious exercises over the previous two years owing to financial cuts, both the amphibious and landing forces demonstrated a high level of expertise on this operation. This was largely thanks to a bedrock of many years of experience on amphibious exercises by commanders and staffs especially in 3 Commando Brigade. This enabled the Amphibious and Landing Forces to carry out a night landing without having had even a turn-away rehearsal in daylight. Not surprisingly, this expertise was almost totally lacking in 5 Infantry Brigade. The numerous errors and ponderous procedures that manifested themselves in this brigade whenever they were deployed by sea, or required to interface with the maritime element were proof of this. No blame can be attributed to any of the commanders or soldiers; through no fault of theirs they were simply out of their depth. A good example was provided by the shooting down by the *Cardiff* of a 5 Infantry Brigade light helicopter carrying their OC Headquarters and Signal Squadron on a reconnaissance. 5 Infantry Brigade had failed to warn anybody that the helicopter was flying well forward of friendly forces, possibly because it never occurred to

them that such a precaution was necessary. The helicopter was, unfortunately, exactly on a route the Navy expected Argentine C-130s to take to resupply Stanley.

Deception

Deception operations were mounted before and during the landings at San Carlos. These included:

- Dummy landings by ships of the Carrier Battle Group approaching likely beachheads in a landing formation, and emitting radio traffic to simulate an approaching amphibious force.

- Ship-shore bombardment to simulate pre-landing fire plans.

- An attack on Darwin by an SAS squadron on the night of 20/21 May (D-Day) while landings were in progress at San Carlos to keep the garrison occupied and in the hope that the enemy would think a major landing was in progress near them.

It is difficult to assess how successful these deception measures were.

Air Superiority

Air superiority was not achieved until several days after D-Day, and air supremacy was never attained. Landing without achieving air superiority was a risky undertaking, and should not be repeated in future unless it is absolutely unavoidable, as was the case in this operation. Fortunately the enemy did not exploit the situation to the full. Their targeting and attack procedures were faulty. They did not use the aircraft positioned in the Falkland Islands, Pucaras and Aermacchis, to interdict the very vulnerable helicopter supply routes. We may not be so lucky next time.

At night the enemy were able to fly C-130 aircraft in and out of Stanley with impunity, and, despite the efforts of some escorts, did so right up to the last night of the war.

Naval Gunfire Support

Naval Gunfire Support (NGS) was invaluable. From the moment of the arrival of the Carrier Battle Group in the theatre of operations, NGS was used to harass targets ashore. During

the landing at San Carlos, a potential enemy gun position was neutralised by NGS, and destroyers and frigates were tasked to provide on-call fire support in the beachhead if required on D-Day and on subsequent days. In the event the on-call missions were not required.

NGS was used at Darwin during the opening phase of the attack by 2nd Battalion The Parachute Regiment. Because of the enemy air threat (see above), the supporting ship had to leave the gunline off Darwin by first light to avoid being exposed to air attack. Therefore her invaluable support was not available during the later, and more critical phases of the battle.

NGS was employed to support the offensives in the land campaign thereafter, but only at night, for the same reason as above. In retrospect, less ammunition should have been expended on harassing fire tasks early in the war, as most of these were of doubtful value. More NGS should have been used on targets in depth during the assaults on enemy positions in the vicinity of Stanley, and in particular in the counter-battery role on enemy artillery positions.

There appeared to be little understanding of the capabilities of NGS at the Headquarters at Northwood. A signal from that headquarters was received by the amphibious and landing force task group commanders which included the phrase, 'Static defensive positions there [at Port Stanley] will be destroyed piecemeal making maximum use of artillery, NGS...'

Apart from the fact that it is difficult to imagine any defensive position that would not be static, since the enemy did not possess any armour capable of operating across country and thus conducting a mobile defence, the author of this signal was clearly unaware, or had forgotten, that light artillery, and even 4.5-inch armour-piercing shells are incapable of 'destroying' well prepared defensive positions. Both are of course capable of neutralising an enemy in defensive positions, demoralising him, and 'keeping his head down', during an assault by infantry. Individual artillery and mortar pieces and ammunition can of course be destroyed by a direct hit, and their crews killed, wounded and demoralised by shrapnel from air burst.

Navy and Landing Force Integration

As alluded to earlier, Navy and Landing Force integration worked well between the Amphibious Group and the 3rd Commando Brigade, but less well between the Amphibious Group and 5 Infantry Brigade. The latter deficiency was solely because of the lack of amphibious training and experience in 5 Infantry Brigade.

Navy and landing force integration between the carricr battle group and the landing force was minimal.

Top-Down Planning

Top-Down planning only applied from the level of the Amphibious and Landing Force Task Group commanders and below. As discussed earlier, because there was no campaign plan and no initiating directive, Top-Down planning from Northwood to the level of these task groups did not exist. The only discussions with the superior headquarters on the ampibious plan took place when Major General Moore visited the Amphibious and Landing Force Commanders before the amphibious group sailed from Ascension Island. He was briefed on the preferred landing plan, and returned to UK with the details. The plan was made by the commanders and staffs of the amphibious and landing force task groups acting entirely alone, and unguided in what can only be described as a 'planning vacuum'.

Commanders and Staffs Same Locality

The co-location of the commanders and staffs of the ampibious and landing forces in the LPD HMS *Fearless* for some seven weeks, was absolutely critical to the success of the operation.

Commando Logistic Regiment at work unloading supplies along the shore line. (IWM)

When Major General Moore and his staff arrived, they were permanently based in the LPD and the situation described above did not arise in quite the same way, except when General Moore found it essential to operate forward leaving a logistic support staff on board.

Logistics

The original plan for logistics was sea-basing, to land the minimum. This was arrived at while the amphibious and landing force commanders were still under the impression that air superiority would be achieved before a landing would be attempted; having been assured of this on no less than three occasions by the Task Force Commander personally. By the time it became clear that this highly desireable state of affairs would not be achieved, all the logistic ships had been loaded and sailed from Ascension ahead of the main body of the amphibious group.

After the first day of air attacks in the beachhead it was decided to offload the bulk of logistic supplies and the medical facility into the Brigade Maintenance Area (BMA) in the beachhead. Some combat supplies were kept loaded in LSLs for subsequent movement to Teal Inlet when this was opened as the 3 Commando Brigade Forward Brigade Maintenance Area (FBMA). The total lack of roads, and consequently reliance on helicopter lift of combat supplies forward of the beachhead, combined with the paucity of medium lift helicopters, made supply forward a slow and laborious process. Logistic lift took priority over tactical lift of troops.

Once the landing began, the shortcomings of the landing force circuits in the *Fearless*, made command of the landing force nigh impossible, and the only remedy was command from a forward location ashore and frequent visits by the commander by helicopter.

The arrangements for a 'Rear HQ' staff on board the LPD to work with the amphibious task group commander were unsatisfactory, and both the Amphibious and the Landing Force Commanders should have given the matter more thought in order to arrive at a better solution. Until the amphibious phase is concluded, although the landing force commander may wish, and indeed have, to command from ashore, he must try and visit the amphibious commander more frequently than was the case on this operation, and make provision for a strong team from his own headquarters to remain on board to support the amphibious commander.

As mentioned earlier, a key logistic move was to open the FBMA at Teal Inlet. A similar facility was subsequently opened for 5 Infantry Brigade at Fitzroy. However, the brigade had come south with inadequate logistic resources, and the 3 Commando Brigade Logistic Regiment was ordered to make up the shortfall.

Summary

The Falklands Operation was a classic amphibious operation, conducted at a distance of over 8,000 miles from the home base with only the airfield and anchorage at Ascension Island as a staging post half way down the route. It was a maritime operation from first to last, albeit with the indispensible support of the Royal Air Force who provided both logistic and carrier-based combat support. The air bridge from the UK to Ascension was critical, as was the ability to drop light spares by parachute direct to the Task Force in the South Atlantic by parachute.

The amphibious operation to recapture the Falkland Islands could not have been carried out without specialist amphibious shipping and ship-shore movement assets, these were in short supply but thankfully there were enough - just. The amphibious expertise of the Royal Marines combined with the small residue of amphibious-trained Naval personnel still serving after savage defence cuts was absolutely vital to success. Without them the operation would not have been possible.

J Company, 42 Commando outside Government House in Port Stanley. In the process of raising the Falkland Islands flag. (IWM)

The unhappy experience of 5 Infantry Brigade showed that there is no substitute for a well trained and practised formation if one is to carry out an amphibious as opposed to a sea-transported operation. The training of staffs and leaders at all levels is critical. There is an irreduceable minimum of amphibious assets below which a brigade-level amphibious operation cannot be carried out. It could be argued that minimum was what was available in the Falklands Operation.

Key Lessons

- Well trained troops and ship's companies trained for inshore maritime operations needed for amphibious operations.
- Need for purpose-built amphibious assets.
- Need for well trained joint staffs at all levels of command from Northwood to Task Group.
- Establish air superiority before carrying out an amphibious operation.
- A LPH is essential if helicopter assets are to be fully exploited in an assault from the sea.

- Commanders must be co-located.
- Good communications to all concerned essential.
- The value of NGS.
- The need for dedicated advance force assets (SBS/SAS) who train with the amphibious and landing forces.

Principles Neglected

- Need to follow laid-down and well understood command structure.
- Need for an in-theatre overall commander.
- Need for a campaign plan.
- Laid-down procedures such as issuing of Initiating Directive ignored.
- Top-down planning.

Further Reading

Clapp, Micheal & Southby-Tailyour, Ewen, *Amphibious Assault Falklands: The Battle of San Carlos Water*, (Leo Cooper, 1996)

Middlebrook, Martin, *The Falklands War 1982*, (Penguin, 2001)

Southby-Tailyour, Ewen, *Reasons in Writing: A Commando's View of the Falklands War*, (Leo Cooper, 1993)

Thompson, Julian, *No Picnic*, (Cassell & Co, 2001)

Biography

Major General Julian Thompson joined the Royal Marines a month after his 18th birthday and served for 34 years, in the Near, Middle and Far East, and the Southern and Northern Regions of Europe and commanded on operations in all ranks from platoon commander to major general. He commanded 40 Commando Royal Marines for two and a half years, and 3 Commando Brigade for two years. The latter period of command included the Falklands War of 1982, in which his brigade carried out the initial landings and fought the majority of the land battles. He is a graduate of the British Army Staff College, and later instructed there. He graduated from the Royal College of Defence Studies in 1980. He has published; *The Lifeblood of War: Logistics in Armed Conflict: The Imperial War Museum Book of Victory in Europe: 1944-45: The Imperial War Museum Book of the War at Sea: The Royal Navy in the Second World War; The Imperial War Museum Book of War Behind Enemy Lines; The Royal Marines: From Sea Soldiers to a Special Force; The Imperial War Museum Book of Modern Warfare (Ed); The Imperial War Museum Book of the War in Burma 1942-45; The Imperial War Museum Book of the War at Sea 1914-18* and *The Victory in Europe Experience.* He regularly appears on the BBC presenting on defence and military matters, for which the documentary team received a BAFTA.

Amphibious Operations in the Gulf War
Operation DESERT SHIELD, 1990-1991

XXXVII

By Lieutenant Colonel H Thomas Hayden USMC (Rtd)

Definition:

US Marine Corps amphibious doctrine in 1990 recognised four types of amphibious operations:

1. **Assaults.** Landings from the sea to make forcible entry onto a hostile shore.

2. **Raids.** Surprise attacks from the sea of limited duration with limited objectives.

3. **Withdrawals.** The removal of friendly forces from a hostile shore.

4. **Demonstrations.** Actions to deceive the enemy using a seaborne show of force. (The Navy and Marine Corps team have developed proficiency in two other amphibious operations: non-combatant evacuation operations (NEO) and sea based humanitarian relief operations (HRO)).

Operation DESERT SHIELD

Following the invasion of Kuwait by Saddam Hussein's Armed Forces on 2 August 1990, in consultation with the government of Saudi Arabia, the President of the United States ordered US forces to deploy to Saudi Arabia, which were led by elements of the 82nd Airborne Division (82nd Abn) and the 7th Marine Expeditionary Brigade (7th MEB). The 7th MEB began deployment to Saudi Arabia on 8 August 1990. The Command Element and initial ground and air units, loaded in USAF C-141 & C-5 aircraft and Marine Corps KC-130 aircraft, air-landed at Dhahran Air Base, Saudi Arabia, on 14 August. Marines would later be off-loaded at Al Jubail Naval Air Base, Saudi Arabia.

The 7th MEB was soon followed by the 1st MEB, from Hawaii with additional MPF shipping. The 4th MEB, from Camp Lejeune had been ordered to embark in amphibious shipping and deploy to the Gulf of Arabia. On 2 September, the I Marine Expeditionary Force (I MEF) assumed operational control of all Marine Corps forces ashore in the Kuwait Theatre of Operation (KTO). On 6 September, 7th MEB and 1st MEB were 'composited' into the 1st Marine Division, and by 6 September, the major subordinate commands of I MEF, 1st MARDIV, 3rd MAW and 1st FSSG, were combat ready. The first amphibious forces to arrive in the Arabia Sea, to join the US Carrier Strike Groups already in the area, were the 13th MEU (SOC) and the five-ship flotilla of Seventh Fleet's Amphibious Ready Group Alpha (ARG Alpha) on 7 September 1990. There were three potential avenues of Iraqi attack into Saudi Arabia from Kuwait. The most likely axis of advance was straight down the coastal highway from Kuwait City all the way to Dharan. A super highway runs north and south, which leads to the industrial and commercial ports of Al Jubail and then on to the industrial complex at Dharan. Two alternate attack routes were further inland.

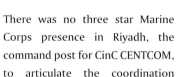

By the first week in September, the Marine forces in-country included more than 30,000 personnel. Offshore, the 4th MEB and 13th MEU(SOC) had 12,737 embarked. At no time during Operation DESERT SHIELD and DESERT STORM did 4th MEB and embarked Marines come under the direct operational control of the I MEF commanding general. However, all planning was done in support of I MEF/Marine Central Command (MARCENT). Forces

afloat came under the Amphibious Task Force (ATF) commander and ultimately the Seventh Fleet/Navy Central Command (NAVCENT).

There was no three star Marine Corps presence in Riyadh, the command post for CinC CENTCOM, to articulate the coordination of Marine forces ashore and amphibious capabilities and their contribution to tactical or operational manoeuvre by CENTCOM forces. The senior Marine in the KTO maintained a dual role as CG I MEF and COMUSMARCENT. The CG I MEF/MARCENT was located at his forward headquarters in Al Jubail and left his Deputy Commander MARCENT (two star), to act as liaison between I MEF/MARCENT and CENTCOM. Not the best of organisational and operational principles. Initially the Navy/Marine team established a joint plan that outlined two amphibious assaults, a series of raids, and an administrative offload. Amphibious assaults were planned to attack behind Iraqi forces that came into Saudi Arabia to interdict Iraqi supply lines or raids that would draw Iraq attention away from their axis of advance. The first line of defence was to protect the industrial complex of Al Jubail. The first of three-scheduled exercises of embarked Marines was called SEA SOLDIER I, with the Omanis, 29 September to 5 October, with both 4th MEB and 13th MEU (SOC). Company D, BLT 1/4, 13th MEU (SOC) conducted a night raid as the final part of the exercise.

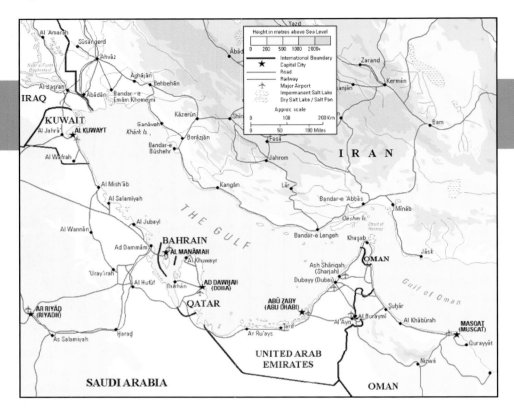

Maritime Interdiction Operations

UN Resolution 661, 5 August 1990, placed a trade embargo on Iraq and the Coalition naval forces formed a Maritime Interdiction Force (MIF). The MIF mission was to challenge, stop, and search Iraqi ships in the Red Sea and the Arabian Sea. The first Maritime Special Purpose Force (MSPF) operations in support of the MIF was with the Iraqi ships *Al Wastti* and *Tadmur* which both refused to slow or allow inspection teams to board. Helicopter insertions were conducted to gain control of the ships.

In another case, 28 October, HMLA-267, AH-1W Sea Cobras, drew Iraqis attention pointing machineguns and rockets at the bridge. While the Iraqis were focused on the gun-ships, a CH-46 Sea Knight from HMM-146 delivered the boarding party.

IMMINENT THUNDER

The first major joint/combined training exercise was called IMMINENT THUNDER. The exercise fully integrated multinational air, ground, and naval forces in a single exercise. The international news media closely watched this exercise, which may have led to later accusations that General Schwarzkopf made them an 'unwilling partner' in what became one of the most successful deceptions in history.

On 13 October, the 5th MEB, Camp Pendleton, California, was officially notified that it would deploy to the Arabian Gulf on PhibGru 3. The mission of the 5th MEB was to be the same as the 4th MEB. However, most thought that both MEBs would be 'composited' into a separate division size landing force. Exercise SEA SOLDIER IV was the last major amphibious exercise in the KTO and was the only time the 4th and 5th MEBs had a chance to exercise together. SEA SOLDIER IV was a rehearsal for an amphibious assault into Kuwait. The world press gave ample coverage to all events.

Operation EASTERN EXIT

While most national civilian leaders and the CENTCOM planners were focused on the KTO, a second regional crisis unfolded in Somalia. The Ambassador requested that the Embassy staff and other international embassy personnel be removed from Mogadishu, Somalia. The BSSG-4 commander was designated the Special MAGTF commander for the NEO. A two-ship amphibious task group departed the Masirah, Oman, area at 2230 Local, 2 January 1991. The first impression was that the NEO would be in a 'permissive' environment, but the Ambassador declared the situation desperate and needed immediate help. Marine CH-53E Sea Stallion helicopters would fly the 900 miles to Mogadishu, conduct the NEO and fly back which called for four aerial refuellings and a flight time of over 16 hours. Upon arrival of the CH-53Es at Mogadishu the Ambassador was reported to have said that when he saw 'Marines' on the side of the first helicopter to land, he knew they would be safe.

The CH-53Es took-off from the Embassy compound at 0700 with 61 civilians aboard, the Marines and SEALs remained behind to organise the Evacuation Coordination Centre (ECC) for the NEO. The return flight was 400 miles with multiple in-flight refuelling. After debriefing the Marine CH-53E flight crews a second CH-53E flight was scheduled to return to Mogadishu. The official report described the decision to scrub the second flight as 'crew fatigue and stabilisation of the situation in Mogadishu.' The facts may have been something else. The CH-46 crew had not

A CH-53E Super Stallion lifts cargo from the underway USS Gunston Hall (LSD44) operating in the Persian Gulf. (USN)

Below: M-60 Battle Tanks driven off a utility landing craft from the amphibious assault ship USS Nassau as 4th MEB conduct a beach assault. (USN)

had their chance at the rescue mission. CH-46s did not have a refuelling probe and had to wait until the Task Force was within range to launch the CH-46s. After the last evacuation by CH-46s the NEO was declared over. The evacuees came from 31 countries and totalled 281 people but the number was raised to 282 when a baby was delivered aboard the Guam.

DESERT STORM

The original plan for Operation DESERT SHIELD was to protect Saudi Arabia and deter Iraq from advancing into the Arabia Peninsula. The President later approved Operation DESERT STORM, to eject Iraq from Kuwait, and the forces were assigned to CENTCOM for this mission. Over 620,000 US forces (94,000 US Marines and 82,000 US Navy) would be in place before the attack. One amphibious assault after another had been on the planning table. One assigned the Marines to land on the heavily defended beaches of Kuwait, another Bubiyan Island, another Faylakah Island, and another Iraq's Al Faw Peninsula.

Coalition intelligence reported that the northern Gulf had been seeded with a mixture of deep-water, near-shore and inshore mines. Also, intelligence estimates reported approximately 550,000 Iraqi troops in southern Iraq or Kuwait, with the remainder of Saddam's armed forces (total believed to be at 1.2 million) to back them up. The Iraqis in Kuwait were reported to have over 200 tanks and 350 artillery pieces. Chemical and biological weapons were highly anticipated. The Centre for Naval Analysis predicted 9,000 to 10,000 Marine casualties if the campaign

lasted more than a week. The amphibious assault initiating directive of 14 January 1991, directed the Marines to 'seize the Ash Shuaybah port, south of Kuwait City, in order to maintain a flow of logistics ashore'. The original I MEF Operations Order 91-0001 envisaged a link-up by I MEF attacking from the south and the amphibious landing on the Kuwaiti coast. Countermine operation needed to ensure a reasonably successful amphibious assault. The US Navy reported that it would take a week to two weeks to have 80 percent assurance of sea mine clearance with no mention of surf zone or beach exits.

After months of unsuccessful diplomatic manoeuvring, President George H. W. Bush directed General Schwarzkopf to commence offensive operations on 16 January. The first Marine Corps action commenced at 0400, 17 January, in a coordinated night air attack against strategic targets in southern Iraq, which was the largest flown by Marines since World War

II. Daily Air Tasking Orders (ATO) from the Joint Forces Air Component Commander (JFACC) coordinated all in-theatre air missions except helicopters. The size of the ATO was immense. The ATO for 17 January ran to over 700 pages. In reality, the 3rd MAW's operations staff had to do some creative scheduling to meet the MARCENT commander's requirements. Nearly all missions flow by Marines after the first week involved tactical targets in the KTO.

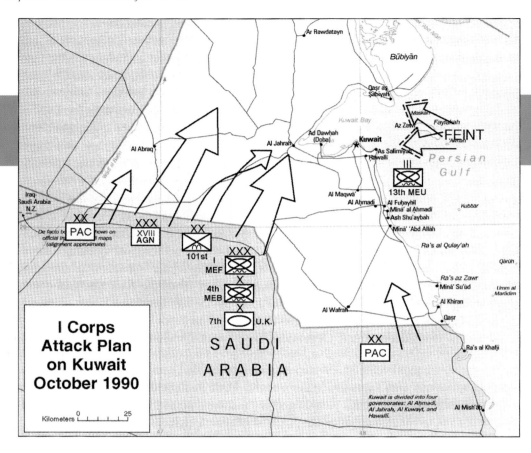

Left: I Corps attack plan on Kuwait 1990. (USMC)

Right: Marines arrive from landing craft from the Nassau. (USN)

The first major ground combat action occurred on 29 January, when Iraqi armoured and mechanised forces attacked into Saudi Arabia at four locations. An Iraqi brigade attacked the coastal city of Al Khafji; however, the main engagement involving Marines was 80 kilometres west. There were three attacks into the MARCENT positions. The primary attack was a brigade-sized force against a general outpost (GOP) for I MEF, Task Force Shepherd, a battalion-sized unit of infantry with light armored vehicles (LAV)s.

The Battle for Al Khafji lasted until 1 February when a Saudi and Qatari force recaptured the city with friendly casualties at 15 KIA and 28 WIA. They captured 642 Iraqi troops, which eliminated

any doubt of the fighting capabilities of the Arab units. Also, on 29 January, the 13th MEU (SOC) conducted Operation DESERT STING, an amphibious raid on the Iraqi occupied Kuwait island of Maradim. Unfortunately, Al Khafji over shadowed the Marine's amphibious operation. Attacks on Iraqi trench lines by Marine air brought enemy soldiers out of their holes with white flags. Marine helicopters were directed to the Iraqi positions and using loud speakers, the enemy troops were told to march south toward Coalition positions.

On 6 February, the Amphibious Task Force commander issued a warning order to begin planning for an amphibious raid on Faylakah Island. The admiral issued an execute order

on 11 February which caused much consternation and misunderstanding at the CENTCOM headquarters. The order was actually, in naval terms, a movement order directing the start of mine clearing operations. General Schwarzkopf and his staff misunderstood the message. A flash message directed a cease and desist. When the fog of war was lifted the admiral was ordered to Riyadh to present a new plan of operation. On 18 February, Amphibious Task Force Operations Order 1-91 was issued for RLT-2 (-) to conduct a simultaneous surface and heliborne assault east of Ras Al Qulayhah, just north of the Kuwait/Saudi border. Unfortunately, an explosion blew a 20-foot hole in the USS *Tripoli* (LPH-10), and later that same morning an Aegis cruiser, a sea bottom 'influence mine' disabled the USS *Princeton*. In less than four hours the Coalition mine clearing operations had become a disaster, effectively halting the Faylakah Island raid and depriving the marines of an amphibious assault ship.

I MEF decided to scrap the link-up plan and opted to move the two Marine divisions to the Kuwait 'elbow,' conduct the breach, capture Al Jaber Air Base in Kuwait, and then attack north to seize the road junctions leading out of Kuwait City. The liberation of Kuwait City was left to Arab Coalition forces. The amphibious assault into Kuwait began to look unnecessary to the CG I MEF scheme of manoeuvre.

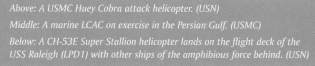

Above: A USMC Huey Cobra attack helicopter. (USN)

Middle: A marine LCAC on exercise in the Persian Gulf. (USMC)

Below: A CH-53E Super Stallion helicopter lands on the flight deck of the USS Raleigh (LPD1) with other ships of the amphibious force behind. (USN)

General Schwarzkopf directed the execution of the ground offensive of Operations DESERT STORM, at 0400, 24 February. The I MEF mission, as described by CENTCOM, was a 'supporting attack' to destroy Iraqi forces in zone and secure key objectives to prevent Iraqi forces from hindering the 'main attack' by the US Army or the coastal attack by Arab forces. I MEF was then to establish blocking positions to stop the retreat of Iraqi forces out of Kuwait. Rain and burning oil fields obscured the vision of the Marines on the ground and in the air.

The 13th MEU(SOC), on 24 February, was tasked to conduct a deception operation in the vicinity of Ash Shuaybah, Kuwait, to hold Iraqi defenders in position. The operation began at 0300, 25 February, and once the helicopters reached their turnaround point, climbed to higher altitude to be illuminated by Iraqi radars, dropped under the enemy radars and returned to their ships. It was all over within an hour. This deception and the total demonstration of the Navy and Marine forces were very effective.

Helicopters from MAG-40 and of HMM-164, 13th MEU (SOC), played a major role in the amphibious demonstration. The helicopters conducted airborne deception operations on G-Day through G+2 and helped to tie up around 40,000 Iraqis in useless defensive positions along the beaches awaiting a surface amphibious assault that never came.

Another deception operation was directed at Bubiyan Island, to distract other Iraqi forces in northern Kuwait. The Iraqis took the bait and the southern end of the island was lit up with radar, flares and anti-aircraft fire. An attack on Faylakah Island actually involved Marine attack AH-1Ns from HMLA-269, with rockets firing at Iraqi positions. Although major combat operations ended on 28 February, there was one more mission for the 13th MEU (SOC). On 1 March, the day after the cease-fire went into effect, the 13th MEU (SOC) was directed to evacuate the remaining Iraqi forces from Kuwaiti islands in the North Arabian Sea. The 5th MEB participated in both the amphibious demonstration and ground operations. RLT-5 came ashore by helicopter lift on G-Day in order to screen the I MEF right flank and protect the extended supply lines. MAG-50 moved ashore and added combat aviation support. BLT 3/1, 5th MEB, engaged Iraqi forces in the Al Wafrah Forest, and then moved north to join 2nd MARDIV.

There had been a number of plans for amphibious assaults, raids and feints from the Kuwaiti/Saudi border to the Iraqi/Iran border. However, the final mission for the Amphibious Task Force was to create a demonstration, a feint, to convince the Iraqis that an amphibious assault was in fact in progress on the Kuwaiti coast. This they achieved most effectively throughout the period of Operations DESERT SHIELD and DESERT STORM, proving the value of an effective Amphibious demonstration.

Above: Barbed wire, mines, and other obstacles along the shoreline during the Iraqi occupation of Kuwait. (USN)

Below: USMC leaflet distributed along the Kuwait coast and at Faylakah Island. (USMC)

Further Reading

JCS Pub 3-07, *Joint Doctrine for Amphibious Operations*, (The Joint Chiefs of Staff, Washington, D.C., November 1986)

Alexander, Joseph H. and Bartlett, Merrill L., *SEA SOLDIERS in the Cold War: Amphibious Warfare 1945-1991*, (Naval Institute Press, Annapolis, MD, 1995)

U.S. Marines in the Persian Gulf, 1990-1999, 9 Volumes. (Washington, DC, History and Museum Division, Washington, D.C., 1992-1999). Anthology and Annotated Bibliography, 1992.

Cordesman, Anthony H. and Wagner, Abraham R., *The Lessons of Modern War Volume IV: The Gulf War,* (Boulder, Colorado: Westview Press, 1996)

Finlan, Alastair, *The Gulf War 1991,* (Oxford: Osprey, 2003)

Pokrant, Marvin, *Desert Shield at Sea: What the Navy Really Did,* (Westport, Connecticut: Greenwood Press, 1999)

Biography

Lieutenant Colonel H Thomas Hayden recently concluded over 35 years of service, which included working in the Agency for International Development, the US Marine Corps, and the Pentagon. His specialties are Intelligence, Counterinsurgency Operations, Counter-terrorism, and Joint Concepts Development and Experimentation. His Marine Corps assignments have included command of two separate battalions; working as a Staff Officer in the 4th Marine Division; Branch Head at the Headquarters US Marine Corps and later Special Assistant to the Assistant Secretary of Defense for Special Operations and Low Intensity Conflict; and Senior Program Analysts with the Joint Staff at the Pentagon. He spent two years in Southeast Asia (1967-1969), and other assignments including, Japan & Okinawa, Europe, Central America, Saudi Arabia and Kuwait, Somalia, Singapore, Philippines, and Colombia. He has an MBA (Pepperdine) and an MA in International Relations (University of Southern California). He has written two books, *Shadow War: Special Operations and Low Intensive Conflict* (Pacific Aero Press, 1991) and the popular *Warfighting: Maneuver Warfare in the U.S. Marine Corps* (Greenhill Books, 1995).

Iraq
Operation TELIC, March 2003

Al Faw Landings - Post-Modern Amphibious Operations?

By Brigadier Jeremy Robbins MBE RM

'Although not doctrinally set piece, this was an amphibious operation'[1]

'The enemy ... failed largely because of his inability to prosecute the 'all arms battle'. I am convinced that this was in no small part attributable to the surprise engendered by the speed and violence of our assault.'[2]

On superficial examination the operations of 3 Commando Brigade Royal Marines from March to May 2003 during Operation TELIC, the UK contribution to Operation IRAQI FREEDOM (OIF), may appear to be a poor example for a case study of amphibious assault in relation to manoeuvre warfare. They were of course only a small part in the combat phase of an overall operation that was predominantly land/air and U.S. dominated; and at a military strategic and operational level the combat phase of OIF was a striking illustration of the operational success that can accrue from the manoeuvrist approach - a fact in danger of being overshadowed by subsequent hostilities. However, the Brigade's tactical operations eschewed many of the long held principles and tenets of amphibious operations, enshrined in such tomes as Allied Tactical Publication 8 (Amphibious Operations) and the UK Approach to Amphibious Operations. Much of the Brigade mounted by air and launched operations from an established land base. Little of the amphibious Command

and Control model applied, with the Brigade Headquarters established ashore prior to operations, already chopped to the Land Component Commander, whilst the Amphibious Task Group commander was afloat embarked in HMS *Ark Royal*. There was no Amphibious Objective Area (AOA) established to provide unity of Command and Control across what was the most complex area of Joint battlespace, the juxtaposition of Land, Maritime, and Special Operations Components, overflown by major Air Component air corridors. Finally, operations could perhaps best be described as land operations **supported** rather than **mounted** from the sea.

Furthermore, many of the principles of the manoeuvrist approach also appeared to be foregone. At a strategic level the build up towards operations was hardly a surprise to the Saddam regime. Coalition operational and tactical objectives were easily identifiable by the Iraqis, with few options available for an indirect approach. Impossible to disguise, the generation and deployment of the UK Amphibious Task Group was clearly reported in the media, with surprisingly informed and accurate speculation on their likely tactical employment options. Finally geography, with a very short Iraqi coastline bounded by the border with Iran and the Shatt Al Arab to the East, and the border with Kuwait and the Khawr Abd Allah to the West (see overleaf), limited amphibious opportunities to the Al Faw peninsula.

And yet, as the quotations at the head of this chapter indicate, this case study will illustrate that at the tactical level the Al Faw operations were both amphibious and manoeuvrist, linked to - but not slavishly following - the doctrinal models for both. Furthermore, they followed a recent pattern of U.S. and UK

(Crown Copyright)

(and other national) operations using amphibious forces, which have been conducted across the operational spectrum, from Humanitarian through Peace Support to Warfighting operations[3]. Based upon amphibious forces and procedures, they have established a new model - one of broad extemporisation, far removed from the classic amphibious model examples of the Pacific Islands campaign, or even the Falklands War. They can best be characterised as **post-modern amphibious operations**, selectively applying amphibious procedures to the particular circumstances and task. Such use of amphibious forces, with their inherent ability to transition in-stride from deployment to sustained tactical operations achieving land effect, typifies and represents the cutting edge of wider Maritime and Joint expeditionary[4] capability.

---

[1] Op TELIC - 3 Cdo Bde RM Post Operational Report.

[2] Overview by Commander 3 Cdo Bde RM to Op TELIC - 3 Commando Brigade's Desert War.

[3] Other most recent examples include: Op TELLAR (HMS OCEAN & 45 Commando in Honduras/Nicaragua 1999), Ops PALLISER & SILKMAN (HMS OCEAN & 42 Commando in Sierra Leone 2000), Op RHINO (USMC Task Force 58 deployment from Indian Ocean into Afghanistan 2001/02), Op VERITAS & DAMIEN (HMS ILLUSTRIOUS & 40 Commando in Afghanistan 2001/02) and Op LICORNE (French deployment in Ivory Coast 2002/3).

[4] 'forces projected from the home base capable of sustained operations' Joint Warfare Publication 0-01.1.

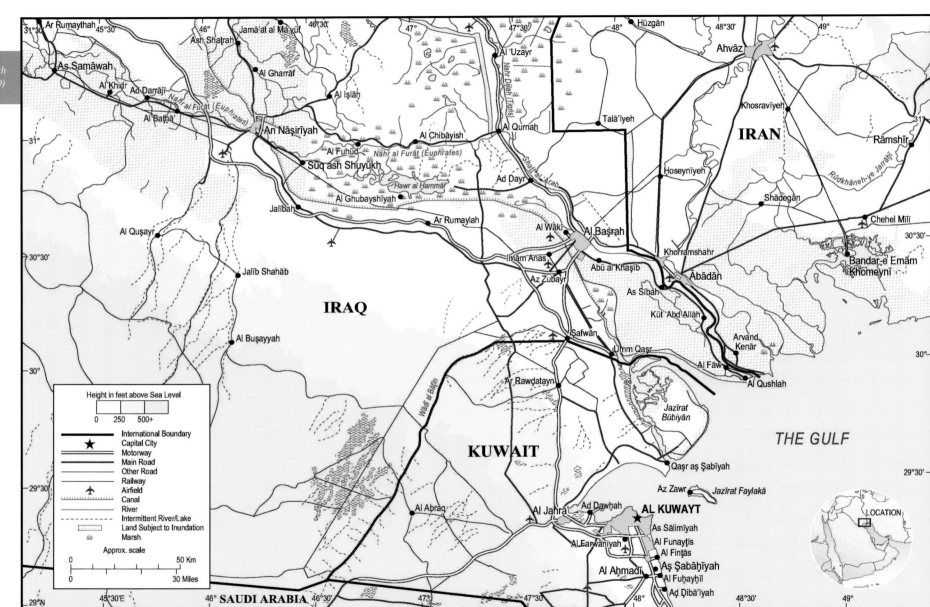

Height in feet above Sea Level

| 0 | 250 | 500+ |

	International Boundary
★	Capital City
	Motorway
	Main Road
	Other Road
	Railway
✈	Airfield
	Canal
	River
	Intermittent River/Lake
	Land Subject to Inundation
	Marsh

Approx. scale

| 0 | | | | | 50 Km |
| 0 | | | | 30 Miles |

CFJFC   Coalition Forces Joint Force Commander
CF   Coalition Forces
LCC   Land Component Commander
SOCC   Special Operations Component Commander
MCC   Maritime Component Commander
ACC   Air Component Commander
CTG   Carrier Task Group
MEF   Marine Expeditionary Force
OPCON   Operational Control
AA   Air Assault
ANGLICO Air, Naval and Gunfire Liaison Companies

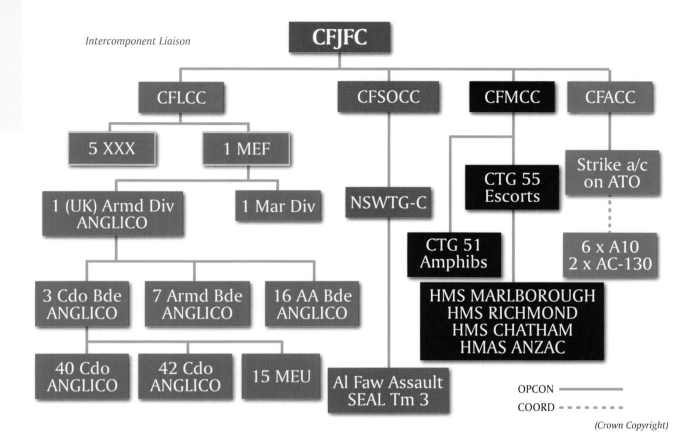

Intercomponent Liaison

OPCON ————
COORD ━ ━ ━ ━

(Crown Copyright)

Op TELIC - The Background To Amphibious Operations

Contingency planning for what became the Al Faw operation began as far back as September 2002. The initial Landing Force task was to support maritime operations clearing the waterway of the Khawr Abd Allah (KAA) and access to Iraq's only deep-water port at Umm Qasr, a major route for grain import in the UN Oil for Food programme. The Landing Force task was to provide flank protection to Mine Countermeasure (MM) vessels operating in the constrained waterway, and planning was based upon a single Commando mounted from an Amphibious Task Group, deconflicted from the build up of land forces in Kuwait (at this stage these were U.S. forces only, as UK land plans were based upon operations in Northern Iraq). However, increasing realisation that securing the Al Faw oil infrastructure was a key strategic objective, and estimates on enemy strength, were to change the plan and priorities.

Mindful of the environmental damage caused in the 1991 Gulf War by destruction of oil wells, and with increasing realisation of the need to preserve the oil infrastructure intact as the basis for reconstruction of the Iraqi economy, oil installations became strategic high priority objectives. The Manifold and Metering Station near the base of the Al Faw peninsula, and the 48 inch pipelines which ran out to Gas Oil platforms 25 miles out to sea, became objectives for the U.S. Navy Special Warfare Group SEALs, supported by the Landing Force. In addition estimates

of enemy force levels were increasing and supported the requirement for increased force levels, leading to the addition of a further Commando and Brigade Troops, with the full Brigade Headquarters in command. Finally, the requirement to near simultaneously secure the Port of Umm Qasr saw the attachment of the USMC 15 Marine Expeditionary Unit (MEU) under command of 3 Commando Brigade, and by mid-December the task organisation was fixed as shown above.

At this stage of planning 3 Commando Brigade represented the only UK land forces operating in Southern Iraq, and plans were

developed under the direct command of 1st Marine Expeditionary Force (I MEF), a 3 Star Corps equivalent command. Crucially these covered air and fires support and coordination, copying USMC Fires best practice and incorporating early attachments from the USMC 1st ANGLICO[5]. Planning also involved intimate coordination with the Navy Special Warfare Group 2 (NAVSPECWARGRU2) for the seizure of the oil installations. In early January 2003 UK Land plans switched from Northern Iraq, and 1 (UK) Armoured Division were allocated to the South under command of I MEF, with 3 Commando Brigade now one of 3 brigades subordinate to the UK Division. Nevertheless, the direct links to I MEF and

---

[5]The USMC are the acknowledged leaders in close all arms fires integration with ground manoeuvre, and provide access to these fires through their Air, Naval and Gunfire Liaison Companies.

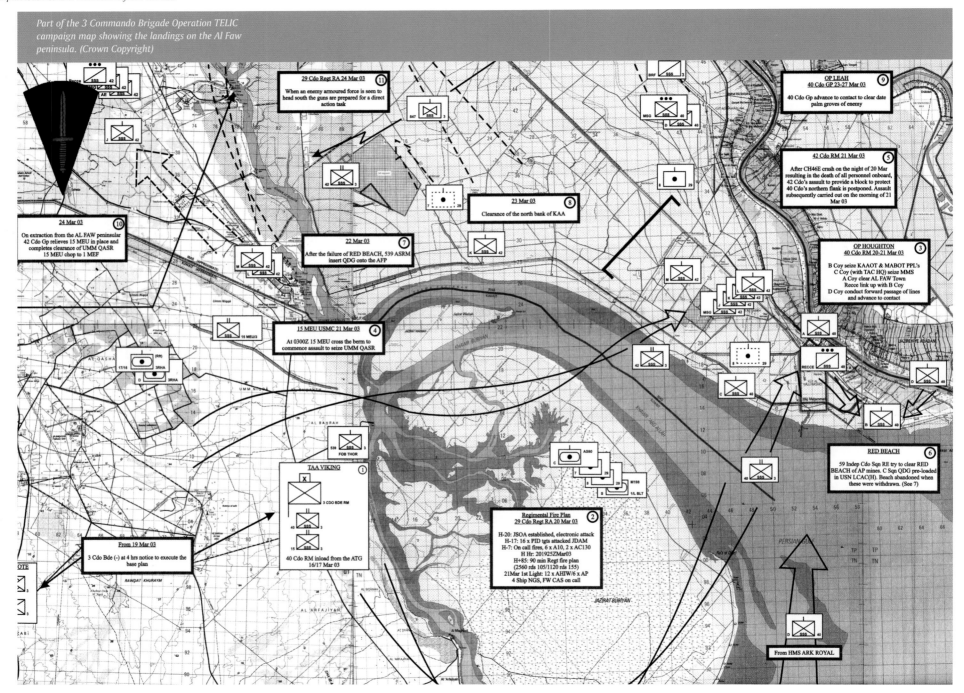

Part of the 3 Commando Brigade Operation TELIC campaign map showing the landings on the Al Faw peninsula. (Crown Copyright)

29 Cdo Regt RA 24 Mar 03 (11)

When an enemy armoured force is seen to head south the guns are prepared for a direct action task

OP LEAH (9)
40 Cdo GP 23-27 Mar 03

40 Cdo Gp advance to contact to clear date palm groves of enemy

42 Cdo RM 21 Mar 03 (5)

After CH46E crash on the night of 20 Mar resulting in the death of all personnel onboard, 42 Cdo's assault to provide a block to protect 40 Cdo's northern flank is postponed. Assault subsequently carried out on the morning of 21 Mar 03

23 Mar 03 (8)

Clearance of the north bank of KAA

OP HOUGHTON (3)
40 Cdo RM 20-21 Mar 03

B Coy seize KAAOT & MABOT PPL's
C Coy (with TAC HQ) seize MMS
A Coy clear AL FAW Town
Recce link up with B Coy
D Coy conduct forward passage of lines and advance to contact

24 Mar 03 (10)

On extraction from the AL FAW peninsular 42 Cdo Gp relieves 15 MEU in place and completes clearance of UMM QASR
15 MEU chop to 1 MEF

22 Mar 03 (7)

After the failure of RED BEACH, 539 ASRM insert QDG onto the AFP

15 MEU USMC 21 Mar 03 (4)

At 0300Z 15 MEU cross the berm to commence assault to seize UMM QASR

RED BEACH (6)

59 Indep Cdo Sqn RE try to clear RED BEACH of AP mines. C Sqn QDG pre-loaded in USN LCAC(H). Beach abandoned when these were withdrawn. (See 7)

TAA VIKING (1)

3 CDO BDE RM

40 Cdo RM inload from the ATG
16/17 Mar 03

From 19 Mar 03

3 Cdo Bde (-) at 4 hrs notice to execute the base plan

Regimental Fire Plan (2)
29 Cdo Regt RA 20 Mar 03

H-20: JSOA established, electronic attack
H-17: 16 x PID tgts attacked JDAM
H-7: On call fires, 6 x A10, 2 x AC130
H Hr: 201925ZMar03
H+85: 90 min Regt fire plan (2560 rds 105/1120 rds 155)
21Mar 1st Light: 12 x AH1W/6 x AP
4 Ship NGS, FW CAS on call

From HMS ARK ROYAL

SSS	Royal Marines Commando
CLR	Commando Logistic Regiment
CHF	Commando Helicopter Force
BRF	Brigade Recce Force
MEU	Marine Expeditionary Unit
DWR	Duke of Wellington's Regiment
RSDG	Royal Scots Dragoon Guards
QDG	Queen's Dragoon Guards
RTR	Royal Tank Regiment
EOD	Explosive Ordnance Disposal

Other Abbreviations appear in the Glossary

3 Cdo Bde RM ORBAT
(Crown Copyright)

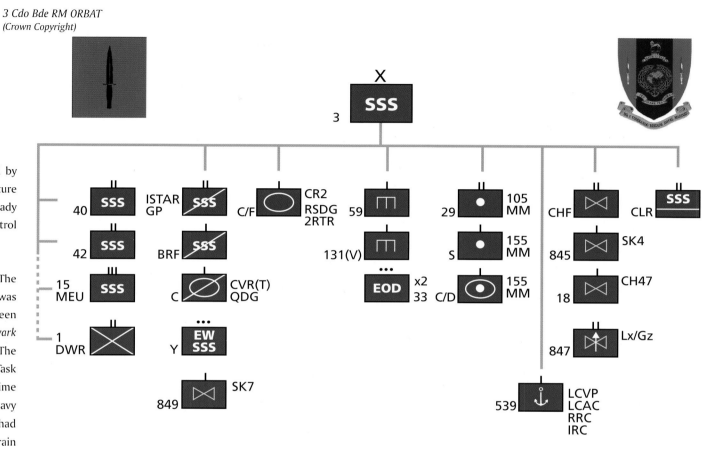

NAVSPECWARGRU2 were retained and actively encouraged by the Division, recognising the complex cross component nature of the Al Faw operations and the extensive planning already completed. A summary of the complex Command and Control architecture is shown.

Maritime planning had been developed in parallel. The availability of UK amphibious shipping in Autumn 2002 was at a nadir – the LPDs[6] HMS *Fearless* and *Intrepid* had both been decommissioned, their replacements HMS *Albion* and *Bulwark* were yet to enter service, and HMS *Ocean* was in refit. The decision was therefore taken to centre the Amphibious Task Group on HMS *Ark Royal*, reconfigured in the LPH[7] role. Maritime Plans were again developed in close liaison with the U.S. Navy and with the UK Maritime Component Commander, who had been collocated with the U.S. Commander 5th FLEET in Bahrain since November 2001 as part of the wider Operation VERITAS War on Terrorism[8]. U.S. amphibious shipping was to be used primarily as transports, offloading most embarked capability and support into Kuwait, and then used in a 'lily pad' role for air and aviation. U.S. maritime Task Forces were functionally rather than task[9] organised, and this dictated a wide web of liaison and coordination to bring task orientated groups together. The UK Amphibious Task Group had its own escorts to act as 'baby sitters' and to provide Naval Fires Support, but

did not command the Mine Counter Measure group. Critically the U.S. Land and Maritime Component Commanders had also decided that the high water mark would be the Inter-Component boundary, making it impossible to define the usual maritime/land/air battlespace of an Amphibious Objective Area, under the control of the Amphibious commander. Given the complexity of operations involving all Components this was an understandable decision, but further complicated the already wide web of liaison and co-ordination required.

Conduct Of Operations

On 12 January 2003 the Brigade Headquarters advance party flew to Kuwait. In the UK the Amphibious Task Group, centred on HMS *Ark Royal* and HMS *Ocean* (which had been rushed out of her refit), assembled and embarked 40 Commando, together with most of the Brigade's equipment and logistic support, sailing under the thinly disguised cover of a previously planned Naval Task Group deployment. By the end of January the Brigade Headquarters main body had flown to Kuwait, closely followed

[6]Landing Platform Docks.

[7]The UK Aircraft Carrier ASW (CVS) can be re-roled as a Landing Platform Helicopter, a role in which HMS ILLUSTRIOUS was employed during Op VERITAS and HMS ARK ROYAL during Op TELIC.

[8]The US Commander 5th FLEET was the Coalition Forces Maritime Component Commander (CFMCC). The collocated UK 2* Maritime Commander was the Deputy CFMCC, the UK Maritime Component Commander for Ops ORACLE and VERITAS, and the UK Maritime Contingent Commmander for Op TELIC.

[9]Organised according to functional groupings e.g. MMs, escorts, amphibious ships, rather than as mission orientated task groups.

Joint operations in action: an RAF Chinook in close support at sea, moving in the Light Guns of 29 Commando Regiment, Royal Artillery. (Crown Copyright)

by 42 Commando, whilst the Amphibious Task Group transited the Mediterranean, conducting amphibious training (a WADER package) in Cyprus and further air group training in UAE, arriving in the North Arabian Gulf (or NAG) by 15 February to meet the required initial operating capability target of 18 February. The next month was spent in continued refinement and finalisation of operational plans, training and operational rehearsals, and build up of logistic capability. Intensive surveillance effort was made to establish enemy positions and intentions, tapping wherever possible into operational and strategic resources. Finally the period allowed a succession of briefings, ROC[10] drills and commander's conferences, including all important tie up between the Commander of the Brigade, Brigadier Jim Dutton, and the Commander Amphibious Task Group, Commodore Jamie Miller, as well as with the UK Maritime Contingent Commander.

On 19 March the Brigade was brought to 4 hours notice to move. After days of bad weather, with low cloud and sand storms, the weather and light conditions were marginal. However, the strategic imperative to seize the oil infrastructure as part of the wider campaign synchronisation meant there was no flexibility in the decision to assault. H Hour was set at 2200 hours local on 20 March. A short but intense bombardment hit known enemy positions. Launching from assembly area VIKING in Kuwait and from HMS *Ark Royal*, 40 Commando conducted a classic night helicopter commando opposed assault onto the Al Faw, the first conventional force ground action of the war

(and the first UK opposed helicopter assault since Suez in 1956, see Chapter XXXIII). Positions continued to be engaged by fires from naval gunfire, artillery, aviation and air, and despite a heavier than expected enemy presence, positions were quickly overrun. Together, U.S. Navy SEALs and 40 Commando had seized all 3 strategic objectives intact, despite enemy preparations for demolition, killing over 30 enemy and taking some 230 prisoners for no loss.

Nevertheless, the Brigade had a tenuous foothold on the Al Faw. The best part of an Iraqi Division and Corps HQ was known to be based in and around Basrah and it was essential to ensure that no counter attack could be mounted. A follow on aviation assault by 42 Commando was planned to follow 40 Commando by an hour, to land just to the North on the Al Faw, destroy an enemy artillery battery which threatened the oil infrastructure, and secure 40 Commando's flank. Landing sites were prepared by heavy bombardment from UK and U.S. artillery and naval gunfire from two British and one Australian ship. In deteriorating conditions the lead assault elements of

42 Commando were just launching from assembly area COYOTE when a returning USMC CH46 helicopter, carrying the HQ of the Brigade Recce Force, crashed, tragically killing all on board. The insertion of 42 Commando by U.S. helicopters was aborted, whilst the Brigade HQ rapidly re-planned a dawn insertion using UK Chinooks.

The landings took place 6 hours late, onto insecure and unprepared landing sites, some of them kilometres away from those previously planned. The Commando almost immediately encountered small pockets of enemy putting up stiff but uncoordinated and ineffective resistance, which was rapidly overcome, overwhelming the enemy with artillery and Close Air Support, and determined infantry action.

---

[10]US term - rehearsal of concept.

Almost simultaneously with 42 Commando's assault, in the early hours of the morning of 21 March, 15 MEU launched aviation and ground assault operations to seize the new port at Umm Qasr, meeting some hard but localised resistance from forces bypassed by the rapid advance to the West of the U.S. 1st Marine Division and the UK 7th Armoured Brigade. By the evening of 21 March the Brigade had established a significant footprint on the Al Faw and secured initial objectives, including early coalition strategic objectives, intact.

It is not the subject of this chapter to detail 3 Commando Brigade's subsequent operations. However, in outline 15 MEU was chopped back to I MEF command on 25 March, and the Brigade subsequently advanced North. 40 Commando, clearing up the Al Faw peninsula through the date groves banking the Shatt Al Arab, were involved in a series of engagements, culminating in the 2 day battle for Abu Al Khasib (Operation JAMES) on the South East approaches to Basrah 30/31 March, which helped precipitate the fall of the City. 42 Commando cleared and secured Umm Qasr, and provided flank security to the Maritime mine clearance operations in the Khawr Abd Allah, culminating in the high profile arrival of the LSL *Sir Galahad* in Umm Qasr on 28 March. On 6 April 42 Commando seized the Basrah Presidential Palace, and the Brigade subsequently prepared to reconfigure in both posture and location, including attachment of 1st Battalion Duke of Wellington's Regiment, securing the Rumaylah oilfields and transitioning from a warfighting to a Peace Support footing.

Amphibious Or Not?

Although D Company 40 Commando was launched from HMS *Ark Royal*, the decision was made not to launch the majority of the assault waves from the amphibious shipping. A continuing coastal radar and mine threat meant that the ships had to operate some way offshore. Together with limited deck helicopter spot space it was realised that a greater simultaneous lift, and a higher tempo in turnaround, could be achieved launching helicopter operations from tactical assembly areas in Kuwait closer to the objectives.

Realising the dependence on helicopters, both to insert and then sustain the force, it had also been intended to open a beach - RED Beach - close to the Manifold and Metering Station. Restricted by shallow beach gradient to the use of hovercraft, U.S. Navy heavy lift LCAC(H)[11] were to carry the much needed Scimitar light armoured reconnaissance vehicles of the Queen's

Dragoon Guards (QDG) to land on the Al Faw peninsula. Unfortunately, despite sterling efforts by Royal Engineers and mine clearance divers to clear the beach, the threat of remaining anti-personnel mines was deemed too great and the U.S. LCAC were withdrawn. The QDG unloaded from USS *Rushmore* back into Kuwait and crossed onto the Al Faw a day later to take up screening positions on the exposed salt marshes to the South of Basrah. Notwithstanding the above, the operations would not have been possible without being mounted, and relying on support, from the Amphibious Task Group. They provided a base for 40 Commando until 48 hours before the assault, and for the majority of their vehicles and stores. They provided basing and maintenance facilities for Seaking, Lynx and Gazelle helicopters, from where they achieved significantly greater availability than those that were ground based. Furthermore, the established amphibious Command and Control procedures following a landing, which link the Brigade Commander and his headquarters

---

[11] Landing Craft Air Cushion (Heavy).

Subsequent operations in the suburbs of Basra: A map showing the 42 Commando area of operations near the Basra Palace. (Capt. T D O'Keefe RM)

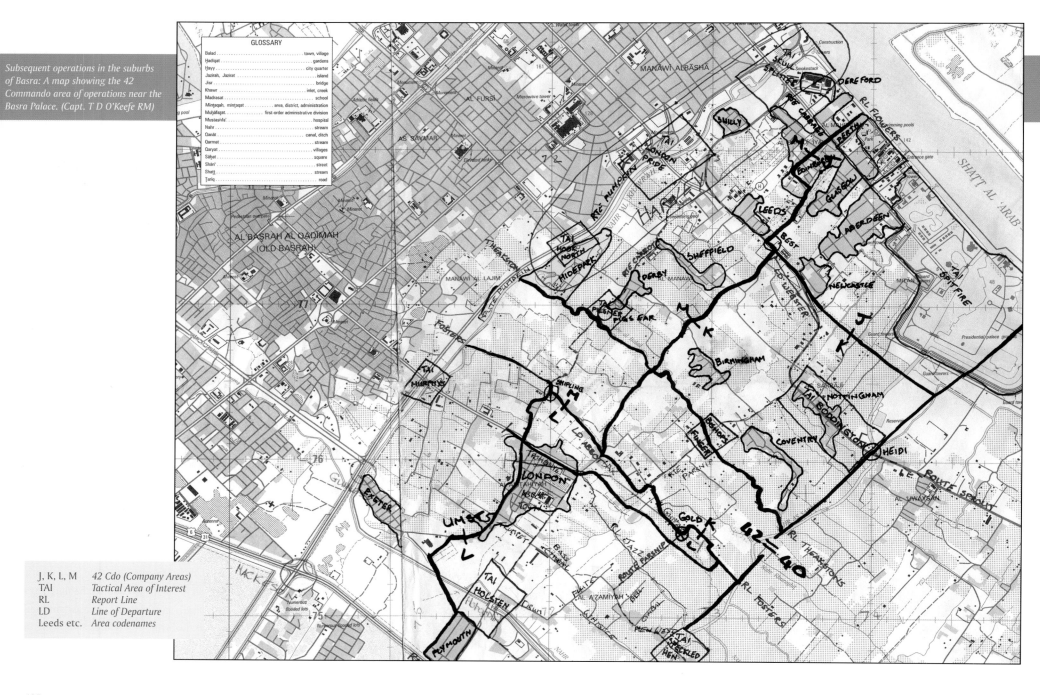

J, K, L, M	42 Cdo (Company Areas)
TAI	Tactical Area of Interest
RL	Report Line
LD	Line of Departure
Leeds etc.	Area codenames

HMS Ocean, photographed in the Arabian sea, with an LCVP from 9 Assault Squadron Royal Marines. (Crown Copyright)

amphibious operations, using further illustrative examples from Operation TELIC. These principles, tenets and considerations are shown below, along with their national origin, and have been effectively grouped under the UK Functions in Combat (Information, Command & Control, Firepower, Protection, Sustainment and Manoeuvre).

INFORMATION -
Sound Intelligence (US/UK)

It is as much a truism today as it was in the time of Wellington that the ability to see 'what lies on the other side of the hill' is the starting point for successful operations. Without intelligence and the intelligence cycle a Commander is fighting blind and has little ability to fight any, let alone a manoeuvrist battle. Prior to operations in Iraq a range of stand-off ISTAR[12] technology was accessed. During operations the eventual ability to find the enemy was achieved by a combination of manned reconnaissance and stand off sensors. No one sensor or system proved decisive, rather it was a web of multi-spectral sensors, ranging from satellite to aircraft to electronic sensor to human that provided what approximated to a consolidated picture, and visual reconnaissance and surveillance deployed in depth still proved better at supporting the close battle. The 3 Commando Brigade ISTAR Group concept, directing and coordinating organic assets, and tapping into other available operational and strategic sensors and sources, proved to be most effective, and cued the Command and Strike functions. As an example, on one occasion 42 Commando received fire from Iraqi Type 59 artillery; weapon

the operations would not have been possible without being mounted, and relying on support, from the Amphibious Task Group

ashore with the Commander Amphibious Task Group (COMATG) afloat, were critical. Through them Fires Support, including naval gunfire which had the range and trajectory to reach the East Al Faw, were coordinated. Through them coordination was achieved with the MM mine clearance operations being conducted in the Khawr Abd Allah approaches to Umm Qasr. Through them Seaking 7 with its Searchwater radar were tasked to conduct ground surveillance tasks. Through them continued helicopter

support was coordinated, and logistic and medical support provided. Finally, but most importantly for UK Joint operations, afloat stocks, initially configured to support 3 Commando Brigade alone, sustained much of 1 (UK) Armoured Division and the wider UK Joint Force in Kuwait in some critical areas, including ammunition and NBC stores. This was a testament to the value of the logistic sea base.

Were The Al Faw Operations Manoeuvrist?

The remainder of this chapter will discuss the Al Faw operations in relation to selected principles and tenets of manoeuvre warfare, principles of war, and U.S. and UK considerations for

---

[12]Intelligence, Surveillance and Target Acquisition.

No one sensor or system proved decisive, rather it was a web of multi-spectral sensors

locating radar identified the firing point; maritime airborne surveillance from *Ark Royal* tracked their hasty withdrawal; PHOENIX unmanned aerial vehicle tracked them to a secondary position; the Strike cell coordinated Air Interdiction to destroy them; and PHOENIX provided the battle damage assessment. However, notwithstanding the technology available, there were still significant gaps in coverage and fidelity. In particular the processing of raw information to provide timely, concise and relevant intelligence, and how it is passed to or made available at the point of need, remains a challenge.

COMMAND & CONTROL - Cooperation (UK); Unity of Effort & Operational Coherence (US/UK); Command and Staffs same locality (US); Navy and Land Force Integration (US)

As already described, the Al Faw was probably the most complex area of battlespace of the War, astride three Components, with the fourth overhead. Amphibious doctrine addresses this dilemma by designating an Amphibious Objective Area (AOA), which defines 3 dimensional maritime, land and airspace within which the Amphibious Task Force Commander coordinates all activity. Given the strategic importance and variety of different Component objectives in this one area, it is understandable

that coordination was not delegated below Component level[13]. However, this created a plethora of coordination challenges. Firstly it demanded overall campaign synchronisation between strategic objectives: was security of the oil infrastructure more important than strategic air strikes? This decision rested at Capital and CENTCOM[14] level, and was only resolved in the hours before operations commenced. There was a concomitant requirement for a wide web of exchange and liaison officers, with appropriate communications, to ensure inter-component and lower level coordination. For the initial U.S. Navy SEAL and 40 Commando operation this was achieved by collocating the HQs

of NAVSPECWARGRU2 and 3 Commando Brigade. In some cases there was a breakdown in effective coordination, for example in plans for Umm Qasr, where a plethora of organisations were involved once opened for humanitarian operations; still within the Brigade area of operations, it fell to the Deputy Commander to coordinate and pull together the efforts of those with different and often competing priorities.

Finally, the traditional collocation of Amphibious and Landing Force Commanders was broken from early January, with the forward deployment to Kuwait of HQ 3 Commando Brigade and

---

[13]By contrast a Component level Joint Special Operations Area (JSOA) was established over the Al Faw for the first 40 minutes of the operation.
[14]US Central Command, commanded by Gen Tommy Franks USA, the overall Joint Force Coalition Commander.

42 Commando operating in the Al Faw and Umm Qasr. (Crown Copyright)

the sailing of the Amphibious Task Group. In order to provide essential linkage between the two, and ensure congruence in land and supporting amphibious plans and operations, the Deputy Commander 3 Commando Brigade and a small staff were embarked alongside Commodore Jamie Miller in HMS *Ark Royal* throughout the deployment and initial operations. Similarly the traditional primacy of the Amphibious Commander was also broken, and the more flexible supporting/supported relationship adopted, in which the Landing Force Commander was in effect the supported commander throughout, a model adopted in recent U.S. Operations[15].

attacking Iraqi Command and Control was at the centre of Coalition strategy

Conversely, attacking Iraqi Command and Control was at the centre of Coalition strategy. At the Operational level a combination of Information Operations and air strikes as part of Op SOUTHERN WATCH progressively attacked the Iraqi command chain and communication nodes prior to 19 March. Once tactical operations started it was clear that whilst there were some pockets of determined resistance that led to sustained and heavy engagements, the enemy lacked 'the tactical competence and effective command and control to offer an effective, coordinated defence'[16].

FIREPOWER - Supporting Arms/ Fires/NGS (US/UK)

The application and concentration of fires, including artillery, aviation, air and naval gunfire support, was the determining factor in both physical destruction of the enemy, and just as significantly in destroying his will to fight. It was also a most effective means by which to achieve force protection. Here, dedicated and timely support was critical, contributing to rapid shock effect and maintaining tempo and momentum (through speed and weight of fire) with which the enemy was unable to cope. As described above, the application of Fires was closely coordinated with and cued by the ISTAR Group. Direct fire and in particular Crew Served Weapons (CSW) were 'central to the success of the operation. Crucially, the firepower of CSW ensured overmatch and they were invariably the weapons of choice when engaging the enemy'[17] and snipers also provided considerable force multiplication. For reasons discussed earlier, armoured reconnaissance and armour were not used in the initial assault, but were of great significance in the subsequent Brigade land battle where, despite disparity in mobility, they were integrated

most successfully into Commando Group operations, and proved their utility even in small numbers. Throughout, other non-kinetic effects were considered and balanced alongside physical attack, in particular in the later transition to a peace support posture.

PROTECTION - Sea Control/Air Superiority/Security (UK)

Force Protection is an ever present command imperative, balanced against affordable risk, and it is perhaps surprising that it does not appear in any guise in the top level U.S. Amphibious principles. There was a presumption of both Sea Control and Air Superiority in early planning for Op TELIC, both of which were to be found

[15]The Op RHINO USMC deployment from the Indian Ocean into Afghanistan was commanded by a USMC 1* TF Comd.
[16]Overview by Commander 3 Cdo Bde RM to Op TELIC - 3 Commando Brigade's Desert War.
[17]Op TELIC - 3 Cdo Bde RM Post Operational Report.

the mobility offered by helicopter aviation was key

less certain in practice, and both primarily from low cost or old technology threats that were almost asymmetric in effect. At sea the low cost/low technology mine threat was a constant concern. The Tanker War experiences of the Iran/Iraq War and the damage to the USS *Samuel B Roberts* in April 1988 from Iranian mine laying had highlighted superpower vulnerability in constrained Gulf waters. Captured Iraqi mine laying vessels proved this was a well founded concern, and there had been the potential for similar disruption in the NAG, which could have seriously affected the flow of shipping, forces and their support into Kuwait. Similarly, whilst the threat from ballistic missile attack was well covered by anti-missile Patriot, the old technology Iraqi anti-ship Seersucker missile, fired without guidance much as a WWII doodlebug, presented a threat to land as well as maritime forces, and also to the Kuwaiti population.

Ironically there is a strong parallel between the use of such low cost/high impact asymmetric attack and manoeuvrist thinking - both are based upon identifying vulnerability and offer the opportunity for disproportionate results. Here there is a

reminder that the enemy may also embrace the manoeuvrist approach, and attempt to do unto you as you intend to do unto him.

SUSTAINABILITY - Logistics (UK/US)

Again it is a truism that logistics are *The Lifeblood of War* (the title of a book by the author of an earlier chapter, and the commander and architect of success in the Falklands War, Major General Julian Thompson, see Chapter XXXVI).[18] The Amphibious Task Group deployed with afloat stocks to support 3 Commando Brigade, but as already described sea based logistics proved essential not just to 3 Commando Brigade, but to the whole UK Joint effort, providing the only timely source of some critical operational stocks without which operational readiness deadlines would not have been met. As with the Brigade combat elements, much of the combat service support was offloaded into Kuwait prior to operations, although key areas continued to be supported from the sea base, including medical support and aviation. Whilst Forward Operating Bases (FOBs) were established ashore, ship based aviation support and maintenance achieved significantly greater availability than those that were ground based. On a more general level it was the sea line of communication, enabled by maritime force protection, that allowed the deployment of a further 60 commercially chartered ships to deploy the bulk of the UK Joint force.

MANOEUVRE – Generating Tempo/ Surprise & Boldness (UK/US)

In UK doctrine there is a danger of muddling manoeuvre, as in the manoeuvrist approach, with tactical manoeuvre - the combination of fires and movement, although there is a recognised overlap. The ability to apply fires has already been discussed, but it is allying those fires to rapid and bold movement that was particularly significant in the initial Al Faw assault and subsequent operations. Here the mobility offered by helicopter aviation was key. Whilst there can have been little Iraqi surprise at the strategic and operational levels about the imminence of the coalition attack, at the tactical level on the Al Faw surprise was achieved through a combination of the speed enabled by aviation (manoeuvre) and the violence (fires) of the assault once launched. It was this that dislocated the enemy, and led to their generally uncoordinated resistance. Notwithstanding the success of aviation helicopter support, subsequent operations highlighted some of the frontline mobility shortfalls within the brigade, many of which will be redressed with the introduction of VIKING protected mobility. Finally, it is left to the reader to assess whether the following selected attributes of the UK manoeuvrist approach apply in the above case study.

- Attacking cohesion/command and will to fight.
- Strength against vulnerability.
- Shock action and Surprise.
- Momentum (speed and weight) and tempo.

---

[18]The Lifeblood of War - Logistics in Armed Conflict, Julian Thompson, Brasseys, 91.

*Such a departure from doctrinal teaching
is entirely in keeping with the 'application
of manoeuvrist thinking to warfighting
... seeking originality combined with a
ruthless determination to succeed'*

CONCLUSION

The operations on the Al Faw took place in the most complex battlespace of the War, straddling the environmental divide of maritime, land, air and special forces operations. Whilst conducted at the tactical level, they had early strategic impact and effect, securing key Southern Iraqi oil infrastructure, both avoiding an environmental disaster which could have had regional consequences, and preserving the engine of eventual Iraqi economic recovery. They delivered some notable 'firsts' and achievements:

- The first conventional ground force action of the war.

- A two Commando Group aviation assault.

- An opposed landing – contrary to UK Defence Planning Assumptions.

- The first use of Naval Gunfire Support by the UK since the Falklands War (and since the Vietnam War for Australia).

- 40 Commando provided support to U.S. Special Forces.

- U.S. Forces (15 MEU) were placed under British tactical command.

- Proved the sea-basing concept for aviation and logistics.

The Al Faw operations did not follow the doctrinal templates of amphibious operations or the manoeuvrist approach, although both provided a basis upon which to extemporise. Such a departure from doctrinal teaching is entirely in keeping with the 'application of manoeuvrist thinking to warfighting ... seeking originality combined with a ruthless determination to succeed'[19], and is the difference between the practical application of doctrine and rigid adherence to dogma. It characterises recent amphibious experience across a range of operations, in what can be termed post-modern amphibious operations.

It rightly places amphibious forces back at the forefront of national short-notice and rapidly deployable Joint expeditionary capability, fulfilling Basil Liddell Hart's oft quoted observation on the '...British traditional employment in amphibious operations

*Frontline mobility shortfalls
are addressed with the
introduction of VIKING.
(Crown Copyright)*

[19]Joint Warfare Publication 0-01- UK British Defence Doctrine.

through which the mobility given by command of the sea could be exploited. A small but highly trained force striking 'out of the blue' at a vital spot can produce a strategic effect out of all proportion to its slight numbers'[20].

Finally the Al Faw operations proved once again the truism that War is about people as much as about process or technology. It is the quality of the individual at all levels, in particular those in the face of combat, their training, ethos and ability to operate together towards a common aim which, combined with process and technology, delivers success on the battlefield. In all three areas the Iraqis were found wanting in Warfighting.

Further Reading

MoD Booklets/Pamphlets:

Operations in Iraq - First Reflections - DCCS Media - Jul 2003.

Operations in Iraq - Lessons for the Future - DGCC - Dec 2003.

Operation TELIC - 3 Commando Brigade's Desert War - RN Graphic Centre, Portsmouth 04/44.

Operation TELIC - The Royal Navy's Contribution - A Versatile Maritime Force - DCCS Media for DCC(N) 10/03.

Royal Marines Operation TELIC - Back Pocket Brief Jan 2004.

Books:

Fox, Robert, *Iraq Campaign 2003 - Royal Navy and Royal Marines,* (Agenda Publishing, London, Nov 2003)

Articles:

Operation TELIC - A perspective from the (UK) Maritime Commander by Rear Admiral David Snelson Royal Navy - *The Association of Royal Navy Officers Journal* 2004.

Operation TELIC - 42 Command Group in Iraq by Lieutenant Colonel Buster Howes OBE Royal Marines - *Ibid.*

Biography

Brigadier Jeremy Robbins joined the Royal Marines in 1978, joining 45 Commando RM in 1980, which included Norway deployments and a tour in Belfast. He then served with 42 Commando, in Norway, Canada and a further NI tour. Moving to the USA in 1987, he served as Military Assistant to the Head British Defence Staff in the British Embassy. Returning to the UK, he was appointed Second in Command 3 Commando Brigade Headquarters and Signal Squadron before attending the Army Staff College at Camberley. In 1997 he had the tri-service lead for Northern Ireland operations, for which he was awarded an MBE. In 1999 he moved to the NATO Headquarters in Naples as Assistant Chief of Staff Expeditionary Operations, which included supporting operations in Kosovo, as well as deployments throughout the Mediterranean and Black Sea. In 2002 he attended the Higher Command and Staff Course and then went on to become the Chief of Staff for the Commander United Kingdom Amphibious Force. In 2003 he deployed as the Deputy and then Senior British Land Advisor to the US Coalition Forces Commander in Kuwait. Prior to his latest posting in Australia he was the Deputy Commander of 3 Commando Brigade and Commanding Officer of Royal Marines Stonehouse.

[20]History of the First World War, B H Liddell Hart, 1934.

Conclusion

XXXIX

By Major General Julian Thompson CB OBE (Rtd)

Attempting to cover every lesson that emerges in the preceding 38 chapters would result in a series of one-liners, risking a repetition of what has already been covered in detail. Instead, this conclusion is aimed at generating thought and discussion, by concentrating on some of the fundamentals that emerge from the amphibious operations covered in this book.

Professional Knowledge and the Amphibious Art

Amphibious landings have been rightly described as the most complicated operation of war. It follows that to conduct them successfully; the practitioner must be thoroughly professional.

Professional knowledge is acquired through regular amphibious exercises and training, education, and experience. The Gallipoli operation is an example of failure because all three ingredients above were missing. At that time no large-scale amphibious landing by British troops against a hostile shore defended by an enemy with modern weapons had occurred within the living memory of Hamilton, nor his commanders, nor their staffs. The World's most powerful navy in 1915, the Royal Navy, had no doctrine, procedures, and practice in amphibious operations against a first class enemy. Apart from steam picket boats to tow rowing boats, British amphibious techniques had not advanced since the landings at Aboukir in Egypt over a century earlier. As an art it had atrophied.

Some landing barges had been built by early 1915, but were not available in the Dardanelles theatre of operations, until the landings at Suvla in August 1915. These vessels were the brainchild of Fisher, the First Sea Lord, constructed as part of his scheme to land troops on the Baltic coast of Germany. How troop transports and escorts were to penetrate the heavily mined, confined waters of the Baltic *and* survive the attentions of the High Seas Fleet transferred from their North Sea base through the Kiel Canal was left unsaid. Neither were there any plans formulated for the employment of troops once ashore, in the unlikely event of there being any survivors to land on the north German coast. Not surprisingly, the Army would have nothing to do with it. These failings were the outcome of lack of joint discussion between the Navy and the Army, lack of an experienced staff at the Admiralty, and because although Fisher was a brilliant technocrat and innovator, he was no strategist, and lacked practical experience at the operational level of command.

There have been other periods in our history when amphibious operations have been accorded low priority. For example between the two World Wars, when as late as 1938, Admiral of the Fleet Sir Roger Backhouse, First Sea Lord indicated to his fellow members of the Chiefs of Staff Committee that he could not visualise any combined operation taking place in the next war. Field Marshal Viscount Gort, the Chief of the Imperial General Staff (CIGS), stated that plans for a combined operations

No landing in memory: Commodore Keyes, Vice Admiral de Robeck and General Sir Ian Hamilton in the Dardanelles. (NHB)

landing in the face of strong opposition were not contemplated.[1] There were others, such as the three service Staff Colleges, and Admiral Madden's Committee, who foresaw the need for amphibious operations in the future, and paradoxically, 1938 saw the establishment of the Inter-Service Training and Development Centre (ISTDC) tasked with producing doctrinal pamphlets, working on procedures, and furthering trials and development of equipment such as landing craft. They did good work that was to bear fruit later. On the outbreak of war in 1939, the ISTDC was closed. Fortunately the Army member remained in post and was able to re-establish the Centre in November 1939.

---

[1] Both the First Sea Lord and CIGS were using 'combined' in its contemporary sense that is an operation involving more than one service, in the way we now use 'joint'.

Left: As an art it had atrophied - Landing craft at Gallipoli. (IWM Q13637)

Specialised shipping: HM[S] Fearless and landing cra[ft] (Crown Copyright)

In the late 1970s and early 1980s, preceding the Falklands War of 1982, and amazingly even in the years following that war, there was distinct possibility that the shipping for amphibious operations would be disposed of without replacement, and hence the Royal Marines would be without the means to carry out their primary role. Fortunately there was sufficient residual expertise in the Royal Navy and especially the Royal Marines, with just enough specialised shipping to make the Falklands operation possible. What does this tell us? Amphibious expertise and support for amphibious operations cannot be taken for granted. The art needs constant nurturing, practice and study, and it only survives if it forms part of the nation's policy for defence.

The Combined and Joint Nature of Amphibious Operations

An amphibious operation will involve at least two participants: the Royal Navy and the Royal Marines, and often the Army and RAF in large numbers in addition. As well as being joint, an amphibious operation may be combined; with allies; the most recent example among many being Operation TELIC. It follows that those involved in amphibious operations should be thoroughly aware of the limitations, and strengths that other services and nations bring to the enterprise. There is

a need for tolerance and understanding, while maintaining a professional approach in order to engender respect in one's own ability among the other participants. When participating in a national joint amphibious operation that is part of a larger allied operation, for example an amphibious hook by a portion of the force in the context of a major land offensive, it is important that the overall commander, who may be a ground or air force officer, is aware of the limitations and strengths of the amphibious force.

A good example of underestimating, or possibly just overlooking, the value of amphibious operations occurred in Sicily in 1943 (examined in Chapter XV). Montgomery failed to use his considerable amphibious assets to block the narrow gap between Mount Etna and the coast north of Catania, to speed up the tempo, restore manoeuvre, and provide an anvil against

which his main force could have destroyed the German army. Instead he butted against the Germans in a series of costly attacks, and the bulk of the enemy escaped across the Straits of Messina to confront the Allies in Italy. Montgomery did of course learn the lesson, and the amphibious hook at Termoli was one outcome (Chapter XVII).

On the other hand, in the First World War, Haig whose name is not popularly associated with 'lateral thinking', several times discussed the possibility of an amphibious hook on the Belgian coast with Vice Admiral Sir Reginald Bacon, Flag Officer Dover Patrol. These discussions included using the threat of an amphibious assault to draw off enemy troops facing the BEF in Flanders, and on another occasion suggesting that Bacon experiment with special 'flat bottomed boats' to land tanks with a view to breaking through the wire and enemy's defences.

Surprise is based on speed, secrecy, and deception - which failed at Dieppe, but is addressed by the current concept of STOM. (NHB & Crown Copyright)

Surprise

'Surprise is based on speed, secrecy, and deception. It means doing the unexpected thing, which in turn normally means doing the more difficult thing in hope that the enemy will not expect it. This is the genesis of manoeuvre – to circumvent the enemy's strength to strike him where he is not prepared'.

General Alfred M Gray and Major John Schmitt, *Warfighting*, United States Marines Corps, 1989.

The amphibious operation by 3 Commando Brigade at Al Faw in March 2003 is a classic example of the way that surprise, and speed reap their reward. In doing so it set the tone for the future, as made clear by Colonel Robbins in Chapter XXXVIII. In a way it also has echoes of the past. In Italy on 2 April 1945, manoeuvre was restored during British Eighth Army's battle of the Argenta Gap by an amphibious assault across the River Reno and Lake Comacchio by 2 Commando Brigade (numbers 2, 9, 40 (RM) and 43(RM) Commandos). The operation was mounted from land using amphibious tractors, and although perhaps not doctrinally 'amphibious' in every aspect, it nevertheless incorporated many of the features of an amphibious operation including: deception, surprise, the need for trained amphibious troops, reconnaissance and terminal guidance by special forces in folboats (canoes).

Gallipoli and Dieppe provide examples of the perils of ignoring surprise, and especially secrecy and good security; and above all

the penalty for doing the obvious thing. In these respects, both repay study in order to provide a list of 'what not to do'.

The need to maintain surprise raises the questions of, such matters as:

- Whether or not to have a pre-bombardment, and in weighing up the advantages and disadvantages one should bear in mind the lessons learned by the Americans where lack of pre-bombardment in order to maintain surprise nearly led to defeat in Sicily, and again at Salerno.

- Should the landing be conducted at night or in daylight?

- Is it possible to avoid the beach altogether, the Ship to Objective Manoeuvre (STOM) concept?

Every operation will differ from the last, and what is good for one, may not be good for the next. Achieving surprise is rarely the result of a flash of inspiration, but rather of excellent intelligence, and painstaking preparation, coupled with good training and leadership.

Air and Sea Control

The British in the Second World War, for example in Norway 1940, Crete in 1941 and the Aegean in 1943 (at Leros especially), learned the bitter lesson that conducting amphibious operations, albeit in the above examples, withdrawals, without air control, could be disastrous. As time passes there is a danger that this lesson will be forgotten. It was sharply rammed home in 1982 in the Falklands War, when on D-Day alone, every escort in the AOA was sunk or damaged by air attack. If the operational area is out of range of land-based aircraft, carrier-based aircraft will be indispensable to success. Equally important is sea control. Considerable efforts may have to be made to establish sea control before an amphibious operation, and this may take time. Until total air and sea control are established, it may not be possible to use charter shipping and aircraft to support the operation. In which case British Flag shipping may have to be taken up from trade (STUFT), and similarly British Flag aircraft taken into service, and the numbers available and other considerations including their crews willingness, or otherwise, to enter the war zone, may impose logistic constraints.

Specialised Shipping and Ship-Shore Movement Assets

Without specialised shipping and ship-shore movement assets, a true amphibious as opposed to a sea-transported operation is impossible. The scale of these assets required will of course depend upon a number of variables, including the size of the landing force, the task, terrain, strength of the opposition, and type of operation. A landing in the vicinity of strongly-held enemy localities will demand a scale and category of ship-shore movement assets that may not be necessary in the case of landings conducted well away from enemy defences, and out of range of their artillery and immediate counter-attack.

Specialised shipping will include vessels for:

- Command and control facilities for the amphibious task group and landing force commanders (LPD or specialised command ship).

- Launching and recovering helicopters (LPH).

- Docking down facility to launch and recover landing craft including LCACs.

- Naval Gunfire Support.

- Launching and recovering combat aircraft (aircraft carrier).

- Logistic shipping.

- Mine Counter Measures/Mine Clearance.

Specialised ship-shore movement assets include:

- Landing craft for personnel and vehicles.

- Landing craft for armour, able if necessary to land armour first.

- Powered pontoons (MEXEFLOTE type).

- Helicopters, both heavy and medium lift.

Although to the practitioner of amphibious operations the above constitutes a 'blinding glimpse of the obvious', in the author's experience this insight is not necessarily vouchsafed to those whose acquaintance with the amphibious art is rudimentary or non-existent, especially to those who confuse a sea transported move to a 'red carpet' destination with an amphibious operation. Those who labour under this misapprehension may include one's allies, and even one's fellow countrymen. By 'red carpet', we mean a locality held by a friendly power, with little or no threat of air, ground, and sea attack, in which host nation support in the form of dock facilities, airfields, fuel, and transport are present in abundance. This is very different from having to fight one's way in under attack, bringing everything with you to an area without docks, airfields, and infrastructure. Readers of this book may find themselves having to make this point at some time in the future.

Logistics

There may be a need to unload stores across the beach if a harbour is not available, cannot be seized early in the operation, or is rendered inoperable because of bomb damage or by the enemy. If the air and sea situation allows, it may be possible to sea-base combat supplies thereby reducing the need for extensive logistic facilities ashore. Both these options are only possible with sufficient ship-shore movement assets.

Command and Control

The chain of command must be clear and unambiguous, under an in-theatre joint task force commander. The overall campaign plan should be made clear to the CATF/CATG and CLF before they draw up the amphibious plan. The amphibious plan must be designed by the CATF/CATG and CLF, not by some outside commander who will not have access to all the information

Command and Control:
Left: USS Augusta, Op TORCH. (NARA)
Right: HMS Albion on exercise.
(Crown Copyright)

including force levels/capabilities, assets and last minute changes to these. The CATF/CATG and CLF should travel together in a dedicated command ship with good command, control, communications and intelligence facilities; and control the landing from that ship together. The point at which command chops from CATF/CATG to CLF must be unequivocal and agreed.

All the foregoing are laid down in the relevant publications, and appear obvious, but in the past have been ignored on occasions, sometimes with unhappy or potentially unhappy results. Two examples of poor location of commanders from the past include Hamilton and de Robeck attempting to command the landings at Gallipoli on 25 April 1915 from the battleship *Queen Elizabeth*. She had a shore-bombardment role, and went where her bombarding duties demanded, not where Hamilton needed to be. Her communications to the landing force were inadequate, and Hamilton did not take all his staff with him. He was not therefore best placed to influence events ashore, even if he had been inclined to, which he was not.

Patton commanding the Western Assault Force in the 1942 North Africa landings with Rear Admiral Hewitt in the cruiser *Augusta* was carted out to sea when the ship was diverted to meet an enemy surface threat, just as Patton was preparing to go ashore (described in Chapter XIII).

Advance Force Operations:
Special Boat Service

Advance Force Operations

Advance force operations for beach reconnaissance, intelligence gathering and terminal guidance to beaches and landing zones are an inseparable part of an amphibious operation, not just a 'nice to have if available' asset. Special force or reconnaissance specialists should ideally be an integral part of the landing force orbat. This ensures common SOPs, and procedures. If not already under command, higher formation headquarters must provide the necessary special force assets. If they do not, it must be made clear that the success of the operation is being put at risk. If it is apparent that special forces assets will not be available, and time permits, 'in house' arrangements for reconnaissance must be made. It may be necessary to train one's own reconnaissance troops in beach

reconnaissance and related skills in anticipation of being refused special forces when an operation appears imminent.

Leadership

Ultimately, as in all military operations, one of the key ingredients in success will be leadership by commanders at all levels. Good training, thorough briefing, and confidence will enable the landing force to overcome problems caused by the enemy, casualties, the weather, and other mishaps resulting from 'friction' that is endemic in war. Well-briefed commanders will be able to use their initiative to overcome the difficulties and achieve their objectives. Nowhere was this demonstrated better than at Port en Bessin (Chapter XXIV).

The LPDs HMS Bulwark (right) and HMS Albion have as a primary function to act as the afloat command platform for the Commander Amphibious Task Force (CATF). With an Embarked Military Force (EMF) of 305 troops, and more extensive command, control and communications, the new ships are a major improvement over the ones which they replace. (Crown Copyright)

The Future

Whatever the future holds in terms of the nature of the threat, there will always be a requirement to maintain a capability to launch an assault from the sea. Amphibious landings present a number of unique warfighting challenges, since they bridge the maritime, land and air environments. The operations examined within this book highlight the most important factors which a commander needs to consider. It is unlikely that the same set of circumstances will ever present itself in the future. Therefore, in order to be prepared it is important that commanders are familiar with these lessons to ensure their operations are successful and incur the minimum number of casualties possible. All those elements worth considering have been experienced before, and it is the duty of all potential commanders to ensure that they are as informed as possible. By being conversant with the material in these pages a firm foundation of knowledge can be developed. With further training and experience the expertise so acquired enables commanders to overcome the unpredictable nature of war in the littoral.

Major General Julian Thompson's Biography appears on page 468.

Right: HMS Albion and LCAC from 539 Assault Squadron RM. (Crown Copyright)

glossary
bibliography
index

Glossary
Principal Abbreviations and Short Titles

AA Bde	Air Assault Brigade	Bn	Battalion	COMUKTG	Commander U.K. Task Group
AA	Anti Aircraft	BPT	Brigade Patrol Troop	COMUSMACV	Commander U.S. Military Assistance Command
AAV	Amphibious Assault Vehicle	BRF	Brigade Reconnaissance Force	COMUSMARCENT	Commander U.S. Marine Central Command
AAW	Anti Air Warfare	BRNC	Britannia Royal Naval College	COMUSNAVCENT	Commander U.S. Navy Central Command
AB	Airborne Brigade	BSSG-4	Brigade Service Support Group-4	COPP	Combined Operations Pilotage Party
ABDA	American, British, Dutch, Australian	CAF	Combined Amphibious Force	COR	Combined Operations Room
AC-130	Hercules Aircraft	CAP	Combined Action Programme/Combat Air Patrol	COS	Chief of Staff
ACC	Air Component Commander	CAS	Close Air Support	COSSAC	Chief of Staff to the Supreme Allied Commander
ACNS(H)	Assistant Chief of the Naval Staff (Home)	CATF	Commander Amphibious Task Force	CPT	Central Pacific Theatre
ACP	Airspace Control Plan/Air Control Post	CATG	Commander Amphibious Task Group	CS	Combat Support
ADP	Army Doctrine Publication	CB	Companion of the Order of the Bath	CSG	Command Support Group
AE	Assault Echelon	CBE	Commander of the Order of the British Empire	CSS	Combat Service Support
AEF	American Expeditionary Force	CCO	Chief of Combined Operations	CSW	Crew Served Weapons
AF	Amphibious Force	CCS	Combined Chiefs of Staff	CTCRM	Commando Training Centre Royal Marines
AFHQ	Allied Force Headquarters	CENTCOM	U.S. Central Command	CTG	Carrier Task Group
AFNOS	Amphibious Force Notes and Orders	CENTO	Central Treaty Organisation	CVR(T)	Combat Vehicle Reconnaissance (Tracked)
AFOE	Assault follow-on echelon	CF	Coalition Forces	CVS	Carrier Vessel Anti-Submarine
AH	Attack Helicopters	CFACC	Coalition Forces Air Component Commander	DCO	Directorate/Director of Combined Operations
AIB	Allied Intelligence Branch/Bureau	CFJFC	Coalition Forces Joint Force Commander	DD Tank	Duplex-Drive (Amphibian) Tank
ANGLICO	Air & Naval Gunfire Liaison Company	CFLCC	Coalition Forces Land Component Commander	DGC	Defence Graphics Centre
ANZAC	Australia and New Zealand Army Corps	CFMCC	Coalition Forces Maritime Component Commander	DMZ	De-militarized Zone
AOA	Amphibious Objective Area	CFSOCC	Coalition Forces Special Operations Component Commander	DoD	US Department of Defence
APC	Armoured Personnel Carrier			DOT	U.S. Division of Operations and Training
ARG	Amphibious Ready Group	CGRM	Commandant General Royal Marines	DSO	Distinguished Service Order
ASRM	Assault Squadron Royal Marines	CH47	Chinook Helicopter	DUKW	Amphibious 6-wheeled Truck
ATC	Armoured Troop Carrier	CHF	Commando Helicopter Force	DWR	Duke of Wellington's Regiment
ATG	Amphibious Task Group	CIGS	Chief of the Imperial General Staff	ECC	Evacuation Coordination Centre
ATO	Air Tasking Order	CinCUSCENTCOM	Commander-in-Chief, U.S. Central Command	ELINT	Electronic Intelligence
AVRE	Armoured Vehicles Royal Engineers	CLF	Commander Landing Force	EMF	Embarked Military Force
AW	Amphibious Warfare	CLR	Commando Logistic Regiment	EMPRA	Embarkation, Movement, Planning, Rehearsal, Assault
AWC	Amphibious Warfare Commander	CMB	Coastal Motor Boat		
BARV	Beach Armoured Recovery Vehicle	CO	Commanding Officer	EOD	Explosive Ordnance Disposal
BCT	Battalion Combat Team	COHQ	Combined Operations Headquarters	ETF	Eastern Task Force
BEF	British Expeditionary Force	COMATG	Commander Amphibious Task Group	EUSAK	8th U.S. Army, Korea
BJ	Beach Jumpers	COMSEC	Communication Security	EW	Electronic Warfare
BLO	Bombardment Liaison Officer	COMSEVENFLT	Commander U.S. Seventh Fleet	FGA	Fighter Ground Attack
BMA	Brigade Maintenance Area	COMUKAMPHIBFOR	Commander U.K. Amphibious Force	FIE	Fly-in Echelon

FMB	Forward Mounting Base	LC(FF)	Landing Craft, (Flotilla Flagship)	LCU	Landing Craft, Utility
FMF	Fleet Marine Force	LCA	Landing Craft, Assault	LCV	Landing Craft, Vehicle
FOB	Forward Operating Base	LCA(FT)	Landing Craft, Assault (Flame Thrower)	LCVP	Landing Craft, Vehicle Personnel
FOO	Forward Observation Officer	LCA(OC)	Landing Craft, Assault (Obstacle Clearing)	LD	Line of Departure
FUSAG	First United States Army Group	LCAC	Landing Craft, Air Cushioned	LF	Landing Force
GAF	German Air Force	LCAC(H)	Landing Craft, Air Cushioned (Heavy)	LF7F	Landing Force Seventh Fleet
GCHQ	Government Communications Headquarters	LCAC(L)	Landing Craft Air Cushion (Light)	LFATGW	Light Forces Anti-Tank Guided Weapon
GHQ	General Headquarters	LCC	Land Component Commander	LFS	Landing Force, Support
GOC	General Officer Commanding	LCC	Landing Craft, Control	LitM	Littoral Manoeuvre
GOP	General Outpost	LCF	Landing Craft, Flak	LPD	Landing Platform Dock
GSM	General Service Medal	LCG(L)	Landing Craft, Gun (Large)	LPH	Landing Platform Helicopter
Gz	Gazelle Helicopter	LCG(M)	Landing Craft, Gun (Medium)	LPT	Landing Priority Table
HAC	Honourable Artillery Company	LCH	Landing Craft, Headquarters (or Hospital)	LRR	Long-Range Rifle
HE	High Explosive	LCI	Landing Craft, Infantry	LSB	Landing Ship, Bombardment
HMG	Heavy Machine Gun	LCI(D)	Landing Craft, Infantry (Demolition)	LSC	Landing Ship, Carrier (Derrick Hoisting)
HMS	Her Majesty's Ship	LCI(G)	Landing Craft, Infantry (Gun)	LSD	Landing Ship Dock
HNS	Host Nation Support	LCI(M)	Landing Craft, Infantry (Mortar)	LSD(A)	Landing Ship Dock (Auxiliary)
HRO	Humanitarian Relief Operations	LCI(R)	Landing Craft, Infantry (Rocket)	LSH	Landing Ship, Headquarters
Ike	General Dwight D. Eisenhower	LCI(S)	Landing Craft, Infantry (Small)	LSI(H)	Landing Ship, Infantry (Hand hoisting)
IRC	Inflatable Raiding Craft	LCL	Landing Craft, Logistic	LSI(L)	Landing Ship, Infantry (Large)
ISTAR	Intelligence, Surveillance, Target Acquisition, and Reconnaissance	LCM	Landing Craft, Mechanised	LSI(M)	Landing Ship, Infantry (Medium)
		LCM(G)	Landing Craft, Mechanised (Gunboat)	LSI(S)	Landing Ship, Infantry (Small)
ISTDC	Inter-Services Training and Development Centre	LCM(R)	Landing Craft, Mechanised (Rocket)	LSM	Landing Ship Medium
IWM	Imperial War Museum	LCN	Landing Craft, Navigation	LSM(R)	Landing Ship Medium (Rocket)
JC	Joint Commander	LCP	Landing Craft, Personnel	LSP	Landing Ship, Personnel
JCS	United States Joint Chiefs of Staff	LCP(L)	Landing Craft, Personnel (Large)	LST	Landing Ship, Tank
JEHU	Joint Experimental Helicopter Unit	LCP(M)	Landing Craft, Personnel (Medium)	LSV	Landing Ship, Vehicle
JFACC	Joint Forces Air Component Commander	LCP(R)	Landing Craft, Personnel (Ramped)	LVT	Landing Vehicle, Tracked
JFC	Joint Force Commander	LCP(Sy)	Landing Craft, Personnel (Survey)	LVT(A)	LVT (Armoured)('Water Buffalo')
JIC	Joint Intelligence Committee	LCP(U)	Landing Craft, Personnel (Utility)	LVT(A)1	LVT (Armoured, + 37mm cannon)
JOA	Joint Operating Area	LCS(L)	Landing Craft, Support (Large)	LVT(A) 4	LVT (Armoured, + 75mm howitzer)
JSCSC	Joint Services Command and Staff College	LCS(M)	Landing Craft, Support (Medium)	Lx	Lynx Helicopter
JSOA	Joint Special Operations Area	LCS(R)	Landing Craft, Support (Rocket)	MAB	Marine Amphibious Brigade
KIA	Killed in Action	LCT	Landing Craft, Tank	MAF	Marine Amphibious Force
KMT	Kuomintang	LCT(A)	Landing Craft, Tank (Armoured)	MAG-40	Marine Aircraft Group-40
KTO	Kuwait Theatre of Operation	LCT(H)	Landing Craft, Tank (Hospital)	MAGTF	Marine Air-Ground Task Force
LBF	Landing Barge, Flak	LCT(R)	Landing Craft, Tank (Rocket)	MarDiv	Marine Division

MAU	Marine Amphibious Unit	OIF	Operation Iraqi Freedom	SAS	Special Air Service
MBE	Member of the Order of the British Empire	OKH	Ger: Oberkommando des Heeres	SBS	Special Boat Service
MC	Military Cross	OKW	Ger: Oberkommando der Wehrmacht	SCAF	Supreme Commander Allied Expeditionary Force
MCC	Maritime Component Commander	OMFTS	Operational Manoeuvre from the Sea	SCAP	Supreme Commander Allied Powers
MCJO	Maritime Contribution to Joint Operations	ONI	Office of Naval Intelligence	SEAL	U.S. Special Forces (Sea, Air, Land)
MCMV	Mine Counter Measures Vessel	OODA	Observation, Orientation, Decision, Action	SF	Special Forces
MEB	Marine Expeditionary Brigade	ORBAT	Order of Battle	SH	Support Helicopters
MEF	Marine Expeditionary Force	OTH	Over the Horizon	SIGINT	Signal Intelligence
MEU	Marine Expeditionary Unit	PERMA	Planning, Embarkation, Rehearsal, Movement, Assault	SK4	Sea King Mk IV Helicopter
MGB	Motor Gun Boat			SLF	Special Landing Force
MGC	U.S. Major General Commandant	PhibGru 2	Amphibious Ready Group 2	SLOC	Sea Lines of Communication
MIF	Maritime Interdiction Force	PJHQ	Permanent Joint Headquarters	SNOL	Senior Naval Officer Landings
ML	Motor Launch/Mountain Leader	PLUTO	Pipeline Under The Ocean	SOC	Special Operations Capable
MLC	Motor Landing Craft	PM	Prime Minister	SOCC	Special Operations Component Commander
MM	Mine Countermeasure	PSO	Peace Support Operations	SOE	Special Operations Executive
MOD	Ministry of Defence	QDG	Queen's Dragoon Guards	SOP	Standard Operating Procedure
MPF	Maritime Pre-positioned Force	RA	Royal Artillery	SSB	Special Service Brigade
MRF	Mobile Riverine Force	RAF	Royal Air Force	SSS	Map Marking Symbol for Commando
MSC	Military Sealift Command	RAP	Regimental Aid Post	STOM	Ship to Objective Manoeuvre
MSPF	Maritime Special Purpose Force	RCT	Regimental Combat Team	STUFT	Ships Taken Up From Trade
MTB	Motor Torpedo Boat	RE	Royal Engineers	SWPT	Southwest Pacific Theatre
NA	U.K. National Archives, Kew	RFA	Royal Fleet Auxiliary	TACON	Tactical Control
NAAFI	Navy, Army, Air Force, Institute	RL	Report Line	TAI	Tactical Area of Interest
NAG	North Arabian Gulf	RLT	Regimental Landing Team	TF	Task Force
NARA	U.S. National Archives and Records	RM	Royal Marines	UAV	Unmanned Aerial Vehicles
NATO	North Atlantic Treaty Organisation	RMM	Royal Marines Museum	UDG/T	Underwater Demolition Group/Team
NAVSPECWARGRU2	Navy Special Warfare Group 2	RN	Royal Navy	UKAF	United Kingdom Amphibious Force
NEO	Non-combatant Evacuation Operations	RNLMC	Royal Netherlands Marine Corps	UN	United Nations
NGFO	Naval Gunfire Forward Observation	RNVR	Royal Navy Volunteer Reserve	USAF	United States Air Force
NGS	Naval Gunfire Support	ROC	Rehearsal of Concept	USMC	United States Marine Corps
NHB	Naval Historical Branch	ROK	Republic of Korea	USN	United States Navy
NID	Naval Intelligence Division	ROKA	Republic of Korea Army	VAC	5th Amphibious Corps
NKPA	North Korean Peoples' Army	RRC	Rigid Raiding Craft	VC	Victoria Cross
NL	Netherlands	RSDG	Royal Scots Dragoon Guards	VC	Viet Cong
NTF	Naval Task Force	RTR	Royal Tank Regiment	WD	War Department
NVA	North Vietnamese Army	SACEUR	Supreme Allied Commander Europe	WIA	Wounded in action
OBE	Officer of the Order of the British Empire	SACMED	Supreme Allied Commander Mediterranean	WTF	Western Task Force

Bibliography

40 Commando War Diary ADM 202/87

Achkasov, V. I. and Pavlovich, N. B., *Soviet Naval Operations in the Great Patriotic War, 1941-1945*, (Annapolis, Maryland: Naval Institute Press, 1973)

Alani, Mustafa, *Operation Vantage. British Military Intervention in Kuwait, 1961*, (Surbiton: LAAM, 1990)

Alexander, Joseph H. and Bartlett, Merrill L., *Sea Soldiers in the Cold War: Amphibious Warfare 1945-1991*, (Annapolis, Maryland: Naval Institute Press, 1995)

Alexander, Joseph H., *Across the Reef: The Marine Assault of Tarawa, Marines in World War II Commemorative Series*, (Washington, D.C.: MCHC, 1993)

Alexander, Joseph H., *Storm Landings: Epic Amphibious Battles in the Central Pacific*, (Annapolis, Maryland: Naval Institute Press, 1997)

Alexander, Joseph H., *Utmost Savagery: The Three Days of Tarawa*, (New York: Ivy Books, 1995)

Ambrose, Stephen, *D-Day, June 6th 1944: The Climactic Battle of World War II*, (New York: Touchstone, 1995)

Anderson, Duncan, *The Falklands War 1982*, (Oxford: Osprey, 2002)

Army Center for Military History, *Aleutian Islands*, (Washington, D.C.: United States Army Center for Military History, 1992)

Ash, Bernard, *Norway 1940*, (London: Cassell, 1964)

Aston, Brigadier-General George, *Letters on Amphibious Wars*, (London: John Murray, 1911)

Aston, Sir George, (Colonel of Royal Marine Artillery), *Sea, Land, and Air Strategy: A Comparison*, (1914)

Atkin, Ronald, *Dieppe 1942: The Jubilee Disaster*, (London: Book Club Associates, 1980)

Atkinson, Rick, *An Army at Dawn: The War in North Africa, 1942-1943*, (New York: Henry Holt, 2002)

Badsey, Stephen, *Normandy 1944: Allied Landings and Breakout*, (London: Osprey, 1990)

Badsey, Stephen, *Normandy: UTAH Beach*, (Sutton, 2004)

Ballard, John R., *Operation Chromite: Counterattack at Inchon*, (Joint Forces Quarterly Spring/Summer 2001)

Ballendorf, Dirk A. and Bartlett, Merrill L., *Pete Ellis: An Amphibious Warfare Prophet, 1880-1923*, (Annapolis: Naval Institute Press, 1997)

Barbey, D. E., *MacArthur's Amphibious Navy*, (Annapolis, Maryland: Naval Institute Press, 1969)

Barnett, Correlli, *Engage the Enemy More Closely*, (London: Penguin, 2000) (Reprint)

Bartlett, Merrill L, *Lejeune: A Marine's Life, 1867-1942*, (Columbia: University of South Carolina Press, 1991; reprint ed., Annapolis: Naval Institute Press, 1991)

Bartlett, Merrill L. ed., *Assault From the Sea: Essays on the History of Amphibious Warfare*, (Annapolis, Maryland: Naval Institute Press, 1983)

Beadle, J.C., *The Light Blue Lanyard – 50 Years with 40 Commando Royal Marines*, (Worcester: Square One, 1992)

Beaufre, Andre, *The Suez Expedition 1956*, (London: Faber and Faber, 1969)

Blumenson, Martin, *Sicily: Whose Victory?* (London: Macdonald & Co, 1969)

Bradley, James, *Flyboys: A True Story of Courage*, (London: Aurum Press, 2004)

Bradley, Omar, *A Soldier's Story of the Allied Campaigns from Tunis to the Elbe*, (London: Eyre & Spottiswoode Ltd., 1951)

Breuer, William B., *Agony at Anzio*, (London: Robert Hale, 1989)

Breuer, William B., *Drop Zone Sicily: Allied Airborne Strike, July 1943*, (Novato CA: Presidio Press, 1983)

Breuer, William B., *Retaking the Philippines*, (New York: St. Martin's Press, 1986)

Bruce, Colin John, *Invaders: British and American Experience of Seaborne Landings 1939-1945*, (London: Chatham, 1999)

Buckley, Christopher, *Five Ventures: Iraq-Syria-Persia-Madagascar-Dodecanese*, (London: HMSO. 1954)

Buckley, Christopher, *Norway: The Commandos: Dieppe*, (London: HMSO, 1951)

Burdick, Charles B., *The Japanese Siege of Tsingtao: World War I in Asia*, (Hamden, 1976)

Butler, Rupert, *Hand of Steel*, (London: Hamlyn, 1980)

C.B. 3081 (27), Battle Summary No. 35, *The Invasion of Sicily: Operation HUSKY*, (T.S.D. 21/46, Naval Staff, Admiralty, S.W.1., February 1946)

Cable, James, *Gunboat Diplomacy 1919-1979: Political Applications of Limited Naval Force*, (Basingstoke: Macmillan, 1981)

Callwell, C.E., *Military Operations and Maritime Preponderance: Their Relations and Interdependence*, (1905, reprinted Annapolis, Maryland: Naval Institute Press, 1996)

Cannon, M. Hamlin, *Leyte: the Return to the Philippines*, (Washington D.C.: United States Army, 1993)

Carlyon, L. A., *Gallipoli*, (London: Doubleday, 2002)

Carpenter, Alfred B., *The Blocking of Zeebrugge*, (London: Herbert Jenkins, 1925)

Carver, Field Marshal Lord, *The Imperial War Museum Book of the War in Italy, 1943-1945*, (London: Pan, 2001)

Chapin, John C., *Breaking the Outer Ring: Marine Landings in the Marshall Islands. Marines in World War II Commemorative Series*, (Washington, D.C.: MCHC, 1994)

Chappell, Mike, *Army Commandos, 1940-45*, (London: Osprey Publishing, 1996)

Churchill, Thomas B. L., *Commando Crusade*, (London: William Kimber, 1987)

Churchill, Winston S., *The Second World War: Vol. V, Closing the Ring*, (London: Cassell, 1966)

Clapp, Michael & Southby-Tailyour, Ewen, *Amphibious Assault Falklands: The Battle of San Carlos Water* (London: Leo Cooper, 1996)

Clark, General Mark, *Calculated Risk: His Personal Story of the War in North Africa and Italy*, (London: Harrap, 1951)

Clausewitz, Carl von, *On War*, (Ware: Wordsworth, 1997)

COHQ Bulletin Y/48' *US Operations in the Marianas June to August, 1944*, (London: Combined Operations Headquarters, 1945)

Collier, Basil, *The Defence of the United Kingdom*, (London: HMSO, 1957)

Conn, Stetson Engleman, Rose C. and Fairchild, Byron, *The United States Army in World War II: Guarding the United States and Its Outposts*, (Washington, D.C.: United States Army Center for Military History, 1962)

Connaughton, R. M., *The War of the Rising Sun and the Tumbling Bear: A Military History of the Russo-Japanese War, 1904-5*, (London: Routledge, 1989)

Corbett, Julian S., *Maritime Operations in the Russo-Japanese War, 1904-1905*, 2 Volumes, (Annapolis, Maryland: United States Naval Institute Press, 1994)

Corbett, Julian S., *Some Principles of Maritime Strategy*, (Longmans, 1911)

Cordesman, Anthony H. and Wagner, Abraham R., *The Lessons of Modern War Volume IV: the Gulf War* (Boulder, Colorado: Westview Press, 1996)

Cosmas, Graham A., and Shulimson, Jack, "The Culebra Maneuver and the Formation of the U. S. Marine Corps' Advance Base Force", in Robert W. Love, Jr. et al, ed., *Changing Interpretations and New Sources in Naval History*, (New York and London: Garland, 1980)

Courtney, G.B., *SBS in World War Two: The Story of the Original Special Boat Section of the Army Commandos*, (London: Robert Hale, 1983)

Cox, Richard ed., *Operation Sealion*, (London: Thornton Cox, 1974)

Coyle, Brendan, *War on Our Doorstep: The Unknown Campaign on North America's West Coast*, (Surrey, British Columbia: Heritage House, 2002)

Craven W.F. and Cate J.L. (Eds.), *The Army Air Forces in World War Two, Vol. 2: Torch to Pointblank, August 1942 to December 1943*, (Washington: Office of Air Force History, 1983)

Creswell, Captain John, *Generals and Admirals: The Story of Amphibious Command*, (London: Longmans, 1952)

Croizat, Victor, J., *Across the Reef: The Amphibious Tracked Vehicle at War*, (Quantico, VA: Marine Corps Association, 1992)

Crowl, Philip A. and Edmund G. Love, *The War in the Pacific: Seizure of the Gilberts and Marshalls. U.S. Army in World War II*, (Washington, D.C.: Department of the Army, 1955)

Cruikshank, C., *Deception in World War II*, (Oxford: OUP, 1979)

Cull, Brian, *Wings over Suez: The First Authoritative Account of Air Operations During the Sinai and Suez Wars of 1956*, (London: Grub Street, 1996)

Cunningham, of Hyndhope, Admiral of the Fleet Viscount, *A Sailor's Odyssey*, (London: Hutchinson, 1951)

D'Este, Carlo, *Bitter Victory: The Battle for Sicily 1943*, (London: Collins, 1988)

D'Este, Carlo, *Decision in Normandy: The Unwritten Story of Montgomery and the Allied Campaign*, (New York: Harper Perennial, 1991)

D'Este, Carlo, *Eisenhower: A Soldier's Life*, (New York: Henry Holt, 2002)

D'Este, Carlo, *Fatal Decision: Anzio and the Battle for Rome*, (London: Fontana, 1992)

D'Este, Carlo, *Patton: A Genius for War*, (New York: Harper Collins, 1995)

Darby, Phillip, *British Defence Policy East of Suez 1947-1968*, (London: Oxford University Press, 1973)

Derry, T. K., *The Campaign in Norway*, (London: HMSO, 1952)

Dorrian, James, *Storming St Nazaire: The Gripping Story of the Dock-Busting Raid March, 1942*, (London: Leo Cooper, 1998)

Doughty, Robert Allen, *The Seeds of Disaster: The Development of French Army Doctrine, 1919-1939* (Hamden: The Shoe String Press, 1985)

Drea, E., *MacArthur's Ultra*, (Kansas: University Press of Kansas, 1992)

Drea, Edward J., 'The Development of Imperial Japanese Army Amphibious Warfare Doctrine', in *idem*, *In the Service of the Emperor: Essays on the Imperial Japanese Army*, (Lincoln: University of Nebraska Press, 1998)

Dunning, James, *The Fighting Fourth: No.4 Commando at War, 1940-45*, (Gloucestershire: Sutton Publishing Ltd, 2003)

Dunstan, Simon, *Commandos: Churchill's Hand of Steel*, (London: Ian Allan Publishing Ltd., 2003)

Durnford-Slater, John, *Commando*, (London: William Kimber & Co Ltd, 1953)

Edmonds, James E., *A Short History of World War I*, (London: Oxford University Press, 1951)

Eisenhower, Dwight D., *Crusade in Europe*, (New York: Doubleday, 1948)

Eisenhower, Dwight D., *D Day to VE Day; Official Report*, (London: HMSO, 2000) (Reprint)

Ellis, L F., *Victory in the West, Volume 2, The Defeat of Germany*, (London: HMSO, 1968)

Ellis, L F., *Victory in the West, Volume I, The Battle of Normandy*, (London: HMSO, 1960)

Evans, Colonel M.H.H., *Amphibious Operations: The Projection of Sea Power Ashore*, (Brasseys, 1990)

Evans, David C. and Peattie, Mark R., *Kaigun: Strategy, Tactics, and Technology in the Imperial Japanese Navy, 1887-1941*, (Annapolis, Maryland: United States Naval Institute Press, 1997)

Farran, Roy, *Winged Dagger: Adventures on Special Service*, (London: Cassell, 1998. Reprint)

Farrar-Hockley, Anthony, *Official History: The British part in the Korean War: Volume 1 A Distant Obligation*, (London: HMSO, 1990)

Fergusson, Bernard, *The Watery Maze: The Story of Combined Operations*, (London: Collins, 1961)

Finlan, Alastair, *The Gulf War 1991*, (Oxford: Osprey, 2003)

Fleming, Peter, *Invasion 1940: An Account of the German Preparations and the British Counter-Measures*, (London: Rupert Hart-Davis, 1957)

FMFM 1, *Warfighting*, (Washington, D.C.: Department of the Navy, Headquarters Marine Corps, March 1989)

FMFM 1-1, *Campaigning*, (Washington, D. C.: Department of the Navy, Headquarters Marine Corps, January 1990)

FMFM 1-3, *Tactics*, (Washington, D.C.: Department of the Navy, Headquarters Marine Corps, June 1991)

Forfar, John, *From Omaha to the Scheldt, The Story of 47 Royal Marine Commando*, (East Lothian, Scotland: Tuckwell Press, 2001)

Forfar, John, *Towards Victory in Europe, the Battle for Walcheren*, (Proceedings of the Royal College of Physicians of Edinburgh; 25: 451-475, 623-628. 1995.)

Fox, Robert, *Iraq Campaign 2003 - Royal Navy and Royal Marines*, (London: Agenda Publishing, Nov 2003)

Fullick, Roy and Powell, Geoffery, *Suez: The Double War*, (Hamish Hamilton, 1979)

Ganz, A. Harding, *ALBION – The Baltic Islands Operation*, (Military Affairs Vol. XLII 1978)

Garfield, Brian, *The Thousand-Mile War: World War II in Alaska and the Aleutians*, (Garden City, New York: Doubleday and Company, 1969)

Garland, Albert N. Lt. Col., & Mc Gaw Smyth, Howard, *U.S. Army in World War II, The Mediterranean Theater of Operations: Sicily and the Surrender of Italy*, (Washington, D.C.: Office of the Chief of Military History, Dept. of the Army, 1965)

Gatchel, Theodore L., *At the Water's Edge: Defending Against the Modern Amphibious Assault*, (Annapolis, Maryland: Naval Institute Press, 1996)

Gilbert, Martin, *First World War*, (London: Weidenfeld and Nicolson, 1994)

Gordon, Andrew, *The Rules of the Game: Jutland and British Naval Command*, (London: John Murray Publishers Ltd., 1996)

Greene, Jack and Alessandro Massignani, *The Naval War in the Mediterranean, 1940-1943*, (London: Chatham Publishing, 1998)

Grove, Eric J., *Vanguard to Trident: British Naval Policy Since World War II*, (London: Bodley Head, 1987)

Grove, Mark J., 'The Development of Japanese Amphibious Warfare 1874 to 1942', in Geoffrey Till, Theo Farrell, and Mark J. Grove, *Amphibious Operations*, (Camberley: Strategic and Combat Studies Institute, 1997)

Guingand, Major General Sir Francis de, *Operation Victory*, (London: Hodder and Stoughton, 1947)

Hagan, Professor Kenneth, *This People's Navy: The Making of American Seapower*, (The Free Press, 1992)

Halpern, Paul G., *A Naval History of World War I*, (Annapolis, Maryland: Naval Institute Press, 1994)

Hamilton, Nigel, *Monty: Master of the Battlefield 1942-1944*, (London: Hamish Hamilton, 1983)

Hamilton, Nigel, *Monty: the Field-Marshal 1944-1976*, (London: Hamish Hamilton, 1986)

Hamilton, Nigel, *Monty: The Making of a General 1887-1942*, (London: Hamish Hamilton, 1981)

Hampshire, Cecil A., *The Beachhead Commandos*, (William Kimber, 1978)

Harries, Meirion & Susie, *Soldiers of the Sun: The Rise and Fall of the Imperial Japanese Army 1868-1945*, (London: Heinemann, 1991)

Hastings, Max, *Overlord: D-Day and the Battle for Normandy*, (London: Guild Publishing, 1984)

Hattendorf, John B., *The Limitations of Military Power*, (Basingstoke: Macmillan, 1990)

Hayden, Lieutenant Colonel, H.T., *Warfighting: Maneuver Warfare in the US Marine Corps*, (Greenhill Books, 1995)

Hayes, Grace Person, *The History of the Joint Chiefs of Staff in World War II: The War Against Japan*, (Annapolis, Maryland: Naval Institute Press, 1982)

Hays, Jr., Otis, *Alaska's Hidden War: Secret Campaigns on the North Pacific Rim*, (Fairbanks: University of Alaska Press, 2004)

Haythornthwaite, Philip J., *Gallipoli 1915: Frontal Assault on Turkey*, (London: Osprey, 1991)

Heinl, Robert D., Jr., and John A. Crown, *The Marshalls: Increasing the Tempo*, (Washington, D.C.: MCHC, 1954)

Hesketh, Roger, *Fortitude: The D-Day Deception Campaign*, (New York: Overlook, 2002)

Hewitt, H. Kent, *The Memoirs of Admiral H. Kent Hewitt*. Edited by Evelyn M. Cherpak, (Newport, RI: Naval War College Press, 2002)

Hickey, Michael, *Gallipoli*, (London: John Murray, 1995)

Hickey, Michael, *The Korean War: The West Confronts Communism 1950-1953*, (London: John Murray, 1999)

Hickey, Michael, *The Unforgettable Army: Slim's XIVth Army in Burma*, (Kent: Spellmount Ltd., 2002)

Higgins, Trumbull, *Soft Underbelly: The Anglo-American Controversey over the Italian Campaign, 1939-1945*, (London: Collier-Macmillan Ltd., 1968)

History of the Commandos in the Mediterranean Sept. 1943 to May 1945, HMSO, Combined Operations, 1940-42, (London: HMSO, 1943)

Hooker, Richard D., (Ed.), *Maneuver Warfare: An Anthology*, (Novato: Presidio, 1993)

Hough, Frank, *Pearl Harbor to Guadalcanal*, (Washington DC: US Marine Corps, 1958)

Howard, Michael, *The Mediterranean Strategy in the Second World War*, (New York: Praeger, 1968)

Howes, Buster, *Operation Telic – 42 Command Group in Iraq*, (The Association of Royal Navy Officers Journal 2004)

Hunter, Robin, *True Stories of the Commandos*, (London: Virgin, 2000)

Isby, D.C. (ed.), *Fighting the Invasion: The German Army at D-Day*, (London: Greenhill, 2000)

Isely, Jeter A. and Philip A. Crowl, *The U.S. Marines and Amphibious War: Its Theory, and Its Practice in the Pacific*, (Princeton, NJ: Princeton University Press, 1951)

Jackson, Robert, *Suez 1956: Operation Musketeer*, (London: Ian Allan, 1980)

James, Robert Rhodes, *Gallipoli*, (London: B. T. Batsford, 1965)

Jentschura, Hansgearg Jung, Dieter Mickel, Peter, (Translated by Antony Preston and J. D. Brown), *Warships of the Imperial Japanese Navy, 1869-1945*, (London: Arms & Armour Press, 1977; reprinted 1996)

Keegan, John, *The Second World War*, (London: Pimlico, 1997)

Kersandy, François, *Norway 1940*, (London: Collins, 1990)

Kesselring, Albert, *The Memoirs of Field Marshal Kesselring*, (London: William Kimber, 1954)

Keyes, Admiral of the Fleet, The Lord, *Amphibious Warfare and Combined Operations*, (Cambridge: 1943)

Keyes, Roger, *The Naval Memoirs of Admiral of the Fleet Sir Roger Keyes: Scapa Flow to the Dover Straits 1916-1918*, (London: Thornton Butterworth, 1935)

Khamalov, Kh., *Naval Infantry in Combat for the Motherland*, (Moscow: Military Publishing House, 1966)

Kieser. Egbert, *Hitler on the Doorstep. Operation "Sea Lion": the German Plan to Invade Britain, 1940*, (London: Arms and Armour, 1997)

Kipp, Jacob W., "The Second Arm and the Problem of Combined Operations: The Russian-Soviet Experience, 1853-1945." In Philip S. Gillette and Willard C. Frank, Jr., Eds. *The Sources of Soviet Naval Conduct*, (Lexington, MA: Lexington Books, D.C. Heath and Co., 1990)

Krueger, Walter, *From Down Under to Nippon*, (Washington D.C.: Combat Forces Press, 1953)

Kyle, Keith, *Suez*, (New York : St. Martin's Press, 1991)

Ladd, James, *Commandos and Rangers of World War 2*, (London: Macdonald and Jane's, 1978)

Ladd, James, *SBS the Invisible Raiders: The History of the Special Boat Squadron from World War Two to the Present*, (London: Book Club Associates, 1983)

Ladd, James, *The Royal Marines, 1919-1980, An Authorised History*, (London: Jane's Publishing Company, 1980)

Laffin, John, *Damn the Dardanelles! The Agony of Gallipoli*, (Stroud: Budding Books, 1997)

Laffin, John, *Raiders: Elite Forces Attacks*, (Gloucestershire: Sutton Publishing Ltd, 1999)

Lake, Deborah, *The Zeebrugge and Ostend Raids*, (Barnsley: Leo Cooper, 2002)

Lee, David, *A History of the Royal Air Force in the Arabian Peninsula and Adjacent Territories 1945-1962*, (London: HMSO, 1980)

Lee, David, *Beachhead Assault: The Story of the Royal Navy Commandos in World War II*, (Greenhill Books, 2004)

Leonhard, Robert R., *Fighting by Minutes*, (Westport, Connecticut: Praeger, 1994)

Leonhard, Robert R., *The Art of Maneuver: Maneuver-Warfare Theory and Air Land Battle*, (Novato, California: Presidio, 1991)

Liddell Hart, Basil H., *History of the Second World War*, (London: Cassell, 1970)

Lind, William S., *Maneuver Warfare Handbook*, (Boulder: Westview, 1985)

Linnell, T G., *48 Royal Marine Commando, The Story*, (Published privately, 1946)

Lockhart, Robert Bruce, *The Marines Were There: The Story of the Royal Marines in the Second World War*, (Putnam, 1950)

Lord, Walter, *Lonely Vigil Coast Watchers*, (New York: Viking, 1977)

Lorelli, John A., *To Foreign Shores: U.S. Amphibious Operations in World War II*, (Annapolis, Maryland: Naval Institute Press, 1995)

Loxton, Bruce, *The Shame of Savo: Anatomy of a Naval Disaster*, (St. Leonards, NSW, Australia: Allen & Unwin, 1994)

Lucas, James, *Hitler's Mountain Troops*, (London: Arms and Armour, 1992)

MacArthur, Douglas, *Reminiscences*, (New York: McGraw Hill, 1964)

MacGarrigle, George L., *The US Army Campaigns of World War II: Aleutian Islands*, (Washington D.C.: US Army Center for Military History, 1992)

Macintyre, Donald, *Narvik*, (London: Evans Brothers, 1959)

Macksey, Kenneth, *Commando: Hit-and-Run Combat in World War II*, (NY: Jove Books, 1991)

Maguire, Eric, *Dieppe: August 1942*, (London: Jonathan Cape, 1963)

Manchester, William, *American Caesar*, (Boston: Little, Brown and Company, 1978)

Mason, David, *Raid on St Nazaire*, (London: Macdonald, 1970)

Maund, Rear Admiral L., *Assault from the Sea*, (Methuen, 1949)

Meister, Jürg, *Der Seekrieg in den osteuropäischen Gewässern 1941-45*, (München: J.F. Lehmanns Verlag, 1958)

Melson, Charles D., *The Marine Corps in Vietnam*, (Oxford: Osprey, 1998)

Messenger, Charles, *The Commandos, 1940-1946*, (London: William Kimber & Co. Limited, 1985)

Middlebrook, Martin, *The Falklands War 1982*, (London: Penguin, 2001)

Miller, John, *Guadalcanal: The First Offensive*, (Washington DC: US Army, 1949)

Millett, Allan R., and Shulimson, Jack, ed., *Commandants of the Marine Corps*, (Annapolis: Naval Institute Press, 2004)

Millett, Allan R., 'Assault from the Sea: The Development of Amphibious Warfare between the Wars, the American, British and Japanese Experiences', in Williamson Murray and Allan R. Millett (eds.), *Military Innovation in the Interwar Period*, (Cambridge: Cambridge University Press, 1996)

Millett, Allan R., *Semper Fidelis: The History of the United States Marine Corps*, (New York and London: Macmillan, 1980)

Mitchell, Donald W., *A History of Russian and Soviet Sea Power*, (New York: MacMillan, 1974)

Mitchell, Raymond, *Marine Commando: Sicily and Salerno, 1943 with 41 Royal Marines Commando* (London: Robert Hale, 1988)

Mitchell, Raymond, *They Did What Was Asked of Them: 41 (Royal Marines) Commando*, (Firebird books, P.O. Books, Poole, Dorset, BH15 2RG, 1996)

Montagu, Ewen, *The Man Who Never Was*, (London: Evans Brothers Ltd., 1953)

Montgomery of Alamein, Field Marshal B., Viscount, *The Memoirs of Field Marshall Montgomery*, (London: Collins, 1958)

Moorehead, Alan, *Gallipoli*, (London: Hamish Hamilton, 1956)

Mordal, Jacques, *Dieppe: The Dawn of Decision*, (London: Souvenir Press, 1962)

Morison, Samuel Eliot, *Aleutians, Gilberts and Marshalls, June 1942-April 1944*, Vol. 7 of *History of United States Naval Operations in World War II*, (Boston: Little, Brown and Co., 1951)

Morison, Samuel Eliot, New Guinea and the Marianas March *1944 – August 1944*, Vol. 8 of *History of United States Naval Operations in World War II*, (London: Oxford University Press, 1953)

Morison, Samuel Eliot, *Operations in North African Waters, October 1942-June 1943*, Vol. 2 of *History of United States Naval Operations in World War II*, (Campaign, IL: The University of Illinois Press, 2001)

Morison, Samuel Eliot, *Sicily-Salerno-Anzio January 1943 – June 1944*, Vol. 9 of *History of United States Naval Operations in World War II*, (London: Oxford University Press, 1954)

Morison, Samuel Eliot, *The Struggle for Guadalcanal, August 1942-February 1943*, Vol. 5 of *History of United States Naval Operations in World War II*. (London: Oxford University Press, 1949)

Morris, E., *Churchill's Private Armies: British Special Forces in Europe, 1939-1942*, (London: Hutchinson Ltd, 1986)

Moulton, J. L., *Haste to the Battle*, (Cassell: London, 1963)

Moulton, J. L., *The Battle for Antwerp*, (Ian Allan Ltd: London, 1978)

Moulton, J. L., *The Norwegian Campaign of 1940* (London: Eyre and Spottiswode, 1966)

Mueller, Joseph N., *Guadalcanal 1942: The Marines Strike Back*, (London: Osprey, 1992)

Nargele, Dominik George, "The Soviet Naval Infantry: An Evolving Instrument of State Power." (Georgetown University, PhD dissertation, 1983)

Naval Historical Center, *The Aleutians Campaign, June 1942-August 1943*, (Washington, D.C.: Naval Historical Center, 1993; reprint, Washington, D.C.: Office of Naval Intelligence, 1945)

Neave-Hill, W.B.R., *British Support of the Amir of Kuwait 1961*, (The Historical Section, Ministry of Defence Library, 1968)

Neillands, Robin, *By Sea and Land: The Royal Marines Commandos: A History, 1942-1982*, (Casemate, 1987)

Neillands, Robin, *The Dieppe Raid*, (London: Aurum Press, 2005)

Neillands, Robin, *The Raiders: The Army Commandos, 1940-1945*, (London: George Weidenfeld & Nicolson Ltd; 1989)

NWP-22 (B)/LFM-01, *Doctrine for Amphibious Operations*.

Pack, S.W.C., *Operation HUSKY: The Allied Invasion of Sicily*, (London: David & Charles, 1977)

Page, Captain Christopher, R.N., *Command in the Royal Naval Division*, (Spellmount, 1999)

Perras, Galen Roger, *Stepping Stones to Nowhere: The Aleutian Islands, Alaska, and American Military Strategy, 1867-1945*, (Vancouver: University of British Columbia Press, 2003)

Phillips, C. E., Lucas, *The Greatest Raid of All*, (London: Heinemann, 1958)

Pimlott, John, *The Viking Atlas of World War II*, (London: Viking, 1995)

Pitt, Barrie, *Zeebrugge: St Georges Day 1918*, (London: Cassell, 1958)

Pokrant, Marvin, *Desert Shield at Sea: What the Navy Really Did*, (Westport, Connecticut: Greenwood Press, 1999)

Polmar, Norman & Mersky, Peter B., *Amphibious Warfare: An Illustrated History*, (London: Blandford Press, 1988)

Pond, Hugh, *Salerno*, (London: William Kimber, 1961)

Porch, Douglas, *The Path to Victory: The Mediterranean Theater in World War II*, (New York: Farrar, Straus and Giroux, 2004)

Prefer, N., *MacArthur's New Guinea Campaign*, (Pennsylvania: Combined Books, 1995)

Rawling, Gerald, *Cinderella Operation*, (Cassell: London, 1980)

Reynolds, Clark G., *The Fast Carriers: The Forging of an Air Navy*, (Annapolis, Maryland: Naval Institute Press, 1992)

Robertson, Terence, *Dieppe: The Shame and the Glory*, (London: Hutchinson, 1963)

Roskill, Captain S. W., *The War at Sea, 1939-1945: Volume II, The Period of Balance*, (London: HMSO, 1956)

Roskill, Captain S.W., *The Strategy of Sea Power: Its Development and Application*, (Collins, 1962)

Rottman, Gordon L., *The Marshall Islands, 1944: Operation Flintlock, the Capture of Kwajalein and Eniwetok*, (Oxford: Osprey, 2004)

Ruge, Friedrich, *The Soviets as Naval Opponents, 1941-1945*, (Annapolis, Maryland: Naval Institute Press, 1979)

Ryder, R. E. D., *The Attack on St. Nazaire*, (London: John Murray, 1947)

Saunders, Hilary St George, *The Green Beret – The Story of the Commandos*, (London: Michael Joseph, 1949)

Schenk, Peter, *Invasion of England 1940: The Planning of Operation Sealion*, (London: Conway, 1990)

Seaton, Albert, *The Russo-German War, 1941-45*, (New York and Washington: Praeger, 1971)

Seymour, William, *British Special Forces: The Story of Britain's Undercover Soldiers*, (London: Sidgwick and Jackson Ltd., 1985)

Shaw, Henry I., Bernard C. Nalty, and Edwin T. Turnbladh, *Central Pacific Drive*. Vol. 3 of *History of United States Marine Corps Operations in World War II*, (Washington, D.C.: MCHC, 1966)

Sheffield, G.D., (Ed.), *Leadership and Command: The Anglo-American Experience Since 1861*, (London: Brassey's, 1997)

Sherrod, Robert, *On To Westward: War in the Central Pacific*, (New York: Duell, Sloan, and Pearce, 1945)

Sherrod, Robert, *Tarawa: The Story of A Battle*, (New York: Duell, Sloan, and Pearce, 1944)

Simmons, Edwin Howard, *The United States Marines: A History*, (Annapolis, Maryland: Naval Institute Press, 1998)

Slim, Field-Marshal Viscount, *Defeat into Victory*, (London: Papermac, 1986)

Snelson, David, *Operation TELIC – A Perspective from the (UK) Maritime Commander*, (The Association of Royal Navy Officers Journal 2004)

Southby-Tailyour, Ewen, *Reasons in Writing: A Commando's View of the Falklands War*, (London: Leo Cooper, 1993)

Special Forces in the Desert War 1940-1943, (Richmond, Surrey: Public Record Office, 2001)

Spector, Ronald H., *Eagle Against the Sun*, (New York: Macmillan, 1985)

Speller, Ian and Tuck, Christopher, *Strategy and Tactics: Amphibious Warfare*, (Staplehurst, Kent: Spellmount, 2001)

Speller, Ian, *The Role of Amphibious Warfare in British Defence Policy, 1945-1956*, (Basingstoke: Palgrave, 2001)

Steel, Nigel and Hart, Peter, *Defeat at Gallipoli*, (London: Macmillan, 1994)

Stockman, James R., *The Battle for Tarawa*, (Washington, D.C.: MCHC, 1947)

Strawson, John, *The Italian Campaign*, (London: Secker and Warburg, 1987)

Tassigny, Marshal de Lattre de, *The history of the French First Army*, (London: Allen and Unwin, 1952)

Tedder, Marshal of the Royal Air Force, *With Prejudice: The War Memoirs*, (London: Cassel & Co. Ltd., 1966)

The Joint Chiefs of Staff, *Joint Doctrine for Amphibious Operations*, (Washington, D.C.: JCS Pub 3-07, November 1986)

The Marines in Vietnam 1954-1973: An Anthology and Annotated Bibliography. (Washington, D.C.: History and Museums Division, Headquarters Marine Corps,1974)

The Vietnam War: The History of America's Conflict in South East Asia, *(London: Salamander Books, 1996)*

Thompson, Julian, *No Picnic:3 Commando Brigade in the South Atlantic, 1982*, (London: Cassell & Co, 2001)

Thompson, Julian, *The Royal Marines: From Sea Soldiers to a Special Force*, (London: Sidgwick & Jackson, 2000)

Thomson, R. W., *The Eighty Five Days*, (Hutchinson: London, 1957)

Till, Geoffrey, *Seapower: A Guide for the 21st Century*, (London: Frank Cass, 2003)

Till, Geoffrey, Series Editor of the Frank Cass Naval History and Policy series; *Amphibious Warfare*, (Leicester: SCSI, 1997)

Till, Geoffrey, with G.D. Sheffield (Eds.), *Challenges of High Command in the Twentieth Century*, (London: Macmillan/Palgrave, 2003)

Till, Geoffrey,ed., *Seapower: Theory and Practice*, (London: Frank Cass, 1994)

Tomblin, Barbara Brooks, *With Utmost Spirit: Allied Naval Operations in the Mediterranean, 1942-1945*, (Lexington, KY: The University Press of Kentucky, 2004)

Travers, Tim, *Gallipoli 1915*, (Stroud, Gloucestershire: Tempus, 2001)

Trew, Simon, *100 Years of Conflict*, (co-editor with Dr Gary Sheffield; Sutton Publishing 2000)

Trew, Simon, *The Hutchinson Atlas of Battle Plans* (Helicon 1999)

U.S. Marines in the Persian Gulf, 1990-1999, 9 Volumes, (Washington, D.C.: Headquarters Marine Corps, History and Museum Division, 1992-1999)

U.S. Marines in Vietnam, 1954-1975, 9 Volumes, (Washington, D. C.: History and Museums Division, Headquarters Marine Corps, 1977-1997)

Vagts, Alfred, *Landing Operations: Strategy, Psychology, Tactics, and Politics from Antiquity to 1945* (Harrisburg, PA: Military Service Publishing Company, 1952)

Van Creveld, Martin, *Command in War*, (Harvard University Press, 1987)

Van Creveld, Martin, *The Art of War: Warfare and Military Thought*, (Cassel, 2000)

Van Creveld, Martin, *Transformation of War*, (Free Press, 1990)

Van Der Vat, Dan, *The Pacific Campaign*, (Edinburgh: Birlinn, 2001)

Varble, Derek, *The Suez Crisis*, (Oxford: Osprey, 2003)

Vaux, Nick, *March to the South Atlantic: 42 Commando, Royal Marines, in the Falklands War*, (London: Buchan & Enright, 1986)

Villa, Brian, *Unauthorised Action: Mountbatten and the Dieppe Raid*, (Oxford: Oxford University Press, 1989)

Von Senger und Etterlin, General Frido, *Neither Fear Nor Hope: The Wartime Career of General von Senger und Etterlin Defender of Cassino*, (London: Macdonald, 1964)

War Department, *The Capture of Attu: As Told by the Men Who Fought There*, (Washington, D.C.: Department of War, 1944)

Warner, Denis and Peggy, *The Tide at Sunrise: A History of the Russo-Japanese War, 1904-1905*, (London: Angus and Robertson, 1975)

Warner, Philip, *Invasion Road*, (London: Cassell, 1980)

Warner, Philip, *The Zeebrugge Raid*, (London: William Kimber, 1978)

Wheatley, Ronald, *Operation Sea Lion: German Plans for the Invasion of England 1939-1942*, (Oxford: Clarendon Press, 1958)

Whitaker, W D & S., *The Battle of the Scheldt*, (Souvenir Press: London, 1984)

Whitehouse, Arch, *Amphibious Operations*, (Frederick Muller, 1963)

Whiting, Charles, *Slaughter over Sicily*, (London: Leo Cooper, 1992)

Willoughby, Charles A. and Chamberlain, John, *MacArthur 1941-51: Victory in the Pacific*, (London: William Heinemann, 1956)

Wilmot, Chester, *The Struggle for Europe*, (London: Collins, 1952)

Wilmott, H. P., *Empires in the Balance: Japanese and Allied Pacific Strategies to April 1942*, (Annapolis, Maryland: Naval Institute Press, 1982)

Winton, John, *Cunningham: The Greatest Admiral Since Nelson*, (London: John Murray, 1998)

Wright, Derrick, *Tarawa 1943: The Turning of the Tide*, (Oxford: Osprey, 2000)

Young, David, *Four-Five: The Story of 45 Commando Royal Marines, 1943-1971*, (Cooper, 1972)

Young, Peter, *Commando*, (London: Ballantine Books Ltd, 1974)

Young, Peter, *Storm from the Sea*, (London: Greenhill Books, 1989)

MoD Booklets/Pamphlets:

British Defence Doctrine, 2nd Edition, (JWP 0-01), (JDCC, 2001)

British Maritime Doctrine, 3rd Edition (BR 1806), (Norwich: TSO, 2004)

United Kingdom Approach to Amphibious Operations, (MWC/HQRM, 1997)

The Application of Force, *An Introduction to Army Doctrine and the Conduct of Military Operations*, (Norwich: TSO, 2002)

Operations in Iraq – First Reflections, (DCCS Media, Jul 2003)

Operations in Iraq – Lessons for the Future, (DGCC – Dec 2003)

Operation TELIC 3 Commando Brigade's Desert War, (Portsmouth: RN Graphic Centre 04/44)

Operation TELIC – The Royal Navy's Contribution – A Versatile Maritime Force, (DCCS Media for DCC(N) 10/03)

Royal Marines Operation TELIC, (Back Pocket Brief Jan 2004)

Index